DICTIONARY OF
THE HISTORY OF IDEAS

DICTIONARY OF THE HISTORY OF IDEAS

Studies of Selected Pivotal Ideas

PHILIP P. WIENER

EDITOR IN CHIEF

VOLUME II

Despotism

TO

Law, Common

CHARLES SCRIBNER'S SONS · NEW YORK

The Publishers are grateful for permission to quote from
previously published works in the following articles:

"Iconography"

   from *Myth and Allegory in Ancient Art*, by Roger Hinks, copyright
   1939, by permission of The Warburg Institute

"Musical Genius"

   from "Musical Genius—Evolution and Origins of a Concept,"
   by Edward Lowinsky, © 1964, by permission of *The Musical
   Quarterly*

PRINTED IN THE UNITED STATES OF AMERICA

Library of Congress Catalog Card Number 72-7943

SBN 684-16422-1 (pbk.)   Volume I
SBN 684-16423-X (pbk.)   Volume II
SBN 684-16424-8 (pbk.)   Volume III
SBN 684-16425-6 (pbk.)   Volume IV
SBN 684-16426-4 (pbk.)   Index
SBN 684-16418-3 (pbk.)   Set

DICTIONARY OF
THE HISTORY OF IDEAS

DESPOTISM

THE CONCEPT of despotism is perhaps the least known of that family which includes tyranny, autocracy, absolutism, dictatorship (in its modern usage), and totalitarianism. Although nearly contemporary with "tyranny," the concept of despotism has not been as significant in the history of political thought. Nevertheless at some times, and in the work of some of the greatest political philosophers, the concept of despotism has been sharply distinguished from other members of its family, and has attained an unusual prominence, as when Montesquieu made it into one of the three fundamental types of government. It was in the eighteenth century, and particularly in France, that despotism supplanted tyranny as the term most often used to characterize a system of total domination, as distinguished from the exceptional abuse of power by a ruler. The temporary success of the term led to its conflation with tyranny, as in the Declaration of Independence where in successive sentences, "absolute Despotism" and "absolute Tyranny" are used as synonyms. In 1835 Tocqueville expressed the opinion that after the French Revolution, modern politics and society had taken on a character that rendered both concepts inadequate. Today their usage suggests archaism: controversies over twentieth-century forms of total domination have centered on the concepts of dictatorship and totalitarianism.

Despotism is a concept that has been used to describe and compare polities, as a weapon in both domestic and international politics, and as an expression, usually although not invariably, in negative form, of an author's political preferences. Because of the use to which it has been put as a category for sorting out and classifying the salient characteristics of one among the forms of government, despotism belongs to the terminology of comparative politics and historical sociology, or at least to their history. But rarely has it been deployed for purely untendentious analysis. A very few authors such as Hobbes have assigned positive connotations to the term; some others such as Bodin, Grotius, and Pufendorf have treated despotism as a legitimate relationship on the basis of legal precedents they did not care to repudiate. But most often despotism has been a label applied, not only in a polemical spirit, but with a set of practical purposes in view: to identify and discredit arrangements antithetical to or incompatible with those regarded by the analyst as making for political freedom. In France during the seventeenth and eighteenth centuries, the aristocratic opposition to the crown made use of the concept of despotism to distinguish between its own model of the French monarchy's constitution and the purported violation of it by those who sought an Oriental mode of domination. Like other classifications of its family, despotism is usually linked to some particular conception of liberty. This connection is usually so close that analysts ought to study together conceptualizations of freedom and arrangements said to be incompatible with it. This has not been the case. Freedom has been much studied; antithetical conceptions, little. This may be due to the assumption, stated by Aristotle in his study of tyranny, and by Montesquieu in his treatment of despotism, that on such forms there is not much to be said. Those forms of rule considered to be incompatible with liberty are represented as simple; those that incorporate it, as complex. The difficulties caused by this assumption have rarely been explored.

The concept of despotism began as a distinctively European perception of Asian governments and practices: Europeans as such were considered to be free by nature, in contrast to the servile nature of Orientals. Concepts of despotism have frequently been linked to justifications, explanations, or arraignments of slavery, conquest, and colonial or imperial domination. The attribution of despotism to an enemy may be employed to mobilize the members of a political unit, or those of a regional area. Thus the Greeks stigmatized the Persians as despotic in much the same way that Christian writers were to treat the Turks. By an irony not always perceived either by the purported champions of liberty against despotism, or by their historians, such arguments often became the rationale, as in Aristotle, for the domination by those with a tradition of liberty over those others who had never enjoyed that happy condition. That chain of ideas is easily visible in Algernon Sidney, as well as in not a few other republican expansionists.

The treatment that follows will be broken down into seven parts: (1) the Greek theory, which represents natural slavery as the basis of absolute rule by an Oriental monarch regarded as legitimate by his subjects; (2) the medieval treatment of despotism as one variety of kingship, as distinguished from the royal and the tyrannical variants of that form; (3) the new setting of the theory in the sixteenth and seventeenth centuries, when beginning with Bodin, despotism was defined as that form of rule which comes into being as the result of the victor's rights over the conquered in a just war, including the right to enslave him and to confiscate his property, or as the result of the conquered party's consent to be enslaved in return for being spared by the victor; (4) those seventeenth- and eighteenth-century writers, for the most part French, who although they began by identifying despotism with absolute Oriental regimes, nevertheless transformed the concept into one that may be applied to total domination anywhere, and indeed according to them, accurately characterized the degree of centralization

1

and monopolization of power achieved under Louis XIV; (5) Montesquieu's formulation of despotism as one of the three basic types of government; (6) the eighteenth-century extensions and critiques of Montesquieu; (7) subsequent developments in the use of the term by Robespierre and St. Just; Madame de Staël and Benjamin Constant; Hegel and Marx; and, finally, Tocqueville, with his vision of the possibility of a qualitatively new form of despotism in the democratic society he held to be inevitable.

1. The history of the concept of despotism begins with the Greeks. The root meanings of the term *despótēs* (δεσπότης) were those of (1) the head of a family, or *père de famille;* (2) the master of slaves. (3) As a political term, despotism was extended to cover a type of kingship, in which the power of the monarch over his subjects, although indistinguishable from that exercised by a master (*despótēs*) over slaves, nevertheless was considered by the ruled as sanctified by custom, and hence legitimate. As Aristotle wrote, "The authority of the statesman (*polítikos*) is exercised over men who are by nature free; that of the master (*despótēs*) over men who are by nature slave" (*Politics* I. 1255b). Both slavery and despotism were said to rest upon the same distinctive type of human relationship, and this was inappropriate to a community of free men. From the time of the Persian Wars, the Greeks considered despotism to be a set of arrangements characteristic of non-Hellenic or barbarian peoples thought to be slaves by nature, a form of kingship practiced by Asians, and the most notable example of which was to be found in the Persian Achaemenid Empire (559–330 B.C.). At the time of the Persian wars, most mainland Greeks were repelled by the Oriental notion of a sun-king, embodying divine law, and hence absolute. As for themselves, they thought, as Herodotus reported, that they were free because subject only to the laws of their respective city-states, rather than to any Asian ruler, before whom his subjects prostrated themselves. Free men do not render such homage to mortals. The only earthly *despótēs* they may acknowledge is the law to which they have consented. Thus the term received still another extension and this became its fourth sense, and was so used by Herodotus, Xenophon, and Plato.

Of all the Greek political writers, Aristotle wrote with the most detail, was the most concerned to compare and contrast despotism with tyranny, and was the most influential.

On the one hand, Asiatic despotism is based, Aristotle asserts, not on force, but on consent. Hence fear cannot be said to be its motive force. Despotism is a form of constitutional monarchy, based on the observance by the king of existing law, rather than the mere assertion of his arbitrary will. Nor do despotisms have the problem of succession that confront tyrannies. In contrast to tyranny, reigns of long duration and stable government characterize despotism. Nor are foreign troops needed to put down the opposition of the ruled (*Politics* III. ix. 1285a).

On the other hand, there is a powerful indictment of despotism latent in the link Aristotle established between it and tyranny. If the power wielded by Asian monarchs was royal, it was also tyrannical: it partook of the nature of royalty because despots ruled in accordance with law and over willing subjects; but such power also partook "of the nature of tyranny because they ruled despotically and according to their own judgment" (*Politics* IV. viii. 1295a). Aristotle, further, employs the word *despotikos* whenever he depicts the vitiated stage of each of the three forms of government (*Politics* III. viii. 1279b; IV. iv. 1292a; V. vi. 1306b). Aristotle established another sinister similarity between despotism and tyranny when discussing the devices requisite for their preservation. Although associated with the tyrant, Periander of Corinth, Aristotle added, such means were also practices of the Persian empire (*Politics* V. ix. 1313a).

Despotism, although rule according to law, is not rule in the common interest. All constitutions that aim at the rulers' advantage "have an element of despotism, whereas a *polis* is a partnership of free men" (*Politics* III. iv. 7), held together by the ties of friendship and justice. But these cannot exist when there is nothing in common between ruler and ruled, as is the case under both tyranny and despotism, where the relationship is equivalent to that "between a craftsman and his tool, or between the soul and the body [or between master (*despótēs*) and slave]: . . . there can be no friendship, nor justice towards inanimate things, indeed not even towards a horse or ox, nor yet towards a slave as a slave. For master and slave have nothing in common; a slave is a living tool, just as a tool is an inanimate slave" (*Nicomachean Ethics* VIII. xi).

Thus in Aristotle, the institution of slavery is related to the political form of despotism, and this in terms of the human relationships characteristic of both. Here Aristotle specifically distinguished between Greek and barbarian. Among the Greeks, there is a free class capable of holding office and ruling and being ruled in turn; among the barbarians, all are slaves by nature. Aristotle goes on to draw two significant conclusions: first, that contrary to nature, among the barbarians, the female and slave occupy the same position (the reason being that no naturally ruling element exists among them, and the conjugal union thus comes to be a union of a female who is a slave with a male who is also a slave); second, that it follows that the

Greeks who possess such a free class, ought to rule over the barbarians. Aristotle here cites the poet who wrote, "Meet it is that barbarous people should be governed by the Greeks" (*Politics* I. i. 1252b).

Another difference Aristotle claimed to have established was that based on climates. The peoples of cold countries, especially those of Europe, are full of spirit, but deficient in skill and intelligence; the peoples of Asia, although endowed with skill and intelligence, are deficient in spirit, and hence are subjects and slaves. Possessing both spirit and intelligence the Greeks can continue to be free and indeed to govern other peoples (*Politics* VII. vi. 327b). It has thus seemed plausible to many commentators that Aristotle in his lost exhortation "On Colonies" did indeed recommend to his student, Alexander the Great, that he rule the Greeks as leader (*hêgêmon*) and the barbarians as master (*despótēs*) (*Politics*, ed. and trans. Ernest Barker, New York [1946], p. lix).

2. In the late Middle Ages, the concept of despotism was revived as the result of the translation of Aristotle's *Politics* by William of Moerbeke, who rendered those words that derived from *despótēs* as *principatus despoticus, monarchia despotica, despotice principari, despoticum,* and *despotizare.* Some medieval writers sought to understand and make use of Aristotle's concept of despotism despite the differences separating their own political, legal, social, and religious arrangements from those of the Greek *polis.* Why did Charles V of France (1337–80) go to the trouble of commissioning a translation into Old French of Aristotle's *Politics* by Nicole Oresme, a great savant and scientist? What in the concept of despotism seemed useful to William of Ockham and Marsilius of Padua?

Nicole Oresme was associated with Charles V in his struggle against the Avignon Papacy. His argument resembled those of Ockham and Marsilius, who from their refuge at the court of the Holy Roman Empire, used the concept of despotism in their effort to discredit the complete power (*plenitudo potestatis*) claimed by the papacy in all matters spiritual and temporal. Oresme was a Gallican and a proponent of the conciliar view of church government; he was accused by papal inquisition of having been the French translator of the *Defensor Pacis.* Aristotle was also used to strengthen the position of secular kings and the Holy Roman Emperor, who wished to be regarded not as a proprietor among proprietors, but as a unique public power which had been ordained for the welfare of the entire community.

No other medieval writer made greater or more precise use of the concept of despotism than did William of Ockham, who did so both in his theory of kingship, and his delimitation of papal power. All polities, principates, and prelacies may be divided into two types, one ruled in the common interest, the other, in the ruler's interest only. Kingship in the common interest is royal monarchy; subjects enjoy natural liberty. It has two variants: (1) the ruler has full power and is not bound by positive human laws or customs, although he is subject to natural law; (2) one man rules in the common interest, but is bound by laws and customs that he swears to maintain. The two other types of kingship, the despotic and tyrannical, are both defined by Ockham as rule in the interest of the monarch alone. Despotic kingship is exercised over men who are slaves, and who consent; it must be distinguished from tyrannical kingship: "a bad king becomes a tyrant . . . if in accordance with the law he begins to rule his subjects against their will for his own good . . . ; but if he begins to rule them with their consent for his own good, he becomes, properly speaking, a despot" (*Dialogus*, Part 3, Tract 1, Book 2, Ch. 6, trans. Ewart Lewis, *Medieval Political Ideas*, London [1954], I, 301–02). At issue in Ockham's classification are the rights, personal and property, of kings and subjects in each of the three forms.

Ockham also used the concept of despotism to delimit the powers of the papacy. Christ did not give unlimited power to Peter. Otherwise all men would have been made into slaves of the Pope, who has "no power to abolish or disturb the rights and liberties of others, especially those of emperors, kings, princes, or other laymen." The papal principate was established only for the salvation of believers, not for the Pope's honor or advantage. His rule, properly understood, is not "dominative or despotic, but ministerial,"

. . . the kind of principate one has over slaves; . . . Christ did not give to the apostles, but a ministerial principate . . . over free men, and which is much nobler and greater in dignity than a dominative principate even though it is not so great in extent of power . . . even as a principate over men is nobler than a principate over beasts (*De imperatorum et pontificum potestate*, Ch. VII, trans. E. Lewis, II, 609).

Marsilius of Padua used the concept of despotism phrased somewhat differently, both to establish the positive principles that ought to prevail in the makeup of a state and to attack the Pope:

. . . for since the state is a community of free men, as is written in the *Politics* . . . , every citizen must be free, and not undergo another's despotism (*despociam*), that is slavish dominion (*Defensor Pacis*, trans. Gewirth, I, xII, 6, p. 47).

Because of excessive obedience on the part of Christians and the falsehoods put together by certain clerics, the Pope now exerted an unjust despotism over Christian believers (. . . *suam injustam despociam in-*

duxerunt super Christi fideles sua simplicate credentes . . . ; ibid, II, 1). Marsilius had found in Aristotle this term associated with slavish barbarians. Addressing free men in his own part of the world, Marsilius found the concept of despotism advantageous in attacking institutions and practices of European origin. Like Ockham, he did not follow Aristotle's practice of restricting despotism to exotic practices, while applying to abuses at home the name of tyranny.

3. In the sixteenth century Jean Bodin redefined the theory of despotism in a way that made it a central theme in the discussions of sovereignty, slavery, and conquest by Grotius, Pufendorf, Filmer, Hobbes, Locke, and Rousseau. Yet Bodin did not himself employ either the Latin equivalents for *despótēs* (*despotia, principatus despoticus*) introduced by William of Moerbeke or those in French (*princey despotique, despotic, despotes*) coined by Nicole Oresme.

One demonstration of the progress made by early Renaissance humanists was the retranslation from the Greek into Latin of Aristotle's *Politics* by the Florentine, Leonardo Bruni, early in the fifteenth century. Leonardo Bruni replaced Moerbeke's equivalents by Latin words connected for the most part with *dominus* and *dominatio*. Although Leonardo Bruni's rejection of words based upon *despótēs* prevailed, later scholars substituted for terms based on *dominus* those Latin words *erus* and *erilis* (*herus, herilis*) which referred to a master of slaves and his relationship to them. Jean Bodin adopted the term *seigneur* as the equivalent of *despótēs* for one of his three varieties of government in the French version of the *Six livres de la République* (1576); while in his Latin version (1586) he used *dominatus*.

The theory of despotic government in Bodin must be understood in terms of three aspects of his political thought: his theory of sovereignty, his distinction between the forms of states or commonwealths and the forms of governments; and the relationship he asserted to exist between the forms of states and climate. "Sovereignty is that absolute and perpetual power vested in a commonwealth. . . ." In the case of a monarchy, although the ruler of a commonwealth (*république, res publica*) is above human, positive law, he is subject to divine and natural law. But is not monarchy so defined identical with despotic rule? Bodin found his answer in the second of his innovations, the sharp distinction he drew between forms of state and forms of government. In his treatment of monarchy, for instance, Bodin both distinguished the three forms of government and made it clear that despotical rule could occur in aristocratic or popular states.

Bodin introduced several departures in the theory of despotism. Principal among them was his use of the term to designate a theory first found in the Roman Law by which slavery and appropriation of property was justified by reference to the rights of conquerors in a just war—a momentous step that in large part was responsible for the interest shown in despotism by Grotius, Pufendorf, Hobbes, Locke, and Rousseau. He thus gave a new turn to the ancient connection between despotism, slavery, and the rights of conquest. Furthermore, Bodin by identifying the Turkish Empire with Oriental despotism implanted the notion that under this form of government private and property rights were unknown, and that the despot was the legal owner of all individuals and goods which he could treat as he liked. This view, later adopted by Montesquieu, was to be challenged as a matter of fact in the great eighteenth-century debate about the validity of the concept of despotism. Bodin made the first attempt to place despotic monarchy within a chronological scheme (a step to be repeated with individual variations by Boulanger, Constant, Hegel, and Marx). Bodin considered despotic monarchy to have been the first form of government known to men. To Aristotle's view that the first kings were elected, Bodin opposed the theory stated in the canon law that lordship began with Nimrod, and originated in human iniquity. Bodin, like Aristotle, believed that "the peoples of Europe are prouder and more belligerent than inhabitants of Asia and Africa."

Bodin followed Aristotle in his belief that "tyrannies quickly come to ruin, but . . . despotic states and despotic monarchies have proved both great and enduring." But Bodin passed over Aristotle's emphasis upon the tacit consent of subjects and the consequent legitimacy of despotism for Asians. Nor was Bodin's lack of interest in consent accidental. His own theory of sovereignty was calculated to undermine theories that derived the legitimacy of rule from the consent of the governed, a doctrine the implications of which had been made clear in his own time by the Monarchomachs.

Hugo Grotius and Samuel Pufendorf knew and significantly used the concept of despotism both as formulated by classical writers, and as rephrased by Bodin. In his *De iure belli ac pacis* (1625), Grotius designated despotism by the word *herilis,* as in *imperium herile;* as did Pufendorf, in his *De iure naturae et gentium libri octo* (1673), a chapter of which is called *De potestate herili. Herilis* was rendered as *despotique* by Jean Barbeyrac, who by his annotated translations and commentaries made Grotius and Pufendorf into authors familiar to every French reader concerned with political thought. Of these, perhaps the most attentive to these two authors and critical of them was Rousseau, whose *Contrat social* may be understood as a response, M. Derathé tells us, to Pufendorf's brief and abstract digest, *De officio hominis et civis* (1673), also translated by Barbeyrac. Arguments, sometimes defining, sometimes justifying despotic rule figure prominently in discussions by Grotius and Pufendorf of slavery, conquest, and sovereignty. Through them, the concept of despotism was made into a theme central to political writing in the seventeenth and eighteenth centuries. Grotius provided the justification for slavery used by Bossuet and was carefully considered by Robert Filmer and Hobbes. Locke owned almost all of Pufendorf's works and corresponded with Barbeyrac; Peter Laslett has suggested that Locke's concern with Hobbes probably stemmed from Pufendorf's critique of Hobbes.

Although representing himself as the founder of a natural and international law based upon the nature of man and of reason, Grotius in practice subordinated questions of right to maxims of the civil law, to historical precedents, all of which he regarded as of equal value. This juristic relativism was prominent in his justifications of despotic rule and slavery. A people may be rightfully enslaved in two ways: (1) by the law of nature it is free to decide to exchange its liberty for subsistence or security; (2) by the law of nations, conquerors in a just war may grant life to the defeated people in exchange for their perpetual enslavement. In the first case, a people may give up its liberty voluntarily because its members are, as Aristotle demonstrated, slaves by nature. Grotius carefully assembled all the classical texts ascribing a servile nature to Orientals, to which he added Hebrew kingship (imitated from such neighbors as the Persians, which may explain divine opposition to Israel taking a king). Grotius, when treating the rights of conquerors in a just war, takes a position that reduces Bodin's category of despotical government to one of three possible outcomes. A conqueror may reduce men to a subjection purely civil, purely personal (despotic), or mixed. A people defeated in a just war may be treated in any of these ways and remain a state, or may lose that status, and become the property of a master who treats his subjects as slaves, whose interest he may rightfully subordinate to his own. Such rule is characteristic of despotism, not civil authority among free peoples (Grotius: *quod herilis est imperii non civilis;* Barbeyrac: *ce qui, selon Aristote, est le caractère distinctif du Pouvoir Despotique par opposition au Gouvernement Civil*).

Grotius refused to condemn slavery in all its forms, defining complete servitude, which consists of serving a master in return for being provided with all necessities. "If this form of subjection . . . is kept within the limits of Nature, there is nothing excessively severe

about it. For the lifelong obligation to work is repaid by the lifelong certainty of support, which is often lacking to those who work for hire by the day" (*De iure*, II, v, xxv).

Grotius certified as legitimate any enslavement consented to freely by a naturally servile people, or one willing to sacrifice its liberty for other advantages. Although identifying Orientals as naturally servile, Grotius did not confine despotism to them. His second form of despotic rule based on the rights of conquerors was from one point of view, a theory of consent, but one which recognized as valid obligations those promises made because of threat to life or security. Hobbes took the same position, but based it unequivocally on consent.

Pufendorf attempted to justify slavery and despotic rule simply on the basis of consent. The absolute power of a conqueror over the defeated, of master over slaves, or of a sovereign over his subjects are equally legitimate if based upon pacts of submission. Pufendorf stated that "although the consent of the subjects is required for the establishment of any kind of legitimate authority, . . . sometimes a people is required by the violence of war to consent to the authority of the victor." He added that the war must be just. A kingdom so gained is held as a patrimony, which by the caprice of the ruler may be divided, alienated, or transferred to anyone he pleases, for by arms, he has gained a people of his own. These prerogatives do not belong to kings who have been chosen by the will of the people (*De officio*, II, ix).

Pufendorf was so confident about his argument justifying despotic rule on the basis of consent that he rejected the Aristotelian case for natural slavery. Men by nature, Pufendorf asserted, enjoy equal liberty. If this is to be curtailed, their consent must be secured, whether that consent be express, tacit, or interpretative, or else they must have done something whereby others have secured the right to deprive them of their equality (*De iure*, III, II, 8).

Because of the political struggles waged in early seventeenth-century England, Bodin's theory of sovereignty was of great interest, and was translated by Richard Knolles in 1606 from a conflation of the French and Latin texts of the *Republic*. *Monarchie seigneurale* and *dominatus* were rendered as "lordly monarchy," as distinguished from the "royall" and "tirannical" varieties. But Hobbes restored the original Greek form and gave it a prominent place in his system at a time when other writers and his audience regarded the term as pejorative; Locke found that by distinguishing "paternal, political, and despotical power," he could strike directly at his principal target, Filmer, and indirectly at Hobbes. By the end of the century

5

Locke had succeeded in restoring its pejorative sense to the word despot and its derivatives.

Hobbes in part followed Bodin's treatment of despotical government, and in part diverged from it in ways that clearly show the thrust of his own thought. From Bodin, Hobbes derived the theory of a type of government that originated in the submission of the conquered to the conqueror and thus legitimately held sovereignty or absolute power. And although Bodin did give Oriental examples of this form, he did not limit it to any one form of state, or to Orientals. Hobbes followed him in this as well. But Bodin had restricted legitimacy to those conquerors only who had participated in a just war, and placed no emphasis whatever on the consent of the conquered to serve as slaves in return for their lives being spared. Hobbes, on the contrary, omitted any mention of the just war, which figured in the formulations of Bodin, Grotius, and Pufendorf. And Hobbes chose as the binding element in dominion, not victory and the rights it confers, but covenant, the consent of the defeated. That such consent derives from fear does not distinguish it, in Hobbes's view, from the origin of any other type of government. A man becomes subject to another from the fear of not preserving himself. Hobbes's formulation may explain why Montesquieu later chose to designate fear as the principle or operative passion of despotism.

Hobbes treated despotic government in *The Elements of Law* (first version, 1640), in *De cive* (1642), and in the *Leviathan* (1651), but he did not adopt Bodin's distinction between types of commonwealth and types of government. Already in the *Elements* Hobbes was concerned to discredit Aristotle's distinction between good and vitiated governments: "that there is one government for the good of him who governeth, and another for the good of them that be governed, whereof the former is despotical (that is lordly), the other a government of freemen." When Hobbes insisted that there are but three types of commonwealth, monarchy, aristocracy, and democracy, depending upon how many held sovereignty, he did not deviate from Bodin (Part II, Ch. 5, no. 1). But in rejecting the types of government, Hobbes was clearly breaking down whatever elements of censure could be derived even from Bodin, whose view of tyrannical government involved a condemnation of it. Hobbes could brook not even this: ". . . the name of tyranny signifies nothing more, nor less, than the name of sovereignty, be it in one or many men, saving that they that use the former word, are understood to be angry with them they call tyrants" (*Leviathan*, ed. Michael Oakeshott, Oxford [1947], p. 463).

Beginning with the *Elements*, Hobbes distinguished between commonwealths created by institution, that form of union whereby many because they fear one another cede sovereignty to an individual or council by mutual agreement; and bodies politic patrimonial and despotic because of fear of an invader, to whom they subject themselves. In Hobbes's preface to his Latin treatise, *De cive*, he repeated the distinction between states originating in *dominium paternum et despoticum*, which he called *naturale*, and another type of *dominium* established by institution, called *politicum* created by artifice. Chapter 20 of the second part of *Leviathan*, "Of Dominion Paternal, and Despotical," treats commonwealth by acquisition, as distinguished from commonwealth by institution, the subject of the previous chapter. In both types, men choose their sovereign out of fear and consent to obey him unconditionally. But in a commonwealth by acquisition, subjects fear him to whom they cede sovereignty; in a commonwealth by institution, the subjects fear one another.

Within this scheme, Hobbes defined despotical dominion (in the Latin version; *dominium herile in servos*):

Dominion acquired by conquest, or victory is that which some writers call *despotical*, from Δεσπότης which signifieth a *lord* or *master;* and is the dominion of the master over the servant. . . . It is not . . . the victory that giveth the right of dominion over the vanquished, but his own covenant.

Hobbes created a greater gap than had thus far existed between the Greek and medieval concepts of despotism, and the sixteenth- and seventeenth-century formulation of it. Total submission derived from fear thereby was made into the sole basis of political obligation. In his "Review and Conclusion" to *Leviathan*, Hobbes made clear the importance he attributed to despotical dominion: whoever conquered and could provide peace and union ought to be obeyed.

Locke's concept of despotical power was deployed against his principal target, Filmer, and only secondarily against Hobbes. At the beginning of his second *Treatise* (*Two Treatises of Government*, 1690), Locke urges the necessity of distinguishing political power, properly so-called, the "power of a *Magistrate* over a Subject . . . from that of a *Father* over his children, a *Master* over his Servant, a *Husband* over his Wife, and a *Lord* over his Slave. After defining political power, and considering it apart from other types of power, Locke in Chapter XV returned to ". . . Paternal, Political, and Despotical Power, considered together." Paternal power was dismissed by Locke, as a temporary power exerted by parents over children during the time when they were not yet capable of living as freemen. In order to contrast political with despotical power, Locke recapitulated:

Political Power is that Power which every Man, having in the state of Nature, has given up into the hands of the Society, and therein to the Gouvernors, whom the Society hath set over itself, with this express or tacit Trust, That it shall be employed for their good, and the preservation of their Property.

Thus political power, which must originate from compact, agreement, and mutual consent, cannot be an absolute, arbitrary power over the lives and fortunes of those who comprise a society.

By contrast to political power, despotical power is defined by Locke as a condition in which not property but persons only are at the Master's complete disposal. Despotical power is exerted by Lords in an absolute and arbitrary fashion for their own benefit over such as are stripped of all property because they have forfeited all rights by being aggressors in an unjust war. Locke thus contradicts in a number of ways Hobbes's assertion that despotical dominion does not differ qualitatively from any other legitimate form. For Locke defines despotical power as "an Absolute, Arbitrary Power one Man has over another to take away his Life, whenever he pleases." This is aimed against Hobbes's interpretation of despotical power as involving on the conqueror's side, the renunciation of his right to kill the defeated. But Locke denies that despotical power can be created as the result of a covenant, which alone can make it equivalent with other forms of legitimate rule (*Locke's Two Treatises of Government*, ed. Peter Laslett, Cambridge [1963], para. 172).

Locke rejected the notion that men could be rightly enslaved merely as the result of conquest. His feelings ran strongest when considering the application of such a doctrine to his own country: "Slavery is so vile and miserable an Estate of Man, and so directly opposite to the generous Temper and Courage of our Nation; that 'tis hardly to be conceived that an *Englishman*, much less a *Gentleman* should plead for 't." These words begin the first *Treatise*, and are aimed at Filmer. Because both *Treatises* were occasional pieces, they did not take up the full range of questions treated by Bodin, Grotius, Hobbes, and Pufendorf. Locke has but one brief chapter on slavery. Anticipating his subsequent treatment of despotical power, Locke concluded that freedom from absolute, arbitrary power is so joined to self-preservation that "a man, not having the power of his own Life, *cannot*, by Compact, or his own consent, *enslave himself* to any one . . ." (para. 23). But there appears to be an inconsistency between both his indignant rejection of the notion that Englishmen could ever be rightfully enslaved, and his careful circumscription of the rights of victory in a just war, on the one side; and his practice as an administrator concerned with slave-owning colonies in North America

on the other. The *Fundamental Constitutions of Carolina* provide that every freeman "shall have absolute power and authority over his negro slaves." In 1698 Locke helped draft the Instructions to Governor Nicholson of Virginia. These treat slaves as rightly so because they were captives in a just war, who had forfeited their lives by some act that deserved death. This would imply Locke's commitment to the belief that all slaves captured and sold in Africa were guilty of such acts, and that those Europeans engaged in the slave trade were carrying on a just war. But when arguing against Filmer about the rights of Englishmen, Locke was quite capable of seeing that a title gained by "Bargain and Money," rests not on natural law, but on quite another basis.

As Polin has remarked, Locke's theory should logically have led him to a categorical condemnation of slavery. Given the actual practice of the slave trade, it was indefensible for Locke to justify Negro slavery in North America as meeting his criterion of personal punishment for aggression in an unjust war. Nor did any of Locke's arguments justify ownership by men who had simply paid money for slaves who had never damaged them, nor perpetual enslavement of the children of slaves. The contrast between Locke's sensitivity to the freedom of Englishmen and his sophistries about Africans recalls the comparable attitude of Aristotle in relation to Greeks and barbarians. Algernon Sidney, who also wrote to refute Filmer, was overtly contemptuous of Asians and Africans, and argued that the superiority of a free people can be demonstrated from its capacity to conquer those who are naturally unfree.

4. It was in the seventeenth century that French writers began to show some interest in both the cluster of concepts associated with despotic government and in the Greek form of the word instead of accepting Loys Le Roy and Bodin's use of the word *seigneurale* as the French equivalent. New political circumstances, both at home and abroad contributed to the shift towards revival of terms connected with *despotique*, one of the 450 neologisms successfully introduced into French by Nicole Oresme in his translations of Aristotle. Within France domestic resistance to the Crown by aristocrats and Huguenots, categories by no means mutually exclusive, coincided with the identification of the Ottoman Empire as the seat of Oriental despotism. During the Fronde, the type of royal power exercised by the Sultan was called *despotique*, and distinguished from that recognized by French constitutional usage: "Not all monarchies are *despotiques;* only the Turkish is of that kind" (Derathé, "Les philosophes . . . ," p. 61).

After the revocation of the Edict of Nantes, French Huguenots in Holland and England began to use the term *despotique* for the polemical purpose of compar-

7

ing the absolutism of Louis XIV to that of the Turkish Grand Seigneur. In the famous anonymous pamphlets, *Les soupirs de la France esclave* (1689–90), its author noted with satisfaction the Glorious Revolution in England, and hoped that this would spur the rebirth in France of *l'amour pour la patrie*. This phrase was used in virtually the same sense in La Bruyère's *Les caractères*, where it is contrasted with *le despotique: Il n'y a point de patrie dans le despotique, d'autre choses y suppléent: l'intérêt, la gloire, le service du prince.* This conjunction between Anglophile Huguenot exiles on the one side and the aristocratic opposition to Louis XIV on the other, culminated in Montesquieu's use of the term *le despotisme* to characterize a distinctive type of government, incompatible with monarchy, whether of the tolerant, limited, and parliamentary type victorious in England, or with that known to the ancient French constitution as interpreted by nobles, *parlements*, and corporations hostile to royal centralization.

The author of the *Soupirs* declared that the King had replaced the state, that the Church, the *parlements*, the nobility, and the cities were all oppressed by an arbitrary power just as despotic as that of the Grand Seigneur. This *puissance despotique* was contrary to reason, humanity, the spirit of Christianity itself. The despotic spirit was manifest in the revocation of the Edict of Nantes, in royal distribution of offices by appointment to new men, in its management of finances, and its constant resort to war. The author drew conclusions of great significance, although they were to be generally acknowledged only after the publication of *De l'esprit des lois* (1748): a tyrannical government, he argued, was less dangerous than one that was despotic. For a tyranny is limited to the individual deviation of a ruler, but a despotic government is a system, once found only among Orientals, but now becoming established in France. Its subjects are "in a condition of servitude, they own nothing, their property and their lives, are always up in the air, depending upon the caprice of a single man."

The step from *le despotique* to *le despotisme* was taken by Pierre Bayle and Fénelon. Bayle, who opposed the calls to action of his archenemy, Pierre Jurieu, and of the author of the *Soupirs*, argued against the notion that a sharp distinction separated despotism from monarchy. Anticipating Voltaire's critique of Montesquieu, Bayle contended that the Grand Seigneur observed laws, just as did the Grand Monarque; there are more and less absolute kings, but the notion of the despot corresponds to no known reality, and is but a political weapon.

This was not the view of those highly placed aristocrats who deplored the increase in royal power, and

who sought to prepare in secret for the successor to Louis XIV, a group which included Fénelon, Louis de Saint-Simon, and Henri de Boulainvilliers. During the Regency Montesquieu was to meet Boulainvilliers and the Abbé Saint-Pierre. In contrast to his opponent, Bossuet, Fénelon espoused the rights of the feudal aristocracy, denounced royal centralization, mercantilism, and constant resort to war. In France, no one speaks of the state and its rules, but only of the king and his pleasure. In *Télémaque*, Fénelon has Mentor preach that absolute power creates not subjects, but slaves. Sovereigns who take sole possession of the state ultimately ruin it. Elsewhere Fénelon denounced both *le despotisme* of sovereigns and that of the people. Wisdom in government consists in finding a mean between these two extremes, that is, in *une liberté modérée par la seule autorité des lois*. When *le despotisme* is at its height, it acts more speedily and effectively than any *gouvernement modéré*; when exhausted and bankrupt, no one will come to its defense. In 1712 Saint-Simon compared the unprecedented authority exercised by Louis XIV with that of Oriental rulers, a comparison further accentuated by reference to his isolation by his ministers from the public. This image of Louis XIV as the Grand Seigneur or other Oriental despot was completed by the Abbé Saint-Pierre in his *Polysynodie* (1718), where he described the *visirat*, the delegation of power to a minister by an absolute ruler, or the alternative *demi-visirat*, where the ruler shares authority with two or more ministers, "much as did Louis XIV with Colbert and Louvois," as Rousseau wrote in his extract.

5. By choosing despotism as one of the three basic types of government, Montesquieu made the term into one of the central issues in eighteenth-century political thought. In part this was due to the fact that Montesquieu's views served the purposes of important groups with important interests; *De l'esprit des lois* was regarded as the statement of the most distinguished thinker associated with the *thèse nobiliare*. The informed reader could not miss the affinities between Montesquieu, Fénelon, Saint-Simon, Boulainvilliers, and the Abbé Saint-Pierre; not to mention spokesmen for the *parlements* after Montesquieu's death. Yet Montesquieu's theory of despotism appealed directly to Rousseau, Robespierre, and Saint-Just, whose sympathies were not identified with the *parlements* and hereditary aristocracy. Montesquieu has some claim to have transcended the mere interests of his class; any such case must be based on the demonstration that his theory of despotism served nobler purposes than the rationalization of prejudices of a privileged caste.

In his treatment, Montesquieu took into account virtually every development of the concept of despotism from its formulation in Greece to its identification with slavery, and its most recent form as a system of government. Like the other two types of government, despotism had to be analyzed in terms of its nature or structure, and its principle or operative passion. As a concept, despotism was an ideal type, a concept built by logic to assist investigation. It is not expected that such an analytical construct will be found to be empirically embodied in all its aspects. An ideal type is designed to determine the extent to which any actual state of affairs approximates to, or diverges from a postulated model. Montesquieu makes this point clearly about despotism:

It would be an error to believe that there has ever existed anywhere in the world a human authority that is despotic in all its aspects. . . . Even the greatest power is limited in some way. If the Grand Seigneur . . . were to attempt to impose some new tax, the resulting outcry would be such as to make him observe the limits to which he had not known he was subject. Although the King of Persia may be able to force a son to kill his father . . . , the same King cannot force his subjects to drink wine. Every nation is dominated by a general spirit, on which its very power is founded. Anything undertaken in defiance of that spirit is a blow against that power, and as such must necessarily come to a stop (Considérations, XIII).

Although a number of the strands previously associated with the concept of despotism recur in Montesquieu's formulation, it shares the significant innovations made in his way of theorizing about politics. Thus despotism was for him, not simply a structure of state power and offices, but a system with a characteristic social organization propelled by fear, a passion peculiar to it. Montesquieu refused to reduce social organization to political form, or political form to social organization. In his view, both the political institutions and the social organization of despotic societies are simple, while those of a monarchy as he defines it, are complex. This he argues in a number of ways: an analysis of the ties uniting despotic and free societies; as well as by contrasting with free societies, the characteristics peculiar to despotism; its suppression of conflict in the name of order; its refusal to recognize the legal status of intermediate groups and classes; and finally its insistence upon immediate and unquestioned obedience to commands. In a free society, the texture of relations among persons and groups is much looser than in a despotism. Disagreements and even conflict are essential to the one, fatal to the other (Considérations, IX).

Montesquieu contrasted the distinctive modes of obedience requisite to despotic governments on the one side, and free governments on the other. The positive side of Montesquieu's political thought cannot be understood without reference to the characteristics of despotism. Many who have declared unsatisfactory Montesquieu's definition of freedom as security from fear, have not grasped his contrast with despotism, which he saw as actuated precisely by that passion. Similarly, the essential features of politics in a free government are the limitation of power, the recognition and accommodation of groups conceded to have some autonomy, the regular discussion between them and the sovereign of alternatives to proposals judged to be adverse to their interests by the parties affected by legislation, and the preference for obedience based on consent (De l'esprit des lois, III, x).

Passive obedience presupposes education of a kind peculiar to despotism: the subject must be ignorant, timid, broken in spirit, requiring little legislation. Social relations must also follow a pattern: in a despotism, every family is, as a matter of policy, isolated from every other. Only religion and custom can moderate despotism, and these are at once less effective and less regular in their operation than the effect of basic laws that limit governments which willingly observe them. Even in the sphere of economic life, despotism exerts noxious effects. The general uncertainty created by the caprice of the despot and his viziers impoverishes the mass of men; commerce is unrewarding, the products of labor, incalculable.

Because of his method, Montesquieu was able to develop the psychological dimensions of despotism. Fear, the principle or passion imputed to despotism, is treated with a subtlety and depth previously unknown. Hobbes, who had founded so much on fear, as the principle underlying all politics was much in Montesquieu's mind, when he argued that no such system can satisfy its members. The units of despotism are the despot himself; his viziers or ministers, to whom he confides administration; and his subjects, equal in their total subjugation and terror. In the Persian Letters (Lettres persanes, 1721), Montesquieu depicted despotism as a system of fear, jealousy, and mutual suspicion. This is illustrated in the relationships among the master of the seraglio, absent in Paris; his eunuchs, who have been sacrificed to the execution of his wishes and the maintenance of order; and his wives. This triangular relationship, because of its inhumanity, absence of liberty, the use of force and fear in a relationship where love ought to rule, fails to provide even its ostensible beneficiary, the master of the seraglio, with the fulfilment he sought. The ultimate paradox is that the master is incapable of enforcing or enjoying his unlimited power; he cannot satisfy himself.

Yet in the final analysis, Montesquieu condemned not only despotism, as conceived by the members of his class, but also slavery and all other forms of total domination as incompatible with human nature, natu-

9

ral law, and the interests of all parties linked in such relationships. No political philosopher prior to Montesquieu had taken such an uncompromising view; no other thinker of his century condemned slavery with greater vehemence than did Montesquieu, a fact which explains in part the respect Voltaire and Rousseau had for him.

In Book XV of *De l'esprit des lois*, Montesquieu set out to refute the justifications of slavery, conquest, and colonialism found in theorists of despotism from Bodin on. Slavery, the absolute right held by a master over the life and property of a slave, is contrary to nature. Nor is it justifiable even on utilitarian grounds. Its effects are deleterious to master and slave alike. No matter what the climate, all necessary work can be performed by freemen. Slavery is in the long run fatal to both monarchies and republics.

Nor did Montesquieu accept any of the justifications for total domination given in the Roman Law or by later jurists. He denied that the claim to enslave men could be justified by attributing pity to conquerors. The reasons given by jurists were absurd. Even in war, only necessity can create the right to kill. A victor has no right to murder a captive in cold blood. Nor does a man have a right to sell himself into slavery. Such a sale presupposes a price. But to give up one's status as a freeman is an act of such extravagance that it cannot be supposed to be the act of a rational being. And how can the enslavement of children as yet unborn be justified by any act or promise on the part of their parents or ancestors? Slavery violates both the natural and the civil law. A criminal may be justly punished because the law he has violated has been made in his favor, and he had benefited from it. But the same cannot be true of the slave, to whom law can never serve any purpose. This violates the fundamental principle underlying all human societies.

As for other arguments offered in defense of slavery, Montesquieu riddled them with scorn. Often they derived from nothing more than the contempt felt by one nation for another with different customs; often, from the absurd pretension that a nation could be reduced to slavery in order to simplify the task of converting it to the true faith. Such reasoning had encouraged those who had ravaged the Americas to believe that they merited absolute power. How pleasant to act as a bandit and to be considered a good Christian. Slavery derives from the desire of a few for unlimited voluptuousness and luxury; slavery appeals to the basest of human passions. Whose desires would not be kindled by the prospect of becoming the absolute master of another's life, virtue, and property? As for Negro slavery, it derives not only from such passions thinly disguised by sophisms, but from the most contemptible of human prejudices. To unmask those who defended the African slave trade, Montesquieu reverted to the irony of the *Persian Letters* (XV, v). This section, together with that deriding the Inquisition, is incompatible with the image of Montesquieu as a self-serving *parlementaire* concerned to defend the privileges of his class.

6. (a) How prominent was the concept of despotism in French eighteenth-century thought after Montesquieu? In the analytical index to the *Encyclopédie*, the entry for *despotisme* runs to sixty-one lines; that for *tyrannie*, to twenty-eight. The Chevalier de Jaucourt, who wrote the principal entry, was a disciple of Montesquieu, as well as one of the editors' principal collaborators. The *Encyclopédie* helped to popularize Montesquieu in a way that, because it made his theories appear to be compatible with those of Diderot and D'Alembert, did not always coincide with Montesquieu's own intentions. Then in the eleventh volume, Diderot introduced an abridgment of Boulanger's *Recherches sur l'origine du despotisme oriental* under the title of *L'Oeconomie politique*. Boulanger (who will be discussed below) was dead, but his manuscripts were being circulated by Holbach because Boulanger had attributed the origin of despotism to a primitive theocracy based upon fear. In this way, despotism was turned into a concept that could be used against the Church.

This was not enough to redeem this aspect of Montesquieu for Voltaire, whose attitude was highly ambivalent, condemning Montesquieu's theory of despotism, but applauding his attack upon slavery. Against Montesquieu's position that despotism is a type of government qualitatively different from monarchy, Voltaire maintained: (1) that an extraordinary violation of historical usage was involved in Montesquieu's designation, now all too generally accepted, of the great empires of Asia and Africa as *despotiques*. In his *L'A.B.C.* (1768), Voltaire engaged in an etymology of *le despotisme*. It had been used in Greek only as *père de famille;* was unauthorized by Latin usage; in short, was an innovation in political language that was both unjustified and recent. (2) Montesquieu's image of the despot was a pure creation of his imagination: "a ferocious madman, who listens only to caprice; a barbarian whose courtiers prostrate themselves before him; and who diverts himself by having his agents strangle and impale [subjects] on all sides" (*Commentaire sur quelques maximes de l'Esprit des Lois*, III). (3) Voltaire disputed the accuracy of Montesquieu's data and citations, particularly those used to support his characterization of China as despotic: "It is regrettable that so intelligent a man engaged in sheer surmises supported by false citations" (*Oeuvres* [1785],

40, 94). (4) Voltaire, who believed in an absolute monarchy that would remove the hereditary privileges of the aristocracy, and in the *thèse royale* about the French constitution, objected to the political implications of Montesquieu's distinction between despotism and monarchy; whatever is valid in Montesquieu's theory is best described by distinguishing between monarchy and its abuses. And there is no reason whatever to make essential to the definition of monarchy its recognition of the rights of a self-seeking hereditary nobility, which belongs to feudalism, for which there is not much to be said (*Commentaire* . . . , III).

If Voltaire thought the concept of despotism to be an aristocratic invention, it was more than balanced in his mind by Montesquieu's attack on slavery. On balance, Voltaire declared *De l'esprit des lois* to be "the code of reason and liberty" (*Commentaire* . . .).

(b) It was precisely in this way that Rousseau was most affected by the concept of despotism. Every major statement of his political theory begins by refuting the apologies for slavery he found in Grotius, Pufendorf, and Hobbes. Like Voltaire, Rousseau did not use *le despotisme* to designate the type of dominion said to justify the enslavement of those conquered in a just war. But the concept of the master-slave relationship became connected in his mind with despotism.

Despotisme figured in Rousseau's thought in three further ways: (1) in his angry rejection of the Physiocratic term *le despotisme légal*, which will be treated in connection with the Physiocrats, and (2) in his partially sympathetic comments upon the French aristocratic use of *despotisme* to characterize an absolute political system on the Oriental model that had been imposed upon a European state. This usage occurs principally in his judgment upon the Abbé Saint-Pierre's model of the *visirat*, recapitulated by Rousseau as "a gross and barbaric form of government, pernicious to peoples, dangerous for kings, fatal to royal houses . . . the last resort of a decaying state" (*Oeuvres complètes*, Pléiade (Paris, 1959—), III, 644).

But Saint-Pierre's positive proposals were rejected because they would favor the privileges of hereditary aristocracy, which Rousseau called the worst of all forms of sovereignty. Rousseau commented that "a thousand readers will find this in contradiction with the *Contrat social*. This proves that there are even more readers who ought to learn to read than authors who ought to learn to be consistent" (ibid., 643). Rousseau's challenge is directly related to his statements defining despotism. He distinguished sovereignty, the legislative power, from government, the executive power which carries out the law. In the *Contrat social*, Rousseau divided aristocracies into three kinds: natural, elective, and hereditary. Hereditary aristocracy is the worst of

all governments; elective aristocracy, the best (III, v). In Rousseau's view there is an inherent tendency for government to seize sovereignty, for the Prince to oppress the sovereign, that is, the people, to become its master constraining it by force alone—acts which dissolve the social pact that alone morally obligates citizens to obey. It is here that Rousseau makes his principal and third use of *le despotisme*. Thus (3) is the distinction made between *Despote* and *Tyran*, which appears to rest upon much the same usage as *le despotisme* in the *Discours sur l'origine et les fondemens de l'inégalité parmi les hommes* (*Oeuvres*, op. cit., III, 190–91).

In the *Contrat social*, Rousseau resorts to his distinction in the chapter called, "The Abuse of Government and its Tendency to Degenerate" (III, x):

> In order to give different names to different things, I shall call any usurper of royal authority, a *tyrant;* and any usurper of the sovereign authority, a *despot*. The tyrant is he, who contrary to law, assumes the power to govern, and then follows the law; the despot puts himself above the laws themselves. Thus the tyrant may not be a despot, but a despot is always a tyrant.

In the *Discours sur* . . . *l'inégalité*, Rousseau sketched three stages, the third of which is the changing of legitimate into arbitrary power, the recognition of that distinction between master and slave, which is the final stage of inequality. Out of the disorders that preceded it arises gradually the "hideous head of despotism," which finally succeeds in trampling underfoot the laws and the people, and in establishing itself upon the ruins of the republic. The subjects of despotism become subject to the will of their master, who follows only his own passions. Thus Rousseau again has assigned the name of despotism to the extreme point of corruption, at which the social pact is broken. Thereafter "the despot is the master only so long as he is the strongest, and as soon as he can be driven out, he cannot protest against violence. The uprising that ends by strangling or dethroning a sultan is as lawful an act, as those by which he disposed . . . of the lives and goods of his subjects" (*Oeuvres*, III, 191).

Rousseau's way of distinguishing tyrant from despot is peculiar to himself, and is adapted to the categories of his own thought. He may have been the first to deny legitimacy to any king. This was not Montesquieu's position on monarchy. As for tyranny, Montesquieu had defined it as meaning "the intention to overthrow the established power, above all in a democracy. This was the sense it had for the Greeks and Romans" (*De l'esprit des lois*, XIV, xiv, a). Again Rousseau's notion that despotism originated in corruption resembled Montesquieu's, but departed from it in a way that reveals **11**

Rousseau's intentions. Montesquieu believed that every form of government could degenerate into a despotism characteristic of it. Thus democracy could become the despotism of all (*De l'esprit des lois,* VIII, vi). Rousseau denied this: "Any condition imposed by all upon each cannot be onerous to anyone" (*Lettres écrites de la montagne,* Lettre VIII, *Oeuvres,* III, 842).

(c) It is now generally agreed that there is no body of political ideas in the eighteenth century that can accurately be described as "enlightened despotism," a term invented by nineteenth-century German historians. A recent survey of the subject concluded:

'Enlightened despotism' is an unfortunate expression in three ways: it yokes together a disparate group of rulers who have far less in common than the collective name implies; it burdens them with the disparaging name of despot, which was already negatively charged in the eighteenth century, thus anticipating what needs to be proved; and it links these rulers, with its adjective more closely to the Enlightenment than in fact they were (Peter Gay, *The Enlightenment,* II, New York [1969], 682).

The idea of legal despotism" was explicitly formulated by Le Mercier de la Rivière in his *L'ordre naturel et essentiel des sociétés politiques* (1767), and Du Pont de Nemours in his *Origine et progrès d'une science nouvelle* (1768). Although they all favored an hereditary and powerful monarchy, the Physiocrats' theory of *despotisme légal* contained strong elements of constitutional and legal limitation on the monarch; they distinguished their theory from *despotisme arbitraire.* This in effect was Montesquieu's Oriental despotism, which by destroying all private property, destroys all the sources of wealth and industry. *Le despotisme légal* is not rule by the arbitrary will of the despot, but by the weight of evidence about the nature of things. Thus the sovereign does not express his will, but declares what seems in accord with the laws of social order. Le Mercier de la Rivière took Euclid as his model of the legal despot, who by the irresistible force of evidence, has ruled without contradiction over all enlightened peoples.

None of the distinctions and qualifications made by the Physiocrats protected them against the counter-arguments of Mably, Holbach, Rousseau, Raynal, and Turgot. Holbach wrote that "A legal despotism is a contradiction in terms" (*Système social,* London [1773], II, xiii). So great was the impression that had been made by Montesquieu. Rousseau attacked the Physiocratic doctrine on three points: (1) that the notion of basing politics on incontrovertible evidence is naive. "The science of government is nothing but a science of combinations [of elements], of applications, and exceptions according to times, places and circum-

stances." (2) Like the Abbé Saint-Pierre, the Physiocrats believe in the progressive advance of reason, although there is no cumulative progress. (3) Legal despotism is utopian because it simply assumes that a despot will rule according to his interests as the Physiocrats define them, that is in harmony with law and the interests of all. Rousseau concluded that almost all men know their interests and nevertheless disregard them: "Gentlemen, permit me to tell you, you assign too much weight to your calculations, and not enough to the inclinations of the human heart and the play of its passions. Your system is too good for the inhabitants of Utopia: it has no value whatever for the children of Adam" (C. E. Vaughan, ed., *Political Writings of Rousseau,* Cambridge [1915], II, 159–61).

(d) Nicolas-Antoine Boulanger's *Recherches sur l'origine du despotisme oriental* was published posthumously by Holbach in 1761 in Geneva, and was translated by John Wilkes in 1764 in London. Boulanger was an engineer, who constructed a theory of the development of religion and society after a universal deluge. Boulanger sought to work out a scheme of historical stages from theocracy to despotism, republic, monarchy, thus providing a philosophical and historical justification for Montesquieu's theory of despotism. Boulanger ascribed its origins to primitive idolatry and theocracy, animated by the spirit of terror which was later maintained in despotism. In theocracy, it is the gods who are given supreme power. Sacerdotal governments are regarded as the physical manifestation of the supernatural government; the invisible master assumed human form in the reign of priests who became legislators. Despotic government followed the sacerdotal, and with it recorded history begins. Boulanger was implying, and this was why he was taken up by Diderot and Holbach, that religious beliefs originated in the fears and hopes of those who survived the great deluge. He also hoped to discover the origin of the forms of government. His thesis is that after the initial terror caused by the deluge, human history would be a struggle between man and the false idea he carries within him, the idea that political institutions ought to express the only true authority, which is that of God. Holbach expressed similar views in *La contagion sacrée* and *Le système social.*

Thus it may appear that politically the concept was at its zenith, pressed into service as a political weapon, and, intellectually, equally in vogue, as for example with the impressive array of students of human history and society produced by the Scottish Enlightenment. Adam Ferguson called the final part of his *Essay on the History of Civil Society* (1767), "Of Corruption and Political Slavery," and the last chapter "Of the Progress and Termination of Despotism." Ferguson, however, showed how the conceptions of corruption and despotism could be combined with optimism about the future:

> National poverty . . . and the suppression of commerce are the means by which despotism comes to accomplish its own destruction. . . . When human nature appears in the utmost state of corruption, it has actually begun to reform. . . . Men of real fortitude, integrity, and ability are well placed in every scene; . . . the states they compose . . . survive, and . . . prosper (Edinburgh [1966], pp. 278–80).

Yet the doctrine of despotism, when utilized for so many purposes by such heterogeneous groups, began to become increasingly vague as it came into general usage. And the evidence upon which the concept was based had begun to be seriously challenged, first by Voltaire, and then with much more weight by Abraham-Hyacinthe Anquetil-Duperron (1731–1805), a pioneer student of Oriental languages and history. The attack he launched on Montesquieu and the theory of despotism considered as an empirical theory applicable to the Oriental empires classified as despotic was so serious that it probably merited the abandonment of the concept, at least until much more reliable work had been done than was then available. It is interesting to speculate what Hegel, Marx, and Engels would have written about despotism, had they known of Anquetil-Duperron's *Législation orientale* (1778). For this was an authentic work of the Enlightenment, cosmopolitan in its respect for other civilizations, while Hegel, Marx, and Engels regarded the Orient as inferior to Europe, which alone possessed the principle of progress.

(f) Anquetil-Duperron, a grocer's son, had become fascinated by references to the Avesta, the sacred document of the religion of Zoroaster, who founded the religion professed by the Iranians at the time of the Achaemenidae. This was the dynasty that was in the minds of the Greeks when they first coined the term despotism. No one in eighteenth-century Europe could translate the language in which the Avesta was written. Anquetil made his way to India, persuaded the Parsees to teach him what they knew about their sacred book, and after living in India from 1755 to 1761, returned to France, where he published his translation. But he found the minds of most Europeans closed to new knowledge about the Orient by the obsessive image of despotism enshrined in Montesquieu. Anquetil argued that there was no basis in fact for attributing despotism to Turkey, Persia, and India, where private property existed, and rulers were bound by codes of written laws. On the basis of inaccurate reports, which he was not trained to assess, Montesquieu had selected evidence to suit his own purposes. Nor was the issue merely of historical interest. Anquetil asserted that this

distorted image of the Orient had provided the excuse for Europeans such as the English in India to confiscate native lands and wealth. If no private property existed under despotism, then the conqueror could take everything in the country because it had belonged to the defeated despot. In his *Législation orientale* (1778), Anquetil denounced foreign exploitation of the peoples of Hindustan, to whom he dedicated his book.

Anquetil censured the arrogance as well as the rapacity of the West, which believed that it knew everything, when in fact it knew nothing about the rest of the world. From the height of the pyramid built upon the classical learning of the Greeks and Romans, the Europeans scorned those other civilizations, which, however, they condescended to despoil. There was a considerable degree of irony in the fact that the concept of despotism from its beginning had been based on the Persians as the model for those barbarians who consent to be thus ruled because they are slaves by nature. Anquetil, who learned the language of the ancient Persians and their history was confronting the concept of despotism after a long development.

Anquetil undertook to support by positive evidence the position anticipated by Bayle and Voltaire: despotism is not a distinctive form of government, but a violation of monarchy and its own constitutional principles. Anquetil did not defend all the practices of Asiatic rulers. What he argued was that the facts demonstrated that their abuses ran contrary to what made their authority legitimate. In this respect, there was no difference between Asia and Europe.

7. (a) Given the prominence of the concept of despotism in the political vocabulary of those hostile to the French monarchy in the eighteenth century, it is not surprising that the term was deployed by many of those who wished to justify all or some part of the Revolution. But few could have predicted that the Terror would be defended in such terms by Robespierre, Saint-Just, and Marat, while it turned out to be equally inviting to liberal critics of the Terror and Napoleon such as Madame de Staël and Constant.

The characterization of the Terror as "the despotism of liberty," came not from its enemies, but from Robespierre, who sought to prove that terror and virtue both were necessary; "If the spring of popular government in time of peace is virtue; its spring in time of revolution is simultaneously virtue and terror. Without virtue, terror is deadly; without terror, virtue has no power" (Report to the Convention, Feb. 5, 1794). Robespierre adapted the concepts of despotism he found in both Montesquieu and Rousseau. Montesquieu had attributed to each type of government a principle or operative passion: that of republics was civic virtue; that of despotism, fear. Robespierre substituted *la*   13 *terreur* for Montesquieu's *la crainte*, as though acknowledging that the terror being practiced was at once greater and more active. Robespierre himself asked whether its use of terror did not stamp the Committee of Public Safety as a despotism:

> It has been said that terror is the spring of despotic government. Does yours, then, resemble despotism? Yes, in just the way that the sword which gleams in the hands of liberty's heroes resembles that of tyranny's satellites. When the despot uses terror to govern his brutalized subjects, he is right as a despot; when you use terror to daunt the enemies of liberty, you are right as founders of the Republic. The government of the Revolution is the despotism of liberty over tyranny. Was force meant only to protect crime? (ibid.)

Robespierre defended terror as self-defense, as vengeance for centuries of oppression, as preparation for profound change. But he did so within the vocabulary of despotism: referring to that "public virtue which has produced so many wonders," the superiority of free peoples over all others, the memories of the triumph of Athens and Sparta over the tyrants of Asia (a conflation of tyranny and despotism); the connection between corruption and despotism in terms that recall Rousseau: "a nation is truly corrupted when, after having by degrees lost its character and its liberty, it passes from democracy to aristocracy or monarchy; it is the death of the body politic by decrepitude" (ibid.).

Saint-Just used a different formula: "A republican government has virtue for its principle, or else terror" (*Oeuvres complètes de Saint-Just*, ed. Charles Valley, 2 vols., Paris [1908], II, 538). Terror temporarily compensates for the absence of those institutions the Republic will create to repress bad habits created by corruption and despotism. Thus terror makes possible republican regeneration. Marat's formulation was closer to Robespierre's: "It is by violence that liberty ought to be established, and the moment has come to organize temporarily the despotism of liberty in order to wipe out the despotism of kings" (Soboul, *Histoire de la révolution française*, Paris [1970], I, 358).

(b) In Madame de Staël the aristocratic and the Protestant concepts of despotism were adapted to take into account the Revolution, Reign of Terror, and Bonapartism. The *thèse nobiliaire* resounds in her maxim that in Europe "liberty is ancient, and despotism, modern"; only there has liberty developed (*Considérations sur la révolution française*, I, Ch. II.). "Asia has always been lost in despotism, and what civilization there was remained stationary" (ibid., Ch. I). In her view of French history, the great despots are Louis XIV and Napoleon, because of their attacks upon liberty at home, and their constant resort to war in the name of national glory. To those who represented the

reign of Louis XIV as tranquil and glorious, she recalled all his acts of cruelty and violence, including the revocation of the Edict of Nantes, a precedent for punishing an entire category of persons, which the Convention followed in its actions against émigrés and aristocrats. The cause of the Revolution was ultimately the despotism and wars of Louis XIV; it was he who was Napoleon's model: both knew that despotism in France required foreign wars; one left France bankrupt and organized for despotism; the other, defeated and humiliated. A despot should not be judged by temporary military victories but by the condition in which he leaves his country.

Napoleon completed the organization of despotism in France. By eradicating all *corps intermédiaires*, by destroying freedom of the press, and by turning the people into his servile flatterers, he made it impossible for anyone to tell him the truth. This, Madame de Staël wrote, led to his downfall in Russia. At home he had sought to be the sole ruler, but he could not escape the logic of despotism. He had to retail his power to his venal agents, whom he then had to bribe. The military despotism he created made the prospects for liberty in France even more dismal than after Louis XIV. "Tyranny is a *parvenu;* despotism is a *grand seigneur;* but both are incompatible with human reason" (*Considérations*, II, Part VI, Ch. 12). Madame de Staël concluded that liberty, which had begun as aristocratic privilege, must be reconciled with that passion for equality that had inspired the Revolution. In the nineteenth century it would no longer be possible to defend a partial liberty without reference to its advantages for all.

Although Madame de Staël thus saw liberty as something that had to be adapted to the spirit of the new century, her view of Bonapartism did not stress its novelty. Despotism remained a relatively static rather than an evolving concept. The stagnation allegedly produced by Oriental despotism, the consequences produced by its structure and principle, are represented as eternal. She saw a continuity, rather than a sharp break between Louis XIV and Napoleon.

Benjamin Constant, however, stressed other and novel elements in the Terror and the Empire. In his *De l'esprit de la conquête* (1813), Constant for the first time suggested that despotism is an antiquated and static form of domination. What had occurred in the Terror and under Napoleon was a more active regime that penetrated more deeply and had a new basis for its power because of its revolutionary and democratic elements. Constant therefore coined the term "usurpation" for describing the form of rule exercised by Napoleon, and declared it to be worse than despotism. Although not always precise in his formulation of terms, Constant implied that usurpation used the despotic structures that already existed, but did so in its own distinctive way, creating a new type of oppression made possible by demagoguery, propaganda, democratic slogans, mass military mobilization, and the breakdown of the structures of a simpler society.

Yet his final judgment was that usurpation, like the spirit of conquest and the system of despotism, were all anachronistic, incompatible with the commercial spirit and pacifism of modern society. And he attributed the Terror to its unrealizable ideals formulated by imitators of ancient republics such as Rousseau and Mably, who did not understand the differences separating ancient from modern societies. The partisans of ancient political virtue found that the sort of liberty they sought could be attained only by despotism. And this involved them in fatal contradictions, which produced a more thorough control of thought and expression, a far more deliberate effort to use the state to terrorize its citizens than had the despotism of the old regime. Napoleon took advantage of these new devices, and also profited from the disgust felt by the populace at their use. The fear of Jacobinism was among his greatest assets.

Despotism for Constant carried the overtones of an older, more static form of rule, which reigning in silence prohibits all the forms of liberty, interdicts discussion, and demands passive obedience. But despotism at least allows its subjects to remain silent; usurpation "condemns him to speak, it pursues him into the intimate sanctuary of his thought; and forcing him to lie to his conscience, seizes from him the last consolation of the oppressed" (*Oeuvres*, ed. Alfred Roulin, Paris [1957], pp. 1004–45).

(c) Hegel assigned an important place to the concept of despotism, but that place was at the beginning of history. In his *Philosophy of History*, Hegel declared:

The history of the World travels from East to West, for Europe is absolutely the end of history. . . . The East knows and to the present day knows only that *One* is free; the Greek and Roman world, that *some* are free; the German world knows that *all* are free. The first political form therefore we observe in history, is *Despotism*, the second *Democracy* and *Aristocracy*, the third *Monarchy* (trans. J. Sibree, London [1905], pp. 109–10).

Hegel thus placed the concept of despotism within a framework of stages; his teleology culminated in Europe.

Hegel declared Oriental experience "unhistorical," despite its stability, a quality previously admired by Aristotle:

On the one side we see duration, stability—Empires belonging to mere space as it were—unhistorical history.

The States in question, without undergoing any change in themselves, or in the principle of their existence . . . are in ceaseless conflict, which brings rapid destruction. This history too . . . is really unhistorical, for it is only the repetition of the same majestic ruin (*Philosophy of History*, pp. 105–06).

Despite his low evaluation of the Oriental world, Hegel devoted not inconsiderable attention to it. In the East we find a political liberty which develops subjective freedom, but not conscience and duty. In the law men recognize, not their own will, but one entirely foreign to them.

Among Asian nations, Hegel grants only Persia a role in world history: it provides the external transition to Greek life, while the internal transition is provided by Egypt. Egypt and Persia together comprise a riddle, the solution of which is found in the Greek world.

The Persian Wars are treated by Hegel as the decisive period when the Greek spirit encountered the previous world-historical people:

Oriental despotism—a world united under one lord and sovereign—on the one side, and separate states—insignificant in extent and resources, but animated by free individuality—on the other side stood front. . . . Never in history has the superiority of spiritual power over material bulk . . . been made so gloriously manifest (ibid., p. 268).

Hegel employs the concept of despotism (*Despotismus*) in three ways: (1) generalizations derived from his view of the history and internal structure of Oriental despotism; (2) an ideal type of despotism in general, which could characterize any government; (3) identification with systems of domination such as master-slave (*Herrschaft-Slaverei*), or master-vassal (*Herrschaft-Knechtschaft*). Such divisions are for expository purposes only; they would have been rejected by Hegel, whose philosophical method had committed him to attempting to synthesize his philosophy of history and phenomenology of spirit with his study of the state and its forms. The *Philosophie des Rechts* not only ends with sections on the phases of mind (para. 352–53), but identifies each of them with a world-historical stage or realm, the first of which is the Oriental (para. 355).

(1) In an essay written during his Frankfurt period, Hegel wrote that Orientals have a fixed character, which never changes. The essence of the Oriental mind is force; one rules and the rest succumb. Their narrowness of character does not admit love; hence subjects must be bound by law that is external to them. Thus in the Orient two apparently contradictory tendencies are perfectly blended; the lust for domination over all and the voluntary submission to all forms of slavery. Over both reigns the law of necessity (Karl Rosenkranz, *Hegels Leben*, Berlin [1844], pp. 515–18). Hegel had

combined both Aristotle's definition of despotism as based on natural servility, and Montesquieu's treatment of the absence of love in the Oriental seraglio. The "form of government is theocratic, the ruler being regarded as a high priest of God himself; constitution and legislation are at the same time religion" (*Philosophie des Rechts*, para. 355). Distinctions based on superstitious ceremonies, the accidents of personal power, arbitrary rule, and class differences become crystallized into hereditary castes. The history of despotism is a tale of the vicissitudes of revolt, monarchical violence, civil war, and the overthrow of the state at home and abroad (ibid., para. 286).

(2) Hegel wished to distinguish sovereignty in his sense from despotism, which does not possess the essential qualities of constitutional monarchy and rational bureaucracy. Sovereignty must be distinguished from might and pure arbitrariness, or despotism which means: ". . . any state of affairs where law has disappeared and where the particular will as such, whether of a monarch or a mob (ochlocracy), counts as law or rather takes the place of law . . ." (ibid., para. 278). Constitutional monarchy is the reign of liberty and laws, to which the king is subject; despotism, that of the unrestrained will of a single man (*Encyklopädie der philosophischen Wissenschaften*, para. 544E).

(3) It has already been noted that with Oriental despotism Hegel associated a particular system of domination. There is an extended section dealing with the Master-Slave or Master-Servant relationship in the *Phänomenologie des Geistes* (IV, A) and another on the relationship between absolute freedom and terror, where another kind of total domination is attained (VI, B, III), although Hegel does not refer to the "despotism of liberty." In the *Philosophie des Rechts* Hegel considered the moral status of slavery. Characteristically he condemned as inadequate both justifications of slavery by reference to "physical force, capture in war, saving and preservation of life, upkeep, education, philanthropy, the slave's own acquiescence," and arguments for the absolute injustice of slavery (para. 57). According to Hegel, not until we recognize that the idea of freedom can be realized only through the state, can we arrive at an adequate basis for condemning slavery.

Two other positions taken in the *Philosophie des Rechts* merit attention: (1) the suggestion that the "inner dialectic of civil society thus drives it—or at any rate drives a specific civil society—to push beyond its own limits and seek markets, and so its necessary means of subsistence in other lands which are either deficient in the goods it has over-produced, or else generally backward in industry, etc." (para. 246). (2)

Hegel speaks of "the absolute right . . . of heroes to found states" (para. 350). "The same consideration justifies civilized nations in regarding and treating as barbarians those who lag behind them in institutions. . . . The civilized nation is conscious that the rights of barbarians are unequal to its own and treats their autonomy only as a formality" (para. 351). Hegel's insights into the dynamics and justification of colonialism were to be developed in his own way by Marx.

Marx was not interested in Oriental societies for their own sake. His first reference to them occurred in the *Communist Manifesto* (1848):

The bourgeoisie cannot exist without constantly revolutionizing the instruments of production, and with them the whole relations of society. . . . [I]t has made barbarian and semi-barbarian countries dependent on the civilized ones, nations of peasants on nations of bourgeois, the East on the West (Ch. I).

The unit of analysis was vague: "the East," "barbarian and semi-barbarian nations"; European capitalism held the center of the stage. Marx's story was told in Hegel's terms: "The Oriental empires always show an unchanging social infrastructure coupled with unceasing change in the persons and tribes who manage to ascribe to themselves the political superstructure" (Avineri, *Karl Marx on Colonialism*, p. 9).

Marx made but one attempt in the Hegelian style to fit Asia into his general scheme of development. In *A Contribution to the Critique of Political Economy* (1859), Marx wrote: "In broad outline we can designate the Asiatic, the ancient, the feudal, and the modern bourgeois methods of production as so many epochs in the progress of the economic formation of society" (Avineri, pp. 33–34).

Marx assumed rather than proved the similarity among all the societies he lumped together as sharing the Asiatic or Oriental mode of production. On the assumption that there was no private property in land, Marx developed the theory of a despotic centralized state power carrying out indispensable public works notably irrigation because of needs attributable to the climate. This political organization was based upon a mode of production distinguished by its self-sufficient villages. In *Das Kapital* Marx discussed the self-sufficing villages that were the other part of his model: "The simplicity of the organization of production in these self-sufficing communities . . . supplies the key to the unchangeableness of Asiatic societies . . ." (Vol. I, Ch. 14, sec. 4). Perhaps Marx's most sophisticated model came in the *Grundrisse der Kritik der Politischen Ökonomie*. There Marx explained how above the village community, there is a higher unity, which performs such functions as irrigation and providing transportation. The surplus product of the community is in turn appropriated by this higher unity in the form of tribute, and in common works for the glorification of the unity: in part the real despot, in part the imaginary tribal being, the god. Thus Oriental despotism appears to lead to an absence of property; in fact its foundation is tribal or common property (Karl Marx, *Pre-Capitalist Economic Formations,* ed. E. J. Hobsbawm, New York [1965], pp. 69–71).

Because of his analysis Marx had to conclude that the Oriental society cannot develop internally. He then described European colonial expansion as a cruel but necessary step towards world socialism. Just as Engels had written that "The conquest of Algeria is an important and fortunate fact for the progress of civilization" (Avineri, p. 43), so Marx said of India: "England has to fulfill a double mission in India: one destructive, the other regenerating—the annihilation of old Asiatic society, and the laying of the material foundation of Western society in Asia" (ibid., p. 125). Marx never approved of cruelty to Asians or their exploitation, but he does not seem to have thought that they were losing much when their country was subjugated and their culture destroyed. For Marx shared Hegel's purely European perspective. Both used sources condemned by Anquetil-Duperron: both regarded all the high cultures of Asia as barbaric or semi-barbaric when compared to Europe. To this Anquetil had answered:

What is meant by *barbaric peoples?* Despite all our knowledge, all our manners, all our *civilization,* the ancient Greeks, if they were to reappear, would treat us as barbarians. Would they be right to do so? Let us abandon such partisan terms. Let us believe that every people, however different from us, is capable of being truly valuable, of possessing reasonable laws, usages, and opinions (*Législation orientale,* v).

(d) At some point in the nineteenth century, the concept of despotism began to appear archaic to some thinkers who felt that it had no reference to the most significant political problems of the century. It was not that absolute power, whether in the hands of a government or a society itself, had ceased to present a threat. Rather the complex of elements that had gone into the concept of despotism no longer seemed to be those most worth taking into account. Although Constant had said something like this, it was Tocqueville who presented it in its most striking form.

In one of the best-known sections of *De la démocratie en Amérique,* Tocqueville warned democratic societies against the domination of the majority in matters of opinion. In the first part of his work (1835), Tocqueville could not decide whether to call this new form of social domination the despotism or the tyranny of the major-

ity. He used the terms interchangeably. In the closing chapters of the second part that appeared five years later, Tocqueville had both enlarged his vision of the greatest danger confronting democratic societies and decided that a new name was needed for a new phenomenon:

Thus I think that the sort of oppression that threatens democratic peoples is unlike anything ever before known. . . . I myself have sought a word that would carry precisely the idea I seek to express. But such old words as "despotism" and "tyranny" are inadequate. The thing is new. Since I cannot give it a name, I must seek to define it (ed. J. P. Mayer, Paris [1951], Vol. 2, Part 4, Ch. 6).

Tocqueville then proceeded to sketch the dangers with a complexity far exceeding that found in the first part of the *Démocratie:* to the invisible but potent effects of public opinion in a democracy upon the nonconforming minority, he added the prospect of an impersonal and benevolent centralized power appealing to the individualism and the passion for material comforts of a society in which all are equal. What might occur, were the dangers not to be recognized and countered, would be a compromise between administrative despotism and the sovereignty of the people. There could be worse outcomes for a democracy. Of these the worst conceivable democratic despotism would be the concentration of all the people's powers in the hands of an individual or body responsible to no one. Tocqueville had the Terror and the Empire in mind. But neither of these sorts of servitude was inevitable. Tocqueville ended his book by pointing out what was necessary in order to prevent them from occurring. Nevertheless despotism as known in the *Ancien Régime* was no longer a significant threat to freedom.

BIBLIOGRAPHY

Shlomo Avineri, ed., *Karl Marx on Colonialism and Modernization* (New York, 1968). Robert Derathé, "Les philosophes et le despotisme," in *Utopie et institutions au xviiie siècle; le pragmatisme des lumières,* ed. Pierre Francastel (The Hague and Paris, 1963). R. Koebner, "Despot and Despotism: Vicissitudes of a Political Term," *Journal of the Warburg and Courtauld Institutes,* 14 (1951), 275–302. George Lichtheim, "Oriental Despotism," in *The Concept of Ideology and Other Essays* (New York, 1967). Donald M. Lowe, *The Function of 'China' in Marx, Lenin, and Mao* (Berkeley, 1966). Sven Stelling-Michaud, "Le mythe du despotisme oriental," *Schweizer Beiträge zur Allgemeinen Geschichte,* 18/19 (1960–61), 328–46. Franco Venturi, "Oriental Despotism," *Journal of the History of Ideas,* 24 (1963), 133–42. E. V. Walter, "Policies of Violence: From Montesquieu to the Terrorists," in *The Critical Spirit. Essays in Honor of Herbert Marcuse,* ed. Kurt H. Wolff and

Barrington Moore, Jr. (Boston, 1967). Françoise Weil, "Montesquieu et le despotisme," in *Actes du Congrès Montesquieu* (Bordeaux, 1956), pp. 191–215. Karl A. Wittfogel, *Oriental Despotism. A Comparative Study of Total Power* (New Haven, 1957).

Translations, unless otherwise identified, are by the author of the article.

MELVIN RICHTER

[See also Anarchism; **Authority**; Freedom; Revolution; State; **Totalitarianism**.]

DETERMINISM IN HISTORY

I. MEANINGS OF "DETERMINISM" IN HISTORIOGRAPHY

1. Universal Determinism and Deterministic Systems. Determinism, so say determinists, is misunderstood and misrepresented by its adversaries; and nowhere more than in historiography. Although antideterminists justly retort that their position has fared no better, they cannot well deny the determinists' complaint. The English word "determinism," like its French, German, and Italian counterparts, is of seventeenth- and eighteenth-century coinage. It was introduced as a name for two different, but related, doctrines. One, the doctrine that choice between different courses of action can, in all cases, be fully accounted for by psychological and other conditions, has as yet played little part in historiography. The other, which, to avoid ambiguity, may also be called "universal determinism," is the doctrine that everything that happens constitutes a chain of causation, a doctrine which obviously implies that human history forms part of such a chain.

Universal determinism depends on a concept of causation that was not generally adopted until after the seventeenth-century "scientific revolution." In ancient and medieval philosophy, a cause was conceived simply as that which produces an effect. Some causes were taken to produce their effects necessarily, as a moving hand holding a stick necessarily moves that stick. Others were taken to have the power to produce an effect, which they might exercise or not without necessitation, as a man without necessitation exercises or does not exercise his power to move his hand. Most ancient and medieval philosophers accepted the principle that every event has a cause. But since most of them took some happenings or events (namely, human or divine actions), to be caused by agents and not by other events, they held that some causes (namely, human or divine actions), are not themselves events

in a causal chain. Hence they were not determinists.

The Greek atomists suggested another feature of the concept of causation, which the work of Galileo, Descartes (even though he was not an atomist), and Newton was to establish in natural science. On this concept, every event in nature is a stage in a process the course of which is determined by laws of nature, and can be considered a necessary consequence, according to those laws, of earlier stages in that process. A cause of an event is simply a set of initial conditions that are, according to laws of nature, jointly sufficient for its occurrence.

This concept of causation underlies Laplace's striking formulation of universal determinism, in the Introduction to his *Essai philosophique sur les probabilités* (1814). Treating the history of the universe as a single process, he maintained that, from a complete specification of the state of the universe at a given instant (initial positions and velocities of all bodies), a superhuman intelligence knowing the laws of nature could infer all past and all future states of the universe. Laplace assumed that mass, position, velocity (the terms of Newtonian physics) would suffice for the required specification. Since it is doubtful, however, not only whether the terms of Newtonian physics or any possible future physics would suffice, but also whether even a superhuman mind could specify, in any terms, a state of the whole universe, Laplace's formulation has been rejected by many determinists. It is now more promising to define universal determinism as the doctrine that every event in principle falls within some deterministic system.

A deterministic system, in the sense here considered, is a system of things in the universe. For any such system there is a set of characteristics, each of which is truly or falsely predicable of each thing in the system, and some of which allow of variation in magnitude or intensity (the variables of the system) such that a state of the system is specified by a description of everything in it in terms of all the characteristics in that set. An event in the system may be defined as any persistence or change in any of its states, in any respect during a temporal interval. Such a deterministic system must, in addition, satisfy three conditions: (1) all events in it must in principle be explicable according to fundamental laws, which (2) mention no characteristics except those in terms of which states of the system are specified, (3) the explanations being such as refer to no thing or event outside the system. Bergmann has usefully labelled the second of these conditions as "completeness" and the third as "closure." Deterministic systems, in this sense, are inevitably abstract. The solar gravitational system, for example, consists of the sun, the planets, and so forth, considered solely with respect to the characteristics taken account of in gravitation theory, and not as concrete objects. The duration of such systems is normally limited: thus, according to astronomers, the solar system had a beginning, and will have an end. It is a fallacy to infer that, because such systems are abstract and impermanent, they are not real.

The complexity of a given deterministic system sets a limit on how adequate a theory can be developed of it. The Newtonian theory of the solar gravitational system, which inspired Laplace's formulation of universal determinism, is almost uniquely adequate because the solar system is, in two respects, almost uniquely simple: both the number of bodies composing it—sun, planets, comets and so forth, and the number of variables by which its states are defined, are comparatively few. Hence, it is practicable not only to establish its state at the present time, but also, by the Newtonian laws, to compute with reasonable accuracy its past and future states. By contrast, it would be utterly impracticable to attempt a similarly adequate theory of the earth's geological history; for the geological state of the entire earth at a given time would be far too complex to define, and the variables determining geological change are more numerous. Geologists accordingly simplify. They explain geological changes by constructing simplified models representing states of the earth or of parts of it at different times, and showing how, according to established laws of nature, the forces at work within one simplified model would bring about a transition to another. For more complex systems, we must be content with even less adequate sketches of a theory.

The concept of a deterministic system has led to extensions in the meaning of "determinism" and its cognates in the following way. One who maintains that a system S is deterministic, or that a set of events K falls within some deterministic system, is naturally said to have embraced determinism with respect to S or K. Such extended special usages are more common in historiography than the general philosophical ones hitherto considered. Thus Pieter Geyl has described determinism as "represent[ing] the historical process as a concatenation of events, one following upon the other inevitably, caused as they all are by a superhuman force or by impersonal forces working in society independently from the wishes or efforts of individuals" (*Debates with Historians*, p. 238). He appears to have in mind the view, accepted by not a few historians, that social systems are, or are parts of, deterministic systems, even if individual human actions are undetermined.

Such views as that a given system of things in the universe is deterministic, or that a given set of events falls within a deterministic system, will hereafter be referred to as "special determinist doctrines," by contrast with universal determinism or the doctrine that every event in the universe falls within some deterministic system. Two elementary facts about the logical relations between universal determinism and special determinist doctrines are often neglected. First, universal determinism does not entail any special determinist doctrine. In particular, universal determinism does not entail the special doctrine which Geyl calls "determinism": it implies that human actions have a place in the causal series, but has nothing to say about what that place is. It is compatible both with the doctrine that the wishes and efforts of individuals cannot affect large-scale historical processes, and with the doctrine that they can and do. Secondly, special determinist doctrines do not necessarily imply or presuppose universal determinism. Thus, the special form of determinism mentioned by Geyl appears to allow that the wishes and efforts of individuals may not fall within a deterministic system. The classical example of this logical independence, however, is found in the philosophy of Descartes, who considered the system of motion and rest in the realm of matter (*res extensa*) to be deterministic, except when changes in it were caused by the activity of thought (*res cogitans*) which he took to be physically undetermined. In a Cartesian universe, even though virtually all happenings in the *material* world fall within a deterministic system, universal determinism fails to hold for acts of the mind.

2. Views Improperly Classified as Determinist. (a) "Logical Determinism" and Predestinarianism. "Logical determinism" is the doctrine that the future is as fixed and unchangeable as the past: that just as what has been, has been and cannot be altered; so what will be will be, despite anything anybody may do. In the classical "logical determinist" argument stated and criticized in Aristotle's *De interpretatione* (18b 9–16) this is said to follow from the premiss that, when it is made, a prediction is necessarily either true or false. Aristotle rejected this premiss as false; and A. C. Danto has pointed out that, if Aristotle was right in doing so, then historical foreknowledge is in principle impossible. If that is so, then it follows that neither universal determinism nor any special determinist doctrine in historiography can be true.

Predestinarianism, sometimes called "theological determinism," is the doctrine that from all eternity God has foreordained everything that happens. It has influenced Christian historiography, although most Christian historians have accepted Saint Augustine's view, in *De civitate Dei*, that divine revelation has to do with the fortunes of the heavenly rather than of the earthly city.

Both universal determinism and all special determinist historical theories treat historical events as falling within a universal or a limited deterministic system. Neither logical determinism nor predestinarianism does so. Logical determinism is independent of any causal theory at all; and predestinarianism is not only consistent with, but is usually held together with, the doctrine of special providence, according to which the foreordained future contains undetermined interventions by God into the normal course of events. It can, therefore, produce nothing but confusion to classify these doctrines as determinist.

(b) Absolute Idealism and "Historism." Absolute (or, *honoris causa*, German) idealism reached its consummation in G. W. F. Hegel's doctrine that the true theodicy, or justification of God to man, is to be found in the philosophy of history. History is the process in which Spirit (*Geist*), or God, or the Idea, carries out its self-appointed task of attaining self-knowledge: first externalizing itself in Nature, and then overcoming that externalization. The working of Spirit manifests itself at different times in different peoples and cultures, it being for Hegel a commonplace that, in his own time, it was doing so chiefly in the Western (*Germanisch*) world, especially in its Protestant parts. But although Hegel thought it dialectically necessary that the self-development of Spirit should in his time have culminated in the western Protestant constitutional state, dialectical necessity is not deterministic. This is shown by Hegel's repudiation of historical prophecy, the possibility of which is implicit in determinism in both its universal and its special forms. "Philosophy," he declared, ". . . appears only when actuality is already there cut and dried after its process of formation has been completed" (*Philosophy of Right* [1822], Preface). It is even more evident from the nature of historical development as Hegel conceived it. It is axiomatic with him that what is real is rational. Hence to exhibit the present as the highest stage yet reached by Spirit is not only the task of philosophy of history, but also the mark of its success. To suspect that the present is less than this betrays a shallowness of mind characteristic of abstract thinking.

Hegel did not notice that the dialectical necessity he professed to find in history simply reflected his axiom. His belief that his philosophical theory of history was confirmed by his ability to interpret his abundant store of historical information in accordance with it is therefore a delusion. Any historian of moderate parts, once assured that the present is the highest stage reached by Spirit, could discover in the course of history a main line of development culminating in it. But such a line of development would not be deterministic. It is not intelligible in the way in which

changes in a deterministic system are, which in principle are calculable in advance. Rather, it is intelligible in the same way as, say, the development of sonata form down to Haydn, which historians of music could not possibly discern unless they were acquainted with Haydn's work.

Although the main tradition of nineteenth-century European historiography rejected the absolute idealist conception of historical development, and affirmed, with Leopold von Ranke, that every epoch is "immediate to God," its value residing in itself, it nevertheless inherited two fatal legacies from absolute idealism. The reality of any historical epoch is of course concrete; and historians who reflected philosophically on their work generally agreed with the idealists (1) that to describe the concrete in terms of abstract concepts must falsify it, and (2) that no aspect of anything concrete can be correctly understood except in relation to all its other aspects. These two doctrines are fused in the motto used by F. Meinecke for his *Die Entstehung des Historismus* (1936), *Individuum est ineffabile*.

Until the mid-1940's, this historiographical tradition, known in Germany as *Historismus*, on the infrequent occasions on which it was referred to in English was mostly called "historism." That usage will be adopted in this article, although "historicism" has become the commoner rendering since the appearance of F. Engel-Janosi's much-cited *The Growth of German Historicism* (1944).

Because of its tenet that every aspect of life in a given historical situation is conditioned by every other, historism is sometimes held to be determinist. As the historians who embraced historism themselves perceived, if all institutions and ideas are to be understood only in terms of their historical context, then the value of each is relative to that context: there is neither absolute good or evil nor absolute truth. Such relativism is suicidal. No theory which implies that there is no absolute truth can present itself as absolutely true. Yet although historism is relativist in this way, it is not determinist. The "historists" did not think that an institution or an idea is conditioned by its historical context in the determinist sense of being a causally necessary response to it, but only in the much weaker sense of being an intelligible response to it.

In sum, absolute idealism and historism are not forms of determinism: neither the dialectical necessity of one nor the historical relativism of the other is determinist.

(c) "Historicism" and Historical Inevitability. In a series of papers written in the late 1930's, and published in 1944–45, Sir Karl Popper introduced the then unfamiliar word "historicism" as a label for what he later described as

. . . an approach to the social sciences which assumes that *historical prediction* is their principal aim, and which assumes that this aim is attainable by discovering the "rhythms" or the "patterns," the "laws" or the "trends" that underlie the evolution of history

(*The Poverty of Historicism*, 1957). Popper sharply distinguished historicism from *Historismus*, which as was usual when he wrote, he called "historism." Historicism, in Popper's sense, was a fashionable position in the 1930's, and it has a long history, even though Popper classified some philosophers as historicists who were not (e.g., Hegel). There is an enormous variety of historicist positions, some of which are determinist and some not. An historicist position is determinist if and only if the historical patterns or trends the existence of which it affirms are conceived as falling within a deterministic system. Theological predestinarians are historicists, because they make predictions on the basis of historical patterns which they take to be revealed by God; but, since they do not think those patterns to fall within any deterministic system, they are not determinists.

For this reason, determinism must be distinguished from the thesis that what happens in history happens inevitably. Historical inevitability may be asserted on either determinist or nondeterminist grounds. Those fatalists who hold that the future can be predicted by magic, accept historical inevitability; but they are not determinists, for reasons given above.

II. DOES SCIENTIFIC HISTORIOGRAPHY PRESUPPOSE DETERMINISM?

The truth of universal determinism is still disputed. It is usually advocated on naturalist or materialist grounds, and assailed on the ground that it is incompatible with the freedom of the will, and therefore with moral responsibility. Those issues are treated elsewhere in this work; but they are neglected by most historians, whose interest in determinism is confined to its applications in history. Pieter Geyl spoke for the antideterminists among them when he described his position as "not that *determinism* is a fallacy, but that *to apply determinism to history* is an impossible and necessarily misleading method" (*Debates with Historians*, p. 239). Even if universal determinism were true, it would not follow that any special determinist theory of history is true.

In consequence, determinism in history is usually defended philosophically, not by inferences from universal determinism, but by methodological arguments that scientific historiography presupposes it.

In *A Study of History*, Vol. IX (1954), Toynbee acknowledges that "antinomian" modern historians consider "Man in Process of Civilization" to be a province of the universe that is not subject to laws of nature, and observes that such a view must be reprobated as "blasphemy" by all right-minded devotees of natural science. There are, Toynbee declares, only two possibilities: the province of man in process of civilization is either one of "Order" or it is one of "Chaos." If of Order, then processes in it are subject to laws of nature; if of Chaos, then processes in it are unintelligible: history is "just one damned thing after another." Now, whatever their antinomian professions, historians do not in practice treat history as a Chaos. They profess to find intelligible patterns in it, and even to furnish explanations. Hence, Toynbee concludes, historians methodologically presuppose that history is a province of Order: that is, that historical events are subject to laws of nature.

When the determinist implications of this conclusion were made clear to Toynbee, he repudiated them, and announced that, although he cannot alter the laws of nonhuman nature, man can alter the laws of his own nature with God's help. Toynbee appears to have remained unaware that this implies that man in process of civilization is not subject to laws of nature—the very blasphemy against science he had denounced in antinomian historians! Of course, his implicit recantation does not invalidate his original argument.

Toynbee makes several questionable assumptions: such as, that the only intelligible order there can be in human history must be of the kind discovered by science in natural processes. To state this assumption is to throw doubt upon it. Like all social scientists, historians seek order in what they study. They classify, compare, and generalize. But not all classifications are of natural kinds, and very few generalizations even remotely resemble putative laws of nature. In their present state, it is plausible neither that the social sciences have as their sole scientific function to establish the lawful determinants of the events they study, nor even that they presuppose that all human actions have lawful determinants.

III. SPECIAL DETERMINIST DOCTRINES IN HISTORIOGRAPHY

In most special determinist doctrines that have commanded serious attention from historians, some kind of social group is singled out as the intelligible unit of historical study. States, nations, races, cultures, classes, civilizations, and organized religions have all been accounted such units; and determinist theories have been offered both about conditions that occur in them, and about their courses of development.

As put forward by social scientists, hypotheses about causal factors in the occurrence of this or that social condition usually fall short of determinism: that is, of the form, *whenever a condition of the kind C_1 occurs in a group of the kind G, then a condition of the kind C_2, must, other things being equal, follow.* Yet, in popular presentations, they often assume this form. Thus race and physical environment, which obviously have some causal significance, have from ancient times cropped up in determinist theories. That the powers of Western Europe developed in the nineteenth century conditions that enabled them to dominate the world was commonly believed to be an inevitable consequence of the nature of the "white race." Sophisticated historians like H. T. Buckle persuaded themselves that the irregular work habits then characteristic of Spaniards, by contrast with the steady ones of the English, were consequences of an extreme as opposed to a moderate climate. Both racialist and environmentalist forms of determinism are now discredited; for geographers have produced abundant evidence with which neither can be reconciled. No special determinist theory relying on other alleged causal factors is even superficially plausible.

The numerous determinist theories of historical development can be classified as cyclical or noncyclical.

1. Cyclical Theories. In his *Republic*, Book VIII Plato taught that even the ideal state is subject to decay; and, in decaying, would pass through the stages: timocracy, oligarchy, democracy, tyranny. *Prima facie*, this is an early cyclical determinist theory, although many Platonic scholars interpret it as no more than an ethical parable. Of the innumerable later cyclical theories, three are still discussed by historians: those of Giambattista Vico, of Oswald Spengler, and of A. J. Toynbee.

In his *Principles of a New Science . . . concerning the Common Nature of the Nations* (1st ed. 1725, 3rd ed. 1744), Vico maintained that in the development of their customs, laws, governments, languages, and modes of thought, all nations except the divinely chosen Israel pass through a course (*corso*) of three stages: first divine or religious, then heroic, then human. Although it is the highest, the human stage is not stable. Having reached it, nations become dissolute, and return to barbarism; whereupon there is a recourse (*ricorso*) of the same three stages. Even the true Christian religion has been established by divine providence "according to the natural course of human institutions themselves," in the return of "truly divine times" that followed the disintegration of the Roman Empire (*New Science*, par. 1047).

Spengler took the intelligible units of historical development to be, not nations as Vico had thought, but cultures, which he defined as groups of individuals sharing a common conception of the world in which they live, and especially of its space. In *The Decline of the West* (Vol. I, 1918; Vol. II, 1922; rev. ed., 1923), he described such cultures as growing in the aimless wilderness of the human past like flowers in a field, each independently of every other. Nine of them he identified, while allowing that there may have been more; but he closely studied only two: the "Apollonian" culture of ancient Greece and Rome, and the "Faustian" culture of the medieval and modern West. Each culture has a life of about a thousand years, in which it passes through four stages, comparable to the four seasons; an agricultural and heroic spring; an aristocratic summer in which towns emerge; an autumn in which cities grow, absolute monarchies subdue aristocracies, and philosophy and science flourish; then finally, a winter of plutocracy and political tyranny, made possible by advanced technology and public administration. Having fulfilled the possibilities of its fourth stage, a culture develops no more. It is dead, even though, like late imperial China, its corpse may long continue in existence.

Toynbee's theory of historical development in the first ten volumes of *A Study of History* (12 vols., 1934–61) is not without qualification determinist: like his view about the presuppositions of scientific history, it is inconsistent. However, it has a determinist side, which is as follows.

The intelligible units of historical study are neither nations nor cultures, but societies, and especially those that are civilized, which, by contrast with primitive ones, are not only relatively long-lived and spatially extensive, but also relatively few. They are not necessarily independent, as Spengler thought cultures are, but one may be the offspring of another. Toynbee distinguished twenty-one known civilizations, which he allotted to three generations; primary, secondary, and tertiary. Of the eight surviving in the present century, five are tertiary (Western, main Orthodox Christian, Russian Orthodox Christian, Iranic, Arabic), and three are secondary (Hindu, main Far Eastern, Japanese Far Eastern). Each of the five tertiary civilizations is affiliated to one of two extinct secondary civilizations, the Hellenic and the Syriac, both of which are affiliated to the same primary civilization, the Minoan. Each of the three surviving secondary civilizations is affiliated to one of the two extinct primary ones: the Sinic and the Indic. In addition, there are four extinct primary civilizations: two of them perished without issue; and the other two each had two secondary offspring, all four of which perished without issue. Finally, Toynbee counted ten other civilizations that were not only barren but necessarily so, being either abortive, or arrested, or fossils.

According to Toynbee, a civilization comes into being when a society responds successfully to a challenge thrown down by its physical or human environment; and it grows as long as it continues successfully to respond to the new challenges to which every successful response must lead. In a growing civilization, successful responses originate in a creative minority, which is imitated by an uncreative majority. When a civilization responds inadequately to a challenge, it breaks down, and a process of disintegration begins. The unsuccessful response alienates the majority from the minority it formerly imitated; but that minority, although no longer creative, establishes itself as dominant. The majority is thus degraded to a proletariat, either internal or external. Disintegration proceeds in a succession of routs (times of troubles) and rallies, usually three of each, terminated by a decisive rout. The last rally of all civilizations now extinct was to form a "universal state"; and all surviving civilizations except the Iranic-Arabic and the Western have already formed such a state.

When seeking inductively based laws of historical development, Toynbee treated civilizations as deterministic systems, each of which necessarily passes through the stages described above. It follows that Western civilization, like all others, will break down and disintegrate; the important question is whether it has broken down already, and, if so, how far it has disintegrated. In the first six volumes of *A Study of History*, Toynbee decided that whether it has already broken down is an open question; but in the last four he explicitly repudiated the conception of civilizations as deterministic systems, and implicitly abandoned his search for the laws of their development. At one point, he suggested that only the disintegration of a civilization might be determined, not its growth and breakdown. Even more important, his principal interest came to be teleological: What is the point, *sub specie aeterni*, of the system of civilizations itself? In his first six volumes the function of the higher religions is to bring certain tertiary civilizations to birth from their secondary parents; in his last six, civilizations exist in order to foster the higher religions.

Historically, Toynbee's is the most impressive of the cyclical theories; philosophically, it is not. His confessed inability to answer the question whether Western civilization has yet broken down, since it cannot be excused on the plea of insufficiency of evidence, betrays a radical unclarity in his concept of a breakdown. The internal links between the concepts *response, growth, creativeness, dominance,* and *breakdown* are plain enough; but what states of affairs in the world any one of them describes is obscure. Although Vico's and Spengler's theories are less objectionable in this respect, all three have been severely criticized both philosophically and historically. Most of the philosophical criticisms are weak. The commonest is the charge that they involve universal determinism, which we have already shown to be false: a nondeterministic world may contain deterministic systems. Another common objection is that Spengler and Toynbee especially generalize from too few cases; but Kepler obtained his laws of planetary motion from even fewer. R. G. Collingwood denounced Spengler for not "working at" history but only talking about it, on the ground that he relied on others for information about individual facts; and for not "determining either past or future," but only "attaching labels" to them, on the ground that, in making such predictions as that, between A.D. 2,000 and 2,200 somebody will arise in the Faustian culture corresponding to Julius Caesar in the Apollonian one, he did not tell us who that person would be. Yet Collingwood would hardly have taxed Kepler with not working at astronomy, because he relied on Tycho for astronomical observations; or Adams and Leverrier with only "attaching labels" to space, because, in predicting that a planet of specified mass and orbit would be at a certain position at a certain time, they could not have told you that that planet would be the concrete object we know as "Neptune."

The cyclical theories of Vico, Spengler, and Toynbee have been refuted not by philosophers, but by historians. Each, as elaborated by its author, contains radical errors of historical fact; and none has found a defender capable of revising it to accord with the facts established by its critics. It is as though every known theory of the solar planetary system as deterministic had been shown to contain radical errors about the orbits of several of the planets.

2. Noncyclical Theories. As they lost the Christian hope of a glorious resurrection, many thinkers of the eighteenth-century Enlightenment, and of the American and French revolutionary movements that grew out of it, came to believe not only that man was perfectible, but that in history he was being perfected. Hence, when Michelet's translations, *Oeuvres choisies de Vico* (2 vols., 1835), made Vico's work known outside Italy, thinkers in the Enlightenment and revolutionary traditions, while hailing him for treating historical events as subject to fixed laws, substituted continuous progress for Vico's cycles as their model of historical development.

In his *Cours de philosophie positive* (6 vols., 1830–42), Auguste Comte sought an explanation of this progressive development; and, conceiving the level of civilization at any given time to be a function of the level reached at that time in the various branches of knowledge, he thought he had found the explanation in his Law of the Three Stages: that each branch of knowledge passes successively through three different theoretical conditions: the theological, or fictitious; the metaphysical, or abstract; and the scientific, or positive. Human civilization must pass through the same three stages. The theological stage, which he subdivided into fetishist, polytheist, and monotheist phases, Comte considered to have ended about A.D. 1400; and he was in hopes that, when he wrote, the succeeding metaphysical stage was in its last throes. Since he believed positive knowledge to be cumulative, he therefore concluded that, in the future as in the past, the movement of history would necessarily be progressive. In drawing this conclusion, he assumed that the development of thought according to the Law of the Three Stages cannot be thwarted by other historical processes, i.e., that it is an independent variable.

Darwin's *Origin of Species* (1859) tempted some of those who believed that history is progressive to look to biology for an alternative to the Comtist foundation for their faith. Among those who succumbed was Herbert Spencer, who had earlier, in *Social Statics* (1851), asserted on teleological grounds that the ultimate emergence of the ideal man is "logically certain." In *First Principles* (1861) and subsequent books, however, he inferred the progress of humanity as a necessary consequence of a universal evolutionary movement from homogeneity to heterogeneity: an idea he obtained by generalizing a law of the pioneer embryologist von Baer. Such a movement cannot be inferred from the Darwinian theory of natural selection; but Spencer got over that difficulty by retaining Lamarck's doctrine, now exploded, that acquired characters can be genetically transmitted.

Both the Comtist and evolutionist theories of progress are philosophically vulnerable. Even if the Law of the Three Stages were true, it would not follow that theology and metaphysics are misguided: the Law might be a law of degeneration. And even if Darwinian natural selection ensures evolution by "the survival of the fittest" (a phrase coined by Spencer), acute biologists like T. H. Huxley saw that what is biologically fittest may not be so by other standards of value.

In *A Letter to Teachers of American History* (1910), the deeply skeptical Henry Adams, writing as a former president of the American Historical Association, maintained that, according to the second Law of Thermodynamics, biological evolution is only an aspect of a more fundamental process of dissipation of energy. It is evident that human knowledge has increased, but may not that gain have been bought by a loss in vitality?

Within his "degradationist" hypothesis, Adams constructed an ingenious special determinist theory of history in terms of a conception of human development

the germ of which he professed to find in the Phase Rule of Willard Gibbs. Gibbs's Rule has to do with conditions of equilibrium in systems consisting of substances which may pass through a specified number of three phases: solid, liquid, and gaseous. In *The Rule of Phase Applied to History* (1909), Adams declared that recent science had disclosed phases besides Gibbs's three: in one passage he listed electricity, ether, space, and hyper-space; but in his theory itself he treated the last three as one, the Ethereal, and identified it with pure consciousness. He proceeded to assume that the history of human thought is the history of its phases, and, by a quite unfounded analogy, that in its successive phases, the movement of thought accelerates according to a law of squares. The phase about which we are best informed began with the Scientific Revolution, and was ending, if it had not already ended, in the twentieth century. Describing it as the "Mechanical phase," Adams dated it from A.D. 1600 to 1900, and calculated by his law of squares that its predecessor should have endured for 90,000 years. The findings of history and archaeology, he claimed, confirm this: they make it probable that the thought-life of man in the 100,000 years preceding the Scientific Revolution was a single Religious phase, which was not transcended even in classical Greece. In the twentieth century, the Mechanical phase passed, or would soon pass, into an Electrical phase, which would be succeeded by an Ethereal phase. If his dates for the Mechanical phase are correct, and he thought that the margin of error could not be greater than a century, the Electrical phase will last only $\sqrt{300}$, or 17.5 years, and the Ethereal only $\sqrt{17.5}$, or about four years. Even allowing for error, this would "bring thought to the limit of its possibilities" between 1921 and 2025.

It cannot be denied that Adams correctly prophesied that in the twentieth century there would be a series of scientific revolutions. Yet, shorn of its fanciful catalogue of phases, and its even more fanciful law of squares, his theory plainly is, as indeed he acknowledged, a sophisticated version of Comte's. Like Comte's, it rests on the intrinsically dubious assumption that the development of thought is historically an independent variable.

The final noncyclical theory that merits consideration arose within the Marxist movement. At Marx's graveside in 1883, Engels declared that "Just as Darwin discovered the law of development of organic nature, so Marx discovered the law of development of human history." Yet Marx's original position was not determinist: it was avowedly a radical version of Hegelianism, in which the self-alienated God of Hegel's *Phenomenology* became self-alienated productive man.

In all societies except the most primitive, Marx held

that down to his own time production had involved the division of labor and private property. Hence labor had been alienated from the worker: its products do not belong to him, and he does not labor for labor's sake. The prevailing mode of production determines the social system—the classes of society and the relations between them. Every social system that arises from the alienation of labor is divided into two antagonistic classes: those who alienate their labor, and those who control the labor alienated. Slavery, feudal serfdom, and working for wages are different forms of alienation, each of which determines a different form of class-division: master and slave, feudal lord and serf, bourgeois and proletarian.

Although in the *Communist Manifesto* (1848) Marx and Engels declared it to be inevitable that the proletariat would soon overthrow bourgeois society, they did not describe it as a stage in a deterministic process. Like Hegel, they treated history as the history of man, and man as essentially rational: when he perceives that he, or his society, is pursuing contradictory ends, he strives to overcome the contradiction. Every change from one form of class division to another has come about because the superseded system was breaking down under the burden of its contradictions, and a class identified with a mode of production in which those contradictions could be overcome seized its opportunity. In the *Theses on Feuerbach* (1845) Marx wrote that the point is not to understand the world, but to change it: theory is a tool of action. The *Manifesto* showed the proletariat what it could do, and what, being human, it inevitably would do: the contradictions of bourgeois society were reaching a crisis; and the nature of capitalist production is such that the destruction of bourgeois society by the proletariat will end man's alienation from himself, i.e., from his own labor. For the first time in history, man will be both highly productive and free.

The conversion of Marx's union of theory and practice into a determinist theory was begun by Engels in *Anti-Dühring* (1877), and completed by Kautsky and the German Marxists. They conceived human societies as deterministic systems, in which change can be explained according to two fundamental laws: that less advanced modes of production generate higher modes (the hand-mill leads to the water-mill, the water-mill to the steam-mill); and that, when a social system is in conflict with the mode of production that prevails in it, it is overthrown, and replaced by a social system that is not. This deterministic theory, which its authors styled "scientific socialism," has for half a century hung like an albatross from the neck of the Marxist movement.

The principal objections to noncyclical determinist theories of history, like those to cyclical ones, are historical. Historical investigation has shown all of them to be radically irreconcilable with what has actually happened. In each, it is usually possible to identify a major thesis that is the source of error: for example, in both Comte's and Engels' theories, it is that some historical variable is independent of the others, namely, the development either of knowledge or of production. That all special determinist theories hitherto advanced in history have turned out false does not show that all those yet to be advanced will do likewise; but it is a reason for skepticism.

BIBLIOGRAPHY

Universal determinism is analyzed in Gustav Bergmann, *Philosophy of Science* (Madison, 1957), and Ernest Nagel, *The Structure of Science* (New York, 1961). Whether scientific history presupposes determinism is discussed in A. C. Danto, *Analytical Philosophy of History* (Cambridge and New York, 1965); W. H. Dray, *Philosophy of History* (Englewood Cliffs, N.J., 1964); and Morton White, *The Foundations of Historical Knowledge* (New York, 1965); and also in articles in Patrick Gardiner, ed., *Theories of History* (Glencoe, Ill., 1959), and W. H. Dray, ed. *Philosophical Analysis and History* (New York, 1966). On special determinist theories see especially Henry Adams, *The Degradation of the Democratic Dogma* (New York, 1919); Isaiah Berlin, *Historical Inevitability* (London and New York, 1954); J. B. Bury, *The Idea of Progress* (1920; American ed., New York, 1932 and reprints); R. G. Collingwood, *The Idea of History* (Oxford and New York, 1946), and R. G. Collingwood, *Essays in the Philosophy of History*, ed. W. Debbins (Austin, 1965); George Lichtheim, *Marxism* (New York, 1961); M. F. Ashley Montagu, ed., *Toynbee and History* (Boston, 1956).

ALAN DONAGAN

[See also **Causation in History;** Free Will; Hegelian . . . ; **Historicism;** Theodicy.]

DETERMINISM IN THEOLOGY: PREDESTINATION

DETERMINISM IS an obvious possible deduction from the definition of the divinity or God in most systems of theology. These systems normally define God as a being who is omnipotent, who is omniscient, and whose omniscience includes foreknowledge of all future events. It would seem that any being who possessed these characteristics fully would have to be ultimately responsible for every event that occurs in the universe. Thus no individual lesser being, such as a man, could be truly free to act or to make a decision on any matter, important or trivial, at any time, in any place, in any conceivable circumstances.

This deduction, however, carries certain disturbing implications, and even provokes contradictions in many systems of theology. For most of these systems also include in their normal definitions of God the idea that He is infinitely good, and the ultimate source of all that is good in the universe. This creates the serious problem of explaining the evil that seems to be such an obvious and recurrent feature of all experience. It creates the particularly serious problem of explaining the ultimate forms of evil forecast by certain systems of theology, such as the eternal damnation of the souls of a high percentage of the entire human race. If God is truly omnipotent and truly good, how can He permit evil to exist, particularly forms of evil which are completely catastrophic and irreversible, such as the eternal damnation of a human soul?

There are several fairly obvious possible logical escapes from this dilemma. One can conclude, as believers in many primitive religions do, that God is evil or neutral. One can conclude, as many modern liberal believers in progress do, that God is not omnipotent at every point in history. Or one can argue that evil is really an illusion, and that everything which seems evil serves some ultimate good purpose.

These logical escapes do not satisfy most theologians. They do not seem to them to be confirmed either by experience or by revealed truth. Most theological systems thus seek to face the dilemma by creating a theodicy, or defense of God's goodness and omnipotence despite the existence of evil. And most theologians, aware of this dilemma, shrink from endorsing determinism. Those who emphasize God's omnipotence, and particularly His role in the salvation of individual human souls, may approach determinism closely. But they hesitate to endorse it openly and frankly. The term "determinism" tends to be used in theology mostly as a polemicist's epithet, directed against theological arguments which are charged with overemphasizing divine omnipotence. It is thus more precise to speak of approaches to determinism in theology, rather than actual determinism.

I. CHRISTIAN DETERMINISM

In the Christian tradition, the nearest approaches to determinism are to be found more in ideas about man's ultimate destiny than in ideas about the course of man's life in this world. They are to be found particularly within systems derived from the thought of Saint Augustine of Hippo, the greatest early theologian of the Western Church. They have been derived most commonly from Augustine's doctrines of original sin and predestination. These doctrines Augustine devel-

oped from his reading of the Pauline epistles in the Christian New Testament. In developing his interpretation, Augustine (354–430) was almost certainly influenced by the preaching of Saint Ambrose (ca. 340–97), and other prominent earlier Western theologians. He departed from the views of influential Eastern theologians such as Saint John Chrysostom. But he reacted most explicitly against the teachings of his contemporaries, the British monk Pelagius and his associates.

Pelagius seems to have been an austere moralist, who worked hard to convince Christians of their duty to lead good lives. The Pelagians argued that the evil, particularly the moral evil, which they acknowledged to be endemic in the world was due to free acts of will by individual human beings. Men decide freely to perform wicked deeds, in full knowledge of the fact that these deeds are wicked and that those who do them incur punishments decreed by God. This wickedness, or sin, became pervasive, as men imitated each other and became the slaves of sinful habits. God punishes wicked acts in a variety of ways, partly in this life through natural disasters like illness, partly in the life to come by eternal punishment of the souls of the sinful. If a man wants to escape from sin, and its many unpleasant consequences, he can do so by the exercise of his reason and will, in imitation of Jesus Christ, who led a perfectly good life. Man can thus decide to avoid sin and do good. He can thus escape punishment and win rewards. He can even escape the ultimate punishment of eternal damnation and win the ultimate reward of eternal bliss in heaven. God gave man the faculties of reason and will for these purposes. God also gave man freedom to use these faculties as he wished, and made man responsible if he did not use them as he should.

These arguments horrified many Christians, of whom Augustine was the most articulate. They did not seem consonant either with the revealed truths of Scripture or with human experience. They seemed to diminish the power and majesty of God, to make Him something less than an omnipotent being. They made it possible for an individual man to decide freely whether to be good or bad, and thus to tell God whether to send him to heaven or hell. And that was an intolerable denial of divine omnipotence, an insult to divine majesty. In short it was a heresy, a belief so dangerous that it doomed its adherents to damnation.

In arguing against the Pelagians, Augustine developed his doctrine of original sin. He insisted that a sin is not one in a series of separate acts, based on erroneous decisions. Sin is rather a radical defect of human character, from which no man can escape by his own efforts. It is a defect which first became apparent in the first man, Adam, when he defied God by violating very explicit instructions, and was thrown out of the Garden of Eden and condemned to a painful life and death as a result. This defect is passed on to every man born into this world by the very way in which he is created, by the marital act, accompanied as it inevitably is by shame and lust. Every man is thus a sinner, even before he is born, incapable of doing anything that is good, doomed to do nothing but evil deeds and to suffer the full consequences for this evil doing. This is the true explanation for the evil we see to be endemic and uncontrollable in the world about us.

God did not intend that all men remain in this desperate state, however. He did develop one, and only one, way for escape from sin and its consequences. This was through His grace, made available to man through the life and passion of Christ. By grace a few men are purged of original sin, and left free to live the good lives which merit eternal rewards. This grace is a free gift. No man can ask for it, or decide to appropriate it, or do anything to deserve it. Grace is given only to a small fixed number of men, the "elect" or "saints." Others are called to the good life, but do not receive the grace to take advantage of the call. God, furthermore, decided which individuals would receive grace before any of them were even born. They are thus predestined to salvation. He endowed these fortunate individuals with perseverance, so that they would inevitably lead the good lives which merit eternal rewards. Every other member of the human race will inevitably remain in the corrupt state in which all are born, will find it impossible to avoid doing sinful acts, and will suffer the eternal punishment which God decrees for the sinner.

These arguments are developed in their most extreme form in Augustine's anti-Pelagian tracts. There are scholars who would argue that Augustine's true opinions are better revealed in his earlier works, which allow a more significant role for human free will. Other scholars would argue that the two strains in Augustine's thought can be synthesized, and that there are elements of both free will and determinism in his thought. The texts of the anti-Pelagian tracts themselves, however, come close to asserting a consistent determinism of man's ultimate destiny. Augustine's successors in the Christian West were aware of this, and either used these tracts to approach determinism themselves, or tried to find ways of attenuating his doctrines so that the rigor of a full determinism could be avoided.

Augustine's theology was tremendously influential. It came to be the most significant single theological system in western Europe for more than a millennium. And with the rest of the system, the doctrine of predestination, with its deterministic implications, came

to be generally accepted. However it also came to be a rather controversial doctrine. It made many theologians uneasy because it seemed to make God the author of evil. If God predestines the elect to salvation, it was felt that He must logically predestine the rest of mankind to live in sin and be damned. And this conclusion was difficult to reconcile with God's ultimately good and loving nature. Consequently a number of theologians in succeeding centuries proposed modifications of the Augustinian doctrine of predestination, designed to introduce some element of human responsibility for sin and damnation. To the extent that they did so, these modifications obviously reduced the degree of determinism in the doctrine. Against these modifications, other theologians worked out the Augustinian doctrine in ever more rigorous and detailed forms. Their modifications tended to bring the doctrine closer to determinism. However a number of them explicitly denied the charge that they were adopting determinism.

This process of modification and counter-modification continued for several centuries. It probably reached its climax in the sixteenth and seventeenth centuries. The great Protestant Reformers were saturated in Augustinian theology. Luther had been educated as an Augustinian monk, and traces of that education remained with him throughout his life. Calvin's education had been secular, in classics and in law, but his writings reveal that he, too, had soaked himself in the writings of Augustine. For Calvin the doctrine of predestination came to be particularly important. In the controversies surrounding it during his career and among his successors, it was reworked and developed into particularly extreme forms. Many of these forms had medieval antecedents, although Calvin and his successors were not always aware of them.

One possible modification was the argument that while God predestines the saints to salvation, He is not actively responsible for the fate of the damned. Human will is too weak to choose the good, and thus merit salvation. But it remains strong enough to choose the sinful way, and thus deserve punishment. This version is labeled the doctrine of single predestination, and it received wide support in influential circles. Against it, the rigorous Augustinians argued that logic requires double predestination, both of the saved and of the damned. God could not give away to men the power to will actively to be damned and still remain omnipotent. Early disciples of Augustine, like Gottschalk of Orbais in the ninth century, read their master in this way. So did Calvin.

A second possible modification was the argument that while God predestines both the saved and the damned to their respective fates, He does it only because He knows, as a result of His foreknowledge, that 27 the saints will lead lives that will merit salvation and the rest will lead lives that will deserve eternal punishment. The rigorists rejected this modification, also, as undercutting divine omnipotence in yet another way. They insisted that an omnipotent God must plot the course of every human life, as well as deciding its ultimate result. Or they argued that God's decisions about each man's destiny could not have followed His acquisition of knowledge about each man's behavior, but must have come first or concurrently.

A third possible modification was the argument that God made His decisions to save some and damn others after the creation of Adam, the first man. God endowed the first human creation, made in His own image, with complete freedom. Only when He saw how badly Adam used his freedom, did God take it away, and decree that all of Adam's descendants would lead sinful and miserable lives, meriting eternal damnation, except for the small number of saints God chose to exempt from this fate. This view, that God enacted His predestinating decrees only after Adam's fall, has been labeled infralapsarian or sublapsarian. It tended to make divine determinism a historic event, introduced into history at a definable point, after an attempt to grant free will to man failed. However it also tended to make divine omnipotence a historic event, suspended at the creation of Adam, only to be reintroduced following his fall. The rigorists consequently rejected this modification too, advancing an argument labeled supralapsarian. They insisted that God's decrees of predestination were enacted before the creation of the first man, even before the beginning of time. They are part of the eternal structure of the universe. God could not suspend them, without denying an essential part of his own nature. This view was advanced by several medieval theologians, by Calvin, and, most vehemently, by his seventeenth-century Flemish disciple Francis Gomarus.

A fourth possible modification was the argument that while it was God's initiative which saved or damned a man, man had to react to this initiative, or at least had to be prepared passively to receive it. The decision as to whether any individual was saved or damned, therefore, was a joint decision, for which both God and man shared responsibility. This argument, often labeled synergism, has a long history, and one can find traces of it in some of Augustine's Greek predecessors. One can find it again in many medieval theologians and also in theologians of the Reformation such as Philip Melanchthon. But for the rigorists this, too, was an unwarranted denial of God's omnipotence and exaltation of man's powers. Hence they rejected it.

The whole debate over predestination came to one of its historic climaxes in the Netherlands during the early seventeenth century. The protagonists in this debate were two Calvinist professors of theology at the University of Leiden, Jacob Arminius and Francis Gomarus. Arminius, who had studied in Geneva with Calvin's own successors, tried to modify Calvinist doctrine in order to reduce its harshness and create some role in it for human responsibility. Gomarus went beyond Calvin himself in insisting on all the harshest logical consequences of his system. The views of Arminius were most succinctly stated after his death, in a five-point *Remonstrance* drafted by his followers in 1610. This document urged: (1) that God's decree of salvation is conditional, benefiting only those who by an act of will accept and persevere in faith; (2) that God's universal love is reflected in the fact that Christ died for all men, although only believers are benefited; (3) that man can truly do good, after he is born again through the Holy Spirit; (4) that man can perversely resist God's offer of grace; (5) that the faithful receive divine assistance in leading the good life, but only if they want this assistance and do not remain inactive.

The *Remonstrance* provoked a bitter controversy, in which the Gomarists led the attack. It spread beyond the Netherlands to other countries in which Calvinist influences had been strong. The controversy was finally settled, at least temporarily, in a general synod of representatives of all the Reformed churches, held in Dort, 1618–19. The synod of Dort was dominated by the Gomarists. It adopted a five-point retort to the *Remonstrance* which has come to be called the Five Points of Calvinism: (1) Unconditional election—God's predestinating decrees derive solely from his decisions, and do not in any way depend on the beliefs or the behavior of individuals; (2) Limited atonement—Christ died for the elect alone, not for all mankind; (3) Total depravity—man in his natural state is so totally corrupt and helpless that he is incapable even of desiring salvation; (4) Irresistible grace—once God decides to save a man he is helpless to resist, and automatically is saved; (5) Perseverance of the saints—God so assists His elect to adopt the correct beliefs and live the proper kinds of life that it is impossible for them to fall from grace. This is sometimes called the TULIP formula, an acronym based on the initial letters of the five points. The formula obviously approaches determinism very closely, since every point limits man's freedom and exalts God's power. Yet even the canons of Dort cannot be called completely and consistently deterministic. For, despite the urgings of Gomarus, the assembly dominated by his followers refused to adopt a clearly supralapsarian formula, but instead settled on one with infralapsarian elements.

Since the seventeenth century, there has been a

general decline in the acceptance of Christian theological doctrines that imply determinism. Among groups that have remained relatively orthodox, semi-Pelagianism has become widespread and Arminianism has won many adherents. And there have been frequent attempts to break loose from all forms of orthodoxy, and to revise Christian doctrine radically, in order to make it more credible to minds shaped by the revolutionary discoveries of modern science and to make it more relevant to men preoccupied by the problems of their own societies. Adherence to the traditional theological doctrines implying determinism has been limited to relatively small groups of churchmen who have remained faithful to a really strict historic theological system, like Calvinism.

The twentieth century, however, has witnessed some recrudescence of these doctrines. This is particularly true of that variety of twentieth-century theology labeled neo-orthodox, and dominated by the thinking of the American Reinhold Niebuhr and the Swiss Karl Barth. In the systems of the neo-orthodox one finds a significant place for the doctrine of original sin, which had fallen out of favor among nineteenth-century theological liberals. Original sin tends to be rooted less in human lust, as in Augustine, than in human finitude. But the fact that man is a finite creature does, it is argued, create a radical defect in his nature. It makes it impossible for him to be truly good, for being invariably good in one's dealings with other men requires a knowledge of their inner problems and needs which no individual can ever achieve. Thus man remains in need of help from some exterior and transcendental source, if he is to avoid evil. Furthermore, for Barth at least, man cannot seek for this external help and appropriate it to himself. It must be freely offered by God alone, without any initiative from man.

In Barth's system one even finds a significant doctrine of double predestination. The doctrine is deliberately made quite distinct from that of Calvin, whose thought Barth knew intimately and generally admired a great deal. For Barth predestination is essentially Christological. Jesus Christ is both the electing God and the elected man. In Christ, God Himself has both suffered rejection and enjoyed salvation. All who are in Christ will benefit from these experiences. This view tends to make of predestination to damnation an ephemeral historic event, occurring in the past with the crucifixion of Christ, while predestination to salvation is a present reality, which will be assigned to true believers.

To the extent that these doctrines of original sin and predestination limit human free will and exalt divine power, the modern systems of the neo-orthodox, like those of their predecessors, approach determinism.

II. NON-CHRISTIAN DETERMINISM

In non-Christian traditions, there are approaches to determinism which resemble closely those one finds in Christian theology. There are also objections to systems approaching determinism which are quite similar to ones found among Christians. The theology of Islam provides a particularly important place for determinism. This is reflected above all in the history of the concept of *kadar*, or divine decree, which is closely analogous to the Christian concept of predestination. The position of Muhammad, the Prophet, as reflected in the Koran, is ambiguous on the problem, although it seems clear that he developed a real predestinarian position late in his life. The earliest Islamic tradition built on this position by developing a strong belief in uncompromising fatalism. By the beginning of the eighth century, however, some Muslims began to question this dogma, particularly the members of the *Kadariya* sect. In reaction to their questioning, a sect of extreme predestinarians formed, called the *Djabriya*. They argued that man bears no responsibility of any kind for any of the actions which seem to proceed from him. This makes of man an automaton, and was too extreme for most Muslims. So intermediate positions generally prevailed.

Those Muslims who have defended human free will, do so basically for ethical reasons. They argue that Allah cannot be just if man does not possess moral responsibility for his actions. Those who have defended *kadar* grapple with the problem of explaining man's apparent consciousness of free choice. This phenomenon is sometimes explained as an illusion, sometimes explained as applying only to unimportant decisions and not to those of ultimate importance.

The mature position of Islamic orthodoxy, however, continues to endorse a strong measure of determinism.

The theology of Judaism provides less room for approaches to determinism than either Christianity or Islam. But it does provide some. The doctrine of predestination is of particularly little importance, partly because of the great importance Judaism assigns to the necessity for ethical behavior among humans, partly because Judaism did not continue to accept an elaborate eschatology. Even among the Jews, however, there have been some groups which have adopted a doctrine of predestination. According to Josephus, this was a cardinal tenet of the ascetic Essene sect.

In general, however, a more significant approach to determinism in Judaism can be found in the widely-held doctrine of providence. Since biblical times, many Jews have believed that God controls the universe in ways which benefit His chosen people, both as individuals and as a group. In general, they believe that this control is made most evident in the temporal life of man on this earth, rather than being postponed until some post-temporal life, after death. The Jews, of course, given their history, have had ample reason to be aware of the existence of evil and pain in this temporal life. Such evil is sometimes explained as a prophylactic or purge, designed by God to prepare man for a good greater than that to which he would otherwise be entitled. Or evil can be explained away as an illusion, or a step in a process ultimately issuing in something good. Arguments of this sort can easily be squared with belief in a Jehovah who is omnipotent and omniscient and who rules the world through His providence. But evil is often explained by Jewish thinkers as a punishment administered to man by God for his wicked behavior, an explanation which would place full responsibility on man for the evil that befalls him, but which diminishes the full plenitude of divine power. In popular Judaism, the dilemma is generally evaded, with both the doctrine of providence and the moral responsibility of man being taught.

III. SOCIAL CONSEQUENCES OF DETERMINISM

It is a common reaction to systems including determinism that they should induce fatalism, passivity, a complete conservatism. For if man can achieve nothing on his own initiative, why should he try to exercise any initiative? It is a similar reaction that these systems should induce amorality, even immorality. For if man can achieve no reward or recognition for good conduct, why should he be good? These tend to be the reactions of neutral observers, however, not those of believers in theological systems containing elements of determinism. In actual fact, these systems have often been associated with socially active, even militant, religious groups, which often demanded a puritanical moralism of their members. In Christian Europe, the Augustinian West has been usually more militant than the Orthodox East, despite the East's greater emphasis on human free will. The difference was reflected at a fairly early point in the ecclesiastical history of the two areas. The churches in the East submitted to the control of secular governments, first the control of the Greek emperors headquartered in Constantinople, later the control of the Russian tsars headquartered in Moscow or St. Petersburg. Forms of cesaropapism thus have often characterized the Eastern churches. The churches in the West, meanwhile, led by the Roman pontiff, claimed a considerable independence from the secular states, and often made such claims good. On occasion the papacy even claimed a measure of control over the secular states.

In more modern times, predestinarian Calvinist churches were the most militant and puritanical prod-

uct of the Protestant Reformation. When the religious tensions created by the Reformation became so acute that they boiled over into open warfare, it was most often the Calvinists who took the leadership of the Protestant cause. This bellicosity was first evident among the Swiss cantons, in Zwingli's day, even before Calvin became the recognized principal leader of the movement. It became even more pronounced and large-scale in France, where Calvinist Huguenots helped to plunge the nation into more than thirty years of religious wars beginning in 1562. It was repeated in the Netherlands, where the Calvinist Beggars helped provoke the eighty-years' war for Dutch independence in 1572. Also in Germany the Calvinists of the Palatinate organized a Protestant Union, which helped push all central Europe into the Thirty Years' War in 1618. In England the Calvinist Puritans won control of Parliament, and then tried to change the form of government by force, from 1640 to 1660.

Even in the twentieth century, neo-orthodox theologians with elements of determinism in their thought have been noted for their concern with social problems and morality. Both Niebuhr and Barth have been sensitive to the need for large-scale reforms which is most commonly exploited by socialists. Both were also early to recognize the great moral evil of fascism and to urge that Christians resist it with force, even war when that seemed necessary.

The correlation between determinism and militancy in Christian civilization is not, to be sure, a perfect one. In the Catholic Counter-Reformation of the seventeenth century, the neo-Augustinian Jansenist movement was in most respects markedly less militant even though markedly more puritanical than its chief opponent, the Society of Jesus. But in general the correlation between Christian determinism and militancy is striking and surely significant.

Similar historical examples of a correlation between determinism and militancy can be found in other systems. They are particularly striking in Islam. The centuries after the Prophet's death when the doctrine of *kadar* was generally accepted were the very years when Islam generated its most explosive force, conquering large parts of the Near East, the Middle East, Africa, and India. The recrudescence of Muslim militancy with the arrival of the Turks several centuries later, seems to have coincided with a revival of a kind of determinism. It took a Turkic form in the doctrine of *kismet*, a form of fatalism about the development of this temporal world, not necessarily connected to questions of man's eternal destiny.

This frequent correlation between theological determinism and social militancy poses problems of great psychological and cultural interest. They may be beyond the competence of a historian of ideas. But there clearly seems to be something about the beliefs that there is a God who controls the universe completely and that those who believe in Him are His chosen instruments, which induces a social activism which can become militant, even frantic, even fanatic.

BIBLIOGRAPHY

Useful introductions can be found in several encyclopedias and dictionaries of religious thought, especially in articles on the histories of doctrines like predestination and providence. See in particular the articles on predestination in *The Jewish Encyclopedia,* on *kadar* in the *Encyclopédie de l'Islam,* and on predestination and providence in the *Dictionnaire de théologie catholique.* The latter two articles, by Reginald Garrigou-Lagrange, were developed into books and translated, as *Providence* (St. Louis and London, 1951), and *Predestination* (St. Louis and London, 1953). Further introductory material can be found in handbooks of dogmatic history. For the Christian tradition, see in particular Reinhold Seeberg, *Lehrbuch der Dogmengeschichte* (Darmstadt, 1959–65, 4 vols. in 5, reprint of the third edition of 1920–23); an English translation is available under the title *Text-Book of the History of Doctrines* (Grand Rapids, Mich., 1966, seventh printing), but is based on the substantially shorter first German edition. The bibliography of specialized monographs and articles on the subject is very large. Some useful examples: Georges de Plinval, "Aspects du déterminisme et de la liberté dans la doctrine de saint Augustin," *Revue des études augustiniennes,* **1,** 4 (1955), 345–78; J. Bohatec, "Calvins Vorsehungslehre," in J. Bohatec, ed., *Calvinstudien* (Leipzig, 1900), pp. 339–441; Paul Jacobs, *Prädestination und Verantwortlichkeit bei Calvin* (Darmstadt, 1937; 1968); John T. McNeill, *The History and Character of Calvinism* (New York, 1954); G. C. Berkouwer, *The Triumph of Grace in the Theology of Karl Barth* (Grand Rapids, Mich., 1956). Almost all of these studies concentrate quite strictly on the history of doctrines, and do not consider the historical circumstances in which they arose and spread. A partial exception is the McNeill book.

ROBERT M. KINGDON

[See also **Evil; Free Will in Theology; God;** Islamic Conception; Necessity; Reformation; **Religious Toleration;** Sin and Salvation; Theodicy.]

DOUBLE TRUTH

THE DOCTRINE of double truth first appears in 1277 as part of the introduction to a Church condemnation of heterodox ideas. In this document the Bishop of Paris, Stephen Tempier, declares that certain masters in the Parisian Arts Faculty "hold that something is true according to philosophy but not according to the Catholic faith, as if there are two contrary truths, and as if in contradiction to the truth of Sacred Scripture there is a truth in the doctrines of the accursed pagans." The same proposition may be true and false simultaneously, true in philosophy and false in theology—such is the condemned doctrine of double truth. Unready to accept this denial of the law of contradiction, which he sees as a device to assert heresy, the bishop then lists 219 condemned errors. The masters of arts are warned not to teach them on pain of excommunication. Although the thirteenth-century Averroist Siger of Brabant, and his contemporary Boethius of Dacia are the only two masters mentioned by name in the condemnation, the list of heterodox propositions is so broad that it includes doctrines taught by Saint Thomas.

In two senses the condemnation represents a crisis in the Western Latin mind. In the narrower sense, it is an attempt on the part of the Parisian Faculty of Theology to stop philosophical speculation in the Faculty of Arts, especially when that speculation abandons the traditional guidance of theology and openly professes heterodox doctrines. At the time of the organization of the University in 1200, the greater part of Aristotle's works was already available in Latin translation. As the higher of the two faculties, the Faculty of Theology wished to assert its control over the study of these new doctrines, particularly the dangerous ideas found in the *libri naturales* and the *Metaphysics.* From the very beginning theologians were suspicious of their contents. In 1210 and again in 1215 the public and private teaching (though not private reading) of Aristotle's works was banned at the University. Yet the theologians themselves soon began to be impressed with the tremendous power and comprehensiveness of Aristotle's doctrines, and in 1231 Pope Gregory IX decided that Aristotle might be taught at Paris if his errors were first expurgated. With this limited approval, the knowledge of Aristotle increased and by 1243 the commentaries of Averroës became known. Although the ban against an unexpurgated Aristotle was still in effect at the University in the 1240's, it was not always upheld. For example, in 1245 Roger Bacon lectured in the Arts Faculty on the complete *Physics* and *Metaphysics.* Nevertheless conflict did not break out between the two faculties, probably because the masters of arts continued to quote Saint Augustine with respect, and to dismiss discreetly any heterodox doctrine of Averroës or Aristotle. When the split finally opened in the 1260's, the cause was not difficult to find. Led by Siger of Brabant, the masters of arts were openly professing heterodox Arabic-Aristotelian concepts in disregard of the doctrines of revelation. Thirteen doctrines, condemned in 1270, were included in the great condemnation of 1277.

In the larger sense, the condemnation represents more than the professional rivalry of two faculties. For the theologians were the guardians of the Augustinian tradition which had been dominant in medieval thought up to this time. Augustinianism had made its peace with pagan philosophy by absorbing the spiritual orientation of Neo-Platonism while subordinating it to Christian revelation. The Augustinian universe consists of a static, hierarchically ordered series of beings culminating in the Supreme Being who has created all from nothing. Through his omniscience, the Divine Being knows all; through His mercy He provides for all; through His freedom He orders all to His will. The Arabic-Aristotelian view, now championed in the Faculty of Arts, stands in dramatic opposition to this. The universe is moved by the Prime Being, the first of the separated Intelligences. Emanating from this Intelligence are the other Intelligences, the heavenly spheres, and finally the earth as the arena of generation and decay. The entire emanation proceeds by an eternal, necessary movement, controlling the Prime Mover Himself. Such a God can only produce an effect similar to Himself: a unique, undifferentiated substance. The multiplicity of effects in the world, then, presupposes the multiplicity of intermediary causes, rather than the direct activity of God. It follows that God acts through the heavenly Intelligences which in turn produce the multiplicity of things on the earth. The Intelligences thus become the immediate causes of earthly effects.

Here then we have a dramatic contrast: a free, personal deity as opposed to an impersonal deity moved by necessary causes; a created universe as opposed to an eternally emanating one; a knowing God as opposed to one who knows only himself; a being who acts directly on the earth as opposed to one who acts through the intermediaries of the Intelligences.

To illustrate this crisis more concretely and to show the origin of the doctrine of double truth, we must isolate several of the condemned propositions. As we have seen, Aristotle and Averroës held the eternity of the world; it was moved by a Prime Mover who activates necessarily the Intelligences of the heavenly spheres. This denied creation *ex nihilo* of Genesis, and the freedom and providence of a personal deity. Moreover, an eternal movement is constant and absolute, and the nature produced from such a movement exhibits the same features: there can be no interruption of the laws of nature. Hence there can be no miracles performed by a personal God or His messengers.

In the second place, Aristotelian psychology, at least as interpreted by Averroës, denied the immortality of the individual soul. For Averroës the only immortal

soul is a divine intellect which at times unites itself to man. This union produces an "acquired intellect" which gives man the power to know. As the title "acquired" makes clear, this intellect—the only human one which knows—is not intrinsic to man. In other words the intellect for man is not an inherent form but an assisting form. Since the "acquired intellect" is produced only when the vegetative and sensitive functions operate, their cessation at death entails the destruction of the "acquired intellect" and the whole human soul. Only the divine intellect remains and is immortal. It is the one, true intellect for all men. This is the famous doctrine of the unity of the intellect, a doctrine which destroys the Christian concepts of personal immortality, salvation, and resurrection.

Finally, other condemned ideas attack the very basis of the Christian religion by asserting that philosophy is the highest wisdom. In contrast, Christianity is pictured as containing falsehoods "like all other religions" and is held to be based on myths and fables. Although the notion that philosophy is the supreme wisdom is found in some thirteenth-century thinkers, the idea that Christianity is false or mythical only appears for the first time with John of Jandun in the early fourteenth century.

What did the masters of arts actually say in professing these doctrines of the "accursed pagans"? Did they attempt to avoid conflict with revelation by saying that there are two contradictory truths?

There is no doubt that the most famous master of arts, Siger of Brabant, taught many of the condemned doctrines. At various stages of his career, he held the unity of the intellect and consequent mortality of the soul, the eternity of the world, and the regularity of natural change prohibiting miraculous interruption. Though his attitude shifted at various times (usually under the pressure of attacks from the Faculty of Theology), he never admitted the possibility of two contradictory truths. Nowhere in his writings does the term "double truth" appear, nor do we ever find the statement of two contrary truths as set down in the 1277 condemnation. On the other hand, there is a good deal of evidence to indicate that Siger upheld the law of contradiction, thus explicitly denying the possibility of a double truth. In his *Questions* on *Metaphysics IV*, he says that we cannot maintain contradictory points simultaneously for that is to deny what we affirm. The mind itself, he holds, will not allow adherence to contradictory propositions. Even God does not produce such contradictions for He will not make man into an ass. With this explicit acceptance of the law of contradiction, the problem remains of Siger's acceptance of the teachings of Greco-Arabic philosophy and his simultaneous insistence on the validity of Christian revelation.

Siger's solution to this problem consists of three different attitudes adopted at various points in his teaching. The first attitude, common throughout his work, is the assertion that faith is true while the doctrines of Aristotle are merely the conclusions of philosophy and reason. The word "truth" always appears associated with faith and in opposition to the teachings of Aristotle and reason. Prescinding from faith, Siger argues, we must investigate nature with Averroës and Aristotle as our guides. Our conclusions, however, are not true but simply the rational deductions of pagan philosophers. In its most radical form, this attitude expresses itself as the reduction of philosophical inquiry to the doctrinal history of previous thinkers. When we proceed philosophically, says Siger, we examine the opinions of the philosophers, not the truth of the matter.

But this attitude did not always satisfy him. Time and again we find the assertion that the doctrines of nature are not simply those of Aristotle and Averroës but also the conclusions of reason. Unlike the first attitude which tends to identify reason with the doctrines of Aristotelians, here reason becomes separated from the philosophers; it produces a knowledge independent of their teachings. At times the arguments of natural reason appear "almost irrefutable." Yet faith contradicts them, and we must accept many things on faith which "human reason leads us to deny." A strict antinomy develops between knowledge and faith: "I know one thing; I believe another," says Siger. There is an epistemological basis for this attitude. Natural philosophy, according to Siger, presents us only with those laws established by human reason. Because God is above rational laws, it follows that He may interrupt them, not to produce absurdities but to complete the inadequacies of human reason. The truth of faith is not denied by contrary assertions of natural reason because revelation itself derives from a source inaccessible to human reason.

Siger's insistence on the great value of autonomous philosophy and the wisdom it produces leads him to adopt still a third position. Impressed with the nature of philosophy, Siger does not always reserve the word truth for faith alone and he seems at least implicitly to assert a double truth. In the *Commentary* on the *Metaphysics*, he says: "The knowledge of truth belongs principally to philosophy because it has for its object the first causes and the first principles—thus the first truths." And in the *Commentary* on the *De anima*, he holds that the knowledge of the soul gained by philosophy is important for truth. If philosophy establishes true principles and faith is still true, it seems difficult, in cases of specific doctrinal conflict, to avoid the statement that two contradictory truths actually exist. The solution to this dilemma stems once more from

epistemological considerations. The highest truth, Siger holds, can only result from the knowledge of causes in themselves and not as they are inferred from effects; in Siger's language we must have knowledge of causes per se. Now all arguments of reason are generalizations from sense perception which enable us to describe nature not through its own causes but only through effects registered on the mind. When set down into laws, such effects can never provide final certainty because they do not establish the causes per se of the things they purport to describe. This reduces all philosophical knowledge to a probable or hypothetical status.

In effect Siger has established degrees of certitude. Faith is absolutely certain even though it is not demonstrable to reason. Rational inquiry limited, as it is, to God's effects cannot attain to the causes per se of these effects. For we cannot describe the mode of God's activity per se which in the end is the cause of the principles of nature. Rational demonstrations therefore which appear final and irrefutable are such only within natural limits, and consequently their demonstrative status is only probable. In several places, Siger endorses this probabilism: "We have demonstrated above that the effect of God is eternal; this conclusion is probable but not necessary"; "The argument of Aristotle is probable; it is not necessary"; "Although the argument of the Commentator has probability, it is not true" (Muller, 1938).

The second thinker mentioned in the 1277 condemnation, Boethius of Dacia, adopted essentially the same attitude as Siger. The method of natural philosophy must limit itself to natural causes and principles. On these principles alone, we must accept the eternity of the world, says Boethius. Although these principles hold within the natural order, supernatural principles may suspend them, not by demonstrating their falsity (that is impossible) but by asserting the opposite on grounds of revelation. Again we are faced with relative degrees of certitude rather than the absolute validity of contradictory truths. Even though Boethius praised the life of philosophy in his *De summo bono* as the pursuit of speculative truth and as the worthiest life for man, we must bear in mind that these concepts are relative to the natural order of philosophy. Nowhere are they asserted absolutely as the 1277 condemnation claims.

There appears to be no reason to doubt the sincerity of Siger and Boethius in their proclamations of loyalty to the Christian religion. They were not secret atheists or rationalists. Sincere Christians, they were confronted with a dramatic gulf between their deeply held religious beliefs and the conclusions of their philosophical pursuits. They adjusted the conflict by setting the Christian God totally outside the natural order. Then they declared all descriptions of that order, produced by philosophy, to be statements of a limited, probable, and hypothetical nature. The doctrine of double truth or two contradictory truths was imposed on them by their adversaries who, by reading it into their statements, hoped to end speculation they considered heretical.

The 1277 condemnation effectively ended philosophical speculation in the Faculty of Arts until the end of the century. In the fourteenth century, however, the masters of arts were once again allowed to take up the doctrine of the Stagirite and his commentators. On the testimony of two chancellors of the University, Jean Gerson and John Buridan, we learn that the masters of the Faculty of Arts were permitted to consider these doctrines provided they took an oath swearing to uphold the doctrines of revelation. When expounding pagan ideas contrary to faith, the Parisian masters had to swear that they would demonstrate the falsity of those views in conflict with faith. In order to do this the masters asserted the necessity of giving a complete exposition of pagan doctrines.

The situation can be well illustrated by considering the thought of John Buridan, onetime chancellor of the University, and one of the most influential scholastics of the century. Like Siger, Buridan accepts the mortality of the soul and the eternity of the world as the doctrines of philosophy. Establishing these doctrines, however, requires that we understand the nature of philosophical statements. All such statements are merely probable because philosophical inquiry proceeds by three modes of understanding—experience, memory, and induction—which derive from sense perception. Since Buridan grants a realm of final truth above sense perception, it is clear that empirical knowledge does not arrive at ultimate certainty.

When we compare the probable philosophical theses of Siger and Buridan, the major difference we discover is the growth in Buridan of a natural philosophy independent of Aristotle. The tendency of separating reason and nature from the ideas of the philosophers—already apparent in Siger—is much more marked in Buridan. As a result, it is impossible for Buridan to argue that he is merely reporting the opinions of previous philosophers. From his many criticisms of Aristotle, it is quite evident that he intends to establish an independent and objective natural science. The assertions of philosophy become the descriptions of nature, and Aristotle himself is often rejected in the name of natural reason. Nevertheless, Aristotle's authority still stands so high that only when Buridan agrees with the Stagirite does he vigorously defend a philosophical position in sharp opposition to faith.

The development of a philosophical probabilism can be seen in Buridan's treatment of creation *ex nihilo*. Creation out of a void, he holds, must be accepted on faith but the notion that every existing being implies a preexisting being is valid for philosophy. Thus, according to philosophy, we must hold the eternity of the world which, in turn, throws into question the immortality of the soul. For if the world is eternal and souls immortal, an infinite number of souls will be wandering around the universe. To avoid this absurdity, the logic of natural philosophy demands that we deny the immortality of the soul. On the basis of natural philosophy, arguments for mortality may be derived either from Averroës' view of the unity of the intellect or the Aristotelian Commentator Alexander of Aphrodisias' (fl. 200) view of the corruptibility of individual souls. Buridan chooses the Alexandrist position: the soul is a form educed from the potency of matter, extended to the extension of matter, multiplied in distinct bodies, and finally generated and corrupted. This is the objectively correct doctrine of natural philosophy. However, Buridan decides that the doctrine of faith is true: the soul inheres in matter but is eternally immortal after death. For the argument of natural philosophy, he concludes, is only probable and must give way before the irrefutable truths of divine revelation.

The most radical Parisian master of the fourteenth century, John of Jandun (d. 1328), continues the tradition of Siger in several ways. Jandun upholds individual mortality on Averroistic grounds, explicitly rejecting the "vile error" of Alexander that the soul actually informs the body. The soul is not created but coeternal with the world. The opposite view of faith, while not demonstrable to reason, is true. God produces this by a miracle not apparent to sense perception: He makes the corruptible soul immortal.

In Jandun, the status of natural philosophy is also raised, as in Buridan, to that of an independent, objective description of nature. Thus the doctrines of natural reason, derived ultimately from sense perception, provide philosophic proofs whose demonstrative status is logical not simply historical: these are not merely the proofs of Averroës and Aristotle, but the independent conclusions of reason. Precisely because these laws are derived from rational demonstrations based on sense perceptions, they are not absolutely true. They must be rejected when they conflict with revelation.

Despite differences in the interpretation of the doctrine of the soul, both Buridan and Jandun subscribed to Siger's original division of probable philosophical demonstration vs. absolute revealed truth. A new element, however, enters with Jandun. We find the first written statements of those condemned propositions of 1277 which spoke of Christianity as full of errors and based on fables and myths. In his *Commentary* on

Aristotle's *De anima*, Jandun notes that Averroës attacks the strength of custom. It is custom alone, says the Commentator, which accounts for the strength of religions. Men come to accept the fables and puerile notions inherent in religious belief only because they have heard them from childhood. And in the Commentary on the *De caelo et mundo*, Jandun notes that Averroës refers to religion in a derogatory sense in his prologue to Aristotle's *Physics*, Book III. There the Commentator holds that the doctrines of religion are apologies established by religious lawmakers for the control of the common people; these doctrines corrupt necessary principles and are "removed from truth and the human mind." The Commentator, Jandun adds, is speaking of the Muslim religion, "and if he should speak of our religion he would lie because all things in our religion are true and proved by the miracles of God and the glory of the Creator." It is important to note that Jandun may be perfectly sincere in this statement. And it is equally important to say that once stated, the notion that religious belief is a human invention reinforced by conventional usage would gain increasing currency.

We can begin to see this development in the late fourteenth and early fifteenth centuries. Particularly at the northern Italian Universities, organized without faculties of theology, we find an increasing emphasis not only on independent philosophical speculation but also on philosophical attacks on religious truth. Most thinkers continued to adhere sincerely to the earlier divisions which established for the masters of arts a method distinct from that of theology. But there were some who denied the probable nature of philosophical conclusions, asserting instead the absolute truth of philosophy, and thus turning philosophical criticism against Christianity itself.

Perhaps the outstanding example of this development is Blasius of Parma (d. 1416). Active in Pavia, Padua, and Bologna in the late fourteenth century, Blasius was professor of astronomy, mathematics, and philosophy. He establishes the mortality of the soul by proving that the soul has no function independent of bodily powers. Knowing, the highest function of the soul, depends on the continuous operation of the sensitive powers; and the eventual dissolution of the sensitive powers carries with it the disruption and disintegration of the mind. Since a function independent of the body is the one feature Aristotle had declared as proof of immortality, Blasius claims that mortality is proved. This proof has Alexandrist features and is not new. But when Blasius announces that mortality is not merely probable but must be accepted absolutely we are in the presence of a new attitude of mind. The development of this stance is worth examining.

Like his predecessors, Blasius sharply separates knowledge and belief. To know something, he declares, is to have arguments based on evidence; to believe something, knowledge is not necessary, and in the case of faith must be set aside. Unlike earlier thinkers he appears to reject the notion of asserting and denying at the same time with different degrees of certitude. We cannot have a probable scientific deduction in conflict with an absolute religious truth. Rather we must choose one or the other. "When you intend to support faith which is believed," contends Blasius, "you must reject the habit of philosophy which insists on evidence, and where the reverse occurs, you must reject the Christian faith."

The question of course remains: Does Blasius reject Christian faith absolutely or merely as irrelevant to philosophy? Perhaps he is insisting with Jandun that the modes of inquiry proper to faith and reason are radically different and cannot be combined; each must pursue a separate path. From Blasius' discussion of the soul, however, it begins to appear that he favors an absolute rejection of faith. He introduces the notion that the soul can be created by spontaneous generation from waste, as is the case in lower forms of life. The method of arriving at this conclusion is quite as interesting as the conclusion itself. Discussing the biblical story of the flood, Blasius points out that all life must have been destroyed when waters covered the earth for forty days. "Nor in this matter," he warns, "should you believe the tales of women that Noah made an ark in which he placed all the animals" (Maier, 1949). Quite the contrary, all human and animal life was destroyed. Man was created anew from the waste products and the appropriate constellation of the stars. It is from this startling discussion that Blasius concludes that the soul is mortal—produced from matter as other generable and corruptible things. Now this is not a probable doctrine of philosophy: Blasius contends that it must be conceded absolutely.

The suspicions raised by the critique of the Bible and the absolute assertion of mortality are confirmed by Blasius' discussion of the origin of religions. The issue is no longer the status of any particular Christian belief but the value of Christianity itself. Following the astrological book *De magnis coniunctionibus* of Albumazar (805–85), Blasius explains that the diversity of religious belief arises from the conjunction of Jupiter with different planets. These in turn produce the different religious sects. The Jewish sect, for example, is produced from the conjunction of Jupiter with Saturn, while the sect of the Saracens is caused by the union of Jupiter with Venus. And "from the union of Jupiter with Mercury the Christian sect is produced." Christianity here originates from the same natural forces which produce the other religions. This extreme astrological determinism eliminates free choice in religious matters. Men no longer choose their religions freely; they are naturally inclined to a particular sect by the conjunction of the planets.

After some trouble with Church authorities and a forced recantation, Blasius gave a later lecture in which he denied these views. In this lecture he warns that the views of Albumazar are erroneous and false, denying specifically that the conjunctions of Jupiter with the other planets produce the various religions. He insists furthermore that a wise man will supersede the knowledge of the stars in deciding his own religious belief. Despite this denial, obviously produced under pressure from Church authorities, it appears that Blasius accepts all these philosophical doctrines as certain. He criticizes religious doctrines on philosophical grounds, attacks biblical miracles, and reverses the traditional degrees of certitude in religion and philosophy. For Blasius truth appears to be on the side of philosophy which claims the privilege of explaining the origin of religion itself as a natural phenomenon. Siger's probable philosophical statements are now transformed into an absolute philosophical certitude, bowing before religious belief and its representatives only out of tactical necessity.

The full development of Blasius' doctrines appears in the sixteenth century, which marks the final liberation of philosophy from its subordination to revelation. In the Aristotelian tradition most thinkers continued to maintain sincerely the traditional distinctions between probable philosophical statements and absolute religious truth. Some professors in the Italian universities, however, developed the dramatic shift in viewpoint already expressed by Blasius. Reacting quickly to this, the Fifth Lateran Council of 1513 revived the traditional oath of the Parisian masters of arts; it declared that all discussions of philosophical positions opposed to faith had to include both a defense of revelation and a reasoned argument against heterodox notions. The theologians of the Council defended orthodoxy with a proclamation of the immortality of the soul as a dogma and the condemnation of three errors: the unity of the intellect, the mortality of the soul, and the idea that such doctrines were true "at least in philosophy." "Truth does not contradict truth," said the theologians, echoing the 1277 condemnation. In the works of the professors of philosophy we do not find the open admission, as the Council charged, of two contradictory truths. But doubtless there were some who were guilty of asserting the absolute truth of philosophy while paying perfunctory obeisance to the "truth" of revelation. An outstanding

example of this attitude can be found in the works of Pietro Pomponazzi (1462–1525).

Teaching natural philosophy at Padua, Ferrara, and Bologna, Pomponazzi summarizes and reshapes the more radical conclusions of his predecessors in the Aristotelian tradition. Of the philosophical themes we have traced Pomponazzi concerns himself primarily with three: the mortality of the soul, the regularity and universality of natural laws, and the nature of religious doctrine. In his immortality treatises—*De immortalitate animae*, *Apologia*, and *Defensorium*—he proves the mortality of the soul. The proof is original only in the sense that it unites many formerly disparate elements. With Alexander of Aphrodisias, he insists that the soul inheres in the body and is forever bound to its material foundation; the corruption of the material foundation entails the destruction of the soul. With Blasius, he finds that no function of the soul can exist without some relation to bodily powers; for even the highest function of thought is part of an interlocking chain of powers based on corruptible matter. With Scotus, he argues against Thomas Aquinas that the soul cannot simultaneously be an immaterial substance and the act of the body; an immaterial substance is separate and separable from the body while an act is a process perfecting bodily operations. Since Aristotle had always defined the soul as the act of the body, we must hold that it is always bound to the powers it perfects; hence it is mortal, Pomponazzi concludes.

In the *De incantationibus*, Pomponazzi discovers natural causes for "miraculous occurrences." Cures, visions, and the raising of the dead are all explained in three ways: as human inventions, the effects of occult powers (found in plants, animals, and men), or the results of the activity of the heavenly Intelligences. Miracles are reduced to unusual events which only the trained mind can trace to their natural causes. The clear conclusion is that there are no miracles produced by angels or demons because there are no interruptions of the natural processes of birth, growth, and decay.

After Pomponazzi establishes these doctrines as the findings of philosophy and natural reason, he applies the usual distinctions which have been traditional for three centuries. These are the findings of natural reason, he says, but they must be suspended by faith. The Church teaches immortality as well as miracles produced by God, demons, and angels. We must accept all this as true, rejecting the conclusions of reason. Although not demonstrable by reason, the truth of faith is superior to the findings of reason. For God, who is the creator of nature, may suspend its principles. In these apologetic statements, Pomponazzi appears to be very close to Siger, Boethius of Dacia, and Buridan.

Closer examination, however, reveals that he follows the path of Blasius. Like Jandun, Pomponazzi knows and lectures on Averroës' prologue to *Physics*, Book III. In these lectures, he proclaims in the name of the Commentator that "truth is the end of philosophy while the end of the religious lawgiver is neither truth nor falsehood but to make men good and well-behaved." He takes the precaution, as did Jandun, of associating these views with Averroës, and finally condemns them as false. But in his own name in his published works there are striking instances of Pomponazzi's acceptance of philosophy as absolute truth, and his discovery of a human origin for religious doctrines. Immortality, he comes to state, is an invention of religious lawmakers who proclaim this doctrine "not caring for truth." Clearly the truth they do not "care for" is the doctrine of mortality as proved by philosophy. Demons and angels, which he apparently has accepted as the Church's teaching, he finds were also invented by men "who knew very well that they did not exist."

Finally, Pomponazzi holds that Christianity is not the gift of an eternal God but merely the product of impersonal heavenly forces. These forces, the heavenly Intelligences, produce life-cycles for all religions, including Christianity. In fact, Christianity itself, he explains, is approaching its death which is why the Intelligences produce so few "miracles" at the present time. If the origin of Christianity is temporally conditioned, so are its doctrines. Far from eternal verities, they are the inventions of religious lawmakers who seek to control a bestial human nature through the fear of hell and the hope of heaven. The philosopher who does not need such restraints, Pomponazzi continues, may nevertheless understand their purpose and approve of them for the masses.

These doctrines mark the beginning of the end of theological dominance in the West. Philosophy is no longer a collection of probable statements but an absolute truth subjecting all doctrines to its powerful analysis. It begins to dislodge theology from its position as queen of the sciences.

If we glance briefly over the history we have discussed, we can see that the masters in the Faculty of Arts at Paris initiated a tradition which lasted over four centuries in the universities of Europe among those philosophers who were professionally concerned with Aristotle and his commentators. Refusing to find or to force agreement between pagan doctrines and revelation, the Parisian masters raised, in its most extreme form, the problem of the precise relationship of philosophical inquiry to revealed truth. Moreover they did this at a time when revealed truth had the strongest institutional sanctions. The history of the idea of double truth is thus really the history of the relationship of philosophy to theology among professional philosophers in the Aristotelian tradition. By carving out an independent domain of inquiry for philosophy, the earlier thinkers, led by Siger, freed philosophy from the necessity of theological guidance. This made possible its ultimate escape from religious domination. Siger, Boethius of Dacia, Jandun, and Buridan all sincerely accepted the one supreme truth of theology. Yet it was probably to be expected that some thinkers in this tradition, confronted constantly with the un-Christian naturalism of Aristotle, would one day proclaim the Stagirite's doctrines as the highest truth, and turn this truth against theology itself.

BIBLIOGRAPHY

The text of the 1277 condemnation is found in H. Denifle and A. Chatelain, *Chartularium universitatis pariensus* (Paris, 1889), I, 543–55. See also: W. Bentzendörfer, *Die Lehre von der zweifachen Wahrheit bei Petrus Pomponatius* (Tübingen, 1919). G. Di Napoli, *L'Immortalità dell'anima nel Rinascimento* (Turin, 1963). Pierre Duhem, *Système du monde*, Vol. V (Paris, 1954). É. Gilson, "La doctrine de la double vérité," *Études de philosophie médiévale* (Strasbourg, 1921), pp. 51–69; idem, *History of Christian Philosophy in the Middle Ages* (New York, 1955). T. Gregory, "Discussioni sulla 'doppia verità,'" *Cultura e Scuola*, **2** (1962), 99–106. P. O. Kristeller, "Paduan Averroism and Alexandrism in the Light of Recent Studies," *Atti del XII Congresso Internazionale di Filosofia*, **9** (1960), 147–55. S. MacClintock, *Perversity and Error: Studies on the "Averroist" John of Jandun* (Bloomington, Ind., 1956). A. Maier, *Studien zur Naturphilosophie der Spätscholastik*, Vol. I: *Die Vorläufer Galileis im 14 Jahrundert* (Rome, 1949), 279–99; Vol. IV: *Metaphysische Hintergrunde der spätscholastischen Naturphilosophie* (Rome, 1955), 3–45. A. Maurer, "Between Reason and Faith: Siger of Brabant and Pomponazzi on the Magic Arts," *Medieval Studies*, **18** (1956), 1–18. J. P. Muller, "Philosophie et foi chez Siger de Brabant: La Théorie de la double vérité," *Studia anselmiana*, **7-8** (1938), 35–50. B. Nardi, *Studi su Pomponazzi* (Florence, 1965). A. Pacchi, "Sul Commento al 'De anima' de G. di Jandun, IV: La Questione della Doppia Verità," *Rivista critica di storia della filosofia*, **15** (1960), 354–75. M. Pine, "Pietro Pomponazzi and the Problem of Double Truth," *Journal of the History of Ideas*, **29** (1968), 163–76. L. Thorndike, *A History of Magic and Experimental Science*, Vol. IV (New York, 1934), 64–79; Vol. V (New York, 1941), 94–110. F. Van Steenberghen, *Siger de Brabant* (Brussels, 1938); idem, *Aristotle in the West* (Louvain, 1955); idem, *La Philosophie au XIIIe siècle* (Louvain, 1966).

MARTIN PINE

[See also Astrology; Certainty; Creation; Death and Immortality; **Dualism;** God.]

DUALISM IN PHILOSOPHY AND RELIGION

A DUALIST is one who believes that the facts which he considers—whether they be the facts of the world in general or a particular class of them—cannot be explained except by supposing ultimately the existence of two different and irreducible principles. For example, dualists in anthropology explain facts about man by two fundamental causes: reason and the passions, soul and body, or freedom and determinism; in the theory of knowledge, dualists explain knowledge by the meeting of two different realities: subject and object; in religious cosmology, they picture the world as dominated by the perpetual conflict of a good and an evil power, both of which have always existed.

There are various kinds of dualism, depending on the different subjects of reflection or research. However, the subjects in which the term dualism is most often employed are the history of religions and philosophy. Thomas Hyde seems to have invented the term "dualist," which he uses in his history of the religion of the ancient Persians (*Historia religionis veterum Persarum*, 1700) in order to designate the men who think that God and the devil are two coeternal principles. The term was later used in this same sense by Pierre Bayle and by Leibniz. Christian Wolff first applied it to the philosophers who considered the body and the soul as two distinct substances: "The dualists (*dualistae*) are those who admit the existence of both material and immaterial substances, that is, they concede the real existence of bodies outside the ideas of the souls and defend the immateriality of these souls" (*Psychologia rationalis* [1734], Sec. 39). Most philosophers employ the word in Wolff's sense, whereas most historians of religions have retained the meaning of "dualism" which it had in Hyde.

The word "dualism" then has two principal meanings: (1) religious and (2) philosophical. In sense (1) it designates religions such as Zoroastrianism of the later Avesta and of the Pahlavi books; in sense (2) dualism applies to philosophies such as Cartesianism. It must be noted that these are very different doctrines, from which it would be possible to draw even contradictory consequences. For example, the dualism of soul and body or of mind and matter might lead to the denial of the existence of an absolutely evil mind (the devil) and even of an evil principle. Matter is not in itself evil for the dualistic philosophers; and a pure mind can hardly be evil for those who think that the cause of error, and consequently of evil, is the mixture of mind with matter or the inversion of their legitimate hierarchic order.

Since the two doctrines are distinct, we must consider them separately. However, it may seem that they are united in some systems, for instance in Manicheism, in which God's adversary is often personified but is also identified with matter. But in Manicheism there is something else, in addition to these two forms of dualism. Manicheism proceeds from Gnosticism, and Gnostic dualism—although some scholars held it to be a synthesis of Hellenic (that is to say of philosophical) and of Zoroastrian dualism—is neither exactly a philosophical dualism, nor a religious one belonging to the Zoroastrian type, nor a synthesis of both. It is in fact a third genus, which consists essentially in the opposition of God and the world. We shall therefore handle it in a third section. This peculiar form of dualism may be considered as belonging principally to the history of Christian theology.

I. DUALISM IN THE HISTORY OF RELIGIONS

Primitive Religions. A religion is not dualistic simply because it admits the existence of good and evil spirits. In animism both good and evil spirits are still considered to belong to the same genus. They all belong to the forces of nature that can be both good and bad: good in certain respects and bad in other respects, good in certain circumstances and bad in other circumstances. These powers are concerned with what serves or injures them rather than with good for the sake of good or evil for the sake of evil.

Certain so-called primitive religions recognize a supreme spirit, a great God, and certain among them represent this God as the principal but not the only creator of the world. According to stories that are found among the North American Indians and in central and north Asia, a second being intervened in the creation and caused the institution of death. The world had been created all good, without evil or death, but this second being (who is either an adversary or a clumsy collaborator of the supreme God) did something malicious or stupid which led to irreparable harm. These stories seem to express the astonishment of man in the presence of evil and death, and the tendency to believe that these do not belong to the essence of things but are rather the result of an accident which cannot be due to the supreme deity. A germ of dualism resides in that idea. But nowhere is the independent origin of the second being positively expressed; sometimes he is a creature of the good god, sometimes nothing is said of his origin.

Religions in Antiquity. In ancient Egypt a dualistic tendency appears, on the one hand, in the religion of the sun-god Rē, the principle of life and truth, who has a perpetual adversary, Apophis, the gigantic serpent of darkness; on the other hand, a similar tendency appears in the legend of Osiris, in which Set is the adversary who kills Osiris and constantly opposes Isis and Horus. However, Rē (or another good god) might be represented as the universal creator. As for Set, who had been the principal god in certain provinces, he was for a long time regarded as capable of doing good in certain respects; only in a later epoch did he become the personification of evil. Moreover, he was regarded as the brother of Osiris, which means they had a common origin.

In the Vedic hymns we find two groups of divinities who, though both were equally venerated, are sometimes conceived as opposed to one another: the *deva* and the *asura*. In the Brāhmana, the *deva* remain as gods, but the *asura* became demons. However, these Indian demons are unorganized, scattered, without a leader, and nothing is said about their origin. We also find in the Veda a greatly stressed antithesis between order (or truth, *ṛta*) and falsity (*druh*); but this opposition is not the basis of the entire religion, as it is in Zoroastrianism.

Various ancient mythologies present a picture of a tremendous battle between the gods and the giants, monsters, or demons. Babylonian mythology tells of the war of Marduk against Tiāmat. The Bible mentions Leviathan, a sea monster of chaos, that God has vanquished and will kill. Greek mythology relates the battle of Zeus against the Titans. The mythology of the Germans includes the past and future struggles of the gods against the giants and against the demonic powers, offspring of Loki. (German myths refer also to the war of the Ases and Vanes, but this war seems to be of a different kind, since Ases and Vanes seem to be complementary forces whose struggle ends in a reconciliation.) The Indian epic narrates the war of the Pāndava, born of the gods, against the army of their demon cousin; now this story is perhaps the transposition of an older story in which the gods themselves fought the demons. These pictures of a gigantic drama might suggest a dualism, but in none of these examples is the dualism complete or systematic. The two parties are always descended from one another or from the same principle. Marduk is a descendent of Tiāmat; Zeus and the Titans have the same origin; Leviathan was created by God; the combatants of Mahābhārata are in the same family; Loki is an Ase like Odin who has a certain friendship for him.

Zoroastrianism. The Iranian dualism differs from the others because of its systematic character. It implies a concentration of all that is good around the great god Ahura Mazdā or Ohrmazd, principle of truth; all that is evil is concentrated around the Evil Spirit, Ahra Mainyu or Ahriman, the power of falsehood. This dualism establishes a nearly perfect symmetry between the forces of good and those of evil, and the whole religion is based on the idea of their incessant warfare. Only at the end of time will the Evil Spirit be vanquished completely.

According to tradition, this religion was founded by Zoroaster who, if he is not a legendary figure, may have lived at the latest around 600 B.C. but might have been much older. The most general opinion is that he reformed the old Indo-Iranian religion. In fact, there are in the *Gāthās* of the Avesta indications of a profound transformation. The word *daēva*, the Iranian form of the root which among the Indo-Europeans designated the gods, in the Avesta designates demons, and some of the ancient rites witnessed by the Veda are attacked. Certain customs practiced by the Magi, and which other peoples regarded as impious (exposing corpses to birds or dogs, consanguineous marriage), seem to indicate a radical break with ancient beliefs. Above all, there is in the *Gāthās* a constant aspiration for a transformation, for a "renovation" of existence, a renovation requiring struggles which will be terminated only in the future. In all these hymns one feels a constant concern to vanquish enemies, to convert people to a certain doctrine, to combat a religion taken to be false, and to fight against social forces taken to be violent and oppressive. This systematic dualism, dividing all of the world's creatures into good and evil beings, could express the intransigence and the intolerance of the revolutionary reformer preaching a new order.

Was the Evil Spirit for Zoroaster completely independent of Ahura Mazdā and co-eternal with him? We cannot be sure of this. In one text of the *Gāthās*, the Good Spirit (Spenta Mainyu) and the Evil One are called "twins" and are said to "choose" truth and evil respectively. According to certain scholars this shows that the two spirits have the same origin and that the evil one became evil by choice. According to other scholars the word "twins" implies perhaps only a kind of parallelism, and they remark that these two spirits are represented as being from the beginning one good and the other evil. (In fact the *Gāthās* do not distinguish clearly between choosing evil and being by nature bad; the *daēva* and the wicked are said sometimes to choose evil and sometimes to be sons of evil.) Whatever the case may be, the Evil Spirit, in the formulas of the *Gāthās*, is opposed to the Good Spirit but not directly to Ahura Mazdā. It is true that the latter seems at times to be identified with the Good Spirit, but the two are sometimes distinguished from one another. Perhaps, therefore, Ahura Mazdā was in primitive Zoroastrianism above the battle.

But in later Zoroastrianism, Ohrmazd is completely identified with the Good Spirit, and henceforth the Evil

One confronts him directly on the same plane. The authors of the Pahlavi books (ninth century A.D.) assert the independent origin of the two principles. This evolution was justified moreover by the spirit of the *Gāthās,* for the warlike atmosphere of irreconcilable opposition that pervades these hymns should lead one to deny any link between the adversaries.

The religion of Zoroaster is indeed a religion of struggle; hence it is not a gentle one. "The one who is good for the wicked is wicked" (*Yasna,* 46, 6). Certain beings in the world are regarded as the creation of Ahriman, which practically amounts to being regarded as completely wicked. The basis of Zoroastrianism is morality, but it is a harsh morality which demands above all, it seems, social discipline. The religious duty of the Zoroastrian consisted in fulfilling his function in society in the best possible manner. Submission and work were the great virtues. In reciprocation this religion seems to have been concerned with the protection of the workers against the forces of anarchy, the protection of the farmer and shepherd against the undisciplined warrior. There was a strong hope that an improved order would be established. Zoroastrianism is directed towards the future, it aspires to progress, and includes an eschatology. The Zoroastrian rites symbolize and prepare the great future "renovation" which will drive evil away once and for all and unify the world.

Under the Sassanids a monistic trend developed in the speculation called "Zurvanism." According to the Zurvanite myth Ohrmazd and Ahriman are both sons of Zurvān, Infinite Time (that is to say, eternity). However, some recent studies tend to show that Zurvanism was not generally taken to be a heresy, and was able to mingle with orthodox Zoroastrianism. After all, to say that Ohrmazd and Ahriman are sons of eternity was perhaps a way of saying that they are eternal. In any case, Zurvān was too abstract and too indeterminate to establish a real unity above the two opposing principles.

The case is different with modern Parsees. They have really become monists. They think that Ahriman is only the symbol of what is evil in man. They reject what is nevertheless the most fascinating characteristic of Zoroastrianism: relating human goodness or badness to cosmic powers, the human struggle to a struggle of the whole universe, and not attenuating by any considerations the opposition of good and evil.

II. DUALISM IN PHILOSOPHY

Western Philosophy. Pythagoras may already have been a dualist, in two senses. On the one hand, the Pythagoreans taught that all things are composed of contraries: the one and the many, the limited and the unlimited, the odd and the even, right and left, masculine and feminine, rest and motion, the straight line and the curve, light and darkness, good and evil, etc. Now, these opposites seem to have been the various forms of a single fundamental relation of contrariety. On the other hand, they distinguished profoundly soul and body, as is shown by their theory of the transmigration of souls and by the dictum attributed to them as well as to the Orphics: "The body is a tomb."

Heraclitus and Parmenides appear to have attacked Pythagorean dualism, at least the dualism of contraries. Heraclitus showed that the contraries are inseparable and form a unity; Parmenides proclaimed that only the one, immobile, eternal Being exists, whereas the many, the moving, perishable things do not exist in true reality.

Empedocles, on the contrary, continued to maintain the two Pythagorean kinds of dualism. For him the world is dominated alternately by two opposing principles, Love and Hate, which produce respectively unity and multiplicity. Furthermore, the soul for him has a different nature than the body, and he tells of a soul which, having fallen from the world of the gods, moaned at seeing itself in "this unaccustomed place" (frags. 118, 119).

Anaxagoras, in his turn, clearly distinguished two kinds of beings: elements in general, that are mixtures in which everything is mingled with everything else, on the one hand, and on the other, the mind (νοῦς) which alone exists apart, is pure, without admixture, and which, on coming into the chaos of the elements, puts order into them.

Plato does not teach any dogmas, but his dialogues tend to support the view that the soul exists independently of the body and that the intelligible world is independent of the world perceived by the senses. It is true that the latter world cannot be said really to be, for only the intelligible, the Idea, constitutes true Being. Yet the world of sense has also a kind of existence. In the myth of the creation of the world, the Demiurge, the good "Worker," is not the only cause of the universe; there is also another cause, namely, Necessity. The Demiurge "persuades" Necessity to direct most things towards the Good, but its power is not unlimited (*Timaeus* 47e–48a). In the *Republic* (379b–380c), Socrates says that God is not the cause of everything, but only of what is good. In the *Theaetetus* (176a), he says: "It is necessary that there should always be something contrary to the good."

It has sometimes been supposed that Zoroastrianism influenced Pythagorean and Platonic thought, but it is hardly probable. The wicked soul mentioned in

Plato's *Laws* (896e–898c) does not appear as a cosmic soul, and in the *Statesman* (270a), he repels the idea that the world could be governed by two opposing deities. Moral evil, for Plato, is due to the ignorance produced in the soul by its union with the body.

Aristotle is much more of a monist than his teacher Plato, whom he criticizes for having "separated" the Idea from sensible things. He tries to restore a continuity between the lower and the higher life; matter is, for him, already potentially what form is in actuality. He ties the soul in an intimate relationship to the body when he defines it as the form or entelechy of a natural body potentially possessing life. Yet there remains in Aristotle something of the Platonic dualism, particularly in his theory of the prime mover, an incorporeal and separate substance; also in his theory of the intellect which he seems to hold as separate from all the other faculties of the soul, entering it as though it were from the outside.

After Aristotle the Stoics and Epicureans are more thorough monists, the first school having a spiritualistic monism according to which the whole world is mind or reason, the second having a materialistic monism which reduces everything to atoms.

Christian philosophy at first leaned principally on Plato, but from the thirteenth century onwards, theologians made use chiefly of Aristotle, not without modifying some of his theories in order to bring them into harmony with Christianity.

In the Renaissance period Plato returned, and with him dualism was revived. In the seventeenth century Descartes sharply divided reality by defining mind exclusively as a substance that thinks, and matter exclusively as an extended substance, thus distinguishing them radically from one another. This distinction, which excludes any intermediary, allowed Descartes to establish a clear, wholly mathematical science of physics. Every fact in the material world was to be explained solely by geometry and mechanics.

Descartes' successors did not tolerate this bifurcation of reality into two substances. Spinoza made extension and thought no longer two substances but two attributes of the one substance God. Leibniz, although he distinguished in a certain way the soul from the body, pictured all reality on the model of thought.

Kant, in his chapter of the *Critique of Pure Reason* entitled "Paralogism of the Ideality of the External World" (Transcendental Dialectic, Book II), criticized dualism insofar as it signified that thinking substance and extended substance are things in themselves, but he admitted it insofar as it could signify that subject and object are quite distinct phenomena. To this division within phenomena he added the distinction of phenomena and things in themselves. For Kant there are somehow two worlds: one is the world of phenomena and the other, known only through consciousness of moral duty, is reality in itself.

Philosophers coming after Kant tried to do away with these profound divisions. Fichte made the free subject the basis of everything, the ground for the existence of the universe. Hegel brought the whole of reality into a single chain by making contradiction, first posited and then transcended, the law of all thought and of all nature.

Thus the history of Western philosophy appears to be an alternation of dualism and monism. On several occasions philosophy has been renovated by a very dualistic doctrine: Platonism, Cartesianism, and Kantianism have initiated such renovations. However, dualism was soon overcome and submerged by more or less monistic doctrines. The teacher is a dualist, but his pupils are not. It seems as though there was something too harsh and rough in dualism for most philosophers to bear. They wish to reconcile everything, and dualism disappoints them by the very fact that it posits two principles and not one alone. They believe that dualism is a failure, that it does not succeed in unifying all of reality; they expect philosophy to unify everything. But the dualistic philosophers have perhaps judged that the human condition requires us only to think and act well in the present; they have tried, above all, to justify the clearest method of thinking and the most certain morality. To confuse the body more or less with thought is to lodge in the body a mysterious force, which is impenetrable to clear science, and which destroys the will to govern the body.

In our own twentieth century, Lovejoy has described, under the title *The Revolt Against Dualism*, the many attempts of contemporary philosophers to refute or to avoid dualism; he believes that they have all failed. Alain (1868–1951) has taught the moral value of dualism in Cartesianism and maintained that dualism is not a fault in a philosophy but, on the contrary, is the most vigorous trait, revealing the energy which makes sound thinking. Philosophical dualism does not imply the condemnation of certain beings outside one's self, but expresses a will to govern one's self.

Indian Philosophy. The dominant and best known philosophy of India is the monistic Vedanta. But India also has its dualistic philosophies. In particular, the very ancient and very important Sāmkhya teaches that both matter (or nature) and the Spirit have existed throughout eternity.

Chinese Philosophy. The oldest Chinese distinguish two fundamental powers, *Yang* and *Yin*. *Yang* is the celestial principle, luminous, warm, masculine, active, and creative; *Yin* is earthly, dark, cold, feminine, passive, and receptive. But the Chinese philosophers represent them generally as manifestations of the same principle.

III. DUALISM IN THEOLOGY

Pre-Gnostic Dualism. Around the beginning of the Christian era, dualistic ideas appeared in Judaism, in which, however, they remain limited by the rigorous monotheism. Whether due to the influence of the Iranian religion or to the autonomous development of Judaism, Jewish writers teach that God acts and even has created the world by means of two opposing powers. According to the *Rule* of Qumrān (III–IV), two spirits created by God, the Prince of Lights and the Angel of Darkness, dominate the world. Philo (ca. 13 B.C.–ca. A.D. 50) says, though only in a single text, that God created the world by means of two powers, one of which is the cause of good things, the other of evil things (*Quaestiones in Exodum*, I, 23). Philo is, moreover, a Platonist, and it is not certain that for him matter was created by God. The Jewish Apocalyptic opposes the present to the future world in a sort of temporal dualism. But nowhere in Judaism is the denial of the value of the world carried to the point to which Gnosticism went and where even certain texts of early Christianity extended. The Qumrān's angel of darkness is not the "prince of the world"; the two spirits are in the world "in equal proportion."

Gnostic Dualism. Historians gave the name "Gnosticism" at first to a group of Christian heresies which appeared towards the end of the first century. These various and numerous heresies had in common their rejection of the Old Testament and especially of the biblical doctrine of creation. The world is neither created nor governed directly by God, but by inferior blind powers that do not know God. The Yahweh of the Bible, creator of the world, is only the chief of these lower powers; he created without knowing the true Good. The world is not of God (directly), and the soul, a spark of the divine, is not of this world. The soul, enslaved in this world, can be freed, become conscious of its origin, and ascend to God only by grace of *gnosis*, the supernatural knowledge brought by the divine Savior.

To some extent, therefore, the Gnostics attributed an origin to the world different from the soul's origin. Moreover, they employed the Greek dualism of soul and matter. Yet they were not completely dualistic, for according to them the Creator was somehow related to the true God, as one of His angels or as an offspring in the genealogy of emanations. Besides, the true God, if He had not wished the Creation, had at least permitted it. Thus their dualism was neither absolute nor systematic. It resided above all in a feeling that the world is alien to God, and that there is between God and nature a gulf which cannot be crossed except by God.

Gnosticism was particularly vigorous in the second century. But, condemned by the Church of Rome toward the middle of that century, it became more and more syncretist. The later Gnostics, inheritors of a Christianity detached from the Old Testament, saw no difficulty in uniting it with pagan traditions (Platonism, the Mysteries, Oriental religions). On the other hand, from about the middle of the second century, we meet ideas of a Gnostic nature no longer only among the Christians, but in writings which seem to be pagan, for example, the *Hermetica*. Gnostic ideas are also found later in Islam, and in Judaism in the Kabbala.

Thus, after a certain epoch, Gnostic ideas seem to be no longer tied necessarily to Christianity. This permits many modern scholars to hold that Gnosticism was not essentially a Christian heresy; that from its origin, contrary to what the Church Fathers believed, it was a great current of thought which, while mingling with Christianity, existed apart from it and perhaps even before it. These scholars have searched for its origins principally in Zoroastrianism, in Hellenism, or in certain trends of Judaism. Nevertheless, these researches have not yet resulted in conclusions of any certainty. The problem of the origins of Gnosticism is still ardently discussed. It is true that after a certain epoch Gnostic ideas spread beyond Christian circles, but still one cannot be at all sure that these ideas were not born there. No Gnostic text before Christianity is known, and the most ancient known Gnostics are Christians. In addition, it seems even more difficult to explain the profound opposition between God and the world by Hellenism, Zoroastrianism, or Judaism than by the New Testament. In the fourth Gospel, for example, the opposition between God and the world is already emphasized nearly as much as among the Gnostics.

It is possible that the crucifixion of Christ, that is to say, the defeat of the Just One in the world, caused this deep pessimism with regard to the world. Besides, the Paulinist and Johannist idea that one could not be saved except by divine Grace means that there is a deep separation between nature and salvation.

Manicheism. Founded in the third century of our era by the Persian Mani, Manicheism is one of the late, syncretist forms of Gnosticism. Mani wanted to unite Christianity (under its Gnostic form) with Zoroastrianism, Buddhism, and Greek philosophy. In fact, the part played by Gnostic Christianity is by far the most im-

42

portant part of his doctrine. But he made Gnostic dualism more rigid and more systematic, reinforcing it on the model of Zoroastrian dualism. With him the two principles are truly independent and co-eternal. Evil for him was identical with matter, but he described evil as having traits which reminded one of Ahriman.

Nobody was as consciously and voluntarily a dualist as Mani. For him the positing of two principles was the foundation of all true religion. By assembling Gnostic myths, he constructed a great myth which described the primitive separation of the two principles (Light, the substance of the soul, and Darkness, that is to say, matter); then their mixture, after Darkness attacked Light and engulfed some of its parts; then the way the particles of Light (souls) can be freed from Darkness and return to their source. He announced that some day all creatures would be brought back to their origin, that the principles would once again be separated, this time forever.

It is often believed that the Manicheans divided all the creatures of the world into absolutely good or absolutely evil beings. This tendency is, however, rather typical of the Zoroastrians. For the Manicheans, everything in the world was a mixture; pure goodness and evil existed only in the principles. Moreover, the Manicheans were neither violent nor intolerant; they adapted their language to that of other religions, thinking that there was something good in nearly all of them. Salvation for them did not consist in fighting against certain beings, but in fighting against matter (Darkness) in themselves, and in escaping from the world.

Dualistic Heresies of the Middle Ages. The dualistic heresies of the Middle Ages—that of the Paulicians, who flourished in Armenia and Asia Minor between the seventh and the tenth centuries, and continued later in the Balkans; that of the Bogomils, whose doctrine started in Bulgaria and spread in the Balkans between the tenth and the fifteenth centuries; that of the Cathari, who flourished in Western Europe in the twelfth and the thirteenth centuries—probably sprang not from Manicheism but, like Manicheism itself, from Gnosticism, which had continued in the Orient. The principle of all these dualisms is still the profound distinction between God and the world.

Augustinian Theology. It has sometimes been held that Manicheism exerted some influence on the theology of Saint Augustine, who, in his youth, was a Manichean for nine years. But whatever there is of dualism in him seems rather to come from Saint Paul and Saint John the Evangelist, who, without themselves being Gnostics, may have been the principal inspirers

of Gnosticism. Be that as it may, Saint Augustine kept alive in occidental theology a rather strong dualistic trend by his deep separation of Nature from Grace. We find this sort of dualism again in Luther and in the Jansenists.

BIBLIOGRAPHY

1. U. Bianchi, *Il dualismo religioso* (Rome, 1958). J. Duchesne-Guillemin, *Ormazd et Ahriman, l'aventure dualiste dans l'antiquité* (Paris, 1953); idem, *La religion de l'Iran ancien* (Paris, 1962). G. Dumézil, *Les dieux des Germains* (Paris, 1959). A. V. W. Jackson, *Zoroastrian Studies* (New York, 1928). P.-J. de Ménasce, "Note sur le dualisme mazdéen," *Études carmélitaines*, **6** (1948), 130–35. M. Molé, *Culte, mythe et cosmologie dans l'Iran ancien* (Paris, 1963). H. Te Velde, *Seth, God of Confusion* (Leyden, 1967). G. Widengren, *Die Religionen Irans* (Stuttgart, 1965). R. C. Zaehner, *The Teachings of the Magi, a Compendium of Zoroastrian Beliefs* (London and New York, 1956); idem, *The Dawn and Twilight of Zoroastrianism* (London, 1961).

2. Alain, *Étude sur Descartes* (Paris, 1928). Fêng (Yu-lan), *A History of Chinese Philosophy*, trans. D. Bodde (Peiping and London, 1937). A. O. Lovejoy, *The Revolt against Dualism* (LaSalle, Ill. and London, 1930). S. Pétrement, *Le dualisme dans l'histoire de la philosophie et des religions* (Paris, 1946); idem, *Le dualisme chez Platon, les gnostiques et les manichéens* (Paris, 1947). L. Renou and J. Filliozat, *L'Inde classique* (Paris, 1947–53). A. Schweitzer, *The Philosophy of Civilization*, Vol. II: *Civilization and Ethics*, 3rd ed., trans. C. T. Campion, revised by Mrs. Ch. E. B. Russell (London, 1946).

3. S. Aalen, *Die Begriffe "Licht" und "Finsternis" im Alten Testament, im Spätjudentum und im Rabbinismus* (Oslo, 1951). A. Adam, "Der manichäische Ursprung der Lehre von den zwei Reichen bei Augustin," *Theologische Literaturzeitung*, **77** (1952), 385–90. G. Aulén, *Christus victor*, trans. A. G. Hebert (London, New York, and Toronto, 1931). U. Bianchi, ed., *The Origins of Gnosticism, Colloquium of Messina* (Leyden, 1967). O. Böcher, *Der johanneische Dualismus* (Gütersloh, 1965). A. Borst, *Die Katharer* (Stuttgart, 1953). W. Bousset, *Hauptprobleme der Gnosis* (Göttingen, 1907). E. Bring, *Dualismen hos Luther* (Stockholm, 1929). F. C. Burkitt, *The Religion of the Manichees* (Cambridge, 1925). R. M. Grant, *Gnosticism and Early Christianity*, 2nd ed. (New York, 1966). H. W. Huppenbauer, *Der Mensch zwischen zwei Welten* (Zurich, 1959). H. Jonas, *Gnosis und spätantiker Geist* (Göttingen, I, 1934; II, 1, 1954); idem, *The Gnostic Religion* (Boston, 1958; reprint, 1963). H. Langerbeck, *Aufsätze zur Gnosis* (Göttingen, 1967). S. Pétrement, "La notion de gnosticisme," *Revue de Métaphysique et de Morale*, **65** (1960), 385–421; idem, "Le Colloque de Messine et le problème du gnosticisme," ibid., **72** (1967), 344–73. H.-Ch. Puech, *Le manichéisme* (Paris, 1949). S. Runciman, *The Medieval Manichee* (Cambridge, 1947). H. Söderberg, *La religion des Cathares* (Uppsala, 1949). P. Volz, *Die Eschatologie der jüdischen Gemeinde im*

43

neutestamentlichen Zeitalter, 2nd ed. (Tübingen, 1934). G. Widengren, *Mani und der Manichäismus* (Stuttgart, 1961). R. McL. Wilson, *The Gnostic Problem* (London and Naperville, Ill., 1958); idem, *Gnosis and the New Testament* (Oxford, 1968).

SIMONE PÉTREMENT

[See also Epicureanism; **Gnosticism;** God; Heresy; **Hermeticism;** Myth in Antiquity; Platonism; Pythagorean Doctrines; Right and Good; Sin and Salvation; Stoicism.]

ECONOMIC HISTORY

The Meaning of the Topic. The title refers to the history of the science dealing with the general and hence abstract principles of "economic" conduct and of the free "economic" social order, based on exchange—rather than with the concrete history of either subject matter. "Pivotal ideas" include a large part of the important things to be said about modern "liberal" civilization, a revolutionary development in Western Europe following the Middle Ages. As the adjective in quotation marks indicates, the central and distinctive feature of this civilization is *liberty,* or the closely synonymous term, "freedom." About that, of course, many books have been written, and many more will be. Briefly, it refers here to the comparative absence or minimizing of "compulsory" control over personal conduct by "society"—its governmental agents and laws enforced by penalties for infraction—interfering with people doing as they like and associating on terms initially agreed upon. Freedom does not mean absence of "natural" obstacles to action, relative to a person's "power" to act, which is taken as "given." It implies absence of arbitrary interference by other persons, which liberalism views as the primary function of coercive law and government to prevent, to assure maximum freedom for all.

The freedom in question applies in three major forms, which are inseparable. Primary is freedom of thought and expression, which largely entails freedom of action or conduct; and these freedoms are meant to be assured by political freedom, or "democracy" in the modern meaning of the term. All exist in an "institutional" social order—partly compulsory in a broad "moral" meaning, but largely consisting of usage established by custom and mostly followed automatically or by voluntary choice. The type of these laws is that of the language current in a society, but will include its accepted proprieties or "manners." Men feel in varying degree restrained and compelled by custom as such, as well as by the agencies which have evolved

for securing conformity, chiefly government and religion. There is some plausibility in Rousseau's famous statement that men are born free but are everywhere in chains; but the first part of the statement asserting natural freedom, though repeated by Jefferson and Lincoln, is manifestly false or without practical meaning; for a newborn babe has neither will nor power to act. And in general, the idea of human beings living outside of limiting social conditions is so unrealistic as to be essentially self-contradictory.

Institutions, or in the aggregate a "culture," are of the essence—the primary distinctive human trait. (The word "freedom" is used with respect to animals, plants, and even inanimate objects; but this meaning must not be confused with that of the human freedom in question here. The word "economy" is also used in connection with living organisms, though not with inert objects. This causes confusion only as implying a kind of purposiveness, which dogmatic devotees of mechanistic science often deny—even to human beings—though the denial itself is a purposive act.)

The problems of a free society, both of explanation and of guiding its policies in acting as a unit, focus in the relations among the three main social expressions or embodiments of freedom—the democratic state, an "economic" organization through exchange of goods and services, and the general freedom of communication and association by voluntary assent and agreement. Logically, and especially in a historical view, the first requirement for freedom is religious, i.e., absence of exercise of power by persons or a "mob" ostensibly acting for a supernatural source. This calls for notice especially because modern free society developed out of an antecedent medieval social order explicitly based on religion—and practically because of the persistence of such presuppositions in the short modern epoch in which democratic ideals have been nominally accepted. These were first effectively born in seventeenth-century Britain, out of a three-cornered struggle for power between a sovereign claiming to rule by divine right, a partly representative Parliament, and a judiciary and legal profession.

Many features had existed before in varying degree, in Greece and Rome and even in medieval Europe (and some non-European lands)—notably the rule of law in contrast with government by arbitrary command; but the "pivotal idea" of free society is government by consent of the governed, or in ideal terms, self-rule. For a group this is possible in only one way, by having the laws made and enforced by the people subject to them, as far as possible; i.e., by agents chosen by a majority, under free and equal suffrage. Majority tyranny is limited only by moral forces and finally overt resistance.

The analytical science of economics, under its present name, goes back less than a century. The discipline, in its most distinctive features, is about a generation older; it grew out of the preceding "political economy," which arose in the late eighteenth century as an aspect of the "Enlightenment" and revolutionary period, marked by the American and French Revolutions; it is also called the Age of Reason. This period of individualism followed a few centuries of "nationalism" beginning at the "Renaissance" with the founding of modern states as monarchies, through concentration of feudal power. This individualistic efflorescence, along with modern science, led to the Protestant Revolt and Wars of Religion, resulting in displacement of the Church as the supreme authority by a plurality of states. Renaissance civilization was as much, if not more a new birth as a rebirth (of classical antiquity). Its most "pivotal" concrete aspect was surely the launching or impetus given to modern science through the work of Copernicus (1543) and Galileo (ca. 1610) in astronomy and mechanics, and of Vesalius (also 1543) in anatomy. Growth of trade, after the Crusades, was an important stimulus to liberalization. A major forerunner was Leonardo da Vinci (d. 1519). Newton, roughly speaking, completed the movement in physical science, and in mathematics; René Descartes should be named, but after the beginning in Italy and Germany, the main development was British. The effective religious revolt started, of course, in Germany with Luther, but England had important forerunners of both aspects, in John Wycliffe and Sir William Gilbert.

The Idea of Economics. The history of analytical economics should begin with the coining by Plato's contemporary, Xenophon, of the word *oikonomikos*. It combines two words meaning a house, household or estate, and a verb, to manage, or rule. In the Middle Ages, the Latin form was used with several meanings, one theological. In the seventeenth century the concept began to be applied to the management of a "state"— under the French name *économie politique;* this followed when the establishment of absolute monarchy made the state the "estate" of the king. In German, the doctrine was called "cameralism." At about the same time, the word "economy" and its relatives began to take on the general meaning it now bears—the "effective" use of means to achieve an end, both means and end being "given." The doctrine of the preceding nationalistic literature is commonly called "mercantilism," because the writers advocated increase of national wealth by an excess of exports over imports, the difference to be received in "money" (gold or silver). Exposure of the fallacy of confusing money with wealth, especially in the *Essays* of David Hume, at the middle of the eighteenth century, is important for the transition to political economy, later replaced by economics.

During the mercantilistic period, apart from the propaganda for a "favorable" balance of trade, some writers in England discussed governmental activities more descriptively, and with some reference to policy. They also broached topics which were to become central later, notably the meaning and determination of economic value. The leader along this line was Sir William Petty, who wrote in the latter part of the seventeenth century. He is most famous for his *Political Arithmetick* (1691), which founded the modern science of statistics. He and contemporaries, such as John Locke, discussed taxes, interest, and money, and also wages. The mercantilists held that both wages and interest should be low, to favor effective trade rivalry with other nations. Toward the end of the same century, writers began to advocate liberalizing international trade—sometimes twisting the balance-of-trade argument to serve this cause. Notable for reasonable views on trade policy was the work, *Discourses on Trade* (1691; ed. J. H. Hollander, 1935), by Sir Dudley North, as discovered by modern scholarship.

The Modern Cultural Revolution. What "fundamentally" happened in this transition was a culture-historical or "spiritual" revolution, a "conversion" in the general mental and social attitude. Such events are characteristic of the history of Western Europe. Politically, its civilization first blossomed in Greek city-states, which were succeeded by Hellenistic and Roman empires—these in turn by the church-religion culture of the Middle Ages joined with politico-economic feudalism; this feudal order gave place in the Renaissance to monarchic "stat-ism." The Enlightenment replaced the idea of *"L'État, c'est moi"* with the radically new idea of individualism, i.e., freedom. The twin value of freedom was progress—the two combined as progress through freedom and freedom for progress, directed by intelligence. This "Liberal Revolution" is perhaps the greatest cultural overturn of history. A major result is that modern men, set relatively free from tradition and authority, are largely motivated by rivalry. But this is in large part turned to constructive action by several "invisible hands": mutual "material" advantage, sportsmanship, workmanship, and scientific curiosity—along with public spirit, sympathy, and benevolence. None of these factors was entirely new, but the degree to which they burst forth and their combination constituted a historical revolution.

The new "science" of political-economy was introduced in 1776 by the Scot, Adam Smith, with his famous book, *The Wealth of Nations.* Its main thesis was practical and it dominated its field until about **45**

1870, when the modern analytical science of economics began substantially to develop. The pivotal idea of the new movement also is freedom, but now as a scientific postulate based on reason—the (inseparable) economic and political aspects are more directly pertinent here, though humanly less important than the religious and cultural. (Smith's great manifesto for economic freedom was nearly simultaneous with Jefferson's Declaration of American Independence, its counterpart in the political field.) Apart from the fact that freedom itself is a negative idea—the absence of coercion—it will be more realistic and more in point to consider as pivotal the fallacious ideas replaced rather than the essentially obvious ones introduced.

A major lesson to be learned from the history of ideas is to realize the "glacial" tardiness of men, including the best minds, in seeing what it later seems should have been obvious at the first look. This is strikingly illustrated by the concept of economy. People have always practiced it—have "economized," in many connections—but have been unaware of the principle, much as the famous M. Jourdain in Molière's *Le Bourgeois Gentilhomme* had talked prose from childhood but was surprised to learn the fact. People have even specialized, and exchanged products in crude markets, and for millenniums have used "money" of some form. But in physical nature it also took many centuries to grasp the idea of "inertia," a fact seriously encountered constantly in everyday life; Aristotle and later great thinkers thought that any motion once started would cease unless maintained by the continuous action of some force—until Galileo showed the opposite to be the case.

Adam Smith did not entitle his book "political economy," presumably because this had recently been used by his countryman Sir James Denham Steuart for a major work, *Inquiry into the Principles of Political Economy* (1767), which properly belonged more to the preceding "mercantilist" school. Both economic and political freedom had been developing through "historical forces" for over a century, notably in Britain, and Smith's book was essentially "propaganda" for more complete economic freedom (later called "laisser-faire," now "laissez-faire"). Neither he nor his political-economist followers argued their case in terms of what is now considered rational economic analysis. They had no conception of a maximum return from resources, specifically as obtained through correct allocation among alternative uses. (And they took little notice of "technology," though they wrote at the height of the "industrial revolution," in which that was the major factor, and it is surely the crucial fact in the popular conception of economy.) The two main themes of economic analysis, price and distribution, were approached by way of absurd presuppositions, especially the second, which the writers failed to see as a matter of pricing the means of production. They adopted a moralistic or social-empirical conception of a division of the social product into three "shares," wages, landrent, and "profit," the three forms of income popularly recognized, which were wrongly assumed to come from three distinct sources and to be received by three different social classes.

Epochs in the Evolution of Economic Thought. Before taking up the transition to analytical economics, it seems in order to relate the whole development to West-European history by distinguishing its main stages. Such a scheme will fit the recognized historical periods, and happens to present a neat cross-dichotomy —two main divisions, each with two subdivisions, which may be labelled I-A, I-B, and II-A and II-B. The main changes affect the objectives attributed to people by writers and thought to be proper as ends of social policy. In the first major epoch, extending from the beginnings in Greece through the Middle Ages (I-A and I-B), the aim was social and may be called idealistic or spiritual, in contrast with later "individualism" and "materialism." Ends were stressed, rather than means. (Max Weber thought the Greek spirit that of comrades in arms.) Writers looked to the persistence and prosperity of the small city-state with its culture, which bequeathed to later times a great literature and art—and the word "democracy," though not the fact as now conceived.

The next sub-epoch (I-B) begins with the decline of imperial Rome and conversion to mystery cults, finally to ecclesiastical Christianity. (Gibbon called it the triumph of barbarism and religion.) The purported end of living was "salvation," for a future eternal life, this world being given up as a vale of tears and man as born to sin, curable only by supernatural action. The political order—while waiting for the Parousia (Second Coming, end of the world) was a theocracy, i.e., a clerocracy, headed by the autocratic Pope of Rome. As typical for authoritarian regimes, its first real concern was its own power. In the West, "feudalism" was variously joined with this; in the East, several patriarchates were subject to the Emperor in Constantinople (new Rome) until the rise of Islam. This church-state conquered most of the old Roman empire, though turned back by the Franks at Tours in 732; in 1453 the Turks took Constantinople, ending the Byzantine Empire (and for some it marks the end of the Middle Ages).

The transition to the second major epoch (II-A) was made at the "Renaissance"—in many ways more a new birth than a rebirth. In Northern Europe it was marked by the Protestant Revolt ("Reformation"). Feudal power became concentrated in nominally "absolute" monarchies, and in the ensuing Wars of Religion, political (and economic) interests increasingly predominated. None of the protagonists wanted religious toleration, let alone general freedom, and the main result was a transfer of authority from the Church to new states, monarchies under sovereign by divine right. Social thinking became state centered, aimed at national aggrandizement. However, the states were several, and rivalry for power forced them to tolerate, even encourage, freedom in trade and industry and hence in science, for the sake of the new wealth they yielded, which the monarchs could tax.

Political authority, though also historically sacred, has been less bound by sanctity than the priestly, and secularism increased. Passing over details of the history, most pertinent here is the fact that for a few centuries "economic" thought was nationalistic—the doctrine of mercantilism, noticed before. But policy and formal government were gradually liberalized, specifically in Britain, notably by the victory of Parliament, defeating Stuart absolutism, in the Civil War, the "glorious revolution" of 1688, and the ensuing settlement.

The next stage (sub-epoch II-B) begins at the Enlightenment, the late eighteenth century, centered largely in France; with American independence, that new nation took the lead, while in France, revolution was followed by reaction, causing a setback for liberalism in Britain.

It is the age of individualism, hence of freedom, and in economic thought, of "laissez-faire." But from this viewpoint, it should be subdivided: first came a century of "political economy"—propaganda for laissez-faire—extending from Smith's *Wealth of Nations* of 1776 to the rise of objective economic analysis in the "subjective-value revolution" of around 1870—promoted independently by W. S. Jevons, Carl Menger, and Léon Walras. The major premiss of individualistic philosophy is that the only value is personal well-being, and each is the best judge of his own and of the action that will promote it—particularly in contrast with the state. (Other groups, notably churches, were in liberal theory reduced to voluntary associations, without authority—science and criticism having destroyed the supernatural appeal.) The state is practically a means only, its chief function to maintain freedom by preventing "predation" i.e., force and fraud. (Adam Smith had added two other functions, defense and "certain public works.") In politics, liberalism introduced democracy—self-government through laws made by freely chosen representatives—meant chiefly to prevent government from trespassing on liberty, and at the time to reduce greatly its scope of action with that of law. Necessary sweeping qualifications of the liberal credo have been recognized and will be noticed here in due course.

The Major Fallacy of the Political Economists.

Pivotal, as the fountainhead of analytical fallacy, was an apparent mental fixation on *labor* as alone really productive. (The idea came from folklore; cf. Genesis 3:19.) Smith began his book with the statement that "The annual *labor* of every *nation* [italics added] . . . originally supplies it with all the necessaries and conveniences which it annually consumes. . . ." He at once qualified this to read "useful" labor—a part of that performed by the fraction of the people who work at all—later defined in a confusing way. The main determinant of the productivity of labor is the proportion of those who perform useful labor. His first chapter is to deal with the "greatest improvement," which is specialization (he calls it "division of labor," though other means of production are as much specialized). This, he says, works in three ways: to increase skill, to save the time of shifting from one task to another, and to increase the application of proper machinery. (This is a main component of "capital," but generations were required to correct the classical view of that concept—and much of the world still views "property" as a means for exploiting workers; even the free nations commonly impute all "productivity" to labor.) "Stock" (capital) is the subject of Book II; it is defined as support for laborers, chiefly food, "advanced" by persons who have a surplus beyond their own needs for consumption. Book III ("Of the Different Progress of Opulence in Different Nations") is short and chiefly historical and propagandistic.

The main thesis of the whole work is found in Book IV, on "Systems of Political Economy," and is practical, not analytical. Two systems, the commercial or mercantile, and the agricultural, are considered and condemned, on vague grounds, so that "the obvious and simple system of natural liberty establishes itself of its own accord" (Modern Library [1937], p. 651). However, Smith at once introduces three qualifications, as tasks (and "expenses") of the sovereign: "defense," an exact system of justice, and maintaining certain public works. These might be construed to allow an indefinite scope of public action, but the author's long discussions need not be considered in detail. (Especially noteworthy is an eloquent, almost florid plea for a little rudimentary education, by local parishes, to offset the evil effects on human beings of extreme specialization.)

Returning to Book I, Chapters II and III continue with the division of labor. Chapter IV treats the "origin and use of money," but is chiefly remarkable because the author turns abruptly at the end to discuss exchange value, and introduces the labor theory. Contrasting exchange value and use value, he rejects the latter as a cause, noting that things which have the greatest

47

value in use have frequently little or no value in exchange (and conversely), illustrated by the famous contrast between water and diamonds. And his political-economist followers followed this lead for nearly a century. "Utility" was held to be a condition of value, but not a cause—or measure, two things which were badly confused. Ignored were the two essential and obtrusive facts: first, that prices pertain to units of goods, which men buy and sell, not whole categories; and secondly, that the use value of a unit decreases as the quantity of the good increases. A buyer adds and a seller subtracts an "increment" of a stock (perhaps beginning or ending with none). The comparison is between having a little more or less of one good and of the other, making incremental utility relative.

However, but for the fact of separately diminishing marginal utility, one's purchasing power would all be spent on the good with the greatest initial appeal. Furthermore, the law of decrease holds under any realistic conditions; the want for (satisfying power of) any good is progressively satiable. Discovery (effective recognition) of this obvious fact came nearly a century after Smith. It will be stressed as the pivotal idea marking the break from political economy to economics, and still later it was gradually seen that a parallel principle holds for applying resources in production.

Smith's Chapter V of Book I—on "Real and Nominal Price"—constantly asserts the labor theory, and confuses value measurement with its causality. "Equal quantities of labor," we read, are of equal value to the laborer. This is false for exchange value and hardly makes sense. One might rate two tasks as (about) equally irksome, but could hardly pronounce one a numerical multiple of the other in that respect; and where different workers are involved, any comparison becomes dubious. However, there is sense in Smith's proposal to take the customary day's wage for common labor as indicating the relative value of money in comparable situations separated in space or time. A statistical tabular standard (index number) of prices was suggested after Smith's death in 1790, but was rejected by David Ricardo (Smith's most famous follower) as not measuring production cost (in labor or wages), by which he practically measured and defined economic value.

To Smith's credit, his further discussion of value (Book I, Chapters VI, VII) though imputing the whole product to labor, with other shares as deductions, qualifies labor cost for differences in irksomeness and skill and also restricts the labor theory of value to a (fictitious) primitive society. Then, when "stock" has accumulated and land been appropriated, the product must be shared with their owners, and these payments enter into exchange value. (Of course it is the scarcity

of land and competition between uses, not private ownership, which makes rent a cost.) The view of labor as the essence of value is replaced by the more realistic one that the precise worth of a thing is its real cost, consisting of the rent, wages, and profit that must be paid to bring it to market (op. cit., p. 55). This is the "natural" price, which Smith indicates (correctly and pivotally, if not too clearly) will in fact be set in the long run by movement of some resources from uses of less to greater yield. Demand and supply may temporarily fix a "market" price somewhat lower or higher. Or a "monopoly" may exist, always charging "the highest price which can be got" (op. cit., p. 61). This "pivotal absurdity" was repeated by Ricardo, who added two others (*Principles*, Groffa and Dorr ed., I, 249).

A pivotal error in the labor-cost theory (and others) is the failure to see that no cost directly affects price, if men act with economic rationality. Cost enters into price only as limiting supply and is the value of resources for other uses, including direct enjoyment outside the market; this is the meaning of the irksomeness of work, and it applies also to nonhuman agents. The true relation between cost and price, a pivotal idea, was stressed in general terms by N. W. Senior, in his *Outline of Political Economy*, in 1836. Senior also stated the underlying pivotal idea of "diminishing utility," but these insights were not recognized until much later. Senior became famous for introducing the idea of "abstinence" as a "subjective cost," along with labor, to explain profit, and this *was* endorsed by J. S. Mill. Both used it to define "capital," but did not treat it as a determinant of the supply of the latter and the price of its use. This came much later, and gradually—perhaps most clearly stated by Irving Fisher.

"Abstinence" tended to be replaced by "waiting" (notably with Alfred Marshall). This implies two fallacies: first, that of a "production period"—meaning that an investment regularly is returned at a later date, with an increase; and second, that production goods are produced by primary factors—labor and capital. People more typically save as social accumulation requires—for an increased future income of indefinite duration; thus the waiting is perpetual, i.e., is abstinence. Further analysis of these phenomena belongs to a later point. Senior gave a brief and general statement, correct as far as it goes, of the role of capital as the use of the produce of industry to increase production in the future.

Returning to Smith, it is to be noted that he turned, in Book I, Chapters VI to XI, to a general discussion of his "component parts of price" (the costs of production): wages, profits, and rent. Some advance toward analytical economics is made in his Chapter X, "Wages and Profits in Different Employments of Labor and Stock." Here he makes his nearest approach to a theory of "distribution" as now conceived, but he strangely fails to consider rent. His short Book II deals with the Nature, Accumulation, and Employment of Stock. First, under "Divisions," he distinguishes arbitrarily between "Circulating" and "Fixed" capital. The former consists of goods for the owner's consumption, or purchased for sale at a profit or for productive use by employing workers. The second includes improvement of land, and all instruments of production, including buildings which yield revenue, and also the "acquired and useful abilities" of the population. Circulating capital further includes money—specie or paper, separately discussed at length in Chapter II—with "provisions," and partial or complete manufactures.

Especially interesting, and historically pivotal, is Chapter III, "Of the Accumulation of Capital *or of Productive and Unproductive Labor*" [italics added]. Smith states clearly that productive and unproductive do not mean useful and useless, but refer only to whether the worker reproduces the "capital" he consumes. (The importance of maintaining capital is well emphasized in this fallacious view of it.) The main concern is with the amount of "circulating" capital—an aspect of the fallacious view just noted—and with the increase of this through saving ("frugality"). "The uniform, constant and uninterrupted effort of every man to better his condition" (op. cit., p. 326) is stressed as an offset to the extravagance of government and errors of administration, and also the inclination of the rich to spend on luxuries (especially on "menial servants," rather a pet aversion of his). The "pivotal fallacy" that a given amount of capital in any form can maintain a definite amount of labor or industry, reflects an assumption that workers have a fixed living requirement; and also the "Malthusian" population theory, which implied that their numerical increase keeps wages at this level, regardless of the amount assigned to their support. (And this was sometimes fallaciously treated as a fixed "wages fund.") Diminishing returns to labor and capital applied to land was also assumed—perhaps first explicitly stated by Malthus. Only generations later it was recognized as valid only if technological advance is ignored, also that such a law holds for the use of any factor in increasing ratio to others. The historical fact has of course been a vast rise of wages, in spite of redoubling of numbers of workers.

Adam Smith's treatment of prices as in effect explained by money cost of production—composed of wages, profit, and rent—implies relations so obvious for a modern reader that it is rather his failure to state them clearly that seems to call for explanation. When we turn to the treatment of these incomes themselves and look for a tenable view of "distribution," there is little to be found. Again to Smith's credit, there is little of the absurdity introduced by Ricardo (taken from Malthus and others) that became a cornerstone of classical political economy—the "residual" or surplus view of rent, with the idea that the main problem is "to determine the laws which regulate the distribution" of the social product among three "classes," landlords, owners of capital, and laborers (Ricardo, *Principles,* original Preface). Smith does speak of distribution among "ranks and conditions of men" (Part I, v. iii) and later of the "three great constituent orders . . . of every civilized society (op. cit., p. 248). Such statements shed no light on the distribution that is of interest today—payments for productive agents, which are incomes to their owners, and determine their scale of living.

The "class" distribution idea may derive in part from the French "Physiocratic" school. It calls for mention here because it was taken over from Ricardo or his followers as the basis of Marxism. Marx's pivotal idea, quite logical, is that since only labor produces, receiving income from property is robbery of the workers—Proudhon's famous dictum that property is "theft."

The Marxist (pseudo) economic analysis follows Ricardo logically, drawing the opposite policy implication, the attack on versus the support of property and market freedom. Both ignored the distinct role of the "entrepreneur," imputing it to owners of wealth. Both held a subsistence theory of wages and a Malthus-Ricardo view of land and its rent (but for Marx all property income is filched from laborers). Profit (including interest) arises because labor produces more than is required for its support. This was most clearly stated by J. S. Mill (*Principles of Political Economy,* Ashley edition, p. 416). By Mill's time, "rent" was under fire; Mill called it a "surplus," but opposed current confiscation yet favored that of future increase—a palpably absurd distinction. Land value is speculative; any prospect of increase enters into present value, and as in gambling, is generally overestimated, so that on the whole losses exceed gains.

The treatment of income distribution in the political-economy classics consists of chapters on the three "shares," which have little bearing on people's relative means of support or provision for the future. The distinction between income and wealth was ignored or confused; only J. S. Mill discussed "property." The three kinds of income were wrongly conceived though at the time they bore a vague relation to population sectors with some "class" attributes; and they mean even less today. As with water and diamonds, land, labor, and capital are not marketed as categories, but by bits and discrete items which differ vastly within each class.

No orderly relation among the shares appears; that inferred now by analysis centers in a few dogmas—first, the three "factors," implicitly distinct and homogeneous. Labor, applied to land, is supported by "capital" as provisions advanced—at a subsistence level, due to the "Malthusian" pressure of population, and "diminishing returns." Machinery and other forms of capital were mentioned—chiefly by Smith and J. S. Mill, but never fitted into the concept. (By Ricardo, machinery is mentioned in a puzzling chapter, XXXI, added in his third edition; and his Chapter XX on Value and Riches also defies interpretation.) A generous reading assigns to wages-and-profit what would now be called their (joint) "marginal" product, of which labor gets subsistence, capital the rest, and land (the owners en bloc) take the "surplus." As simple economic analysis shows, this is the marginal product of the land, taken empirically, in small units; and in production land stands in a symmetrical relation with other kinds of agents (as does any kind with all others). The chapters dealing with the "shares" state various conditions tending to make each larger or smaller (logically in varying degree).

Economics as a Science. Economics, as noted before, describes "economic" behavior and an "economic" social organization, *insofar as* human conduct conforms to certain rules, assumed to be known axiomatically, but *not* excluding other motives. Since its root idea is "economy," which is relative to *intentions* and these are not observed by the senses, it is *not* a strictly empirical or inductive science. People economize—use means more or less effectively to achieve ends—but as certainly, they do not succeed completely in achieving their ends to the maximum degree possible with the means under their control; and the ends may not be ideally good. Ignorance and error play much the role of "friction" in mechanics, to which science the study of economics bears a fairly close analogy in methodology. Motives play the role of forces, which also are metaphysical, not observed but inferred from effects—though the basis of knowledge is different in the two cases. (Friction may be useful, and "efficiency," the objective in economizing, is harmful if the end is bad.) To reduce economic friction (ignorance), men develop the role of "expert," and agency relations permeate free society. Freedom relates largely to choice of agents, in economics and politics. The main source of economic knowledge, i.e., of people's minds, is communication, chiefly by language—the rational use of which is the special attribute, and mystery, of man.

The pivotal new logical idea of the subjective-value revolution is what came to be called "marginalism," which happened to be "discovered" first in consumption (later seen to hold in production also). It dawned on a few minds that the classical rejection of use-value as a cause of price had been an error because the economic value of a good reflects the use-value of an increment (acquired or given up), not that of the commodity in the abstract; also that this value depends on the amount of the good used or transferred, decreasing as this amount increases. That is, wants are satiable (the want for any one good, "other things being equal").

This may (and should) seem trivial, but its publication started controversy, and not all the implications are yet settled. The simplicity is marred by the fact (finally recognized) that any good is wanted (used) in combination with others, hence an increase or decrease in quantity is a change in proportions, and goods may be complementary or antagonistic. This does not weaken the principle of appraisal "at the margin," which is valid under all conditions. Proportioning to equalize marginal utilities clearly "maximizes" the total: if an increment yields more satisfaction in one use than in another, the total will be increased by moving some of it into the field of greater yield, until equality, for equal indivisible increments, is reached. The principle had really been expressed by several writers decades before it got wide recognition through the works of William Stanley Jevons, Carl Menger, and Léon Walras—most notably perhaps by N. W. Senior and W. F. Lloyd in Oxford (in the 1830's); also earlier by Jules Dupuit and C. J. Garnier in France, H. H. Gossen in Germany (1854), and others.

In this period also the idea found parallel application in the field of production and the yield of productive services—distribution in the modern and relevant meaning. Diminishing returns (incremental yield—often misstated as proportional yield even by Alfred Marshall, in his *Principles of Economics* [1890], p. 153) from increasing application of one agent to a given combination of others takes the place of diminishing marginal utility. The increments of physical yield decline, and the value product still more. (In this connection notable contributions had been stated by Senior, the German J. H. v. Thünen, and M. Longfield, to be recognized later.) Near the end of the century, the incremental principle was applied especially to distribution by P. H. Wicksteed in England and J. B. Clark in the U.S.A., Wicksteed for the three traditional "factors," Clark for two, labor and capital. A controversy arose as to whether payment by marginal increments would exactly exhaust the product. This is strictly true only under subtle mathematical conditions; it is roughly true empirically, since producers must act on the principle, and the product does get distributed—after a fashion.

The Fallacy of Three Productive Factors. The most important defect in the traditional theory is that its "factors" are unreal. Persons (as productive) and "natural agents" both largely qualify as "capital goods." They have been produced at a cost and require maintenance and replacement. Natural agents cost investment in exploration and development, a distinctly speculative activity; the classical "land" as "original and indestructible" is unknown on the market, and these qualities pertain separately, in different ways and degrees to all concrete productive agents—even including human beings. And all kinds, however distinguished, are mutually complementary in use. Differences economically significant for classification may be alleged first in the conditions of supply, *by investment* affected by luck. These involve varying durability and the possibility, and cost, of reduplication or production of agents equivalent or more or less similar in function; also differences in transferability among a range of uses, but this is largely a matter of obsolescence and replacement, i.e., transfer of the "investment in" the agents, without moving these themselves. Typical in a progressive economy is mobility, in effect, through differential increase. No general classification by economic qualities is realistic, since differences are a matter of indefinite detail. Laborers *in a free society* are, in human and social terms, a category distinct from "property," i.e., "capital goods"; but further classification depends on law and morals, or on technology.

The principle of "decreasing returns" relates to any kind of productive agent applied in increasing proportions to any combination of kinds. And all "means" are means of production. There is no corresponding law of "increasing returns" except, rigorously speaking, for a short threshold on a minimal dosing of one kind of means onto others. The expression "increasing returns" is confusingly used for an increasing ratio of output to inputs with an expanding scale of units in organizations, due to increasing specialization so made possible. The "unit" in production has various meanings. The subject calls for mention because the two expressions falsely suggest antithesis; but more especially because of the tendency of many people, and some economists, to think that increasing returns with larger scale is also a general law. It holds only for an early stage in a hypothetical expansion of a "unit," beginning at zero. The gains from more minute specialization are soon offset by increased difficulty of coordination, unwieldiness, and costs of management. And if the market conditions do not call for a large number of units of roughly the size of greatest efficiency, competition is impossible; the result will be

monopoly, or "oligopoly." The one gives rise to an abstractly simple price problem, while the other term may stand for a group of vague monopoloid situations, given inconvenient Greek names by Edward H. Chamberlin (*The Theory of Monopolistic Competition*, Cambridge, Mass. [1933], and revisions).

Greater output from equal resources results from use of better technology, which calls for mention of a pivotal fact: that new technology is usually created by investment. Such investment, however, is very different from the production of more productive agents of kinds already in use, or kinds already known. It calls for "invention," a creative act, perceiving and solving a problem. Here the end cannot possibly be known in advance, and so the activity cannot be "economic" in the strict meaning; in many cases such efforts fail outright. The fact of technological progress suggests that on the whole, the results of research and development are worth more than they cost. But much cost is unrecorded and unknown, and this holds in part for the results also. For progress is no definable equilibrium position, and the product value may exceed or fall below its cost in particular cases.

What is true of invention holds also for exploration for natural resources; the significance of this hardly needs detailed explanation, or in particular its bearing on the "classical" theory of rent. Statistics—grouping cases—may reduce the error or "chance" but never remove it. And all economic activities are affected by some uncertainty, with general consequences that must be taken up later. (It is somewhat puzzling that statistics and probability theory apply to real "error," and even crime, as well as purely chance events, but the fact is familiar.)

The Concept of an Economic System. The pivotal idea in the next great advance of economic science to be noticed here is that of an economic system, or the concept of a general equilibrium relation among all the main variables—prices and quantities—treated in economic analysis. This results from combining and interrelating the several "partial equilibria" typified by demand and supply, the quantities offered and purchased of a particular good, in relation to its price. On the analogy of mechanics, mentioned before, change is explained by an imbalance of forces causing movement toward a balance. The basic fact is that over a period of time the quantity of a good sold must equal the quantity bought; hence if at a moment, buyers (say) will take more or less than sellers offer, market competition will raise or lower the price as long as there is a difference. Utility theory explains why less will generally be bought at a higher price than at a lower, and more sold (of an existing supply in the hands of owners—or in a longer view, more will generally be 51 produced; but exceptions here require explanation).

The concept of a unitary economic system results from recognizing that different consumables are mostly produced by the same fund of resources which an entrepreneur producing any good acquires by outbidding those who want them for making other goods. The payments made are his costs of production, while to those who sell him the productive services they are income, which they use to buy portions of the joint social real product, thus performing the function of distribution. The idea of a system was perhaps first effectively proposed, in the form of a crude system of equations, by L. Walras, in his *Éléments d'économie politique pure* of 1874 and 1877 (where he also independently stated the principle of utility theory).

Divisions of Modern Economic Science. It seems fitting at this point to turn from history to outline the *content* of modern analytical economics in terms of its pivotal ideas. This content happens, like the history, to fall naturally into four parts, forming a cross dichotomy; i.e., there are two main divisions, each with two subdivisions, which may be schematized as I-A, I-B, and II-A and II-B. The first main division deals with the economic conduct of an individual, first (I-A) under fixed general conditions, and second (I-B) with these subject to change through economic conduct by the acting person. The two together are introductory to the main subject matter, which fills the second major division. This describes the social organization of economic conduct (a national economy), as worked out under mutual freedom, through exchange of goods and services in markets. The second main part has similar subdivisions, the first assuming fixed general conditions, the second dealing with economic activity partly directed to changing these. The given conditions in question are wants and the resources available to the person or persons acting for satisfying them; the resources used are internal or external to the persons. They include a stock of technical knowledge (and "know-how"), which may either be considered as an internal resource or treated as a third main datum. (Economic conduct which changes basic conditions presumably causes progress, here meaning fuller satisfaction of given wants; action to improve wants—one's own or another's—does not fit the general concept of economy.)

The task of the first main division (two sub-parts) is to analyze the economic conduct of an isolated person (a "Crusoe" economy), abstracting from all social interests and relations. This is necessary in order to avoid serious fallacies that pervade economic discussion, particularly of economic progress, achieved through saving and investing. A full treatment would require much explanation and qualification. Economic

analysis is abstract; it says nothing about "what" wants are felt or what concrete means are used to gratify them—except for the triad of personal capacity, external means and materials, and "technology" (if this is distinguished from "labor-power," which there are good reasons for doing). Nonhuman agents call for most comment, first because the tradition has made a false distinction between "land" and other "capital goods," and secondly because of failure to relate these clearly to "capital."

The first subhead—the Crusoe economy under given conditions—can be treated briefly. Differences between different forms of productive capacity as to conditions of maintaining a constant supply do not justify the recognition of productive factors but some differences cannot be ignored; this would not be too unrealistic for labor-power and technology; but nonhuman agents present the same problem of choice for maintenance as for growth, and the two will best be considered together, later. Much of what is commonly called production of such indirect goods is not capital creation but maintenance of an existing stock, hence is assumed with stationary conditions. To begin with, productive capacity might, for simplicity, be arbitrarily treated as a unit, making it Crusoe's problem to apportion it among the uses known to him so as to achieve maximum total want-satisfaction. The relevant general principles have been stated above. They are summed up in (a) diminishing "marginal utility" and (b) apportionment so that equal units (of negligible size) make equal additions to total satisfaction in all uses. The name comes from an early translation of the German *Grenz* (meaning boundary). The three discoverers used other names: Jevons had called it "final degree of utility," Menger simply "importance" or "meaning" (*Wichtigkeit* or *Bedeutung*), and Walras "scarcity" (*rareté*).

The precise meaning and conditions of validity have been controversial; subtleties may be ignored here, but the discovery was pivotal for the transition from political economy to analytical economics, and (as also noted before) it was later recognized that parallel principles hold for apportioning productive resources— diminishing marginal productivity and equalization for final units in all uses. The principles hold for the allocation of any single kind of good—added to a complex of others, assuming "correct" combination, recognizing complementarities and antagonisms. In social life analysis of consumption is much simplified by the intervention of money, an *income* as a fluid resource to be apportioned in purchasing various consumables available, at their prices. More precisely, that part of a person's income that is devoted to consumption—for the whole is commonly divided between this use and *investment* for future increase. Treatment of this apportionment belongs under the next heading.

The Crusoe Economy with Planned, Net Investing.
It is, of course, "income" which people consume or live on—with occasional, mostly temporary, additions from "disinvesting" *capital* previously accumulated. Theoretical analysis commonly assumes that consumption, at some time, is the sole end of economic activity—making increased future consumption the end of saving and investing. (Smith, op. cit., p. 625; but on p. 352 national power is the end of policy, and on p. 397 there are "two distinct objects," revenue for the people, and for support of the public services, in which "defence is much more important than opulence," p. 431.) In social life, consumption is by no means the whole end, even if we add the security that wealth gives against events that may disrupt one's income, which might bulk large with a Crusoe. Social motives such as rivalry and prestige would be absent, but he would presumably wish to be purposely active, and would have many reasons for raising his scale of living—if not explicitly for the distant future.

Detailed speculation on this point would not be useful here, and it is simply postulated that he invests for progress as well as to prevent decline. The usual assumption makes progress mean an increasing consumable income (also available for further investment). In a stationary economy, only income is really produced; reproduction is a part of maintenance. Income consists of *services*, rendered by persons or by "property" (wealth, capital goods)—only "scarce" things having economic value. Logically, persons, as yielding valuable services, are property, but entailed as to ownership. (Where there are slaves, they class with work animals or machines.) In a free society, persons are not bought and sold, thus are not effectively capitalized and are reasonably not counted as wealth; but, to repeat, they are essentially like (other) capital goods economically. Some personal earnings are in effect capitalized through contracts for services, and other obligations; but enforcement of these is limited as a protection to general freedom.

As just indicated, *capital* is primarily "capitalized income," the present value embodied in a capital-good. A Crusoe might need the capital concept, if he actively decided to maintain a constant income, and it is required for any rational decision on net investment. In society, there are other facts, especially the *production* for sale of income sources, that make it necessary to know the "present-value" of a future stream or flow of income. Such production, by net investment, implies a value result in excess of *cost*, which must also be known. As investing requires time, it involves a *rate of growth*, which is that of the income to be had by

stopping further investment at any point. This concept is most familiar as the compound-interest formula and curve, but applies as well to growth of any population, and elsewhere. It is pivotal for the understanding of economic analysis.

Simple compounding by years (or other periods) is expressed by the formula, $A = (1 + r)^n$, where A is the amount accumulated by one dollar in n years at the simple interest rate r, the growth for a year. This r includes some interest-on-interest as well as on the principal. To separate the two, compounding should be *continuous*, the period being reduced to zero. (The formula becomes e^{nr}, where r and n have the former meaning, e^{nr} replacing $(1 + r)^n$; e is the number $2.7182818 \ldots$, a mathematical constant, the base of "natural" logarithms.) A present-value is found by *discounting* the future income, using the same formula in reverse (and same rate) to find the investment that will yield the income stream in question.

Rational investing calls for using that available opportunity which affords the highest rate-of-growth. The discounting is simple where the future income is to be perpetual (the normal case, as will be shown). Then the present value is simply $\frac{1}{4}$ per income unit, the annual yield divided by the rate as a percentage. (A dollar per year in perpetuity at 5% annually is worth $20.) For a time-limited future income, use of the formula involves some algebra, but that need not be explained here.

Investment theory is abstract and unrealistic, in that an investor could never have the knowledge required for accurate calculation; but (to repeat) that is at least as true of mechanics, where the procedure is not questioned. In a social economy, money is used and is lent at interest, which introduces complications, calling for further analysis, best taken up under the next heading. The need to analyze the growth rate of investment apart from lending and interest is a main reason for considering the Crusoe economy, where this is obviously excluded.

The Free Social-Economic Order, Assuming Stationary Conditions. Under this head, II-A in the suggested scheme, what is to be considered is the stationary economy (or stationary state) which was much discussed early in the present century, especially in the American economic literature. It was pioneered by John Bates Clark, whose book, *The Distribution of Wealth*, was published in 1899, following earlier articles. Clark's main object was to advocate the marginal-productivity theory of income-distribution and defend it ethically. He assumed two productive factors, labor and capital, including land in the latter. About the same time, Alfred Marshall, of Cambridge University, published a more realistic, though less systematic,

53

treatment in connection with discussion of price-determination over long and short periods. He extended the former to include "secular changes" in conditions of demand and supply, but did not explicitly work out this concept. (See his *Principles of Economics*, Book V, p. 379 in the sixth edition, little changed in his "final" eighth edition.) However, the subject comes up again in his treatment of "Distribution" in Book VI, which involves fallacies that must be pointed out.

It may be Marshall's (obvious) veneration of his classical forebears, especially Ricardo, that led him to commit himself to the idea of a real stationary-state in the future—implied by ultimate equilibrium rates of wages and interest—which implies the same as regards "rent." He said (following Ricardo) that land is (approximately) fixed in supply (most explicitly on p. 170; cf. also pp. 534–36) and called its rent a "surplus" (p. 429, Glossary). Of land *acreage* this is true; of the economic land that is leased or bought and sold, not true at all. Ricardo's land, as "original and indestructible," never existed since human beings have planned economically. Imagination can by abstraction form an idea of such "powers of the soil," but they cannot be separated in practice from "artificial" ones, in various meanings, and evidence shows that these account for most or all of present land value; in fact, past investment probably exceeds this, on the average. Moreover these elements exist in all productive agents. As to the "surplus" theory, reasoning at an arithmetical level shows that rent viewed as a surplus *is* the marginal product, and either theory applies to any "factor of production." (Marshall improved on J. S. Mill in seeing that the increase in land value is not free of cost.)

Marshall's main error, as regards stationary conditions (from which Clark can be exonerated) also results from following the "classicals," specifically in neglecting the nature and the consequences of technological progress. This of course has offset any tendency to "diminishing returns" from labor or capital or both. Wages have risen manifold, in the face of a similar population growth; the rate of interest has shown something of a seesaw, moving upward or downward at different periods (but not very much) with the fluctuating growth of investment opportunity, which in principle fixes it. The most serious error, still common in economic writings since Marshall, is failure to note that new technology is chiefly produced by investment, which increases the yield of and demand for all kinds of productive services, however these may be classified. Moreover, this field of investment shows the opposite of diminishing returns; scientific and technical progress constantly opens the way to more progress, with no assignable limit. (And it also changes the character of both labor and economic land.)

One can use the concept of a stationary economy as a postulate useful for analysis (which Clark perhaps meant, and which can be read into Marshall's words), but should make it clear that asserting a tendency towards a long-run equilibrium assumes "other things equal" which could not be, and that such tendencies are more than offset by others making for indefinite cumulative change. Clark also failed to recognize this. The exposition has already trespassed on the subject matter of the next section where, incidentally, it will be shown that even in a social economy, if stationary, there would be little occasion for the lending of money.

The Market Economic Order with Growth: Capital and Interest; Rent, Wages, and Profit. Discussion of section II-B needs as introduction a brief description of the economic order under which modern progress has occurred, which should begin with a historical note. The "existing order" is a mixture of organization forms, mainly based on free exchange, especially two which arose out of feudalism in roughly historical sequence. The enterprise system was preceded by a handicraft stage, with marketing of products but little dealing in the means of production. To be pictured are families—perhaps with one or more apprentices—each specializing in a final product, using simple tools owned by the users. The product is sold in a market for money, with which are bought for consumption various products of other family units. Each of these maintains its own productive capacity, of person and property, and may increase this more or less, as in the Crusoe economy. This system survives to a substantial extent, in farming, repair work, and professional services. (Our familiar social-ethical problems due to inequality, wealth, and poverty, could arise in such a system—and did, in history.)

The past few centuries have seen handicraft progressively replaced by a much more complex system, rooted in a higher order of specialization. In an enterprise-economy, production of any final good is carried on by an organization of persons and equipment, with much internal specialization of roles. This enterprise is legally owned by a person or small group, the "entrepreneur," who buys from outside owners most of the labor power and property services it uses. The entrepreneur may also own any part of the property it uses—often subject to creditor claims, a complication to be considered in due course. The simplest arrangement is for the entrepreneur to hire property services, paying *rent;* the correct meaning of that term applies to all property alike, the traditional limitation to "land" being a misuse of words. (The term "rent" might well apply to the hiring of persons, where the payment happens to be called "wages"—or, it would make for clear thinking if a common word, such as "hire" were used for both.)

The working of the system is explained by describing the general equilibrium which "economic forces" tend to establish, relative to given conditions—as to persons and their wants, resources, and technology—or, in Marshall's words, "would bring about if the conditions of life were stationary long enough for them to work out their full effect" (op. cit., p. 347). Some limitations of this tendency will call for notice. At equilibrium, *simultaneously* all consumer expenditures would buy at the margin equal increments of satisfaction and all productive resources would yield (marginally) equal increments of value product, all prices being equal to costs (ignoring monopoly). The economic forces are human preferences, expressed in partly rational choices. This conclusion should be qualified by the fact that the system pictured embodies "feedback" principles, and as in a mechanical situation, these typically produce oscillations, where responses are not instantaneous—and they do so in economic affairs, creating serious problems.

Enterprise organization is inevitable, if men strive to get ahead, which they often do (not universally, as Adam Smith strangely assumed). It can hardly be imagined without use of money, as a unit of value and intermediary in exchange. (But, to repeat, money-*lending* is not inevitable, since a loan is always equivalent to another transaction, a lease or sale.) The main economic decisions are made formally by entrepreneurs, interacting with their opposite numbers in markets, and acting directly or through agents whom they hire. But they are finally responsible to consumers and owners of productive agents—act in a real sense as agents of both, and "at equilibrium" have no power at all. (Describing the system as "consumer sovereignty" states a half truth.)

Both business and politics are dominated by the agency relation. Personal freedom is mostly freedom to choose agents—usually among competing seekers of the role. The entrepreneur is the central figure of the modern economy. Each buys productive services, makes products, and sells both in markets, in competition with all others, hoping to make some *profit*. This profit is an element in the entrepreneur's own income (along with the earnings of his own services or property); but it is as likely to be negative, i.e., a loss, as a gain, which the word "profit" misleadingly suggests. The profit-system should be called profit-seeking, or "profit-and-loss." As noted above, the classical political-economists misconceived profit, failed to distinguish the entrepreneur function, and only incidentally recognized loan interest. Even J. S. Mill merely divided "gross profit" into three parts (op. cit., p. 407), and then endorsed (on p. 416) the Ricardian theory. (This system was taken over by the Marxists and used logically in propaganda for a social revolution—in place

of its strange use as a basis for a doctrine of laissez-faire; in the case of "rent" it served, also logically, in propaganda for land-value confiscation—by some political unit itself without the individual owner's essentially valid claim—which Marshall recognized.)

Profit, correctly defined (including loss), is clearly the result of an imperfect working of the competitive market system, due in turn to the uncertainty of the future and the limited foresight of entrepreneurs. (If any one of them knew the future, he would not suffer loss, and if his competitors knew, he could not make a gain.) Uncertainty can often (in practice not always) be reduced by insurance or dealing with cases in groups, but never eliminated. To understand enterprise and profit, it is useful first to imagine a situation in which labor alone is productive and where just two persons wish to cooperate. The matters on which they must agree—what to produce, by what procedure, and the division of the joint result—might conceivably be settled by negotiation. But this would be difficult, and it seems more reasonable to expect formation of a partnership, in which one party will make the decisions and grant to the other a stated amount of the product, himself taking any excess over the agreed share, and making up the loss if there is a deficit. The "active" partner is then an entrepreneur, paying wages and receiving profit, or incurring loss. (The entrepreneur might consider what he could have made by working alone as wages and view profit as only the difference between this and what he realizes.) No new principle is introduced if either or both parties also furnish the services of nonhuman productive agents which they may own; payment for the use of any such item will be a rent.

The next step in the explanatory hypothesis has been suggested, and is a pivotal idea. Instead of a lease for any nonhuman agent, the parties may agree on a sale, the previous owner taking a "note" for the price, and receiving interest instead of rent. Under theoretically ideal conditions—perfect knowledge and economic rationality—the sale price and interest rate would make the payment (per time unit) the same as in the other case. Under conditions resembling those of real life, the actual figures would be fixed by the best opportunity open for investment, the principal being the cost of creating a new income source with the same yield as that whose use is being transferred. Shifting attention from the two-person situation to a competitive economy, intelligent selection of opportunities in the market will fix a uniform rate—after allowance for costs, uncertainties, attitudes towards risk-taking, and especially for complications due to the use of money.

If a temporary arrangement is desired, an agreement for later resale will still make the two arrangements fully interchangeable. The result will differ if risk attitudes differ—or as will be explained, if the actual risk differs for the two parties. The latter is the case in real social life, and this is the main general reason why the lease procedure is used in some cases and the sale in others.

In a social economy, income-yielding assets are bought and sold, at prices which strongly tend to equal their expected yield capitalized at the going interest rate, which in turn strongly tends to equal the rate to be expected on the best new investment opportunities open. But these prices are affected by numberless uncertainties, and any rise or fall in the value of an asset impinges on the formal owner. Hence if the prospective user of a given asset is on any ground more optimistic as to its future market value than is the current owner, who turns it over to him for use, they will agree on a price making a sale with a loan preferable to both parties over any lease on which they can agree, and conversely for the opposite situation.

However, the motive for lending money, rather than leasing some income source, is vastly strengthened in the major type of cases where it is done in modern life, that is, not in connection with the transfer for use of existing assets, but with investment by one party to create a new source of income to be used by another. This again could be arranged, by the first party making the investment himself and leasing the result to the other; but the two must then agree on the kind of capital good to fit the needs of the prospective user, and for obvious reasons they usually agree on a loan of money. In fact, of course, lending money to entrepreneurs for "real" investment has become a major vocation—that which now best defines the "capitalist." Thus the act of investing is divided: owners of abstract wealth held in the form of money (itself to them an investment) invests the money financially by lending to entrepreneurs who invest materially by buying productive services and creating income sources. (Other complications arise, but need not be considered here.) Each mode of investing may involve a "profit" (or loss), i.e., may yield more or less than might have been had through perfect foresight.

Some lending and borrowing is done for other purposes, notably consumption in anticipation of receiving income, or to avoid a sale of assets. This consumption loan is unimportant in the market, and finally comes under the same principles—apart from a motive of charity. Any economic loan must have *security* and is always an alternative to the sale or lease of the asset in question. In a progressive society, a person's consumption of capital merely subtracts something from its growth in the whole economy. (Net social disinvestment hardly occurs, or does so only under disorganization by a crisis.)

It has been held that as investment grows the yield-rate must tend to fall—due to diminishing returns. As noted above, this ignores the fact that much investment increases the yield of capital-goods by creating new knowledge, a field of investment that shows no tendency to exhaustion but rather the contrary—and also goes into more people, and useful human qualities other than technical knowledge. And much goes into exploration for natural resources. These familiar fields perhaps tend to become at some time fully known, but not in combination with new knowledge, and exhaustive knowledge cannot be foreseen. As to the yield-rate, the reasonable expectation is more of what has happened through modern history, some "seesaw" in the rate of yield as opening of new investments runs ahead of or falls behind exhaustion of old. Moreover, "the" rate in any market at any time is a complex of "pure interest" and numerous other factors (risk, transaction cost, etc., and especially the monetary situation and business prospects), so that the true rate is not definitely determinate.

A pivotal idea in the published discussion of interest theory has been the "dogma" that interest is paid because human nature systematically prefers present goods to future goods of like kind and amount. This is a fallacy because it overlooks two patent facts: first, that while one does not want to postpone today's consumption until tomorrow, neither does one want to consume tomorrow's provisions today; and further, that perpetual postponement of all consumption is impossible. Given provisions for two days, there seems to be no economic principle or general fact of psychology to determine the precise distribution between the two. Abstract rationality would surely call for something near uniformity over time, but some persons will diverge in one direction and some in the other. Of this, Alfred Marshall gave the homely illustration of boys eating a plum pudding: some will pick out the plums and eat them first, some will save them to the last, and others eat them as they come to them. An intelligent person of means (not on the point of suicide) will certainly consume some of his income (or wealth, by disinvestment) day by day, and keep some provision for the future; but as to how much of the latter he will invest for a future increase, again no general principle can say.

It surely seems reasonable to prefer enjoyment while one is alive rather than after death; but, as remarked before, people do deliberately leave accumulated wealth at death—and significant net social accumulation depends on the wide prevalence of such conduct. Economic science can say only that decision between consuming and investing some part of one's means is a matter of taste, not arguable—like consumption choices—(ignoring contracted obligations) and that rational conduct dictates making any investment that is made at the going rate; i.e., at the margin of growth of capital wealth in the society at the time, or in some newly discovered better opportunity—where the return above the going rate would be profit.

Two Major Qualifications of General Economic Analysis. The treatment thus far has dealt with "pure" theory, oversimplified in two respects in particular, where it must be supplemented, though very briefly. One of the two is monopoly—including "monopoloid" situations where either sellers or buyers are too few for effective competition—the other, *money* and problems due to its use. The former may be more quickly disposed of as to main essentials. Historically, as observed earlier, the founders, Smith and Ricardo, wrote "nonsense" about monopoly pricing; and J. S. Mill was little better. By 1890, Alfred Marshall had stated the principle correctly, in words and mathematically. (A mathematical study had been published in French by A. A. Cournot in 1838, but it received general notice only when rediscovered and published in English, in 1897, as *Researches Into the Mathematical Principles of Wealth*, with a bibliography of mathematical economics by Irving Fisher.)

The monopolist's interest plainly is to adjust the supply and through it the price so as to maximize his total net revenue or profit (*not* to maximize the price). Monopoly is less important in fact than it is psychologically because the public greatly exaggerates both its prevalence and still more the real evil. Much monopoly is "natural," even inevitable, and more is beneficial. Governments grant temporary monopolies by patent, copyright, etc., to encourage useful innovations, and a large share of those privately set up work in the same way. On the other hand, the public encourages costly monopolies in the fields of labor and agriculture, and in foreign trade, though "protection" does not directly establish monopoly, as early writers said.

Exaggeration of the occurrence of monopoly is a common ground for condemning free enterprise —alleging that market competition is unreal or ineffective. This ignores bankruptcy figures and other facts proving the contrary. Pointing out the error does not imply that business monopolies do not exist or present no serious public problems, but public action itself causes restrictions more costly to society. The classical political economists thought monopoly bad, but proposed no action except negatively not to establish them. In modern times "anti-trust" laws have become familiar, but in the United States they exempt highly restrictive labor unions, and "administered" prices.

Money and Interest. The Business Cycle. It is hard to say briefly anything objective and useful about money, even ignoring all the preaching about its evils. Denunciation is largely based on confusing it with wealth, and wealth (also commonly confused with income) is merely one form of power. Here the classical political economists deserve credit; they tried to get behind its mask or "veil," though, as has been shown, what they said about economic reality was largely fallacy. And they strangely ignored for the most part the main problem that arises from the use of money. That problem is the periodic occurrence of "hard times," alternating somewhat cyclically with prosperous periods. Some exception is called for by J. S. Mill's treatment of speculation and crises (op. cit., Book III, Ch. XII). "Mercantilist" writers had held that abundance of money causes good business, either directly or by way of lower interest rates. In the 1740's, David Hume published his *Essays* with the pivotal idea that with an *increasing* quantity of money, selling prices rise more rapidly than cost prices, thus raising profits, and conversely for falling prices—which causes business prosperity and depression, the latter with unemployment and misery.

From the sixteenth century, writers noticed the effect of rising prices (due to influx of silver and gold from the New World) in favoring debtors at the expense of creditors. Adam Smith noted the loss incurred by receivers of feudal rents, etc., which had been converted into cash from payment in kind. The inflation of the period of the French Revolutionary and Napoleonic wars led to demands that obligations be repaid in money of the same value as that in which they were contracted. Meanwhile, John Locke and others had been developing in explanation the "quantity theory of money"—or quantity and circulation velocity, as even Locke recognized the role of the latter.

A pivotal idea for cycle (or "conjuncture") theory, but slow to be recognized, is the general fact already mentioned, that supply-and-demand adjustments work on the "feedback" principle, like a speed-governor on an engine, a thermostat, etc., and that all such mechanisms produce oscillations. Thus any price normally shows cycles of rise and decline, more or less regular, extensive and prolonged—as normal-price theory should recognize. The basis of the phenomenon is "lag" in response of an effect to its cause. When the production of "x" is profitable (say of hats, an example from Russian propaganda) it tends to expand, but time is required for new supply to reach the market and reduce the price, and, meanwhile, under individualistic control, the movement tends to be overdone, "glutting" the market and reversing itself. (This *is* abstractly an argument for central advance planning and control—*if* 57 it could be guided by complete foresight and were free from evils of its own.) The cycles for an item will be longer as it takes longer to expand production *or* to exhaust an existing supply or its sources. Further, a price bulge that would naturally be temporary is likely to be mistaken for a trend, prolonging the effects through reduction of current output to prepare for a later increase. This is obvious with livestock, when animals that would have been marketed are held back for breeding purposes; similar causes operate elsewhere.

Familiar facts make the value of money an extreme case for oscillation. The current "price"—the reciprocal of the general price-level—is not conspicuous, and the position of equilibrium is vague in comparison with commodities which have an organized market or a known cost of production. And, more important, the self-perpetuation and self-aggravating tendency of price-movements is magnified. Rising prices make it seem preferable to hold goods rather than money and so to speed up the turnover of money; this stimulates real production, especially through bank loans, creating deposits which circulate as equivalent to more money. Hence further rise of prices and greater profit margins, and so on. But shortage of labor and decrease of its quality, along with rising wages, help bring the boom to an end—which tends to be precipitate and may cause a panic in the loan market. Typical and pivotal is a sharp contraction in the capital-goods industries, spreading to those serving consumption. In the depression of the 1930's about half the calamitous unemployment occurred in the field of "durables," which had furnished about a fifth of the total employment.

In general, what happens at the peak of a boom—its collapse and a drastic reversal of the trend—is readily explained and even predictable; and in principle the boom is largely remediable through monetary and fiscal action. But no one knows just when to act or how much action to take, and the public mind opposes "killing prosperity," and in any case tends to blame the "money power" for the unfavorable consequences. At the bottom of the cycle the situation is very different. It is not clear why the decline stops just where it does, or why the pickup is slow, which gives many observers the impression of a stable equilibrium along with extensive idleness of labor and other resources. This is self-contradictory, but explanation of the situation involves many factors and discussion beyond the scope of this article. Adjustments, including liquidations, must be carried out, requiring time; and an essential fact is that potential investment opportunities must be seen far ahead, and seized by individuals. On the whole subject, controversy is abundant.

A major aspect is the relation between monetary phenomena and the interest rate—or rates. Boom con-

ditions raise the demand for money in the investment market and throughout the economy. At the time of a collapse, the need for "cash" to meet commitments may create a "panic" or near panic, causing a demand for loans at fantastically high rates, not connected with the long-run determination of the rate by investment opportunities. Under such conditions one can hardly speak of "the" rate of interest. Where the security seems good, loans may be available at very low rates, and otherwise only at very high rates, or not at all, forcing bankruptcies. A full discussion would prompt analysis of the Great Depression of the 1930's, the "New Deal" measures, and the role of the ideas publicized especially by John Maynard Keynes (later Lord Keynes), who stressed the aspect of interest as a rent on cash, rightly as regards very short-period changes.

From the pivotal fact of the wide instability of the general price level and its consequences follow two others: first, that money, and circulating credit, must be "managed"—a policy of laissez-faire here has "intolerable" results; but secondly, that the management cannot be very effective, consistently with social freedom in economic and other respects. The measures taken under the "New Deal" administration of the 1930's to deal with unemployment and distress ("pump priming" through public make-work projects) were ineffective; unemployment was finally cured by the outbreak in Europe of World War II.

Movements Opposed to Analytical Economics. Many aspersions have been cast on "political economy" since Carlyle referred to it as "that dismal science." This attitude may be found in the New Testament condemnation of the desire for riches and money. But to idealists all science is dismal, since it describes the real, in contrast with the ideal or perfect. And economics is an extreme case, because it deals with cost, the need to give up one good to get another; and the same prejudice doubtless underlies the popular condemnation of trade, and the market organization of production and distribution.

There is a special ground for disliking historical economic thought in its advocacy (overt, implied or imputed) of the policy of laissez-faire. The earliest public opposition to Adam Smith's teaching rested on humanitarian grounds. It is pointed up by the reversal of position by the Italian scholar, Jean Charles Léonard de Sismondi, who first supported Adam Smith, in a book, *De la richesse commerciale* (1803), but in 1819 revolted against the position in his *Nouveaux principes d'économie politique.* His second position was sound and well taken, for, as noted earlier, Smith's great work was one-sided propaganda for "natural liberty," with little argument either way from economic analysis. He never spelled out the meaning of the "invisible hand" said to harmonize the individual interest with that of society. Nor did he recognize the real logic of his position, the view that there is no real social interest, that society is merely an organization of individuals for mutual economic advantage. The state is viewed as a means, never an end with values of its own—except perhaps as implied by the recognition of "defence," rated as "much more important than opulence" (op. cit., p. 431). The "hand" should not be interpreted as "Providence," or a mystical force, as is often done.

However, laissez-faire (an expression not used by Smith or Ricardo) is not an economic doctrine, but a political one. As already explained, the validity of economic freedom as a policy depends on that of the social ethics of utilitarian (instrumentalist) individualism, which has serious limitations. This policy issue has nothing to do with economics as a science, which assumes only the partial (analytical) descriptive truth of its principles, not their ethical rightness—any more than the assumption of "frictionless conditions" in mechanics implies that friction (and other qualifications) should be ignored by engineers in applying the principles. The common accusation of "unreality" of economic theory is as valid for theoretical mechanics.

On the other hand, the critics (on the ground in question) are open to the criticism that merely abstract repudiation of laissez-faire means anarchism and ignores stated qualifications. Smith listed and developed three general exceptions to the system of natural liberty, as tasks of the sovereign (op. cit., p. 351). Any constructive criticism of laissez-faire must point out concrete evils of freedom and at least indicate in general terms feasible measures for the control and supplementation of free-market relations that can reasonably be expected to remedy or mitigate them. Taking measures implies a political order; and modern Western nations are committed to "democratic" government—law making and enforcement by representatives of the citizen body, chosen by majority vote, the citizens including all normal adults. (Smith and his early followers said nothing about the form of government, the nature of the "sovereign.") In the modern West, the primary task of government is to define and maintain the maximum *permissible* freedoms, notably market freedom, freedom presupposing a fair degree of legal order. (The second of Smith's exceptions, after defence, was to maintain "an exact administration of justice" in Book IV, Ch. IX.) This would now include much more than he intended, though much might be read into his treatment of this and the other two exceptions, or that of taxation. The democratic political order and the economic order of markets and enterprise are now each a part of the other—all based on "cultural" freedom, religion included.

The most extreme opponents of the market economic order, and of the science which analyzes it, are the Marxists, who repudiate democracy also, in favor of nothing, i.e., anarchism, as far as the documents state. The original and still sacred "scripture," the *Communist Manifesto*, demands the "violent overthrow of all existing [*bisherige*] social order," by and for the workers of the world, who "have nothing to lose but their chains [and] have a world to gain." Marx defined government as the agency by which a ruling class, of owners, exploits the workers. The revolution should establish a "dictatorship of the proletariat," giving no indication of its organization for unitary action. This has worked out in fact as the dictatorship of a self-perpetuating clique, led by a "chairman"; it is miscalled a "party" and the system is miscalled "communism." In Russia, where its advocates came to power—against Marxist predictions—the regime is much farther from communism than is the (also misnamed) "capitalism" of the free nations. But the doctrine (in essence an application of Ricardian economics) has been embraced by innumerable bright minds and has conquered over half of the world.

More reasonable, being more moderate, is the opposition movement called "socialism." Its advocates have stood for a democratic government, making the problem again one of politics. They have generally accepted the main body of economic science, but have advocated governmental ownership and management of the bulk of income-yielding wealth (by some political body), with "just" distribution of burdens and benefits. Political control of income distribution would separate this from payment for productive services, and destroy the free economic system. In the case of labor, as an incentive, pay might correspond to some extent with productive contribution, hence with the scarcity of particular abilities. Socialists have also been vague about the productive organization, as well as on justice, and disagree widely on details; they agree chiefly in denouncing capitalism. The word "socialism" replaced "Owenism," stigmatized by Marx as "utopian"—along with other early schemes, in contrast with his own so-called "scientific" socialism. Claim to this description rested on the "materialistic interpretation of history," which is neither materialistic nor scientific—nor even "economic," as it is often called—but dialectical, in an inverse-Hegelian sense; but it did logically imply inevitability.

The first socialists to be called such, as a school, were the "Ricardian" group. They are so named because they based their teaching on the labor theory of production, drawing the common inference, the right of 59 laborers to the whole product. A book with this title, *The Right to the Whole Produce of Labor* (1899) by an Austrian, Anton Menger, has in the English translation an Introduction by H. S. Foxwell, which gives perhaps the best account of the group. They were theorists not, like Owen, reformers. Some Owenites tried to put the labor theory into practice by setting up labor-exchanges, stores where workmen brought products to receive "scrip" stating their labor-time value, to be sold to others on the same terms; they were short-lived. Owen, Charles Fourier, Étienne Cabet, and other utopians established communistic colonies in America, attracted by cheap land; some became famous, but all failed.

The first Ricardian Socialist, in time, was William Thompson (1785?–1833) whose *Principles of the Distribution of Wealth* appeared in 1824. He was perhaps also the most influential, since Marx is thought to have taken from his book the idea of surplus-value. (He might have gotten it from J. S. Mill by merely renaming what Mill defined as profit.) John Gray and J. S. Bray argued on similar lines, holding that property is stored-up labor, and an owner should receive only postponed wages for its labor cost. (Marx's labor-cost theory would take account of the labor-cost of producing laborers.)

To the criticism that socialists have offered no plan for the organization of an economy without private ownership, a few exceptions should be noted, notably "The Webbs" (Sidney and Beatrice), *Outline for a Socialist Constitution for Great Britain*, and G. D. H. Cole, *Guild Socialism Restated* (both London, 1920). Also a book by Carl Landauer, *Theory of National Economic Planning* (1944, p. 47), and others, might be named. Of late there has been a tendency to use "planned economy" in place of "socialism," as more appealing. Whatever the name, the general issue of socialism versus free enterprise is a matter of degree and of details; as the Prince of Wales, later King Edward VII, said in 1895, "We are all socialists now." It is pointless to argue for either system in general; but for the modern Western mind there is a presumption in favor of the market order, unless there is a good reason to the contrary, since it affords more freedom.

There is a question "how" socialistic a nation could become and still preserve democratic forms, i.e., not lead to a dictatorship. To repeat, the problem is one of politics, having little to do with economics as a science. Of this, the most general principles are valid for any social order; while (somewhat) intelligent beings engage in production, distribution, and consumption and form a society, "economic" decisions will be made, by some units and for some units—wisely or otherwise—and details do not affect the abstract theory. The concept covers all more or less effective means-ends relations, including "function" in sub-human life.

The intellectually more serious opposition to "orthodox" economics has been "historicism." Its contention is methodological—that the proper subject matter of economics is not inferences from familiar principles of economy, but description and induction from current facts and history. This doctrine originated in Germany and is characteristically German, as the more prevalent one is British. The alternative view has had advocates in English works; of these writers, T. E. Cliffe-Leslie is perhaps most important, though Sir William Ashley and many other economic historians might be named; also perhaps, R. H. Tawney, who was more socialistic. His book, *Equality* (London, 1929), raises a serious problem for advocates of freedom, since inequality of power limits effective freedom. And inequality tends to grow, since power can be used to get more power, and this is conspicuously true of economic power. Its growth has been largely checked by differential taxation, public education, and other measures, and by some natural counter-tendencies.

German historical economics was doubtless suggested by the historical jurisprudence of Friedrich K. von Savigny and others. Montesquieu was a cultural forerunner. Two German historical schools are commonly recognized—the first led by W. Roscher, B. Hildebrand, and K. Knies, the second by Gustav Schmoller. This last was a "tsar" and censor of German university economics for a generation, under the Empire of 1871. He was important as a historian as well as a propagandist. Karl Bücher and others of the "schools" were more interested in history than in conceptual or mathematical analysis.

The anti-deductivist writers called for a science not of wealth alone but of life—as Othmar Spann, a romantic adherent stated it (*Tote und lebendige Wissenschaft*, 2nd ed., 1928)—with only special attention to the economic aspect; i.e., they opposed the "narrowness" and the unreality of analysis and specialization. (One might ask, why only "life," not the world, since man is a part of it, and high authorities say that life is nothing but physics and chemistry.)

An offshoot of the German movement was American "Institutionalism" which flourished around the turn into the twentieth century. Thorstein Veblen was its best known champion—writing satire along with science—and had a devoted follower in Clarence E. Ayres. John R. Commons wrote on economic institutions chiefly from a legal standpoint, and Wesley C. Mitchell was sympathetic; he was claimed as an institutionalist, but his main work, on money, statistics, and business cycles, belongs to "orthodox" economics.

What should be said about these opposition movements is that there is no conflict at all with orthodoxy. One can advocate a policy or write historical or sociological economics at will, distinguishing the result from history or sociology as far as possible. There was little excuse for a "methods quarrel" (*Methodenstreit*) such as raged in Germany and Austria after the publication of Carl Menger's *Untersuchungen* ("Inquiries into Methods") in 1883—chiefly between him and Gustav Schmoller. One may contend that inductive treatment is superior, or even that no other economics should be written. But it remains true that price theory yields laws more useful for guiding action than any other comparably simple view of social phenomena (e.g., criminology). There has been much effort to find predictive historical laws, but success has been sadly limited. Perhaps the major achievement has been Sir Henry Sumner Maine's formula, "from status to contract" (*Ancient Law* [1930], p. 182). Hegel used somewhat similar words, but with a very different meaning. Doubtless enough has been said about the conflicting approaches; but a final word may revert to the parallelism of economic theory with the science of mechanics, where the abstraction and unrealism are greater, but their necessity and usefulness are not questioned.

BIBLIOGRAPHY

Background for this topic, and important bibliographies, can be found especially in Joseph A. Schumpeter, *History of Economic Analysis* (New York, 1954; published posthumously), and Edmund Whittaker, *A History of Economic Ideas* (New York, 1939). Other useful volumes are: Eric Roll, *A History of Economic Thought* (New York, 1939; 3rd ed., 1942); J. F. Bell, *History of Economic Thought* (New York, 1953); Alexander Gray, *The Development of Economic Doctrine* (London and New York, 1931); the last is less comprehensive than the others. Valuable for the history of "laissez-faire" are D. H. Macgregor, *Economic Thought and Policy* (Oxford, 1949); and Edward R. Kittrell, "'Laissez-Faire' in English Classical Economics," *Journal of the History of Ideas*, **27** (1966), 610–20. Additional studies are Edwin Cannan, *A History of the Theories of Production and Distribution in English Political Economy from 1776 to 1848*, 3rd ed. (London, 1924); Mark Blaug, *Ricardian Economics: A Historical Study* (New Haven and London, 1958); and Paul T. Homan, *Contemporary Thought* (New York, 1928).

The following are the best editions of economic classics. Adam Smith, *The Wealth of Nations*, ed. Edwin Cannan, 2 vols. (London and New York, 1904). It is available in reprints, and in a useful abridgment of W. J. Ashley, *Selected Chapters and Passages from The Wealth of Nations* (London, 1895; 1906). David Ricardo, *Principles of Political Economy and Taxation*, Vol. I of *Works and Correspondence*, ed. P. Sraffa and M. H. Dobb, 10 vols. (Cambridge, 1951–55). John Stuart Mill, *Principles of Political Economy*, ed. W. J. Ashley (London and New York, 1909). A new version has an introduction by V. W. Bladen, textual editor J. M. Robson, 2 vols. (Toronto, 1965). E. von Böhm-Bawerk's chief works are *Kapital and Kapitalzins*, Vol. I, *Geschichte und Kritik der Kapitalzinstheorien* (Innsbruck, 1884), trans. William Smart as *Capital and Interest* (London, 1890; 1932); Vol. II, *Positive Theories des Kapitals* (Innsbruck, 1889), trans. William Smart as *The Positive Theory of Capital* (London, 1891; 1923).

On Socialism the following are recommended: Alexander Gray, *The Socialist Tradition, Moses to Lenin* (London and New York, 1946; reprint 1968); and Harry W. Laidler, *History of Socialism*, rev. ed. (New York, 1968).

Still useful is R. H. I. Palgrave, *Dictionary of Political Economy*, ed. Henry Higgs, 3 vols. (London and New York, 1926).

FRANK H. KNIGHT

[See also Anarchism; Authority; Cycles; Democracy; **Economic Theory of Natural Liberty;** Enlightenment; Equality; Freedom; Individualism; **Liberalism;** Marxism; Nationalism; Progress; **Property;** Socialism; State.]

ECONOMIC THEORY OF NATURAL LIBERTY

"NATURAL LIBERTY" is an expression associated particularly with Adam Smith in his *Inquiry into the Nature and Causes of the Wealth of Nations* (1776). It is often associated with the idea of laissez-faire, or the doctrine that government should intervene as little as possible in the affairs of its citizens, especially in matters relating to economic life. In the hands of Adam Smith, however, "natural liberty" is a much more subtle and realistic concept than laissez-faire and indeed is the basis of a whole theory of social organization. "Natural liberty" implies the ability of each individual to do what seems to him best in the circumstances in which he finds himself without fear of threat or reprisal.

Political philosophers from Plato to Hobbes saw society organized primarily through what might be called legitimated threat. They were all convinced that if everybody did what he pleased society would rapidly fall apart and that the only thing that held it together was the organization of a credible threat system in the hands of the state. This would dissuade people from doing antisocial things that they wanted to do, because if they did so, they believed they would suffer penalties inflicted by the state. The idea that society might be held together by mutual self interest would probably not have occurred to anybody earlier than the eighteenth century.

61

We can perhaps trace some origins of the idea in the medieval and even later concepts of natural law or of natural rights. These relations, however, are tenuous. Christianity, it is true, did introduce the idea that there was a higher law than that of the state, which was the law of God. The enforcement even of the law of God, however, depended on the fear of Hell—a spiritual threat system of considerable credibility—and while this undoubtedly operated to mollify the harshness of the material threat system, it is still a very long way from the idea of natural liberty. Hobbes, indeed, makes an important contribution by breaking away from the spiritual threat system and supposing that the state is a purely human institution which we put up with for fear of finding something worse. Hobbes, however, was very insistent that his "Leviathan" must exercise a monopoly of coercive power without which society would fall apart into the state of nature in which life would be ". . . nasty, brutish, mean, and short." It would certainly never have occurred to Hobbes that a man by following his own interests could enhance the welfare of all.

Locke comes closer to the idea of natural liberty in his concept of limited government and society based on property. He comes close also to anticipating a labor theory of value, which is an important element of Adam Smith. He still gives a very large role to government, however, and he lacks Adam Smith's extraordinary insight on how society is organized through exchange.

Other possible origins of the idea may be found in the Newtonian celestial mechanics with its concept of the universe ruled by differential equations rather than by angels. The hope of discovering a celestial mechanics of society was close to the minds of the eighteenth century and undoubtedly influenced Adam Smith. Another possible source would be Rousseau, with his idealization of the noble savage and his feeling that the coercive system of civilization thwarts and distorts the natural harmonies of mankind. This sentiment is not wholly foreign to the optimistic bias of Adam Smith, although he is too much of a canny Scotchman to be taken in by it very much.

The most direct antecedent of Adam Smith's concept of "natural liberty" is the doctrine of the physiocrats or *économistes* of France. The very name "Physiocracy" means the rule of nature. The physiocrats made a particularly important contribution in seeing society as a whole of interrelated parts. François Quesnay, in the *Tableau économique* (1758), develops the first concept of national income as the sum of the geometric series of continually smaller reactions, and so anticipated in a certain degree the Keynesian concept of the multiplier. The peculiar physiocratic doctrine, however, that all economic surpluses arose from agriculture and that manufacturing was "sterile," prevented them from achieving a complete theory of economic equilibrium. Of the French thinkers at the time A. R. J. Turgot had the most direct influence on Adam Smith and may well have influenced Adam Smith's ideas on the self-regulating character of the economy. The physiocrats, however, still believed that an absolute monarchy was the only means of reconciling the internal conflicts of a society and they did not have a clear picture of the self-regulating character of a price system.

We must conclude, therefore, that the idea of natural liberty as a self-adjusting process in society, whereby each individual by following his own interests or bent promotes the total welfare, is an idea which owes so much to Adam Smith that it seems only fair to give him most of the credit for it.

The Wealth of Nations is rightly regarded as the first great systematic exposition of economics and it is essentially a study of how society is organized through exchange. Adam Smith, oddly enough, does not have any good theory about the origins of exchange, which he attributes to some mysterious "propensity to truck," and it was not until a hundred years later that the utility theorists achieved a reasonably satisfactory explanation of how exchange originates, even though the study of the social conditions under which exchange becomes legitimate is still very underdeveloped and requires much further work. His vagueness about the origins of exchange, however, did not hamper Adam Smith in discussing the consequences of exchange. He sees very clearly that exchange develops a division of labor, that the division of labor itself widens the market, and that the widening of the market promotes further exchange and further division of labor. We have here a process with what today we call "positive feedback" and which leads, therefore, into "development," that is, a steady increase in productivity, in specialization, in the extent of the market and in the total per capita output of commodities, which Smith regards as the principal measure for the wealth of nations.

This process operates through the price system; that is, the total set of all prices or ratios of exchange which determines the terms of trade of any individual conducting exchanges. Since an individual has an output of the things which he sells into the market and an input from the market of the things that he buys, his terms of trade are the ratio of the quantity of what he buys to the quantity of what he sells. In these days we would describe this by some kind of index number. Adam Smith did not have this device; nevertheless, his concept is fairly clear. Whether a person will go on producing what he is producing and exchanging it, depends on the terms of trade which he experiences. If these terms are poor, that is, if he is giving out a lot and not getting very much in return, then he will tend to shift his occupation to one in which the terms are more favorable. This change of occupation, however, will have an effect on the terms of trade themselves, improving the terms of trade in the occupation which he has left and worsening the terms of trade in the one to which he has gone. This process will tend to go on until nobody feels he can better his condition by shifting to another occupation, or, more accurately, until in each occupation the amount of resources entering the occupation is just equal to the amount leaving it. The price structure, which produced this situation would be an equilibrium price structure, or a structure of "natural prices" as Adam Smith called them. We notice that the word "natural" here is not merely a vague appeal to some divine order or order of nature, but is a quite specific equilibrium concept in the sense that if price structure is not at its natural level, people will perceive those occupations with "high prices" as unusually profitable and will move into them, which will bring the price down, and will perceive those occupations with "low prices" as unusually unprofitable and will move out of them, which will bring the prices up. The natural price system, therefore, is a system of mechanical equilibrium and is in a very real sense a kind of celestial mechanics of the social system.

In its sharpness, clarity, and operationalism, this concept is far removed from the vague concept of natural law and natural rights. It is this equilibrium system, and not any presumed intervention from God or nature, which constitutes the famous "invisible hand" which turns the pursuit of private gain into public welfare. This "invisible hand" has two aspects. In the first place, it organizes the productive activities of society so that people produce on the whole what people want. Thus, if there is a shift in demand, say from tea to coffee, the price of coffee will rise and the price of tea will fall, production of coffee will become unusually profitable and this will attract people into it, production of tea will become unprofitable and that will chase people out of it. Eventually the production of coffee will be expanded and tea will contract until the new structure of demand is satisfied and the production of coffee and tea are once more equally profitable or at least equal enough so that there is no movement of resources from one to the other. By contrast, if the visible hand of government attempts to distribute commodities to people in accordance with their demand, by some sort of rationing, in the absence of any price-profit equilibrium mechanism, many demands will be undersatisfied or overfulfilled, and the political feedback from these dissatisfactions will be slow and uncertain.

The second function of the "invisible hand" is to promote economic development. It does this if it is profitable to direct activity towards making things more cheaply, that is, towards getting more output per unit of input in production. If the price structure is adapted to a previous level of technology, then the innovators of superior technology profit because the price, at least temporarily, will be higher than its eventual new equilibrium. There is a certain dilemma here in that if new processes can be imitated very rapidly, there may be no advantage in introducing them; they will be imitated so rapidly that the price will fall immediately to the point where it is not profitable to innovate. It is for this reason that we have introduced a coercive, that is, a non-exchange element into the system, such as the patent law or copyright, which can protect the innovator against too rapid imitation.

Adam Smith applied the concept of "natural liberty" far beyond the realm of commodity exchange. He applied it in Book Five of The Wealth of Nations to education, to religion, and even to some extent to the judiciary. In education, the idea that teaching is most likely to be effective if the teacher is paid by results is highly unpalatable to the educational establishment, which has always looked with horror on the idea of a free market in education. Nevertheless, Adam Smith's arguments cannot be dismissed easily. If the teacher's income does not depend on the performance of his duties, there is a strong temptation for the students to be neglected. At eighteenth century Oxford and Cambridge, indeed, as Adam Smith observes "the greater part of the public professors have for these many years given up altogether the pretense of teaching" (1937, p. 718). By contrast, he observes that:

Those parts of education, it is to be observed, for which there are no public institutions are generally the best taught. When a young man goes to a fencing or a dancing school, he does not always learn to fence or to dance very well, but he seldom fails in learning to fence or to dance (1937, p. 721).

The so-called "elective system" by which a student at the university is free to choose whatever courses he wishes, as long as he completes a sufficient number of hours at sufficiently high quality, is a good example of "natural liberty," and the idea owes a good deal to Adam Smith. The criticisms of the elective system— they give a cafeteria education without consistency or structure, and that the student could not be trusted to know what was essential and what was nonessential— led to substantial modifications of it in American

63

universities, which interestingly enough were challenged again during the 1960's in the name of liberty by the student generation. This illustrates perhaps some of the difficulties of the "natural liberty" concept.

In religion, also, Adam Smith advocated a separation of church and state, and full religious freedom which would allow any sect the right to compete in the market of religious ideas for adherents. An established religion violates natural liberty because it prohibits people from going to "the church of their choice." Adam Smith, as a good eighteenth-century deist, was suspicious of the excesses of enthusiasm in religion, as indeed was his friend David Hume. Hume, however, argued that the way to protect society against the excesses of religious zeal was to set up an established church in which the clergy were not dependent upon the goodwill of the congregation for their pay, but on the goodwill of the established order. Under these circumstances there would be no payoffs for excessive zeal on the part of the clergy and the church could be relied on to be an instrument of the establishment. By contrast, Adam Smith argued that free competition in religion would force preachers to moderate their views in order to attract new members to their congregation, and that competition of churches for adherents would force them to line up somewhere near the reasonable middle. Thus he says:

The teachers of each little sect finding themselves almost alone would be obliged to respect those of almost every other sect and the concessions which they would mutually find it both convenient and agreeable to make to one another might in time probably reduce the doctrine of the greater part of them to that pure and rational religion, free from every mixture of absurdity and postural fanaticism such as wise men have in all ages of the world wished to see established, but such as positive law has perhaps never yet established and probably never will establish in any country, because with regard to religion positive law always and probably always will be more or less influenced by popular superstition and enthusiasm (1937, p. 745).

In some degree both Adam Smith and Hume may have been right. The state church, as in Scandinavia, is apt to be an efficient producer of religious apathy, and free competition in religion, as in the United States, has tended to make the competing churches more alike in the middle, though perhaps more extreme at the edge. The history of religion in the United States, however, also supports Adam Smith's contention that natural liberty will lead to development, for in the United States the rise of religion under a regime of free competition has been spectacular, church membership having risen from perhaps 7 per cent in the time of the revolution to about 64 per cent in the 1960's. There can hardly be a greater contrast indeed

between, say, the dead and formal Lutheran Church where it is established in Scandinavian countries and the vigorous and aggressive Lutheran Church of the United States. Thus, in a field far removed from ordinary economic activity we find substantial evidence for the virtues of natural liberty and for the use of exchange rather than coercion as a social organizer.

Natural liberty, however, has its limits, which are fully recognized in principle by Adam Smith, though modern economists and social thinkers might not agree with him about exactly where the limits should be drawn. Thus, he argues against allowing bankers to issue notes of small denominations as follows:

To restrain private people, it may be said, from receiving in payment the promissory notes of a banker, for any sum whether great or small, when they themselves are willing to receive them; or, to restrain a banker from issuing such notes, when all his neighbours are willing to accept of them, is a manifest violation of that natural liberty which is the proper business of law, not to infringe, but to support. Such regulations may, no doubt, be considered as in some respect a violation of natural liberty. But those exertions of the natural liberty of a few individuals, which might endanger the security of the whole society, are, and ought to be, restrained by the laws of all governments; of the most free, as well as of the most despotical. The obligation of building party walls, in order to prevent the communication of fire, is a violation of natural liberty, exactly of the same kind with the regulations of the banking trade which are here proposed (1937, p. 308).

The problem which Adam Smith is raising here is one which economists later discussed very extensively under the title of "externality." The freedom of all individuals to produce and exchange anything they like with anyone they like at whatever price they can get, only promotes the general welfare if there are no effects outside the exchanging parties. If, for instance, a man produces something to sell, but in the course of producing it he creates a negative commodity, such as air or water pollution which injures somebody else, he should clearly be charged for this, if necessary through the tax system. On the other side, if there are activities which produce benefits to people for which the producer cannot charge them, then, unless some arrangement is made for compensating the producer, he will not produce enough of this commodity because he is only producing enough to meet the demands that can be paid for. It is this kind of consideration which has generally led to the subsidization of education, which is supposed to be an industry which produces benefits above and beyond the private benefits which the educated person enjoys. Adam Smith recognized this indeed and proposed that the state should subsidize education of the poor.

Another possible case is that of public works, enterprises which either cannot be charged for easily or which require a magnitude of enterprise which the private sector is incapable of providing. Adam Smith took rather an unfavorable view of private joint stock companies which, he thought, were only capable of dealing in occupations in which the operations could be reduced to a routine. He did not anticipate the enormous growth of the corporation, although oddly enough for very good reasons. If it had not been indeed for what Boulding has called the "organization revolution" (1968), that is, the marked increase in the economies of scale (that is, the ability to increase the size of an organization without diminishing its efficiency) which came about 1870 with the invention of the typewriter, the telephone, and other means of internal communication, as well as certain social inventions in regard to corporate organizational structure, Adam Smith would probably have been right.

The classic summary of his position comes on page 651 of *The Wealth of Nations* and it is worth quoting it in full:

All systems either of preference or of restraint, therefore, being thus completely taken away, the obvious and simple system of natural liberty establishes itself of its own accord. Every man, as long as he does not violate the laws of justice, is left perfectly free to pursue his own interest his own way, and to bring both his industry and capital into competition with those of any other man, or order of men. The sovereign is completely discharged from a duty, in the attempting to perform which he must always be exposed to innumerable delusions, and for the proper performance of which no human wisdom or knowledge could ever be sufficient; the duty of superintending the industry of private people, and of directing it towards the employments most suitable to the interest of the society. According to the system of natural liberty, the sovereign has only three duties to attend to; three duties of great importance, indeed, but plain and intelligible to common understandings: first, the duty of protecting the society from the violence and invasion of other independent societies; secondly, the duty of protecting, as far as possible, every member of the society from the injustice or oppression of every other member of it, or the duty of establishing an exact administration of justice; and, thirdly, the duty of erecting and maintaining certain public works and certain public institutions, which it can never be for the interest of any individual, or small number of individuals, to erect and maintain; because the profit could never repay the expence [sic] to any individual or small number of individuals, though it may frequently do much more than repay it to a great society.

Another major criticism of the regime of natural liberty is that it inevitably leads to a distribution of power, income, and wealth in society which is unacceptably concentrated and unequal. The regime of "natural liberty," certainly as Adam Smith envisioned it, implies private property in the means of production, except, presumably, in human minds and bodies. Adam Smith indeed took a very unfavorable view of slavery even though it might be argued that the prohibition of slavery involved a restriction on the natural liberty of a man to sell himself for the compounded value of his future labor. This, however, represents for Adam Smith one of the desirable infringements on natural liberty simply because he believed that slavery inevitably produced economic stagnation and hence was socially undesirable. This objection, however, did not apply to private property in physical capital and buildings, machines, and even in land. Here there was every inducement for the owner to deal with his property in the most profitable way, which usually meant to improve it and to innovate with it.

Nevertheless, it is often claimed that while private property in the means of production, especially given a widespread achievement orientation in the society, is highly favorable to the development process, the price of this development is the increasing concentration of property and power in the hands of a few. There are many reasons for supposing this, the most significant being perhaps that the rich man finds it easier to save both as a proportion of his income and as an absolute amount than a poor man. A man who is living at the bare minimum level of subsistence cannot save at all and hence cannot accumulate property in any form or improve his condition. A man whose income is above this level is able to save, and the more he saves, the larger his income and the more he is able to save. This tendency is accentuated if, under the laws of inheritance, estates are unequally divided among inheritors, as they are under conditions of primogeniture. It is accentuated if the rich are infertile as they frequently are. As the statistician Francis Galton pointed out, heiresses are frequently infertile, for this is why they are heiresses. In rich but fertile families the riches tend to be dissipated among the multitude of descendants. Economists have never worked out an exact model which governs the dynamic process of the entire distribution of wealth. However, in the absence of positive intervention in the shape of progressive income and inheritance taxation, the tendency for wealth to accumulate into fewer and fewer hands and its distribution to become more unequal seems to be quite strong and this is frequently used as a justification for the restriction of the natural liberty of the property-holder.

It is interesting to note that Adam Smith did not hold this view and felt that development would actually increase equality. There is an extraordinary passage in Adam Smith's *Theory of Moral Sentiments* (1759) in which he uses for the first time the expression, the "invisible hand":

It is to no purpose that the proud and unfeeling landlord views his extensive fields, and without a thought for the wants of his brethren, in imagination consumes himself the whole harvest that grows upon them. The homely and vulgar proverb, that the eye is larger than the belly, never was more fully verified than with regard to him. The capacity of his stomach bears no proportion to the immensity of his desires, and will receive no more than that of the meanest peasant. The rest he is obliged to distribute among those who prepare, in the nicest manner, that little which he himself makes use of, among those who fit up the palace in which this little is to be consumed, among those who provide and keep in order all the different baubles and trinkets which are employed in the economy of greatness; all of whom thus derive from his luxury and caprice that share of the necessaries of life which they would in vain have expected from his humanity or his justice. The produce of the soil maintains at all times nearly that number of inhabitants which it is capable of maintaining. The rich only select from the heap what is most precious and agreeable. They consume little more than the poor; and in spite of their natural selfishness and rapacity, though they mean only their own conveniency, though the sole end which they propose from the labours of all the thousands whom they employ be the gratification of their own vain and insatiable desires, they divide with the poor the produce of all their improvements. They are led by an invisible hand to make nearly the same distribution of the necessaries of life which would have been made had the earth been divided into equal portions among all its inhabitants; and thus, without intending it, without knowing it, advance the interest of the society, and afford means to the multiplication of the species. When providence divided the earth among a few lordly masters, it neither forgot nor abandoned those who seemed to have been left out in the partition. These last, too, enjoy their share of all that it produces. In what constitutes the real happiness of human life, they are in no respect inferior to those who would seem to be much above them. In ease of body and peace of mind, all the different ranks of life are nearly upon a level, and the beggar, who suns himself by the side of the highway, possesses that security which kings are fighting for (1966, pp. 264–65).

To the modern mind in the light of slums and ghettos, famine, and destitution in many parts of the world this sunny eighteenth-century optimism seems a little unreal. Nevertheless, the point which Smith is making cannot be dismissed as absurd. The principle that the limits of the capacity of the belly makes it impossible for the rich man to eat even five or ten times as much food as the poor man applies increasingly with the development of the mass production of commodities. Thus, the same "capacity" principle applies to clothing. One certainly has to look carefully these days to tell

a rich man from a poor man by his clothing. It applies even to automobiles, where again there is a strong tendency towards rough equality of distribution; the rich man may have three or four superior cars, but he cannot personally use one hundred times as many automobiles as the poor man. With housing likewise, the ever increasing cost of servants and maintenance has made the palaces of the eighteenth century impossible to maintain, and outside of the bottom 10 or 20 per cent of incomes, the United States has achieved a rough equality in the amenity of the dwelling. In the mass production society, just as practically everybody has an automobile, so practically everybody has a bathroom, just because this is the only way of disposing of the automobiles and bathrooms that are produced. This is not to argue against progressive taxation or inheritance taxes or other devices for ameliorating the tendency of a market society to increase inequalities of wealth and income. It is worth pointing out, however, that the real inequalities of income are much less than they seem in money terms. Henry Ford may have had a money income ten thousand times that of his average worker, but he certainly did not live on ten thousand times the scale.

The above considerations perhaps do not meet another more subtle, but perhaps more fundamental criticism of the regime of "natural liberty" which is that it leads to a concentration of private and irresponsible power. Even though the rich may not constitute a very large burden on the developed society, the concentration of the ownership of physical capital is much greater than the concentration of incomes, simply because such a large proportion of total income, something like 80 per cent, is derived from labor. The rich property owners do exercise a power in society which is disproportionate even to their income. This power, it is argued, is essentially private and irresponsible, and without the checks and balances of political administration. This irresponsibility of private power is particularly noticeable where it is based on monopoly. Under a regime of perfect competition, private economic power is very severely limited by erosion through market forces. Under these circumstances, the owners of private capital simply have to do what the market orders, otherwise, they will take losses and will lose their capital. It has been pointed out, for instance, by J. K. Galbraith in *The New Industrial State* (1967) that under modern conditions with large corporations and large concentrations of private economic power, what he calls the "accepted sequence," by which the desires of consumers are supposed to govern the structure of production, no longer operates as well and is replaced in part at least by what Galbraith calls the "revised sequence." According to this, producers produce what is convenient for them to produce and then through the arts of advertising and mass persuasion they persuade the consumers to take whatever the producers have produced. The introduction of advertising and mass persuasion certainly alters the regime of "natural liberty" in a way that Adam Smith would never have imagined.

We see the same phenomenon in government where according to the "accepted sequence" in a democratic government, government is supposed to carry out the will of the people as expressed by the voters. Under the revised sequence the government decides what it wants to do and proceeds to sell its people on its policies in order to achieve their consent.

The existence of the "revised sequence" can hardly be doubted; what is hard to evaluate is its quantitative importance. It can be argued, for instance, that a good deal of persuasive advertising is persuading consumers to do what they want to do anyway, that is, by revealing previously unawakened desires. Whether it is a good thing to awaken unawakened desires, of course, is another matter altogether. Similarly, in the case of government, there may be decisions and policies where expertise is necessary for decision-making, and where the general public do not possess this expertise. Hence, the people either have to trust their government or else have the policies "sold" to them by propaganda. Furthermore, there have been some notable failures of the "revised sequence" of which the Edsel automobile is the classical example in the private sector and perhaps the Vietnam war in the public sector. Certainly there was no grass-roots demand among the voters for a war in Vietnam and the attempts to sell it to the American people by the arts of persuasion did not seem to be particularly successful.

Another aspect of the regime of "natural liberty" which has received severe, and again not always justified, criticism is the famous argument for free trade. Tariffs, and still more, quantitative restrictions, such as quotas and licensing, are an interference with the "natural liberty" of exchange, and Adam Smith, of course, devotes a great deal of his argument to demolishing the mercantilist case for extensive government intervention in international trade relations. There are two aspects of this intervention; the first is concerned with the balance of trade or the balance of payments, and the second with the protection of domestic industry. By the balance of trade, economists usually mean the excess of the value of exports of goods and services over the value of the imports of goods and services for a particular country. The balance of payments includes items which are not payments for exports or imports, such as the purchase or sale of securities, so that in effect the balance of payments represents the excess of payments in over payments out and hence is equivalent to the increase in the country's liquid assets on international account.

In regard to the argument about the balance of trade or the balance of payments, Adam Smith argues with great persuasiveness that the international payments system is self-adjusting and requires very little attention from government.

This part of the argument was made even more clearly by David Ricardo, who demonstrated that there was an equilibrium system at work in distributing the money stock of the world among the nations. A nation, for instance, which had an outflow of money, and a consequent diminution in its money stock, would have an internal deflation, to use the modern term, which would discourage imports into it and encourage exports out of it which would soon stop or even reverse the drain of money. Similarly, a country with a positive balance of payments, and which therefore is increasing its money stock, would have some inflation which would encourage imports and discourage exports and again would stop or even reverse the flow of money into it. Thus, movements in the balance of payments tend to be self-correcting.

The structure of balance of payments simply reflects the shift of liquid assets among owners. If a person or a group or a nation has a positive balance of payments, this means that its expenditure of liquid assets (money) is less than its receipts and he is increasing his total stock of money. Similarly, if his balance is negative, it means that he is decreasing his total stock of money. If the total stock of money owned by all holders together were constant, then the structure of balance of payments would simply reflect the "surge" of money stocks out of some pockets into others, as at Christmas, for instance, household balances tend to decrease and department store balances increase.

The view that these movements are self-correcting has much to recommend it. The actual mechanism by which these corrections were made, however is still somewhat in dispute, particularly the relative role of price changes and income changes. The processes of adjustment themselves may also cause trouble. Even in a homogeneous society with a common money, if one person or a group is suffering from a negative balance while another group has a positive balance, the first group is likely to correct this by diminishing its expenditures and the second is likely to correct their situation by increasing their expenditures. Difficulties may arise if these two reactions are not symmetrical, as they may not be, for a negative balance produces a greater sense of urgency than a positive balance. In the international system, national economies may be insulated from changes in the international balance of payments by the national fiscal and monetary system, especially by the respective Central Banks. Under these circumstances, "natural liberty" may lead to perverse consequences. The more extreme supporters of "natural liberty," such as Milton Friedman of the University of Chicago, have argued that if free markets were allowed in foreign exchanges so that exchange rates between different currencies could fluctuate according to market forces, all balance of payments problems would automatically be solved. This, indeed, may well be true, but further questions arise as to whether speculative movements in foreign exchange markets would not create even greater difficulties in the system of international trade.

The problem of "protection" is quite different conceptually from that of the regulation of the balance of payments, although the two are sometimes confused in practice. In its most general meaning "protection" means the establishment or preservation of a certain proportionate structure of industries in an economy by means of government intervention. The intervention may take the form of tariffs, imports, quotas, and quantitative restrictions, especially on imports, or direct subsidies—"bounties" as Adam Smith calls them—or taxes. Perhaps Adam Smith's greatest contribution to this controversy is a clear perception of the economy as involving a total allocation among different industries of rather fixed resources, so that if one industry expands, another somewhere in the system must contract. Hence he sees the problem not in terms of the support or penalization of particular industries but in terms of the distribution of industries in the total economy. If, for instance, by imposing a tariff a country expands a particular industry and so makes it larger than it otherwise would be, Adam Smith sees clearly that because this industry is larger something else must be smaller.

In effect, what Adam Smith is saying is that the burden of proof lies on those who would distort the proportionate industrial structure of any economy away from natural liberty. He does not say that no distortions are permissible. Indeed, he is quite clear that an absolutely free market society does not result in the optimum proportional industrial structure of the economy. He defends, for instance, the Navigation Acts, on the grounds that a merchant marine larger than the free market would give, is necessary for defense. He likewise argues for subsidization of education, or even of public entertainments in a gloomy country like Scotland! He insists, however, that these distortions must be justified in terms of the welfare of the society as a whole, and not in terms of the welfare of particular industries.

Ricardo again clarified the argument further in the theory of comparative advantage, in which he pointed out that import duties and other interferences with international trade forced a country to diminish its specialization in those industries in which it had the best terms of trade.

Later, more sophisticated arguments for protection, such as those of Friedrich List, do not for the most part differ from Adam Smith in principle. List argued, for instance, that certain industries contributed more to the general development of a society than others, and hence should be expanded through protection. This argument is used frequently in the case of poor countries today who are seeking development. The facts of each case may be difficult to establish, but Adam Smith could not object to the principle. It is indeed a special application of the principle of externality, as noted above.

The possibility of purely speculative fluctuations in prices and speculative distortions in the price structure suggests still another possibly pathological condition of the regime of natural liberty.

Organized markets, both in durable commodities such as wheat and in financial instruments such as stocks and bonds, are subject to speculative fluctuations which may not correspond to any significant conditions outside the markets themselves. The price of a commodity or financial instrument in an organized market tends to be that at which the market is "cleared," that is, at which the owners of the item in question in toto have no desire either to get rid of it or to accumulate it. If there is increased aggregate desire to accumulate the item, its price will rise. If then a rise in price produces expectation for further rise, this will further increase the desire to hold the item and it may increase the price still further. This process of self-justified expectations may go on until at some point people realize that the price is "too high," and the reverse process easily sets in. This will force the price down until it reaches some kind of floor at which the whole process begins again. These speculative movements introduce a degree of uncertainty into the productive process which is most undesirable, and a strong case can be made for some kind of "counter-speculation," some agency, for instance, which will buy and sell the item at a fixed price for limited periods of time to prevent these speculative changes.

The old gold standard itself was one such "counter-speculative" arrangement under which the monetary authorities effectively fixed the price of gold in terms of the national currency within fairly small limits by offering to buy and sell gold for the national currency at a fixed price in unlimited quantities. This system broke down eventually because it was increasingly felt that it interfered with the "natural liberty" of governments to pursue other economic policies which they regarded as more favorable to their people. If, however, we look at something like the price supports for agricultural commodities which have been imposed in the United States for the last thirty years, there is a good deal of evidence that the reduction of uncertainty for the producer which has resulted from the interference of "natural liberty" of free markets has actually created a very rapid rate of technological development in American agriculture which might not have taken place under the free market regime. These interferences with "natural liberty" are not, as Adam Smith himself pointed out, necessarily inimical to the principle. They represent the correction of defects in the system rather than a repudiation of the system itself.

Since the day of Adam Smith, the history of the idea of natural liberty has been somewhat checkered. The classical economists such as Ricardo, Nassau Senior, and James Mill, of the generation after Adam Smith, accepted the idea perhaps even more enthusiastically than Adam Smith himself. Its impact on economic policy, especially in Britain and in France, was considerable, culminating in England in the repeal in 1846 of the Corn Laws, which had imposed a protective tariff on the import of cereals. Even from the early decades of the nineteenth century, however, we find a rising tide of sentiment in favor of protection, especially in the United States and later in Germany. Nevertheless, it was the mid-nineteenth century that saw perhaps the greatest apostle of natural liberty, the Frenchman, Frédéric Bastiat, whose pamphlets are still classics of economic rhetoric, but who carried a belief in laissez-faire far beyond the cautious limits of Adam Smith. From the middle of the nineteenth century, however, natural liberty not only comes into increasing disfavor as a principle of government policy, but is subject to increasing attacks both from the Protectionists and from the Marxists.

The most severe criticism of the system of "natural liberty" itself has come from the socialists, and especially from the Marxists. The socialist criticism is many-sided and its psychological roots may be very different from its formal intellectual exposition. Some of it is a modern version of a very ancient feeling that exchange is in some sense degrading, partly because of its calculatedness, partly because it seems to be unproductive in the sense that it seems to produce no physical embodiment of value, especially where it looks as if equal values are exchanged. The farmer or the peasant, for instance, frequently feels that he is the "real" producer and that the merchant is merely trickily getting a profit out of moving around among owners the real wheat or potatoes which the farmer has actually produced. There is also a lingering feeling from medieval times that trade is ignoble, that it is unheroic and that the good man, whether the saint or the soldier, acts for love or for glory and not for money. The feeling that money is somehow grubby and ignoble goes back a long way in history. Insofar, therefore, as the regime of natural liberty is virtually co-terminous with the organization of society through free exchange, the delegitimation of exchange itself also attacks the regime of "natural liberty."

The Marxist criticism is more specific but also rather less convincing than the more psychological reasons for rejecting the exchange economy listed above. Marx, in effect, turned the labor theory of value, which in the hands of Ricardo was a rather sophisticated explanation of what determined the equilibrium structure of relative prices, into the theory of production and exploitation. His argument roughly is that as it is active labor that ultimately produces everything, labor is in some sense entitled to the whole product; therefore the income which accrues to the owners of capital as profit or interest is derived from exploitation, that is, it represents in reality a one-way transfer or a kind of tribute which arises out of the peculiar power position of the capitalist. Marx, then, is able to draw quite effective pictures of the worker working twelve hours a day, producing products of which he only gets, say, half, because in effect he is working six hours for himself and six hours for the boss. This is indeed a radical criticism of the system of natural liberty and it has resulted in the destruction of that system over a considerable part of the world and its replacement by centrally planned economies through a communist revolution. Private property, at least in the means of production, is expropriated by the state, acting, it believes, on behalf of the working class. The state then becomes the sole capitalist and the society becomes, in effect, a one-firm state, or the state becomes a giant corporation encompassing all economic activity.

The ultimate social balance sheet of the centrally planned economies still remains to be drawn. They have succeeded in creating a rate of development approximately equal to the rate which the successful capitalist countries have maintained at about the same level of income. In some cases a communist revolution and the establishment of a centrally planned economy, especially in Eastern Europe, seem to have resulted in a marked acceleration of the rate of development, the earlier regimes having been remarkably incompetent leftovers from feudal times. On the other side of the ledger the human cost of the centrally planned economy has often been very high. It has not solved the problem of concentration of economic power. Indeed, it has accentuated the problem, as in fact all power is concentrated in the one corporation of the state. Such a system slips easily into tyranny as it did under Stalinism in the Soviet Union, and under Mao Tse Tung in China. Capitalist societies, it should also be said, are also capable of falling into tyranny, as, for instance, in Haiti or Nazi Germany. This always seems to go hand in hand, however, with a virtual abandonment of the regime of "natural liberty," and the development of extensive governmental intervention in the price system, especially through quantitative restrictions. One could argue indeed that it is quantitative restrictions that create the danger of tyranny whether in capitalist or in socialist countries.

In recent years there has been an interesting move within socialist countries towards what might almost be described as a socialist version of "natural liberty," particularly in Yugoslavia, where the various enterprises have been given a great deal of independence and are linked together by strictly market relationships. In all socialist countries, furthermore, it has never been possible to destroy either the consumer markets or the labor markets, although there is not much consumer sovereignty or labor sovereignty. Under socialism the "revised sequence" of Galbraith operates with full force, and consumers, while they have some freedom of individual choice, in the mass have to accept what the planners decide is good for them. The workers also, while they have some freedom of occupational choice, are severely restricted in their choice by the national economic plan. The drawing up of the plans, of course, is consummated by a great deal of public discussion and supposedly by public modification. One suspects, however, that a great deal of this talk by the "people's representatives" is a political ritual designed to legitimate the plan rather than to modify it, just as all too often a voting system in a capitalist democracy serves to legitimate the continuing policies of government rather than to change them. The "rediscovery" of the price system in the socialist countries, however, by such economists as E. G. Liberman of the Soviet Union, is a sign that the concept of natural liberty and the organization of the society through free exchange is not dead, even in the socialist world.

The rise of Keynesian economics in the capitalist world has had an important effect in blunting the socialist criticism and in correcting what may have been the most serious defect in a purely market-oriented society, which has been in the past the tendency of these societies to slip down at intervals into unemployment and depression. The Great Depression of the 1930's was the culminating example of this kind of defect. By 1933 in the United States, for instance, unemployment was 25 per cent of the labor force. This represented not only a serious waste in product unrealized, but it was a social disaster in terms of disorganized lives, unnecessary poverty, and the loss of a role in society which a job gives to a large portion of the population. If this had persisted, there is little doubt that the socialist criticism would have become unanswerable, and that the defects of socialist societies would have seemed mild in comparison to this overwhelming defect of a market-based economy.

The challenge, however, produced a response in the shape of what has come to be called the "Keynesian Revolution," even though J. M. (later Lord) Keynes contributed to this revolution in the economic policy of capitalist countries in a rather confused or at least a confusing way. Nevertheless, an important revolution in economic policy has taken place in the capitalist world, based perhaps on two social inventions, the first that of national income statistics which gave the policy maker for the first time a reasonably clear picture of what was happening in the total economy, and the second, a very simple Keynesian-type model which suggested that if the Gross National Product at full employment was not absorbed in some way by household purchases, government purchases, voluntary business investment, that is, the willingness of businesses to increase the total stock of capital, and the international balance, then forces would be set in motion to reduce the GNP and create unemployment. Three major policies were suggested by this model. The first was the use of a deliberate government deficit (excess of expenditure over receipts) to increase total consumption when needed, and similarly, a surplus (excess of receipts over expenditures) to diminish consumption when the need is to prevent inflation. The second was the use of the Central Bank and the monetary system to encourage or discourage business investment. The third was the direct increase or decrease of government expenditure. The foreign balance is usually a small item, but may cause trouble in preventing the other adjustments.

The results of this revolution in policy may be judged in part by contrasting the experience of the twenty years following the end of the First World War with the twenty years following the end of the Second. The first period (1919–39) was a disaster; it produced the Great Depression, Hitler, and ended in the Second World War. The second period has not had a great depression, the rich countries indeed have enjoyed unprecedented rates of development, and though the international system is almost unbearably costly and very unsatisfactory, at least it has not yet degenerated into another world war. The success of the last twenty or twenty-five years, in comparison with the '20's and '30's, cannot all be attributed to Keynesian modification of the regime of "natural liberty," but some of it at any rate must be attributed to this. It is important to realize, however, that Keynesian-type intervention is in the interest again of correcting a defect in the system of "natural liberty," as expressed in its tendency if uncorrected to fall into deflation, depression, and unemployment, and has the result indeed of restoring something much more like the classical economics. It is something of a paradox, for instance, that the success of a full employment policy reestablishes a regime of scarcity in which it becomes highly apparent that an increase in a military dollar, for instance, comes out of something and somebody else and does not simply come out of unemployment. Under Keynesian manipulation, therefore, the economy looks much more like the world of the classical economists than it did in the doleful '30's, and the virtues of organization through the market become all the more apparent. It is interesting indeed that there has been a revival of interest in the use of the market in fields like education, income maintenance, and public works, where it has previously been much neglected. After nearly two hundred years, therefore, we can claim that the regime of "natural liberty" is by no means dead. It has been many times transformed but its transformations made it stronger and more relevant.

"Natural liberty," like many other institutions and conditions of society, may have more to fear from its self-appointed friends than from its enemies. The free exchange of privately owned commodities through mutually accepted bargains is a powerful organizer in society, as we have seen, and there is no sense in despising it or throwing it out of the window. On the other hand, it is absurd to claim that the "market" can do everything. It is dangerous to claim that it can do more than in fact it can. Market institutions in society must constantly be supplemented by institutions involving legitimated threat, as in the law, and by institutions which create legitimacy and community. Without a setting of law and legitimacy, indeed, the market institutions cannot function and will destroy themselves. Furthermore, the market is subject to pathologies of its own and there must be other institutions in society outside the market which can correct these. Government may not be the only one of these institutions for correcting the deficiencies of the market, but it is certainly the most important. Both the invisible hand and the visible hand are necessary for the healthy functioning of society.

BIBLIOGRAPHY

Kenneth E. Boulding, *The Organizational Revolution: A Study in the Ethics of Economic Organization* (New York, 1954). John Kenneth Galbraith, *The New Industrial State* (Boston, 1967). Friedrich List, *The National System of Political Economy* (German ed., 1840; London, 1904; 1928). David Ricardo, *On the Principles of Political Economy and Taxation* (1817; London, 1917). Nassau W. Senior, *An Outline of the Science of Political Economy* (1836; New York, 1951). Adam Smith, *An Inquiry into the Nature and Causes of the Wealth of Nations* (1776; New York, 1937, Modern Library); idem, *The Theory of Moral Sentiments* (1759; New York, 1966).

KENNETH E. BOULDING

[See also **Economic History; Individualism;** Law, Natural; Marxism; Property; Socialism; **State;** Totalitarianism; Work.]

EDUCATION

I

WE MAY begin with the word "education." Through the Latin it is related both to the notion of bringing up or rearing and to that of bringing out or leading forth, but during the centuries its meaning, and that of its equivalents in other languages, has become even more complex. In relatively recent times, "education" has come to stand, as "philosophy" and "psychology" do, for a discipline or field of studies, once called "pedagogics," often set up as a department or school within a college or university, and thought of as subject matter to be taught and developed by further research. One of our tendencies is to make everything just another subject in the educational curriculum, and we have now done this with education itself.

In some uses, however, "education" stands, as it always did until recently, not for the discipline just referred to, but for the enterprise it studies and reflects on. In this sense, which is the more important one for the history of ideas, education is not a study or field of inquiry but an activity or endeavor of a very different kind, one that is related to the discipline of education and the disciplines supporting it (philosophy, psychology, etc.) in something like the way in which building bridges and rockets is related to what is done in engineering schools and science classrooms and laboratories. This enterprise needs theory and science to guide it, once it has developed beyond unreflective practice, and it is the task of the discipline, with the help of other disciplines, to provide this. But it is itself a kind of action, not of theory or science. What makes it interesting for the history of ideas, however, is the ideas—the concepts and theories—behind it, and especially the fact that both it and they have involved so many other fields, including philosophy, that are not themselves primarily concerned with education.

For, as Moses Hadas says, ". . . education is man's most important enterprise" (*Old Wine, New Bottles* 71

[1963], p. 3). If we include self-education, then on it depends "all that makes a man"; everything that raises man above or puts him ahead of the other animals. As Kant put it, "Man can only become man by education. He is merely what education makes of him" (*Education* [1960], p. 3). The example of wolf-children shows this, though it has always been true. It is only recently that someone was able to add that education is also man's biggest business—and, indeed, educators are beginning to use language borrowed from commerce and industry. We even speak now of "international education," and, as noted, have whole schools and institutes to develop and teach the discipline of education. The economics of education has become an important study, and people debate the question whether education is a profession.

Even if we consider only formal instruction, it is not too much to say that the enterprise of education either has come to involve everyone alive or is expected to, that every other human endeavor of any importance depends on and is served by it, and that almost every other such enterprise is stimulated by it and plays a role with respect to it, either as a source for its premisses and methods, as part of its curriculum, or as one of its aims. In short, the idea of education behind it, if there is one, is one of the oldest and most important energizing and organizing ideas in Western culture—ranking with those of government, morality, science, and technology.

The word "idea" may stand either for a concept or for a doctrine or proposition. Thus, "the idea of progress" may denote either the concept of a certain kind of change, i.e., a constant change for the better, or the belief that history actually embodies a change of that kind. And "an idea of man" may mean either a concept of man as a certain kind of animal or being, e.g., as a rational animal or featherless biped, or a belief or set of beliefs about such an animal or being, e.g., the Christian idea of man. Coming to the phrase "idea of education," we find that it has at least four uses: (1) "*the* idea of education" may mean either (a) the concept of education, or (b) the belief or faith in education; (2) "*an* idea of education" may denote either (a) *a* concept of education, i.e., a suggested definition of education, or (b) a belief or set of beliefs about education, about its aims, forms, means, etc. A large part of our task is to analyze, perhaps somewhat roughly but still helpfully, the four categories thus distinguished. Those referred to in (1a) and (2a) can be discussed together, for an idea of education that really proposes a definition of education is simply an attempt to give an analysis of the idea of education.

It may be argued at once that there is no such thing as *the* idea or concept of education that underlies or

defines the educational enterprise, that there are only *ideas* of education such as are referred to in (2a) and (2b), for example, President Garfield's idea of education as a log with a student on one end and Mark Hopkins on the other. In fact, this is virtually what T. S. Eliot contends, coming to the conclusion that "education does not appear to be definable" (*To Criticize the Critic, and other Writings* [1965], p. 120). Actually, he is closer to the truth when he says, somewhat in passing, that we all mean by education some training of the mind or body (p. 75). It is true that the term "education" is ambiguous and vague, or "wobbly" as Eliot so nicely puts it, but its uses do have more clarity and unity than he recognizes. The enterprise of education, as his own passing remark suggests, consists in all forms and places of activity in which some individual or group fosters or seeks to foster in some individual or group some ability, belief, knowledge, habit, skill, trait of character, or "value," and does so by the use of certain methods. There is always someone doing the educating, someone being educated, something being fostered in the second by the first, by some method or combination of methods.

Thus we can and do think of education in different but related ways: (1) as the activity of the one doing the educating, the act or process of *educating* or *teaching* engaged in by the educator, (2) as the process or experience of *being educated* or *learning* that goes on in the one being educated, and (3) as the *result* produced in the one being educated by the double process of educating and being educated, i.e., the combination of abilities, etc., that are produced in him or that are possessed by him when he has been educated. In these three uses of "education" we are referring to the enterprise of education in one way or another, but we also think of education in a fourth way, namely, (4) as the discipline or study discussed earlier.

Two comments are in order. (a) The individual or group doing the educating and the one being educated may be the same, as they are in any process of self-education. (b) Education in sense (4) can be defined as the study of (1), (2), and (3); education in sense (3) as the result of (1) and (2); and education in sense (2) as the reverse side of (1). Thus, though the four senses are distinct, there is a nice kind of unity among them.

It will be convenient to use the word "disposition" to denote all of the abilities, beliefs, habits, knowledges, skills, traits, or "values" that education may seek to foster by activities of the kinds just indicated, as Dewey sometimes does, though he elsewhere prefers the term "habit." This is a somewhat extended and unusual use of the word "disposition," since it means designating as dispositions not only things like cheerfulness, but also things like an ability to act, a knowledge of physics, or a belief in God or education. But we need some single term here and any ordinary word we choose must be extended to cover the very varied things under discussion.

We may say, then, that the idea of education is the idea of someone fostering dispositions in someone by activities of certain sorts. More formally, the idea of education may be at least partly explicated as follows:

X educates Y only if X fosters disposition W in Y by method Z. Strictly, of course, this is an explication only of education in sense (1), but we have already seen that education in the other three senses can be defined in terms of this one. To this extent the formula just given does represent a concept that may be called *the* idea of education. However, we do not yet have a complete analysis of this concept; to achieve this we must know something more, something about the ranges of the variables involved. May we put just anything in the places of X and Y, any disposition in the place of W, and any method in the place of Z, and still say that *education* is going on? Rousseau (writing in 1762) talks as if we may when he says that education comes to us from three sources, from nature, from men, and from things, since they all do something for us (*Émile* [1962], p. 11). It should be observed that our question here is not normative but conceptual. For example, we are not asking, as if education were already defined, what dispositions it should cultivate or what methods it should use; we are still defining it and are asking whether any restrictions on the dispositions that might be cultivated or the means that might be employed are to be built into the very concept of education (i.e., put into our definition).

In reply R. S. Peters has argued very cogently that, unless we extend the term education as Rousseau does, we would not say that X is educating Y if he is fostering undesirable and morally objectionable dispositions or using undesirable and morally objectionable methods; for example, if he is helping Y to form bad habits and false beliefs, or if he is using harmful drugs, brain-washing, or hypnotic suggestion (*Concept of Education* [1967], pp. 1–6). This seems to be correct. It is true we may say that what X is doing then is "bad education," but we would be more likely to say it is not education at all. Education is, normally at least, a laudatory term and its laudatoriness seems to be built into it. If one says that X is educating Y, one must be thinking that X is cultivating desirable and morally unobjectionable dispositions (excellences) by similar means. Education must foster dispositions and use methods that are desirable and morally unobjectionable, or at least regarded as such, otherwise it is not education.

Does the concept of education impose any further restrictions on the dispositions and methods to be pursued? May or should we build anything more about them into the definition of education? It is sometimes assumed that education is by definition concerned only to promote knowledge and intellectual excellences. Thus, R. M. Hutchins writes, "Education implies teaching. Teaching implies knowledge" (*The Higher Learning* [1962], p. 66). And again, "Education deals with the development of the intellectual powers of men. Their moral and spiritual powers are the sphere of the family and the church" (*Conflict in Education* [1953], p. 69).

One can, of course, so define education, but it is a rather arbitrary limitation of the concept, since we do ordinarily include moral and religious education within it. If one says that such cultivation of moral and spiritual powers is not education, but something else, however desirable it may be, one not only rejects our usual way of speaking; one forces us to look for some other term that covers the whole idea we have throughout history been using "education" and its equivalents to mean.

Peters has also sought to build further criteria into the concept of education. He argues that education is going on only if X is initiating Y into some form of activity, some body of knowledge or mode of conduct that is governed by public standards enshrined in a public language to which both teacher and learner must give allegiance. Education "consists in initiating others into activities, modes of conduct and thought which have standards written into them by reference to which it is possible to act, think, and feel with varying degrees of skill, relevance, and taste" (*Education as Initiation* [1964], p. 41).

Peters contends, furthermore, that education implies that the teacher and learner both know what they are doing, at least in an embryonic way, and care about it; that, though education does include the cultivation of moral and spiritual powers as well as intellectual ones, it always entails some kind of cognitive or intellectual development, some kind of "knowing-that" as well as "knowing-how"; and that the methods it uses must be appropriate to the dispositions involved in the kind of initiation described, as well as compatible with the learner's knowing what he is doing and caring about it. This is a more adequate view than that of Hutchins, and one is tempted to accept it, at least if it can be made to cover the cultivation of bodily skills, manual training, aesthetic education, and vocational preparation, all of which we ordinarily cover by the word "education."

On the other hand, it is not entirely clear that Peters' definition will cover all of these things. Moreover, he appears to be thinking that the forms of activity and thought into which X is to initiate Y must have been developed in the past and in some public way, and so, though he does try to provide for the teaching of critical thinking, he seems to exclude from education the possibility that X might initiate Y into some new mode of activity or thought with standards not yet publicly accepted—or possibly into some "form of Life" that involves no standards at all or only those Y comes to regard as his "own thing" or commits himself to by some act of "choice" or "decision." Such possibilities seem to be envisaged by those who are presently advocating a "new" or "free" education, and it does seem a bit arbitrary to say that what they are envisaging just is not a form of education, even if it turns out to be desirable and morally unobjectionable (as it very well may not).

The much-discussed question of the relation of in-doctrination to education is relevant here. Indoc-trination appears to be one way in which the young might be made to acquire at least some of the disposi-tions Peters has in mind, though he may be meaning to rule out its use in education by his criterion that the learner must see, if only as a child, what he is doing and why it is desirable. What seems crucial in the debate about it, however, is not whether indoctrination passes this criterion but whether its use is desirable and morally unobjectionable. Those who think it is never so tend to deny that indoctrination is a form of education, while those who think it sometimes is so tend to hold that indoctrination is a kind of educa-tion, even if they limit its use. This suggests that we rule indoctrination and other doubtful methods out of education by definition, if and only if we regard them as undesirable or morally objectionable. Should we rule them out of education on any other grounds? To say no here has the disadvantage that, if we find promoting good dispositions by drug, pill, electrode, or hypnotism to be feasible and unobjectionable, then we must rec-ognize such methods as properly educational, which many are admittedly reluctant to do. On the other hand, perhaps we are reluctant to recognize them as educational only because we are certain that they are morally or otherwise objectionable—or simply so incapable of producing desirable dispositions as not to deserve consideration at all.

So far as the ranges of W and Z go, then, it is not clear that we should build into the definition of educa-tion anything more than the requirement that the dispositions sought and the means employed must be desirable on some ground or other and morally unob-jectionable. As for the conceptual question about the ranges of X and Y, it seems fairly clear that we would think that X is educating Y only if X and Y both have minds of a human level. It is true that Rousseau says

we are educated by nature and things as well as by men, and that his way of speaking is not entirely unnatural. Still he is stretching the range of X too far. It is only when "exempt from public haunts" that we find "tongues in trees, books in the running brooks," and "sermons in stones." We do, of course, "learn" from our experience with things, but to call them our "teachers" is surely some kind of metonymy at best; if there is a teacher here it is ourselves. What Heidi's grandfather learned from the eagle he taught himself. As for Rousseau's talk about education by nature—this is simply a mistake. By it he means the fruition of innate dispositions that would take place in our lives if it were not for the action of men and things on us. But automatic realization of dispositions when no one is doing anything to bring it about, not even oneself, is not education but something else. Rousseau's philos-ophy of education is a philosophy of *education* only because he thinks that we have to do something to prevent unnatural dispositions from being formed through our experience of men and things. This pre-vention *is* a kind of educational activity. But the natu-ral evolution of innate dispositions as such is not, even if they are desirable, as Rousseau assumes.

Some would say that X may be a superhuman being; in *The Idea of Christian Education* (1957, pp. 255–65), S. F. Bayne says that the basic idea of Christian educa-tion is that God is our teacher. Now, if God really does, by some special act on his part (and not just through our own use of our natural faculties), "reveal" things to us, then He can be said to teach us. If X reveals to Y the way to set up a tent he is teaching Y something. Thus the Psalmist writes, "Teach me thy way, O Lord; I will walk in thy truth . . . ," and, again, "Teach me good judgment and knowledge. . . ." One may then say that God educates man, if one chooses, and if one believes that such special divine revelation is available to us. It seems better, however, to follow Plato's *Meno* in limiting the term "educating" to human activities like practicing and instructing, and to think of God's acts of revelation and regeneration as "gifts," as Christianity itself usually does—as some kind of divine aid to education rather than as education itself. This would, among other things, accord with Aquinas' doctrine that faith, hope, and love are not acquired by teaching but by divine infusion. One can still argue then, as religious people often have, that education is important only because it is necessary or at least helpful as a preparation for God's act of grace; because it enables one to understand His revelation, or because it equips one to do His work in the world.

If what has been said is accepted, then it follows that the concept of education is a normative concept that is open-textured at two points, since it restricts the ranges of W and Z to what is desirable and morally unobjectionable or judged to be so, but imposes no other restrictions upon them. It also follows that all education is, strictly speaking, "education of men"—of and by, if not necessarily *for,* men—that the idea of education is the idea of a distinctively human activity or enterprise of forming desirable dispositions or excellences by morally unobjectionable means.

Whatever may be thought of this discussion of the conceptual ranges of X, Y, W, and Z, it remains true that the idea of education is the idea of an enterprise in which someone fosters certain dispositions in someone by methods of certain sorts. We may now observe that anyone who consciously embarks upon this enterprise must not only have this concept, he must also have certain beliefs or postulates—a certain minimal philosophy, if you will. This is made clear by the discussion in Plato's *Meno.* These presuppositions are: (a) that some set of dispositions is desirable, (b) that they are not innate or just naturally or automatically acquired (as Rousseau thought they might be), (c) that they are not all acquired wholly by luck or by divine gift, (d) that they may (some of them perhaps wholly, others at least in part) be acquired or passed on by humanly instituted activities of an educational kind, e.g., by practice or instruction, though possibly only "wid a little bit o' luck" or a bounteous divine aid. Actually, there is another presupposition, not envisaged in the *Meno,* namely, (e) that they are not simply created in oneself by an act of choice or decision, out of whole cloth as it were (as so many seemed to think in the 1960's).

One might, of course, *conceive* of education without making these assumptions, but then it would be the idea of a purely hypothetical endeavor. Any X who actually engages in the enterprise of education can do it only under these presuppositions, for, if they are false, then education is either impossible, unnecessary, or so uncertain of success as to be pointless. X may be relatively optimistic or relatively pessimistic about education, but if he engages in it at all, he must make these assumptions.

We see then that there is such a thing as *the* idea of education and that it is possible to give something more nearly approaching a definition of it than T. S. Eliot realized. To say that X educates or is educating Y is to say at least that X is fostering desirable and morally unobjectionable dispositions in Y by the use of methods that are also desirable and morally unobjectionable, or at least that X is cultivating dispositions in Y by certain methods. This idea (concept) of education is common to all of the different ideas (doctrines, theories) of education held by Plato, Kant, Dewey, President Garfield, or the Chinese. They all mean by

"education" (or its equivalents in their languages) a process, involving an X (educator) and a Y (educated), of forming desirable dispositions by desirable methods. They have different beliefs about education—about what it should be like—but they mean the same thing by it. There are also different *kinds* of education—physical, moral, vocational, public, etc.—but these all involve the forming of desirable dispositions by desirable methods. The same basic concept underlies all kinds and theories of education. All kinds and theories of education have the same five basic presuppositions.

We may end our account of the concept of education with a word about its emergence in the history of Western thought. Eliot talks as if our notion of education has undergone a kind of evolution through the centuries, but all he shows is that we have had changing views about what X, Y, Z, and W should be, which is true but does not mean that our basic concept itself has changed. Actually, according to the above account, the concept of education was fully conceived when some individual or people first consciously judged that a certain set of dispositions was desirable, that they were not innate or automatically acquired, nor matters of fortune or divine gift, and that they could (some of them at least in part) be acquired or passed on by some human program of teaching or practice. Just when and where this was we cannot say for certain, even if we consider only the Western world. We must suppose that some kind of education or *paideia* has been going on since the beginning of human history. The self-making of man, of which Kant speaks, may not be as old as the hills but it must be as old as man. Education must then have been in the world before the concept of it came to anyone's consciousness in an explicit way. As Eliot says, ". . . a long tradition and many educational institutions preceded the time at which the question, 'What is education?' needed to be asked" (p. 121).

By Pindar's day, however, antidemocratic spokesmen were arguing that some men have aretē ("excellence") by nature and others do not, and that for the former education is unnecessary, while for the others it is of no avail. Here we find the concept of education as we have defined it becoming clear. It came completely out in the open in the days of Socrates and the Sophists, when the Greek air was full of debate about education, as is shown by the discussion Plato purports to describe in the *Protagoras* and *Meno* about the teachability of aretē. For Meno begins by asking how aretē is acquired and he lists four alternatives: (a) that it is acquired by teaching, (b) that it is acquired by practice, (c) that it is acquired by fortune or divine gift, (d) that it is possessed by nature. The ostensible conclusion is that (c) is true and hence that aretē is unhappily *not* acquired by education, but the point is that education is being definitely conceived as the attempt to foster excellences by such methods as teaching and practice. Thus the idea of education is here essentially complete and its postulates understood. This discussion, whenever it first took place, marks the real beginning of the philosophy of education. Indeed, it took place precisely because philosophy was beginning to take a hand in the educational enterprise.

II

Differing ideas of or views about education must agree with much of what has been said, particularly with the general outlines of the analysis given of the idea of education and with the statement of the presuppositions of any educational enterprise. They may include different views about the ranges of X, Y, W, and Z to be built into the idea or definition of education. However, even if they agree completely about conceptual matters, they may and do still differ about substantive issues. In fact, as Eliot sees, it is precisely these further substantive questions that have been and are the historically and practically most important ones. These substantive questions, which remain open on any plausible definition of education, roughly stated, are: (1) Are the postulates of education true? Are the excellences cultivatible by education? Need they be so cultivated? (2) What dispositions are desirable and to be fostered by education? What dispositions are excellences? (3) By what means or in what ways should education (educators) seek to foster these desirable dispositions? (4) Who is to be educated? How should educational opportunity be distributed? (5) Who should educate?

Actually each of these questions is a family or group of questions. They are, moreover, interrelated and hence cannot be answered in entire independence of one another, e.g., (1) and (2), (2) and (4), (3) and (4), and (4) and (5). In what follows, however, we shall have to keep them somewhat separate. It should also be noted that the last four questions are normative, since they ask what should be done, or what is desirable, while the first is not.

The main point for our purposes now, however, is the fact that theories and philosophies of education arise as answers to these substantive questions and, apart from conceptual or definitional preliminaries like the above, consist of and are distinguished by their answers to them. Before we discuss the questions and the issues involved in answering them, we must stop to look at such substantive theories and philosophies, to see what they are like, what they include, and how they are or should be put together; this is the second main part of our task—to analyze the kind of idea of education referred to earlier in (2b).

A theory of education, then, is a set of answers to the above five questions. Since it includes answers to the last four it will be normative, saying what education should be like, not just descriptive, explanatory, or predictive, as a psychological theory of learning or child development would be. In J. S. Mill's language (*A System of Logic* [1843], Book VI, Chs. V, XII), education is not a science, but an art. It may, however, and no doubt should, make use of such scientific theories of development and learning as a basis for some of its normative conclusions; in fact, Mill thought educational theories should rest their normative "precepts" entirely on such premises as psychology alone can provide, except for the one basic normative premiss supplied by ethics, which for him was the principle of utility.

What is usually called a philosophy of education is a theory in this normative sense, but not every such theory is properly called a philosophy. For a theory of education might simply assume, without argument, that the dispositions to be promoted and the methods to be used are those regarded as desirable by the society or individual the education is to serve, and then it can be called a philosophy of education only by extreme courtesy. It is better regarded as a minimal theory of education, reserving the title of philosophy of education for fuller theories that provide a reasoned justification for their answers to normative questions about education.

Every theory of education in our sense will, then, assume an affirmative answer to the first question, though it may do so dogmatically, without discussion. That is, it assumes that the acquisition of desirable dispositions is not wholly a matter of nature, luck, divine gift, or choice, but is in part or to some extent amenable to educational programming. If it seeks to defend these assumptions, it must list these dispositions, analyze them, and show that the claims made in the assumptions are true. In other words, it must establish certain facts about human nature and about the world. To do this it may appeal to science, to metaphysics, or to theology—different thinkers will have different views about what is to be appealed to, views that will depend on their general philosophical orientations.

What means, methods, or practices education is to make use of—e.g., just what the teacher is to do in the classroom—will appear in answer to question (3). Even a minimal theory of education may try to give a reasoned reply to this question by seeking to justify its recommendations. How then may a precept about the method of teaching something be justified? Suppose one maintains, as the Greeks did, that in order to foster the moral virtues we should use music of certain sorts, at least during a certain stage in a child's life (a belief that was for the most part given up in the Hellenistic

Period, though parents even in the twentieth century sometimes wonder about the possible moral effects of some new combinations of sound that some of their children listen to). To justify this claim one must use an argument something like this: (a) Education should cultivate moral virtue. (b) The hearing of such and such kinds of music is conducive to moral virtue. (c) Therefore education should make use of music of those kinds. Or suppose we use the dictum that, no matter what disposition is being fostered, learning is by doing. Then our reasoning must be along these lines: (a) Education should foster an understanding of music. (b) Any disposition is more effectively fostered if some relevant "doing" on the part of the student is arranged for. (c) Therefore education should include learning to sing or play an instrument.

Thus, in order to justify any normative conclusion in answer to question (3), whether this is specific or general, one must make use of a normative premiss like (a) in these examples, which says something about dispositions to be promoted, and of a factual premiss like (b) which says that a certain method or practice is necessary, sufficient, or at least helpful for the promotion of those dispositions.

Two things about premisses like (b) should be noted. In the first place, even if they are simply assumed or borrowed from common sense or tradition, they are empirical statements that may in principle be verified by empirical observation and scientific testing, and any theory that seeks to justify them must appeal to experience or to some empirical science. In the second place, they may be of different kinds depending on whether they assert that a certain practice is necessary, sufficient, or neither necessary nor sufficient but still helpful, for the fostering of the disposition referred to in premiss (a), or simply that it is more effective in doing so than other methods are; and the conclusion in (c) must be understood differently, depending on which of these claims they make, though the argument may in each case be read as establishing that the practice in question has some value or desirability.

Arguments like those illustrated do not, however, establish that the practices they defend ought to be employed unless they show the practices to be necessary. Take the following argument: (a) Education should foster citizenship. (b) Indoctrination is conducive to citizenship. (c) Therefore education should include indoctrination. Even if one accepts its premisses one may reject the conclusion because one does not regard citizenship as having top priority; but, even if one gives citizenship first place, one may reject it because one regards indoctrination as morally wrong. Of course, if one believes that citizenship must be given first place in education, and that indoctrination is necessary for promoting citizenship, then one must con-

clude that indoctrination should be used. But then one will not regard its use as morally objectionable. This example shows that ethical considerations are important in connection with question (3) as well as scientific ones, since methods must be shown to be morally unobjectionable as well as effective or helpful in producing desirable dispositions before we can consider them justified.

Still, except when ethical premisses by themselves dictate something about educational methods, e.g., that educators should not use lies (except in cases in which lying is morally excusable, if there are any), the justification of answers to question (3) will include a premiss like (a) in our examples that presupposes an answer to question (2), plus, of course, a factual premiss like (b). In this sense, (2) is the central normative question in any theory of education, and the central part of any such theory is a list and description of the dispositions to be fostered by education. How then is one to justify saying that a certain disposition (which is not simply a matter of nature, luck, divine gift, or choice) should be cultivated by education? From what has been said, it follows that one must show that the disposition is desirable on some ground and that it is not morally objectionable. In order to show that it is not morally reprehensible he must, of course, appeal to some ethical premiss about what is or is not morally wrong, bad, or vicious, and at least sometimes also to a factual premiss. For example, to show that a liking for the kinds of music Plato and Aristotle banned from education is not morally bad, one would have to use a premiss telling us what moral virtues we should have and a factual one to the effect that a liking for those kinds of music does not conflict with the acquisition of those virtues.

In order to show that it is desirable to foster a certain morally innocuous disposition by education, one must, again, use premisses of two kinds, namely, ethical or other value premisses stating more ultimate aims or principles of education, and factual ones stating that the disposition in question is necessary, sufficient, or at least helpful in relation to them. For example, one might accept, as many would, the three aims of education discussed by Eliot (p. 69): 1. To prepare a child to make a living (for a vocation). 2. To equip him to be a good citizen. 3. To develop his powers and so enable him to enjoy a good life. Then to show that education should foster a certain disposition one would show that its acquisition or possession is required by or at least conducive to one of these ends (and not inconsistent with a more important end). The argument would have this form: (a) Education should promote such and such an end (or principle). (b) Disposition W is conducive to this end. (c) Therefore education should foster W. Here (a) is a normative or value premiss; it belongs to one's ethical or value theory, more specifically, to one's political or social philosophy. Political or social philosophy is thus shown to be of crucial importance in the theory of education. As Aristotle said, it is *politike*

that ordains which of the sciences are to exist in states, and what branches of knowledge the different classes of citizens are to learn, and up to what point . . . (*Ethics* I, 2).

Then (b) is a factual premiss, saying that a certain disposition is necessary, sufficient, or at least helpful in achieving a certain end (or living by a certain principle); it will usually be of a kind that depends on experience and science for its verification, but in some theories of education it might come from metaphysics or theology.

Thus, answers to question (3) depend on answers to question (2)—which give us the "proximate" aims of education—and answers to question (2) depend on answers to a more basic question which give us the more "ultimate" aims or principles of education, factual premises appearing in both cases. How then are answers to this more basic question, statements about the more ultimate aims of education, to be justified? An educational theorist might stop at this point and refer us to a philosopher or theologian, but, if he is offering us a full-fledged philosophy of education, he will try to justify his statement in (a) of our last example. Then, again, he must appeal to premises of two kinds: first, a still more basic normative or value premiss, and, second, a still more basic factual one. There is no one form his reasoning must take, but he will make use of premises like the following: We ought always to do what will bring about the greatest general balance of good over evil (the principle of utility); Society ought to be just; Pleasure is the end of life; Contemplating the heavens with understanding is good in itself; Belief in Jesus Christ is necessary for salvation; Making a living (having a vocation) is necessary both for life and for the good life; This life is all there is. Such premises contain no explicit reference to education, and hence do not belong specifically to the philosophy of education but to other branches of philosophy, to science, or to theology. One may, of course, seek to justify them in turn by appeal to more basic premises, until one finally comes to one's most basic ethical or value premises and one's most basic beliefs about man and the universe.

To illustrate what has been said, one relatively complete line of argument in education might proceed as follows: (a) Other things being equal, what is good in itself should be pursued and promoted. (b) Contemplating the heavens with understanding is good in itself. (c) Therefore the contemplative understanding of the heavens should be pursued and promoted. (d) This entails acquiring and fostering the knowledge of astronomy (the disposition called a knowledge of astronomy). (e) This can be done by education and by education alone. (f) Therefore education should foster a knowledge of astronomy (other things being equal). (g) In order to do this it is necessary, among other things, to initiate people into the use of the telescope. (h) Therefore education should initiate the young into the use of the telescope. Granting the premises, this is, as far as it goes, a good argument for its conclusions in (c), (f), and (h).

It is not final, however, for the acquisition of a mastery of astronomy might be incompatible with that of more important dispositions. But arguments to show this would have a somewhat similar structure, and so this example can be used as a basis for a number of points. (1) Both factual and normative premises are necessary to answer normative questions about education. (2) Among the factual premises must be some empirical or scientific ones, e.g., (e), (g), and possibly (d). (3) Epistemological premises are neither necessary nor sufficient to establish educational conclusions, as so many twentieth-century writers on the philosophy of education seem to assume. (4) Specifically religious, theological, or metaphysical premises are also neither necessary nor sufficient, as Eliot and many others allege. (5) The philosophy of education is not autonomous, for it depends on premises from other fields. (6) What is basic and central in the philosophy of education is such normative inquiries as ethics, value theory, and social philosophy, as is shown by the role of premises like (a) and (b) and conclusions like (c) and (f). (7) Philosophers of education might content themselves with establishing conclusions like (c) and (f), leaving more practical steps like (g) and (h) to educational scientists and practitioners, but they have usually attempted to supply such steps too.

Four points should be added. (8) Eliot and others who hold that a philosophy of education must ultimately rest on religious or theological premises assume that the final premises one appeals to are religious or theological just because they are normative, because they are about the nature of man and the universe, or because they are ultimate. But to say that they must *therefore* be religious or theological and not just ethical, axiological, philosophical, or scientific is to make them religious or theological simply by a kind of baptism. For then atheism, naturalism, secularism, cynicism, hedonism, perhaps even skepticism, all become forms of religion without undergoing any conversion and without relaxing their opposition to theism or to what usually counts as religious or theological belief; and nothing is gained but a Pyrrhic victory. (9) One may insist that specifically theistic beliefs must be brought to bear on educational arguments like the above, e.g., in connection with premises (b), (d), or (e), but this is not obvious and it is not logically necessary; in fact, one can agree to this only if one already shares such theistic beliefs. (10) It remains true that religious, epistemological, and metaphysical premises may, so far as the logic of the matter goes, be relevant to the justification of educational conclusions. If one believes, as Thomas Merton did, that the whole work of man in this life is to find God, one may and, indeed, must use this belief as the basis of one's philosophy of education. That epistemological premises may be *relevant* even though they are neither *necessary* or *sufficient* is shown by one of Cardinal Newman's arguments (1852) for teaching theology in universities: (a) A university should teach knowledge. (b) Theology is a form of knowledge. (c) Therefore a university should teach theology (*The Idea of a University* [1959], Ch. II). Here (b) is an epistemological claim. Incidentally, it should be noticed that neither of Newman's premises is specifically religious or theological. (11) Thus, a full normative philosophy of education will contain the following kinds of statements, in addition to definitions, distinctions, and other bits of analysis: 1. Normative premises like (a) and (b) in the longer of our last two examples. 2. Factual premises like (d), (e), and (g), including at least some empirical or scientific ones. 3. Normative conclusions answering questions (2) and (3) like (c), (f), and (h). It may include epistemological, metaphysical, or religious premises, though it need not; if so, they will belong under the second heading (unless they are normative).

This brings us to questions (4) and (5) on our earlier list. Answers to these questions are somewhat interwoven with answers to questions (2) and (3), as has been observed, but it is clear that in general they too will depend on premises of the two kinds already distinguished, normative and factual, and that political and social philosophy in particular will play an important part in establishing them. Among the factual premises there will be empirical or scientific judgments, for example, about the capacities, needs, and responses of different groups of children, or about the effectiveness of different sorts of teacher training.

III

The third part of our task is to make, in the light of our analyses thus far, some clarifications of and comments on the "history of educational ideas" and on the chief issues involved in it. Such a history should be distinguished, more than it sometimes is, from a history of education. The former is a history of certain ideas, of certain concepts and theories, and is a part of the general history of thought or ideas; the latter is a history of certain actions, institutions, and practices, and is a part of the general history of what human beings have done and how they did it. The two histories are, of course, very intimately connected, but they should not be confused.

In any case, however, a complete history of theories of education will include, in one way or another, histories of the four kinds of "ideas of education" distinguished early in Section I. The history of *the* idea of education would be the story, if it can be told, of the emergence into full consciousness of the concept of education we tried to analyze in the rest of that Section. The closely related history of proposed analyses or definitions of that concept would be a part of the history of analytical philosophy of education, and so might be of interest both for the theory of definition and for the history of ideas. It would certainly appear, if what was said in Section I is correct, that many proposed definitions of education are faulty, and that many apparent definitions are really disguised normative theories about what the aims and means of education should be, in which case they belong to the history of such theories.

The third of our histories would be a history of "the belief (or faith) in education" that has characterized some thinkers and epochs in our culture, and it or parts of it have often been told. Here we can only analyze the belief. It is not a normative belief about the ends or means of education, but a factual conviction about its efficacy and results, such as Socrates sometimes appeared not to have. It entails a belief in the presuppositions of education formulated in Section I, but it goes beyond them, not just to a confidence that education can in fact produce the dispositions it seeks to produce, but to a conviction that the acquisition of these dispositions will have certain hoped for results. In modern times it has been associated with the idea of progress, and has taken the form of a belief that, through the spread of education, man as a race can and will progress steadily either toward material prosperity or toward some more ideal goal.

It may, however, take two more individualistic forms: the belief that education is the key to an individual's getting ahead or succeeding in the world, or the belief that education is his way to a more ideal happiness, to perfection, or to salvation. An example of the last is Plato's view in the *Symposium* that the right kind of child-leading will lead him to immortality. In effect, then, the belief in education splits into four beliefs, viz., two kinds of social faith, one idealistic and one materialistic, and two corresponding kinds of individual faith. Perhaps we should also recognize a fifth form of the belief—the belief in education as a panacea, said to be especially characteristic of Americans, at least until the 1960's.

It is, however, especially about the history of normative theories of education that we are now concerned. Perhaps it is possible to find implicit theories of this sort in Homer and other descriptions of Greek education, but, at any rate, more conscious and fuller theories arose in Greece through a conjunction of two developments—the rise of philosophy or what Aristophanes called the "Think Shop" and tried to laugh out of existence, and the breakdown of the traditional or "old" educational system. In a real sense, philosophy and thinking about education arose together; philosophers at once set themselves up as teachers and critics, and education gave them a profession and problems to think about.

Between the many ideas of education that have appeared in our history there have been a great many issues of debate of various kinds, more or less independent of or interdependent on one another, but all related in some manner to our schema of analysis. We must now try to identify and analyze them, make some historical remarks about them, and relate them to our schema—all as an aid to understanding the issues and their history, and to our own thinking about them.

Some of these "great debates" have been more or less perennial; others can be roughly dated in the sense that they peaked early or only recently. One could then take them up in some kind of chronological order. One can, however, also take them up in a more logical order dictated by their relation to our schema of questions. Here they will be dealt with in a mixture of these ways. Some of them are specifically educational, since what is at issue is some normative question explicitly about education, but others are meta-normative rather than normative—the debate is about the method to be used in determining the answer, say, to question (2) in Section II, or about the kinds of factual premisses that are admissible. Still others are about substantive factual or normative questions that are not specifically about education, though they are relevant to it. In each case, our concern here is primarily analytical and secondarily historical; we cannot attempt to settle the issues involved.

We may begin with three ancient debates.

(1) The discussion in the *Meno* and *Protagoras* has already been referred to. Is a virtue somehow amenable to cultivation by education or is it not? The question was not whether education is effective in fostering any desirable dispositions whatsoever. This is a much more radical question, which might perhaps also be discussed, but Socrates had no doubt that some knowledge and skills could be taught. The question was about a particular set of desirable dispositions, namely, those

the Greeks included in aretē, and about the efficacy of traditional methods of moral education in promoting them (one feels that Socrates has some notion of a new method that will be effective where the old ones were not). But it can be asked for any other proposed set of desirable dispositions and for any other proposed methods of education—and one might wish to add that it makes a difference who the pupil and the teacher are (Plato obviously thought that Socrates could teach virtue to at least some young men). If a certain disposition cannot be fostered in anyone by anyone by any educational method, it cannot realistically be taken as a goal in education anywhere. Even in his own context Socrates did not state the question accurately enough, as Protagoras partly sees. For he does not distinguish, as we have seen one must, between asking whether education is *necessary* for the acquisition of virtue, whether it is *sufficient*, or whether it is *relevant* at all. At most Socrates' crude evidence would show only that it is not sufficient, not that it is not necessary or helpful as far as it goes, in at least some cases. His evidence does not even show that it is not sufficient in some cases.

Before we leave the *Meno* it will be interesting to notice that later theories of education have approximated more or less closely to one or another of the alternatives, which, accepted without qualification, would make the great enterprise of education "turn awry, and lose the name of action." This is possible within the framework of the five postulates of any educational endeavor (Section I). Thus, Rousseau and the followers of nature in education stay as close as possible to the alternative that the dispositions to be sought in education are in us by nature and are automatically realized if nothing interferes; traditional Christian theory holds that the most desirable dispositions—faith, hope, and love—are mainly or wholly a matter of divine gift; and Kant makes the most crucial of them—good will or moral virtue—a matter of free noumenal choice that is not determined by anything that goes on in time or space, while the existentialists and their followers come close to making such a "decision" a necessary and sufficient condition of the possession of any disposition whatsoever, thus rendering the very possibility of education problematic.

(2) The debate highlighted by the *Meno* was connected with another which Plato calls "the ancient war between the poets and the philosophers," itself highlighted in his *Republic* and in Aristophanes' *The Clouds*. Ostensibly this was a debate over the question who should teach, that is, who should be the ultimate educator—the poet, who was also the theologian and historian of Greece, and who depends on divine inspiration, or the philosopher, who was also the scientist

of Greece, and, who depends on reason or thinking. It may also be thought of as an issue between two "unified curricula," two unified sets of dispositions, both aiming at truth and virtue, but involving the two radically different approaches indicated. In both of these aspects, it has been continued ever since, especially in the patristic and medieval periods, by the debate in educational theory between the theologians on one side and philosophers and scientists on the other. The high point on the philosophical side was reached in the educational thinking of Socrates, Plato, and Aristotle—or, as some would say in the twentieth century, in that of Dewey. Aquinas' philosophy of education represents the most influential synthesis of the opposing positions. By that time, however, what we usually call poetry had virtually dropped out of contention, except that its study continued to be a part of the educational curriculum, as it still is. Now its scope has been extended to include modern literature and all of the arts, and, as Lionel Trilling has pointed out (*Beyond Culture* [1965], p. 219), in spite of the recent conflict of "the two cultures" it bids fair, for good or for ill, to be the most important educational influence of the period since World War II.

The debate had another aspect in terms of our schema, for it also involves the question of the source of the basic premises of any educational theory. Do they come from some kind of inspiration or revelation or are they reached by some human effort of critical and systematic reflection? Here the question is not whether we are to teach poetry or philosophy, religion or science, but whether our conclusions about what to teach, whatever it may be, must be grounded on premises from one source or from the other. This again is an issue that we still have with us, as Eliot's essay shows. And it is not only religious thinkers who put themselves on the side of the "poets"; a basic anti-rationalism infects a large part of contemporary educational thinking, especially that of the very "newest" writers—and it is closely connected with developments in the arts.

(3) A third ancient debate concerning education, related to both of the others, took place between the Sophists and Socrates, and was continued by Plato, Aristotle, and other philosophers on one side, and Isocrates, Quintilian, and other orators and rhetoricians on the other, with Cicero seeking a synthesis of sorts (one might think of this as one aspect of a three-sided war between poets, philosophers, and sophists). At issue here, for one thing, was Protagoras' thesis that education should be based on a study of the poets. But more important was the Sophist tendency to conceive of areté or excellence as consisting of a number of skills, which they claimed to be able to teach, and which

could be used to achieve some end or other, or could be enjoyed for their own sakes, but which had no essential reference to truth or moral virtue. For Socrates, Plato, and Aristotle skills that could be used for or against the true or the good were unimportant; what really mattered in education was the moral and intellectual virtues proper, which they conceived of as essentially directed to the good or the true.

This opposition represents one of the main watersheds in the history of educational thinking, for very different visions of education emerge on the two sides. It too is still with us in the question whether the emphasis in education should be on method or skill or on knowledge and truth. It is not unrelated to the question of liberal versus vocational education; at any rate, many "consumers," if not thinkers about education, seem to conceive of it as a tool or a toy, much as the Sophists did.

What was said is roughly true of the Sophists, but it will hardly do for the orators, Isocrates and Quintilian, since they thought of the orator not only as the possessor of a number of skills, but as essentially concerned with truth and virtue. They were, however, relatively antiphilosophical, and did not make anything much in the way of either philosophy or theology a part of education as they conceived of it, as Plato, Aristotle, and other philosophers did. For them, education centered, not in philosophy or theology, but in the liberal arts, the trivium and quadrivium of the Middle Ages—which were roughly speaking originated by the Sophists, and came to form the perennial curriculum of education. For it was not the poets or the philosophers who won that ancient war, or even the theologians though they ruled for centuries, but the Sophists and their followers, those who believed in a curriculum consisting of a number of arts, disciplines, or sciences.

Ultimately everything else was simply added to the number. For long there were only the liberal arts and classical studies, plus the faculties of law, medicine, and theology; but slowly, in fact only recently, the natural and social sciences, modern history, language, and literature, and other arts, were added to the curriculum—and many other things, including, as was mentioned, education itself—with nothing dominating the whole as the poets, philosophers, and theologians had each hoped their subject would; though some now think, as Herbert Spencer did (*Education* [1884], Ch. I) and as C. P. Snow does (*The Two Cultures*, 1959), that science ought to dominate if it does not do so already. Given this conception of education, of course, the main remaining questions are: Who studies which subject and by what compulsion, if any, must he?

Thus these three Greek debates about education 81

were somewhat complex, involving a number of issues, and, in one form or another, had important subsequent histories. Let us now approach other issues in a more logical manner.

(4) As we saw, the central problem in the theory of education is question (2): What dispositions are to be fostered? But this question immediately raises another: How are we to determine what dispositions education should foster? For some the answer is relatively easy. They assume that education is to promote the dispositions regarded as desirable by the society in which it is going on. Or they look at the various arts, disciplines, and sciences referred to a moment ago—all there, like mountains to be climbed—and juggle them into a curriculum or simply let students "elect" from among them. Such approaches have their practical advantages. But a less minimal theory of education must give more of a rationale than this, and how is it to proceed?

The usual method is to look for "the aims of education." But this method has been much criticized by Dewey (*Democracy and Education* [1916], Chs. 4, 8, 18) and his followers and more recently by analytical philosophers like Peters (*Authority* . . . [1959], Ch. 7). Especially objected to is the notion that education has an end beyond or external to itself. Aims *in* education, and even *criteria* or *principles* of education, are not under attack, only "aims of" or "external" to education. For education is life and life can hardly have an aim external to itself. Comment here must be brief.

To begin with, education in sense (1), i.e., the activity of the educator, does and must have an end beyond *itself*, viz., the fostering of a disposition in the one being educated. There are criteria for determining whether he is educating and principles according to which he must act, but his actions must have an aim—a proximate aim—to foster some ability, belief, knowledge, skill, trait, or value. One may also say that the aim of education in sense (1), as distinguished earlier, is education in senses (2) and (3). The question is whether it must have any aim beyond that of forming desirable dispositions, whether the dispositions are somehow means to something further. Some certainly are, for example, the habit of brushing one's teeth. Here the activity in which the disposition manifests itself has value only or at least primarily as a means. The same is true, as Aristotle argued, of the activities in which any *technē* like a mastery of carpentry manifests itself; they have an end, which is to build things like houses. On the other hand, the exercise of some dispositions like an ability to play a flute or a knowledge of geometry may or may not have an end beyond itself—it may be engaged in simply for its own sake, because it is worthwhile in itself. But even then one

may say that the earlier activity of the educator and of the one being educated have the aim of putting the latter in a position of being able to engage in those activities at will, and so have an end beyond themselves, though not necessarily one external to the latter's life. Whether they must also have an end external to his life, as Eliot (pp. 75, 109, 117) and Marrou think (*History of Education* [1964], pp. 307f.), is another question, the answer to which depends on one's most basic factual and normative beliefs.

It remains true that one's ultimate normative premisses need not be statements about aims or ends to be pursued. They might be principles like Kant's first or second forms of the categorical imperative, which serve as the bases of his philosophy of education. Which form they take depends on one's ethical theory. Even so, it is hard to see how one can avoid saying that some experiences and activities are worthwhile in themselves or, as Dewey prefers to say, consummatory—and what is this but to say that we should *aim* at having or engaging in them, and at helping others to have or engage in them?

(5) Another meta-normative issue that runs through the history of educational theory has to do with the question concerning what kinds of premisses may or must be appealed to in determining what dispositions are to be formed by education: ethical, epistemological, metaphysical, scientific, or theological. This issue has already been touched on more than once, but we may add that theories of education may be classified according to the kinds of premisses they appeal to. Thus a "scientistic" theory will ultimately appeal only to scientific premisses, claiming, as Dewey does, that ethical judgments rest or should rest on scientific ones. A positivistic theory, like Mill's, may deny this claim, but will insist that, apart from one's normative premisses, one should appeal only to scientific ones. A religious theory would contend, as Eliot does, that theological premisses must, or at least may and should be appealed to. And so on. It should be repeated, however, that though the issues between such opposing views are relevant to educational conclusions, and philosophers of education must be prepared to discuss them, they belong to philosophy generally, and not specifically to the philosophy of education.

(6) Another relatively abstract, though normative, issue or group of issues, very crucial in the history of educational ideas, is that between the Absolutists and the Relativists. The Absolutists maintain that there is a certain set of dispositions (they may differ about what it is) that ought to be fostered by education, or by some central part or kind of education (e.g., liberal or general education), everywhere and at all times, in everyone capable of acquiring these dispositions and to the ex-

tent to which he is capable of acquiring them. This contention, of course, presupposes that human beings all have the same basic nature and differ only in the degree in which they have it (and in "accidental" ways, like sex or color of skin), though one may accept this presupposition and yet not be an Absolutist in educational theory—Aristotle accepts it (with some doubts about barbarians, slaves, and women) but he holds that education should be relative to the political constitution of the state, and, even in the case of the ideal state, offers rather different kinds of education to freemen, slaves, workers, and women.

Though philosophers have a natural penchant for being Absolutists when they write about education, it is surprisingly hard to find good examples of this position—was Plato an Absolutist?—but we may cite R. M. Hutchins, M. J. Adler, and perhaps Kant (though he too had doubts about women).

Relativists about education may be and have been of many different kinds, depending on what they hold education should be relative to. They all hold that no important kind or part of education need or should be the same everywhere and at all times, that every kind or part of education of any significance must and should vary according to some principle, i.e., should cultivate different dispositions. The following principles at least have all had followings: (a) that education should be relative to the desires or value-judgments of the society in question, e.g., perhaps, H. I. Marrou and W. H. Woodward; (b) that it should follow the flag in the sense of varying with the political constitution of the state, and cultivate, not "the virtues of the good man" but "the virtues of the good citizen" as defined by that constitution; this was Aristotle's view and in places Rousseau's, and seems to be that of those who think that American or democratic education must take a different form from other educations, including possibly Dewey; (c) that it should vary with vocation or station in life, e.g., Rousseau in other places; (d) that it should be relative to the historical situation in which it goes on or to the problems facing society and its members at the time, e.g., Theodore Brameld and other "reconstructionists," and, in some passages, P. H. Phenix; (e) that it should be relative to individual capacity, commitments, interests, needs, native dispositions, or decisions, e.g., Rousseau, in still other places, and other proponents of "child-centered" education.

Further discussion is hardly possible, but a few comments are necessary. This debate shows the central role of political and social philosophy and of psychology and conceptions of human nature. One may, of course, hold some kind of combination of views, one for one kind or part of education, and another for another. One might, for example, be an Absolutist about liberal and a Relativist about vocational education. One can also be an Absolutist about the dispositions to be promoted, but hold that the methods to be used are relative in one of the ways indicated. If Dewey's view is not wholly relativist in sense (3), then he is most likely holding that all education should foster certain dispositions (e.g., scientific intelligence) but that it should gear its methods to the capacities and interests of the individual child.

(7) One of the modern educational wars has been what Dewey called "the case of Child vs. Curriculum" that accompanied one of the four main revolutions in the theory of education of modern times, the shift from subject-centeredness to child-centeredness. We may distinguish at least the following issues in this debate, which is an aspect of the one just described: (a) Are the dispositions to be fostered in a child to be determined by *him,* i.e., by his own choice or decision? There is a strong tendency today to say yes to this question—in existentialism, "the new morality," "free" education, and "do-your-own-thingism." (b) Are these dispositions to be determined by the *educator* but wholly through a study of the child's desires, needs, capacities, experience, situation, welfare, etc? If so, is the educator, to consider only "present" interests, etc., or also the child's future? (c) Are they to be determined by the educator and the educated *jointly,* by mutual participation and agreement alone, no matter how young the latter is? If not, at what age is the line to be drawn and on what basis? (d) The question corresponding to (a) about the methods to be used. (e) The question corresponding to (b) about the methods to be used. (f) The question corresponding to (c) about the methods to be used. It should be observed that these questions, some of which overlap, are normative and must be answered, as indicated earlier, on the basis of normative premises from ethics and social philosophy and factual premises from the empirical sciences and any other source thought to be available. In any case, they are clearly the most pressing educational questions of the present time. Closely related to them, of course, is the question whether any part or kind of education is to be compulsory or not.

(8) We saw that reasoned answers to question (2) presuppose normative premises stating the more ultimate aims or principles of education, and that these in turn depend on yet more basic normative premises that do not mention education, like the principle of utility and Kant's categorical imperative. Here is a large area for debate, of course, but since the basic issues are not specifically educational, we can hardly stop to look at them, except to say that they will be of two kinds in a way that is not always noticed. We must distinguish, at least prima facie, between what

is morally good or morally right and what is good in a nonmoral sense; between the morally good life and a life that is desirable, good, or worthwhile in itself in the sense in which a pleasant, happy, contemplative life, or a life of excellent activity or exercises of one's powers, may and have been said to be the good life; in this sense it is not a pleonasm to say, as many have, that the morally virtuous life is the good or best life.

There is, of course, the view that the morally good or right way for a person to live simply *is* to do what will give him the good life in this sense, but this view (ethical egoism) is only one among many possible positions, and a dubious one at that. Except on this view, at any rate, there will be two kinds of ultimate normative issues, moral ones and nonmoral ones. The former are illustrated by the debate in ethics between the utilitarians, the ethical egoists, and deontologists like Kant, the latter by the debate in value theory about the good—whether it is pleasure, excellent activity, virtue, self-realization, etc.

However these two sorts of issues are resolved, there is likely to be agreement that education, considered as a whole, should foster both the dispositions required by or conducive to the moral life and those required by or conducive to the good life, whatever these are. The most serious disagreement with this position would come from certain Relativists, e.g., from those who hold, as Aristotle does, that the virtues of the good citizen and those involved in the moral life or in the good life do not coincide, and that, when they do not, the former must be given precedence in education. This is why Eliot, who rather surprisingly accepts the principle of "the relativity of educational theory and practice to a prevailing order" (p. 95), tries so hard to show that the good citizen and the good man are the same in any society. If one adds, as it is plausible to do, that, inasmuch as being alive, healthy, and able to make a living are conditions of leading a moral life and of having a good one, education should also foster certain physical and vocational dispositions. Then one arrives at the threefold view of the aims of education borrowed earlier from Eliot. Even if one accepts this rather common view one is not out of the woods, however; one must still wrestle, as Eliot so helpfully does, with the problem of the interrelation and possible conflict of the three aims, and also of the means of realizing them. For example, one must decide what, if anything, is the primary aim of education: character, knowledge, excellence, the general good, personal fulfilment, success, or pleasure.

(9) More specific matters relating to the aims and means of education in connection with questions (2) and (3) we must leave untouched, for example, questions about the curriculum, about the places of the arts, humanities, and sciences, about teaching methods, or about stages in the ordering of education. But we must at least mention some issues relating to questions (4) and (5). If we list the outstanding revolutions in educational theory of modern times, then, besides the movement toward child-centeredness, the rise of secularism, and the introduction of science and other modern subjects into the curriculum, we must add the advent of a belief in universal education as an answer to question (4). For, until relatively recently, Occidental education was always thought of as virtually a prerogative of a larger or smaller male, white, elite class, defined in one way or another. The adoption of a belief in universal education, generally thought of as in large part compulsory, free, and public, is one of the reasons our educational theory is so much of a problem. In a sense, all societies have always provided everyone—women, slaves, peasants—with some kind of education. They have all been taught to walk erect, to speak a language, to obey instructions, to cook, to hunt, to farm, to practice certain rites, and so on. Again, the example of wolf children proves this. The issue is not whether everyone is to be educated, but what education each is to have, and how much choice he is to have in the matter. What is special about the doctrine of universal education is the belief that everyone is to have or at least to be offered a formal education of one or another of a few general types, at least up to a certain age or stage, the main differences of opinion being about the cost to him, the amount of compulsion involved, just what kinds of education to provide, and where to set the point at which one is on one's own.

As for question (5)—one aspect of it is whether education or a certain kind or part of education should be public or not, whether the state should be an educator in the sense of regulating and supporting some or all of the educational enterprise within its bounds. The Greeks tended to answer in the affirmative, the Romans in the negative. The typical modern answer is that at least a large part of education should be public, making it a question whether this part of education can be in any way religious, and whether private systems of education should be left free in their choice of dispositions to be fostered or of means to be used in doing so.

Other problems relating to question (5) are those of the amount and kind of training educators are to have, how teachers are to be recruited, what salaries and what status they are to receive. As has been indicated, however, the most crucial problem here is the extent to which each one of us, however young, is to be his own educator—how far Bianca in *The Taming of the Shrew* is right for all children when she says,

Why, gentlemen, you do me double wrong,
To strive for that which resteth in my choice.
I am no breeching scholar in the schools;
I'll not be tied to hours nor 'pointed times,
But learn my lessons as I please myself
(III, i, lines 16–20).

BIBLIOGRAPHY

Background material, historical or systematic, may be found in E. P. Cubberly, *The History of Education* (New York, 1920); S. J. Curtis and M. E. A. Boultwood, *A Short History of Educational Ideas,* 3rd ed. (London, 1961); W. K. Frankena, *Three Historical Philosophies of Education* (Chicago, 1965); J. W. Tibble, *The Study of Education* (London, 1966).

Works referred to in the text are: M. J. Adler, "In Defense of the Philosophy of Education," *41st Yearbook of National Society for Study of Education,* Part I (Chicago, 1942). Aristotle, *Nicomachean Ethics; Politics;* any edition. Theodore Brameld, *Education as Power* (New York, 1965). John Dewey, *Democracy and Education* (New York, 1916). T. S. Eliot, *To Criticize the Critic, and Other Writings* (New York, 1965). Moses Hadas, *Old Wine, New Bottles* (New York, 1963). R. M. Hutchins, *The Conflict in Education* (New York, 1953); *The Higher Learning in America* (New Haven, 1962). W. Jaeger, *Paideia: The Ideals of Greek Culture,* trans. Gilbert Highet, 3 vols. (New York, 1939–44). Immanuel Kant, *Education* (Ann Arbor, Mich., 1960). H. I. Marrou, *A History of Education in Antiquity* (New York, 1964). J. S. Mill, *A System of Logic* (London, 1843). J. H. Newman, *The Idea of a University* (1852; Garden City, N.Y., 1959). R. S. Peters, *Education as Initiation* (London, 1964); idem, *The Concept of Education* (London and New York, 1967); idem, *Authority, Responsibility, and Education* (London, 1959; New York, 1966). P. H. Phenix, *Education and the Common Good* (New York, 1961). Plato, *Meno; Protagoras; Republic;* many editions. J. J. Rousseau, *Émile* (1762), trans. and ed. W. Boyd (New York, 1962). C. P. Snow, *The Two Cultures and the Scientific Revolution* (Cambridge and New York, 1959). Herbert Spencer, *Education: Intellectual, Moral, and Physical* (1861; New York, 1884). Lionel Trilling, *Beyond Culture* (New York, 1965). W. H. Woodward, *Studies in Education during the Age of the Renaissance, 1400–1600* (New York, 1967).

WILLIAM K. FRANKENA

[See also **Imprinting;** Irrationalism; Pre-Platonic Conceptions; Progress; **Psychological Theories;** Right and Good; **Utilitarianism.**]

EMPATHY

EMPATHY IS the idea that the vital properties which we experience in or attribute to any person or object outside ourselves are the projections of our own feelings and thoughts.

The idea was first elaborated by Robert Vischer in *Das optische Formgefühl* (1872) as a psychological theory of art which asserts that because the dynamics of the formal relations in a work of art suggest muscular and emotional attitudes in a viewing subject, that subject experiences those feelings as qualities of the object. Aesthetic pleasure may thus be explained as objectified self-enjoyment in which subject and object are fused.

In the social sciences a similar conception called in English "empathic understanding" refers to our deliberate attempts to identify ourselves with another, accounting for his actions by our own immediate experience of our motivations and attitudes in similar circumstances as we remember or imagine them. The English term is a translation of the German *nacherleben* as used in the works of Max Weber and Wilhelm Dilthey (cf. Maurice Natanson, *Philosophy of the Social Sciences: A Reader,* 1963). All general behavior-maxims are the results of an investigator's ability to "relive" a situation. This idea is accepted by many social scientists as the basis of a method claimed to be unique to those sciences. Empathic understanding has been made the ground for ethics and personality theory as well as for historical and sociological explanations.

In popular usage the idea refers to the emotional resonance between two people, when, like strings tuned to the same frequency, each responds in perfect sympathy to the other and each reinforces the responses of the other. A good example of this occurs in the statement: "Aleatoric concert music, like jazz, demands a strong empathy between performer and listener" (Houkom, p. 10).

The word "empathy" (feeling-in) was coined by the American psychologist, Edward Titchener, as a translation of the German *Einfühlung.*

The theory of *Einfühlung* arose in the latter part of the nineteenth century in Germany, and, like most German thought of that century had its roots in Kantian philosophy. Kant's assertion that pure beauty is the beauty of form was variously interpreted. Those who developed the notion of empathy refused to find the source of our aesthetic pleasure in form considered solely as mathematical relations, as the Herbartians did, or in form as the bearer of Idea, as the Hegelians did. They saw form as the vehicle for the expression of feelings and emotions. Kant also declared that the judgment of beauty is grounded in the subject making the judgment, not in the object (Kant, pp. 45–46). With this notion as well as with his assumption that the mind's objects must agree with the forms and categories of the mind he enunciated ideas which, as their full import and romantic interpretations, such as Schiller's, unfolded, were to characterize later German philosophy and aesthetics. Thenceforth the new philosophy explored the formative activities of the mind, and the new aesthetics elucidated the process of artistic creation and the resulting work of art primarily in relation to the human subject. This new orientation meant that aesthetics turned away from the classical idea of imitation, which explained art in its relation to nature. The theorists who believed the content of art was human feelings and emotions found their main problem was that of expression. They viewed the aesthetic problem as part of a larger question. Not only works of art but the forms of nature are incapable of experiencing human feelings. How, then, can they express them?

In 1872 Robert Vischer, following a suggestion of his father, Friedrich Vischer, proposed an answer. The explanation, he said, must lie in some unconscious process of the person who views these forms. He must endow them with their vital content by an involuntary act of transference of which he is not at the time aware. He named this process *Einfühlung*.

The *Ästhetik* (1903–06) of Theodor Lipps is the most extensive analysis of empathy, presented with a host of examples from the visual arts. Lipps thought of psychology as philosophy made scientific. Its business was the uncovering and describing of one's inner experiences. Yet his analysis of empathy is laden with the vestiges of philosophical speculation and his thought is frequently unclear.

All that I experience, he says, is permeated by my own life. Why? Because an object as it exists for me is the resultant of two factors, something sensuously given and my own activity. The first is merely the material that my activity uses to construct the object as it is for me. Consequently my experience of that object is an experience of a self-activity projected as an attribute of the object. This is the first fact of empathy.

The sensible appearance of an object originates activity in me. It asks to be "apperceived" in a particular way. If it is a line it asks me to apprehend the bend of its curvature; if a large hall, I grasp its spaciousness through a feeling of expansion. If I see a tree swaying in the breeze I carry out its movements in imaginative imitative activities. In these responsive actions not only do I feel alive, for activity is associated with life, but I also enliven the object by my vital actions. These actions, being incipient, are actually tendencies of my will. Empathy is the projection of my feeling and willing ego in an object. But there is no twofold consciousness of self and object. Empathy, he says, is the intuited fact that object and self are one.

If the elicited responses are in accord with my incli-

nations, I experience feelings of pleasure and freedom. This harmony between stimulus and my own inner urges is positive empathy. If the responses are contrary to my basic drives I feel displeasure and the empathy is negative. It is important to recognize negative empathy. One must account for displeasure by the same principle that accounts for pleasure. But if an object can elicit a response which is appropriate to it but contrary to my inclinations it would seem the material of appearance must have far greater active power than Lipps has assigned to it.

He mentions three levels of empathy. The first is general apperceptive empathy when the form of a common object evokes a unique recreative activity, and the object presents itself merely to be perceived. The second is natural empathy. Here objects summon from my understanding the willful, striving activity of fitting them into a scheme of reality or a causal order. This is the level where natural objects are humanized. The highest level is empathy for the sensible appearance of a human being, when we respond to the gestures, facial expressions, and tone of voice in another.

Each of these levels is exploited in art and exhibited in our responses to art. But the way I attend to a work of art is different from my experience of an object in the natural world. Before a work of art an ideal self, existent only in the act of aesthetic contemplation, experiences an ideal world. This is Lipps' way of accounting for the difference in reactions one might have to a painting of a raging storm, and to a raging storm itself.

An Englishwoman, Violet Paget (1856–1935), who wrote under the name of Vernon Lee, presented the notion of empathic projection independently of Lipps. Her description is not entangled with metaphysical notions of the self, or with the identity of self and object. Her early ideas, first stated in "Beauty and Ugliness," which was written in collaboration with C. Anstruther-Thompson (*Contemporary Review*, **72** [Oct. and Nov. 1897], 544–69, 669–88), limit empathy to the projection of our own body sensations, particularly the imagined muscular adjustments we tend to make before a work of art. Later, influenced by Lipps, she considered these muscular accommodations as symptoms of emotions and ideas, which are our ejects. Actions like raising our eyes and lifting our heads when we look at a mountain towering above us give us an awareness of rising which then coalesces with the object of our attention. The general idea of rising which has accumulated in our minds from this and past experiences and from anticipated future ones, is finally transferred to the mountain and occasions a resulting emotional fullness.

Wilhelm Dilthey and Max Weber along with some

other German philosophers who were interested in the special problems of the *Geisteswissenschaften* ("humanistic and social studies") advanced the method of empathic understanding at about the same time Lipps was presenting his theory of empathy. Probably the source of both ideas lay in the statement made in the beginning of the eighteenth century by Giambattista Vico that man knows only what he makes, his history, his art, his languages, his customs; and in Vico's attempt to understand the poetry and customs of the men of the past by the reconstruction of circumstances of the past.

The basis of the method depends upon an investigator's sympathetic identification with the point of view and motivations of the human subjects of his study. An historian, seeking to explain the actions of someone in the past on a certain occasion should first project himself imaginatively into the situation that confronted that person. Discovering his own imaginative reactions in those circumstances as vicariously relived, the investigator has a basis for explaining the actions of his subject. One understands why Caesar crossed the Rubicon by becoming Caesar. Or, as Croce says, to understand a Sicilian first make yourself into a Sicilian. Historical novelists adopt this method as a device for artistic purposes to provide them with materials for convincing character portraits.

The differences between empathic understanding and the first conception of empathy are two. Empathic understanding derives from an alleged re-experiencing of the motivations and mental purposes of another and on this basis makes a knowledge claim about the causes of that person's action. The original notion of empathy with another person limits its identification to the feelings and emotions of the other, and makes no knowledge claim. When I identify in feeling with a laughing countenance I do not claim to use the laughter to tell me something about the laughing person.

The nontechnical, popular idea of empathy appears to presuppose even more than the other two conceptions. It refers to that immediacy of communication between two people that dispenses with the need of conceptualization through abstract ideas conveyed by language. It is part of the anti-intellectualist current which has risen so strongly in our century that emphasizes the greater importance of sublogical, nonconceptual "thinking" over intellectualization. Deeper knowledge, it claims, is "co-naissance." It is also part of the mid-twentieth-century emphasis on communication, as this term refers to the dynamic interrelationships between mind and mind that language and outward signs fail to convey. A good actor, knowing that one does not project an emotional state to an audience merely by imitating the actions of one in that state, "lives" his part, becoming the character he portrays, directly experiencing states of feeling but keeping some residue of objectivity to prevent his behavior from disintegrating altogether. Doing this he affects his audience more successfully.

In talking of our response to drama we often refer to one's identification with the characters of a play as an empathic response. However, this is actually a case in which the spectator is not projecting his own feelings into the characters but is experiencing feelings of the characters as though they were his own. He projects himself into a character through an imaginative identification. This has been our traditional response to Western drama since the time of Aristotle. One does not merely witness a drama; he experiences it with personal involvement. Though Bertolt Brecht with his theory of the epic theater repudiated this tradition, asking his actors to recount the drama like epic storytellers and expecting his audience to think about the problem a drama presents, the continued persistence of audiences to respond emotionally to the characters in his plays attests to the strength of this long habit of response.

Empathy is a latecomer to our stock of ideas, being scarcely a hundred years old. But its origins are diverse. One could call it primitive animism made sophisticated by reformulation as a psychological theory, at least as far as feeling into natural objects goes. Poets have always enlivened the world of our experience by humanizing it. Animism is the root of poetic metaphor. Aristotle foreshadowed a discussion of empathy when he remarked how often Homer described some physical object with an adjective appropriate only to a living thing. He cites passages, such as those where the poet speaks of the arrow as "bitter," or "flying on eagerly," or "panting" (*Rhetoric* 1411b). Empathy theory interprets the affective part of all experience as the unconscious creation of metaphor.

The belief that, when one is in affective communion with another, subject and object become merged is recognized at least as early as Plato, who says of the beloved that "his lover is the mirror in whom he is beholding himself, but he is not aware of it" (*Phaedrus* 255, Jowett translation).

Sometimes the idea of sympathy, as developed in the eighteenth century by such writers as Kames and Gerard, is cited as a source of the idea of empathy. Actually the two notions are different. Empathy supposes a fusion of subject and object, while sympathy supposes a parallelism between them in which I am aware of the distinction between myself and the other. In sympathy I feel with; in empathy I feel in. Popular thought often does not respect the difference, using empathy where sympathy is meant.

The insistence by some that the distinguishing characteristic of empathy is the merging of subject and object has not seemed by others to be the important requirement. Living in the experience of another only means being in perfect sympathy with him; when one identifies with another it means he has the same kind of feelings. What is the relation of empathy to British associationism, in the context of which the theory of sympathy developed?

Lipps insisted that empathy was independent of the association of ideas. One does not first see a form and then associate emotional content with it, he says; the perception and the emotion are indistinguishable. But we do know that Lipps was a great admirer of the psychology of Hume and translated some of Hume's writings into German. It is not surprising, therefore, to find a basis for conjecturing some influence. Hume's notion that certain qualities of things are naturally fitted to produce particular feelings in us might have been the basis of Lipps' idea that sensible appearances generate appropriate activities in us. The fact that he never explained how the appearances do this leads us to assume that he never supposed there was a question here. Again, he declares that though a subject experiences vitality, power, and feeling in himself, he finds the empathic content in what is outside him. The "raging" is in the storm, he says. He then contents himself with observing that it is a remarkable fact that what we can feel only in ourselves we can again find in something else. This observation asserts that we must first experience the raging in ourselves, then, upon seeing the energy of natural forces of a storm, we apprehend it in those forces. But the present raging is not identical with past raging. They are only similar, and may be connected by association.

On the other hand, empathy repudiates two assumptions inherent in the British tradition. One is the passivity of the subject of experience. Associationism made the active work of the mind as automatic as if it were a reflex movement responding to the contiguity and succession of impressions. Empathy gives the subject all the activity which it denies, or at least reduces to a minimum, in the object. The other is the claim that the humanizing of nature is a fallacy. Ruskin described this "pathetic fallacy" which occurs when we see something under the influence of emotion or contemplative fancy. "Cruel, crawling foam" is an untrue description of foam, for there is no such power in the foam. It is falsely imputed. Empathy accepts the imputation but does not call it a fallacy.

Empathy enjoyed its greatest acceptance as a fundamental principle of the theory of art in the early part of this century. Variations of it appeared in the writings of Karl Groos and Johannes Volkelt in Germany, Victor Basch in France, and Herbert Langfeld in America. It has a common ground with Santayana's definition of beauty as "pleasure objectified." It was congenial to the voluntaristic activism that the Nietzschean and Bergsonian philosophies were popularizing. It was accepted as accounting for the appeal of the new decorative style of *l'art nouveau*. One of the leaders of the *Jugendstil* in Germany, August Endell, was a student of Lipps. With the increasing dehumanization of content as twentieth-century art developed, empathy was first reduced to equal acceptance with the new principle of abstraction. It has come under strong criticism by those influenced by Gestalt psychology. They object to the assumption that the expressive character of an object is not inherent in its form. Those who accept empathy today generally concede it is only one factor accounting for our responses.

Empathic understanding has also met sharp criticism. One cannot identify one's self with another. Consequently there can be no resulting verifiable knowledge of the kind a science seeks. One can only claim at best a possibility. In spite of such criticism empathic understanding has strong supporters.

Empathy remains an idea to be reckoned with in our traffic with art, with nature, in our interpersonal relations, and in our inquiries in the social sciences.

BIBLIOGRAPHY

The classical works for the development of empathy in Germany are Robert Vischer, *Das optische Formgefühl*, reprinted in *Drei Schriften zum ästhetischen Formproblem* (Halle, 1927), and Theodor Lipps, *Raumästhetik und geometrisch-optische Täuschungen* (Leipzig, 1897), and *Ästhetik*, 2 vols. (Hamburg and Leipzig, 1903–06; 2nd ed. 1914–20). Vernon Lee [Violet Paget], *Beauty and Ugliness and other Studies in Psychological Aesthetics* (London and New York, 1912), written with C. Anstruther-Thompson; and *The Beautiful* (Cambridge, 1913) are the sources for her form of the theory. Herbert Langfeld, *The Aesthetic Attitude* (New York, 1920), is the best introduction in English. The fullest recent consideration is David A. Stewart, *Preface to Empathy* (New York, 1956).

Shorter selections of Lipps translated into English may be found in E. F. Carritt, *Philosophies of Beauty* (London and New York, 1930) pp. 252–58; Melvin Rader, *A Modern Book of Aesthetics*, 3rd ed. (New York, 1960), pp. 574–82; and Karl Aschenbrenner and Arnold Isenberg, *Aesthetic Theories* (Englewood Cliffs, N.J., 1965), pp. 403–12.

For further reference see Wilhelm Worringer, *Abstraction and Empathy* (New York, 1953); Victor Basch, *Essai critique sur l'esthétique de Kant* (Paris 1927); I. Kant, *Critique of Judgment*, trans. J. H. Bernard (New York, 1951), pp. 45–46.

The development of the method of *Verstehen* and empathic understanding occurs in Wilhelm Dilthey, *Ideen über einer beschreibende und zergliedernde Psychologie* (Leipzig, 1894); and Max Weber, *Gesammelte Aufsätze zur*

Wissenschaftslehre (Tübingen, 1920). The best short statement and analysis of the idea occurs in Theodore Abel, "The Operation Called 'Verstehen'," in the *American Journal of Sociology*, **54** (1948–49), 211–18, reprinted in Edward H. Madden, ed., *The Structure of Scientific Thought* (Boston, 1960), pp. 158–66. The full reference for Houkom is Alf S. Houkom, "Lucas Foss and Chance Music," *Music: the A.G.O. and R.C.C.O. Magazine*, **2**, no. 2 (Feb. 1968), 10.

CHARLES EDWARD GAUSS

[See also Iconography; **Impressionism;** Metaphor; **Mimesis;** Psychological Schools; *Ut pictura poesis*.]

ENLIGHTENMENT

ENGLISH writers of the period speak of "enlightening" and "enlightened peoples," also of the "historical age"; in French *l'âge de lumière, l'âge philosophique, siècle des lumières, siècle de la bienfaisance, siècle de l'humanité;* in German *Aufklärung* and *Zeitalter der Kritik;* in Italian *Illuminismo.* Enlightenment denotes a historical period in the same sense as the terms Reformation, Renaissance, and Baroque. It is broadly co-extensive with the eighteenth century, beginning with the Glorious Revolution of 1688, the writings of Locke and Bayle, and ending with either the Declaration of Independence of 1776 or the French Revolution of 1789 or the defeat of postrevolutionary France in 1815 and the romantic reaction. Some historians, following Troeltsch, regard the eighteenth century (rather than the sixteenth) as the beginning of modern history. In this view, the individualism and toleration of the Renaissance and Reformation, the cosmopolitanism following the opening up of the New World and the East as well as the scientific advances of the seventeenth century were merely programmatic and did not lead to significant social, cultural, and political changes until the eighteenth century. Naturally there is no monolithic spirit of the age to be discerned; traditional ideas persisted, while the tendencies of romanticism made their appearance and left a strong imprint. The Enlightenment then represents a movement within the period to which it lent its name and to which it imparted its lasting significance. Its aspirations and anxieties, its debates and methods are still with us in their original form; though its values have been belittled by subsequent reaction, they appear increasingly meaningful to the survivors of the catastrophes of recent history. The Enlightenment from the outset has been a European movement. Unlike earlier periods, which affected particular aspects of life or certain classes of the population, it witnessed and heralded sweeping social change. It did not become effective at the same rate in the various countries of Europe.

It originated in England both as regards structural change and the reform of intellectual and moral ideas. While it was a reality in the English-speaking world, it remained a program and sometimes a utopia in other parts of Europe. The Enlightenment was a self-conscious and highly articulate movement, presenting common basic conceptions, a common methodological approach, and reform proposals based on commonly held values. Its thought is basically a social philosophy, starting from social premises, concerned with social ends, and viewing even religion and art in social terms. (This article is devoted to a delineation of the basic tenets of this philosophy; it does not offer a circumstantial account of the course of the Enlightenment in different countries, nor does it deal in detail with the fields of art, religion, and natural science.) The Enlightenment reached its climax in the mid-eighteenth century in Paris and Scotland; in both these centers coordinated fellowships of thinkers and men of the world developed the body of thought which is peculiar to the Enlightenment. The ideas and quotations in this article are therefore derived from the writings of the *philosophes* responsible for Diderot's and D'Alembert's *Encyclopédie* of 1751 and of the Scottish thinkers from Francis Hutcheson and David Hume onwards, including their English followers Edward Gibbon and Jeremy Bentham. The thought of the Italian and German Enlightenment, though distinguished by outstanding contributors, was derivative, starting from English and French models and merging them with the respective national traditions. In Italy Cesare Beccaria and Pietro and Alessandro Verri followed in the footsteps of Steele and Addison's *Spectator* and *Tatler,* of Montesquieu, Hume, and the *Encyclopédie.* In Germany the Enlightenment, though never dominant, was largely influenced by the University of Göttingen founded by George II of England in 1734, whose historians and students (including Justus Möser and Freiherr vom Stein) echoed the thought of David Hume, William Robertson, Adam Ferguson, Gibbon, and Adam Smith; Johann Christoph Gottsched started by translating the *Spectator,* the young Lessing translated Francis Hutcheson and Diderot; Kant set out, after Leibniz, from Hume and Rousseau, Mendelssohn from Locke and Shaftesbury; Winckelmann was steeped in English thought, and so was Herder in addition to his debt to the French life sciences.

Forerunners. According to D'Alembert's "Discours préliminaire" to the *Encyclopédie,* the Enlightenment brought to fruition the aspirations of two earlier periods of enlightenment, namely, classical Greece and the Renaissance and Reformation. Greek ideas, supported by such Latin authors as Seneca and Vergil, made a great impact upon the thought of the eighteenth century. While the old metaphysics, Hobbes's "Aristotelity," was relegated to the background, the individualism and the conception of knowledge as being merely provisional, the Platonic application of mathematics, his Eros and Kalokagathia, an Aristotelian conception of nature, the anthropology and ethics of Stoic philosophy, a Protagorean humanism as well as Plutarch's notions of nation and liberty—echoes of all these views reveal the continuity of the thought of the period with the past. However, in contrast to Renaissance and humanism, the interest in classical models was not a matter of imitation of the Ancients. The *"Querelle des Anciens et des Modernes"* had exposed the treasures of classical art and scholarship to a new critical evaluation of their intrinsic value. Voltaire and his followers went so far as to reject the Greek heritage because of its failure to order its social and political problems; others found refuge from the discontents of their own time in its beauty and thought. A spate of outstanding writing on the history of Greece and Rome all through the period serves as witness to the living presence of the classical world. The young Gibbon gave expression to the representative modern attitude: "I think that the study of literature, that habit of alternatively becoming a Greek or a Roman, a disciple of Zeno or of Epicurus, is admirably adapted to develop and exercise . . . the rare power of going back to simple ideas, of seizing and combining first principles" (Gibbon, *Essai sur l'étude de la littérature* [1761], Para. XLVII).

Traces of the thought of medieval forerunners from Roger Bacon onwards can be widely discerned in Enlightenment writings. The decisive forerunners were Descartes, Leibniz, and Newton in the field of methodology, Francis Bacon and Locke both for their substantive philosophy and their empirical approach, Grotius, Bodin, and Hobbes for their social and political thought. In general terms, the period was characterized by a shift of emphasis from old to new anthropological metaphysics, from the preoccupation with natural science to history and the social and life sciences, a turning away from dogma and traditional conventions, a critical reappraisal of established authority in the fields of religion, politics, philosophy, and the arts. The human situation and man's liberty, the place of man in society, the interrelation of social and natural phenomena, their "uniformity amidst variety" come to condition the guiding lines of thought. The Enlightenment was an iconoclastic movement intent both on interpreting and ushering in social change. Radical

structural changes were occurring in society; they help to explain why certain ideas came to be regarded as relevant while others were rejected. In England the new ideas were largely an expression of contemporary reality; elsewhere, by way of reforms, and often only of utopias, they merely gave evidence of a challenge to a historical situation which lagged behind a new consciousness of what was possible and desirable.

Underlying Structural Change. Gibbon, in *The History of the Decline and Fall of the Roman Empire* (1776–88), Ch. 38, distinguished three levels of social change: the technological improvements, the legal-political-economic infrastructure, and the representative achievements of culture. There was visible change occurring in the first level throughout the period. The scientific inventions, especially of the seventeenth century, found their practical application in an increasing control of the forces of nature. The employment of new techniques and tools produced greater efficiency in agriculture. The modes of industrial production changed gradually from manufacture to "machinofacture." New roads and canals were constructed to carry the growing internal and foreign trade. The improved communications opened up an era of travel (including the Grand Tour) all over Europe. The advances in navigation and the art of war brought the continents of the earth within regular and easy reach of one another, thus consummating the previous great discoveries. These technological advances represented clearly "more and better" in comparison with earlier times; there was visible a well-defined progress which gave its imprint to a distinct stage of historical development or evolution. The traditional organization of society proved to be inadequate in the face of technological change. Small agricultural holdings gave place to large-scale farming, and surplus rural population converged on the towns. Competition and the division of labor made the security and rigidity of the guild system obsolete. The new commercial ventures involved risk-taking by individuals; but individual initiative, though unbounded in its aspirations, found itself hemmed in by a network of governmental regulations and inhibitions. Thus the power of the state came to be felt as abuse and was assailed by reform proposals and by rebellion.

Legal, fiscal, administrative, political, religious, and educational reforms were put into practice, by parliament and private initiative in Britain and the small republics, and elsewhere by enlightened despots like Frederick the Great, Joseph II, Leopold II, and Catherine. Many reform proposals, from the Abbé St. Pierre to Bentham, remained only on paper. Where the new aspirations were blocked (as, e.g., Turgot's reform in 1776) rebellions resulted, and finally, the

French Revolution. While technological change proceeded under its own momentum, the reform of institutions involved human judgment and needed action to give it direction. The desirability and possible scope of reform posed questions which could not be evaded.

The traditional class structure was being eroded in the process. The circle of citizens with a say in public affairs widened with the rise of the new bourgeoisie and its growing affluence. The progressive levelling of the distinctions of rank was visibly preparing the ground for the polarization of the population into the two classes of the rich, the employers, the exploiters and the poor, the employed, the exploited. The new middle class was imposing its values upon society, using commerce and education as vehicles of social change. In effect a new society came into being. Voltaire observed it in London in 1734 (*Lettres philosophiques*, Lettre X), and Hume, in his seminal essay "On National Characters" in 1748, described England as "a mixture of monarchy, aristocracy, and democracy. The people in authority are composed of gentry and merchants. All sects of religion are to be found among them; and the great liberty which every man enjoys, allows him to display the manners peculiar to him. Hence the English, of any people in the universe, have the least national character, unless this very singularity may pass for such" (Hume, *Essays Moral and Political* [1741–42], 3rd ed. [1748], Essay XXI).

Alessandro Verri noted in 1766 that in London tolerance and civil liberties were a reality while in Paris they remained philosophical ideas (quoted by Sergio Romagnoli, ed., *Il Caffè* [reprint 1960], p. XLVI). On the cultural plane, far-reaching structural changes accompanied the rise of the new social order, affecting the substance and teaching of scientific thought, of religion, and of art. The man of letters and the artist acquired a measure of freedom from court and clerical patronage, and emerged as new professional groups. The hold of clericalism lessened, and so did papal domination following the widespread elimination of the Jesuit order. Dissent was thriving in the new, less hierarchical society; religion gained a new and deepened meaning in various strata of society, from philosophical deism and Rousseau's *religion de Genève* to the popular revival movements of Pietism and Methodism.

These currents were advanced by the development of the printed media of communication which, like other earlier inventions and discoveries, assumed only now their full potential. A spate of printed material sprang up, periodicals, encyclopedias, novels, histories, newspapers as well as book clubs and circulating libraries. Periodicals were numbered by the hundreds;

in 1776, the year of American independence and Adam Smith's *Inquiry into the Nature and Causes of the Wealth of Nations*, a daily average of 33,000 copies of newspapers was sold in Britain; Voltaire's books reached a sale of one and a half million copies within seven years. Instant translations and personal contact between authors of different nations effected a cosmopolitanism far beyond that achieved in previous periods by the common use of Latin and French. Steele's and Addison's periodicals, *The Tatler* (1709–11) and *The Spectator* (1711–12), exerted an epoch-making influence as models of truly civilized living; they were soon imitated in Germany, France, and Italy. The universities in general were not instrumental in fostering change, largely because of their ties with the established churches. Where these commitments were loose, as in Scotland and Göttingen, they played a leading role.

Intellectuals overcame their isolation by forming circles and meeting in coffeehouses and, in France, in salons. Thus the French *philosophes* combined in producing the Enlightenment's central enterprise, the *Encyclopédie* edited by Diderot and D'Alembert from 1751 onwards. The leading French authors, scientists, architects, artists, from Voltaire to Rousseau, from Buffon to Lamarck, took a hand in the enterprise. Previously established encyclopedias, in particular Louis Moreri's *Grand dictionnaire historique* (1674), had devoted their space mainly to biographical, genealogical, mythological, theological, geographical, and military-historical entries. (Even Bayle's *Dictionnaire historique et critique*, 1695–97, though contemptuous of Moreri, did not break with the established tradition.) By contrast, the *Encyclopédie* contained systematic and analytical articles on "Man," "Society," "Method," "Nature," as well as on the natural and social sciences and the various handicrafts. Like all the literature treated in this article, the *Encyclopédie* was an avant-garde piece of writing, the contents of which allow us to reconstruct a profile of the Enlightenment as a movement. (Side by side with these productions, the period witnessed the growth of a new cheap entertainment literature as well as a greater diffusion of writings in the old tradition, which aimed at the new enlarged reading public. Although popular reading habits and crowd behavior have come to fascinate some modern historians, such publications are ignored here, as they hardly contributed to the march of ideas, that is, to the *incivilimento* due to man's creative liberty.)

The Science of Human Nature and the Science of Legislation. Continental thinkers like to take as the starting-point of modern thought man's three "humiliations," namely, the recognition that the earth is not the center of the universe; that man, rather than being created in the divine image, is a creature of nature like the other animals; and that his reason is subject to the passions and subconscious urges. In the view of the Enlightenment these "humiliations" appear as intellectual conquests which spell out man's peculiar responsibilities: these are the scientific discovery of truths, the realization of individual happiness in a viable society, and the exploration of the conditions and limits of liberty. In place of a static conception of a divine, immutable order a new sociological perspective takes over; society and culture are regarded as products of history, i.e., of man's free and creative will, and as subject to change. The existence of man in society, what he is, and what he can do, become the basic questions to be explored. "Instead of following the high *a priori* road [of metaphysical enquiry], would it not be better humbly to investigate the desires, fears, passions and opinions of the human being, and to discover from them what means an able legislator can employ to connect the private happiness of each individual with the observance of those laws which secure the well-being of the whole?" (Gibbon, "Abstract of Blackstone's Commentaries," quoted by William Holdsworth, *A History of English Law*, London [1938], XII, 753).

The *Encyclopédie* views man as "a feeling, deliberating, thinking being who walks freely the surface of the world . . . the first . . . among all other animals, who lives in society, has invented sciences and arts, has a goodness and malevolence quite his own, has given himself masters, has made laws for himself . . . to know him in all his qualities one must know him in his passion" (article "Homme"). Man is the product of nature and of history, as Hume points out in his epoch-making *Treatise of Human Nature* (1739); "There is a general course of nature in human actions . . . There are also characters peculiar to different nations and particular persons, as well as common to mankind . . . the different stations of life influence the whole fabric, external and internal. . . . Man cannot live without society, and cannot be associated without government . . . [whose] actions and objects cause such a diversity, and at the same time maintain such an uniformity in human life" (Book II, Part III, Sec. I).

The course of nature, individual and national character, the inequality of classes, man's sociability, uniformity amidst variety—these notions of the science of human nature enter into the modern social sciences as basic propositions. It is necessary to know man's natural propensities and his historical achievements. They teach, however, that "man may mistake the objects of his pursuit; he may misapply his industry, and misplace his improvements. . . . [Therefore] it is of more importance to know the condition to which we ourselves should aspire than that which our ancestors may be supposed to have left" (Adam Ferguson, *An Essay on the History of Civil Society* [1767], Part I, Sec. I). It is not enough to ask what man is and what he can do. The answers to these questions supply the raw material for the crucial enterprise of giving direction to human activity or at least preventing it from self-destruction. Within the limits set by nature and history there is a dichotomy between what *is* and what *ought* to be. Men "cannot change their natures. All that they can do is to change their situation" (Hume, *Treatise*, Book III [1740], Part II, Sec. VII).

The *ought* of the Enlightenment is therefore not an appeal so much to the individual, the product of nature and history, as to the advisors of the legislator who can change the environment in which men and nations live. Thus Adam Smith defines "political economy . . . as a branch of the science of a statesman or legislator" (Book IV, Introduction), who must have the welfare of both the individual and society in mind, must balance and protect the concerns of various groups of people and of various localities with a view to adjudicating what the state should take upon itself and what it should leave to individual initiative. If the article "Homme" in the *Encyclopédie* had dealt with facts of nature and history, that on "Société" establishes the general principle of social action: "The rationale of human society is based upon this general and simple principle: I want to be happy; but I live with men who, like myself, want to be happy as well, each according to his own light: let us then search for the means of procuring our happiness by procuring theirs, or at least without ever harming it." The balanced emphasis on both man and society preserved Enlightenment thought from the extremes of nineteenth-century individualism and holism.

Progress and Perfectibility. "Man is susceptible of improvement and has in himself a principle of progression and a desire for perfection. . . . He is in some measure the artificer of his own frame as well as his fortune, and is destined from the first age of his being to invent and contrive. . . . He is perpetually busied in reformations, and is continually wedded to his errors" (Ferguson [1767], Part I, Sec. I). The human condition is not necessarily immutable or retrogressive owing to the Fall. On the contrary, undeniable and cumulative progress can be seen to occur in the fields of science, technology, and the applied arts. Progress is a fact of history. The cosmos evolves, the species is transformed, the individual grows from helpless imperfection to his full stature. Mechanical and biological models and analogies irresistibly influence the understanding of the historical process. What distinguishes mankind particularly from the animal world, says Buffon, is the perfectibility of the species and of the institutions of society (Buffon, *Histoire naturelle*, XIII, Paris [1765], 3–4). The concept of perfectibility as a process implies the actual imperfection of society, just as enlightenment, according to Kant (*Was ist Aufklärung?*, 1784) denotes a process rather than an end product. In his influential writings on history, Turgot compares progress to a storm-lashed sea; men must commit a thousand errors to arrive at the truth ("Plan de deux discours sur l'histoire universelle" [1751], in *Oeuvres de Turgot*, Paris, I [1913], 277, 314). D'Alembert emphasizes the provisional and, perhaps, exceptional character of enlightened progress: "It took centuries to make a beginning; it will take centuries to bring it to an end. . . . Barbarism lasts for centuries; it seems to be our natural element; reason and good taste are only passing" (Discours préliminaire, *Encyclopédie*, 1751). "Man's progress . . . has been irregular and various . . . yet the experience of four thousand years should enlarge our hopes and diminish our apprehensions . . . [though] the merit of discovery has too often been stained with cruelty and fanaticism: and the intercourse of nations has produced the communication of disease and prejudice" (Gibbon, *Decline and Fall*, Ch. 38). Bentham expressly rejects Dr. Priestley's "expectation that man will ultimately attain a degree of happiness and knowledge which far surpasses our present conditions. . . . Perfect happiness belongs to the imaginary regions of philosophy . . . it may be possible to diminish the influence of, but not to destroy, the sad and mischievous passions" (*Influence of Time and Place in Matters of Legislation* [1802], Ch. V, *Works*, I, 193–94). The conception of progress is based upon historical experience, and not any longer on metaphysical speculation; therefore it is not necessarily cyclical or unilinear; it is a matter of judgment and probabilities like all other phenomena.

Stages of Evolution. Antoine Yves Goguet (*De l'Origine des loix, des arts, et des sciences*, Paris [1758], I, 16) distinguished two classes of positive (historical) laws, namely, those "which are, or at least ought to be, common to all the different kinds of society," and those "which are peculiar to a society which has made some progress in agriculture and commerce and in the more refined arts of life." The reconstruction of the stages of human evolution is a means of determining one's own place in the history of civilization. The task is undertaken on the basis of historical research as well as comparative and ethnological observations; where there are missing links in the record, judicious conjectures have to complement the picture. Hume, Montesquieu, Rousseau, Adam Smith, Adam Ferguson, John Millar, and others delineate subsequent stages of evolution. According to Smith "the natural course of

things is first agriculture, then manufactures, and finally foreign commerce [though] this order has been in many respects inverted" (Book III, Ch. I). Millar distinguishes the stages of barbarism and matriarchy, the pastoral age, the age of agriculture, that of the useful arts and manufactures, and finally "great opulence and the culture of the elegant arts." The tripartition, later used by Comte and Hegel, is rather usual.

"Conjectural history" does not imply a purely logical reconstruction of the origins (as has been frequently suggested). Rousseau's account of the evolution of society owes something to the uncontrolled flights of the imagination. However, in general, the conjectures used by Montesquieu, Smith, Robertson, Ferguson, et al., are not the "large" ones which are used to prove a case, but conjectures of detail based upon experience and historical probability, in the sense in which Niebuhr was to say in 1804: "I am a historian, for I can trace a complete picture from individual extant data, and I know where parts are missing and how to complement them" (*Die Briefe Barthold Georg Niebuhrs*, Berlin [1926], I, 317). Annals may be written without conjectures, history requires a judicious sense of what is possible and probable, "a just observation" and "the knowledge of important consequences" of the progress of mankind which "they build in every subsequent age on foundations formerly laid" (Ferguson [1767], Part I, Sec. I). In this sense Robertson was one of the first to trace the history of the Middle Ages as a step in the history of European civilization. The introduction of the concepts of progress and evolution did not entail a deterministic or teleological philosophy of history. In the hands of the authors of the Enlightenment, most highly developed by Millar, it amounted to a taxonomy dealing with the accumulative character of objective knowledge and rational technique, a sober illustration of especially important types of structural innovation in the course of social change.

In particular, the conception of evolutionary stages served to combat the naive attribution of cultural, political, and social innovation to the legendary legislators of previous historiography. In the process of historical reconstruction all relevant variables have to be taken into account, whether technological and biological, structural or cultural. An "infinite variety of circumstances" (Turgot) determines the organic growth of society which arises "from the instincts, not from the speculations of men . . . the circumstances in which [they] are placed . . . the result from human action, but not the executions of human design" (Ferguson; similarly Hume). Human contrivance leads to unforeseen consequences (the "heterogeneity of ends"—following Wilhelm Wundt's psychological terminology). However, this insight does not entail the helpless acceptance by *Historismus* of the status quo. For the Enlightenment it establishes the need for a closer analysis of historical sequences; it calls for the development of the theoretical social sciences whose task it is, in the words of Karl Popper, "to try to anticipate the unintended consequences of our actions" (Popper, "Reason or Revolution?," *European Journal of Sociology* [1970], 260).

Nature. Nature, reason, liberty, and utility are preeminently among the most used keywords of the period. "There is scarcely a word that is used in a vaguer way than that of Nature . . . hardly ever does it attach itself to a precise idea (*Oeuvres diverses de M. Pierre Bayle*, [1727], III, 713). The *Encyclopédie* emphasizes the many different uses of the term, ranging from physical necessity to utopian idolization, from Hobbes's awareness of man's animality to an Aristotelian conception of "what every being is in its most perfect state." One speaks of nature and natural history in the context of religion, the soul, the law, reason, sentiment, taste, virtue, happiness, innocence, society, providence, physical necessity, order, and liberty. The concept is brandished as a weapon in the urge to free mankind from the curse of original sin, against the world of conventions and of tradition, as, e.g., superstition, prejudice, the belief in miracles and the reliance on grace and revelation, the hierarchical order of society and governmental constraints of all kinds; all these are rejected as being unnatural. At the same time, nature imposes its own constraints, not only through physical necessity, not only by way of an aristocratic Epicureanism, but in the Puritan values of the rising commercial bourgeoisie; work, frugality, usefulness, sexual morality, and benevolence are regarded as natural, while passions are not.

However, in the view of the Scots and the *Encyclopédie*, nature is neutral in the sense that it needs to be explored to provide the empirical foundation of the social sciences. Hume defines the term according to the context in which it is used: justice is an *artificial* in contrast to a *natural* virtue, artificial yet not *arbitrary;* it is both socially determined and a *sine qua non* for the preservation of society. But "in another sense of the word, as no principle of the human mind is more natural than a sense of virtue, so no virtue is more natural than justice" (Hume, *Treatise*, Book III, Part II, Sec. I).

The desire for justice, that is, the awareness of suffering inflicted and the urge to restore happiness, as well as the tendencies to improvement and cultivation, are natural propensities in man which serve "to obviate the casual abuses of passion" which itself, however, is natural as well. "If we are asked therefore, where the state of nature is to be found? we may

answer, it is here; and it matters not whether we are understood to speak in the island of Great Britain, at the Cape of Good Hope, or in the Straits of Magellan" (Ferguson, 1767). The hut is as natural as the palace; the physical attributes of man are as natural as his intellectual and moral propensities and the laws which may be observed to obtain in physical and social relations. Nature is the raw material on which the science of human nature is based, and from which the understanding of the necessity, the possibility, and the limitation of the science of the legislator is derived. In Baconian terms, we must know nature in order to control it.

Liberty. The concept of liberty is hardly less ambiguous than that of nature. For some thinkers of the eighteenth century like Mandeville, Helvétius, and de Sade, it means the negative freedom from constraint and the right to self-realization. For others, like Schiller, it is self-perfection. There is a rather general consensus that the progress of civilization is due to individual initiative and spontaneous inventiveness. Liberty of action and of thought are the prerequisites for bringing about great things. However, in contrast with the rhetoric of Rousseau and the French Revolution, liberty is not regarded as an attribute of human nature. It is a gift of culture, inseparable from civilized society, the great achievement of European history since the Italian late twelfth century. According to Voltaire (*Essai sur les moeurs et l'esprit des nations* [1756], Ch. LXXXIII), the *citadins* of Italy were different from the *bourgeois* of the northern countries of Europe in that they admitted loyalty only to their own republic rather than to feudal masters. William Robertson (*A View of the Progress of Society in Europe* [1769], *Works* [1834], III, 129ff., 274ff.) and Gibbon (*Decline and Fall*, Ch. 56) take up the same theme, which is developed with greater theoretical finesse by John Millar (*The Origin of the Distinction of Ranks* [1778], Ch. V, Sec. III) and especially by Adam Smith in the *Wealth of Nations*, Book III, Ch. III: "On the Rise and Progress of Cities and Towns after the Fall of the Roman Empire"; Smith ascribes also "the present grandeur of Holland" to its "republican form of government" (Book V, Ch. II, Article IV). Rousseau in the *Second Discourse* (1755) and the *Lettre à D'Alembert* (1758) and Jean-Louis Delolme in his *Constitution de l'Angleterre* (1771) feel authorized to pronounce on questions of liberty because of their experience as citizens of the small republic of Geneva. All are agreed that the process which started in the city republics has come to its perfection in the England of the day, the only large country ever to have secured liberty to its citizens. This widespread literature dealing with the constitutions of the free peoples found its culmination in Jean Charles Léonard Simonde de Sismondi's *Histoire des républiques italiennes au moyen âge* (*History of the Italian Republics*, 1803–18), which treats history as the history of liberty, a notion which inspired the work of Benjamin Constant, Auguste Comte, and Hegel.

Though a precious gift of culture, liberty, for the Enlightenment, is not an end in itself. It is a means to the attainment of happiness, a necessary, though not a sufficient, condition of the good life. However, if the individual is to be free from restraint, is liberty not incompatible with order and good government? Locke had already rejected Filmer's definition of "'liberty' for everyone to do as he lists, to live as he pleases, and not to be tied by any law"; he called such a condition "the perfect condition of slavery." In Locke's view, "Liberty is to be free from restraint and violence from others, which cannot be where there is no law" (*Of Civil Government* [1690], Book II, Chs. IV and VI). According to Hume only the madman is fully free; the absence of law and good government entails lack of liberty and security of individuals. Montesquieu disparages absolute liberty as a merely rhetorical notion and defines a free people as "that which enjoys a form of government established by law" (*Mes pensées*, Ch. XXII, No. 631). The *Encyclopédie* distinguishes moral, natural, civil, political liberty, and liberty of thought. Natural liberty is the individuals' right to happiness and self-fulfilment "under the condition that they don't abuse it to the detriment of others"; civil liberty "to live under the rule of law; the better the laws, the better the liberty"; political or English liberty exists when everyone is conscious of his security . . . "good civil and public laws safeguard this liberty" (article "Liberté"). Liberties, rather than liberty in the abstract, are predicated by the writers of the Enlightenment including Adam Smith, the protagonist of laissez-faire under the rule of law, who, following Hume, sees "a continuous state of war with their neighbours, and of servile dependency upon their superiors" as the alternative to "order and good government" (Smith, Book III, Ch. IV). Liberty requires and justifies the reform of onerous laws, but not individual license; it aims at reconciling the duties and rights of the individual with his role as a citizen. However, this prevailing conception of liberty is opposed to that of the later Diderot who makes allowances for a capricious liberty of the artist which resembles closely the self-willed arbitrariness of the masters of feudal courts with their admiring and sycophantic followers. It is equally at variance with the tendencies of popular eighteenth-century writers who, unlike the Scottish historians and Voltaire, instead of following Thucydides and Xenophon, turned "to the extravagant representations of Plutarch, Diodorus Curtius and other romancers of the same class (who) ranted about liberty and patriotism . . . (as) something eternally and intrinsically good, distinct from the blessings which it generally produced" (Macaulay, "On Mitford's History of Greece" [1824] in *Complete Works*, London [1879], VII, 686). Historians like Charles Rollin and political writers like H. F. Daguesseau thus aspired to a revival of republican Rome, holding up an idealized vision of a political order which was certainly not based on the insights of the science of human nature. Though the vision was unrealistic, it contributed effectively to the breakup of the existing order.

Reason. The Enlightenment has frequently been arraigned for its overemphasis on abstract reason and its neglect of imagination. Its representative thinkers break with the rationalism and the *esprit de système* of those who precede them. Locke's philosophy is their philosophical bible, just as the detractors of the Enlightenment later agree with de Maistre's verdict that "philosophy begins with contempt for Locke." "The word *reason* . . . has different significations: sometimes it is taken for true and clear principles; sometimes for clear and fair deductions from those principles; and sometimes for the cause, and particularly the final cause. But the consideration I shall have of it here is a signification different from all these . . ." (Locke, *An Essay concerning Human Understanding* [1690], Book IV, Ch. XVII, Para. 1). Locke's concern is with "the original certainty, evidence and extent of human knowledge, together with the grounds and degrees of Belief, Opinion and Assent," in short, with reasoning or the discursive faculty, with proof, classification, and deduction. There are marginal intimations of the power of reason to provide a Baconian art of discovery (*ars inveniendi*). On the whole, however, Locke dwells on the *limits* of reason:

It is of great use to the sailor to know the length of his line, though he cannot with it fathom all the depths of the ocean. It is well he knows that it is long enough to reach the bottom at such places as are necessary to direct his voyage, and caution him against running upon shoals that may ruin him. Our business here is not to know all things, but those which concern our conduct. If we can find out those measures whereby a rational creature, put in that state which man is in in this world, may and ought to govern his opinions, and actions depending thereon, we need not be troubled that some other things escape our knowledge (Book I, Ch. I, Para. 6).

Locke's investigation of human understanding is thus part of the science of human nature which comes to characterize the Enlightenment: It serves as the basis for practical conduct; and though the formulation here given seems to point to individual conduct, in practice, **95** because of the weaknesses inherent in individual reasoning, it points to the science of the legislator as the only area in which contriving and reforming man is not necessarily out of his depth.

There is another, epistemological aspect to Locke's philosophy which expresses itself in his idealism and sensationalism, an aspect which interests professional philosophers, and which was to make a great impact on the theory of art and nineteenth-century materialism (beginning with eighteenth-century sensationalists like Condillac and La Mettrie). However, for the social philosophers of the Enlightenment, the discovery that moral and material qualities are "not qualities in objects, but perceptions of the mind . . . has little or no influence on practice" (Hume, *Treatise,* Book III, Part I, Sec. I). What counts, is the rejection of metaphysical first causes which results in the setting free of the "plain, historical method" of experience, observation, and experiment.

This consideration applies also to Hume's skeptical view of the limitations of reason. "Reason is nothing but a wonderful and unintelligible instinct . . . this instinct . . . arises from past observation and experience. . . . Reason is the discovery of truth and falsehood . . . our passions, volitions and actions . . . [cannot] be pronounced either true or false . . . reason . . . can have an influence only after two ways: either when it excites a passion, by informing us of the existence of something which is a proper object of it; or when it discovers the connection of causes and effects. . . . All knowledge resolves itself into probability . . . ," that is, the experience of many, of the past, and of Trial and Error. Though "understanding, when it acts alone, and according to its most general principles, entirely subverts itself," yet "when reason is lively and mixes itself with some propensity it ought to be assented to" (Hume, *Treatise,* Book I, Part III, Sec. XVI; Book III, Part I, Sec. I; Book I, Part IV, Sec. VII). For the alternative to reason is imagination which, when acting unchecked by reason, leads into superstition, illusion, and fanaticism. Imagination controlled by reason, the creative human nature protected from its destructive propensities by the legislator and by education—this is the gist of the theory of knowledge underlying the quest of the good society of the reformers in the Enlightenment.

The awareness of the limitations of the human understanding rather than its overestimation determines also the attitude of the *Encyclopédie.* "All certitude which is not mathematical demonstration, is only extreme probability. There is no other historical certitude" (article "Histoire"). D'Alembert in the "Discours préliminaire" of the *Encyclopédie* denigrates Descartes' "believing he could explain everything," and extols

Newton's insistence that scientific knowledge is merely provisional, and that conjectures and hypotheses must be presented as such and subjected to tests. He disapproves the application of logic and the "spirit of discussion" to the fields of literature and art because "the passions and tastes have their own sort of logic" (specifically Pascal's *logique du coeur*). The dissection of the psychology of love (by Marivaux, Prévost, and others) has ushered in a "species of the metaphysics of the heart," and "this 'anatomy of the soul' has even slipped into our conversations; people make dissertations, they no longer converse; and our societies have lost their principal ornaments—warmth and gaiety" (ibid.). Diderot contrasts reason "coldly perceived" unfavorably with the "brilliant and sublime" imagination: "Locke has seen, Shaftesbury has created" (article "Génie"). He calls mathematicians "bad metaphysicians . . . bad actors . . . bad politicians . . . such things cannot be expressed in terms of X and Y. They depend on a judicious observation of the intricate flow of life" (undated letter, in *Lettres à Sophie Volland,* Paris [1930], III, 279).

Whatever their weaknesses, the thinkers of the Enlightenment pondered the problem of knowledge more seriously than the thinkers of possibly any other period. The customary strictures of their work are largely derived from nonrational "flights of the imagination" and from the wish to defend old bastions and temples. Far from being an abstract rationalist, Diderot goes rather to the extreme of spontaneous, personal knowledge. In the article "Éclecticisme" in the *Encyclopédie* he foreshadows "the end of all schools" of modern philosophy. Prejudice, tradition, antiquity, and public opinion must be subjected by the philosopher to a rational analysis and experience, "peculiarly and personally his own." This view has been said (by Paul Hazard, *La Pensée européenne au XVIIIe siècle,* Paris [1946], II, 48) to blink at the problem of solipsism. However, the article as a whole makes it clear that eclecticism requires both imaginative genius, the gift to combine and explain, and the ability to gather evidence and to put facts to the test; only he who combines (objective) experimental and (subjective) systematic eclecticism, like Democritus, Aristotle, and Bacon, may claim to be a truly eclectic philosopher in Diderot's sense.

Happiness and Utility. The science of human nature and the science of the legislator supply the key also to the ethics and politics of the Enlightenment. Its moral thought is based upon the principle of utility, the greatest happiness of the greatest number. For Locke, the fundamental interests (he expresses them still in terms of the law of nature) are the preservation of the individual and of mankind. To that end, freedom under the law, equality of individuals, and justice among them (*pacta sunt servanda*) are required: ". . . being all equal and independent, no one ought to harm another in life, health, liberty or possessions" (*Of Civil Government*, Book II, Ch. II). The science of human nature lays bare man's basic propensities, namely self-interest and sympathy. Both these qualities, says Hume, are useful to the individual and to society, and it is their utility that makes people virtuous. Like Liberty, "Virtue is considered as means to an end" (Hume, *Treatise*, Book III, Part III, Sec. VI), namely the happiness or well-being of the individuals composing society.

For the thinkers in the utilitarian mainstream there is no identity of human desires or interests. Man's selfishness, his insatiable avidity for acquiring power and possessions for himself and his group, if left to itself, is destructive of society. Therefore, it must be restrained and regulated through institutions governing property, rights, obligations, etc.; it is the science of the legislator, based on experience and reflection, which suggests the right balance between warring interests. Adam Smith (in the *Wealth of Nations*, Book IV, Chs. IX, V, II; Book I, Ch. VI; Book III, Ch. I) extols "the natural effort of every individual to better his condition, when suffered to exert itself with freedom and security . . . in a well-governed society . . . in a civilised country . . . as long as he does not violate the laws of justice. . . ." Provided security is created by the legislator without unduly restraining spontaneous individual activity, "an invisible hand" leads man "to promote an end which was no part of his intention," that is, socially desirable ends. What ends are conducive to the well-being of society, can be discerned from past general and national experience and the observation of consequences; on this basis it is possible to advise the legislator on what regulations to promote and which to avoid. However, what acts are conducive to the perfection of the individual except in his role of a citizen, is no concern of the legislator, nor does utilitarianism have much to offer on this subject (despite attempts like Adam Smith's *Theory of Moral Sentiments*, 1759). Man's nature is inscrutable, his motives and intentions are manifold and complex, and it is therefore overambitious for the philosopher to pronounce on his self-regarding morality.

Voltaire gives expression to the philosophical anthropology of the period in typical passages:

L'homme, étranger à soi, de l'homme est ignoré.
Que suis-je, où suis-je, où vais-je, et d'où suis-je tiré?
("Man, stranger to himself, does not know himself. What am I, where am I, where am I going, and from where have I come?"; *Poème sur le désastre de Lisbonne*, 1756)

Le ciel, en nous formant, mélangea notre vie
De désirs, de dégoûts, de raison, de folie,

De moments de plaisir, et de jours de tourments,
De notre être imparfait voilà les éléments . . .
("Heaven, in creating us, made our life a blend/ Of desires, of loathing, of reason, of madness,/ Of moments of pleasure, and of days of torment,/ Of our imperfect being these are the elements"; *Discours en vers sur l'homme* [1738], Premier Discours)

Our exploration of human nature serves to contain, not to change it. Man's hope of salvation must come from religion or his own creativeness and discipline. The utilitarian may judge actions, but not the agent. He is restricted to the exploration of human propensities and their consequences, and to the demarcation of social (and only indirectly of individual) good. Utilitarianism is a *public* philosophy, not a purely personal ethics. Therefore there is no contradiction contained in Bentham's famous statement that it is for our "two sovereign masters, pain and pleasure . . . to point out what we ought to do as well as to determine what we shall do." What we shall do, follows from our instincts and passions. What we ought to do, "is determined by and proportional to the tendency which (the utilitarian) conceives to have to augment or to diminish the happiness of the community" (*Introduction to the Principles of Morals and Legislation* [1789], Ch. I, Para. 1, 9).

It is true that there was an alternative influential philosophy, that of Lord Shaftesbury, who put the emphasis on the perfection of the individual rather than on the reform of society. It is echoed in Diderot's aesthetics, and, allied with the predominant Neo-Platonic and Pietist tradition, it helped to thwart the short-lived German Enlightenment. According to Shaftesbury's Hellenic or aristocratic philosophy (*Characteristicks of Men, Manners, Opinions, Times*, 1711), the Beautiful, the Good and the True are equally expressions of the sense of harmony and proportion. While rejecting the Promethean dogma of human corruption, he proclaims the benevolence of nature and the identity of human interests. The Eros of contemplation elevates the cultivation of taste, and the felicity derived from the gemlike flame of vital experience, to the level of virtue. Accordingly, in life, as in art, the end can be neglected; it is subordinated to the intensity of contemplation, passion, and action (though Shaftesbury, in his scintillating and confused work, speaks also of the controlling power of the intellect and of the public interest).

In the English-speaking world, however, Francis Hutcheson's philanthropic and democratic thought, intentionally developed against Shaftesbury, has dominated the philosophical, literary, and aesthetic scene. In Hutcheson's view the sense of beauty and the moral sense are not the same. Harmony, rather than being natural and good in itself, is the concord of individual character with the social good. "Uniformity amidst variety," i.e., order and proportion find their perfect expression in the reign of the moral law, in "the love of humanity, gratitude, compassion, a study of the good of others and a deep delight in their happiness" (Hutcheson, *An Inquiry into the Original of our Ideas of Beauty and Virtue* [1725], Treatise I, Para. 2; Treatise II, Para. 1).

Politics. The guiding ideas of utilitarianism bear also upon the principles of politics and education. In political thought the widely used concepts of the social contract and of natural law give a misleading impression of continuity with previous thought. Actually they provide an obsolete vocabulary for a theory of individual and social interests, which is based upon historical experience and the consciousness of a new historical situation. Going beyond Montesquieu's classification of political and legal institutions, and, like Rousseau, starting from the problem how liberty can exist in a large country (as contrasted with the small city-state), Delolme and John Millar subject the British constitution to penetrating sociological scrutiny. Political thinking advances from a merely institutional to a behavioral approach, from a mere theory of government to political theory. The outstanding new criteria are the displacement of the state by society and the substitution of the citizen for the subject. Adam Smith and his followers fight the power of the state in the name of the individual, but never society. The formal constitution of the state is only one of the various factors which must be taken into account in assessing the condition of a nation. The new commercial society is comparatively classless within the confines of the ruling groups which are spread widely and demarcated only faintly. Voltaire's (1734) and Hume's (1748) observations have been quoted above, in the section on "Underlying Structural Change."

Rather than in the profuse clamor for natural rights and revolutionary measures, the real innovation of the time consists in the consciousness of the identity of rulers and ruled (except for the laboring classes which were then not part of the political process). The traditional problems of rebellion and of the assertion of the individual against the metaphysical state are transmuted into the need for defining a balance among the divergent interests of the individuals whose totality forms society. Rebellion and revolution in the circumstances are liable to become self-destructive by definition. For Hobbes, self-mastery still meant the stoic acceptance of necessity imposed by nature and the sovereign. Now self-mastery is a question of political behavior. It presupposes self-scrutiny, an understanding of one's own propensities and interests in their relation to those of one's fellow men; in short, it calls for the insights of the science of human nature and the precepts of the science of the legislator. In this sense Bentham's and Kant's political maxims are to be understood: "Under a government of Laws . . . obey punctually . . . censure freely" (*A Fragment on Government* [1776], Preface, Para. 16), and: "Criticize as much as you like, if only you obey" (*Was ist Aufklärung?*).

Institutions must be criticized because they tend to determine the rules of behavior. If they concentrate power in individuals or in office, they may deprive the mass of individuals of the safeguards for their security and give free rein to the violent passions of the privileged. As human nature is not obviously susceptible of change, an appropriate institutional framework is needed and must be based less "on abstract and refined speculation" than on "a study and delineation of things passing in the moral world. . . . The question now afloat in the world respecting THINGS AS THEY ARE is the most interesting . . . to the human mind" (William Godwin, *The Adventures of Caleb Williams* [1794], Preface). Institutions both express the existing structure of society and, in turn, present a challenge to things as they are. It is therefore necessary to scrutinize the functions and dysfunctions of social, legal, and political institutions. Considering that society was still largely agricultural, this sociological scrutiny reached its climax in the investigation of rural morphology.

Modern sociological methods were being applied, including highly developed questionnaires, in assessing the respective merits of large-scale and peasant-type holdings. Theoretical findings were being put to practical tests in the agricultural reforms introduced in Britain, Tuscany, France, and elsewhere, often under the guidance of Agricultural Academies which sprang up all over Europe. The theoretical side of this movement was started by Turgot and Pierre Samuel Du Pont de Nemours, especially in the *Ephémérides du citoyen* (from 1765). Soon it found its master in Arthur Young who, from 1768, toured Britain, France, and Italy, on horseback, indefatigably surveying all aspects of farming and the farming population. One of the great Scottish pioneers, Sir John Sinclair, as the first head of the English Board of Agriculture, created in the 1790's a detailed survey of the agricultural structure of the various counties which set the tone for later sociological investigations (and was soon imitated by Jean Chaptal, Comte de Chanteloup as the basis of the Napoleonic *Statistique de la France*). Highlights of the considerable new sociological literature were Sir Frederick Morton Eden's *The State of the Poor . . .* (1797) and Sismondi's *Tableau de l'agriculture toscane*

(1801) and *Statistique du Département du Léman* (1803).

Critique of Society. Society is seen both as a boon and as a burden. It supplies that "additional force, ability and security without which individual life could not persist" (Hume, *Treatise*, Book III, Part II, Sec. II). However, society requires organization by law which safeguards the liberty of the individual by curbing his license. Some persons are strong and some are weak; there is both biological and sociological inequality. Society can therefore be oppressive, and the legislator must take steps to protect the weak and safeguard equality of opportunity for all individuals.

The critique of society in the eighteenth century takes up prophetic and Stoic themes. In this sense it is a critique of the human situation in general, a part of the eternally recurring revolt against civilization and its discontents. A judicious investigation of late eighteenth-century popular English novels of the period has led Lois Whitney to this conclusion:

Common to them all . . . is the conviction that the time . . . is out of joint; that what is wrong with it is due to an abnormal complexity and sophistication in the life of civilized man, to the pathological multiplicity and emulativeness of his desires and the oppressive over-abundance of his belongings, and the factitiousness and want of inner spontaneity of his emotions; that "art", the work of man has corrupted "nature" . . . (*Primitivism and the Idea of Progress*, London [1934], p. xiv).

This lament of man's lost innocence (the Fall, Prometheus, Pandora's Box) spills over into the anxieties of the romantics, of Marx, Kierkegaard, Nietzsche, Kafka, and so on. Critique of society is inextricably mixed with that of the human situation.

By contrast, the thinkers in the mainstream of the Enlightenment restrict themselves (for the reasons set out in the section above on Happiness) to the critique of society to the extent that it is sociologically determined. "No society," says Adam Smith, "can surely be flourishing and happy, of which the greater part of the members are poor and miserable" (Smith, Book I, Ch. VIII). The division of labor not only produces prosperity but is also the source of inequality, far beyond the biological inequality of talents. It "destroys intellectual, social and martial virtues unless government takes pains to prevent it" (Book V, Ch. I, Part III, Article II). Traditionally, government has been on the side "of the rich against the poor" in the defense of property. It is therefore necessary to counteract the dangers inherent in the commercial and industrial state by means of public education and other appropriate agenda of the state designed to redress the social imbalance which competition and the division of labor

have created. This analysis of the *Wealth of Nations* finds its parallels in the writings of D'Alembert, Rousseau, Adam Ferguson, John Millar, and Dugald Stewart who all emphasize both the good and deleterious effects of commercial and industrial society, and, in particular, what has come to be called the social and economic alienation of man, i.e., the freezing of the individual in a rigid system of role allocation. According to John Millar, for example,

. . . competitions and rivalships, which contract the heart and set mankind at variance . . . , [arouse] envy, resentment and other malignant passions . . . the pursuit of riches becomes a scramble, in which the hand of every man is against every other. . . . The class of mechanics and labourers, by far the most numerous in a commercial nation . . . become like machines . . . are . . . debarred from extensive information . . . in danger of losing their importance, of becoming the dupes of their superiors and of being degraded . . . (*An Historical View of the English Government* [1787, London, 1803 ed.], IV, 248, 249, 146, 156).

Specific criticisms of the capitalist order are also advanced by Jean Meslier, Morelly, G. B. de Mably, S. N. H. Linguet, William Godwin, Thomas Paine, and others.

Education. The aim of education is to prepare the individual to make the best of the spontaneity and initiative which allow him to play his full part in society. If he is restricted in his self-expression owing to the division of labor, education must supply him with the facilities and the vicarious experience which make up a full personality. Plato's concern with the "citizen" must be complemented by the concern with Rousseau's "man" (*homme*). "Life," says Rousseau in *Émile*, "is the trade I would teach him (my pupil). When he leaves me, . . . he will be neither a magistrate, a soldier, nor a priest; he will be a man" (*Oeuvres complètes*, IV, Paris [1969], 252). Pestalozzi translates Rousseau's educational ideas into practice, and his assistant-masters, Philipp Emanuel von Fellenberg and Friedrich Wilhelm Froebel, spread them all over Europe. Professional education, foreshadowed by the emphasis of the *Encyclopédie* and the resulting innovations, becomes universal. Education for citizenship comes to complement economic and political reform where there is a politically active and emancipated citizenry, as in England (where Fellenberg's methods were introduced by Lord Brougham). Where there is little political participation, as in Germany, education, like art and historiography, provides a haven for those who resign themselves to "seeking Greece with their souls" rather than putting into practice the reformist aspirations of Faust and Wilhelm Meister.

Uniformity amidst Variety. The educational process needed to make society inhabitable by man is the 99

common task of science (especially the science of society), of art, of religion, and of education in the technical sense. Unity and correlation supply principal themes in this respect. The interrelation and mutual dependence of institutions, of people, and of nations, the unity and hierarchy of the sciences are widely discussed. The *Encyclopédie*, starting from and complementing Bacon's logical classification of the sciences by an historical arrangement, brings into view Francis Hutcheson's principle of uniformity amidst variety, the significance of the interconnection of the parts with the whole. Hume's science of human nature is an attempt at basing all the sciences on a common methodology; his *Treatise of Human Nature* has the subtitle "being an attempt to introduce the experimental method [of Bacon and Newton] into moral subjects." At the end of the period, Dugald Stewart, in his "Preliminary Dissertation, containing some critical Remarks on the Discourse prefixed to the French Encyclopedia" (*Philosophical Essays* [1810], in *Works*, V, Edinburgh [1855], 5–54), adds a functional approach to the merely classificatory, earlier arrangements of the sciences of matter and mind. The full title of Montesquieu's *Esprit des lois* emphasizes the rapport of the legal system with the constitution, the manners, the climate, the religion, the commerce, etc. of a people. In 1800 Madame de Staël published her *De la Littérature considérée dans ses rapports avec les institutions sociales*. The structure and historical totality and cohesion of social units supplies the raison d'être of Universal Histories and the national histories of the Scottish school and its followers. Vico's *Scienza nuova* (1725) maps out both the common fundamental principles of mankind and the historical "philology" of individual peoples, i.e., the contribution of their free and creative will. Hume provides a definitive methodological basis for a macrosociological theory in his essay "On National Characters" (1748).

Comparative historical and anthropological studies confirm the interaction of nations as an enrichment of national character. "By comparing among all nations laws with laws, talents with talents, and manners with manners, nations will find so little reason to prefer themselves to others, that if they preserve for their own country that love which is the fruit of self-interest, at least they will lose that fanaticism which is the fruit of exclusive self-esteem" (*Encyclopédie*, article "Législateur"). D'Alembert, in *De la Liberté de la musique*, exemplifies the interchangeability and interaction of forms of art as means of expression. Cosmopolitanism, toleration, universality are qualities closely bound up with this interest in common roots and functions, and characterize the leading ideas of the Enlightenment.

BIBLIOGRAPHY

G. Bryson, *Man and Society, The Scottish Inquiry of the Eighteenth Century* (Princeton, 1945). E. Cassirer, *Die Philosophie der Aufklärung* (Tübingen, 1932), trans. F. C. A. Koelln and James P. Pettegrove as *The Philosophy of the Enlightenment* (Princeton, 1951). A. Cobban, *In Search of Humanity* (London and New York, 1960). G. R. Cragg, *The Church and the Age of Reason* (London, 1960). J. Ehrard, *L'Idée de la nature en France* (Paris, 1963), with bibliography. P. Gay, *The Enlightenment: an Interpretation*, 2 vols. (New York, 1966–69; London, 1967–70), with bibliography. P. Hazard, *La Pensée européene au XVIIIe siècle* (1946), trans. as *European Thought in the Eighteenth Century* (London, 1954); Vol. III of French edition contains bibliography. R. Hubert, *Les Sciences sociales dans l'Encyclopédie* (Paris, 1923). A. O. Lovejoy, *Essays in the History of Ideas* (Baltimore, 1948). F. E. Manuel, *The Eighteenth Century Confronts the Gods* (Cambridge, Mass., 1959). P. Mantoux, *The Industrial Revolution in the Eighteenth Century*, 2nd ed. (London, 1928; reprint 1961). Kingsley Martin, *French Liberal Thought in the Eighteenth Century* (1929; New York and London, 1962). R. Mauzi, *L'Idée du bonheur . . .* (Paris, 1960). F. Meinecke, *Die Entstehung des Historismus*, 2 vols. (1936; 2nd ed. Munich, 1946). J. Roger, *Les Sciences de la vie dans la pensée française au XVIIIe siècle* (Paris, 1963). R. V. Sampson, *Progress in the Age of Reason* (London, 1956). Preserved Smith, *A History of Modern Culture*, Vol. II: *The Enlightenment 1687–1776* (New York and London, 1930). J. Starobinski, *The Invention of Liberty* (Geneva, 1964). F. Venturi, *Settecento Riformatore* (Turin, 1969). B. Willey, *The Eighteenth Century Background* (London, 1950).

HELLMUT O. PAPPE

[See also Ancients and Moderns; Classicism; **Counter-Enlightenment; Perfectibility;** Progress; Religious Enlightenment; **Religious Toleration;** Social Contract; **Utilitarianism.**]

THE COUNTER-ENLIGHTENMENT

I

OPPOSITION to the central ideas of the French Enlightenment, and of its allies and disciples in other European countries, is as old as the movement itself. The proclamation of the autonomy of reason and the methods of the natural sciences based on observation as the sole reliable method of knowledge, and the consequent rejection of the authority of revelation, sacred writings and their accepted interpreters, tradition, prescription, and every form of nonrational and transcendent sources of knowledge, was naturally opposed by the churches and religious thinkers of many persuasions. But such opposition, largely because of the absence of common ground between them and the philosophers of the Enlightenment, made relatively little headway, save by stimulating repressive steps against the spreading of ideas regarded as dangerous to the authority of Church or State. More formidable was the relativist and skeptical tradition that went back to the ancient world. The central doctrines of the progressive French thinkers, whatever their disagreements among themselves, rested on the belief, rooted in the ancient doctrine of Natural Law, that human nature was fundamentally the same in all times and places; that local and historical variations were unimportant compared with the constant central core in terms of which human beings could be defined as a species, like animals, or plants, or minerals; that there were universal human goals; that a logically connected structure of laws and generalizations susceptible of demonstration and verification could be constructed and replace the chaotic amalgam of ignorance, mental laziness, guesswork, superstition, prejudice, dogma, fantasy, and, above all, the "interested error," maintained by the rulers of mankind and largely responsible for the blunders, vices, and misfortunes of humanity.

It was further believed that the methods similar to those of Newtonian physics which had achieved such triumphs in the realm of inanimate nature could be applied with equal success to the fields of ethics, politics, and human relationships in general, in which little progress had been made; with the corollary that once this had been effected, it would sweep away irrational and oppressive legal systems and economic policies the replacement of which by the rule of reason would rescue men from political and moral injustice and misery and set them on the path of wisdom, happiness, and virtue. Against this, there persisted the doctrine that went back to the Greek Sophists, Protagoras, Antiphon, and Critias, that beliefs involving value-judgments, and the institutions founded upon them, rested not on discoveries of objective and unalterable natural facts, but on human opinion, which was variable and differed between different societies and at different times; that moral and political values, and in particular justice and social arrangements in general rested on fluctuating human convention. This was summed up by the Sophist quoted by Aristotle who declared that whereas fire burned both here and in Persia, human institutions change under our very eyes. It seemed to follow that no universal truths established by scientific methods, that is, truths that anyone could verify by the use of proper methods, anywhere, at any time, could in principle be established in human affairs.

This tradition reasserted itself strongly in the writings of such sixteenth-century skeptics as Cornelius

Agrippa, Montaigne, and Pierre Charron whose influence is discernible in the sentiments of thinkers and poets in the Elizabethan and Jacobean age. Such skepticism came to the aid of those who denied the claims of the natural sciences or of other universal rational schemas and advocated salvation in pure faith, like the great Protestant reformers and their followers, and the Jansenist wing of the Roman Church. The rationalist belief in a single coherent body of logically deduced conclusions, arrived at by universally valid principles of thought and founded upon carefully sifted data of observation or experiment, was further shaken by sociologically minded thinkers from Bodin (1530–96) to Montesquieu (1689–1755). These writers, using the evidence of both history and the new literature of travel and exploration in newly discovered lands, Asia and the Americas, emphasized the variety of human customs and especially the influence of dissimilar natural factors, particularly geographical ones, upon the development of different human societies, leading to differences of institutions and outlook, which in their turn generated wide differences of belief and behavior. This was powerfully reinforced by the revolutionary doctrines of David Hume, especially by his demonstration that no logical links existed between truths of fact, and such *a priori* truths as those of logic or mathematics, which tended to weaken or dissolve the hopes of those who, under the influence of Descartes and his followers, thought that a single system of knowledge, embracing all provinces and answering all questions, could be established by unbreakable chains of logical argument from universally valid axioms, not subject to refutation or modification by any experience of an empirical kind.

Nevertheless, no matter how deeply relativity about human values or the interpretation of social, including historical, facts entered the thought of social thinkers of this type, they, too, retained a common core of conviction that the ultimate ends of all men at all times were, in effect, identical: all men sought the satisfaction of basic physical and biological needs, such as food, shelter, security, and also peace, happiness, justice, the harmonious development of their natural faculties, truth, and, somewhat more vaguely, virtue, moral perfection, and what the Romans had called *humanitas*. Means might differ in cold and hot climates, mountainous countries and flat plains, and no universal formula could fit all cases without Procrustean results, but the ultimate ends were fundamentally similar. Such influential writers as Voltaire, D'Alembert, and Condorcet believed that the development of the arts and sciences were the most powerful human weapons in attaining these ends, and the sharpest weapons in the fight against ignorance, superstition, fanaticism, 101 oppression, and barbarism which crippled human effort and frustrated men's search for truth and rational self-direction. Rousseau and Mably believed, on the contrary, that the institutions of civilization were themselves a major factor in the corruption of men and their alienation from nature, from simplicity, purity of heart and the life of natural justice, social equality, and spontaneous human feeling; artificial man had imprisoned, enslaved, and ruined natural man. Nevertheless, despite profound differences of outlook, there was a wide area of agreement about fundamental points: the reality of Natural Law (no longer formulated in the language of orthodox Catholic or Protestant doctrine), of eternal principles by following which alone men could become wise, happy, virtuous, and free. One set of universal and unalterable principles governed the world for theists, deists, and atheists, for optimists and pessimists, puritans, primitivists, and believers in progress and the richest fruits of science and culture; these laws governed inanimate and animate nature, facts and events, means and ends, private life and public, all societies, epochs, and civilizations; it was solely by departing from them that men fell into crime, vice, misery. Thinkers might differ about what these laws were, or how to discover them, or who were qualified to expound them; that these laws were real, and could be known, whether with certainty, or only probability, remained the central dogma of the entire Enlightenment. It was the attack upon this that constitutes the most formidable reaction against this dominant body of belief.

II

A thinker who might have had a decisive role in this counter-movement, if anyone outside his native country had read him, was the Neapolitan philosopher Giambattista Vico (1668–1744). With extraordinary originality Vico maintained, especially in the last work of his life, *Scienza nuova* (1725; radically altered 1731), that the Cartesians were profoundly mistaken about the role of mathematics as the science of sciences; that mathematics was certain only because it was a human invention. It did not, as they supposed, correspond to an objective structure of reality; it was a method and not a body of truths; with its help we could plot regularities—the occurrence of phenomena in the external world—but not discover why they occurred as they did, or to what end. This could be known only to God, for only those who make things can truly know what they are and for what purpose they have been made. Hence we do not, in this sense, know the external world—Nature—for we have not made it; only God who created it, knows it in this fashion. But since men are directly acquainted with human motives, purposes, hopes, fears which are their own, they can know human affairs as they cannot know Nature.

According to Vico, our lives and activities collectively and individually are expressions of our attempts to survive, satisfy our desires, understand each other and the past out of which we emerge. A utilitarian interpretation of the most essential human activities is misleading. They are, in the first place, purely expressive; to sing, to dance, to worship, to speak, to fight, and the institutions which embody these activities, comprise a vision of the world. Language, religious rites, myths, laws, social, religious, juridical institutions, are forms of self-expression, of wishing to convey what one is and strives for; they obey intelligible patterns, and for that reason it is possible to reconstruct the life of other societies, even those remote in time and place and utterly primitive, by asking oneself what kind of framework of human ideas, feelings, acts could have generated the poetry, the monuments, the mythology which were their natural expression. Men grow individually and socially; the world of men who composed the Homeric poems was plainly very different from that of the Hebrews to whom God had spoken through their sacred books, or that of the Roman Republic, or medieval Christianity, or Naples under the Bourbons. Patterns of growth are traceable.

Myths are not, as enlightened thinkers believe, false statements about reality corrected by later rational criticism, nor is poetry mere embellishment of what could equally well be stated in ordinary prose. The myths and poetry of antiquity embody a vision of the world as authentic as that of Greek philosophy, or Roman Law, or the poetry and culture of our own enlightened age, earlier, cruder, remote from us, but with its own voice, as we hear it in the *Iliad* or the Twelve Tables, belonging uniquely to its own culture, and with a sublimity which cannot be reproduced by a later, more sophisticated culture. Each culture expresses its own collective experience, each step on the ladder of human development has its own equally authentic means of expression.

Vico's theory of cycles of cultural development became celebrated, but it is not his most original contribution to the understanding of society or history. His revolutionary move is to have denied the doctrine of a timeless Natural Law the truths of which could have been known in principle to any man, at any time, anywhere. Vico boldly denied this doctrine which has formed the heart of the Western tradition from Aristotle to our own day. He preached the notion of the uniqueness of cultures, however they might resemble each other in their relationship to their antecedents and successors, and the notion of a single style that pervades all the activities and manifestations of societies of human beings at a particular stage of development. Thereby he laid the foundations at once of comparative cultural anthropology and of comparative historical linguistics, aesthetics, jurisprudence; language, ritual, monuments, and especially mythology, were the sole reliable keys to what later scholars and critics conceived as altering forms of collective consciousness. Such historicism was plainly not compatible with the view that there was only one standard of truth or beauty or goodness, which some cultures or individuals approached more closely than others, and which it was the business of thinkers to establish and men of action to realize. The Homeric poems were an unsurpassable masterpiece, but they could only spring from a brutal, stern, oligarchical, "heroic" society, and later civilizations, however superior in other respects, did not and could not produce an art necessarily superior to Homer. This doctrine struck a powerful blow at the notion of timeless truths and steady progress, interrupted by occasional periods of retrogression into barbarism, and drew a sharp line between the natural sciences which dealt with the relatively unaltering nature of the physical world viewed from "outside," and humane studies which viewed social evolution from "inside" by a species of empathetic insight, for which the establishment of texts or dates by scientific criticism was a necessary, but not a sufficient, condition. Vico's unsystematic works dealt with many other matters, but his importance in the history of the Enlightenment consists in his insistence on the plurality of cultures and on the consequently fallacious character of the idea that there is one and only one structure of reality which the enlightened philosopher can see as it truly is, and which he can (at least in principle) describe in logically perfect language—a vision that has obsessed thinkers from Plato to Leibniz, Condillac, Bertrand Russell and his more faithful followers. For Vico men ask different questions of the Universe, and their answers are shaped accordingly: such questions, and the symbols or acts that express them, alter or become obsolete in the course of cultural development; to understand the answers one must understand the questions that preoccupy an age or a culture; they are not constant nor necessarily more profound because they resemble our own more than others that are less familiar to us. Vico's relativity went further than Montesquieu's. If his view was correct, it was subversive of the very notion of absolute truths and of a perfect society founded on them, not merely in practice but in principle. However, Vico was little read, and the question of how much influence he had had, before his *New Science* was revived by Michelet a century after it was written, is still uncertain.

If Vico wished to shake the pillars on which the Enlightenment of his times rested, the Königsberg theologian and philosopher, J. G. Hamann, wished to smash them. Hamann was brought up as a Pietist, a member of the most introspective and self-absorbed of all the Lutheran sects, intent upon the direct communion of the individual soul with God, bitterly antirationalist, liable to emotional excess, preoccupied with the stern demands of moral obligation and the needs for severe self-discipline. The attempt of Frederick the Great in the middle years of the eighteenth century to introduce French culture and a degree of rationalization, economic and social as well as military, into East Prussia, the most backward part of his provinces, provoked a peculiarly violent reaction in this pious, semi-feudal, traditional Protestant society (which also gave birth to Herder and Kant). Hamann began as a disciple of the Enlightenment, but, after a profound spiritual crisis, turned against it, and published a series of polemical attacks written in a highly idiosyncratic, perversely allusive, contorted, deliberately obscure style, as remote as he could make it from the, to him, detestable elegance, clarity, and smooth superficiality of the bland and arrogant French dictators of taste and thought. Hamann's theses rested on the conviction that all truth is particular, never general; that reason is impotent to demonstrate the existence of anything and is an instrument only for conveniently classifying and arranging data in patterns to which nothing in reality corresponds; that to understand is to be communicated with, by men or by God. The universe for him, as for the older German mystical tradition, is itself a kind of language. Things and plants and animals are themselves symbols with which God communicates with his creatures. Everything rests on faith; faith is as basic an organ of acquaintance with reality as the senses. To read the Bible is to hear the voice of God, who speaks in a language which he has given man the grace to understand. Some men are endowed with the gift of understanding his ways. of looking at the universe which is his book no less than the revelations of the Bible and the Fathers and saints of the Church. Only love—for a person or an object—can reveal the true nature of anything. It is not possible to love formulae, general propositions, laws, the abstractions of science, the vast system of concepts and categories—symbols too general to be close to reality—with which the French *lumières* have blinded themselves to concrete reality, to the real experience which only direct acquaintance, especially by the senses provide.

Hamann glories in the fact that Hume has successfully destroyed the rationalist claim that there is an *a priori* route to reality, insisting that all knowledge and belief ultimately rest on acquaintance with the 103 data of direct perception. Hume rightly supposes that he could not eat an egg or drink a glass of water if he did not believe in their existence; the data of belief—what Hamann prefers to call faith—rest on grounds and require evidence as little as taste or any other sensation. True knowledge is direct perception of individual entities, and concepts are never, no matter how specific they may be, wholly adequate to the fullness of the individual experience. *"Individuum est ineffabile,"* wrote Goethe to the physiognomist J. K. Lavater in the spirit of Hamann whom Goethe profoundly admired. The sciences may be of use in practical matters; but no concatenation of concepts will give one an understanding of a man, of a work of art, of what is conveyed by gestures, symbols, verbal and nonverbal, of the style, the spiritual essence, of a human being, a movement, a culture; nor for that matter of the Deity which speaks to one everywhere if only one has ears to hear and eyes to see. What is real is individual, that is, is what it is in virtue of its uniqueness, its differences from other things, events, thoughts, and not in virtue of what it has in common with them, which is all that the generalizing sciences seek to record. "Feeling alone," said Hamann, "gives to abstract terms . . . hands, feet, wings"; and again "God speaks to us in poetical words, addressed to the senses, not in abstractions for the learned," and so must anyone who has something to say that matters, who speaks to another person.

Hamann took little interest in theories or speculations about the external world; he cared only for the inner personal life of the individual, and therefore only for art, religious experience, the senses, personal relationships, which the analytic truths of scientific reason seemed to him to reduce to meaningless ciphers. "God is a poet, not a mathematician," and it is men who, like Kant, suffer from a "gnostic hatred of matter" that provide us with endless verbal constructions—words that are taken for concepts, and worse still, concepts that are taken for real things. Scientists invent systems, philosophers rearrange reality into artificial patterns, shut their eyes to reality, and build castles in the air. "When *data* are given you, why do you seek for *ficta?*" Systems are mere prisons of the spirit, and they lead not only to distortion in the sphere of knowledge, but to the erection of monstrous bureaucratic machines, built in accordance with the rules that ignore the teeming variety of the living world, the untidy and asymmetrical inner lives of men, and crush them into conformity for the sake of some ideological chimera unrelated to the union of spirit and flesh that constitutes the real world. "What is this much lauded reason with its universality, infallibility . . . certainty, overweening claims, but an *ens rationis,* a stuffed dummy

. . . endowed with divine attributes?" History alone yields concrete truth, and in particular the poets describe their world in the language of passion and inspired imagination. "The entire treasure of human knowledge and happiness lies in images"; that is why the language of primitive man, sensuous and imaginative, is poetical and irrational. "Poetry is the native language of mankind, and gardening is more ancient than agriculture, painting than writing, song than recitation, proverbs than rational conclusions, barter than trade." Originality, genius, direct expression, the Bible or Shakespeare fashion the color, shape, living flesh of the world, which analytical science, revealing only the skeleton, cannot begin to do.

Hamann is first in the line of thinkers who accuse rationalism and scientism of using analysis to distort reality: he is followed by Herder, Jacobi, Möser who were influenced by Shaftesbury, Young, and Burke's anti-intellectualist diatribes, and they, in their turn, were echoed by romantic writers in many lands. The most eloquent spokesman of this attitude is Schelling, whose thought was reproduced vividly by Bergson at the beginning of this century. He is the father of those antirationalist thinkers for whom the seamless whole of reality in its unanalyzable flow is misrepresented by the static, spatial metaphors of mathematics and the natural sciences. That to dissect is to murder is a romantic pronouncement which is the motto of an entire nineteenth-century movement of which Hamann was a most passionate and implacable forerunner. Scientific dissection leads to cold political dehumanization, to the straitjacket of lifeless French rules in which the living body of passionate and poetical Germans is to be held fast by the Solomon of Prussia, Frederick the Great, who knows so much and understands so little. The archenemy is Voltaire, whom Herder called a "senile child" with a corrosive wit in place of human feeling. The influence of Rousseau, particularly of his early writings, on this movement in Germany, which came to be called *Sturm und Drang,* was profound. Rousseau's impassioned pleas for direct vision and natural feeling, his denunciation of the artificial social roles which civilization forces men to play against the true ends and needs of their natures, his idealization of more primitive, spontaneous human societies, his contrast between natural self-expression and the crippling artificiality of social divisions and conventions which rob men of dignity and freedom, and promote privilege, power, and arbitrary bullying at one, and humiliating obsequiousness at the other, end of the human scale, and so distorts all human relations, appealed to Hamann and his followers. But even Rousseau did not seem to them to go far enough. Despite everything, Rousseau believed in a timeless set of truths which all men could read, for they were engraved on their hearts in letters more durable than bronze, thereby conceding the authority of Natural Law, a vast, cold, empty abstraction. To Hamann and his followers all rules or precepts are deadly; they may be necessary for the conduct of day-to-day life, but nothing great was ever achieved by following them. English critics were right in supposing that originality entailed breaking rules, that every creative act, every illuminating insight, is obtained by ignoring the rules of despotic legislators. Rules, he declared, are vestal virgins: unless they are violated there will be no issue. Nature is capable of wild fantasy, and it is mere childish presumption to seek to imprison her in the narrow rationalist categories of "puny" and desiccated philosophers. Nature is a wild dance, and so-called practical men are like sleepwalkers who are secure and successful because they are blind to reality; if they saw reality as it truly is, they might go out of their minds.

Language is the direct expression of the historical life of societies and peoples: "every court, every school, every profession, every corporation, every sect has its own language"; we penetrate the meaning of this language by "the passion" of "a lover, a friend, an intimate," not by rules, imaginary universal keys which open nothing. The French *philosophes* and their English followers tell us that men seek only to obtain pleasure and avoid pain, but this is absurd. Men seek to live, create, love, hate, eat, drink, worship, sacrifice, understand, and they seek this because they cannot help it. Life is action. It is knowable only by those who look within themselves and perform the "hell-ride" (*Höllenfahrt*) of self-examination, as the great founders of Pietism—Spener, Francke, Bengel—have taught us. Before a man has liberated himself from the deathly embrace of impersonal, scientific thought which robs all it touches of life and individuality, he cannot understand himself or others, or how or why we come to be what we are.

While Hamann spoke in irregular, isolated flashes of insight, his disciple J. G. von Herder (1744–1803), attempted to construct a coherent system to explain the nature of man and his experience in history. While profoundly interested in the natural sciences and eagerly profiting by their findings, particularly in biology and physiology, and conceding a good deal more to the French than the fanatical Hamann was willing to do, Herder in that part of his doctrine which entered into the texture of the thought of the movements that he inspired, deliberately aimed against the sociological assumptions of the French Enlightenment. He believed that to understand anything was to understand it in its individuality and development, and that this required a capacity which he called *Einfühlung* ("feeling

into") the outlook, the individual character of an artistic tradition, a literature, a social organization, a people, a culture, a period of history. To understand the actions of individuals, we must understand the "organic" structure of the society in terms of which alone the minds and activities and habits of its members can be understood. Like Vico, he believed that to understand a religion, or a work of art, or a national character, one must "enter into" the unique conditions of its life: those who have been storm-tossed on the waves of the North Sea (as he was during his voyage to the West) can fully understand the songs of the old Skalds as those who have never seen grim northern sailors coping with the elements never will; the Bible can truly be understood only by those who attempt to enter into the experience of primitive shepherds in the Judean hills. To grade the merits of cultural wholes, of the legacy of entire traditions, by applying a collection of dogmatic rules claiming universal validity, enunciated by the Parisian arbiters of taste, is vanity and blindness. Every culture has its own unique *Schwerpunkt* ("center of gravity") and unless we grasp it we cannot understand its character or value. From this spring Herder's passionate concern with the preservation of primitive cultures which have a unique contribution to make, his love of almost every expression of the human spirit, work of the imagination, for simply being what it is. Art, morality, custom, religion, national life grow out of immemorial tradition, are created by entire societies living an integrated communal life. The frontiers and divisions drawn between and within such unitary expressions of collective imaginative response to common experience are nothing but artificial and distorting categorizations by the dull, dogmatic pedants of a later age.

Who are the authors of the songs, the epics, the myths, the temples, the mores of a people, the clothes they wear, the language they use? The people itself, the entire soul of which is poured out in all they are and do. Nothing is more barbarous than to ignore or trample on a cultural heritage. Hence Herder's condemnation of the Romans for crushing native civilizations, or of the Church (despite the fact that he was himself a Lutheran clergyman) for forcibly baptizing the Balts and so forcing them into a Christian mold alien to their natural traditions, or of British missionaries for doing this to the Indians and other inhabitants of Asia whose exquisite native cultures were being ruthlessly destroyed by the imposition of alien social systems, religions, forms of education that were not theirs and could only warp their natural development. Herder was no nationalist: he supposed that different cultures could and should flourish fruitfully side by side like so many peaceful flowers in the great human garden; nevertheless, the seeds of nationalism are unmistakably present in his fervid attacks on hollow cosmopolitanism and universalism (with which he charged the French *philosophes*); they grew apace among his aggressive nineteenth-century disciples.

Herder is the greatest inspirer of cultural nationalism among the nationalities oppressed by the Austro-Hungarian, Turkish, and Russian empires, and ultimately of direct political nationalism as well, much as he abhorred it, in Austria and Germany, and by infectious reaction, in other lands as well. He rejected the absolute criteria of progress then fashionable in Paris: no culture is a mere means towards another; every human achievement, every human society is to be judged by its own internal standards. In spite of the fact that in later life he attempted to construct a theory of history in which the whole of mankind, in a somewhat vague fashion, is represented as developing towards a common *Humanität* which embraces all men and all the arts and all the sciences, it is his earlier, relativistic passion for the individual essence and flavor of each culture that most profoundly influenced the European imagination. For Voltaire, Diderot, Helvétius, Holbach, Condorcet, there is only universal civilization of which now one nation, now another, represents the richest flowering. For Herder there is a plurality of incommensurable cultures. To belong to a given community, to be connected with its members by indissoluble and impalpable ties of common language, historical memory, habit, tradition, and feeling, is a basic human need no less natural than that for food or drink or security or procreation. One nation can understand and sympathize with the institutions of another only because it knows how much its own mean to itself. Cosmopolitanism is the shedding of all that makes one most human, most oneself. Hence the attack upon what is regarded as the false mechanical model of mankind used by scientifically minded French *philosophes* (Herder makes an exception for Diderot alone, with whose writings, wayward and imaginative and full of sudden insights, he felt a genuine affinity) who understand only machine-like, causal factors, or the arbitrary will of individual kings and legislators and commanders, sometimes wise and virtuous and altruistic, at other times, self-interested or corrupt or stupid or vicious. But the forces that shape men are far more complex, and differ from age to age and culture to culture and cannot be contained in these simple cut-and-dried formulae. "I am always frightened when I hear a whole nation or period characterized in a few short words; for what a vast multitude of differences is embraced by the word 'nation,' or 'the Middle Ages,' or 'ancient and modern times.'" Germans can be truly creative only among Germans; Jews only if they are restored to the ancient soil of Palestine. Those who are forcibly pulled up by the roots wither in a foreign environment when they survive at all: Europeans lose their virtue in America, Icelanders decay in Denmark. Imitation of models (unlike unconscious, unperceived, spontaneous influences by one society on another) leads to artificiality, feeble imitativeness, degraded art and life. Germans must be Germans and not third-rate Frenchmen; life lies in remaining steeped in one's own language, tradition, local feeling; uniformity is death. The tree of (science-dominated) knowledge kills the tree of life.

So, too, Herder's contemporary, Justus Möser (1720–94), the first historical sociologist, who wrote about the old life of his native region of Osnabrück in Western Germany, said that "every age had its own style," every war has its own particular tone, the affairs of State have a specific coloring, dress and manner have inner connections with religion and the sciences; that *Zeitstil* and *Volksstil* are everything; that there is a "local reason" for this or that institution that is not and cannot be universal. Möser maintained that societies and persons could be understood only by means of "a total impression," not by isolation of element from element in the manner of analytical chemists; this, he tells us, is what Voltaire had not grasped when he mocked the fact that a law which applied in one German village was contradicted by another in a neighboring one: it is by such rich variety, founded upon ancient, unbroken tradition that the tyrannies of uniform systems, such as those of Louis XIV or Frederick the Great, were avoided; it is so that freedoms were preserved.

Although the influence was not direct, these are the very tones one hears in the works of Edmund Burke and many later romantic, vitalistic, intuitionist, and irrationalist writers, both conservative and socialist, who defend the value of organic forms of social life. Burke's famous onslaught on the principles of the French revolutionaries was founded upon the self-same appeal to the "myriad strands" that bind human beings into a historically hallowed whole, contrasted with the utilitarian model of society as a trading company held together solely by contractual obligations, the world of "economists, sophisters, and calculators" who are blind and deaf to the unanalyzable relationships that make a family, a tribe, a nation, a movement, any association of human beings held together by something more than a quest for mutual advantage, or by force, or by anything that is not mutual love, loyalty, common history, emotion, and outlook. This emphasis in the last half of the eighteenth century on nonrational factors, whether connected with specific religious beliefs or not, which stresses the value of the individual, the peculiar (*das Eigentümliche*), the impalpable, and appeals to ancient historical roots and immemorial custom, to the wisdom of simple, sturdy peasants uncorrupted by the sophistries of subtle "reasoners," has strongly conservative and, indeed, reactionary implications. Whether stated by the enthusiastic populist Herder with his acute dislike for political coercion, empires, political authority, and all forms of imposed organization; or by Möser, moderate Hanoverian conservative; or by Lavater, altogether unconcerned with politics; or by Burke, brought up in a different tradition, respectful towards Church and State and the authority of aristocracies and *élites* sanctified by history, these doctrines clearly constitute a resistance to attempts at a rational reorganization of society in the name of universal moral and intellectual ideals.

At the same time abhorrence of scientific expertise inspired radical protest in the works of William Blake, of the young Schiller, and of populist writers in Eastern Europe. Above all, it contributed to unpolitical turbulence in Germany in the second third of the eighteenth century: the plays of such leaders of the *Sturm und Drang* as J. M. R. Lenz, F. M. von Klinger, H. W. von Gerstenberg, and J. A. Leisewitz are outbursts against every form of organized social or political life. What provoked them may have been the asphyxiating philistinism of the German middle class, or the cruel injustices of the small and stuffy courts of stupid and arbitrary German princelings, but what they attacked with equal violence was the entire tidy ordering of life by the principles of reason and scientific knowledge advocated by the progressive thinkers of France, England, and Italy. Lenz regards nature as a wild whirlpool into which a man of feeling and temperament will throw himself if he is to experience the fullness of life; for him, for C. F. D. Schubart, and for Leisewitz art and, in particular, literature are passionate forms of self-assertion which look on all acceptance of conventional forms as but "delayed death." Nothing is more characteristic of the entire *Sturm und Drang* movement than Herder's cry "I am not here to think, but to be, feel, live!", or "heart! warmth! blood! humanity! life!" French reasoning is pale and ghostly. It is this that inspired Goethe's reaction in the seventies to Holbach's *Système de la nature* as a repulsive, "Cimmerian, corpse-like" treatise, which had no relation to the marvellous, inexhaustibly rich vitality of the Gothic cathedral at Strasbourg, in which, under Herder's guidance, he saw one of the noblest expressions of the German spirit in the Middle Ages, of which the critics of the Augustan age understood nothing. J. J. W. Heinse in his fantasy *Ardinghello*

und die glückseligen Inseln (1787; trans. as *Ardinghello; or an Artist's Rambles in Sicily,* 1839), leads his central characters after a bloodstained succession of wild experiences of more than "Gothic" intensity, to an island where there is total freedom in personal relations, all rules and conventions have finally been flung to the winds, where man in an anarchist-communist society can at last stretch himself to his full stature as a sublime creative artist. The inspiration of this work is a violent, radical individualism, which represents an early form, not unlike the contemporary erotic fantasies of the Marquis de Sade, of a craving for escape from imposed rules and laws whether of scientific reason or of political or ecclesiastical authority, royalist or republican, despotic or democratic.

By an odd paradox, it is the profoundly rational, exact, unromantic Kant, with his lifelong hatred of all forms of *Schwärmerei*, who is in part, through exaggeration and distortion of at least one of his doctrines, one of the fathers of this unbridled individualism. Kant's moral doctrines stressed the fact that determinism was not compatible with morality, since only those who are the true authors of their own acts, which they are free to perform or not perform, can be praised or blamed for what they do. Since responsibility entails power of choice, those who cannot freely choose are morally no more accountable than stocks and stones. Thereby Kant initiated a cult of moral autonomy, according to which only those who act and are not acted upon, whose actions spring from a decision of the moral will to be guided by freely adopted principles, if need be against inclination, and not from the inescapable causal pressure of factors beyond their control—physical, physiological, psychological (such as emotion, desire, habit)—can properly be considered to be free or, indeed, moral agents at all. Kant acknowledged a profound debt to Rousseau who, particularly in the "profession of faith of the Savoyard vicar" in the fourth book of his *Émile,* spoke of man as an active being in contrast with the passivity of material nature, a possessor of a will which makes him free to resist the temptations of the senses. "I am a slave through my vices and free through my remorse"; it is the active will, made known directly by "feeling," which for Rousseau is "stronger than reason [i.e. prudential argument] which fights against it," that enables man to choose the good; he acts, if need be, against "the laws of the body," and so makes himself worthy of happiness. But although this doctrine of the will as a capacity not determined by the causal stream is directed against the sensationalist positivism of Helvétius or Condillac, and has an affinity to Kant's free moral will, it does not leave the objective framework of Natural Law which governs things as well as persons, and prescribes the same immutable, universal goals to all men.

This emphasis upon the will at the expense of contemplative thought and perception, which function within the predetermined grooves of the categories of the mind that man cannot escape, enters deeply into the German conception of moral freedom as entailing resistance to nature and not harmonious collusion with her overcoming of natural inclination, and rising to Promethean resistance to coercion, whether by things or by men. This, in its turn, led to the rejection of the doctrine that to understand is to accept the view that knowledge demonstrates the rational necessity and therefore the value of what, in his irrational state, may have seemed to man mere obstacles in his path. This conception opposed as it is to reconciliation with reality, in its later, romantic form, favored the unending fight, at times ending in tragic defeat, against the forces of blind nature, which cares nothing for human ideals, and against the accumulated weight of authority and tradition—the vast incubus of the uncriticized past, made concrete in the oppressive institutions of the present. Thus, when William Blake denounces Newton and Locke as the great enemies, it is because he accuses them of seeking to imprison the free human spirit in constricting, intellectual machines; when he says "Robin Redbreast in a cage/ Sets all Heaven in a rage," the cage is none other than Newtonian physics that crushes the life out of the free, spontaneous life of the untrammeled human spirit. "Art is the Tree of Life, Science is the Tree of Death"; Locke, Newton, the French *raisonneurs*, the reign of cautious, pragmatic respectability and Pitt's police were all, for him, parts of the same nightmare. There is something of this, too, in Schiller's early play *Die Räuber* (1781), where the violent protest of the tragic hero Karl Moor, which ends in failure, crime, and death, cannot be averted by mere knowledge, by a better understanding of human nature or of social conditions or of anything else; knowledge is not enough. The doctrine of the Enlightenment that we can discover what men truly want and can provide technical means and rules of conduct for their greatest permanent satisfaction and that this is what leads to wisdom, virtue, happiness is not compatible with Karl Moor's proud and stormy spirit which rejects the ideals of his *milieu*, and will not be assuaged by the reformist gradualism and belief in rational organization advocated by, say, the *Aufklärung* of the previous generation. "Law has distorted to a snail's pace what could have been an eagle's flight" (*The Robbers*, Act I, Scene 2). Human nature is no longer conceived of as, in principle, capable of being brought into harmony with the natural world: for Schiller some fatal Rous-

seauian break between spirit and nature has occurred, a wound has been inflicted on humanity which art seeks to avenge, but knows it cannot fully heal.

Friedrich Heinrich Jacobi, a mystical metaphysician deeply influenced by Hamann, cannot reconcile the demands of the soul and the intellect: "The light is in my heart: as soon as I try to carry it to my intellect, it goes out." Spinoza was for him the greatest master since Plato of the rational vision of the universe; but for Jacobi this is death in life: it does not answer the burning questions of the soul whose homelessness in the chilly world of the intellect only self-surrender to faith in a transcendent God will remedy.

Schelling was perhaps the most eloquent of all the philosophers who represented the Universe as the self-development of a primal, nonrational force that can be grasped only by intuitive powers of men of imaginative genius—poets, philosophers, theologians, or statesmen. Nature, a living organism, responds to questions put by the man of genius, while the man of genius responds to the questions put by nature, for they conspire with each other; imaginative insight alone, no matter whose—an artist's, a seer's, a thinker's—becomes conscious of the contours of the future, of which the mere calculating intellect and analytic capacity of the natural scientist or the politician, or any other earthbound empiricist has no conception. This faith in a peculiar, intuitive, spiritual faculty which goes by various names—reason, understanding, primary imagination—but is always differentiated from the critical analytic intellect favored by the Enlightenment, the contrast between it and the analytic faculty or method that collects, classifies, experiments, takes to pieces, reassembles, defines, deduces, and establishes probabilities, becomes a commonplace used thereafter by Fichte, Hegel, Wordsworth, Coleridge, Goethe, Carlyle, Schopenhauer, and other antirationalist thinkers of the nineteenth century, culminating in Bergson and later antipositivist schools.

This, too, is the source of that stream in the great river of romanticism which looks upon every human activity as a form of individual self-expression, and on art, and indeed every creative activity, as a stamping of a unique personality, individual or collective, conscious or unconscious, upon the matter or the medium in and upon which it functions, seeking to realize values which are themselves not given but generated by the process of creation itself. Hence the denial, both in theory and in practice, of the central doctrine of the Enlightenment according to which the rules in accordance with which men should live and act and create are pre-established, dictated by nature herself. For Joshua Reynolds, for example, "The Great Style" is the realization of the artist's vision of eternal forms, prototypes beyond the confusions of ordinary experience, which his genius enables him to discern and which he seeks to reproduce, with all the techniques at his command, on his canvas or in marble or bronze. Such *mimesis* or copying from ideal patterns, is, for those who derive from the German tradition of revolt against French classicism, not true creation. Creation is creation of ends as well as means, of values as well as their embodiments; the vision that I seek to translate into colors or sounds is generated by me, and peculiar to me, unlike anything that has ever been, or will be, above all, not something that is common to me and other men seeking to realize a common, shared, universal, because rational, ideal. The notion that a work of art (or any other work of man) is creation in accordance with rules dictated by objective nature, and therefore binding for all practitioners of it, as Boileau or the Abbé Batteux had taught, is rejected in toto. Rules may be an aid here or there, but the least spark of genius destroys them, and creates its own practice, which uncreative craftsmen may imitate and so be saying nothing of their own. I create as I do, whether I am an artist, a philosopher, a statesman, because the goal that I seek to realize is my own, not because it is objectively beautiful, or true, or virtuous, or approved by public opinion or demanded by majorities or tradition, but because it is my own.

What this creative self may be differs according to doctrine. Some regard it as a transcendent entity to be identified with a cosmic spirit, a divine principle to which finite men aspire as sparks do to the great central flame; others identify it with their own individual, mortal, flesh and blood selves, like Byron, or Hugo, or other defiantly romantic writers and painters. Others, again, identified the creative self with a super-personal "organism" of which they saw themselves as elements or members—nation, or church, or culture, or class, or History itself, a mighty force of which they conceived their earthly selves as emanations. Aggressive nationalism, self-identification with the interests of the class, the culture or the race, or the forces of progress—with the wave of a future-directed dynamism of history, something that at once explains and justifies acts which might be abhorred or despised if committed from calculation of selfish advantage or some other mundane motive—this family of political and moral conceptions is so many expressions of a doctrine of self-realization based on defiant rejection of the central theses of the Enlightenment according to which what is true, or right, or good, or beautiful, can be shown to be valid for all men by the correct application of objective methods of discovery and interpretation, open to anyone to use and verify. In its full romantic guise, this attitude is an open declaration of war upon the very heart of the rational and experimental method which Descartes and Galileo had inaugurated, and which for all their doubts and qualifications even such sharp deviationists as Montesquieu, or Hume and Rousseau and Kant, fully and firmly accepted. For the truly ardent opponents of classicism, values are not found but made, not discovered but created; they are to be realized because they are mine, or ours, whatever the nature of the true self is pronounced to be by this or that metaphysical doctrine.

The most extravagant of the German romantics, Novalis or Tieck, looked on the Universe not as a structure that can be studied or described by whatever methods are most appropriate, but as a perpetual activity of the spirit and of nature which is the selfsame spirit in a dormant state; of this constant upward movement the man of genius is the most conscious agent who thus embodies the forward activity that advances the life of the spirit most significantly. While some, like Schelling and Coleridge, conceive this activity as the gradual growth into self-consciousness of the world spirit that is perpetually moving towards self-perfection, others conceive the cosmic process as having no goal, as a purposeless and meaningless movement, which men, because they cannot face this bleak and despair-inducing truth, seek to hide from themselves by constructing comforting illusions in the form of religions that promise rewards in another life, or metaphysical systems that claim to provide rational justification both for what there is in the world and for what men do and can do and should do; or scientific systems that perform the task of appearing to give sense to a process that is, in fact, purposeless, a formless flux which is what it is, a brute fact, signifying nothing. This doctrine, elaborated by Schopenhauer, lies at the root of much modern existentialism and of the cultivation of the absurd in art and thought, as well as of the extremes of egoistic anarchism driven to their furthest lengths by Max Stirner and, in some of his moods, by Nietzsche, Kierkegaard (Hamann's most brilliant and profound disciple), and modern irrationalists.

The rejection of the central principles of the Enlightenment—universality, objectivity, rationality, and the capacity to provide permanent solutions to all genuine problems of life or thought, and (not less important) accessibility of rational methods to any thinker armed with adequate powers of observation and logical thinking—occurred in various forms, conservative or liberal, reactionary or revolutionary, depending on which systematic order was being attacked. Those, for example, like Adam Müller or Friedrich Schlegel, and in some moods, Coleridge or William Cobbett, to whom the principles of the French Revolution or the Napoleonic organization came to seem the most fatal obstacles to free human self-expression, adopted conservative or reactionary forms of irrationalism and at times looked back with nostalgia towards some golden past, such as the prescientific ages of faith, and tended (not always continuously or consistently) to support clerical and aristocratic resistance to modernization and the mechanization of life by industrialism and the new hierarchies of power and authority. Those who looked upon the traditional forces of authority or hierarchical organization as the most oppressive of social forces—Byron, for example, or George Sand, or, so far as they can be called romantic, Shelley or Georg Büchner—formed the "left wing" of the romantic revolt. Others despised public life in principle, and occupied themselves with the cultivation of the inner spirit. In all cases the organization of life by the application of rational or scientific methods, any form of regimentation or conscription of men for utilitarian ends or organized happiness, was regarded as the philistine enemy.

What the entire Enlightenment has in common is denial of the central Christian doctrine of original sin, believing instead that man is born either innocent and good, or morally neutral and malleable by education or environment, or, at worst, deeply defective but capable of radical and indefinite improvement by rational education in favorable circumstances, or by a revolutionary reorganization of society as demanded, for example, by Rousseau. It is this denial of original sin that the Church condemned most severely in Rousseau's *Émile,* despite its attack on materialism, utilitarianism, and atheism. It is the powerful reaffirmation of this Pauline and Augustinian doctrine that is the sharpest single weapon in the root and branch attack on the entire Enlightenment by the French counterrevolutionary writers, de Maistre, Bonald, and Chateaubriand, at the turn of the century.

One of the darkest of the reactionary forms of the fight against the Enlightenment, as well as one of the most interesting and influential, is to be found in the doctrines of Joseph de Maistre and his followers and allies who formed the spearhead of the counterrevolution in the early nineteenth century in Europe. De Maistre held the Enlightenment to be one of the most foolish, as well as the most ruinous, forms of social thinking. The conception of man as naturally disposed to benevolence, cooperation, and peace, or, at any rate, capable of being shaped in this direction by appropriate education or legislation, is for him shallow and false. The benevolent Dame Nature of Hume, Holbach, and Helvétius is an absurd figment. History and zoology are the most reliable guides to Nature: they show her to be a field of unceasing slaughter. Men are by

nature aggressive and destructive; they rebel over trifles—the change to the Gregorian calendar in the mid-eighteenth century, or Peter the Great's decision to shave the boyars' beards, provoke violent resistance, at times dangerous rebellions. But when men are sent to war, to exterminate beings as innocent as themselves for no purpose that either army can grasp, they go obediently to their deaths and scarcely ever mutiny. When the destructive instinct is evoked men feel exalted and fulfilled. Men do not come together, as the Enlightenment teaches, for mutual cooperation and peaceful happiness, when history makes it clear that they are never so united as when given a common altar upon which to immolate themselves. This is so because the desire to sacrifice themselves or others is at least as strong as any pacific or constructive impulse. De Maistre felt that men are by nature, evil, self-destructive animals, full of conflicting drives, who do not know what they want, want what they do not want, do not want what they want, and it is only when they are kept under constant control and rigorous discipline by some authoritarian elite—a church, a state, or some other body from whose decisions there is no appeal—that they can hope to survive and be saved. Reasoning, analysis, criticism shake the foundations and destroy the fabric of society. If the source of authority is declared to be rational, it invites questioning and doubt; but if it is questioned it may be argued away; its authority is undermined by able sophists, and this accelerates the forces of chaos, as in France during the reign of the weak and liberal Louis XVI. If the State is to survive and frustrate the fools and knaves who will always seek to destroy it, the source of authority must be absolute, so terrifying, indeed, that the least attempt to question it must entail immediate and terrible sanctions: only then will men learn to obey it. Without a clear hierarchy of authority—awe-inspiring power—men's incurably destructive instincts will breed chaos and mutual extermination. The supreme power—especially the Church—must never seek to explain or justify itself in rational terms; for what one man can demonstrate, another may be able to refute. Reason is the thinnest of walls against the raging seas of violent emotion: on so insecure a basis no permanent structure can ever be erected. Irrationality, so far from being an obstacle, has historically led to peace, security, and strength, and is indispensable to society: it is rational institutions—republics, elective monarchies, democracies, associations founded on the enlightened principles of free love—that collapse soonest; authoritarian churches, hereditary monarchies and aristocracies, traditional forms of life, like the highly irrational institution of the family founded on lifelong marriage—it is they that persist.

The *philosophes* proposed to rationalize communication by inventing a universal language free from the irrational survivals, the idiosyncratic twists and turns, the capricious peculiarities of existing tongues; if they succeed, this would be disastrous, for it is precisely the individual historical development of a language that belongs to a people that absorbs, enshrines, and incapsulates a vast wealth of half-conscious, half-remembered collective experience. What men call superstition and prejudice are but the crust of custom which by sheer survival has showed itself proof against the ravages and vicissitudes of its long life; to lose it is to lose the shield that protects men's national existence, their spirit, the habits, memories, faith that have made them what they are. The conception of human nature which the radical critics have promulgated and on which their whole house of cards rests is an infantile fantasy. Rousseau asks why it is that man who was born free is nevertheless everywhere in chains; one might as well ask, says de Maistre, why it is that sheep who are born carnivorous, nevertheless everywhere nibble grass. Men are not made for freedom, nor for peace. Such freedom and peace as they have had was obtained only under wisely authoritarian governments that have repressed the destructive critical intellect and its socially disintegrating effects. Scientists, intellectuals, lawyers, journalists, democrats, Jansenists, Protestants, Jews, atheists, these are the sleepless enemy that never ceases to gnaw at the vitals of society. The best government the world has ever known was that of the Romans: they were too wise to be scientists themselves: for this purpose they hired the clever, volatile, politically incapable Greeks. Not the luminous intellect, but dark instincts govern man and societies; only elites which understand this, and keep the people from too much secular education that is bound to make them over-critical and discontented, can give to men as much happiness and justice and freedom as, in this vale of tears, men can expect to have. But at the back of everything, must lurk the potentiality of force, of coercive power.

In a striking image de Maistre says that all social order in the end rests upon one man, the executioner. Nobody wishes to associate with this hideous figure, yet on him, so long as men are weak, sinful, unable to control their passions, constantly lured to their doom by evil temptations or foolish dreams, rests all order, all peace, all society. The notion that reason is sufficient to educate or control the passions is ridiculous. When there is a vacuum, power rushes in; even the bloodstained monster Robespierre, a scourge sent by the Lord to punish a country that had departed from the true faith, is more to be admired—because he did hold France together and repelled her enemies, and created

armies that, drunk with blood and passion, preserved France—than liberal fumbling and bungling. Louis XIV ignored the clever reasoners of his time, suppressed heresy, and died full of glory in his own bed. Louis XVI played amiably with subversive ideologists who had drunk at the poisoned well of Voltaire, and died on the scaffold. Repression, censorship, absolute sovereignty, judgments from which there is no appeal, these are the only methods of governing creatures whom de Maistre described as half men, half beasts, monstrous Centaurs at once seeking after God and fighting Him, longing to love and create, but in perpetual danger of falling victims to their own blindly destructive drives, held in check by a combination of force and traditional authority and, above all, a faith incarnated in historically hallowed institutions that reason dare not touch. Nation and race are realities; the artificial creations of constitution-mongers are bound to collapse. "Nations," said de Maistre, "are born and die like individuals. . . . They have a common soul, especially visible in their language." And since they are individuals, they should endeavor to remain "of one race." So, too, Bonald regrets that the French nation has abandoned its ideal of racial purity, thus weakening itself. The question of whether the French are descended from Franks or Gauls, whether their institutions are Roman or German in origin, with the implication that this could dictate a form of life in the present, although it has its roots in political controversies in the sixteenth, seventeenth, and early eighteenth centuries, now takes the color of mystical organicism which transcends, and is proof against, all forms of discursive reasoning. Natural growth alone is real. Only time, only history, can create authority that men can worship and obey: mere military dictatorship, a work of individual human hands, is brutal force without spiritual power: he calls it *bâtonocratie*, and predicts the end of Napoleon. His closest intellectual ally was Bonald, who in similar strain denounced individualism whether as a social doctrine or an intellectual method of analyzing historical phenomena. The inventions of man, he declared, are precarious aids compared to divinely ordained institutions that penetrate man's very being, language, family, the worship of God. By whom were they invented? Whenever a child is born there are father, mother, family, God; this is the basis of all that is genuine and lasting, not the arrangements of men drawn from the world of shopkeepers, with their contracts, or promises, or utility, or material goods. Liberal individualism inspired by the insolent self-confidence of mutinous intellectuals has led to the inhuman competition of bourgeois society in which the strongest and the fastest win and the weak go to the wall. Only the Church can organize a society in which

111

the ablest are held back so that the whole of society can progress and the weakest and least greedy also reach the goal.

These gloomy doctrines became the inspiration of monarchist politics in France, and together with the notion of romantic heroism and the sharp contrast between creative and uncreative, historic and unhistorical individuals and nations, duly inspired nationalism, imperialism, and finally, in their most violent and pathological form, fascist and totalitarian doctrines in the twentieth century.

The failure of the French Revolution to bring about the greater portion of its declared ends marks the end of the French Enlightenment as a movement and a system. Its heirs and counter-movements that, to some degree, they stimulated and affected in their turn, romantic and irrational creeds and movements, political and aesthetic, violent and peaceful, individualist and collective, anarchic and totalitarian, and their impact, belong to another page of history.

BIBLIOGRAPHY

M. H. Abrams, *The Mirror and the Lamp* (Oxford and New York, 1953). R. Ayroult, *La genèse du romantisme allemand,* 2 vols. (Paris, 1961). M. Beyer-Froelich, *Die Entwicklung des deutschen Selbstzeugnisse:* Vol. 7, *Pietismus und Rationalismus* (Leipzig, 1933), Vol. 9, *Empfindsamkeit, Sturm und Drang* (Leipzig, 1936). H. Brunschwig, *La crise de l'état prussien à la fin du XVIIIe siècle et la genèse de la mentalité romantique* (Paris, 1947). L. G. A. de Bonald, *Oeuvres complètes* (Paris, 1859). A. Cobban, *Edmund Burke and the Revolt Against the Eighteenth Century* (London, 1929). Lester G. Crocker, *Nature and Culture* (Baltimore, 1963), Ch. 6. Joseph de Maistre, *Les soirées de Saint-Pétersbourg,* 2 vols. (Paris, 1821); idem, *Considérations sur la France* (Paris, 1821); idem, *Lettres et opuscules* (Paris, 1861); idem, *Oeuvres complètes,* 14 vols. (Lyons, 1884–87); idem, *The Works of Joseph de Maistre,* trans. J. Lively (London, 1965). J. G. Fichte, *Die Bestimmung des Menschen* (1800), ed. F. Medicus (Leipzig, 1921), trans. William Smith as *The Vocation of Man* (LaSalle, Ill., 1906); idem, *Reden an die deutsche Nation* (1807–08; Leipzig, 1921), trans. R. F. Jones and G. H. Turnbull as *Addresses to the German Nation* (Chicago, 1922); on Fichte: Xavier Léon, *Fichte et son temps,* 2 vols. (Paris, 1922–24; 1954–59). J. C. Hamann, *Werke,* ed. J. Nadler, 6 vols. (Vienna, 1949–57); idem, *Briefwechsel,* ed. W. Ziesemer and A. Henkel, 8 vols. (Wiesbaden, 1955—); works on Hamann: W. M. Alexander, *Johann Georg Hamann* (The Hague, 1966); J. Blum, *La vie et l'oeuvre de J. G. Hamann* (Paris, 1912); R. Knoll, *J. G. Hamann und F. H. Jacobi* (Heidelberg, 1963); W. Leibrecht, *Gott und Mensch bei J. G. Hamann* (Güttersloh, 1958), trans. J. H. Stam and M. H. Bertram as *God and Man in the Thought of Hamann* (Philadelphia, 1966); P. Merlan, "From Hume to Hamann," *The Personalist,* **32** (1859); idem, "Parva Hamanniana," *Journal of the History of Ideas,* **9** (1948), 380–84, **10** (1949), 567–74; idem, "Hamann et les dialogues de Hume," *Revue de métaphysique et de morale,* **59** (1954); J. Nadler, *J. G. Hamann* (Salzburg, 1949); J. C. O'Flaherty, *Hamann's Socratic Memorabilia* (Baltimore, 1967); idem, *Unity and Language. A Study in the Philosophy of Johann Georg Hamann* (Chapel Hill, 1952); R. Unger, *Hamann und die Aufklärung,* 2 vols. (Halle, 1925; Tübingen, 1963). Hiram Haydn, *The Counter-Renaissance* (New York, 1950; 1960). J. G. von Herder, *Sämtliche Werke,* ed. B. Suphan, 33 vols. (Berlin, 1877–1913). F. H. Jacobi, *Jacobis Werke,* ed. F. Roth, 6 vols. (Leipzig, 1812–25); idem, *Briefwechsel,* ed. F. Roth, 2 vols. (Bern, 1825–27); on Jacobi: L. Lévy-Bruhl, *La philosophie de F. H. Jacobi* (Paris, 1894). H. Kindermann, *Entwicklung der Sturm- und Drangbewegung* (Vienna, 1925); idem, *J. M. R. Lenz und die deutsche Romantik* (Vienna, 1925); idem, *Von deutscher Art und Kunst, Deutsche Literatur, Irrationalismus,* Vol. 6 (Leipzig, 1935). A. Koyré, *La philosophie de Jacob Boehme* (Paris, 1929). A. O. Lovejoy, *The Reason, the Understanding, and Time* (Baltimore, 1961). F. Meinecke, *Die Entstehung des Historismus,* 2 vols. (Munich and Berlin, 1936), trans. J. E. Anderson as *Historism* (London, 1972). E. Neff, *The Poetry of History* (New York, 1947; 1971). R. Pascal, *The German Sturm und Drang* (Manchester, 1951). M. Peckham, *Man's Rage for Chaos* (Philadelphia, 1965). K. J. Pinson, *Modern Germany, Its History and Civilization* (New York, 1954; 2nd ed. 1966). J. Roos, *Aspects littéraires du mysticisme philosophique* (Blake, Novalis, Ballanche), (Strasbourg, 1951). F. Schlegel, *Lucinde* (Jena, 1807). F. Schleiermacher, *Vertraute Briefe über Friedrich Schlegels Lucinde* (Berlin, 1807). C. Schmitt-Dorotic, *Politische Romantik* (Munich and Leipzig, 1925). Shaftesbury, Third Earl of, *A Letter Concerning Enthusiasm* (London, 1708); idem, *The Moralists* (London, 1708); idem, *Characteristicks of Men, Manners, Opinions, Times* (1711), ed. J. M. Robertson (London, 1900). E. Spenle, *La pensée allemande de Luther à Nietzsche,* 4th ed. (Paris, 1949). J. Starobinski, *Jean-Jacques Rousseau, la transparence et l'obstacle* (Paris, 1957). A. Viatte, *Les sources occultes du romantisme,* 2 vols. (Paris, 1928). G. B. Vico, *Opere,* one-volume ed., F. Nicolini (Milan and Naples, 1953); idem, *La Scienza nuova* (1725; rev. 1730, 1744), trans. T. H. Bergin and M. H. Fisch as *The New Science* (Ithaca, 1948; New York, 1961); see the collections entitled *Omaggio a Vico* (Naples, 1968) and *Giambattista Vico,* ed. G. Tagliacozzo and H. V. White (Baltimore, 1969).

See also the collections *Sturm und Drang: Kritische Schriften* (Heidelberg, 1962; 1963), and *Sturm und Drang: Dramatische Schriften,* 2 vols. (Berlin, 1958).

ISAIAH BERLIN

[See also **Enlightenment;** Irrationalism; Organicism; **Romanticism;** *Volksgeist; Zeitgeist.*]

ENTROPY

1. The Thermodynamic Definition. The idea of entropy as a measure of the mechanical unavailability of energy—that is, of that part of a given amount of energy which cannot be transformed into useful mechanical work and is therefore lost or dissipated for all practical purposes—originated in early nineteenth-century studies on the efficiency of steam engines. The first to raise the question of maximum efficiency in steam-power engineering was Nicolas Léonard Sadi Carnot (1769–1832). In a famous memoir he asked: "How can we know that the steam is used in the most advantageous way possible to produce motive power?" (Carnot, 1824). Carnot studied heat engines whose thermal interaction with their surroundings consists only in the exchange (absorption or rejection) of heat with appropriate reservoirs of fixed temperatures, and he showed that the reversibly operating engine is more efficient than its irreversible counterpart when working between the same temperatures. He derived this conclusion, which became known as "Carnot's Theorem," on the basis of the caloric theory according to which heat is regarded as a fluid. As scattered statements in the literature of that period indicate, Carnot and some of his contemporaries have been fully aware that in any practical transformation of heat into mechanical work part of the stored energy is always dissipated. The exact answer as to precisely what part is necessarily lost could not be given before the Second Law of Thermodynamics was explicitly stated.

During the years 1840–48 J. P. Joule, J. R. Mayer, and H. von Helmholtz discovered the equivalence between heat and work and thus established the First Law of Thermodynamics (conservation of energy in a closed system). It invalidated Carnot's assumptions but not his conclusions. Referring to the conflict between Carnot and Joule, William Thomson (Lord Kelvin, 1824–1907) declared that further experiments were needed to resolve this dilemma (Thomson, 1849). But only one year later Rudolf Julius Emmanuel Clausius (1822–88) showed without the benefit of further experimentation that the issue can be resolved by either taking "Carnot's Theorem" as an independent principle or by deriving it from the First Law of Thermodynamics in conjunction with the premiss that "heat always shows a tendency to equalize temperature differences and therefore to pass from *hotter* to *colder* bodies" (Italics in the original; Clausius, 1850).

With these words Clausius introduced rather casually the Second Law of Thermodynamics, namely, that it is impossible for a self-acting cyclic machine, unaided by any external agency, to convey heat from one body at a given temperature to another at a higher temperature, a statement which Max Planck later called "the Clausius Formulation of the Second Law." Gibbs rightly remarked that with Clausius' memoir of 1850 "the science of thermodynamics came into existence" (Gibbs, 1889). In fact, it was the first paper to contain

the two principal laws of thermodynamics. Thomson derived Carnot's Theorem from the First Law and the premiss that "it is impossible by means of inanimate material agency to derive mechanical effect from any portion of matter by cooling it below the temperature of the coldest of the surrounding objects" (Thomson, 1851). It is easy to show that the Kelvin Formulation of the Second Law, as Planck called the preceding statement (impossibility of perpetual motion of the second kind), is fully equivalent to the Clausius formulation (Huang, 1963). In a second paper Thomson discussed the cosmological implications of the Second Law and concluded that "within a finite period of time past, the earth must have been, and within a finite period of time to come the earth must again be, unfit for the habitation of man as at present constituted, unless operations have been, or are to be performed, which are impossible under the laws to which the known operations going on at present in the material world are subject" (Thomson, 1852).

Although the preceding formulations of the Second Law as well as Thomson's sweeping generalization expressed essentially what subsequently became known as "the entropy principle," the concept of entropy as such was still unknown. Its definition was made possible only after Clausius demonstrated the following theorem: if in a cyclic transformation q_i denotes the quantity of heat drawn from (positive), or rejected by (negative), a heat reservoir at the (absolute) temperature T_i, then the expression $\Sigma q_i / T_i$ is equal to zero for reversible cycles and negative for irreversible ones. The first part of this statement was found independently also by Thomson. In fact, as Planck showed in a critical analysis of Clausius' paper (Planck, 1879), Thomson's derivation of the so-called "Clausius Equality" $\Sigma q_i / T_i = 0$, or in the limit of infinitesimal quantities of heat

$$\phi \int \frac{\delta q}{T} = 0 \qquad (1)$$

for reversible (more precisely, quasi-static) closed-cycle processes, was logically superior. Nevertheless, it was Clausius who first realized in the same paper (Clausius, 1854) that for reversible processes $\delta q / T$ is a total (or exact) differential, or equivalently that T^{-1} is an integrating factor. The line integral of a total differential, as shown in the calculus, depends only on the limits of integration and not on the particular path chosen for the integration. In other words, it defines a point function or, in thermodynamics, a state function; that is, a function which depends on the thermodynamic variables, like volume or temperature, of the state under consideration.

It took another eleven years for Clausius to realize the importance of the state function defined by the

113

above-mentioned total differential. Writing $dS = \delta q/T$ and integrating, he obtained

$$\int_A^B \delta q/T = S_B - S_A \qquad (2)$$

where the path of integration corresponds to a reversible transformation from the thermodynamic state A to the thermodynamic state B. By combining an irreversible transformation from A to B with a reversible one from B to A and taking notion of the "Clausius Theorem," he concluded that

$$\int_A^B \delta q/T < S_B - S_A \qquad (3)$$

Looking for an appropriate name for the state function S, Clausius remarked that just as the (inner) energy U signifies the heat and work content (*Wärme- und Werkinhalt*) of the system, so S, in view of the preceding results, denotes its "transformation content" (*Verwandlungsinhalt*). "But as I hold it to be better," he continued "to borrow terms for important magnitudes from the ancient languages, so that they may be adopted unchanged in all modern languages, I propose to call the magnitude S the *entropy* of the body, from the Greek word τροπή, transformation. I have intentionally formed the word *entropy* so as to be as similar as possible to the word *energy*, for the two magnitudes to be denoted by these words are so nearly allied in their physical meanings, that a certain similarity in designation appears to be desirable" (Clausius, 1865).

Clausius' thermodynamic definition of entropy, based as it is ultimately on a certain existence theorem in the theory of differentials, is obviously rather abstract and far removed from visualizability, in spite of the fact that the differential expression under discussion reflects an operational result in steam-power engineering. As the preceding equations (1) and (2) show, the entropy of a closed (adiabatically isolated—change of state without transfer of heat) system can never decrease, for $\delta q/T = 0$ implies $S_B \geq S_A$. Extrapolating this result for the universe as a whole, Clausius concluded his paper with the famous words: "The energy of the universe is constant—the entropy of the universe tends toward a maximum."

That irreversibility indeed entails increase of entropy—the so-called "entropy principle"—follows logically from the two statements, (1) that the entropy of the universe never decreases, and (2) that a process, accompanied by entropy increase, is irreversible (Gatlin, 1966).

The fundamental importance of the entropy concept was soon understood to lie in the fact that it makes it possible to predict whether an energy transformation is reversible $(dS = \delta q/T)$, irreversible $(dS > \delta q/T)$, or impossible $(dS < \delta q/T)$, even if the total energy involved is conserved. Moreover, with the help of the entropy concept other thermodynamic state functions could be defined, such as the *Helmholtz free energy* or the *Gibbs thermodynamic potential*, which proved extremely useful for the calculation of the maximum attainable work under conditions of constant temperature or constant temperature and constant pressure, respectively.

2. A Modernized Version of the Thermodynamic Definition of Entropy. With the extension of thermodynamics at the end of the last century to electrical and magnetic phenomena, to elastic processes, phase changes, and chemical reactions—the result of researches by J. W. Gibbs, Helmholtz, H. A. Lorentz, P. Duhem, W. H. Nernst, and others—it was felt unsatisfactory that a science of such astounding generality, and especially such central conceptions as that of entropy, should be based on engineering experience with heat engines and their cycles. L. J. Henderson's critical remark, that "the steam engine did much more for science than science ever did for the steam engine," served as a serious challenge for those concerned with foundational research. Stimulated by Max Born, who as a student had criticized the conventional approach as deviating "too much from the ordinary methods of physics" (Born, 1921), Constantin Carathéodory replaced this approach in 1908 by a purely axiomatic treatment, based on the integrability properties of Pfaffian differentials (Carathéodory, 1909). His "principle of adiabatic unattainability"—according to which adiabatically inaccessible equilibrium states exist in the neighborhood of any equilibrium state, this being a mathematical reformulation of the impossibility of a perpetual motion of the second kind—implies the existence of an integrating divisor only temperature-dependent and hence of the entropy S. Due to the mathematical intricacies of Carathéodory's ideas, they were generally ignored in spite of the enthusiastic acceptance by Born, A. Landé, S. Chandrasekhar, and H. A. Buchdahl. Since 1958, however, primarily after having been simplified by L. A. Turner, F. W. Sears, and P. T. Landsberg, Carathéodory's approach became more popular, and his definition of entropy is now presented even in textbooks of thermodynamics (P. T. Landsberg, 1961; I. P. Bazarov, 1964).

3. The Kinetic Definition of Entropy. Another definition of entropy, which we owe to Ludwig Boltzmann, has been provided by the kinetic theory of gases. Elaborating on J. C. Maxwell's famous statistical derivation of the velocity distribution of gas molecules under equilibrium conditions, Boltzmann studied the change of this distribution $f(v)$ under equilibrium approach and showed that $f(v)$ always tends toward the Maxwellian form (Boltzmann, 1872). Boltzmann obtained this result by introducing a certain one-valued function of the instantaneous state distribution of the molecules, which he called the E-function and later the H-function (Burbury, 1890), and of which he could show, apparently on the basis of pure mechanics alone, that it decreases until $f(v)$ reaches the Maxwellian form. His proof relied on the simple fact that the expression $(x - y) (\log y - \log x)$ is always negative for positive numbers x and y. Since under equilibrium conditions E turned out to be proportional to the thermodynamic entropy, Boltzmann realized that his E-function (or H-function) provides an extension of the definition of entropy to nonequilibrium states not covered by the thermodynamic definition.

4. *The Statistical Definition of Entropy.* Boltzmann's H-Theorem, that is, his conclusion that, for nonequilibrium systems, H is a decreasing function in time, was bound to raise questions concerning the nature of irreversibility of physical systems and its compatibility with the principles of mechanics. Boltzmann, fully aware of these problems, tried therefore to base his conclusion on more general grounds by taking into consideration the relative frequencies of equilibrium states compared to nonequilibrium distributions. In 1877 he showed that if W denotes the number of states in which each molecule has a specified position and velocity (so-called "micro-states") which describe the same given macroscopic state defined by measurable thermodynamic variables like pressure or temperature (so-called "macro-states"), then the entropy of the system (gas) is proportional to the logarithm of W (Boltzmann, 1877a). The introduction of the logarithm followed from the fact that for two independent systems the total entropy is the sum of the individual entropies while the total probability is the product of the individual probabilities:

$$S = S_1 + S_2 = f(W_1) + f(W_2) = f(W_1 \, W_2)$$

implies that $S =$ constant log W. It is clear that a given macro-state can be realized by a large number of different micro-states, for the interchange of two molecules, for example, does not alter the density distribution in the least. If therefore the number W of micro-states corresponding to a given macro-state is regarded as a measure of the probability of occurrence of the thermodynamic state, this statistical conception of entropy provides an immediately visualizable interpretation of the concept: it measures the probability for the occurrence of the state; and the fact that in adiabatically closed systems S increases toward a maximum at thermodynamic equilibrium means that the system tends toward a state of maximum probability.

Finally, since ordered arrangements of molecules (e.g., when the molecules in one part of a container all move very fast—corresponding to a high temperature—and those in another part all move very slowly—corresponding to a low temperature ζ) have a much smaller probability of occurrence than disordered or random arrangements, the increase of entropy signifies increase of disorganization or of randomness (equalization of temperature).

5. *Immediate Consequences of the Entropy Conception.* Boltzmann's statistical interpretation of entropy, based as it was on probabilistic considerations, had to regard the principle of entropy increase as a statistical law rather than as a strict law of nature as originally maintained by thermodynamics. The conclusion that a spontaneous change toward a state of smaller entropy or increased order, though extremely improbable, is no longer an impossibility had, as we shall see, important implications for the cosmological applications of the concept of entropy.

The first to draw cosmological conclusions from thermodynamics was, as we have seen, Thomson in 1852. Two years later, Helmholtz discussed the dissipation principle and formulated the so-called "theory of thermal death," or "heat death" (Helmholtz, 1854). Eventually, Helmholtz declared, the universe would run down to a state of uniform temperature and "be condemned to a state of eternal rest." These arguments by Thomson and Helmholtz implied also the existence of an initial state of minimum entropy and hence a distinctive beginning "which must have been produced by other than the now acting causes"; they challenged therefore uniformitarian geology (James Hutton, Charles Lyell) and its denial of large-scale catastrophic changes in the past. Since, moreover, the Darwinian theory of biological evolution relied at that time considerably on the uniformitarian doctrine, it was only natural that the religious controversy about Darwinism embraced also the discussion on entropy.

The principle of entropy increase was also carried over into social philosophy, primarily by Herbert Spencer. His *First Principles* (1862), published three years after Darwin's *Origin of Species* and aimed at interpreting life, mind, and society in terms of matter, motion, and energy (force), had as its central thesis the instability of homogeneity and its trend toward heterogeneity as a characteristic of evolution in all its phases, whether of individual organisms, groups of organisms, the earth, the solar system, or the whole universe. These developments, however, were held as incidental to a more fundamental process, namely, "the integration of matter and the concomitant dissipation of motion" (Spencer, 1862). That Spencer's social physicalism and its alleged implications for human history had been directly influenced by the principle of energy dissipation is shown by the fact that in the fifth edition of *First Principles* (1887) Spencer made an explicit reference to Helmholtz' essay on "The Interaction of Natural Forces." Spencer's conclusion that the total degradation of energy in the cosmos is followed, due to a process of concentration under gravitation, by a renewed dispersion and evolution so that eras of dissolution and evolution alternate, found but little approval by contemporary scientists like John Tyndall and James Clerk Maxwell (Brush, 1967).

A most remarkable application of the notion of entropy to history was made by Henry Adams. Trying like others of his generation to establish history as a science, and prompted by the conceptual similarity between history and irreversibility, Adams attempted to describe human history in terms of socio-physical or rather socio-thermodynamical laws (Adams, 1919). Stimulated by Andrew Gray's study of Lord Kelvin (Samuels, 1964) and, in particular, by Gray's discussion of the social implications of "Kelvin's great generalization" (energy dissipation) and the idea of the ultimate heat death which had been popularized meanwhile by H. G. Wells in *The Time Machine* (1895), Adams referred to Auguste Comte's teachings that the human mind had passed through three phases, the theological, metaphysical, and positive; these phases Adams compared with the chemical phases of solid, liquid, and gaseous, subject to Gibbs's phase rule, and claimed that these "three phases always exist together in equilibrium; but their limits on either side are fixed by changes of temperature and pressure, manifesting themselves in changes of Direction or Form." The Renaissance, for example, with its marked change in direction, form, and level of what Adams called "spiritual energy," was for him but a phase transition in accordance with Gibbs's rule. Adams concluded that the future historian "must seek his education in the world of mathematical physics" and, in particular, in the teachings of Kelvin, Maxwell, and Gibbs.

6. Restrictions of the Conception. Even before the appearance of Boltzmann's statistical interpretation of entropy, which, as we have seen, questioned the universal validity of the entropy principle, doubts had been voiced whether the principle applies unrestrictedly to small-scale phenomena. One of the earliest devices conceived to this effect was the "sorting demon," first mentioned by Maxwell in a letter of 11 December 1867 to P. G. Tait (Knott, 1911) and published in Maxwell's *Theory of Heat* (1871). Referring to a vessel containing a gas at thermodynamic equilibrium, and "divided into two portions A and B, by a division in which there is a small hole," Maxwell imagined a being "whose faculties are so sharpened

that he can follow every molecule on its course," and who "opens and closes this hole, so as to allow only the swifter molecules to pass from A to B, and only the slower ones to pass from B to A. He will then, without expenditure of work, raise the temperature of B and lower that of A, in contradiction to the second law of thermodynamics" (Maxwell, 1871). The gist of this device, which Kelvin "nicknamed" "Maxwell's Demon," was of course the idea that through the intervention of an intelligent being, capable of sorting physical systems of molecular size merely "by simple inspection," as Maxwell put it, the entropy principle could be violated.

The problem raised by Maxwell's demon became the subject of much discussion (Whiting, 1885), especially when it was subsequently generalized to molecular fluctuations and quasi-macroscopic manipulations (Smoluchowski, 1914). After the rise of quantum mechanics John Slater claimed that the idea of Maxwell's demon must become nugatory through W. Heisenberg's indeterminacy relations (Slater, 1939). However, N. L. Balazs showed that for nondegenerate systems of relatively heavy particles with small concentrations and high temperatures quantum effects do not affect the demon's mode of operation and that, consequently, Slater's view was erroneous (Balazs, 1953). Leo Szilard offered a satisfactory solution of the problem raised by Maxwell's demon. He showed that the process of "inspection" (observation or measurement), necessarily preceding the sorting operation, is not at all so "simple" as Maxwell believed; rather it is inevitably associated with an entropy increase which, at least, compensates the decrease under discussion (Szilard, 1929). Szilard's investigation was followed by a series of studies on the relation between entropy and measurement which culminated in Claude Shannon's fundamental contribution (Shannon, 1948) to the modern theory of information and the notion of "negentropy" (negative entropy) as a measure of information, just as entropy measures lack of information about the structure of a system. In 1951 Leon Brillouin proposed an information theoretical refutation of Maxwell's demon (Brillouin, 1951), and since then entropy, as a logical device for the generation of probability distributions, has been applied also in decision theory, reliability engineering, and other technical disciplines. By regarding statistical mechanics as a form of statistical inference rather than as a physical theory E. T. Jaynes greatly generalized the usage of the concept of entropy (Jaynes, 1957). Moreover, M. Tribus demonstrated the possibility of retrieving the thermodynamical concept of entropy from the information-theoretical notion of entropy for both closed and open systems (Tribus, 1961).

A few years after Maxwell's invention of the demon another attempt to avoid the consequences of the entropy principle was advanced, first by Thomson (Thomson, 1874), and two years later, in greater detail, by Josef Loschmidt, with whose name this so-called "reversibility objection" (*Umkehreinwand*) is usually associated (Loschmidt, 1876). It emphasized the inconsistency of irreversibility with the time reversal invariance of Newtonian mechanics and its laws of (molecular) collisions which underlie Boltzmann's derivation of the *H*-Theorem. It claimed that for any motion or sequence of states of the system in which *H* decreases there exists, under time reversal, another motion in precisely the opposite way in which *H* increases. Consequently, Loschmidt declared, a purely mechanical proof of the Second Law of Thermodynamics or of the principle of entropy increase cannot be given. To counter this objection Boltzmann argued statistically that of all state distributions having the same energy, the Maxwell distribution corresponding to equilibrium has an overwhelming probability, so that a randomly chosen initial state is almost certain to evolve into the equilibrium state under increase of entropy (Boltzmann, 1877b). In fact, Boltzmann's statistical definition of entropy (Boltzmann, 1877a) was a by-product of his attempt to rebut Loschmidt's objection. Later on, when the problem of mechanics and irreversibility became a major issue before the British Association for the Advancement of Science at its Cardiff meeting (August 1891), and its Oxford meeting (August 1894) which Boltzmann attended, he revised the result of his *H*-Theorem by ascribing the *H*-curve certain discontinuity properties (Boltzmann, 1895). In a celebrated *Encyklopädie* article on the foundations of statistical mechanics Paul and Tatiana Ehrenfest demonstrated by a profound analysis of the problem that Boltzmann's arguments could not be considered as a rigorous proof of his contention (Ehrenfest, 1911).

Meanwhile Henri Poincaré had published his famous prize essay on the three-body problem (Poincaré, 1890), in which he proved that a finite energy system, confined to a finite volume, returns in the course of a sufficiently long time-interval to an arbitrarily small neighborhood of almost every given initial state. Poincaré saw in this theorem support for the thesis of the stability of the solar system in the tradition of Lagrange, Laplace, and Poisson; in spite of his great interest in fundamental questions in thermodynamics he does not seem to have noticed its applicability to systems of molecules and the mechanical theory of heat. It was only in 1896 that Ernst Zermelo made use of Poincaré's theorem for his so-called "recurrence objection" (*Wiederkehreinwand*) to challenge Boltzmann's derivation of the entropy principle. Zermelo claimed that in view of Poincaré's result all molecular configurations are (almost) cyclic or periodic and hence periods of entropy increase must alternate with periods of entropy decrease. The ancient idea of an eternal recurrence, inherited from primitive religions, resuscitated by certain Greek cosmologies, such as the Platonic conception of the "Great Year" or Pythagorean and Stoic cosmology, and revived in the nineteenth century especially by Friedrich Nietzsche, now seemed to Zermelo to be a scientifically demonstrable thesis. In his reply Boltzmann admitted the *mathematical* correctness of Poincaré's theorem and of Zermelo's contention, but rejected their *physical* significance on the grounds that the recurrence time would be inconceivably long (Boltzmann, 1896). In fact, as M. Smoluchowski showed a few years later, the mean recurrence time for a one per cent fluctuation of the average density in a sphere with a radius of 5×10^{-5} cm. in an ideal gas under standard conditions would amount to 10^{68} seconds or approximately 3×10^{60} years. The time interval between two large fluctuations, the so-called "Poincaré cycle," turned out to be $10^{10^{23}}$ ages of the universe, the age of the universe taken as 10^{10} years (Smoluchowski, 1915).

7. Applicability Limits of the Concept of Entropy. These time intervals, though enormously great, are yet finite and cannot therefore be ignored in cosmological considerations. In applying the notion of entropy to the universe at large, Boltzmann, following a suggestion made by his long-time assistant L. Schuetz, described the universe as follows: though generally in thermal equilibrium "and therefore dead," it contains "here and there small regions of the same size as our galaxy which, during the relative short time of eons, fluctuate noticeably from thermal equilibrium" and in which the entropy "will be equally likely to increase or decrease" (Boltzmann, 1896–98). In recent years the applicability of the entropy concept to such cosmological considerations has been repeatedly questioned (Plotkin, 1950; Milne, 1952). Whether the introduction of an upper boundary to the applicability of the entropy concept—like that of its lower boundary (Maxwell's demon)—will eventually be refuted remains an open question.

Nor has a unanimous answer been obtained to the problem whether the notion of entropy fully applies also to biology. Helmholtz had envisaged the possibility of cytological processes being associated with entropy decrease, a thesis which subsequently was given limited support by H. Zwaardemaker, but rejected by the majority of contemporary biologists. It gained a revival of interest when in 1910 Felix Auerbach, an ardent proponent of biological entropy decrease, adopted from G. Hirth (Hirth, 1900) the notion of "ectropy" as the biological antithesis of entropy, and promulgated this concept in his popular work *Ektropismus oder die physikalische Theorie des Lebens* (Auerbach, 1910). The issue is of course intimately connected with the conflict between biological mechanism, according to which biological phenomena can be exclusively explained in physicochemical terms, and vitalism, according to which the processes of life have a character *sui generis*.

8. The Boltzmann Problem. What may be called "the Boltzmann problem," namely the question as to the minimum additional assumption, if any, necessary to derive macroscopic irreversibility from pure mechanics, is also philosophically of great importance. On the solution of this problem depends decisively whether a purely mechanistic explanation of nonelectromagnetic phenomena is possible. Until quite recently the conceptual difficulties were usually overcome by the introduction of probabilistic assumptions *a priori*, such as Boltzmann's hypothesis of a molecular chaos in his *Stosszahlansatz*. It was soon understood, however, that these assumptions, though not inconsistent with the principles of pure mechanics, are nevertheless not derivable from them. A general tendency arose to banish probability from statistical mechanics as far as possible.

With the advent of quantum mechanics, which like classical mechanics is time reversal invariant, it seemed for some time, as shown in a paper published by W. Pauli in 1928, that the above-mentioned probabilistic hypotheses could be derived from the statistical aspects inherent in the very foundations of the quantum theory. A certain equation, derived on the basis of Dirac's perturbation theory, which describes the transition probabilities between quantum mechanical states, appeared appropriate for the treatment of irreversible processes. This so-called "master equation" (T. Prigogine, P. Résibois) in conjunction with the Hermiticity assumption of perturbation operators, made it possible to derive all laws of thermodynamics as well as the phenomenological equations for thermal conduction, diffusion, and even the Onsager reciprocity relations, without major difficulties (R. T. Cox, 1950, 1952; E. C. G. Stueckelberg, 1952; J. S. Thomsen, 1953; N. C. van Kampen, 1954).

Since 1958, however, the logical legitimacy of using perturbation theory in this context has been seriously questioned, and new attempts to solve this problem were made in the so-called "thermodynamics of irreversible processes." In 1968 it became apparent that irreversibility is intimately connected with the coexistence of phases in equilibrium and occurs whenever a thermodynamic variable is coupled through an equilibrium process to another independent variable. (See D. G. Schweitzer, "The Origin of Irreversibility from

Conventional Equilibrium Concepts," *Physics Letters 27a* [1968], 402–04.)

Contemporary investigations of the "Boltzmann problem" are very important also for foundational research on quantum mechanics and, especially, on its theory of measurement, since here quantal phenomena are coupled with macroscopic irreversible processes that occur in the measuring device (G. Ludwig, P. Bocchieri, A. Loinger, G. M. Prospèri). Also Louis de Broglie's (1964) reinterpretation of quantum mechanics as a hidden thermodynamics (*thermodynamique cachée des particules*) will be greatly affected by the outcome of these investigations.

9. Extrascientific Applications. In summary, it should be remarked that the notion of entropy or, equivalently, the Second Law of Thermodynamics, "the most metaphysical law of nature" (Henri Bergson, *Creative Evolution*), had considerable influence also on extrascientific considerations. Because of their proximity to cosmological speculations, philosophy and theology were of course most affected.

Ever since Boltzmann (1895), in his rebuttal of Zermelo's recurrence objection, reduced (local) anisotropy of time (the "arrow of time") to statistical irreversibility, the entropy concept has played an important role in philosophical discussions on the nature of time (A. S. Eddington, H. Reichenbach, A. Grünbaum, H. Mehlberg, P. W. Bridgman, K. R. Popper). The concept became also a battleground between idealism (Jeans, 1930) and materialism (Kannegiesser, 1961).

The dysteleological tenet of the energy dissipation principle and its gloomy prediction of a heat death touched upon profound religious issues, and was bound to provoke theological polemics. Examples of such controversies on the acceptability of theological consequences from the entropy principle are the discussion between Abel Rey (Rey, 1904) and Pierre Duhem (Duhem, 1906) and the published correspondence between Arnold Lunn and J. B. S. Haldane (Lunn, 1935).

BIBLIOGRAPHY

Henry Adams, *The Degradation of the Democratic Dogma*, with an introduction by Brooks Adams (New York, 1919), esp. "The Rule of Phase Applied to History," pp. 267–311. F. Auerbach, *Ektropismus oder die physikalische Theorie des Lebens* (Leipzig, 1910); cf. also his popular *Die Grundbegriffe der modernen Naturlehre* (Leipzig and Berlin, 1902; 1926). N. L. Balazs, "Les relations d'incertitude d'Heisenberg empêchent-elles le démon de Maxwell d'opérer?," *Comptes Rendus,* **236** (Paris, 1953), 998–1000; idem, "L'effet des statistiques sur le démon de Maxwell," ibid., 2385–86. I. P. Bazarov, *Thermodynamics* (Oxford, 1964). Ludwig Boltzmann, "Weitere Studien über Wärmegleichgewicht unter Gasmolekülen," *Wiener Berichte,* **66** (1872), 275–370, repr. in Boltzmann's *Wissenschaftliche Abhandlungen* (Leipzig, 1909; New York, 1968), I, 316–402; trans. "Further Studies on the Thermal Equilibrium of Gas Molecules," *Kinetic Theory,* ed. S. G. Brush, 2 vols. (Oxford, 1966), II, 88–175; idem, "Über die Beziehung zwischen dem zweiten Hauptsatze der mechanischen Wärmetheorie und der Wahrscheinlichkeitsrechnung, respektive den Sätzen über das Wärmegleichgewicht," *Wiener Berichte,* **76** (1877a), 373–435, *Abhandlungen,* II, 164–223; idem, "Über die Beziehung eines allgemeinen mechanischen Satzes zum zweiten Hauptsatze der Wärmetheorie," in "Bemerkungen über einige Probleme der mechanischen Wärmetheorie," *Wiener Berichte,* **75** (1887b), 62–100, *Abhandlungen,* II, 112–48; trans. in *Kinetic Theory,* II, 188–93; idem, "On Certain Questions of the Theory of Gases," *Nature,* **51** (1895), 413–15; "Erwiderung an Culverwell," ibid., 581, *Abhandlungen,* III, 535–44, 545; idem, "Entgegnung auf die wärmetheoretischen Betrachtungen des Hrn. E. Zermelo," *Annalen der Physik,* **57** (1896), 773–84, *Abhandlungen,* III, 567–78; trans. in *Kinetic Theory,* II, 218–28; idem, *Vorlesungen über Gastheorie,* 2 vols. (Leipzig, 1896–98), sec. 90; trans. as *Lectures on Gas Theory* (Berkeley and Los Angeles, 1964), "Applications to the Universe." M. Born, "Kritische Betrachtungen zur traditionellen Darstellung der Thermodynamik," *Physikalische Zeitschrift,* **22** (1921), 218–24, 249–54, 282–86; idem, *Natural Philosophy of Cause and Chance* (Oxford, 1949; New York, 1964), p. 38. L. Brillouin, "Maxwell's Demon Cannot Operate—Information and Entropy I," *Journal of Applied Physics,* **22** (1951), 334–43. H. Burbury, "On Some Problems in the Kinetic Theory of Gases," *Philosophical Magazine,* **30** (1890), 301–17. This paper seems to have been the first to use *H* instead of *E.* G. S. Brush, "Thermodynamics and History," *The Graduate Journal,* **7** (1967), 477–565. C. Carathéodory, "Untersuchungen über die Grundlagen der Thermodynamik," *Mathematische Annalen,* **67** (1909), 355–86, repr. in *Gesammelte Mathematische Schriften* (Munich, 1955), pp. 131–66. N. L. S. Carnot, *Réflexions sur la puissance motrice du feu et sur les machines propres à développer cette puissance* (Paris, 1824; 1878); trans. in *Reflections on the Motive Power of Fire, by Sadi Carnot; and other papers on the Second Law of Thermodynamics by E. Clapeyron and R. Clausius* (New York, 1960); cf. also W. F. Magie, *A Source Book in Physics* (New York, 1935), pp. 221–28, and idem, *The Second Law of Thermodynamics* (New York, 1899), pp. 3–60. R. Clausius, "Über die bewegende Kraft der Wärme und die Gesetze welche sich daraus für die Wärmelehre selbst ableiten lassen," *Poggendorffs Annalen der Physik und Chemie,* **79** (1850), 368–97, 500–24; repr. in idem, *Abhandlungen über die mechanische Wärmetheorie* (Brunswick, 1864), Part 1, pp. 16–78; also in *Ostwalds Klassiker No. 99* (Leipzig, 1898); trans. in W. F. Magie, *The Second Law of Thermodynamics* (New York, 1899), pp. 65–107; in *Reflections* (New York, 1960), pp. 107–52; and in Clausius, *The Mechanical Theory of Heat* (London, 1867), pp. 14–69; idem, "Über eine veränderte Form des zweiten Hauptsatzes der mechanischen Wärmetheorie," *Poggendorffs Annalen,* **93** (1854), 480–506; *Abhandlungen,* Part 1, pp. 127–54; idem, "Über verschiedene für die Anwendung bequeme Formen der Hauptgleichungen der mechanischen Wärmetheorie," *Poggendorffs Annalen,* **125** (1865), 353–400, originally delivered as an address at the Philosophical Society in Zurich on 24 April 1865; trans. as "On Several Convenient Forms of the Fundamental Equations of the Mechanical Theory of Heat," in *The Mechanical Theory of Heat* (London, 1867), pp. 327–65. R. T. Cox, "The Statistical Method of Gibbs in Irreversible Changes," *Reviews of Modern Physics,* **22** (1950), 238–48. A. Daneri, A. Loinger, and G. M. Prosperi, "Quantum Theory of Measurement and Ergodicity Conditions," *Nuclear Physics,* **33** (1962), 297–319. L. de Broglie, *Thermodynamique de la particule isolée, ou thermodynamique cachée des particules* (Paris, 1964). Pierre Duhem, *La Théorie physique—son objet, sa structure* (Paris, 1906; 1914); trans. as *The Aim and Structure of Physical Theory* (Princeton, 1954), esp. the Appendix, "Physics of a Believer," first pub. in *Annales de Philosophie chrétienne,* **77** (1905). P. and T. Ehrenfest, "Begriffliche Grundlagen der statistischen Auffassung in der Mechanik," *Encyklopädie der mathematischen Wissenschaften* (Leipzig, 1911), Vol. 4, Part 32; trans. as *The Conceptual Foundations of the Statistical Approach in Mechanics* (Ithaca, N.Y., 1959). L. L. Gatlin, "Logical Proof of the Entropy Principle," *American Journal of Physics,* **34** (1966), 1–2. J. W. Gibbs, "Rudolf Julius Emanuel Clausius," *Proceedings of the American Academy,* **16** (1889), 458–65; repr. in *The Scientific Papers of J. Willard Gibbs* (London, 1906), 2, 262. H. von Helmholtz, "Über die Wechselwirkung der Naturkräfte und die darauf bezüglichen neuesten Ermittlungen der Physik" [lecture delivered on 7 February 1854 at Königsberg, Prussia], pub. in *Populäre wissenschaftliche Vorträge,* 2nd. ed. (Brunswick, 1876), pp. 91–136; trans. in *Popular Scientific Lectures,* ed. M. Klein (New York, 1961). G. Hirth, *Die Ektropie der Keimsysteme* (Munich, 1900). K. Huang, *Statistical Mechanics* (New York, 1963), pp. 10–11. E. T. Jaynes, "Information Theory and Statistical Mechanics," *Physical Review,* **106** (1957), 620–30; **108** (1957), 171–90. J. H. Jeans, *The Mysterious Universe* (New York, 1930). K. H. Kannegiesser, "Zum zweiten Hauptsatz der Thermodynamik," *Deutsche Zeitschrift für Philosophie,* **9** (1961), 841–59. C. G. Knott, *Life and Scientific Work of Peter Guthrie Tait* (Cambridge, 1911), Supplementary Vol., pp. 213–14. P. T. Landsberg, *Thermodynamics* (London, 1961). J. Loschmidt, "Über den Zustand des Wärmegleichgewichtes eines Systems von Körpern mit Rücksicht auf die Schwere," *Wiener Berichte,* **73** (1876), 128–42; **75** (1877), 287–99; **76** (1877), 204–25. G. Ludwig, "Der Messprozess," *Zeitschrift für Physik,* **135** (1963), 483–511. A. Lunn and J. B. S. Haldane, *Science and the Supernatural: A Correspondence* (London, 1935); cf. also E. W. Hiebert, "The Uses and Abuses of Thermodynamics in Religion," *Daedalus,* **95** (1966), 1046–80, esp. sec. 9. J. Clerk Maxwell, *Theory of Heat,* 10th ed. (London, 1891), pp. 338–39. E. A. Milne, *Modern Cosmology and the Christian Idea of God* (Oxford, 1952), p. 148. W. Pauli, "Über das H-Theorem vom Anwachsen der Entropie vom Standpunkt der neueren Quantenmechanik," *Probleme der modernen Physik,* Sommerfeld Festschrift (Leipzig, 1928), pp. 30–45. Max Planck, *Über den zweiten Hauptsatz der mechanischen*

Wärmetheorie (Munich, 1879). I. R. Plotkin, "Increase of Entropy in an Infinite Universe," *Journal of Experimental and Theoretical Physics* [USSR, in Russian], **20** (1950), 1051–54. Henri Poincaré, "Sur le problème des trois corps et les équations de la dynamique," *Acta Mathematica*, **13** (1890), 1–270, esp. sec. 8, "Usage des invariants intégraux," pp. 67–72; repr. in *Oeuvres de Henri Poincaré* (Paris, 1952), 7, 262–479. A. Rey, "La philosophie scientifique de M. Duhem," *Revue de Métaphysique et de Morale*, **12** (1904), 699–744. E. Samuels, *Henry Adams: The Major Phase* (Cambridge, Mass., 1964) esp. pp. 463–96; cf. also H. Wasser, *The Scientific Thought of Henry Adams* (Thessaloniki, 1956). Claude Shannon, "A Mathematical Theory of Communication," *The Bell System Technical Journal*, **27** (1948), 379–423. John Slater, *Introduction to Chemical Physics* (New York, 1939), pp. 45–46. M. von Smoluchowski, *Vorträge über die kinetische Theorie der Materie und Elektrizität* (Leipzig, 1914); idem, "Molekulartheoretische Studien über Umkehr thermodynamisch irreversibler Vorgänge und über die Wiederkehr abnormer Zustände," *Wiener Berichte*, **124** (1915), 339–68. Herbert Spencer, *First Principles*, 5th ed. (London, 1887), p. 527. E. C. G. Stueckelberg, "Théorème H et unitarité S," *Helvetica Physica Acta*, **25** (1952), 577–80. Leo Szilard, "Über die Entropieverminderung in einem thermodynamischen System bei Eingriffen intelligenter Wesen," *Zeitschrift für Physik*, **53** (1929), 840–56; P. Clausing's criticism of Szilard's reasoning, published under the same title in *Zeitschrift für Physik*, **56** (1929), 671–72, proved untenable. J. S. Thomsen, "Logical Relations Among the Principles of Statistical Mechanics and Thermodynamics," *Physical Review*, **91** (1953), 1263–66. W. Thomson (Lord Kelvin), "An Account of Carnot's Theory of the Motive Power of Heat," *Transactions of the Edinburgh Royal Society*, **16** (1849) 541–63; repr. in *Mathematical and Physical Papers of Lord Kelvin* (London, 1911), 1, 113–35; idem, "On the Dynamical Theory of Heat," *Transactions of the Royal Society of Edinburgh*, **18** (1851); *Papers*, op. cit., 1, 174–316; extracts also in W. F. Magie, *The Second Law of Thermodynamics* (New York, 1899), pp. 109–47; and in W. F. Magie, *A Source Book in Physics* (New York, 1935), p. 244; idem, "On a Universal Tendency in Nature to the Dissipation of Mechanical Energy," *Proceedings of the Royal Society of Edinburgh*, **3** (1852), 139–42; *Philosophical Magazine*, **4** (1852), 304–06; *Papers*, 1, 511–14; idem, "The Kinetic Theory of the Dissipation of Energy," *Proceedings of the Royal Society of Edinburgh*, **8** (1874), 325–37. M. Tribus, "Information Theory as the Basis for Thermostatics and Thermodynamics," *Journal of Applied Mathematics*, **28** (1961), 1–8. N. G. van Kampen, "Quantum Statistics of Irreversible Processes," *Physica*, **20** (1954), 603–22. H. Whiting, "Maxwell's Demons," *Science*, **6** (1885), 83–85. E. Zermelo, "Über einen Satz der Dynamik und die mechanische Wärmetheorie," *Annalen der Physik*, **57** (1896), 485–94; trans. as "On a Theorem of Dynamics and the Mechanical Theory of Heat," in *Kinetic Theory*, ed. S. G. Brush (Oxford, 1966), II, 208–17.

MAX JAMMER

[See also Cosmology; Evolutionism; **Indeterminacy in Physics**; Time; Uniformitarianism and Catastrophism.]

ENVIRONMENT

Environment Versus Organism. There seems to be no difficulty at first glance in differentiating between organism and environment. As commonly used, the word "environment" refers to the setting in which the organism develops and functions; more specifically, it denotes all the known factors of the external world as well as those not yet recognized that impinge on the organism and thus affect its biological nature. According to this definition, the cellular wall, just like the human skin, sharply separates the organism—microbe or man—from the external world.

The distinction between organism and environment becomes quite blurred, however, when one considers biological nature and external world not as separate static entities, but as interacting components in complex dynamic systems. Before discussing the knowledge derived from the natural sciences that bears on the interplay between environment and organism, it may be useful to introduce the problem from the opposite points of view identified (since the seventeenth century, if we limit ourselves historically to the modern era) with the philosophies of John Locke and Bishop George Berkeley.

For the modern philosophers of Locke's persuasion, all our knowledge comes from sensations and through ideas of reflection on our sensations. Sensation begets memory; memory or internal reflection begets ideas. Since only material things can affect our senses, it follows that mind cannot be separated from the external world. John Locke follows Aristotle and Thomas Aquinas in believing that there is nothing in the mind except what was first in the senses. Bishop Berkeley argued in contrast, that if our knowledge of anything is merely our sensations of it, and if our ideas are derived from these sensations, then a "thing" has no objective reality; so that nothing exists "without the mind." A thing is merely a bundle of perceptions—that is, of sensations that have been classified and interpreted by the mind. Matter, as far as we know it, would then be nothing but a mental construct. Berkeley's point of view makes it just as difficult as John Locke's to differentiate between organism and the external world.

The Locke-Berkeley controversy could be profitably followed through the views of David Hume, Immanuel Kant, and all the other philosophers who have tried to understand how man's mind relates to the rest of the universe. But on the whole professional scientists have not been much concerned with these problems. They believe in the reality of the external world and in the possibility of making some kind of sense out of its manifestations. This attitude of pragmatic realism, however, is not without ambiguity as was recently brought out by Michael Polanyi, who was a scientist before becoming a philosopher.

The way we see an object, Polanyi points out, (in a lecture before the American Academy of Arts and Sciences in 1968) is determined by events inside our body of which we are aware only through the position, shape, size, and motion of the very object to which we are attending. We are attending *from* these internal processes *to* the things outside; their qualities are what these internal processes *mean* to us. We know the external environment by attending to it *from* our body, more specifically from our internal environment. Furthermore, we know our body by attending *from* its attributes to the events of the outside world. This is precisely what it means to live in our body. Our very participation in the act of knowing then conflicts with the attitude of scientific detachment and therefore with objectivity. For this reason, according to Polanyi, biologists cannot inquire into the functions of organisms without keeping in mind the purpose these functions serve in a particular environment; sociologists cannot ignore the power of ideals in their analysis of social problems.

The organismic view of biology, as opposed to the purely chemical view, gives hope that the knowledge derived from the natural sciences can be related to the preoccupations of the philosophers who are concerned with the environment versus organism problem.

On the one hand, the very process of living transforms the environment profoundly and lastingly, and this is particularly true of man's activities. All organisms impose on their environment characteristics that reflect their own biological and social nature.

On the other hand, man's perceptual apparatus is shaped by the environment. Although we obviously perceive the outside world through our sense organs, what we perceive, and the way we perceive it, are conditioned not only by the evolutionary experiences of the human species, but also by each person's existential experiences. Because of this inescapable conditioning, the conversion of environmental stimuli into shapes, colors, sounds, smells, and other purely sensual impressions can never be completely objective. Since our individual modes of perception have been produced during evolutionary development and are continuously being altered during experiential life, they always intervene between us and the external environment.

Fitness. The changes that occur in organism and environment as a consequence of the interplay between the two may be beneficial or detrimental to one or both components of the system. The quality of fitness expresses the beneficial results of this interplay.

As used by theoretical biologists, the word "fitness" denotes the set of attributes enabling a particular organism to function effectively and to reproduce abundantly in a particular environment. Such fitness is progressively achieved through the multifarious adaptive responses that the organism continuously makes to environmental forces in the course of its life span.

The Harvard chemist and physiologist Lawrence J. Henderson considered the problem of fitness from a point of view which appears at first glance different from that of the biologist, but is in reality complementary to it. Instead of concerning himself with the attributes of organisms, Henderson placed emphasis on the characteristics of the earth which are essential for life. In his book *The Fitness of the Environment* (1913), he pointed out that life as we know it implies the existence of a certain set of physicochemical properties in both the organism and the environment. He defended the thesis furthermore that the physicochemical conditions prevailing on the crust of the earth are ideally suited—and perhaps uniquely so—for the emergence and maintenance of life. The fitness of the earth environment for life has developed progressively in the course of cosmic evolution. In Henderson's own words, "Darwinian fitness is compounded of a mutual relationship between the organism and the environment. Of this, fitness of environment is quite as essential a component as the fitness which arises in the process of organic evolution."

The use of the same word—fitness—to designate the beneficial consequences of two sets of processes as different as the organic evolution of living things and the cosmic evolution of the earth may appear a semantic artifact and indeed misleading. Yet, it has a justification that transcends verbal analogy. As already mentioned, organisms become transformed by responding to environmental stimuli, and they simultaneously transform the environment which harbors them. Some of the physicochemical conditions that are now regarded as essential for most forms of life were in fact created by living things. For example, the chemical composition and physical structure of the soil are determined not only by its mineral basis and by the effects on it of atmospheric elements, but also by the effects of the animal, plant, and microbial life it harbors. Even more striking is the fact that the concentrations of free oxygen and carbon dioxide that exist today in the atmosphere of the earth differ profoundly from those that prevailed before the appearance of life. Our present atmosphere is the product of biochemical phenomena that have been going on since the beginning of life on earth. The compositions and structure of the soil and of the atmosphere determine in turn the kind of microbial, plant, and animal life that can become established, prosper, and multiply in a given area of the earth at a given time. Thus, life and environment evolve simultaneously through a series of feedback processes.

ENVIRONMENT

It is impossible at present to understand how the organism-environment interplay began, since nothing is known concerning the origin of life—unless one counts as knowledge the crude, vague, and unsubstantiated hypotheses that have recently been formulated to explain how precellular, self-duplicating, organic systems originally emerged from inanimate matter. It is relatively easy, however, to imagine what kind of feedback processes took place between even very primitive cellular organisms and the physicochemical environment that prevailed during the early biological history of the earth's crust. Darwinian fitness now implies a complex system of mutual relationships between organism and environment progressively reached through the evolutionary mechanisms guided by natural selection. But, as pointed out by L. J. Henderson, "Fitness of the environment is quite as essential . . . as the fitness which arises in the process of organic evolution" (p. v).

As everyone knows, the earth environment is becoming further and further removed from the ideal of fitness that Henderson had in mind. Most societies seem willing to sacrifice environmental quality at the altar of economic wealth and political power. Wherever conditions are suitable for technological development, the earth is losing not only its ecological balance and pristine beauty, but also its fitness for biological and mental health. The deterioration of the earth is so rapid that environmentalists are now concerned less with fitness than with the social and biological dangers of modern life, in other words with the destructive aspects of the environmental problem. In fact, the word "environment" now evokes almost automatically pollution of air, food, and water; wastage of natural resources; exposure to excessive and abnormal stimuli; the desecration of natural and humanized landscapes; in brief, the thousand devils of the ecologic crisis. Yet, there are other aspects of the relations of the environment to life that are at least as interesting scientifically, and as important practically, as are the nefarious effects of human activities on environmental conditions.

Environmental factors exert such a powerful governing influence on the development of all human characteristics that they literally shape the body and the mind. The adaptive responses that man makes to the physicochemical, behavioral, cultural, and even historic stimuli that he experiences during the formative stages of his development constitute the mechanisms through which he achieves biological and mental fitness to his surroundings.

Most ancient people had empirically acquired the poetical faith that health depends upon ways of life in harmony with the natural world and the social environment. In The Yellow Emperor's classic of internal medicine—the oldest medical treatise in the Chinese language—men are admonished to live in accordance with the laws of the seasons, and with the doctrine of the yin and the yang (Huang . . . , 1949). Half a century ago, the Navajo Indians spoke in a similar vein of their wish to live "in accord with the mountain soil, the pollen of the native plants, and all other sacred things." And comparable expressions of man's personal and indeed intimate relationship with his total environment can be found in the legends and mythologies of all archaic people.

The theme of man's dependence on his environment pervaded the religious as well as the rational aspects of early Greek civilizations. Hygeia, from whose name our word "hygiene" is derived, was one of the personifications of Athena, the goddess of wisdom. She symbolized the belief that men would retain physical and mental health if they lived within the golden rule, and according to the laws of reason. In a more concrete manner, the physicians of the Hippocratic school taught that man's well-being is influenced by the quality of air, water, and food; by the topography of the land and the direction of the predominating winds; and by his general living habits. The fundamental principle of the Hippocratic doctrine was that health can be achieved only by conducting life in accordance with natural laws and in such a manner that the body and mind are in harmonious equilibrium with the total environment.

The Greek philosophers and physicians were also the first to realize clearly, or at least to communicate to us explicitly, that man's relationships to his environment go much beyond the problems of health and disease. In a prophetic passage of his treatise, "Of Airs, Waters, and Places," Hippocrates asserts boldly that food, water, climate, soil, and topography affect not only man's biological welfare, but also his physical stature, temperament, behavioral patterns, military prowess, and even political institutions.

Until late in the nineteenth century, most European physicians held to the Hippocratic view that human characteristics, in health and in disease, are profoundly influenced by the external environment and therefore could be manipulated and improved by sending patients to appropriate climates, altitudes, or geographic situations. Needless to say, this belief was not limited to medical circles. It was shared by many philosophers, historians, and critics who believed that man was as much a product of his environment as of his genetic endowment. To illustrate the point of view of those who took the side of the environmentalists in the nature versus nurture controversy, it will suffice to quote here a passage from the essay "Uses of Great Men" by Ralph Waldo Emerson: "There are vices and follies incident to whole populations and ages. Men resemble their contemporaries even more than their progenitors."

We resemble our progenitors because we inherit from them our genetic endowment. But we resemble our contemporaries even more, because, within a given social environment, most members of a given generation are exposed to the same forces in early life. The human genetic pool remains essentially the same from one generation to the next, but its phenotypic expressions change rapidly because the surroundings and events that shape physiological characteristics and behavioral patterns differ from place to place and from one person to another.

As a moralist, Emerson was concerned with the intellectual and emotional attributes of human beings, but his aphorism is just as valid for anatomical and physiological attributes, as can readily be illustrated by examples taken from recent history and modern life.

The Total Environment. The phrase "surroundings and events" has been used in the preceding paragraph in an attempt to convey the multiplicity and complexity of the factors covered by the word "environment."

The total environment refers of course to the complete physicochemical and social setting in which the organism develops and functions; it includes elements that may have no biological effect whatever, and also elements that are biologically active but have not yet been defined. In describing the physicochemical environment, one usually ignores the whole electromagnetic spectrum except for the wavelengths of light. Yet it is sufficient to take a radio or a Geiger counter into a natural situation to realize that there are in the environment all sorts of forces that are not detected by the senses; some of them presumably have important biologic effects. It is only during the past few decades that reliable observations have been made, for example, on the responses of plants, animals, and men to the cosmic forces that are responsible for the diurnal, lunar, and seasonal cycles.

Biologists have so far studied chiefly the environmental factors that are intercepted by the sense organs, and that constitute therefore the perceptual environment. But our perceptual environment should not be regarded as representing the total environment. Each living thing inhabits a perceptual world of its own. A dog, sniffing the breezes or the traces of a rabbit on the earth, lives in a world that a man or a frog hardly perceives. An insect moving at night toward a potential mate, a salmon crossing oceans toward its mating ground, or a bird exploring the soil or a dead tree for an insect, uses clues that are nonexistent for another species. Much of animal and human behavior is thus influenced by stimuli which make the perceptual

environment differ from species to species and indeed from one individual organism to another.

It is being realized more and more that the responses of organisms to their total environment embrace much that seemed paranormal but a few decades ago. Animals have been shown to receive information through many unfamiliar ways such as pheromones (substances excreted from the body and perceived by animals of the same species), ultra sound waves (in bats), and infrared waves (in moths and pit-vipers). Men also are sensitive to radio waves and magnetic fields. Weather changes have been reported to affect the autonomic nervous systems and various physiologic processes such as blood clotting and blood pressure. It is also likely that man, like other organisms, uses exo-hormones for communication at the biological level. For this reason, parapsychologists have suggested that extrasensory perception "is merely a 'crypto-sensory response.'" There is no doubt, in any case, that various unfamiliar channels of communication, once dismissed as nonexistent and indeed impossible, enable us to acquire information from our environment and from each other without awakening in us a conscious awareness of the process.

In addition to the factors that are inherent in nature and can—or eventually could—be identified by physicochemical methods, the total environment includes elements that exist only in man's mind. For most archaic people, on a Micronesian atoll for example, the environment does not consist only of sea, land, and sky, but also of a host of "spirits" that lurk everywhere. These factors of the Micronesian conceptual environment do not have less influence on the inhabitants of the atoll for having no concrete existence. The "spirits" are generally innocuous, but they become malevolent if not properly treated, and can then elicit behavioral responses that may be even more dangerous than wounds inflicted by sharks or moray eels.

Nor is the conceptual environment of less importance in industrialized societies. Whether learned and sophisticated, or archaic and ignorant, every human being lives in a conceptual environment of his own which conditions all his responses to physicochemical, biological, and social stimuli. These responses eventually contribute in turn to the manner in which he shapes his surroundings and ways of life. In our societies, the conceptual environment is becoming increasingly powerful as a mediator between man and external nature.

The phrase "conceptual environment" is almost synonymous with what psychoanalysts call superego and even more with what anthropologists call culture. Its only merit, perhaps, is to help make clear that the total environment involves much more than the effects of natural forces on man's body: it is a determinant of human behavior and evolution as well as a product of human intervention.

There is no doubt in any case that for thousands upon thousands of years, human activities have played an immense role in shaping the appearance and the productivity of the earth's crust. Many areas commonly assumed to be "natural" in reality acquired some of the characteristics by which they are known today in the course of civilization. The valleys of the Euphrates and the Nile were profoundly transformed by human labor during the Neolithic period. Since that time, all over the inhabited parts of the globe, arable lands have been created by clearing primeval forests or irrigating desert areas. The character of the vegetation is also largely man-made. Many plants now regarded as typical of the Mediterranean landscape—the olive tree, for example—were introduced from Iran; and the tulip was first introduced into Holland from Turkey as late as 1675. The moors of England, so celebrated in literature, used to be covered with forests: they became deforested through the grazing and farming practices of the medieval monks, and then again later when the construction of tunnels by the mining industry created large demands for timber.

Agrarian and urban areas long retain the characters imposed on them by the conditions that prevailed during their early development. The growth of cities is inevitably influenced by the networks of waterways, streets, and roads as well as by the kinds of activities that existed at their beginnings. This shaping of the natural world by man, in turn conditions his activities and thereby his biological and mental nature.

In civilized life as well as in plant and animal life, organism and environment continuously transform each other as a result of their mutual relationships. Although it is impossible to dissociate organism from environment, the choices made by living things, and by man in particular, exert a directive influence that guides the organism-environment system into channels from which there is hardly ever any retreat, and that imposes a pattern on the development of both.

Internal and External Environment—Le Milieu Intérieur. Human history during the past two hundred years provides striking examples of man's desire and ability to change the trend of his relationships with environmental forces.

Throughout the nineteenth century, one of the manifestations of the Hippocratic doctrine, according to which man can escape disease by living reasonably, was the interest that prevailed throughout Europe in the health and ways of life of the noble savage. The illusion (and it still persists!) was that civilized man could recapture biological and mental sanity by re-

turning to the ways of primitive life in nature. Naive as it was, and contradicted by epidemiological facts, this attitude was of practical importance nevertheless because it created an intellectual climate favorable for the Sanitary Revolution of the mid-nineteenth century.

If ever men lived under environmental conditions completely removed from the ways of nature, and deleterious to health in all ways, it was the proletariat of the first phase of the Industrial Revolution. Physicians and enlightened citizens could not help noticing that biological and mental degeneration always accompanied dirt, want, and other aspects of the appalling conditions that prevailed in the factories, shops, and tenements of industrial cities. This awareness led to the conclusion that it was a social responsibility to provide the multitudes with pure air, pure water, pure food, and pleasant surroundings. In Munich, the chemist Max von Pettenkoffer, who was city administrator, practiced with astonishing success the policies of sanitation that he formulated later in his pamphlet, "The Value of Health to a City," consisting of two popular lectures delivered on March 26 and 29, 1873. For him, collective cleanliness was the surest way to health and happiness. The sanitary movement in England generated the "Health and Town Association," which took as a goal "to bring home to the poorest . . . the simple blessings which ignorance and negligence have long combined to limit or spoil: *Air, Water, Light.*" In 1876, the English physician Benjamin Ward Richardson published his book *Hygeia: A City of Health* describing a utopia based on what he regarded as rational control of the environment by social regulations.

The publication of von Pettenkoffer's "The Value of Health to a City" and of Richardson's *Hygeia* marks the height of the nineteenth-century sanitary revolution. But, paradoxically enough, it also marks its end because, as these books were being published, the environmental philosophy that they advocated was beginning to be overshadowed by the more precise environmental knowledge derived from laboratory science. As a result of the discoveries made in the 1870's, especially by bacteriologists and nutritionists, the cleansing of the environment rapidly lost the limelight to chemical disinfection, vaccination, drugs, and vitamins. Charles V. Chapin, the Health Commissioner of Providence, Rhode Island, symbolized this change of attitude by stating that it mattered little from the point of view of hygiene whether city streets were clean or not, provided microbes were kept under control and people were protected against infection by the proper vaccines. Environmental control of health was being replaced by laboratory control.

The laboratory scientists, who superseded the nineteenth-century sanitarians on the health scene, worked on the assumption that each particular disease could be equated with the effect of a specific causative agent—whether this be a microbial pathogen, a nutritional deficiency, a metabolic defect, or a mental stress. The evidence in favor of the doctrine of specific etiology is so impressive indeed that it appears to leave no place for the rather vague Hippocratic hypothesis according to which disease results from the breakdown of the harmonious equilibrium that exists in the state of health between organism and environment. Hippocratic doctrine has acquired a new and more profound significance during recent years from the broad implications of the concepts identified with the names of Charles Darwin and Claude Bernard. Interestingly enough, these new concepts were first being formulated a century ago, precisely at the time when the doctrine of specific etiology was beginning to gain momentum.

Darwinian evolution through natural selection implies that an organism cannot be biologically successful unless it is well adapted to its external environment. Genetic science has defined furthermore how this adaptation is achieved through selective processes which are under the control of environmental forces. As is now well understood, mutation and selection provide the mechanisms which make for adaptation to the environment and which progressively become incorporated in the genetic apparatus of the species.

While mutation and natural selection account for the evolutionary evolution of species, these processes contribute little to the understanding of the precise mechanisms through which each individual organism responds adaptively to its environment. This complementary knowledge has evolved in large part from Claude Bernard's visionary concepts regarding the interplay between the external environment and what he called the *internal* environment. Claude Bernard formulated the hypothesis that organisms could not maintain their individuality and could not survive if they did not have mechanisms enabling them to resist the impact of the outside world. Whether man, animal, plant, or microbe, the organism can function only if its internal environment remains stable, at least within narrow limits. The constancy of the internal environment determines in fact the organism's individuality. In the case of man, it involves not only biological attributes but also mental characteristics.

The recognition that the internal environment must remain essentially stable, even when the external environment fluctuates widely, constitutes such an important landmark in biological thought that Claude Bernard's phrase "milieu intérieur" has gained acceptance in the English language. The most commonly quoted expression of his law is: "The constancy of the *milieu intérieur* is the essential condition of inde-

pendent life." But its most complete expression occurs in the *Leçons sur les phénomènes de la vie communs aux animaux et aux végétaux* (1878–79):

The fixity of the *milieu intérieur* supposes a perfection of the organism such that the external variations are at each instant compensated for and equilibrated. Therefore, far from being indifferent to the external world, the higher animal is on the contrary constrained in a close and masterful [*savante*] relation with it, of such fashion that its equilibrium results from a continuous and delicate compensation established as if by the most sensitive of balances. . . . All of the vital mechanisms, however varied they may be, have always but one goal, to maintain the uniformity of the conditions of life in the internal environment (Holmes, in Grande and Visscher, p. 188).

William James was one of the first to recognize the philosophical importance of the *milieu intérieur* concept and he referred to it in an editorial in the *North American Review* as early as 1868. But it was probably Lawrence J. Henderson who did most to make scientists aware of the concept by discussing it in the introductory chapter of his book *Blood, A Study in General Physiology* (New Haven, 1928).

Homeostasis, Homeokinesis, and Individuality. In his book on living phenomena common to animals and vegetation, mentioned above, Claude Bernard had guessed that the maintenance of stable conditions in the body fluids and cells was in some way dependent upon neural control: "In the animal which has attained a completely independent life, the nervous system is called upon to achieve harmony among all these conditions" (Olmsted, in Grande and Visscher, p. 27).

This view was developed much further by the physiologist Walter B. Cannon in his classical work on the role played by the sympathetic nervous system in maintaining the internal equilibrium of the body. Cannon introduced the word "homeostasis" to describe this phenomenon in his *The Wisdom of the Body* (1932).

Homeostatic mechanisms are not merely passive. They involve on the part of the body and the mind powerful reactions which aim at warding off the environmental threat, or at repairing the damage it has done. In this respect the concept of homeostasis recalls the Hippocratic view that disease involves not only suffering (*pathos*) but also work (*ponos*). *Ponos* is the work expended by the organism in its attempts to maintain its identity in an ever-changing world.

The responses to biological and mental environmental changes must naturally help the organism to function adequately under the changed conditions; but, as already mentioned, the adjustments must remain within limits precisely defined for each organism. These two demands apply to populations as well as to individual organisms. Whatever its complexity, a biological system can continue to exist only if it possesses mechanisms that enable it, on the one hand, to maintain its identity despite the endless pressure of external forces, and, on the other hand, to respond adaptively to these forces. The complementary concepts of homeostasis and adaptation are valid at all levels of biological organization; they apply to large social groups as well as to unicellular organisms.

A further elaboration of the *milieu intérieur* concept, providing a link with cybernetics, was formulated by Norbert Wiener when he wrote:

Walter Cannon, going back to Claude Bernard, emphasized that the health and even the very existence of the body depends on what are called homeostatic processes . . . that is, the apparent equilibrium of life is an active equilibrium, in which each deviation from the norm brings on a reaction in the opposite direction, which is of the nature of what we call negative feedback (Wiener [1956], p. 291).

Both the theory of evolution (Darwin, Mendel, and the Neo-Darwinians) and the cybernetic theory of physiological responses (Bernard, Cannon, Wiener) provide a dynamic approach to some of the problems posed by the interplay between man and his environment. But neither theory deals with the mechanisms through which each individual person becomes what he is and behaves as he does in response to the environmental forces that have impinged on him in the course of his development.

The shape of our biological and mental individuality is influenced by forces which do not affect genetic constitution, but act on our organism at the critical periods of development.

W. B. Cannon's and Norbert Wiener's self-correcting cybernetic feedback represents sophisticated expressions of Claude Bernard's constancy of the *milieu intérieur* concept. Unfortunately, an uncritical belief in the efficacy of homeostatic processes tends to create the impression that all is for the best in the best of all worlds. The very word "homeostasis" seems indeed to imply that nature in its wisdom elicits responses that always bring back the organism to the same ideal condition. There is no mention of disease in Cannon's *The Wisdom of the Body*—as if the homeostatic negative feedback was always successful in preventing the nefarious effects of environmental influences, and in assuring healthy development. This is, of course, far from the truth.

Furthermore, if it were true that the cybernetic feedback always returns the organism to its original state, individual development would be impossible. But in fact, the situation is very different. Most responses to environmental stimuli leave a permanent imprint on the organism, thus changing it irreversibly. It is now

obvious that if an organism were truly in a state of complete equilibrium, it could not develop. What characterizes living processes is *homeokinesis* and not homeostasis.

Individuality develops step by step throughout life, in part as a result of physiological processes which are encoded in the genetic constitution, and in part also because the total environment has formative and repressive effects on developmental processes. Most responses to environmental stimuli leave an imprint on the body and the mind, thereby conditioning subsequent responses to the same and other stimuli. The so-called reticulo-endothelial system acts as a memory organ for those responses which manifest themselves in the form of immune and allergic phenomena, whereas the brain is of course the memory organ for mental processes.

Individuality, therefore, reflects the evolutionary past as encoded in the genetic apparatus and the experiential past inscribed in the bodily structures that store biological and mental memories. Since biological and mental attributes include at any given time all the inherited potentialities that have been made functional by life experiences, and since they are irreversibly altered by most responses to environmental stimuli, individuality might be defined as the continuously evolving phenotype of each individual person. It consists, so to speak, in the incarnation of those aspects of the environment to which the organism has responded during its evolutionary and experiential past.

The influence of environmental factors on the phenotypic expression of the genetic endowment is particularly striking and lasting during the formative stages of prenatal and early postnatal life. As commonly used, the phrase "early influences" denotes the conditioning of emotional attitudes and behavioral patterns by the experiences of early life. But such conditioning also affects many other biological characteristics, indeed almost every phenotypic expression of the adult.

The effects of environmental factors on the development of individuality are complicated by the fact that man tends to symbolize everything that happens to him and then to react to the symbols themselves as much as to external reality. All perceptions and apprehensions of the mind can thus generate organic processes of which the environmental cause is often extremely indirect and remote. In many cases, furthermore, the person does not create the symbols to which he responds; he receives them from his group. His views of the physical and social universe are impressed upon him very early in life by ritual and myth, taboos and parental training, traditions and education. These acquired attitudes constitute the basic premises according to which he organizes his inner and outer worlds, in other words his conceptual environment.

Whether this conceptual environment is acquired from the social group, or whether it develops from individual experiences, the body and the mind are simultaneously affected by any stimulus—physico-chemical or mental—that impinges on the organism.

Like the evolutionary development of mankind, the experiential development of each individual consists therefore in an integrated series of responses to environmental stimuli. Man cannot perceive the external world objectively without concepts because his perceptual apparatus is shaped by the environment.

BIBLIOGRAPHY

Claude Bernard, *An Introduction to the Study of Experimental Medicine*, trans. H. C. Greene (New York, 1927; 2nd ed., 1949); idem, *Leçons sur les phénomènes de la vie communs aux animaux et aux végétaux* (Paris, 1878–79). W. B. Cannon, *The Wisdom of the Body* (New York, 1932). René Dubos, *Man Adapting* (New Haven, 1965); idem, *So Human an Animal* (New York, 1968). L. J. Henderson, *The Fitness of the Environment* (New York, 1913); idem, *Blood, A Study in General Physiology* (New Haven, 1928). Frederic L. Holmes, "Origins of the Concept of the Milieu Intérieur," *Claude Bernard and Experimental Medicine*, eds. F. Grande and M. Visscher (Cambridge, Mass., 1967). Hippocrates, *Of Airs, Water, and Places*, trans. W. Jones (New York, 1931). Huang Ti Nei Ching Su Wen, *The Yellow Emperor's Classic of Internal Medicine*, trans. Veith Ilza (Baltimore, 1949). E. Harris Olmsted, "Historical Phrases in the Influence of Bernard's Scientific Generalizations in England and America," *Claude Bernard and Experimental Medicine*, eds. F. Grande and M. Visscher (Cambridge, Mass., 1967). Max von Pettenkoffer, "The Value of Health to a City," *Bulletin of the History of Medicine*, 10 (1941), 487–503. Benjamin Ward Richardson, *Hygeia: A City of Health* (London, 1876). Norbert Wiener, "The Concept of Homeostasis in Medicine," *Transactions and Studies of the College of Physicians in Philadelphia*, 20 (1953), 87–93; idem, *I Am A Mathematician* (New York, 1956).

RENÉ DUBOS

[See also **Biological Models**; Conservation; **Environment and Culture**; Evolutionism; **Genetic Continuity**; Primitivism; Psychological Theories.]

ENVIRONMENT AND CULTURE

I

IDEAS CONCERNING the relation of the physical environment to culture have their roots in at least three broad areas of Western thought. Their lineage is ancient, their scope broad, and an article of this length can aspire only to general exposition, a prolegomenon to a complex subject ranging widely in theology, philosophy, the biological and the social sciences, and the humanities (Glacken, 1967; Wright, 1966).

First there are those ideas about culture and environment which are constituent parts of religion and philosophy, especially questions concerning the creator, and the manner and the nature of the creation. These include God's care for the world, His ordered creative acts as evidenced by the distribution and adaptability of life, and the creation of human society dependent upon nature for its support. This is the literature of natural and physico-theology devoted to proving God's existence—and His goodness—in the order and beauty of the creation.

Second, there are the ideas in which the world of nature is the point of departure. It is to the earth that man is bound; he is subject to the influences of winds, waters, the seasons, and climatic change throughout history. Distinct but often intricately intermeshed with this set of ideas are those of a more subjective nature; the influence of the external world, the effects of aspects of nature on the mind and the emotions; communion with nature; empathy between man and nature in which the joys and sorrows of man find reflection in it and natural phenomena assume human attributes —notions ridiculed with obvious pleasure by Ruskin who classified them under the rubric of the Pathetic Fallacy (*Modern Painters*, Part IV, Ch. 12).

Third, there are the ideas in which man and his activities are the center of interest. These may have their sources in a religious or philosophical view of man as God's vicar on earth, dominant over all nature by His will, in scientific studies showing man's effects on the balance of nature, nature being viewed as an ecosystem, or on man as *homo faber*, a creator of a technological apparatus with which he overcomes environmental limitations, for example by building a bridge or installing a television circuit.

II

The first body of thought in all its variant forms can be traced in such representative texts as Plato's *Timaeus*, the Stoic presentation in Cicero's *De natura deorum*, the first chapter of Genesis, the hexaemeral literature, especially the *Hexaemeron* of Basil the Great, in many passages of Saint Augustine, Saint Thomas Aquinas, the Cambridge Platonists, John Ray, Bernardin de Saint-Pierre, William Paley, and the nineteenth-century controversial literature over evolution. Such philosophies make·man a part of and yet distinct from nature, his life cycle attesting to the former, his uniqueness because of the manner of his creation to the latter. It is further assumed that man and nature do not work at cross purposes, an assumption which has rapidly broken down during the last one hundred years (Marsh's *Man and Nature*, 1864, is an excellent landmark) with accumulating knowledge of man's destructiveness of the natural environment.

The unity, order, and harmony of nature are assumed because the creator is wise, reasonable, and no lover of chaos. The idea of adaptability is the keystone of this arch because it explicates and throws light on final causes: adaptability of environment to man, as evidenced by the multifarious uses to which it is put, and of man to environment as is clearly evidenced by environmental limitations on human settlement or on procuring food, clothing, shelter. Furthermore, the extraordinarily wide distribution of the human race compared with that of individual species of plants or animals like the cactus or the polar bear, show the intricacy of this adaptability, reflecting the God-given superior endowments of man. Before the attacks made upon the idea of design in the late seventeenth and eighteenth centuries, and its replacement by nineteenth-century evolutionary theory (with a stern Malthusian message from the social world), it was an exalted, almost universally accepted, all-embracing generalization, accounting for the distribution of all forms of life, their relation to one another, and for differences among peoples. It was truly holistic, and it is noteworthy that with the general collapse of teleological explanation at least in physical science, the history of the last century has been one of attempts to create with some variant of ecological theory a holistic conception which, like the old, could embrace the whole of nature from the attitudes of man to a glaciated Swiss valley.

Although essentially earthbound, the generalization could be reconciled with eschatology (the earth still is the abode of man even though a temporary one) on the one hand, and concepts of an order and harmony in nature on the other. Nature is fundamentally kind; J. G. von Herder in the eighteenth century and Carl Ritter in the nineteenth likened it to a nursery or a school for man. This conception offered opportunities for ideas stressing the intimate organic relationships between man and his surroundings which, even with the collapse of religious teleology, could still thrive in Friedrich Ratzel's *Anthropogeographie* which reflects the new thought engendered by the Darwinian theory. It could stress earth-boundedness; it could also find a place for human inventiveness and skill. In seventeenth-century design arguments of men like Leibniz and John Ray, theoretical knowledge gained from the new science leads to practical knowledge and control of the natural environment. Deep probing into the secrets of

nature increases one's respect for and love of the Creator and enables man, made in His image, to complete the creation in myriad ways—by agriculture, drainage, town and city building. It possessed a religious inspiration from the texts of the Psalms and of Romans 1:20; it found in nature a home for man; it had a place for technology, and for homilies on the compatibility of religion and science.

This teleological view of nature and man's place in it was dominant until the era of critical questioning and analysis of final causes, conspicuously by Spinoza in his *Ethics* (Part I, Appendix), by Hume in his *Dialogues Concerning Natural Religion* (1779), and by Kant in his *Critique of Judgment* (1790). It foundered badly even before the losing battles of the controversy over evolution, both in the writings of Buffon in which unity and harmony of the natural world, but not the teleological explanation, are accepted, and in the writings of Alexander von Humboldt, a good example being his introduction to the *Kosmos* (1845–62). The Darwinian theory of evolution offered another alternative in which adaptation and interrelationships in nature were not neglected. Phrases like "struggle for existence" and "natural selection" obscure the fact that the idea of the web of life (expressed in less pugnacious and bloodthirsty language) replaced old notions of interrelationships by design, and provided a basis in evolutionary theory for modern ideas of ecology, the biotic community, the biocenose, and its fashionable and contemporary theoretical expression, the ecosystem. If we wish to take the long view, both the design argument and ecological theory were attempts to formulate the conception of an order of nature as well as the nature of human participation in it.

If this analysis is correct, there has been a historical continuity from the idea of design—nature created by God with love, reason, and foresight—to a concept of harmony and balance in nature, for example, in the writings of Buffon and von Humboldt, in which teleology is eliminated or perhaps persists only in metaphorical language. Then the concept of balance and harmony based on the idea of a web of life, itself the result of evolutionary forces, ironically prepared the way for the view widely held today of the fragility of nature—nature as an ecosystem—in relation to human power, in short, a nature at the mercy of man. The reasons for preserving it are not based on religion or anything transcendental but arise from values created by society. What started with God has ended with man. Basically this newer conception is a consequence of the power of the human race to produce cumulative modifications of the physical environment—from primordial practices like clearing and starting fires to bombs and defoliants—and of the interpretations which have been made of this power. We shall return to this question in discussing the third idea, the force of human agency.

III

Theories of geographic influence historically have played an important role in the study of culture. They appear in secular form, but they are amenable to the first, the teleological, idea because of the vital role of adaptation, and they may be combined with the third, the idea of human agency, in studies of reciprocal influences. The idea that cultural differences may be caused by environment appears first in elaborate form in the *Airs, Waters, Places* of the Hippocratic Corpus (the ideas probably date from the fifth century B.C.). Judging by this essay, speculation about the influence of environment was stimulated by the cultural diversity of the eastern Mediterranean and regions accessible to it—the Greeks, the non-Greeks of Asia Minor, the Scythians, the Egyptians, and their varying environments. The thought progression in *Airs, Waters, Places* and other texts of the Hippocratic Corpus such as *Ancient Medicine* seems to have been (1) denial of the divine cause of disease, (2) the effect of natural conditions, of the atmosphere, of waters, and of places on the causes of disease, (3) their effects on the mind, and finally, (4) extrapolating these effects to whole peoples, thus formulating early generalizations about the relation between environment and national character. The essay does not deal with environmental questions alone, although these influenced later thinkers, climate often being especially singled out; cultural differences are also ascribed to occupation, government, and custom. Many classical writers commented, seldom with any depth, on these matters: some mentioned the role of the environment in creating areas of isolation where peoples, deprived of cultural contact, preserved their old ways; others remarked on cosmopolitan—often wicked—areas like harbors on the seacoast where people could mix and learn one another's vices. Some thinkers, among them Herodotus, Polybius, and Strabo, pointed also to the force of custom in the molding of peoples.

In the Middle Ages, milestones in the history of these environmental theories are the *De natura locorum* of Albertus Magnus and Thomas Aquinas' *On Kingship, To the King of Cyprus*. Both are of interest mainly for showing continuity with classical sources; environmental influences are secondary causes operating on an earth which is the handiwork of God and under His continuous governance. *The Methodus* (1566) and *The Republic* (1576) of Jean Bodin (especially the former) are valuable sources for such ideas and their influence in the Renaissance. Bodin is important as a

comprehensive expositor of classical ideas and medieval echoes rather than as an innovator; he, however, applied his principles to contemporary life, for like Plato, Thomas Aquinas, and later Montesquieu, Bodin thought that knowledge about the environment is vital for rulers seeking wisdom in governing. In Bodin the thought is complicated by large doses of astrological ethnology.

Speculations continued unabated from the publication of Bodin's *Methodus* to Montesquieu's *Esprit des lois* (1748). In Books XIV–XVIII Montesquieu restates the case for the influence of climate, soils, and physical configuration, relying in part on John Arbuthnot's *An Essay Concerning the Effects of Air on Human Bodies* (1733) and on classical traditions, based mainly on Hippocrates. In pithy and often witty sentences, Montesquieu ranged widely to show the force of these influences on national character, religion, the position of women, slavery, diet, and even on the opera. Montesquieu's forceful arguments made strong friends and strong enemies, and for good reason: he posed very clearly and trenchantly the questions based on environmental versus social causation. Does climate influence religion? Are society's ills to be blamed on climate or on the deadweight of custom, and on oppressive governments and religions? It was in answer to Montesquieu that Voltaire, in one of his milder dissents, said "climate has some influence, government a hundred times more; religion and government combined, more still" ("Climate," usually printed in the *Philosophical Dictionary*). Montesquieu indeed became a source for what was already a body of thought in its own right, but he was equally important for the criticism his ideas evoked, not only from Voltaire, but from Hume in his essay "Of National Characters" (1748), both emphasizing the force of moral causes. These books read alone, however, overemphasize the deterministic character of Montesquieu's thinking; his treatment of population in Book XXIII, one of the best in his work, brings out clearly the social and religious influences on human compared to animal populations.

Herder's *Outlines of a Philosophy of the History of Man* (1784–91) sets off in new directions; one could maintain that modern cultural geography started with him. He considered the whole earth and all mankind, past and present. Whereas Montesquieu, like his predecessors, was more interested in correlations, Herder stressed organic ties and blood relationships between man and the earth. Herder's view of man and nature was typical in more than one way of many ideas of romantic thinkers. He used the design argument to show that the earth is a fit environment for mankind whose unity he assumed and whose cultural differences he explained by the "situation and wants of the place, 129 the circumstances and occasions of the times and the native or generated character of the people" (Book XII, Ch. 6). But Herder also noted that man takes an active part in reshaping and transforming the earth, for as a student of Europe's past Herder had also read accounts of the clearing of the woods of the New World (Glacken, 1967).

Carl Ritter is conventionally regarded along with von Humboldt as a founder of modern geography, but if one comes to Ritter after Herder there are few surprises. In his *Comparative Geography* (1852), Ritter presented the all-embracing design argument in the tradition of Leibniz, Ray, and Herder. Ritter greatly admired science and the scientific method, as they increased knowledge and helped in the explication of final causes. Like Herder, Ritter strove to show the deep ties between man and nature. Both illustrated very well how the idea of design could embrace concepts of environmental influence, of man as a modifier of nature.

The humanistic writings of Alexander von Humboldt are of far greater interest than those of Ritter; he was at home in the thought of the Enlightenment, the pre-romantics, and the romantics, and many of his ideas were based on personal observation made in his travels; e.g., his (and Aimé de Bonpland's) *Essai sur la géographie des plantes* (1805), which is a miniature human geography: man's modifications of heath vegetation; comments on the absence of pastoral nomadism in the New World; contrasts in mountain settlement between the Alps and the Andes; human beings as world disseminators of plants; the influence of plants on man's imagination and sensitivity.

Von Humboldt also saw the fundamental importance of the history of ideas. In the *Kosmos*, he made magnificent surveys of the history of the subjective contemplation of nature, stimulated by descriptions of nature in literature, by landscape painting, and by exhibitions of exotic plants; and then of the objective understanding of nature attained through meditation, reason, enlarged horizons resulting from exploration, and invention. Von Humboldt is loath to divorce the humanistic appreciation of nature through poetry, travel, and landscape painting from the objective scientific investigation of nature's laws. The two, aesthetic appreciation and scientific understanding of nature, are not antagonistic; they reinforce one another. He was encouraged that a modern literature concerned with the psychological interactions between men's minds and the external aspects of nature, the power of natural surroundings to evoke moods and feelings, was coming into being, stressing, as Buckle did later in the introduction to his *History of Civilization in England* (Vol. I, 1857), the differential character of environments in their ability to overawe men.

There is good reason for distinguishing between environmental theories current before and after Darwin. The Darwinian theory, inspired in part by Malthus, in pointing to the enormous reproductive power of living things compared with the food available for their sustenance, called dramatic attention to the survival value of adaptation of organisms to the environment. Nature, the physical environment, acquired a new and dynamic force. In her *Modern Geography* (1911, p. 11), Marion Newbigin wrote that evolution was a great unifying principle: Darwin had shown that there is a delicately adjusted balance between organisms and their surroundings. Throughout earth history, slight changes in physical conditions and the effort of organisms to readjust to the disturbed balance have been factors in evolution. Thus in part at least the characters of organisms can be explained by the nature of their surroundings. In this respect human societies and settlements, she argued, behave like organisms. Cultural differences can therefore be explained, at least partially, by minor differences in physical conditions. This unifying and coordinating principle, she thought, has enabled geography to comprehend vast accumulations of facts, and for the first time raised it to the level of a science. The new principle also reinforced older ideas of environmental influence; it led in geography to concepts of the struggle for "living space," the roots of twentieth-century geopolitics, as it did in sociology to a literature now called Social Darwinism.

Friedrich Ratzel's criticism of Darwin is most instructive in this connection: Darwin erred in his conception of the struggle for existence in nature, for "nature" concealed the fact that the earth was not uniform, but consisted of all kinds of environments, some far more favorable to life, to progress, and to survival than others (Ratzel [1899], Vol. I).

Ratzel in fact introduced a new era in environmental thinking; we may single out one of his key ideas, the importance of movement or of migrations in history. Two great forces are at work here: the mobility of man and the stability of the earth. Migration is especially characteristic of the earlier stages of human culture; it is limited and in fact controlled by the physical configuration of the earth which provides distribution routes by land or sea, thus exercising a decisive influence over where men go, on the density of population, and ultimately on the world distribution of man. As mankind develops, however, into a life less migratory, more sedentary, the process of becoming rooted in the soil (*Einwurzelung*) begins, and the higher the development the greater and deeper is this binding relationship. A people and its land are indivisible; one cannot be understood without the other. Ratzel thus set himself firmly against any philosophy of history that sees progress in terms of a gradual divorce from the controls of nature characteristic of the earlier stages of human development. It is only fair to add that Ratzel was not a systematic environmentalist; he saw clearly that the powerful forces of human agency were at work in his own times and in the past, but this body of thought did not achieve the organization and coherence in his thinking that ideas in the environmental tradition did.

To a considerable degree Ratzel's influence in the English-speaking world owed much to Ellen Semple, his American student, who consciously avoided many of his more speculative and mystical ideas like the organic theory of the state; her *Influences of Geographic Environment* (1911), an independent work based on the principles of Ratzel's *Anthropogeographie*, reveals on almost every page the influence of evolutionary theories as unifying principles in explaining the relation of culture to environment.

The period from Ratzel's day to the present resists summarizing; during that time materials pertinent to our theme have accumulated in greater volume and wider scope than in all previous periods combined. We may, however, hazard certain broad generalizations. There has been a loss of faith in environmentalistic explanation, but this should be qualified by saying that even among the most deterministic thinkers there had always been loopholes for nonenvironmental influences (Claval, 1964; Hartshorne, 1959; Taylor, 1957). The partisans of environmentalism simply did not select the human factors for special study. The shifts in interest and the trend away from environmentalism have been sensitively described by Carl Sauer, himself a leader in a new conception of cultural geography (Sauer, 1931). The disenchantment with environmental theories led to greater emphasis on man—his culture and his power to modify nature. The best known example of this shift is the work of the French geographers, Paul Vidal de la Blache, Jean Brunhes, and Lucian Febvre, whose *Geographical Introduction to History* (1925) is a skillful exposition of their philosophy. The rejection of environmental determinism, the insistence on the permissiveness of the environment—it offered possibilities and opportunities, not commands, hence the association of this school with the word "possibilism"—were not bold and revolutionary manifestos but evidences that academic discussions of culture and environment could no longer ignore what was obvious to an intelligent and open-eyed observer. It was absurd to emphasize man's adaptation to the environment when overwhelming evidence from all over the world showed that the human transformation of the environment, now being seen in better historical perspective, was one of the great processes in human history, that changes were accelerating at an unheard-of rate. Dis-

tinct ways of life (*genres de vie*) developed in various parts of the earth due to such factors as environment, traditional occupations, and historical circumstances.

Second, holistic concepts of environment, based on some form of ecological theory, a trend already apparent in Ratzel's *Anthropogeographie*, reflect the growing importance of biogeography and ecological principles upon which it is based. The concept of natural regions among the French geographers, for example, is based on biogeography and ecological theory as they were understood around the turn of the century (Febvre, 1925).

Despite the widespread rejection of environmentalism, the writings of Ellsworth Huntington, Arnold Toynbee, and other contemporary writers in their reexaminations of concepts have kept alive these persistent and vexing questions concerning the nature of environmental influences. Huntington was concerned basically with two broad fields: (1) the relation of the distribution of civilization (as he defined it) to the geographic distribution of climatic areas favorable (again by his definition) to high energy, creativity, productivity, and the like; and (2) the role of climatic change in the history of civilization (Huntington, 1945). Huntington's work was not done in isolation but in the mainstream of wide-ranging research which had been conducted vigorously since the latter part of the nineteenth century on the relation of environment —particularly climate—to health and disease, diet, creativity, labor efficiency, mental diseases, genius and intelligence, race, social and political organization, national character, the suitability of the tropics to white settlement, and climatic factors including climatic change in the rise and fall of civilizations (Glacken, 1956, on climatic change).

Huntington was not an environmental monist, nor did he deny the operation of many other factors. It was the climatic factor that enchanted him. His influence extended far beyond his own discipline; like Montesquieu, Buckle, Spengler, and Toynbee, not the least of his merits was the exegetical literature his many books produced.

More recently, Arnold Toynbee, examining the question whether certain environments present conditions favorable to the genesis of civilizations, has dismissed the environment as a causative factor; he has also rejected race. His discussions, however (1961), of "the challenge of the environment" (the stimulus of hard countries, of new ground, of blows, pressures) have provoked charges of environmentalism, for example, by O. H. K. Spate in an article on Toynbee and Huntington (*Geographical Journal*, 118 [1952], 406–28).

In the years following World War II, British and American geographers, especially, have shown considerable interest in analyzing the semantics of environmental theory, and the meaning of such words as "environment," "possibilism," and "determinism." This discussion has grown out of the vagueness in usage, the accretions of time, often inconsistent with one another, and out of the fear that a cultural was supplanting an environmental determinism. Fear also of being accused of environmental determinism meant that important and legitimate areas of inquiry were ignored or at best neglected (Lewthwaite, 1966; Spate, 1968).

IV

A distinction should be made between two concepts of man as a modifier of nature, for they have had a separate, though often interlocking history: (1) man as a planner of environmental change, as in constructing a dam—evidence of this inventive, purposive behavior and its effects (often called "control over nature") has generally come from the history of applied science and technology; and (2) the idea of the indirect and the unconscious modifier, which has come mainly from the literature of natural history. That man is an unconscious disturber of nature, an indirect transformer because of his ignorance of the causal chain of interferences, was observed long before the development of modern ecology. According to a note in William Derham's *Physico-Theology* (1798 ed.), colonists in America tried to exterminate crows because the birds harmed the corn, with the result that worms, caterpillars, and beetles increased. When the war on crows stopped, they were relieved of the plague of insects (Glacken, 1967).

The idea that men are bringers of order into the natural world appears deeply imbedded in human thought. Mircea Eliade, for example, in *Cosmos and History. The Myth of the Eternal Return* (trans. W. Trask, 1959), has called attention to the act of "cosmicizing" the environment: areas outside of man's ken, remote from his settlement, are areas of chaos. With settlement, with possession, a sacred and creative act, the bringing of order, takes place. "The uncultivated zone is first 'cosmicized,' then inhabited."

In classical times, the conception of man as a controller of other kinds of life, as an intermediary governing and curbing the powers of plants and animals, is clearly formulated. Without human control weeds, brambles, and thickets might cover the earth; wild and voracious animals, their numbers unchecked, do as they will. How can man impose his will on the animals, the docile and the ferocious alike? Philo the Jew (ca. 50 B.C.–A.D. 45) was obviously impressed by this power; man is like a governor or a ship's pilot in guiding other forms of life. In Judeo-Christian theology, the uniqueness of man, created by God in his image, gives him power over the whole creation. It is indisputable that the unique position of man in the creation—he was the only creature in whom God took a strong personal interest and made in his own image—has emphasized in Christian thought the environment as a utility created for man. Man has also been considered a finisher of nature; God created the earth, and the results were good but there was still opportunity for man to develop his skills, accommodating the earth to his needs and preferences.

In the Middle Ages, there were many observed instances of unfavorable environmental changes as a result of the exercise of customary rights of grazing and forest clearance, but these cases were local in nature and produced no synthesis. The most profound contributions to this idea came in modern times. Buffon made a remarkable interpretation of the effects of human agency. He was impressed by the landscapes of Europe transformed by man in contrast to the thinly populated areas of the largely virgin New World. He postulated (1778) seven epochs in the history of the earth, the last being characterized by the active participation of man in bringing it to its present state. Man is thus an intruder in a natural order already established in the previous six epochs. Though often a destroyer, he is generally portrayed as an embellisher of nature. Buffon had no taste for the state of nature, and it was not difficult for him to choose between a beautiful cultivated landscape in the French countryside and a dense uninhabited forest of the New World.

The idea of the intruder was also basic to the work of the American George P. Marsh, *Man and Nature* (1864); but man appeared to him predominantly as a destroyer of his natural environment. Marsh's ideas of the power of human intrusions in the natural order opposed the view that man is a weak geological agent compared to other geological forces changing the earth—volcanoes, earthquakes, streams—and objected to the environmentalists who insisted upon the influence of environment on man as an organizing principle in the study of man's relation to nature. Marsh's *Man and Nature* assumed a primordial balance in nature, which without man's interference tends to self-restoration—even with great natural catastrophes upsetting the balance—with plants and animals, participating in the healing process, for unlike man they do not initiate irreversible processes. Thus human history may be viewed as a continuous series of intrusions—often irreversible—into the natural order, first by means of plant and animal domestication, then by clearing the woods, and by interfering with the waters, as in stream diversion, or with the sands as in dune fixation (Marsh, 1965; Lowenthal, 1958).

Though Marsh seems to have arrived at his idea of a balance in nature independently of Darwin, it is similar to the web of life concept; but Darwin is basically concerned with the web of life as a product of evolution, Marsh as a basis from which to measure the influences of man. The web of life, the biocenose, the biotic community, the ecosystem—all terms relating to the same kinds of concept—have broadened and deepened the opportunities for studying the relation of nature and culture, particularly changes in the natural order. New perspectives were opened up: (1) in these circumstances, balance and harmony implied fragility, delicacy, and susceptibility so that man, far from being overwhelmed by the environment, could initiate irreversible processes that would destroy the environment for human use and thus make man the victim of a new environment brought into being by him; (2) since he was an intruder in an order tending toward harmony and balance, science and ethics, as well as concern for his own well-being, called upon him to be a steward of nature whose power in the creation of changes entailed responsibilities; and (3) it called attention not only to the directive force of man on the evolution of animals, plants, and man himself, but also to the continuously intensifying imprint of human values on the landscape. With accumulating knowledge of the long history of environmental changes by human agency, students increasingly have described them in ecological terms. By the first decade of the twentieth century—scarcely seventy years after Sir Charles Lyell had described man as a weak geological agent—several geologists were calling man the dominant geological force of the planet. Terms like the "psychozoic era," "anthropozoic era," and "the mental era" were used to characterize this new geological period, anticipating the thesis of Edouard Le Roy, W. I. Vernadsky, and Pierre Teilhard de Chardin a generation later that the world was no longer a biosphere but a noösphere (Glacken, 1956). Carl Ortwin Sauer's writings (selections in *Land and Life; Agricultural Origins and Dispersals,* 1963) made important contributions to the study of modifications of nature by man; he consistently emphasized their antiquity, the significance of fire, the wider implications of domestication, the role of human agency in disseminating plants and animals, and man as a highly selective appraiser of resources. Finally, Chardin, in many of his writings, notably *The Phenomenon of Man,* employed the word noösphere to describe the "humanized" earth as a planet now under the directive force of mind; to him, the human race, in the time perspective of earth history, is still relatively new and inexperienced, and Chardin can thus reserve judgment on the enormous volume of pessimistic literature and

observation which has accumulated since the days of Marsh, attaining new momentum with the Midwest dust storms of 1934, and the broadening scope of post-World War II developments.

Many contemporary ideas have grown out of the unparalleled destruction of the last hundred years—of primitive peoples and wildlife, out of deforestation and soil erosion, and as a result of the creation of industrial landscapes, we have witnessed the deterioration of urban environments. Accompanying these changes has been a growing understanding of them because of the gradual refinement of ecological ideas and the ecosystem concept as it is understood today. The changes do not appear as unrelated and discrete events. One must, however, distinguish between understanding and its dissemination, for ecologic theory still had an extremely limited influence on the world until the 1960's. Among thinkers friendly to the ecological point of view, viz., that the power of human agency has been so great and all-pervading, there has been a reversal of roles; the ecosystem concept is used very frequently to dramatize the fragility of nature, a natural environment at the mercy of human needs expressed in economic systems, cultural factors, religious belief, values, or lack of them. It is a moving experience to compare Marsh's *Man and Nature* with the symposium volume, dedicated to him, *Man's Role in Changing the Face of the Earth* which appeared in 1956.

Under these circumstances it is not surprising that there should be interest also in environmental questions other than those of an economic, utilitarian, or purely scientific nature, that there should be interest in environmental perception, nature imagery, in scenery, in preservation, whether it is an old quarter in a city or an old oak. The desire to preserve unique forms, whether wilderness, redwoods, or erratic blocks left by glaciers, would seem to be a recognition of variety and historical depth as indispensable elements of civilization. Moreover, the interest in wilderness, Roderick Nash's *Wilderness and the American Mind* (1967), for example, has reopened questions about the meaning of nature to man which hitherto had been prominent only in anthologies on romanticism. The present-day concern for aesthetics of landscape (e.g., Paul Shepard's *Man in the Landscape,* 1967) may be compared with the same kinds of questions raised by the romantics and by men like John Ruskin and William Morris, by the creation of industrial landscapes like the Coketown which Dickens described in the fifth chapter of *Hard Times* (Burton, 1968; Lowenthal, 1961).

There is every indication that the literature concerned with the relation of culture to environment will appear in ever-increasing volume. The more thoughtful and more profound of these writings will be concerned, 133 as they have been in the past, with the meaning and value not only of human but of all life, with the environments that support them, and with deeper understandings of the dazzling variety in attitudes toward nature still held throughout the world today.

BIBLIOGRAPHY

Ian Burton, "The Quality of the Environment: A Review," *Geographical Review*, **58** (1968), 472–81, provides current discussions of environmental quality, imagery, perception, attitudes to nature, and is well documented. Paul Claval, *Essai sur l'évolution de la géographie humaine*, Annales littéraires de l'université de Besançon, Vol. 67 (Paris, 1964), is a history of human geography, including contemporary world developments with references in English, French, and German. T. W. Freeman, *A Hundred Years of Geography* (Chicago, 1962), includes discussion of geographers, methodology, and environmental theories. Clarence J. Glacken, "Changing Ideas of the Habitable World," *Man's Role in Changing the Face of the Earth*, ed. William L. Thomas, Jr. (Chicago, 1956), pp. 70–92, discusses the history of the idea of man as a modifier of nature, and has many references. Materials discussed in this article up to the early nineteenth century are based on idem, *Traces on the Rhodian Shore. Nature and Culture in Western Thought from Ancient Times to the End of the Eighteenth Century* (Berkeley and Los Angeles, 1967), which provides references to the sources and important secondary works; see p. 423 for eighteenth-century ecology. Richard Hartshorne, *Perspective on the Nature of Geography* (Chicago, 1959), has revisions and amplifications of his *Nature of Geography* (1939). Ellsworth Huntington, *Mainsprings of Civilization* (New York, 1945), is a summary of Huntington's life work, with a full bibliography including references to Huntington's earlier writings; see especially Part III, "Physical Environment and Human Activity." Gordon R. Lewthwaite, "Environmentalism and Determinism: A Search for Clarification," *Annals of the Association of American Geographers*, **56** (1966), 1–23, is a valuable discussion of environmental concepts, especially for the 1950's and early 1960's with full citations chiefly to sources in English. David Lowenthal, "Geography, Experience, and Imagination: Towards a Geographical Epistemology," *Annals of the Association of American Geographers*, **51** (1961), 241–60, is an essay "in the theory of geographical knowledge," on the relation of man's perception of environments and his interpretations of them, with valuable notes; idem, *George Perkins Marsh. Versatile Vermonter* (New York, 1958), is indispensable for understanding a key figure in the history of attitudes to environment. George P. Marsh, *Man and Nature*, ed. David Lowenthal (Cambridge, Mass., 1965), is an excellent edition (with an introduction) of Marsh's work, first published in 1864. Friedrich Ratzel, *Anthropogeographie. Erster Teil*, 2nd ed. (Stuttgart, 1899); idem, *Zweiter Teil*, 3rd ed., 2 vols. (Stuttgart, 1922), is a basic work on modern human geography, Vol. I of which has an interesting historical introduction; for criticism of Darwin, see I, xxiv–xxvi; and for a discussion of people's roots in the soil, see I, 195. Carl O. Sauer, "Cultural Geography," *Encyclopedia of the Social Sciences*, 15 vols. (New York, 1931), VI, 621–24, discusses the decline of modern environmentalism and its replacement by newer concepts in cultural geography. Ellen C. Semple, *Influences of Geographic Environment, on the Basis of Ratzel's System of Anthropo-geography* (New York, 1911), was in its time probably the most influential single work on this subject in English. O. H. K. Spate, "Environmentalism," *International Encyclopedia of the Social Sciences*, 17 vols. (New York, 1968), V, 93–97, is particularly informative, with excellent bibliography on contemporary discussions of environment and ideas of determinism, possibilism, and probabilism, with semantics of these words and comments on quantification. Johannes Steinmetzler, *Die Anthropogeographie Friedrich Ratzels und ihre ideengeschichtlichen Wurzeln*, Bonner Geographische Abhandlungen, Heft 19 (Bonn, 1956), provides Ratzel's basis ideas in anthropogeography including his relationship to Herder and Ritter, and a valuable bibliography of German secondary works. Griffith Taylor, ed., *Geography in the Twentieth Century*, 3rd ed. (New York, 1957), is an excellent source for nineteenth- and twentieth-century concepts of environment, determinism, possibilism, as well as for French and German developments. William L. Thomas, Jr., ed., *Man's Role in Changing the Face of the Earth* (Chicago, 1956), consists of fifty-two articles with discussions based on an International Symposium of the same name, and is dedicated to George P. Marsh. Arnold J. Toynbee, *A Study of History*, 2nd ed., Vol. I, (London, 1935), discusses environment and the genesis of civilizations and challenge and response; ibid., Vol. XII, *Reconsiderations* (London, New York, and Toronto, 1961), answers the critics of his treatment of environment, 146–48, 254–58, 314–27. Harriet Wanklyn, *Friedrich Ratzel. A Biographical Memoir and Bibliography* (Cambridge, 1961), is a short but well-balanced appraisal of Ratzel with a bibliography of his works. John Kirtland Wright, *Human Nature in Geography . . .* (Cambridge, Mass., 1966), is an admirable selection from Wright's essays on environment and culture. D. O. Zöckler, *Geschichte der Beziehungen zwischen Theologie und Naturwissenschaft mit besondrer Rücksicht auf Schöpfungsgeschichte. Erste Abtheilung: Von den Anfängen der christlichen Kirche bis auf Newton und Leibnitz. Zweite Abtheilung: Von Newton und Leibnitz bis zur Gegenwart*, 2 vols. (Gütersloh, 1877–79), is a fundamental work on natural and physicotheology by one sympathetic to the design argument.

CLARENCE J. GLACKEN

[See also Causation; **Conservation;** Continuity; Creation; Design Argument; **Environment;** Evolutionism; God; **Mountains;** Progress; **Uniformitarianism.**]

EPICUREANISM AND FREE WILL

THE EPICUREANS were followers of Epicurus, a Greek philosopher who lived from 341 to 270 B.C. The most important of them to us is Lucretius, a Roman poet of the first century B.C., whose *De rerum natura* is the fullest account of Epicurus' philosophy that we possess. Nearly all Epicurus' own writings are lost. One problem raised by them is that of free will, the problem whether a man's actions are entirely determined by his inherited characteristics, his past experience, and his present circumstances, or whether sometimes at least he has a free choice between alternative courses of action. The word "will" must not be pressed here: indeed the Greeks had no word exactly equivalent to it, but the problem is one that they were able to understand and formulate without difficulty. It is independent of any particular psychological terminology.

Many modern philosophers have written about this problem. Some say that freedom is an illusion, and that all our actions are determined; others deny this, and try to show how determinism can be avoided, while a third group argues that determinism and freedom are in fact compatible, and only seem to be opposed. But they are all agreed that there at least appears to be a problem, and the intelligent layman also sees the difficulty, for it arises from assumptions that he takes for granted. The earlier Greek philosophers, however, do not seem to have been aware of any such problem, although they were familiar with the elements of it. Plato, for instance, in the *Republic* (II–III, esp. 416; IV 429–30; V 458–61; VI 490–92), discusses a program for breeding human beings which implies that he believed in the influence of heredity, and a program for educating them which implies that he believed in the influence of training, but he does not generalize from these two points and conclude that a man's actions are entirely the result of these and other external factors. Both Plato, in the *Laws,* and Aristotle, in the *Nicomachean Ethics,* discuss problems of punishment and voluntary action from a legalistic standpoint, and in their discussion they touch on a number of arguments that, if followed up, might lead to thoroughgoing determinism, but such arguments are not taken very seriously. This is not surprising. Both men were concerned with limited problems bearing on practical issues—good government and law—and did not go beyond them. One very good reason for this, mentioned by Aristotle, is that thoroughgoing determinism destroys the natural basis for a distinction between voluntary and involuntary actions: all actions become involuntary because a man cannot help but do them. But for the purposes of the law it is vital to be able to regard some actions as voluntary, for it is only these that can justifiably be punished. For Aristotle, this argument seemed to be final.

Epicurus was different. Like Aristotle, he was interested in the applicability of punishment, advice, and similar concepts, but he was not content to accept Aristotle's approach. One reason was that he had taken

over from the great atomist philosopher, Democritus (ca. 460–390 B.C.), an account of the nature of the universe which seemed to involve determinism and at the same time simplified, or perhaps oversimplified, the issues. According to Democritus, the universe consisted solely of atoms of solid matter moving through empty space. Every large-scale object, including gods and men, was made up entirely of such atoms and the spaces between them. Being of different shapes, atoms could combine with each other in many ways, and the differences between one thing and another could be accounted for entirely in terms of such combinations. Even the soul was material, though composed of the finest and most easily moving atoms. All observable changes were to be explained by changes in the atomic microstructure, and all these were changes in the spatial relations of atoms among themselves: atoms could not change internally. This theory involved determinism, because given the original shape, speed, and direction of the atoms, or their shape, speed, and direction at any single moment of time, all later states of the universe would necessarily follow, including all the states and actions of every individual man. Not only this, but the theory also reduced psychological causation to mechanical or physical causation, and so simplified the issues. It was possible for earlier thinkers, including Plato and Aristotle, to treat psychology as an independent field, as indeed we frequently do today. But if minds are no more than combinations of atoms, they are bound by the laws of atomic behavior, and if atomic behavior is fully determined, then so is psychology. Hence the issues presented themselves with peculiar sharpness.

The fact that all men's actions would thus be completely determined does not seem to have worried Democritus, but for Epicurus it was a stumbling-block. Indeed he says explicitly that "it would be better to follow the myths about the gods than to be a slave to the determinism (*heimarmene*, εἱμαρμένη) of the physicists. For you can hope to appease the gods with worship, but you cannot appease necessity" (*Letter to Menoecus,* 134). He had two main reasons for believing in free will. The first was that he observed a kind of spontaneity in human beings—and perhaps in some animals—which appeared to consist in the ability to originate actions. The second was that he believed that praise and blame, reward and punishment, advice and reproach, which men use freely in their relations with one another, are out of place unless men are genuinely free to choose one course of action rather than another. For you cannot blame or punish a man for something he cannot help doing.

Unfortunately we have lost nearly all of Epicurus' writings, and those that we have tell us little about the first point. But there are some detailed examples of it in Lucretius, whose long poem is an account of the system of Epicurus, and follows Epicurus very closely.

His first example of spontaneity seems, surprisingly, to be about the behavior of horses at the start of a race (*De rerum natura* II, 263–71). This raises difficulties, as in some of his fragmentary works Epicurus seems to deny that animals can have free will, and it may be that this passage of Lucretius has come down to us in a corrupt form. The second example is of a man who is pushed or dragged headlong by some external force, but is able to oppose it and stand his ground because of something within his breast which has the power to do so (II, 277–87).

If we are to take these examples seriously Epicurus was not here concerned with moral decisions, but with the ability men—and perhaps animals—have to make a fresh start in many kinds of situations. This ability was something that he believed one could observe. But moral issues were also relevant, and these are indicated in a point made by Epicurus himself in a work that has come down to us only in fragments, his *On Nature*. There he speaks of men "admonishing one another and struggling and trying to change each others' ways as having a causal principle in themselves, and not only in their original constitution and in the necessity of that which surrounds and enters them according to its own laws" (31.27, 3–9, Arrighetti). This is the clearest fragment we have on this point from the remains of two books of the *On Nature* that were probably on this subject. Epicurus seems to have argued several times that all men, including strict determinists like Democritus, tried to affect others by reproaching them for their vices and other similar means, but this would be pointless if in fact men had no power to change their ways.

Although the evidence is confused in places, there is no real ground for doubt that Epicurus believed in free will for these reasons, and could not accept complete determinism because he thought it inconsistent with such free will. He therefore introduced some modifications into Democritus' system. One change was indeed independent of these issues, but has a bearing on what follows. Democritus had held, as far as we can tell from the evidence that we have, that the atoms moved in all directions, upwards, downwards, or sideways, but Epicurus said that their natural movement was downwards, and that all would fall at the same speed. Atoms moving continually at the same speed and in the same direction would however never collide and so start off the combined motions by which larger objects could come into being. To meet this difficulty he added that any atom might swerve a hairsbreadth from its straight path and so eventually collide with another, which, rebounding, might affect a third, and

so on. In addition, the swerve (*clinamen*, παρέγκλισις) would be uncaused and unpredictable, and this was the innovation that he thought would allow for free will. For it would break the strict chain of causation found in Democritus' system, and in his own original version of that system.

At this point we encounter great difficulty. There is no ancient evidence that tells us clearly and in detail how Epicurus thought the swerve affected human decisions. Indeed the swerve is not even mentioned in any of his tolerably complete surviving works though it may have been in a missing part of the *Letter to Herodotus*. But the evidence of Lucretius and some other writers is at least enough to show that Epicurus did introduce the swerve, and did use it to solve the problem of free will. Or rather he tried to solve the problem, because no satisfactory solution of this kind is possible. The swerve provides a break in the causal chain, but does not provide for the kind of rational freedom that is needed. What is required is the freedom to choose the right or prudent course even though one's constitution and experience incline one to do what is wrong or imprudent. But the atomic swerve will only produce a random change in the course of events, which need not, and probably will not, have any bearing on morality. Somehow Epicurus must have presented his views in such a way that this was not too obvious.

From the fragments of the *On Nature* it emerges that Epicurus recognized two causal factors in a man's decisions, the mind's original constitution and the pressure of external circumstances. But he insisted that one should also distinguish a third, called, in rather obscure technical terminology, "the generated" (*to apogegennemenon*), and that this was the seat of freedom. Beyond this we can only go by conjecture. Somehow he must have linked "the generated" and the swerve, but we do not know how. Perhaps, for the reason suggested above, and because the matter is almost impossibly difficult, he said very little more. It may be that he held that when a man acted freely there might be no more than a single swerve in a single atom, which would break the causal chain only to the extent of slightly changing the pattern of the atomic dance, and so producing an action that was free but still in character (Furley, 1967). But the difficulty of principle remains. What we now have is a choice that is fully determined except in a single respect, and that single respect is a random event.

Epicurus' importance lies therefore far more in his recognition of a problem than in the solution he gave to it. It is probable, though the evidence is slight, that as soon as he had formulated it it was taken up by philosophers of many different schools, and particularly by the Stoics. They did not accept atomism, but had their own peculiar blend of determinism and fatalism that seemed to rule out the possibility of free action. From this time onwards universal causation seems to have been taken for granted in a way far removed from Aristotle's outlook. We even find Cicero, in his *On Fate* (*De fato*, 44 B.C.), laughing at Epicurus for introducing the swerve because it was uncaused, and an uncaused event was ridiculous. Epicurus' presuppositions were accepted, even if his solution was rejected.

It does not do, however, to see his problem solely in the way we have done so far. It was complicated for him by an argument of a quite different kind, turning on a logical point. It had been much discussed by philosophers from Aristotle downwards at the end of the fourth century B.C., and ran something like this: any statement is either true or false. In particular, any statement about the future is either true or false. But we can form disjunctions of contradictories about the future, like "I will die tomorrow or I will not die tomorrow." Of these contradictories one must be true and the other false. Therefore some statements about the future must be true. And if, for instance, it is true that I will die tomorrow, then it is determined that I will die tomorrow. And, in general, the future is determined.

Epicurus, like many others, seems to have felt that this was a serious argument in favor of determinism which had to be rebutted. Cicero must be mistaken in saying that Epicurus brought in the swerve of the atoms to solve it: rather he met it by the strictly logical contention that in a disjunction of contradictories neither contradictory is either true or false. (Aristotle, however, did say that statements about the future were neither true nor false.)

However this may have been an academic answer to what he regarded as an academic problem, and his major interest was in the reconciling of physical determinism and free will. Unfortunately our information about the later history of his doctrine is scanty, but it may be more than a coincidence that Saint Augustine's account of free will in the fifth century resembles Epicurus' in many respects, though it is set against a theological and not a physical background. In distinguishing between animals and men because only the latter have free will, in saying that a man's actions may be due solely to the "weight" of his natural impulses but that he also has a power of acting voluntarily, and in maintaining that praise and blame are appropriate only to voluntary action, Augustine is making points that are all found in Epicurus' *On Nature*. This does not mean that he had read Epicurus, but suggests that the latter's ideas were by now common currency.

Epicurus urged men to use their freedom to seek pleasure and avoid pain. But the pleasure he advocated was a state of serene freedom from pain which could best be attained by leading a quiet and virtuous life. In ancient times the Epicureans were attacked on two levels: they were vilified as gross sensualists by those who misunderstood them, or who took as typical the many who called themselves Epicureans without fully understanding the doctrine, and they were criticized by serious philosophers because they used the word "pleasure" to cover two distinct things, freedom from pain as well as positive pleasure, and because the former should not be called pleasure at all; more seriously, men were born for something higher than the pursuit of pleasure (Cicero, *De finibus* I and II).

In Christian times the Epicureans were frowned upon as atheists, and little read. But in the Renaissance, through Cicero, Diogenes Laërtius, and Lucretius himself they were rediscovered, and in humanist Italy it was possible for a man like Lorenzo Valla (ca. 1400–57) both to write in praise of Epicurus and to be made apostolic secretary by Pope Nicholas V. Since then followers of Epicurus have fallen into two main classes, those who tried to reconcile his teachings with Christianity, and those who regarded him as the first of a line of enlightened thinkers whose views were incompatible with Christianity. Among the former were Pierre Gassendi (1592–1655), priest as well as scholar and mathematician, who combined atomism with a belief in the immortality of the soul. Through him atomism became known to Robert Boyle and then to Newton, whose language in his description of atoms shows the influence of Lucretius; Gassendi also revived interest in Epicurus' hedonism. Again, in the nineteenth century Walter Pater (1839–94), in his *Marius the Epicurean* showed a sensitivity to the highest as well as the lowest in Epicureanism, which was not incompatible with at least an aesthetic interest in Christianity. On the other hand the freethinking tradition of modern Europe derives at least in part from Epicurus. Thomas Hobbes, though he does not mention Epicurus, must have known of him through Francis Bacon, and Giordano Bruno (ca. 1548–1600) was burnt as a heretic partly at least for setting out the Epicurean doctrine of the infinity of the Universe. In seventeenth-century France Saint-Évremond was one of several professed Epicureans, and Fontenelle carried a similar outlook into the middle of the eighteenth century. Even Voltaire, too much of a fighter to be a true Epicurean, recognized that the secret of happiness might lie in cultivating one's own garden (*Candide*, 1759). The utilitarians, too, though primarily social reformers with keen consciences, recognized Epicurus as one of their forerunners (J. S. Mill, *Utilitarianism*, Ch. I).

137

BIBLIOGRAPHY

The major sources: Epicuro, *Opere*, a cura di G. Arrighetti (Turin, 1960) has the Greek text of all Epicurus' works and fragments, with an Italian translation; C. Diano, *Epicuri ethica* (Florence, 1946) has all the ethical works and fragments; C. Bailey, *Epicurus* (Oxford, 1926) has a text (omitting the Herculaneum fragments) with English translation and commentary; Lucretius, *De rerum natura* has been edited and translated many times. C. Bailey's edition (Oxford, 1947) has text, English translation and commentary. See also, G. D. Hadzsits, *Lucretius and His Influence* (New York, 1963).

Modern commentary includes: C. Bailey, *The Greek Atomists and Epicurus* (Oxford, 1928), Part II, Chs. V and VIII; C. Diano, "La psicologia d'Epicuro e la teoria delle passioni," *Giornale Critico della Filosofia Italiana* (1939), 105–45; (1940), 151–65; (1941), 5–34; (1942), 5–49, 121–50; D. J. Furley, *Two Studies in the Greek Atomists* (Princeton, 1967), Study II, "Aristotle and Epicurus on Voluntary Action"; M. Hadas, *A History of Greek Literature* (New York, 1950), and idem, *A History of Latin Literature* (New York, 1952); P. M. Huby, "The First Discovery of the Freewill Problem," *Philosophy*, **42** (1967), 353–62, and idem, "The Epicureans, Animals, and Freewill," *Apeiron*, **3** (1969), 17–19.

PAMELA M. HUBY

[See also Atomism; Causation; **Free Will; Stoicism.**]

EQUALITY

EQUALITY, as an idea, consists in the belief that things can be alike and when alike should receive similar treatment. It involves, therefore, both ontological and ethical judgments. In the present article it is human equality that is in question. The affirmation of human equality is a profound and recurrent phenomenon, especially in Western civilization, where it is documented as early as the fifth century B.C. in the surviving Greek and Hebrew writings. With the Protestant Reformation, and more especially with the Enlightenment and the French Revolution, the idea of equality began to be a major force for institutional change in Europe and North America, and as such has passed in the twentieth century to the non-European world also. It is a complex and elusive idea, related to many other pivotal ideas. We begin with theoretical considerations and then proceed with an historical survey.

Conceptions of human equality seem to have depended ultimately on views of the world as a whole. The world must be seen as more than appearances, by which no two things are wholly alike. The sense of an overpowering greatness of a single God, as with the Hebrews, may produce a sense that all men are equally his creatures. Equality is also by origin a mathematical concept. In a cosmos perceived as a multiplicity of qualitatively different objects, higher or lower, fine or gross, noble or base, the stress is on hierarchic order in a series of levels. It seems more than chance that the Greek assertions of human equality coincide in time with the geometric axioms of Euclid. In general, however, with the Aristotelian and Ptolemaic traditions, the idea of a qualitative universe of earth and heavens persisted in Europe until the seventeenth century, along with hierarchic ideas of man and society. With Galileo, the ultimate attributes of matter, motion, and force were seen as quantitative and measurable. At the same time, with the English Revolution (1640–60), we find clear statements of human equality and begin to hear arguments for political representation in proportion to numbers.

Equality, even in human affairs, by no means need refer to human equality or equality of persons. The principle of equal treatment has been applied through the history of the idea, and is applied today to associated entities or groups that are thought to require similar consideration, without regard to numbers of persons which the group may include. Thus, in classical Greece, each city in the Aetolian and Achaean leagues had an equal vote, and the states in the American Union are equal in the Senate today. At the origin of the English House of Commons each town of any importance, large or small, received an equal right of representation as a borough, as did each county; and as the three-estates system crystallized on the Continent, the clergy, the nobility, and the "third" estate were regarded as, in a sense, equals, though persons within these estates had different rights. The European kings recognized each other as equals, while observing a certain precedence, as did the sovereign states which emerged in the European state-system after the Peace of Westphalia. Today, by extension, more than a hundred independent nations are legally equal in the General Assembly of the United Nations.

At a more commonplace level, for certain purposes of consultation if not of power, labor and management may be equally represented, or faculty and students in a university committee, or Protestant, Catholic, and Jewish clergymen on occasions of public ceremonial in the United States. In such cases it is groups or interests or functions that receive equal recognition, somewhat as in the estates-system of Europe before the democratic movement overthrew it. When enough individuals feel damaged by such corporate representation, the cry is heard for representation by numbers, of persons as persons, with "vote by head" instead of "vote by order." Meanwhile, in the European tradition (with the conspicuous exception of Poland), even in bodies not themselves representing numbers, a principle of majority rule established itself, in the place of a general consensus or of determination by a *melior et sanior pars* ("the better and sounder part"). Decision by majority required the counting of all voting members as equal, whatever their differences in importance, wealth, or wisdom.

The claim to equality, in these cases, does not assert that the things compared are wholly alike, but only that they are alike in certain respects or for certain purposes. The same is true of human equality, or the belief in equality of human beings as persons, which is no more incredible than the equality of Connecticut and Nevada. "Equality," said Aristotle, "consists in the same treatment of similar persons" (*Politics* VII. 14). Everything here depends on what is meant by "similar." The difficulty is that all human beings are in fact different, that each individual is unique, that each embodies his own combination of qualities or the lack of them—genetic, environmental, or cultural in origin—such as strength, health, learning ability, courage, persistence, sex, race, moral virtues, nationality, economic role, wealth, status, or power.

Individuals thus infinitely various can nevertheless be grouped into classes and categories within which they receive similar treatment as similar persons. Distinctions are thus drawn between male and female, slave and free, citizen and alien, noble and common, black and white, rich and poor, worker and bourgeois, bright children and stupid children in school, those who pass and those who fail an examination, or those who qualify and those who do not qualify under certain standards of skill or employment. Such distinctions when first made are thought to be valid, in accord with fact or justice. As conditions change they may come to be thought unjust, or untrue, or irrelevant in fact, or in conflict with a higher social or divine purpose, or in violation of a higher category into which individuals may also be put, such as children of God, or human beings, or citizens.

In any case, given the actual disparities among persons, belief in equality requires an act of choice, by which some differences are minimized or ignored, while others are maximized and allowed to develop. Thus, on the current American scene, differences of race may be minimized, and differences of aptitude or performance highly valued, with persons of similar aptitude or performance of whatever race receiving similar treatment. Or the differences of aptitude or performance may be brushed aside, and differences of race endowed with higher value, so that persons of similar race are considered alike and receive similar treatment. One way lies "integration"; the other way

both white ascendancy and black nationalism, or at most a form of pluralism with a "separate but equal" doctrine. Either may fall within Aristotle's brief definition of equality.

Equality may be thought of as a fact: that men in some respects *are* alike, theologically, metaphysically, or in the eyes of the biologist, the psychologist, and the physician. Or it may be thought of as a value; that those respects in which men are alike should be the ones chosen for emphasis, or that men should become more nearly equal in more respects than they now are. Where men in important ways are already equal, remaining distinctions may seem to be unjustified barriers. Thus Tocqueville identified as a cause of the French Revolution the fact that men of the upper middle class had become like the nobles except in having inferior rights; and in the United States, as members of ethnic minorities come in fact to resemble the dominant population, the distinctions against them lose their force and are seen as unfair discrimination. On the other hand, persons not really equal, that is enjoying less than others in education, wealth, income, respect, or way of life, may wish to become more nearly equal in the possession of such goods. For them it is not so much a question of removing barriers to opportunity as of creating the conditions in which opportunity may exist. When seen as a value, something of which there ought to be more, equality presupposes belief in the changeability of society and of individual behavior. Questions arise also of the conflict of values, as abundantly evidenced in analytic and polemical literature. Moves to obtain more equality (or at times to restrict or reduce equalities already enjoyed) may conflict with the values of social peace, lawful order, individual liberty, or objective excellence and achievement.

If the philosophical questions are whether men are, can be, or ought to be equal, and if so in what respects and at the expense of what other values, the historical question is to examine how men in some societies, at some periods of time, assert or demand this or that form of equality, and to see what they are thereby protesting against, and what ends they hope to obtain. There is also the larger historical question of whether equality increases, or is more widely diffused, with the passage of time. Broadly speaking, one sees a change from a time when primitive tribes recognized only fellow tribesmen as "men," which is to say that they had no abstract conception of "man" at all, to a time when all human beings are seen as variants of a single mankind, though the wanton extermination of some human beings by others, of which the twentieth century has furnished examples, has occurred throughout the historical record.

139

In the Greek democracies, as is well known, the citizens were equal in the possession of liberty, and largely equal in other respects, but they formed only one category of the population, from which women, metics (aliens), and slaves were excluded. To Aristotle it was evident that slaves and free men differed by nature. A similar insuperable distinction obtained between rulers and ruled in the ideal state projected by Plato. For Aristotle equality required that each should receive his just due, a doctrine of *suum cuique,* or equality for equals, which was perfectly compatible with an unequal ordering of social groups. In declaring that "inequality is everywhere a cause of revolution" (*Politics.* V. 1), Aristotle meant that turmoil ensues when persons who are not really equal demand equality of treatment, or when some among a group of equals demand more than their share, as of power within the state.

Signs of a wider sense of equality are found among the Greeks even before Plato and Aristotle, significantly in a religious connection, as when Euripides has Jocasta say that "nature gave men the law of equal rights," and that "we are but stewards of the gifts of God" (*Phoenician Maidens,* in Abernethy, p. 36). As time passed, the Stoics, drawing on Greek science, reached a conception of cosmic law, or a law of nature to which all men were subject alike, and embodying a universal reason, of which all men, slave and free, possessed some spark. By this spark of reason all men resembled each other, and differed from animals. In the first century A.D. Seneca observed that no man was more noble than another except in being more right-minded or capable of good actions, since "the world is the one parent of all" (*De beneficiis,* III, 28). In the second century Roman lawyers pronounced men equal by nature. Thus was launched a very long-lived conception; the Universal Declaration of Human Rights, proclaimed by the United Nations in 1948, justifies human equality by the statement that all human beings "are endowed with reason and conscience." But for a long time such views had little practical impact. Stoicism offered a philosophy of calm withdrawal, of aloofness from pain, care, selfish struggle, and popular illusion. For lawyers, the natural law remained only a basis on which actual laws could be examined, and positive rights were understood to depend not on nature but on civil society.

The Hebrews saw man as created in the "image of God"—male and female, and as Thomas Paine remarked over two millenniums later, quoting this passage, "no other distinction is even implied" (*Rights of Man* [1791]; in *Writings,* ed. M. D. Conway, II, 305). These words from Genesis, as we have them, probably date from the sixth or fifth century B.C. In Judaism, their implications were developed by the prophets and thereafter. Jesus further expressed the same insights. While he could hardly use the abstract Latinism "equality," he saw men as children of one Father, declared an offense even to the "least of these" to be an offense to himself and to God, preached love of one's neighbor as the truest sign of love of God (Matthew 5:44–45). In Saint Paul these Judaic teachings were reinforced by Hellenistic and Roman conceptions. Breaking with ethnic Jewry, Paul launched with a new force the message of universalism. He ordered the slave to return to his master. But despite all differences the similarities among human beings were of more importance. Paul wrote to the Galatian Christians about A.D. 50: "There is neither Jew nor Greek, there is neither bond nor free, there is neither male nor female: for ye are all one in Christ Jesus" (Galatians 3:28). He repeated the same thought to the Colossians: in the new man, or in the divine image, "there is neither Greek nor Jew, circumcision nor uncircumcision, barbarian, Scythian, bond nor free . . ." (Colossians' 3:10–11). "Barbarian" here means civilized but not Greek, "Scythian" means what the modern languages call "barbarian." Differences of sex, language, culture, and social position were transcended. All were alike as persons, all dependent on the same God, all laboring under sin, all suffering the same psychic stresses of will and reason, all potential vehicles of divine grace, all capable of salvation if they would only accept it.

The rise of such ideas must be attributed to the decline of the ancient Mediterranean civilization, or at least of the beliefs by which it lived. The failures of the Greek city-state, as much as the growth of science and mathematics, turned men either to skepticism or to monotheism and universal law. It became impossible to believe in inherited myth, local deities, or merely civic religion. In the new view, slaves were not slavish by nature, or the Roman Emperor divine. Populations became very mixed, especially in the great cities; men also became more mobile. Both Stoicism and Christianity reflected the growth of the Roman Empire, in the universality of their doctrines and in the geographical extension of their adherents. As the Empire, beginning in the third century A.D., fell into confusion and violence, with consequent personal insecurity, anxiety, and doubt about the world's future, even the rich and the philosophical turned increasingly to the Christian religion. As formulated by Augustine, whose *City of God* was written early in the fifth century, Christianity gave the assurance that, while the world itself might be going to pieces, a higher realm of rightness and justice remained intact.

With Augustine also came the development of the predestinarian idea: that God gave saving grace to some, but not to others. A new kind of inequality was thus introduced. The elect were equal to each other but superior to the damned. If this predestination raised problems concerning divine justice, it seemed at least to have some correspondence to the facts, by which some men were observed to be more insensitive, more willful, more frivolous, or more vicious than others. Inequality between the elect and the damned, depending only on God's will, was in any case not due to human ordinance or to nature. The Church, as it spread throughout Europe, preserved a kind of ultimate kernel of belief in human equality. Slavery disappeared, at least among Christians. The intensity of the belief that all souls were equally deserving of salvation produced the missionary efforts by which Northern Europe and the more inaccessible rural populations of the former Empire, the *pagani*, were Christianized. By the twelfth century all Europeans except the Jews were supposed, or indeed were required, to be adherents of the Christian faith. The result, though later frowned upon as intolerance, was to produce a certain uniformity, or equality in some respects, among Europeans of a kind not so commonly found in Asia, where the most highly civilized areas might exist side by side with primitive tribal peoples, or where, as in the case of India, religious castes continued to be dominant social and cultural institutions.

With the Germanic migrations and spread of Germanic tribal law and of feudalism, very marked social inequalities were introduced in Europe, originally at bottom those between fighters and workers, later formulated as hereditary distinctions between noble and common. The Church long reflected these differences. But nothing in church law ever prevented intermarriage between Christians of whatever class or ethnic group, or acceptance of lowborn persons into the priesthood, or their elevation in the ecclesiastical hierarchy. The Church remained the most usual avenue for upward social mobility well into modern times.

On the other hand, the Church, as it developed in the Middle Ages, produced new inequalities against which later generations were to rebel. By the doctrine of apostolic succession, it was held that the Christian message had been transmitted most especially to the clergy, and among them to the bishops, and among them to the bishop of Rome, or Pope. By administration of the sacraments, the clergy provided the means of salvation to laymen. In addition, since the time of the Emperor Constantine in the fourth century, the Church has been associated with the civil power. Then for several centuries the clergy were the only literate persons, and their influence expanded accordingly. As the Church adapted to medieval society its clergy came to be considered an estate of the realm,

a legal order, the first estate. The clergy grew rich through pious benefactions, bureaucratic through worldly success and responsibility, and divided by deep inequalities within itself. Even at its height as an organized body in the Middle Ages, the Church had to contend with temporal monarchs, sectarian heretics, and occasional undeclared atheists. In the sixteenth century reformers attacked the idea of a special priesthood on whose mediation the laity must depend for salvation. By the time of the French Revolution the attack was directed against the whole association of church and state, including the notion that any religion should be compulsory for all members of society.

In general, throughout antiquity and the Middle Ages, the insistence upon human equality led to no corresponding social change. If it influenced action, it did so only for individuals in their own lives. It is possible that Christianity made the powerful a little less self-satisfied or relentless, and the weak and the poor a little less hopeless and brutalized. From its religion, European culture may have acquired traits of compassion, or depths of private psychology and habits of examination of conscience. Yet human differences and pretensions continued to flourish. Men were equal, but only "in heaven," as it seemed to indignant radicals of later times. Or equality might be located in a golden or patriarchal age of the remote past. Or it might actually exist in small, self-selecting, and self-isolating communities, as with the very first Christians or monastic groups in the Middle Ages. It went along with ideas of poverty and self-abnegation. Equality was neither demanded nor expected for men as a whole in the affairs of the world. Society remained hierarchic, an ascending series of acknowledged ranks with differential advantages.

The Protestant reformers asserted the equality of Christian believers as a means of overthrowing the special position of the papacy and the priesthood. Luther considered all men equally capable of spiritual life, repentance, and hence salvation. They differed in worldly function, but could lead equally holy lives in any calling.

It is pure invention that popes, bishops, priests and monks are to be called the "spiritual estate"; princes, lords, artisans and farmers the "temporal estate". . . . There is really no difference . . . except that of office and work, but not of "estate". . . . Again, it is intolerable that in the canon law so much importance is attached to the freedom, life, property of the clergy. . . . Why are your life and limb, property and honor so free, and mine not?. . . If a priest is killed, the land is laid under interdict—why not when a peasant is killed? Whence comes this great distinction between those who are equally Christian? Only from human laws and inventions! (*To the Christian Nobility* . . . , in *Three Treatises* [1520], pp. 14–19).

In these words, written in 1520, Luther anticipated ideas that were to spread in Catholic as well as Protestant countries, and be basic to the modernizing of Europe—an ethics of work, classification of persons according to occupation, dissolution of the medieval institution of "estate" or "order," equality of persons in the eyes of the law, and attribution of undesired differences to "human invention," that is to a social environment that human beings could modify. To overthrow the traditional priesthood and establish a spiritual equality of believers, Luther welcomed an increase of power in the hands of ruling princes, who could exercise the force necessary for institutional change. The Peasant Rebellion, which broke out in the 1520's, and which horrified Luther, confirmed him in his reliance on the power of government.

The Peasant Rebellion was directed against the inequalities of serfdom, but drew inspiration and confidence from the religious agitation prevalent in Germany in the 1520's. The religious radicals, generically called Anabaptists, went beyond Luther in their understanding of the equality of believers, which for them meant not only an equality of laity with ecclesiastics, but an equality of poor and simple men with the learned and well-to-do. They insisted on a direct, mystical, and personal revelation from God, which need not be mediated through any sophisticated exegesis of Scripture. Some were content to form small peaceful communities—Hutterite, Moravian, or Mennonite—in which worldly goods might be shared by a select few. Others, notably Thomas Münzer, intended a wider application of a doctrine in which Marxists and others have seen the first announcement of a kind of communist movement in practice. Münzer led a group of organized followers, united as he thought in a suffering that made them the equals of Christ, who regarded the existing social order as wholly unjustified, and acted as a group of prophets to bring about a real equality for all men in this world. As agents of the true Spirit they could not tolerate compromise, and they accepted conflict, violence, and even the extermination of adversaries as a means to reach the goal which God himself prescribed. Münzer thus appears as the first avowed revolutionary extremist in a movement of equalitarian revolution.

Most revolutions of the following centuries, notably the Dutch, English, and American, owed more to Calvin. Since Calvin neither opposed private property, nor had any confidence in the untutored common people, nor believed that depravity could be overcome by purely human exertion, he has sometimes been seen by recent students as a conservative (Lakoff, pp. 38–48). He was radical with respect to the inequalities by which educated or middle-class persons then felt offended. He went further than Luther in equating the laity with the clergy, he rejected the institution of bishops and the hierarchic ordering of the clergy themselves, he further reduced the office of priest to that of pastor or minister, and he refused to allow any determination of church affairs by government, especially by princes. He strongly contributed to the republican tradition, which was the strongest revolutionary force for three centuries after his death. Calvinist groups developed procedures for government of the church by consent, which were readily transferred to the political sphere. Calvin insisted also, more than Luther, on the predestination by which God alone gave grace or withheld it. He even went so far as to say: "All are not created on equal terms, but some are preordained to eternal life, others to eternal damnation" (*Institutes,* III, 21, para. 5). No one owed his superiority to his own merits. In thus humbling his followers before God, Calvin may have made them more inclined to see each other as equals. At the same time, they looked down on the worldly, disliked pomp, and were suspicious of power.

Calvinist and Anabaptist ideas, along with more purely political forces, came together in the English or Puritan revolution of the seventeenth century. For the main body of these Puritans equality was not much of an issue, though in the course of their struggle with Charles I they abolished the episcopacy, the House of Lords, and the monarchy itself. They appealed, not to human rights, but to the traditional law of England and rights of Englishmen as they understood them. A more equalitarian note was struck by John Lilburne, a spokesman for the group known as Levellers by its enemies, who, arguing from the "image of God" in Genesis, found it "unnatural, irrational, sinful, wicked, unjust, devilish and tyrannical" for any man to exercise power over others without their consent (Abernethy, p. 95). Cromwell repressed Lilburne, but some of the civilian-soldiers in Cromwell's army took up the Leveller cause. In their proposed Agreement of the People, and in the famous debates to which it led at Putney in 1647, they offered the earliest public program of what may be called political democracy. They argued partly from divine and natural law, and partly in the practical contexts of representation in Parliament and of providing adequate authority for the laws. "For really I think," said Colonel Rainborough, "that the poorest he that is in England hath a life to live, as the greatest he . . . that the poorest man in England is not at all bound in a strict sense to that government that he hath not had a voice to put himself under. . . . I do not find anything in the Law of God, that a lord shall choose twenty burgesses, and a gentleman but two, or a poor man shall choose none. . . . But I do find that all Englishmen must be subject to English laws, and . . . that the foundation of all laws lies in the people . . ." (Abernethy, pp. 101–03). It was objected to Rainborough that such a program would endanger property. And indeed a small group, the Diggers, did repudiate the private ownership of land. Their spokesman, Gerrard Winstanley, saw no need of a difference between rich and poor, believed that the riches of some arise from the poverty of others, and argued that "one man hath as much rights to the earth as another" (Abernethy, p. 126).

The main ideas of the Puritan Revolution were driven underground at the Restoration. The Revolution of 1689 vindicated a form of constitutional government in which equality was of slight importance. Nevertheless the Puritan Revolution and Commonwealth, and notably the Levellers, raised the issues in terms of which equality was chiefly debated for the next two hundred years. Mostly, from the 1640's to the 1840's the question was one of government, or political jurisdiction and authority, and hence of constitutional forms. But the issues were by no means purely political, for they involved the claims of government to regulate religious practice, the press, and individual thought and expression; government was itself viewed as a source of economic wealth for those who took part in it, or for those whom it favored by successful war, lucrative appointments, commercial regulations, land grants, privileges, sinecure, taxation, or pensions. The age of the "bourgeois revolution," as these two centuries have often been called since the 1830's, took no narrow view of equality. The somewhat disparaging term "bourgeois equality" arose in the socialist critiques of the mid-nineteenth century. Some forms of socialism became preoccupied with economic equality. In others, equality was not of major importance. The two centuries following the English Revolution were in fact the classic period for consideration of equality in human society. It was in this period that the interlocking triad of Liberty, Equality, and Fraternity was invented.

In England ideas like those of the Levellers, though not acknowledged as theirs since the term was pejorative, continued to be expressed in the eighteenth century, were actively advanced by English "Jacobins" at the time of the French Revolution, inspired Parliamentary reform, and animated the Chartists in the nineteenth century. They maintained a continuous life in the British colonies in America, especially in New England. This originally English radicalism may have had more influence than John Locke in preparing the American Revolution (Bailyn, 1967). Mixing with Continental thought, it entered into the Enlightenment and so into the French Revolution and the general democratic revolutionary movement which swept over the Western world at the close of the eighteenth century (Palmer, 1959; 1964).

The principal new thought which the Enlightenment had to contribute, with respect to equality, was the idea of environmentalism, the belief that men became what circumstances and education made them. The ancient idea that men were equal at birth, or by nature, or in the eyes of God, was thus enriched by the further idea that they were potentially equal in earthly life if only environmental influences could be altered. A sense of the relativity of all institutions developed among Europeans as they became more familiar with Asia and America. The state of nature, long an abstract legal postulate, was seen more concretely in the lives of the Huron Indians or the Tahitians. Social critics used it to argue that existing society in Europe was artificial, and that prevailing ideas were largely prejudices instilled by wrong education. The work of John Locke was of the utmost importance, his *Essay Concerning Human Understanding* (1690) even more so than his *Two Treatises of Government* (1698). Locke's repudiation of innate ideas, his belief that the mind of every human being was shaped by experience after birth, was taken up in France by Condillac and Helvétius, and widely formulated as the associationist psychology, which became a premiss of educational and other reform. Thus the basis of traditional, customary, and hereditary inequalities was undermined. At the same time, a strong current of humanitarianism began to flow. For reasons that are hard to explain, and which did not arise from pure reason, men were more shocked by cruelty, sensitive to injustice, insistent on the dignity of all human beings, eager to alleviate misery and raise the level to which all could aspire.

During the Enlightenment equality not only ramified as an idea, but received an emotional charge such as it had not had since the early Christians. Not everyone believed in it; some insisted on aristocratic values, corporate rights, and hereditary status; such views were made into a philosophy at the close of the century by Edmund Burke. Equality became a burning question precisely because inequality was so strongly asserted as a necessity of civilized living and even of a free society (Palmer, 1959).

Among the French *philosophes*, Montesquieu upheld the need for unequal corporate groups, such as the nobility and privileged towns, as a bulwark against tyrannical government. Voltaire and most others were more inclined to denounce "feudalism" and "privilege." Rousseau was the main philosopher of equality. He did not regard it as a fact of nature. "It is precisely because the force of *things* always tends to destroy equality that the force of *legislation* should always tend to maintain it" (*Social contract*, Book II, Ch. 11, italics

143

supplied). In his *Discourse on the Origins of Inequality* (1754) Rousseau argued that men were indeed equal in a state of nature, though somewhat brutish, but that as their minds developed they also developed qualities of pride, arrogance, domination, the love of show and of material goods, together with a desire to outdo their neighbors and to be admired for their own superiority.

The advent of property inflamed these proclivities and perpetuated inequality from one generation to the next. The conclusion, for Rousseau, was neither a return to nature nor an abolition of property, but a realization of the social, psychological, and moral costs at which civilization was maintained. In the *Social Contract* (1762), Rousseau raised the problem of Rainborough and the Levellers, without their concern for equality of representation: how could a man be obedient to law and yet remain a free moral agent? Here he argued, much like Hobbes, that the state of nature was ruled by force alone. By the social contract each individual, by becoming a citizen in a civil state, and sharing in a "general will," became sovereign and subject at the same time. In such a state all public authority would be exercised by delegation only. No one would be born as ruler or into a ruling class. Equality meant chiefly an equality of respect and participation among citizens, but some degree of economic equality was required—none must be "so rich as to be able to buy another, and none so poor as to have to sell himself" (*Social Contract*, II, 11). In his *Government of Poland*, which he wrote in 1771 (published in 1782) at the request of certain Poles for advice on how to prevent the partition of their country, Rousseau urged the need of more equal participation in a strong and ineradicable national character.

There were pragmatic reasons for the extension of equality also. Governments, under what has been called enlightened despotism, found it useful for fiscal reasons to reduce the tax privileges of the nobility, to equalize the tax liability as between various provinces, to bring religious minorities more fully into the civil community, and to weaken or abolish the guild system, which discouraged new enterprise, protected established interests, and allowed some while forbidding others to enter upon certain kinds of occupation, manufacture, or trade. Military requirements also promoted civil equality. In Austria and Prussia the governments tried to alleviate serfdom, by making the peasantry into subjects of the state rather than of their lords, both for humanitarian reasons and as a means of facilitating military conscription and training. The need for intelligent and technically qualified officers, in these countries as well as in France and Great Britain, opened careers for persons of middle class as well as of noble birth.

The French Revolution in part continued these equalitarian trends that existed in governments before 1789, and in part proceeded to implement the ideas of social critics, and, in the crisis of events, to go beyond them. The new doctrine was set forth in the Declaration of Rights of 1789, significantly called the rights not only of "man" but of the "citizen." "Men are born and remain free and equal in rights," according to Article I. "These rights are liberty, security, property, and resistance to oppression." There followed the "abolition of feudalism," of the difference between noble and commoner, of inheritance of legal social rank and of public office, together with legislation to provide equality of rights, equality before the law, equality of punishment for the same offense, equality of taxation for persons of the same income, equality of access to public office depending only on "virtues and talents," equality of civil rights for Catholic, Protestant, Jew, and nonbeliever, equality of property in the formal sense that all real property was of the same kind (no longer seigneurial and common), economic equalities in opportunities for employment or investment following an abolition of the guilds, equalities as between geographical areas within the state, and equality of representation with constituencies based primarily on numbers. Equality of educational opportunity, and sometimes equality of women with men, were proposed but not implemented during the Revolution.

Racial equality was advanced in 1791, when free blacks received the same rights as whites; slavery in the French colonies was abolished in 1794. In 1793, in the crisis of war and invasion, inflation and security, the artisan and laboring classes made a strong bid for both political and economic equality. The war also advanced equality by producing the first large-scale citizen army. Herodotus, twenty-three centuries before, had said that the Greeks made better soldiers because they were free and equal citizens. Robespierre said much the same in 1793, declaring that the European powers would be defeated because the Revolution had given the ordinary Frenchman something to fight for. Kosciuszko echoed the same thought when he tried to abolish serfdom in Poland during the attempted revolution and struggle against the Russians in 1794.

The meaning of equality in the French Revolution was brilliantly set forth by Condorcet, in his *Progress of the Human Mind* (1794), which concluded with the enraptured vision of a highly secularized Saint Paul. To the kinds of equality already enumerated he added others. He saw an eventual equality among all races and nations, in which those still backward, being already potentially equal, would one day join in a common, uniform civilization throughout the world. He prophesied that by way of universal education, public hygiene, scientific agriculture, and social insurance there would at last emerge an equality of fact as the final objective of the "social art."

The American Revolution had meanwhile launched a similar message of equality, though less urgently and over a narrower range, since except for blacks and Indians there were fewer inequalities to combat in America than in Europe. The armies of the French Revolution took the new ideas to many parts of Europe, where there were eager sympathizers to receive them and to work for change in their own countries. There were many such in Britain and Ireland also, where, however, the successful reformers came to prefer the ostensibly more empirical views of Jeremy Bentham. Bentham scorned the French Revolution and the very idea of "rights," but he shared its disaffection with the old social order and advanced his own equalitarian doctrine with his principle that, in planning reform on utilitarian lines, each should count for one and none for more than one.

Even during the French Revolution, except for Robespierre and a few others, and except during the crisis of 1792–95, there was no acceptance of political democracy in the sense of universal male suffrage. The vote was thought of as a kind of office for which a certain capacity was required. It was by emphasis on their common features as substantial citizens and taxpayers that older inequalities among Frenchmen were to be erased. The economic changes, including the abolition of guilds, the reshaping of property law, and the resale of real estate confiscated from the church and the émigrés, were especially useful to those who owned property or were sufficiently enterprising, thrifty, astute, or fortunate to acquire it. The very removal of other differences accentuated the difference between rich and poor. Property, not rank or status, was legally inherited. Quantitative differences in worldly possessions became more important than ever before in the determination of family standing and social class. The bourgeoisie came to signify those who possessed property, whether their ancestors had been noble or common. The poor had neither property, nor the vote, nor even that participation in civic activity and the national culture which both the Enlightenment and the Revolution had recommended. These differences between "bourgeois" and "proletarian" were made worse by changes which were incident to the Industrial Revolution.

Equality in the nineteenth and twentieth centuries therefore came increasingly to mean economic equality, or, more exactly, a reduction of the difference between the extremes of rich and poor, since only a few doctrinaires ever demanded a literal equality of incomes. It was furthered by the growth of democracy

and socialism. Democracy was now equated with a universal and equal suffrage, with the vote justified not by any particular qualification, but as a means by which everyone, however poor or uninformed on political issues, could make his needs known, his wishes heard, and his weight felt in the political process. The results were variously seen in the recognition of labor unions, mass parties, the progressive income tax, parliamentary socialism, and the welfare state. Some early socialists were political democrats, but most of them had little faith or interest in the political order, however reformed. For some, true equality could be attained only by the ancient idea of small colonies set apart from the world. For others, in an anarchist vein, the questions of classical political theory which were very much alive through the French Revolution, involving power, authority, law, and obedience, were dismissed as unnecessary, or ignored. For still others, as with Marx, such questions were relatively superficial, since law and government were a superstructure of which economic relationships were the foundation.

The revolutionary socialism of the nineteenth century aimed at an equality beyond that attained in the French Revolution. It found its precursor in "Gracchus" Babeuf, executed in 1797 for planning an insurrection against the French Directory. In his Conspiracy of Equals, Babeuf had projected a genuine and total equality, in which each person delivered the product of his labor to a common store, and withdrew from it an equal income, with no difference allowed for differences of productivity or skill. Stressing the resemblance between human beings in basic needs— "stomachs are equal," as he put it—Babeuf was willing to ignore, in the allocation of rewards, the differences of talent or effort (*Manifeste des plébéiens*, in Mazauric, pp. 204–19). Few later forms of socialism went so far. The admiration for Babeuf felt by socialists, and more recently communists, was due less to his "communism" than to other qualities in his enterprise. He designed his plan for a whole country, he felt himself to be part of an ongoing revolutionary movement, and he organized a small insurrectionary party, or vanguard, for the seizure of power and overthrow of the state.

The most serious socialists of the nineteenth century, while moved by the gross inequalities from which the poor suffered, aimed less at an ideal equality in the manner of Condorcet than at a coordination of the economic system. They objected to its wild cyclical fluctuations, its unemployment and waste of human lives, its starvation wages alongside conspicuous luxury, its dependence on the market, the profit motive, the machine, and the need of immediate payoff on capital investment. For Marx, equality was not so much a goal to be worked for as a consequence that would follow from the operation of social forces. Capitalism, in his view—that is, the private ownership of the means of production and the purchase of labor for wages— generated by its very nature two social classes, the bourgeoisie and the proletariat, whose mutual estrangement would become more acute until the proletariat took over and the bourgeoisie disappeared. A classless society would follow, since "class" meant by definition groupings as they arose from capitalistic production. Differences of function and of income would remain under socialism, but they would not be differences of class, would not be transmitted by inheritance of property, and would be justified by differences of individual talent or usefulness. Equality meant classlessness. It could be scientifically expected to follow from the facts themselves—from history. As Engels wrote:

From the moment when the bourgeois demand for the abolition of class privileges was put forward, alongside it appeared the proletarian demand for the abolition of *classes themselves*—at first in religious form, basing itself on primitive Christianity, and later drawing support from the bourgeois equalitarian theories themselves. The proletarians took the bourgeoisie at their word: equality must not be merely apparent, must not merely apply to the sphere of the state, but must also be real, must be extended to the social and economic sphere.

But the worker must neither imagine that any real equality was possible in a class system, nor expect that under socialism all persons would be treated alike. "The real content of the proletarian demand for equality is the *abolition of classes*. Any demand for equality which goes beyond that, of necessity passes into absurdity" (*Anti-Dühring*, in Abernethy, pp. 199–200).

It was left for liberals, in the nineteenth and twentieth centuries, to work toward greater equality in a society which continued to recognize the permanency of social classes. Unlike conservatives, and in common with democrats and socialists, most liberals accepted the goals of the French Revolution, while deploring its violence. Many, however, especially with the rise of socialism, came to see a conflict between liberty and equality. Where socialists argued that liberty for the capitalists made equality impossible for others, liberals feared that equality if carried beyond a certain point, would become a menace to liberty, not only of economic enterprise but in other spheres. The classic expression of this concern was given by Alexis de Tocqueville. He saw in the movement toward equality the key to all European history since the Middle Ages. He accepted it as providential and just. He thought, however, that the end product might be a society of

equally small, helpless, and unorganized individuals over whom despotism, or an over-strong central government, could be easily exercised. He feared also that similarity of ideas and achievement might be so highly prized that all forms of excellence, or freedom of opinion, would disappear under a general cloud of mediocrity or in a tyranny of the majority. Tocqueville wrote his *Democracy in America* (original French, 1835) in part to trace the impact of equality upon the American behavior and character, and in part to find out how the less desirable consequences of equality were avoided by the Americans. The safeguards in America, he thought, lay in the decentralized federal system, the vitality of religion, and the love of liberty itself. John Stuart Mill, while finding Tocqueville's alarm somewhat exaggerated, and having more confidence in the good effects of education, felt much the same apprehensions. He too believed that all history moved toward equality, that as it had been with the loss of distinction of patricians and plebeians, so it would be, "and in part already is, with the aristocracies of color, race and sex" (*Utilitarianism*, in Abernethy, p. 192).

Liberal views on equality, into the twentieth century, can essentially be analyzed into two kinds. One assumes an existing amount of human capacity, widely different among individuals; the problem is to allow maximum fulfilment of his capacity for each person, either as an act of justice, or to prevent frustration and social disaffection, or to make maximum use of human talents for society as a whole. Equality of right is upheld; inequality of fact is accepted. The key words are fair competition, equality of opportunity, reward for merit, and careers open to talent. There is a contest open to all, in which the same rules and prizes obtain; standards and criteria are the same for all, relating only to the matter in hand, without regard to personal traits deemed irrelevant, or, in the American phrase, regardless of "race, creed, or color." The purpose is to give encouragement to the able. There is upward mobility for the able few. The social value lies in this degree of mobility, and in the maintenance of high standards of skill and performance. A vast apparatus of testing and examination, of sifting, sorting, elimination, and legitimate discrimination, has arisen to serve these purposes and these values. The difficulty in such a system is that there are more losers than winners, and that each person can blame only himself, or his own shortcomings, for his failure to reach the top. Those disadvantaged at the start remain disadvantaged throughout the contest. These problems, long ago perceived by others, are wittily illuminated by the British sociologist, Michael Young, in his *Rise of the Meritocracy* (1958). The book describes the horrors of a future utopia in which each person, at each moment of his life, really enjoys only what he exactly deserves under a perfected system of testing, classification, and assignments of social roles.

The other view, which owes as much historically to democracy and socialism as to liberalism, is most recently illustrated in America in the movement for racial equality. It was expressed forty years ago in R. H. Tawney's remark that mere equality of opportunity may be a cruel jest, like an invitation to dinner sent by a wealthy person to one who is in no position to accept it. In this view people must be prepared for opportunities, not merely presented with them. Capacity must be instilled, not merely liberated from obstacles. The pool of capacities for the entire population must be enlarged. Thus the American colleges, more selective in their admissions, and business firms committed to equal opportunity in employment, pass beyond the stage of merely selecting the already most qualified persons; at a further stage they attempt to produce the qualifications themselves, by preliminary training, in persons who do not yet possess them. There may even be a reverse favoritism, or privilege, or restitution for former injustice, in giving more than usual attention to persons more than usually disadvantaged. The maintenance of high standards remains important. But the need is seen also to provide for those who do not excel. Each is encouraged to reach his own ceiling. But the floor is also raised, below which none should fall. Liberalism of this kind looks to education, not only for the production of an elite, but for forms of schooling useful and relevant to everyone; and in an increasingly productive society it devises such projects as the reverse income tax to provide minimum income even for those who are unable to earn it. Equality of right moves toward a greater equality of fact, as demanded by the liberal Condorcet, the collectivist Babeuf, and the socialists who came after them. Both forms of equality are now argued for, even in relatively conservative quarters, not merely on humanitarian grounds, but as a means of obtaining social peace and maximizing manpower resources which a wealthy society can in any case afford.

Equality, like democracy, is a value which no developed or civilized country in the mid-twentieth century will explicitly deny. It is upheld in the Soviet Union as in the United States, in "people's democracies" as in the "free world." Each country realizes it in its own way and in varying degree, and each has its own kinds of inequality which still remain. The demand for equality is still heard, as between rich and poor, between subjects and rulers, between races in the same country, between races and nations in the world. The demand always signifies a sense of inequality or injustice, a belief that differences exist which should and could be removed.

It would be idle to pretend that equality is not in conflict with other values. It may conflict with superiority of achievement if it ignores the differences in talents. It may conflict with liberty if liberty means the right to do as one pleases. Equality can be assured only if the liberties of some to impose inequality on others are restricted. Equality exists not by nature, nor for "man" except on a religious or metaphysical plane; it exists in civil society, by law, and by the form and policies of the state. No rights are very useful except those that the state will enforce. So much is evident from the difference of impact between the rights of man as declared by the United Nations in 1948, and those of man—"and citizen"—as declared by the French revolutionary assembly in 1789. Anarchy is the form of human association in which equality would the soonest disappear. It is only as citizens, as well as men, by belonging to an organized community and having a share in the public power, that human beings can assert or advance their rights, or aspire with any chance of success to an equality either of right or of fact.

BIBLIOGRAPHY

A convenient collection of extracts from ancient to recent times, though least adequate on French writers, is provided by G. L. Abernethy, *The Idea of Equality: An Anthology* (Richmond, Va., 1959). For an analytic treatment of ideas since the sixteenth century see S. A. Lakoff, *Equality in Political Philosophy* (Cambridge, Mass., 1964). Also: R. H. Tawney, *Equality* (London, 1929, and later eds.); D. Thomson, *Equality* (Cambridge, 1949); L. Bryson et al., eds., *Human Equality: Fifteenth Symposium of the Conference on Science, Philosophy and Religion* (New York, 1956), including nineteen papers on a wide array of topics; S. I. Benn, "Equality, Moral and Social," *Encyclopedia of Philosophy* (New York, 1967), III, 38–41, a compact analysis, with bibliography.

For selected histories bearing on certain periods see G. P. Gooch, *English Democratic Ideas in the Seventeenth Century*, 2nd ed. (London, 1927); R. R. Palmer, *The Age of the Democratic Revolution: A Political History of Europe and America, 1760–1800*, 2 vols. (Princeton, 1959; 1964); B. Bailyn, *Ideological Origins of the American Revolution* (Cambridge, Mass., 1967). Of serious import is the satirical utopia, presented as history, by M. Young, *The Rise of the Meritocracy, 1870–2033: An Essay on Education and Equality* (London, 1958; later eds.).

Documentary sources mentioned above may be consulted in Abernethy; in M. Luther, *Three Treatises* (Philadelphia, 1960); C. E. Vaughan, ed., *Political Writings of J. J. Rousseau*, 2 vols. (Cambridge, 1915); M. de Condorcet, *Sketch for a Historical Picture of the Progress of the Human Mind* (New York, 1955); C. Mazauric, *Babeuf: Textes choisis* (Paris,

1965). A. de Tocqueville, *De la démocratie en Amérique* (Paris, 1835); trans. as *Democracy in America*, (various reprints), is in effect a treatise on equality.

R. R. PALMER

[See also Anarchism; Democracy; **Enlightenment; Equity; General Will;** Hierarchy; Individualism; Justice; **Marxism;** Nature; Perfectibility; Property; Reformation; Religious Toleration; Revolution; Social Contract; Socialism; State; **Stoicism;** Utilitarianism.]

EQUITY IN LAW AND ETHICS

"Equity" is a term widely used in ethics, law, and jurisprudence, with connotations that suggest or invoke ideals of justice, fairness, equality, mercy, judgment according to law, as well as judgment that bypasses or transcends strict law in the interest of conscience, humanity, natural law, or natural justice (as distinguished from justice according to law): judgment according to the spirit, rather than the letter, of the law. Equity is also a term used to denominate a special system of law in England and the United States differentiated from the common law.

In addition, equity is used to refer to an economic interest—e.g., the equity of the redemption of the mortgagor; or, more broadly conceived, as one's fair economic share in an enterprise—for instance, in the 1967 strike of the American automobile workers, it was stated that the workers "are going to insist that [they get] the equity that flows from increased productivity in Ford"; or equity may be used to point to a kind of property which does not lend itself to precise definition, and must remain suggestive and detached—e.g., equity is the interest in a corporation vested in an owner of shares of common stock. What these uses of the term have in common is the notion that equity is a claim or a right not known to the strict law, yet one which the law does or ought to recognize.

Equity thus suggests that the law may not always be perfect, that the enforcement of legal rights and duties may fall short of justice, that there may be conflicts between the demands of conventional or legal justice and natural justice or justice according to conscience or reason.

I

Plato. Classical Greek philosophy fully recognized this duality of claims. Plato, ever sensitive of the impossibility of ideals fulfilling themselves, saw the necessity of counterweights to the law and expressed

the essence of the idea of equity (*epiekeia, επιέκεια*) in the *Statesman* (or *Politicus*):

Stranger: There can be no doubt that legislation is in a manner the business of a King, and yet the best thing of all is not that the law should rule, but that a man should rule, supposing him to have wisdom and royal power. . . . Because the law cannot comprehend exactly what is noblest or most just, or at once ordain what is best for all. The differences of men and actions, and the endless irregular movements of human things, do not admit of any universal and simple rule. No art can lay down any rule which will last forever. . . . But this the law seeks to accomplish; like an obstinate and ignorant tyrant, who will not allow anything to be done contrary to his appointment or any question to be asked—not even in sudden changes of circumstances, when something happens to be better than what he commanded for someone. . . . A perfectly simple principle can never be applied to a state of things which is the reverse of simple (Jowett trans. 294 a).

The law, then, is not the perfection of right. The rule of a wise ruler, possessing royal power, is better than the rule of law. But since such a god or superman cannot be found, it is good not to allow the claim to be free from the guidance of laws—a claim which implies possession of perfect knowledge and wisdom with respect to every question or issue. The alternative to the ideal is to require strict guidance of the laws and to disallow their correction in particular cases by judicial or executive action. It cannot be assumed that the legislator will sit at the judge's side and direct him to the exact particulars of his duty. This does not mean, however, that laws are immutable; but until properly, wisely altered, to violate the laws, "which are based upon long experience, and the wisdom of counsellors who have graciously recommended them and persuaded the multitude to pass them . . . would be a far greater and more ruinous error than any adherence to written law" (ibid., 300). Once we depart from the ideal polity, rulers are bound by the principle to do nothing contrary to their own written laws and national customs; and the judge is only the guardian of these laws and has no legislative, innovative, or amending powers (ibid., 305). The emphasis, however, in this dialogue is clearly antinomian, for the ideal statesman "will do many things within his own sphere of action by his art without regard to the laws, when he is of opinion that something other than that which he has written down and enjoined to be observed . . . would be better" (ibid., 300).

This dialogue, which belongs to Plato's post-*Republic* period (375–368 B.C.; Taylor, p. 19; Field, p. 209), looks in two directions: back to the strict antinomianism of the *Republic*, and ahead to the rule of law in *The Laws*, probably Plato's last work. But the *Statesman*, as the above discussion shows, clearly articulates the problem of equity: the conflict between the need to administer and apply the law in its general terms, and the demands of justice or conscience in a particular case, which point to the law as it should be.

In *The Laws* Plato still maintains that "No law or ordinance whatever has the right to sovereignty over true knowledge" (*The Laws*, 875, Taylor trans.). Since, however, such insight is nowhere attainable in its perfection, "we must choose the second-best [i.e.,] ordinance and law." After ten years of experiment with the code of laws, changes shall be possible only if approved by all the magistrates, the popular assembly, and the representatives of the oracular shrines. Any one of these authorities shall have a veto power (ibid., 772).

Plato, however, left some room for equity. His most notable and influential provision in this respect is that the entire code should be preceded by a preamble, and many specific laws should likewise be introduced by preambles, which would be expositions of what the legislator accounts laudable or the reverse (ibid., 822–23). These preambles should be carefully distinguished from the laws proper; their purpose is to educate and persuade. The proposal was a novel one for its time, and has implicit in it the possibility of distinguishing the spirit of a law from its letter, and in some way presages what came to be known as the equity of a statute (Cairns, pp. 154–56). Plato's preambles, however, differ from later proposals and uses in that they appeal to ultimate rather than immediate and particular ends; but in any case preambles are bound to be used as aids to interpretations, and make possible interpretations that go beyond the strict letter of the law to its deeper rationale (Morrow, p. 555). For the law (*nomos*) ought always to approximate reason (*nous*), its source and justification.

In Plato's scheme for a society subject to the rule of law, there are other doors left open for equity to enter, though covertly and interstitially. In judging, Plato recognizes the difference between the question of fact and the question of law. The judge does not make the law—that is for the legislator. But the judge finds the facts, and then imposes the punishment, with respect to which, Plato acknowledges, he must have some discretion. "You and I," he says, "are about to fix the penalty or fine to be inflicted on him who wounds another, or does him a hurt. Now it is, of course, a proper and obvious comment to make at this point, to say: 'Wounds? Yes, but wounds whom, and where and how and when? The different cases are countless and their circumstances are widely unlike.' So it is equally impossible to leave everything to the discretion of the courts and to leave nothing" (*The Laws*, 875). The judge, then, has discretion in finding the answers to the issues of fact. And if the judges are properly trained, and are removed from the passions which sway Attic dicasts who form a jury, we ought not to impose on them by statute "the numerous and important" rules which they may discover by insight, "for attaching to the particular offences the penalty merited by the wrong committed and hurt inflicted" (ibid., 876). Since legislators "can consider most cases and provide for them, but not all [cases]," the code of laws of "the second-best" society can be nothing more than "an outline of law with samples of penalties" to which the judges can look for guidance as to a model (ibid., 876–77, 934).

Perhaps the calmest and most comfortable way to admit equity into the legal order is to assume that there is a body of unwritten law, divine in nature, which may not be contradicted with impunity by legislator or judge. Thus, Plato assumes that the "law of our forefathers" is what "mankind at large" calls the "unwritten law," and which is "a true corpus of ancestral and primitive tradition which, rightly instituted and duly followed in practice, will serve as a sure shield for all the statutes . . . committed to writing." These customs, practices, traditions, these unwritten laws, are "the mortises of a constitution" (ibid., 793). Whatever else they accomplish, these unwritten laws make possible the work of equity when the judge finds it necessary or advisable to avoid the written law; for law, gropingly or directly, must try to satisfy the demands of justice, reason, or conscience. *Nomos* must approximate to *nous*.

Aristotle. In the development of the idea of equity, Aristotle was far more influential than Plato. In his *Ethics* Aristotle formulated the idea of *epiekeia* in terms that made it, for future philosophers and jurists, the *locus classicus* of the notion of equity.

Aristotle defines equity as the correction of the law in cases in which the law is found to be deficient by reason of its generality. Equity and law are, says Aristotle, not entirely the same, nor are they entirely different. Both are right and praiseworthy; they are not opposed to one another; each is a kind of justice; but the equitable is superior as a good. There are the legally just and the equitable just, and the latter is a correction of the former.

But why should the legally just ever need correction? The reason, says Aristotle, is that all law is universal, but about some things it is impossible to make a correct universal statement; yet the law will make it, knowing, however, that there is the possibility of error by reason of the law's generality. No one is to blame for this state of affairs, neither the legislature nor the law itself. For the law must speak universally; but life will thrust 149 forth cases not covered by the universal statement; then it becomes necessary to correct the omission, "to say what the legislator himself would have said, and would have put into his law if he had known." The equitable is, therefore, "not better than absolute justice but better than the error that arises from the absoluteness of the statement [of the law]. And this is the nature of the equitable, a correction of law where it is defective owing to its universality" (*Ethics*, Book V, Ch. 10).

The problem as formulated by Aristotle is not essentially different from Plato's formulation in the *Statesman*, but its articulation in the *Ethics* has a sharper juristic edge, and characteristically combines the practical with the theoretical. While most discussions of equity disregard Plato's contribution, no scholar fails to mention Aristotle's discussion of the subject.

In the *Rhetoric*, Aristotle repeats and somewhat refines the same conception of equity. It is, he says, "justice that goes beyond the written law" because there are omissions from the written law. Some actions may have escaped the notice of the legislators, and in some cases it was simply impossible for them to define all cases, yet they felt obliged to formulate a general law which would be applicable to most but not all cases; then Aristotle cites an example, which has found a place in the literature on equity and legislation: the legislators provide against infliction of a wound with an iron instrument. A man wearing an iron ring strikes another man. According to the written law, he is guilty of wrongdoing, "but in reality he is not; and this," says Aristotle, "is a case for Equity." Aristotle then adds that actions which should be treated with leniency are cases for equity, and among such actions he includes those that are the consequence of misfortune, error, and human weakness. In such cases one should look to the intention of the legislator and not to the letter of the law; one should look, he says (Freese trans. I. xii. 13–19):

not to the action itself, but to the moral purpose; not to the part, but to the whole; not to what a man is now, but to what he has been, always or generally; . . . to prefer arbitration to the law court, for the arbitrator keeps equity in view, whereas the dicast looks only to the law, and the reason why arbitrators were appointed was that equity might prevail.

In the same treatise, when examining the application of these notions to forensic oratory, Aristotle advises that when the written law is against us, we should have recourse to "the general law and equity as more in accordance with justice"; that we should contend that while written laws often vary, equity is constant; for, like the unwritten law which Antigone used to justify her having buried Polynices contrary to the law of Creon, equity is based on nature; it is a part of genuine, not spurious, justice (I. xv. 1–9).

There is no doubt that Aristotle's observations on the forensic use of equity reflected a common practice; for Greek orators appealed to equity, especially when they faced archaic or rigid statutes, and particularly as these laws applied to wills and contracts. Since there were in ancient Athens 6,000 dicasts, who could be chosen by lot to sit as judges, the heliastic courts (which used the dicasts) in fact were a popular institution representing the sovereign people, who possessed the prerogative of the sovereign, and could therefore dispense justice without regard to technicalities. Thus equity was no abstract conception but an essential part of Greek justice and its practical administration (Vinogradoff, II, 63–69).

II

Cicero quoted as a saying familiar in his time, *Summum jus summa injuria*. Through oversubtle and even fraudulent construction of law, he said, much wrong was committed (*De officiis* I. X. 33). Indeed, in *De legibus*, Cicero goes so far as to say that it is only "the crowd's definition of law" which identifies law with written decrees in which the people issue commands and prohibitions as they please (I. vi. 19). Law for Cicero is the voice of reason and of nature; action according to virtue is action according to the law; an enactment which commands an injustice is not truly a law. The most foolish notion of all, he says, is the belief that everything in the customs or laws of nations is just. "For Justice is one; it binds all human society, and is based on one Law, which is right reason applied to command and prohibition. Whoever knows not this Law, whether it has been recorded in writing anywhere or not, is without Justice" (*De legibus* I. xv. 42).

Cicero obviously was influenced by the teachings of Plato and the Stoics, in which the dichotomy between written and unwritten law stands out prominently. Institutionally, however, Roman law seems to have had a development which did not lean on Greek precedents. The praetor, Roman chief magistrate, readily developed *aequitas* as the *jus honorarium*. Since his power was supreme, the praetor found no obstacle in his way. Without annulling the *jus civile* the praetor introduced principles which allowed equitable defences or remedies. Praetorian law took a specially productive turn in the form of equity when, in the third century B.C., a *praetor peregrinus* was named to exercise jurisdiction in cases involving foreigners, who were attracted by Rome's commercial activity. The *praetor peregrinus* introduced principles and rules more liberal than those found in the *jus civile*. The equitable principles which the *praetor peregrinus* substituted for the *rigor juris* influenced the *praetor urbanus* to make available to Roman citizens principles which could not be the exclusive privilege of foreigners. The principles were those which, the praetors believed, were the bases on which the law could be built—and in this respect their action was influenced by Greek philosophical ideas. For the leading jurisconsults were closely associated with Greek philosophy, especially with Stoicism, and it was they who came to see in the *jus gentium*, the law common to nations, an expression of the Stoic law of nature; and it was precisely through equity that the *jus gentium* and the law of nature touched and blended. It was, Sir Henry Maine observed, the *levelling* tendency of the *jus gentium* that became the characteristic of the praetorian system of equity (Maine, Ch. III). Principles such as *aequitas, aequum et bonum*, and *bona fides* became prominent in Roman jurisprudence (Allen, pp. 377, 381). There were, of course, those who objected to this development; e.g., Quintilian, in the first century A.D., argued that if the court "is always to be spending its time turning statutes inside out to discover what is just and what is equitable . . . well, then there might as well be no statutes at all." In A.D. 125, Hadrian, to end the powers of the praetor, asked Julian to edit the praetorian edicts and put them in final form, and when this was accomplished, further alterations were prohibited.

III

Yosher. In the Hebrew Scriptures there is no one term that is uniformly translated as equity; however, the Hebrew term (*yosher*) and its derivatives, perhaps more frequently than others, is given the meaning of equity or equitable. When Isaiah describes the ideal ruler, he says that he shall judge the poor with righteousness, "and decide with equity [with *yosher*] for the meek of the lands" (11:4). So, too, the psalmist (98:9) proclaims that the Lord "is come to judge the earth; He will judge the world with righteousness, And the peoples with equity [with *yosher*]." The term is, however, often used synonymously with words connoting righteousness or justice or virtue.

When judged by today's moral standards, some of the biblical laws seem unduly harsh and even unjust; but the Jewish tradition has consistently held to the belief that in addition to the written law, there is an oral tradition, and that the latter is primary and the written text secondary. The *lex talionis* means fair or monetary compensation in place of wild revenge; the *value* of *one* eye, not two, for an eye. It enjoins the principle of an equitable relation between the crime and the punishment, and the principle that all men are equal before the law and are to be judged by the same standard. In brief, the interpretation of the text

rejects literalism; the oral tradition admits judgment according to the voice of justice, humanity, righteousness, fairness, or equity. The basic commandment is not to observe the letter of the law in all its strictness but, rather, "Justice, justice shalt thou follow" (Deuteronomy 16:20); and justice is often used in ways which suggest its link with loving-kindness or grace.

In his *Mishneh Torah*, the classic code of Jewish law, Maimonides (twelfth century) states that at the outset of a trial the judges should inquire whether the litigants desire adjudication according to law or settlement by arbitration. A court, says Maimonides (pp. 66–67),

. . . that always resorts to arbitration is praiseworthy. Concerning such a court, it is said: *Execute the justice of . . . peace in your gates* (Zechariah 8:16). What is the kind of justice which carries peace with it? Undoubtedly, it is arbitration. So, too, with reference to David it is said: *And David executed justice and charity unto all his people* (2 Samuel 8:15). What is the kind of justice which carries charity with it? Undoubtedly, it is arbitration, i.e., compromise.

While strict constructionists—like the Sadducees and the school of Shammai—could support their conservative, literalist approach by citing the text (Deuteronomy 4:2), "You shall not add to the word which I command you, nor take from it," the liberal Pharisees and the school of Hillel could cite as support for *their* creative, and even innovating, approach the text (Deuteronomy 17:8–13) which commands the submission of difficult cases to whoever is judge at the time, and to do according to what he decides: "You shall not turn aside from the verdict which they [the judges] declare to you, either to the right hand or to the left." In the spirit of the latter view, the Jewish authorities at times proceeded in the face of expressly contrary laws. Maimonides put the rationale as follows (p. 141): "Even as a physician will amputate the hand or the foot of a patient in order to save his life, so the court may advocate, when an emergency arises, the temporary disregard of some of the commandments, that the commandments as a whole may be preserved."

Thus, despite the fact that the written law provides for capital punishment for numerous crimes, every effort was made to circumvent the letter of the law; and the *Mishnah*—basic compilation of the oral law, prepared in the second century A.D. from an earlier compilation by Akiba—reports that a court which imposed the death penalty once in seven years was called a court of destroyers, that Rabbi Elizer ben Azariah said that it was a court of destroyers if it put one man to death even in seventy years, and that Rabbi Tarphon and Rabbi Akiba said that if they were mem-

151

bers of the Sanhedrin, never would a person be put to death (*Mishnah*, 403).

Since the Hebrew Scriptures and classical, Pharisaic Judaism fail to make a distinction between religion, law, custom, and morals, and since the Bible places such stress on equity that the word for it became a name for Israel—Jeshurun, Yosherun (Deuteronomy 32:15; 33:5, 26)—equity jurisdiction could not become separately institutionalized but had to be woven into the very fabric of rabbinic jurisprudence.

IV

While the rationale, the maxims, and the precedents for equitable adjudication are all part of our ancient Hebraic-Greek-Roman heritage, which flowed directly into the canon law, and into the secular law where the Church had influence, it was in the Anglo-Norman and Anglo-American legal systems that equity won its clearest formulation.

Before the Norman conquest, the courts of the Angles, the Saxons, and the other peoples of England administered the tribal, customary laws peculiar to each tribe or social group. With the Normans came the feudal social order, and beginning in 1178 the successors of William organized royal courts to administer the King's justice according to the law common to all England—perhaps something comparable to the Roman conception of *jus gentium,* "the sum of the common ingredients in the customs of the old Italian tribes" (Maine, p. 29)—what came to be known as "the common law." These courts exercised considerable discretion out of a sense of equity or fairness, and adopted procedures to meet new conditions. But in the middle of the fourteenth century the expansion of the common law seems to have stopped, and the courts said that if the law is to be altered in any respect, Parliament must take the initiative.

Parliament did not respond to the challenge; yet considerations of equity could not be indefinitely repressed or repulsed. The stultification of law in the royal courts created the royal remedy: the Chancellor, the surrogate for the King in the administration of the government, established in his office—the Chancery—an agency to hear grievances which the royal courts administering common law would not hear. The Chancellor said that, when he took jurisdiction of a cause, it was a matter of grace or conscience, and that he would render justice, not according to the technicalities of the common law but according to the dictates of equity. Since the Chancellor was usually a cleric—the last clerical Chancellor was Bishop John Williams (1621–25)—he was naturally much more familiar with the equitable principles of the canon law of the Church and with the praetorian edicts in Roman law than with

the law and legal forms administered by the King's Bench. The equitable basis of the Chancellor's jurisdiction was marked by the basic guideline that equity could be sought only in cases where the common law remedy was inadequate.

The common law courts exercised their jurisdiction through "writs" which directed the sheriff to seize the defendant's property and use it to satisfy a judgment against him, or through other writs which affected rights *in rem;* but Chancery acted only *in personam,* on the person directly. This was consistent with the theory that equity makes its appeal to the conscience of the party. A disobedient party was held by the Chancellor to be in contempt of the King, and thus in a way a rebel. Since the Chancellor could order the parties before him to do what equity demanded, he could keep a matter in controversy indefinitely before him, and decree various steps or actions affecting it. Thus he could order specific performance of a contract, while a court of law could only award damages for a breach. Unlike the King's courts of law, Chancery could enforce trusts by compelling the trustee to act in accordance with the demands of fairness or conscience. In due course, certain maxims came to be associated with equitable jurisdiction, among them: "He who seeks equity must do equity." "He who comes into equity must come with clean hands." "Equity suffers not a right to be without a remedy."

There was, naturally, criticism of a court that candidly admitted that it sought guidance in conscience, as, in the famous statement by John Selden in the seventeenth century (Selden's *Table Talk,* 1689):

Equity is a roguish thing. For Law we have a measure, know what to trust to. Equity is according to the conscience of him that is Chancellor, and as that is larger or narrower, so is Equity. 'Tis all one as if they should make the standard for the measure we call a 'foot' a Chancellor's foot; what an uncertain measure that would be! One Chancellor has a long foot, another a short foot, a third an indifferent foot. 'Tis the same thing in the Chancellor's conscience.

In the reign of James I the contest between the common law courts and Chancery broke out in the open, and the King himself, in 1616, resolved it by throwing his weight on the side of the latter. Equity, however, now began to restrain itself and to impose an order on its work. Francis Bacon, as Chancellor (1617–21), contributed to this effort. Before long equity itself became a system of precedents and itself began to suffer from *rigor juris.* The conscience of the Chancellor was, it was said in 1672 by Lord Chancellor Nottingham, not his natural or personal, but his civil and official, conscience.

After the Puritan Revolution, when the struggle

between royal power and Parliament was resolved in favor of the latter, the Chancellor, as the voice of the King's conscience, naturally declined; the common law courts, which had sided with Parliament, gained in prestige and authority. They now benefited from Sir Edward Coke's earlier struggle against James I, in which Coke was the champion of the supremacy of the common law against prerogative.

Beginning in the eighteenth century the common law courts proceeded to introduce doctrines and procedures which for centuries had been limited to Chancery. These reforms were effected sometimes by statute and sometimes by court decision. In time it became apparent that there was little if any justification for the two systems of courts, and a movement got under way to combine the two into a single court system. This was accomplished by the Judicature Acts of 1873 and 1875, which, among other things, fused law and equity.

V

The American colonists lost no love on the King's courts or the King's conscience. Remembering the oppression suffered at the hands of some judges following the Restoration, and that equity was somehow associated with royal prerogative, they looked with more favor on the law of the Hebrew Scriptures than on the common law and equity of England. Thus, when the Constitution of the United States was framed, it provided for a single system of federal courts, with power as to both law and equity; and some states also adopted this pattern. However, this did not mean the fusion of the two systems of law. It only meant that at times the court sat as a court of law and at times as a court of equity. But this device, adopted in part because it was more economical than two separate courts, could not but contribute in time toward a fusion. Some states set up entirely separate courts of equity and of law. New York State in 1848 broke new ground by adopting the code drafted by David Dudley Field, which effectively merged the two systems. In 1938 the federal courts adopted the essentials of the Field Code, and in 1948 New Jersey, by then the only state with a Court of Chancery, also effected a merger of the separate courts. The right to equitable relief, however, is still based on the inadequacy of "legal" relief; equity's principles, maxims, and precedents remain relevant.

VI

While equitable principles and procedures are still identified as such, their force is now largely historical, professional, and institutional, rather than moral. Lord Chancellor Nottingham would note that their force

flows from the official and impersonal conscience of the judge and not from his personal and moral conscience. In part this has become possible because legislatures and courts generally have learned from equity the need constantly to reform the law, substantively and procedurally, and they do so, though the bench and bar remain on the whole conservative. But judges no longer speak of the demands of conscience. They use formulas more acceptable to a secular, democratic society, and to a learned profession. But like Molière's character who spoke prose for more than forty years without knowing it, Anglo-American judges and lawyers speak equity on many occasions without knowing it—when they protect victims of fraud; when they protect married women in their separate property rights; when they seek relief from distress, mistake or misfortune; when they seek an injunction or an order for specific performance of a contract; when they argue that substance is more important than form; when they try to evade the technicality of the law in the interest of the intent of the law; when they seek to compel a party to do that which he should have done—they in fact follow precedents laid down by the great Chancellors, like Thomas More, Lord Ellesmere, Francis Bacon, Lord Cowper, Lord Harcourt, Lord Hardwicke, and Lord Eldon. Equity remains the spirit by which the law is reformed, in one way or another, to become more responsive to the moral demands of society.

This spirit manifests itself under other names than equity, and at times goes much further than any chancellor could have anticipated. For example, Jerome Frank's early and influential work, *Law and the Modern Mind* (1930) is extremely skeptical of the effectiveness of laws formulated in general terms, and places almost exclusive reliance on fact-finding. The result seems to be a reversal of Aristotle's formulation: the exception is, in fact, the rule; each case is or should be decided on its own facts. What Aristotle admitted only reluctantly and guardedly, Frank and the rule-skeptics accepted as the very core and crown of the judicial process: judges are at their best when they consciously exercise their discretion and their power to "individualize" justice.

A similar denigration of general rules, a stress on fact situations, and a belief that exceptions are in fact the rule can be found in contemporary moral theory—e.g., Paul Lehmann's *Ethics in a Christian Context* (1963), Bishop John A. T. Robinson's *Honest to God* (1963) and *Christian Morals Today* (1964), and Joseph Fletcher's *Situation Ethics* (1966). Interestingly, this antinomian, "situational," "contextual" approach has been developed mainly by theologians—a development that recalls the fact that at least in England equity

153

was first projected by chancellors who were churchmen to whom the theological and philosophical conception of conscience was quite familiar and congenial, and to whom "the law of conscience" was, in theory and in fact, law. But it is doubtful if the chancellors would wish to take credit for developments which give central place to facts rather than to rules, and which seem to replace the rule of law with the rule of the exception—the rule of equity.

BIBLIOGRAPHY

Carleton Kemp Allen, *Law in the Making,* 6th ed. (Oxford, 1958). Aristotle, *Nicomachean Ethics,* trans. H. Rackham, Loeb Classical Library, revised ed. (London and Cambridge, Mass., 1934); idem, *The "Art" of Rhetoric,* trans. John Henry Freese, Loeb Classical Library (London and Cambridge, Mass., 1926). William W. Buckland, *Equity in Roman Law* (London, 1911). Huntington Cairns, *Legal Philosophy from Plato to Hegel* (Baltimore, 1949). Cicero, *De republica—De legibus,* trans. Clinton W. Keyes, Loeb Classical Library (London and Cambridge, Mass., 1938). Boaz Cohen, *Law and Tradition in Judaism* (New York, 1959); idem, "Letter and Spirit in Jewish and Roman Law," *Mordecai M. Kaplan Jubilee Volume* (New York, 1953). David Daube, *Studies in Biblical Law* (Cambridge, 1947). G. C. Field, *The Philosophy of Plato* (Oxford and New York, 1949). William S. Holdsworth, *A History of English Law,* 16 vols. (London, 1903–66), esp. 3rd ed. (1945), Vol. V. James Willard Hurst, *Growth of American Law: The Law Makers* (Boston, 1950). John W. Jones, *Law and Legal Theory of the Greeks* (Oxford, 1956). Maimonides, *Code,* Book 14, *The Book of Judges,* trans. Abraham M. Hershman (New Haven, 1949). M. R. Konvitz, "Law and Morals in the Hebrew Scriptures, Plato, and Aristotle," in *Social Responsibility in an Age of Revolution,* ed. L. Finkelstein (New York, 1971). Henry Maine, *Ancient Law* (London, 1861), Ch. III. Frederic W. Maitland, *Sketch of English Legal History* (New York, 1915); idem, *Equity, also Forms of Action at Common Law,* eds. A. H. Chaytor and W. J. Wittaker (Cambridge, 1909). *Mishnah,* trans. Herbert Danby, Makkoth I. 10 (Oxford, 1933). Glenn R. Morrow, *Plato's Cretan City* (Princeton, 1960). Plato, *Dialogues,* trans. Benjamin Jowett (Oxford, 1892); idem, *The Laws,* trans. A. E. Taylor (London, 1934). Theodore F. T. Plucknett, *Concise History of the Common Law,* 5th ed. (London, 1956). Frederick Pollock, *Essays in the Law* (London, 1922), Ch. VII. Max Radin, *Handbook of Anglo-American Legal History* (St. Paul, 1936). *Select Essays in Anglo-American Legal History,* by various authors (Boston, 1908), Vol. II, Part IV. A. E. Taylor, *Plato: the Man and His Work,* 6th ed. (New York, 1952). Paul Vinogradoff, *Outlines of Historical Jurisprudence,* 2 vols. (London, 1920–22).

MILTON R. KONVITZ

[See also Equality; Justice; Law, Common, **Natural**; Legal **Precedent**; Stoicism.]

ESCHATOLOGY

The Concept. Eschatology, or "the doctrine of last things," is today often employed as a comprehensive term for all religious ideas of the afterlife. In the following, however, we shall employ the concept Eschatology in its original sense: eschatology describes and explains the goal and ultimate destiny of human history. Eschatology thus presupposes a unique linear flow of history from the beginning to the end of temporal history.

Apocalyptics. There are myths among many peoples of the collapse of the world, sometimes also of a time of redemption to be expected upon the ending of the world; and in these, of course, Christian influences are often present. The eschatological beliefs of Western as well as of Islamic cultural history are rooted in late Jewish apocalyptics in which the historical perspectives of the Old Testament are fused with aspects of Iranian eschatology.

Generally speaking, the idea was widespread in antiquity that time proceeds cyclically, just as nature does: history returns, after the expiration of a cosmic year—or aeon—to its beginning; events repeat themselves in perpetual reiteration. In Iran, on the other hand, the notion of a circular pattern was abandoned quite early. History was viewed as a straight line. The content of world events is the battle for men between the good god and the evil spirit. At the end of the world the dead are awakened and judged, the evil spirit is destroyed by the hosts of the good god, and there begins an eternally blessed existence on an earth freed from all evil. This blissful period heralds the finale, the *eschaton* of history; nothing is said of a repetition of the battle between light and darkness, even if the thought is borrowed from the cyclical view that the *eschaton* corresponds to the felicitous beginnings of the world.

This Iranian belief concerning the end of time encountered Old Testament piety and was thereby introduced into Jewish thought. This was all the more readily possible because the cyclical view of history had been alien to the Old Testament from time immemorial. God, the Creator of the world, guides the history of His chosen people along a straight line of historical development toward specific goals: He furnishes the Promised Land; He leads them through the catastrophe of exile into a new period of redemption; He promises the people a powerful Prince of Peace out of the House of David, etc. But these ideas were not eschatological to the extent that they were not connected with the idea of the final end of all history.

Under the influence of Iranian eschatology this Old Testament view of history was developed in time into an apocalyptic eschatology, the oldest documents of which still made their way into the Old Testament canon (Daniel; Isaiah 24–26). This apocalyptic view now includes not only the history of the children of Israel, but the whole of world history with all its people. Simultaneously, in place of the fluctuating this-worldly ideas of the goals of Israelite history, it substitutes the expectation of a cosmic catastrophe that leads to the end of the old aeon and of its master, the Devil, and passing through an eschatological period of redemption yields to a new world of absolute and perfect salvation. The depiction of the old aeon can in consequence borrow its coloration from the cyclical view of history, and the history of the expiring world can be seen as a process of decline from a Golden Age. But the apocalyptic conflagration of the world at the end of the old epoch does not introduce any repetition of events but, in accordance with dualistic thought, leads into an ahistorical new aeon. The subjects of history are no longer primarily peoples, but individual persons who, if they have already died, are consequently to be raised to judgment at the end of the old aeon. The time and manner of the eschatological turning point are decided by God alone as the master of history, but to some scattered prophetic figures the course of history to its end, as well as the eschatological outcome, has been revealed by God himself in advance (hence apocalypse, from the Greek *apokalyptein,* "to reveal"). Thus the process of history unfolds inalterably in accordance with a plan laid down by God.

Not infrequently a balance is struck between the historically immanent Old Testament hope and the transcendental apocalyptic expectation such that the apocalyptic end of history is preceded by a final messianic reign *within* history; hence an interregnum between the old and the new aeons in which the elect rule together with the Messiah. Texts such as Revelation 20 have perceptibly influenced the history of the West in expecting a thousand-year interregnum (chiliasm); for although the eschatological interregnum is conceived as historically immanent, revolutionary movements have often been fired in anticipation of it.

Gnosticism. At about the same time as the Hebrew apocalyptics, and not without some interchange with it, another manifestation of eschatological world perspective arose in the confluence of Iranian and Greek spiritual thought, viz., Gnosticism. Gnosticism is likewise associated with the Iranian dualism of a good and evil God. On this view, a personage from the world of Light fell under the power of Darkness during the battle between the two principles in primeval times. The evil powers then created the world as a place of sojourn and human bodies as prisons to hold this figure of Light captured and divided by them into so many

separate sparks of light. The good god now sets into motion the process of redemption in order to liberate the sparks of light from the power of Darkness and to return them to the world of Light. As soon as this process of redemption is completed the world will collapse into Nothing again, so that history comes definitively to an end.

While for apocalyptics God controls the old aeon, it is nonetheless subject to the power of sin so that for the Gnostic the world and history are represented mostly as a work of the Devil. Thus though one cannot properly speak of a goal of history in Gnosticism, yet the notion of an end of history is at the root of Gnostic thought. One can therefore speak of an unhistorical Gnostic eschatology, and the asceticism of this life becomes an adequate expression of an eschatological self-consciousness that strives for liberation from the world itself.

Gnosticism, which was a serious competitor of Christianity well into the fourth century, certainly influenced the thought of the West (e.g., Neo-Platonism), yet in both the West and the East, in opposition to anti-Gnostic dualism, the quest for the meaning and the goal of world history *controlled by God* proved victorious. The answer given by apocalyptics, that the meaning of history lies concealed in its eschatological goal, incited powerful historically effective forces in the West above all, and influenced both spiritual and world history. The philosophy of history, a branch of inquiry still unknown to Greek antiquity, could spring up only on a biblical foundation. Every current quest for the ultimate meaning of world history springs from biblical faith.

Primitive Christianity. Jesus was an apocalyptic. He was not indeed interested in elaborating the depiction of the final apocalyptic drama, but he foretold the beginning of last events in the imminent future. His exorcisms heralded the end of the old aeon. Even to the impious, provided they were repentant, his preaching opened the way at the last minute to salvation under God's reign, which very soon, without human participation, would appear throughout the earth as a bolt of lightning from God's hand.

When the Crucified One appeared to His disciples after His death, they interpreted Jesus' resurrection as the beginning of the universal resurrection of the dead, i.e., as the onset of last events. Jesus is the first of all the dead to be resurrected (I Corinthians 15:20). It is true that the consummation of apocalyptic last things did not follow; nonetheless early Christianity continued to understand the events surrounding Christ as God's eschatological redemptive act, themselves as a community of the redeemed, and their age as a time of eschatological redemption. In other words: "The

155

primitive Christian community did not understand itself as an historical, but as an eschatological, phenomenon. It already no longer belongs to this world, but to the future ahistorical era that is dawning" (R. Bultmann, p. 42). Out of this consciousness, and in view of the subsequent course of history, the problem arose how the eschatological community of the redeemed should live in history, and how historical time should be denominated from an eschatological point of view. As a solution of this problem there emerged the extraordinary dialectic of the primitive Christian concept of time, characterized as it is by the conflict of "It is here now" and "Not yet" when speaking of eschatological redemption. Paul and John dwelt with particular intensity on this problem and each gave it expression after his own manner.

Both understood their time as an age amid ages: the faithful lives *already now* in the new aeon, even though he is *not yet* free of the danger of relapse into the old aeon. The unfaithful still belongs to the expiring world, but by faith may still find access to the community of the redeemed. "Faith" means the abandonment of the material word as the basis of life, and living in the grace of God encountered by man in Christ. This faith redeems life: it brings righteousness and peace and joy (Romans 14:17). The faithful is a new creature (II Corinthians 5:17). To him is come the day of salvation (II Corinthians 6:2), he lives in love (I Corinthians 13), and lives and dies unto the Lord (Romans 14:7–9). The demonic forces of the expiring aeon have already been obliged to surrender their power to Christ.

The delay in the definitive consummation of last events is not felt to be a difficult problem in view of this conception. It is even possible for John to renounce altogether the apocalyptic eschatology of the future including the return of Christ to which Paul clings: the believer has already been judged (John 3:18); it is true that he still lives *in* the world, but he is no longer *of* the world (John 17:11–16).

The Christian Church. The primitive Christian understanding of the present as eschatological time is soon clearly weakened in the Church. The present simply becomes a time of preparation for the future salvation promised by the sacraments. Hope for the future is less connected with the end of the world than with the salvation of the individual soul after death. The doctrine of purgatory, in which individual souls are purified, displaces the expectation of a cosmic conflagration at the end of time; the Day of Judgment loses ground in favor of individual judgment after death and the tenets of penitence and indulgence connected with it. The teleological mode of historical thought survives all the same, and apocalyptic eschatology is not abandoned, but the end of time is postponed to some indeterminate temporal distance. Already by the time of II Peter 3:8 we read that with the Lord a thousand years are as one day.

At first the Church kept eschatological anticipation alive with the injunction to keep ever watchful for *no man* knows the day and hour of the end (Mark 13:32f.). But the triumph of the Church in the Roman state caused interest in an *indeterminate eschaton* to decline. As a legally constituted instrument of salvation the Church bridges the period from the first Coming of Jesus until the end of history on his return. Ticonius and Augustine both equate the thousand-year interregnum that is to precede the actual *eschaton* with the age of the Church, and thus delay the end of the world by a great interval, even if the number 1000 is not taken literally. The Church has in general regarded with suspicion and has restrained any heightened interest in eschatology and in the revolutionary pathos easily associated with it. All the same, *one* apocalyptic book, the Revelation of Saint John, finally made its way into the canon of the New Testament in the fourth century despite widespread opposition.

Thus apocalyptic eschatology as the goal of history has remained a significant feature of the New Testament and part of dogma, and can thus reappear in the foreground from time to time. It becomes manifest again in the Montanism of the second century with its acute expectation of an imminent end, but even at this time was viewed critically by the greater Church. Around the year 1000 many awaited the end of the thousand-year reign and therewith the end of the world; as a result there was a temporary increase of interest in the Day of Judgment (Peter Lombard). Joachim of Floris (d. 1202) recalculated the epochs of history in the light of the dogma of the Trinity and anticipated that, following the age of the Father and that of the Son, the onset of the age of the Holy Ghost as the epoch assuring complete salvation would come in 1260. Nicholas of Lyra likewise counts on the imminent beginning of the last events in his commentary on the Revelation of Saint John, written in 1329. In pre-Reformation times apocalyptic speculations were awakened particularly among those theologians who suffered acutely from the unsatisfactory conditions in the Church. Pre-Reformation and Reformation figures saw in the Pope the Antichrist who would appear before the end; thus Luther is able to announce the end of the world as imminent, just as many of the reformers inclined to call their age the final age, the twilight of the world. Under the influence of the humanists, apocalyptic thought retreated wholly in Zwingli, and eschatological fanatics, associated in some places with groups of enthusiasts and the Anabaptist movement seeking to install the Kingdom of God for the time being by force of arms, soon discredited all radical speculations concerning the end of time in the eyes of all the reformers. Reformation catechisms contained hardly any eschatological propositions of an apocalyptic nature: Article XVII of the Augsburg Confession denounces the chiliasm of the fanatics as a Jewish doctrine. Luther dissociated himself sharply from the social revolutionary thoughts of Thomas Münzer (who died in the Peasant War in 1525), from Melchior Hofmann, the inspired prophet of the end of time, and from the communistic fanaticism of Bernard Rottmann and his friends in Münster. Despite this, apocalyptic anticipations of the end remained alive and were augmented in times of plague, in the Thirty Years' War, and indeed everywhere that, from the time of the Counter-Reformation, minorities lived under repression and persecution and hoped for redemption from their plight. Above all in Pietistic circles all kinds of speculations concerning the onset of the thousand-year reign constantly reappeared. Following the precedent of Jacob Böhme, Philipp Jacob Spener, for example, combined exegesis of Revelation 20 with the optimistic expectation of a better time for the Church in the future; and the Swabian Pietist, Friedrich Christoph Oetinger drew the entire universe into this hope of historical salvation: for, he says, "carnality is the end of God's ways."

Many contemporary sects derive from speculations concerning the end of the world in the near future. The group of Adventists, for example, was formed on the basis of the American William Miller's computations that Christ would return in 1843–44 to found the thousand-year reign. In the origination of such Catholic-Apostolics as the New Apostolic Communion lies the conviction that in preparation for the return of Christ twelve apostles must stand ready; these indeed met in 1835 and together awaited last events. The Jehovah's Witness movement was based on the assertion of another American, Charles T. Russell, that Christ returned in secret in 1874 and would begin his thousand-year reign in 1914. Similar expectations of the imminent approach of the end recur frequently, particularly in times of catastrophe and often on the basis of fantastic interpretations of Revelation, without however at once leading to the stable formation of sects.

The remarkable increase in apocalyptic fanaticism since the eighteenth century is connected with the universal emergence of historical consciousness that took place at that time; this in turn led to numerous conceptions of an eschatologically oriented salvationist theology; in the eighteenth century, for example, in J. A. Bengel, who computed the date of the end of the world as 3836, and in J. J. Hess, who—a clear sign of historical interest—was the author of the first *Life of Jesus* (3 vols., 1768–72), and in 1774 wrote a work of salvationist dogmatics entitled *Of the Kingdom of God. An Essay on the Plan of God's Provisions and Revelations;* in the nineteenth century, J. C. K. Hofmann, among others, organized the whole of history on the basis of the Bible into a scheme of prophecy and fulfillment; more recently, in O. Cullmann, above all, who takes Christ as the "Center of Time," ebbing in undulating lines toward its end.

Among the influential theologians of the present whose suppositions are markedly determined by apocalyptic eschatology are W. Pannenberg and J. Moltmann. Pannenberg sees the resurrection of Jesus as a prolepsis of final events. Anyone who relies on the resurrection of Jesus is thus enabled in advance to view it to its end, and hence to grasp history as meaningful including that part of it not yet played out. Beginning with the resurrection of Jesus, Moltmann, in his *Evangelische Kommentare* (1968), erects a theology of hope teaching that all our forces are to be concentrated on the final apocalyptic goal of history, for Jesus' resurrection heralds the end of the world as the end of misery, injustice, and mortality. "The social revolution of unjust conditions is the immanent obverse of transcendent hope in the resurrection." Among philosophers, G. Krüger and K. Löwith, for example, associate themselves closely with the traditional biblical eschatology. In all the scholars mentioned, there is, of course, a more or less pronounced association of the idea of progress that has appeared in modern times with apocalyptic eschatology. The conception of the sudden end of history is replaced by the interpretation of history as a process aspiring to a climax.

Idealism. One stream of thought running in opposition to the activation of apocalyptic eschatology is represented by its idealization. By the time of the Alexandrian theologians of the third century, Clement and Origen had already banished any sensual eschatological expectations under Platonic and Gnostic influence. For them, all Being is spiritual. The souls of men are in increasing measure purified and by stages returned to their goal, divinity; until finally all are saved and the old order of the world, the material world, ends.

Such thoughts remained alive in some places in mystical circles, in which there is often some association between the actual withdrawal of spirit from history and apocalyptic conceptions of the end of history. In such circles Luke 17:21 plays a major role: "The kingdom of God is within you." The authentic eschatological event lies in the union of the soul with God (J. Arndt). Apocalyptics are therefore only of marginal interest: "We have enough on the sabbath of a new rebirth . . . the other we can well consign to God's omnipotence" (J. Böhme). Thus in the last analysis mysticism takes the place of eschatology: "When I abandon time I am myself eternity/ and enclose myself in God, and God enclose in me" (Angelus Silesius).

For Fichte likewise, a leading representative of so-called "German idealism," man can here on earth everywhere and always, so long as this is his own desire, attain to the rest, peace, and blessedness of the Kingdom of God by conceiving of himself in his own spirit as a part of the Absolute and can thus abide and rest in the *One*. Still Fichte combines this pure idealism with eschatological aspects: the more men realize the Kingdom of God as a moral and spiritual realm within themselves, the more will it then manifest itself in the world of appearances also. Men must therefore form themselves in accordance with reason "until the species actually exists as a perfected copy of its eternal prototype in reason, and thus the purpose of earthly life would be attained, its goal manifest, and mankind would enter upon the higher spheres of eternity"; ". . . for in the end everything must surely flow into the safe harbor of eternal rest and blessedness; in the end the Kingdom of God must appear, and His strength, and His power, and His glory" (*Werke*, V, 260f.).

Following the lines of the Alexandrian theologians, Hegel also found that the Real, the Absolute-Divine, is Spirit. But here, as opposed to Origen, Spirit does not stand as a general idea in relation to natural reality; rather it realizes itself *in* the particular: everything real is spiritual, everything spiritual is real. In the self-consciousness of the thinking spirit there is a reconciliation in an ideal unity of the "for-itself" of universal spirit here and the particular which derives from it there. "The goal, which is Absolute Knowledge or Spirit knowing itself as Spirit, finds its pathway in the recollection of spiritual forms as they are in themselves and as they accomplish the organization of their spiritual kingdom," Hegel says in the final chapter of the *Phenomenology of Mind*. This process of the self-unfolding of Spirit thus takes place historically, and indeed in accordance with inalterable laws, just as in apocalyptics; but God does not write its laws from without, but the spirit immanent within history writes them from within. Instead of divine providence we find the "cunning of (spiritual) reason," which is even able to make humans act unconsciously and render seemingly senseless or destructive actions in history serviceable for the purposes of Spirit. The end of history is attained when Spirit comes into its own in self-conscious thought, when it gains absolute knowledge

of itself in man, i.e., for all practical purposes in Hegel's own Christian philosophy of religion, on the basis of which both Church and State will be consolidated in a rational social order. The eschatological judgment of the world collapses in unison with world history.

The idealistic view of the Kingdom of God, deriving from Fichte and Hegel, surrenders the notion of a sudden reversal of cosmic conditions by the intervention of God, and favors instead the idea of progress. Furthermore, interest in the definitive end of history diminishes altogether, and is replaced by the construction of a course of history striving to attain its culminating climax. God functions as Spirit *in* this progressive historical development. The theology of the nineteenth century, from Schleiermacher down to so-called liberal theology, similarly shows itself markedly under idealistic influence. At least the idea of progress exercises great influence. R. Rothe felt he could expect the Christian state, the *civitas Dei*, as the perfected form of the Kingdom of God. For A. Ritschl the Kingdom of God, the perfection of which certainly lies in the remote future, comes to realization in the expanding community of those acting morally out of neighborly love.

Secularization. The awakening historical consciousness that advanced salvationist schemes in theology since the eighteenth century led in the course of a general secularization of culture to a secular idea of eschatology also. Although faith was maintained in the thought of the end or of the goal of history proceeding in linear fashion, no further consideration was given to divine intervention in the course of history; the goal of history was thought of as purely immanent.

The path to this goal was in part seen as progress to ever greater perfection of the human condition; and—where it clung more firmly to biblical modes of thought—it was interpreted or promoted as a sudden revolutionary incursion. The pioneers of this development were the humanists, above all, Erasmus of Rotterdam, who wanted to see the Kingdom of God as a universal realm of peace already realized in earthly society. Movements of chiliasm and pacifism, with their intensive expectation of such an earthly realm of peace, have thus prepared the ground since the time of the Reformation for the complete secularization of eschatology; Thomas Münzer is one of the "saints" of communism.

The Enlightenment, which led the battle of reason against unreason, was able to view, to the extent that it was open to historical thinking, the worldwide triumph of human reason as the necessary outcome of historical development—not that of history itself (Turgot, Condorcet, the positivists). Compare also Lessing's essay on "The Education of the Human Species." Under the spell of the Enlightenment Kant expects the Kingdom of God in the guise of a worldwide ethical commonwealth, in any case as the end of a "progression stretching to eternity" of mankind involved in "the continuous progress and approach to the highest good possible on earth." In calling this view "chiliasm" Kant correctly observes the close connection between the devout pietistic and the secularized Enlightenment eschatology of the eighteenth century (*Critique of Practical Reason*, Book II, Ch. II, Sec. 5).

It is apparent that marked secular influences were at work even in the idealistic systems described above, for in these ideas the divine spirit is identical with the human spirit so that the eschatological climax of history can only be attained by means of human activity, and is therefore conceived of as "this-worldly." In his book *The Kingdom of Christ* (1842; 1959), F. D. Maurice takes up the idealistic concept of the Kingdom of God and awaits the onset of God's reign in the immanent moral perfection of mankind. Influenced by Maurice, Charles Kingsley, for example, hopes for the progress of the Kingdom of God in the improvement of the social order. The influence of secularized eschatology had its impact also on so-called liberal theology of the last century which expected progress in human civilization to come about through the education of individual personality after the example of the absolute personality of Jesus, and equated such progress with the Kingdom of God, which it saw in consequence as moral grandeur. Even Nietzsche's hero (*Übermensch*) quiet naturally represents a secularized form of the "new creature" of Christian hope for the end of time.

The most influential proposal for secularized eschatology to be found after Hegel was advanced by Karl Marx. History develops for him, as for the apocalyptics, with ineluctable lawlikeness. The impelling force of history is neither God nor, as in Hegel, the absolute World Spirit, but instead the process of production with economic contradictions obtaining at any given time, and in connection with which the development of social classes and heightening of class conflict are played out. The ultimate class in world history is the proletariat. The proletarian revolution heralds the end of class conflict and therewith, so to speak, the end of history. Marxist theory computes the objective goal of the course of history in advance: the victorious class establishes the classless society. It renews and redeems the world. With it will come the realm of freedom for all individuals, the end of exploitation as primeval evil, the triumph of the good, the reconciliation of all contradiction between light and darkness, the Kingdom of God without God. The very concept of revolution, hitherto an expression for political upheavals in general, takes on an explicitly eschatological sense in Marx.

But while Marx saw history striving with the necessity of a natural law toward the proletarian revolution as its eschatological goal, many of his followers expect the classless society as the outcome of a world revolution consciously provoked by men. These modern Marxist theories of revolution are the most utterly explicit expression of secularized biblical eschatology.

In the 1960's the Marxist Ernst Bloch, in *The Principle of Hope* (1959), offers the most impressive account of the connection between Marxist expectations for the future and the hopes of religious apocalypse. He interprets Marxist thought about the future as the real sense of Judeo-Christian eschatology, just as, conversely, religious socialism could for a time represent socialist hopes for the appropriate temporal form of the biblical hope for the Kingdom of God. Even at the present time the "feedback" from Marxist eschatology to theology is in some places considerable; above all in connection with the so-called "God is dead" theology, hope of social justice is considered to be the only meaningful form of eschatological hope (Harvey Cox). Increasingly expanded planning for the future, so necessary in the modern world, with the aid of scientific prognosis ("futurology"), is in itself not eschatological, but reinforces the effectiveness of secularized eschatological world perspectives, above all, of communism and socialism.

Evolution. Since the Enlightenment the optimism concerning progress already founded in humanism has broken new ground and, coupled with awakening historical thought, leads to the idea that history strives toward its goal of salvation in constant or in undulating development. This notion of development can be connected, as we have seen, with the apocalyptic idea of the sudden end of history. In idealism it clearly leaves virtually no room for apocalyptic eschatology, and even in secular eschatology ideas of evolution and revolution are in mutual contention.

Evolutionary ideas were particularly stimulated (mostly they had sought the felicitous outcome of history in a remote future, and originally they were based solely on the philosophy of history) in the nineteenth century by Darwin's scientific theories of evolution and by the enormous advances of modern technology. The incorporation of the totality of Nature in an eschatology assimilated to apocalyptic accounts had already been initiated by Oetinger and in Schelling's philosophy of nature, although it had appeared also in a number of Enlightenment figures; and thus combinations of hopes for the Kingdom of God and technological utopias are to be found since the Renaissance. Darwin's doctrine of the higher development of species as well as faith in technological progress then led in the nineteenth century, on the one hand, to purely secularized hopes for the *Übermensch* and a perfected society liberated from material need, and, on the other hand, to theological attempts to reconcile the evolutionary ideas of natural science with the superseded eschatology. Mention should be made in this connection, for example, of the Scotsman James McCosh (d. 1894), the Unitarian Minot J. Savage (d. 1918), and also the English theologian Henry Drummond (d. 1897), on whose views God reveals Himself in a natural evolution that is to lead to a "more divine" man. By comparing the evolution of creation with a column topped by a capital, Drummond takes Christian salvationism as the pinnacle of universal evolution. Among others thinking along the same lines in the twentieth century are the German philosopher Leopold Ziegler and the French Jesuit and anthropologist Teilhard de Chardin, who associates the "God from above" with the "God striving forward," and whose thinking is not only regarded highly in Christian circles, but also plays an important role in the Christian-Marxist dialogue whenever revolutionary Marxist pathos is corrected by evolutionary thought.

The Abandonment of Eschatology. In the idealization of eschatology under the influence of Greek thought and in its modern secularization there remains, despite the overwhelming role of the idea of evolution, some trace of the influence of biblical thought: the course of history is viewed as goal-directed, and history is therefore viewed as meaningful.

Nonetheless, over the last 200 years there has been, to an increasing extent in some intellectual movements, an abandonment of *every* form of eschatology. History has lost the structure of a goal-directed process; inquiry into the meaning of history has become meaningless. This abandonment of eschatology in general is to be ascribed in the first place to the scientific mode of thought derived from British empiricism (Bacon, Hobbes, Locke, Hume) which, through its views on the death of the world by entropy, by cosmic collision, and the possibility of atomic disintegration, have supplied only a meager alternative to traditional eschatology. With this must be associated, after the rise of historical consciousness and the collapse of the optimistic Enlightenment belief in progress, a form of historical relativism which accepts only discrete causally connected historical events, but rejects any meaningful pattern in the totality of history, all philosophies of history, and all eschatological beliefs (J. Burckhardt, F. Nietzsche). Historical interest can thus be focussed solely on the past and on the modest inquiry: "How things actually were" (positivistic historiography). Or history is understood—mainly aesthetically—as an expression of a unified intellectual and spiritual life (W. Dilthey). When this relativism was converted, as not infrequently was the case, into pessimism viewing history as hastening toward catastrophe (e.g., O. Spengler, *Decline of the West,* 1918–22; Eng. trans., 1926–28) there was a revival of the cyclical thought of pagan antiquity (as adopted by Nietzsche in his doctrine of the Eternal Return) rather than of the eschatological consciousness of the Bible.

Renewal of New Testament Eschatology. The very meaning of history appears to vanish when, on the one hand, hope for the end of sacred history by the intervention of an external source fades away, and at the same time the optimistic secular eschatology of progress also dwindles; when, on the other hand, the whole question of an eschatological goal for history is abandoned. To the extent that nihilism appears appropriate we come closer to a return to the biblical view of history in which Jesus Christ represents the turning point of the aeon, so that the present at any given period is denominated an eschatological time. This eschatological interpretation of history has manifested its vigor in the course of Church history particularly among those theologians most indebted to biblical thought. Thus for Augustine the battle in world history between the *civitas terrena* and the *civitas Dei* is fought out in the history of the individual in such a manner that Christ is already here and now able to live as a citizen of the Kingdom of God through his "rebirth," even though the palpable worldwide victory of the city of God is still lacking.

Luther's conviction of standing at the end of time is rooted in the existential experience of his own death consummated in the death of Christ; that is, the death of the "old Adam" enslaved in sin; or, as the case may be, in assumption of the freedom guaranteed to the child of God in the sense of the Pauline utterance: "Therefore being justified by faith, we have [eschatological!] peace with God through our Lord Jesus Christ" (Romans 5:1). Luther is able to place in the future the *present* eschatological gift of salvation by forgiving grace *because* it is present *in faith,* that is, it is simply an *unmerited* gift of God, and thus can *now* be seized.

In the twentieth century, so-called dialectical theology relying on Luther and Kierkegaard returned to the dialectical interpretation of eschatology in the New Testament, following on the rediscovery in New Testament scholarship, toward the end of the nineteenth century, of the primarily apocalyptic character of the biblical message concerning the Kingdom of God (J. Weiss, A. Schweitzer). Karl Barth defines the acknowledgment of Christian revelation as an insight into the existential truth "that time becomes as eternity, and eternity as this moment." Time, for faith, is "the eternal moment, the Now, in which past and future come to rest." The present at any given moment is thus eschatological time, and in this sense Barth writes: "Christianity that is not wholly, simply, and totally eschatology has wholly, simply, and totally nothing to do with Christ."

Above all R. Bultmann, relying on aspects of Heidegger's existential philosophy (itself in turn markedly influenced by the New Testament, Luther, and Kierkegaard), has fallen back on New Testament eschatology. According to Bultmann substantial passages in the New Testament treat the events surrounding Christ as God's ultimately valid act of salvation. The annunciation of these events thus denominates every present moment as eschatological time. For it liberates man from himself, that is, from the sinful compulsion to locate his life in the actuality of *his* past and the possibilities of *his* future, by bestowing on him life out of god's charismatic future. Such existence drawn out of God's future is eschatological existence, for with its coming all temporal history is at an end. Each moment is possessed of the possibility of being an eschatological moment; the faithful actualizes this possibility. The *eschaton* eventuates constantly *in* history from *beyond* history. To the extent that apocalyptic eschatology is retained in the New Testament this mythological conception has the existential meaning of representing futurity, that is, the charismatic, or the character of grace of God's liberating word: new life fulfills itself solely in the acceptance of the "freedom of the children of God."

Summary. The following may be said in summing up: the problem of eschatology is inquiry into the end as the goal and meaning of history. Since man as an historical being never confronts history but is always moving *in* history he is never able to answer the question about the *eschaton* objectively, i.e., as a neutral observer. His judgment concerning the *eschaton* of history always implies a judgment about himself as an historical being. Regardless of whatever solution has been or will be given to the problem of eschatology we conclude: since history is still an ongoing process at the present time, and nobody is in a position to scan history from its beginning to its definitive outcome, and since the course of history does not itself indicate what its end and goal might be, the question of eschatology remains open as a subject for systematic inquiry and can only be answered as a matter of personal decision.

BIBLIOGRAPHY

E. Benz, *Evolution and Christian Hope*, trans. H. G. Frankl (New York, 1966). W. Bousset, *Die Religion des Judentums im späthellenistischen Zeitalter*, 3rd. ed. (Tübingen, 1925). R. Bultmann, *History and Eschatology* (London, 1957; New York, 1962). R. G. Collingwood, *The Idea of History* (London and New York, 1946). B. Croce, *La Storia come pensiero e come azione* (Bari, 1938); trans. Douglas Ainslie as *History: Its Theory and Practice* (1916; New York, 1960). O. Cullmann, *Heil als Geschichte* (Tübingen, 1965); trans. as *Salvation in History* (New York, 1967). J. G. Fichte, *Werke*, ed. F. Medicus, 6 vols. (Leipzig, 1908–12; reprinted, 1954—). G. Krüger, *Geschichte und Tradition* (Stuttgart, 1949). K. Löwith, *Meaning in History. The Theological Implications of the Philosophy of History* (Chicago, 1957). H.-J. Marrou, *La Connaissance historique* (Paris, 1956); trans. as *The Meaning of History* (New York, 1965). J. Moltmann, *Theologie der Hoffnung* (Munich, 1964). W. Pannenberg, *Offenbarung als Geschichte* (Göttingen, 1961). O. Plöger, *Theokratie und Eschatologie*, 2nd ed. (Neukirchen, 1962). E. Staehelin, *Die Verkündigung des Reiches Gottes in der Kirche Jesu Christi*, 7 vols. (Basel, 1951; 1965). A. J. Toynbee, *A Study of History*, 12 vols. (London and New York, 1934–61).

WALTER SCHMITHALS

[See also **Dualism**; Existentialism; **Gnosticism**; God; Hegelian . . . ; Marxism; **Millenarianism**; Perfectibility; Progress; Sin and Salvation.]

PROBLEM OF EVIL

THE IDEA of evil and the problems which it has presented to thinkers throughout history have expressed incisively the great divide in men's outlooks on nature and on human experience: the fundamental philosophical distinction between a natural-scientific and a spiritual-religious attitude. Scientific naturalism has been concerned with description and explanation and on principle has been neutral to any basic evaluation. But religion, men's deepest response to the Highest, has been essentially and thoroughly evaluative. Going beyond the domain of description and explanation its judgments have been verdicts either of worship or of condemnation.

In a religious perspective the idea of reality has been completely imbued with the idea of perfection: *ens realissimum ens perfectissimum*. First and last, religion has set out with a primal and ultimate recognition of consummate perfection in all its aspects. Men have exalted their conviction of the essential supremacy of their ideals and have proclaimed them as divine in origin, sanction, and final justification. The maturing development of men's ideas of God has been due to man's progress in evaluative insight and vision.

The very growth in spiritual intelligence has emphasized the radical problem of evil. In its devout conviction religion has declared: "Great is truth and it will prevail"—and likewise for the other supreme values. But do the facts of life really and finally sustain this belief in man's status in the universe? Is external nature really attuned to our highest values, or is it neutral to them, or even, in a sort of counter-religious demonic outlook, is it actually malign? The confirmation of religious assurance hangs upon the settlement of these issues. The actuality of evils demands reconciliation with the prevailing reality of the Divine. The problem of evil is imposed by our experienced frustration of values, by the clash between what ought to be and what actually is. Religious reflection has not been able to shirk this problem. Even a brief consideration of its treatment in the ancient religions would disclose its abysmal character. Modern philosophy and literature have expressed the persistent embroilment of secular thought in the issues of the traditional theodicies. The words of Charles Bernard Renouvier are brought to our attention: "Life can concern a thinker only as he seeks to resolve the problem of evil" (Lasbax, p. 1).

Religious thought in India, Brahmanic and Buddhist, set out with a firm conviction of the evil in the whole world of finite existence, but these two religions entertained different explanations of evil and different prospects of deliverance. Brahmanic pantheism contemplated the world and ourselves in it as manifestations of the Infinite Brahman. Everything whatever, in its inmost reality or soul, Atman, is one with the Infinite; but considered in their apparent multiplicity, things and persons are corrupt and illusory. Man's only hope is in his eventual saintly deliverance from the veil of illusion and the cycle of rebirth, in his absorption in Brahman. The Brahmanic sages were reluctant to confront resolutely the basic questions which embroiled their theodicy: Why should Brahman be manifested in this world of delusion and evil? Does not this propensity towards finite existence stain the perfection of the Infinite?

Buddhist reflection followed the more radical course of avoiding the pitfalls of theodicy by a fundamental atheism. It rejected all substantial existence as illusory, Brahman and Atman alike, infinite or finite. There are no real substances; there are only processes, but all of them are processes operating in strict retribution, Karma. The course of human existence is a wretched round of evils and miseries. This universal woe is due to men's deluded and futile attachment to the lusts and interests of their imagined soul or self. The deliverance from this evil state is possible only through the extinction of self-engrossment. To these three cardinal truths or convictions the Buddha added a fourth: his program of a life of progressive liberation from egoism, leading towards the utterly selfless blessedness of Nirvana.

To Zarathustra (Zoroaster) in ancient Iran the basic fact of existence, and thus the first principle of cosmic interpretation, was the universal opposition of good and evil. This radical conflict, evident throughout nature and in human life, indicated a cleavage reaching to the very roots of being, a fundamental dualism. In the Zoroastrian theology the perfect creation by God, (or Ohrmazd), Ahura-Mazdā was countered at each turn by Ahriman's evil work: darkness against light, corruption and banes against all purity and health and life. The daily conflicts between good and evil in our character and careers are only incidents in the universal war between the two creative cosmic powers. True religion is in man's loyal cowarriorship with the Lord, Ahura-Mazdā, in every thought and word and deed that resist and defeat and destroy Ahriman's evil creation: in industrious and productive labor, in pure conduct, truthful speech, saintly thought. This world conflict, though immemorial, was regarded by Zarathustra as destined to end in the final overthrow and fiery destruction of Ahriman's entire evil creation. Thus the initial and basic dualism of good and evil in Zoroastrian theology reached its climax, not merely in an assured meliorism, but in the conviction of a finally perfect world order.

Unlike the sages of India, Greek thinkers were at home in this world and did not seek deliverance from evil through escape from finite existence. Beginning with the sixth century, philosophical reflection turned away from the traditional polytheistic mythology towards the ideal of ultimate divine unity, contemplated as perfect and sovereign Reason. Most emphatically in Platonism, this rationalism was decisive in the theory of knowledge, in ethics, in metaphysics. Truth and perfection and abiding reality are all rational. Error and evil and unstable multiplicity are in the material world and in processes of sense-impressions, desires, and impulses. Our human nature is a tangle of appetites and a dynamic drive of energies, but it also possesses intelligence and should be controlled and directed by rational judgment. In the words of Socrates, the unexamined, unintelligent life is not worth living. Plato portrayed the process of rational mastery, aristocracy (dominance of the best), as the right fulfillment and self-realization of personality. This positive Higher Naturalism of the Platonic philosophy of life did not quite silence the tragic note in his theodicy, but it would not yield to final negation. In human life and in finite reality there was always the drag of corrupt matter. Plato was no docile optimist; he declared: "Evils can never pass away; for there must always remain something which is antagonistic to good" (*Theaetetus* 176; trans. B. Jowett). But he resolutely rejected any cosmic despair: God desired that all things should be good and nothing bad "as far as this was attainable." God alone is absolutely perfect; any finite world would of necessity have its strains of imperfection. So corruption and evils are actual: to be recognized and confronted and, within the range of our rational powers, to be overcome. In Greek ethics, this is the problem of reason and the passions; in Greek philosophy of religion, we may note here a trend in theodicy which is to find its concluding classical expression in the *Enneads* of Plotinus.

Between Plato and Plotinus, Greek philosophers with one notable exception exalted reason as the mark of the supreme and perfect reality. The exception is the Epicurean materialistic view of the world process and human existence as a scrambling and unscrambling of atomic configurations and motions. So-called good and evil alike are in the mechanical contacts and reactions of our sense organs, in pleasure and pain.

Against this atomism, the Stoic sages of Greece and Rome contemplated the material world itself as manifesting a hierarchical order, from the most rudimentary dust to the highest rational perfection of God. In this cosmic scale of being, men may yield to the drag of lower desires and passions or, resisting all evil lures, the sage would follow the lead of rational intelligence, in apathy, the passionless life of godlike serenity which alone is virtuous and truly good.

Before Epicurus and the Stoics, Aristotle pursued the course of realistic rationalism. He contemplated nature as a cosmic process of the hierarchical realization of potentialities: each type of existence is the Form or fulfillment of capacities of a lower order and in turn has the potential capacity to serve as the Matter of a higher order of being. Aristotle's God is Pure Form or creative reason in eternal self-contemplation. In human nature and experience, the curve of perfection ascends from Matter, bodily desires, and inordinate passions towards the realized Form and harmonious fulfillment of our humanity in balanced rational expression. This Aristotelian distinction of the evil and good aspects or stages of human experience was positive but also coolly objective, without the tragic overtones of reflection that mark any ecclesiastical demand for a theodicy.

Philosophical theodicy finds its classical version, both its consummation and its self-criticism, in the Neo-Platonism of Plotinus. The Plotinian cosmology contemplated the entire course of nature as the self-manifestation of God. The thorny problem, why or how perfect Deity should be manifested in such an imperfect world, was not evaded by Plotinus. He met it by a reinterpretation of the process of self-manifestation. God alone is absolutely perfect; the divine perfection radiates or emanates in nature, through the zones of Reason and Soul, to the outermost rim of least self-manifestation, in the world of Matter. These are all degrees of perfection, but, being emanations, they are not and cannot be consummately perfect. They are less and less luminous as they radiate towards the outer darkness or the abyss of material existence and its corruptions and evils. Our human career is a contention between the urge godward and the evil drag of sensuality. Plotinus resists any cosmic pessimism: each level or zone of emanation has its appropriate perfection, but what is appropriate to animal or plant or other material existence is not befitting the life and career of men. Our true fulfillment is in turning godward, towards the life of reason, and even beyond reason, towards the mystical ascent in ecstasy.

The intensified gravity of the problem of evil in monotheistic worship is evidenced strikingly in the Hebrew religious development. The prophetic reformation, starting in the eighth century B.C., advanced from the tribal monolatry of the popular cults towards ethical monotheism and personal worship. The fuller attainment of this religious maturity by the prophet Jeremiah, in the days of the siege and destruction of Jerusalem and the Babylonian exile of the people of Judah, raised grave perplexities in the traditional doctrine of men's covenant or contractual relation to God: of God's justice in rewarding the righteous man with prosperity and other blessings and punishing the wicked for their evils. Against the confident recital of the first Psalm were the tragic facts of Hebrew life. Bad men as well as good escaped the horrors of the national ruin; and what multitudes of choice worshipers of Yahweh were driven into exile by the godless Babylonians!

This predicament and quandary of religious thinkers provided the setting for the Book of Job: the probing of the problem of evil as evidenced in the undeserved misery and ruin of righteous men. The nameless poet of the Hebrew dramatic masterpiece proposes in searching dialogue alternative answers to the questions which perplex theodicy. He portrays an outstanding righteous and prosperous Job, who is laid low and stricken with ills, a mass of sores on the trash heap of the countryside. The longest dialogues consider the traditional doctrine, expounded by Job's prosperous friends, that God brings evil to men justly, as punishment for their sins, and that Job must therefore confess his hidden misdeeds and repent. Against their orthodox pronouncements stands God's own recorded praise of Job as his choicest worshiper. Are we, then, to follow Satan, the Adversary in God's cabinet, and regard Job's sufferings as a testing of his righteousness, as gold is tested by fire? But Job's firm loyalty has already been declared by omniscient Deity. Or are the tribulations

163

of the righteous a mystery in the vast universe of mysteries? The poet of the drama has no formulated solution of the abysmal problem, but he does portray the right way in which men should confront it—in forthright integrity.

The Book of Ecclesiastes is a sardonic reflection of another side of the problem of evil: not the unmerited sufferings of righteous men but the final futility and vanity of all so-called attainments and satisfactions of human life. They are all vanity of vanities, a striving after wind. Good men and evil, winners and losers, all of them "go unto one place; all are of the dust, and all turn to dust again" (Ecclesiastes 3:20). This is the dour and sour negation of any abiding worth: value skepticism.

Christianity was fundamentally a gospel of salvation of sinful men. The conviction of sin, the vilest evil in existence, and of man's own utter incapacity to surmount it set the conditions of any orthodox Christian theodicy. Any depreciation of the radical depravity and any moral self-reliance were impious insults to the solemnity of Divine Grace. In thus concentrating its view of evil on sin, Christian theology depreciated other ills, to be endured or even welcomed by the repentant and saintly soul, ready to suffer and be persecuted for righteousness' sake. In this radical transvaluation and spiritualizing of all worth, the problem of evil became a problem of interpreting sin: its essential nature, its origin and ground in God's perfect creation, the blessed redemption from it for a saintly minority, and the everlasting damnation of countless unsaved multitudes.

According to Saint Paul, the essential evil, sin, is in man's straying from the straight path of righteousness into the erring ways of the flesh. Paul's initial education was classical, but we are not to regard his contrast of the spiritual and the carnal as a mere rephrasing of the Greek dualism of reason and matter. Nor are we justified in interpreting the Christian ideal, the contempt of this world for the love of Christ, as explicitly ascetic. The sinful life in detail is worldly and carnal, but sin essentially is man's perverse scorn of God's will.

The radical depravity vitiates even that which, in its right measure, is good, when it is set above its better and higher values. "He that loveth father and mother *more than me* is not worthy of me." While ascetic saintliness did become exalted in Christian monasticism, the basic Christian idea was not a stark antithesis of the spirit and the flesh. The antithesis was directional and gradational; the good was always in the upward reach, the evil in the downward drag. Nowise asserting this as a rigid formula, we may yet recognize that, while asceticism did gain ascendency in traditional Christian devotion, the fundamental Christian idea was not a reduction of the evil to the carnal. Whether manifested in sensuality or in vain pride or ambition, the basic evil, sin, is always in the depraved straying of man's will from the higher to the lower. So we find it affirmed by the two pillars of orthodoxy. Saint Aquinas declared: sin is essentially *aversio*, man's turning or straying from the immutable Good to some mutable good. And more than eight centuries before him, Saint Augustine, in his *City of God*, had given the finest expression of this Christian conviction: "When the will abandons the higher, and turns to what is lower, it becomes evil—not because that is evil to which it turns, but because the turning is perverse (*sed quia perversa est ipsa conversio*)."

The recognition of the fundamental nature of evil, of man's sinful bondage, and of his only hope of redemption through Divine Grace, accentuated the other demand of Christian theodicy, to explain this evil depravity of man as nowise compromising the absolute perfection of man's Creator. Augustine's version of orthodoxy reflected his strong reaction against the Manichaean heresy, to which he had been attached for some ten years prior to his conversion. Manichaeism, fusing the Zoroastrian antithesis of good and evil with the Greek dualism of reason and matter, ascribed the evil strains in human life to man's inherently corrupt bodily nature. Against Manichaeism, Augustine upheld the Christian truth that God is the sole creator of all existence, creator of the material world, and that everything in nature, as the above quoted passage maintains, is essentially good in its place and role in creation. Evil is in the will's perverse misdirection of choice. But Augustine rejected also the opposite Pelagian heresy, that our will, though inclined to sin, has also the capacity to choose the good. Between these two counter-fallacies, Augustinian theodicy pointed to the source of evil in Adam's original disobedience to God's will. The possibility of Adam's evil choice was allowed by God, else it would have lacked the quality of a free and morally responsible act. But that choice, when once made, that original sin involved in its dire consequences all of us, tainted children of Adam. Left to its own resources, our will is bound to sin and to its ruinous retribution. Our only possible refuge, wholly unmerited, is in God's grace.

Augustinian theodicy has largely set the direction of later Christian doctrine but has also aroused much criticism and controversy. It has been restated more rigidly, e.g., in Calvinism, or it has been revised so as to allow some semi-Pelagian implications. Augustine's critics have pressed the point that Adam's fateful choice, while freely his own, was yet representative of his character, and they have raised the question whether God could not have created an Adam that would have freely made a good choice, as he did actually create an Adam that freely chose evil. Furthermore, how are the rest of us, countless multitudes, justly punishable through all eternity for our sinful wills, sinful through no decisive choice of ours but due to our evil inheritance as children of Adam?

Ethical theories have been distinguished by their alternative views of the Highest Good. Religious tradition adoring all supreme perfection as Divine, has contemplated with dismay its demonic counterparts of utter evil. Embattled against the blessed angelic and archangelic host are the wicked cohorts of the Lords of Darkness. Kinships as well as differences in the various faiths have found expression in their views of the Evil One. The extensive study of them would comprise an important part of the history of religions. Mara the Tempter tried to dissuade the Buddha from his holy mission, even as Jesus was tempted by the Devil in the wilderness. Most terrifying in evil majesty was the Zoroastrian Ahriman, and it has been conjectured that the grim dualism of the *Zendavesta* may have had some influence on Jewish and Christian demonological speculation.

Popular superstition and folklore, hagiography and solemn theology teem with stories of demonic incursion. With their protean and tireless wiles the countless devils hold in bondage the unregenerate multitude, and they are ever ready to invade the cells of devout monks and nuns, to assume priestly vestment and desecrate the eucharist itself. Most of these stories are medieval. Modern Christian piety has been engrossed in its struggle with definite evils to be overcome and vicious tendencies to be curbed, but it has shown a steady decline of interest in the traditional demonology. The idea of the Devil, however, has stirred the imagination of great poets to dramatic expression of the problem of evil. Three outstanding works of genius should be noted here, however, briefly: Milton's *Paradise Lost*, Byron's drama, *Cain*, and Goethe's *Faust*.

Milton's Satan is an archangel fallen and depraved. The noble qualities of his erstwhile supernal character are not extinct, but they have been perverted by misdirection to evil ends and have made his spiritual downfall the more abysmal. The firm courage, heroic devotion, and pure loyalty of an archangelic character have been corrupted into desperate temerity and rebellious unyielding arrogance, a resolution indomitably malign. In Milton's moral philosophy good and evil are determined by opposite directions of the will: towards devotion to high ideals which mark the truly intelligent spirit, or in the downward sweep of lusts and perverse drives.

The most significant difference between Byron's Lucifer and Milton's Satan is in the evaluation of their characters. Byron seems to praise what Milton stigmatizes. Satan's rebellious disdain appears in Byron's Lucifer as indomitable pride; furious violence is romantically exalted as heroic ardor. Byron's tragedy also expresses the forthright, though futile, refusal to worship mere omnipotence. It ends on a note of final moral chaos, when Cain's revolt against a God who demands cruel animal sacrifice sweeps him to blind fury in which he slays his own brother Abel.

The philosophy of life in Goethe's *Faust* defies any cursory formulation, but the poet's guiding idea of good and evil can be recognized clearly. Goethe portrays man as seeking a finality of achievement and satisfaction which no experience in life can yield. It is this sense of eventual frustration which leads Faust to barter his soul's salvation to the devil for one moment of supreme and consummate bliss. But the dramatic career through which Mephistopheles leads him teaches Faust in the end that the true value of life is not in the ardor of gratified desires or in any seemingly final achievement, but rather in the creative pursuit itself, in high endeavor and noble hazard:

Of life and freedom only he's deserving
Who daily must win them anew (Part II, Act V, Scene vi).

Against this heroic dynamism of Goethe's ideal of the good we have his portrayal of radical evil in the moral nihilism of Mephistopheles, who recognizes no degrees of worth:

Step down here! I could also say: Step up!
'Twere all the same (Part II, Act I, Scene v).

Within but also beyond the theological demand, insistent in religions of salvation, to reconcile the evils and the sinful corruption of creation with the infinite perfection of the Creator, philosophical thinkers have sought a basic evaluation of existence. The alternative appraisals, optimism and pessimism, have been entertained in their literal meaning, to signify views of the world as the best or the worst possible, but more generally they have expressed a fundamentally approving or a condemnatory evaluation. Philosophical reflection has rarely proceeded to unqualified eulogy or stark malediction, but the intensity of poetic speech has not stopped short of either extreme. Examples of both are not lacking; the following two may suffice. On the one hand, Pope's firm complacency:

All nature is but art unknown to thee;
All chance, direction which thou canst not see;
All discord, harmony not understood;
All partial evil, universal good;
And spite of pride, in erring reason's spite,
One truth is clear, Whatever is, is right.

On the other hand are black pages of utter despair, as by Giacomo Leopardi:

> Nought is worthy
> Thine agonies, earth merits not thy sighing.
> Mere bitterness and tedium
> Is life, nought else; the world is dust and ashes.
> . . . Scorn all, for all is infinitely vain.

The cloudless noon of philosophical optimism was the early eighteenth century. Its leaders were Leibniz and Shaftesbury; the latter comes close to unqualified laudation of all existence. In contrast to them was the darkening outlook on life which marked later eighteenth-century thought and the systematic pessimism of some nineteenth-century philosophers, Schopenhauer and Hartmann, and most desolate of all, Julius Bahnsen.

Shaftesbury's optimism led him from the particular apparent evils and woes of daily life to the universal system in which they are all transcended as elements in the cosmic perfection. Evils and woes are like the shadows that set off the light and beauty of the whole picture or like the discords which swell the fuller harmony of the composer's masterpiece.

Leibniz is less rhapsodic but no less assured in his philosophical theodicy, which he would justify on rational grounds. He distinguishes three principal kinds of evil: physical evil, or suffering; moral evil, sin; and what he calls metaphysical evil, that is, the imperfection which is inevitable in finite existence. He depreciates the gravity of bodily aches and woes as less common and severe than grumblers aver, as largely avoidable or due to intemperance or other vices, to moral evil. The problem of moral evil involves Leibniz' theodicy. He cannot regard moral evil as an imperfection staining the Creator's own activity, and he prefers to interpret it as due to metaphysical evil, the imperfection characteristic of all finite existence. Leibniz' appeal here is to his principle of the "compossibility" of God's attributes. God in His omniscience recognizes what we ourselves must understand, that any created world would have some imperfection. In His infinite goodness he has chosen the least imperfect world, and by his omnipotence he has created it, "the best of all possible worlds."

Leibniz' theodicy was judged as precarious in its theological implications. If our woes and sins are basically due to our essential imperfections as God's creatures, we cannot complain of the Creator; but can He then rightly condemn us for being such as He has created us? Leibniz' reduction of the moral antithesis, good-evil, to a metaphysical one, infinite-finite, has been criticized as compromising ethical judgment and all basic valuation, human or divine. And has Leibniz'

optimistic intention been realized? Voltaire's irony may be recalled here: "If this is the best of all possible worlds, what must the others be like?"

The outstanding systematic doctrine of pessimism in the nineteenth century was Schopenhauer's philosophy. In sharp opposition to all rationalism, Schopenhauer regarded nature as reasonless at the core, as a blind drive or urge or craving which he called the Will-to-live. It is manifested at every level of existence. In human life it is active as insatiate desire. All our experience is a form of craving concerned with attack or defence; our intelligence is a tool of the Will-to-live; it is analogous to the dog's keen scent or even to the snake's venom. In all his greeds and lusts man is ever wanting, insatiate and ungratified. The distress of unsatisfied desires may occasionally be allayed by the pleasure of some fulfilled want, but only to be rearoused by a new greed. Thus our life is a continual round of frustration: selfish, ruthless, wretched, and futile, a bankrupt enterprise.

Schopenhauer's pessimism is not absolute. He pointed out two ways of escape from the wretched tangle of will-driven existence. One of them is in the disinterested contemplation of aesthetic experience. In creating or in beholding art, intelligence regards or reveals things as they are and not as objects of our desires. This artistic emancipation from selfish craving, however, is transitory. A more radical denial of the Will-to-live is achieved in the morality of compassion. Evil conduct is most usually due to selfishness. Less common but more wicked is malice, which is not merely callous to the woes of others but actually gloats over them. Virtue and good conduct can only be in the curbing of these vices: in justice which is willingness to bear our own burdens, and in humane lovingkindness which moves us to relieve the woes of others. But in this benevolent sympathy the moral saint is led to recognize the fundamental evil in life, the will-driven craving itself. So he may proceed to ascetic negation of all desires and ambitions, to the selfless extinction of the Will-to-live, Nirvana.

This proposed aesthetic, moral, ascetic deliverance has been criticized as inconsistent with Schopenhauer's metaphysics. If the ultimate reality is the Will-to-live, how is the alleged desireless contemplation possible in art? If man is by nature a tissue of selfish and ruthless desires, how can he ever act with genuine compassion? How can the ultimate Will-to-live be denied, in ascetic saintliness? Schopenhauer's successors have had to grapple with the fundamental discrepancy of the two sides of his pessimism.

In the most distinguished revision of the philosophy of the Will-to-live, Eduard von Hartmann maintained that neither the irrationalism of Schopenhauer's metaphysics nor the rationalism of Hegel explain adequately the complexity of nature, which is unconscious urge with the capacity for conscious and intelligent manifestation. So in interpreting human nature we should recognize the tangle of will-driven greeds but also the positive values attainable by our intelligence: logical, aesthetic, moral, religious values, genuine and maturing in our development. Thus Hartmann described himself as an evolutionary optimist, but the dark pessimistic tone prevailed in his account of the human quest for happiness—a deluded and futile misdirection. He distinguished three stages of Man's Great Illusion. In classical antiquity men sought happiness in their own lives on earth. Disenchanted in this vain pursuit, men turned to the Christian gospel of immortality. The modern advance of knowledge disabused this baseless longing for personal happiness after death. Then men pinned their faith on a new ideal of social progress and well-being in the future. But the course of history is once more undeceiving men. We are bound to face the grim truth; while we may and should promote the values of civilization, riper intelligence should lead us to abandon the delusion of attainable happiness, to recognize the essentially tragic course of human existence. Hartmann even entertained the ideal—today we regard it as a constant menace—of man's eventual universal self-extinction.

Most dreary of all pessimists, Julius Bahnsen rejected all gospels of deliverance as weak palliatives. He would not yield to any optimistic concessions and held firmly to his desolate outlook: there is no way out. Our life, and nature altogether, are hopeless tangles of self-rending activities, ruling out any rational direction or organization. For Bahnsen, Macbeth's dismal soliloquy closed the entire argument:

> Life's but a walking shadow . . .
> . . . it is a tale
> Told by an idiot, full of sound and fury,
> Signifying nothing (Act V, Scene 5).

As has been noted in our brief survey of the thought of classical antiquity, the basic ideas of good and evil have been expressed in various theories of ethics. Ethical reflection has tended to concentrate on the problems of the moral standard and the Highest Good, and any review of the principal alternative theories would take us to other articles. But one doctrine of widespread modern development that should be noted has given a seemingly plain account of good and evil: a critical revision of the old Epicurean hedonism. Reaffirming the reduction of good and evil to pleasure or happiness and pain or displeasure, modern utilitarianism answered the old question, whose pleasure?, by an altruistic answer: the greatest happiness of the greatest number. There was disagreement regarding the other disturbing question, what kind of pleasure or pain? Jeremy Bentham was concerned with quantitative valuation and proposed a hedonistic calculus of pleasures and pains as a guide in moral deliberation and choice. But John Stuart Mill emphasized the importance of distinguishing the quality of pleasures and pains in evaluating the good and evil in various proposed actions or experiences: "Better to be a Socrates dissatisfied than a fool satisfied." This radical revision affected the entire basis of strictly hedonistic valuation, for as Mill recognized, the qualitative appraisal depended on intelligent judgment.

The issue between optimism and pessimism which signalizes the fateful importance of the right choice of values, and thus of the basic role of intelligence in valuation, leads us to recognize a related and more general issue which has affected our basic ideas of good and evil. The history of thought manifests repeatedly a correlation of optimism with rationalism, and of pessimism with irrationalism and skepticism. This correlation is not hard to explain. One side of the argument is expressed in Hegel's magisterial pronouncement, "The Real is the Rational, and the Rational is the Real." But doubting Thomases may still press the decisive question, whether our intelligence does have this alleged rational capacity to comprehend Reality. If we recall the first sentence in Aristotle's *Metaphysics*, "All men by nature desire to know," and if we recognize the urge for understanding as man's distinctive characteristic, then any denial or doubt regarding the attainability of this fundamental value would signalize human life as a losing venture. Skepticism exposes the radical evil of irrational and meaningless existence, especially when it results in the annihilation of values. More dismally than any philosophical formulation, poetic outburst has expressed this "sense more tragic than defeat and blight," as in James Thomson's *City of Dreadful Night*:

> The sense that every struggle brings defeat
> Because Fate holds no prize to crown success;
> That all the oracles are dumb or cheat
> Because they have no secret to express;
> That none can pierce the vast black veil uncertain
> Because there is no light behind the curtain;
> That all is vanity and nothingness.

Men's reactions towards this skeptical outlook have varied. Some minds have recognized our inconclusive and downright incompetent thinking but have refused to be tragic about it. Montaigne was explicit but also genial about his motto, *Que sçais-je?* ("What do I know?"). Disavowing any claims to real understanding, he was content to tread the twilit alleys of human experience, an aimless pilgrimage but most interesting withal. Life and the world offer us no ground of reliance, but no reason for fear or complaint either. We take things as they come, serene in fortuitousness.

Genial skepticism was intolerable to minds committed to the demand for understanding. So Pascal, while assured about the valid theorems of the geometric method, recognized the incapacity of reason to answer reliably the ultimate questions which most concern us: about the existence of God, about man's moral career and final destiny. "When I consider the short span of my life, . . . I am dismayed to find myself here rather than there; . . . Who has put me here? By whose order and direction has this place and time been allotted to me?" (*Pensées*, No. 205). Pascal admitted this, his basic incertitude, but he refused to accept it. His attitude towards his tragic skepticism varied. He sought deliverance from the doubts of the intellect in the insistent demands of the heart. "The heart has its reasons which reason does not know at all." In his tragic perplexity, confronted with the dual hazards of belief and unbelief, his will inclined him to wager on the problematical but infinitely momentous alternatives of faith. But again, his searching reason would refuse to surrender its quest: "All our dignity . . . lies in our thought. . . . Let us therefore strive to think well: such is the foundation of moral life."

In our day existentialism has reaffirmed the quandaries of rational intelligence, but in its search for alternatives to it has followed different paths. Against all rationalistic reliance on theology, dogmatic or philosophical, Kierkegaard had emphasized an existential dialectic, a living truth expressed in the unique reality of his own spiritual crisis, which he did not merely know, which possessed him in consecration, in life and death. He would thus face God in self-penetrating encounter, and would not merely be doctrinally conversant about God.

This surrender of rational proof to the demands of living conviction has been reaffirmed as repossession of orthodox verities by the pious fiat of unquestioning devotion, itself due not to any wisdom or merit of ours but to the working of God's grace in us. Thus, according to Karl Barth, we are raised from the evil vanity of rational self-reliance to the godly refuge of faith and consecration.

But the existential dialectic may proceed in an opposite direction. Disavowing all faith in God or in any supreme values as unwarranted, Sartre, starting with explicit atheism, begins with the primal existential reality, oneself. I am myself, I am what I choose and become. That is my freedom and my engagement in this world of reasonless and unprincipled process. It is a nauseating bewilderment, but it is also a respon-

sibility without contrition. If I am judged, it is by a court of my own self, of my own continually self-propelled career. Without any moral *corpus juris* of genuinely positive and negative values, good or evil, we have here only one's own continual self-assertion and self-attestation, the freedom to which one is always condemning and entrusting oneself.

The idea of evil has been expressed forcibly in the counter-appraisals of the historical process: the affirmation or the denial of social progress. The cult of progress has been called the modern man's religion, or the new superstition. The citing of evidence on the opposite sides of the controversy has been an assessment of modern ideas of the positive and negative values of life, good and evil in social perspectives.

The optimist's inventory emphasizes modern technological improvements in every field of the social economy. We hear, as it were, modern versions of the great soliloquy of Prometheus. Past ages were cramped and crude in their isolation and short-fingered indigence. But modern knowledge, expanded research, and perfected technical mastery have unlocked boundless resources in nature for our advantage and well-being. We have shrunk the barriers of space and time and achieved instant communication on earth and beyond earth. The advance in curative and preventive medicine has eliminated one burden after another and has lengthened man's life span. Our public education, already universal in the West, is radiating its enlightenment and bringing the gifts of trained intelligence to vast areas of formerly dark ignorance.

Against this technological eulogy of the modern age, social-historical pessimists have cited our glaring spiritual barrenness, the vulgarity and corruption, the inequity and violence of modern life, the disastrous turns in our contemporary crisis which threaten not only the well-being but the very existence of humanity.

The disdain and despair of civilization as a corrupting process were expressed with romantic fervor two centuries ago by Jean Jacques Rousseau. He flouted the cultivation of the arts and sciences as pandering to the luxury and idle curiosity of the rich, who thrive on the miserable toil of the masses. The entire social system, with its governments that sustain exploitation and oppression, was denounced by Rousseau as a wicked fraud.

Of more recent memory is Tolstoy's condemnation of our social system as un-Christian and wicked. Our civilization does not unite men in true Christian brotherhood. We exalt self-gratification and self-aggrandizement. We not only condone sensuality but pander to it in our art and literature. We profess a concern for peace but gird ourselves for war and tax ourselves to build the most destructive armaments. We not only accept but also support and promote an economic system which exploits the masses for the enrichment of the few. This unjust system has entangled us all, so that even the few of us who aspire to a better way of life are made willy-nilly participants in manifold social evils. In all this advocacy of a radical social reform and reconstruction, Tolstoy was appealing to the teachings in the Sermon on the Mount. In his stern verdict on our civilization he was also criticizing himself. His refusal to participate in the evils of our social system marked the thoroughgoing change in his own later course of life.

The world crisis in our time has aggravated the confusion in our social outlook. On all sides we hear the warnings and the ominous blasts of the prophets of doom. Two disastrous wars and the postwar piling up of defensive and offensive armament have poured out our treasure that, rightly spent, might already have served to wipe out poverty and revitalize and raise culture throughout the world. As it is, aggressive nationalism and racial or religious hostility are violently ranging nations and social classes against each other. Ironically, the very advances of knowledge and technology are aggravating some of our social problems. The population explosion which menaces us with global starvation is partly due to the reduction of infant mortality and the improvement in sanitation achieved by modern medical science.

Between placid optimism and the pessimistic doom, the ongoing historical course, from primitive and barbaric stages to the widening scope of civilization, has been recognized as an expanding range of the fields in which human values may be pursued and realized, or frustrated. Spreading civilization shows how much higher and higher men can rise, or how much lower and lower they might sink, each depending on the wise or misdirected choice of values. Our present nuclear age sets out these alternatives of good and evil with crucial momentous clarity. We have split the atom, but we have not united men in a humane social order. Our present atomic technology can enable us to achieve a civilization of unimagined progress, but we might also blow ourselves to ashes.

The evaluation of the principal versions of the idea of evil inclines us to a gradational view. Value judgments are seen as forming a hierarchy which consists of choices which are not on a par but are lower or higher. In its choice between them, good and evil are rightly conceived as directional, and at every level of experience men may contemplate the prospect of a higher attainment, but also face the hazard of degradation. In philosophy and literature this idea of the issue between good and evil has found reasoned or imaginative utterance. Religious meditation has no better expression of this conviction than the passage from Saint Augustine's *City of God* cited above, which may well be recalled here: "When the will abandons the higher, and turns to what is lower, it becomes evil—not because that is evil to which it turns, but because the turning itself is perverse."

BIBLIOGRAPHY

E. M. Caro, *Le pessimisme au XIXe siècle* (Paris, 1876). Paul Claudel, et al., *Le mal est parmi nous* (Paris, 1948). Paul Haberlin, *Das Böse* (Bern, 1960). Eduard von Hartmann, *The Philosophy of the Unconscious*, trans. E. C. Coupland, new ed. (London, 1931); idem, *Zur Geschichte und Begründung des Pessimismus* (Leipzig, 1891). William King, *An Essay on the Origin of Evil* (Cambridge, 1739). Émile Lasbax, *Le problème du mal* (Paris, 1919). G. W. Leibniz, *La théodicée* (1710), in *Leibnitii Opera*, ed. J. E. Erdmann (Berlin, 1840). Ernest Naville, *Le problème du mal* (Geneva, 1868). Plato, *Dialogues of Plato*, trans. Benjamin Jowett, 3rd ed. (Oxford, 1892). Josiah Royce, *Studies in Good and Evil* (New York, 1898). Arthur Schopenhauer, *The World as Will and Idea*, trans. R. B. Haldane and J. Kemp, 6th ed., 3 vols. (London, 1907); idem, *The Basis of Morality*, trans. A. B. Bullock (London, 1903); idem, *Studies in Pessimism*, trans. T. B. Saunders, 4th ed. (London, 1893). A. G. Sertillanges, *Le problème du mal*, 2 vols. (Paris, 1948–51). Paul Siwek, *The Philosophy of Evil* (New York, 1951). James Sully, *Pessimism* (London, 1871). Radoslav A. Tsanoff, *The Nature of Evil* (New York, 1931; 1971). R. M. Wenley, *Aspects of Pessimism* (Edinburgh and London, 1894). Charles Werner, *Le problème du mal dans la pensée humaine* (Lausanne, 1946).

RADOSLAV A. TSANOFF

[See also Buddhism; Demonology; **Dualism; Existentialism;** God; Happiness and Pleasure; Hierarchy; Neo-Platonism; **Right and Good; Sin and Salvation; Theodicy;** Utilitarianism.]

EVOLUTION OF LITERATURE

THE IDEA OF an evolution of literature dates back at least as far as Aristotle's *Poetics* (Chapter IV). There we are told that the origin of tragedy is in the dithyramb, and of comedy in phallic songs, and then Aristotle continues: "From its early form tragedy was developed little by little as the authors added what presented itself to them. After going through many alterations, tragedy ceased to change, having come to its full natural stature" (trans. Allan Gilbert, quoted from *Literary Criticism: Plato to Dryden*, New York [1940], p. 74). The analogy between the history of tragedy and the life-cycle of a living organism is here asserted for the first time.

Tragedy reached maturity, "natural stature," beyond which it could not grow, as man cannot grow after he has reached the age of twenty-one. Evolution is conceived (as everywhere in Aristotle) as a teleological process in time directed toward one and only one absolutely predetermined goal.

Antiquity applied Aristotle's insight extensively: thus Dionysius of Halicarnassus traced the evolution of Greek oratory towards the supreme model of Demosthenes, and Quintilian did the same for Roman eloquence culminating in Cicero. (See J. W. H. Atkins, *Literary Criticism in Antiquity,* Cambridge [1934], II, 123, 281.) Velleius Paterculus, in a passage quoted throughout the history of criticism, even as late as by Sainte-Beuve, asserted the alternation of periods of flowering and exhaustion, the impossibility of lasting perfection, the fatal necessity of decay. (See J. Kamerbeek Jr.,"Legatum Velleianum," in *Levenden Tale,* No. 177 [December, 1954], pp. 476–90; reprinted in *Creative Wedijver,* Amsterdam [1962]. Sainte-Beuve quotes the passage in *Nouveaux Lundis,* 9 [January, 1865], 290.)

These ancient ideas were taken up by Renaissance and neo-classical criticism: echoes can be found everywhere, but no systematic application to the history of literature was made before the middle of the eighteenth century, when the growth of biological and sociological speculation (in Vico, Buffon, and Rousseau) stimulated analogous thinking about literature. John Brown (1715–66) wrote a general history of poetry, *A Dissertation on the Rise, Union, and Power, the Progressions, Separations, and Corruptions of Poetry and Music* (London, 1763), which expounds an elaborate evolutionary scheme: a union of song, dance, and poetry is assumed among primitive nations, and all subsequent history is described as a separation of the arts, a dissolution of each art into genres, a process of fission and specialization, of degeneration linked to a general corruption of pristine manners. Brown's scheme, marred as it is by his illogical recommendation of a return to the original union of the arts, still foreshadows the later concept of an internal development of poetry. Brown writes a "history without names," in blocks and masses, seen in a perspective which embraces the oral poetry of all known nations.

Brown's sketch was published the year before J. J. Winckelmann's *Geschichte der Kunst des Alterthums* (1764), the first history of an art which traced an evolutionary scheme with a wealth of concrete knowledge. Within an overall analogy of growth and decline, Winckelmann describes four stages of Greek sculpture: the grand youthful style of the earliest time, the mature perfection of the Periclean climax, the decline with its imitators, the sad end with late Hellenistic manner-

ism. Both Herder and Friedrich Schlegel proclaimed an ambition to become the Winckelmann of literature. In Herder's many sketches of literary history and in Friedrich Schlegel's fragmentary histories of Greek poetry (in *Griechen and Römer* [1797], which contains a long paper, "Über das Studium der griechischen Poesie," written in 1794–95, and in *Geschichte der Poesie der Griechen und Römer* [1798]), the "organological" concept of evolution is employed with skill and consistency. Both Herder and Schlegel assume throughout a principle of continuity, the adage *natura non facit saltum* ("nature makes no leap"), which in Germany had been immeasurably strengthened by the philosophy of Leibniz. But in detail, Herder, Schlegel, and their many followers vary in their attitudes toward the future and the implicit consequences of the determinism implied in their scheme. Thus Herder teaches that poetry must decline from the glories of primitive song, but at the time he believes that poetry, at least in Germany, can be saved from the blight of classical civilization and be returned to the racial wellspring of its power. Friedrich Schlegel conceives of Greek poetry as a complete array of all the different genres in a natural order of evolution. The evolution is described in terms of growth, proliferation, blossoming, maturing, hardening, and final dissolution, and it is thought of as necessary and fated. But this closed cycle is completed only in Greece—modern poetry is rather "universal progressive poetry," an open system, perfectible almost limitlessly. In the Grimms, the process is one of irreversible decay: there has been in the dim past the glory of natural poetry, and modern poetry is but its sorry detritus. What is common to all of these conceptions is the assumption of slow, steady change on the analogy of animal growth, of an evolutionary substratum in the main types of literature, of a determinism which minimizes the role of the individual, and of purely literary evolution in the general process of history.

Hegel introduced a strikingly different concept of evolution. Dialectics replaces the principle of continuity. Sudden revolutionary changes, reversals into opposites, annulments, and, simultaneously, preservations constitute the dynamics of history. The "objective spirit" (of which poetry is only a phase) differs profoundly from nature. The biological analogy is dropped. Poetry is conceived as self-developing, in constant give-and-take with society and history, but distinct and even profoundly different, as a product of the spirit must be, from the processes of nature. But in his *Vorlesungen über Aesthetik* (pub. 1835; lectures given in the preceding decade) Hegel does not apply his method consistently: he makes many concessions to the older, "organological" point of view which he has met in the Schlegels. Though he traces an involved scheme of triads, from epic through lyric to a synthesis in tragedy, and from symbolic through classical to romantic art, the *Lectures* remain largely a poetics and aesthetics and do not incorporate history successfully, as they should according to his theory. Hegel's followers tried to apply his scheme to literary history, but most of them succeeded only in discrediting his method by forcing the complexities of reality into Hegelian formulas. (Cf., e.g., Karl Rosenkranz, *Handbuch einer allgemeinen Geschichte der Poesie*, 3 vols., Halle [1832], and the much later writings of the St. Louis Hegelians, Denton Snider, W. T. Harris on Dante, Shakespeare, and Goethe.)

With the advent of Darwin and Spencer evolutionism revived. Spencer himself suggested how the development of literature could be conceived in terms of a law of progression from the simple to the complex. (See "Progress: its Law and Cause" [1857], in *Illustrations of Universal Progress*, New York [1880], pp. 24–30, and *First Principles* [1862; New York, 1891], pp. 354–58.) In many countries the ideas of the new evolutionism were eagerly applied to literary history. But it seems difficult to decide exact priorities and to distinguish the new, Darwinian and Spencerian, *motifs* from returns to ideas of "organological" or of Hegelian evolution. The exact share of these three conceptions needs detailed investigation in the case of each writer on the subject. In Germany, for instance, where the romantic tradition was very strong, it would be almost impossible to disentangle the different strands in the writings on *Völkerpsychologie* of H. Steinthal and M. Lazarus, or in those on the history of German literature and on poetics of Wilhelm Dilthey and Wilhelm Scherer. (See Erich Rothacker, *Einleitung in die Geisteswissenschaften*, 2nd ed., Tübingen [1930], pp. 80n. and 215, for good comments on Steinthal, Lazarus, Wilhelm Scherer, and Dilthey.) Evolutionism is Darwinian only when it implies the mechanistic explanation of the process (which was Darwin's special contribution) and when it uses such ideas as "survival of the fittest," "natural selection," "transformation of species."

In England, John Addington Symonds applied the biological analogy to the history of Elizabethan drama (1884) with ruthless consistency. He argues that Elizabethan drama runs a well-defined course of germination, expansion, efflorescence, and decay. This development is described as "e-volution," as an unfolding of embryonic elements to which nothing can be added and which run their course with iron necessity to their predestined exhaustion. The initiative of the individual is completely denied. Genius is incapable of altering the sequence of the stages. Even the individuality of

different cycles of evolution disappears: Italian painting passes through exactly the same stages as Elizabethan drama. Literary history becomes a collection of cases which serve as documents to illustrate a general scientific law. In practice, Symonds escaped some of the rigidities of his scheme by his aesthetic sense and by such a device as the concept of the "hybrid," which allows for the blurring of types which would otherwise be made to appear too sharply distinct. In the preface to *Shakspere's Predecessors in the English Drama* (London, 1884) Symonds says, that he wrote the book substantially in 1862–65. "On the Application of Evolutionary Principles to Art and Literature," in *Essays Speculative and Suggestive* (London, 1890), I, 42–83, contains a theoretical defense of his method.

After Symonds, Richard Green Moulton applied evolutionism to *Shakespeare as a Dramatic Artist* (1885) and reiterated his faith in the principle as late as 1915, in *The Modern Study of Literature*. There is hardly any English or American book in these decades which deals with oral literature and is not based on Darwinian conceptions. H. M. Posnett treated *Comparative Literature* (1886) as a Spencerian progress from communal to individual life. F. Gummere's *Beginnings of Poetry* (1901) and A. S. Mackenzie's *The Evolution of Literature* (1911) may serve as later examples by American authors.

In France the two leading critics of the period, Hippolyte Taine and Ferdinand Brunetière, were preoccupied with the problem of evolution. Taine, however, is not a naturalistic positivist: in spite of many terminological borrowings from physiology and biology, his concept of evolution remained purely Hegelian. He definitely disapproved of Comte and Spencer. Hegel, whom he read as a student, "taught him to conceive of historical periods as moments, to look for internal causes, spontaneous development, the incessant becoming of things." (On Taine and Comte, see besides his article in *Journal des Débats* [July 6, 1864] reproduced in V. Giraud, *Essai sur Taine*, 6th ed., Paris [1912], p. 232, D. D. Rosca, *L'Influence de Hegel sur Taine*, Paris [1928], p. 262n. On Spencer and Hegel, see *Derniers Essais de critique et de l'histoire*, 3rd ed. [1903], pp. 198–202.) But Taine never thinks of evolution as a separate literary evolution. Literature is part of the general historical process conceived as an organized unity. Literature is dependent on society, represents society. It is also dependent on the *moment*, but *moment* for Taine usually means the "spirit of the age." Only once in all his writings does Taine think of *moment* as the position of a writer in a merely literary evolution. He contrasts French tragedy under Corneille and under Voltaire, the Greek theater under Aeschylus and under Euripides, and Latin poetry under Lucretius

171

and under Claudian, in order to illustrate the difference between precursors and successors (Introduction to *Histoire de la littérature anglaise*, 2nd ed. [1866], I, xxx).

Ferdinand Brunetière (1849–1906) finds his starting point in this very passage. *Moment* with him takes precedence over *milieu* and *race*. He resolutely envisages the ideal of an internal history of literature which "has in itself the sufficient principle of development" (*Études critiques sur l'histoire de la littérature française*, Paris [1890], III, 4). What is to be established is the inner causality. "In considering all the influences which operate in the history of literature, the influence of works on works is the main one" (Preface to *Manuel de l'histoire de la littérature française*, Paris [1898], p. iii). It is a double influence, positive and negative: we imitate or reject. Literature moves by action and reaction, convention and revolt. Novelty or originality, is the criterion which changes the direction of development. Literary history is the method which defines the points of change. So far Brunetière could be a Tainian or even an Hegelian. But he has also tried to transfer specifically biological concepts from Darwinism. He believes in the reality of genres as if they were biological species. He constantly parallels the history of genres with the history of human beings. French tragedy was born with Jodelle, matured with Corneille, aged with Voltaire, and died before Hugo. He cannot see that the analogy breaks down on every point; that French tragedies were not born with Jodelle but just were not written before him, and that they died only in the sense that *important* tragedies, according to Brunetière's definition, were not written after Lemercier. Racine's *Phèdre*, in Brunetière's scheme, stands at the beginning of the decline of tragedy, but it will strike us as young and fresh compared to the frigid Renaissance tragedies which, according to the scheme, represent the "youth" of French tragedy. Brunetière in his genre histories even uses the analogy of the struggle for existence to describe the rivalry of genres and argues that some genres are transmuted into other genres. French pulpit oratory of the seventeenth and eighteenth centuries was thus changed into the lyrical poetry of the romantic movement. But the analogy will not withstand close inspection: at most, one could say that pulpit oratory expresses similar feelings (e.g., about the transience of things human) or fulfills similar social functions (the articulation of the mystery behind our lives). But surely no genre has literally changed into another. Nor can one be satisfied with Brunetière's attempt to compare the role of genius in literature, its innovative effect, to that of the Darwinian "sport," the mechanistic variation of character traits. (See E. R. Curtius, *Ferdinand Brunetière*, Strassburg, 1914.)

Brunetière's followers pushed his schematism often to absurd extremes: thus Louis Maigron, in his *Le Roman historique* (1898), simply declares one book, Mérimée's *Chronique de Charles IX* (1829), to be the culmination point of the French historical novel, to which those preceding it (such as Vigny's *Cinq-mars*, 1826) provide the stepping-stones, while all those which follow (such as Hugo's *Notre Dame de Paris*, 1831) demonstrate only slow decadence. Chronology is king: a neat gradation and recession must be construed at any price.

Later attempts to modernize and modify the concept of literary evolution failed. Thus John Matthews Manly was deeply impressed by the mutation theory of De Vries and proposed its application to literary history and especially to the history of medieval drama ("Literary Forms and the New Theory of the Origin of Species," in *Modern Philology*, 4 [1907], 577–95). But "mutation" turns out to be simply the introduction of new principles which suddenly crystallize new types. Evolution, in the sense of slow continuous development, is given up in favor of an anomalous principle of special creation.

Evolutionism, especially in the form in which it was formulated by Brunetière, was widely criticized and rejected, in part, of course, simply in the name of genius and impressionistic appreciation. But the reaction in the early twentieth century has deeper roots and raises new issues. It was powerfully supported by the new philosophies of Bergson and Croce. Bergson's concept of creative evolution, its intuitive act of true duration, rejected the whole idea of a chronological order. It is no accident that his central book, *Evolution créatrice* (1907), ends with an attack on Spencer. Also Croce's onslaught on the very concept of genre was almost universally convincing. His arguments for the uniqueness of every work of art and his rejection of artistic devices, procedures, and styles (even as topics of history) destroyed, in the eyes of many, the very basis of all evolutionism. Croce's prediction and hope that literary history would come to consist entirely of essays and monographs (or handbooks and compendia of information) is being fulfilled ("La Riforma della storia artistica e letteraria," in *Nuovi saggi di estetica*, 2nd ed., Bari [1927], pp. 157–80; and "Categorismo e psicologismo nella storia della poesia," in *Ultimi Saggi*, Bari [1935], pp. 373–79).

All over the West, the anti-historical point of view in criticism reasserted itself at about the same time. It was in part a reaction against critical relativism, against the whole anarchy of values to which nineteenth-century historicism had led, and in part a new belief in a hierarchy of absolute values, a revival of classicism. T. S. Eliot has most memorably formulated his sense of the simultaneity of all literature, the feeling of a poet "that the whole of the literature of Europe from Homer and within it the whole of the literature of his own country has a simultaneous existence and composes a simultaneous order" ("Tradition and the Individual Talent" [1917] in *Selected Essays*, London [1932], p. 14). This sense of the timelessness of literature (which Eliot oddly calls the "historical sense") is only another name for classicism and tradition.

Eliot's view has been followed by almost all recent English and American critics. On occasion they may recognize the illumination which criticism derives from literary history and history in general. (See William K. Wimsatt, Jr., "History and Criticism: A Problematic Relationship," in *The Verbal Icon*, Louisville, Ky. [1954], pp. 253–66.) But they have on the whole ignored the problem of an internal literary historiography and evolution. Histories of literature and of literary genres are being written without any allusion to the concept and apparently with no awareness of it. F. W. Bateson's *English Poetry and the English Language* (Oxford, 1934) and *English Poetry: A Critical Introduction* (London, 1950) are attempts to trace the history of English poetry as a mirror of either linguistic or of social evolution. The statistical investigations of Josephine Miles (*The Vocabulary of Poetry*, Berkeley, 1946; *The Continuity of Poetic Language*, Berkeley, 1951; *Eras and Modes in English Poetry*, Berkeley, 1956, new ed. 1963) which trace the changes in key words and sentence patterns aim finally at an evolutionary scheme. But these are isolated instances.

The story has been very different in Russia. There Spencerian evolutionism was stated most impressively in the grandiose attempts of Aleksandr Veselovsky (1838–1906) to write a historical poetics on a worldwide scale. Veselovsky had been a pupil of Steinthal in 1862 in Berlin; he drew evolutionism also from many other sources, including the English ethnographers. More concretely, and with a much wider command of literatures and languages than anybody in the West, he traces the history of poetic devices, themes, and genres throughout oral and medieval literature. Yet Veselovsky's theoretical assumptions are extremely rigid. Content and form are sharply divorced. Poetic language is assumed as something given since immemorial times: it changes only under the impact of social and ideological changes. Veselovsky traces the breakup of the syncretism of original oral poetry and always looks for survivals of animism, myth, ritual, or customs in conventional poetic language. All poetic creativity is viewed as occurring in prehistoric times when man created language. Since then the role of the individual has been limited to modifying the inherited poetic language in order to give expression to the changed content of his own time. On the one hand Veselovsky conducts a genetic inquiry into the dim origins of poetry, on the other he studies "comparative literature," migrations and radiations of devices and *motifs*.

His shortcomings are those of his period: he worships fact and science so excessively that he has no use for aesthetic value; he views the work of art far too atomistically, dividing it into form and content, *motifs* and plots, metaphors and meters. (On Veselovsky see Victor Erlich, *Russian Formalism: History—Doctrine*, The Hague, 1955; in Russian see B. M. Engel'gardt, *A. N. Veselovskij*, Petrograd, 1924; and V. Žirmunskij's long introduction to Veselovskij, *Istoričeskaja Poètika*, Leningrad, 1940.)

Deservedly Veselovsky enjoyed enormous academic prestige and thus imposed the problem of literary evolution on the Russian Formalists. They shared his emphasis on the work of literature, his preoccupation with formal devices, his interest in the "morphology" of literary types. But his view of evolution was unacceptable. They had grown up in a revolutionary atmosphere which radically rejected the past, even in the arts. Their allies were the Futurist poets. In contemporary Marxist criticism art had lost all autonomy and was reduced to a passive reflection of social and economic change. The Formalists rejected this reduction of literature. But they could accept the Hegelian view of evolution: its basic principle of an immanent, dialectical alteration of old into new and back again. They interpreted this for literature largely as a wearing out or "automatization" of poetic conventions and then the "actualization" of such conventions by a new school using radically new and opposite procedures. Novelty became the only criterion of value. (On the Russian Formalists Erlich's book is the most informative, not only in English.)

Jan Mukařovský (born in 1891), a follower of the Russian Formalists in Czechoslovakia who developed their theories more coherently, with a great awareness of philosophical issues, formulated the theory very clearly: "A work of art will appear as positive value when it regroups the structure of the preceding period, it will appear as a negative value if it takes over the structure without changing it" (*Kapitoly z české poetiky, Chapters from Czech Poetics*, Prague [1948], II, 100–01). A divorce between literary history and criticism is advocated. Purely aesthetic evaluation is the business of criticism. In literary history there is only one criterion of interest: the degree of novelty.

On many occasions René Wellek, who was a member of the Prague Linguistic Circle in the thirties, argued (e.g., in "The Theory of Literary History," in *Travaux du Cercle Linguistique de Prague*, Vol. V [1936]) against this divorce between criticism and history pointing out that works of art are assemblings of values which constitute their very nature, and are not merely structures analyzable descriptively. In his view works of art are not simple members of a series, links in a chain. Still, he wanted to salvage the concept of literary evolution, the whole problem of an internal history of literature by pointing to a modern concept of time. Man is not merely in the present reacting against the immediate past (as the evolutionists assume) but lives simultaneously in three times: in the past through memory, in the present, and, through anticipations, plans, and hopes, in the future. He may reach, at any moment, into his own remote past or into the remotest past of humanity. An artist does not necessarily develop toward a single future goal: he can reach back to something he may have conceived twenty, thirty, or forty years ago. He can start on a completely different track. His reaching out into the past for models or stimuli, abroad or at home, in art or in life, in another art or in thought, is a free decision, a choice of values which constitutes his own personal hierarchy of values, and will be thus reflected in the hierarchy of values implied in his works of art. This multiple relationship to past and present can be paralleled in larger groupings of works of art, in a period and hence in the whole evolution of art and literature. The interpenetration of the causal order in experience and memory refutes the simplicist schemes of evolution but does not dispose of the complex problem of the evolution of art and literature. It is still unsolved, if not in theory, then certainly in the practice of literary historians.

BIBLIOGRAPHY

No history of evolutionism in literature is known to exist. For earlier treatments of this theme see René Wellek, "The Theory of Literary History," in *Travaux du Cercle Linguistique de Prague*, **6** (1936), 173-91; idem, *Theory of Literature*, with Austin Warren (New York, 1949); and idem, "The Concept of Evolution in Literary History," in *For Roman Jakobson* (The Hague, 1956), pp. 653-61, reprinted in *Concepts of Criticism* (New Haven, 1963), pp. 37–53. For evolutionary concepts in historiography and philosophy see Ernst Troeltsch, *Der Historismus und seine Probleme* (Tübingen, 1922); F. S. C. Northrop, "Evolution in its Relation to the Philosophy of Nature and the Philosophy of Culture," in *Evolutionary Thought in America*, ed. Stow Persons (New Haven, 1950), pp. 44–84; and Hans Meyerhoff, *Time in Literature* (Berkeley, 1955).

RENÉ WELLEK

[See also Continuity; **Evolutionism;** Historicism; **Literature; Periodization in Literature.**]

EVOLUTIONISM

EVOLUTIONISM IS a family of ideas which affirm that the universe and some or all of its parts have undergone irreversible, cumulative changes such that the number, variety, and complexity of the parts have increased. Evolutionism is thus opposed to the belief that the universe and its parts are eternally the same; or that they have been the same since they were created; or that they are now the same as they have been periodically in the past; or that they are emanations from a higher and perfect source. If only living things are included, theories of organic evolution result. These theories may embrace accounts of human, mental, moral, and cultural evolution. If nonliving things are included, there result theories of physical evolution which may embrace the earth, the solar system, and the spatiotemporal cosmos. If what is included is the universe as a whole, or everything that is held to be real, metaphysical theories of evolution result. Hence many differences occur within the one family of ideas. Early theories tend to be simple, vague, and speculative. Later theories, particularly when given a scientific formulation, are more intricate, exact, and verifiable. There are many disagreements, however, about such issues as the origin, character, and causes of evolutionary processes. In the present article some of the main stages in the history of this family of ideas will be discussed.

I. PROTO-EVOLUTIONISM

Proto-evolutionary ideas occur very early in man's thinking about the world. They were perhaps suggested to him by the observation of processes of growth in plants and animals. Such phenomena seem to have served as a model for speculations about how the world began and how it acquired the features it has. Evolutionary cosmogonies, largely mythical in content, appear in ancient Chinese and Indian cultures. Confucius, for example, is said to have held the view that "things were originated from a single, simple source through gradual unfolding and branching" (Chen, 1929). By others it was believed that the primary elements of the universe—water, fire, wood, metal, earth—had come into being in an evolutionary order under the influence of natural forces. Furthermore, "the Taoists elaborated what comes very near to a statement of a theory of evolution. At least they firmly denied the fixity of biological species" (Needham, 1956). In early Indian thought, one of the Buddhist groups affirmed "that nature . . . is a unitary entity which evolves into varying forms, including minds (here regarded as distinct from underlying souls)" (Smart, 1964). The term "evolution" (*parināma*) in this context is said to imply that nature successively manifests new properties as a result of a process which began when an initial state of equilibrium was disturbed. Yet the novelty involved at each stage is only apparent, for whatever manifests itself must have been implicit in unitary nature from the start.

Ideas similar to these were advanced by early Greek thinkers. Among the pre-Socratic philosophers, evolutionary doctrines predominated and were largely detached from mythical elements. The world-order was represented as having come into existence by virtue of the generative power of nature (*physis*). What took place was without design (*technē*), and exemplified the presence either of chance or of blind, irrational necessity. Nature was assumed by some to be literally alive. Like an organism it can initiate changes to which it is itself subject. From this assumption it was only a short step to an evolutionary conception of plants and animals.

Both Anaximander and Anaximenes put forward the view that living things were generated spontaneously by the action of the sun's warmth on a primordial moist element. Empedocles and Democritus regarded the element as moist earth or slime. Such views were undoubtedly influenced by the observation of flies, maggots, and worms appearing on decomposed organic matter (e.g., meat), and by the mistaken idea that this phenomenon was a spontaneous generation of life. The pre-Socratics did not limit the application of this idea to simple organisms, but applied it speculatively in such a way as to allow fanciful and fantastic discontinuities in the history of living things. Thus Anaximenes believed that plants, animals, and men appeared on the earth in that order. But each was generated directly from the primordial element. Democritus likewise seems to have countenanced the ancient idea that men originated from the earth. Empedocles proposed that men had been formed by the random coming together of separate limbs and organs which had been produced spontaneously. Some of the combinations proved to be viable and others perished. Anaximander thought that men first developed inside a fish-like creature, from which they emerged to live on dry land. These and other ideas were mere hints of a theory of evolution as it was later to be understood.

In Democritus there occur the rudiments of a doctrine of social and cultural evolution. The ideas involved were, however, not original with him, for they were widely current in the fifth century and had largely replaced earlier poetic and religious ideas of a "golden age" in the past (Guthrie, 1962). According to the evolutionary view, the first men lived like solitary animals, without technical skills or social organization. Their manner of life was highly precarious, and so the need to survive forced them to band together into societies. Here they developed the practical, and eventually the fine arts, and achieved a measure of civilization. Human culture was thus the daughter of necessity. Democritus called attention to the importance of the evolution of language in this process. He was among the earliest proponents of the view that words have a conventional origin. They began as sounds related quite arbitrarily to things or notions by men who felt the need for a means of communication more comprehensive and subtle than grunts or animal cries. The growth of language in turn accelerated the evolution of culture.

II. ANTI-EVOLUTIONISM

The impetus of evolutionary thinking among the Greeks was brought to an abrupt halt by the work of Plato and Aristotle. Both of these influential thinkers held views that were incompatible with any conception of irreversible, cumulative changes taking place in the real world. Plato maintained that the real world is a realm of unchanging forms or archetypes apprehended solely by thought. Things perceived by the senses are imperfect copies of forms and are less than fully real. When applied to living organisms this conception had anti-evolutionary consequences. It implied that the characteristics of organisms are to be explained by resemblance to ideal archetypes, not by descent from ancestors who had undergone changes of form and function over long periods of time. Furthermore, this Platonistic conception became a basis for classical taxonomy in which plants and animals were classified into kinds that are sharply demarcated and allow no intergrading. This typological classification acted as a block to the idea of a gradual transmutation of one species into another. Evolutionary taxonomy is still in the process of detaching itself from the influence of Platonism (Simpson, 1961).

Aristotle represented the real world as a hierarchy of kinds of things, each of which combines form and matter. In his biological writings, however, he recognizes that living organisms are not sharply classifiable into kinds, for there are many intermediate types which blur the lines of demarcation. He even says in one place that "nature passes from lifeless objects to animals in an unbroken sequence." These views have led some students to conclude that Aristotle must have been an evolutionist. But such a conclusion is mistaken. It wrongly supposes that because the affirmation of continuity in the living world is incompatible with a belief in sharply discrete kinds, it implies that a historical derivation of one kind from another must have taken place. Aristotle certainly did not think that the intergrading of organisms had come about historically. It would have been inconceivable to him that one species of animal could slowly change into another species, just as it would have been inconceivable that the complex hierarchy of nature could have been gradually developed from simple beginnings. For him the universe is eternal and unchanging. In it every thing has its fixed nature which remains unaffected by the motion which brings about its actuality from a state of potency. **175**

The profoundly anti-evolutionary character of Aristotelianism helped to arrest all forms of evolutionism for nearly two thousand years.

Another influence that worked in the same direction during this period was Christianity. After the time of Aristotle, there were occasional revivals of the idea that living things had arisen naturally from terrestrial elements and that human society had developed from a state of barbarism. Lucretius, Cicero, and Horace all advocated views of this kind. But such views were eclipsed when the Christian world-outlook became predominant in Europe. An essential part of this outlook was the biblical story of creation, according to which the universe was brought into being by an all-powerful God who had made it complete in every detail, with each kind of creature occupying its proper place in the whole. The period since the creation was relatively brief, being only a few thousand years. Adam, the first man, was created by God in His image, and hence could not possibly have had ancestors. The human race is, indeed, central to the cosmic drama which is being worked out according to the divine plan. The rest of the universe merely forms the background for what is taking place. Thus the static creationism taught by Christianity made it difficult for any idea of evolution to arise, let alone be defended.

III. EVOLUTIONISM REBORN

The rebirth of evolutionism is associated with the advance of the natural sciences in the period after the Renaissance. Several stages in the process of rebirth can be distinguished. The first was a result of the new cosmogony. Theories of how the physical universe, including the solar system, had been or might have been produced in accordance with mechanical laws were set forth by René Descartes in his *Principles of Philosophy* (1644), by Immanuel Kant in his *Universal Natural History and Theory of the Heavens* (1755), and by Pierre Simon de Laplace in his *Exposition of the System of the World* (1796). As a consequence, the idea that nature had a history emerged as a powerful rival to the dogma of special creation, even though Descartes presented his theory as a purely imaginative exercise which was not intended to contradict the first chapter of Genesis. Furthermore, the new cosmogony supposed that originally the matter of the universe was in a chaotic, nebular state from which it passed through a succession of orderly changes to its existing complex structure. Isaac Newton's *Principia Mathematica* (1687) had given a definitive account of that structure, but had said nothing about how nature developed. Yet it was an obvious move to apply Newtonian principles to cosmogonic problems, and thereby bring to the fore

the idea that the universe had developed in an orderly way from an unorganized state.

A second phase in the rebirth of evolutionism was due to the rise of geology and paleontology. These sciences established three conclusions that were essential to the revival of evolutionary views.

(1) The changes in the surface features of the earth through the ages are the result of physical forces whose operation has been gradual and broadly constant. This uniformitarian doctrine replaced the ancient biblical story of the Flood, and also the conception that the earth's surface had been subject to periodic catastrophes. The classical version of uniformitarianism appeared in Sir Charles Lyell's *Principles of Geology* (1830), a work that profoundly influenced the thought of Charles Darwin.

(2) The age of the earth is far greater than biblical chronology allowed. In 1650 Archbishop Ussher calculated that the Creation took place in 4004 B.C. A century later, Buffon conjectured that some seventy thousand years had elapsed since the molten earth began to cool. By the beginning of the nineteenth century, the age of the earth was estimated in millions rather than thousands of years. This expansion of the terrestrial time scale provided the setting needed for the doctrine that biological evolution tends to take place slowly.

(3) The fossils or "figured stones" which had been noticed in the earth's crust ever since antiquity and which posed an enigma to nonevolutionists, are in fact the remains of organisms that lived in the past. One of the first to support this conclusion was Leibniz (*Protogaea*, 1680), although he did not surmise how much time was needed for petrifactive processes to occur. Later, Buffon and Maillet formulated geological theories to account for the presence of fossils, but their views were subjected to ridicule by Voltaire who was hostile to the idea of development in nature (Haber, 1959). By Lyell's day, however, it was clearly understood that many fossils were relics of species long extinct, and that observed or reconstructed sequences of fossils were direct evidence for evolution.

IV. EIGHTEENTH-CENTURY EVOLUTIONISM

During the eighteenth century evolutionary ideas in the biological sciences gradually matured, despite strong opposition. The history of what happened is complex, but broadly speaking, there were changes in basic theoretical or philosophical principles, and new empirical discoveries made in those sciences. On the theoretical side, they were influenced by the doctrine of continuity which had a considerable vogue at the time. They were also influenced by the nominalism which had become a feature of contemporary philosophy. These doctrines encouraged biologists to question Platonistic conceptions of species, and to investigate the anatomy, embryonic development and variability of individual organisms. Likewise, the theoretical model of nature as a mechanical system governed by external laws was confronted with a rival model, due in part to Leibniz, of nature as a self-organizing system functioning in accordance with inner dynamic forces. On the empirical side, the biological sciences brought forward new interpretations of observed facts in comparative anatomy, embryology, and genetics which stimulated maturing evolutionism. Three influential figures whose work embodies these ideas were Buffon, Maupertuis, and Diderot.

Buffon's vast *Histoire naturelle*, in 44 volumes (1749–1804), contains material which, as Lovejoy has said, "both fostered and hindered the propagation of evolutionary ideas in biology" (Lovejoy [1959], p. 111). The contribution of Buffon's geological views has already been mentioned. In addition, he stated quite explicitly the hypothesis of organic evolution, without actually espousing it. He even suggested "that man and ape have a common origin; that, in fact, all the families among plants as well as animals, have come from a common stock" (Buffon [1783], IV, 382). His knowledge of anatomical homologies and of individual variations inclined him to espouse evolutionism. Yet on the other hand, he publicly denied that species are mutable. They are "perduring entities, as ancient, as permanent, as Nature herself." In holding this view, however, Buffon differed sharply from his contemporary, Carl von Linnaeus, who had defined a species Platonistically in terms of invariant characteristics. Buffon defined a species in terms of the relation of interbreeding, so that two animals of opposite sex belong to the same species if their offspring are fertile, and belong to different species if they fail to produce offspring or produce offspring that are sterile. It has sometimes been said that his refusal to espouse the transmutation of species was due to his desire to avoid the hostility of the Church. This may have been partly the case; but he does offer arguments in support of his position drawn from the biological knowledge of his day (cf. Lovejoy, 1959).

The importance of Maupertuis for evolutionism lies in the fact that he not only envisaged the transmutation and diversification of species, but also sketched an explanation of how these processes might have come about. His study of embryogeny impressed on him the frequent occurrence of deviations from the norm in individual development. "Errors" arise that produce new characteristics of organisms and are then transmitted to offspring. If these characteristics enable the organisms to adapt to the environment more success-

fully than their predecessors, a new species will result. Repeated deviations could lead to a diversification of species such as now obtains on the earth. The whole process might even have started "from two individuals alone." Furthermore, since the developmental "errors" may be attributed to fortuitous rearrangements of the basic hereditary particles, no design or teleology need be postulated. This explanation appears to anticipate in outline much later accounts of evolution which appeal to genetic mutations and natural selection. Yet Maupertuis' approach was more speculative than empirical, and his ideas remained rather vague. Hence, despite his importance, it is overstating the case to say that "he must be ranked above all the precursors of Darwin" (Glass [1959], p. 74; cf. Lovejoy, 1950).

Diderot was influenced by Buffon's *Histoire naturelle* and by Maupertuis' *Système de la nature* (1751). He recognized that the anatomical homologies mentioned in Buffon's work supported the idea that species evolve. He also recognized the value of Maupertuis' conjecture that variations which occur in individual development might, given sufficient time, lead to an immense diversification of species. He shared with both men a predilection for the idea of spontaneous generation, although he did not accept Buffon's concept of "organic molecules" or Maupertuis' speculation that the basic hereditary particles had some rudimentary form of intelligence. The most he was prepared to admit was that "sensitivity" is either an inherent property of matter or a property which it acquires when it reaches a stage of sufficient organization.

The distinctive feature of Diderot's transformism is that it is part of an evolutionary metaphysics. Like Spencer a century later, but much less systematically, he aimed to explain how the universe had evolved from a primitive state towards increasing complexity and specialization. Unlike Spencer, however, he espoused a thoroughgoing, dynamic materialism. Matter with its inherent property of motion, and perhaps of sensitivity, accounts for all that has come to be. The universe is a self-organizing whole whose parts are interconnected and ceaselessly changing. In the course of "millions of years," living things have undergone "an infinite number of successive organizations and developments." These have brought about the existence of sensations, thoughts, languages, laws, sciences, and arts on the earth. Living things have "perhaps still other developments to undergo which are unknown to us." The process of universal change is neither purposive nor mechanical but organic. Like the life-cycle of plants and animals, it may well be subject to dissolution as well as evolution.

These formulations of evolutionism in eighteenth-century biology met resistance from within the science

177

itself. The chief resistance came from embryology which was then dominated by the version of preformationism known as the "encapsulation (*emboîtement*) theory," defended with powerful arguments by Charles Bonnet in his *Considérations sur les corps organisés* (1762). This was one of the first works to use the term "evolution" in a biological sense. For Bonnet, however, "evolution" designated the process of ontogenesis interpreted as the development of an individual organism from a germ in which it, and all its potential descendants, were contained. When the world was created, all future generations of living things were "encapsulated" in a set of primordial germs. Preformationism thus implied that the boundaries between species were permanently fixed. The counter-theory of epigenesis, accepted by Maupertuis, Diderot, and K. F. Wolff, was favorable to transformism because epigenesists regarded hereditary variations as adding characteristics to living things in the course of their development. But epigenesis had become linked with the notion of spontaneous generation, and was discredited along with that notion by the experiments of Lazaro Spallanzani (1729–99) and others. Hence the temporary triumph of preformationism arrested biological evolutionism until the period of Lamarck. This situation may have had something to do with the fact that even so eminent a figure as Kant, who was vaguely attracted to evolutionistic modes of thought, rejected the idea that species can change.

V. PROGRESSIONISM

A new version of evolutionism began to make its appearance in the latter half of the eighteenth century. This was the metaphysical doctrine of universal progress, or progressionism. It resulted in large measure from what Lovejoy has called "the temporalizing of the Chain of Being" (Lovejoy [1936], Ch. ix). According to a conception derived from Platonic and Neo-Platonic philosophy, the universe is a completed hierarchy or "chain" which extends from entities having a minimal degree of being, through all possible forms, to the *ens perfectissimum*. This conception underwent a modification which made its first appearance in Leibniz. The stages of the hierarchy were regarded as coming into existence successively in time, starting with the lowest; and the movement towards the higher stages was regarded as unfinished and as continually producing new and diverse forms. Thus the conception of a static chain of being became that of a unilinear process of ascent to greater perfection.

The details of progressionism were worked out in many different ways. Thus, Jean Jacques Rousseau and Lord James Barrett Monboddo limited the scope of the doctrine to man's advance from a primitive to a civilized state. This formulation not only gave a new impetus to the idea of social or cultural evolution, but also contained the radical suggestion that man was derived from apelike ancestors, such as the orangutans, with whom he forms a single species. Yet neither Rousseau nor Monboddo accepted transformism. The development of man did not imply for them that any species-barriers were passed in the rise from animality to humanity.

Another formulation of progressionism centered around the idea that a single, basic prototype had been more and more fully actualized in the history of nature. This idea was clearly stated by Robinet in his *De la nature* (1761). "A stone, an oak, a horse, a monkey, a man are graduated variations of the prototype which began to form itself with the least possible number of elements" in the remote past. The succession of variations has been "so many steps towards the being of humanity." Herder advanced a similar idea in his *Ideen zu einer Philosophie der Geschichte der Menschheit* (1784–91), although he gave more emphasis to the standard form (*Hauptform*) which is diversified in the animal kingdom and most perfectly exemplified in man. These ideas represented a response of speculative minds to the facts of vertebrate homologies discussed by Buffon and Louis Jean Marie Daubenton. The conclusions of the new science of comparative anatomy were translated into terms of a teleological scheme according to which the production of man has been aimed at from the start and has been achieved by a gradual perfecting of one prototype that appears in all living things.

Various metaphysical explanations of this perfecting process were offered. Robinet posited a "creative power" (*puissance active*) that increased in strength through the ages and produced higher forms despite the resistance of brute matter. Herder attributed the perfecting to vaguely conceived "purposes" of Nature which have been realized in a necessary historical order. Exponents of *Naturphilosophie*, such F. W. J. Schelling and L. O. Oken, for whom progressionism had a strong appeal, had recourse to the belief that a divine power is expressed in the succession of forms. God is gradually revealing his nature in the history of the cosmos, and man is the being in whom at last divinity is fully manifested. These teleological explanation-schemes, especially the ones advocated by the German *Naturphilosophen*, embodied the notion of successive creation or spontaneous generation of kinds, and hence were not transformist. They were rather explanations which were strongly tinged with Neo-Platonism, and formulated by minds of a romantic rather than a scientific cast. Yet the biological sciences in the early nineteenth century were much influenced by such romantic speculations (cf. Nordenskiöld [1929], Ch. xiv).

The linking of progressionism and transformism was mainly due to Erasmus Darwin and Lamarck. These men accepted the idea of a broad historical advance of living things from simple to complex. But they rejected the idea of a successive creation of kinds in favor of the view that later kinds had descended with modifications from earlier ones. Both men held that what had occurred at successive stages of this descent is amenable to explanation in natural terms. Erasmus Darwin's explanation was sketchy and quasi-poetic; Lamarck's explanation was more detailed and quasi-scientific. The general pattern was similar in the two cases. It invoked the notion that living things, by virtue of an internal vital power, respond to the changing environment in such a way as to satisfy their wants or needs. As a result of this process, somatic characteristics are developed which meet those wants or needs, and are passed on to successive generations of offspring. Thus in the course of time the organisms concerned undergo alterations of form and function. The alterations, however, are not random, for they are phases of the progressive advance of living things from lower to higher types.

Although Erasmus Darwin and Lamarck helped to pave the way for the work of Charles Darwin, their evolutionism was very different from his. They were eighteenth-century deists, for whom the history of the cosmos is the actualizing of a divine plan established at creation. Deism and evolutionism were readily combined in the view that God had so designed the universe that evolution is the means by which His plan is executed without miraculous intervention. The historical succession of forms obeys the laws ordained by God in the beginning. A basic aim of Erasmus Darwin in his *Zoonomia* (1794–96), of Lamarck in his *Philosophie zoologique* (1809), and somewhat later, of Robert Chambers in his popular *Vestiges of the Natural History of Creation* (1844), was to advocate deistic evolutionism. All these works did indeed invoke empirical facts. But the facts were introduced not to support specific biological hypotheses, as was the case with Charles Darwin. They were introduced to support a general philosophy of nature. Furthermore, little reference was made to the problem of the origin of species. Erasmus Darwin scarcely mentions species, whereas Lamarck took the position that since only individual organisms exist in nature, species are arbitrary groupings which men establish. Moreover, individual organisms are parts of a continuous, changing process, which is constantly creating life at the bottom of the scale and raising it upwards to more perfect forms of organization (cf. Gillispie, 1959).

In the early nineteenth century biological progressionism came under attack. The anatomist and paleontologist, Cuvier, denied that living things can be arranged in a unilinear sequence. He contended that there are four fundamental groups of animals, so different that they cannot be integrated into an ascending taxonomic scheme or regarded as belonging to one historical series in which a single basic prototype was gradually perfected. The embryologist, Karl E. von Baer, and the paleontologist, Louis Agassiz, supported these contentions. Von Baer argued that the developmental processes in the four groups bear no significant embryological relationships to each other. Serious doubt was thus cast not only on the idea that living things had evolved in a unilinear way, but also on the idea that they had evolved at all. For Cuvier, von Baer, and Agassiz rejected the notion of the mutability of species. They were anti-evolutionists as well as anti-progressionists. This fact tended to obscure the logical point that since biological evolutionism does not entail progressionism, it is quite possible to subscribe to the former without subscribing to the latter. Hence in much nineteenth-century thought evolution was mistakenly identified with progress, not only in biology but also in other disciplines.

The work of Cuvier and von Baer helped to undermine the influence of the idea of a great chain or scale of beings. As zoological evidence accumulated, it became hard to accept the progressionists' view that living things form a single, tidy, unilinear series. Lamarck, who was widely familiar with the evidence, admitted that such a series could only be formed by abstracting characteristics common to animal groups. By the time of Charles Darwin, another metaphor had come to the fore, namely, that of "a great tree" whose twigs, branches, boughs, etc., represent respectively species, genera, families, etc., of living things, ramifying in a complex, irregular way from a single trunk, or from two main trunks at the base. This figure of the tree of life became a new paradigm in evolutionary biology, bringing with it a shift in thought which allowed account to be taken of the facts pointed out by Cuvier and von Baer without rejecting the transmutation of species. The book that accomplished this revolutionary shift in thought was Charles Darwin's *On the Origin of Species* (1859).

VI. DARWINISM

All the versions of evolutionism prior to 1859 suffered from two major limitations. They were not able to produce a well-organized body of evidence to show that evolution had occurred, and they were not able to formulate a verifiable explanation of how it had occurred. Darwin did both things for the theory

179

of organic evolution. His *Origin of Species* is, as he says, "one long argument" which combines hypotheses, deductions, and observations to support three major propositions: (1) all species of organisms now on earth have descended by a long, gradual process of modification from a small number of very different species in the remote past; (2) the chief cause of the transmutation of species is natural selection which acts on populations of organisms having varying and inheritable characteristics and as a result there is differential survival and reproduction in the population, depending on the extent to which the characteristics favor or handicap the organisms in the struggle for existence; (3) natural selection accounts for the adaptations of viable organisms to widely different conditions of life; it also tends to improve those adaptations, and conversely, it leads to the extinction of poorly adapted species. Darwin did not profess to have invented any of these ideas, and he was particularly cognizant of his indebtedness to Thomas Malthus and Lyell. What he did was to make evolutionism for the first time a testable theory and to offer a powerful body of evidence in its support. Consequently, before long it was accepted by the whole scientific community. There was indeed a "triumph of the Darwinian method" (cf. Ghiselin, 1969).

Darwinism had a revolutionary impact on many aspects of Western intellectual culture. It destroyed the quasi-theological frame of mind in the sciences, so that biologists no longer concerned themselves with the biblical story of the creation of species, or geologists with the story of the Flood. Darwin's proof that species change in a gradual, orderly way under the influence of natural causes utilized the same uniformitarian principle by which Lyell had made geology a science. The adaptations of plants and animals to their environments, cited by William Paley in his *Natural Theology* (1802) as evidence of providential design in the world, were accounted for by Darwin without any reference to divine purposes. Thus the living world became amenable to explanation in mechanistic, or more accurately naturalistic terms, just as the nonliving world was. A new scientific outlook, altogether free of theological presuppositions, was strongly reinforced by Darwinism.

Of even greater importance was the impact of Darwinism on man's conception of himself. It was a clear implication of the *Origin of Species* that human beings had descended not from an historical Adam created by God in 4004 B.C., but from remote, prehuman ancestors. T. H. Huxley developed this implication with reference to bodily traits in *Man's Place in Nature* (1863). Darwin developed it with reference to mental, moral, and social traits in *The Descent of Man*

(1871). Once again it was not so much the novelty of these ideas as the arguments offered in support of them that caused a shock. Even some of Darwin's allies, such as Lyell, Alfred Russel Wallace, George Romanes, and Asa Gray, were unwilling to accept the conclusion that the powers of the mind were evolutionary products. Huxley came to believe that there was a fundamental conflict between the operation of natural selection and the ethical values cherished by men. Nevertheless, by the end of the nineteenth century the force of the Darwinian argument was augmented by the discovery of various proto-human fossil remains, and the "death of Adam" was widely admitted (cf. Greene, 1959).

The Darwinian theory excited bitter theological and popular opposition, especially in England. Its opponents were mainly members of the privileged upper classes who regarded the theory as a threat to the Establishment. They associated the doctrine of evolution with the atheistic materialism which had been part of the ideology of the French Revolution. The *ancien régime* had been overthrown by those who held that man can improve his lot and perfect himself by his own efforts. Darwinism was believed to belong to this same family of radical ideas. More than half a century before its appearance, the influence of those ideas in England had been counteracted by Malthus' *Essay on Population* (1798) and by Paley's *Natural Theology*. Malthus had contended that the improvement of man's lot is made impossible by the rate of population increase and the consequent need to keep the population in check by a high rate of mortality in the struggle for existence. But Darwin had shown that it was precisely mortality in the struggle for existence that enabled natural selection to improve adaptation among those that survived. Furthermore, Darwin had exploded Paley's claim that the existence of adaptations is evidence of the providential ordering of the world. To Victorian conservatives all this proved that the doctrine of evolution by natural selection was a threat to Church and State which had to be resisted. Nor would they have been reassured by the fact that Darwin had declined Marx's invitation to allow Volume I of *Das Kapital* to be dedicated to him (de Beer [1965], p. 266).

In the later nineteenth century, attempts were made to use Darwinism to support the system of laissez-faire capitalism which had become dominant in the Western world. Those who reaped the benefits of the system but who were aware of its inequities, argued that it conformed to a primal law of evolution. For since, as Darwin had shown, competition in the struggle for existence results in the survival of the fittest, the rich are simply better adapted than the poor to the conditions of social life. To remove or even mitigate competition would be to go against nature. This doctrine, somewhat inappropriately called "Social Darwinism," was used to oppose government intervention in economic affairs, the growth of trade unions, and the rising tide of socialist ideas. Leading protagonists of the doctrine were Herbert Spencer in England and J. D. Rockefeller and W. G. Sumner in the United States. But Social Darwinism also had its critics, among whom were C. S. Peirce, and also Peter Kropotkin, the author of *Mutual Aid* (1907). The question of the bearing of evolutionary theory on social philosophy and ethics was much debated at this time, and is still being discussed (cf. Waddington, 1960; Flew, 1967).

The success of the Darwinian explanation scheme in biology called attention to certain methodological features of it which influenced subsequent science. (1) Darwin showed that explanation can be historical without losing its scientific character. For in biology one is often able to explain phenomena by showing how they originated and developed. To understand "the tree of life" one has to understand how it grew. (2) By getting rid of Platonistic elements in his treatment of natural selection, Darwin established evolutionary science on a nominalistic basis. He then introduced statistical or "population" conceptions to permit generalizations to be made about the changes which selection produces in individuals. (3) The *Origin of Species* explained what happened in evolution as an outcome of accidental and orderly events combined. Natural selection is an order-generating process. The occurrence of variations, the survival and reproductive success of organisms, etc., are matters of accident or chance. It thus became clear that a discipline does not need to establish what must necessarily happen according to universal laws in order to be a science. (4) The Darwinian explanation showed that although adaptations are not the result of design, they are nevertheless purposive. They serve certain ends and must be so studied. Thus a scientific concept of teleology can be admitted at the same time that theological and metaphysical teleology are rejected.

These Darwinian ideas spread rapidly into the whole intellectual domain. The social sciences, for example, became strongly evolutionary. Facets of human culture came to be investigated in terms of their origin, development, and survival or disappearance. The word "evolution" began to appear in the titles of works by anthropologists, psychologists, sociologists, historians of moral, legal, and political institutions, and so on. Indeed, "it was not long before the lesson of evolution filtered through to all fields of human endeavour, including literature, art, music, and the history of ideas in general" (de Beer [1965], p. 216). Darwinism excited the interest and frequently the antipathy of English

men of letters, such as Tennyson, Samuel Butler, and George Bernard Shaw. Above all it gave a renewed impetus to cosmogonic speculation in philosophy. As a result various systems of metaphysical evolutionism were constructed after 1859.

VII. METAPHYSICAL EVOLUTIONISM

Although Darwin himself disavowed any intention to draw philosophical conclusions, it was clear that his ideas could be readily generalized so as to constitute a world-outlook. The final sentence of the *Origin of Species* remarked on the "grandeur of this view of life," and thereby invited a metaphysical interpretation of the book's conclusions. Such metaphysical interpretations not only generalized those conclusions, but also tended to deal with questions that Darwin legitimately bypassed. Among these were the question of how life began, why it started to evolve, whether evolution had always been continuous, and to what extent naturalistic principles adequately accounted for cosmic order, teleology in nature, the appearance of the human mind, ostensible freedom of action, and human knowledge. In taking up these matters, evolutionary philosophies sometimes tried to anticipate the findings of the sciences, sometimes offered speculative answers to nonscientific questions, and sometimes undertook conceptual analysis and redefinition of terms. Occasionally there was a failure of nerve in the face of the Darwinian challenge, so that an anti-evolutionary position ultimately emerged. It will be convenient to deal with a few of the major evolutionary philosophies under four headings: mechanistic evolutionism, vitalistic evolutionism, emergent evolutionism, and pragmatic evolutionism.

Mechanistic Evolutionism. According to one generalized doctrine, the total universe has evolved as a consequence of its basic stuff being acted on by extrinsic forces or laws. The biologist Ernst Haeckel, Darwin's vigorous champion in Germany, expounded this doctrine in his popular work, *The Riddle of the Universe* (London, 1899), Chs. I and XIII. "Evolution" was for him the magic conception which could lead to the solution of every cosmic riddle. All natural phenomena, he contended, "from the motion of heavenly bodies . . . to the growth of plants and the consciousness of man, obey one and the same great law of causation." It produces "a vast, uniform, uninterrupted process of development." In the process countless types of organization arise, but "all may be ultimately referred to the mechanics of atoms." Yet since continuity prevails throughout, the atoms which constitute the world-stuff must be supposed to have a rudimentary consciousness or "soul" from which the consciousness of man was evolved. Hence atoms are 181 not just bits of physical matter. Haeckel therefore referred to his doctrine as "monism," not materialism. It may be viewed as a philosophically crude but influential attempt to unite Darwinism with the cosmogony initiated by Descartes, Kant, and Laplace.

A more sophisticated version of mechanistic evolutionism was formulated by Herbert Spencer in *A System of Synthetic Philosophy* (1862–93). He had published an attack on the idea of fixed, created species, and a defense of transmutation, in his essay, "The Development Hypothesis" (1852). When the *Origin of Species* appeared Spencer accepted its contention that existing forms of life had descended with modifications from common ancestors. He even coined the phrase "survival of the fittest" which Darwin unwisely adopted as a synonym for natural selection.

Yet Spencer was not a Darwinian. The general definition of evolution he formulated was inspired by von Baer's description of embryological development, and also by Lamarckian progressionism. Evolution is defined as "an integration of matter and a concomitant dissipation of motion; during which the matter passes from a relatively indefinite, incoherent homogeneity to a relatively definite, coherent heterogeneity; and during which the retained motion undergoes a parallel transformation" (*First Principles*, 6th ed., p. 144). The causes of this movement are mechanical, being extrinsic to matter and motion. Spencer undertook to apply his definition to all phenomena, from the formation of the solar system out of a primitive nebula to the rise of civilization out of primitive human associations. The enterprise needed ten large volumes and thirty years to complete. In its day it was world-famous.

Part of the reason for its fame was that the *Synthetic Philosophy* proposed to reconcile science and religion. But in doing so it largely negated evolutionism. For in his opening volume, *First Principles* (1862), Spencer adopted an epistemological premiss from Mansel's *The Limits of Religious Thought* (1858) according to which ultimate reality cannot be known. Now religion involves the consciousness of an Incomprehensible Power behind phenomena, and science, since it is only concerned with phenomena, can acknowledge that they are manifestations of an unknowable reality. Hence there need be no opposition between the respective claims of religion and science. But it follows that the process of evolution is a feature of phenomena alone. Ultimate reality does not evolve. Moreover, even in the domain of phenomena evolution is not all-pervasive. For it is essentially a rearrangement of enduring matter and motion in various sectors— inorganic, organic, and super-organic. The mechanical causes that operate are likewise enduring. And,

Spencer declares, more forthrightly than Diderot, universal development will eventually run its course. It will then be followed by the reverse process of retrogression and dissolution in the grand cosmic cycle. Thus despite the wealth of detail it encompasses, the *Synthetic Philosophy* turns out to be an anti-evolutionary system or, as Henri Bergson put it, "evolutionism only in name."

Vitalistic Evolutionism. The ancient idea that organisms are animated by a vital force not found in inorganic matter had been invoked to account for the history of life by advocates of progressionism and *Naturphilosophie* in the eighteenth century. The influence of these romantic speculations did not end with the appearance of the *Origin of Species*, however, but continued to be manifested in metaphysical doctrines hostile to Darwinism. No objection was raised to the conclusion that evolution had occurred. What was objected to was the philosophical adequacy of mechanistic or naturalistic explanations of evolution. The issue of teleology, largely ignored by Haeckel and Spencer, came in for much attention, as did the question of why organisms had become ever more diversified and complex since arising on the earth. Answers to such questions in terms of a generalized vitalism, with strong romantic overtones, were offered by Schopenhauer and Bergson.

The importance of Schopenhauer for the history of evolutionism was first pointed out by Lovejoy (see Lovejoy, 1911). The relevant material occurs mainly in a late work, *Zur Philosophie und Wissenschaft der Natur* (1850), which Schopenhauer wrote under the influence of Chambers' *Vestiges of the Natural History of Creation*, a book that prefigured many Darwinian arguments for the theory of descent. Schopenhauer used Chambers' ideas to develop an evolutionary philosophy of nature as a final supplement to the earlier system which Schopenhauer had worked out in *Die Welt als Wille und Vorstellung* (1818). According to that system, absolute reality is Will, an unconscious, striving, irrational power, beyond space and time, which "objectifies" itself in the phenomenal world. By 1850 Schopenhauer construed this objectification as a process of cosmic, geological, and biological evolution. Each individual in the process embodies the will to live. The general diversification of types and the movement through sudden saltations towards complexity are explicable in terms of a striving of the Will for maximum expression. This is an "end" determined by its nature, though not consciously pursued. Hence the whole process is teleological, not mechanical. Yet like Spencer, Schopenhauer refused to give ontological primacy to evolution. For the Will in itself is timeless, complete, and inscrutable. As Lovejoy remarks, "both systems consist of an evolutionary philosophy of nature, projected against the background of an essentially mystical and negative metaphysics" (Lovejoy [1911], p. 214).

A thoroughgoing evolutionary metaphysics was set forth by Bergson in *L'évolution créatrice* (1907; trans. as *Creative Evolution*, 1911). This ingenious speculative work proclaimed the ontological priority of time and becoming over being. It attributed the history of organisms and their living properties to the activity of a primordial impulse (*élan vital; poussée vitale*) which infused inert matter, created organic structures, and endowed organisms with the capacity to grow and adapt to the environment. The vital impulse freely created forms in ever-increasing diversity, at each stage "engrafting on to the necessity of physical forces the largest possible amount of indetermination." Like his eighteenth-century predecessor, Robinet, Bergson supposed that inert matter resisted the vital impulse, so that there is a constant tendency for organisms to relapse into repetitive, devitalized routines. Eventually, the individual organism dies, but the "current of life" passes on to succeeding generations and gives rise to unpredictable novelties. At bottom, the vital impulse is "a current of consciousness" which has found expression in human intelligence as a result of "a sudden leap from animal to man" (*Creative Evolution*, p. 195).

Bergson contended that this doctrine provided a far more adequate account of evolutionary phenomena than either Darwinism or Spencerian mechanism. These theories, he held, failed to make intelligible the springing up of new organic types, the drive towards ever-increasing complexity of structure, and the preservation of adaptive functioning through phases of rapid change. Such phenomena become intelligible if they are regarded as consequences of the action of a vital impulse. It works purposively to sustain each organism for a short period, but it does not pursue any final goal. There is "teleology without design" which results in continuous progress, indefinitely pursued. Man is the growing tip of this progressive movement. In him true freedom is realized; and he has access to ultimate reality in his intuition of time.

Bergson's evolutionism was attractive to those who were in revolt against mechanistic and materialistic ideas at the start of the twentieth century. Many welcomed the important place he gave to mind in the evolutionary picture. Philosophers such as William James, and writers such as Marcel Proust, André Gide, and Shaw were influenced by his emphasis on creativity, freedom, novelty, and the flow of consciousness. His defense of metaphysics challenged the positivism of Hippolyte Taine which had dominated French intellectual life for some years before Bergson's works

appeared. Yet it was the romantic, imaginative quality of those works rather than the presence in them of cogent arguments and supporting evidence that made Bergsonian evolutionism popular.

Emergent Evolutionism. A central theme in the *Origin of Species* was that no abrupt changes had taken place in the history of life. That history conformed to the principle, *natura non facit saltum* ("nature makes no leap"), and hence all evolutionary changes in organisms were gradual. Some of Darwin's supporters considered that his espousal of this principle was ill-advised since it is not an essential part of his theory. Thus, T. H. Huxley affirmed in *Collected Essays* (9 vols., 1893–94) "that Nature does make jumps now and then, and a recognition of the fact is of no small importance in disposing of minor objections to the doctrine of transmutation" (II, 77). A Darwinian could accept the view that sudden novelties had arisen in evolution, although it was not clear how he could then escape from accepting the unpalatable conclusion of thinkers like Schopenhauer and Bergson that the "leaps" to novelty are due to a vital force. The conceptual difficulties here were resolved by the formulation of the doctrine of emergent evolutionism.

In its full statement emergent evolutionism is a metaphysical doctrine. But one of its contentions is empirical, namely, that emergent events can be observed in nature. The results of certain chemical reactions which happen suddenly provide a simple example. Hence the claim that nature makes no leaps is empirically false. Furthermore, when they first occur, these emergent events add something new to the sum-total of existence, and being genuinely novel, they are unpredictable in principle. Emergents can also be noted in the history of life at those points where new organic types appeared on the scene. Their emergence is a natural fact which does not require the postulation of a vital impulse. The fact is, however, incompatible with mechanistic, reductionist, or preformationist interpretations of what took place. It is likewise incompatible with some, but not all, interpretations of the causal principle. The emergence of novelties in biological evolution illustrates the cumulative aspect of the process.

These contentions were embodied in systems of metaphysical evolutionism by Lloyd Morgan in *Emergent Evolution* (1923) and by Samuel Alexander in *Space, Time and Deity* (1920). They construed "emergence" as applying not to individual events or to particular organic forms, but to broad "levels" of being. Lloyd Morgan affirmed that the universe had evolved by generating four temporally successive levels: psycho-physical events, life, mind, and spirit or God. Alexander distinguished five levels of complexes and their qualities: space-time, matter, life, mind, and deity. The supervening of each level on its predecessors was declared to be inexplicable, a fact to be accepted with "natural piety." Other exponents of the doctrine objected to this conclusion, and undertook to show that emergents can be given a rational explanation *ex post facto*, without denying that when they occur they are unpredictable novelties. There is no consensus about how many or what kinds of levels cosmic evolution has produced. By no means do all emergent evolutionists accept the view that one of the levels can be called God. Naturalistic formulations of the doctrine have been given in which the main categories are physical, e.g., elementary particles, atoms, molecules, cells, organisms, and societies.

The notion of emergence has been accepted by many biologists as a valid description of what happened at critical stages of terrestrial evolution. The notion has also been found useful as a device for integrating biological evolution and the unique products of mental, moral, and cultural evolution that have enriched the sum of things on the earth. These applications accord with the view that discontinuities exist among living systems because of the different degrees of complexity in their organization. The metaphysical extension of this view, however, is problematic. It requires the postulation of such highly controversial ideas as an overall, cosmic evolution, pervasive levels of being, and an inherent tendency of the cosmos to produce novelties. Furthermore, the model or paradigm associated with these ideas is obscure. Emergent evolution is envisaged neither as a temporal building up of a scale of nature, nor as a temporalized chain of beings. For it is said that each level which emerges "contains within it" all earlier levels, and also that the supervening of a level on others may engender novel qualities at one or more of those other levels. The model here would seem to be that of a developing organism which during embryogenesis can be observed to manifest new structures within which earlier structures are contained. Emergent evolutionism has, indeed, an affinity for organismic and epigenetic ideas, which have sometimes been combined with it.

Pragmatic Evolutionism. A distinctive generalization of Darwinian conceptions took place in connection with the rise of pragmatism in America. The initiators of this doctrine accepted Darwin's view that evolution is continuous. But they broadened his theory of chance variations and natural selection so as to explain the role of human thought and its multifarious creations. Out of this explanation there developed a reconstruction of traditional philosophy. Its primary concern was not with abstract speculation but with reflection on concrete problems of scientific method, education,

jurisprudence, and social ethics. Pragmatism thus provided a way of understanding how cultural evolution is related to biological evolution. At the same time, pragmatic evolutionism did involve a world view, a predominantly empirical and naturalistic metaphysics, in which no appeal was made to cosmic purposes, vitalistic agencies, or mechanistic laws.

On the pragmatic approach, man is recognized to be engaged, like every other living thing, in a constant process of adapting to his environment. His mental capacities are, therefore, adaptive devices which serve him well or ill in this process. Ideas are instruments for coping with the world, and must be tested by observation and experiment to determine their worth. Thought and action, when functioning properly, are inseparable, for man adapts to an existing situation either by making his behavior conform to it or by actively changing the situation to meet his needs. This pragmatic approach to mind had its roots not only in Darwinism but also in Bain's conception of belief as a "preparation to act," in Chauncey Wright's view of scientific principles as "working hypotheses," and in Peirce's contention in *Collected Papers* (8 vols., 1931–58) that "the elements of every concept enter into logical thought at the gate of perception and make their exit at the gate of purposive action" (*Collected Papers* [1934], V, 212). John Dewey developed these notions into a full-blown evolutionary logic in his *Logic: The Theory of Inquiry* (1938). Another pragmatist, G. H. Mead, put the matter strikingly when he said that "the scientific method is, after all, only the evolutionary process grown self-conscious" (*Movements of Thought in the Nineteenth Century* [1936], p. 364). For in the history of science ideas, like somatic variations in the history of life, have been subject to a selective process which has resulted in a survival of the fittest.

The world view which pragmatic evolutionism involved was, with one notable exception, pluralistic and open-ended. "Nature" was the basic ontological category which embraced the multiplicity of events whose interactions are sometimes regular and sometimes random. There is no fixed cosmic order and no overall direction in cosmic history. Yet a cumulative, determinate past is being built up by the actualization of some events out of the array of indeterminate possibilities. Wright compared the physical history of the universe to meteorological phenomena, in his doctrine of "cosmic weather," where what happens is causally determined but shows no dominant trend. William James, in opposing the Hegelian "block universe," suggested that world events are "only strung along, not rounded in and closed." Dewey urged, in *The Influence of Darwin on Philosophy*, that a philosopher who has learned the lesson of Darwinism will "forswear inquiry after absolute origins and absolute finalities in order to explore specific values and the specific conditions that generate them" (1910, p. 13). Pragmatism can find no meaning in a "wholesale theory" of first and last things.

The exception to all this was the speculative evolutionism of Peirce. Although he had a sound grasp of the logic of Darwinism, recognizing as few did its use of the statistical method, he never accepted the theory as a complete explanation of either biological or cultural evolution. Thus he held that the diversification which has occurred among organisms cannot be accounted for by any lawlike mechanism such as natural selection. It points rather to the operation of an intrinsic spontaneity in the universe. Furthermore, the principle of continuity implies that evolution is *growth* in the widest sense of the word. But whatever grows must be present in the process from the start. Hence such phenomena as feeling and thought, so far from being late arrivals on the evolutionary scene, have always been in existence, at least in an inchoate form, throughout the cosmos. In man these phenomena have developed through the forming of habits, especially habits involving the use of signs and symbols, to their present state. Accordingly, man's adaptation is primarily to a semiotic environment and only secondarily to a bio-physical one. An adequate pragmatism will therefore conclude that the purposive action into which thought passes, is directed to the increase of concrete reasonableness, and is not simply a bodily response.

Peirce generalized these themes into a "cosmogonic" evolutionism reminiscent of Schelling, to whom he acknowledged his indebtedness. The universe is represented as growing from a state of total randomness in the infinitely distant past towards a state of total order in the infinitely distant future. Cosmic evolution is also represented as beginning with "a chaos of unpersonalized feeling" and ending with "an absolutely perfect, rational, and symmetrical system" in which mind becomes "at last crystallized." What happens in this process is not causally necessitated. Yet it is destined or "fated" to occur, partly because it involves a progressive unfolding of God's purpose in nature. These and other descriptions can hardly be said to form a perspicuous and logically consistent doctrine. In this area of his thought, Peirce's transcendental and religious predilections often led him to make vague, grandiose claims. These claims were not only at variance with the philosophical method he advocated elsewhere, but were also at variance with the principles that guided other pragmatic evolutionists (cf. Wiener, 1949; Goudge, 1950).

VIII. LITERARY EVOLUTIONISM

The influence of the idea of evolution outside the sciences and philosophy is well illustrated by the work of Samuel Butler, Friedrich Nietzsche, and George Bernard Shaw. They were primarily men of letters, and may be taken to represent respectively the fields of the novel, classical philology, and drama. All accepted the idea of descent with modification, but all were hostile to Darwinism and favorable to Lamarckism. They did not, however, embody their objections in scientific or philosophical arguments. They used various literary forms for the expression of their views, and often mingled rhetoric and invective with exposition.

Four broad themes appear in the writings of these literary evolutionists.

(1) They objected to Darwin's admission of chance or accident as an element in the evolutionary process. Butler contended in his *Evolution, Old and New* (1879) that a theory which invoked the notion of accidental variations ultimately failed to account for the origin of species. Erasmus Darwin and Lamarck were, he held, on much firmer ground when they attributed variations to the purposive activity of organisms. Shaw echoed Butler's contention in the Preface to his play, *Back to Methuselah* (1921). The underlying concern appears to have been to block any suggestion that man's mental powers arose by chance, by affirming that like all other organic attributes they are the outcome of what living things have done to meet their needs in the course of evolution.

(2) The literary evolutionists rejected Darwin's theory of natural selection as a mechanistic misconception which assigned far too much importance to the environment. "The influence of 'environment' is nonsensically *over-rated* in Darwin," Nietzsche wrote. "The essential factor in the process of life is precisely the tremendous inner power to shape and create new forms, which merely *uses, exploits* 'environment'" (*The Will to Power*, II, Sec. 647). Butler asserts in *Luck or Cunning?* (1887) that living forms "design themselves . . . into physical conformity with their own intentions." They do so by means of "unconscious memory" which binds the generations together, allowing each to profit from the experience of its ancestors. Shaw ridicules the Darwinian theory which he calls "Circumstantial Selection." It ignores "the simple fact" that the impulse which produces evolution is creative. No matter what the environment, "the will to do anything can and does, at a certain pitch of intensity . . . create and organize new tissue to do it with" (Preface, *Back to Methuselah*).

(3) These vitalistic views were part of the basis on which Nietzsche and Shaw envisaged the possibility of the evolutionary improvement of man. Unlike pre-

Darwinian advocates of human perfectibility, they believed that man has the capacity to surpass himself and to become a new species. But this development will not take place automatically. It has to be initiated by men as they are now. Both writers were vague about the steps needed to set the development going, and also about the distinctive qualities that are to characterize the new type of *homo*—referred to as the *Übermensch* by Nietzsche and as the superman by Shaw. In the Prologue to *Also Sprach Zarathustra* (1883), Nietzsche urged that man must be seen as a transitional being, "a rope tied between beast and *Übermensch*—a rope across an abyss. . . . What is great in man is that he is a bridge and not a goal." Shaw rejected the idea that the superman can be brought about by any program of social reform. What is needed is a profound collaboration with the creative impulse or Life Force whose purposes are being realized in the evolutionary process. Behind this theme lay the recognition that evolutionism, by dissolving the conception of a fixed human essence, had opened up the possibility for man so to arrange things that his descendants will become beings far superior to himself.

(4) Shaw regarded his doctrine of the Life Force as an evolutionary theology. In his plays, prefaces, and speeches he identified the Life Force with God who is striving to make himself. God is affirmed to be not an infinite, omnipotent, and perfect being, but a finite power, limited to working through the process of evolution. The only method he can use in the effort to become perfect is that of trial and error. This accounts for the many failures which mark the history of life. Man is the latest experiment to be tried, and he is still on probation. If he fails to advance God's purpose he will be scrapped, as the numerous extinct species were. "We are not very successful attempts at God," Shaw declared; but we can nevertheless "work towards that ideal, until we get to be supermen, and then super-supermen, and then a world of organisms who have achieved and realized God" ("The Religion of the Future" [1911], p. 35).

Shaw's evolutionary theology was one of a number of formulations of the idea of a finite, developing God advocated in the twentieth century. The idea occurs in William James, Bergson, Samuel Alexander, A. N. Whitehead, and others. It appeared to provide a way of reconciling the presence of a divine power in the world with the suffering, cruelty, and waste exhibited by the evolutionary process. The reconciliation is in fact difficult to achieve. But the attempt to undertake it shows how profoundly evolutionism had penetrated the thought of the times.

IX. RECENT EVOLUTIONISM

During recent decades the explanatory range of the doctrine of evolution has expanded, its conceptual structure has become more intricate, and several further attempts have been made to give it a metaphysical formulation. Evolutionary explanations now occur in biochemistry, cultural anthropology, and relativistic cosmology as well as in biology. Classical Darwinism has been replaced by an enlarged theory of natural selection which does greater justice to the facts of the living world. The changes that have taken place in the history of life are recognized to be extremely complex, and a corresponding complexity has had to be introduced into the conceptual schemes employed to account for those changes. At the same time, interest in schemes of metaphysical evolutionism has continued, especially among philosophically-minded biologists. A brief account of these trends will conclude the present article.

In Darwin's day there was little knowledge of the causes and the nature of variations which occur in populations. The laws of heredity were first worked out by Mendel in 1865, but they did not become widely known until 1900. The laws provided the basis for the science of genetics which advanced rapidly in the first three decades of the twentieth century. During that period geneticists were indifferent or hostile to Darwinian selection. By the fourth decade, however, a theoretical breakthrough had been achieved which enabled R. A. Fisher (1930) and J. B. S. Haldane (1932) to restate the doctrine of natural selection so as to reconcile it with the principles of genetics. The result has come to be known as the "synthetic theory" of evolution which is now generally accepted (J. Huxley, 1943; B. Rensch, 1947; G. G. Simpson, 1949).

The new synthetic theory, like classical Darwinism, undertakes to explain evolutionary changes in naturalistic terms. But it avoids past oversimplifications by correlating a number of causal factors to account for those changes. Hence the theory admits phenomena unrecognized by the Darwinians, such as different rates and levels of evolution, different degrees of selection pressure, evolution without speciation, etc. Furthermore, in the new theory the central feature of selection is differential reproduction, not individual survival. Hence the struggle for existence, the destruction of the unfit, and the survival of the fit become special cases of selection rather than identical with it. T. H. Huxley's "gladiatorial theory of existence" can now be characterized as a Victorian myth (Simpson, 1949).

The causal factors assembled by the synthetic theory purport to explain pre-human biological evolution, but they do not purport to explain what happened after man emerged. For it is conceded that human evolution has been powerfully influenced by cultural factors that man himself has produced. Hence his history has been quite unique among living things. Other animals have been made by natural processes acting on them. Man has very largely made himself by means of culture, a new kind of adaptive mechanism. These facts were systematically underlined by the rise of evolutionary cultural anthropology in the nineteenth century. Works such as Sir Henry Maine's *Ancient Law* (1861), E. B. Tylor's *Primitive Culture* (1871), and Lewis Henry Morgan's *Ancient Society* (1877) laid some of the foundations for a science of cultural evolution. After the turn of the century, interest in this subject waned for a time, but it has recently been revived by the writings of L. A. White (1949), V. G. Childe (1936; 1951), and J. H. Steward (1955). The subject contains many unsolved problems, but evolutionary explanations appear to provide one fruitful way of tackling them (see Dobzhansky, 1962).

At the other end of the scale, evolutionary explanations have been introduced into discussions of the origin of life. Innumerable accounts of how the first living things came to be occurred in ancient religious traditions. But the subject eluded a scientific treatment, so that Darwin could say as late as 1863, "it is mere rubbish, thinking at present of the origin of life." Nevertheless, T. H. Huxley dealt with it in 1868, as did John Tyndall in his Belfast address of 1874. With the rise of twentieth-century biochemistry an evolutionary approach to the subject became possible. A most influential hypothesis was stated by A. I. Oparin (1924; trans. as *The Origin of Life*, New York, 1938) and by Haldane (1929). According to a recent modified version of this hypothesis, life originated by a process of chemical evolution on the earth, before there was free oxygen in its atmosphere. Through the action of ultraviolet light, inorganic material gave rise to organic molecules, which in turn evolved into complex biological polymers having a primitive capacity to reproduce. From these diffused polymers, specific closed organisms developed, culminating in the nucleated cell. At this stage chemical evolution was succeeded by organic evolution (see Bernal, 1967).

This speculative reconstruction recognizes a substantial difference between chemical and organic evolution. Yet the two processes are assumed to have some formal elements in common. "One of these is the concept of the survival of the fittest, of the maintenance of one particular molecular pathway as against others for which certain material substances proved to be lacking" (Bernal, p. 30). It is supposed that random combinations of inorganic elements were subject to a kind of natural selection by which increasingly complex and efficient aggregations were built up. Ultimately one type of aggregation survived, and gave rise to proto-life. Many unsolved problems remain in this area, including that of explaining how the capacity for molecular replication or reproduction could have evolved.

Evolutionary conceptions figure in modern astronomy at two points. (1) There is a well-grounded theory of stellar evolution which concerns the life-cycle of main sequence stars. A developmental pattern has been worked out that specifies a regular succession of phases in a normal star's history. (2) There is also a group of cosmological theories—relativistic descendants of the cosmologies of Descartes, Kant, and Laplace—which are based on evolutionary models. Here accounts of the evolution of the nebulae from a primordial, hyper-dense mass are proposed. These accounts are based partly on mathematical deductions from observations and partly on purely hypothetical interpolations that are not in conflict with observations. Yet as in the case of the origin of life, cosmological evolution is a subject containing many disputed issues.

The spread of evolutionary ideas in the sciences has kept alive an interest in giving the ideas a metaphysical generalization. This interest has been mainly manifested, however, among workers in the life sciences rather than among professional philosophers whose anti-speculative predilections have been strong in recent decades. Accordingly, generalized evolutionism has tended to be lacking in philosophical finesse, and has been little more than a semi-popular extension of scientific material.

In various publications, Sir Julian Huxley has contended that evolution encompasses "all the historical processes of change and development at work in the universe: in fact, it *is* the universe historically regarded" (1960, pp. 20–21). The overall process from "cosmic star-dust to human society" is continuous, yet it has three distinguishable phases which have supervened in the course of time: the cosmological, the biological, and the psycho-social. Each of the phases has its own self-transforming mechanisms, which display increasing efficiency, and so ensure genuine evolutionary progress. Basically, what undergoes evolution, Huxley contends, is "the world stuff." It is per se neither mental nor material, but it has mental and material aspects or "potentialities." Prior to the psycho-social phase, the universe was devoid of purpose. With the appearance of *homo sapiens*, however, purposes entered the cosmic scene. Human purposes allow men to influence the course of evolution, if they so decide, and hence man has become "the sole agent of future evolutionary advance" (1953, p. 132).

187

A materialistic form of evolutionism is advocated by Simpson (1949; 1964). He distinguishes (a) the nonevolutionary dimension of the universe—the enduring properties of matter-energy—from (b) the evolutionary dimension—the temporally successive, cumulative changes of configuration or structure that make up the history of life. The properties in (a) constitute the ultimate causal explanation of events, but historical explanations do have a limited place in relation to (b). Man is unique in being "the highest form of organization of matter and energy" (1949, p. 344). He is the result of a purposeless, materialistic process. But he does exhibit some behavior that is purposeful, and that can be influenced by "an ethical need" within and peculiar to himself. The need impels him to adopt ethical standards for the guidance of his conduct in society, but these standards are relative to changing circumstances, and are never absolute. Simpson stresses man's basic trait of "responsibility." It is through the exercise of this trait at the present critical point of human affairs that *homo sapiens* can ensure either the future welfare of the species or its early extinction. As to whether mankind will face up to that responsibility, Simpson finds no reason for despair, "but a good deal of reason for pessimism."

A more optimistic, religiously-oriented form of evolutionism is presented in the posthumous writings of the Jesuit paleoanthropologist, Teilhard de Chardin (1955 ff.). Like Julian Huxley, he has espoused a grandiose vision of cosmic evolution, or "cosmogenesis," which is orthogenetic in the sense that it depicts evolution as having been marked by a steady increase in the complexity and concentration of the stuff of the universe. This stuff has an external "material face," but inwardly it is psychical or spiritual. In its evolution, successive thresholds of integration have been passed, so that each later level is more intensely concentrated or "involuted" than its predecessors. The human level has added to the planet a new envelope, the "noosphere," which has been superimposed on the biosphere. The concentration engendered by the noosphere will make possible further human evolution. Its outer manifestation will be the forming of a single world-culture, and its inner state will be the melding of individual consciousnesses in a Hyper-Personal Consciousness "at a point which we might call Omega." Teilhard's concept of Point Omega is obscure, like much else in his evolutionism. Apparently, Omega is God, insofar as He determines the direction and constitutes the goal of cosmic history. The melding of personal consciousnesses at Omega will be achieved by the power of love, which forms *"le Milieu divin"* within which evolution takes place. All this represents the expression of a mystical outlook having little concern with precise ideas or with the relation of what is affirmed to any evidence.

It is plain that evolutionism is a family of conceptions having great vitality and viability. Its long, influential history is likely to be matched by its continuing future impact on man's thinking about the world and about himself.

BIBLIOGRAPHY

J. D. Bernal, *The Origin of Life* (Cleveland and New York, 1967). Chapter 2 contains an interesting account of the history of ideas on the origin of life. G. L. L., Comte de Buffon, *Histoire naturelle générale et particulière* (Paris, 1783), IV, 382. Tze Tuan Chen, "Twenty Five Centuries Before Charles Darwin," *The Scientific Monthly,* **29** (1929), 49–52. V. G. Childe, *Man Makes Himself* (London, 1936); idem, *Social Evolution* (London, 1951). Sir Gavin de Beer, *Charles Darwin,* Natural History Library edition (New York, 1965), by far the best available account of Darwin's work. T. Dobzhansky, *Mankind Evolving* (New Haven and London, 1962), a comprehensive discussion with numerous historical references. L. Eiseley, *Darwin's Century: Evolution and the Men Who Discovered It* (New York, 1958), an excellent, brief history of evolutionary thought. A. G. N. Flew, *Evolutionary Ethics* (London, 1967). Sir R. A. Fisher, *The Genetical Theory of Natural Selection* (Oxford, 1930). M. T. Ghiselin, *The Triumph of the Darwinian Method* (Berkeley and Los Angeles, 1969). C. C. Gillispie, *Genesis and Geology* (Cambridge, Mass., 1951); idem, "Lamarck and Darwin in the History of Science," *Forerunners of Darwin* (Baltimore, 1959), pp. 265–91; idem, *The Edge of Objectivity* (Princeton, 1960). Chapters VII and VIII are particularly relevant to the present article. B. Glass, O. Temkin, and W. L. Straus, Jr., eds., *Forerunners of Darwin: 1745–1859* (Baltimore, 1959). The fifteen essays in this book are indispensable for the understanding of evolutionism in the century before Darwin. B. Glass, "Maupertuis, Pioneer of Genetics and Evolution," *Forerunners of Darwin,* pp. 51–83. T. A. Goudge, *The Thought of C. S. Peirce* (Toronto, 1950); idem, *The Ascent of Life: A Philosophical Study of the Theory of Evolution* (London and Toronto, 1961). J. C. Greene, *The Death of Adam: Evolution and Its Impact on Western Thought* (Ames, Iowa, 1959). A well-documented history. W. K. C. Guthrie, *A History of Greek Philosophy,* Vol. I (Cambridge, 1962). F. C. Haber, *The Ages of the World: Moses to Darwin* (Baltimore, 1959). J. B. S. Haldane, *The Causes of Evolution* (London, 1932); idem, "The Origin of Life" (1929), in *Science and Life: Essays of a Rationalist* (London, 1968), pp. 1–11. Sir Julian Huxley, *Evolution: The Modern Synthesis* (London, 1943); idem, *Evolution in Action* (London, 1953); idem, *Knowledge, Morality and Destiny* (New York, 1960), also published with the title *New Bottles for New Wine* (New York, 1957). A. O. Lovejoy, "Buffon and the Problem of Species," *Forerunners of Darwin,* pp. 84–113; idem, "Some Eighteenth Century Evolutionists," *The Scientific Monthly,* **71** (1950), 162–78; idem, *The Great Chain of Being* (Cambridge, Mass., 1936); idem, "Schopenhauer as an Evolutionist," *The Monist,* **21** (1911), 195–222. These works are examples of the history of ideas at its best. J. Needham, *Science and Civilization in China,* Vol. II, *History of Scientific Thought* (Cambridge, 1956). E. Nordenskiöld, *Biologins Historia,* 3 vols. (Stockholm, 1920–24), trans. as *The History of Biology* (New York, 1929). Despite some inaccuracies, this work is a valuable source of ideas on the interrelations of biology, philosophy, and cultural history. B. Rensch, *Neuere Probleme der Abstammungslehre* (Stuttgart, 1947), trans. of the 2nd ed., *Evolution Above the Species Level* (New York, 1960). G. B. Shaw, *The Prefaces* (London, 1934); idem, *The Religious Speeches of Bernard Shaw* (University Park, Pa., 1963), contains the essay, "The Religion of the Future" (1911). G. G. Simpson, *The Meaning of Evolution* (New Haven, 1949; rev. ed. 1967), the best introduction to the new synthetic theory of evolution; idem, *The Principles of Animal Taxonomy* (New York, 1961); idem, *This View of Life: The World of an Evolutionist* (New York, 1964). Part One contains interesting material on the history of the doctrine of evolution. N. Smart, *Doctrine and Argument in Indian Philosophy* (London, 1964). J. H. Steward, *Theory of Culture Change* (Urbana, 1955). P. Teilhard de Chardin, *Oeuvres,* 9 vols. to date (Paris, 1955 ff.). The most widely read of the works is probably *Le Phénomène humain* (1955); trans. Bernard Wall as *The Phenomenon of Man* (New York and London, 1959). C. H. Waddington, *The Ethical Animal* (London, 1960). L. A. White, *The Science of Culture* (New York, 1949). P. P. Wiener, *Evolution and the Founders of Pragmatism* (Cambridge, Mass., 1949).

THOMAS A. GOUDGE

[See also **Biological Conceptions in Antiquity;** Chain of Being; Evolution of Literature; **Genetic Continuity;** God; Inheritance Through Pangenesis; Pragmatism; **Progress; Recapitulation;** Spontaneous Generation; Uniformitarianism.]

EXISTENTIALISM

A PHILOSOPHICAL movement is often named not by the philosophers who are taken to be its representatives, but rather by its opponents, by those who observe from the outside a community of thought amongst certain thinkers, and who give the name to what they regard as a trend in order to be able to refute or attack it. It is only the minor followers, usually not the great innovators, who adopt the label of their own accord. This is certainly the case with existentialism; indeed the name has more often been applied as a term of abuse than as a neutral description. There would, however, be general agreement that the three major figures to whom the term "existentialist" can rightly be applied are Soren Kierkegaard, Martin Heidegger, and Jean-Paul Sartre. Kierkegaard did not use the term,

and would probably not have thought of himself as a philosopher; Heidegger has stated that his "philosophical tendencies cannot be classed as existentialism"; Sartre, we are told by Merleau-Ponty, only admitted to being an existentialist because he was so frequently called one that he felt that it was his duty to accept the label. Thus it is impossible to look for a definition of the term from any of the major proponents of the doctrine, though Sartre has come closest to providing one in his lecture *L'Existentialisme est un humanisme* of 1946, which was intended as a general description rather than a statement of his own views. It is in this lecture, later published as a book with the same title, that occurs the famous phrase "Existence is prior to essence," which is explained as meaning that subjectivity must be the starting-point of philosophy, that the human individual is the central concern of all legitimate metaphysical thinking.

Once any philosophical statement has been made it is possible to find hints of it in previous writers, to attribute priority to anyone who used similar forms of words, even though their main line of thought in reality had been very different. However, it is only in the writings of Kierkegaard that there can be detected a distinctive philosophical viewpoint that stresses the existence of the individual as against his essence, the particular character of a man as opposed to what he shares with all other men. It is to this that the name "existentialism" will be given here. Certainly many philosophers and religious thinkers, such as Saint Augustine in his *Confessions,* and Pascal in his *Pensées,* lay stress on individual responsibility, though they do this in the context of a universal metaphysics. Kierkegaard is the first to assert that "Truth is subjectivity," that "All essential knowledge relates to existence, or only such knowledge as has an essential relationship to existence is essential knowledge" (*CUPS,* p. 176). He also emphasizes the absurdity of this knowledge; the notion of the absurd being another feature which unites thinkers who can be called existentialist. For Kierkegaard this absurdity is manifest in the doctrines of Christianity: "The absurd is—that the eternal truth has come into being in time, that God has come into being, has been born, has grown up, and so forth, precisely like any other individual human being . . ." (*CUPS,* p. 188).

The emphasis on individuality and on absurdity has frequently led to a romantic element in existentialist writing, and has partly been the source of its popular appeal. It is no accident that many existentialists are literary figures as well as philosophers, Sartre being perhaps the most conspicuous example, though Gabriel Marcel has written many plays, and Albert Camus was better known for his literary than for his theoretical works. Critics of existentialists claim that their writings are full of exaggerations. Their tendency to think in terms of individuals, frequently in extreme situations which are one of the staples of the novel and the drama, the appeal of their arguments to the emotions rather than to the reason of the reader, have given weight to the charge. Though Kierkegaard wrote no novels, his style is intensely personal and is connected with the central drama of his life to an extent unknown in most philosophers. This drama was his engagement to a young girl, Regina Olsen, with whom he was deeply in love and who reciprocated his affection. However, Kierkegaard was convinced that he should not marry, owing to his father's sin and his own sense of mission. He persuaded her to break off the engagement by convincing her that he was unworthy. Much of his voluminous writing is connected with this episode, and many of the books were dedicated to Regina; indeed, knowledge of this episode is necessary to understand both the contents and the elaborate pseudonyms under which many were published, though there were also philosophic reasons for the latter. To an unsympathetic reader, Kierkegaard's whole attitude seems morbid and unhealthy, and the same charge has been brought against other existentialists. One writer has even said: "I should be inclined to regard it almost as a touchstone or criterion of an author's being classifiable as an Existentialist, that a reader may get impatient and accuse him of gross exaggeration and pretentiousness; that the reader may be inclined to deflate him and 'boil down' what he seems to be saying to some true but absolutely platitudinous remark" (Mary Warnock, *Existentialist Ethics* [1967], p. 6). To some extent this remark would be accepted by existentialists, for one of their targets has always been complacency, the attitude that the world is basically in order as it is. Kierkegaard attacked the "Christians" of his day, who thought that baptism and confirmation were sure evidence of Christianity and who failed to realize the paradox and difficulty of true faith. Heidegger and Sartre also mocked the complacent. The aim of all three, and of most others who can be described as "existentialists," was to expose the illusions of everyday life and recall men to a more serious view of their responsibilities. For this purpose exaggeration and paradox, concentration on the seamier side of life, are obvious techniques; an appeal to the emotions of the reader is as important as to his reason. Hence even the philosophers among the existentialists employ techniques rejected by those who regard reason as the only element in man worthy of attention, and who think of the emotions as merely distracting to the intellect.

It is this concentration on the emotional, the subjective element, that gives, or has given, existentialism its popular appeal. And the resentment which the movement has aroused in many philosophers of other schools is partly due to their jealousy of such a mass appeal. Sartre's famous example of the uselessness of moral rules to a man in an extreme situation is obviously capable of speaking to many to whom the detailed analyses of traditional moral philosophy would be boring or unhelpful. Sartre takes the case of the young man who, after the fall of France in 1940, is faced with the dilemma whether to escape to England to carry on the fight with the Free French Forces or to stay and look after his mother, who is in need of his attention if she is to survive the hardships of the time. The moral rules "Do your duty to your country" and "Honor thy father and mother" here come into conflict, and there is no *superior* moral rule which can be invoked to decide between them. If there were, there would be no problem. What advice could Sartre (or anyone else) offer? In one sense even the act of asking for advice is not a neutral matter, for the choice of an advisor is also the choice of the kind of advice that will be given; a priest who has preached obedience to the new government will tell him to stay, as his higher duty lies with his mother. A member of the Resistance will tell him to try and leave the country. Any attempt to take advice as if it were neutral will in fact be a decision. In the last resort the young man can only decide, choose one moral rule to be followed and the other to be disobeyed. And this example is to be seen as the true model of all moral choices. The smug, the comfortable, and the bourgeois pretend that there are moral rules written into the nature of things, but this is a device of *bad faith* or *inauthenticity*, an attempt to hide from one's self the agony of choosing.

Kierkegaard's attack upon Christendom contained similar elements. The comfortable Christians of his day failed to realize the paradoxical nature of their belief in Christ, to see the difficulty of claiming that the infinite Creator had come to earth in the form of a man. Further, such a belief must make a radical difference to the believer's life; it could not be satisfied in perfunctory attendance at church one day a week. What was needed was *authentic* Christianity, as distinct from the watered-down version preached from the Danish pulpits of his time. Here again the authentic individual is the one who stands out from the crowd, who does not try to escape from the burden of choice by doing what everyone else does. In fact Kierkegaard was among the first to stress the growth of the anonymous crowd and the dangers to individuality arising from it.

This concentration on the personal, the subjective, the authentic individual who makes his choice without reference to "what *they* will think," made existentialism popular in times of crisis; it is no accident that the movement had its greatest appeal in wartime and in the immediate postwar period, particularly in France. The stress on individual choice was obviously relevant to the many Frenchmen who found themselves in the same position as Sartre's young man. With the return of more settled social conditions, the need for such agonizing personal choices became rarer; at the same time it became evident that the state of the world is too complex for the isolated individual to affect it by his own action, that some sort of concerted effort is needed. Sartre's own development reflects this; he begins with an almost anarchic individualism, in which the moral soundness of the person is all that matters, and progresses to a modified Marxism, wherein his earlier existentialism is reduced to a mere facet of the total system of thought. Authenticity comes to seem impossible unless social conditions are appropriate: "In a curved space it is impossible to draw a straight line," as one of the characters in Simone de Beauvoir's novel *Les Mandarins* expresses it. De Beauvoir's writings are very similar to those of Sartre himself.

What is remarkable about existentialism is the extent to which a movement whose central figures were often obscure and technical in their writings should appeal to a large number of people who normally would have shown no interest in philosophical works. No doubt many of them failed to understand the details of the discussion; certainly more people bought copies of *L'Etre et le néant* or of *Sein und Zeit* than could have fully understood them. But for a considerable period of the twentieth century, existentialism was a philosophical movement that numbered many nonphilosophically trained people among its adherents. Certainly the plays and novels of Sartre were important in this popularizing, but they were so because the central themes of authenticity and moral choice, of the individual as isolated in a hostile world, seemed to reflect the experience of the period.

From an Anglo-Saxon point of view it may have seemed that all Continental philosophy was existentialist in character; this of course is an illusion. Throughout the period the majority of academic philosophers in Europe were pursuing their own lines of thought, even though "intellectual circles" in those countries were thinking in existentialist terms. This wide popularity no longer exists, though there are still those who find existentialist writers have something important to say to them. Hence it is possible, at least in outline, to trace the rise and fall of existentialism as an intellectual movement in the persons of its central proponents. To do this in full would require a detailed examination of the influence of the events of their day on the

thinkers in question, as well as their influence on the events. However, here their main lines of thought are sketched and it is indicated why existentialism had the effects it did.

Though Kierkegaard can be called the founder of the movement, his views did not penetrate the intellectual world immediately; this was partly because the time was not ripe for them to have an effect, and partly because he wrote in Danish and it was some time before German or other translations were available. English versions of his writings only appeared in the thirties and forties of the twentieth century. Kierkegaard's influence was not always decisive; Marcel reached his main conclusions before he had read the Danish thinker. Kierkegaard only turned to philosophy because of an objection to the way religion, or more specifically Christianity, was treated in the work of Hegel. To an extent which it is hard to realize nowadays, Hegel's was the dominant philosophy of the age; attacks on his system were thought to be attacks on philosophy itself. He claimed that philosophy, as the science of sciences, transcended and incorporated all other modes of thought, including art and religion. Christianity was, as it were, rationally reconstructed to take its place in the vast structure. Even those who objected tended to write in Hegelian terms, as is obvious in the case of both Marx and Engels and of Kierkegaard himself. Instead of the dialectical progress of Hegel, Kierkegaard substituted a series of dialectical leaps. In 1843 Kierkegaard, as well as Engels, attended lectures in Berlin by Schelling, who had been appointed by the Prussian government in an attempt to undo Hegel's influence. Some features of Kierkegaard's thought, such as the notion of man being his own choice, were derived from these lectures, though the particular cast given them was his.

His basic idea is that personal existence cannot be comprehended in a system; he compares Hegel to a man who constructs a vast palace and then lives in a hovel at its gates. For "existence corresponds to the individual thing," and in such a system there is no room for the individual, only for abstract concepts. He summed it up: "A logical system is possible, an existential system impossible." Whatever universal rules may be established, the following of a rule is always a matter of individual decision. In fact the ethical represents the universal; it refers man to a set of rules which render his conduct comprehensible to observers. When Agamemnon sacrificed Iphigenia in order that the fleet could sail for Troy, or Brutus ordered the execution of his traitorous sons, they made a hard or tragic choice. Even though their actions were commanded by laws publicly acknowledged, it was still open to them to hold back; their obedience gave their actions a heroic character. But what they did was public, could be understood by others because it was done in accordance with public rules, even if those others would have been incapable of emulating them. But when Abraham decided to sacrifice Isaac, Kierkegaard claims in *Fear and Trembling*, the situation was totally different. There were no public reasons for the deed, no obvious external ends to be gained by it, nor were the reasons which he could have given ones which others could have acknowledged, for he had a private command from God. Whatever may be the function of the story in the Old Testament, Kierkegaard takes it as the prime example of what he calls "the teleological suspension of the ethical." For the ethical demands that the father should love his son, the religious that he should sacrifice him; the religious command is "higher" and so must be obeyed. Kierkegaard's own refusal to marry Regina, in spite of his praise of marriage in *Either/Or* is relevant here.

The whole of the relation of an individual to God is an example of this suspension of the ethical or universal; for if God were an object whose existence could be established in the normal way, then we should *know* that He existed. There would be no virtue in such a belief; it would not differ from that in any natural object. For the central feature of religious belief is a relation between the individual and God; hence public standards of proof are out of place. Hence "Faith is this paradox, that the individual as the particular is higher than the universal, is justified over against it. . . . This position cannot be mediated, for all mediation comes about precisely by virtue of the universal" (*FT*, p. 66). The knowledge obtained in this way makes the individual what he really is; it is existential knowledge. The paradox is manifest in that faith involves a relation between the temporal and the eternal, both in the story of the life and passion of Christ and in the fact that faith involves a relation between the finite believer and an infinite God. This can only come about by a "leap" of faith: "But can anyone comprehend this Christian doctrine? By no means. . . . It must be believed. Comprehension is coterminous with man's relation to the human, but faith is man's relation to the Divine" (*SD*, p. 226). There can be no rational justification of faith to the nonbeliever, and the believer needs none, unless the passionate choice itself is considered a justification. In this sense truth is subjectivity.

Many theologians have developed views based on Kierkegaard; notable examples of such "existential theologizing" are Karl Barth, Rudolf Bultmann, Paul Tillich, and Dietrich Bonhoeffer. In various ways these have attempted to strip Christianity of the metaphysical accretions which they regard as inessential, and to put emphasis on some kind of relation, an "existential" one, between man and God. To many Christians their views seem to be near atheism, for the kind of "demythologizing" which they have found necessary in order to give Christianity a meaning in the modern world has similarities with Kierkegaard's "attack on Christendom," and, as in his case, there is an inevitable suspicion that the baby has been thrown out with the bath water. Some sayings of Kierkegaard seem very close to atheism, for example the remark in his diary: "When a concrete individual lacks faith, then neither does God exist, nor is God present, albeit God, eternally understood, is eternal." It is not difficult to understand why Kierkegaard can be held partially responsible for the atheistic trend of many who followed him, notably Heidegger and Sartre.

For to make the relation between man and God into something purely individual, mediated by no organization or body of public standards, is to be in danger of making Him into something like the choice of a person rather than an independently existing Being. If the "leap of faith" is a private and unjustifiable act, validated only by what happens after the leap is taken, the status of God becomes peculiar; certainly no evidence of His existence can be sought in the world. This is not to claim that Kierkegaard is responsible for the atheism of other philosophers, but only to point out that the ambiguous character of his religiosity makes it possible for much of what he says to be incorporated into a system which is fundamentally atheist, such as that of Sartre. Indeed, Sartre's arguments against the existence of God might be seen as taking what Kierkegaard demanded and claiming that it was in principle unsatisfiable. Nietzsche talked of the "Death of God" in the modern world, by which he meant that the existence of God was no longer a simple and natural fact as it was for men in earlier centuries; Kierkegaard's frantic search for faith can be seen as an expression of the same feeling.

One important difference between Kierkegaard and Heidegger and Sartre is that they are professional philosophers, concerned with teaching the subject and with presenting their ideas in a form which will be acceptable to their colleagues. Hence their writings contain reference to other philosophers and discussions of questions which might not have appeared to Kierkegaard relevant to the matter in hand. For another central influence on both Heidegger and Sartre was the phenomenologist, Edmund Husserl, who formalized the philosophic method both men later used. Heidegger was Husserl's pupil and later succeeded him in the chair at Freiburg.

In spite of his disclaimers, Heidegger's *Sein und Zeit* (*Being and Time*) has had a wide influence as an existentialist work. In this book the central concern is the analysis of *Dasein*, an almost untranslatable term which refers to the way in which human beings, as distinct from things, exist. It is this analysis which has facilitated the existentialist reading. For *Dasein* can only be understood in terms of human existence, the way in which it lives its life, never in terms of its essence. Normally this life is "inauthentic." Heidegger claims that this is not a moral term, though the use he makes of it shows that an inauthentic life is lacking in important respects.

Dasein has three important characteristics; the first is "facticity," the fact that I exist in an already existing world which is *my* world, which could no more exist without me than could I without it. Things in the world are not experienced as mere material objects but as tools, things "ready to hand" to be used in ways which are defined for me by the structure of this world. Heidegger also talks of this as *Geworfenheit*, "thrownness," the fact that I am born into a world which I did not make and which hence sets limits for me.

The second feature is "existentiality": "*Dasein* is not a thing which has additionally the gift of being able to do something, but it is primarily possibility." I live my life as a series of "projects," and so in the future as much as in the present. My life is "transcendent" in the sense of always going beyond the merely given. My personal time is different from that marked by watches and calendars; a future event (or a past one) may be more "present" to me than that which is chronologically present.

Thirdly there is "forfeiture," the way in which *Dasein* is distracted from the realization of its true being by the claims of everyday life, of the trivial and the inessential. We live mostly in the inauthentic world of *das Man*, "one" or "they" as in "They expect it of me." The analyses of this anonymous crowd which plays such a part in our lives is a striking feature of *Sein und Zeit*.

Dasein is free, yet in everyday life it is enslaved. But unless there were some central "I" there would be nothing to be enslaved; the reality of *Dasein* may be hidden by the everydayness of the world, it cannot be extinguished. Two things reveal *Dasein*, dread (*Angst*) and death. These involve a relation to *Nothing*. Heidegger's talk of "nothing" as if it were a kind of thing has often been criticized by analytic philosophers; it has been compared to the King's mistake in *Alice through the Looking-Glass* of talking of "nobody" as if it were the name of a person. It is possible to see why Heidegger, and later Sartre in a slightly different manner, found it necessary to use the term. It should be remembered that many mystics have also found it necessary to use the term in connection with the "Dark night of the soul." Dread, as distinct from

normal emotions, is not directed to any particular thing; it is, as Kierkegaard said in the *Concept of Dread*, dread of no thing, of *nothing*. Further, for Heidegger, human freedom or "transcendence" involves nothingness; in that *Dasein* is not determined in its actions, the human project is free: "Without this original manifest character of Nothing there is no selfhood and no freedom." Sartre later characterizes human reality in a similar way, as that being "who is not what he is and is what he is not," again to stress the openness of human existence, its freedom. Further, for Heidegger dread is connected with death; the only thing which each person must do for himself alone is to die. The contemplation of my ultimate possibility, death, is an essential feature of authentic living; the realization of the fact that I must die makes possible a proper understanding of my own *Dasein*. Dread is not a morbid state to be avoided. A fictional representation similar to Heidegger's analysis of the way in which the contemplation of death can alter a whole attitude to life is given in Tolstoy's story *The Death of Ivan Ilyitch*.

It is now possible to see the relation between Heidegger's thought and Husserl's phenomenology. Husserl's motto was "Back to the things themselves," by which he meant back to our actual experience without the layer of common sense and scientific presuppositions which hide the "experienced phenomena" from us. Dread is something which we experience and hence must be described with as much care as would normally be spent on more "objective" experiences. Again, that material objects present themselves as tools first, as material objects only as the result of thought, is a result of the phenomenological method, namely, of inspecting experience. Heidegger's use of phenomenology was criticized by Husserl, but it is clear that the attempt to view experience without the normal presuppositions was an essential element of *Sein und Zeit* and one factor making for its appeal.

One important point stands out: Heidegger's man is an essentially solitary individual whose relations with his fellows only occur at the level of forfeiture, as part of the anonymous world of *das Man*. Each person must seek his own relation with Being via the contemplation of his own death. Here, and in his emphasis on dread, Heidegger is like Kierkegaard. The difference between them lies in the fact that the relation to Being is not at all like that to a personal God; indeed, it is not clear from *Sein und Zeit* what this relation should be. It is only when it is read in the context of Heidegger's later works that his central point becomes clear. It was the negative analyses of human experience which struck the readers of the book in the years following its publication and which made Heidegger into an influential existentialist despite his expressed intention.

Jean-Paul Sartre is in one respect the most significant of those considered here, for his development has been a move from a full-blooded existentialism to a modified Marxism. His reasons were basically a dissatisfaction with extreme individualism as a guide to moral choice. For Sartre is first and foremost a moralist, even though his major early work *L'Etre et le néant* is described as an "essay in phenomenological ontology." The influence of Husserl and Heidegger is always visible, though he is often critical of them. Authenticity is the aim of life, and it is clear that for Sartre it is a moral value. Its opposite is "bad faith," the attempt to claim that values or personality are given, are part of the order of nature instead of the result of choice. The waiter in a café, in a famous analysis, is shown to be "playing at being a waiter," trying to conceal from himself the fact that it is his own choice which drives him to work for long hours, etc. The striking analyses which occur in *L'Etre et le néant* are paralleled in many cases by fictional representations in Sartre's large output of plays and novels. For many people the first introduction to existentialism has been through these, rather than through his more philosophical writings. However, Sartre is too good a writer to transfer his philosophy direct to the stage; to take the expressions of the characters in plays and novels as statements of his philosophical views often leads to error. The remark at the end of *Huis clos*, "Hell is other people," is not his considered judgment on the world but is meant as evidence of the bad faith of the character uttering it.

Bad faith is a belief in the lack of freedom: that a person acts as he does because of his character or because of his situation, the position into which he was born. Sartre wished to assert an absolute freedom, to regard everything that is done as the result of a choice. Material objects are what they are, can only behave in circumscribed ways; human beings contain nothingness, are separate from their situation in that they can imagine alternatives. It is his "project" that makes a man what he is, and the fundamental project is "choice of one's self." Orthodox psychoanalysis is wrong to think of complexes as existing in the unconscious; they are really choices which bad faith has suppressed. Sartre's "existential psychoanalysis" has as its object the uncovering of the fundamental project to enable it to be changed. Detailed examples of the procedure are given in his books on Baudelaire and Genet.

A person might also seem to be limited by his situation, by the fact that he was born at such a time of such parents and possesses such physical characteristics. Sartre argues that these are not really limitations if viewed correctly. To take an extreme case, a physical disability is not a limitation, but a particular way of existing in the world. The only possible existence for human beings is embodied existence, and to have a body is to have limitations. Given our original body it is how we react to it, whether we make it an excuse for failure or treat it as an obstacle to overcome, which manifests our freedom. We can only exist in an environment, and every environment gives a full range of human possibilities. It might seem that gravitation is a restriction on freedom of action, but in fact without it it is almost impossible to *do* anything at all; without some resistance or friction there is nothing to push against. Similarly, choice can only take place in a concrete situation; we may imagine that if some things were different our life would be easier, but this is due to the incompleteness of the imagined life.

Values also are chosen, not given. The young man already mentioned chooses not just a course of action by deciding to join the Free French Forces, but a *value*, in that his choice is implicitly of what anyone in the same situation should do. It is this that makes it a choice rather than an arbitrary act. If there were a given set of values, it would be possible to choose in accordance with them, but Sartre wishes to represent all, or all important, choices as choice of values. Hence no rational argument in favor of one choice over against another can be given. This view is often regarded as irrationalism, but Sartre's point is that even criteria of rationality are not given by the nature of the universe, they also have to be chosen. Sartre refers to those who believe that values are given in the same way as physical facts as *salauds* and equates them with the bourgeois. Thus his attack on this class precedes his Marxism; to a great extent he is following the attitude of many French writers and artists of the late nineteenth and early twentieth centuries who felt it necessary to *épater les bourgeois*. He is attacking a mental attitude rather than an economic group, a belief that basically everything is in order as it is, that man possesses rights in the way in which objects possess properties. This belief is a failure to glimpse the nothingness that lies at the heart of man.

Sartre, like Heidegger, provided a devastating negative analysis of the human condition. With great skill he shows up the shifts and evasions that are ordinarily used to escape responsibility, to cover up the fact of choice. Everyone is shown to be infected with bad faith. But when the time comes for advice, for instruction on how an authentic choice is to be made, Sartre seems to confine himself to the bare command to choose. Because of the analysis he has given, no positive recommendations can be made, for these would themselves become given values and so a source of bad faith. It is significant that *L'Etre et le néant* closes with the words: "These questions . . . can be answered only on a moral level. I will devote my next work to them." No such work has so far appeared; also, the fourth volume of the series of novels *Paths to Freedom* (*Les Chemins de la liberté*), which was to show how the characters whose inauthenticity had been exposed in the first three books managed at last to achieve authenticity, has never been completed in spite of Sartre's efforts to do so. Sartre has found it easier to show what is wrong with everyday human life than to provide a sketch of the right way to live. Heidegger evades this issue by a shift of interest to the question of Being, whereas Sartre's solution is more traditional, invoking the concept of cooperative action. Authentic existence can only be shared by a group. It is this which leads to his modified Marxism, which is certainly not that of the normal party member. His relations with the Party have been complex; he has often been attacked for his "bourgeois idealism." He looks on Marxism as primarily a moral doctrine, and as political only insofar as just political conditions are necessary for moral action to become possible. In *Critique de la raison dialectique*, existentialism is reduced to the level of an "ideology," something limited in contrast to Marxism which is the "unsurpassable philosophy of our time." Many of the earlier insights seem to have been denied.

In many ways Sartre's abandonment of existentialism in the late nineteen-fifties can be seen as the end of the movement, and his conversion to Marxism as a recognition that more is needed than analyses of the human condition. Not all of those who earlier followed him have taken the same path as Sartre, but the defection of the man who was the most popular of all existentialists is bound to make a significant difference to them. Existentialism never was an organized movement, but was a loose grouping of like-thinking people who found the analyses given by the writers discussed here appropriate to the historical circumstances in which they found themselves. In one sense there have been as many existentialisms as existentialists. That such a movement should have arisen is itself significant, and in spite of its ambiguous nature, twentieth-century thought would have been different and less interesting without it.

BIBLIOGRAPHY

General Works. H. J. Blackham, *Six Existentialist Thinkers* (London, 1952), and F. H. Heinemann, *Existentialism and the Modern Predicament* (London, 1953), give good accounts. R. G. Olson, *An Introduction to Existentialism* (New York, 1962), compares the existentialists with the American pragmatists. Mary Warnock, *Existentialist Ethics* (London and New York, 1967), is a good brief survey (57 pages). A special number of the *Revue Internationale de Philosophie* (1949) contains bibliographies of the subject.

Kierkegaard. The standard life of Kierkegaard is W. Lowrie, *Kierkegaard* (London and New York, 1938). It contains a bibliography. G. E. and G. B. Arbaugh, *Kierkegaard's Authorship* (London, 1968), contains summaries of all his books. Kierkegaard's own comments are contained in *The Point of View for My Work as an Author* (1859), trans. W. Lowrie (Princeton, 1939; reprint New York, 1962). Works mentioned in the text: *The Concept of Dread* (1844), trans. W. Lowrie (Princeton, 1944); *Concluding Unscientific Postscript* (1846), trans. D. Swenson (Princeton, 1941); *Fear and Trembling* (1843), trans., with *The Sickness unto Death* (1849), W. Lowrie (Princeton, 1941); *Either/Or* (1843), Vol. I, trans. D. & L. Swenson; Vol. II, W. Lowrie (Princeton, 1944).

Heidegger. His major work on which the existentialist interpretation rests is *Sein und Zeit* (Halle, 1927); *Being and Time* (London and New York, 1962), trans. Macquarrie and E. Robinson. A summary of *Sein und Zeit* together with translations of some of his later works is given in: Martin Heidegger, *Existence and Being*, introduction by W. Brock (London, 1949). A short account occurs in M. Grene, *Martin Heidegger* (Cambridge, 1957).

Sartre. F. Jeanson, *Le problème moral et la pensée de Sartre* (Paris, 1947, new edition Paris, 1967), has won the approval of Sartre. There are several English works on Sartre: Anthony Manser, *Sartre* (London, 1966; New York, 1967), contains a complete bibliography of Sartre's writings up to 1964. Works mentioned in the text are: *L'Etre et le néant* (Paris, 1943), trans. H. Barnes as *Being and Nothingness* (New York, 1956); *L'Existentialisme est un humanisme* (Paris, 1946), trans. B. Frechtmann as *Existentialism* (New York, 1947); *Huis clos* (Paris, 1947), trans. S. Gilbert as *In Camera* (London, 1946), as *No Exit* (New York, 1947); *Baudelaire* (Paris, 1947), trans. M. Turnell (New York, 1950); *Saint Genet* (Paris, 1952), trans. B. Frechtmann (New York, 1963); *Critique de la raison dialectique* (Paris, 1960); *Les Chemins de la liberté: L'Age de raison* (Paris, 1945), trans. E. Sutton (New York, 1947); *Le Sursis* (Paris, 1945), trans. E. Sutton as *Reprieve* (New York, 1947); *La Mort dans l'âme* (Paris, 1949), trans. G. Hopkins as *Iron in the Soul* (London, 1950), and as *Troubled Sleep*, (New York, 1951); *Drôle d'amitié* (*Temps Modernes*, Nos. 49 & 50); this is part of the projected fourth volume, *La Dernière chance*.

Camus. J. Cruickshank, *Albert Camus and the Literature of Revolt* (Oxford, 1959), discusses how far he can be regarded as an existentialist.

Marcel. *Etre et avoir* (Paris, 1935), trans. K. Farrer as *Being and Having* (London, 1949); *Homo Viator* (Paris, 1944), trans. E. Crauford (London, 1951; reprint New York).

ANTHONY MANSER

[See also God; Irrationalism; **Marxism; Romanticism.**]

EXPERIMENTAL SCIENCE AND MECHANICS IN THE MIDDLE AGES

THE SCIENTIFIC revolution of the seventeenth century had its remote antecedents in Greek and early medieval thought. In the period from the thirteenth to the sixteenth centuries, this heritage gradually took shape in a series of methods and ideas that formed the background for the emergence of modern science. The methods adumbrated were mainly those of experimentation and mathematical analysis, while the concepts were primarily, though not exclusively, those of the developing science of mechanics. The history of their evolution may be divided conveniently on the basis of centuries: (1) the thirteenth, a period of beginnings and reformulation; (2) the fourteenth, a period of development and culmination; and (3) the fifteenth and sixteenth, a period of dissemination and transition. By the onset of the seventeenth century considerable material was at hand for a new synthesis of methods and ideas, namely that of classical science.

I

Experimental science owes its beginnings in Western Europe to the influx of treatises from the Near East, by way of translations from Greek and Arabic, which gradually acquainted the Schoolmen with the entire Aristotelian corpus and with the computational techniques of antiquity. The new knowledge merged with an Augustinian tradition prevalent in the universities, notably at Oxford and at Paris, deriving from the Church Fathers; this tradition owed much to Platonism and Neo-Platonism, and already was favorably disposed toward a mathematical view of reality. The empirical orientation and systematization of Aristotle were welcomed for their value in organizing the natural history and observational data that had survived the Dark Ages through the efforts of encyclopedists, while the new methods of calculation found a ready reception among those with mathematical interests. The result was the appearance of works, first at Oxford and then at Paris, which heralded the beginnings of modern science in the Middle Ages.

1. Origins at Oxford. Aristotle's science and his methodology could not be appreciated until his *Physics* and *Posterior Analytics* had been read and understood in the universities. Among the earliest Latin commentators to make the works of Aristotle thus available was Robert Grosseteste, who composed the first full-length exposition of the *Posterior Analytics* shortly after 1200. This work, plus a briefer commentary on the *Physics* and the series of opuscula on such topics as light and the rainbow, served as the stimulus for other scientific writings at Oxford. Taken collectively, their

authors formed a school whose philosophical orientation has been characterized as the "metaphysics of light," but which did not preclude their doing pioneer work in experimental methodology.

The basis for the theory of science that developed in the Oxford school under Grosseteste's inspiration was Aristotle's distinction between knowledge of the fact (*quia*) and knowledge of the reason for the fact (*propter quid*). In attempting to make the passage from the one to the other type of knowledge, these writers, implicitly at least, touched on three methodological techniques that have come to typify modern science, namely inductive, experimental, and mathematical.

Grosseteste, for example, treated induction as a discovery of causes from the study of effects, which are presented to the senses as particular physical facts. The inductive process became, for him, one of resolving the composite objects of sense perception into their principles, or elements, or causes—essentially an abstractive process. A scientific explanation would result from this when one could recompose the abstracted factors to show their causal connection with the observed facts. The complete process was referred to as "resolution and composition," a methodological expression that was to be employed in schools such as Padua until the time of Galileo.

Grosseteste further was aware that one might not be able to follow such an orderly procedure and then would have to resort to intuition or conjecture to provide a scientific explanation. This gave rise to the problem of how to discern a true from a false theory. It was in this context that the Oxford school worked out primitive experiments, particularly in optics, designed to falsify theories. They also employed observational procedures for verification and falsification when treating of comets and heavenly phenomena that could not be subjected to human control.

The mathematical component of this school's methodology was inspired by its metaphysics of light. Convinced that light (*lux*) was the first form that came to primary matter at creation, and that the entire structure of the universe resulted from the propagation of luminous *species* according to geometrical laws, they sought *propter quid* explanations for physical phenomena in mathematics, and mainly in classical geometry. Thus they focused interest on mathematics as well as on experimentation, although they themselves contributed little to the development of new methods of analysis.

2. Science on the Continent. The mathematicist orientation of the Oxford school foreshadowed in some ways the Neo-Pythagoreanism and rationalism of the seventeenth century. This aspect of their thought was generally rejected, however, by their contemporaries at the University of Paris, especially Albertus Magnus and Thomas Aquinas. Both of the latter likewise composed lengthy commentaries on the *Posterior Analytics* and on the physical works of Aristotle, primarily to put the Stagirite's thought at the service of Christian theology, but also to aid their students in uncovering nature's secrets. Not convinced of an underlying mathematical structure of reality, they placed more stress on the empirical component of their scientific methodology than on the mathematical.

Albertus Magnus is particularly noteworthy for his skill at observation and systematic classification. He was an assiduous student of nature, intent on ascertaining the facts, and not infrequently certifying observations with his *Fui et vidi experiri* ("I was there and saw it for myself"). He recognized the difficulty of accurate observation and experimentation, and urged repetition under a variety of conditions to ensure accuracy. He was painfully aware of and remonstrated against the common failing of the Schoolmen, i.e., their uncritical reliance on authority, including that of Aristotle. Among his own contributions were experiments on the thermal effects of sunlight, which A. C. Crombie has noted employed the method of agreement and difference later to be formulated by J. S. Mill; the classification of some hundred minerals, with notes on the properties of each; a detailed comparative study of plants, with digressions that show a remarkable sense of morphology and ecology; and studies in embryology and reproduction, which show that he experimented with insects and the lower animals (Crombie, 1953). Albert also had theoretical and mathematical interests, stimulating later thinkers such as William of Ockham and Walter Burley with his analysis of motion, and doing much to advance the Ptolemaic conception of the structure of the universe over the more orthodox Aristotelian views of his contemporaries.

The best experimental contribution of this period, however, was that of Peter Peregrinus of Maricourt, whose *Epistola de magnete* (1269) reveals a sound empirical knowledge of magnetic phenomena. Peter explained how to differentiate the magnet's north pole from its south, stated the rule for the attraction and repulsion of poles, knew the fundamentals of magnetic induction, and discussed the possibility of breaking magnets into smaller pieces that would become magnets in turn. He understood the workings of the magnetic compass, viewing magnetism as a cosmic force somewhat as Kepler was later to do. His work seems to be the basis for Roger Bacon's extolling the experimental method, and it was praised by William Gilbert (1540–1603) as "a pretty erudite book considering the time."

3. *Use of Calculation.* Mathematical analysis was not entirely lacking from scientific investigation in the thirteenth century. One unexpected source came at the end of the century in the work of Arnald of Villanova, who combined alchemical pursuits with those of pharmacy and medicine. Arnald was interested in quantifying the qualitative effects of compound medicines, and refined and clarified a proposal of the Arabian philosopher Alkindi (ninth century) that linked a geometric increase in the number of parts of a quality to an arithmetic increase in its sensed effect. The exponential function this implies has been seen by some as a precursor of the function later used by Thomas Bradwardine (d. 1349) in his dynamic analysis of local motion (McVaugh, 1967).

A more noteworthy mathematical contribution was found, however, in earlier work on mechanics, particularly in statics and kinematics, that definitely came to fruition in the fourteenth century. Jordanus Nemorarius and his school took up and developed (though not from original sources) the mechanical teachings of antiquity, exemplified by Aristotle's justification of the lever principle, by Archimedes' axiomatic treatment of the lever and the center of gravity, and by Hero's study of simple machines. They formulated the concept of "positional gravity" (*gravitas secundum situm*), with its implied component forces, and used a principle analogous to that of virtual displacements or of virtual work to prove the law of the lever. Gerard of Brussels was similarly heir to the kinematics of antiquity. In his *De motu* he attempted to reduce various possible curvilinear velocities of lines, surfaces, and solids to the uniform rectilinear velocity of a moving point. In the process he anticipated the "mean-speed theorem" later used by the Mertonians, successfully equating the varying rotational motion of a circle's radius with a uniform translational motion of its midpoint.

Other conceptual work in the study of motive powers and resistances, made in the context of Aristotle's rules for the comparison of motions, laid the groundwork for the gradual substitution of the notion of force (as exemplified by *vis insita* and *vis impressa*) for that of cause, thereby preparing for later more sophisticated analyses of gravitational and projectile motion.

II

The more valuable scientific contributions of the thirteenth century were in most instances those of isolated individuals, who reformulated the science of antiquity and made new beginnings in both experimentation and mathematical analysis. The fourteenth century saw a fuller development along these same lines, culminating in important schools at both Oxford and Paris whose members are commonly regarded as the "precursors of Galileo."

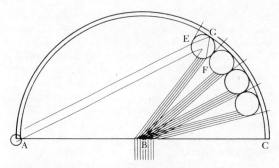

FIGURE 1. The formation of the primary or lower rainbow, showing the much magnified drops (or collection of drops) that produce the four colors Dietrich held were present in the bow. The sun is at *A*, the observer at *B*, and a point directly in front of the observer on the horizon at *C*. Rays from the sun enter the uppermost drop (or drops) at *E*, are refracted there, then are internally reflected within the drop at *G*, and finally are refracted again at *F* and transmitted to the eye of the observer. Each drop (or group of drops) reflects a different color at the eye position.

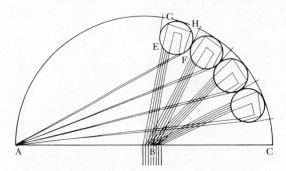

FIGURE 2. The formation of the secondary or upper rainbow, showing the four drops (or collection of drops) that produce the four colors Dietrich held were present in this bow also. *A*, *B*, and *C* are as in Figure 1. Rays from the sun enter the uppermost drop (or drops) at *F*, are refracted there, then are internally reflected within the drop twice, at *H* and *G*, before being finally refracted at *E* and transmitted to the eye of the observer. These drops reflect the same colors, but in the reverse order to those in Figure 1.

1. Theory and Experiment. These precursors worked primarily in the area of mechanics, concentrating on logical and mathematical analyses that led to somewhat abstract formulations, only much later put to experimental test. They never reached the stage of active interchange between theory and experiment that characterizes twentieth-century science, and that could only be begun in earnest with the mechanical investigations of Galileo and Newton. In another area of study, however, a beginning was made even in this type of methodology; the area, predictably enough, was optics, which from antiquity had been emerging, along with mechanics, as an independent branch of physics.

The reasons for the privileged position enjoyed by optics in the late thirteenth and early fourteenth centuries are many. One was the eminence it earlier had come to enjoy among the Greeks and the Arabs. Another was its easy assimilation within the theological context of "Let there be light" (*Fiat lux*) and the philosophical context of the "metaphysics of light" already alluded to. Yet other reasons can be traced in the striking appearances of spectra, rainbows, halos, and other optical phenomena in the upper atmosphere, in the perplexity aroused by optical delusions or by an awareness of their possibility, and above all in the applicability of a simple geometry toward the solution of optical problems.

Whatever the reasons, the fact is that considerable progress had already been made in both catoptrics, the study of reflected light, and dioptrics, the study of refraction. In the former, the works of Euclid, Ptolemy, and Alhazen (d. 1038) had shown that the angles of incidence and reflection from plane surfaces are equal; they also explained how images are formed in plane mirrors and, in the case of Alhazen, gave exhaustive and accurate analyses of reflection from spherical and parabolic mirrors. Similarly in dioptrics Ptolemy and Alhazen had measured angles of incidence and refraction, and knew in a qualitative way the difference between refraction away from, and refraction toward, the normal, depending on the media through which the light ray passed. Grosseteste even attempted a quantitative description of the phenomenon, proposing that the angle of refraction equals half the angle of incidence, which is, of course, erroneous. In this way, however, the stage was gradually set for more substantial advances in optics by Witelo and Dietrich von Freiberg. Perhaps the most remarkable was Dietrich's work on the rainbow (*De iride*), composed shortly after 1304, wherein he explained the production of the bow through the refraction and reflection of light rays.

Dietrich's treatise is lengthy and shows considerable expertise in both experimentation and theory, as well as the ability to relate the two. On the experimental side Dietrich passed light rays through a wide variety of prisms and crystalline spheres to study the production of spectra. He traced their paths through flasks filled with water, using opaque surfaces to block out unwanted rays, and obtained knowledge of angles of refraction at the various surfaces on which the rays in which he was interested were incident, as well as the mechanics of their internal reflection within the flask. Using such techniques he worked out the first essentially correct explanation of the formation of the primary and secondary rainbows (Figures 1 and 2). The theoretical insight that lay behind this work, and that had escaped all of his predecessors, was that a globe of water could be thought of—not as a diminutive watery cloud, as others viewed it—but as a magnified raindrop. This, plus the recognition that the bow is actually the cumulative effect of radiation from many drops, provided the principles basic to his solution. Dietrich's experimental genius enabled him to utilize these principles in a striking way: the first to immobilize the raindrop, in magnified form, in what would later be called a "laboratory" situation, he was able to examine leisurely and at length the various components involved in the rainbow's production.

Dietrich proposed the foregoing methodology as an application of Aristotle's *Posterior Analytics* wherein he identified the causes of the bow and demonstrated its properties using a process of resolution and composition. In attempting to explain the origin and ordering of the bow's colors, however, he engaged in a far more hypothetical type of reasoning, and coupled this with experiments designed to verify and falsify his alternative hypotheses. This work, while closer methodologically to that of modern science, was not successful. There were errors too in his geometry, and in some of his measurements; these were corrected in succeeding centuries, mainly by Descartes and Newton. Dietrich's contribution, withal, was truly monumental, and represents the best interplay between theory and experiment known in the high Middle Ages.

2. Nominalism and Its Influence. Most historians are agreed that some break with Aristotle was necessary before the transition could be made from natural philosophy to science in the classical sense. One step toward such a break came with the condemnation, in 1277, by Étienne Tempier, Bishop of Paris, of 219 articles many of which were linked to an Aristotelian-Averroist cosmology. Concerned over God's omnipotence, the bishop effectively proclaimed that several worlds could exist, and that the ensemble of celestial spheres could, without contradiction, be moved (by God) in a straight line. The general effect of his condemnation was to cause many who were uncritically accepting Aristotle's conclusions as demonstrated and necessarily true to question these. The way was thus opened for the proposal and defense of non-Aristotelian theses concerning the cosmos and local motion, some with important scientific ramifications.

Another step came with the rise of nominalism or terminism in the universities. Under the auspices of William of Ockham and his school, this movement developed in an Aristotelian thought context but quickly led to distinctive views in logic and natural philosophy. Its theory of supposition questioned the reality of universals or "common natures," generally admitted by Aristotelians, and restricted the ascription of reality to individual "absolute things" (*res absolutae*), which could be only particular substances or qualities. Quantity, in Ockham's system, became merely an ab-stract noun: it cannot exist by itself; it can increase or decrease without affecting the substance, as is seen in the phenomena of rarefaction and condensation; and by God's absolute power it can even be made to disappear entirely, as is known from the mystery of the Eucharist. Thus, with Ockham, quantity became a problem more of language than of physical science; his followers soon were involved in all manner of linguistic analyses relating to quantity, but not infrequently the physical problems involved got lost in a maze of logical subtleties.

Ockham's treatment of motion went along similar lines. Convinced that the term "local motion" designates only the state of a physical body that may be negatively described as not at rest, he effectively denied the reality of motion. Moreover, since motion is not a real effect, it does not require a cause, and hence the Aristotelian rule "whatever moves is moved by another" (*quidquid movetur ab alio movetur*) is no longer applicable to it. Some have seen in this rejection of motor causality a foreshadowing of the law of inertia or even the principle of relativity (Sir Edmund Whittaker, E. J. Dijksterhuis). Undoubtedly there are some affinities between Ockham's analysis and those of classical and modern mechanicians, but the identification need not be pressed. Ockham's more direct contribution would seem to lie in his preparing the way for sophisticated, if highly imaginative, calculations of spatiotemporal relationships between motions with various velocities. These calculations opened the path to considerable advances in kinematics, soon to be made at Merton College in Oxford.

Nominalism quickly spread from Oxford to the universities on the Continent, where it merged its thought patterns with both "orthodox" and "heterodox" (from the viewpoint of the Christian faith) schools of Aristotelianism. From this amalgam came a renewed interest in the problems of physical science, a considerably revised conceptual structure for their solution, and a growing tolerance of skepticism and eclecticism. Most of the fruits were borne in mechanics and astronomy, but some were seen in new solutions to the problems of the continuum and of infinity. Nicholas of Autrecourt is worthy of mention for his advocacy of atomism—at a time when Democritus' thought was otherwise consistently rejected—and for his holding a particulate theory of light. His skepticism generally has led him to be styled as a "medieval Hume" and as a forerunner of positivism.

3. Merton College and Kinematics. One of the most significant contributors to the mathematical preparation for the modern science of mechanics was Thomas Bradwardine, fellow of Merton College and theologian of sufficient renown to be mentioned by Chaucer in his *Nun's Priest's Tale*. While at Oxford Bradwardine composed treatises on speculative arithmetic and geometry wherein he not only summarized the works of Boethius and Euclid, but expanded their treatments of ratios (*proportiones*) and proportions (*proportionalitates*) to include new materials from the Arabs Thâbit and Ahmad ibn Yusuf. He then applied this teaching to a problem in dynamics in his *Treatise on the ratios of velocities in motions* (*Tractatus de proportionibus velocitatum in motibus*) composed in 1328. By this time various Arab and Latin writers had been interpreting Aristotle's statements (mostly in Books 4 and 7 of the *Physics*) relating to the comparability of motions to mean that the velocity V of a motion is directly proportional to the weight or force F causing it and inversely proportional to the resistance R of the medium impeding it. This posed a problem when taken in conjunction with another Aristotelian statement to the effect that no motion should result when an applied force F is equal to or less than the resistance R encountered. In modern notation, V should equal 0 when $F \leqslant R$, and this is clearly not the case if $V \propto F/R$, since V becomes finite for all cases except $F = 0$ and $R = \infty$.

In an ingenious attempt to formulate a mathematical relationship that would remove this inconsistency, Bradwardine equivalently proposed an exponential law of motion that may be written

$$\left(\frac{F_2}{R_2}\right) = \left(\frac{F_1}{R_1}\right)^{V_2/V_1}.$$

Referred to as the "ratio of ratios" (*proportio proportionum*), Bradwardine's law came to be widely accepted among Schoolmen up to the sixteenth century. It never was put to experimental test, although it is easily shown to be false from Newtonian dynamics. Its significance lies in its representing, in a moderately complex function, instantaneous changes rather than completed changes (as hitherto had been done), thereby preparing the way for the concepts of the infinitesimal calculus.

Bradwardine composed also a treatise on the continuum (*Tractatus de continuo*) which contains a detailed discussion of geometrical refutations of mathematical atomism. Again, in a theological work he analyzed the concept of infinity, using a type of one-to-one correspondence to show that a part of an infinite set is itself infinite; the context of this analysis is a proof showing that the world cannot be eternal. In such ways Bradwardine made use of mathematics in physics and theology, and stimulated later thinkers to make similar applications.

Although occasioned by a problem in dynamics, Bradwardine's treatise on ratios actually resulted in more substantial contributions to kinematics by other Oxonians, many of whom were fellows of Merton College in the generation after him. Principal among these were William of Heytesbury, John of Dumbleton, and Richard Swineshead. All writing towards the middle of the fourteenth century, they presupposed the validity of Bradwardine's dynamic function and turned their attention to a fuller examination of the comparability of all types of motions, or changes, in its light. They did this in the context of discussions on the "intension and remission of forms" or the "latitude of forms," conceiving all changes (qualitative as well as quantitative) as traversing a distance or "latitude" which is readily quantifiable. They generally employed a "letter-calculus" wherein letters of the alphabet represented ideas (not magnitudes), which lent itself to subtle logical arguments referred to as "calculatory sophisms." These were later decried by humanists and more traditional Scholastics, who found the arguments incomprehensible, partly, at least, because of their mathematical complexity.

One problem to which these Mertonians addressed themselves was how to "denominate" or reckon the degree of heat of a body whose parts are heated not uniformly but to varying degrees. Swineshead devoted a section of his *Book of Calculations* (*Liber calculationum*) to solve this problem for a body A which has greater and greater heat, increasing arithmetically by units to infinity, in its decreasing proportional parts (Figure 3). He was able to show that A should be denominated as having the same heat as another body B which is heated to two degrees throughout its entire length, thus equivalently demonstrating that the sum of the series $1 + \frac{1}{2} + \frac{1}{4} + \frac{1}{8} \ldots$ converges to the value 2. Swineshead considerably advanced Bradwardine's analysis relating to instantaneous velocity and other concepts necessary for the calculus; significantly his work was known to Leibniz, who wished to have it republished.

Motion was regarded by these thinkers as merely another quality whose latitude or mean degree could be calculated. This type of consideration led Heytesbury to formulate one of the most important kinematical rules to come out of the fourteenth century, a rule that has since come to be known as the Mertonian "mean-speed theorem." The theorem states that a uniformly accelerated motion is equivalent, so far as the space traversed in a given time is concerned, to a uniform motion whose velocity is equal throughout to the instantaneous velocity of the uniformly accelerating body at the middle instant of the period of its acceleration. The theorem was formulated during the early 1330's, and at least four attempts to prove it arithmetically were detailed at Oxford before 1350. As in the previous case of Bradwardine's function, no

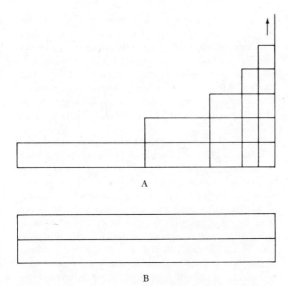

FIGURE 3. A schematic representation showing how a nonuniform heat in body *A*, with one degree in the first half of its length, two degrees in the next quarter, three degrees in the next eighth, etc., may be reckoned to have the same heat as a body *B* of equal length which is uniformly heated to two degrees throughout. Similar diagrams appear in the margin of a fourteenth-century manuscript of Swineshead's *Calculations*, Paris BN Lat. 9558, fol. 6r, and the person who drew them was apparently familiar with Oresme's configurational geometry (see Figure 4).

attempt was made at an experimental proof, nor was it seen (so far as is known) that the rule could be applied to the case of falling bodies. The "Calculatores," as these writers are called, restricted their attention to imaginative cases conceived in abstract terms: they spoke of magnitudes and moving points, and various types of resistive media, but usually in a mathematical way and without reference to nature or the physical universe. When they discussed falling bodies, as did Swineshead (fl. 1350) in his chapter "On the Place of an Element" (*De loco elementi*), it was primarily to show that mathematical techniques are inapplicable to natural motions of this type (Hoskin and Molland, 1966).

A final development among the Mertonians that is worthy of mention for its later importance is their attempts at clarifying the expression "quantity of matter" (*quantitas materiae*), which seems to be genetically related to the Newtonian concept of mass. Swineshead took up the question of the "latitude" of rarity and density, and in so doing answered implicitly how one could go about determining the meaning of "amount of matter" or "quantity of matter." His definition of *quantitas materiae*, it has been argued, is not signifi-

cantly different from Newton's "the measure of the same arising from its density and magnitude conjointly" (Weisheipl, 1963).

4. Paris and the Growth of Dynamics. As in the thirteenth century an interest in science with emphasis on the mathematical began at Oxford, to be followed by a similar interest with emphasis on the physical at Paris, so in the fourteenth century an analogous pattern appeared. The works of the English Calculatores were read and understood on the Continent shortly after the mid-fourteenth century by such thinkers as John of Holland at the University of Prague and Albert of Saxony at the University of Paris. Under less pronounced nominalist influence than the Mertonians, and generally convinced of the reality of motion, the Continental philosophers again took up the problems of the causes and effects of local motion. Particularly at Paris, in a setting where both Aristotelian and terminist views were tolerated, "calculatory" techniques were applied to natural and violent motions and new advances were made in both terrestrial and celestial dynamics.

The first concept of significance to emerge from this was that of impetus, which has been seen by historians of medieval science, such as Duhem, as a forerunner of the modern concept of inertia. The idea of impetus was not completely new on the fourteenth-century scene; the term had been used in biblical and Roman literature in the general sense of a thrust toward some goal, and John Philoponus, a Greek commentator on Aristotle, had written in the sixth century of an "incorporeal kinetic force" impressed on a projectile as the cause of its motion. Again Arabs such as Avicenna and Abū'l-Barakāt had used equivalent Arabic terminology to express the same idea, and thirteenth-century Scholastics took note of impetus as a possible explanation (which they rejected) of violent motion. What was new about the fourteenth-century development was the technical significance given to the concept in contexts that more closely approximate later discussions of inertial and gravitational motion.

The first to speak of impetus in such a context seems to have been the Italian Scotist Franciscus de Marchia. While discussing the causality of the Sacraments in a commentary on the *Sentences* (1323), Franciscus employed impetus to explain how both projectiles and the Sacraments produced effects through a certain power resident within them; in the former case, the projector leaves a force in the projectile that is the principal continuer of its motion, although it also leaves a force in the medium that helps the motion along. The principal mover is the "force left behind" (*virtus derelicta*) in the projectile—not a permanent quality, but something temporary ("for a time"), like

201

heat induced in a body by fire, and this even apart from external retarding influences. The nature of the movement is determined by the *virtus:* in one case it can maintain an upward motion, in another a sideways motion, and in yet another a circular motion. The last case allowed Franciscus to explain the motion of the celestial spheres in terms of an impetus impressed in them by their "intelligences"—an important innovation in that it bridged the Peripatetic gap between the earthly and the heavenly, and prepared for a mechanics that could embrace both terrestrial and celestial phenomena.

A more systematic elaborator of the impetus concept was John Buridan, rector of the University of Paris and founder of a school there that soon rivaled in importance the school of Bradwardine at Oxford. Buridan, perhaps independently of Franciscus de Marchia, saw the necessity of some type of motive force within the projectile; he regarded it as a permanent quality, however, and gave it a rudimentary quantification in terms of the primary matter of the projectile and the velocity imparted to it. Although he offered no formal discussion of its mathematical properties, Buridan thought that the impetus would vary directly as the velocity imparted and as the quantity of matter put in motion; in this respect, at least, his concept was similar to Galileo's *impeto* and to Newton's "quantity of motion." The permanence of the impetus, in Buridan's view, was such that it was really distinct from the motion produced and would last indefinitely (*ad infinitum*) if not diminished by contrary influences. Buridan also explained the movement of the heavens by the imposition of impetus on them by God at the time of the world's creation. Again, and in this he was anticipated by Abū'l-Barakāt, Buridan used his impetus concept to explain the acceleration of falling bodies: continued acceleration results because the gravity of the body impresses more and more impetus.

Despite some similarities between impetus and inertia, critical historians such as A. Maier have warned against too facile an identification. Buridan's concept, for example, was proposed as a further development of Aristotle's theory of motion, wherein the distinction between natural and violent (compulsory) still obtained. A much greater conceptual revolution was required before this distinction would be abandoned and the principle of inertia, in its classical understanding, would become accepted among physicists.

Buridan's students, Albert of Saxony and Marsilius of Inghen, popularized his theory and continued to speak of impetus as an "accidental and extrinsic force," thereby preserving the Aristotelian notions of nature and violence. Albert is important for his statements regarding the free fall of bodies, wherein he speculates

that the velocity of fall could increase in direct proportion to the distance of fall or to the time of fall, without seemingly recognizing that the alternatives are mutually exclusive. (This confusion was to continue in later authors such as Leonardo da Vinci and the young Galileo.) Albert himself seems to have favored distance as the independent variable, and thus cannot be regarded as a precursor of the correct "law of falling bodies."

Perhaps the most original thinker of the Paris school was Nicole Oresme. Examples of his novel approach are his explanation of the motion of the heavens using the metaphor of a mechanical clock, and his speculations concerning the possible existence of a plurality of worlds. An ardent opponent of astrology, he developed Bradwardine's doctrine on ratios to include irrational fractional exponents relating pairs of whole-number ratios, and proceeded to argue that the ratio of any two unknown celestial ratios is probably irrational. This probability, in his view, rendered all astrological prediction fallacious in principle. Oresme held that impetus is not permanent, but is self-expending in its very production of motion; he apparently associated impetus with acceleration, moreover, and not with sustaining a uniform velocity. In discussing falling bodies, he seems to suggest that the speed of fall is directly proportional to the time (and not the distance) of fall, but he did not apply the Mertonian mean-speed theorem to this case, although he knew the theorem and in fact gave the first geometrical proof for it. Further he conceived the imaginary situation of the earth's being pierced all the way through; a falling body would then acquire an *impétuosité* that would carry it beyond the center, and thereafter would oscillate in gradually decreasing amplitudes until it came to rest. A final and extremely important contribution was Oresme's use of a two-dimensional figure to plot a distribution of the intensity of a quality in a subject or of velocity variation with time (Figure 4). Possibly this method of graphical representation was anticipated by the Italian Franciscan Giovanni di Casali, but Oresme perfected it considerably, and on this account is commonly regarded as a precursor of Descartes' analytic geometry.

III

The fourteenth century marked the high point in optical experimentation and in the conceptual development of mechanics during the late Middle Ages. The fifteenth and sixteenth centuries served mainly as periods of transition, where the underlying ideas were diffused throughout Europe, entered into combination with those of other cultures, and provided the proximate setting for the emergence of classical science.

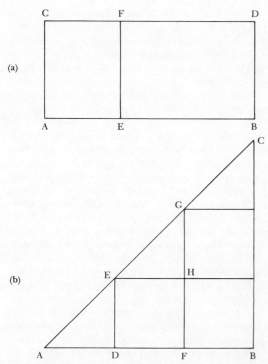

FIGURE 4. In Oresme's system, the rectangle (a) and the right triangle (b) above measures the quantity of some quality (or motion). Line *AB* in each case represents the extension of the quality in the subject, whereas perpendiculars erected to this base line, e.g., *AC*, *EF*, and *BD* in (a) and *DE*, *FG*, and *BC* in (b), represent the intensity of the quality at a particular point. Oresme designated the limiting line *CD* in (a) and *AC* in (b) as the "line of the summit" or the "line of intensity." This is comparable to a "curve" in modern analytic geometry, while the figures themselves are comparable to the "areas under curves."

Much of this interplay took place in Italy, although France and Spain also figured in it to a limited extent.

1. Italy and Renaissance Influences. The tradition perhaps most opposed to Scholasticism was that of humanism, with its interest in classical antiquity, its emphasis on the arts, and its general preference for Plato over Aristotle. Writers such as Marsilio Ficino and Erasmus ridiculed, respectively, the Paduan Schoolmen and the "calculatory sophisms" of their Parisian counterparts. Their overriding interest in philology, moreover, led humanists to make much of original texts, and, even in the case of Aristotle, to confer unprecedented force on arguments from the authority of the classical author. Yet they did make available, in Greek and in accurate translation, the mathematical and mechanical treatises of Euclid, Archimedes, Apollonius, Pappus, Diophantus, and

Ptolemy—works that perforce had a salutary effect in preparing for the new scientific mentality.

The writings of particular authors also contributed in different ways to the coming revolution. Nicholas of Cusa is important for his use of mathematical ideas in elaborating his metaphysics, which prepared for the transition, in Koyré's apt expression, "from the closed world to the infinite universe." He also placed great emphasis on measurement, and preserved elements of the medieval experimental tradition in his treatise on "Experiments with Scales" (*De staticis experimentis*)—this despite the fact that most of his experiments are purely fictitious and not one mentions a numerical result. Leonardo da Vinci is perhaps overrated for his contributions to science, since his was more the mentality of the engineer; his notebooks are neither systematic nor lucid expositions of physical concepts. Yet he too supplied an important ingredient, wrestling as he did with practical problems of mechanics with great genius and technical ability. He brought alive again the tradition of Jordanus Nemorarius and Albert of Saxony, and his speculations on kinematics and dynamics, if inconclusive, reveal how difficult and elusive were the conceptual foundations of mechanics for its early practitioners. Giordano Bruno may also be mentioned as a supporter and successor of Nicholas of Cusa; his works abound in Neo-Platonism and mysticism, and show a heavy reliance on Renaissance magic and the Hermetic-Cabalist tradition. Of little importance for mechanics, his ideas are significant mainly for the support they gave to Copernicanism and to the concept of an infinite universe.

Of more direct influence, on the other hand, was work done at the University of Padua under Averroist and terminist influences. Aristotelianism flourished there long after it had gone into eclipse at Oxford and Paris, not so much in subordination to theology as it was among Thomists, but rather under the patronage of the Arab Averroës or of Alexander of Aphrodisias, a Greek commentator on Aristotle. The Averroists were Neo-Platonic in their interpretation of Aristotle, whereas the Alexandrists placed emphasis instead on his original text. Again, at Padua the arts faculty was complemented not by the theology faculty but by the medical faculty; in this more secularized atmosphere the scientific writings of Aristotle could be studied closely in relation to medical problems and with much aid from Arab commentators.

The result was the formation of a new body of ideas within the Aristotelian framework that fostered, rather than impeded, the scientific revival soon to be pioneered by the Paduan professor, Galileo Galilei. Among these ideas some were methodological. They

203

derived from extended discussions of what Galileo would refer to as the "method of analysis" (*metodo risolutivo*) and the "method of synthesis" (*metodo compositivo*). Writers such as Jacopo Zabarella systematized these results, showing how they could be applied to detailed problems in physical science, thereby bringing to perfection the methodology outlined by Grosseteste, which has already been discussed.

More than a century before Zabarella, Paul of Venice (Paolo Nicoletti), who had studied at Oxford in the late fourteenth century, returned to Padua and propagated Mertonian ideas among his students. A number of these wrote commentaries on Heytesbury that were published and widely disseminated throughout Europe. Noteworthy is the commentary of Gaetano da Thiene, who illustrated much of Heytesbury's abstract reasoning on uniform and difform motions with examples drawn from nature and from artifacts that might be constructed from materials close at hand. As far as is known this fifteenth-century group performed no experiments or measurements, but they took a step closer to their realization by showing how "calculatory" techniques were relevant in physical and medical investigations.

2. Paris and the Spanish Universities. The Paduan school exerted considerable influence throughout northern Italy; it also stimulated a renewed interest in Mertonian ideas at the University of Paris at the beginning of the sixteenth century. The group in which this renewal took place centered around John Major (or Jean Mair), the Scottish nominalist, who numbered among his students John Dullaert of Ghent, Alvaro Thomaz, and Juan de Celaya. Dullaert edited many of the works of Paul of Venice, while he and the others were generally familiar with the "calculatory" writings of Paul's students. Major's group was eclectic in its philosophy, and saw no inconsistency in making a fusion of nominalist and realist currents, the former embracing Oxonian and Parisian terminist thought and the latter including Thomist and Scotist as well as Averroist views. The Spaniard Gaspar Lax and the Portuguese Alvaro Thomaz supplied the mathematical expertise necessary to understand Bradwardine's, Swineshead's, and Oresme's more technical writings. Several good physics texts came out of this group; especially noteworthy is that of Juan de Celaya, who inserted lengthy excerpts from the Mertonians and Paduans, seemingly as organized and systematized by Thomaz, into his exposition of Aristotle's *Physics* (1517). Celaya treated both dynamical and kinematical questions, as by then had become the custom, and thus transmitted much of the late medieval development in mechanics (statics excluded) to sixteenth-century scholars.

Celaya was but one of many Spanish professors at Paris in this period; these attracted large numbers of Spanish students, who later returned to Spain and were influential in modeling Spanish universities such as Alcalá and Salamanca after the University of Paris. An edition of Swineshead's *Liber calculationum* was edited by Juan Martinez Silíceo and published at Salamanca in 1520; this was followed by a number of texts written (some poorly) in the "calculatory" tradition. Theologians who were attempting to build their lectures around Thomist, Scotist, and nominalist concepts soon complained over their students' lack of adequate preparation in logic and natural philosophy. It was such a situation that led Domingo de Soto, a Dominican theologian and political theorist who had studied under Celaya at Paris as a layman, to prepare a series of textbooks for use at the University of Salamanca. Among these were a commentary and a "questionary" on Aristotle's *Physics;* the latter, appearing in its first complete edition in 1551, was a much simplified and abridged version of the type of physics text that was used at Paris in the first decades of the sixteenth century. It reflected the same concern for both realist and "calculatory" interests, but with changes of emphasis dictated by Soto's pedagogical aims.

One innovation in Soto's work has claimed the attention of historians of science. In furnishing examples of motions that are "uniformly difform" (i.e., uniformly accelerated) with respect to time, Soto explicitly mentions that freely falling bodies accelerate uniformly as they fall and that projectiles (presumably thrown upward) undergo a uniform deceleration; thus he saw the distance in both cases to be a function of the time of travel. He includes numerical examples that show he applied the Mertonian "mean-speed theorem" to the case of free fall, and on this basis, at the present state of knowledge, he is the first to have adumbrated the correct law of falling bodies. As far as is known, Soto performed no measurements, although he did discuss what later thinkers have called "thought experiments," particularly relating to the vacuum. An extensive survey of all physics books known to be in use in France and Spain at the time has failed to uncover similar instance of this type, and one can only speculate as to the source of Soto's examples.

3. Italy Again: Galileo. With Soto, the conceptual development of medieval mechanics reached its term. What was needed was an explicit concern with measurement and experimentation to complement the mathematical reasoning that had been developed along "calculatory" and Archimedean lines. This final development took place in northern Italy, again mainly at Padua, while Galileo was teaching there. The stage was set by works of considerable mathematical sophistication, under the inspiration of Archimedes, by sixteenth-century authors such as Geronimo Cardano, Nicolo Tartaglia, and Giovanni Battista Benedetti. Also the technical arts had gradually been perfected, and materials were at hand from which instruments and experimental apparatus could be constructed.

The person of Galileo provided the catalyst and the genius to coordinate these elements and educe from them a new kind of synthesis that would reach perfection with Isaac Newton. Galileo received his early university training at Pisa around 1584, where his student notebooks (*Juvenilia*) reveal an acquaintance with many Schoolmen, including Soto, an edition of whose *Physics* appeared at Venice in 1582. Galileo used their terminology in an early treatise *On Motion* (*De motu*), and only gradually departed from it. His teacher at Pisa, Francesco Buonamici, himself a classical Aristotelian, seemingly gave a muddled account of the medieval tradition, and it is difficult to know how well Galileo understood what was presented. Actually this matters little; what is important is that the ideas that contributed to the developing science of mechanics were at hand for himself or another to use. Classical science did not spring perfect and complete, as Athena from the head of Zeus, from the mind of Galileo or any of his contemporaries. When it did arrive, it was a revolution, and no one can deny this, but it was a revolution preceded by a strenuous effort of thought. The genesis of that thought makes an absorbing, if little known, chapter in the history of ideas.

BIBLIOGRAPHY

The principal sources and bibliography are given in M. Clagett, *The Science of Mechanics in the Middle Ages* (Madison, 1959); also E. A. Moody and M. Clagett, eds., *The Medieval Science of Weights* (Madison, 1952). See too A. C. Crombie, *Robert Grosseteste and the Origins of Experimental Science, 1100–1700* (Oxford, 1953), p. 195; idem, *Medieval and Early Modern Science*, 2nd rev. ed., 2 vols. (Cambridge, Mass., 1961); E. J. Dijksterhuis, *The Mechanization of the World Picture*, trans. C. Dikshoorn (Oxford, 1961); J. A. Weisheipl, *The Development of Physical Theory in the Middle Ages* (New York, 1959); P. Duhem, *Études sur Léonard de Vinci*, 3 vols. (Paris, 1906–13; reprint 1955), a pioneer work of great scope, but requires revision in light of the researches of A. Maier in her *Studien zur Naturphilosophie der Spätscholastik*, 5 vols. (Rome, 1949–58), especially Vol. I, *Die Vorläufer Galileis im 14 Jahrhundert* (Rome, 1949) and Vol. V, *Zwischen Philosophie und Mechanik* (Rome, 1958). See also: P. Duhem *Le Système du monde*, 10 vols. (Paris, 1913–59); idem, *To Save the Phenomena*, trans E. Doland and C. Maschler (Chicago, 1969; original in French, 1908).

Special studies include C. B. Boyer, *The Rainbow: From Myth to Mathematics* (New York, 1959); Jean Buridan, *Quaestiones super libros quattuor de caelo et mundo*, ed. E. A. Moody (Cambridge, Mass., 1942); M. Clagett, *Archimedes in the Middle ages*, Vol. I. *The Arabo-Latin Tradition* (Madison, 1964); idem, *Nicole Oresme and the Medieval Geometry of Qualities and Motions* (Madison, 1968); H. L. Crosby, Jr., ed. and trans., *Thomas of Bradwardine, His "Tractatus de Proportionibus," Its Significance for the Development of Mathematical Physics* (Madison, 1955); S. Drake and I. E. Drabkin, eds. and trans., *Mechanics in Sixteenth Century Italy* (Madison, 1969); H. Élie, "Quelques Maîtres de l'université de Paris vers l'an 1500," *Archives d'histoire doctrinale et littéraire du moyen âge*, 18 (1950–51), 193–243; N. W. Gilbert, *Renaissance Concepts of Method* (New York, 1960); E. Grant, ed. and trans., Nicole Oresme, *De proportionibus proportionum* and *Ad pauca respicientes* (Madison, 1966); M. A. Hoskin and A. G. Molland, "Swineshead on Falling Bodies: An Example of Fourteenth-Century Physics," *The British Journal for the History of Science*, 3 (1966), 150–82; A. Koyré, *From the Closed World to the Infinite Universe* (Baltimore, 1957), and idem, *Études galiléennes*, 3 vols. (Paris, 1939), much of which is summarized in idem, *Metaphysics and Measurement: Essays in the Scientific Revolution* (Cambridge, Mass., 1968); E. McMullin, ed., *Galileo: Man of Science* (New York, 1967); M. McVaugh, "Arnald of Villanova and Bradwardine's Law," *Isis*, 58 (1967), 56–64; A. D. Menut and A. J. Denomy, eds., Eng. trans. by Menut, *Nicole Oresme, Le Livre du ciel et du monde* (Madison, 1968); E. A. Moody, "Galileo and His Precursors," *Galileo Reappraised*, ed. C. L. Golino (Berkeley, 1966), pp. 23–43; idem, "Galileo and Avempace: The Dynamics of the Leaning Tower Experiment," *Journal of the History of Ideas*, 12 (1951), 163–93, 375–422. J. E. Murdoch, *"Rationes Mathematice": Un Aspect du rapport des mathématiques et de la philosophie au moyen âge* (Paris, 1962); J. H. Randall, Jr., *The School of Padua and the Emergence of Modern Science* (Padua, 1961); C. B. Schmitt, "Experimental Evidence for and against a Void: The Sixteenth-Century Arguments," *Isis*, 58 (1967), 352–66; W. A. Wallace, *The Scientific Methodology of Theodoric of Freiberg* (Fribourg, 1959); idem, "The Enigma of Domingo de Soto: *Uniformiter Difformis* and Falling Bodies in Late Medieval Physics," *Isis*, 59 (1968), 384–401; idem, "The 'Calculatores' in Early Sixteenth-Century Physics," *The British Journal for the History of Science*, 4 (1969), 231–32; idem, "Mechanics from Bradwardine to Galileo," *Journal of the History of Ideas*, 32 (1971), 15–28; J. A. Weisheipl, "The Concept of Matter in Fourteenth Century Science," in *The Concept of Matter*, ed. E. McMullin (Notre Dame, 1963), pp. 319–41; C. Wilson, *William Heytesbury: Medieval Logic and the Rise of Mathematical Physics* (Madison, 1960).

WILLIAM A. WALLACE

[See also **Abstraction;** Alchemy; Astrology; Authority; Causation; **Continuity; Islamic Conception;** Neo-Platonism; **Optics;** Renaissance Humanism.]

EXPRESSIONISM IN LITERATURE

AMONG THE areas of knowledge and scholarly inquiry listed by Lovejoy in his essay "The Historiography of Ideas," we note his reference to "Literary history, as it is commonly presented, namely, the history of the literatures of particular nations or in particular languages—in so far as the literary historians interest themselves . . . in the thought-content of literature" (*Essays in the History of Ideas*, p. 1). It is with the explicit or implicit thought content of German literary expressionism that our survey is primarily concerned. However, Lovejoy disparaged the study of literary and artistic movements as "units" of the history of ideas; for, according to him, "the doctrines and tendencies that are designated by familiar names ending in -ism or -ity, though they occasionally may be, usually are not of the sort which the historian of ideas seeks to discriminate" (*The Great Chain of Being*, p. 5). Yet he devoted considerable time and effort to the discrimination of romanticisms. Still, the history of ideas, rather than dealing with philosophical systems or esthetic currents, isolates the components or elements (also called the unit ideas) of which such thought structures are made up. It does so knowing full well that "the seeming novelty of many a system is due solely to the novelty of the application or arrangement of the old elements which enter into it" (ibid., p. 4).

In dealing with German literary expressionism as intellectual historians, we are fortunate in facing a situation compatible with Lovejoy's strictures. For unlike naturalism and surrealism in literature and impressionism in painting, literary expressionism was not a movement in the strict sense of the word, i.e., to use René Wellek's definition, a body of "self-conscious and self-critical activities" resulting in "consciously formulated programs." It was, rather, a syndrome of thoughts and feelings—in short: a *Weltanschauung*—giving rise to certain techniques and engendering a preference for certain types of subject matter, such as the conflict of generations. Unlike their activist contemporaries (Franz Pfemfert and Kurt Hiller, to name only two of the most prominent ones), who shared a common sociopolitical, humanist-pacifist goal and expressed their views in periodicals like *Die Aktion, Das Ziel,* and *Die weissen Blätter,* all the expressionists proper seem to have had in common was, in the words of Gottfried Benn, their urge for *Wirklichkeitszertrümmerung* ("destruction of external reality"). *Intensität* ("intensity") is, in fact, another of those "sacred words and phrases" which Lovejoy wished to see dissected. As early as 1915, Otto Flake, writing in *Die neue Rundschau* (XXVI, 1276–87), used

it to label the most recent literature, and Kurt Pinthus, editor of the paradigmatic anthology *Menschheitsdämmerung* (Berlin, 1920; "The Twilight of Mankind"), singled out the same phenomenon as characterizing the work of the poets included in his collection.

The basic difference between expressionism and activism (which Wolfgang Paulsen made the subject of a still cogent monograph) is well explained by Max Krell, who writes:

Expressionism—a collective term for a complex of feelings and ideas (*Gefühls- und Anschauungskomplex*)—is not a program. There is a league of Activists, but not of Expressionists. There the goal is *Bindung* (adherence to a common cause), here it is *Lösung* (detachment). Whatever force seeks to compel intellectuals, artists and creators to subscribe to an identical program is to be condemned. A program implies bias (*Tendenz*), obligation. Obligation means death of the self. The self: adventure of spiritual loneliness. This loneliness gives birth to the work of art" (*Über neue Prosa*, pp. 11f.).

So diverse have been the opinions, still held by the artists themselves as well as by literary historians and critics, as to who should, and who should not, be regarded as an expressionist that no universally accepted grouping is available. For example, Georg Trakl, several of whose poems appear in *Menschheitsdämmerung* and who is now sometimes designated as a proto-expressionist, would seem to belong, in part, to a completely different tradition which, on occasion, has been called surrealist. Similarly, the writings of the German dadaists are usually discussed in the standard surveys of expressionism, although the ties are very tenuous—at least esthetically speaking. Ernst Barlach, the "existential" expressionist par excellence, was shocked to see his plays staged expressionistically. However, Rainer Maria Rilke, some of whose later poems—including certain aspects of the *Duino Elegies* and the *Sonnets to Orpheus*—display stylistic mannerisms of the kind we tend to associate with expressionism, is rarely discussed in this particular context. What is more, it would be downright foolish to think that an author's entire oeuvre could be regarded as belonging, fairly and squarely, to expressionism. Those who wish to discuss this complex literary phenomenon are, therefore, well advised to concentrate on specific works or groups of works.

Historically, expressionism in art and literature must be seen as one of many manifestations, in the arts, the sciences, philosophy, religion, and so forth, which were symptomatic of the revolt against positivism, a revolt which erupted shortly after 1900. Like the cubists and the futurists—from whom they were only tentatively and inadequately distinguished by such perceptive contemporary critics as Theodor Däubler and Hermann Bahr—the expressionists despised the realistic-naturalistic approach to art which, as a final, glorious offshoot, had recently produced the sensuous surface portrayals of impressionism. Following Cézanne, the cubists aimed at stabilizing and eternalizing impressionism by transforming it into an "art of the museums" (Cézanne's formulation) bordering on, but never actually resulting in, geometrical abstraction. The futurists, glorifying speed and idolizing the machine, indulged in a kind of accelerated impressionism using hardened particles and centering in the notion of simultaneity. The expressionists, finally, pitted their own brand of emotional but, characteristically, nonsensuous and nonerotic subjectivism against the imitative art of the nineteenth century.

With Kasimir Edschmid, one of their chief literary spokesmen, the expressionists in Platonic fashion believed that to reproduce an already existing reality was a waste of creative strength: "The world is there; so why should we repeat it?" (*Über den Expressionismus in der Literatur und die neue Dichtung*, p. 56). Emphasis was not to be placed on *Sehen* ("observation of visual details") but on *Schauen* ("visionary experiences"), in an effort to gain mystical access to permanent values and thus merge the subjective with the objective. The program which the expressionists unwittingly embraced was formulated by Vincent van Gogh in several letters to his brother Theo, written between 1886 and 1888. In one of these, dated mid-August, 1888, we encounter the following exemplary passage:

Because instead of trying to reproduce exactly what I have before my eyes, I use color more arbitrarily so as to express myself more forcefully. . . . I should like to paint the portrait of an artist friend, a man who dreams great dreams, who works as the nightingale sings, because it is his nature. He'll be a fair man. I want to put into the picture my appreciation, the love that I have for him. So I paint him as he is, as faithfully as I can, to begin with.

But the picture is not finished yet. To finish it I am now going to be the arbitrary colorist. I exaggerate the fairness of the hair, I get to orange tones, chromes and pale lemon yellows.

Beyond the head, instead of painting the ordinary wall of the mean room, I paint infinity, a plain background of the richest, intensest blue that I can contrive, and by this simple combination the bright head illuminated against a rich blue background acquires a mysterious effect, like the star in the depths of an azure sky (*Letters*, p. 277).

Substituting definition for description, Herbert Read called expressionism an art seeking to reproduce "not the objective reality of the world, but the subjective reality of the feeling which objects and events arouse in us" (*The Philosophy of Modern Art*, p. 51). Much

the same was said by John Galsworthy who, in his Presidential Address to the English Association (1924) entitled "On Expression," quotes a "great good painter" as ironically stating that

Expressionism meant expressing the inside of a phenomenon without depicting its outside in a way that could be recognized. That is to say, if you wanted to express an apple-tree you drew and coloured one vertical and three fairly horizontal lines, attached a small coloured circle to one of those, and wrote the word "Fruity" in the catalogue. . . (*Castles in Spain* [1927], p. 89).

Although Galsworthy may have spoken with a degree of levity, this deliberate emphasis on the inside of phenomena led to the serious and dogged attempt, on the part of many expressionists, to breathe a soul (*beseelen*) not only into animals and plants, but into inanimate objects as well. Thus, Franz Marc wished to portray a horse or an eagle not as he saw them but as they would see and feel themselves; and Theodor Däubler referred to Robert Delaunay's painted Eiffel Tower as an expressionist, or even the father of Delaunay (Däubler, p. 182). This spiritualizing tendency marks one of the strongest contrasts between expressionism on the one hand and all the other major nineteenth- and twentieth-century movements (including surrealism) on the other.

Although, as we have already indicated, no one individual connected with expressionism wrote a program or offered a theory that was binding for the entire "movement," one work in particular exerted a powerful influence on many artists: Wilhelm Worringer's book *Abstraktion und Einfühlung* ("Abstraction and Empathy") which, originally written as a dissertation, was not published until 1908. In this treatise, Worringer, speaking as an art historian, champions the nonnaturalistic and anticlassical phases in the history of the plastic arts. After refuting the empathetic mode of creation and perception he finds to have prevailed in these eras, he introduces the concept of *Kunstwollen* ("artistic volition") in contrast to the notion of art as a skill (*Können*) dependent on the artist's technical expertise and the nature of his materials.

Kunstwollen, which disregards all conventional canons of beauty, asserts itself most forcefully in primitive and highly sophisticated ages when man is either still afraid of his natural environment or has already transcended it spiritually. Rejecting the art of the Renaissance, neo-classicism, and realism-naturalism, Worringer praises the Middle Ages—especially the Gothic style—the baroque, and romanticism, during which periods, according to him and his followers, the urge for transcendence and spiritualization made itself felt, without quite succeeding in breaking through the

207

barrier of material life. It is precisely these three eras (notably the baroque and romanticism) which the expressionists exalted for similar reasons.

Although, in *Abstraktion und Einfühlung*, Worringer does not refer to contemporary art, his provocative study was shortly to be regarded as the Bible of expressionism. Without this model, for instance, Wassily Kandinsky's essay *Über das Geistige in der Kunst* (1912; "Concerning the Spiritual in Art") would not have been written, at least not in its present form. Here the father of abstract ("nonobjective") art, writing in 1910, invokes the principle of Spiritual Necessity, his equivalent of Worringer's *Kunstwollen*. Renouncing any claims to universal beauty, Kandinsky states that "internal beauty is achieved through necessity and renunciation of the conventionally beautiful. To those who are not accustomed to it it appears as ugliness." But Kandinsky's link with expressionism is a weak one, for the style he developed after 1910 is of the serene, post-empathetic and Oriental-decorative kind, whereas, on the whole, the expressionists (such as the members of the Dresden *Brücke*) were drawn toward the neo-primitive.

Geist ("spirit"), by the way, was the expressionists' favorite catchword, although occasionally they confused or contaminated it with *Seele* ("soul"), which suggests a more religious outlook than they usually had in mind. *Geist*, at any rate, was preferred to intellect or reason and was always stressed at the expense of *Körper* ("body") or *Materie* ("matter").

The intensity of the experiences which the expressionistic writers sought to convey was frequently hinted at by such synonyms as *Ballung* ("agglomeration or concentration") and *Spitzen* ("peaks"), both of which terms play a crucial role in the dialogue of Georg Kaiser's drama *Von Morgens bis Mitternachts* (1916; *From Morn to Midnight*). Elsewhere, phrases like *Höhe des Gefühls* ("height of feeling") and *Berge des Herzens* ("mountains of the heart," a metaphorical expression coined by Rilke) prepare one for the typically expressionistic situation of *Aufbruch* ("departure") signaling the emergence of the projected New Man.

Trying to pierce the surface of things, the expressionists intuitively grasped for essences. *Mensch, werde wesentlich!*—the opening lines of a famous epigram by the seventeenth-century poet Angelus Silesius—served as an inspiration for a whole generation of poets and playwrights, among them the proto-expressionist Ernst Stadler, whose poem "Der Spruch" ("Epigram") incorporating this dictum, has an almost programmatic ring. Like *Wesen* ("essence"), *Kern* ("core") is a term which crops up incessantly in expressionism, for instance, in Reinhard Goering's drama *Seeschlacht* ("Naval Engagement"), which contains a whole reper-

tory of phrases relevant to our survey. In this work, *Kern* primarily refers to that which all human beings, irrespective of their race, creed, social status, or mentality have in common. It is an attribute of *Mensch* (man seen abstractly and universally) rather than *Mann* (man seen as a concrete and unique individual).

The replacement of concrete particulars by quasi-abstractions bordering, at times, upon allegorical forms, is another distinct feature of literary expressionism. Thus Goering's play is significantly entitled *Seeschlacht* rather than *Die Seeschlacht* or *Die Schlacht am Skagerrak*. The poet August Stramm displayed an increasingly radical tendency toward nounalization on the one hand and reduction of syntax to its bare essentials on the other; and even Trakl—whose ties with expressionism are so brittle—distinctly preferred nounalized adjectives, such as *ein Weisses* ("a white thing"), to less generalized, and hence less abstract, designations. In summarizing this significant trend, Edschmid claims that, in the context of expressionism, "the rhythmic construction of the sentences is different," in so far as they serve "the same spiritual urge which renders only the essential" (op. cit., p. 65).

Although the term "expressionism" and its cognates were occasionally used before the turn of the century (as Armin Arnold has shown in the opening chapter of his book *Die Literatur des Expressionismus*), the most appropriate point of departure for a semantic history is the exhibition held in 1901 at the Salon des Indépendants in Paris, which included several canvases grouped together under the title "Expressionisme" by the otherwise unknown painter Julien Auguste Hervé. (The term was never popular in France, where a kind of decorative expressionism—that of *Les Fauves*—flourished around 1905.)

In Germany, the term was first applied to painting in 1911, in connection with an exhibition staged by the Berlin *Sezession*. It was quickly popularized by influential critics like Karl Scheffler and Worringer. (The latter's *Abstraktion und Einfühlung* came to the attention of T. E. Hulme, who transmitted some of the key notions to Wyndham Lewis and the group of vorticists gathered around Ezra Pound and the short-lived periodical *Blast*, which became the voice of English expressionism—in reality, a blend of expressionist, cubist, and futurist ideas.) Generally speaking, expressionism had little impact on English drama, whereas American playwrights like Eugene O'Neill (*The Emperor Jones* and *The Hairy Ape*) and Elmer Rice (*The Adding Machine*) were strongly influenced by Georg Kaiser.

Although "expressionism" had been applied to literature as early as 1911 (by Kurt Hiller), it did not gain currency until 1915 when Otto Flake published the review article mentioned above. In the fall of 1917, however, Kasimir Edschmid denounced those imitators of the expressionistic style who sought to reproduce its external features without sharing the underlying world view. And by April, 1922, Kurt Pinthus, prefacing the second edition of *Menschheitsdämmerung,* could assert, in good faith, that in the intervening two-and-one-half years no poetry begging for inclusion in his anthology had appeared. Indeed, what around 1917 had been true of expressionistic prose and poetry could now be said to apply to expressionistic drama as well; for, along with Goering's *Seeschlacht,* Georg Kaiser's most significant plays, although written several years earlier, had been premiered in quick succession, among them *Die Bürger von Calais* (1914), *Von Morgens bis Mitternachts* (1916), *Die Koralle* (1917), and *Gas* (1918). The first version of Bertolt Brecht's *Baal* was also written in 1918. Thus expressionism had run its course, covering a time span extending over the decade from 1910 to 1920, a decade which Gottfried Benn was justified in calling *das expressionistische Jahrzehnt.* Perhaps the lustrum beginning in 1921 might be included by extension, although by 1923 the dominant style of the twenties, *Neue Sachlichkeit* (New Objectivity, or functionalism) had acquired full momentum through the activities of the *Bauhaus.*

BIBLIOGRAPHY

A. Arnold, *Die Literatur des Expressionismus: Sprachliche und thematische Quellen* (Stuttgart, 1966). H. Bahr, *Expressionismus* (Munich, 1916). Th. Däubler, *Der neue Standpunkt* (Dresden, 1916). H. Denkler, *Drama des Expressionismus* (Munich, 1967). B. Diebold, *Anarchie im Drama* (Frankfurt, 1921). K. Edschmid, *Über den Expressionismus in der Literatur und die neue Dichtung* (Berlin, 1919); idem, ed., *Schöpferische Konfession* (Berlin, 1920). M. Hamburger, *Reason and Energy* (New York, 1957), essays on Trakl, Benn, and "1912." C. Hill and R. Ley, *The Drama of German Expressionism: A Bibliography* (Chapel Hill, 1960). W. Kandinsky, *Über das Geistige in der Kunst* (Munich, 1912), trans. as *Concerning the Spiritual in Art . . .* (New York, 1947). A. Klarmann, "Expressionism in German Literature: A Retrospect of a Half Century," *Modern Language Quarterly,* **26** (1965), 62–92. M. Krell, *Über neue Prosa* (Berlin, 1919). M. Niedermayer, ed., *Lyrik des expressionistischen Jahrzehnts* (Munich, 1962). W. Paulsen, *Aktivismus und Expressionismus: Eine typologische Untersuchung* (Berne and Leipzig, 1935); idem, ed., *Aspekte des Expressionismus* (Heidelberg, 1968). K. Pinthus, ed., *Menschheitsdämmerung* (Berlin, 1920; new ed., Hamburg, 1959). W. Rothe, ed., *Expressionismus als Literatur* (Berne, 1969). R. Samuel and R. H. Thomas, *Expressionism in German Life, Literature and the Theatre* (Cambridge, 1939). W. Sokel, *The Writer in Extremis* (Stanford, 1959); idem, *Expressionismus in Kunst und Literatur 1910–1923* (Munich, 1960). H. Steffen, ed., *Der deutsche Expressionismus* (Göttingen, 1965). Vincent van Gogh, *Letters of Vincent Van Gogh,* ed. Mark Roskill (New York, 1963). U. Weisstein, "Vorticism: Expressionism English Style," *Yearbook of Comparative and General Literature,* **13** (1964), 28–40; idem, "Expressionism: Style or Weltanschauung?," *Criticism,* **9** (1967), 42–62. W. Worringer, *Abstraktion und Einfühlung* (Munich, 1908; new ed. 1948), trans. as *Abstraction and Empathy* (New York, 1953).

ULRICH WEISSTEIN

[See also **Empathy; Impressionism; Naturalism in Art; Romanticism.**]

FAITH, HOPE, AND CHARITY

THE CONCEPTS of faith, hope, and charity are profoundly interrelated and in reality not clearly distinguishable. The object of this article is not to detail their history—a process which would be impossible in so short a space. Rather, the article will attempt to illumine some of the points of interrelatedness frequently overlooked in historical surveys—interrelatedness among these concepts themselves in their development and between them and other phenomena—political, social, and psychological.

The connections among the ideas of faith, hope, and charity are problematic to many scholars. The problem can be seen as rooted to some extent in the conflict between two distinct conceptions of love—eros and agapē—which were united in the Christian conception of charity.

The idea of eros was derived largely from the philosophy of Plato, for whom it meant a love of man for the divine, a desire by which man seeks a contemplation which will be wholly satisfying (*Symposium* 210A–E). The contemplation or possession of the Good, according to Plato, is attained by a difficult ascent above the transient things of the world. Eros, then, is an appetite for the Good, which is sought not for its own sake but in order to satisfy spiritual desire. Since this yearning is basically for the extension of one's own being, it may in this sense be called egocentric.

In the New Testament eros is largely overlooked in favor of *agapē.* The latter is not simply another Greek term for love. What is being conveyed is a very distinct attitude. In the fullest sense *agapē* is God's love. It is generous love, not appetitive in the sense that there is need to satisfy that in oneself which is incomplete, not stimulated by or dependent upon that which is loved. It is indifferent to value, seeking to confer good, rather than to obtain it. It is therefore spontaneous and creative, and it is rooted in abundance rather than in poverty. In this sense God himself is called love (I John 4:8). The use of the *agapē* idea to convey the Christian's attitude toward God is therefore problematic. There are a few passages in the Pauline epistles in which *agapē* is used in the sense of love toward God (e.g., Romans 8:28; I Corinthians 2:9; 8:3; Ephesians 6:24). Nevertheless, the use of the term in this sense is infrequent in Paul. He does use it frequently to denote the Christian attitude to one's neighbor, however.

Recognizing the problem involved in describing the Christian's attitude toward God by the term *"agapē,"* a controversial scholar argued that in the epistles of Paul, especially, man's attitude of response to God is more clearly expressed by the word "faith." "Faith includes in itself the whole devotion of love, while emphasizing that it has the character of a response, that it is reciprocated love" (Nygren [1953], p. 127). While this interpretation can be and has been debated, it indicates the inseparability of the ideas of faith and love and the futility of divisions and distinctions which are too neat and simplified.

In the writings of the Church Fathers new developments can be seen. In some of these writings eros seems to come to the fore in the interpretation of Christian love of God. That is, there is a tendency to speak primarily in terms of possession of God. Related to this is a tendency to distinguish between "mere faith" and Christian "gnosis." Within this frame of reference, the mere believer is understood to have what is essentially necessary for salvation, that is, he has been brought into relationship with God, but his understanding is superficial. In contrast to this, gnosis implies a kind of possession, that is, true knowledge of God. Thus Clement of Alexandria wrote that faith points beyond itself to a higher and more perfect stage, that is, gnosis (*Stromata* VII, Ch. x. 55, 3). According to this view, then, there are two stages of development, and the true Gnostic is the Christian who has reached a higher plane of vision. Since he has true insight into Scripture, he does not depend upon external authority as does the mere believer. This pattern of thinking is strongly reflected also in Origen, whose notion of Christian love is developed in terms of eros. Characteristically he also described two levels of the Christian life, that of mere faith and that of gnosis.

A synthesis of the eros theme and the *agapē* theme was achieved by Augustine in his development of the conception of Christian charity. The combination of these two themes is suggested by the fact that he was able to write of an "ascent" of the soul toward a "vision" of God (by a "ladder" of virtue, speculation, and mysticism) and yet also to affirm the utter sovereignty, gratuitousness, and spontaneity of divine love and grace. There is rich content in Augustine's view

of love—God's love, love of God, love of neighbor— but the most usual meaning of charity for him is man's love of God. This charity is absolutely central to the Christian life. Without it, faith and hope cannot establish the right relationship to God. The following statement is significant: "When it is asked whether a man is good, one does not ask what he believes or hopes, but what he loves" (*Enchiridion*, Ch. cxvii. 31).

Augustine's problematic synthesis was the major source of medieval speculation on faith, hope, and charity. While this is generally recognized, it would be misleading to assume that there were not other influences upon medieval thought. One of the most important was an author known as "Pseudo-Dionysius," who wrote about the year 500 A.D. What comes through most strongly in the works of this author is the idea of love (eros) as a unifying and cohesive force pervading the whole universe (*De divinis nominibus*, Ch. iv, n. xv). He strongly emphasizes the symbolism of ascent to God by the ladder of virtue, speculation, and mysticism. The ideas of Dionysius began to have impact upon the West in the ninth century, largely through the work of John Scotus Erigena, who stresses the idea that God is eros to himself, and when we love God it is really God loving himself through us.

In the Middle Ages the most cohesive and original synthesis of Christian thought on the virtues of faith, hope, and charity is most probably that of Thomas Aquinas, who conceptualizes them as three distinct but interdependent supernatural, infused, "theological" virtues directing man to God. Thomas's doctrine later became officially accepted in Roman Catholicism. Like Bonaventure and the medieval Augustinians he considered himself a disciple of Augustine, but Aquinas is too complex a thinker to be classified simply in this manner. What is radically different in his thought stems from a conscious choice to adopt Aristotelianism into his synthesis, and this marriage of Aristotelian philosophy with Augustinian Platonism profoundly affected the course of Christian thought for centuries to come. Although Thomas treats of faith, hope, and charity in that order, there is some point in focusing first upon what he does with the idea of charity and then seeing the other concepts in relation to this.

In his analysis of charity, Thomas follows Aristotle's distinction between love of concupiscence, which he takes to mean desire of the other's good for oneself, and love of benevolence, according to which the other's good is willed for his own (the other's) sake. Within this context, friendship is understood as mutual love of benevolence. Friendship, however, does not precisely exclude concupiscence. Rather, because of a similarity perceived between the self and the other, one is able to expand his "selfish" love, the benevolence that he has for himself, to the other. In his doctrine on charity, what Thomas does is to extend the Aristotelian notion of friendship into the "supernatural" order, so that charity is seen as friendship of man for God. He does not intend to minimize the infinite distance between man and God. Indeed, the charity of which he speaks is the result of grace; it is infused with sanctifying grace, a totally gratuitous gift of God by which man is enabled supernaturally to participate in the divine life. As a result of this divine self-communication man is "to the likeness of God" in a special way. He is *raised* to a state of friendship with God and is supernaturally united to God (*Summa Theologica*, II-II, q. 23, a. 1 and 2).

For Thomas, charity is not only the most excellent of the virtues but also the "form" of all the others, so that without charity they cannot be strictly true virtues (*Summa Theologica*, II-II, q. 23, a. 7 and 8). It exists in the will of those who have sanctifying grace ("will" is understood as a faculty of the soul distinct from the intellect) and it extends to one's neighbor as well as to God, since what one wills to one's neighbor is that he may be in God. Although Thomas has been criticized for his insertion of charity into the seemingly mundane category of friendship, it is evident that there was no intent to detract from the absolute sovereignty of God's grace but rather to cope with the difficult problem of reconciling man's basic drive for self-fulfillment with the traditional doctrine of the totally gratuitous quality of God's gift of grace and the virtues.

The inherent difficulties in Thomas's treatment of the theological virtues show up more clearly in his handling of faith and hope. Since for him the basic thrust of the will toward God made possible by grace is charity, faith is understood as a virtue in the intellect. However, since there is a lack of evidence, since the object of faith is unseen, the act of faith requires also a will act. Thus he can say that "to believe is to think with assent" (*Summa Theologica*, II-II, q. 2, a. 1). Although Thomas's thought is far more subtle and complex than that of most of his disciples and of the great body of Catholic theologians in recent centuries, it is undeniable that this notion of faith invites deterioration into what has rightly been called a distortion of faith—"the will to believe." The distortion has been aptly described by theologian Paul Tillich:

In classical Roman Catholic theology the "will to believe" is not an act which originates in man's striving, but it is given by grace to him whose will is moved by God to accept the truth of what the Church teaches. . . . This kind of interpretation agrees with the authoritarian attitude of the Roman Church (Tillich [1957], p. 36).

This tendency to deterioration from a profound and authentic inner commitment of the personality into a "thinking with assent" to certain propositions on authority involves a surrender of autonomy, a descent into a heteronomous, or "other-directed" situation. At its worst, this means that the capacity for intellectual honesty as well as for religious experience is profoundly damaged and psychic infantilism in religious matters is encouraged. It means also that the sense of relativity is lost and that religious symbols cannot be appreciated as such. Then dogmatic literalism or verbal fundamentalism becomes the believer's surrogate for deep religious awareness.

Closely related to the idea of the act of faith as thinking with assent is the distinction between explicit and implicit faith. It is not surprising that Thomas keeps this distinction, maintaining that "men of higher degree, whose business is to teach others, are under obligation to have fuller knowledge of matters of faith, and to believe them more explicitly" (*Summa Theologica*, II-II, q. 2, a. 6). This distinction has been characteristic of Roman Catholic theology ever since, and it implies that for the masses of people subjection of personal judgment to religious authority is necessary. As Max Weber pointed out, *fides implicita* really involves a placing of confidence in and dedication to a prophet or to the authority of a structured institution. Weber maintains that the faith of Abraham, Jesus, and Paul had the central significance of reliance upon the promises of God, and was no intellectual assertion of dogmas. When it becomes an assertion of dogmas and when the distinction between explicit and implicit faith is made, it works out that the institutional church, with its hierarchy of priests and preachers, gains great power.

Also interrelated with Thomas's conception of the act of faith, and with his distinction between explicit and implicit faith, is his handling of the problem of man's knowledge of God. Whereas in the Augustinian-Anselmian tradition God's existence was considered to be self-evident, Thomas rejected this idea of God's self-evidence to us and proposed elaborate demonstrations based in large measure upon Aristotelian principles. Because of this complexity, it was natural to conclude that "the truth about God such as reason could discover would only be known by a few, and that after a long time, and with the admixture of many errors" (*Summa Theologica*, I, q. 1, a. 1). This meant that for most men, incapable of such mediating discourse, ecclesiastical authority came to be judged necessary for knowledge even of God's existence.

Thomas's idea of hope as a supernaturally infused virtue in the will is also problematic. For him, the proper and principal object of this virtue is eternal happiness, seen as attainable through divine assistance, although we may hope for other things secondarily and as related to eternal happiness (*Summa Theologica*, II-II, q. 17, a. 2). Although many Christians have found this idea meaningful in itself, there are basic difficulties which are attached more to what is not said than to what is actually said. This presentation of hope reflects the fundamentally otherworldly mentality of the Middle Ages—a mentality which was insensitive to the facts of social injustice and of human suffering because it saw these facts as universal and unchangeable. The medieval mind tended to view this world essentially as a vale of tears, the injustices of which would be remedied in the life to come. It saw the universe and society as hierarchical. Each person, whether he was noble or peasant, cleric or layman, had his state of life assigned to him by divine providence, and everything would be satisfactorily explained at the Last Judgment. There was little experience or conception of social mobility and basically no conception of radical social reform. This general outlook helped to form Thomas's view of hope.

It would not be farfetched to infer that there are psychological connections between this otherworldly conception of hope and the idea of faith as an assent to propositions, with its subsequent distinction into explicit and implicit faith. Both ideas reflect and reinforce a conditioning process by which subjection to authority, particularly to ecclesiastical authority, is made acceptable. Moreover, this conception of hope is related to the stress on union with God in the Thomistic idea of charity. On the whole, then, it must be concluded that in the Thomistic synthesis human transcendence is seen primarily in terms of reaching out toward attainment of infinite Good, rather than in terms of creative effort to transform the human situation in this world.

The Protestant Reformation, of course, brought a strong reaction against medieval thought. Luther objected violently to what appeared to him to be the egocentric character of the medieval ideas of the theological virtues. He was repulsed by the idea, so strongly expressed in Thomas, of friendship with God on God's level made possible by transforming grace. Luther's basic objection was to any implication that man is loved by God because of man's own worth. He wished above all to stress the unmotivated character of God's love and the continued sinfulness of the justified sinner. He therefore struggled against the "ladder" symbolism of medieval piety. For Luther, the Christian receives God's love by faith and then mediates this to his neighbor. When he insisted upon justification by faith alone he wished to stress that God's love for man is completely unmerited.

The problems raised by the medieval synthesis of the virtues of faith, hope, and charity and by Luther's critique are complex and have wide ramifications for ethics and politics as well as for theology.

First of all, there is the problem of moral insensitivity in relation to social structures. The Catholic stress upon faith as thinking with assent, and upon the distinction between explicit and implicit faith, although it was hardly conducive to revolutionary activity as regards the church's structures, could induce a certain independence of the secular power, particularly if that power were not supported by the church. An acute observer of this phenomenon, the seventeenth-century philosopher Thomas Hobbes, wrote, in regard to the doctrines of infused virtue and of transubstantiation: "For who will endeavor to obey the laws, if he expect obedience to be poured or blown into him? Or who will not obey a priest, that can make God, rather than his sovereign; nay than God himself?" (*Leviathan*, IV, 46). However, basically this idea of faith worked for the established order insofar as that order was supported by the church. The medieval church and Catholicism for centuries afterward saw social and political reform as superfluous.

On the other hand, critical analysis of Luther's doctrine also uncovers serious problems of ethical motivation, since stress is placed upon salvation by faith alone. Max Weber points out that, given this frame of reference, "every rational and planned procedure for achieving salvation, every reliance on good works, and above all every effort to surpass normal ethical behavior by ascetic achievement, is regarded by religion based on faith as a wicked preoccupation with purely human powers" (Weber [1963], p. 198). According to Weber's analysis what happens is a complicated series of phenomena. Transworldly asceticism and monasticism tend to be rejected when salvation by faith is stressed, and as a result there may be an increased emphasis upon vocational activity within the world. However, the emphasis upon personal religious relationship to God tends to be accompanied by an attitude of individualism in pursuit of such worldly vocational activity. The consequence is an attitude of patient resignation regarding institutional structures, both worldly and churchly. Thus Lutheranism too lacked motivation toward revolutionary activity in society.

A second serious difficulty closely related to this, and inherent both in the medieval synthesis and in the Protestant ethic is the deterioration of the meaning of charity into the sense it may have in such expressions as "charity bazaar" or "charity case." What is involved in this deterioration, aside from a delusory idealizing of selflessness vis-à-vis less fortunate neighbors, is a lack of concern for the transformation of the alienating structures themselves which are at the root of social injustice. It is noteworthy that both Augustine and Thomas accepted the institution of slavery, and that Thomas, in the same work in which he developed his long treatise on charity, upheld the idea that slavery is in some way natural, and that the master has a special right of domination, including the right to beat his slave (*Summa Theologica*, II-II, q. 57, a. 3 and 4; q. 65, a. 2). "Charity" then becomes a substitute for political, economic, and social reform, and the church functions as a distraction from commitment to such reform.

A third difficulty, also closely interrelated with the others has to do with the exclusiveness which is inherent in a notion of faith which is somehow reducible to a "will to believe," whether it be the idea of faith as assent to propositions mediated by the church's authority, which was the distortion growing out of medieval catholicism, or whether it be the Protestant version of "will to believe," characteristic of the notion of faith found in Karl Barth and Rudolf Bultmann. The most scathing criticism of the latter was expressed by philosopher Karl Jaspers, who wrote of Bultmann's idea of justification by faith in the redemptive history: "For a philosopher this is the most alienating, the most outlandish of beliefs—this Lutheran dogma with its terrible consequences scarcely seems any longer even denotative existentially" (Jaspers [1958], p. 50). The basic reason for Jaspers' objection to this idea of faith is its lack of universality. He sees this chiefly in terms of the fact that the doctrine as presented does not correspond to universal human experience, and in terms of the fact that it excludes the possibility of faith or revelation for those who have not received the biblical message. This exclusiveness has been noted with alarm by others as well. Indeed, so widespread is the conception of Christianity as exclusive that a historian of the stature of Arnold Toynbee has seen intolerance as one of the outstanding characteristics of Christianity.

It is not surprising, then, that in modern times there have been violent reactions to Christian belief. Modern atheism has in large measure been a revolt against the distortions of faith, hope, and charity in traditional Christianity. When in the nineteenth century Nietzsche proclaimed the "death of God" he was not merely declaring that the age of unbelief in an entity named "God" had arrived. Rather, the "death of God" served as a symbolic means of conveying the impending death of an entire world view, of a static, otherworldly vision of reality. Included in that vision which Nietzsche so violently rejected was the hypocrisy of traditional Christian morality—which he labeled "slave morality." Other major thinkers of modern and contemporary

times, such as Feuerbach, Freud, Camus, and Sartre, have rejected Christianity for a variety of reasons, but all share a fundamental antipathy to a world view which they have seen as basically at odds with man's deepest striving toward a validly human realization of faith, hope, and love. Many Christians too, while retaining their identity as such, have shared to some extent this widespread disillusionment. Theologian Dietrich Bonhoeffer, for example, declared that he considered the attack of Christianity upon the adulthood of the world to be in the first place pointless, in the second ignoble, and in the third un-Christian. Of all modern critiques of Christianity, however, probably that which is most directly relevant to the ideas of faith, hope, and charity is that which has developed out of Marxism. This is particularly important in view of the cross-fertilization process which is now taking place through Christian-Marxist dialogue, and which has contributed to the development of a new theology of hope.

Marxism has atheism as a presupposition; its primary concern is man. It defines man as a working being who enters into his humanity by transforming the world. The Marxist does not see transcendence as an act of God calling man; rather he sees it as a dimension of man's own activity reaching out beyond itself. Contemporary Marxist theoreticians such as Roger Garaudy are concerned to maintain an absolute openness to the future. Their attitude is one of creative hope, but it is a purely human hope, not utopian or content with the world as it is, but bent upon transformation of the world, and upon the liberation of man from all alienation, material and moral. One might ask why atheism appears to them to be necessary for the attainment of this goal. Garaudy, one of those Marxists who are most able to communicate with progressive Christian theologians, suggests the answer:

If we reject the very name of God, it is because the name implies a presence, a reality, whereas it is only an exigency which we live, a never-satisfied exigency of totality and absoluteness, of omnipotence as to nature and of perfect loving reciprocity of consciousness (Garaudy [1966], p. 94).

In effect, Garaudy distinguishes his position on man's hope from that of even the most progressive Christian thinkers by saying that the exigency of the Christian for the infinite is experienced or expressed as presence, whereas for him it is absence. This philosophical attitude is similar to that of another influential Marxist, Ernst Bloch, who also rejects the Christian tendency to hypostatize the future into an already existing God.

Aside from this metaphysical difference, there is also an undisguised distrust for Christianity because of its historical record of teaching resignation in the face of exploitation and oppression. The support given in the past and still given by the churches to the forces that exploit and oppress human beings is an acknowledged obstacle even for the more open Marxists to acceptance of the Christian contribution to human progress. Some of them, however, have overcome confusion between the deep nature of faith as commitment to transcendence and the transitory expressions and ideologies in which it is encased. These few avant-garde Marxists, such as Bloch and Garaudy, may have been helped in this respect by dialogue with some avant-garde theologians. In any case they are in advance of the vast body both of Christians and of Marxists.

The criticisms of modern secular humanists and in particular of modern day Marxists have not been lost upon some Christian thinkers, who have taken upon themselves the task of rethinking the Christian tradition for those living in the age of "the death of God." It is not by accident that the most powerful recent trend in theology has been a new "theology of hope," rather than a "theology of faith" or of charity. This does not by any means signify a minimizing of these latter ideas; rather, it indicates the central focus of interest in contemporary theology and in the contemporary consciousness: the future.

One of the first Christian thinkers to confront the Marxist criticism was the Jesuit scientist, poet, philosopher, and theologian Pierre Teilhard de Chardin. Teilhard proclaimed almost poetically his sense of belonging to that half of mankind which sees the seemingly fixed and random universe as moving forward, and expressed his anguish at the failure of traditional Christianity to proclaim this evolutionary vision. At the heart of the modern religious crisis he saw a conflict within faith between the "forward" impulse toward progress in humanization of this planet and the traditional "upward" impulse of religious worship. He saw this conflict as an apparent rather than a real contradiction because it is the inherent task and function of the church to Christianize *all* that is human in man. Yet since church authority has in fact failed to embrace everything that is human on earth, the unity of which we dream seems to beckon us in two different directions. Thus "we see the dramatic growth of a whole race of 'spiritual expatriates'—human beings torn between a Marxism whose depersonalizing effect revolts them and a Christianity so lukewarm in human terms that it sickens them" (Teilhard de Chardin [1964], p. 268). Teilhard's prophetic vision reached out toward a synthesis to be attained in the future through the interaction of Marxism and Christianity—toward the birth of a faith that would embrace total commitment both to the world and to God.

In the 1960's the theologians of hope began to formulate in a more precise way the implications of such insights. Johannes Metz—a German theologian who communicates well with American intellectuals—stresses the character of Christian hope as creative rather than passive wishful thinking. This hope is by no means utopian; in its attempt to reform the world it recognizes the inseparability of the cross and the resurrection. It recognizes the reality of human alienation, of the pain of finiteness, of death. It strives to look steadily at these realities and to work through them; hence its characteristic of being a hope-against-hope. Rather than being a purely individualistic hope for personal salvation abstracted from the realities of this world, it is of a radically social and political nature, attempting to reach out toward the "God of Abraham"—the "God before us"—through commitment to transformation of the alienating structures of this world. For Metz, the responsibility of Christian hope towards the world, then, implies the idea of a "political theology" and of "creative eschatology."

Another important voice among the future-oriented theologians is Wolfgang Pannenberg, whose highly speculative work reconsiders some of the basic assumptions of Hellenized theological tradition. The list of ground-breaking thinkers also includes Leslie Dewart and Harvey Cox. However, there is no major theologian in this area to whom indebtedness is more universally acknowledged than Jürgen Moltmann, author of *Theologie der Hoffnung*. While it would be impossible to summarize here the wealth of his thought, a few points can be made. For Moltmann, the eschatological is the medium of the Christian faith as such, the key in which everything in it is set. Since Christian faith lives in hope, there is only one real problem in Christian theology—the problem of the future—and hope is the foundation of theological thinking as such. Moltmann takes a strong stand against the mysticism of being because he thinks it presupposes an immediacy to God which the faith that believes in God on the ground of Christ cannot validly adopt. Future-oriented, he rejects much of the Hellenic world view. For him, all knowledge in faith is anticipatory and fragmentary; its mobilizing force is hope, through the medium of which all theological judgments function as showing reality its future possibilities. Moreover, "creative action springing from faith is impossible without new thinking and planning that springs from hope" (Moltmann [1967], p. 35). Moltmann's theology of hope understands history as a reality instituted by promise. That is, there is a relation between *promissio* and *missio* such that the Christian consciousness of history is a consciousness of mission. In this view, then, the reality of man is historic and progressive, and revelation too is progressive in that it creates progress.

However promising may be the work of the theologians of hope, however, it should be recognized that the number of people alienated from Christianity is enormous. To countless educated persons the various forms of secular humanism—scientific, ethical, and political—continue to seem more authentic than even the most enlightened manifestations of Christianity. Indeed, the quest for authenticity in faith, hope, and love is a notable characteristic of the contemporary attitude, particularly among the young. It is perhaps for this reason that a thinker such as Albert Camus continues to have such influence. In *The Myth of Sisyphus* he sets forth a powerful symbol in the figure of Sisyphus the absurd hero, doomed for eternity to push a rock up a hill, only to have it roll down again, and who yet is greater than his fate because he is conscious of it, conscious that he has no hope of succeeding. When Camus claims that there is but one serious philosophical problem, namely suicide, his intention is to face up to the hopelessness of finitude. Philosophical suicide, the irrationalist's leap of faith, is rejected as an inadequate response to the problem of the absurd. The only adequate response is to live in the face of the absurd, refusing to escape.

The theologians of hope are attempting to take into account this modern demand for utter honesty and authenticity. Hence the repeated insistence that Christian hope is not utopian, that it is hope "in spite of," that it is hope-against-hope. Having absorbed into its consciousness the full weight of modern man's sense of ambiguity and having proclaimed that all religious understanding is fragmentary and anticipatory, creative modern theology appears to have made a qualitative leap beyond the dogmatism of the past. However, there is room for serious doubt about whether institutional religion will be able to meet the challenge of change.

A central difficulty lies in the fact that institutional religion is subject to a process of routinization, by which structures, persons, places, and things become sacralized and faith itself becomes transformed into a thing or object. One author notes with amazement the way in which this objectification has occurred in Christianity: "The peculiarity of the place given to belief in Christian history is a monumental matter whose importance and whose relative uniqueness must be appreciated" (Smith [1963], p. 180). In fact, most Westerners are unsuspecting about this and tend to think of the question of belief as a primary one. In any event, institutionalized Christianity has tended to lose sight of the original revelatory experience which gave it its being and to focus upon transitory ideologies and structures as if these were ultimate.

Catholicism especially has in recent centuries re-acted against modernity in a manner typical of severely threatened communities. The Roman Index of Forbidden Books, the Syllabus of Errors, the Anti-Modernist Oath, all reflected this sense of threat. Its defensiveness expressed itself in a kind of hyper-rationalism and a verbal fundamentalism which functioned to separate true believers from heretics, the sheep from the goats. Yet if Catholicism has displayed a marked tendency toward ossification, it has also managed to preserve the Christian symbols. By contrast, Protestantism, which to a greater extent has sustained a spirit of self-criticism, has tended to experience the death of religious symbols and fatal acculturation. Indeed, since the Reformation, Catholicism and Protestantism have functioned as separate historical embodiments of different and complementary aspects of Christian faith. It is coming to be recognized that continued reactualization of this faith, motivated by creative hope, will require a meeting of these opposites in striving toward a qualitatively higher union than has existed in the past, in order that those who still call themselves Christians may dare to speak to the modern world again about charity.

BIBLIOGRAPHY

The principal biblical and patristic texts are discussed in A. Nygren, *Den kristna kärlekstanden genom tiderna* (Stockholm, 1936); trans. P. S. Watson as *Agape and Eros* (Philadelphia, 1953). See also especially P. Berger, *The Sacred Canopy* (New York, 1967); E. Bloch, *Das Princip Hoffnung* (Frankfurt, 1959); A. Camus, *Le mythe de Sisyphe* (Paris, 1942), trans. as *The Myth of Sisyphus & Other Essays* (New York, 1955; and repr.); *Cross Currents*, **18**, 3 (1968); R. Garaudy, *De l'anathème au dialogue* (Paris, 1965), trans. L. O'Neill as *From Anathema to Dialogue* (New York, 1966); K. Jaspers and R. Bultmann, *Die Frage der Entmythologisierung* (Munich, 1954), trans. as *Myth and Christianity* (New York, 1958); M. Marty and D. Peerman, eds., *New Theology No. 5* (New York, 1968); J. Moltmann, *Theologie der Hoffnung* (Munich, 1965), trans. J. Leitch as *Theology of Hope* (New York, 1967); T. O'Dea, *The Catholic Crisis* (Boston, 1968); W. C. Smith, *The Meaning and End of Religion. A New Approach to the Religious Tradition of Mankind* (New York, 1963); T. Steeman, "The Underground Church: The Forms and Dynamics of Change in Contemporary Catholicism," *The Religious Situation: 1969*, ed. D. Cutler (Boston, 1969), pp. 713–48; P. Teilhard de Chardin, *L'avenir de l'homme* (Paris, 1959), trans. N. Denny as *The Future of Man* (New York, 1964); P. Tillich, *The Courage to Be* (New Haven, 1952); idem, *Dynamics of Faith* (New York, 1957); idem, *The Protestant Era*, trans. J. L. Adams (Chicago, 1948); A. Toynbee, *Christianity among the Religions of the World* (New York, 1957); E. Troeltsch, *Die Soziallehren der christlichen Kirchen und Gruppen* (Tübingen, 1911), trans. O. Wyon as *The Social Teaching* *of the Christian Churches*, 2 vols. (1931; reprint New York, 1960); M. Weber, "Religionssoziologie," *Wirtschaft und Gesellschaft* (Tübingen, 1922; 1956), trans. E. Fischoff as *Sociology of Religion* (Boston, 1963).

MARY DALY

[See also Authority; **Church as an Institution;** Gnosticism; God; **Love;** Reformation; Socialism; Women.]

FORM IN THE HISTORY OF AESTHETICS

FEW TERMS have lasted as long as "form"; it has been in existence since the Romans. And few terms are as international: the Latin *forma* has been accepted in many modern languages, in Italian, Spanish, Polish, and Russian without change, in others with slight alteration (in French *forme*, in English "form," and in German *Form*).

However, the ambiguity of the term is as great as its persistence. From the outset the Latin *forma* replaced two Greek words: *morphē* and *eidos;* the first applied primarily to visible forms, the second to conceptual forms. This double heritage contributed considerably to the diversity of meanings of "form."

The many opposites of form (content, matter, element, subject matter, and others) reveal its numerous meanings. If content is taken as the opposite, then form means external appearance or style; if matter is the opposite, then form is regarded as shape; if element is considered opposite, then form is tantamount to the disposition or arrangement of parts.

The history of aesthetics reveals at least five different meanings of form, all of them important for a proper understanding of art.

(1) First, form is equivalent to the *disposition, arrangement, or order of parts*, which will be called *form A*. In this case the opposites to form are elements, components, or parts which form A unites or welds into a whole. The form of a portico is the arrangement of its columns; the form of a melody is the order of sounds.

(2) When the term form is applied to what is *directly given to the senses*, we shall call it *form B*. Its opposite then is content. In this sense, the sound of words in poetry is its form, and their meaning its content.

These two meanings, form A and form B, are at times confusingly identified, but this should be avoided. Form A is an abstraction; a work of art is never just a disposition but consists of parts in a certain arrangement of order. Form B, on the other hand, is by definition

concrete, "given to the senses." Of course, we can combine forms A and B by using the term "form" to refer to the order (form A) of what is directly perceived (form B), form to the second power, as it were.

(3) Form may mean the boundary or contour of an object. Let us call it *form C*. Its opposite and correlate is matter or substance. In this sense, frequently used in everyday speech, form is similar to, but by no means identical with, form B: colors and contours perceived together belong to form B, but contour alone pertains to form C.

The above three ideas of form (A, B, and C) are the creations of aesthetics itself. On the other hand, the remaining two concepts of form arose within general philosophy and then passed into aesthetics.

(4) One of them—we shall call it *form D*—was invented by Aristotle. Here form means the *conceptual essence* of an object; another Aristotelian name for this form is "entelechy." The opposites and correlates of form D are the accidental features of objects. Most modern aestheticians dispense with this idea of form, but his has not always been so. In the history of aesthetics, form D is as old as form A and even older than the ideas of B and C.

(5) The fifth meaning, which we shall call *form E*, was used by Kant. For him and his followers it meant a *contribution of the mind* to the perceived object. The opposite and correlate of the Kantian form consists in what is not produced and introduced by the mind but is given to it from without through experience.

Each of these five forms has a different history, which will be presented here as they occur in aesthetics and the theory of art. The five forms appear historically not only under the name "form" but also under many different synonyms, e.g., *figura* and *species* in Latin, or shape and figure in English.

We are concerned here not only with the history of the concept but also with the history of theories of form, including not only the question of when and in what meaning form appeared in theories of art, but also when and in which meanings it was regarded as an essential factor of art.

The History of Form A. Words which the ancient Greeks used to name beauty etymologically meant pattern or proportion of parts. For visible beauty, for works of architecture or sculpture, *symmetria*, that is, commensurability, was the principal term; for audible beauty, for musical works it was *harmonia*, that is, consonance. The word *taxis*, that is, order, had a similar meaning. Such were the ancient synonyms of form A, the disposition or order of parts. These terms were not accidental: the Greeks used them because they were convinced that beauty—particularly of the visible and audible kind—*consists in* an arrangement and proportion of parts, in *form*. This was their great contribution to aesthetic theory.

This aesthetic theory, as testified by Aristotle, originated among Pythagoreans, probably in the fifth century B.C., and claimed that beauty consists in a well-defined simple proportion of parts. Strings produce harmonious sounds when their length is in proportion to the relatively simple ratio of one to two (octave) or two to three (fifth). A portico of a temple is perfect if its height, width, and the arrangement of columns are computed according to the accepted module (in the Doric temples architects regarded five to eight as the correct ratio of the width of columns to the space between). A man, as well as a monument, is beautiful when his proportions are correct; sculptors observed the one to eight ratio of the head to the body and one to three of the forehead to the face.

The Pythagoreans, convinced that beauty depends on proportions, expressed this in a very general formula: "order and proportion are beautiful and useful" (Stobaeus IV, 1, 40). "No art comes about without proportion. All art therefore arises through number. So there is a certain proportion in sculpture and also in painting. Generally speaking, every art is a system of perceptions, and a system implies number; one can therefore justly say: things look beautiful by virtue of number" (Sextus Empiricus VII, 106).

The Pythagorean point of view was maintained by Plato: "It is always beautiful and virtuous to preserve measure and proportions" (*Philebus* 64E). "Ugliness means simply a lack of measure" (*Sophist* 228A). Aristotle's view was similar: "Beauty consists in magnitude and ordered arrangement" (*Poetics* 1450b 38). Just as the Stoics thought: "Bodily beauty is the proportion of limbs in their mutual relation and in relation to the whole; so is it the case with the beauty of the soul" (Stobaeus II, 62, 15). Cicero thought similarly: "Harmonious symmetry of limbs engages the attention and delights the eye" (*De officiis* I, 28, 98). Of the six qualities of architecture that Vitruvius recognized as many as four (*ordinatio, dispositio, eurythmia, symmetria*) consist in the correct arrangement or disposition of parts (*De architectura* I, 2, 1). It is rather unusual for a general theory to meet with such a universal acceptance over so long a period of time. A nineteenth-century historian of aesthetics, R. Zimmermann, maintained that the principle of ancient art was form (Zimmermann, p. 192). This view is correct, and refers to the meaning of form as an orderly disposition and proportion of parts.

The privileged position of form as orderly disposition was not called in question until Plotinus, at the close of antiquity in the third century A.D. While agreeing that the proportion of parts is the basis of beauty he disputed whether proportion is regarded as its only basis (*Enneads* I 6, 1; VI 7, 22). Had that been the case, only composite things could then be beautiful, whereas there are things which though simple are yet beautiful, e.g., the sun, light, gold. Beauty therefore, as Plotinus said, lies not only in proportions but in the luster of things as well. Since that time the position of form A, although still privileged in the theory of art, has ceased to be exclusive.

In the Middle Ages aesthetics had appeared in not one but *two* varieties. According to the one which was true to the ancient Greek tradition, beauty and art consisted in form alone. Saint Augustine supported and upheld this theory: "Every thing pleases only by beauty; in beauty, by shapes; in shapes, by proportions; and in proportions, by numbers" (*De ordine* II 15, 42). No Greek in classical antiquity ever expressed this old Hellenic idea more emphatically than this Father of the Church. "There is no ordered thing which is not beautiful" (*De vera religione* XLI, 77). And again: "Beautiful things please us by their number" (*De musica* VI 12, 38). And lastly: "The more measure, shape, and order there is in all things, the more they have that is good" (*De natura boni* 3). This triad (*modus, species, ordo*) became the formula of medieval aesthetics and survived a thousand years. It was repeated literally in the thirteenth century by the great scholastic compendium *Summa Alexandri:* "A thing is said to be beautiful in the world when it observes the proper measure, form, and order—*modum, speciem, et ordinem*" (Quaracchi ed., II, 103). Taken together they were synonyms of what we call form.

In the Middle Ages the principal term for form A was *figura* (from the Latin *fingere*, to shape). Abélard defined it as a disposition of the body (*compositio corporis*), both of the model and of the work of art (ed. Geyer, p. 236). However, the term *forma* was also used in this meaning. As early as in the sixth century Isidore of Seville composed both terms *figura* and *forma* (*Differentiae*, Ch. 1). In the twelfth century Gilbert de la Porrée wrote: "Form is used in many meanings; also in the meaning of the figure of bodies" (Porretanus, p. 1138). The treatise *Sententiae divinitatis* (ed. Geyer, p. 101), dating from the same century, stressed the distinction between the conceptual form (form D) and visual form (form A). Clarembaldus of Arras defined form (A) as follows: "Form is the appropriate arrangement of parts in material things" (ed. Jansen, p. 91). Alain of Lille considered as synonyms: form, shape (*figura*), measure, number, connection (*Patrologia Latina*, Vol. 210, col. 504). The ancient symmetry, harmony, proportion was called form.

This usage lasted until the end of the Middle Ages. As Duns Scotus formulated it: "Form and figure are

217

the external disposition of things" (ed. Garcia, p. 281). Also, in the works of Ockham it was part of their regular terminology: form was on a par with figure (ed. Baudry, p. 225 and p. 94).

The adjective *formosus* was, fairly early, incorporated into the language of art. This adjective meant the same as shapely, well-proportioned, beautiful; it conveyed a favorable aesthetic judgment, and was a sign of the appreciation of form in the Middle Ages. Then followed the noun *formositas* ("shapeliness"), which meant the same as beauty. The negative adjective *deformis* ("shapeless," "ugly") was also used. In Bernard of Clairvaux we find a play on the words *formosa deformitas* and *deformis formositas* which he used to describe the art of his time (*Patrologia Latina*, Vol. 182, col. 915).

In its second variety, medieval aesthetics followed Plotinus with his dualistic conception: beauty consists in form but not exclusively in form. Just as Augustine championed the first conception, Pseudo-Dionysius advocated the second (*De divinis nominibus* IV, 7). He is the author of the dual criterion of "proportion and luster" (*proportio et claritas*), a conception of beauty which also had many followers. Robert Grosseteste described beauty as proportion, but concerning the beauty of light he maintained that "it is based not on number, not on measure, and not on weight or anything else like that, but on sight" (*Hexaemeron* 147 v). The second conception won the support of Saint Thomas Aquinas in his early commentary on *In divina nomina* (Ch. IV, lect. 5), and in his *Summa theologica* (II-a IIae.180 a.2 ad3): "Beauty consists in a certain luster and proportion" (*Pulchrum consistit in quadam claritate et proportione*).

Both trends in aesthetics, with their different approaches to form A, persisted during the Renaissance. The line advocated by Pseudo-Dionysius was kept alive by the Platonic Academy in Florence. Its head, Marsilio Ficino remarked: "Some regard beauty as an arrangement of component parts, or to use their own words, commensurability and proportion. . . . We do not accept this view because this kind of arrangement occurs only in composites and, therefore, no simple thing can be beautiful. However, pure colors, lights, separate sounds, the glitter of gold and silver, knowledge, the soul, are all called beautiful and are all pure and simple" (*Convivium* V 1). This was in agreement with the beliefs of Plotinus and his medieval followers. Pico della Mirandola's pronouncements were similar. However, the representatives of this dualistic conception were in a minority during the Renaissance.

It was the classical theory which again became predominant; namely, that beauty consists exclusively in the disposition and proportion of parts, in form (A). This was the case in Alberti's treatises which formu-

lated the Renaissance theory of beauty and art: "Beauty is a harmony of all the mutually adapted parts" (*De re aedificatoria* VI 2); ". . . beauty is a concordance and mutual attunement of parts." The consonance of parts determining beauty was called by Alberti *conserto, consenso, concordantia, corrispondenza*, and particularly *concinnitas*. Following Alberti the last term was most commonly used in the Renaissance to describe perfect form. Nevertheless, Alberti used other names too: *ordine, numero, grandezza, collocatione e forma* (ibid., IX 5).

Alberti had followers. In 1525 Cardinal Bembo wrote: "The body is beautiful when its members are in proportion to each other, just as with the soul whose virtues are in mutual harmony" (*Gli Asolani* I). The great Palladio saw the excellence of architecture in *forme belle e regolate* (Palladio, I, 1, p. 6). And the philosopher-mathematician Cardano explained once more that beauty depends on simple proportions (*De subtilitate*, p. 275).

This conception of art based on form persisted in seventeenth-century France. It is most clearly stated by Nicolas Poussin. It appears also in the French Academy, where a particular stress was placed on the *rules* which govern form. We find it in the writings of the academic theorists André Félibien, Abraham Bosse, Charles Alphonse Du Fresnoy, Henri Testelin (Tatarkiewicz, *Historia Estetyki*, III, 389, n. 471). The classical conception was advanced by François Blondel, author of a classic work on architecture; according to him, in a building the following are essential: "l'ordre, la situation, l'arrangement, la *forme*, le *nombre*, la proportion" (Blondel, p. 785).

The supremacy of form—if form is understood as a simple, conspicuous disposition of parts which can be defined in numbers—declined in the eighteenth century under the spell of romanticism. Nevertheless, it soon revived, in the neo-classicism of the end of the century, in the writings of Johann Joachim Winckelmann and Quatremère de Quincy. De Quincy (p. 66) proclaimed true beauty to be "geometrical." And independently of all artistic trends, of classicism and romanticism, Kant declared in 1790 that "in all the fine arts the essential element consists, of course, in form" (*Kritik der Urteilskraft*, sec. 52).

In the first half of the nineteenth century *idealische Schönheit* ("ideal Beauty") distracted aestheticians away from form but only briefly. The term embodying the concept of form A reappeared in J. F. Herbart's aesthetics and especially in the writings of his disciple, R. Zimmermann, whose entire aesthetics was conceived as *Formwissenschaft* ("science of form"), precisely in the sense of form A, that is, of the interrelation of elements.

The recognition of the importance of formal relations in the arts is not a modern achievement; formal relations were the foundation of Greek aesthetics. On the other hand, it is indeed true to say that in certain trends in art and art theory, the twentieth century has again brought form to the fore in several meanings of the term, including that of form A. Stanislaw I. Witkiewicz and the adherents of "formism" and pure form defended form A in Poland, Clive Bell and Roger Fry in England. Emotions connected with figurative art, Fry said, quickly evaporate and those which remain spring from a purely formal relation: "what remains, what never grows less nor evaporates, are the feelings dependent on the *purely formal relation.*"

Twentieth-century artists and theoreticians concur on this point even when some of them use different terminology. Instead of "form" Charles Jeanneret (Le Corbusier) said "invariants" (*Esprit Nouveau*, 1921). He also said: *la science et l'art ont l'idéal commun de généraliser, ce qui est la plus haute fin de l'esprit* ("science and art share the common ideal of generalizing, which is the highest goal of the mind").

Among those who in the twentieth century have been concerned with the problem of form in art some, like E. Monod-Herzen, give it a purely geometrical interpretation, and others, like M. Ghyka, a mystical one. The ancients, especially the Pythagoreans, were familiar with both interpretations. While the whole ancient theory of art attached particular importance to form, the twentieth century sees only some movements in art theory doing the same, but in a more radical way.

A noted contemporary American aesthetician, Karl Aschenbrenner, has offered the following solution to the controversy over form: form alone (meaning form A) does not determine the aesthetic impact of a work of art, which is also composed of elements, but only form can be analyzed adequately and is, therefore, alone fit to be the subject of aesthetic theory. This view is a new solution to the old problem.

Surveying two thousand years of the history of form A, we notice another point; namely, form used to mean either *any* arrangement of parts or more exclusively, a *correct*, beautiful, harmonious, and orderly arrangement; synonyms of this narrower sense of form A were *symmetria, concordantia, concinnitas*. Particularly with the Pythagoreans and Augustine, form used to mean an arrangement or order which is *rational*, regular, and expressible by *numbers*; this more specific meaning explains the Greek and scholastic synonyms of form, e.g., *numerus* and *ordo*. A more thorough analysis will therefore distinguish any arrangement (form A) from a harmonious or regular order (a subspecies, form A_1).

The narrowing of the concept of form A to the more specific form A_1, in the sense that only an outstanding form is worthy of its name, may be illustrated in many fields. In Latin paleography, from the thirteenth to the fifteenth century, a certain style of writing was called *littera formata*, but only when it was used for the copying of important, biblical and liturgical texts, and had a ceremonial character. Furthermore, in ordinary everyday handwriting, *littera cursiva*, a refined variant appeared around 1400 and was called *cursiva formata*.

"Structure" is an often used term in recent years, and its meaning is close to that of form A. However, it usually refers only to nonaccidental forms created by inner forces or internal drives. Consequently it applies rather to biological or geological structures; but recently, the term and concept of structure have been adopted in the theory of art. This usage expresses the tendency to regard forms of works of art as products of natural processes. If we are to include structures in the "family" of forms, they may be considered closely related to form A, particularly to form A_1, but *sui generis* are a second subspecies, form A_2.

The History of Form B. While the first sense of form (A) refers to arrangement or order, the second sense (B) refers to the *appearance* of things. The correlates of form A are component elements, parts, colors in painting, sounds in music; in form B, the correlates are content, import, meaning. The impressionists stress the importance of form in appearance, and the abstract painters stress form in arrangement.

Formalists have been advocating both form A and form B, and occasionally confound the two concepts. Yet as early as the thirteenth century, Saint Bonaventura drew a clear line of division, using *figura* as a synonym of form: *Figura dicitur . . . uno modo dispositio ex clausione linearum . . . secundo modo exterior rei facies sive pulchritudo* (Quaracchi ed., V, 393). Here "form" (*figura*) has a twofold meaning: first, it is an arrangement enclosed within boundary lines; secondly, it is an external appearance or beauty of a thing.

(1) The ancient Sophists were the first to single out form B and to emphasize its importance, e.g., in the realm of poetry by separating the "sound of words" from their "significant content"; the "sound of words" and "beautiful rhythm" constituted the form in poetry. The distinction between form and content was preserved in Hellenistic poetics. Posidonius' definition of poetry distinguished the word from its meaning, or "verbal expression" from its "content" (in Philodemus, ed. Jansen, p. 25). Following Demetrius another formula contrasting form with content was used: "*what* the work communicates" and "*how* it communicates it" (*De elecutione* [1508], p. 75). This formula is the vaguest and most flexible of all.

Some trends of poetics in late antiquity not only selected "wording" as form, but attached special importance to it as the very essence of poetry. Cicero and Quintilian believed that "judgment of the ears" 219 (*aurium judicium*) is important in oratory and poetry; even as early as the third century B.C., for some Greek scholars the judgment of the ears was the only judgment that mattered. The names of these ancient formalists are known; one of them, Crates, maintained that pleasant sound makes the only difference between good and bad poetry; Heracleodor was even more specific when he considered good poetry as a pleasing *arrangement* of sounds, thus uniting forms A and B. Hellenistic scholars not only contrasted form with content in poetry, but also regarded form as superior.

In the Middle Ages, form (*compositio verborum*) and content (*sententia veritatis*) were even more sharply opposed to one another, as *external* and *internal* factors of poetry. The scholastics called content "the internal sense" (*sententia interior*) and form "the external verbal ornament" (*superficialis ornatus verborum*). They distinguished two kinds of form: one purely sensory, i.e., acoustic (*quae mulcet aurem*) or musical (*suavitas cantilenae*); the other, mental or conceptual form, the manner of expression (*modus dicendi*), embraced tropes and metaphors and was on the whole optical in kind, employing images and constituting the *visual* aspect of poetry. These *distinctiones* were elaborated chiefly by Mathieu of Vendôme (*Ars . . .* , ed. Faral, p. 153). Form B thus includes *ornatus verborum* and *modus dicendi*.

In medieval poetics beside two kinds of form there were two kinds of content (*sententia interior*); one comprised the subject of a work (*fondus rerum*) and the plot of the events narrated, the other consisted of the ideological content, the religious or metaphysical import.

In Renaissance poetics the dividing line between form and content was just as distinct. The terms used were *verba* and *res*. Invention (*inventio*) and thought (*sententia*) were included in content; wording (*elocutio*) belonged to form. Some writers like Fracastoro and Castelvetro called form an instrument (*stromento*), intimating thereby an inferior role for form (B. Weinberg). On the other hand, writers like Robortello saw the real purpose and value of poetry in beautifully and properly ordered words, that is, in form B.

Form acquired a still higher status in the aesthetics of literary mannerism; while one trend within mannerism, called *conceptismo*, aimed at subtlety of thought (that is, of content), another (*culturanismo*) strove for subtlety of language—that is, of Form B (Gracián). However, if we are to contrast form with content in line with Demetrius' formula ("what is said" and "how it is said"), then we notice that the whole movement of literary mannerism was centered on form exclusively. However, the term "form" was rarely used because the Aristotelians in taking possession of it

employed it in a different sense (discussed below as form D). The ideas of form (B) and its content were employed only in poetics, in which domain they were used for many centuries and occupied a position of paramount importance.

(2) In the eighteenth century the problem of the relation of form to content ceased attracting attention; in the meantime other problems came to the fore. The term "form" and its synonyms were seldom encountered in poetics. The problem was revived in the nineteenth century not only in poetics but in the theory of all arts. By the middle of that century "form" (i.e., form B) appeared in the theory of music (E. Hanslick) and soon after in the theory of fine arts. This change was fundamental because previously the concept of form B had been applied only to poetics.

In the art of the word, form and content were two separate items because only in this art do they form two different, clearly divided, and very dissimilar strata, viz., words and things (*verba* and *res*). Here the form is linguistic, the content material. The reader is presented directly only with words by means of which he may indirectly represent things. Such a duality of form and content does not exist in other arts.

However, musical works express something; works of painting and sculpture express, mean, or denote something, and what they express, mean, or denote seems to constitute their content and not their form. Nevertheless, the situation is different in these arts because in none of them can we find two strata as dissimilar as words and things. The content of a novel lies beyond the printed page seen by the reader; on the other hand, the content of a picture (for instance the river Seine in Monet's picture), is seen *in* the picture. What lies beyond the picture is not the content but its subject, its model, or whatever the painter imitated.

The concepts of form (B) and its correlated content changed when applied to the visual arts; one might even say that next to the old concept of form in poetics, a new concept of form (B₁), more universal and vague, came into existence. For a long time no occasion arose to confuse these two concepts, form A and form B, because the first was applied mainly to the visual arts and the second only to poetry. Confusion arose when form B was introduced to the theory of the visual arts in addition to form A. "Form" was then used in both senses at the same time. "Only form is important" intimated, first, that only the appearance (not the content) is important, and, secondly, that within the appearance only arrangement (not the elements); that is, only form B matters, but also form A within form B, thus overlooking the distinction between the two meanings of "form."

(3) Another important turning point in the history of form B occurred when a new question was raised: Which is the *more important* in art, form or content? Formerly considered equally necessary and complementary, form and content, in the nineteenth and especially in the twentieth century, began to compete with each other. The debate was intensified by radical supporters of "pure" form; the years 1920–39 heralded the ideas of formalism, suprematism, unism, purism, neo-plasticism; also, Malevitch's pronouncements in Russia, Clive Bell's in England, Le Corbusier's in France, the formists' in Poland, P. Mondrian's in Holland.

The moderate statement of formalism appears in a formulation like Le Corbusier's that in a true work of art "form is the *most important thing*." According to extreme formalism *only* form is important, or stated negatively, content does not matter. The extreme view implies that the subject, narrative content, correspondence with reality, the idea itself, the thing represented by the work of art, and even the feelings expressed by it are all unimportant. In extreme formalism content is unnecessary, only form is needed; content will not help but may harm art. According to the formula of H. Focillon, forms are neither signs nor images since they signify and express only themselves. On the other hand, W. Kandinsky remarked: "Form without content is not a hand but an empty glove filled with air. An artist loves form passionately just as he loves his tools or the smell of turpentine, because they are all powerful means in the service of content" (*Cahiers d'art*, **1** [1935], 4).

Finally, an important distinction between two kinds of form was made: those with a corresponding content and those having none. In fact there are *figurative* forms representative of things, or reproducing objective forms, and forms which are abstract or nonrepresentative. This duality of forms had been noticed as long ago as Plato, who contrasted "the beauty of living beings" with "the beauty of a straight line and circle" (*Philebus* 51C). In the eighteenth century this duality of form had been recognized in the theory of art; Kant distinguished between free (*freie*) and dependent beauty (*anhängende Schönheit*), and Home similarly had discriminated between "intrinsic" and "relative beauty."

However, the sharp contrast between the two kinds of form has been questioned; Kandinsky, himself an abstract painter, regarded abstract form as no more than an extreme link in a continuous chain of forms from the purely representative to the abstract. To say nothing of the fact that various abstract forms are inspired by real objects and that the effect of abstract forms on the viewer is frequently due to associations with real objects. In any case, the twentieth century has seen form B elevated to the highest place in the theory of art.

The History of Form C. In many dictionaries the explanation of form begins with a third meaning given here of this term. A. Lalande's French dictionary of philosophy gives as a first definition of form: "a geometrical figure made up of the contours of objects." Similarly, in P. Robert's dictionary of the French language, the long list of meanings of the term begins with the definition: form is a "set of contours of objects."

In everyday speech "form" frequently has this meaning, which seems to be the original and natural one, compared with which all the others appear metaphorical or at least derivative. Thus conceived this sense of form (form C) is synonymous with contour, figure, and shape; its meaning is close to that of surface outline.

Form C is known also outside of everyday speech; it is used in art, specifically in visual arts where it is applied to the works of architects, sculptors, painters. These comprise the artists who attempt to reproduce or construct forms conceived as contours. If form B is a natural concept in poetics, form C is the natural one for the visual arts, which are concerned with spatial forms.

Form C played an important part in the history of the theory of art only from the fifteenth to the eighteenth century, but it was indeed the basic idea during that period. It also appeared under the names "figure" or "drawing" (in Latin texts *figura* predominated; in Italian writers *disegno* was more popular). "Form" was used in those centuries rather with the different shade of meaning discussed below as form D (substantial form). "Drawing" was the natural synonym for form as contour. G. Vasari in his *Lives of the Painters* (*Vite . . .* , I, 168) considered drawing as similar to a form (*simile a una forma*). Another late Renaissance writer, F. Zuccaro, defined drawing as *a form without bodily substance*.

Form C concerns only drawing, not color, and there lies the obvious difference between forms C and B. For sixteenth-century writers contour (form C) and color represented two opposite extremes in painting. Paolo Pino wrote about it in 1548 in his *Dialogo di pittura*. In the seventeenth century a rivalry ensued in the visual arts between form and color. Drawing was considered more important, particularly in academic circles: "Let the drawing always point the way and serve as a compass," Lebrun said; he was the dictator in art during the reign of Louis XIV (Lebrun, pp. 36, 38). H. Testelin, the historiographer, declared to the French Academy of Painting and Sculpture: "A good and competent draughtsman, even if he is a

221

mediocre colorist deserves more respect than one who paints beautiful colors but draws badly" (*Sentiments . . .* , p. 37).

The supremacy of form as drawing ended at the start of the eighteenth century, when, with the emergence of Roger de Piles and the Rubenists, color gained a position parallel to that of drawing. The rivalry and arguments died down, and the contrasting of form (C) with color lost its topical interest.

Comparing the three histories, briefly given above, we may note that the most long-lived one was that of form A as arrangement, followed by form B as appearance, and form C as drawing. In antiquity particular value was attached to form A, in the Renaissance form C was favored, and in the twentieth century form B was stressed.

When critics at times write that a work "lacks form," we may well wonder whether it is possible for a work of art, or for that matter, for any object to be without form? The correct answer will be that it depends on what we understand by "form." Objects cannot be without form A because their parts must be arranged in some way. However, this arrangement may not be an orderly or harmonious one, and therefore may lack form in sense A_1. So likewise with forms B and C, since no material object can exist without appearance or contour. On the other hand, not every object has an important or, to use Clive Bell's expression, "significant form." W. Strzemiński (a Polish painter and theorist) insisted on the "inequality of 'form'," its "knots," and "voids."

We recall the words of the distinguished philosopher Ernst Cassirer who declared that to see the *forms* of things (*rerum videre formas*) is a no less important and indispensable task than to know the causes of things (*rerum cognoscere causas*) (*Essay on Man*, sec. 9). Though beautiful this formula is not quite precise because it is unclear which of the three concepts of form Cassirer means.

The History of Form D (Substantial Form). The fourth concept of form was initiated by Aristotle. He used *morphē* for form in various senses, e.g., shape or figure, but primarily as a synonym for his particular concept of *eidos, entelechia*. He thus regarded form as the essence of a thing, its nonaccidental component: "By form I mean the essence of each thing" (*Metaphysics* 1032b 1, trans. W. D. Ross; see also 1050b 2; 1041b 8; 1034a 43). He identified form with act, energy, aim, and with the dynamic element of existence. This use of form may appear metaphorical to us but it was not so in antiquity. It was basic in Aristotle's metaphysics, but neither he nor his followers in antiquity ever used it in aesthetics.

However, in the Middle Ages, when in the thirteenth century the scholastics accepted the Aristotelian concept of substantial form, they introduced it into aesthetics. They did it in connection with the old idea derived from Pseudo-Dionysius that beauty consists in both the right proportion and luster (*claritas, splendor*) of objects. "Luster" became identified with Aristotelian form, and what resulted was the peculiar idea that the beauty of an object depends on its metaphysical essence when revealed in its appearance. The first to offer this interpretation was probably Albert the Great; for him beauty consisted in the luster of substantial form (form D) revealing itself in matter, but only when it has the right proportion (form A) (ed. Mandonnet, V, 420–21).

This viewpoint was maintained by the Albertine school, in particular, by Ulrich of Strassburg, who tersely wrote: "substantial form is the beauty of every object" (ed. Grabmann, pp. 73–74). Other contemporary schools, such as the Franciscan and Augustinian, thought the same way. Bonaventura accepted this view and inferred that since beauty consists in substantial form, and since every being, has such a form, every being is beautiful: *omne quod est ens habet aliquam formam, omne autem quod habet aliquam formam habet pulchritudinem* (Quaracchi ed., II, 814).

The use of form D in aesthetics reached its zenith but also its end in the thirteenth century: though characteristic of the high Middle Ages, it did not survive. "Substantial form" along with the whole of Aristotelian philosophy lasted until the sixteenth century but least of all in aesthetics. Some traces could still be found, e.g., in the writings of Vincenzo Danti, a scholar in the sixteenth century who said that shape in art originates in a *perfetta forma intenzionale* (Danti, Book I, Ch. 11); also in the theories of the painter Federigo Zuccaro, who identified drawing with form and form with idea, rule, knowledge (Book I, Ch. 2). These traces of Aristotelian form in aesthetics became extinct in the seventeenth and eighteenth centuries. F. Baldinucci, in his dictionary (1681), describes form as a philosophical but not aesthetic term, and so does Richelet (1719). Form D ceased as an aesthetic meaning, and was certainly not used in the nineteenth century.

However, in the twentieth century, this conception under different names seems to be revived in the works of abstract painters, such as P. Mondrian or Ben Nicholson. When Mondrian writes that ". . . a modern artist knows that the feeling of beauty is cosmic and universal," or that new art "expresses a universal element of things because it reconstructs *cosmic relations*" (Seuphor, p. 144), then he is praising a sense of form similar to what the Aristotelians called "substantial form."

The historian of aesthetics will note also that "form" was used not only for Aristotle's entelechies but also for Plato's Ideas. Medieval translators of Plato's works did so, and they were followed by translators of Plato into modern languages. Translating "idea" by "form" is justified to some extent by the fact that in everyday Greek, "idea" meant shape, approaching form B, but a different meaning was introduced then by Plato. The translators, however, followed the original everyday meaning of idea as form. As a result, "form" acquired another metaphysical meaning, which never achieved the same currency as form D, entelechy, in aesthetics. Of course, the Platonic Idea has played a considerable role in the history of aesthetics but not under the name "form."

The History of Form E (A Priori Form). The fifth concept of form was created by Kant. He described form as a property of mind which compels us to experience things in a particular "form." This Kantian form (here called form E) is the *a priori* sense of form; we find it in objects only because it is *imposed* upon them *by the subject.* Thanks to its subjective origin, form E is endowed with the unusual attributes of universality and necessity.

(1) Did Kant have any precursors? Was his concept of form known to anyone before? The Marburg School attributed this concept to Plato, claiming that his *a priori* approach was similar to Kant's, and that Plato understood "ideas" as forms of the mind. Plato's *Theaetetus* appears to confirm this interpretation; however, a more ontological conception dominated his works.

Nicholas of Cusa (Cusanus), an early Renaissance thinker and follower of Plato, reflected over the nature of form in art: "Forms originate only through human art. . . . An artist does not imitate shapes of natural objects; he only renders matter capable of accepting the form of art"; and further: "Every visible form will constitute the likeness and image of the true and invisible form existing in the mind" (Cusanus, p. 219). This formulation in the pre-Kantian theory of art is probably closest to the Kantian meaning of form.

(2) Kant himself prepares a surprise for us. In his *Critique of Pure Reason* he discovered the *a priori* forms of knowledge in the mind: forms of space and time and categories like substance and causality. When later he embarked upon the critique of aesthetic valuation in his *Critique of Judgment* (1790), one might have expected that he would have also discovered in the mind permanent, universal, and necessary forms. But surprisingly enough, he did not detect in aesthetics any *a priori* forms analogous to those he found in the theory of knowledge. He did not think that beauty was determined by permanent forms of mind but by unique gifts of artistic talent. Essential forms (form E) of beauty do not exist, for Kant; beauty has been, and

always will be, created anew by geniuses. In short, in aesthetics *a priori* forms (D) play no role.

(3) The successors of Kant who developed his theories in the nineteenth century also failed to detect any *a priori* forms in aesthetics. However, such forms were discovered in the last quarter of the century, in 1887, by Konrad Fiedler, a thinker who was not a Kantian; in philosophy he followed J. F. Herbart. Vision had for him its universal form, just as knowledge had its *a priori* form for Kant. Fiedler admitted that men may lose the right form of vision; however, artists preserve it in their work. Artistic vision and visual arts are not results of free play of the imagination, as Kant thought: they are governed by the laws and forms of vision.

Fiedler's understanding of the forms of vision was still vague. A clearer definition was given by his disciples and successors: the sculptor A. von Hildebrand, two art historians, A. Riegl and H. Wölfflin, and the philosopher A. Riehl. Hildebrand's *Problem der Form* (1893) was an important turning point. He made a distinction between *two forms* of *visual images:* the nearby (*Nahbild*) and the distant (*Fernbild*). A clear image can be seen only from a distance; only then does a distinct and consolidated form appear which the work of art requires and which can provide aesthetic satisfaction.

The rapidity of changes in artistic trends, especially during the nineteenth century, could not but produce skeptical feelings about any single form of artistic vision; there must be more than one such form; in the history of art a variety of forms succeed one another in coming to the fore. As a result a pluralistic conception of the *a priori* form E of art came into existence, and became characteristic of art theories in the first half of the twentieth century, particularly in Central Europe. Consequently, form E has many alternative forms; they are not timeless, permanent as in Fiedler, but correspond to, and change with, the times. This conception is best known in Wölfflin's formulation. He illustrated the alternative variety of forms in the transition from the Renaissance to the baroque, from the linear to the plastic form, from the closed to the open form. The Austrian school, under A. Riegl's leadership, demonstrated the fluctuations of art between the optical and haptic (tactile or kinesthetic) forms. J. Schlosser, close to this school, contrasted crystalline form with organic form; W. Worringer, abstract with empathetic form (*Abstraction und Einfühling*); W. Deonna, primitive with classical form. Though they differed they accepted form E in its pluralism.

The History of Other Forms. There are still other meanings of form which, though less important, are used in the theory and practice of the arts.

(1) The name "form" is sometimes given to tools **223**

which serve to produce forms, e.g., the forms used by sculptors, potters, tinners, and others. We may call them forms F; they are employed in making forms, and at the same time are forms. Often, as in the case of sculptor's forms, they are negatives of the forms which will be created with their help. Some of them, namely, sculptors' and potters' forms, are used for shaping the form we have called form C, whereas others, such as the tinctorial and printing forms, give objects color as well as shape, thus producing forms in the meaning of form A. History shows that the importance of form F in art is increasing. Even architects are now making use of such forms in the production of prefabricated elements for the construction and facing of buildings.

(2) In the history of the visual arts, as in the history of music or literature, forms are frequently discussed in yet another meaning: conventional, traditionally or commonly accepted forms, binding on the composer or writer who uses them. Once accepted, for whatever reason, they are ready and waiting to be used. These forms, which we may call form G, are exemplified in literature by the forms of the sonnet or of tragedy with the "three unities" (place, time, and action); in music, the forms of the fugue or sonata; in architecture, the *peripteros* ("array of columns") or the Ionic order; the bosquet form in Italian and French gardening; the *zwiebelmuster* ("onion pattern") design in Saxon porcelain. These forms are partly structural and partly ornamental. Though they are all forms A, a few of them are forms G. Many forms G have a long and venerable history, their Golden Age going back to antiquity when almost every variety of art was enclosed within such forms. Medieval art was also restricted by such controlling forms, as was also eighteenth-century classicism. Romanticism undermined the old forms, but also created new ones in their place. In avant-garde art the departure from stable and conventional forms seems thoroughgoing: every artist wishes to have his own way. History appears to show that art moves way from forms G. It is, however, possible for new stable forms to be created.

(3) "Form" of art may also mean a kind or variety of that art. In an expression like "new forms of painting" form is used in the same sense as that in a "form of government" or a "form of disease." The term is used but does not belong in the theory of art; it is simply a convenient way of expressing the multiplicity of the arts: *Ars una, species mille.* In our catalogue of forms, we may list it as form H.

Nor are all the meanings of "form" in art exhausted by the above. Their great number has been known and remarked upon long ago. In the twelfth century Gilbert de la Porrée wrote: "one talks about form in many meanings." In the thirteenth century Robert Grosseteste (p. 109) distinguished three meanings: (a) as a model, e.g., a sandal used as a form (pattern) for making sandals; (b) as a casting mold, e.g., for a statue; (c) as an image in the mind of an artist. Bonaventura's distinction between two meanings of form was given above.

Some of the concepts of form discussed above have disappeared and belong to the past; the concept of form D is not needed by modern aestheticians, and form E has acquired new names. Form F is used rather in artists' workshops than in art theory; form G is a technical expression of theoreticians of art; form H may easily be replaced by other expressions. In all these cases there is no danger of confusing their respective meanings. However, concepts A, B, and C are closely related and are likely to be mixed up; and yet since they are so intimately linked with the name "form" it would be wrong to deprive them of that usage. Thus there does not appear to be any prospect of eliminating the ambiguity of "form" in aesthetics and in the theory of art. But once we are aware of the various meanings of the term, it ceases to be harmful.

Summary. The history of the five conceptions of form developed along diverse lines. For an astonishingly long time form A has been the basic concept in art theory. Form B has been sporadically contrasted with and placed above content in works of art, for example, in the Hellenistic period, but never to such an extent as in the twentieth century. Form C was peculiar to art in the sixteenth and seventeenth centuries. Form D was a distinctive feature of high scholasticism. Form E aroused no interest until the end of the nineteenth century.

BIBLIOGRAPHY

Pierre Abélard, *Logica "Ingredientibus,"* ed. B. Geyer, in *Beiträge zur Geschichte der Philosophie und Theologie des Mittelalters,* Vol. XXI, Nos. 1–3 (Münster, 1933). Alanus ab Insulis, *Anticlaudianus, Patrologia Latina* (Paris, 1844–64), 210, 504. L. B. Alberti, *De re aedificatoria* (Florence, 1485), Book VI, Ch. 2; Book IX, Ch. 5. Albertus Magnus, *Opusculum de pulchro et bono,* ed. P. Mandonnet, in *Santi Thomae Aquinatis Opuscula omnia,* Vol. V (Paris, 1927). Alexander of Hales, *Summa Alexandri* (Quaracchi, 1882), II, 103, sec. 175. Aristotle, *Metaphysics,* trans. W. D. Ross (Oxford, 1908); idem, *Poetics,* trans. S. H. Butcher as *Aristotle's Theory of Poetry and Fine Art, with a Critical Text and Translation of The Poetics,* 4th ed. (London, 1920). K. Aschenbrenner, "Forma i formalizm," *Studia Estetyczne,* **6** (Warsaw, 1969). Saint Augustine, *De ordine,* II 15, 42; idem, *De vera religione,* XCI 77; idem, *De musica,* VI 12, 38; idem, *De natura boni,* 3; English trans. in The Library of Christian Classics. F. Baldinucci, *Vocabolario toscano dell'arte del disegno* (Florence, 1681). Monroe Beardsley, *Aesthetics from*

Classical Greece to the Present (New York and London, 1966). Clive Bell, *Art* (London, 1914). P. Bembo, *Gli Asolani* (1525; Turin, 1932). Bernard of Clairvaux, *Apologia ad Guillelmum*, in *Opp. S. Bernhardi*, ed. J. Mabillon, 6 vols. (Paris, 1667–90). Saint Bonaventura, *Opera*, 10 vols., II Sent. D. 34a. 2q. 3 (Quaracchi, 1882–1904), II, 814. G. Cardano, *De subtilitate* (Nuremberg, 1550), p. 275. E. Cassirer, *Essay on Man*, 2nd ed. (New York, 1953). Clarembaldus of Arras, *Expositio super libros Boetii De Trinitate*, ed. W. Jansen, in *Der Kommentar des Clarembaldus von Arras zu Boethius De Trinitate, ein Werk aus der Schule von Chartres im 12 Jahrh.* (Breslau, 1926), p. 91. N. Cusanus, *De ludo globi*, in *Opera omnia* (Basel, 1565), p. 219. V. Danti, *Trattato della perfetta proporzione* (Florence, 1567). L. Dolce, *Dialogo della pittura intitolato l'Aretino* (Venice, 1557). Demetrius, *De elocutione* (Venice, 1508). Marsilio Ficino, *Commentarium in Convivium*, in *Opera* (Basel, 1561), p. 1336. K. Fiedler, *Schriften über Kunst* (Munich, 1913–14). H. Focillon, *La vie des formes* (Paris, 1934). Roger Fry, *Vision and Design* (London, 1920; reprint New York, 1956). M. G. Ghyka, *Esthétique des proportions dans la nature et dans les arts* (Paris, 1927); idem, *Le nombre d'or* (Paris, 1931). B. Gracián, *Agudeza y arte del ingenio* (Huesca, 1648). Robert Grosseteste, *Hexaemeron*, MS, British Museum, p. 147ᵛ. cf. E. de Bruyne, *Études d'esthétique médiévale* (Ghent, 1946), III, 133. A. von Hildebrand, *Das Problem der Form* . . . (Strasbourg, 1893), trans. M. Meyer and R. M. Ogden (New York, 1907). R. Ingarden, "On Form and Content of a Literary Work of Art," *Studia z Estetyki*, **2** (Warsaw, 1958), distinguishes nine meanings of "form" in contemporary usage. Isidore of Seville, *Sententiae*, Ch. I, 8, 18, in *Patrologia Latina*, ed. J. P. Migne, 83, 551; idem, *Differentiae*, ibid., pp. 1–59. W. Kandinsky, *Ueber das Geistige in der Kunst* (Munich, 1910), trans. M. T. H. Sadler, as *The Art of Spiritual Harmony* (London, 1914). I. Kant, *Critique of Judgment* (1790), trans. J. H. Bernard (London, 1914), sec. 52. A. Lalande, *Vocabulaire philosophique*, 9th ed. (Paris, 1962), article on "Forme." Ch. Le Brun, *Conférence sur l'expression générale et particulière des passions* (Paris, 1715). Le Corbusier (Charles Jeanneret), "Les yeux qui ne voient pas," *Esprit Nouveau*, **8** (1921), 10. G. P. Lomazzo, *Trattato della pittura, scultura et architettura* (Milan, 1584), trans. R. H. Student (1598); idem, *Idea del tempio della pittura* (Milan, 1590). Mathieu of Vendôme, *Ars versificatoria*, in E. Faral, *Les arts poétiques du XIIe et du XIIIe siècle* (Paris, 1924). P. Mondrian, "De nieuwe Beeldjng in de Schilderkunst," *De Stijl* (1917, 1918); cf. M. Seuphor, *Piet Mondrian, Life and Work* (New York, 1958), p. 144. E. Monod-Herzen, *Principes de morphologie générale*, Vol. I (Paris, 1956). G. Morpurgo-Tagliabue, *L'esthétique contemporaine* (Milan, 1960). William of Ockham, *Summulae in libros physicorum*, Book III, Ch. 17, p. 69, cf. L. Baudry, *Le Tractatus de principiis theologiae attribué à Guillaume d'Occam* (Paris, 1936); idem, *Guillaume d'Occam, sa vie, ses oeuvres, ses idées* (Paris, 1950). A. Palladio, *Quattro libri dell'architettura* (Venice, 1570). Philodemus, *Herculaneum papyri*, 2, XI, 165, in Ch. Jensen, *Philodemos über die Gedichte* (Leipzig, 1923). Plato, *Philebus, Sophist*, in *Plato's Dialogues*, trans. B. Jowett, 4th ed. (Oxford, 1953).

Plotinus, *The Enneads*, trans. S. MacKenna, 5 vols. (London, 1917–30). G. Porretanus, *In Boethii De Trinitate* (Basel, 1570), p. 1138. Duns Scotus, *Super praedicamenta*, q. 36. n. 14, in *Opera omnia*, ed. L. Vivès (Paris, 1891–95), I, 436f. Sextus Empiricus, *Adversus mathematicos* VII, 106. Stobaeus, *Eclogue* IV 1, 40. W. Tatarkiewicz, *History of Aesthetics*, 2 vols. (The Hague and Paris, 1970). H. Testelin, *Sentiments . . . sur la pratique de la peinture et sculpture* (Paris, 1680), p. 37. Thomas Aquinas, *In divinis nominibus*, c. IV, lect. 5, ed. P. Mandonnet (Paris, 1910), p. 363; idem, *Summa theologiae*, II a IIae, 180a. 2 ad 3. Ulrich of Strassburg, *De pulchro*, ed. M. Grabmann, in *Sitzungsberichte der bayerischen Akademie der Wissenschaften*, Philos.-philol. Klasse, Jahrgang 1925 (Munich, 1926). Vitruvius, *De architectura*. I 2, 1–9. B. Weinberg, *A History of Literary Criticism in the Italian Renaissance*, 2 vols. (Chicago, 1961). St. I. Witkiewicz, *Nowe formy w malarstie* (Warsaw, 1919; 1959). H. Wölfflin, *Renaissance und Barock* (1888; Basel, 1961); idem, *Kunstgeschichtliche Grundbegriffe* (1915; 6th ed. Munich, 1923), trans. as *Principles of Art History* (London 1923; New York, 1929). cf. idem, *The Sense of Form in Art* (New York, 1958). W. Worringer, *Abstraktion und Einfühling* (Munich, 1908). R. Zimmerman, *Geschichte der Aesthetik* (Vienna, 1958); idem, *Allgemeine Aesthetik als Formwissenschaft* (Vienna, 1965). F. Zuccaro, *L'idea de' pittori, scultori, ed architetti* (Turin, 1607).

W. TATARKIEWICZ

[See also **Beauty;** Iconography; Impressionism; Naturalism in Art; **Structuralism;** Style.]

FORTUNE, FATE, AND CHANCE

THE FUNCTION of indeterminism or the element of chance in the universe is a theme which runs from antiquity to modern times. It enters unavoidably into modern scientific developments. "No matter how far one goes in the expression of the laws of nature, the results will always depend in an unavoidable way on essentially independent contingencies which exist outside the context under investigation" (Bohm [1957], p. 158). But scientific indeterminism is much beyond the scope of this survey. Our purpose is to trace the meanings assigned historically to the various expressions of the element of chance in the universe, in order to understand the concept in all its ramifications. The most common recurring terms indicating different aspects of the element of chance are Fortune, Fate, and Chance itself, although other terms such as Necessity, Destiny, Providence, Predestination, Virtue, Luck, etc. also enter into the discussion. This survey will deal primarily with Fortune, Fate, and Chance from early Greek philosophy to the rise of Humanism.

In its popular representations, in which reasoning

and superstition overlap, Fortune assumed numerous forms historically. In Roman times in particular, Fortune appears as a deity worshiped under various forms and names. Basically all the forms represented an unknown power whose effects seemed to escape the regularity of recognized laws of causality. That power was feared and consequently worshiped. As Fortune, it was personified into a divinity guarding the individual in a situation whose outcome was in doubt, such as a storm, a trip, a financial venture, an amorous experience, etc.

If the laws of the universe work with unfailing regularity based on antecedent causes, a complete knowledge of all factors regulating an outcome would unfailingly lead to a knowledge of the outcome itself. If observations prove that such unfailing regularity does not obtain in the laws of the universe, there must be some element which breaks that regularity, and that element may be due to the observer or inherent in the laws themselves. This element, generally known as chance, could conceivably be the failure of man to know all possible factors affecting an outcome, thereby leading to the conclusion that the greater the increase in human knowledge, the lesser the sphere of the indeterminate. On the other hand, if the element of indeterminateness is inherent in the very laws of causality, it would remain in spite of the most complete knowledge; the laws of the universe would be a summary of the highest probabilities affecting an outcome.

One of the earliest explanations of the workings of the element of chance in the universe is attributable to Democritus, in the fifth century B.C. Referring to his ideas, Aristotle states (*Physics* II. iv): "Some indeed attribute our Heaven and all the worlds to chance happenings, saying that the vortex and shifting that disentangled the chaos and established the cosmic order came by chance." Here indeterminism is present in the creation of the cosmos as an actual element connoting the absence of organized purpose. On the other hand, once the cosmos is established, natural causality obtains and, as Aristotle further explains (ibid., 196a 28ff.): "here below, plants and animals proceed from a definite antecedent cause, and each thing springs from the appropriate seed, so that an olive tree will reproduce an olive tree and a man will beget a man, not as a result of Chance but of Nature or of Mind." In the Democritean or atomistic cosmology, though chance may have been present at the formation of the cosmos, once the heavens and all the worlds have come into being, chance ceases to function, because everything proceeds from an antecedent cause as a predictable and hence necessary result. In the world known to man indeterminism disappears except as the subjective insufficiency of knowledge on the part of man, but it still appears in ideas about the formation of the universe.

Such is the element of chance as represented in the Democritean system. Other thinkers sought explanations of the workings of the universe by personifying the element of causality which brought about events necessarily and unavoidably; that element of necessary sequence of cause and effect was symbolized in Fate, known as *Ananke* or *Heimarmene*. The notion of Fate could well have arisen from the observation of the inexorability of death. Among the Orphics Fate was viewed as the law which controls the conditions of our birth, death, and successive reincarnations. The belief in the process of a constant, monotonous, and unavoidable return to the point of departure came to be symbolically represented in the revolution of a wheel. The wheel of Fate was considered as regulating the course of humanity through the process of birth, death, and reincarnation. Plato gathered myths and beliefs concerning Fate, and reshaped them in a certain order which was to be adhered to closely by subsequent thinkers. In his works, therefore, we can establish the stage and the implications which had been reached concerning Fate and its relation to Fortune.

Since a pictorial symbol tends to be a substitute for reasoning, Fate came to be identified with Necessity because of the unceasing revolution of its wheel. With Necessity as the essential ingredient of Fate, the question of free will came to constitute a fundamental problem of ethics. How could the unceasing revolution of the wheel be interrupted so as to make it possible for man to exercise free volition? As developed by Plato in the *Timaeus* (41E), the laws of Fate are the divine decrees whereby the animal universe is produced out of successive reincarnations of man, who, however, determines the nature of each successive reincarnation by the manner of his actions or volitions. In the Timean conception, the Creator first portioned off souls and distributed one to each star and then He showed them the nature of the universe and spoke to them of the fated laws. The fated laws were spoken by the Creator, and Fate as *Heimarmene* is considered a *logos*. Later the Latin word *fatum* was to be connected with the verb *fari*. The relations of the soul to the body are determined by the nature of the particular star, and Fate designated the laws which govern the succeeding reincarnations. Man's soul has been created by God, but his first bodily differentiation has been entrusted to the astral powers. Fate becomes the instrument of perpetuation of the animal Universe obtained through successive palingeneses (*Laws* 904E 5ff.).

The well-being of the Universe is the supreme concern of the Deity, and to this end the welfare of individuals is subordinated and made instrumental. The law of *Heimarmene* or Fate is the power which keeps order in the Universe. In the *Timaeus* and in the *Republic* the course of successive reincarnations which is basic to this concept of the Universe is accomplished by the choices which man makes through the compelling power of the stars, but in conformity with the divine will. The souls originally assigned to astrally differentiated bodies have further differentiated themselves by their own actions. Different roles have been assigned to the stars and, under their influence, to man, in order to safeguard the fixed needs of the Universe. Within that framework, in order to maintain some freedom of action for man, chance is made operative. The patterns of life are submitted for selection to the souls present for the exercise of their free will in their choice, but the order in which the souls exercise their choice is determined by lot. It is by chance, therefore, that the number of patterns available to the soul at the time of choice is determined. This chance element, viewed subjectively from the point of view of the soul, becomes Fortune. Following Fate, which is the law and order of the Universe, the soul is transformed as a result of its free choice of life, but that free choice may itself be limited by the individual's Fortune (Cioffari [1935], pp. 34–42).

Aristotle accepts the existence of the chance event and proceeds to explain how the belief comes about. The Greeks grouped chance events under *Tyche* or *Automaton,* which operates in nature and in human affairs, personified as a mysterious deity worshiped accordingly. *Tyche* ("Fortune") is used in the more general sense including the chance element in human affairs as well as the deity itself, and *Automaton* ("Chance") is used in the causal scheme in relation to purposes or values. He proceeds to determine the value of occurrences controlled by Chance relative to a happy life; the etiological inquiry turns into a consideration of human and religious values. Neutral Fortune resolves itself into good Fortune and bad Fortune when viewed by the individual affected by this chain of accidental occurrences. When Fortune attaches itself to the cause, it is Mind itself insofar as it confronts accidental causes. In such a role Fortune is either guidance by the divinity or providential interference. When Chance attaches itself to the cause, it is Nature insofar as accidents are causes. As such, chance negates the possibility of predicting the outcome, but does not affect the human or religious values of the outcome. Therefore, in the ethical works of Aristotle Fortune assumes a definite function as conditioning the happiness of life, but Chance in its restricted sense does not enter into this sort of evaluative consideration.

Philosophically luck has been resolved into causes which are independent of Reason and Nature; yet we observe that there are men who, with natural aptitude and with good reasoning, strive to attain success but fail, while others with no such qualifications succeed. In the ethical treatises, either written by Aristotle or attributable to his school of thought, these questions are treated in full. In the *Eudemian Ethics* luck is analyzed as operating through a personal instinct which guides man to a desired success at the opportune moment and under the most favored circumstances, and does so in defiance of good reasoning, or rather by making bad reasoning come out right (1247b 34ff.). This personal instinct is also operative in those who attain an end not even considered by them and therefore without any reliance on Reason or Nature. The personal instinct which guides man, when traced back to its very beginning, must resolve itself into that which is higher than thought, and consequently it must be God who moves all things within us. The naturally lucky man is the one, therefore, whose desires are prompted and guided by the deity. The Scholastics' view of this divine luck as Providence is introduced into the world, and good Fortune is seen thus as partially disconnected from Fortune in general. However, two questions remain unanswered: (1) How is it possible for the deity to bring luck to the undeserving? (2) Why is bad luck visited upon those who deserve good luck? These questions become the main task of later writers, particularly in scholastic philosophy.

In the *Magna moralia* luck is connected with Nature rather than with the deity. The lucky man is defined as "the one who has an impulse without reason toward goals which he actually gets, and such an impulse is natural," since by nature there is in our soul something in virtue of which we are impelled toward things for which we are well fitted (1207a 16). The man who is actuated by such an impulse behaves as though he were beside himself, unconscious of what he is doing. Beside this form of luck as a natural impulse, there is another luck—independent of any impulse—which enables us to get praeter-rationally goods that have not even been considered as desired. Thus in the *Eudemian Ethics* luck is viewed as a superrational impulse and in the *Magna moralia* as a natural, but praeter-rational impulse in the province of psychology. If the lucky ones had a reason for what they do, then luck would constitute an art: all people would learn how to be lucky and all science would be lucky pursuits. In either case irrationality lies at the base of Fortune.

Aristotle analyzes the realm of Fortune in terms often repeated in the Middle·Ages, and which explain the many later usages of Fortune, Fate, and Chance. He explains that good things have been divided into three classes: external goods, goods of the soul, and goods of the body. The external goods constitute the realm of Fortune. Under external goods are grouped noble birth, wealth, power (both political and otherwise), friends, good children, beauty, and in general, good luck and bad luck (which include all other undefined external goods). There is an overlapping between the goods of the body and external goods in the matter of goods ascribable to heredity, such as personal attractiveness or beauty, but there is no confusion between external goods and goods of the soul. Consequently the realm of Fortune which is transmitted to later philosophers is the realm of external goods as opposed to goods of the soul. Fortune comes to be viewed not just as an indeterminate cause, but as a power which controls external goods and arranges their distribution among human beings in such a way as to affect their happiness. "Since our discussion is about happiness, it will be connected with the preceding to speak about good fortune. For the majority think that the happy life must be the fortunate one, or not apart from good fortune, and perhaps they are right in thinking so. For it is not possible to be happy without external goods, over which fortune is supreme" (*Magna moralia* 1206b 30ff.).

In understanding the relation of the fortuitous to God, it became necessary to trace the causal chain leading from God to the accidental event affecting man's existence and thereby to integrate Fortune into Divine Providence. Among the Stoics in particular the necessity arose to account for bad luck in a providentially ruled world. In Greek tragedy Fate had been considered a deterministic power ruling both men and gods. In Seneca God and Nature became identical, and Destiny was identical to both. Fate was the word of God, which once spoken had to be obeyed (*De providentia* V). In Apuleius Providence is the Divine Plan and Fate is the law regulating the unfolding of that plan (*De Platone et eius dogmate*, I. 12.205). Fate itself is necessity and order, but as such it is the law which governs variations. The cyclical, eternally recurrent character of Fate accounts for its necessity and order. Mythology combines with philosophy to account for the tripartite division of Fate into the Parca: Clotho, Lachesis, and Atropos, with Lachesis controlling the future. Control implies accompanying necessity, leaving a residuum of free will and chance to be accounted for. In Simplicius Fate is the chain of causal concatenation which is inherent in the seed and therefore considered the *ratio seminalis.* It is the law of individual aberration made to control human actions. The Stoics considered Fate as an incomplete comprehension of causal concatenation. However, if Fate is defined as a cause unknown to human understanding, it can have no reality of its own. As such, it can no longer be suspended from God.

The problem of maintaining both free will and fated causality was at the root of explanations of the fortuitous in a providential universe. In Proclus Divine Providence includes Fate and is superior to it. Fate acts as a providentially ruled nature, i.e., as a divine incorporeal nature; through it bodies are united in time and space, but Fate itself transcends connection and, as the mover, is independent of the thing moved. The difference between Fate and Nature lies in the fact that Fate is the only one of the two which controls external goods such as noble birth, reputation, and wealth. As such, its domain is that which was assigned to Fortune by Aristotle; Fate and Fortune become interchangeable terms, but only in the particular sense that Fortune is that part of the total chain which controls external goods. All things in the universe are divided into three classes: the intellectual, the corporeal, and the animal. The life of sense, or the corporeal, is more subject to Fate and the life of the intellect is less subject to it. Fate guards the interest of the universal over the interest of the individual. Fortune acts like the daemon which governs our inner movements, with the distinction that the daemon works out the adaptation of the soul to the universe, and Fortune works out the adaptation of the universe to the soul.

In Simplicius Fortune moves from the cold, philosophical indeterminism of Aristotle's second book of *Physics* into an all-embracing power controlling all things which are in need of attainment. Fortune (*Tyche*) is the divine power that controls success, both intended and unintended. In the universe all things are in need of attainment which need to participate in something, and all things need to participate in something when they are severed from one another. The celestial spheres, although separate from each other, are not severed because there is consubstantiation among them and not participation from one to the other. *Tyche* is operative among the celestial spheres as it is everywhere, but its power is not manifest because the necessity and constant attainment operating in them removes from our mind the concept of attainment. However, for all things in the sublunar world there is danger that the needed attainment may fail to occur because of the concourse of indeterminable causes. *Tyche* is the power which conjoins all causes so that each thing may not miss but will have its fitting outcome. It shows its power best when mind (or something like it) is not directly causative, but, rather, when indeterminable causes are at work. Therefore *Tyche*, although always operative, is particularly obvious in the case of those occurrences in which we see no other cause. Fortune or *Tyche* has the function to guide everything in nature which is in process of coming together into the proper order, and consequently it is represented as the helmsman—*Fortuna gubernans*—which steers all that crosses the sea of becoming.

The philosophic implications of Fortune and Fate are clear in some of the pictorial or mythological representations. In Martianus Capella (fifth century A.D.) the universe is governed by a celestial Senate, in whose inner consistory are present Adrasteia, Heimarmene, and the Fates, right next to Zeus and Hera. These powers abide with Zeus. Adrasteia sets down the laws operating above the material world and binding on the gods as well; Heimarmene indicates the law which operates in the material world; and the three Fates are the ministers of Zeus whose job is to determine and record his mandates when the gathering takes place (*De nuptialis philologiae* [*On the Marriage of Philology*], I. 64ff.). The Fates indicate the laws of the events which must necessarily follow at the bidding of Zeus. Fortune is represented as a celestial deity who comes into the conclave shocking everyone with her unexpected behavior. She interferes with the recording Fates by introducing sudden and unforeseen outbursts. Not satisfied with the control of unforeseeable occurrences, she claims some control over predictable causality, thereby becoming identified with Nemesis, the goddess of retribution, in a way which will recur frequently in later writers.

As we approach Christian philosophy, the problem of integrating the element of chance into a providentially governed universe becomes paramount. The Neo-Platonic Chalcidius, in his *Commentary on the Timaeus* (Ch. 145) enumerates and arranges the different causes of being. He tells us that some things come from Providence alone, some from Fate, some from free will, some from Fortune, and some from Chance. Thus all causes and outcomes are accounted for, both those which are determinate and those which are indeterminate. All existence proceeds from God in one eternal, uninterrupted flow whose regularity is the expression of God's will and understanding. In immediate sequence to God is Providence, which the Greeks called *Nous* and which is the intelligible essence of Goodness, ever turned toward God as the Highest, who showers His goodness through Providence to all beings. Its name does not imply seeing the future in advance, but rather the act of understanding of all things as a property of the Divine Mind. Next in sequence comes Fate, which is the law of the world soul; it is the unchanging law of change, which rules all things according to their nature. Fate, which makes room for free will, contains Fortune within itself, because in the occurrences of elemental nature we have frequency and not constant regularity. Fortune is the power that controls the residuum between constancy and the rare or unusual occurrences. Having accounted for the occurrences which are under the power of Fortune, Chalcidius includes the Aristotelian distinction between Fortune and Chance, since they are both undetermined causes of undesigned results. However, while in Aristotle the causes for Fortune are Mind (for Fortune) and Nature (for Chance), in Chalcidius the principal cause of both Fortune and Chance is Fate.

The influence of Chalcidius on Christian thought is profound. In his view Fate is controlled by Providence, which means that no occurrence in the universe is outside of the sphere of God's Will. Fate as the divine law inherent in the world-soul and carrying out the order of Nature carries a connotation of the spoken mandate of God as well as a connotation of unavoidability or necessity. The sphere of domain of the world-soul consists of three parts: (1) the *aplanes* or sphere of fixed stars, (2) the planetary spheres, and (3) the elemental world. In the heavens regularity and unfailing necessity obtain, and therefore Fate is determinate. But in occurrences which depart from unfailing regularity, namely in those events which have normality or frequency rather than constancy, Fate actually exercises its power. Here Fate regulates motion and is viewed as the unchanging law of change. Since there is an infinite variety of accidental causes and an infinite series of temporal points at which they can occur, Fate is the determinate law of the series regulating these changes, for all things which take place in the heavens or on earth return cyclically to their point of departure.

In order to establish some harmony between human conduct and Fate, Chalcidius has recourse to a distinction of causes in the series which comprises the total power of Fate; they are the causes which are *ex praecessione* and those which are *secundum praecessionem*. Fate operates in human conduct on condition that we deduce it from certain antecedents. These postulated antecedents are our merits. There is freedom of choice at the start, but once a choice is made, necessity comes into control. Events are fateful only after the exercise of free will; otherwise there could be no rewards or punishments and consequently no moral law. Fate from this point of view becomes no more deterministic than any other law. The law is there, but it is in our power to initiate or not to initiate the action which will set off the application of the law. Divine foreknowledge does not imply determinism, for knowledge on the part of God is proportionate to the thing known: necessary knowledge for necessary things and contingent knowledge for contingent things. This concept becomes basic in the conciliation between free will and the element of chance in Christian doctrine.

Fate thus related to free will contains Fortune within

229

itself. In sequence, the powers that are subject to Providence through Fate are as follows: (1) the rational soul, (2) Nature, (3) Fortune, (4) Chance (in the restricted sense), (5) *daemones*. As stated, the control of Fate is proportionate to the nature of the things controlled. Among heavenly things Fate operates with constant regularity. On earth, however, the constant regularity is not free from exceptions and it is in this residuum that Fortune has its control. Because Art imitates Nature, the same elements in the occurrences of Nature are to be found in Art. Although Fortune operates in events involving human choice and Chance in lower animals or inanimate things, both are accidental causes and as such they have to be derived from principal causes. In Chalcidius the sum total of principal causes constitutes Fate, and therefore both Fortune and Chance derive from Fate. However, in addition to the Aristotelian explanations described, Chalcidius considers Fortune as the cause which brings together two actions or occurrences which, in appearance at least, are totally disconnected. His final definition of Fortune, and one which recurs frequently in scholastic philosophy is (Ch. 159): *Concursus simul cadentium causarum duarum, originem ex proposito trahentium, ex quo concurso provenit aliquid praeter spem cum admiratione* ("There must be a concurrence of two causes, each arising from an act of free will, and the concurrence must produce an unexpected result"). Such are the elements which constitute Fortune in the Christian tradition.

The Christian doctrine becomes firmly entrenched in Saint Augustine. With him there is no question but that Providence controls all things, for it is inconceivable that God, who provided for everything in the universe, should wish that any part of it escape the rule of Providence (*De civitate Dei*, Book V, Ch. 11). Any cause which is beyond the control of Providence cannot be accepted. Hence Fate as a necessary cause over and beyond Providence, or any astral determinism independent of God's Will, cannot possibly exist, for that would be tantamount to a denial that everything in the universe takes place only according to God's Will.

Yet Augustine realizes that terms such as Fate, Fortune, and Chance do exist and that, without a logical basis for their existence, they would have disappeared. He therefore proceeds to present reasonable explanations. Starting from the premiss that God, in His omnipotence and foreknowledge, permitted nothing to be without order, that order of the universe might well be called Fate, since the Stoics had already explained Fate as the order and connection of all causes inherent in the universe. This order and connection is now attributable to the will and power of the transcendent Christian God, but within that concept Fate as the order of the universe can well remain. In fact, Augustine states that the word Fate is misused and that one should speak of God's Will instead (ibid., Book V, Ch. 1). God's foreknowledge would tend to imply a deterministic system, but free will is maintained by the fact that our wills are included in the order of causes and effects and consequently they form part of God's foreknowledge in which temporal sequences do not apply. The necessity which would control results contrary to our wills is no more cogent than the necessity which controls them in conformity with our wills. The necessity implied in the order of causes which we term Fate is such only when viewed as a sequence of cause and effect; when viewed without the element of sequence it is timeless and hence not outside the realm of God's Providence (ibid., Book V, Ch. 9).

In such a providential system the causeless does not actually exist. Occurrences which are not preceded by a natural cause or are not purposed by our will do actually have a cause, but it is not manifest to our mind. Augustinian philosophy does away with indeterminism in the universe by the assumption that there can be nothing causeless in the providential order. However, this does not mean that every cause is determined insofar as human beings are concerned. There are fortuitous along with natural causes, and causes which are the result of will. The fortuitous causes are those which are concealed from human understanding because of its insufficiency and are consequently assigned to Fortune and Chance. The Aristotelian accidental causes were concealed from human understanding because of their unpredictable nature. The Augustinian fortuitous causes would disappear as such if man had complete knowledge of all causality in the universe. The Aristotelian fortuitous causes could never disappear entirely because there is actually an element of indeterminism in the universe.

The Augustinian explanation of Fate, Fortune, and Chance falls into a difficulty which will become quite common both among Christian philosophers and literary writers. The fact that logically there is no place for Fortune or Chance in his providential system does not prevent Augustine from using these terms as popular designations of accepted concepts. However, the existence of Fortune as a divinity has to be repudiated, for if it were a divinity and could systematically favor its worshipers, it would cease being inconstant and therefore would cease being Fortune (ibid., Book IV, Ch. 18). No religion can purify the language of the common crowd and eliminate all words which in any way refer to occult causes, but of one thing we can be sure: the reason that any cause is fortuitous is simply because it is concealed from us. An all-embracing providential tutelage in control of all individual actions leaves no room for undesigned, unmoderated, uncontrolled occurrences. Yet the fact that Augustine eliminated Fortune from his providential system does not mean that as a divinity it disappeared from Christian concepts. It rather became fixed as the power to which were ascribed all occurrences which did not fit logically into a providentially ruled universe.

The Augustinian providential system does not question the existence of causality itself. However, in theories where the power of causality is denied to created beings and is exercised only by God directly, the problem of chance assumes a different solution. In the Epicurean system events were not causally connected and happened either as a result of chance or of undetermined free will. In the Philonic system, in which God is either the remote or immediate cause of all that happens, it is God himself who "breaks the chain of secondary causes or deviates from the continuity of His own direct creation" (H. A. Wolfson [1961], pp. 198ff.). Just as God performed major miracles in the creation of the universe, so He continues to perform minor miracles which break the continuity of causation by endowing man with a touch of His own miraculous power through free will. The break in the continuity of causation for purposeful action is due directly to God's intervention; the break in that continuity for occurrences which are not attributable to any human cause must come also directly from God. Fortune in the Philonic sense is really "the 'divine *Logos*,' namely the providence of a God who is not bound by any fixed laws of nature, but who can upset these laws of nature fixed by himself" (H. A. Wolfson, *Philo*, 4th ed. [1968], II, 422).

The whole question of the fortuitous is treated comprehensively by Boethius. His explanation of the element of chance in the universe closely follows the Aristotelian explanation. He subdivides all occurrences into constant, frequent, rare, and even (half-and-half). The constant occurrences are assigned to the heavens, the frequent or regular are assigned to Nature, the even (half-and-half) are assigned to free will, and the rare are assigned to Fortune or Chance. Moreover causes are subdivided into two major classifications, those which have a purpose and those which do not. Since both Nature and Mind act teleologically, that is with a purpose, rare occurrences of teleological import may occur in either realm. The element of chance operates among occurrences which have a purpose provided they are rare. Boethius consequently explains Chance as follows: Chance and the fortuitous occur in those events which, although occurring rarely, come about through accident and are done with a purpose. Boethius fails to account for the Aristotelian argument

of finality in the chance event itself, for in Aristotle, if the chance meeting of two lines of action is devoid of purpose, the occurrence cannot be ascribed to Chance (*Physics* II.V, 196b 35).

The interpretation of the chance occurrence as the apparently undesigned meeting of unconnected lines of action does occur in Boethius, again with the qualification that, although the chance occurrence may be undesigned, it is not uncaused. The actual *concursus* or concurrence of these causes has its own appropriate causes, and it is their unexpected and unforeseen conjunction which seems to have brought forth Chance. However, the chance occurrences, or the goods or things unexpectedly attained or unintentionally missed, belong to the world external to man. Boethius accepts the Aristotelian separation of all goods into goods of the mind, goods of the body, and external goods in order to delineate the sphere of action of Fortune. Fortune is most powerful over external goods, has some effect over goods of the body, but has no power over goods of the mind.

The external goods over which Fortune has control are (1) wealth in all its varieties, (2) dignity, and (3) power. There is never any question but that wealth or material goods belong to the realm of Fortune. However, dignity and power come in different proportions under the aegis of goods of the body and goods of the mind; they will be attributed differently to the power of Fortune or to the power of Virtue, as we shall see in later writers. Boethius himself adds mundane glory as one of the further divisions of external goods which are under the power of Fortune. Once Boethius has established the existence of the chance event, he proceeds to clarify the sphere of action of the power that controls it.

Like Augustine, Boethius proceeds to the justification of the workings of the Fortune in a divinely governed universe. The world of becoming or of change, in other words the physical world, derives its causes, order, and form from the motionless Mind of the Deity. This Deity, one and undivided, wills the *modus* of multiplicity as the regime of the universe. This *modus* of multiplicity, when viewed in the purity of Divine Intelligence, is called Providence. When it operates in the world of motion and becomes order in time and space, it is called Fate; Fate in turn governs Chance by joining the acts and the fortunes of men, even though acts proceed from free will and fortunes may proceed from other causes including Chance. Fortune may seem to move at random, but in actuality it does submit to a control and moves according to law.

The moral question which arises with Boethius was initially answered in Plato's *Laws* (903C): How can we admit of Providence when we see Fortune harassing good men and favoring evil ones? If Providence by its very nature has to be good, how can it tolerate evil? The answer is that Fortune is always good, regardless of the way it appears to us. This is the element of faith and resignation, which permeates the explanations of Fortune in Christian philosophy.

The personification of *Fortuna* is more important in Boethius than in any previous writer. The various characteristics assigned historically to *Fortuna* appear as aspects of this personification. The instability of Fortune, its alterations, its slippery ways, its flattery, its irrationality, its temperament—all form part of the Boethian figuration of *Fortuna*. Philosophic concepts merge with popular beliefs to produce a figure which approaches a divinity and yet retains all the elements which contributed toward its conceptual development. Basically, the Boethian figuration remains the core of pictorial representations through the Middle Ages and early Renaissance.

With Albertus Magnus and Saint Thomas Aquinas there is a return to the Aristotelian explanations of Fate, Fortune, and Chance as a function of causality. In Albertus Magnus the Aristotelian definition of Fate is influenced not only by the Stoic position, but by the astrological theories which had developed through writers such as Hermes Trismegistus, Firmicius Maternus, and Apuleius. In his fusion of many doctrines Albertus presents a descending determinism from Providence to the new creature at the time of birth. Fatal causality flows from celestial bodies down to the embryo. Albertus postulates two different types of Fortune: the Fortune of causality and the Fortune of astrology. The Fortune of causality is the last link in the chain unfolding from the Divine Mind, through Providence, through Fate, to the chance event. In the unfolding of the chain of causality first come necessary causes, which produce effects with unfailing regularity; next come those causes which act with normal regularity; then those which act with halfway regularity; and finally the rare occurrences, in which the fortuitous is observed. When causality is viewed as a force differentiated among individual beings, it is Fortune; when it is viewed as the entire process from necessary causes to rare occurrences, it is Fate. Thus in Albertus Magnus, as in Augustine and Boethius, Fortune and Fate are different aspects of the total chain of causality.

In Saint Thomas the existence of Chance is not questioned; it is accepted and explained as an integral part of the providential system of the universe. Assuming that the Divine Ordainer cannot possibly be Chance because effects cannot proceed except from a direct cause, we may look for Chance anywhere in the universe except in God himself. Chance must arise

somewhere between God's knowledge, which is all-encompassing and timeless, and our own knowledge, which is derived from causality and is limited by temporal relations. Things which we see only in causes, God sees in existence. Since for God knowledge and foreknowledge are the same, the element of chance, which involves a sequence of cause and effect, does not enter into His foreknowledge. Fortune, or the element of chance, exists only in relation to something else in the universe, not in relation to God. If Fortune is analyzed as the absence of intentionality either in the cause or in the effect, the absence of intentionality may be in relation to immediate prior causes, but not in relation to the ultimate superior cause. The order of human events, among which are the fortuitous, is comparable to a procession in which one event succeeds the previous one simply because they are observed in their temporal sequence; for God, who is above the temporal procession and sees the sequence both in cause and effect without relation to time, the sequence constitutes no necessity. In the same manner, human events have a causal sequence only from the point of view of man's knowledge, so that for necessary effects there are necessary causes and for contingent effects there are contingent causes.

Since fortuitous events involve human choice, the manner in which human choice enters the chain of causality is significant. It is important to coordinate the scheme of causality and the element of chance in relation to the celestial bodies, the angels, and God. In referring human things to higher causes, the following conditions and limitations prevail (*Summa contra gentiles* III. 91): (1) volitions and choices are disposed immediately by God, without intermediary; (2) human knowledge is disposed by God through the medium of the angels; (3) bodily goods are disposed through the angels and celestial bodies. Celestial bodies influence volitions and choices by acting upon our bodies by intellectual consideration without passion. Volitions and choices which act without man's intention and without his knowledge are what we call Fortune. Angels illumine our minds to make appropriate choices; therefore the custodian angel is the cause of what we call *fortuna*. Similarly, impressions from the celestial spheres cause natural body dispositions which affect choices and volitions. Fortune in the latter case is a natural disposition, as opposed to Fortune coming through the angels illumining our minds. The Aristotelian impulse toward achieving desired goals or success which was not even desired has taken its proper place in the Thomistic providential system. But the astrological determinism which still survived in Albertus has now been absorbed entirely in the providential universe of God, the angels, and the celestial bodies. If the impulse which makes a person fortunate is referred higher than the celestial spheres and the angels, then it is found to emanate directly from God himself. Through our will, which is disposed immediately by God, God himself is the only *causa per se* of our Fortune.

Dante as the poet who synthesized previous philosophic, literary, and popular ideas brings a vast eclecticism into the concepts of Fortune, Fate, and Chance. In his philosophic work, the *Convivio*, he limits the influence of the fortuitous to the realm of the accidental, as it was in Aristotle's *Physics*. Fortune is a cause concealed from human understanding, yet not without *divino imperio*, as it was in Saint Thomas. Its irrationality is translated into a simile: "the more man is subject to the intellect, the less he is subject to Fortune" (*Convivio* IV. xi.9). Fortune appears as the Chalcidian *concursus causarum*, which is accompanied by the least amount of mind or reason. Fortune as the impulse of the Aristotelian ethical treatises appears as Fortune aided by reason or Fortune the aider of reason. It appears as the divine power that controls attainment or success, as it was in Simplicius. The astrological Fortune of Albertus Magnus appears as personal destiny transmitted through the constellation or the individual star. The element of chance is explained in Aristotelian fashion as the *causa per accidens* annexed either to the agent or to the effect. Fortune appears as the cause which opposes the regularity of Nature. The element of Fortune in the individual enters as the impression from the spheres which causes bodily dispositions. Yet all of the various elements which have historically been assigned to Fortune, Fate, and Chance are gathered into a single providential system of which the fortuitous is a part.

All the various aspects of the fortuitous are personified in a deity which in Thomistic philosophy is classified as a divine Intelligence. In Dante this newly created Intelligence is termed *Fortuna*. Since *Fortuna* is a personification of the fortuitous, and the fortuitous is a branch of the chain of causality, its normal place in the providential scheme is within the realm of Fate, which is the unfolding of Providence in multiplicity and time. The gradation from the Divine Mind to the individual event is therefore: God, Providence, Fate, and Fortune. Fate includes the regularity of Nature and Fortune includes the irregularity of all chance events.

The poetic figure of *Fortuna* which Dante created personifies all aspects of the fortuitous, from its place in the causal chain proceeding from God to the realm which affects the individual. The distinction between the goods of the soul and the goods of the body, or external goods, is maintained throughout Dante's

works, and Fortune is always in charge of external goods only, never the goods of the soul. Fortune is always viewed as a tool of Providence and never as a master of it (*Paradiso* XXXII. 53). Fortune and Fate become indistinguishable when considered as the individual destiny which affects a person unexpectedly, and usually adversely. This individual destiny is an impression made by the celestial spheres on the bodily dispositions in the form of passions, and it is these bodily dispositions which produce a regularity in the ability or inability to achieve desired goals, or goals which may even be independent of desires. Although astrological destiny as such is denied in Dante's providential system, the influence of constellations is resolved into the impression which in turn guides the individual toward success or failure in accordance with the total plan of the universe.

Fortune in its role as a providential agent foresees, judges, and pursues future events (*Inferno* VII. 69ff.). As a divine Intelligence it has its own beatitude and is consequently unconcerned with the effects of its activity on mankind. Since the activity of Fortune is that part of the Divine Plan dealing with the distribution of external goods, the identification of Fortune with Divine Justice is logical (*Inferno* XXX. 13). Since the variations of Fortune are the basis of its nature, the figure of the wheel remains symbolic of its constant changes. Dante accepts as natural the thesis that if the constant movement of Fortune stopped, it would cease being Fortune. The changes of Fortune find a correlation in the constant and inexorable changes of the moon; hence the correlation with the moon is maintained. The activity of Fortune is *a priori* that part of human activity which is beyond our power to comprehend; hence *Fortuna* remains *oltre la difension di senni umani* (*Inferno* VII. 81). Since Nature follows causality with unfailing regularity, Fortune as a branch of causality is likewise a branch of Nature when the latter is considered as the total circular movements of the heavens. The differentiation which Fortune causes in individuals independent of the moment of birth are a result of this *circular natura* (*Paradiso* VIII. 127). Since virtue is that power of the individual which intentionally guides him toward a desired end, the power which unintentionally drives him away from the desired end (namely *fortuna*) must be a contrary power; hence if one is a friend of virtue (redeeming grace as personified in Beatrice), he is no friend of Fortune (*Inferno* II. 61).

The influence of Fortune in human affairs becomes all important in Boccaccio's artistic world. The function of Fortune is to determine the outcome of a course of action. Boccaccio's universe is strictly providential and God is directly in charge of both favorable and unfavorable circumstances. God is above Fortune and, of course, can do no wrong. Nature and Fortune are both administrators of the Divine Will. Fortune indicates the operation of the heavens in human affairs and the only way that its influence can be forestalled is for free will to act prior to *Fortuna*. Boccaccio accepts with resignation the idea that *Fortuna* influences human affairs, but feels that man can have enough advance notice through his reasoning power to counteract the intended course of Fortune. Boccaccio does not change the popular and accepted idea of Fortune; he simply molds it to fulfill his purpose. Fortune was in charge of external goods; Boccaccio adds sensual pleasures and fame as external goods. Fortune was an impulse whose effects are inescapable; Boccaccio maintains that love is an even more powerful impulse. Stoic Fate which became synonymous with Fortune was considered a test of courage and virtue; Boccaccio assigns to Fortune the power to rescue the weak of heart and inspire him with the courage needed to achieve his goal. The Aristotelian impulse of the moral treatises becomes the impulse that leads the individual toward achievement irrespective of any moral import. In Boccaccio good Fortune is a cause for exaltation and bad Fortune is a cause for complaint, but both types of Fortune are part of the providential system and do not necessarily have any bearing on the moral character of the individual.

With Petrarch the question of Fortune resumes its moral significance. Petrarch's philosophy of life is directly related to his views on the influence of Fortune in human affairs. Aristotelian explanations of the nature of Fortune as a cause have no bearing on Petrarch's views. Petrarch sees no difference between Fortune and Fate, nor does the distinction between *fortuna* and *casus* enter into his considerations. Fortune is God's Will and as such it must prevail, whether we like it or not. The problem is how to best conduct one's life in view of the unquestioned existence of the fortuitous element in human affairs.

Assuming that all things in this world are transitory, the Divine Will regulates this transitoriness through Fortune. The good or bad aspect of Fortune is a human illusion and is basically not a distinction between good and evil, for what is necessary in the nature of the universe cannot possibly be evil. Complete knowledge on the part of man and complete goodness are one and the same. Accepting the traditional view that material goods constitute the domain of Fortune, Petrarch explains that these material goods are God's gifts and their goodness depends on the use which man makes of them. Evil arises not from their possession but from their misuse. The root of bad luck is not any natural disposition, but the blame which Man bears

for misusing God-given gifts. The Stoic concept of Fortune as a test of man's fortitude runs throughout Petrarch's views, but in the Stoics the test has no significance for the afterlife, whereas in Petrarch the test is viewed as a preparation for eternity.

Petrarch resolved man's struggle against *Fortuna* into a system in which the escape from the inevitability of Fortune lies in a disregard of external goods and a withdrawal into contemplation of the goods of the spirit as a preparation for eternal life. The providential system of the universe, of which the element of chance is an integral part, can be maintained only by considering the chance event as an inscrutable part of the universe closed to our understanding as human beings. Yet in Petrarch, as in Dante and Boethius, the allegorical portrayal of Fortune offers again the opportunity to combine all the elements ascribed to Fortune and its kindred powers, and to relate those elements to the philosophic concept. Superstitions and fears about *Fortuna* have been turned into rationalizations which permit man to find relative happiness in a universe in which some elements elude the regularity of deterministic causality.

While Petrarch approaches Fortune from the point of view of its effect on the life of the individual, the philosophic writers continued to search for a system which would account logically for all accepted aspects of Fate, Fortune, and Chance. The *De fato et fortuna* of Coluccio Salutati constitutes a significant stage in the comprehensive summary of the place of Fate, Fortune, and Chance in a universe which is conceived as the unfolding of Divine Providence. In this system, Fate is the operation of God's Providence. Without changing the basic Christian concept which had developed up to that time, Salutati directs that concept toward moral values for a good life. Astrological determinism is again refuted, not as being unverifiable this time, but as having no influence on the rational soul. The providential origin of the fortunate impulse brings even the accidental into the fold of the total good for the universe. This seemingly accidental cause is traceable directly to Divine Providence. Those events which are entirely within man's control are the *bona animi*, but as a corollary those events which are not entirely within man's control are not *bona animi* and therefore mutable or external goods. Such external or mutable goods cannot be pertinent or important to virtue because if they were, they would become *bona animi*. Since those mutable goods do not lead to virtue, the man who is aiming toward a virtuous life must either resist them outright or be indifferent to them. Hence the equation that where there is the greatest prudence there is bound to be the least Fortune.

The moral significance of the acceptance of Fortune

becomes increasingly important in the early humanists. In Poggio Bracciolini's *De fortunae varietate*, for example, we find that the mutability of the goods of Fortune is so baffling that the only recourse for a wise man is to withdraw altogether from worldly goods. The power of Fortune comes from the madness of men in wanting to possess the goods under its control. Therefore the more men attach themselves to goods of the soul by following Virtue, the more the power of Fortune will be broken. The natural conclusion for Bracciolini, as it was for Petrarch, is that the way to virtue is a life which is indifferent to the possession of mutable goods. Following in the same trend, Leon Battista Alberti maintains that Fortune holds in yoke only the man who submits to it. Whereas in the Aristotelian moral treatises Fortune was the impulse toward achieving goals, whether desired or not even envisaged, in Alberti it is Virtue which is the capacity for achieving goals of potential worth. Fortune is still in charge of external goods; however Virtue not only understands the distinction between the *bona animi* and the *bona externa*, but develops techniques for attaining the *bona externa* when their possession can aid the *bona animi*.

From the mobility of external goods which are under the domain of Fortune arises the mobility of human affairs in general. And just as the mobility of external goods is under the domain of Fortune, so the mobility of human affairs is under its domain. If Prudence and Virtue can regulate the mobility of goods, they can also regulate the mobility of human affairs. The treatises on the subject of Fortune take cognizance of this mobility and introduce the element of civil happiness as part of their consideration of Fortune. In Giovanni Pontano's *De fortuna* the distinguishing element of Fortune is the unexpected collision with some human purpose. Fortune is still the personification of all elements which run contrary to the predictable pattern of cause and effect. The difference is attributable to the variation between a steadfast Divine First Cause and variable secondary causes. Sustained good Fortune is an impulse which comes directly from God, whereas rare or intermittent good Fortune can only come from accidental causes. Having assumed the existence of sustained good Fortune as an impulse directly from God, what remains to be explained is the intermittent good Fortune; the only source for the intermittent can be the *causa per accidens*. The astrological influence of Fate on the individual is not discarded because, although it does not fit into the providential system, the denial of its existence would leave a lacuna in the explanation of the universe. Rather loosely, the influence of stars is attributed to Fate and to God; Fortune is considered the handmaid of Fate.

With Machiavelli we reach another important stage in the concepts of Fortune, Fate, and Chance, and with it we shall conclude the present study. The external goods which are the domain of Fortune are expanded to include political power, because civil happiness is considered unattainable without it. Escape from the power of Fortune through disregard of external possessions or through dedication to the goods of the soul is a solution for the contemplative life, but it is no solution for the active life, in which one must still face the influence of Fortune. Machiavelli views Fortune as the compendium of all circumstances regarding the good outside of oneself, or the sum total of all mobility in human affairs. His analysis of Fortune is a rationale of the balance to be maintained between the mobility of human affairs and the ultimate purposes of humanity on this earth, which is the survival of the state as an organism.

Machiavelli's views are centered on the realities of life as they exist rather than on any theological concept of eternal life. There is a conflict between the forces which preserve the organism and the forces which would tend to disrupt it or retard its development, namely between *virtù* on one side and *fortuna* on the other. *Virtù* is considered as the life strength of a state; it is the organized energy which propels the state. Everything in life is in a state of mobility, not only external goods and their possession, but events themselves. In the Machiavellian concept of reality everything is bound to the wheel of Fortune, which symbolizes constant, inexorable change. Control of this mobility can come only through knowledge of the laws regulating it. Therefore, knowing the time and order of things is the best guard against the power of Fortune (*Il Principe* [*The Prince*], XXV).

Contrary to the accepted Christian philosophy, Machiavelli denies any providential character to Fortune; yet in no way does he deny the existence of Fortune itself. Fortune represents all the external forces with which a man must learn to work or must overcome. Recognizing that the circumstances which beset man's path are those which are not under his control, the struggle which arises is between man's personal power and the power of Fortune. From man's point of view, Fortune is the power which acts contrary to his control and therefore capriciously. Fortune is identified with the errors and vices of men, because those are the failings which beset his progress. Fortune is considered prevalent in the affairs of men because it represents a whole set of circumstances against which a single individual must struggle.

Writers prior to Machiavelli had sought ideological solutions to the confrontation between man and Fortune. Machiavelli concentrates on practical solutions based on hard common sense. Recognizing that the reality in which man acts is extremely mobile and changeable, and that by the nature of reality these circumstances are mostly beyond man's control, Machiavelli proceeds to show what man can do in a one-sided struggle, as it were. In philosophic terms, man's free will was the one sure weapon against the irrationality of Fortune. In Machiavelli, man's free will acts through his *virtù*, which is his God-given power to determine a choice and follow it through. Machiavelli assumes that man is conditioned by his nature to act in a certain way, thereby accepting to some extent Fortune or Fate as an impression on the individual to act regularly in a predictable way. However, man does have the power of choice, and through that power he can control his own nature. That power of choice comes from the evaluation of future events in their causes, and that evaluation is really prudence, or the power of reasoning. The prudent man can foresee dangers, forestall them, and thereby gain control of his own destiny. Symbolically, in the personification of Fortune, man can aim at conquering it rather than opposing it. The *virtù* of man can conquer Fortune by the ability to make appropriate choices based on calculations of events and their effects. Most important in the control of Fortune is the choice of the propitious moment or *occasione*, because the mobility of events is such that only one momentary combination of circumstances provides the favorable vantage point of attack. The *concursus causarum* is brought under human control. Machiavelli not only does not deny the existence of Fortune, but he recognizes it as a significant force in human affairs. What he does do is to raise the ability of man to withstand and control the forces of causality.

Fate, Fortune, and Chance as parts of the chain of causality in the universe have been analyzed by natural philosophers, they have been incorporated into providential systems by theologians, they have been personified by poets, and they have entered all types of pictorial figurations. The distinctions between the three terms were rigorously outlined by some philosophers and were completely obliterated by others, to the extent that it is impossible to trace each of the terms individually. However, the element of the fortuitous is concentrated more on the term Fortune than on either Fate or Chance, particularly because of the personification of Fortune and its elevation to the status of a divinity. Treatises continued to be written on Fate, Fortune, and Chance, treating the element of chance primarily as Fortune; as such the topic pervaded the literatures of western Europe long after the early humanists.

BIBLIOGRAPHY

David Bohm, *Causality and Chance in Modern Physics* (Princeton, 1957). V. Cioffari, *Fortune and Fate from Democritus to St. Thomas Aquinas* (New York, 1935); idem, *The Conception of Fortune and Fate in the Works of Dante* (Cambridge, Mass., 1940); idem, *Fortune in Dante's Fourteenth Century Commentators* (Cambridge, Mass., 1944). A. Doren, *Fortuna im Mittelalter und in der Renaissance*, in *Vorträge der Bibliothek Warburg, 1922–23*, Vol. I (Berlin and Leipzig, 1924). K. Heitmann, *Fortuna und Virtus. Eine Studie zu Petrarcas Lebensweisheit* (Cologne, 1957). C. W. Kerr, "The Idea of Fortune in Italian Humanism from Petrarch to Machiavelli" (Ph.D. diss., Harvard University, 1956). E. W. Mayer, *Machiavellis Geschichtsauffassung und sein Begriff virtù* (Munich and Berlin, 1912). M. Santoro, *Fortuna, ragione e prudenza nella civiltà letteraria del Cinquecento* (Naples, 1967). H. A. Wolfson, *Religious Philosophy, A Group of Essays* (Cambridge, Mass., 1961).

VINCENZO CIOFFARI

[See also **Astrology;** Atomism; Causation; **Chance;** Cycles; Epicureanism; **Machiavellism;** Necessity; **Renaissance Humanism;** *Virtù*.]

FREE WILL AND DETERMINISM

THE IDEA of human freedom antedates philosophical speculation on this idea. When philosophers began to inquire into the nature and existence of freedom, they did not initially think of freedom as an attribute of a man's will. For example, no theoretical discussion of the concept of will appears in the works of Plato, and therefore, no talk about the freedom of the will. Nonetheless, Plato had definite ideas regarding the conditions under which a man is free. A man is free when the rational part of his soul governs the other parts, viz., the feelings and passions. A man may thus be enslaved by his feelings or passions if they dominate his being. Governance by reason produces harmony and justice; in the individual, justice is conceived as the state of the soul in which each part performs only its proper function in harmony with all other functions. A man is liable to sin if his soul is unjust; but the sin is involuntary for no man would knowingly choose to be in this state. Nor does a just man choose evil voluntarily for the explanation of this choice is always ignorance. Hence, according to Plato, a person in whom reason reigns, and who possesses knowledge, can do no evil.

Since a man incurs responsibility only for his voluntary actions, Aristotle undertakes an ethical and psychological inquiry into the voluntary. An act is unwilled if its moving principle is outside the person, i.e., the person is acting under compulsion, or if the act can be explained by reference to the person's ignorance. Aristotle makes two qualifications regarding the second way in which an act can be unwilled: (1) if a man does not regret having performed the act once his ignorance is removed, the act may be said to have been involuntary rather than unwilled; (2) the ignorance must be about circumstances and consequences, not moral principles. A man who acts contrary to a moral principle whose truth he refuses to acknowledge is acting willingly (assuming he is not acting under compulsion or through ignorance of circumstances and consequences) and wickedly (Wheelright, p. 203).

If a man chooses to do something out of some desire or even a strong or sudden impulse, the moving principle is in the man and he is, therefore, acting willingly. Aristotle does not require for voluntariness, therefore, what libertarians will later require for freedom; to wit, that the act be caused by the actor or agent rather than some state of the agent, e.g., a desire.

Choice is not identical with desire (choice has to do with matters in our power whereas desire is not so restricted) or with any cognitive state like belief or opinion (choices are good or bad whereas beliefs are true or false). It is a voluntary act preceded by deliberation in which a desire for some end is transformed into a desire for the means deemed appropriate to that end. Assuming that the chosen act is done willingly, it may be a virtuous or a vicious act. Virtue and vice, therefore, are voluntary. Moreover, a man may be responsible for the ignorance that makes his act unwilled and for the original choices that determined his present character, even if it is not now within his power to act contrary to his character.

Neither Plato nor Aristotle philosophized about man's freedom or responsibility in the light of problems that are raised by a conception of the world as a mechanism governed entirely by inviolable laws. The Stoic philosophers confronted this issue, but failed to provide a satisfactory account. They accepted a thoroughgoing materialistic determinism—everything necessarily obeys the order of nature, which was also conceived as Providence and thought of as a material entity. But this determinism turns out not to be really thoroughgoing, for, although man's actions are determined, his attitudes and impressions, particularly his judgments about good and evil, are not. Since a man's attitude or intention is the sole determinant of moral good or evil, what happens to a man or what a man does is morally neutral. Hence, Providence, who determines what happens in the world rather than man's

reaction to it, is absolved from the responsibility for moral evil.

Since a man's attitude or intention determines moral good or evil, i.e., virtue or vice, the only vice is the wrong attitude, i.e., judging that things really are evil. Hence, resignation or subordination to nature is the correct attitude. It is the attitude demanded by man's reason, which is an emanation of Providence. But, of course, man has it within his power to accept or reject the dictates of his own reason. (This conception of freedom is similar to a conception that appears in determinists at several points in the history of philosophy, viz., the idea that freedom is the recognition of necessity, i.e., the acceptance of the world as it has to be. See the discussion below of Spinoza.) This attitude of acceptance requires the suppression of passion and emotion, for these involve mistaken judgments about things, e.g., that some object is intrinsically desirable. This consequence of Stoic doctrine seems to imply a contradiction, however, for a part of nature, man's passionate nature, is being morally condemned. Some Stoics, grappling with the inconsistencies and other problems of their doctrine, attempted solutions. In the third century B.C. Cleanthes, for example, argued that foreordination by Providence does not imply that an action not performed is not possible.

Epicurus had previously believed, however, that the validation of man's sense of freedom requires an indeterministic world. He introduced into the doctrine of atomism, which he accepted, the idea that atoms spontaneously swerve and saw this spontaneity as the basis of a genuine control and direction by a person over his own actions and destiny. As the Epicurean Lucretius (first century B.C.) expressed it, we can act freely because the atoms of which the mind is composed can swerve minutely, transmitting their motion to the body.

The first great Christian philosopher to grapple with the problem of human freedom in the light of Christian theology was Saint Augustine. Since Christianity imposed certain moral obligations on man, it appeared to follow that man's will must be free. For if man's will is under constraint, God cannot legitimately make demands upon him and then punish him if the demands are not satisfied. The fundamental obligation man is under, according to Augustine, is the obligation to turn to and love God. Hence, man's will is free to turn to or turn away from God. The freedom of the will is evident from the fact that man chooses one or the other.

A will that freely turns from God lacks a certain right order. The man himself, not God, is responsible for this absence and God cannot, therefore, be blamed

237

for moral evil, i.e., for the lack in the man's will. But Augustine also maintained that a will cannot have right order without God's grace. A will is motivated by love; hence a good will must be motivated by the love of God. But it is God, through grace, that implants in man the seeds of man's love of God. A creature without grace will delight in the wrong objects. How free is man's will, then, if man depends so completely on God's grace?

Although it is not entirely clear how Augustine dealt with this apparent conflict, he seems to have resolved it in the following way. Since free will is the ability to choose and since men do choose throughout their lives, all men have free will regardless of their state of grace. It is absurd to suggest that an act of will may not be free if freedom is the ability to will. But free will is not useful without grace. Once man is given grace, he has the ability to use his free will to attain union with God. Moreover, the fact that God knows beforehand how man will choose does not negate the freedom of will. To know what a man will do is not to constrain him to do it. God knows how man will freely choose.

Saint Thomas Aquinas also accepted the reality of free will. He believed, as did Augustine, that man's ultimate happiness or fulfillment is found only in God. If all men fully recognized this fact, they would choose God because man's will necessarily chooses what it conceives to be good or desirable. The will's being under this necessity does not preclude its being free for two reasons: (1) the necessity is not coercion since no external agent imposes itself upon the will independent of the will's inclinations. This distinction is similar to a distinction that will become central to the "reconciliationist" approach to free will (the view that there is no incompatibility between determinism and free will) as presented in Hume. As we shall see, Hume distinguishes coercion or compulsion from ordinary causation which, he maintains, involves no objective necessity. (2) Although a man must choose what he deems to be good, his judgment that something is good or bad is not necessitated. Hence the freedom of choice is the freedom of judgment that guides the will.

A choice is free, therefore, if it is the product of deliberation involving free judgments. An animal's judgment is not free because it flows from a natural instinct rather than rational deliberation. The factor in rational deliberation that confers freedom upon the resultant judgment is the lack of a necessary connection between deliberation and judgment. Each potential act may be viewed by the person under its good aspects or under its bad aspects. Although the person must choose the act he believes to be good, he is free to confer this goodness on virtually any object because he is free to view the object in different ways.

In the seventeenth century, the views of Benedict Spinoza on freedom are strikingly similar, in tone and content, to the ideas of the Stoics. Both accepted determinism; but Spinoza, unlike the Stoics, was unwavering in his application of determinism to the psychological domain. The behavior and mental life of human beings are completely determined and cannot, therefore, be different from what they are. We often think we are free or choose freely in a sense implying the absence of causal determination; but this belief is a consequence of our ignorance of the causes that determined our action or choice. Because the term "free will" was often used to explain behavior that was believed to be immune to explanation by underlying causes, Spinoza rejected this view of the concept. Moreover, it is absurd to praise and blame people since they are and do what they must be and do. We should rather seek to understand the causes of their actions and states of mind.

Like the Stoics, Spinoza felt that the wise man would react to universal determinism in two ways: (1) he would, of course, acquiesce; and (2) he would seek knowledge of the causes of his own behavior in order to understand his position in nature. The latter takes on added significance in the light of Spinoza's metaphysical system. He believed that "mind" and "body" are not the names of distinct substances that jointly comprise man, but are rather the names of two different ways of conceiving the unitary man. Hence, every bodily state can be conceived as a mental one, and conversely. The ideas of an ignorant man will not be connected logically because ignorance is the lack of knowledge of causes, and causal knowledge, according to Spinoza, is expressed in a deductive system where ideas depend on one another logically. The bodily aspect of ignorance is the predominance of passive emotions, emotions like love and hate that reflect the passive reaction to things that conduce to or detract from pleasure or vitality. As a man's intelligence increases and his ideas begin to succeed one another logically, his emotions will become active, i.e., they will be generated by mental activity itself. He will pursue his own interests and seek the friendship of others, guided by reason alone. He will be objective, resolute, happy, and free of pettiness. This development also represents an increase in perfection and freedom. Spinoza speaks of freedom because, under man's mental and physical aspects, man will be (relatively) free of external influence, his states and activities resulting rather from his own causal activity. His ideas will be the results of other ideas, and his emotions and actions will be determined by his own mental activity. In general terms, therefore, Spinoza conceived of freedom as self-determinism, not indeterminism.

The views of Gottfried Wilhelm Leibniz on freedom are also intimately bound up with his metaphysical outlook. Like Spinoza, he rejected any conception of freedom based on the assumption that a choice is undetermined (philosophers often call this conception of freedom the "liberty of indifference"). Any choice is determined by a combination of nonrational factors, i.e., feelings, together with a rational appraisal whose purpose is the selection of the act that appears to be for the best. An act is free if the predominant component in its determination is the man's reason or intelligence. But, according to Leibniz' metaphysical system, each individual person's life is the necessary unravelling of his given nature. Thus, all acts are necessary, including, therefore, free acts. Leibniz may be classified as a "reconciliationist" because he tried to reconcile this metaphysical theory of necessity with his belief in freedom. His task was more difficult than the analogous task for reconciliationists like David Hume and Moritz Schlick because the latter two denied the existence of objective necessity. In this regard, Leibniz distinguished necessity from compulsion, the latter, of course, being incompatible with freedom, and made distinctions among different types of necessity (metaphysical, moral, and physical).

John Locke defined freedom as the power a person has to act in accordance with his will. Sense experience does not provide man with a clear idea of *any* power. So reflection, or the mind's experience of its own activities, is the source of all knowledge of power, including, of course, the knowledge of freedom. Freedom is the opposite of necessity; but Locke defines a voluntary act as one that is preferred by the agent even if the act is not free, i.e., even if the act is performed necessarily. Will, like freedom, is defined as a power of a person, to wit, the power to will or to perform that act of preference or thought that sometimes gives rise to the preferred act. Since freedom and will are powers of persons, freedom cannot meaningfully be predicated of the will; hence, there is no genuine concept of free will.

Locke is forced to concede, however, that the concern about free will is genuine because it is the concern about the freedom *to* will rather than the freedom *of* will. Locke initially denies this freedom on the ground that a man *must* choose some alternative in a decision-making situation. Realizing that the question does not concern the freedom to make *some* choice, but rather the freedom to make a *specific* choice, Locke examines the status of the question, "Is he free to will A?" He

concludes that the question is absurd because the answer is a tautology. A man cannot but have it in his power to will what he in fact wills. Locke fails to see that the concern here is not with whether or not a man can will what he does will (since he does will A, he can will A), but whether or not he can will what he does not will. For if willing A is the only act of will in his power, it looks as if the act is not free in some important sense of "free."

Locke added a section on the determination of the will to the second edition of his *Essay Concerning Human Understanding* (1694). His psychology is hedonistic—man's will is always determined by a state of uneasiness and, given that he believes this state can be removed, he will act accordingly, priorities being determined by the relative urgencies of the uneasy states. Into this mechanistic picture, Locke introduced "free-will" as the power to prevent desire or uneasiness from determining the will. But this turns out not to be a concession to indeterminism, but rather to those who identify freedom with rational action, e.g., Leibniz. For the interruption of the mechanical workings of the will is due to a judgment formed as the result of deliberation and consideration of alternative courses of action. Thus, a man may foresee that an act he would perform has an undesirable consequence and this judgment, rather than the uneasiness that would lead to the act, determines the will to refrain from that act. In reply to the charge that a "free-will" is incompatible with a determined will, even if reason determines the will, Locke presents his case against the advocates of the liberty of indifference, arguing that freedom cannot be conceived as the *irrelevance* of our judgments to our will. A conception of freedom similar to Locke's "free-will" was also advanced by René Descartes.

Although the view that determinism is true and compatible with the existence of free will has been held by a number of philosophers, contemporary thinkers associate Hume's name, more than any other, with this doctrine.

The belief that all physical events have causes such that a given physical event must occur if the event that always caused it in the past recurs is a belief that has equal validity in the psychological sphere. We can predict how any human being will behave if we have a complete knowledge of his motives, circumstances, background, etc. Since determinism is true even in psychology, there is no liberty of indifference. But Hume agreed with Locke that the existence of such liberty would not be worthwhile anyway. A man who had this sort of liberty would not be a genuinely responsible agent. It would be pointless, for example, to

239

praise or blame this man, for, since his actions are not regularly connected with his motives, reinforcing or inhibiting certain motives will have no effect. Moreover, a man is held responsible for those acts that reflect his character rather than his casual or unpremeditated acts. The latter two, unlike the former, do not give us insight into the enduring personality and character traits that form the basis of judgments of responsibility. Hence, responsibility requires a regular connection between character and action that leaves no room for the liberty of indifference.

The freedom we do have is the power to act or not to act, depending upon our decision. As Hobbes and Spinoza had pointed out, all human beings possess this power whenever no external impediments stand in their way or whenever they are not being constrained to act in a certain way by an external force. Later reconciliationists will add certain internal constraints, e.g., psychological compulsions like kleptomania, to the list of impediments to liberty.

Finally, freedom is compatible with determinism because a free act is determined by a decision that is itself determined by the operative motives. A free agent, in other words, is one whose acts are caused by his own volitions rather than external sources. Reconciliationism has been and continues to be a subject of heated philosophical debates.

The approach of Immanuel Kant to the free will-determinism problem has reconciliationist aspects in that he wishes to deny neither. Determinism or the view that all events are caused certainly holds in the empirical world, including the psychological domain of inner experience. Like many of his predecessors, Kant was not disturbed by the fact that determinism precludes the liberty of indifference, for the latter notion is not genuine freedom. Freedom does involve the absence of external constraints. Hence, if man's will is free, it is neither subject to external constraints nor are its decisions determined by chance, i.e., by nothing real. Freedom, therefore, must be self-determination, i.e., determination of the will by its own laws. These laws are not natural laws, i.e., laws governing experienced events, for such external determination is incompatible with freedom. Experience tells us that man's decisions are often governed solely by his desires and inclinations, and, on that level, he is not free. Hence, Kant does not agree with those reconciliationists who say that freedom is ordinary determination by desires. Freedom, therefore, must be a special type of causality or determination.

As stated above, experience tells us that human beings are subject to determination by natural law. But this conclusion is formed from the vantage point of judging human beings as empirical occurrences in time

or, in Kant's language, as phenomena. Human beings as noumena, i.e., as things-in-themselves, are outside time and, hence, free from ordinary determination by events. Although we do not know human beings as noumena, they must be noumena to be free. Man as phenomenon is determined; man as noumenon is free.

Although we cannot be conscious of freedom, we can be conscious of the moral law and the moral law implies freedom. Since experience tells us only what is the case, not what must always be or ought always to be the case, moral laws must originate in man's "pure practical reason," i.e., his reason as transcending empirical inclinations. Hence a rational being who acknowledges the moral law must acknowledge that his will is being determined by his practical reason and this is freedom. A moral agent must, therefore, conceive of himself as free. Man, however, is both rational *and* natural, and he, therefore, has natural inclinations that may conflict with the dictates of reason. His experience of morality, therefore, is an experience of obligation to the moral law within his deeper "noumenal" self.

Freedom, in fact, is the essence of morality. For if freedom is determination of the will by the laws of *its own* reason, then freedom is autonomy, legislation by the self for the self. And one of Kant's formulations of the moral law is: act according to the principle that rational beings are lawgivers to themselves, i.e., as autonomous. If human beings do not create the laws they obey, they might be bound to them by an interest (e.g., God's laws might be obeyed in order to go to heaven), in which case morality would not be truly unconditional and necessary.

Many philosophers have rejected as unintelligible Kant's attempt to preserve both freedom and determinism. Since the rational determination of the will of man qua noumenon is always in accordance with morality, it is not clear why men act immorally. Presumably, they act immorally because they are determined to do so by their desires and inclinations. But then only moral acts are free and people ought never to be blamed, therefore, for their immoral acts. Also, since *every* human act is part of the empirical world, it is determined. Hence, all free acts are determined. Now, how can man qua noumenon freely determine the will to perform a specific act that it is necessitated by antecedent conditions to perform?

Nineteenth-century idealists tended to be libertarians on the free-will question, and F. H. Bradley is a good example. (A libertarian identifies man's freedom with his ability to interpose himself into the causal order by directly causing a decision or act. The decision or act is not caused by some state of or occurrence within the self, e.g., a desire or belief, but by the self directly.

Hence, not all occurrences are caused by antecedent conditions, states, or occurrences. Kant is not exactly a libertarian because he did not view self-determination as incompatible with ordinary determination.) Bradley, like many reconciliationists, rejected the liberty of indifference. If a man's choice proceeds not at all from his motives, he is an idiot rather than a responsible agent. If, on the other hand, determinism requires laws that enable prediction of a man's character from data available at birth, determinism too is incompatible with responsibility. The dilemma is resolved by the concept of the self. The accountability of an individual for a past act requires an abiding self, since the man who did the act must be identical with the man held accountable. Hence, responsibility requires a concept of the self as something more than a stream of changing states and experiences. The determinist, who seeks laws connecting these various states and experiences, therefore ignores the self. The self's creation of its character, thus, is not completely determined even if a man's acts can be predicted from a knowledge of his formed character. Even in the case of a formed character, the self can always change it and thereby thwart the determinist.

In the twentieth century, the position of the logical positivists on the free-will problem, viz., reconciliationism, held sway for a number of years. Moritz Schlick, for example, argued that the concern about freedom and responsibility arises from the confused assumption that laws of nature compel or necessitate human beings to behave in certain ways, when in fact these laws just describe what people actually do. Schlick enumerates the typical reconciliationist position: (1) freedom is the absence of compulsion; (2) freedom actually requires, rather than precludes determinism—freedom as the liberty of indifference is neither real nor desirable; (3) determinism is compatible with responsibility because the imputation of responsibility requires only that the man's motives for doing the action be amenable to change by the introduction of rewards and punishments.

In the nineteenth century, John Stuart Mill is perhaps the outstanding representative of reconciliationism. Mill and Schlick agree on fundamental doctrine. Mill does, however, emphasize the fact that we can often modify our character if we wish to do so, a fact whose recognition constitutes the feeling of moral freedom.

C. A. Campbell has argued for libertarianism against Schlick's reconciliationism. He concedes that there is a real difference between causation and compulsion, but insists nonetheless that freedom is incompatible with causation. Freedom requires self-causation and, like Kant, Campbell cites moral experience as the possible source of the knowledge of self-activity. He also agrees with Kant that the experience may be delusive. Unlike Kant, however, Campbell is a genuine libertarian because he maintains that self-activity is incompatible with determinism.

The major difference between Bradley and Campbell has to do with the relation between self and character. For Bradley, man is free because the creation of character by the self cannot be understood deterministically. A man is accountable, therefore, for acts that flow from his formed character. For Campbell self and character are less intimately connected. Self does not create character; it "watches" its creation with delight or dismay. If a man's character disposes him to act in a way his self views as immoral, the self may produce a decision in favor of duty. *Only* when the self overrides character or lets character override it is the man free. Campbell is forced to maintain, therefore, that a man's moral outlook is not determined in the ordinary way in which his character traits are determined.

Most contemporary philosophers conceive of freedom as the power or ability to choose (or act) differently from the way a person actually chooses (or acts). There has been a great deal of debate, therefore, on the meaning of: "He could have acted otherwise." Reconciliationists, like P. H. Nowell-Smith, argue that the expression can be analyzed hypothetically, e.g., "He would have acted differently if he had wanted (or chosen) to." This hypothetical statement is consistent with determinism because it does not preclude the possibility that his actual act was determined by his actual desires or choices. Campbell and others reject hypothetical analyses in favor of analyses (categorical) that make freedom incompatible with determinism.

Many contemporary philosophers reject both reconciliationism and libertarianism and yet claim to find room for freedom. They reject the reconciliationist conception of freedom as action caused by desire and the libertarian conception of self-activity. They view human behavior as explicable in two radically different ways. As movement, it is subject to ordinary determination. But some behavior can be understood as action, as something *done*. Although the movement of a man's arm can be deterministically accounted for in terms of physiological conditions, the explanation of the fact that a man raised his arm in terms of his desires, beliefs, purposes, and intentions, is *not* a deterministic explanation. In fact, it makes no sense to request a deterministic account of action. The libertarian concedes to the determinist the possibility that all actions are determined and then argues that some, the ones caused by the self, are not. According to A. I. Melden, a representative of this approach, this concession is a

241

mistake. The determinist who applies his doctrine to human action is guilty of conceptual confusion.

Melden's position is strikingly similar to Kant's. For Kant a man's decision may be conceived of as part of the phenomenal world, in which case it is determined; and it may be conceived of as part of the noumenal world, in which case it is free. For Melden an arm movement is determined if conceived of as movement, and free if conceived of as action. And both agree with the libertarian against the reconciliationist that man cannot be conceived as just a natural object (albeit quite special) if we are to view him as free.

BIBLIOGRAPHY

Saint Thomas Aquinas, *Basic Writings of Saint Thomas Aquinas*, ed. A. C. Pegis (New York, 1945). Aristotle, *The Nicomachean Ethics*, trans. J. A. K. Thomson (Harmondsworth, 1955), Book III. Saint Augustine, *On Free Will*, in *Augustine, Earlier Writings*, trans. J. H. S. Burleigh (Philadelphia, 1955). F. H. Bradley, *Ethical Studies* (London, 1927), No. 1. C. A. Campbell, *In Defence of Free Will* (Glasgow, 1938). Jonathan Edwards, *Freedom of the Will*, ed. P. Ramsey (New Haven, 1957). Thomas Hobbes, *Of Liberty and Necessity*, in *The English Works of Thomas Hobbes*, ed. Sir William Molesworth, 5 vols. (London, 1839–45), Vols. IV, V. Sidney Hook, ed., *Determinism and Freedom in the Age of Modern Science* (New York, 1961). David Hume, *An Inquiry Concerning Human Understanding* (New York, 1955), Sec. VIII. William James, "The Dilemma of Determinism," in *The Will to Believe* (1897; New York, 1921). Immanuel Kant, *Critique of Practical Reason*, trans. L. W. Beck (Chicago, 1949). G. W. Leibniz, *Selections*, ed. Philip P. Wiener (New York, 1951). John Locke, *An Essay Concerning Human Understanding*, ed. A. C. Fraser, 2 vols. (New York, 1959), Vol. I, Book II, Ch. XXI. A. I. Melden, *Free Action* (New York, 1961). John Stuart Mill, *An Examination of Sir William Hamilton's Philosophy* (London, 1867), Ch. XXVI. P. H. Nowell-Smith, *Ethics* (Harmondsworth, 1954), Chs. XIX, XX. Plato, *The Republic*, trans. F. M. Cornford (London and New York, 1945). Moritz Schlick, *Problems of Ethics*, trans. D. Rynin (New York, 1939), Ch. VII. Benedict Spinoza, *Ethics*, ed. J. Gutmann (New York, 1949). Philip Wheelright, *Aristotle* (New York, 1951).

BERNARD BEROFSKY

[See also Evil; **Freedom;** Indeterminacy; Justice; Nature; Necessity; Newton on Method; Positivism in the Twentieth Century; Right and Good; Stoicism.]

FREE WILL IN THEOLOGY

"FREE WILL" is to be defined in general as intentional action uninhibited, or alternatively as the power so to act. The idea of will adds nothing to the idea of action, so long as action is taken in its full and personal sense; for personal action is such insofar as it is voluntary. To call it voluntary, or the expression of will, is to negate a negation about it—to exclude the suggestion that it is something less than a piece of genuine personal doing. It is a further point of refinement, to take up will, the voluntariness of voluntary action, and to distinguish an exercise of it which is free, from one which is not; a man may act with conscious intention to do what he does, and yet not seem to merit the description of being a free agent. The assertion of free will has no significance, except in relation to some constraint it is intended to exclude. The force of the term has varied, and still does vary, with predominant interest in various types of constraint; and it is this variation which makes the history of the notion.

The notion of freedom as such plainly derives from the distinction between the freeman and the slave. So long as freedom of will is simply equated with freedom of status, no point of philosophical interest arises; freemen are men who do what they like, slaves are men who do what they are told. But reflection will suggest that in many things slaves do what they choose, and in some things freemen are liable to constraint, being subject (for example) to kings. Nor can kings themselves do whatever they wish; they must obey the gods, or suffer the consequences. The development of legal practice leads to systematic thought on the topic. A man is not to be held accountable for actions which were not his own. The slave's action under orders is his master's. But equally on occasion a freeman might be coerced to act against his will; whose, then, is the action, and whose the responsibility?

Sophistic Doctrine. An early Greek philosophical position regarding freedom was the simple denial of all intrinsic limitations upon the pursuit of voluntary aims. Moral convention and social structure are mere conveniences of life, and can be made the instruments of masterminds who know how to get outside them and to manipulate them. Such was, or was said to be (e.g., by Plato, *Republic* 336b ff.) the doctrine of certain fifth-century Greek Sophists who claimed to teach well-placed young men the art of success in public life. In opposition to this doctrine, Socrates and Plato shifted attention from external to internal constraint— from the rub between one's own will and one's neighbor's to the rub between one's reason and one's passion or appetite. A man's true self was his Reason; to be free was to rule one's passions; it was no true freedom to make one's fellowmen the instruments of mindless appetite, or of exorbitant ambition.

Plato and Aristotle. In the *Republic* Plato boldly inverted the historical order. The philosophical notion of inward sovereignty does not arise through the interiorization of political relations; it is the other way about: men acknowledge political sovereignty through first recognizing the intrinsic right of Reason to rule their souls, and then accepting sovereignty in the State—"the individual writ large"—as the outward embodiment of the same Reason (*Republic* 534d). Political sovereignty is to be valued as supporting Reason in the individual, and keeping it on its throne. We are not enslaved by a genuine exterior sovereignty; we are liberated by it. Here is the beginning of that famous philosophical paradox, that a right choice of service is the only freedom.

The model or parable exploited by Plato is hierarchical. Suppose a household presided over by a master capable of finding the path of right reason for himself and the other members of it, while they have no such capacity. If he lets himself be run by his inferiors, he will be enslaved and they (through the resulting chaos) will be unhappy. If he maintains control he will be free, and they will be both outwardly well-circumstanced and inwardly content, for they can feel the intrinsic rightness of rational direction, even though they cannot find it for themselves. Such is the position of the rational self in relation to the passions or appetites. Reason persuades passion; passion merely overbears reason (*Republic* 548b, 554b–d).

Plato and after him Aristotle introduced several refinements into the doctrine in their progressive realization of the necessity for reason to train the passions themselves, and to take them into partnership as fellow initiators of right intentions. It remained that essential freedom was the freedom of thoughtfulness to find the right path; particular and practical choice was to be seen as general reason finding expression under given circumstances. A man had no freedom to invent principles of good life, for they were laid down in the nature of things. Free thought would lead to agreement about the Good, as it would lead to agreement in mathematics (Aristotle, *Nicomachean Ethics* 1106b).

To be rational, then, is to be free. But does it lie within a man's power to be rational? Does effort of will suffice to bring the passions into line? Plato and Aristotle make no such unequivocal claim. They discuss the psychology of struggles for self-mastery (Plato, *Republic* 439e ff., *Phaedrus* 246ff.; Aristotle *Nicom. Ethics* 1145–47); they show how ruinously our very judgment of what is good can be perverted by an ill-formed character (*Nicom. Ethics* 1113a). They feel no concern to enquire whether or not every soul that is capable of hearing the philosophical gospel is capable also of winning her interior battle and finding felicity. Their concern is rather to vindicate the free power of Reason as such to perform its function of moralizing human existence. It is a hopeful enterprise,

even if hope lies rather in conditioning the next generation than in self-culture. Such an attitude was natural, considering that the whole discussion arose out of a critique of city-state life. Reason was to prevail by being socially projected, and embodied in institutions, above all in schools.

Aristotle lived to see the collapse of city-state autonomy; but the cultural mission of his pupil, the all-conquering Alexander, was still conceived as the planting of Greek self-governing cities the world over, to drill men into rational freedom. Plato made some concession to the individual's aspiration after the freedom to save his soul, by the myth of transmigration. One's effort in this life might not take one far; but it might suffice to enable one to make the choice of such an embodiment or destiny in one's next life, as to allow of one's going further (*Republic* 617e).

Later Greek Philosophers. The progressive overshadowing of city autonomy by monarchical empire after Alexander provided a soil for Stoicism, a philosophy which both made the individual the captain of his soul, and at the same time related his strenuous self-government to the governing mind of the Universe. It was still the ideal, to let Reason rule; but Reason was now seen as embodied in the Universal Order, the recurrent cycle of world-process. Since the cycle must fulfill its pattern, and universal Reason (of which the individual's reason is but a function) must prevail, the new problem is theoretically posed, of the relation between the individual's exercise of freedom, and the operation of a universal, rational necessity. The official solution lay in the doctrine of Relaxation—though it is the Universal Reason which functions as our rational mind, it relaxes its operation in us to what is (initially) the mere rudiment of actual rationality; and from that starting-point finds its level in us by and as our personal or free endeavor. So far from feeling himself oppressed by the World-Reason, the Stoic embraced it *con amore* and, by willing in the line of Cosmic Will, enjoyed that freedom which is escape from all frustration. (For the spirit of this ethos, see Marcus Aurelius, passim.) If one asked whether the sinner or fool could *resist* Cosmic Destiny, one was put off with such sayings as that God leads good will by the hand and drags recalcitrance by the hair. In practice a man was offered the choice of being the victim of fate or the partner of providence; how men could have such a choice was, no doubt, theoretically insoluble and must always be so in a strictly pantheist system.

The contemporary rival to Stoicism, the School of Epicurus, taught an out-and-out libertarian individualism (Diogenes Laërtius, X. 133–34). The philosopher shook from his shoulders both the burden of politics and the burden of cosmic destiny, and pursued an amiable, cultured life at his own sweet will, under the leadership of the laudable and tranquil emotions. It must surprise the modern reader to observe that Epicurus supported his doctrine of freedom by a strict atomic materialism. Everything, including the human soul, is a chance constellation of atoms. But he does not conclude "So we do what the atoms make us do." He insists, "Our choices are ours to make." The explanation of the paradox is that the ancients were not obliged to view the movements of matter as the realm of inflexible regularity. Reason it was that imposed order; be rid of Cosmic Reason, leave matter to itself, and there might be scope for the self-determination of a soul which atoms had transiently blown together.

Epicureanism proved to be a deviation which was not followed up. The settlement of world-empire in the seemingly everlasting Roman dominion and the infiltration of oriental attitudes toward divine monarchy favored a philosophical development building on Stoic foundations, but tending towards an elevation of the Supreme Principle into an absolute transcendence over the world. Neo-Platonism, as this development is called, reached maturity in the third century A.D. Insofar as the system viewed the human soul as an emanation from the universal being rather than as a part or function of it, it allowed a more intelligible basis for the substantial distinctness of the human agent and so for his freedom to determine his own relation to the Divine. Emanation proceeded in a cascade of descending steps, and man embraced within his being an epitome of nature's sinking scale, from spirit above to mere matter below. He had in his faculty of desire a corresponding scale of "loves," each with affinity for its own objects. His freedom of choice essentially lay in the power to identify himself with one love or another, and supremely with love for the Supreme.

Christendom. It was as a doctrine of free will that Neo-Platonism was embraced by Saint Augustine at the turn of the fourth to the fifth century. It afforded him deliverance from the crude heresy of Christian Manichaeism. In common with other forms of Gnosticism this sect attributed the genesis of mankind to a cosmic defeat by which elements of "light" were captured and enmeshed in "darkness." The Neo-Platonic psychology gave arms to Augustine in which to appear as the champion of God's good creation. By a shift in the level of his love, man, created in the divine image, had become the author of his own degradation. Being free, he had misused the power of choice (*Confessions* vii 3-21).

So far, Augustine was all for free will. He was soon to face in another direction. There was nothing arbitrary or accidental in his change of front. There were special emphases in biblical and Christian theism

which tipped the balance of the Neo-Platonic system. Neo-Platonic deity is not seen as the Judge of men's souls, fixing their eternal destiny according to their merit; and so there is no urgency in the enquiry about the degree of a man's personal responsibility for his character or attitudes. If men are wise and holy, they are wise and holy; they can be influenced towards such a desirable state, and their own choices or resolves will help. The absolute question, how much could have been expected of any one soul, has no practical importance. It is another thing for the Christian who sees himself placed before the bar of the Eternal Judge.

But while on the one side biblical theism sharpened the sense of a free choice of will determining one's salvation or perdition, on another side it called it in question. The God of the Bible is conceived as sovereign will, the creator of all things by fiat, and the savior of men by interposition. How then can the creature's will be anything but the instrument of the Creator's, and how can the salvation of the elect be the work of any but God? Neo-Platonism conceived of God not as sovereign will, but as supreme perfection; less perfect beings were the outfall and overspill of his being, not the creatures of his will. He was their savior only in the sense that he was their true Good, and that without the pull of his attraction, no one would aspire after him. But equally if one did not aspire, the attraction would have no effect. On these terms it was scarcely meaningful to ask whether the turning of a soul to God was its work or his.

Augustine felt able to save man's free will on the side of the Creatorship of God. The Creator had *chosen* to confer on his human creature much such a free will as Neo-Platonism taught, for had not he created man in his own image? But on the side of Redemption no such concession could be made. Redemption was a rescue of the perishing, a sheer seizure of minds incapable of loving God through their own act or choice. Though created free to love God, man had lost that freedom by his disobedience or irreligion. Mankind, apart from the grace of salvation, was sick or corrupt; it needed to be restored or healed by God, before it regained freedom to love God. Fallen man might indeed exercise free choice in the pursuit of such objectives as he was capable of loving; he could not give himself the higher love. Restored by grace, he would choose freely on all levels, except insofar as his unredeemed condition still hung about him (*De spiritu et litera, De natura et gratia*).

Augustine's teaching provoked vigorous reactions from Christians who feared it would enervate spiritual effort. It would be wiser, said Pelagius and Julian, to see in salvation God's provision of indispensable means, means which it lay in the free choice of man to employ or to neglect. Augustine rejected that doctrine as inadequate to the Christian facts and as conducive to spiritual pride. We do not reach out our hands and take salvation; salvation takes us. The controversy drove him into extremes. God had eternally predestined whom he would elect to salvation and his saving will was irresistible. None who truly aspired to salvation, indeed, were denied it; but their aspiring was by God's predestination and grace.

Augustine carried the day against Pelagianism, but the sharp paradox of human responsibility and divine predestination was found difficult to live with and was soon qualified by the Church. The Scholastics of the high Middle Ages elaborated a subtle account of the cooperation of free will with grace (e.g., Aquinas, *Summa Theologica*, prima secundae Quaest. cix-cxiv). But the balance of interest for them was somewhat shifted by their adoption of a Neo-Aristotelianism drawn from Muhammadan sources. The system derived from Islam an overwhelming concern with the absolute sovereignty of the Creator's will over all created things and events. The human agent, like every other creature, was a secondary cause instrumental to the sole primary cause, God. The Christian philosophers labored to find a place for free will under the all-determining and all-foreseeing mind of God (ibid., pars prima, qu. xiv art. 13, qu. xxii art. 4). Within the created system, says Thomas Aquinas, there are chances genuinely open to the choice exercised by human free will; human decision is as real a cause as any other finite cause. But that does not stand in the way of our acknowledging the whole system, including the human volitions it contains, as the effect of divine ordination. It is a superstition to suppose that a divinely ordained effect must operate by a process of mechanical determination rather than by one of free choice. It would be misleading, then, to say that I was *bound* to do what I freely decided, since there is no binding in the case. It remains that I was *going* to do what I did. It must surely be objected that if this is a harmless tautology, it does not give reality to God's prior causality; while if it is so understood as to do this, it reduces free choice to a subjective illusion. Freely as we may act, we shall be toeing a predetermined line.

The Protestant Reformation rejected the subtleties of Scholastic Aristotelianism together with its metaphysical preoccupations. The interest of Luther and Calvin reverted to Augustine's position on salvation, which they reasserted in all its uncompromisingness. Indeed, the paradox is sharpened, insofar as Augustine is now seen as a commentator on Saint Paul simply, and his Neo-Platonic overtones are lost. The sovereignty of the divine will is conceived as decisive power rather than as self-fulfilling Good and the collision of omnipotent grace with creaturely free will is uncushioned. Salvation is an unmerited gift towards which the fallen will can do nothing. Luther wrote a treatise *Of the Will Enslaved* (*De servo arbitrio*, 1525); Calvin carried the speculation of predestination to unexampled extremes (*Instituta*, iii 21–23; definitive ed., 1559). Reaction was not slow to follow; on the part of the Catholic Church it was immediate (Council of Trent, 1545–63). Within the Calvinist confession Arminius led the revolt. Strict Calvinism has since been reasserted by one reform after another, but on balance has lost ground.

Modern Physicalism. Meanwhile a totally different issue has come to the fore and defined the freewill question as it is now commonly understood. This is the issue raised by the development of scientific materialism. If the activity of the human person is geared to the movements of a physical body, and if that body is a system operating by rules of perfect and as it were mechanical uniformity, how can the apparent freedom of choice be real? Atomistic materialism had been a school of Greek speculation but, as we have seen in the case of Epicurus, carried no necessarily deterministic implications. The parentage of scientific determinism is rather to be found in astronomical studies. It was an ancient and a medieval commonplace that the movements of the heavenly bodies were mathematically exact and ideally predictable. Supposing the "influences" of the stars upon the causality of earthly events to be determinative, human actions will be subject to fate. It was easy to refute the argument by pointing out that the effect of astral influence was highly general; different earthly agents reacted to it variously, and men as they might choose (Aquinas, *Summa Theologica*, prima, qu. cxv). But now the hypothesis of the mathematical physicists was that earthly bodies were composed of constellated atoms or of vortices, of which the motions and mutual influences were as mathematically exact and as predictable as those of the stars. Physical fate seemed to have descended from the skies, and so closed in upon us as to leave no escape.

No conclusion could have been more unwelcome or more out of tune with the times. The new science was the expression of humanist self-assertion, of the resolve of strong minds to make all events, however unpromising, subject to human calculation or control. The method of physical enquiry was the voluntary invention of experimental tests and the forcing of them upon Nature; besides, as Descartes pointed out in his *Meditations* (i, iv, vi), it was only by a constant act of will that one could hold the mathematico-physical hypothesis itself in face of the contrary suasions of one's five senses. What could be more preposterous, therefore, than to make the will to intellectual world conquest the prisoner or even the creature of the mechanism it postulated? Descartes deserves the highest credit for the firmness with which he held to both sides of the duality of free mind or will and of determinate matter; and for the honesty with which he admitted his inability to construe the operative unity of the mind-body person. There were thinkers who took the desperate course of denying free will, e.g., Hobbes or Spinoza; they were violently disliked by their contemporaries.

The Cartesian position treated thought as the activity of a spiritual subject and found the immediate effect of will in the formation of mental decisions. How the clockwork body came to register or execute such decisions was beyond comprehension; all one could study on that side was the mechanism through which it did so. For practical purposes such a division of the ground was not inconvenient, and people could laugh at the rage for consistency which led George Berkeley to rid himself of dualism by reducing material objects to "ideas," thus making will or spirit the sole substance, agent, or cause, subject only to the higher will of God.

It was a more serious matter when the proved fruitfulness of experimental physics began to suggest that its methods and basic conceptions were the models for all factual science, including psychology. It was then not merely a matter of squaring a freely-choosing mind with its mechanistically-conceived embodiment; it was a matter of squaring an experienced exercise of freedom in the mind with a causal explanation of mental experience in terms of invariant regularities. It was David Hume who first rubbed the sore of this problem in his *Treatise of Human Nature* (1739). His subtle thought continues to exercise its spell on English-speaking philosophers, and it is still widely held in academic circles that an empiricist logic distilled from the study of physical phenomena is binding upon all thought about matters of fact; and that its applicability to thinking and to behavior makes determinism in some sense inescapable.

Solutions were bound to be attempted. Immanuel Kant, in his two first *Critiques,* conceded to Newton and to Hume that we are forced to think deterministically about both physical and mental processes, when making them an object of study; but Kant also maintained that our need so to think is an inescapable limitation of the human mind. Reality is not such, as is shown by the fact that we know ourselves called to exercise free and responsible choices in favor of the moral law. How our power so to do fits in with the actual order of nature lies (Kant thought) beyond our comprehension; what we can understand is that the very form of our cognitive processes prevents their attaining the knowledge of things as they are in themselves. Kant's solution is a rational and systematic agnosticism. His German successors attempted more positive answers by advancing bold metaphysical speculations concerning the subjective and the objective poles of existence (Fichte, Schelling, Hegel, Schopenhauer).

Modern defenders of free will insist on the abstract or diagrammatic character of our scientific knowledge but do not need to go all the way with Kant's scientific agnosticism. For the progress of the natural sciences themselves has eased their task. The scientist's model of physical reality is no longer the simple man-made machine. Nature is seen as a complex of forces, which by knotting themselves in combinations of increasing elaborateness develop astonishing new properties of joint action; and so a physical basis for free consciousness becomes less starkly inconceivable.

The Human Sciences. The decreased urgency of the problem on the physical side in the present century has been balanced by increased pressure from historical, social, and psychological science. However little capable these sciences may be of attaining the mathematical rigor pursued in physical enquiry, they disclose a deep and complex conditioning of the individual by background, environment, and subconscious makeup, such as threatens to reduce the exercise of genuine choice to trivial proportions. Several thinkers have been impressed by the predominant effect of one factor or another: Marx by the pressure of economic needs and of the current system for coping with them; Freud by the twists of emotional attitude formed in us during one helpless immaturity; Jung by the individual's inheritance of ancestral archetypes of personal relation or function.

Self-creation. In the face of such considerations men have looked in opposite directions for a vindication of significant free decision. A new and historicized version of the Stoic creed calls on us to identify ourselves with the march of historical process from which we should vainly hope to cut ourselves off; so let us lead it on. Such, broadly, was the attitude of Hegel; such is the attitude of Marxists today, and, in effect, of those Western optimists who are content to back the momentum of scientific and technological advance. By contrast, several schools of existentialism have put forward a parody of Augustinianism—our acknowledged conditionedness by factors of all kinds is a state of subhumanity from which we must be raised into authentic existence by deciding for ourselves what we will be and do. Kierkegaard and the religious existentialists see the challenge to self-creation as the challenge to determine your existence in the face of God; Sartre and the atheists see it as the challenge to be

God to yourself—there being no other God for you.

The call to embrace historical destiny and the call to exercise self-creation, however seemingly opposed, equally exemplify a distinctively modern belief in the openness of the future. The ancients saw free will as freedom to fulfill the determinate requirements of human nature, human nature being a fixed quantity. Insofar as thought later turned in a theistic direction, human nature became a God-given form, articulated in divine commands, and oriented towards God, the immutable living perfection. Even Kant, with his passion for moral autonomy, was still viewing free will as power to impose upon one's conduct a law written into the very structure of one's mind. The two succeeding centuries have dissolved the fixity of the human aim. Romanticism popularized the conception of the artist as a creator of the unique and allowed the individual life or even the common life of an epoch to be seen as an unique invention. Historicism showed the degree to which what passed for human nature had been a cultural product changing with the times. Evolutionism suggested the mutability in principle of the human species, and technology has seemed to put into our hands the means of transforming our existence beyond recognition. In consequence, freedom of will is seen as no longer limited in scope to the fulfillment of human nature, but as the power and the responsibility, whether corporate or individual, to determine in some measure the very nature we are to express.

Linguistic Philosophy. The linguisticism now predominant in American and British academic philosophy offers no contribution, perhaps, to the development of the free will idea; but it offers a fresh approach to the free will-determinism issue, seeing it as a question of adjusting to one another two modes of speech, through a careful study of the natural uses proper to each. We use the language of sheer personal action—with or without implications of alternative choice—and we use the language of event, process, etc. Actions we talk of as what we simply or freely do; events we talk of as happening. To actions we assign intentions, to events we assign causes. Of an event we ask, "What led to it?" Of a man's action, "What is he up to?" The problem of free will (excluding its theological aspects) will be the problem of relating these two ranges of speech to one another.

One point must first be made clear. Language which describes or mentions choiceful action is secondary to language in which we do our choiceful thinking or make our choice itself, as when you say to someone placing alternatives before you "I opt for" A or B (J. L. Austin, *How to Do Things with Words*, Oxford, 1962). Having made this point, we may proceed to show that the correlation of event-style and personal-action-style speech, so far from being an oddity, is common form. In the case of your talking choice, or spoken option, you choose in view of an opinion of facts or events, which, if you do not explicitly state it, you still take for granted. Indeed, your making of your choice is a virtual affirmation of the facts in view of which you make it. Voluntary decision to act upon (supposed) facts will often be taken as a more serious assertion of those facts than a direct statement of them. If you did make the mere statement, it would be in event-style form.

Or take the case in which you are simply describing events or their interrelations. It remains true that you do the describing, and you go about it as you choose, talking backwards, forwards, or across the event-process you describe, picking one word and rejecting another. And if I wish to understand your speech, I do not look for the causes of the vocal inflections, I look to your expressive intention. Whereas, to understand what you are talking about, I attend to the causal sequences you are describing. In fact, I am bound to do both. To understand you as speaking I must understand the facts you state and to understand the facts you state I must understand you as speaking; so inseparably are the two modes or logics connected.

But if the matter is as straightforward as this, how can we ever come to think of denying either mode of speech its rights? Why should anyone dream of reducing voluntary-action statements to the happening-by-cause category? The answer is this. So long as we are talking our way into or through choiceful acts we can use no category but the category proper to such talk—I cannot talk to myself the choice I am making, as being an event which occurs. But often we speak of choiceful actions from outside, as having been done or as likely to be done, and then it is possible for us to switch categories, and to talk of them as events—or, more accurately put, to talk, instead, about the events in which they take effect. And events as such are subject, we assume, to the category of causality—to exposition in terms of uniform sequence—and are in principle predictable from a knowledge of their antecedents. If, then, the event in which a choiceful act takes form is predictable, and causally determinate, how can that act itself be free? Such appears to be the puzzle.

The determinist case is that the causal regularity of choice-produced events should be accepted. There are two stories—one descriptive from "within" of the way in which the choice is made, another descriptive from "outside" of the event's position in the event-sequence. Each story is veridical in its own sphere, and there is no difficulty in letting them run parallel.

The freewill rejoinder is that a solution in that sense

rests on a falsification. Two stories covering the same ground and expressed in different logical idioms may rightly be tolerated when they are both objectively descriptive stories. I may tell a story of past voluntary activity in cold detachment, and feel no great mental discomfort in doubling it with a causal account of the same behavior. But that is because in imagination I degrade a personal story to the level of a story about a process which unrolled as it did unroll. And that is to depersonalize the story. It is only personal insofar as I identify myself in some measure with the characters or agents in it and express them as personally active from "within." And then the acquiescence in a parallel cause-and-effect story becomes impossible.

All the rejoinder achieves is to set aside the determinist's soothing compromise. Three possible positions remain. We may say (1) So much the worse for the ultimate validity of the free-action language—a determinist conclusion; (2) So much the worse for that of the caused-event language—a libertarian conclusion; (3) So much the worse for both, our language in either case having a purely pragmatic value, in serving our purposes—an agnostic conclusion.

The determinist will speak slightingly of the "subjective character" of personal experience and its expressions, the libertarian of the "abstract and diagrammatic character" of causality-constructions; while the agnostic will cite the agelong inconclusiveness of the debate between the two other parties, and the inadequacy of language as such to the nature of things.

The defender of free will ruins his case if he overplays his hand. He must not deny the validity of causal-regularity interpretations so far as they go; but he will maintain that we have no reason to suppose, and much reason to disbelieve, that the grid of natural uniformity fits so tightly upon living processes as to deny scope to free personal action. On the other side of his case, he must avoid exaggerating human liberty. The individual is constantly subject to pressures, visible and invisible, which he often has no motive and sometimes no ability to resist; and the free options he does exercise are mostly within a range of choice narrowly circumscribed by conditions outside his control. So human conduct may often be broadly predictable. On the other hand, the libertarian is not going to admit that all the predictability in a man's conduct is dependent upon the operation of determining causes which restrict his freedom of choice. For in taking a decision, a man will follow his usual policy in such matters unless he now sees reason to revise it. If we, his friends, have formulated his policy to ourselves, we may think of the policy-rule, taken in conjunction with the circumstances invoking its application, as *causing* his action. But voluntary consistency is not subjection to any determining causality. His policy only guides the man because he goes on choosing to maintain it. It is a hard case, if voluntary freedom is only to be evinced by wild and continuous caprice.

Most difficult of solution along linguistic lines is the theological problem of free will in face of a sovereign divine will, insofar as religious conviction puts forward statements about divine initiative in the origination of human free acts which are in formal conflict with statements about the human agent's own initiative. Appeal may be made to the believer's practical understanding of what it is to exercise his will in prolongation (as it were) of God's. But no formal solution can be attempted without a prior examination of the special sense and status of statements about the Divine Subject (traditionally known as the topic of Analogy).

BIBLIOGRAPHY

As will have been seen from the body of the article, the history of the freewill idea is the history of philosophy from a certain angle, and correspondingly difficult to supply with a limited bibliography. Harold Ofstad, *An Inquiry into the Freedom of the Will* (London, 1961) contains a very full bibliography as well as a thorough discussion of the subject from a semi-determinist standpoint. An out-and-out libertarian is Corliss Lamont, *Freedom of Choice Affirmed* (New York, 1967). He offers a good historical survey. Austin Farrer's *Freedom of the Will* (New York, 1960) works largely from linguistic ground.

To turn to historical positions, in addition to references in the article we may cite the following. For a classic defence of the Calvinist position: Jonathan Edwards, *Careful and Strict Enquiry . . .* (1754). For German Idealism, Arthur Schopenhauer, *The World as Will and Idea (Die Welt als Wille und Vorstellung)*, trans. R. B. Haldane and J. Kemp, 3 vols. (London, 1883). For American Pragmatism, William James, "The Dilemma of Determinism" (1884), in *The Will to Believe . . .* (New York, 1897). For Vitalistic Philosophy, Henri Bergson, *Essai sur les données immédiates de la conscience* (Paris, 1889). For Existentialism, J-P. Sartre, *L'Etre et le néant* (Paris, 1943), trans. H. Barnes as *Being and Nothingness* (New York, 1956).

AUSTIN FARRER

[See also Agnosticism; Causation; Dualism; Epicureanism and Free Will; **Existentialism; Free Will and Determinism;** Freedom, Legal Concept of; God; Love; Nature; **Necessity;** Sin and Salvation; **State;** Stoicism.]

LEGAL CONCEPT OF FREEDOM

I

A NUMBER of legal conceptions contribute to the popular notion of freedom. The ordinary man generally associates freedom with the positive idea of liberty to do or not to do something, but to a lawyer such liberty would signify the absence of a duty to refrain from the act or omission in question. Free speech, for example, implies that one is under no duty to keep silent. But freedom means much more than this, and a second idea familiar to both laymen and lawyers is that of a person's immunity from the power of another. Thus, a freeman, as opposed to a slave, is one who is not under someone else's dominion. Yet a third meaning which the word "freedom" implies in law is capacity to perform legal transactions, for example, to vote or make a will; but since this aspect of the idea is not as important as the other two and is in fact consequential on them, it does not merit separate discussion.

Convenient though it is to distinguish between these component ideas of freedom, it must be remembered that they have been interwoven throughout history. This may be why people so often fail to realize that "freedom from" power and "freedom to" assert oneself are not two aspects of one issue, but two separate issues. To gratify a desire for freedom from power does not imply freedom to gratify every desire, otherwise deliverance from the evil of untrammelled power will inevitably end in the evil of untrammelled liberty, and vice versa. There is a point beyond which liberty of action is harmful and needs restraining. For instance, if everyone were free to drive as he pleased on the road the result would be chaos. So, too, in countless other ways one's freedom to do what one will has to be checked in the interest of others; and if restraint is not forthcoming spontaneously it has to be compelled. More troublesome is the question, which the law has sometimes to solve, of how far one should be free to surrender one's freedom or to degrade oneself; and to this there can be no general answer. It may be gathered from all this that freedom in law cannot be isolated from social and moral issues, and we glimpse here the lesson that liberty of action at law can, in the main, be allowed with safety only where there is restraint bred from a spontaneous sense of obligation. The corollary of this would appear to be that a society which relaxes legal restraints without a corresponding measure of individual self-discipline is rushing, like the Gadarene swine, to destruction.

It is clear, then, that a balance has to be found between authority and the individual as reflected in the measure of immunities and liberties accorded to the latter. To guard against the misuse of law, whether in the form of abuse of power or of liberty, men have appealed through the ages to principles of justice and morality and even to some higher law, such as Natural Law. These ideas, however, are so broad as to accommodate divergent interpretations with the result that the history of freedom in law becomes the story of how certain concepts of law and philosophy have been used to satisfy the paramount need of each age.

II

Jewish Law contributed powerfully to the ideal of freedom. The enslavement of the Israelites under the Egyptians led them to found a society in which Pharaohs had no place and in which individuals owed allegiance only to God, thereby obviating the need to depend on any human institution. But their assertion of independence went further, for even the rulership of God had to rest on voluntary acceptance, which is alleged to have occurred in the Covenant with Abraham (Genesis 15:18), and to have been renewed with Isaac and Jacob. This arrangement also set a pattern for the benevolent use of power by the ruler. The later appointment of Saul as king in 1037 B.C. amounted to a rejection of God's rulership, but the king's own position still rested on a contract with his people. The partnership between God and Man in the latter's development towards holiness led to an emphasis on discipline and corresponding restraint on liberties of action. At the same time, be it noted, these ideas must be considered in the light of the social structures of the age, for slavery was recognized, and equality did not obtain between men and women.

Throughout the Greek era the background was one of precarious social stability, which tended to emphasize moderation and preservation of the status quo. Solon, it is true, sought to limit power by means of the idea that men should have a say in selecting those to whom they have to submit—the idea of democracy; but both Plato and Aristotle stressed the need for restraint in action. The former argued that the restraints imposed by society are necessary to develop virtue in those who possess this capacity. Not all men are so endowed, for they differ in this respect just as they differ in physique. Aristotle, for his part, condemned democracies in which people acknowledge no restraints. But it is not enough merely to have laws; they must be just laws, that is, laws which enable virtuous people to achieve as far as possible in the light of their reason the fullness of their nature in society. A just law favors liberty, and freedom and good government go together. To educate is to develop the subject in virtue, so it becomes a prime task of the state to be the school of the citizen. On the other hand, slaves should accept their lot, since some people are slaves by nature. Indeed, it is the very service of wise and virtuous masters that brings out the best in their slaves; and masters should of course treat slaves with kindness.

The achievements of the Romans were practical rather than theoretical. That great repository of Roman Law, the *Corpus Juris Civilis*, contains passages which would support absolute authority (e.g., *Digest* 1.3.31) as well as the authority of law (e.g., *Codex* 1.14.4). It was left to Cicero, who was not strictly a lawyer, to strike off the ringing statement, "We are slaves of the law that we may be free" (*Pro Cluentio* 53.146). But he added that there were limits to the use of law. "True law," he said, "is right reason in agreement with nature" and from it there can be no dispensation either by the Senate or the people (*De republica* III, xxii). This doctrine of Man's nature as the "true" source of law had much influence later. Roman Law recognized slavery throughout, and there were also grades of free men who in varying degrees were less privileged than *cives*, or citizens. Although it was admitted that slavery was contrary to Natural Law, it continued because it suited the economic order. The movement towards freedom is discernible in three ways. (1) In A.D. 212 citizenship was conferred on free men throughout the Empire; (2) increasing restrictions were imposed on the powers of masters over slaves; and (3) there was a preference for freedom rather than slavery in the interpretation of rules concerning a person's status.

Even early Christian philosophy did not condemn slavery, or for that matter condemn authoritarian government. The equality of souls in Heaven did not call for social disruption in order to achieve equality of bodies on earth. So it was that Saint Paul urged a fugitive slave to return to his master (Epistle to Philemon). Saint Augustine, however, sought to explain slavery as a form of collective retribution for original sin. All in all the early Christian concept of freedom was far removed from that of the Jews; it was, in effect, freedom to enter into the bondage of God.

After the Dark Ages, which followed the Roman era, the establishment of order required a power structure, not liberty; the power of monarchs, of the feudal nobility and, from the eleventh century onwards, of the Church. The economic order was the feudal system under which a person was bound to render service to the overlord whose land he held. The trends of the age consolidated power in the sovereign who, on the one hand, sought to entrench his position and, on the other, was looked up to by his subjects in their struggle for freedom from the power of the feudal nobility. Legal theory was adapted to these ends. Niccolò Machiavelli in his *Discourses* characterized republics as superior to princedoms and as requiring high moral quality in citizens. People who lack this must be governed by tyrants, and in his *Prince* he proceeded to analyze and advocate absolute monarchy. Thomas Hobbes in his *Leviathan* turned to Natural Law. Men, he said, in a state of nature were so unprincipled that the life of Man was "solitary, poore, nasty, brutish and short." This ended when all people yielded their rights to a sovereign, who in return for absolute subservience guaranteed order and a measure of freedom for all. The sovereign's external independence and internal

omnipotence posed two serious threats. Under the guise of the "sovereignty of states" the unbridled pursuit of selfish policies soon reduced Europe to a barbarous condition which culminated in the Thirty Years War. Little wonder that voices, notably that of Hugo Grotius, began to be heard urging restraint. A body of duties, known as "International Law," was evolved in the hope of limiting the liberty of action of states. But duties lacking enforceability, which is the case with International Law, are of little avail, and today, when the weapons of war are assuming increasingly monstrous proportions, the continued insistence on the sovereignty of states foreshadows a very bleak future indeed. In the municipal sphere the individual, who had trusted so fondly to his sovereign to be a bulwark against feudal oppression, soon found that he had exchanged one tyrant for another. Accordingly, John Locke was moved to argue that when men in a state of nature entered into the primeval contract with the sovereign, they surrendered to him only the right to preserve order. Personal rights to "life, liberty and estate" could never be surrendered since they were inalienable, and a sovereign who tries to infringe them may be overthrown. Locke thus became the philosopher of the revolution of 1688 in England by which the supremacy of the royal prerogative power was replaced by that of the Crown in Parliament, and his theory also furnished the main arguments in the classic case of *Somersett* ([1772], 20 State Trials, 1) in which English Law set its face against slavery for all time.

In France events took a more drastic turn. Jean Jacques Rousseau imagined a social contract whereby sovereignty was surrendered to society as a whole. This dispensed with the need for a personal sovereign, and within a few years of his death the French Revolution put the theory to sinister effect. Once again the pattern of development was repeated: deliverance from the evil of untrammelled monarchical power led to the evil of untrammelled liberty of popular action, which in turn led to the power of Napoleon.

The problem of protecting the individual was not to be solved merely by giving him immunity from the power of the monarch, for power was thereby only transferred to the faceless institution called "government." Protection against this had to come from an independent judiciary, that is, one which holds itself free to weigh governmental interests against individual interests according to yardsticks of its own. Now, there is always a measure of interpretative discretion left to a judge in the application of any rule, and even with enacted laws a judge can, if he wants, adopt an interpretation favoring the individual. Chief Justice Coke's assertion in 1612 to King James I that the king was under God and the Law, was of the profoundest significance, for it made the people's ultimate protection from power rest on the craftsmanship of the law of which the judges are the exponents, and thereby established one of the proudest traditions of Anglo-American Law.

Where there is a constitution guarded by the courts their protective function is more pronounced. Baron de Montesquieu, in his *Spirit of Laws* (*De l'esprit des lois*, 1748), believed the secret of freedom to lie in vesting the legislative, executive, and judicial powers of government in separate bodies. Under the Constitution of the United States, which embodies this idea, the Supreme Court has frequently declared Acts of Congress to be void for infringing fundamental rights. Yet another way in which the courts might help is by refusing to uphold the exercise of legislative power which, though not unconstitutional, is nevertheless immoral. Discriminatory racial laws are an example. Until now, courts have generally not concerned themselves with the morality of laws, but it is possible to find a basis for at least some judicial control. Nearly every revolution or constitutional settlement takes place as a reaction against an abuse, and the moral objectives behind the new power distribution are built-in limitations on its future exercise. To argue that, no matter what the circumstances of its origin, power somehow becomes absolute, is an illogical assumption and one which has had the sorriest consequences. Whether courts will adopt this line of approach remains to be seen.

III

The problem of preventing the abuse of liberty is graver than that of safeguarding people from the abuse of power, and is far from being solved. It has been pointed out that it would be unwise to relax legal restrictions until people are disciplined to behave with restraint without compulsion. Where is the line to be drawn? John Stuart Mill in his tract *On Liberty* (1859) drew it at harm to others; that is, he would use law only to forbid activities likely to disrupt any and every sort of society. Beyond this, he said, the law has no business to invade privacy. An objection to this is that no sharp distinction can be drawn between "public" and "private" activities. Human behavior is a "seamless web" and in numberless ways what one does in private can have repercussions outside oneself, and vice versa. That is why a British judge, Lord Devlin, argued, in effect, that law may be used even in the sphere of private activities whenever these are capable of undermining the institutions which form the fabric of the particular society (*The Enforcement of Morals*, 1959; 1965). Thus, the monogamous marriage has be-

come an institution of Christian countries and has given rise to certain precepts of moral behavior. Lord Devlin would not place immoral activities, even though they may be conducted in private, outside the reach of the law if by their very nature they threaten the institution which is the foundation of the accepted morality. The danger in this argument is that a blind desire to uphold institutions can so easily shade off into an abuse of power.

It may also be contended that the state has an interest in the moral self-discipline of its subjects. However true and desirable this may be, it is important that convincing reasons be given. As long as religion provides the basis for self-discipline, the law may hold back; but when that influence starts to decline, mere legal compulsion without alternative support, so far from preserving a sense of moral duty, will only appear to perpetuate taboos against which intelligent people are bound to rebel. This does not mean that legal restraints should be relaxed, for to do so at the very time when the hitherto accepted basis of self-discipline is being eroded is like cutting oneself adrift on a perilous tide.

The prerequisite of freedom in the 1960's and early 1970's, then, is the instilling of a new sense of discipline. It poses a problem to which no answer is yet in sight, and as long as this is so, the history of freedom as reflected in law must remain an unfinished story.

BIBLIOGRAPHY

For extracts from the Greek, Roman, medieval, and a few of the more modern authorities mentioned, see *Masters of Political Thought*, eds. E. McC. Sait and W. T. Jones, 3 vols. (London and New York, 1963). The controversy between the followers of J. S. Mill and Lord Devlin is fully dealt with by Basil Mitchell, *Law, Morality and Religion in a Secular Society* (London and New York, 1967); also Patrick Devlin, "The Enforcement of Morals," British Academy Lecture (London and New York, 1959); idem, *The Enforcement of Morals* (London and New York, 1965); this includes additional essays. See also E. S. Corwin, *Liberty against Government* (Baton Rouge, La., 1948); D. V. Cowen, *The Foundations of Freedom* . . . (Cape Town, 1961), Part II; A. T. Denning, *Freedom under the Law* (London, 1949); H. Street, *Freedom, the Individual and the Law* (1954; London, 1963; New Orleans, 1964); C. Wirszubski, *Libertas as a Political Idea at Rome* (Cambridge and New York, 1950). For a technical legal analysis of liberty, see G. L. Williams, "The Concept of Legal Liberty," *Columbia Law Review*, **56** (1956), 1121.

R. W. M. DIAS

[See also Authority; **Democracy;** Equality; **Free Will;** Law, Natural; Social Contract.]

FREEDOM OF SPEECH
IN ANTIQUITY

1. The terminology, theory, and practice of freedom of speech in the modern Anglo-Saxon world is genetically connected with Greek and Latin ideas and institutions. It is therefore not very difficult to recognize in the Greek and Roman world the words, ideologies, and institutions which can legitimately be studied as the classical counterpart of the modern notion of freedom of speech. But the evidence of the classical world presents serious difficulties to the interpreter insofar as it is unevenly distributed, and relates to social and political conditions which are seldom well known. Our main evidence for Greece is confined to Athens from the fifth century B.C. onwards; we know very little about other Greek city-states. The evidence about Rome begins to be entirely reliable only in the second century B.C. This means that for both Greece and Rome the important archaic period, in which institutions and ideas were shaped, is insufficiently known. Even so, one is bound to recognize that much more could be done with the extant evidence if it were properly collected, sifted, and interpreted according to modern methods of social research. The present sketch can only offer a provisional and small map of largely unexplored territory.

The discovery and interpretation of data relating to freedom of speech in the great ancient civilizations of the Near East (Egypt, Mesopotamia, Hittite Kingdom, Persia, Phoenicia, Judea) present far more serious problems because—with the partial exception of the biblical texts—genetical connections with modern ideas and institutions are not apparent. It is even arguable that the whole political and social structure makes it difficult to isolate the very notion of freedom of speech from other political and religious notions. The only field in which analogy of institutions makes comparison easier with the modern world is that of political assemblies.

One general remark may be added. The modern notion of freedom of speech is assumed to include the right of speech in the governing bodies and the right to petition them, the right to relate and publish debates of these bodies, freedom of public meeting, freedom of correspondence, of teaching, of worship, of publishing newspapers and books. Correspondingly, abuse of freedom of speech includes libel, slander, obscenity, blasphemy, sedition. In the classical world all these aspects appear to be present, including a sort of journalism at the end of the Roman Republic and at the beginning of the Empire. However, certain aspects such as the right of petition never became seriously controversial. Others, such as freedom of teaching,

surprisingly enough, were issues only for comparatively brief periods. Furthermore, religious freedom was so clearly subordinated to the notion of impiety and later of heresy as to require special treatment.

2. Though it may be mere pedantry, let us start with some very general remarks on the classification of political assemblies, insofar as it is relevant to the ancient history of the Near East, of Greece, and of Rome. First of all, we must obviously make a distinction between popular assemblies and councils of advisers. Not every popular assembly implies a democracy or indeed even the smallest amount of freedom of speech. The chieftain or king may convene an assembly simply to give orders. In other types of assembly the people are asked to confer power on a sovereign and to sanction decisions previously taken either by the king or by the council of advisers without being given the alternative of refusing to do so. Democracy in its ancient form exists when the popular assembly has power to elect the king or the magistrates, to make war and peace, to enact laws, and to administer justice.

As for the council of advisers, it presented itself in two different forms in the Near East. In tribal societies or in city-states it was normally a council of elders. Membership of the council was often hereditary, less frequently, dependent on some sort of election. In large territorial monarchies the advisers were chosen by the king from among the members of certain families (including his own) and/or among the highest officers of the State: he could dismiss them at will.

Popular assemblies are not to be found in the great monarchies of the Near East, with the partial exception of the Hittite Empire. In the Empires of Egypt, Babylonia, Assyria, and Persia, the monarch ruled despotically and by divine right with the assistance of his officers and advisers. This does not mean that individual cities or villages of these Empires did not have their popular assemblies and councils of elders.

3. Councils of elders and general assemblies of citizens existed in individual cities of Mesopotamia since the third millennium B.C. An episode in the short Sumerian epic poem on Gilgamesh and Agga is regarded as the earliest evidence on record about both councils and assemblies. The extant tablets of the poem were inscribed in the second millennium but reflect the situation of a time not far removed from 3000 B.C. Gilgamesh, the mythical hero and lord of Uruk, addresses the council of elders in order to enlist its support for war. The council turns down his proposal, but another assembly, which is likely to have included all the local arms-bearing males, overrides the opinion of the elders and declares for war. The possibility of disagreement in assemblies is confirmed by an omen of the Old Babylonian Kingdom (ca. 1800 B.C.).

Composition and function of such councils and assemblies naturally varied in time and space. In the Assyrian commercial colony of Kanis in Cappadocia in the nineteenth century B.C. the council of elders apparently divided into three sections while deciding—which might imply a collective vote of each section. In a trial for murder at Nippur about the twentieth century B.C. opposite opinions on the guilt of the culprit are chanted alternately by various members of the judging assembly. Thus military expeditions, trials, relations with local kings all appear to be within the competence of such gatherings. In no case are we sufficiently well informed to visualize the real nature of the activities of these bodies. Even the distinction between councils of elders and popular assemblies is blurred. According to what is now the prevailing opinion among Assyriologists, the Mesopotamian institutions developed from an original basis of primitive military democracy, and the king in Mesopotamia (in contrast to Egypt) was very seldom equated with a god. Indeed even the gods formed a society with some democratic features. The *Enûma Elish* was written in the first half of the second millennium B.C. to explain how Marduk had been elected by the gods to be their king. However powerful the royal palace and the temple might be in a city, the original communal organization survived beside them: it was especially strong in the great commercial centers. The proud sense of autonomy of the citizens of Babylon (who reminded Assurbanipal that even a dog is free when he enters their city) and the elements of social criticism in prayers and epics go well with this communal life. But the history of Babylonia and Assyria in the second and first millennia B.C. is that of centralized empires in which decisions are taken by a king, and his advisers are hardly visible. Intellectual life is directed towards the reiteration of orthodox opinions, not towards expression of dissent. The absence of popular protest against the administration in real life, and the poverty of intellectual controversy in Akkadian literature, have often been noticed. We must assume some freedom of speech behind routine legal and administrative processes: nowhere does it appear as a value or as an art in itself.

The Hittites were the only great state of the Ancient Near East in which the king had to reckon with a central political assembly—not just with local assemblies of individual cities. The *Pankus* is mentioned in the so-called political testament of Hattushilish I (ca. 1650) and in the edict of Telepinush (ca. 1500) regulating the succession to the throne and reforming the judicial system. The etymology of the word *Pankus,* an adjective meaning "entire," is irrelevant to the interpretation of the institution. But a magical text puts the *Pankus* above the court officials, though it places the "kin of the Pankus" below the priests and the military. This can only imply that the *Pankus* was an aristocratic assembly, and indeed there are signs that it had some say in the succession to the throne. Hittite scholars like to think that the *Pankus* was an institution of undeniably Indo-European character, but who has ever seen an Indo-European assembly? Telepinush even extended (or restored) the judicial powers of the *Pankus* to include the trial of a king under specified circumstances. We hear nothing more of the *Pankus* after him. In the next century the builders of the Hittite empire seem to have had an easier time working with a tamer council of court dignitaries. When Shuppiluliumash I (perhaps about 1350) was suddenly faced with the request to provide a husband for the widow of Tutankhamen, "he called the great into council (saying): since of old, such a thing has never happened before me." The "council of the great" is probably something different from the Elders of Hatti who appear in a strange clause of the political testament of Hattushilish I. Hattushilish I appears to be anxious to establish a barrier between his successor-designate and the Elders of Hatti: "The Elders of Hatti shall not speak to you, neither shall a man of . . . , nor of Hemmuva nor of Tamalkiya, nor a man of . . . , nor indeed any of the people of the country speak to you." For the rest we know that the Hittite code recognized the jurisdiction of the elders outside the capital. Naturally the king dealt with councils of elders in occupied territories.

Thus it appears that the Hittite kings came to rely increasingly on a military organization in which decision-making would be characterized by swiftness, secrecy, and deference to the king's will. Hattushilish's move to prevent the elders—and more in general the common people—from approaching his heir is one of the most definite and explicit limitations of freedom of speech we encounter in antiquity. We should like to know whether in the exercise of justice the weak was heard and whether intellectual life included discussion of moral and religious topics. The Hittite texts, such as they are, do not offer much in these directions. A moving soliloquy, the prayer of Kantuzilish for relief from his sufferings, is a sign of reflection and sensitiveness. But independent thinking on either political or social or religious issues does not emerge from the extant Hittite documents.

4. The El-Amarna letters and the Ugaritic texts have shown the presence of councils of elders and less conspicuously of popular assemblies in Syria-Palestine during the second half of the second millennium. It was a world of small city-states in which assemblies made sense. Both councils of elders and popular assemblies seem to have been particularly active when the local king was not present. Letter 254 of El-Amarna very vividly recounts the story of Labaja who addressed the citizens of Gezer. One passage in the Egyptian story of Wen-Amon indicates that in the eleventh century B.C. the King judged cases between foreigners in a popular assembly at Byblos. J. A. Wilson recognized the Phoenician word *mo'ed*, "assembly," in the Egyptian text. The existence of assemblies favored changes of political allegiance in a time of crisis: it favored what we would call propaganda and is better described as inducement to rebellion. According to some El-Amarna letters (74; 81) a rebel against Egypt, Abdiashirta, apparently used political assemblies to spread his call to subversion.

In the old South Arabian states (known to us from documents of the earlier part of the first millennium B.C.) a tribal assembly or council existed and was summoned by the king for the enactment of laws and other decisions.

We have seen from an Egyptian document that the Phoenician cities had popular assemblies and councils of elders as early as the eleventh century B.C. Greek and Latin sources confirm this feature which may be an adaptation to city life of the old tribal assembly and council of the Semites. Unfortunately we have no details. But we do know more about the constitution of Carthage, the Phoenician colony of the Western Mediterranean, because Aristotle was interested in it and described it in some detail. He thought that the constitution of Carthage was similar to that of Greek cities. While the Phoenician cities of the East retained kings, perhaps until after Alexander the Great, Carthage was a republic as early as the fifth century B.C. It was ruled by a mercantile aristocracy through a supreme council of thirty members elected or chosen (we do not know how) for life. Aristotle tells us in a notoriously difficult passage of Book II, 1273a, of his *Politics* that the Carthaginian popular assembly was asked to decide on matters on which the magistrates and the council of the elders had not reached agreement. Indeed, in case of disagreements among the leaders the common people were allowed freedom of discussion. Aristotle remarks: "Anybody who wishes may speak against the proposal introduced, a right that does not exist under the constitutions of Sparta and Crete." Nowhere in the Near East do we find a comparable right. The Carthaginians were in close contact with the Greek colonies of Sicily and may well have learnt something about freedom of speech and collective decision-making from their Greek neighbors.

The Persians, during the Achaemenid period, had certainly no assembly and probably no central council of elders. The kings who were chosen by Ahura Mazdā

never considered themselves gods, but had the truth by divine right and were supposed to fight "the lie." How they ascertained it is a question strictly connected with the nature of the religious beliefs of the Achaemenids about which we know so little. It would appear that the Magi, "a very peculiar race," as Herodotus says, did not invariably function as religious counsellors to the Achaemenids. Whatever their origins, they had become a priestly class which controlled sacrifices and interpreted dreams (Herodotus, I, 107; 140). They could not be ignored, but after the Smerdis affair there were legitimate suspicions. No doubt the king had other advisers. The six helpers of Darius in his struggle for the throne were the originators of families who had free access to the king (ibid., III, 118). These six families may ultimately be identical with the seven chiefs of the Persians and Medes, who according to the Book of Esther could see the face of the king, if we assume that one of the seven was the representative of the family of the king himself. We are also told by Herodotus that during the expedition against Greece, Mardonius was sent by Xerxes to ask the advice of his vassals about the suitability of engaging the Greeks (ibid., VIII, 67–69). Xerxes was pleased with the minority opinion expressed by Artemisia, but decided that the "advice of the greater number should be followed." So he was defeated at Salamis. The considerable decentralization of the Persian state, with its system of satrapies, made it easier for the king to rely on private and individual consultations, though the result often was rebellion. Political debates were not a frequent occurrence with the Achaemenids.

One of the things we learn from the scanty evidence about assemblies and councils of elders in Syria and Palestine is of course that the Hebrew tribes with their assemblies and councils of elders conformed to well-known patterns. Biblical tradition being what it is, we are never quite certain whether our evidence about pre-monarchic institutions (and even monarchic ceremonies) reflects actual events or later idealization and theorization. It is, for instance, suspicious that apparently there is no mention of an assembly of one tribe in the pre-monarchic period. But the picture of the functions of elders and assembly inspires trust even if individual episodes bear the sign of later elaborations. Though we would not take Deuteronomy 5:23 as evidence for the existence of elders in each tribe, elders of Judah (e.g., II Samuel 19:11) are well authenticated. So are the elders of Gilead who made a pact with Jephthah (Judges 11:5f.), not to speak of the elders of individual cities. The elders of each city had jurisdictional functions even during the monarchy. They represented the tribes or the cities: in some texts "men of Israel" and "elders" are used interchangeably (Joshua 24:1-2). The elders had a say in the declaration of wars of the monarchic period (I Kings 20:8) and, what is more, in the election of the first two kings (I Samuel 8:4; II Samuel 5:3). Later, in the post-exilic period, they organized the convocation of the assembly (Ezra 10:8). We do not know who were the heads, the *sarim*, of the elders about whom we hear in various circumstances (e.g., Isaiah 3:14).

The assembly (*ʿedah, Kahal*) had judicial functions, at least in the idealization of later times: the Sabbath violator (Numbers 15:33), the blasphemer (Leviticus 24:14) are brought before it, and it is a touch of realism conforming to popular justice in the Near East that the judges are also the executioners. Women appear before the assembly to ask for the right of inheritance (Numbers 27:2). The *ʿedah* and its obscure "princes" appear in treaties and arbitrations (Joshua 9:15; Judges 20:1). The *ʿedah* proclaims Jeroboam King of Israel (I Kings 12:20). The assembly of Judah is probably implied as partner in the covenant of Josiah after the recovery of the Book of the Law (II Kings 23:1-2). According to Chronicles the *ʿedah* took part in the restoration of the Davidic dynasty with Joash (II Chronicles 23:3) and in the reform of Hezekiah (II Chronicles 29:28f.). It reappears after the exile in legal decisions of basic importance, such as the repudiation of foreign wives (Ezra 10:1-2). As we have already mentioned, it is sometimes difficult to distinguish in the sources the assembly from the elders. In Exodus 19:7-8 Moses puts the words of Yahweh before the elders of Israel, and all the people answer. The elders of Israel make a covenant with David in Hebron on behalf of the people (II Samuel 5:1-3).

Elders and assembly were closely involved in the covenants which characterize the election of leaders and later of kings among the Hebrews, though it would be a waste of time to try to reduce these elections to one pattern. The contractual character of leadership is a notion which underlies much of the biblical thinking about judges and kings and undoubtedly had its roots in historical facts. It has its counterpart in the notion of the covenant between Yahweh and Israel which in various degrees of development is accepted by all our biblical sources from the Yahwist to the Deuteronomist. According to one line of thinking, which did not prevail, the covenant with Yahweh was incompatible with the choice of a king and consequent covenant with him. Thus historical and constitutional thinking in Israel presupposes the existence of assembly and elders and conceives the relation between Israel and its leader (whether human or divine) in terms of a covenant. Indeed a series of covenants with God marks the progressive separation of Israel from the

other nations. There is not much room in the Bible for the notions of amphictyony and divine kingship which modern scholars have tried to introduce into ancient Hebrew thinking.

It is difficult for us to visualize how decisions were taken in a Hebrew council of elders or in assembly either before or during the monarchy. We may have an example of how a council of elders operated in the disagreement between the senior and the junior advisors of Rehoboam at the beginning of the conflict with the northern tribes (I Kings 12:6). And we remember how easily the assembly and the elders of Jezreel condemned Naboth to death according to Jezebel's pleasure (I Kings 21:12). The historical books of the Bible taken as a whole give the impression of informality and outspokenness in the relations between the Hebrew leaders and their followers which agrees with the contractual nature of the relation itself. This impression is confirmed by the few letters of the seventh and sixth centuries B.C. which have so far been discovered (especially the ostraca of Lachish). The man who writes to his superior uses traditional servile formulas, but speaks directly and firmly, and in one case boldly rejects an insinuation.

What characterizes Hebrew life, however, is the intervention of the prophet in the name of Yahweh. Recent concentration on the problem of the relation between cult and prophecy, though understandable as a reaction to the romantic idealization of the prophet as a solitary seer and thinker, obscures the essential. The prophet is the unpredictable messenger of the word of Yahweh. It has been calculated that out of the 241 mentions of the "Word of Yahweh" in the Old Testament, 221 indicate a prophetic utterance. The word of Yahweh manifests itself through the mouth of the prophet. In the Prophetic Books, in the Psalms, and even in the Book of Job (15:8) one finds the notion that Yahweh has his own Council, and the true prophet is a member of it. According to Jeremiah, Yahweh says of the false prophets: "If they stood in my council, then they would have proclaimed my words to my people" (23:22). This notion of a Council of Yahweh is only one instance of the legal thinking which emerges from the Prophetic Books. In some memorable passages the word of Yahweh is an indictment of Israel in proper legal terms for infringement of the Covenant: "Therefore I will surely bring suit against you [Oracle of Yahweh], With your children's children I will contend" (Jeremiah 2:9ff.; cf. Deuteronomy 32; Isaiah 1:2; Micah 6:1).

In other cases, of which Jeremiah 3 and [Deutero-] Isaiah 42:6, 49:8 (whatever the precise meaning of these passages) are the most conspicuous, the prophet is made to announce a new covenant with Israel.

Through the prophet a new legal situation is promised to Israel. But the word of Yahweh does not of course exhaust itself in legal formulations. It introduces into Hebrew life an element of freedom of speech which breaks all the conventions and which the kings may try to suppress or at least to control. As long as prophets operated in their midst, the freedom of speech that the Hebrews knew was the word of God through his prophets. When prophecy lost momentum, the notion of an unchangeable Torah became the center of Jewish life: this implied a profound reorientation. The prophet gave expression to the constant feeling of guilt towards Yahweh which was inherent in the life of the Hebrew tribes. The rabbi, who to a certain extent replaced the prophet as a teacher, was the mediator in a new harmonious relationship between God and man. The task of the rabbi was to define the boundaries of the Torah, in other words, those types of behavior which are *Kiddush Hashem* ("sanctifying God's name") in contrast to *Hillul Hashem* ("profaning God's name"). The rabbi's concern was not freedom of speech, but cooperation with God, hence the danger of heresy.

5. Ancient Egypt from a certain point of view offers the most interesting situation to the student of freedom of speech. Advisers at all levels and village notables existed in Egypt as elsewhere, but there was no place for formal assemblies in a country which had settled for divine kingship and regular bureaucracy before recorded history began. Yet the Egyptians appreciated eloquence and knew the power of words. As the Vizier Prah-hotep said in his Instruction, "Eloquence is more hidden than the emerald, yet it may be found with maidservants at the grindstone." The warning came true in the crisis of the First Intermediate Period (2200–2000 B.C.?). In the Admonition of the Leyden papyrus, Ipu-wer reflects the new discontent: "All female slaves are free with their tongues. When their mistress speaks, it is irksome to the servants." Protests became loud. The "Story of the Eloquent Peasant" has perhaps too much of a happy end to be regarded as a story of social protest. The eloquent peasant, after denouncing injustice in violent terms, not only gets his goods back, but also obtains the patronage of the Chief Steward whom he had accused. Other texts are less ambiguous. The Sage Ipu-wer himself takes advantage of the freedom of speech he notices as a bad symptom in the maidservants. He blames the King. He compels him to defend himself and concludes by saying that what the King has done, though perhaps good, is not good enough. The "Dispute over Suicide" presents suicide as the only remedy for a social situation in which nobody is left worth talking to:

To whom can I speak to-day?
No one thinks of yesterday
No one at this time acts for him who has acted.

The point is made, even if ultimately (but this is not certain) the soul persuades the body to wait for death instead of hastening it by suicide.

This determined questioning of the ordinary assumptions of life was never aimed at political reforms; if anything, it encouraged anarchy, religious skepticism, and enjoyment of whatever pleasure life could offer. Another well-known early text, the "Song of the Harper," is the classic statement of Egyptian hedonism. In later times return to order and power politics took the form of the idealization of silence. The Wise Man of the Post-Hyksos period is a silent man.

In perhaps the fifteenth century B.C. the scribe Ani advised his son: "A man may fall into ruin because of his tongue." The "Hymn by the Scribe to his god Thoth" states: "The silent one comes and finds the well." According to the teaching of Amenemope—one of the late texts which influenced Hebrew Wisdom (or which were influenced by it!)—"the truly silent man holds himself apart. He is like a tree growing in a garden. It flourishes, it doubles its fruits; it stands before the Lord." Egyptian history is a very long history, and it is dangerous to string together texts which are separated by centuries. But the final impression is that in the crisis of the Old Kingdom freedom of speech became an issue. Writers were aware that protesting, debating, and accusing were ways of undermining the existing order. Silence appeared to be the remedy: it became a central virtue in later days. It did not necessarily mean compliance and obedience; it included an element of astuteness and perhaps of concealment. But it implied the essential acceptance of an unmodifiable order. The prospects of freedom of speech had never been brilliant, because there was no institution to which potential reformers could turn when they felt dissatisfied with the Pharaonic administration. There was no regular assembly in which to voice discontent.

6. The development of Greek political assemblies is to a great extent still obscure. We do not know how the majority of Greek assemblies actually functioned at any time of their history. Even for Sparta we are confined to the interpretation of a few (and not very coherent) pieces of evidence. The only assembly we know well is the Athenian *ecclesia*, and even here our evidence begins to be reliable only from the fifth century B.C. Seen from the angle of classical Athens, what characterized a political assembly was the extent of its powers as the legislative, judicial, and policy-making body. Equally remarkable was the extent to which an

ordinary citizen could initiate business or advocate policies from the floor. It may well be that Athens took a lead in the creation of what, in the fifth century B.C., became known as democratic government, though it has been claimed that Athens was preceded by some Ionian cities of Asia Minor. Many of the Greek States (including Sparta) never granted such powers to their assemblies and never allowed comparable freedom of speech in political meetings. The time and modality of the introduction of important parliamentary features, such as the counting of votes, the regularity of meetings, the *quorum* for the validity of certain decisions, the qualifications for participation in the meetings, the formalities of the relations between the general assembly and other bodies (city council, king's advisers, priestly colleges), are either unknown or imperfectly known.

The earliest descriptions of Greek assemblies are of course to be found in Homer. They are a good example of the problems which Greek assemblies pose for the modern researcher. Any reader of the assembly scenes in the *Iliad* is entitled to ask whether such scenes reflect any historical reality: this is a part of a more general question about the value of the *Iliad* as historical evidence. We have less difficulty with the evidence on assemblies provided by the *Odyssey* because it obviously reflects some acquaintance with the political assemblies of the Greek polis of the archaic age. Life in the Greek camp near Troy *may* be the product of the imagination of the poet of the *Iliad*, but the meetings at Ithaca or among the Phaeacians seem to be of the sort a poet might see for himself when he wandered about Greece. The sensible middle way seems to be to use the evidence of the *Iliad* about assemblies only when it is in basic agreement with that of the *Odyssey*. But we must always bear in mind that very little is certain about the historic reality of the institutions described by Homer and that, even in the most optimistic assessment, we are still left in the dark about the time, the places and the coherence of the political experience reflected by the *Odyssey*.

Five features characterize the Homeric assemblies: 1) The assemblies described by Homer are irregular: they are convoked in special circumstances. 2) They may be summoned by "important" individuals: neither kings nor magistrates seem to have the exclusive right to summon an assembly, though it would obviously be unthinkable to have one summoned by ordinary members of the city or of the army. 3) The assembly listens to "important" people and signifies approval or disapproval, but does not vote. 4) Intervention from the floor in the exceptional case of Thersites in the *Iliad* is clearly considered scandalous (yet it does happen).

5) Decision may mean either that dissent is ultimately eliminated by pressure or persuasion or that contrasting groups will ultimately act in contrasting ways. No Homeric assembly ends in civil war, but the danger is implicit in the whole course of action.

7. On the borderline between Greeks and non-Greeks there are the Macedonians. It has been suggested, but it is a suggestion of doubtful value, that the Macedonians preserved features of the "Homeric" institutions. Their kings considered themselves Greek in the fifth and fourth centuries B.C., but the ordinary Macedonians never seem to have shared the ambitions of their kings in this matter. They had a national, perhaps a military, assembly and we know that Philip II and Alexander spoke before it. For the rest, all our evidence concerns the exceptional period when Alexander's generals had to take responsibility for the succession. It has been asserted that every Macedonian soldier was entitled to speak freely in that assembly, and Polybius has been quoted as an authority for this statement. Polybius tells us apropos of the condemnation of Leontius in 218 B.C. that the soldiers sent a deputation to Philip V, begging him not to try the case in their absence. Polybius' comment on the soldiers' message to the king is: "with such freedom (*isegoria*) did the Macedonians always address their kings" (Polybius, 5, 27, 6). Now Polybius mentions Macedonian freedom of speech, not on the occasion of an assembly, but in connection with a deputation. He seems to emphasize the directness with which the Macedonian soldiers treated their kings, not what happened in the Macedonian assembly.

In Spartan political life not all was crude. It has indeed been suggested that with the so-called *Rhetra* of Lycurgus (Plutarch, *Lycurgus* 6), which somehow defined the powers of the *gerousia* (the council of 28 life members to whom the two kings were added), the rule that council should take the responsibility and the initiative for presenting measures to the assembly was introduced into Greek political life for the first time. This would have happened in the eighth or seventh century B.C. The same *Rhetra* gave the assembly power to approve or reject proposals. Even by the beginning of the Peloponnesian war shouting was still the ordinary method of the assembly for the election of magistrates and for the voting on formal proposals (which might involve peace and war). The candidate who got the loudest shout at elections was deemed to have been chosen; and the proposal which had the loudest applause was deemed to have been approved. But at least in the case of voting decrees the extent of the approval represented by the applause could be checked by subsequent division, as happened in 432 B.C.

257

In a disputed passage, Aristotle seems to tell us that there was no freedom of discussion in the assemblies of Sparta and Crete (*Politics* II, 1272a). We cannot say anything very definite about Crete, but in the case of Sparta there is enough evidence to show that, whatever Aristotle may have meant, private individuals could speak in the assembly even in Aristotle's time. Aeschines (I, 180–81) has a story about a disreputable man who spoke in the Spartan assembly and was listened to with attention. Then an elder warned the Spartans that the city could not survive for long if they listened to such advisers. The possibility of speeches by private individuals seems always to have been contemplated by the Spartan constitution. The famous rider to the *Rhetra* in Plutarch (*Lycurgus* 6) enjoins that if the *demos* formulates crooked decisions the *gerontes* and the kings shall decline to accept them. This rider was already known to Tyrtaeus (frag. 3a). Its natural interpretation seems to be that it gives the kings and the *gerontes* power of veto, limiting preexisting rights of the assembly. The veto controls, but does not abolish, the powers of initiative of the assembly. There is, furthermore, evidence in Thucydides and Xenophon that the assembly was an important decision-making body in the fifth and fourth centuries B.C., though it must be emphasized that deciding after listening to opposite opinions is not the same as taking part in the debate. What we really do not know is who at a given time took the initiative and controlled decisions behind the screen of theoretical equality of the Spartiates.

It is a pity that we have so little information about the limits of freedom of speech in other Greek cities for the period in which they were not yet likely to have been influenced by Athens. We know from Thucydides that at Syracuse a magistrate could stop discussion in a way which seems different from Athenian practice. But the archaic assemblies of Ionia remain a mystery, and as long as they remain a mystery it is possible to overrate Athens' contribution to political freedom of speech. It is true, however, as we shall presently see, that at least one of the two technical terms for freedom of speech, *parrhesia*, spread from Athens.

In the matter of freedom of speech much of the constitutional development of Athens is obscure. The rule that people over fifty had priority in speaking is attributed to Solon, and was already obsolete by the fourth century. It shows that private individuals were allowed to speak in the Solonian assembly, which seems to have been open to the fourth class, the *thetes*. It is uncertain when the meetings of the assembly became regular in Athens and when the ordinary citizen was allowed to propose amendments and new resolutions.

But one point is clear. From the end of the sixth century B.C. five hundred Athenian citizens were chosen by lot every year to be members of the Council (*Boule*). Members of this Council were bound to discuss matters freely and in detail during their meetings. After such an experience they could not be expected to keep silent when they returned to the assembly as ordinary citizens. Freedom of speech in the Athenian assembly cannot have been more recent than the reforms of Cleisthenes. It may of course have preceded them. What we know well enough is the state of affairs in the second half of the fifth century B.C.

In the second part of the fifth century and during the greater part of the fourth century every Athenian citizen had the right to speak unless he disqualified himself by certain specified crimes (such as having been a deserter or having beaten his own parents, or having been found guilty three times of illegal proposals). Any citizen could defend his own proposals already submitted to the *boule* and introduced to the *ecclesia* by *probouleuma*, or could submit proposals direct to the *ecclesia*. No citizen could speak more than once in a meeting on the same topic. The only risk a speaker had to face was the possibility of being prosecuted later for having misled the people, a remote possibility even for professional politicians.

We need hardly add that this extraordinary amount of freedom of speech in the assemblies was accompanied by an exceptional amount of freedom of speech in the theater and generally speaking in ordinary life. A fifth-century law which made it illegal to attack people by name in comedies can have been enforced only by fits and starts because our information on it is both vague and contradictory. But there are two remarks which we should like to make about freedom of speech in Athens outside the *ecclesia*. First, personal reputations were protected by various laws against slander. In the fourth century it was an offense even to sneer at any citizen for having worked in the marketplace. Secondly, about 432 B.C., Diopeithes' decree, making it an offense to deny the gods of the city and to teach new doctrines about meteorological phenomena, showed that Athens cared more for political liberty than for intellectual liberty. Anaxagoras, Protagoras, Diagoras, and perhaps Diogenes of Apollonia had to run for their lives. Socrates did not go away and was killed. The suspicion that democracy and philosophy were incompatible could never be dispelled again, with the consequences that are evident in Plato's works.

With this background of political institutions in mind, we shall not be surprised if the notion of freedom of speech turns out to be an Athenian fifth-century idea. In earlier times the notion of liberty (*eleutheria*) did not include freedom of speech: indeed, another important notion of Greek archaic ethics, *aidos* ("modesty, respect"), implied that silence and reticence were characteristic of the good man.

Since Homer (and probably even earlier, in the Mycenaean age) the free man (*eleutheros*) is the opposite of a slave. For Homer the event that stood out as the cause of transition from freedom to slavery was defeat in war, the end of "the free day." This, of course, was a gross simplification of real life with its many varieties of freedom and of slavery. Some archaic poets restricted the meaning of *eleutheros* to indicate the generous man. They paved the way to the later notion cherished by Aristotle that there is an inborn aristocratic quality of the mind which distinguishes the free man from the slave.

On the other hand, Solon perceived that debts can be worse than war in affecting the freedom of the individual. He also associated the notion of *eleutheros* with the notion of law (*nomos*) and regarded tyrants as the enemies of freedom because tyrants do not respect the law. During the Persian Wars, the Persian king appeared as an especially dangerous and powerful tyrant. Liberty—*eleutheria* (now used in the abstract)—came to indicate a collective Greek attitude to political life as opposed to Persian despotism. We do not know where and by whom freedom was first associated with democracy. The connection appears to be current in Athens during the fifth century: it is hinted at by Aeschylus and loudly proclaimed by Euripides; it is clearly familiar to Thucydides who uses it in Pericles' speeches. In democratic thinking freedom of speech appears to be one of the most important and necessary ingredients of *eleutheria*. Aeschylus in the *Suppliants* (now dated after 468 B.C.) names the free mouth as a sign of freedom, whereas Herodotus uses the word *isegoria* (equality in freedom of speech) to indicate Athenian democracy (V, 78).

8. When Thersites spoke, he broke the rules of *aidos*, the aristocratic virtue of respect and self-respect. Homer represents his aristocrats endowed with "gentle aidos" (*Odyssey* VIII, 172). Hesiod, who remembered Homer's lines, described the kings from whom gracious words flow (*Theogony* 84). Theognis has an implicit rebuke for those who believe that *aidos* is a virtue of the eyes only, not also of the mouth. The writers of the fifth century still emphasize the value of *aidos*, insofar as speech is concerned. But in the same century a new notion spread, the notion that freedom of speech is a positive, or at least a remarkable, achievement. Prometheus is affectionately accused: "you speak too boldly." A free tongue is an essential element of the ideal democracy of Aeschylus' *Suppliants*. The same Aeschylus describes in the *Persae* how, among the

Persians, after the defeat of Salamis, "the tongue is no longer in fetters." Pindar, the aristocrat, was obviously suspicious of this change of attitude towards free speech. It has been suggested that when he spoke with horror of *panglossia* in the second Olympian Ode, he had in mind the word *parrhesia*. This may or may not be the case, but certainly *panglossia*, like *parrhesia*, denotes a readiness to utter anything. In another passage of the second Pythian Ode, Pindar is at pains to explain that frankness is free from political connotations. He hated what he called the slander and envy of people.

The word *parrhesia*, however, is to be found neither in Pindar, nor in Aeschylus and Sophocles; and first appears in Euripides' *Hippolytus* (line 422; performed in 428 B.C.) and *Ion* (lines 672, 675; of uncertain date). In both cases the word is used in connection with Athens. In other passages (most notably in the *Electra*, lines 1049, 1056; of uncertain date), Euripides uses *parrhesia* to mean freedom of speech in private relations (cf. also *Orestes*, line 905; *Bacchae*, line 668; *Phoenician Women*, line 391; frag. 737, Nauck, 2nd ed.). But, in his only passage mentioning *parrhesia*, Aristophanes also uses it in a political sense (*Thesmophoriazusae*, line 540). Finally, Democritus says in a fragment (226D) that *parrhesia* is inherent in *eleutheria*. We conclude that in the late fifth century *parrhesia* became a popular word in Athens, denoting freedom of speech chiefly in political matters, but occasionally also in private situations.

If we turn to Herodotus (V, 78) and Pseudo-Xenophon ("the Old Oligarch"), *Constitution of Athens* (1, 12), we find that neither of them uses the word *parrhesia*. Both indicate democracy by the word *isegoria*. *Isegoria* was not necessarily a democratic virtue: it meant equality of rights in the matter of freedom of speech and could easily apply to a restricted number of aristocrats. Isagoras, who was an aristocratic contemporary of Cleisthenes, was probably born about 550. It is hard to believe that his father called him Isagoras because he wanted to encourage democratic virtues in his son. But in the fifth century *isegoria*, like *isonomia*, came to mean democracy. *Parrhesia* represented democracy from the point of view of equality of rights. There was an old-fashioned flavor about *isegoria*. We are not surprised that Herodotus and the Old Oligarch preferred it to *parrhesia*, while Euripides chose the more modern word *parrhesia*.

Thucydides, of course, knew both words and, of course, used neither. Not simply because he was never satisfied with simple formulas. Discussion he appreciated above all things, but he recognized that freedom of speech is inseparable from good faith, both in the speaker and in the listener, and must be used to foster reason against unreason. The debate between Cleon and Diodotus is not only the most profound discussion about imperialism ever held in the ancient world before Saint Augustine; it is also the most searching analysis of the conditions in which discussion is useful in a democracy. If you attack, not the objective validity, but the good faith of your opponent, you introduce an element which will poison democratic proceedings. Even more than Pericles' Funeral Speech, Diodotus' speech represents Thucydides' contribution to the theory of freedom of speech.

In the fourth century *parrhesia* became more popular than *isegoria*. Demosthenes uses *parrhesia* twenty-six times as against three or possibly four instances of *isegoria;* Isocrates has *parrhesia* twenty-two times, *isegoria* only once; Aeschines *parrhesia* eight times, but *isegoria* once. In some of the Demosthenic speeches of doubtful authenticity *parrhesia* is most emphatically *the* right of the Athenian citizen. But other texts say that in Athens everyone enjoyed freedom of speech, including foreigners and slaves. At the same time *parrhesia* was frequently used to mean either the virtue of frankness or the vice of loquacity. Plato, of course, knows *parrhesia* both in the political and in the nonpolitical sense, but Aristotle, remarkably enough, knows *parrhesia* only in the nonpolitical sense, except in an anecdote about Pisistratus (*The Constitution of Athens* 16, 6).

We have learnt from J. Sundwall's epoch-making studies that in the fourth century Athens was ruled by a minority of wealthy people. Both the Macedonian and the anti-Macedonian parties had wealthy leaders. These people emphasized the right to say all that they wanted (*parrhesia*) rather than equality of freedom of speech (*isegoria*). But the interest in democratic institutions was declining. People were more interested in private life and private virtues and vices than in political achievements. Menander replaced Aristophanes, and *parrhesia* as a private virtue replaced *parrhesia* as a political right.

9. At this point we may pause. *Isegoria* implied equality of freedom of speech, but did not necessarily imply the right to say everything. On the other hand, *parrhesia* looks like a word invented by a vigorous man for whom democratic life meant freedom from traditional inhibitions of speech. We doubt whether the word *parrhesia* pleased Cleon, but it must have pleased Euripides and certainly pleased Demosthenes. We are not surprised that Plato disliked it (*Republic* 557e) except when it was granted as a privilege to the wise counsellor (*Laws* 694b; *Laches* 188e). We shall never know about Pericles. The two words *parrhesia* and *isegoria* point to the conflict between democracy as liberty and democracy as equality that was to concern later political thinkers.

After the fourth century B.C. *isegoria* remained a very respectable though not a very common word. It was used by people with a philosophic education, both in the political and in the nonpolitical sense. Polybius used it alone or together with *parrhesia* (never *parrhesia* on its own: 2, 38, 6; 2, 42, 3). He used *isegoria* to describe the state of affairs prevailing in the Achaean League. In this league every member was entitled to speak in the assemblies, though in fact the league was ruled by an oligarchy. Soon afterwards, with the Romans ruling the world, there was little freedom of speech left for Greek political assemblies. Philodemus the Epicurean used *isegoria* in connection with the good king, and Philo considered *isegoria* to be the quality of the serious man. Marcus Aurelius (I, 14) was grateful to one of his teachers for having introduced him to the idea of *isegoria* in politics: it is difficult to imagine what he really meant.

The career of *parrhesia* was more brilliant, because it was not as connected with political institutions. *Parrhesia* became a philosopher's virtue. In the *Nicomachean Ethics* Aristotle included it among the characteristics of the "magnanimous" man (1124b 28–30) and of the good comrade (1165a 9). Diogenes the Cynic made *parrhesia* his watchword (Diog. Laërt., VI, 69). His choice may have discouraged other philosophers from talking about *parrhesia*. As a matter of fact, neither Zeno nor Epicurus seem to have made extensive use of the word. But later Epicureans came to like *parrhesia* as a quality of friendship. Philodemus wrote a book on *parrhesia*, and Horace may have got from him or other Epicureans his *incorrupta fides nudaque veritas* (*parrhesia*) of the ideal friend (Horace, *Carmen*, I, 24). Plutarch defined *parrhesia* as the voice of friendship (*Moralia* 51C). The Cynic Demonax condemned religious mysteries as secretive, and therefore contrary to *parrhesia* (Lucian, *Demonax* 11). Many texts teach us that *parrhesia* signified a courageous behavior towards tyrants and emperors. It was not a revival of the republican or democratic meaning of *parrhesia*, but rather the reaction of philosophically educated men to the flattery and moral degradation inherent in tyranny. The meaning attributed to *libertas* (or even *licentia*) by some Roman writers, including Tacitus, was certainly influenced by the use of *parrhesia*.

10. At this stage the Greek situation becomes practically identical with the Roman situation, and to Rome we may turn to clarify antecedents and to explain what happened in the Roman Empire.

Republican Rome was an aristocratic society in which patricians and plebeians, patrons and clients, rich (*adsidui*) and poor (*proletarii*) were kept apart by law and custom. But patricians, patrons, and rich men were not necessarily the same persons. Different institutions took different notice of the various categories of citizens. Up to the end of the republic, patricians formed a group of their own in the Senate, though of decreasing importance. On the other hand, patricians were never allowed into the influential assembly of the plebeians (*comitia plebis tributa*). In the assembly of the *centuriae* (*comitia centuriata*), the main legislative and electoral assembly, wealth was the main criterion for the classification. Wealth counted in the general assembly of the tribes (*comitia tributa*), but less conspicuously.

The Roman army remained organized according to principles of wealth until the end of the second century B.C. Later it became an army of proletarians. Patronage was recognized in civil law, especially in relation to freed men, who were ipso facto clients of their ex-masters. Patronage operated unofficially in lawsuits, elections, services, etc. Legal regulations and customs affecting freedom of speech in the Roman society of the Republic have to be interpreted against the background of this complex net of relations. According to the most plausible interpretation, one of the laws of the Twelve Tables (fifth Century B.C.) punished slander by death. Aristocrats were likely to derive most advantage from such a provision which can be paralleled in other societies (Anglo-Saxons punished slander by the excision of the tongue). At the end of the third century B.C., the poet Naevius seems to have been prosecuted in accordance with this law when he attacked the powerful Metelli in a theatrical performance (the details are extremely obscure). Later this law fell into desuetude, and slander was prosecuted as *iniuria* which was stretched to cover attacks in theaters against individuals. At least since the time of Augustus (if not of Sulla) offensive words against persons in authority came under the law of *maiestas:* here again details are by no means clear. Foreign philosophers and rhetoricians were thrown out of Rome more than once in the second and first centuries B.C. under the ordinary coercive powers of the magistrates, who had the support of the Senate. This amounted to implicit interference with education.

In the political assemblies (*comitia*) as such there was no place for discussion. Citizens were there to vote. But there was opportunity for discussions in the more informal meetings (*contiones*) which normally preceded the formal *comitia*. The magistrate who presided over the *contiones* had considerable discretionary powers. It seems that he could either throw open the discussion or invite carefully selected individuals to speak. Foreign ambassadors were admitted to speak in such gatherings, and women are known to have spoken in them. In the Senate freedom of speech was complete, but senators were asked to speak in order of rank (which meant that the most influential members, the ex-censors, the ex-consuls, and the consuls-designate spoke first).

The general impression one receives for the last century of the Republic is that in both political and intellectual life tongues moved freely. But this was a period of crisis, and even in this period the beneficiaries must have been a restricted privileged group. Men like Cicero felt that there was less freedom of speech in Rome than in Athens. This admission did not imply any regret. It is typical of Republican Rome that freedom of speech was never directly and precisely connected with the more general notion of *libertas*. The very terminology of freedom of speech, however, pointed to a relationship between freedom in general and freedom of speech in particular: we hear of *libera lingua*, *òratio libera*. It goes without saying that by the first century B.C. Roman terminology was influenced by Greek usage. Yet *parrhesia* never had an exact equivalent in Rome; when it was translated by *licentia*, *contumacia*, an element of criticism was often implied. The general attitude seems to have been that only persons in authority had a right to speak freely: one senses that freedom of speech belongs to the sphere of *auctoritas* just as much as to the sphere of *libertas*.

11. In the Imperial period the connection of freedom of speech with political freedom became generally recognized, for obvious reasons. Paradoxically, Tiberius was one of the first to say so (Suetonius, *Tiberius* 28). Limitation of political discussion even in the Senate and the disappearance of *contiones* before the formal assemblies (followed by the de facto disappearance of the assemblies themselves), political trials, constant intimidation, and eventually elimination of potential rivals left the members of the Roman Empire in no doubt as to the repressive character of the regime established by Augustus. The burning of books and desultory persecution of philosophers (especially under Vespasian and Domitian) more particularly affected the intellectuals. Restrictions in the practice of astrology (Dio Cassius, 56, 25, 5) and frequent expulsions of astrologers from Rome underlined the danger of any enquiry about the future of the government of the Empire. Noises in the circus remained the only impressive (and occasionally effective) form of verbal protest in the Roman Empire. Widespread servility made sensitive people aware that adulation was a characteristic vice of Imperial society—a vice disastrous for the moral fibre of men. In the first century and in the early part of the second, both Roman and Greek writers expressed profound disgust with adulation (Phaedrus, Persius, Quintilian, Juvenal, on the Roman side; Philo, Dio Chrysostom, Plutarch, and Epictetus, on the Greek side). Tacitus, though not without contradictions, gave this feeling its classical expression. His *Annals* are a study in the moral degeneration resulting from the lack of freedom of speech. His *Dialogue on the Orators* examines the relation between decay in eloquence and decline of political liberty.

After the first decades of the second century freedom of speech ceased to be an important issue. It was replaced by the issue of religious toleration raised by the spread of Christianity. As far as we are aware, nobody presented the case for or against Christianity as a question involving the principle of freedom of speech. There is, however, a Christian development of the idea of freedom of speech which deserves our attention and may bring our story to a conclusion.

Parrhesia was one of those words—like *ecclesia, intercessio, suffragium*—which the Christian Church took over from Greek and Latin political language and endowed with a new meaning. The Christians were preceded by the Jews in this reinterpretation. The isolated expression of Isocrates' *Busiris* 40, "liberties towards the gods," was rediscovered and given a positive meaning by Jewish writers such as the Septuagint translators, Philo and Josephus. The Septuagint used *parrhesia* to translate different Hebrew expressions (Leviticus 26:13; Proverbs 1:20, Psalms 93:1, etc.), one of which indicated God's power. *Parrhesia* became the right and the privilege of the believer; already in Philo (*De specialibus legibus* I, 203) and later in the *Testament of the XII Patriarchs* (*Reuben* 4, 2) it is connected with the notion of *syneidesis*, conscience (cf. also Josephus, *Antiquitates iudaicae* 2, 52). In the New Testament, *parrhesia* "in the name of Jesus" is the consequence of conversion. The word occurs most frequently in the Fourth Gospel, in Acts and in Saint Paul. It is the sign of the new hope (II Corinthians 3:12). The believer can speak not only in the name of Jesus, but also to Jesus. He has *parrhesia* towards God. Saint John Chrysostom makes it clear that a catechumen does not enjoy this right (*Homilies* 2, 5, ed. Gaume, X, 506). More particularly, *parrhesia* becomes the right and the privilege of the martyr and of the saint. These have purchased liberty by martyrdom and sanctification, and have a special right to speak to God. They can therefore help other people by speaking to God on their behalf. The Life of Saint Anthony by Athanasius is a conspicuous document testifying to this conception which was to affect the whole outlook of the Middle Ages. On the other hand *parrhesia* is used in monastic texts (for instance, the *Apophthegmata patrum*) to indicate pride and excessive attachment to this world.

We have come a long way from the political *parrhesia* of which the Athenians were proud, but the new *parrhesia* of the Christian martyr and saint contributes to the notion of freedom of conscience. Faith and suffering give a right to speak out—even to God.

BIBLIOGRAPHY

The Oriental texts (with the exception of the biblical ones) quoted above are to be found in J. B. Pritchard, *Ancient Near Eastern Texts*, 3 ed. (Princeton, 1968). Pioneer work on political thinking of the ancient Near East has been done especially by members of the Oriental Institute of Chicago. It will be enough to refer to H. and H. A. Frankfort, J. A. Wilson, Th. Jacobsen, *The Intellectual Adventure of Ancient Man* (Chicago, 1946); reprinted as *Before Philosophy* (Harmondsworth, 1949); H. Frankfort, *Kingship and the Gods* (Chicago, 1948); J. A. Wilson, *The Burden of Egypt* (Chicago, 1951); reprinted as *The Culture of Ancient Egypt* (Chicago, 1956); C. H. Kraeling and R. M. Adams, eds., *City Invincible* (Chicago, 1960); A. L. Oppenheim, *Ancient Mesopotamia* (Chicago, 1964); and the collection of essays by Th. Jacobsen, *Toward the Image of Tammuz and other Essays* (Cambridge, Mass., 1970); some of the most important essays by Jacobsen are quoted below.

On Oriental political assemblies and related problems see especially: G. Buccellati, *Cities and Nations of Ancient Syria* (Rome, 1967). I. M. Diakonoff, "Die hethitische Gesellschaft," *Mitteilungen aus dem Institut für Orientforschung,* **13** (1967), 313–66. G. Evans, "Ancient Mesopotamian Assemblies," *Journal of the American Oriental Society,* **78** (1958), 1–11. A. Falkenstein, "La Cité-temple Sumérienne," *Cahiers d'Histoire Mondiale,* **1** (1954), 784–815. G. Fohrer, "Der Vertrag zwischen König und Volk in Israel," *Zeitschrift für Alttestamentliche Wissenschaft,* **71** (1959), 1–22. P. Garelli, *Les Assyriens en Cappadoce* (Paris, 1963), pp. 171–204; idem, *Le Proche-Orient asiatique* (Paris, 1969), 248–53. R. Gordis, "Democratic Origins in Ancient Israel," *Alexander Marx Jubilee Volume* (New York, 1950), pp. 369–88. O. R. Gurney, *The Hittites*, 2nd ed. (London, 1966). Th. Jacobsen, "Primitive Democracy in Ancient Mesopotamia," *Journal of Near Eastern Studies,* **2** (1943), 159–72; idem, "Early Political Development in Mesopotamia," *Zeitschrift für Assyriologie,* **52** (1957), 91–140. H. Klengel, "Die Rolle der Ältesten . . . im Kleinasien der Hethiterzeit," *Zeitschrift für Assyriologie,* **57** (1965), 223–36. S. N. Kramer, "Gilgamesh and Agga," *American Journal of Archaeology,* **53** (1949), 1–18. J.-R. Kupper, S. N. Kramer, et al., articles on "Vox Populi" in the Ancient Near East, in *Revue d'Assyriologie,* **58** (1964). J. L. McKenzie, "The Elders in the Old Testament," *Analecta Biblica,* **10** (1959), 388–406. S. Moscati, *The World of the Phoenicians* (London, 1968). A. L. Oppenheim, "A New Look at the Structure of Mesopotamian Society," *Journal of Economic and Social History of the Orient,* **10** (1967), 1–16. H. Reviv, "On Urban Representative Institutions and Self-Government in Syria-Palestine in the Second Half of the Second Millennium B.C.," *Journal of Economic and Social History of the Orient,* **12** (1969), 283–97. R. N. Whybray, *The Heavenly Counsellor in Isaiah XL, 13–14* (Cambridge, 1971). G. Widengren, "The Sacred Kingship of Iran," *Numen,* Supp. 4 (1959), 242–57. J. A. Wilson, "The Assembly of a Phoenician City," *Journal of Near Eastern Studies,* **4** (1945), 245. J. A. Wilson et al., *Authority and Law in the Ancient Orient, Journal of the American Oriental Society* (1954), Supp. 17. C. U. Wolf, "Traces of Primitive Democracy in Ancient Israel," *Journal* *of Near Eastern Studies,* **6** (1947), 98–108. R. N. Whybray, *The Heavenly Counsellor in Isaiah XL. 13–14* (Cambridge, 1971).

On Greece and Rome this bibliography is confined to specific works on freedom of speech. For the history of freedom in general refer to R. Klein, ed., *Prinzipat und Freiheit* (Darmstadt, 1969); H. Kloesel, *Libertas* (Breslau, 1935); D. Nestle, *Eleutheria,* Vol. I (Tübingen, 1967); M. Pohlenz, *Die griechische Freiheit* (Heidelberg, 1955); Ch. Wirszubski, *Libertas* (Cambridge, 1950); reviewed by A. Momigliano, *Journal of Roman Studies,* **41** (1951), 146–53. Greece and Rome: J. A. O. Larsen, *Representative Government in Greek and Roman History* (Berkeley, 1955). Greece: A. Andrewes, "The Government of Classical Sparta," in *Ancient Society and Institutions. Studies Presented to V. E. Ehrenberg* (Oxford, 1966), pp. 1–20. V. Ehrenberg, "Isonomia," in Pauly-Wissowa, *Realencyclopädie,* Suppl. VII, (1940), 293–301. G. T. Griffith, "Isegoria in the Assembly at Athens," in *Ancient Society,* op. cit., 115–38. A. H. M. Jones, *Sparta* (Oxford, 1967). J. A. O. Larsen, "Cleisthenes and the Development of the Theory of Democracy in Athens," in *Essays in Political Theory: Presented to George H. Sabine* (Ithaca, 1948), pp. 1–16. M. Radin, "Freedom of Speech in Ancient Athens," *American Journal of Philology,* **48** (1927), 215–20. G. Scarpat, *Parrhesia* (Brescia, 1964). Rome: T. Bollinger, *Theatralis Licentia* (Winterthur, 1969). T. Frank, "Naevius and Free Speech," *American Journal of Philology,* **48** (1927), 105–10. M. Gigante, *Ricerche Filodemee* (Naples, 1969). L. Robinson, *Freedom of Speech in the Roman Republic* (Baltimore, 1940), discussed by A. Momigliano, *Journal of Roman Studies,* **32** (1942), 120–24. Early Christianity: L. J. Engels, *Reallexikon für Antike und Christentum* (Stuttgart, 1968), 7, 839–77. W. Jaeger, "*Parrhesia* et fiducia," in *Studia Patristica,* I (Berlin, 1959), 221–39. E. Peterson, "Zur Bedeutungsgeschichte von *Parrhesia,*" in *Festschrift für R. Seeberg,* I (Berlin, 1929), 283–97. H. Schlier, *Theologisches Wörterbuch zum Neuen Testament* (Stuttgart, 1959), 5, 869–84. W. C. van Unnik, "De semitische achtergrond van *Parrhesia* in het Nieuwe Testament," *Mededelingen Nederlandse Akademie,* N.R. 25 (1962), 585–601.

ARNALDO MOMIGLIANO

[See also Constitutionalism; **Democracy; Equality;** Freedom; **Liberalism;** State.]

GAME THEORY

1. Decisions and Games. Human life is an unbroken sequence of decisions made by the conscious individual. He is continuously confronted with the need for making choices, some of them of narrow, others of very wide scope. In some cases he commands much information about consequences of a particular choice, in most he is quite uncertain. Some affect the immediate present, others commit him for a distant future. Some decisions are entirely his own—whether to have another cup of tea, to go for a walk; some involve other persons—whether to marry X. Many decisions are made with respect to nature: what planting to choose, what weather to expect. Many decisions are made by groups of individuals, and the group decision can be arrived at by a great variety of processes.

Some decisions arise from a logical structure as in law. There are also mathematical and logical decisions; whether π is a transcendental number, or whether to accept a particular proof of the existence of God. Even in mathematics there may be uncertainty, as Gödel has shown.

Decisions must also be made when an individual plays a game. (First, however, he must make the decision to play, which is normally though not necessarily a voluntary one.) In playing the game, the individual follows rules which, together with the decisions made, usually determine the winner. In all cases the desire for optimality (maximum rewards) will arise since clearly a decision is a choice among alternatives and the "best" decision will be preferred over all others. Many different kinds of decisions occur in connection with *games* of various types, the number of different games being indeterminate since always new games can be invented. In order to describe the behavior of individuals and to evaluate their choices, *criteria* have to be known or must be established.

Clearly a comprehensive theory of decision-making would encompass virtually all of voluntary human activity and as such would be an absurd undertaking, given the infinity of human situations. A more reasonable approach is to develop a science, or sciences, dealing with the principles, so as to govern decision-making in well-defined settings. In what follows the structure of that theory will be laid bare as far as this is possible without going into the use of the underlying mathematics.

Game theory represents a rigorous, mathematical approach towards providing concepts and methods for making reasonable decisions in a great variety of human situations. Thus decision theory becomes part of game theory. The basic features of the theory are described in Section 7, below.

2. Historical Considerations. A history of general decision-making is an impossibility, but histories of important decisions in law, military operations, business, etc., is another matter, though none of our concern here. Games on the other hand, as far as both their origin and development is concerned, as well as their scientific analysis, have a long and varied history.

The roots of games go back deep into the animal kingdom and to primitive society. Even the oldest known games of Homo sapiens are abstract creations of surprisingly high order, and justify the expression "Homo ludens." Games are present in all civilizations, not only in great varieties of form, but they also appear in disguises such as in ceremonies, liturgies, diplomatic customs, or war, the latter being especially visible during the time of maintenance of expensive private mercenary armies. In Roman Imperial times public games were a great burden on the state. In modern ages the money transactions, say, in the United Kingdom from football pools, exceed those of some of the largest corporations.

Since games have always occupied man in a very real sense it is curious that it was so long before games became a subject of scientific inquiry, especially in view of the dominating role of uncertainty in games. But finally the fundamental notion of *probability* arose from a study of games of chance and is a creation of the sixteenth century, developed by Girolamo Cardano (cf. Ore, 1953) from which time Galileo, Blaise Pascal, Christiaan Huygens, the Bernoullis, Pierre Simon de Laplace and many others of equal distinction have extended our understanding of this basic concept. It is still the subject of searching mathematical analysis without which it is impossible for modern science even to attempt to describe the physical or social world. Probability theory, not to be discussed further here though to be used in an essential manner, deals in spite of its complexity and high mathematical sophistication with a simpler specialized game situation than that encountered in those games in which true strategic situations occur. These are characterized by the simultaneous appearance of several independent but interacting human agents each pursuing his own goal. Probability theory first explained chances in particular games. But philosophical questions were raised, notably by Laplace. The relationships between those games and situations similar to them, but transcending them in their human significance were subjected to analysis. While some issues were clarified it immediately became clear that buried under the obvious there were further questions which awaited formulation and answer, not all of them posed or given to this day. The application of probability theory to physics, by then an actively developing abstract mathematical discipline, had to wait until the second half of the nineteenth century. Though it originated from the study of a social phenomenon, i.e., from games of chance, the application to social events—except for actuarial purposes (J. Bernoulli)—lagged behind that made to physics and astronomy.

The need for a *theory* of those games for whose outcome probability alone is not decisive was clearly seen, apparently for the first time, by Leibniz (1710) who stated: "Games combining chance and skill give the best representation of human life, particularly of military affairs and of the practice of medicine which necessarily depend partly on skill and partly on chance." Later, in his letter of July 29, 1715 to de Montmort he said . . . *il serait à souhaiter qu'on eut un cours entier des jeux, traités mathématiquement* (". . . it would be desirable to have a complete study made of games, treated mathematically"). Leibniz also foresaw the possibility of *simulation* of real life situations by indicating that naval problems could be studied by moving appropriate units representing ships on maneuver boards. The similarity of chess to some real life situations is obvious and was noted for example as early as 1360 by Jacobus de Cessolis, or in 1404 by Dirk van Delft who saw in that game a microcosm of society. The ancient Chinese game *wei-ch'i*, better known by its Japanese name of *go* was always interpreted as a mirror of complex, primarily military, operations. Later many authors have referred to the "game of politics," "the game of the market," or of the stock-exchange, etc. But it is one thing to observe some similarity and quite another to establish a rigorous and workable theory.

In 1713 when James de Waldegrave analyzed the game "le Her," as quoted in a letter from Pierre Remond de Montmort to Nicholas Bernoulli (Baumol and Goldfeld, 1968), a very different step was taken. This remarkable study anticipated a specific case of what is now known as the (optimal) minimax strategy concept (see Section 7, below) applied to a matrix game without a saddle point. However this matter was entirely forgotten or perhaps never understood, and has only been unearthed recently. Thus de Waldegrave had no influence; also his solution would have remained singular since the mathematics of his time would not have made it possible to prove a generalization of his specific result.

It is a moot question whether mathematics could have developed rapidly in the direction which the theory of games of strategy has taken. The interest of mathematicians was then dominated by the study of analysis, stimulated by the concomitant and inseparable development of mechanics. It can be even argued that it is at any rate largely an accident that the human mind turned early towards the formal science of mathematics and not towards, say, the intriguing task of formalizing law in a similarly rigorous manner.

There is no known record of any deeper scientific concern with games of strategy for about 200 years, though various authors, including C. F. Gauss and others, have from time to time studied certain combinatorial problems arising in chess (e.g., Gauss determined the minimum number of queens needed to control the entire chess board). M. Reiss (1858), who even quoted Leibniz, is apparently the first author who has given an extensive mathematical treatment of a game that is not strictly a chance game. But his is a game of "solitaire" and as such was not of great consequence. It seems that this work too was forgotten and without influence. Among others E. Zermelo (1912) and E. Lasker (1918) advanced the understanding of chess mathematically and philosophically. In 1924–27 É. Borel published papers on a certain two-person game, for which he found an optimal method of playing, but he expressed belief that it would not be possible to arrive at a general theorem. Confirming the well-known danger of making negative statements in science, John von Neumann in his important paper of 1928, "Zur Theorie der Gesellschaftsspiele" (*Mathematische Annalen*, **100**), proved precisely what Borel had thought to be impossible: a general theorem which guarantees that there is always an optimal strategy available for a player: the now famous fundamental and widely influential minimax theorem (cf. 7 below). This paper, though decisive, was again neglected, though in 1938 J. Ville gave a simplified and more general version of the proof of the minimax theorem. In 1944 appeared the *Theory of Games and Economic Behavior* by John von Neumann and Oskar Morgenstern, a large and comprehensive work, which definitely established the field. Since then an immense, steadily growing literature on games and decision theory has arisen in many countries. The theory developed by von Neumann and Morgenstern has been extended, applied and modified, but its basic structure and concepts sustain the new developments. Decision theory in the narrower, principally statistical, sense had developed due to the pioneering work of A. Wald (1950). The minimax theorem is of crucial importance also. The newest modifications and extensions of either game theory or statistical decision theory are manifold, and some brief indications are found in the text below. The history of the theory of games of strategy to 1944 is found in Morgenstern, 1972.

3. Utility. Before discussing games of strategy proper and developing the essence of the theory, a clarification of the medium in which the payoff is made is needed. When a game is played for money then the winnings in money can be taken as the criterion for the outcome, be it a game of chance or of strategy. But when the score is not set in ready-made numerical terms, or even by a simple "win" or "lose" declaration, the matter is more difficult. While it would be possible merely to postulate the existence of a number, it is desirable to show how a numerical criterion of a specifiable character can be established. This was accomplished (von Neumann and Morgenstern, 1944) by showing that "utility" can be defined as a number up

to a positive linear transformation without fixing a unit or a zero. In these terms payoffs will be expressed. The utility concept takes prior rank even over money units, though they be available. Utility thus defined is what the individual will fundamentally aim for when selecting his strategy. The above-mentioned numerical expression is obtained from a small set of plausible axioms by combining probability and an individual's completely ordered set of preferences (fulfilling the Archimedean order property), showing that the individual will think in terms of expected utility. It is proved that these axioms define "utility" and make it numerical in the desired manner. It is an additional step to assume that the individual will endeavor to maximize this utility.

The new utility theory also has given rise to a large literature. Though modifications of the original version have been proposed (e.g., the use of subjective, Bayesian probabilities instead of the frequency concept, etc.) the theory has entered virtually all writings on decision-making and the more modern treatments of economics. The theory has its antecedents in D. Bernoulli's famous treatment of the "St. Petersburg Paradox" (1738; Menger, 1934 and 1967) in which he introduced the notion of moral expectation, i.e., a value concept, in order to account for the fact that in spite of an infinitely large mathematical expectation in that game a person will not risk his entire possessions as a stake in order to be allowed to play this game, even if it could be offered. The second step in the direction of von Neumann-Morgenstern utility theory was taken by F. P. Ramsey in his "Truth and Probability" (1926; 1931); but this paper was only rediscovered after the expected utility theory in the von Neumann-Morgenstern formulation was developed and had become dominant. The use of subjective probability does not invalidate the theory (Pfanzagl, 1962; 1967) as was already noted on the occasion of the original formulation in 1944. The new theory of numerical utility is not identical with theories of "cardinal" or "ordinal" utility of the older and neo-classical economists, nor has it a basis in philosophical or political utilitarianism.

In order to establish further the empirical validity and power of the new theory a great number of experiments have been made—a *novum* in this field. These experiments attempt to test the validity of the underlying axioms, and to clarify the question of how individuals behave typically in situations involving risk. This behavior is clearly a phenomenon that any theory of decision-making has to take into account, given the glaring fact of the prevalence of chance in human affairs.

The development of the new theory of utility definitely advances our ability to analyze decisions (Fishburn, 1970) and raises important philosophical issues (Martin, 1963).

4. Games as Models of Human Actions. Games can be classified into two broad but sharply different categories: (a) games of chance and (b) games of strategy, which contain chance games as a simple, special case. In (a) the outcome is totally independent of the action of the playing individual as, e.g., in roulette. There may nevertheless be different manners of betting on the outcome, e.g., the player must decide whether to place a given stake in one throw, or to distribute it over several places (numbers, colors), or over several plays. These questions lead to important exercises in probability theory but they do not alter the fundamental simple chance character of the game. In (b) the outcome is controlled neither by chance alone, nor by the individual player alone, but by each player to some extent. Chance may (as in poker) or may not (as in chess) be present.

It is the entirety of the actions of the players—and of chance if nature intervenes—which determines the outcome and the equilibria (which the theory is to determine). In the course of a play the interests of the players are sometimes opposed to each other, sometimes parallel.

The significance of game theory is that besides explaining games proper, suitable games can be identified *strictly* with important other human actions which they therefore *model*. This is to be understood in the precise manner in which models are used in science, as when the planets are considered to be mere mass points and a theory of the solar system is built on that basis. In the same manner military, political, economic, and other processes can be identically represented by certain games of strategy. If a theory of such games can be established then a theory for the modeled processes is obtained. Such a theory would necessarily have to be mathematical. Its structure turns out to be quite different from that of classical mechanics and, *a fortiori*, from the differential and integral calculus. This is due to the essentially combinatorial character of the problems encountered and to the wide divergence of the underlying phenomena from physical phenomena. Among molecules or stars there is no cooperation, no opposition of interest, no information processing or withholding, no bluffing, no discrimination, no exploitation. Matter may collide, coalesce, explode, etc., but there is no conscious activity.

It was to be expected that the widespread attempts to use the concepts and techniques that had originated in the natural sciences must ultimately fail when applied to social phenomena. But the acceptance of new approaches is slow and difficult in any field and the impact of natural science thinking is hard to break.

The world of social phenomena is embedded in that of natural phenomena. But the two are different and as a consequence the structure of the sciences dealing with them will differ too. All sciences must, of course, have elements in common such as are dealt with in the theory of knowledge. However, the connections must not be overrated. Montaigne spoke of the need for separate scientific languages and this need has now become quite evident. It can be demonstrated that ultimately different fields of inquiry will generate even their own "logic." For example, the logic of quantum mechanics is best described by a projective geometry in which the distributive law—which in algebra means that $a(b+c) = ab + ac$—does not hold (Birkhoff and von Neumann). It is to be expected that a calculus as germane to the social sciences may someday be developed (or discovered?) as differential calculus is to mechanics. Other parts of the natural sciences show signs of producing their own mathematical disciplines and structures, and this process may repeat itself. One important aspect of game theory is that it has already given rise to considerable, purely mathematical activity. This process is only in its beginning, but proves once more that the development of mathematics is ultimately dependent on the mathematician being involved with empirical problems. Mathematics cannot proceed solely on the basis of purely formalistic and possibly aesthetic grounds. Thus the creation of game theory may be of a significance transcending in that respect its material content.

The essential justification for taking games of strategy as models for large classes of human behavior was already stated in the first paragraph of this section: our acts are interdependent in very complex manners and it is the precise form of this interdependence that has to be established. Interdependence has, of course, been recognized, but even where neo-classical economics of the Walras-Pareto type tried to describe this interdependence, the attempt failed because there was no rigorous method to account for interaction which is evident especially when the number of agents is small, as in oligopoly (few sellers). Instead large numbers of participants were introduced (under the misnomer of "free competition") such that asymptotically none had any perceptible influence on any other participant and consequently not on the outcome, each merely facing fixed conditions. Thus the individual's alleged task was only to maximize his profit or utility rather than to account for the activities of the "others." Instead of solving the empirically given economic problem, it was disputed away; but reality does not disappear. In international politics there are clearly never more than a few states, in parliaments a few parties, in military operations a few armies, divisions, ships, etc. So effective decision units tend to remain small. The interaction of decisions remains more obvious and rigorous theory is wanting.

5. Rational Behavior. A purpose of social science, of law, of philosophy has been for a long time to give meaning to the notion of "rational behavior," to account for "irrationality," to discover, for example in criminal cases, whether a given individual could be considered as having acted rationally or not. In general there appears to exist an intuitive notion of what "rational" must mean. Frequently this notion would be based on experience; but experience varies with each individual, and whether any person has an intuitively clear idea of "rationality" is doubtful. In the simple case in which an individual wishes to maximize a certain quantity, say utility, and *provided* he controls *all* factors or variables on which his utility depends, then we shall not hesitate to say that he acts rationally if he makes decisions such that he actually obtains this maximum, or at least moves stepwise in its direction. Thus, rationality is predicated on two things: (a) the identification of a goal in the form of preferences formed, possibly stated numerically, and (b) control over all the variables that determine the attainment of the goal.

The first condition requires that the individual have a clear notion of what he wants and that he possess sufficient information which will identify the goal he wishes to reach. The second condition requires that the individual be able to determine first the variables, and second the consequences of the changes he may make in setting their values for reaching the intended goal, and finally that he actually can set the values of the variables as it may appear proper to him. The amount of foresight demanded (especially if the goal should be distant) is considerable but this point shall not be considered further. The control factor, however, is of primary concern: if *nature* intervenes in his intended behavior, the individual can control an indifferent nature by means of statistical adjustment; the farmer, for example, can arrange his planting so that on the average neither a very dry nor a very wet summer will hurt him. Whether nature is always indifferent is another question (Morgenstern, 1967). But it is an entirely different matter if among the variables there are some that are controlled by other individuals having opposite aims. This lack of complete control is clearly the case in zero-sum (winnings compensate losses exactly) two-person games of strategy, but also in business, in military combat, in political struggles and the like. It is then *not* possible simply, and in fact, to maximize whatever it may be the individual would like to maximize, for the simple reason that no such maximum exists. It is then not clear intuitively which

course of action is "better" than another for the individual, let alone which one is optimal.

To determine optimal, or "rational" behavior is precisely the task of the mathematical theory of games. *Rational behavior is not an assumption of that theory;* rather, its identification is one of its *outcomes*. What is assumed is that the individual prefers a larger advantage for himself to a smaller one. If these advantages can be described and measured and are understood by the individual, and if he chooses *not* to pursue the required course, then there is a limited definition of *non*rational behavior for such situations. It is assumed that the demonstration (if the theory succeeds) of the optimal course of action is as convincing to the individual as a mathematical proof is in the case of a mathematical problem. But the theory allows that a participant may deviate from his optimal course, in which case an advantage accrues to the others who maintain their optimal strategies.

Prior to the advent of game theory the term "rational" had been used loosely as referring to both of the two conceptually different situations set forth above, as if there were no difference. The transfer of the notion of rationality from the completely controllable maximizing condition to one in which there is no exclusive control over the variables is inadmissible. This has been the cause of innumerable difficulties permeating much of philosophical, political, and economic writing. No side conditions, however complicated, which may be imposed or exist when one is confronted with a clear maximum problem changes the situation conceptually. In the case where full control exists side conditions merely make the task of reaching the maximum more difficult—perhaps even impossible, for example, because it may computationally be out of reach. But even in its most complicated form it is *conceptually* different—and vastly *simpler*—than the problem faced by, say, a chess player or a poker player, and consequently by any one whose activities have to be modeled by games of strategy. The conceptual difference does not lie in numbers of variables or in computational difficulties; but we note that the solution of games becomes extremely difficult both when the number of strategies is large (even with as few players as in chess) and also when the number of participants increases, though each may have only a few strategies.

When there are, say, 100 variables of which one individual controls 99 the other the remaining one, this appears to be a different situation from that when there are only 2 variables and each player controls one. Yet conceptually the two are identical. No practical considerations, such as possibly assigning weights to variables, and the like, in an effort to reduce difficulties of action, will work. The fundamental conceptual difference and difficulty remains and has to be resolved by the theory.

6. Normative or Descriptive Theory. The purpose of a theory of decision-making, or specifically of game theory, is to advise a person how to behave by choosing optimally from the set of his available strategies, in situations subject to the theory. If he decides knowingly to deviate from the indicated course he has either substituted another goal, or dislikes the means (for moral and other reasons). It is then a matter of terminology whether he is still considered to be a rational actor. The theory at any rate can take such deviations into consideration. Clearly, some technically available strategies may be inadmissible in legal, moral, and other respects. In some cases these questions do not arise: chess is played equally whether the opponents are rich, poor, Catholics, Muhammadans, communists or capitalists. But business or political deals are affected by such circumstances. Advice can be given with or without constraints which involve morals or religion.

The theory is also descriptive, as it must be if it is to be used as a model. It might be argued that the theory cannot describe past events since before it was created individuals could not have followed the optimal strategy which only the theory could discover! The answer is that for some situations the individual can find it by trial and error and a tradition of empirical knowledge could develop after repeated trials. However, the same objection applies regarding ordinary maximum problems (provided they are even given): the identification and computation of the maximum was (and in many cases still is) out of reach even for very large organizations; yet they behave as if they could find it and they try to work in that direction.

Theories thus can be viewed as being both descriptive and normative. In the natural sciences a similar apparent conflict shows up in interpreting phenomena as either causally or teleologically related, while in fact this distinction may resolve into merely a matter of how the differential equations are written.

Thus the theory is capable of being used in both manners. Future descriptions of reality will be improved if the concepts of the theory are available and future actions of those who use the theory in order to improve their own rationality will be superior (except in the simplest cases where the correct answer is also intuitively accessible). Clearly, if more and more players act rationally, using the theory, there will be shifts in actual behavior and in real events to be described. This is an interesting phenomenon worth pointing out. It has philosophical significance: progress in the natural sciences does not affect natural phenomena, but the spread of knowledge of the workable social sciences changes social phenomena via changed individual behavior from which fact there may be a feedback into the social sciences (Morgenstern, 1935).

7. Basic Concepts: Game Theory and Social Structure. The description of a game of strategy involves a number of new concepts. Obviously, games are first classified by virtue of the number of players or participants: $1, 2, \ldots, n$. Second, when the winnings of some are compensated exactly by the losses of others, the game is zero-sum. The sum can also be positive (when all gain), negative (when all lose), constant, or variable. Games are "essential," when there is an advantage in forming coalitions, which can happen even in zero-sum games, but only when $n \geq 3$. This expresses advantages in cooperation; it can develop even when there are only two players, but then the game has to be non-zero sum. Games are "inessential" when there is no such advantage, in which case each player proceeds independently for himself. Note, however, that he still does not control the outcome for himself by his actions alone; the "others" are always present, and sometimes also nature is present as an agent.

Games are played according to *rules* which are immutable and must be known to the players. A rule cannot be violated since then the game would cease; it would be abandoned or go over into another game—if that is possible. A tacit assumption is that players agree to play. They do this without doubt when playing for pleasure. When games are used as models, it may however happen that one's participation in the modeled situation is not voluntary. For example, a country may be forced into a military conflict; or, in order to survive and to earn a living a person may have to engage in certain economic activities. Games come to an end; the rules provide for this. Again in the modeled situation one play of a certain game—a play being the concrete, historical occurrence of a game—may follow another play of the same game, or the play of one game may follow that of another game and so on. Sometimes it is possible to view such sequences as supergames and to treat them as an entity. In some games as in chess the players are perfectly informed about all previous moves, in others they have only partial information about them. Sometimes the players are not even fully informed about themselves, as e.g., in bridge, which is a two-player game, but each player (e.g., North and South) plays through two representatives. In this case information about oneself and to oneself is only disclosed by the manner of playing. In addition chance enters, since the cards are dealt at random. This example gives a first indication of the great complexity that confronts any attempt at theory even under simple conditions. In poker, bluffing is added, as the pretense by some players of having certain sets of cards can become an element in the play.

Decisions have to be made, when to bluff in the face of possible bluffs by the other players, how to surmise bluffs by others, and many more such factors.

The rules normally specify sequences of moves, countermoves and tell when the game has terminated. It is possible to view games described in this *"extensive" form* strictly equivalently by introducing the notion of strategies, which are the complete plans made up by each player for such series of moves. Games are then described in the *"normalized" form* and it is thus that they shall be treated in what follows. In choosing a pure strategy, i.e., by specifying the precise complete course of action, the player may or may not be at a disadvantage in expected values if he has to make his choice openly before the other player makes his choice. If there is no disadvantage, then the game has a *saddle point* in the payoff matrix, for if the first player chooses his optimal strategy, then no matter what the second player may do, he cannot depress the first one's expected payoff below a certain value which is the value of the saddle point. Exactly the same is then true conversely for the second player. Games having saddle points in *pure* strategies are strictly determined. In these cases there is no value of information flowing, voluntarily or involuntarily, from one player to the other. Each behaves rationally if in pursuit of his intended maximum benefit he chooses his pure strategy so that he is guaranteed at least as much as corresponds to the value of the saddle point. If the other player deviates from his optimal strategy, i.e., behaves "irrationally," the first one can only gain.

However, games usually have no saddle points in pure strategies. A player forced to disclose his pure strategy would then be at a disadvantage and the question arises whether there is at all an optimal way of playing. The attempt of opponents to outguess each other by the chain of thought: I think that he thinks that I think he thinks . . . will never lead to a resolution of the dilemma exemplified by the Sherlock Holmes—Professor Moriarty pursuit case (Morgenstern, 1928), which corresponds exactly to a qualified game of matching pennies. How then shall one proceed?

John von Neumann proved in 1928 that for these games which are not strictly determined a saddle point *always* exists if the players resort to proper so-called *mixed strategies:* the now famous minimax theorem. A mixed strategy means that instead of selecting a particular pure strategy from the whole set of all available pure strategies, the player must *assign* a specific probability to each one of them such that at least one will be played. A properly chosen chance device will then determine the strategy actually chosen. The player himself will not know which strategy he will actually play; hence he cannot be found

out by his adversary and he cannot even accidentally disclose his choice, which if he did would be disastrous.

The fundamental "Minimax Theorem" assures that the player, using mixed strategies, can always find a correctly computed optimal mixed strategy to protect himself (minimizing the worst in expected values that can happen to him) precisely as in strictly determined games he can identify, and even announce, his optimal *pure* strategy. The original proof of this theorem involved very advanced methods of topology and functional analysis. The theorem is of outstanding importance and has had wide ramifications: the original theory of games for any number of players rests on it. Though the implications of the theorem have often been found uncomfortable (and were termed "pessimistic"), it stands unchallenged. As is often the case in mathematics, other simpler proofs have later been offered, by von Neumann himself as well as by others, such as using concepts from the theory of convex bodies, a theory which in turn has greatly benefited from these developments.

It is necessary to examine the significance of the use of mixed strategies since they involve probabilities in situations in which "rational" behavior is looked for. It seems difficult, at first, to accept the idea that "rationality"—which appears to demand a clear, definite plan, a deterministic resolution—should be achieved by the use of probabilistic devices. Yet precisely such is the case.

In games of chance the task is to determine and then to evaluate probabilities inherent in the game; in games of strategy we *introduce* probability in order to obtain the optimal choice of strategy. This is philosophically of some interest. For example, the French mathematician É. Borel asserted that the human mind cannot produce random sequences of anything; humans need to invent devices which will do this for them. Borel did not and could not give a mathematical proof because his assertion is not a mathematical one. It is noteworthy, incidentally, that recent studies of the brain seem to indicate, however, that some uncertainty and randomness in its operation are essential for its proper functioning.

The identification of the correct probabilities with which to use each pure strategy is a mathematical task—sometimes computationally formidable—and is accomplished by use of rigorous theory. Putting these probabilities to use requires then a suitable physical generating device which always can be constructed. In practice players may merely approximate such devices where these would tend to be very complicated. In some cases they will produce them exactly, as in matching pennies. In this game, on matching either heads or tails, one unit will be paid to the first matching player; when not matching, one unit by the first to the second. This game, clearly zero-sum and of complete antagonism between the two players, is not strictly determined. Hence each will protect himself against being found out. As is well known the optimally correct way of playing is for both players to toss his coin simultaneously with the other player, which is equivalent to choosing each of the only two available strategies with probabilities $\frac{1}{2}$, $\frac{1}{2}$. The coin itself when tossed will either show heads or tails precisely with the required probabilities.

The manner in which this game is played makes it appear to be a game of chance, but in reality it is one of strategy. This incidentally illustrates a grave difficulty of giving correct descriptions of social events! The probabilities of $\frac{1}{2}$, $\frac{1}{2}$, have to be changed if there should be a premium, say, on matching on heads over matching on tails. The new probabilities that secure the saddle point can no longer be guessed at or be found intuitively; they have to be computed from the theory, so quickly does the true, mathematical analysis which requires the full use of the complex theory have to be invoked. When the number of strategies goes beyond two the computational difficulties increase at any rate; the computations may become impossible even when the game is strictly determined, as in chess, where there are about 10^{120} strategies. The existence proofs of optimal strategies are valid nevertheless.

The problem now arises how a *social equilibrium* can be described when there are more than two decision makers. Here only the most basic concepts can be indicated as a full description would require much space and intricate mathematical analysis. The structure is this: when in a zero-sum game $n \geq 3$, then the possibility of cooperation among players arises, and they will form coalitions wherever possible. In order to be considered for inclusion in a coalition a player may offer side payments to other players; some may be admitted under less favorable terms (when $n > 3$) than those set by the initial members of the coalition and the like. When a coalition wins, the proceeds have to be divided among the partners and these then find themselves in the same kind of conflict situation which arises for the players of a zero-sum two-person game.

The totality of all payments to all players is an "imputation." In order to determine an equilibrium it appears to be necessary to find a particular imputation that is "better," that is, more acceptable, from among all possible ones than any other. Such an imputation then "dominates" all other imputations. But that would be the case in inessential games. Only for those is there a *unique* social optimum, a division of the proceeds of the game played by society which cannot be improved upon and which therefore is imposed or imposes itself upon society as the best stable arrangement. But since cooperation is a basic feature of human organization these games are of little interest. No such single imputation exists for essential n-person games. Domination is then not transitive, thus reflecting a well-known condition of social arrangements in which circularity often occurs (as, for instance, in the relative values of teams in sports).

Thus the hope of finding a uniquely best solution for human affairs is in vain: there is no stability for such arrangements. Political, social, and economic schemes have been proposed under the tacit, but frequently even open, assumption that this is possible when men organize themselves freely. Only the isolated individual or a fully centralized (usually dictatorial) society can produce a scheme that it considers better than any other and that it hopes to be able to enforce.

Thus there is, in general, no "best" all dominating scheme of distribution or imputation; but there may be a number of imputations which do *not dominate each other* and which among them dominate everything else. Such imputations, therefore, must be considered by society. They form a special "stable set," originally called the "solution set." Any one of the imputations belonging to this stable set is a possible, acceptable social arrangement.

A stable set is precisely a set S of imputations, no one of which dominates any other, and such that every other possible imputation not in S is dominated by some imputation in S. (Technically, the imputations belonging to each stable or solution set are not even partially ordered and, *a fortiori*, the elements of this set are not comparable with one another.)

The stability that such a set possesses is unlike the more familiar stability of physical equilibria. For no single imputation can be stable by itself; it can always be disturbed, not by "forces" (as a physical equilibrium could be), but by the proposal of a different arrangement by which it is dominated. Such a proposal must necessarily lie outside of S. But for every such proposal, there is always a counter-proposal which dominates the proposal, and which lies in S. Thus a peculiar, delicate but effective equilibrium results which has nothing to do with the usual equilibria of physics; the process of proposal and counter-proposal always leads to an imputation in S. Indeed the present notion differs so profoundly from the usual ideas of stability and equilibrium that one would prefer to avoid even the use of the words. But no better ones have yet been found.

There may exist, even simultaneously, different, conflicting solution sets or standards of behavior, *each* one with any number of different imputations, always more than one, sometimes even infinitely many. But those within the respective solution sets are merely *alternative* to each other; they are not in fundamental conflict as are the different standards.

Clearly, it is difficult to identify solutions, i.e., sets of imputations with the required properties, even from the whole set of all possible imputations. In 1968 W. F. Lucas made the important discovery of a game of 10 players that has no solution (in the so-called characteristic function form). The question is open whether this is a rare case and what modifications in concepts and methods may be necessary to assure solvability. In all other cases so far investigated solutions have been found.

These admittedly difficult notions emerge from the rigorous mathematical theory whose empirical basis is formed by facts that are not questioned even by current social and economic theory, though these theories have not rendered a successful account of the nature of decision-making. The lack of identification of a single settlement or imputation is not a deficiency of game theory. Rather there is herein revealed a fundamental characteristic of social, human organization which cannot be described adequately by other means.

In the light of these considerations one of the standard concepts currently used in describing a social optimum, the so-called Pareto optimum (formulated by V. Pareto, 1909) appears at best to be an oversimplification. That notion says that the optimal point is reached when no one can improve his position without deteriorating that of others. What is lacking in that formulation, among other things, is to account for nonuniqueness, uncertainty, deceit, etc., hence a more comprehensive frame within which individuals make decisions that guarantee a precisely defined but different stability (Morgenstern, 1965).

The appearance of novel and complicated notions is due to a mathematical analysis that is germane to the subject matter and has nothing to do with any ideological or other conception of society. The mathematical analysis unravels implications of some generally accepted facts and observations, axiomatically stated, and then leads via the fundamental minimax theorem to the discovery of relationships in the empirically given social world which without the aid of the new theory have either escaped notice altogether or were at best only vaguely and qualitatively described. Since inventions are possible in the social world this process is an unending one, which means that new concepts and theorems have arisen and more are bound to arise. For example, new concepts of solution structure have emerged. It may even happen that social organizations are proposed that have no stable sets; and that only work in a manner that is quite different

from the original intentions, even though these may have involved sound philosophical and ideological principles.

Physics studies given physical facts and is *not* confronted with this type of creation; it faces in this sense a static world (though it may be expanding!) as far as we can tell. Not all *given* physical facts are known; new effects are constantly being discovered but it is doubtful that they are currently being created, while it is certain that novel forms of social organization are being and will be invented. We know that the life sciences are also, and in fact more clearly, confronted with the evolutionary creation of new phenomena, not only with their discovery, as in the case of physics. But on the other hand, the time spans which are necessary for genetic change are so great as to make this concern with the creation of new phenomena (other than breeding of new plants and animals) to have as yet no practical importance in this context.

This goes to show that the intellectual situation in the social sciences is disquieting even when one abstracts from the further complication presented by the existence of frequently changing ideologies.

There is thus no hope to penetrate into the intricate web of social interdependencies by means of concepts derived from the physical sciences, although thinking along such lines still dominates. This is partly due to the immense success of physics and the slow development even of any proper description of the social world. Where this description has used abstract concepts these were mainly taken from the physical sciences. Thus a recasting of the records of past social events is necessary. The two movements of description and theory formation are as inseparably interrelated as they were in physics and astronomy where the analysis of simple processes, for instance, that of a freely falling body, led to mechanics and to the discovery of the appropriate tool of the differential calculus. Fate will not be easier for the social sciences and in this methodological situation lies the deep philosophical significance of game theory, i.e., of the new analyses of human decision-making and the interlocking of such decisions.

To give but one illustration: a formal system of society may be fully symmetric, i.e., give each member exactly the same possibility, such as laissez-faire, and thereby have provisions of complete freedom and equality. But the possibility of cooperation via coalitions, agreements, and the like produces nonsymmetric arrangements so that the intent of the law-maker cannot be maintained without forbidding coalitions which then would run afoul of the principle of freedom. While this asymmetry is sometimes not very hard to discover there are other, more elusive cases; but in order to be accepted the mathematical theory must first yield results which are also obtainable from common sense experience. However, theory must in addition be able to predict the emerging structures and show how the inner nature of social processes works.

8. Applications. Application is the final test of theories but may be hard to come by. Decision theory and game theory have a potentially wide range of uses. Those already made are limited partly because of the newness of the field, because of computational difficulties, and partly because the theories are in a state of active development which produces new concepts and theorems. The distance in time and difficulty from an abstract theory to application is always large when a fundamentally novel development occurs. This period may stretch over generations. Some directions of application are becoming clear, however. Decision theory is basic for, and indeed inseparable from, modern *statistics*. The use of the minimax theorem has given rise to a new turn in that science (primarily due to A. Wald) and produced a large literature. Noteworthy is a study by J. Milnor (1954) on games against nature in which various possible criteria, due certain authors such as Laplace, A. Wald, L. J. Savage, and L. Hurwicz, were investigated regarding their compatibility. Milnor showed that no criteria satisfy all of a reasonable set of axioms and it is an open problem whether new ideas can be evolved to resolve this impasse. Since this is a game against nature, then our incomplete and changing knowledge of nature's laws also has to be taken into account—a further complication not specifically considered by Milnor or others. Nature may be infinitely complex and therefore can never be "found out" completely.

Game theory has a profound bearing on economics. Many special problems have been attacked such as oligopoly (markets with few sellers) which could never be adequately treated by conventional methods. Particularly noteworthy is the work by Shapley and Shubik (1965 to date). The penetration to other areas such as bargaining, auctions, bidding processes, general equilibrium, etc., is slow but steady. The very structure of existing theory is threatened once it is recognized that there is no determinism and that no one, not even the state, controls all variables, as was explained above. But recognition of this indeterminism demands the scrapping of more than can be immediately replaced, and this causes a profoundly disturbing situation: one shows the logical inadequacy of existing theories but cannot offer a specific immediate and detailed replacement. Also recall that false theories often have had significant workability (Ptolemy) and therefore, though doomed, could live together with their ultimate replacement (Copernicus) for a considerable time.

Sociology, with a less advanced theory than economics will undoubtedly become a fertile field for applications once the connections are seen. In particular the distinction between the rules of games and the standards of behavior (which depend on previously formulated rules but are the *consequences* rather than antecedents of games) offer wide areas for sociological investigations.

In political science there are increasingly many applications. Going back to Condorcet's voting paradox (1785), which is the possibility of an inconsistent collective choice, even when individual choices are consistent, great strides have been made in illuminating voting procedures (Farquharson, 1969), many of these steps resting on the theory of weighted majority games. In addition political power play, with favors granted, side payments made, bluffs, promises kept and broken, is as ideal and fertile a field for the new concepts as one could wish, but the path is thorny, especially because of the preliminary, difficult quantification of matters such as "political advantage" and the like. Of particular significance is the illumination of the bargaining and negotiation process. A considerable literature has emerged which is of great practical value though it is highly technical. One question, for example, is how the contracting parties should deal with disclosure of their own utility functions in the process of negotiating. Another is the proof, given by von Neumann and Morgenstern (1944), that of two bargaining parties the one will get the upper hand which has the finer utility scale, a better discernment of advantages. Negotiation is always possible except when there is full antagonism, which exists only in a zero-sum two person game. In all other cases negotiations are possible, whether the game be zero-sum or not.

The application to military matters is obvious and some possibilities have been explored extensively in many countries. The idea of a "strategy" has after all since ancient times been embedded in military activities, but it is noteworthy that the modern theory did not take its inspiration from the military field but from social games as a far more general and fruitful area from which it could radiate.

Combat and conflict, however, are as deeply rooted in human nature as is cooperation, so that the combination of both, emerging with singular clarity in military affairs, makes this field naturally attractive for study. As a consequence there is now a game theoretic literature concerning combat, deployment, attrition, deterrence, pursuit, and the like. Also the insight that in war—especially in nuclear war—both parties may lose ("Pyrrhic victories") has found precision in the formulation of games with negative payoffs to all. In most cases it is only in the 1960's that all these notions have become precise and were in part successfully applied in a concrete and computational form.

Game theory has also been used in *ethics, biology, physics,* and even *engineering.* This spread of applications is two-fold. First, in *ethics* the problems of decision-making are essential, and it may appear that they consist primarily in imposing constraints on the individual or on society (Braithwaite, 1955). This view would exclude technically feasible strategies for moral reasons (though permitted within the rules of the game). This exclusion of strategies shows how ethical decisions involve other persons, positively or negatively, directly or indirectly, singly or in groups, as well as compromises and commitment. An ethics that considers only a normative system of possible ideals (which can never be fully explicit in view of the infinity of situations that may be encountered), or single decisions by single, isolated individuals is unable to deal with crucial issues of that field. The mere exclusion of a feasible strategy on moral grounds implies that the consequences of its use are known and can be disapproved. But the consequences depend also on the strategies chosen by the others and prediction of this type may be impossible. The moral code may forbid murder but accept killing on command in war, and then try to qualify what kind of commands are valid and which are not. This goes clearly beyond the mere establishment of an abstract normative system, not considered in *action.* Analysis taking into account the above points leads to a probabilistic ethics if only because the not strictly determined games demand the use of mixed strategies. These ideas are now only in the first state of development. They are fundamentally different from previous abortive applications of mathematics to ethics, such as by Spinoza.

Second, in the other areas game theory appears as a mathematical *technique* rather than as a model. Certain processes, say in engineering, can be interpreted *as if* they were games because of a formal correspondence. This then makes the use of the extensive mathematical apparatus of game theory possible. Illustrations would necessarily be of a rather specialized character and are therefore omitted here, though the large field of linear programming with its many variants (of great practical importance) must be mentioned. Game theory and programming theory are closely related by virtue of the well known duality theorem for linear programming.

Biologists (Lewontin, 1961; Slobodkin, 1964) have interpreted evolution in game theoretic terms, in spite of the difficulty for a nonteleological biology to use the purposeful orientation of game theory. By means of appropriate reinterpretation, including that of utility, it is shown that game theory can give answers to problems of evolution not provided for by the theory of population genetics. It is possible to identify an optimal strategy for survival of populations in different environments.

Some of these developments involve game theory strictly as a technology (not as a model) and in some it is still doubtful whether a true model character can be accepted (as possibly in biology). There are here transitional phases of high interest and it is impossible to foresee the development of these tendencies.

9. *Philosophical Aspects.* The appraisal of the philosophical significance of a new field of science, or of a fundamental turn in its treatment, or of the appearance of a new scientific language expressing new concepts, is an extremely delicate matter. Hence little shall be said here as it may be premature to do so. But if we attribute philosophical meaning to the fact that the study of decision-making under a wide set of circumstances has not only affected significantly sciences like statistics, but is spreading to other fields as a new mathematical discipline—game theory—and is influencing even pure mathematics, then we are justified in speaking of a philosophically relevant development.

While raising no claims of equal importance, the development of game theory has created a shift of standpoints in viewing the social world and human behavior, just as relativity theory and quantum mechanics have provided a new outlook on physical reality. It is too early to be very specific: in those other two areas it took years before the strange new concepts of space curvature, of an infinite but bounded space, of the Heisenberg uncertainty relationship, and of Bohr's principle of complementarity (to name only a few) were properly incorporated into philosophy, and it is doubtful whether this process has already come to an end. Consequently it will likewise be many years before the philosophical discussion of the new outlook due to game theory will have crystallized.

In statements about the philosophic significance of a scientific area it would help if it were unambiguously clear what is meant by "philosophy." Philosophy has a difficult but fairly well defined scope when it comes to analyzing problems of knowledge, of verification, of the meaning of truth. But to determine the philosophical meaning of a new scientific development is almost impossible while that change is rapidly progressing. Therefore only some tentative remarks shall be made in which there is no attempt to order them according to their significance or to be exhaustive. Nor can one be sure that the principal philosophical meaning does not lie elsewhere.

(a) We are confronted with a new development concerning our understanding of *reason* and *rationality* as the previous sections have indicated. Both being

273

possible human attributes we are now in possession of precise concepts that were lacking or undefined formerly. We have a mathematical theory that is largely combinatorial in character and whatever ultimate crises mathematics itself may be afflicted with there has never been any doubt cast on the final character of combinatorics. The new light thrown on the problem of rational behavior has shown that there is here not one problem but many, that they inevitably lead to formulations requiring mathematical analysis, that one is now capable of providing such analysis at considerable depth and that actual computations are possible, though limited by physical processes such as speed and memory of the computers.

Mathematics thus has encroached on another field of human activity in a decisive manner, and it is certain that it will never be dislodged from it again. We also note that axiomatics, so far the ultimate formal expression we are capable of giving to theories, has now for the first time firmly established itself in the social sciences.

(b) A further step has been taken in the behavioral sciences by the replacement of *determinism* by the new, extended, role which has been assigned to probability though the indeterminacy introduced is not in all respects that of a probabilistic nature (as is shown, e.g., by the uncertainty regarding which imputation in a solution set in an *n*-person game will be chosen). This also affects the ideas held concerning prediction: neither deterministic nor probabilistic approaches need to work, as uncertainty of a different kind appears to prevail in many social setups and decision situations.

(c) Modern decision theory has thrown new light on the nature and role of *information*, its flow from individual to individual and on the value and cost of obtaining it or preventing it from spreading. In the same spirit mention must be made of the fact that one has gained control—no doubt in an initial manner only—of the troublesome notion of utility by tying it firmly to expectations and various forms of probability.

(d) The immense complexity of social actions and their interplay has been laid bare. It is seen that it is greater by several orders of magnitude over what earlier writers in the social sciences had contemplated, and it has been shown—though only in part and so far mainly indirectly—how and why the classical formalistic approaches must fail. It is probably no exaggeration to state that social science will prove to be far more difficult than physics and that it will require (as indicated earlier) the development of new mathematical disciplines.

There is, in particular, one philosophical consequence that must be stressed because it seems to have escaped proper attention thus far: it was emphasized above that certain formal systems of society will of necessity work in a manner different from the intentions of the designers. More generally we state that *no complete formalization of society is possible:* if a formalization is made, it is either incomplete or self-contradictory. Hence the attempt can only be to formalize as much as possible and to supplement the formalism by new formalistic decisions in those concrete situations where it fails. Every social theory must therefore be dynamic, proceeding from one formalism to another. The axiomatization of games conforms to this fact, since the axioms require neither categoricity nor completeness because new games can always be invented and these can serve as prototypes for new social arrangements.

The theory of finding optimal strategies in decision-making has thus produced a new paradigm for the social and behavioral sciences. It will take considerable time before the full impact of this development is felt. But one philosophical meaning cannot be missed even now: the push towards a more general theory firmly based on combinatorial mathematical concepts and procedures.

However, before philosophy reaches its ultimate state of becoming the most general abstract science, in the sense of Leibniz' *Mathesis universalis,* philosophical activity may itself be viewed as a game. This only appears to be a heretic idea. Plato in *Parmenides* did speak of philosophy as a game and the Sophists engaged openly in philosophical contests. Philosophical schools have always competed with each other, as is the case in all sciences in different stages of their development. The same applies to art; it suffices to recall the contests between Leonardo da Vinci and Michelangelo. With this remark we return to the opening observation in this paper which showed the deep roots of games in human affairs to be such that we may speak rightly of man as Homo ludens.

BIBLIOGRAPHY

R. J. Aumann and M. Maschler, eds., *Recent Advances in Game Theory* (Princeton, 1962). W. J. Baumol and S. M. Goldfeld, eds., *Precursors in Mathematical Economics: An Anthology* (London, 1968), Introduction by H. Kuhn, pp. 1–9. Claude Berge, *Théorie générale des jeux à n-personnes* (Paris, 1957). R. B. Braithwaite, *Theory of Games as a Tool for the Moral Philosopher* (Cambridge, 1955). M. Dresher, L. S. Shapley, and A. W. Tucker, eds., *Advances in Game Theory, Annals of Mathematics Studies,* No. 52 (1964). R. Farquharson, *The Theory of Voting* (New Haven, 1969). M. Fréchet and J. v. Neumann, "Commentary on the Three Notes of Émile Borel," *Econometrica,* **21** (1953), 118–27. P. C. Fishburn, *Utility Theory for Decision Making* (New York, 1970). K. P. Heiss, "Game Theory and Human Conflicts,"

Methods of Operations Research, **5** (1968), 182–204. Johan Huizinga, *Homo Ludens* (Leyden, 1938). G. Klaus, *Spieltheorie in Philosophischer Sicht* (Berlin, 1968). W. Krelle, *Präferenz und Entscheidungstheorie* (Tübingen, 1968). H. W. Kuhn, A. W. Tucker, et al., eds., *Contributions to the Theory of Games,* 4 vols. (Princeton, 1950–59); Bibliography in Vol. IV (1959), compiled by Dorothea M. Thompson and Gerald L. Thompson. G. W. Leibniz, "Annotatio de quibusdam ludis," *Miscellanea Berolinensia* (Berlin, 1710), p. 22. R. C. Lewontin, "Evolution and the Theory of Games," *Journal of Theoretical Biology,* **1** (1961), 382–403. W. F. Lucas, "A Game with No Solutions," *Bulletin of the American Mathematical Society,* **74** (1968), 237–39; idem, "Some Recent Developments in n-Person Game Theory," *SIAM Review,* **13** (1971). R. D. Luce and H. Raiffa, *Games and Decisions* (New York, 1957). Richard M. Martin, *Intension and Decision* (New York, 1963). K. Menger, "Das Unsicherheitsmoment in der Wertlehre," *Zeitschrift für Nationalökonomie,* **5** (1934), 459–85; trans. Wolfgang Schoellkopf, with the assistance of W. Giles Mellon, as "The Role of Uncertainty in Economics," in M. Shubik, ed., *Essays in Mathematical Economics in Honor of Oskar Morgenstern* (Princeton, 1967), pp. 211–31. J. W. Milnor, "Games Against Nature," in R. M. Thrall, C. H. Coombs, and R. L. Davis, eds., *Decision Processes* (New York, 1954). O. Morgenstern, *Wirtschaftsprognose, eine Untersuchung ihrer Voraussetzungen und Möglichkeiten* (Vienna, 1928); idem, "Vollkommene Voraussicht und Wirtschaftliches Gleichgewicht," *Zeitschrift für Nationalökonomie,* **6** (1935), 337–57; idem, "Pareto Optimum and Economic Organization," *Systeme und Methoden in den Wirtschafts und Sozialwissenschaften,* ed. N. Kloten (Tübingen, 1964), pp. 573–86; idem, in preparation, "History of Game Theory to 1944," *International Journal of Game Theory,* **1** (1972). Oskar Morgenstern and John von Neumann, *Theory of Games and Economic Behavior* (1944); 3rd ed. (Princeton, 1953). John von Neumann, "Zur Theorie der Gesellschaftsspiele," *Mathematische Annalen,* **100** (1928), 295–320; trans. Sonya Borgmann, in Kuhn, et al., IV, 13–42. O. Ore, *Cardano, The Gambling Scholar* (Princeton, 1953). V. Pareto, *Manuel d'économie politique* (Paris, 1909). J. Pfanzagl, "Subjective Probability derived from the Morgenstern-von Neumann Utility Concept," in M. Shubik, ed., *Essays in Mathematical Economics . . .* (Princeton, 1967), pp. 237–51. F. P. Ramsey, "Truth and Probability" (1926), reprinted in *The Foundations of Mathematics and Other Logical Essays* (New York, 1931). M. Reiss, "Beiträge zur Theorie des Solitärspiels," *Crelle's Journal,* **54** (1858), 344–79. W. Riker, *The Theory of Political Coalitions* (New Haven, 1962). L. S. Shapley and M. Shubik, *Competition, Welfare and the Theory of Games,* Vol. I, in preparation. M. Shubik, ed., *Game Theory and Related Approaches to Social Behavior* (New York, 1964). L. B. Slobodkin, "The Strategy of Evolution," *American Scientist,* **52**, No. 3 (1964), 342–56. P. Suppes, "The Philosophical Relevance of Decision Theory," *Journal of Philosophy,* **18** (1961), 605–14. J. Ville, "Sur la théorie générale des jeux où intervient l'habilité des joueurs," in Émile Borel, ed., *Traité du calcul des probabilités et de ses applications,* Vol. 4: *Applications diverses et conclusion* (Paris, 1938), 104–13.

A. Wald, *Statistical Decision Functions* (New York, 1950). James Waldegrave, Excerpt from a Letter (1713); see Baumol and Goldfeld, above. E. Zermelo, "Über eine Anwendung der Mengenlehre auf die Theorie des Schachspiels," *Proceedings of the Fifth International Congress of Mathematicians* (Cambridge, 1912), 2, 501–04.

OSKAR MORGENSTERN

[See also Art and Play; Axiomatization; **Chance;** Indeterminacy in Physics; **Probability; Social Welfare;** Utility.]

GENERAL WILL

THE PHRASE "general will" is ineluctably the property of one man, Jean Jacques Rousseau. He did not invent it, but he made its history.

Father Malebranche was the first well-known writer to put the words "general will" to philosophic use. In his first work he spoke of God's general will as accounting for all the laws of the phenomenal world and for grace. Cause and effect in the natural world are merely the "occasions" on which God's general will manifests itself (*De la recherche de la vérité,* Book I, Chs. I–IV; Book V, Chs. I–II). While this notion has little direct bearing upon politics, it is worth noting that from its origins the general will is a legislating organ. It was Montesquieu who transferred it from the theological to the social level. Although he knew Malebranche's work well, he did not find his outlook congenial and it is fairly certain that Montesquieu borrowed the phrase from an Italian jurist, Gian Vincenzo Gravina, who had, in a work on Roman law, spoken of the public or general will as the source of civil law. Montesquieu used the actual phrase *volonté générale* only once, but at a most important point, i.e., in discussing the separation of powers in England. Having explained the special autonomy and safeguards needed in order to keep the judiciary impartial, he turned to the executive and legislative powers, the latter being "the general will of the state, and the other the execution of that general will." Ideally, the legislative power should reside in the whole people, but that is not possible in large modern states, where representatives must act on behalf of the people. This had many advantages, if electoral districts were fairly drawn and if everybody had the vote except people "of so mean a station as to be deemed to have no will of their own" (*De l'esprit des lois* [1748], Part I, Book XI, sec. 6).

Although Rousseau was certainly familiar with and deeply influenced by Montesquieu's writings, he began to consider the notion of the general will together with

Denis Diderot when they were still close associates. In several articles that he wrote for the *Encyclopédie*, Diderot had found the expression useful but he never developed it extensively. In describing the growth of political thinking in Greece, he showed how law gradually came to replace the cycle of revenge. Only when the "general will," which must be opposed to the avenging "particular will," was finally established through law, was there an end to murder, rape, adultery, and parricide. In J. F. de Saint-Lambert's essay on the duties of the legislator, which was once attributed to Diderot, we also hear of the general will as a necessary guide; without it, legislators become tyrants, and "the spirit of community dies." Finally, in an article on Natural Right, to which Rousseau's *Économie politique* was meant to be a companion piece, Diderot defined the general will as the sense of justice shown by all mankind. Justice, he argued, must by definition be a general rule that has a source other than personal inclination. If it is to fix all of men's social duties, it must be universally valid, and it must, therefore, have its roots in the will and welfare of all mankind. It is, in fact, expressed in all actual social rules, however various and inadequate, and it is felt by all men when they express indignation or resentment. As such it is the force that restrains the particular, self-regarding wills in all men, individually and collectively. Fundamentally the general will, for Diderot, was the rule obliging mankind to do unto others as they would have others do unto them ("Grecs," "Droit Naturel," in *Encyclopédie*).

From the first Rousseau rejected the notion of a universal bond obliging mankind. As he reacted against the cosmopolitanism of his friend, he came to insist that a law obliging mankind in general was a fantasy and an evasion of immediate social duties. Only mutual obligations among members of a single civic body are binding and effective, he claimed (*Première version du contrat social*, Book I, Ch. II, pp. 447–54). Thus he returned to Montesquieu's view, that *vox populi* alone expressed *vox dei*, and the general will. It could be meaningful only in the small classical republic in which equality and virtue formed the spirit of the laws. Moreover, this spirit was not just a matter of consent to a form of government. The general will was an articulation of the entire patriotic ethos, of which Sparta was the ultimate symbol. For unlike Montesquieu, Rousseau refused to compromise with aristocratic civil liberty as it existed in modern Europe. Only the civic spirit of antiquity could maintain a general will (*Économie politique*, passim). This social republicanism also separated Rousseau's ideas decisively from the thought of Thomas Hobbes and Samuel von Pufendorf, who had, in the seventeenth century, also spoken of civil society as the creation of a union of wills, and as an artificial body endowed with a single sovereign, law-giving will. In Pufendorf's words, "a state is defined as a composite moral person whose will, intertwined and united by virtue of the compact of the many is regarded as the will of all, so that it can use the powers and resources of all for the common peace and security." This "will of the state" is the source of all public acts (*On the Duty of Man and the Citizen*, trans. F. G. Moore, New York [1927], Book II, Ch. VI, p. 108). For the theorists of monarchical absolutism, the will of the many existed only in order to be delegated. For Rousseau, on the contrary, no man or group ought ever to part with any fraction of the freedom to make its own decisions, because to do so is to renounce one's quality as a man. That is why "we will never be men until we are citizens" (*Première version du contrat social*, Book I, Ch. II, p. 453). Sovereignty, he wrote, is a "mere personification" that stands for the will of all which alone is "the order and supreme rule" in society, and one that the people ought never to delegate (*Lettres écrites de la montagne* [1764], VI, 201; *Contrat social* [1762], Book III, Ch. XV, pp. 95–98). The people, above all, are not everyone and anyone in a given place. They were all those who had no special wealth, talents, or powers (*Émile*, trans. B. Foxley, London [1948], pp. 186–87). In short, the common man alone stood to benefit from the civic republic.

The importance of the will for Rousseau was not merely social, but also psychological. He knew that men behaved differently in groups than in isolation, but "without a perfect knowledge of the inclinations of individuals" one could not understand society (ibid., p. 202). The general will only expressed collectively something that was a vital part of every person's moral life. The ability to make choices, to will one's aims, distinguishes men from other animals even in the state of nature. However, when men form societies they lose the capacity to act independently and sensibly in their own interest. The "situation" of society, while it arouses men's moral faculties, also deprives them of their self-reliance and kindles all kinds of self-destructive inner dispositions. Society stimulates a need for approbation and with it ambition and competition. Inequality and weakness become both personal attitudes and social institutions. The strong and rich strive for power; the weak and poor are driven by envy. Both join to sustain the worst of all social evils: institutionalized inequality. Society is thus a threat to human willpower, and a good education must concentrate on restoring that willpower (*Discours sur l'origine de l'inégalité*, 1754), for it is the sole inner force that men have to counteract the impact of their present social condition which is a mixed one, half natural and half social, and unjust and oppressive at all times.

Like John Locke, Rousseau regarded the will as a power of the mind, a psychological faculty. His contempt for metaphysics and for that part of it which deals with the will was boundless (*Émile*, pp. 236, 253). The function of the will was, according to Rousseau, not to direct specific actions, but to order men's passions. These passions are all good, as long as there is a will to keep them natural and in proper balance. Since happiness is the sole possible object of human striving, a good education develops the capacity to reject avoidable misery. It enforces resignation to necessity, first of all. Natural necessity, within and outside us must be accepted without a murmur. Opinion, however, is to be shaken off as a man pursues his real, rather than falsely defined, interests. Above all, he must be able to liberate his conscience which is an instinct, once it is aroused, and which is experienced just like physical pain or pleasure. Nothing is more satisfying than a sense of one's own goodness, nothing more painful than remorse. A man with a will capable of all that, is his own master. He wills what is necessary for his own felicity and does nothing except what he wills. That is freedom (ibid., p. 48). That is also the way to escape from the present torment of being torn between duty and inclination.

For an individual such freedom may mean withdrawal from society. For "man in general" a social cure for the diseases of inequality would be required. What "men in general" need is a general will to protect them against the general social and emotional forces which tend to victimize them. It is the will against inequality and all that stimulates and sustains it. For without equality there can be no liberty (*Contrat social*, Book II, Ch. IX, p. 61). That is the lesson of history. Only in a small, isolated, agrarian, patriotic republic in which men know each other and live under educative laws, given to them by a great legislator such as Lycurgus, would it be possible for them to be truly at peace with themselves and each other. Only then can vanity be redirected to public ends, xenophobia replace private ambition, and the sense of civic pride undermine that particular will that always seeks privileges. As such the "general will" for Rousseau was far less an historical probability, least of all a likely future, than a judgment against all actual societies. For all actual societies are based on a fraudulent social contract by which the rich dupe the poor into accepting legal restraint while they remain as free as ever to do as they please (ibid., Book I, Ch. IX, p. 39).

The great legislator must liberate a people from history, take them, as it were, right out of it, by steeling their will and character sufficiently to resist the full "force of circumstances," which always tends to inequality (ibid., Book II, Ch. IX, p. 61). That is why the will he instills is far more important than the contract that first creates civil society. All societies, good and bad, are based on generally accepted conventions. That is merely the definition of a society. All have contracts by which mere possession is transformed into socially protected property, but the terms are never really enforced equally or fairly (*Lettres écrites de la montagne*, VI, 199–205). The fact is that most men are stupid and readily deceived into doing what they do not really want to do.

Group pressure is generally irresistible and not only soldiers are moved by an "esprit de corps." All special orders, magistrates, priesthoods, professions, or any elite may be composed of personally upright, excellent members, who would, however, stop at no evil in order to maintain their collective status. Private aggression is not the great problem of society. It is organized, impersonal violence, and group vanity and group wills that lead to incessant war and to the rule of the strong over the weak (*Émile*, pp. 310–20; *Économie politique*, pp. 242–43; *L'État de guerre*, pp. 298–307). That is why in a well-regulated polity every citizen must look into himself and consult his own conscience before voting so that he will not be subject to the pressures of privilege-seeking groups. It is the influence of such pressures that the general will must combat, not the occasional selfishness of individuals or personal errors which cancel each other and are of no consequence. It is the conspiratorial activity of those who organize against equality that is to be dreaded (*Contrat social*, Book II, Ch. III, pp. 42–43). That is why the first condition of an effective social contract is that the rich must never be so rich and the poor so impoverished that the former can buy the latter. There must be no personal subjugation. Secondly, the general will must always be able to assert itself decisively against the magistrates.

The main function of regular assemblies of the citizens is to supervise the structure and performance of the government. The general will *does* very little. There is no need for new legislation. On the contrary, the people must merely hold to its ancient laws and customs which, thanks to the wisdom of the legislator, are the main sources of its well-being. Policy, even in matters of war and peace, is up to the government. The rulers can be counted on to remain patriotic "chiefs," as long as their interests are not allowed to diverge from that of the rest of the citizens. An everwatchful populace, asserting its will against all inequality, maintains that identity of interests (ibid., Book III, Ch. XVIII, pp. 100–04).

The general will is by definition always upright **277**

because it expresses the spirit of the people. Every society is based on public opinion. That is inevitable (ibid., Book IV, Ch. VII, pp. 122–23). The problem is to ensure that opinions beneficial to the people dominate. Now the people have an inherent interest in justice. For they know that exceptions to the rules will never be in their favor, but always in the interest of the few who are strong and shrewd. Injustice is self-injury for the people. Civic education must not only see to it that the people do not falter, but maintain their will, laws, and mores. For though the general will is certainly not the will of all, especially not when the people are corrupt, there can be no effective civic order unless most of the people are inspired by patriotic zeal most of the time. A minority may err; that is not serious, but when the majority ceases to possess a general will, then the republic is dead. Most governments, in their despotic group-urges, see to it that sooner or later this death will occur (ibid., Book III, Ch. XI, pp. 91–92).

The general will is not only "general" because it is the expression of the greatest single social interest of men in general: the inhibition of inequality. It is general also in its scope. It can only will what is genuinely useful to the sovereign people, and that is something the latter must be made to recognize itself. Moreover, the general will can only legislate; that is, create rules that apply impersonally to all citizens in exactly the same way. That is in a sense tautological, since the will to equality cannot, except when ill-informed or misdirected, will privileges. If it weakens, the rule of law is at an end. The *moi commun* of the citizens is overcome by vanity. Then the fraudulent contract of the rich and powerful replaces the sovereignty of the people. In such circumstances men obey, as they must, out of prudence and sensible fear. They continue to have moral obligations, but no civic duties. For no obligation can be binding unless men have accepted it openly and vocally. Tacit consent is meaningful only when it can become vocal at known and regular intervals. If the general will cannot be heard it cannot be said to exist. And in fact, it will be replaced by the rule of personal power which now is so thinly veiled under laws which serve only the rich. The sense of justice remains but its rule is gone (ibid., Book III, Chs. XII–XIV, XVII–XVIII, pp. 92–95, 99–102; Book IV, Chs. I–II, pp. 102–06; *Émile*, pp. 437–39). Unless each citizen is heard with the deference due to a member of the sovereign people and unless a genuine fraternity binds each citizen to every other there is no effective contract (*Économie politique*, passim; *Première version du contrat social*, Book II, Ch. IV, pp. 494–95). And unless there is an effective social contract, sustained by an active general will, political

society is merely a set of chains binding an "aggregation" of men not a genuine "association" fulfilling the deepest interests of ordinary men: peace and abundance. These are the benefits of a society, without the inequalities and oppression which are its usual burdens. That is why the general will is the will against inequality (*Contrat social*, Book II, Ch. I, pp. 39–40).

When it is recognized that the general will is a regulative law-maintaining force and not a governmental will, it is clear that the rights of minorities, other than those seeking to destroy equality, are not threatened by it. An individual may be "forced to be free," that is, made to abide by the conditions he has accepted when he joined the community; for as a lawbreaker he has returned to the rule of force which threatens his and every other citizen's freedom. That is inherent in the contract (ibid., Book II, Ch. VII, p. 36; Book II, Ch. V, pp. 46–48). The social contract may also include a unanimous agreement to accept future majority rule. When outvoted, therefore, a minority need not feel aggrieved. Moreover, any individual must be free to leave, without any difficulty, a society he no longer wishes to share, if he has fulfilled his obligations, which include military service in time of war (ibid., Book III, Ch. VIII, p. 102; Book IV, Ch. II, p. 105). The general will cannot, as the word "will" implies evidently enough, be imposed, but it can be ignored or become feeble in polities, as it does within individuals, when the negative pressures of their "situation" in society overwhelm them.

Rousseau's general will was thus neither a plan for revolution nor a design to say anything about actual societies except that they were irremediably unjust and would remain so as long as civilization continued on its predictable course, for the inherent tendency of inequality is to increase. The general will is not, however, in spite of its decidedly unhistorical character, a "higher" will. It is merely the will that properly educated ordinary people pursuing basic interests would follow if they were to organize themselves into units small and simple enough to suit their very limited political talents. For Rousseau this was the sum of the values that he felt the *philosophes* had rejected in their enthusiasm for an "enlightenment" and for forms of progress which corresponded to their own interests and neglected the real needs of the people among whom he, "the watchman's son," had grown up. That alone sufficed to ensure his continued uniqueness.

The ideological career of the "general will" began with the French Revolution when it became a vital part of public discourse. That accounts for its entire subsequent fate. Liberals never ceased to associate it with the Terror and socialists with the incomplete, merely political, revolution. Radical nationalists im-

278

mediately found some use for the notion and even conservative nationalism eventually discerned an appealing principle of social unity "above classes" in it. However, only the anarchists really believed in Rousseau's original conception, little as they cared for the man whom they, also, took to be the principal ideologist of the Revolution and of the new state that it had brought into being.

To see how the general will acquired its revolutionary reputation, one need only look at Abbé Sieyès' famous pamphlet *What Is the Third Estate?* (1789). The commonalty as a whole is now everything, the nobility no longer anything at all. The people, moreover, have a will to which Sieyès referred as the "national will" or the "will of the community." He may have eschewed the "general will" perhaps because he knew that he was not following Rousseau. For the people that will consists of everyone who happened to live at any given time in France. Rich and poor, ex-noble and commoner, corrupt or civic, all are part of the people, of an undifferentiated whole whose will, moreover, expresses itself indirectly through its government, the elected representatives. The general will was in fact on its way to becoming national self-determination, with one law made for all the citizens by its very own national government.

This course of development can be traced perfectly in the philosophy of J. G. Fichte. In his radical youth he was one of the few thinkers who accepted popular sovereignty as a necessary active force. Even if it could be represented, the common will, the actual will of the whole people, must always have an opportunity to become vocal. A special committee of "Ephors" must be set up to see that when the need arose the whole people would meet to reconsider the basic contract. Rousseau's Spartan republic, moreover, also appealed to him deeply. Even when he abandoned his populism in favor of an isolationist nationalism, which made social unity its highest aim, he retained much of Rousseau's vision of an educative polity that served the needs of the people, even if its voice was no longer to be heard (*Naturrecht*, 1796–97, secs. 16 and 17, trans. as *The Science of Rights;* and *Reden an die Deutsche Nation*, 1808, passim, trans. as *Addresses to the German Nation*). In effect nationalism became for him a means of both creating and expressing the general will after the humiliations of the Napoleonic Wars.

Hegel was perfectly right in recognizing that Fichte remained close to Rousseau because Fichte had no conception of a "higher" will. As such their ideas led directly to the Terror, according to Hegel. However, the "higher" will was not the only road away from radicalism. Benjamin Constant had also criticized Rousseau for ignoring freedom, but he was able to accept his general will as the principle that legitimized constitutional government. He thus simply gave it a new task. The protection of individual freedom replaced the battle against inequality. Constitutional government based on a broad suffrage providing equality before the law and personal freedom through the principle of the separation of powers, was, to Constant, the only alternative to the rule of force. Moreover, he recognized without outrage that the laws enacted and enforced by such a state would be the result of a bargaining process in which individual interests came to terms with each other. The result was superior to the particular will of any monarch or class, and indeed could be said to realize a general will whose sole aim was to permit the greatest degree of individual liberty, especially of intellectual expression (*Principes de politique*, in *Oeuvres*, Paris [1957], pp. 1099–1112, 1132–45).

It was left to Immanuel Kant to make the general will a "higher" will, divorced from the interests, desires, felicities, and other advantages that men might pursue. This was entirely in keeping with his conception of the individual moral will, which was the rational possibility of men's aspiring to moral self-determination in accordance with universally valid rules of conduct. It is a law-giving will that has freedom, conceived as self-imposed duties, as its one aim. And it is a higher will because it aims solely at a moral goodness that is recognized to have a universal human application. In politics that means that freedom was for Kant, as for Constant, the sole justification of the state. Moreover, Kant's legitimate republic is in no way different from Constant's idea of constitutional government. However, it is based not on an actual historical or psychological will, but on a hypothetical general will and social contract. These are the standards for judging the legitimacy of states. They stand for everything to which a people would morally have to agree, not only in domestic but also in international politics. For unlike Rousseau's general will, Kant's has a universal human scope. Equality of rights, impartial justice, and, above all, external freedom are the necessary conditions for realizing the rational moral will of men, but the actual people need not be heard, much less bring its "lower" will to bear directly on legislation. Bargains do not make right any more than force. For the legitimizing general will expresses only a moral aspiration, the will to freedom and to justice, and not the material interests of the people, nor those of the governments that Kant so heartily detested. It is the moral will of the individual applied to the organization of public life (e.g., *Metaphysik der Sitten*, Vol. I, secs. 43–52). It was also the last genuine expression of the original spirit of the Enlightenment.

The general will for Kant had no seat other than the individual, even if it was confined to his highest potentiality, his moral reason. It was only with Hegel that the national will acquired an existence apart from the wills of the citizens who composed the political order. Rejecting the individualism inherent in Rousseau and Kant, Hegel managed to resurrect Leviathan on a new basis. The state is the mind of the nation and its highest ethical will. Unlike Hobbes' artificial body, however, it does not serve men's natural needs for peace and well-being. Its legitimacy is derived from its historical necessity, its part in the development of mankind toward an ever-greater rationality. The state alone, in organizing a people, speaks and wills for it, because it alone gives it a rational form, which is its historically necessary structure. It acts for the people, but never through them. To the extent that individuals make the will of the state their own, they are also rational, but the validity of the state does not depend on this. It is guaranteed by historical forces which the state recognizes and consciously wills and acts upon (*Philosophy of Right*, secs. 257–360).

Such a degree of depersonalization was not altogether acceptable to Hegel's liberal English followers. They, therefore, attempted to reintroduce at least some aspects of the original popular will into the Hegelian state. T. H. Green thus insisted that the legitimacy of the state had to rest on its pursuit of the common good which was a matter of securing, and even enhancing, the rights of each citizen. That did not mean that the will of the majority was needed as an affirmation of the state's legitimacy, but it did recognize the general will as the expression of a valid demand for a common good. Without it only coercive force rules. In short, consent was given a greater part to play in defining the legitimate state (*The Principles of Political Obligation*, London [1941], pp. 80–141). It was, however, a very vaguely defined consent. In this respect Hegel was far less ambiguous. For if he did not make public opinion the final judge of legitimacy, he did not give the state that function either. Only philosophy, as the retrospective recognition of what had been and what had not been historically necessary, can really judge.

The attractions of the general will as a principle of unity in a period of considerable industrial strife, found its final panegyrist in Bernard Bosanquet. The state is the highest, most general organic unit to which men can aspire. It must, therefore, as a matter of sociological and psychological necessity be the source of the highest values. Its history is that of the general will gradually becoming more and more aware of itself as men organize society into an increasingly comprehensive unit, the nation state. It has claims on men above all lesser group and class allegiances, because it is the broadest possible, and therefore universally valid end to which men can direct their political efforts, or their wills. The state is the rational principle of the nation and the sole end of collective self-development (Bernard Bosanquet, *The Philosophic Theory of the State*, 1899).

For all these post-Revolutionary theorists, the general will played a part in the difficult effort to find a consensual basis to legitimize national governments. For the Hegelians, it also had the function of overcoming the narrow scope that liberalism had ascribed to politics. Rousseau was for them a link to the classical tradition that had regarded politics as the highest human activity. However, the revolutionary potentialities of that ideal made it necessary to refashion it, if it was to support the existing state order. That rendered it relatively insignificant also.

Anarchism, especially Pierre Joseph Proudhon's doctrine, for all its un-Rousseauian radicalism, was closest to the original conception. To be sure, Proudhon's faith in progress dampened his voluntarism, as it had Hegel's. Moreover, Proudhon hated Rousseau, whom he took to be the primary ideologue of the "bourgeois" and statist Revolution. What had Rousseau known of economic laws, he asked? However, Proudhon's notion of justice as mutuality, as openly, directly, and continually renewed agreements between members of small groups and among such groups, is just what Rousseau had meant by a living social contract. Not the justice imposed from above, by God or by abstract law or by a state, but only the inherent feeling of community and of clearly understood self-interest expressed in personally made, mutual binding agreements, create true obligations. That was Proudhon's notion of immanent justice no less than Rousseau's. Identity of interests and "the abolition of the opposition of the social law and the will of the individual," Proudhon wrote, must be the basis of a viable social order. He also put his trust in the common people, "as an organized union of wills that are individually free and that can and should voluntarily work together." For Proudhon insisted, as Rousseau had, that the social contract involved not government but the whole social and moral environment in which simple people might live decent and satisfying lives. That is why his form of socialist anarchism was the only real effort to develop Rousseau's idea of the general will, rather than an attempt to integrate it into an inegalitarian order (P. J. Proudhon, *Idée générale de la Révolution au XIXe siècle*, in *Oeuvres complètes*, Paris [1923], pp. 182–236; 267–331; *De la justice*, ibid., I, 420–30).

The overwhelming problem of political thought in the nineteenth century was how to cope with the

Revolution. Rousseau had been remote from that concern, but to the extent that he was taken to speak for the forces of upheaval, his idea of the general will, especially, became a political force that had to be contained or redirected. The result was nothing if not ironic: the last defender of the agrarian republic was transformed into the founding father of the modern nation state, and the general will of the European peasantry was made to serve as the justification for industrial progress and political centralization.

BIBLIOGRAPHY

Translations refer to the editions to which references may be made. There are numerous versions of many standard works cited here.

Bernard Bosanquet, *The Philosophical Theory of the State* (London, 1899; reprint 1965). Benjamin Constant, *Principes de politique* (1815), in *Oeuvres* (Paris, 1957). Denis Diderot, ed., *Encyclopédie* (1751–80), in *Oeuvres complètes* (Paris, 1876), Vols. XIV–XV. J. G. Fichte, *Grundlage des Naturrechts* (1796–97), in *Sämtliche Werke* (Berlin, 1845), Vol. III; idem, *The Science of Rights*, trans. A. E. Kroeger (Philadelphia, 1869; London, 1889); idem, *Der geschlossene Handelsstaat* (1800), in *Sämtliche Werke*, Vol. III; idem, *Addresses to the German Nation*, trans. R. F. Jones and G. H. Turnbull, ed. G. A. Kelly (New York, 1968). T. H. Green, *Lectures on the Principles of Political Obligation* (London, 1882; 1941). G. W. F. Hegel, *The Philosophy of Right* (1821), trans. T. M. Knox (Oxford, 1942). Immanuel Kant, *Über den Gemeinspruch: Das mag in der Theorie richtig sein, taugt aber nichts für die Praxis* (1793), in *Werke* (Berlin, 1914), Vol. VI; idem, *Zum ewigen Frieden* (1795), ibid.; *The Philosophy of Kant*, trans. and ed. C. J. Friedrich (New York, 1949); idem, *Die Metaphysik der Sitten* (1797), in *Werke*, Vol. III; idem, *The Philosophy of Law*, trans. W. Hastie (Edinburgh, 1887). Nicolas de Malebranche, *De la recherche de la vérité* (1674–75; Paris, 1962). Charles de Secondat de Montesquieu, *L'Esprit des lois* (1748), in *Oeuvres complètes* (Paris, 1950), Vol. I; trans. Thomas Nugent as *The Spirit of the Laws* (New York, 1949). P. J. Proudhon, *Idée générale de la révolution au XIXe siècle* (1851), in *Oeuvres complètes* (Paris, 1923), Vol. III; trans. J. B. Robinson as *General Idea of Revolution in the Nineteenth Century* (London, 1923); idem, *De la justice dans la révolution et dans l'église* (1858), in *Oeuvres*, op. cit., Vol. IX. Samuel von Pufendorf, *On the Duty of Man and the Citizen According to the Natural Law* (1673), trans. F. G. Moore (New York, 1927). J. J. Rousseau, *Émile* (1762), trans. B. Foxley (London, 1948); idem, *Political Writings*, ed. C. E. Vaughan, 2 vols. (Cambridge, 1915; reprint Oxford and New York, 1962); idem, *The Social Contract and Discourses*, trans. G. D. H. Cole (London and New York, 1950). Emmanuel Sieyès, *Qu'est-ce que le Tiers État?* (1789; Paris, 1888), trans. H. Blondel as *What Is the Third Estate?* (London, 1963).

Secondary Sources. John Bowle, *Politics and Opinion in the Nineteenth Century* (London and New York, 1954). Ernst Cassirer, *Rousseau, Kant, and Goethe* (Princeton, 1945; also reprint). Alfred Cobban, *Rousseau and the Modern State*, 2nd ed. (London, 1964), contains a history of Rousseau interpretations. Robert Derathé, *Jean-Jacques Rousseau et la science politique de son temps* (Paris, 1950). Ginette Dreyfus, *La volonté selon Malebranche* (Paris, 1958). C. W. Hendel, *Jean-Jacques Rousseau: Moralist*, 2 vols. (London, 1934), Vol. I, Ch. V, a history of the idea of general will. Roger D. Masters, *The Political Philosophy of Rousseau* (Princeton, 1968), has an excellent bibliography.

JUDITH N. SHKLAR

[See also Anarchism; **Democracy;** Equality; Hegelian . . . ; **Liberalism;** Marxism; **Social Contract;** State; *Vox populi*.]

GENETIC CONTINUITY

All Life from Life of Its Own Kind. By genetic continuity we mean not only that all life comes from life (the "Law of Biogenesis"), but more particularly that each organism comes from one or two parents of its own species. It thus inherits its characteristics in unbroken lineage from its ancestors, to the beginning of its species on earth, and, if we accept the Theory of Evolution, to the beginnings of all life on earth.

That living beings come from parents of their own kind is an observation as old as man, but the conviction that they can arise only in that manner was for ages in dispute. The book of Genesis, in relating the Creation Story, says that each creature brought forth "according to its kind." Aristotle, writing in the fourth century B.C., is more specific. In the *Generation of Animals* (Loeb Classical Library, 747b 30–35), he wrote: "In the normal course of nature the offspring which a male and a female of the same species produce is a male or female of that same species—for instance, the offspring of a male dog and a female dog is a male dog or a female dog." Yet the Bible affords witness of the common belief that the lower orders of life could be generated otherwise, as when Samson found "bees" in the carcass of a lion he had killed. Aristotle, too, believed in the spontaneous generation of living things, for in the *History of Animals* he says:

For some plants are generated from the seed of plants, whilst other plants are self-generated through the formation of some elemental principle similar to a seed. . . . So with animals, some spring from parent animals, according to their kind, whilst others grow spontaneously and not from kindred stock; and of these instances of spontaneous generation some come from putrefying earth or vegetable matter, as is the case with a number of insects, while others are spontaneously generated in the inside of animals out of the secretions of their several organs (trans. D'Arcy Thompson, Book V, 539a 16–26).

281

Before men could accept the view that heredity results from a biological mechanism of some sort, the ghost of spontaneous generation had to be laid. For Aristotle, the greatest biologist of ancient times, and for all those who followed his ideas so unhesitatingly until the year 1600 or later, the pattern of development was accounted for by the Final Cause and the Formal Cause, the former being the End for which the organism exists, and the latter being the *logos,* or essential nature of the organism. Of the Greek philosopher's four causes, the Material Cause was supplied by the female parent and the Motive (Efficient) Cause was supplied by the male parent. These two Causes supply substance and energy; but there is no indication that the Formal Cause is in any way transmitted from the parents. It is more allied to the Final Cause, and exists in the very nature of things. Hence, given the presence of the proper Formal and Final Causes, a particular animal might just as readily originate from slime or filth or decaying matter as from the substance and energizing force provided by parents of the same species.

The scientific disproof of the idea of spontaneous generation required a series of investigations extending over two centuries, beginning with the experiments of Francesco Redi in 1668 and ending with those of Louis Pasteur in 1860–64. Redi succeeded in showing that blowflies lay the eggs from which maggots develop in putrefying meat, and that in the absence of the eggs no maggots, and subsequently no flies, make their appearance, even though the meat decays. The method was simple, and affords a fine example of a scientific experiment involving a control. Some vessels containing meat of various kinds were left open; others were closed with paper and sealed. In the former the flies laid eggs, and in due course the maggots made their appearance; the sealed vessels remained free of "worms." Later, in order to answer the objection that the sealing of the vessels might have prevented free access of air, Redi performed other controlled experiments in which some of the vessels were covered with fine Naples netting, that would admit air but exclude flies. In some experiments a double protection was provided by adding a second shelter of net. Flies laid eggs on the meshes of the cloth and the eggs developed into maggots, but if the mesh was fine enough to keep them from dropping through, not a single worm appeared in the putrid meat.

Even so, Redi retained a belief that in certain other cases—the origin of parasites inside the human or animal body or of grubs inside of oak galls—there must be spontaneous generation. Bit by bit the evidence grew against such views. In 1670 Jan Swammerdam, painstaking student of the insect's life cycle, suggested that the grubs in galls were enclosed in them for the sake of nourishment and must come from insects that had inserted their semen or their eggs into the plants. In 1687 Antony (Antonij) van Leeuwenhoek, in one of his famous letters to the newly founded Royal Society in London, described how a surgeon brought to him some excised tissues from the leg of a patient. The tissue had in it worms that the surgeon thought had originated spontaneously. Leeuwenhoek readily recognized them as being insect larvae, removed them to a piece of beef, found they grew and transformed into pupae, and eventually hatched into flies. These, having mated, produced fertile eggs from which maggots like the original ones soon developed. Leeuwenhoek, although he performed no critical experiments to test his belief, strongly denied that any of the microscopic protozoans and bacteria he had discovered arose spontaneously. "No creature takes birth without generation," he wrote in 1694 (Letter 83).

Meanwhile (1700–11), Antonio Vallisneri, who was a student of the great anatomist Marcello Malpighi (1628–94), turned his attention to the nature of plant galls, and proved that Swammerdam had been entirely correct in his conjecture. Galls indeed arise from the stinging of the plant tissues by the ovipositors of female gall wasps, and the egg laid in the plant tissues develops inside the gall into a grub, which eventually emerges full-grown and transformed into a mature gall wasp. Although the mystery of the generation of intestinal worms and the muscle-embedded cysticerci of tapeworms was not to be solved until 1832, it may fairly be said that Redi, Leeuwenhoek, Swammerdam, Malpighi, and Vallisneri wrought a revolution in biological thought hardly second to that of the nineteenth-century theory of organic evolution. The belief in spontaneous generation, though still held by common folk and by some scientists, was disproved in the main and was suspect in entirety. Genetic continuity was established as the normal if not the only pattern of life. Young developing organisms grow into adults like their parents because they have the parents they do. Presumably, then, they inherit some material basis that holds them to the pattern of development that is characteristic of their own species. A new question began to arise: what might this material basis of genetic continuity be?

By 1711, when Vallisneri was completing his studies on the gall wasps, a French biologist, Louis Joblot, was undertaking to test Leeuwenhoek's belief that even protozoans and bacteria arise from parents of their own kind. He prepared a boiled hay infusion, in which these organisms commonly appear. Some vessels were covered with parchment, others were left uncovered. After several days the microorganisms appeared in vast numbers in the infusions left exposed, but not in the closed ones. There was much talk of "vital forces" in those days, so to avoid the criticism that by closing the vessels the hay infusion in them had lost some vital force, Joblot after a time removed the coverings from the closed vessels. These were soon teeming with microorganisms.

Later experimenters, especially John Turberville Needham, were not satisfied. Needham repeated this type of experiment many times (1748–50), using boiled mutton gravy and infusions of boiled seeds. He used corks to close his flasks. The results: bacteria appeared in the corked vessels as well as in the open ones. Spontaneous generation, at least for bacteria, thus remained an unsettled question. Later in the century, in 1765, the Abbé Lazzaro Spallanzani, perhaps the greatest experimental biologist of his time, reinvestigated Needham's results by more refined methods. He found that infusions of seeds, even when most carefully sealed, had to be boiled a long time (e.g., 45 minutes) to remain free of microbial growth. Needham had used corks sealed with mastic, and had merely set his flasks by the fire at a temperature he thought sufficient to kill all organisms. Spallanzani used glass flasks with slender necks that could be fused in a flame and were thus sealed hermetically beyond all doubt. The flasks containing infusion were then immersed in boiling water for 45 minutes. His sealed flasks remained clear and free of organisms; the controls became turbid with bacterial growth. Still the argument was not settled. Needham maintained that the severe heating had destroyed the capacity of the infusions to support life. Spallanzani triumphantly broke the fused necks of the flasks and showed that bacterial growth promptly occurred in them. Then Needham maintained, and quite correctly, that the heating led to the expansion of the air in the flasks prior to the fusion of the necks, and that after cooling there would consequently be a low pressure or partial vacuum in the flasks. When one broke the necks of the sealed flasks one could actually hear the whistle of the entering air. Air is necessary for the generation of life, claimed Needham, and Spallanzani's experiments were therefore not conclusive. There the matter rested for the time being.

When microscopes with achromatic lenses became available in the 1830's, and good resolution at a magnification of 400 diameters was possible, interest focused on the globules always to be seen in fermenting liquors. The earliest conception of the nature of fermentation, from Antoine Lavoisier through J. J. Berzelius to Justus von Liebig, was that it was a strictly chemical process. Then, in 1835 to 1838, Charles Cagniard de Latour and Theodor Schwann independently reported that alcoholic fermentation is invariably associated with, and depends upon, the presence of microscopic yeast cells. These were capable of reproduction and were identified as plant cells. They caused the fermentation of sugar only when they were alive, for Schwann showed that boiling killed them and that neither fermentation nor putrefaction occurred after boiling, if all air admitted to the vessel was heated prior to entry. In similar experiments F. F. Schulze used sulfuric acid to purify the air entering the flasks; and in 1854 H. G. F. Schröder and T. von Dusch introduced the use of plugs of cotton wool, which proved effective in excluding dust and bacteria by mechanically filtering the air admitted to the sterile flasks. The chemists J. J. Berzelius, Friedrich Wöhler, and J. Liebig were not satisfied. Heat, strong chemicals, or even mechanical filtration might in some way denature the air. Liebig admitted that yeast played a role, but he insisted that the fermentation was brought about by some soluble substance formed through decomposition. Louis Pasteur, from 1857 to 1860, disputed with Liebig the issue of a vital versus a purely chemical character of fermentation.

At this time the bacteriologist F. A. Pouchet claimed that he had actually demonstrated the spontaneous origin of microorganisms during fermentation and putrefaction. Pasteur set himself to reexamine the bases of the ancient controversy. From 1861 to 1864 he conducted his crucial experiments. He made microscopic observations of particles trapped from the air and showed that there were many bodies capable of living growth floating in it. He confirmed Schwann's experiments with heated air. Most convincingly, he made flasks with long S-curved necks open to the air at the tips, and demonstrated that liquid media capable of supporting bacterial growth will remain sterile in such flasks after boiling, unless even so little as a drop flows into the final curve of the flask's neck, where dust might have collected, and is then permitted to flow back into the body of the flask. He examined the air on a glacier high on Mont Blanc and found it to be free of floating bacteria. Some of these flasks, with their contents still sterile, are preserved to this day in the Pasteur Institute in Paris. Similar flasks, exposed to the air of the city, became heavily contaminated. Even blood remained sterile when collected with sufficient precautions to exclude bacterial pollution.

On the other hand, Pasteur's methods of sterilization by means of a single exposure to boiling temperature did not always prove effective; and Pouchet, who used hay infusions rather than nutritive broth as a medium, would have won his point—at least for a time—had he not lost his courage or his conviction. John Tyndall in 1877 studied the phenomenon just described, and found that by boiling for intermittent periods of not longer than a minute at intervals of 12 hours, sterilization could be obtained even in cases where a single boiling was ineffective. He was thus led to postulate the existence of highly resistant "germs." Ferdinand Cohn, using similar methods, discovered the formation of spores by *Bacillus subtilis* in hay infusions, and then demonstrated that a single boiling will not kill the spores but that, after these have once germinated, even a very short exposure to a high temperature will kill all the organisms present. Tyndall, who was a physicist, also used optical methods to demonstrate that there is dust in even the stillest air—and asserted that where there is dust there are germs.

The establishment of the Germ Theory of Disease is thus intimately related with the final establishment of the fact of Genetic Continuity. But the fact that there *is* genetic continuity only raises the question of its mechanism. The eighteenth-century preformationists, of whom Spallanzani was one and his friend Charles Bonnet another, were the avowed mechanists of their day. To them the idea that nutritive or hereditary particles, derived either from the environment or from an organism's parents, could of their own accord become organized into all the complexity of a living being was preposterous. Something preorganized must itself be transmitted from parents (or parent) to offspring, to serve as a substructure and guide in the course of development. The preformationists—who were in the great majority among eighteenth-century biologists—were thus convinced that either the ovum or the sperm contains the germ of the future being, just as one finds a small embryo plant within a seed. To some preformationists this conviction meant the presence of a little homunculus within the head of the sperm, while the female parent would supply only nutriment for the growth of the next generation. To others, the ovists, the germ or embryo lay in the egg, and the semen or sperm of the male merely activated its development. The more sophisticated of the preformationists, such as Bonnet, though at first charmed by the idea of the infinite, or nearly infinite, array of embryos within embryos going back to Mother Eve or to the first female of every other species, nevertheless admitted in the face of the evidence of reproduction by budding that such a concept was too crude.

It was in particular the consideration of the formation of buds by *Hydra*, the little freshwater polyp discovered by his cousin Abraham Trembley, that forced Bonnet to a more general conclusion. The hydra's bud can form anywhere on its body and it clearly does not contain parts within it, like the bud of a plant, all ready to expand and unfold. It is a mere bump, an excrescence. Yet, as it grows in size, it puts forth tentacles, develops a mouth between them, and becomes a fully formed polyp of the same species as

the parent. There must then be something, reasoned Bonnet, to make this happen, something that was present from the beginning of the growth of the bud— "certain particles which have been preorganized in such a way that a little polyp results from their development" (*Palingénésie,* "Tableau des Considérations," Art. XV). Since the polyp can regenerate itself from any part of its body when cut into small pieces, the preorganized particles must exist in every part of the whole. The "germ," then, is not necessarily a miniature organism, it is "every preordination, every preformation of parts capable by itself of determining the existence of a Plant or of an Animal" (ibid.). It is, in Bonnet's further words,

. . . the *primordial foundation,* on which the nutritive molecules went to work to increase in every direction the dimensions of the parts. [It is] a network, the elements of which formed the meshes. The nutritive molecules, incorporating themselves into these meshes, tended to enlarge them (*Palingénésie,* Part VII, Ch. IV).

Evidently Bonnet's real opinions were far different from the ludicrous view commonly attributed to him. He clearly saw the need for a material pattern that from the beginning of each life would control the hereditary course of its development, and that would of necessity be transmitted from the parent generation to the offspring. Here, however, lay the unresolved difficulty.

The dilemma was most clearly pointed out in 1745 by Pierre Louis Moreau de Maupertuis, Bonnet's contemporary. There is abundant evidence that in sexually reproducing species the offspring inherit characteristics from both their male and their female parents. In fact, the very same characteristic can be transmitted in one and the same family, at times through the female and at others through the male line. Maupertuis studied the inheritance of polydactyly in a Berlin family over four generations and demonstrated this matter conclusively. How, then, can a preformed embryo, or even a preorganized particulate system, be involved? Whatever is transmitted from parents to offspring, it must be provided equally by both male and female parents.

The facts led Maupertuis to a daring speculation. Let us suppose, he wrote, that particles corresponding to every part of the offspring are provided by each of the parents and that in the generation of the embryo they find their way into the right places by reason of chemical affinity between like particles. Then corresponding particles will unite, and those that should be next to each other to form a part properly will be attracted together and by their union will exclude less appropriate associations. The embryo will thus be built up in the correct hereditary pattern of its species, but since now the paternal and now the maternal particles will be utilized, the hereditary character may resemble the condition in either one of the parents.

Maupertuis' particulate theory of heredity was not accepted in its time, because the very idea of chemical attraction on the basis of affinity was too novel. And to be sure, Maupertuis confused the hereditary particles with the effects they produce and with the parts whose development they control. In those respects Bonnet had clearer insight. But after all, the time was nearly a century before the formulation of the Cell Theory or any recognition of the microscopic elements upon which heredity might depend. To see that at bottom heredity must depend on a sort of organic, chemical memory, and to attribute this capacity to separable particles that maintain their intrinsic nature when in combination was extraordinary enough. This fundamental idea led Maupertuis further to suggest that defective development—leading to the formation of monsters—might arise from excesses in numbers or deficiencies of the particles; that the particles might undergo novel alterations giving rise to new hereditary types; and even that the isolation of these forms in different parts of the earth might lead to the origin of new species.

Although Maupertuis' ideas of heredity were far in advance of the more general notions of a blending of parental characteristics and a loss of hereditary variability in the population through the mere action of interbreeding and hybridization, they had little heuristic value; that is, they stimulated few experiments. In the absence of any chemical and cytological knowledge of the physical basis of heredity they could not be tested, and soon they were forgotten. Similarly, one might say that Bonnet's views prefigure some of the more important modern ideas of the relation of the genetic pattern, or genotype, to the course of development and the production of a phenotype, or assemblage of final characteristics. Again, there was no way to test such ideas until the eventual development of experimental embryology. Yet it may fairly be said that had Darwin and others of his generation had a proper knowledge of the ideas of Maupertuis and Bonnet, much fruitless theoretical speculation about heredity might have been avoided.

Nothing has arisen to disturb the generality of this principle. When plant, animal, and bacterial viruses were discovered (1892–1918), the ghost of spontaneous generation was evoked by some who were puzzled over the release of viruses from healthy organisms. Further investigations, however, disclosed that besides existing in their typical virulent, infectious state, many viruses are capable of adapting themselves so successfully to their hosts that they may live within the host cells in an avirulent, symbiotic or latent condition from which, under appropriate conditions, they may be released after long periods of time. In some cases the latent viruses may even be transmitted from one generation of host organisms to the next by being included in the reproductive cells or buds from which the offspring arise. Thus they become virtually an inherited trait of the host species! Nevertheless, for viruses too, *omnium vivum ex vivo.*

Every Cell from a Cell. The early formulations of the Cell Theory, especially in the classic form stated by Matthias Schleiden and Theodor Schwann in 1839, were not helpful to the development of the concept of genetic continuity. At the turn of the century (1802) K. Sprengel had thought that cells originate inside of other cells in the form of granules or vesicles. He probably mistook starch grains for newly forming cells. Nevertheless, and in spite of criticism by others, this mistaken idea was adopted by others and was accepted even by Schleiden himself as late as 1849. As for Schwann, he seems to have gotten his ideas of the formation of new cells from the notions of Christian Friedrich Wolff almost a century earlier (1759; 1768). Schwann, in brief, thought that new cells might form outside existing cells in the midst of a ground substance supposed to exist between the cells, or alternatively that they might form inside of the older cells by a kind of crystallization from the mother liquor. Better ideas of the genetic continuity of cells were to be based upon the discovery made by Robert Brown, in 1831, that a nucleus is a regular feature of each cell in a flowering plant. (It is not true, though often so stated, that Robert Brown discovered the nuclei of cells. They had been seen many times before. What he actually did was to develop a general concept of the essentiality of the nucleus for the cell.) Schleiden and Schwann recognized the importance of this concept, and Schwann's work on animal cells, such as the cells of the notochord and developing cartilage in embryos, made it possible to extend the concept to the cells of animals as well as of plants.

Cell division had already been observed carefully and critically by a number of workers: by J. P. F. Turpin (1826) and B. C. Dumortier (1823) in filamentous algae, by Hugo von Mohl (1835–39) in filamentous algae and in the club moss *Anthoceros;* by J. Meyen (1830) in green algae, the mycelia of molds, and the terminal buds and root tips of flowering plants; and by C. G. Ehrenberg (1833) in the fission of various protozoans. It was especially Meyen and von Mohl who most vigorously opposed the views of cell formation put forward by Schleiden and Schwann and who maintained that on the contrary cells arise by self-division. Over the two decades from 1840 to 1860, these views were supported on the botanical side by F. Unger and Carl Nägeli, and on the zoological side by A. Kölliker, R. Remak, and Rudolf Virchow. These men first succeeded in obtaining an admission that cells do arise by division, and ultimately that they arise only in that manner. Virchow's aphorism, so often quoted —Omnis cellula e cellula—merely put a period to the long dispute. It is very significant that both Remak and Virchow opposed Schleiden's and Schwann's idea of free cell formation because they regarded it as equivalent to spontaneous generation.

Great changes in point of view rarely occur abruptly. Although Virchow's and Remak's views eventually carried the day and laid the foundation for the concept of cellular continuity that is a basic corollary of overall genetic continuity, the arguments continued for some time after 1855. There were still many biologists who believed that while cells might arise by division of preexisting cells, they could also arise by free cell formation. But slowly the increasing weight of evidence and scientific opinion prevailed.

One of the most important early observations made on the nature of cell divison was Nägeli's observation that the nuclei of the two daughter cells are derived from the division of the parent nucleus. (He saw this in the stamen hairs of the spiderwort Tradescantia, still a classic material for demonstrations of mitosis to biology students of all ages.) Nägeli, however, thought that division of the nucleus was exceptional. By laborious and careful work Wilhelm Hofmeister (in 1848–49), using the same material, detected the breakdown of the nuclear membrane prior to divison of the cell, and with remarkable clarity he figured the presence of a cluster of what were later to be called chromosomes. According to his observations these separated into two groups, each of which became reconstituted into one of the daughter nuclei. Considering that all of this was observed without the benefit of staining and with the imperfect microscopes of the time, it was a truly remarkable achievement. But the fact that others were unable to see nearly as much left them unconvinced that Hofmeister was correct.

It was the zoologists, who were working largely with separate dividing cells, such as blood cells in the chick embryo or the dividing cells of newly fertilized eggs of marine invertebrates, who seem first to have become convinced that nuclear division is invariably a part of cell division. Remak saw the chick's blood cells in late stages of division, when connected by a narrow stalk, and he observed that a fine thread connected the daughter nuclei. He also figured the star-shaped asters in some dividing cells. Some of the animal cytologists became convinced that the original nucleus becomes dissolved in the course of each cell division, and that

the daughter nuclei are reconstituted within each daughter cell; but by 1852 Remak concluded that the nuclear material does in fact persist from one cell generation to the next. A most remarkable failure of interpretation at this time was that of E. G. Balbiani, who in 1861 was one of the very first biologists to apply a fixative and then a stain, carmine, to produce a degree of selective staining of different parts of the cell. Observing ciliate protozoans during their conjugation, he was misled into thinking of them as animals with organ systems analogous to those of multicellular animals. Thus he interpreted the micronuclei as the "testes" of the protozoan and completely missed the significance of the beautiful examples of mitosis which he actually saw and figured.

To sum up, by 1870 it was generally believed that cells arise only from parent cells, but the origin of the daughter nuclei from a parent nucleus remained in some doubt because of the dissolution of the parent nucleus at the commencement of cell division. What was needed was a clear and unmistakable sign that the principal bodies within the nucleus, namely, the chromosomes, possess their own genetic continuity.

Every Chromosome from a Chromosome. In the establishment of the concept of genetic continuity, the decade following 1873 was a crucial period. During these years the details of mitotic cell division were worked out, step by step, by a considerable number of cytologists, among whom Eduard Strasburger, working on plant materials, and Walther Flemming, working on animal materials, were leaders. Many of these researches were closely connected with the study of the events of gametogenesis and fertilization. Here we shall look simply at the discovery of the sequence of events in the division of the cell and its nucleus, a towering achievement of nineteenth-century biology, fully as important as the Cell Theory itself. One may sharply contrast this remarkable development of biological science with the advent of Mendelian genetics, or of Darwin's Theory of the Origin of Species by means of Natural Selection, for both of those achievements were largely the creation of single men, whereas in the unfolding of mitosis many individuals contributed essential parts. In that respect the discovery of mitotic cell division was an advance more like those of genetics in the twentieth century, when the Chromosome Theory of Heredity and the elucidation of the roles of DNA and the nature of the genetic code have required the labors of many persons, even though some individuals may stand out as leaders or originators.

In the year 1900 the American cytologist E. B. Wilson, whose own work on genetic continuity was to be so fruitful, wrote in the first edition of The Cell in Development and Inheritance (p. 46) the following words: "It was not until 1873 that the way was opened for a better understanding of the matter. In this year the discoveries by Anton Schneider, quickly followed by others in the same direction by Otto Bütschli, Hermann Fol, Eduard Strasburger, Eduard van Beneden, Flemming, and Hertwig, showed cell-division to be a far more elaborate process than had been supposed . . ."—supposed, that is, by Remak and others, who thought that nuclear and cell division represented simply a pinching in two of the nucleus and the body of the cell.

First it became evident that cell division is regularly associated with the formation in the cell of an achromatic (nonstainable) figure called the *spindle*. Fol saw the initiation and growth of two asters in each dividing cell of the sea urchin egg, and Otto Bütschli observed that a spindle-shaped structure, also achromatic, is formed between the asters and is eventually cut through by a deepening constriction or furrow around the cell in the plane of the equator of the spindle. By 1875 Strasburger had shown that in the typical plant cell things happen somewhat differently. A spindle is indeed produced, but there are no asters at its poles, and no furrow constricts the dividing cell. Instead, a cell plate is formed across the equator of the spindle, and gradually extends beyond the spindle until it meets the old cell walls on all four sides. The new, rigid cell wall separating the daughter cells is then deposited in layers on either side of the cell plate.

As for the nuclear elements themselves, Fol showed that they can be brought back into view after the nuclear membrane has dissolved, and then in 1873 A. Schneider, and shortly thereafter I. Tschistiakoff, stained and observed the bodies later to be named chromosomes. These structures of the cell were especially well observed in the studies of Strasburger on dividing plant cells and of Balbiani on those of a grasshopper. The stained structures, rodlike in the grasshopper but often angled or V-shaped in the plant material, were found to cluster on the center of the spindle. They then divided—Strasburger thought it to be transversely—and the two parts thus formed moved to opposite poles of the spindle. Oscar Hertwig showed that these two groups of chromosomes reconstitute the nuclei of the daughter cells; and Strasburger showed that in his plant cells, well before the spindle is formed, the chromosomes are to be seen within the nucleus as long, twisted double threads, which later shorten and thicken.

Walther Flemming confirmed that this is also characteristic of animal cells, and in 1879 he added a most significant observation: the division of each chromosome to make two is *longitudinal*, not transverse. The succession of the stages of mitosis deduced from fixed and stained material was shown to be correct by Flemming and W. Schleicher by observing cell division in living material. By 1880 and 1882, when Strasburger's third edition of *Zellbildung und Zelltheilung* ("Cell Structure and Cell Division") and Flemming's *Zellsubstanz, Kern und Zelltheilung* ("Cell Substance, Nucleus, and Cell Division") respectively appeared, the story of mitosis was almost complete. The final proof that the longitudinal halves of each split chromosome separate and move to opposite poles was provided for animal cells by van Beneden in 1883 and for plant cells by F. Heuser in 1884.

It is a striking fact that the two greatest contributors to the unfolding of the nature of the mitotic process, Strasburger and Flemming, were each responsible for a serious misconception that plagued later students for many years. Strasburger's error, the conception of the transverse division of the chromosomes, offered a serious block to recognition that the elements of heredity might be linearly arranged within the chromosomes; for of course, if a chromosome really divided transversely, either its two parts would be genetically different, or else each chromosome could contain only a single genetic element to be duplicated and apportioned to the daughter cells. Strasburger recognized his error, however, in a few years. Flemming, on the other hand, clung to his erroneous view that all the chromosomes are at first united into one long continuous thread, a "spireme," which later breaks up into the separate chromosomes. This conception, which was based simply on inadequate observations of the number of free chromosome ends in the early prophase nuclei, was less in conflict with any of the principles of genetics, and had a much longer life. Even in the middle of the twentieth century, textbooks and teachers could still be found perpetuating this error, in spite of the fact that a careful look at Flemming's own figures of nuclei in early prophase shows quite clearly that more than two chromosome ends are apparent in various prophase nuclei!

Every chromosome from a chromosome—how sharply this continuity contrasts with the mass division of the cytoplasm, which may be very unequal in amount. The significance of this understanding was quickly apparent. Wilhelm Roux in 1883 suggested that the longitudinal splitting of the chromosomes implies the existence of a linear array of different hereditary "qualities" along the length of each chromosome.

In 1884 Carl Nägeli, a botanist noted for his work in plant physiology and plant hybridization, and referred to already, proposed what he called a "mechanistic-physiological theory of descent." In part he was undertaking to criticize Darwin's theory of natural selection, but in part he was also attempting to supply

287

a conceptual scheme for a physical system to account for heredity. Strangely and unaccountably, just as he ignored Mendel's discoveries, he ignored entirely all the contemporary developments in knowledge of the roles of the nuclei of the germ cells during fertilization, as well as the indications of the genetic significance of the chromosomes that were to be drawn from mitotic cell division. Instead, reasoning that the sperm and the egg, in spite of their differences in size, have an equal share in the determination of the hereditary characteristics of the offspring (see Maupertuis), Nägeli concluded that the hereditary material is not the entire substance of the egg but only some special part of it. This restricted hereditary substance he called the "idioplasma." He supposed it to be dispersed in a sort of network through the entire substance of the cell, through nucleus and cytoplasm alike. By division of the fertilized egg into cells, the idioplasm would become distributed to every new cell and give to each its hereditary character. Evolution was thought to take place through changes in the idioplasm, changes going on continuously and impelled by some inherent force toward inevitable change. For a man who so insistently proclaimed that he was a mechanistic biologist, this inconsistency was truly remarkable, but Nägeli did not seem to notice that it was in the least illogical.

Perhaps a word should be permitted to characterize a long, voluminous record of analogies between heredity and memory, best exemplified by a lecture given by the physiologist Ewald Hering in 1870. The dialectic progresses from the idea that memory must have an unconscious organic, or material, basis to the analogous idea that a material basis must be involved in the transmission from one generation of living organisms to the next of the "memory" that guides its development. The weakness is quickly apparent in the purely speculative mechanism, which like Nägeli's was conceived in total disregard of the superb cellular discoveries that at the very time were laying a sound basis for understanding the real nature of genetic continuity. The reason is readily found. Hering clearly hoped to provide an organic basis for his Lamarckian conviction that acquired characteristics can become inherited. Among others, Ernst Haeckel in 1876, Samuel Butler in 1878, H. B. Orr in 1893, and finally R. Semon in 1904 all elaborated magnificent speculations about heredity in the same amazing oblivion of the developing knowledge of cell division, chromosome individuality and persistence, and the Chromosome Theory of Heredity. Like Darwin, in an effort to account for supposed heritable effects of the environment, they assumed the existence of "plastidules" or other living units that could be modified in various body parts, and were then transmitted through the reproductive cells to members of the next generation. Yet unlike Darwin, not one of them made an effort to check his theory by further experiments. Not one of them, in fact, reasoned as clearly or tested his system as carefully against the known facts as Maupertuis had done, over a century before. On the contrary, it seems to have escaped these nature philosophers that memory must at best be a poor analogy for heredity, since memory exists demonstrably only in animals, whereas heredity is just as characteristic of plants. Herbert Spencer, in his *Principles of Biology* (1864), was equally speculative and equally fallow. In postulating biological units determinative of development, he clearly revealed less breadth of knowledge and biological perspicacity than Charles Bonnet had exhibited a century earlier.

It was August Weismann, once a student of Nägeli, who undertook the task of properly relating Nägeli's concept of the idioplasm to the recent developments of cytology. In his first famous paper on the subject of heredity, in 1883, Weismann defined the *germplasm* as the unbroken lineage of cells connecting the fertilized egg from which an individual springs with that individual's own gametes, which through their union form the fertilized eggs of the next generation. "We have an obvious means by which the inheritance of all transmitted peculiarities takes place," he said, "in *the continuity of the substance of the germ cells, or germplasm.*" Weismann stressed two principles about the germplasm. The first principle was the Continuity of the Germplasm. According to this concept, the substance of the body (the somatoplasm) is in each generation produced as an offshoot of the germplasm, or germ-line, so that whatever characteristics are inherited must be transmitted from the germplasm to the somatic part of the body. "Changes in the latter," Weismann stated, "only arise when they have been preceded by corresponding changes in the former." He deduced also that characteristics acquired by the somatic cells cannot be transmitted to the next generation unless there is some physical mechanism to transfer material substances or particles from the somatic cells to the germplasm. Weismann believed that any such transfer of particles was highly improbable, and in subsequent years he set himself to test the inheritance of acquired characteristics by experiment. All of his later work confirmed the noninheritance of whatever characteristics were acquired by the somatic cells, and from this experience he derived his second major principle, the Isolation of the Germplasm. By this he meant that effects of the environment which are inherited must be exerted *directly* on the germplasm and cannot be produced in somatic tissues and thence be transferred to the germplasm.

288

Weismann, like Hertwig and Strasburger, identified Nägeli's idioplasm with the chromosomes, but Weismann extended the conception to the postulate that each chromosome is made up of hereditary elements he called "ids," which in turn are composed of hereditary determinants for each inherited characteristic. During somatic development, the ids were supposed to release their determinants and so to be used up. Only in the germ cells would the undiminished quota of ids be retained. Moreover, in Weismann's view, every chromosome was like every other. In spite of growing evidence of the individuality of the chromosomes, as well as their longitudinal division, already noted, Weismann resisted all objections to his schema. Here, if ever, we have a supreme example of a scientist who commences with great insight and who hardens, in devotion to some favored conceptual model, into dogmatic resistance to all evidence that would force him to change his views!

A theory far more like our modern views was put forward by Hugo de Vries in 1889, under the name of "Intracellular Pangenesis." De Vries wished to restrict the hereditary elements, or pangenes as he called them, to the nucleus and the chromosomes, and also to limit their activities to the particular cell within which they might lie. That was what he meant by "intracellular." De Vries' pangenes differ little from the conceptual genes of the twentieth century. In his view they constituted the chromosomes, but could migrate into the cytoplasm and become active there, thus controlling the development of the cell. A representative group of them, however, would always remain behind within the nucleus, to be handed on by mitotic division to both body cells and gametes. Can one fail to be struck by the profound similarity between these pangenes supposed to remain in the chromosomes and the current concept of genes composed of DNA (deoxyribonucleic acid) and restricted to the chromosomes, or on the other hand between the pangenes supposed to migrate into the cytoplasm in order to regulate development and to control the hereditary characteristics and the current views of messenger RNA (ribonucleic acid)? Since the pangenes were limited to the cell and corresponded one to one with particular hereditary characteristics, and since they were always represented in full measure in the nucleus, the conceptual model developed by de Vries was consonant with the principle of the isolation of the germ-plasm and the noninheritance of acquired characteristics. Unfortunately, the use of the term "pangenes" made everyone recall the speculative theory which Darwin evoked to allow for some supposed inheritance of acquired characteristics. Consequently de Vries is often thought, by persons who have never read his massive volume on *Intracellular Pangenesis*, to have held views quite the opposite of his real ones.

By the turn of the century, when the rediscovery of Gregor Mendel's work really gave birth to modern genetics, the cytological basis of genetic continuity had been established. *Omnis chromosoma e chromosoma:* every chromosome from a chromosome.

Every Gene from a Gene. The line of thought about genetic continuity developed thus far has described an ever-increasing degree of precision in the generation of living forms. Biogenesis becomes reproduction; reproduction becomes cellular; cell division becomes mitotic; chromosomes split longitudinally, or put more accurately, they replicate themselves, since each new chromosome is no *half*-chromosome but a chromosome entire; and finally, the substituent elements of the chromosomes, whether visible chromatids or invisible genes, are held likewise to replicate themselves. During the lengthy period from about 1883 to 1953, a span of 70 years, little was added to this particular line of development of the concept. True, the development of genetics made it clear that one is entitled to say: "Every gene from a gene." But that deduction was made on the basis of evidence that genetic continuity is not interrupted when cells divide, or when gametes are formed, unite, and generate a new individual. One could say where a gene resided in a particular chromosome, but not *what* it was. The gene and its replication remained total abstractions.

Every DNA Molecule from a DNA Molecule. All of this changed in the decade following 1944, when it became evident that the physical material of heredity is not, as had been generally supposed, protein but instead is deoxyribonucleic acid (DNA). The problem of replication again became real when J. D. Watson and F. H. C. Crick in 1953 proposed, on the basis of chemical considerations and X-ray diffraction data, that the DNA molecule is a double helix. Its two strands have -sugar-phosphate-sugar-phosphate- backbones from which paired purine and pyrimidine bases extend inward toward the axis of the helix and are held together by hydrogen bonds that regularly match adenine with thymine and guanine with cytosine. The basic problem of genetic continuity was at once recognized to be the nature of the mechanism whereby the DNA molecule replicates itself (Figure 1).

Several aspects of the model of DNA and its replication need some emphasis. First, the two strands of the double helix are in every detail complementary. They are not identical. A portion of the sequence that in one strand might run -CATCATCAT- in the other would run -GTAGTAGTA- and read in either direction would be quite different from the first. The equivalence in amount of adenine with thymine and of guanine

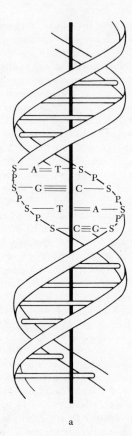

Thymine   Adenine

Cytosine   Guanine

a   b

FIGURE 1.

a. Model of a deoxyribonucleic acid (DNA) molecule. In one portion of the double helix the symbols for the repeating sugar (S) and phosphate (P) groups that constitute the backbone of each strand are shown. The paired bases are A, adenine; T, thymine; G, guanine; and C, cytosine.

b. The molecular structure of the pairs of purine and pyrimidine bases of DNA. Adenine, a purine, regularly pairs with thymine, a pyrimidine, by means of two hydrogen bonds. Guanine, a purine, regularly pairs with cytosine, a pyrimidine, by means of three hydrogen bonds.

with cytosine, so characteristic of all DNA's no matter what their AT:GC ratios may be, is a property of the double helix and not of single-stranded DNA. Similarly, the equality of purine bases to pyrimidine bases is a property of the double helix, not of the single strand. Replication itself is not a process that can be performed in a single step by single-stranded DNA. The single strand makes, or is a template for, a *complementary* strand, with a polarity that runs in the opposite direction along the molecule, since the 3′–5′ phosphate ester linkages are reversed in direction in the two strands. Properly considered, *replication is thus performed only by the double helix*, which upon separation and formation of two complementary strands generates two double helices.

Watson and Crick found that certain evidence ex-

cluded the possibility that the two polynucleotide chains of a DNA molecule are paranemically coiled, that is, are so coiled that they can simply slip into and out of each other. Instead, they were *plectonemically* coiled, like strands of a twisted rope, and therefore, in order to come apart, they must in fact untwist. Since they could not very well be conceived to replicate while bound in the double helix, when every base is paired and held by hydrogen bonds to its partner, it seemed that replication must require a prior untwisting and separation of the strands. As a most important part of their theory of DNA structure, Watson and Crick therefore postulated that replication is preceded by uncoiling of the strands, after which each strand could attract free nucleotides from the metabolic pool. These nucleotides could then become united by phosphate ester linkages so as to form a new strand that would, with the original strand, twist into the double helix again. Thus each of the separated strands of the original double helix would serve as a template, and two double helices would be produced from one.

Step by step, evidence has been found to support the validity of this hypothesis. An important early piece of evidence was Arthur Kornberg's discovery (1956) that for the synthesis of DNA in vitro one must supply a pool of nucleotide triphosphates, that is, nucleotides which are already provided with the high-energy phosphate bonds that enable formation of the phosphate ester linkages to proceed. Calculations by Cyrus Levinthal and H. R. Crane, and by others, showed that the energy required to spin a very long DNA molecule so as to untwist it is not inordinately great but is only a small part of the available nucleotide triphosphate energy of the cell, while the time required would be brief. A model was proposed that envisaged the progressive uncoiling of the double helix from one end and the beginning of replication of the separated strands while the remainder of the double helix was still intact. It was found independently by Paul Doty and J. Marmur that exposure of DNA to critical high temperatures would lead to dissociation of the strands of the double helix and that if cooling thereafter was sufficiently gradual, the strands would in fact reassociate, or "anneal." In this way it was possible to produce certain kinds of hybrid DNA artificially, by bringing about the association, while cooling, of single strands from different sources.

A celebrated experiment of M. Meselson and F. W. Stahl in 1958 provided very convincing evidence of the correctness of the Watson-Crick hypothesis. A culture of the bacterium *Escherichia coli* was first grown in a medium containing heavy nitrogen (N^{15}), until all the DNA was labeled with this isotope. The cells were then transferred to a medium containing ordinary nitrogen (N^{14}) for periods equal to one cell generation and two cell generations. DNA was extracted from a sample of the original N^{15}-labeled cells and subjected to ultracentrifugation in a cesium chloride density gradient, which differentiates molecules by weight. The DNA formed a single band at a characteristic place. DNA from the sample taken after one cell division formed a single band at a different place, while DNA from the sample taken after two divisions revealed two bands, one of them at the same place as in the DNA from cells after the first replication, the other a new band still further displaced from the band characteristic of N^{15}. The interpretation seems clear. When the N^{15}-labeled double helical DNA molecule replicates in medium containing only N^{14}, each new duplex will contain one strand labeled with heavy and one labeled with ordinary nitrogen. There will therefore be only a single band, but it should lie—as indeed it does—just midway between the positions occupied by pure N^{15}-labeled and pure N^{14}-labeled DNA. After a second division, the separation of the double helices will provide in each case one heavy and one ordinary strand as templates. Hence, after replication, duplexes will be formed half of which will contain one heavy and one ordinary strand and half of which will contain two ordinary strands. The latter will form a band at the position characteristic of DNA in which all replication has occurred in medium with ordinary nitrogen.

This experiment not only neatly confirms the Watson-Crick hypothesis of replication, but shows that the process is "semi-conservative," which may be defined in the following way. Once replication has taken place in heavy nitrogen, there will always be some double helices containing one heavy and one ordinary strand when replicating in ordinary medium, but the proportion should decline from one hundred per cent in the first daughter generation to one-half in the next, one-fourth in the third, one-eighth in the fourth, etc. If this is so, the original strand that serves as a template remains intact. Yet we know from Herbert Taylor's studies that the original chromosome does not always remain intact. It may undergo exchange at one or more points with the new sister-chromatid that is formed. There is clearly a discrepancy here; but it serves mainly to emphasize the tremendous shift in dimensions when a DNA double helix is compared with a chromosome. The DNA double helix has a diameter of 20 Å, the completely uncoiled chromosome one of at least 0.2 microns (or 2000 Å), one hundred times greater. Until we know much more about the internal construction of the chromosomes and the exact arrangement of the DNA molecules in them, this hundred-fold difference in dimensions (two orders of magnitude) leaves plenty of scope both for molecules and for imagination. Numerous models have been proposed to explain how the replication of DNA can be semi-conservative while that of the chromosome is not.

In this essay we have sought for the meaning of reproduction in its broadest terms. We began with the idea: all life from life of its own species. We have ended with the replication of the DNA molecule. Reversing the direction of our discourse, we see that the whole of genetic continuity really lies here. Because each DNA molecule can replicate itself, each gene and chromosome undergoes replication. Because, whenever the chromosomes divide, the sister chromatids separate and move by means of the spindle mechanism into the daughter cells, it follows that every cell comes from a cell and contains within it the same genetic heritage.

Because cells arise mitotically from parent cells and because each individual must originate as a single cell or a cluster of cells derived either from two parent organisms or from one, all life comes from life of its own kind.

It remains for us to place this concept, genetic continuity, within a social context. Scientific ideas may lead to technological applications which increase human power and alter the course of civilization. In time, the concept that genetic continuity resides ultimately in the replicating strands of the DNA double helix may assist in the techniques of genetic surgery and manipulation whereby man will some day acquire total control over the evolutionary process and alter hereditary characteristics in selected directions. That time is not yet. On the other hand, the greatest influence of scientific concepts may lie not in the field of technological applications, but rather in the profound alterations of man's philosophical views of nature, life, and man himself. The ultimate concern of man finds voice in the age-old cry: Whence? And whither?

In man's construction of his world view, the refinement of the idea of genetic continuity to a point where it is shown clearly to reside in the replications of a remarkable sort of molecule represents the final step in the validation of J. O. de La Mettrie's "L'Homme Machine." It is the ultimate reduction of life, symbolized by its most unique and characteristic property, *reproduction,* to the physical and chemical behavior of molecules. All the genetically transmitted characteristics and potentialities, both those defining the species and those distinguishing the individual, are coded in the sequence of nucleotides in the DNA molecule and are produced during development through its chemical control over the synthesis of a thousand—ten thousand—proteins in the cells of the growing body. Like the Theory of Organic Evolution, like the Theory of Natural Selection, the full explication of Genetic Continuity is destined to affect most profoundly man's view of man, man's view of life.

Yet the mystery is not quite destroyed, not fully replaced by "L'Homme Machine." One must remember that the DNA double helix cannot replicate outside of its most complex living surroundings. It cannot replicate outside a system that includes not only necessary components such as trinucleotides and necessary sources of energy, such as adenosine triphosphate (ATP); it also cannot replicate without the assistance of a specific enzyme, itself a protein synthesized under the directions of some part of the DNA molecules present in the cell. Life, reproduction, the replicating molecules are after all parts of an integral, complex system; and it is the *system* that lives, reproduces itself, and replicates its genetic code. There is mystery enough here to satisfy anyone who persists in asking: Whence? And whither?

The Principle of Genetic Continuity, in its final refinement, would of itself produce a world of species inalterable, of populations composed only of identical individuals, because the DNA double helix replicates itself so precisely. Yet the actual world is full of different species, and populations belonging to the same species exhibit incessant variety. The representatives of the species Man differ almost as much as they resemble one another. Our world view must therefore accommodate the existence of novelty and change in hereditary characteristics, and the mutations of genes and chromosomes which can be observed must have their final locus in some change of a component of the DNA, some error occurring in the process of exact replication. Admit these alterations of the code, and at once natural selection is supplied the material to play upon. Thus, in our final view, Genetic Continuity and Evolution are the two great themes of life, and are linked through mutation and natural selection. Genetic continuity implies the replication of chance errors as well as the persistence in the main of the old, tried and tested, reasonably successful attributes. Genetic continuity is both the stable element in the nature of man (and all other living species), and also the basis for our hope that change may continue, that new adaptations may be realized, and that a more prescient creature may succeed us in the end.

BIBLIOGRAPHY

Aristotle, *Generation of Animals,* trans. A. L. Peck, Loeb Classical Library (Cambridge, Mass., 1943). Aristotle, *Historia animalium,* trans. D'Arcy Thompson (Oxford, 1910). R. Barthelmess, *Vererbungswissenschaft* (Munich, 1952). C. Bonnet, *Palingénésie philosophique, Oeuvres,* 24 vols. (Neuchatel, 1783), Vol. VII. Y. Delage, *L'Hérédité et les grands problèmes de la biologie générale* (Paris, 1903). L. C. Dunn, *A Short History of Genetics* (New York, 1965). B. Glass, "Evolution and Heredity in the Nineteenth Century," in L. G. Stevenson and R. P. Multhauf, eds., *Medicine, Science, and Culture* (Baltimore, 1968), pp. 209–46. B. Glass, O. Temkin, and W. Straus, Jr., eds., *Forerunners of Darwin* (Baltimore, 1959), Chs. 2, 3, 6. É. Guyénot, *Les Sciences de la vie aux XVIIe et XVIIIe siècles* (Paris, 1941). A. van Leeuwenhoek, *Brieven (seu Werken),* Deel II, Letter 83 (various dates and places); also in Latin, *Opera Omnia* (Lugduni Batavorum [Leyden] 1722), Vol. II. P. L. M. de Maupertuis, *Vénus physique* (1745), in *Oeuvres,* 4 vols. (Lyon, 1756). C. Nägeli, *Mechanisch-physiologische Theorie der Abstammungslehre* (Munich-Leipzig, 1884). E. Nordenskiöld, *The History of Biology* (New York, 1942). H. Stubbe, *Kurze Geschichte der Genetik bis zur Wiederentdeckung der Vererbungsregeln Gregor Mendels,* 2nd ed. (Jena, 1965). J. H. Taylor, ed., *Selected Papers on Molecular Genetics* (New

York and London, 1965), for papers by J. D. Watson and
F. H. C. Crick; M. Meselson and F. W. Stahl; A. Kornberg;
J. H. Taylor. H. de Vries, *Intracellulare Pangenesis* (Jena,
1889). J. D. Watson, *Molecular Biology of the Gene* (New
York and Amsterdam, 1965). A. Weismann, *Ueber die Verer-
bung* (Jena, 1883), trans. as *Essays upon Heredity and Kin-
dred Biological Problems*, 2nd ed. (London, 1891), I, 67–106.
E. B. Wilson, *The Cell in Development and Inheritance* (New
York, 1900).

BENTLEY GLASS

[See also Biological Conceptions, Homologies; **Inheritance;**
Man-Machine; Spontaneous Generation.]

GENIUS
FROM THE RENAISSANCE
TO 1770

I

GENIUS IS relevant to the history of ideas in the following meanings: (1) the designation of superior mental
powers productive of rare superior performances; or
also as the designation of a man possessing these
powers; (2) as the peculiar spiritual character of an
era, of a nation, of a man; (3) as a special talent for
some particular type of performance.

The first designation is basic. Performances considered as products of genius may also belong to politics, warfare, exploration, etc., but such achievements
are regarded primarily as *original* intellectual work,
as discoveries or inventions, and especially as artistic
creations in contrast to imitation. Until the middle of
the eighteenth century, these original activities were
collectively designated by *inventio*, or equivalents of
this term. Their further differentiation (especially of
discoveries from inventions) is frequently ignored.
During the Renaissance (and later), two different Latin
terms were used for genius: *ingenium* and *genius;* they
seem to have first acquired this meaning in Italy, where
corresponding Italian words, *ingegno* and *genio*, were
also used. A fundamental trait of genius is that it is
an *innate* capability, operating with *spontaneous facility*, versus talents which may be taught and learned
by diligence; but, nevertheless, it may need diligence for its development and discipline. Whether this
capability depends on a unique mental power, or on
an assemblage (proportion) of powers, or on a kind
of inward revelation, is a further debatable question.

At first, *irrational* traits attributed to genius are
considered irrelevant; later they are magnified by the
confluence into this idea of the Platonic doctrine of
furor poeticus in poetics. Genius, in this respect, is

sometimes considered as verging on distraction. Also
Platonic is the *divine* character frequently attributed,
metaphorically or not, to genius, because its original
work is compared both with God's creation, and with
what is considered the result of supernatural inspiration. In fact, while *ingenium* is intended to mean
"inventive intelligence," the Latin term *genius* (Italian
genio) in the Renaissance originally refers, metaphorically or not, to a superior spirit inspiring a human
being in the tradition of Socrates' demon or in that
of astrology (astral spirit). Petrarch and Boccaccio had
used *ingenium* in this sense, but still rather atypically;
but Poliziano and Pico stress the element of originality
when they use it. Pico also refers to *genius*, as does
Erasmus in 1528. Castiglione (1528) only uses *ingegno*.
The Portuguese art theorist Hollanda, a pupil of
Michelangelo, stresses (1548) the innate character of
genius (Portuguese *engenho*, *genio*). Alberti, Condivi,
and Vasari point out that genius and diligence are
different qualities, but that they may be profitably
united; the same connection between genius and memory is asserted by Boccaccio, Alberti, Enea Silvio
Piccolomini, Erasmus, Trissino.

Scaliger's doctrine of genius (1561), centering on
poetics, is peculiarly important. Genius (*ingenium*,
genius) is something divine and innate, associated with
enthusiasm (*furor poeticus*); it belongs to both arts and
sciences. Cardano identifies genius with a kind of
spiritus familiaris. For Fracastoro and Giovio, genius
only means a talent in some particular field (Zilsel,
1926; Thüme, 1927). The term "genius" is used by
Adriani (*Manuale*, 1845) as the spirit of a nation.

For Bruno (1585), genius as divine enthusiasm is the
origin of the rules of art (Bruyne, 1951; Thüme, 1927).
But seventeenth-century Italian authors, such as
Galileo, Torricelli, Magalotti, Salvini, exclude from
genio supernatural and enthusiastic traits (Zilsel, 1926).
Pellegrini (1650), Tesauro (1654), and Pagano consider
ingegno in connection with beauty. For Vico, *genio*
is the source of inventions (Croce, 1946; Pagano, 1650).

II

In Spain, Vives (1538) defines *ingenium* as the
strength of the mind (Gracián, 1960); Huarte, in his
famous *Examen de ingenios* (1575), means by *ingenio*
a special talent. Huarte's book stimulated many imita-
tions in all European countries (Lipenius, 1682;
Kahlius, 1740). Herrera (1580) identifies "Plato's genius" (Spanish *genio*) with "Aristotle's active intellect"
as a supernatural power of invention. Rengifo (1592)
and Carvallo (1602) interpret *ingenio* as *furor poeticus*
(Menéndez, 1962). Gracián (1646; 1658) makes a distinction between *genio* and *ingenio:* the first seems to
be (as for other authors) a natural inclination to un-

293

common achievement, the second a peculiar intelligence (*agudeza*) adapted to discover similarities and analogies (Gracián, 1960; Cirot, 1926; Zilsel, 1926).

III

The French Renaissance, aware of the problem of originality and inspiration in poetry (Thüme, 1927), seems, however, to ignore this twofold meaning of the French term *génie; ingenium* is translated into French as *esprit* (Zilsel, 1926), a word having a much wider range of meanings. Descartes employs the term *ingenium* to mean both an unusual capability to discover the truth (viz., new truths) and a special talent (Laporte, 1950). *Génie* appears in seventeenth-century psychology as a kind of inventive instinct which must be ruled by reason and taste; or, as the natural spontaneity of an author, in contrast to science and art. Mairet (1637) calls it *fureur divine* (Zumthor-Sommer, 1950); for Jean-Louis Guez de Balzac (1640) it is a secret force coming from heaven, bestowing greatness and majesty (Bray, 1927). Saint-Evremond regards poetical genius as incompatible with common sense (*bon sens*): sometimes it verges on madness. For Dacier (1681), on the contrary, judgment governs genius but is concealed under inspiration and apparent disorder (Thüme, 1927). Rapin (1686) calls genius *feu céleste* (Bray, 1927), and Bouhours finds it opposed to, but not incompatible with common sense. Boileau contrasts genius with art and its rules. For Perrault (1693) genius (*feu sacré, sainte fureur*) discovers the eternal ideas of beauty (Zumthor-Sommer, 1950). Dubos (1719) takes "genius" to stand for an instinctive and natural capability for original creation, above and sometimes against the rules; it should not be overwhelmed by enthusiasm; genius results from an assemblage of psychophysical powers (Wolf, 1923; Grappin, 1952; Fubini, 1965). For André (1741), genius (*feu de l'esprit*) may infringe the rules of art, but only within certain limits (André, 1843). Vauvenargues (1746) considers genius as depending on the passions, and resulting from an assemblage of powers; its originality does not exclude imitation (Vauvenargues, 1857). Condillac (1746) opposes genius to talent: both are powers of invention, combining ideas received through the senses; but talent does not go beyond natural combinations, while genius is provided with an *esprit créateur* (Condillac, 1803).

In Batteux's opinion (1747), genius should not conflict with natural laws; in fact, it discovers, it does not create. Therefore, it is a superior form of reason imitating nature, and promoted by enthusiasm (Wolf, 1923; Grappin, 1952). Diderot considers genius as a mystery of nature, going beyond imagination and judgment by the force of enthusiasm; this brings about creation, as an idea drawn from experience through

an original process (Dieckmann, 1941; Belaval, 1950). For d'Alembert (1751) genius, the power of original invention in science and art, cannot be taught (d'Alembert, 1930). Cahusac (1757) applies genius to emotion and feeling, as a faculty receptive to and reproductive of impressions. J. F. de Saint-Lambert (1757) opposes genius to taste; genius creates independently of the rules; in philosophy, Shaftesbury is a genius, he has *créé, construit, édifié*—Locke is not, because we owe him only *de grandes vérités froidement aperçues, méthodiquement suivies, froidement annoncées*. Helvétius (1758) gives a mechanical explanation of genius: genius invents by combination, not by creation, and it is a rational power (Wolf, 1923). Voltaire identifies genius with "active imagination"; it ought to be matched by memory and judgment (*Encyclopédie*, 1765). Voltaire, as many others in his time, uses *génie* also to mean the character of an era or of a nation (Tonelli, 1955) as was usual in France, at least after Corneille and Racine (Corneille, 1640–41; Racine, 1669). In this sense, *esprit* is a synonym of *génie*.

IV

In Britain, Barclay mentions a *genius saeculi* ("genius of the age") as early as 1614 (Tonelli, 1955).

The doctrine of originality and divine inspiration especially for poetry is developed during the sixteenth and seventeenth centuries (Thüme, 1927), but the term "genius" is comparatively rarely used in this connection (Latin *ingenium* is frequently translated as "wit," but as such it does not include the idea of creativity). Evelyn refers to Huygens as a "universal Mathematical Genius" (Evelyn, 1662); Wolseley (1685) opposes poetical genius to imitation and to laborious elaboration. Temple (1690) refers genius to "Coelestial Fire or Divine Inspiration," superior to the constraint of the rules. The doctrine of creative imagination and of its superiority to the rules is especially developed in Shakespearean criticism, e.g., by Rymer (Thüme, 1927).

During the eighteenth century British writers begin to theorize about genius, and stress its irrational traits more than elsewhere. For Shaftesbury, a genius is a person who is able to create as nature does: and nature is a revelation of the universal spirit. Therefore a genius is considered as a second deity, or as a Prometheus. Enthusiasm is a condition of creation; nevertheless, a man of genius should not infringe the rules of art: he needs knowledge and good sense, although he avoids minuteness. Addison (1711) considers genius as founded on active imagination, and contrasts it to imitation; but there are two kinds of geniuses: the first, or the natural kind (Homer, Shakespeare) create independently of the rules; the second, or the learned kind

(Plato, Vergil, Bacon, Milton) have been educated and developed through the rules. For Young (1759), genius is divine inspiration; its creation is as spontaneous as that of nature, and the rules are only a hindrance to it. With Young, the interpretation of genius as a sort of irrationality reaches its climax. Gerard (1759; 1774) distinguishes genius from imagination: the second collects new materials, the first orders them into a whole according to judgment and to taste. The work of genius is the original source of rules: it establishes them, but is not constricted by them. Though genius, for Gerard, does not act in a consciously rational way (but rather by inspired enthusiasm), its psychological explanation, through the theory of association of ideas, is completely rational (Wolf, 1923; Thüme, 1927). Duff considers genius as a proportion of different powers, such as inventive imagination, judgment, and taste. In art, the proper manifestation of genius is the sublime (Duff, 1767). For Ogilvie, genius or invention proceeds in science by judgment or understanding, in poetry by imagination; only poetical invention is original and, metaphorically speaking, creative (Ogilvie, 1777).

V

In seventeenth-century Holland, Vossius mentions a *furor* as *ingenii excitatio* for poetry (Bray, 1927). In late sixteenth-century Germany, Castiglione's *ingegno* is translated into German as *ingenium* (Zilsel, 1926). German seventeenth-century treatises in Latin use *ingenium* in its various meanings (Lipenius, 1682); "genius" appears only occasionally (Maior, n.d.). The German term of French origin, *das Genie*, has been known since 1728 (Bertram, 1728), but became of general use only after J. A. Schlegel's translation of Batteux (1751). Bodmer still employs *grosser Kopf*, *grosser Geist* to mean a poetical genius submitted to rules of nature and of reason only, not to those imposed by the critics (Grappin, 1952). *Ingenium* is also translated, e.g., by Chr. Wolff, as *Witz*, but in the very restricted meaning of a power productive of discovery of similarities or analogies (Baeumler, 1923). For Baumgarten and Meier *ingenium latius dictum*, or *Kopf*, is a favorable proportion of mental powers producing superior performances in science or, as *ingenium venustum*, in art; they neither stress the creative aspect of genius, nor admit irrational elements into it (Baeumler, 1923; Wolf, 1923; Grappin, 1952; Tonelli, 1966). Creativity and freedom from the rules were claimed for artistic genius by Gellert in 1751 (Wolf, 1923). Trescho (1754) considers genius to be an instinct providentially inborn in all human beings, as an inclination towards a certain role in life. For Wieland (1755), genius is connected with freedom of imagination and with enthusiasm. Sulzer (1757; 1771) identifies genius with an extraordinary strength of the whole representative faculty, utilizing all its powers; it is a gift of nature and, in art, its task is to reach ideal beauty. The production of genius is partially unconscious; its sudden manifestation generates enthusiasm. Originality (and independency of the rules) is not always connected with genius, but genius should pursue it. Resewitz (1759–60) explains genius through the preponderance over others of a certain aptitude required by some art (but not required in science). In general, a genius must be especially predisposed to intuitive knowledge. For Flögel (1762), genius is a harmony of powers; it is not opposed to the rules. Moses Mendelssohn is convinced that genius corresponds to a state of perfection of all mental powers working in harmony towards a certain aim; if it can control enthusiasm through reason, it may reach sublimity in art. Through genius, nature dictates her own rules; therefore, genius cannot oppose true rules (Wolf, 1923; Grappin, 1952).

Hamann (1760–61), influenced by Young, breaks with the rationalist tradition in the explanation of genius. He regards it as a divine inspiration opposed and superior to reason; creation is brought about by feeling, identified with intuition; its thinking is identified with linguistic expression, and its language is poetry. Genius is considered sometimes as a kind of divine seizure (Grappin, 1952). For Klopstock, artistic genius, a balance of different powers, must be endowed with compassion, which can generate emotion along with moral conscience. It is subject to rules (Grappin, 1952). Lessing's theory is still more rationalistic; genius is a natural facility for discovering the true and reasonable principles of art (Rosenthal, 1933; Grappin, 1952). Riedel (1767) refers to genius as a facility in intuitive knowledge, both in science and in art (Riedel, 1783). Eberhard's interpretation of genius (1776) almost completely excludes irrational elements (Eberhard, 1786).

Genius for Herder means chiefly *national* genius. (*Genie* as the characteristic of an era or of a nation was used by other German authors at that time; however, the term *Geist* was generally preferred for the national characteristic.) Herder refuses to analyze the notion of original genius, but defines it as a natural force. At first, he is inclined to stress the irrational elements of genius, but later he restricts their function (Ernst, 1916; Grappin, 1952). Lavater, in his enthusiastic and rather confused exaltation of genius (1778), stresses its instinctive and extraordinary character (Ernst, 1916).

Between 1770 and 1780, Kant developed a first version of his theory of genius. He distinguished genius from skill or talent, when these are not creative; genius is opposed to diligence, but needs instruction, and is a favorable proportion of four powers: sensibility, judgment, creative spirit, and taste. Its realm is the production of new ideas and ideals. Genius, freedom, and living organisms are elements which cannot be explained mechanically (Tonelli, 1966).

Thus, a rational explanation of the force of genius seems to be largely prevalent in Germany in this period, in spite of the *Sturm und Drang* ideology, developing after 1770: rational elements seem to be prevalent also in Goethe's early theory of genius (Sudheimer, 1935; Grappin, 1952).

BIBLIOGRAPHY

J. Addison, *Spectator*, 160 (3 September, 1711). J. Le Rond d'Alembert, *Discours préliminaire de l'Encyclopédie*, ed. Ducros (Paris, 1930), pp. 47, 53, 64. Y. M. André, *Oeuvres philosophiques*, ed. Cousin (Paris, 1843), p. 59. A. Baeumler, *Kants Kritik der Urteilskraft, ihre Geschichte und Systematik* (Halle, 1923); reprinted as *Das Irrationalitätsproblem in der Aesthetik und Logik des 18. Jahrhunderts bis zur Kritik der Urteilskraft* (Darmstadt, 1967), Part I, A, Ch. 7: pp. 146f., *Witz;* pp. 157f., Baumgarten. Y. Belaval, *L'esthétique sans paradoxe de Diderot* (Paris, 1950), pp. 141, 151f., 156f., 299f. J. F. Bertram, *Einleitung in die sogenannten Schönen Wissenschaften* (Brunswick, 1728), p. 199. R. Bray, *La formation de la doctrine classique en France* (Paris, 1927): Balzac, p. 87; Vossius, p. 88; Rapin, p. 90. E. de Bruyne, *Geschiedenis van de Aesthetica. De Renaissance* (Antwerp and Amsterdam, 1951), p. 142. G. Cirot, review of "B. Gracián, pages caractéristiques," in *Bulletin Hispanique*, 28 (1926), 106f. E. Bonnot de Condillac, *Connoissances humaines*, Part I, Sec. II, #104, in *Oeuvres complètes* (Paris, 1803), I, 147f. P. Corneille, *Cinna* (1640–41), Act II, scene 1. B. Croce, *Estetica come scienza dell'espressione e linguistica generale* (Bari, 1946), "Storia," Ch. III: Pellegrini, Tesauro, p. 207; Vico, p. 253. H. Dieckmann, "Diderot's Conception of Genius," *Journal of the History of Ideas*, 2 (1941), 151–82. W. Duff, *An Essay on Original Genius and Its Various Modes of Exertion in Philosophy and the Fine Arts* (London, 1767), pp. 6, 8, 10, 22, 99. J. A. Eberhard, *Allgemeine Theorie des Denkens und Empfindens* (Berlin, 1786), pp. 208f. *Encyclopédie, ou dictionnaire raisonné des sciences, des arts et des métiers* (Neufchâtel, 1765), Vol. VIII, art. "Imagination." J. Ernst, *Der Geniebegriff der Stürmer und Dränger und der Frühromantiker* (Zurich, 1916): Herder, pp. 25f.; Lavater, pp. 29f. J. Evelyn, *Sculptura: or the history and art of Chalcography and engraving Copper* (London, 1662), p. 74. E. Fubini, *Empirismo e classicismo: saggio sul Dubos* (Turin, 1965), pp. 75f. B. Gracián, *Obras completas*, ed. del Hoyo (Madrid, 1960): Vives, et al., p. 78n.; *genio* and *ingenio*, pp. 78f.; *ingenio* and beauty, pp. 239f. P. Grappin, *La théorie du Génie dans le préclassicisme allemand* (Paris, 1952): Dubos, pp. 112f.; Batteux, pp. 114f.; J. A. Schlegel, pp. 110f.; Bodmer, p. 62; Baumgarten, pp. 91f.; Trescho, pp. 122f.; Wieland, pp. 125f.; Sulzer, pp. 139f.; Resewitz, pp. 128f.; Flögel, pp. 134f.; Mendelssohn, pp. 131f.; Hamann, pp. 187f., 207f.; Klopstock, pp. 254, 259f.; Lessing, pp. 169f.; Herder, pp. 221f., 228f., 247f.; Goethe, pp. 270f. I. M. Kahlius, *Biblioteca philosophica Struvviana* (Göttingen, 1740), II, 82–96. J. Laporte, *Le rationalisme de Descartes* (Paris, 1950), pp. 29f. M. Lipenius, *Bibliotheca realis philosophica* (Frankfurt am Main, 1682; reprint Hildesheim, 1967), I, 731f. I. D. Maior, *Genius errans, sive de ingeniorum in scientiis abusus* (Kiel, n.d.). *Manuale dell'arte greca* (Florence, 1845), p. 15. M. Menéndez Pelayo, *Historia de las ideas estéticas en España* (Madrid, 1962), Vol. II: Huarte, p. 141; Herrera, p. 71; Rengifo, Carvallo, pp. 218f. J. Ogilvie, *Philosophical and Critical Observations on the Nature, Characters and Various Species of Composition* (London, 1774), pp. 46f., 55f., 104f. M. Pagano, *I fonti dell'ingegno ridotti ad arte* (Bologna, 1650). J. Racine, *Britannicus* (1669), Act III, scene 2. F. J. Riedel, *Sämtliche Schriften* (Vienna, 1783), III, 282f. E. Rosenthal, *Der Geniebegriff des Aufklärungszeitalters. Lessing und die Popularphilosophie* (Berlin, 1933). O. Schlapp, *Kants Lehre vom Genie und die Entstehung der "Kritik der Urteilskraft"* (Göttingen, 1901). H. Sudheimer, *Der Geniebegriff des jungen Goethe* (Berlin, 1935), with many references to theories of genius prior to Goethe. H. Thüme, *Beiträge zur Geschichte des Geniebegriffes in England* (Halle, 1927): *Furor poeticus* in the Italian Renaissance, pp. 7f.; Cardano, pp. 17f.; Fracastoro, p. 11; Bruno, pp. 23f.; French Renaissance, pp. 29f.; Saint-Evremond, p. 65; Dacier, pp. 72f.; sixteenth- and seventeenth-century England, pp. 31f., 51f.; Wolseley, Temple, Rymer, pp. 62f.; Shaftesbury, pp. 67f.; Addison, pp. 78f.; Young, pp. 87f. G. Tonelli, *Kant, dall'estetica metafisica all'estetica psicoempirica*, Memorie della Accademia delle Scienze di Torino, Series III, Volume 3, Part II (Turin, 1955): Barclay, Voltaire, p. 115; Kant, p. 61; idem, "Kant's Early Theory of Genius (1770–1779)," *The Journal of the History of Philosophy*, 4 (1966); 217f., on the theory of genius in the eighteenth century; Meier, p. 219. L. de Clapiers de Vauvenargues, *Oeuvres* (Paris, 1857), pp. 20f. O. Walzel, *Das Prometheussymbol von Shaftesbury zu Goethe* (Munich, 1932). R. Wittkower, "Imitation, Eclecticism and Genius," in E. R. Wasserman, ed., *Aspects of the Eighteenth Century* (Baltimore, 1965). H. Wolf, *Versuch einer Geschichte des Geniebegriffes in der deutschen Aesthetik des 18. Jahrhunderts*, Vol. I, *von Gottsched bis auf Lessing* (Heidelberg, 1923): Dubos, pp. 52f.; Batteux, pp. 57f.; Cahusac, pp. 71f.; Saint-Lambert, p. 73; Helvétius, pp. 60f.; Shaftesbury, pp. 17f.; Addison, pp. 24f.; Young, pp. 30f.; Gerard, pp. 37f.; Baumgarten, pp. 101f.; Gellert, pp. 108f.; Wieland, pp. 113f.; Sulzer, pp. 142f.; Resewitz, pp. 115f.; Flögel, pp. 126f.; Mendelssohn, p. 130. E. Zilsel, *Die Entstehung des Geniebegriffes. Ein Beitrag zur Ideengeschichte der Antike und des Frühkapitalismus* (Tübingen, 1926): definition of genius, p. 252; problem of irrationality, p. 269; invention, pp. 272f.; divine, pp. 276f.; Petrarch, pp. 213f.; Boccaccio, pp. 267f.; Poliziano, Pico, Erasmus, pp. 214f.; Hollanda, p. 246; genius and diligence, pp. 266f.; genius and memory, pp. 267f.; Scaliger, pp. 284f.; Cardano, pp. 292f.; Fracastoro, pp. 290f.; Galileo, Torricelli, et al., pp. 296f.; translations of *ingenium* into modern languages, pp. 294f.; Gracián, pp. 297f. P. Zumthor and H. Sommer,

"A propos du mot génie," in *Zeitschrift für romanische Philologie*, **66** (1950): in general, 180f., 186; Mairet, 183; Bouhours, 191; Boileau, 196; Perrault, 197f.

GIORGIO TONELLI

[See also Art and Play; **Beauty; Creativity; Genius, Musical;** Irrationalism.]

GENIUS: INDIVIDUALISM IN ART AND ARTISTS

I. TERMINOLOGY

THE TERMS "individualism" and "genius" have gone through many changes of meaning and cannot even now be used in an unequivocal way. Individualism will here be understood not only as "the individual pursuing his own ends or following his own ideas" (Murray, *A New English Dictionary* [1901], V), but also as the self-conscious, reflective conduct of single persons or groups of persons allied by common interests, ideals, and purposes. Genius is an infinitely more vacillating term, and its many meanings since antiquity have been recorded in Murray's *New English Dictionary*. The concern here is primarily with the meaning the term acquired in the course of the eighteenth century as denoting the creative powers and outstanding originality of uncommonly endowed, exalted individuals. While the modern literature on individualism in general is scarce and unsatisfactory and on individualism in art and artists practically nonexistent, that on genius is vast, diversified, and illuminating. Written mainly by literary critics, it discusses almost exclusively poetry and poets. Since the fifteenth century artists have believed in a close alliance between the sister arts, the word and the picture—the Horatian *ut pictura poesis* had widest currency for over 300 years—and thus a concentration on artistic genius without taking into account literary criticism would tend to distort the historical evolution.

II. INDIVIDUALISM IN ART

Individualism in art and individualism of artists are not necessarily closely related. The first problem, that of individualism in art cannot be divorced from visual evidence, while the second, that of the origin, history, and vicissitudes of the individualist artist is above all a sociological and psychological one. In the following pages the latter problem will be more fully discussed than the former. The entire history of art could, and perhaps should, be written under the heading of "Changing Aspects of Individualism in Art." Since this cannot be done within the compass of this article, only

three topics of particular relevance to the history of ideas have here been singled out for brief consideration: (1) the question of individual styles, (2) that of rapid changes of style within the work of one artist, and (3) that of the *non finito*, the unfinished work of art.

Individual Styles and Rapid Changes of Style. Ever since Johann Joachim Winckelmann and more specifically since the late nineteenth century, under the influence of such scholars as Heinrich Wölfflin and Alois Riegl, the history of art has been equated with the history of styles, and this approach has still a great many advocates in the third quarter of the twentieth century. Starting from Greece and the Italian Renaissance, standards of judgment, terms of reference, and a critical language have been developed, and step by step the history of art of all cultures and periods has been approached and investigated with similar stylistic criteria.

No one can doubt that large cultural areas (such as Europe and China) have developed mutually exclusive artistic conventions to which they have adhered for very long periods of time; that there are national (French, English), regional (Venetian, Neapolitan), and period styles (Gothic, Renaissance), all vastly different; and that these puzzling phenomena may be described as bearing the mark of individualism of peoples, regions, and periods. Nor can one doubt that by a strange emotional and intellectual but basically unconscious submission, creative individuals partake in and, at the same time, become active heralds of the characteristic style of their country, region, and period. Each artist has, in fact, an individual style and a fluctuating degree of freedom within the broader stylistic setting of the national and period styles. It must be admitted, however, that individual styles of artists reveal idiosyncratic traits to a varying extent at different periods and in different cultural contexts and, moreover, that the recognition of personal styles is often dependent not only on the degree of study and empathy but also on the theoretical standpoint of critics and historians. John Ruskin abhorred individualist artists; he loved medieval art and fully accepted the concept of the medieval artist as the servant of God and as such lacking the worldly pride of individualists. In contrast to this view, which is still to be encountered, it is now common knowledge that many masters of the Middle Ages— great as well as mediocre—often had highly individual manners (Schapiro, 1947). How else could we attribute with assurance certain statues of the West porch of Chartres to a great anonymous revolutionary, and lesser statues to his pupils and followers. Attributing works of art—a highly specialized art historical procedure—implies an absolute trust in the individuality of style, without barriers of time and place.

297

But the conception of an individual style, the awareness of it, and the wish to develop it in a definite direction, all this was not conceivable until Renaissance artists began to see themselves as historical beings in a new sense, to which the writing of autobiographies, starting with Lorenzo Ghiberti's, bears witness. It was only then that artists were able to survey the panorama of history and make a considered choice of their allegiance. No medieval artist could have expressed what the architect Filarete (Antonio Averlino) wrote about 1460: "I ask everybody to abandon the modern tradition [i.e., the Gothic style]; do not accept counsel from masters who work in this manner. . . . I praise those who follow the ancients and bless the soul of Brunelleschi who revived in Florence the ancient manner of building" (Oettingen, 1888).

The freedom of choice was accompanied by a freedom to change. It seems that Renaissance artists were the first to bring about controlled changes of their manner, not rarely even from year to year. Without literary evidence and a highly developed technique of analysis it would often be impossible to recognize that a great master's works from different periods of his career are actually by the same hand (Wittkower, "The Young Raphael," 1963). This is true of many artists from Raphael on and particularly so of modern artists. Picasso's ability to switch from a style derived from negro sculpture to one based on Greek vase painting and sculpture illustrates well how the freedom of choice effects radical changes of style.

The change from a comparative stability to a comparative mobility of style is also reflected in a changing approach to the training of artists. For medieval artists the road to eminence lay in the closest possible imitation of one master. Cennino Cennini, in his late medieval artists' manual, warned apprentices against imitating many masters, and advised them to follow one master only, in order to acquire a good style. At the end of the fifteenth century Leonardo reversed this position by counselling that a painter should not attempt to imitate another painter's manner. Medieval workshop practice was eventually replaced by the method of selective borrowing from many masters, a method that from Vasari to the eighteenth century was regarded as style-forming and quality-enhancing, while since the romantic age it has been stigmatized as eclectic. But, in fact, by the very freedom of choice the method implies, it can enhance individualism of style, as it does in Picasso's case.

It is true, however, that the freedom of choice need not necessarily lead to heightened individualism of style. For reasons not easily accounted for, periods pregnant with great individualist artists alternate with others which show a levelling in the individualism of style. Such "lows" may be found in the second half of the sixteenth century in Italy, the second half of the seventeenth in France and, indeed, in most other European countries, and the first half of the eighteenth in England. Somewhat similar observations led Clive Bell, in his spirited and not yet forgotten book *Art* (London, 1914) to the not entirely paradoxical conclusion that Giotto was at once the climax and anticlimax of medieval individualism: "For Giotto heads a movement towards imitation. . . . Before the late noon of the Renaissance, art was almost extinct" (p. 148).

By contrast to the long period of the individualism of style deliberately derived from and based upon the serviceable repertory of a homogeneous artistic culture (fifteenth to eighteenth century), the romantic conception of genius opened new doors to an individual approach to style. Although romantic artists often deluded themselves by believing that their own creations were independent of any tradition, they surely fostered a great richness and variety of personal styles and enhanced the potentiality of unpredictable and sudden changes. Moreover, the fervent romantic belief in the uniqueness and the inviolability of the individual led to the conviction that art is not teachable. This novel creed had important consequences for the future course of the history of art. Even Gustave Courbet, by no means a romantic artist, declared: "I cannot teach my art nor the art of any school, since I deny that art can be taught, or, in other words, I maintain that art is completely individual" (Goldwater and Treves, 1947). Such views help us to understand the peculiar development of art in the nineteenth century, when a gulf opened between the great individualist works of the chosen few and an impersonal art production: the autonomous, creative artist stood aside, while many young artists had to submit to the collective discipline of the academies.

The Non Finito. The *non finito* affords perhaps an even deeper insight into the process of individualization than do problems of style. Unfinished Egyptian, classical, and medieval works have come down to us, but it can be said with complete confidence that they were meant to be finished and remained incomplete for external reasons. With Leonardo and especially Michelangelo the *non finito* enters a new phase, for it now results from internal rather than external causes.

Never before had a tension existed between the conception and the execution of a work. But now self-criticism, dissatisfaction with the imperfect realization of the inner image, the gulf between mind and matter, between the purity of the "Platonic idea" and the baseness of its material realization—often the subject of Michelangelo's sonnets—prevented these masters from finishing some of their works. They would, however, never have claimed that unfinished creations can be regarded as finished (Barocchi, 1962; Tolnay, 1964).

A shift from this position to one intimately connected with expanding individualism culminates in the nineteenth century in the unfinished work by Rodin and others. Here the *non finito* is often due to a deliberate decision to bring the creative process to an end at a moment of the artist's choice, so that the torso, the roughly-hewn work, the half-finished picture, the sketchy execution are the finished product. Rodin commented on his *Balzac:* "The essential things of the modeling are there, and they would be there in less degree if I 'finished' more." Thus the intentional *non finito* requires a new form of self-analysis and introspection, for the work results from a sophisticated control of the act of creation. Moreover, if only half is said and so much hidden and hinted at, the umbilical cord between the work and its maker is never truly severed. In consequence the personality of the artist asserts itself in the work and through the work more demandingly than in any other context and at any other period of the history of art. By the visual evidence of his "unfinished-finished" work the artist requests the public to follow him even where his goal seems indistinct or when he seems beset with problems peculiar to him alone. And the public is prepared to respond and pay due regard to the artist's genius, sure in the conviction that all he creates is important and worth the effort of interpretation and assimilation. Such considerations would seem to blur the dividing line between art and artist. Similarly, some of the points made in the part of this article on Individualism of Artists might, with a slight change of emphasis, have found a place in the present section.

III. INDIVIDUALISM OF ARTISTS

1. Antiquity and Middle Ages. The image of the individualist artist is tied to the elevation of practitioners from the rank of mere craftsmen to the level of emancipated creators. Such a change has come about twice in the history of Western art: in fourth-century Greece and again in fifteenth-century Italy. A process of individualization began even earlier in Greece. Pliny, our main source for Greek artists, reports that the mid-sixth-century B.C. architect and sculptor, Theodoros of Samos, cast a bronze self-portrait "famed as a wondrous likeness" (Pliny, xxxiv, 83; Sellers, 1896). And the fifth century B.C., the classical period of Greek art, saw the rise of a diversified literature by artists on art (Overbeck, 1868; Sellers, 1896; Kalkmann, 1898). Apelles' teacher, Pamphilos (ca. 390–340 B.C.), was the first painter who could boast an all-round education

and a special knowledge in arithmetic and geometry (Pliny, xxxv, 76), and we have it on good authority that artists during this period wanted to appear as gentlemen in dress and mien: Zeuxis is reported to have amassed great wealth and to have displayed his name woven in golden letters into the embroideries of his garments, and his rival, Parrhasios, who lived in luxury, indulged in similar extravagances (Pliny, xxxv, 62, 71). But despite the highly developed self-esteem of artists, public recognition was lacking.

The Greeks felt contempt for those who had to toil with their hands for money; they hardly ranked them higher than slaves. It was the skill of the craftsman that was valued (Poeschel, 1925; Schweitzer, 1925; Zilsel, 1926), and artists, therefore, were mentioned in the company of barbers, cooks, and blacksmiths. Moreover, both Plato and Aristotle assigned to the visual arts a place much below music and poetry. Plato's doctrine of divine enthusiasm had room for poets and musicians but not for artists. Nevertheless, in the fourth century B.C., i.e., in Aristotle's days, the public's attitude began to change.

Characteristically, at the end of the fourth century the historian Duris of Samos wrote a book on the *Lives of Painters and Sculptors* and this work, of which only a few fragments have survived, inaugurated the biographical literature on artists, implying an interest in artists' personalities and individual idiosyncrasies. There are many other indications to show that the respect for the individual creator superseded that for the anonymous craftsman. The Stoics as well as such authors as Philostratus (ca. A.D. 170–245) and Pausanias (late second century A.D.) acknowledged that, just like poets, painters experienced inspiration and ecstasy (Schweitzer, 1925). Masterpieces now found eager bidders; an interest in art and involvement in art criticism became a status symbol. It is credibly reported that Alexander the Great and his court painter Apelles were tied by bonds of friendship (Pliny, xxxv, 85). Later, such Roman emperors as Nero, Hadrian, and Marcus Aurelius regarded painting and sculpting as a suitable pastime for themselves. In spite of all this, the old philosophical and social traditions never ceased to assert themselves; we find them reflected as late as the first century A.D. in Plutarch's well known dictum "We enjoy the work and despise the maker" (*Pericles* i, 4, 5; Dresdner, 1915); or even a hundred years later in Lucian's assessment that by becoming a sculptor "you will be nothing but a labourer . . . one of the swarming rabble . . . whatever your achievement you would be considered an artisan, a craftsman, one who lives by the work of his hands" (*Somnium*, 9).

With the decline and fall of Rome the modest "breakthrough" of the artist was soon forgotten and for many centuries he was once again reduced to the status of artisan and craftsman. This is certainly true, although we now know that the Victorian image of the medieval craftsman, content to be an anonymous member of his lodge and devoted to his work for the glory of God alone, is a myth unsupported by historical facts. Many names of medieval artists have come down to us and even at the darkest period there were masters of distinct individuality such as S. Eligius, who died as Bishop of Noyon in 658; before having taken the vows he had won fame as an artist of remarkable accomplishments. It is recorded that he was a passionate reader, that he loved precious jewelry and gorgeous gowns, that he kept servants, and was surrounded by devoted pupils (Schlosser, 1891). From the eleventh century onward the names of artists abound and, judging from some of their self-laudatory inscriptions—such as those of Rainaldus, one of the architects of Pisa Cathedral (after 1063), or of Lanfrancus, at Modena Cathedral (1099)—we may safely assume that they had a high opinion of their own merits and achievements (Jahn, 1965). Epithets such as *doctus, expertus, probus, sapiens, prudens, praestans*, and *artificiosus*, frequently found in early documents and inscriptions should, however, not be too highly valued as individual characterizations but should, rather, be regarded as referring to the expert handling of execution. While some medieval masters rose to positions of trust and distinction, while some architects in particular attained social advancement and high honors, the rank and file of artists were, in the words of Bishop Otto von Freising (d. 1158), not admitted to higher positions and were kept away "like the plague . . . from more honorable and liberal studies" (Booz, 1956).

When from the thirteenth century onward the urban working population of western Europe became increasingly organized in guilds, artists could not easily assert their individuality; in the fourteenth century and even in the fifteenth the guilds tended to control the whole man, from the education of apprentices to the exercise of jurisdiction. Nor did they omit to look after the physical and moral conduct of their members. Thus there are good grounds to argue that the guilds had an equalizing influence, for artists were de jure and de facto craftsmen with a well-regulated training and a well-regulated daily routine. On the other hand, it cannot be denied that the city breeds individualism, and it is against the very background of the guild-controlled craftsman that the personality problems of Renaissance artists appear revolutionary and emphatically real. It would seem that Jacob Burckhardt's famous thesis of the liberation of the individual in the age of the Renaissance remains valid, especially in the field of the visual arts, although Burckhardt excluded this aspect from his *Civilization of the Renaissance* (1860).

2. Renaissance Individualism. The Renaissance artists' protracted revolt against the guilds was a fight on several fronts: a fight for social recognition, for the recognition of art as an intellectual rather than a manual occupation; a fight for the inclusion of painting, sculpture, and architecture among the disciplines of the liberal arts; a fight, moreover, for the right of free men to look after themselves and act as their consciences dictated. In retrospect, it does not seem astonishing that it was in Florence, the most advanced city-state in Europe, where the individualized artist showing many modern traits first evolved. The new class of merchant patrons with their highly developed individualism, their sense of liberty and enterprise, their progressive and competitive spirit, found in their artists an attitude towards life which they themselves cherished. In this congenial intellectual climate artists first insisted upon their rights as free individuals in a manner that was somewhat unpredictable and not always beyond reproach.

The first memorable case of a challenge of the guild laws is that of the great Filippo Brunelleschi. He refused to pay his dues and on 20 August 1434 was thrown into prison (Fabriczy, 1892). But Brunelleschi's self-assured disobedience ended in victory. He was released after a few days and no interference in his work at the cupola of Florence Cathedral is recorded. This victory had symbolic significance; it was followed by many others. A wealth of documents shows how relentlessly and against what odds the artists carried on their struggle for emancipation. In France the guilds defended their rights stubbornly until Colbert's reorganization in 1663 of the *Académie Royale de Peinture et de Sculpture* (founded in 1635), spelled an end to their power. In England most painters remained low-class tradesmen even longer than in France; as "face-painters" they were organized in the Painter-Stainers Company on an equal footing with coach-painters and house-painters (Wittkower, 1968). Not until well into the eighteenth century, when William Hogarth took up their cause and the Royal Academy was inaugurated with Sir Joshua Reynolds in the President's chair (1768), did British artists achieve a freedom comparable to that of their Italian *confrères* of 200 years before.

The process of individualization, first observable in fifteenth-century Florence, has to be approached from the viewpoint of the artist as well as the public. Early in that century, the painter Cennino Cennini wrote a basically medieval craftsman's manual entitled *Il libro dell'arte*, in which he exhorted his fellow painters to emulate the dignity and temperance of scholars (Cennini, 1932). Otherwise Cennini's work contains mainly technical recipes. But at the same moment in time a new kind of literature on art written by artists arose. Its first product, Leon Battista Alberti's *On Painting* (*De pittura*), written in 1436, a prophetic work of great perspicacity, contains the program of the modern emancipated artist. His art must be given a firm theoretical foundation, for it ranks equal with poetry and the theoretical sciences; and the artist himself has to be a man of immaculate character and great learning. In addition, Alberti regards polite manners and an easy bearing as marks of personality that elevate the artist above the craftsman with his virtues of mere industry and technical skill. Alberti's contemporaries delved into theoretical studies with great eagerness and many tried their hand in the writing of treatises. The sculptor Lorenzo Ghiberti composed a monumental work on art and artists that contains the first autobiography known to have been written by an artist (Schlosser, 1912). This must be regarded as a phenomenon of utmost importance, for an autobiography means looking at one's own life as an observer; it requires the distance of self-reflection, and introspection became an important character trait of the new race of artists.

The new ideal of artistic personality propounded by Alberti adumbrated a conforming, well-adjusted, and socially integrated type, an ideal that was in fact upheld in academic circles through the ages. But at the same time one can also observe the emergence of the nonconforming, alienated artist, and it is this type that is of particular interest in the present context. As early as the fourteenth century a certain class of literary production in Tuscany shows an anecdotal interest in the behavior of artists. In Boccaccio's *Decamerone* and, above all, in the Tuscan *novelle*, artists appear mainly as the perpetrators of entertaining and burlesque practical jokes. For Boccaccio a painter was a man full of fun, high-spirited, quite shrewd, of somewhat lax morals, and not burdened by much learning. And in one of Franco Sacchetti's *novelle* one finds a painter's wife exclaiming: "You painters are all whimsical and of ever-changing mood; you are constantly drunk and are not even ashamed of yourselves!" (Sacchetti, 1946). This remarkable statement sounds like a prophetic definition of the Bohemian artist, and it is certainly true that such anecdotes would have been neither invented nor read if they had not echoed a popular reaction to artists. But in contrast to the anecdotal *topoi* in the Tuscan *novelle* (Kris and Kurz, 1934), the literary image of the artist from the fifteenth century onward loses its jolly and light-hearted connotations and presents us with serious problems of individualization.

Owing to the rich and, as time went on, steadily growing literary production concerning artists, some general observations regarding these problems can safely be made. Instead of being subjected to the regulated routine of the workshop, the Renaissance artist was often on his own and developed characteristics compatible with his freedom. Now periods of most concentrated and intense work often alternated with unpredictable lapses into idleness. The vacillation between obsession with work and creative pauses became the prerogative of free individuals who felt that they were ultimately responsible only to themselves. Vasari, whose *Vite de' più eccellenti pittori, scultori e architetti* (first published in 1550) was the accepted model of historical writing on art for over 200 years, conveys the impression that his Tuscan countrymen showed a greater obsession with their work than others, and since they were the proud and conscious pioneers of an entirely new approach to art, he may not have been wrong at all. The corollary to obsession with one's work is indifference to dress, cleanliness, food, family, public affairs; in short, to everything outside the object of the fixation. Vasari's *Lives* abounds with this theme and consequently many idiosyncratic personalities of artists come to life. Masaccio is described as careless and absentminded, entirely unconcerned about worldly matters; Luca della Robbia, we are told, dedicating himself day and night to his work, patiently bore physical discomfort; Paolo Uccello entirely disregarded the affairs of the world and lived like a hermit, intent only on unravelling the laws of perspective; Bartolomeo Torri from Arezzo, a pupil of Giulio Clovio, had to be turned out of the latter's house because he was so enamored of the study of anatomy that he kept pieces of corpses all over his room and even under his bed. It matters little whether such tales are true or merely anecdotes. For Vasari, his contemporaries, and succeeding generations such anecdotes helped to elucidate individual character traits of artists of distinction.

The emancipated artist needed introspection, and introspection necessitates pauses, often of considerable length. Early reports about such unaccustomed behavior in artists are not very frequent, but some are gratifyingly explicit. A contemporary of Leonardo has left us a vivid description of the latter's procedure when painting the *Last Supper*. According to this eye-witness report Leonardo often stayed on the scaffolding from dawn to dusk without putting down his brush, forgetting to eat and drink, painting all the time. Then, for two, three, or four days he would not touch his work and yet he would stay there, sometimes an hour, sometimes two hours a day wrapped in contemplation (Flora, 1952). Similarly, Jacopo da Pontormo would set out to work in the morning and return in the evening "without having done anything all day but stand lost in thought" (Vasari, VI, 289). The sculptor

Giovan Francesco Rustici, a remarkable individualist who had studied with Leonardo, contrasted the daily toil of workmen with the responsibility of the artist: "Works of art cannot be executed without long reflection" (Vasari, VI, 600). Such a statement, that may nowadays appear hackneyed, could not be experienced and verbalized until the Renaissance emancipation of the artist.

Introspection requires solitude, and solitude and secrecy became the hallmark of many artists. Petrarch as well as Erasmus attest that the intellectual recluse of the Renaissance felt the pangs of isolation. When artists aligned themselves with scholars and poets, they developed symptoms, often to an excessive degree, of the class they joined. Michelangelo never allowed anyone, not even the Pope, to be near him while he worked. Artists like Piero di Cosimo, Pontormo, and many others behaved similarly. Leonardo justified this kind of conduct. "The painter," he wrote, "must live alone, contemplate what his eye perceives and commune with himself" (Ludwig, 1888). And Rustici gave reasons why one should never show one's work to anyone before it was finished (Vasari, VI, 600). A breach of secrecy aroused Franciabigio to such a pitch of anger that he damaged some figures of his fresco of the *Marriage of the Virgin* (SS. Annunziata, Florence) with a bricklayer's hammer. The result can be seen to this day. Tintoretto, a pleasant and gracious person, was of an extremely retiring disposition. He rarely admitted friends to his studio, "let alone other artists, nor did he ever let other painters see him at work" (Ridolfi, 1914). At the threshold of the romantic age Goya talked persuasively about the "looking-into-himself," the spiritual monologue. This attitude would seem a sure sign of a highly developed individualism. No one reveals this more clearly than the most individualistic artist of the Renaissance and maybe of all time, Michelangelo Buonarroti. The essence of the problem that moved him to the core is perhaps contained in the three lines of a sonnet that remained a fragment:

> Entire understanding none can have
> Before he has experienced the immensity
> Of art and life
>
> (Frey [1897], lxxx, 2).

That experience can only be won in isolation, and isolation spells agony. His suffering, his distress of mind is the thread that runs through many of his letters. As a man of seventy-four he writes to a friend: "You will say that I am old and mad; but I answer that there is no better way of keeping sane and free from anxiety than being mad" (Milanesi, 1875). At the same period he put the paradox differently in a famous sonnet:

> Melancholy is my joy
> And discomfort is my rest
>
> (Frey [1897], lxxi).

There is no doubt that the agonized revelling in self-reflection was, at times at least, a satisfying experience for Michelangelo.

Michelangelo's personality hardly less than his art has fascinated and puzzled people for close to 500 years. Every possible epithet has been attached to his name, but in spite of the contradictory light in which he appeared to his contemporaries as well as to posterity, all agree that he was an eccentric endowed with a most difficult nature. "He is terrible, as you can see, and one cannot deal with him," Pope Julius II once said during an audience (Gaye, 1839). Michelangelo's *terribilità* became proverbial, to indicate both the tormented impetuosity of his character and the sublimity of his art.

Eccentricity, however, was not Michelangelo's prerogative, as many tend to believe. From the fifteenth century onward it was regarded as a characteristic of artists as a professional group. The cases of Piero di Cosimo and Pontormo stand out among many others. Both had misanthropic habits of the oddest kind. Piero di Cosimo was held by many to be rather mad, and Pontormo, "solitary beyond belief" was, as his diary kept from 1554 to 1556 reveals, an almost insane hypochondriac. Even minor artists such as Graffione Fiorentino attracted attention because of their eccentric behavior, while others led by a certain Jacone, a pupil of Andrea del Sarto, went all out to *épater le bourgeois*. As their contemporary Vasari (VI, 451) tells ". . . under the pretence of living like philosophers, they lived like swine and brute beasts . . . this miserable existence of theirs . . . was held by them to be the finest in the world."

3. The Post-Renaissance Gentleman-Artist. The list of eccentricities in which artists indulged is long, varied, and well-documented (Wittkower, *Born Under Saturn . . .* , 1963). And the reality of this new type of artist is thrown into relief by the violence of the reaction against it. As early as the middle of the sixteenth century the nonconforming artist with his foibles and extravagances was no longer fashionable. It was then felt that artists should unobtrusively merge with the social and intellectual elite. Vasari himself, to whom any form of excess was anathema, resorted in his biography of Raphael to a technique of idealization: he depicted Raphael as the acme of moral and intellectual perfection. According to him there was no greater contrast than that between Raphael's grace, learning, beauty, modesty, and excellent demeanor and the majority of artists who showed a detachment from reality, and displayed eccentricity admixed with madness and uncouthness (Vasari, IV, 315). Even before this was written, the Portuguese painter Francisco de Hollanda, who was in Rome between 1538 and 1540 and put in literary form the talks he supposedly had with Michelangelo, ascribed the following statement to the great master, surely in order to give it the weight of highest authority:

People spread a thousand pernicious lies about famous painters. They are strange, solitary, and unbearable, it is said, while in fact they are not different from other human beings. Only silly people believe that they are eccentric and capricious (Hollanda, 1899).

In the second half of the sixteenth century the proscription of the eccentric artist was rather general. Most revealing passages are to be found in G. B. Armenini's *Dei veri precetti della pittura* (1587) and G. P. Lomazzo's *Idea del tempio della pittura* (1590). Artists are strongly advised to keep away "from the vices of madness, uncouthness, and extravagance, nor should they aim at originality by acting in a disorderly way and using nauseating language. . . ." Thus from the mid-sixteenth century on writers disavowed artists who displayed conspicuously a nonconforming behavior; instead they created and advocated a new image of the artist: the conforming, well-bred, rational philosopher-artist, who is richly endowed by nature with all the graces and virtues. From then onward artists saw themselves in the role of gentlemen, and the public complied with this idea. Although the anti-conventional artist had come to stay, it may be claimed that great gentlemen and great individualists such as Rubens and Bernini, Lebrun and Reynolds embody most fully the seventeenth- and eighteenth-century ideal of the artist as a versatile, unaffected, well-bred, captivating man of the world. Much as they differed from each other, these masters were all great individualists who left an imprint on their time and later ages, not only because of their art and through their art but also because of their powerful personalities.

As early as the 1540's Francisco de Hollanda makes Vittoria Colonna say that those who knew Michelangelo had greater esteem for his person than for his work. Rubens' affability and prudence, erudition and eloquence, alert mind, broad culture, and all-embracing intellect shine forth after centuries just as does Bernini's spirited Italian individualism, gracing a man of infinite charm, a brilliant and witty talker, fond of conviviality, aristocratic in demeanor and "passionate in his wrath," as his son Domenico reports. Bernini's triumphal procession from Rome to Paris in 1665 at the invitation of Louis XIV was not only an ovation to the greatest artist then alive and to a truly impressive personality, but also illustrates most vividly the revolutionary reassessment of art and artists that had come about in less than 200 years. Indeed, the peak then reached in the estimation of artistic genius has hardly ever again been equalled. Nowadays no government would take so much trouble to look after a traveling artist and architect. Unlike Colbert, prime ministers would scarcely go out of their way to make his stay agreeable.

Among eighteenth-century artists, it was Sir Joshua Reynolds who, in his country, attained a standing and success comparable to Bernini's. Although he came from a family of modest means and although neither lavish praise nor public honors, neither his knighthood nor his presidency of the Royal Academy changed his essentially middle-class bearing, he "certainly contrived"—as his pupil James Northcote wrote—"to move in a higher sphere of society than any other English artist had done before. Thus he procured for Professors of the Arts a consequence, dignity, and reception, which they had never before possessed in this country" (Northcote, 1818). At his death in 1792 a whole nation bowed before the achievement of this great man. Three dukes, two marquesses, three earls, and two lords were his pallbearers; ninety-one carriages, conveying all the members of the Royal Academy and scores of distinguished luminaries followed the body to its resting place in St. Paul's Cathedral.

4. Academicians and Bohemians. The sixteenth century has been called the century of the academies and, indeed, before the end of the century some academies of art were founded. Appropriately, the first one came to life in Florence in 1563 (*Accademia del Disegno*) with Vasari as its initiator and organizer. The new type of gentleman-artist would be unthinkable without the rising social and educational institutions of the art academies which saw their heyday between the seventeenth and the nineteenth centuries. Looking back from the position of the academic artist, the plight of his pre-academic colleague can be more easily understood. Not unlike the medieval artist, the academician enjoyed the benefit of a professional organization, a center toward which his life gravitated. The Renaissance artist, by contrast, partaking no longer in the old and not yet in the new social structure, had to fend for himself. The Renaissance artist's fight for liberation from the encumbrances of the guilds was reenacted in the romantic artist's fight for liberation from the ties of the academy. Just as the individualism of the Renaissance artist put an end to the sheltered position of the late medieval craftsman, so the new

303

romantic vocabulary—enthusiasm, naïveté, spontaneity, feeling, autonomy of artistic creation, intuition, totality of vision, and so forth—reversed many basic tenets of the academic artist. The specter arose of the artist as a kind of being elevated above the rest of mankind, alienated from the world and answerable in thought and deed only to his own genius: the image of the Bohemian took shape, fostered as much by the ideology and conduct of the artist as by the reaction of the society on the fringe of which he lived. Thus we see toward the end of the eighteenth century and at the beginning of the nineteenth problems of personality in the making, which, under kindred circumstances, had beset the artists of the Florentine Renaissance. With good reason, therefore, one may talk of a proto-Bohemian period around and after 1500 separated from the Bohemian era proper by the centuries of the conforming artist.

5. Romanticism and its Aftermath. By and large, Renaissance and post-Renaissance artists regarded the business of art as an intellectual discipline. The intellectual responsibilities artists took upon themselves had a noticeable influence upon forming their minds and personalities. With Michelangelo, they believed that "a man paints with his brain," and with Leonardo they agreed that "painting has to do with natural philosophy," that it is "truly a science," and that a painter had "first to study science and follow with practice based on science." Not until the second half of the eighteenth century does a shift away from intellectualism toward an intuitive approach begin to predominate. The revolt came into its own when an artist such as William Blake vented his scorn against the reign of Reason with these lines:

> All Pictures that's Painted with Sense and
>   with Thought
> Are Painted by Madmen as sure as a Groat
>   (Keynes, p. 660).

Romanticism with its "egomania" brought about a most serious change in the personality of artists. A romantic pedigree is recognizable in the untrammeled individualism of many twentieth-century artists and in their personality and social problems, though it must be admitted that the freedom they arrogate to themselves is in the last analysis derived from the revolution of the Italian Renaissance, the period in history on which they heap the fullness of their scorn.

When the psychologists entered the arena, artists, backed by an "authoritative" analysis of the psyche and armed with an up-to-date vocabulary, could state with confidence the case for self-expression unencumbered by book-learning. Artists of the Freudian and post-Freudian era claim a degree of subjective and

moral freedom that would bewilder even their romantic precursors. When Pablo Picasso says that "the artist is a receptacle of emotions come from no matter where," or Marc Chagall comments on his pictures "I do not understand them at all. . . . They are only pictorial arrangements that obsess me," or Mark Rothko strives to eliminate all obstacles "among others, memory, history, or geometry" (Wittkower, *Born Under Saturn*, 1963), or Jackson Pollock maintains "When I am *in* my painting, I'm not aware of what I am doing" (Read, 1967)—they may emphasize and cultivate the emotional element in their creations, but theirs is a very conscious surrender to the unconscious. Contrary, however, to the artists' own belief, "automatism" in art does lead to a loss of artistic individuality. Nevertheless, even though a doodle by Picasso or Klee may lack a distinct personal quality, one cannot argue that the public is deceiving itself by paying high prices for such works. For, obviously, the public places the artist above the work: it is the name that works the magic. Behind the name looms the man, the great artist, in whose integrity we believe and of whose genius we are convinced.

IV. ART AND GENIUS

In the present context "individualism" and "genius" are sister terms and considerations of the one implicitly illuminate the other. This is particularly striking when we consider some of the roots of the modern conception of genius that emerged in the course of the eighteenth century.

1. Natural Talent. In his *History of Modern Criticism* René Wellek said: "The terms 'genius,' 'inspiration,' *poeta vates, furor poeticus* are the stock in trade of Renaissance poetics, and even the most rigid critic . . . never forgot to say that poets need 'inspiration,' 'imagination,' 'invention'. . . . They believed in a rational theory of poetry but not that poetry was entirely rational." All the terms here mentioned are closely tied up with the concept of genius, but the key to the ideas later associated with original genius is to be found in the irrational element always acknowledged in poetry and art. The idea that the poet is born with his talent had first taken shape in Hellenistic thought, when writers and artists first became conscious of the vital importance of individual artistic endowment (Schweitzer, 1925). The concept appears in the writing about art theory even before the publication in 1554 of Longinus' *Peri hupsous* (*On the Sublime*), which exerted a steadily growing influence on literary criticism (Monk, 1935). According to Leonardo painting "cannot be taught to those not endowed by nature" (Richter, 1939). The great Aretino was a passionate champion of inborn artistic genius; he voiced his view repeatedly and in a letter of 1547 expressed epigrammatically: "Art is the gift of bountiful nature and is given to us in the cradle" (Aretino, 1957). His friend Lodovico Dolce, also a Venetian, in his *Dialogue on Painting* (1557) made this opinion his own, and later art critics such as G. P. Lomazzo (1590) reiterated that "those who are not born painters can never achieve excellence in this art." Thereafter this view became an often repeated *topos* (Kris and Kurz, 1934).

If the artist owes his individual talent to a gift of the gods, his art, too, defies rational analysis. Ancient authors—Cicero, Quintilian, Pliny—made allowance for the irrational element in works of art and called it *venustas* ("grace"). From the sixteenth century onward classical art theory was permeated with this concept. "Grace" for the Italians from Baldassare Castiglione to Vasari and beyond was *un non so che*, which in the French theory of the seventeenth century became the *je ne sais quoi* and in England, in Pope's immortal phrase, "A Grace beyond the Reach of Art" (Monk, 1944).

Critics and artists of the Renaissance had definite ideas of how talent ought to be displayed. Pedantic, slow, laborious execution smacked of the artisan's craft. The work of the artist richly endowed by nature cannot be measured and valued in terms of working hours spent on manual execution. As early as the mid-fifteenth century a distant "rumbling" may be noticed. The Archbishop Saint Antonino of Florence explained: "Painters claim, more or less reasonably, to be paid for their art not only according to the amount of work involved, but rather according to the degree of their application and experience" (Gilbert, 1959). But it was not until well into the sixteenth century that artists stated with vigor that the compensation for a work of art depended on the ingenuity and not on the length of time that had gone into its making. Thus Michelangelo supposedly said to Francisco de Hollanda: "I value highly the work done by a great master even though he may have spent little time over it. Works are not to be judged by the amount of useless labor spent on them but by the worth of the skill and mastery of their author" (Holt, 1947).

The modern artist had to perform in a way that matched his new status, and thus we find from the second half of the sixteenth century onward most theorists insisting on facility of execution, on a manner of painting that would give the impression of rapid work and effortless skill hiding the toil that had gone into the making of the work of art. As early as 1550 Vasari made the memorable observation that "many painters . . . achieve in the first sketch of their work, as though guided by a sort of fire of inspiration . . . a certain measure of boldness; but afterwards, in finish-

ing it, the boldness vanishes" (Wittkower, 1967). Throughout the seventeenth and eighteenth centuries a number of progressive artists attempted to preserve something of the brio of spontaneous creation, with the result that the finish itself became sketchy. The masters working with a free, rapid brushstroke assumed steadily greater importance and led up to the position of painters like Delacroix, for whom the first flash of the idea was "pure expression" and "truth issuing from the soul." It was in the context of this development that the painter's sketch as well as the sculptor's sketchy clay model (*bozzetto*) were conceded the status of works of art in their own right. The appreciation of individual manner and style in the drawing, the sketch, and the *bozzetto*—first savored by the eighteenth-century virtuoso—cannot, of course, be separated from the recognition of genius emerging at the same time.

2. Talent and Genius. But one must be careful not to confuse talent and genius. The qualities with which the term "genius" has been invested ever since the mid-eighteenth century, such as spontaneity, outstanding originality, and exceptional creativity were not implied in the Latin *ingenium* and the Italian *ingegno*, meaning natural disposition, i.e., talent. The Elizabethans still employed the term *ingenium*, or its counterpart at that time, "wit." In the course of the seventeenth century the use of the term genius increased and gradually supplanted "wit," absorbing *ingenium* in the process (Kaufman, 1926). But before the end of the seventeenth century Sir William Temple distinguished between "high flights of wit" and "the pure native force or spirit of genius." Nonetheless talent and genius remained synonyms for a considerable time. It was only after the men of the German "Storm and Stress" had aggressively turned their attention to the comparatively loose English ideas on genius "that the distinction between genius and talent . . . was sharpened into the strong antithesis which is now universally current . . ." (Murray, *New English Dictionary*, IV). Thus we see, about a hundred years after Sir William Temple's time, genius and talent taking on their present-day meanings. William Jackson in *Whether Genius be born or acquired* (1798) declared that "a man of genius must have talents, but talents are possessed by many without it [i.e., genius]. . . . Genius is inventive, a creation of something not before existing; to which talents make no pretence . . ." (Kaufman, 1926). Again, about a hundred years later, the poet James Russell Lowell laid down epigrammatically: "Talent is that which is in a man's power; genius is that in whose power a man·is."

Despite such semantic distinctions the term "talent" has been used in the preceding paragraph to charac- 305 terize the pre-eighteenth-century concept of inborn genius, because during the Renaissance the accretion of distinct ideas defining the modern term genius were still lacking. In the following sections these characteristics will be briefly discussed, one by one.

3. Imitation and Originality. The literary criticism of the sixteenth century knew of no breach between originality and imitation. On the contrary, Marco Girolamo Vida's dictum (1527) that the highest originality was the most ingenious imitation of the ancients, quoted here in lieu of many others, had a long life and also reverberated for a long time in the theory of art. An Aristotelian and pseudo-Aristotelian theory of imitation informed both literary criticism and art theory, and to a certain extent even artistic practice (Wittkower, 1965). It was only in the course of the eighteenth century that some great artists differentiated between copying and imitating (Anton Raphael Mengs) or copying and borrowing (Sir Joshua Reynolds). Borrowing from great masters was, according to Reynolds, "the true and only method by which an artist makes himself master of the profession. . . . Such imitation is so far from . . . the servility of plagiarism, that it is . . . a continual invention." Horace Walpole, in the *Anecdotes of Painting in England* (1762), valiantly rose in defense of the great painter concluding: ". . . a quotation from a great author, with a novel application of the sense, has always been allowed to be an instance of parts and taste; and may have more merit than the original." But in the last decades of the eighteenth century this meant defending a lost position. A growing number of artists were in revolt. Their criticism is epitomized in Chardin's *Singe peintre* (Louvre) showing an ape who copies an antique statue which on his canvas also turns into an ape. Hogarth, in his famous tailpiece of the Spring Gardens Catalogue of 1761, used the same simian formula to ridicule the antiquarian adulation of masters of past ages.

Many artists were clamoring for a new kind of originality, a search for new values independent of imitation. But it was literary critics rather than artists who defined the changed meaning of originality. The primary contribution came from England, perhaps influenced by Giordano Bruno's *Eroici furori*, published in London in 1585 and dedicated to Sir Philip Sidney. Bruno had a clear notion of the character of genius: "The rules are derived from the poetry, and there are as many kinds and sorts of true rules as there are kinds and sorts of true poets." Such a premiss opened up the problem posed by Shakespeare's work: obviously, it could not be fitted into the traditional Aristotelian categories, and the modern alliance of originality and genius was probably due to Shakespearean criticism. Alexander Pope in the preface to his edition of Shakespeare (1715) noted: "If ever any Author deserved the name of an Original it was Shakespeare. . . ." Characteristically, "original" and "original genius" appear in titles of books after 1750 (Edward Young, 1759; William Duff, 1767; Robert Wood, 1769, 1775).

In one of his famous *Spectator* articles on Genius (No. 160, 3 September, 1711), Addison still regarded his subject as "so uncommon." It was only after the mid-century that a vigorous analysis of "genius" was undertaken. Next to Alexander Gerard's, the most remarkable of the many publications was Edward Young's *Conjectures on Original Composition* (1759), in which the aged author intended to show genius the way out of the obstructions of Augustan dogma: the "meddling ape imitation . . . destroys all mental individuality" was the new creed. The little book contains such well-known and often quoted passages as "An *Original* may be said to be of a *vegetable* nature; it rises spontaneously from the vital root of genius; it *grows*, it is not *made*." What has been called Young's "vegetable concept of genius" (Abrams, 1953) has been looked upon askance by some modern critics (Fabian, 1966), because the links to sub-rational processes turned genius into an occult phenomenon. But Young's compelling language and metaphors assured his success. The book was immediately translated twice into German and created—as Herder wrote—an electrifying effect. Young actually adumbrated the notions of the romantic concept of genius. In his claims of originality Young had gone far beyond Duff, the author of *An Essay on Original Genius* (1767), who, despite his adulation of originality and exorcism of imitation, demanded that an exuberant imagination must be restrained by a proportionate share of reason and judgment—herein apparently following Gerard's *An Essay on Genius*, a work largely written in 1758, but not published until 1774 (Fabian, 1966). Already in his *An Essay on Taste* (1759) Gerard had made the point that "Diligence and acquired abilities may assist or improve genius: but a fine imagination alone can produce it."

At the end of the century the radical dedication to original creation found eloquent apostles in John Pinkerton and William Blake; in their revolt against imitation both used violent language unheard before. In his *Letters of Literature* (1785) Pinkerton attacked "the complete folly of instituting Academies of Painting . . . that is, Schools of Imitation. Did ever any one good painter arise from an academy? Never. . . ." And Blake in his utter condemnation of Reynolds' *Discourses* exclaimed "What has Reasoning to do with the Art of Painting?" His dictum "One power alone makes a poet: Imagination, the Divine Vision" contains the gist of his view of genius (Keynes, p. 770).

4. Invention and Creation, Fancy and Imagination, Spontaneity and Inspiration. Blake may be the most violent exponent of spontaneity and divine inspiration but his ideas are less his own than is sometimes believed. He enthroned originality and called it imagination. The terms heading this paragraph have their own complex history and, at the same time, they are all closely interwoven with the growth of the concept of genius.

"Invention," a term of classical rhetoric, one of the pillars of Renaissance literary and art theory (Zilsel, 1926), was, it might be said, demoted in the course of the eighteenth century and increasingly replaced by "creative" and "creation," terms more indicative of the spontaneity of genius. It has been suggested (L. Pearsall Smith) that this changeover began with the critical study of Shakespeare. Dryden, discussing the character of Caliban, said: "Shakespeare seems there to have created a person which was not in Nature, a boldness which, at first sight, would appear intolerable." Yet Alexander Gerard in his *Essay on Taste* (1759) still stated: "The first and leading quality of genius is invention . . . ," and he returned to this in his *Essay on Genius* (1774): while "Genius is properly the faculty of invention," he wrote, "it is imagination that produces genius. . . ." The new concise terminology appeared in the *Essay on Original Genius* (1767) of William Duff, who found that "creative Imagination [was] the distinguishing characteristic of true Genius." Thereafter the concept "creative imagination" was assimilated by the German Storm and Stress movement and became a catchword during the romantic era. Kant in the *Critique of Judgment* (1790) propounded authoritatively: "Creative imagination is the true source of genius and the basis of originality."

German criticism also hammered out the distinction between fancy (*Einbildungskraft*) and imagination (*Phantasie*), the former referring to human awareness and the latter, the higher power, to "divine infusion." Coleridge, steeped in German aesthetic speculations, likewise distinguished genius and imagination from the lower faculties, talent and fancy (Wellek [1955], II). And Ruskin still accepted these distinctions.

It was also in eighteenth-century criticism that the vital function of spontaneity and inspiration was constantly reiterated. William Sharpe in his *Dissertation on Genius* (1755), the first book on the subject, remarked on the natural untrained powers of genius. Edward Young (1759) laid down that genius creates "spontaneously from the vital root" of our individual natures. George Colman in his papers on Genius published in *The St. James Chronicle* (1761–62), claimed that "A Genius is a character purely modern, and of so late an origin that it has never yet been described

or defined. . . ." He recognized egotistical reliance on untutored spontaneity as a hallmark of genius (Kaufman, 1926). William Duff (1767) singled out irresistible spontaneity. This list could be endlessly prolonged, for next to the emphasis on originality and creative imagination, spontaneity and inspiration were basic to the cult of genius. No more need be said here since a great deal of ingenuity has been devoted by modern scholars to an epistemological exploration of these terms. But a few comments on other characteristics of genius are in place.

5. Genius without Learning. While Renaissance and post-Renaissance theory could not envisage great achievement without the control of the reasoning faculties and without solid intellectual grounding, those who shaped the new concept of genius created a thoroughly anti-intellectual image of the select few: they were deemed capable of producing from pure inspiration. Sir William Temple had already suggested that learning might weaken the force of genius (*Of Poetry*, 1690). And Addison made the memorable remark (*Spectator*, No. 160, 3 September, 1711) that genius creates "by the mere Strength of natural Parts and without any Assistance of Arts or learning." By the mid-century this idea must have been current to such extent that Dr. Johnson denounced as "the mental diseases of the present Generation . . . Impatience of Study, Contempt of the great Masters of antient [sic] Wisdom, and a Disposition to rely wholly upon unassisted Genius . . ." (*The Rambler*, No. 154, 7 September, 1751). Literary evidence of this concept abounds in the second half of the century; witness such remarks as the following by George Colman (1761–62): "The Genius . . . needs neither diligence nor assiduity"; or Young (1759), "Many a Genius, probably, there has been, which could neither write, nor read"; "To the neglect of learning, genius sometimes owes its greatest glory." And on to Schiller, Coleridge, and Nietzsche.

It was only natural that primitivism now appeared as an asset favoring original genius. Adam Ferguson had expressed the idea quite simply in *An Essay on the History of Civil Society* (1767, p. 265): a primitive poet is always original because "he delivers the emotions of the heart, in words suggested by the heart: for he knows no other." And in the same year William Duff made the more daring assertion that "original genius will in general be displayed in its utmost vigour in the early and uncultivated periods of society . . . and that it will seldom appear in a very high degree in cultivated life."

It must be emphasized, however, that most practicing artists were rather conservative. Few accepted the extravagant claims made by literary critics for natural genius. Sir Joshua Reynolds, for instance, condemned the opinion "too prevalent among artists, of the imaginary powers of native genius, and its sufficiency in great works." Despite his classic-idealistic convictions, he was not unmoved by the new ideas, but opposed the notion that "rules are the fetters of genius. They are fetters to men without genius." An insistence on freedom tempered, however, by study, learning, and imitation prevailed with other great practitioners. Robert Adam, who almost monopolized important architectural commissions in England between 1760 and 1790, held that the freedom permissible to genius gave him liberty "to transform the beautiful spirit of antiquity with novelty and variety." But at the same time he maintained that architecture needed "to be informed and improved by correct taste," and the models of correct taste were the works of the ancients (*Works*, 1773). Adam's Roman friend, the great Giovanni Battista Piranesi, in his *Parere su l'architettura* (1765) ridiculed reason and rule and advocated imaginative instead of imitative art. But despite this stress put on originality, he admonished his readers: "Let us borrow from their stock" (i.e., that of the ancients). Even Goya, the greatest genius of Blake's generation and, like Blake, an advocate of unfettered imagination, intended to inscribe on the title page to his series of *Caprichos*: "The sleep of reason produces monsters." In his comment to this plate Goya added: "Imagination deserted by reason produces impossible monsters. United with reason, imagination is the mother of the arts and the source of their wonders."

6. The Artist as Second God. The Renaissance concept of the *divino artista* ("the divine artist") had a double root. On the one hand, it was derived from Plato's theory of the *furores*, the inspired madness of which seers and poets are possessed; on the other hand, it looked back to the medieval idea of God the Father as artist, as architect of the universe. When, as early as 1436, Leon Battista Alberti suggested in his treatise *On Painting* that the artist may well consider himself, as it were, another god, an *alter deus*, he was probably prompted by the medieval *deus artifex*. Whatever his source, the simile suggested that the artist was divorced from the rank and file of "normal" people.

The *tertium comparationis* between God and the poet or artist is the act of creation. This was often expressed (for examples, Zilsel, 1926). Leonardo called the artist *signore e Dio* (Ludwig, 1888; Panofsky, 1962), while Scaliger (*Poetics*, 1561) returned to Alberti's dictum: the poet was "as it were a second god" (*velut alter deus*). Similarly, the influential Lomazzo in another work, *Trattato . . .* (1584), regarded the *fare e creare* of the painter as a lower form of divine activity.

The epithet "divine" (*divus, divino*) for living poets or artists appears rarely before the sixteenth century

(Zilsel [1926], p. 276); it becomes more common with the diffusion of Renaissance Neo-Platonism. The supreme example is, of course, Michelangelo, whom Aretino addressed as "divine" and to whose name Ariosto gave a fashionable meaning in the punning verse

> *Michael più che mortal*
> *Angel divino*
> ("Michael more than mortal/ Angel Divine")

that was in every one's mouth and is still a standard quotation. Francisco de Hollanda poignantly characterized the new position by saying: "In Italy one does not care for the renown of great princes, it's a painter only that they call divine."

The concept of the divinity of artistic creation lives on (Kris and Kurz, 1934) and reappears imaginatively and forcefully in Shaftesbury's Platonic vision of artistic inspiration as "divine enthusiasm." Shaftesbury, who according to Ernst Cassirer (1932; 1955) rescued the term "genius" "from the confusion and ambiguity that had previously attached to it," goes on to characterize the inspired poet, the real Master, as "a second Maker; a just Prometheus under Jove." The idea of the divine metaphysical power of genius became an inalienable part of English and also Continental considerations—"Genius has ever been supposed to partake of something Divine," "Genius is from Heaven, Learning from man" (Young, 1759). Meanwhile, the Prometheus motif as presented by Shaftesbury influenced German thought with archetypal power. This story was fully explored in a classic paper by Oskar F. Walzel (1910).

7. Genius, Madness and Melancholy. Plato not only opened up for all times the concept of divine rapture, but was indirectly also responsible for the entrenched alliance between genius and madness. Seneca's often quoted dictum "There never has been great talent without a touch of madness" which referred to the Platonic fire of divine inspiration, was usually misunderstood. Dryden's "Great wits are sure to madness near allied,/ And thin partitions do their bounds divide," and even Schopenhauer's "Genius is nearer to madness than the average intelligence" echo the misinterpreted line from Seneca. But the myth of a close alliance between genius and madness was not buttressed until the nineteenth century by professional psychologists (such as J. Moreau, C. Lombroso, P. J. Moebius, W. Lange-Eichbaum) and pseudo-clinical evidence, so that many great nineteenth-century minds such as Balzac, Rimbaud, and Taine took the supposed connection between mental illness and artistic genius for granted, and the belief in this connection has spread so widely that it has become, in Lionel Trilling's phrase, "one of the characteristic notions of our culture." The catchword "mad artist" of the *vox populi*, however, does not refer simply to lack of mental or emotional stability. The notion nowadays implies "a mythical picture of the creative man: inspired, rebellious, dedicated, obsessive, alienated, as well as neurotic" (Philips, 1957).

For an understanding of the idea of the mad artist before the nineteenth century, familiarity with Aristotle's doctrine of the Saturnine temperament is necessary. Developing the Hippocratian humoral pathology, Aristotle postulated a connection between the melancholic humor and outstanding talent in the arts and sciences. "All extraordinary men distinguished in philosophy, politics, poetry, and the arts," he maintained, "are evidently melancholic." But the melancholy of such men is a precarious gift for, although only the *homo melancholicus* can rise to the loftiest heights, he is also prone to conditions bordering on insanity. It was Marsilio Ficino who, in his *De vita triplici* (1482–89), revived Aristotle's half-forgotten doctrine. Moreover, he took the important step of reconciling Aristotle's and Plato's views by maintaining that melancholy, the ambivalent temperament of those born under the equally ambivalent planet Saturn was simply a metonymy for Plato's divine *mania* (Klibansky, Panofsky, and Saxl, 1964). Ficino's conclusion was widely accepted: only the melancholic temperament was capable of Plato's enthusiasm.

From then on gifted men were categorized as saturnine and, conversely, no outstanding intellectual or artistic achievement was believed possible unless its author was melancholic. In the sixteenth century a veritable wave of "melancholic behavior" swept across Europe (Babb, 1951). Many great artists—and not only they—were described as melancholic, among them Dürer, Raphael, and Michelangelo (Wittkower, *Born Under Saturn*, p. 104). Michelangelo's use of the terms "madness" and "melancholy" in reference to himself will now be more readily understood. They echo Ficino's uniting of Platonic "madness" and Aristotelian "melancholy," and there is reason to assume that it was this alliance that many a Renaissance artist regarded as essential for his own creativity.

But even at the height of the vogue of melancholy, doubts were voiced, and eventually the Renaissance concept of the *melancholicus* was supplanted by the new image of the conforming artist. None of the great seventeenth-century masters—Rubens and Bernini, Rembrandt and Velázquez—was ever described as melancholic and, indeed, showed any traces of the affliction. It was not until the romantic era, with artists such as Caspar David Friedrich (Hartlaub, 1951), that melancholy appears once again as a condition of mental and emotional catharsis. Nevertheless, the Greek humoral pathology was forever dethroned as early as 1697 with the publication of G. E. Stahl's *Lehre von den Temperamenten*.

8. Sanity of Genius. In 1826, at a time when the conviction of the abnormality of genius was widely shared, Charles Lamb raised the voice of common sense in his essay on "The Sanity of True Genius" (1826). Not only did he deny any connection between genius and madness, but even maintained that genius "manifests itself in the admirable balance of all the faculties." Lamb had some following among psychologists and psychiatrists even in the twentieth century (Wittkower, *Born Under Saturn*, pp. 100f.), and what is perhaps more remarkable, took up and continued—maybe unknowingly—ideas well established before him.

Indeed, Leon Battista Alberti in the fifteenth century, Vasari, the Venetian Paolo Pini, and others in the sixteenth had a clear vision of the many accomplishments with which talent must be endowed, and even when the modern conception of genius began to make its entry, it was first the exalted, lofty, and harmonious qualities that were regarded as characteristic of the very greatest. In his *Réflexions critiques sur la poésie et sur la peinture* (1719) the Abbé Du Bos spoke of the nobility of the heart and mind of genius, of the vivacity and delicacy of feeling inseparable from it, and said that the artist of genius must have "much more exquisite sensibility than normal people." Even much later, reasonableness and perfect balance appear as the touchstone of true genius. Thus James Northcote (1818) left the following character sketch of his master Reynolds:

> He had none of those eccentric bursts of action, those fiery impetuosities which are supposed by the vulgar to characterize genius, and which frequently are found to accompany a secondary rank of talent, but are never conjoined with the first. His incessant industry was never wearied into despondency by miscarriage, nor elated into negligence by success. . . .

The concept of the sanity of genius is linked with the idea that exceptional work can only be accomplished by exceptional characters and, moreover, that there is a kind of mirror-image relationship between personality and work. As Vasari informs his readers, the lofty art of Raphael could only result from a lofty soul.

9. Union of, and Dichotomy between, Man and his Work. The mirror-image concept has a pedigree leading back to Plato's *Politeia* and *Gorgias*. Aristotle too believed in a union of the morality of the poet and that of his work. This theory had a long life; we find it in the Stoa, in Cicero, and in Quintilian (Heitmann

[1962], pp. 9ff.). And the Renaissance assimilated it, mainly owing to Marsilio Ficino's *Theologia Platonica*, the cornerstone of Renaissance philosophy. To quote an essential passage: "We can see in them [i.e., paintings and buildings] the attitude and the image, as it were, of his [the artist's] mind; for in these works the mind expresses and reflects itself not otherwise than a mirror reflects the face of a man who looks into it" (Gombrich [1945], p. 59). This ancient conception, which in due course became part and parcel of the humanist Renaissance tradition, can be traced through the sixteenth century (Weinberg, 1961) and even through the seventeenth and into the eighteenth. Boileau, in *L'Art poétique* (1674), expressed firm belief in the correlation of character and artistic qualities:

Que votre âme et vos moeurs peintes dans vos ouvrages
N'offrent jamais de vous que de noble images. . . .

And probably not independent of Boileau, Jonathan Richardson in *An Essay on the Theory of Painting* (1715), a pioneering work for England, enlarged on the topic that "The way to be an Excellent Painter, is to be an Excellent Man." The theory of a mirror-image relationship between character and work has found a following into our own days. In fact, it is often naively applied by art historians, who are forgetting that ambiguity is a specific characteristic of the visual image: what looks chaste to one beholder may appear obscene to the next. Reflections upon the man behind the work must therefore be regarded with considerable skepticism. There are, however, also some deliberate attempts—such as in Hartlaub and Weissenfeld (1958)—to present the old Platonic concept in a modern psychological dress.

This story would not be complete without taking note of the fact that a theory diametrically opposed to that of the mirror image had found advocates at an early date. There are passages in Catullus, Pliny, Apuleius, Ovid, and others (Heitmann [1962], pp. 16f.) denying a connection between the morality of the author and that of his work. And from Boccaccio on, the assertion is repeated that no link exists between the author and the character of the stories told by him. The theory culminates in Diderot's axiom, published in his article "Platonism" in the *Encyclopédie*, that great men may be morally deficient and a burden to those close to them, and that nevertheless their work remains untouched by such personal shortcomings. There is, in short, no link between *grand auteur et homme de bien*. In *Le Neveu de Rameau* Diderot maintained that geniuses are hypertrophically developed in one direction, but are failures as persons: *Ils ne sont bons qu'à une chose, passé cela, rien; ils ne savent ce que c'est d'être citoyens, pères, mères, parents, amis.*

It has been noticed that Diderot's forcefully stated thesis was readily taken up in the nineteenth century: Goethe, Victor Hugo, Paul Bourget, and others learned their lesson from him, and from here, of course, there opened another avenue to the nineteenth-century theme of the alliance of genius and madness. But it has also been shown (Heitmann [1962], pp. 30ff.) that Diderot, far from being a pedant, could happily contradict himself. Discussing François Boucher (whom he detested) in the *Salon* of 1765, Diderot remarked that the degradation of taste, color, composition, etc., resulted from a degraded personality. Other passages too show that he had not entirely dismissed the old mirror-image theory. It is, in fact, remarkable how vigorously the doctrine of a harmony between man and work reasserted itself. This is demonstrated by material collected by M. H. Abrams (1953, Ch. IX) and K. Heitmann (1962).

The apparent impasse that mars a solution to this problem is understandable: common sense insists that every work of art bears the personal stamp of its maker. Nonetheless, it would be absurd to postulate that a fierce brush reveals an unruly temperament or that "tame" painters or writers have gentle characters, are morally healthy, law-abiding, and pleasant to deal with. Diderot himself tried to resolve these contradictions by drawing new conclusions from the Platonic concept of divine frenzy. In *De la poésie dramatique* he submitted that the artist in the ecstasy of creation is a being very different from his normal self. We must clearly differentiate, he argued, between ourselves and

. . . l'homme enthousiaste, qui prend la plume, l'archet, le pinceau. . . . Hors de lui, il est tout ce qu'il plaît à l'art qui le domine. Mais l'instant de l'inspiration passé, il rentre et redevient ce qu'il était; quelquefois un homme commun (Heitmann [1962], p. 20);

(". . . the enthusiast who takes up pen, fiddlestick, paintbrush. . . . When in a frenzy he is everything he desires to be in the art that dominates him. But the very moment the inspiration is over, he returns to earth and becomes what he has been before, quite often an ordinary man"). Basically in the same vein Flaubert postulated much later (1853) the principle *vivre en bourgeois et penser en demi-dieu* ("live like a bourgeois and think like a demi-god"). Baudelaire seems to have deepened this insight by explaining that there are men whose art must be regarded as the result *d'une vaste énergie vitale inoccupée* ("a vast latent vital energy"). Art here assumes a cathartic function, a theme discussed in an illuminating chapter of M. H. Abrams' work (1953). It appears that as early as the 1830's John Keble, who held the Oxford Chair of Poetry, progressed to a "proto-Freudian theory, which conceives of literature as disguised wish-fulfillment. . . ." Psychoanalytical dialectics offer a deepened awareness and new methodology in approaching the problem of interaction between the artist and his work. In psychoanalytical opinion (Kris, 1953) artistic products add a new dimension to the artist's personality, because the works result from the resolution and sublimation of repressions. In this way the unity of work and personality is preserved, for we are made to understand why a retiring character may be a bold artist, or an outgoing artist timid in his work. Discreetly handled, this approach may also throw more light on the still mysterious resources on which artistic genius thrives.

Although we are reminded that the man of the second half of the twentieth century no longer believes in geniuses (Lowinsky, 1964), they can hardly be abolished by an act of "cultural will." Geniuses will appear and be acknowledged both in the arts and sciences as long as Western man regards free development as the inalienable right of the individual. The extreme self-interest normally associated with genius and conceded to it by society without a murmur is and will remain at the very core of the problem of individualism.

BIBLIOGRAPHY

For Parts II and III (Individualism), R. Wittkower, "Individualism in Art and Artists: A Renaissance Problem," *Journal of the History of Ideas*, **22** (1961), 291–302; R. and M. Wittkower, *Born under Saturn. The Character and Conduct of Artists: A Documentary History from Antiquity to the French Revolution* (London and New York, 1963), have been used extensively.

For Part IV (Genius) the following were particularly important: M. H. Abrams, *The Mirror and the Lamp: Romantic Theory and the Critical Tradition* (Oxford, 1953), a standard work; B. Fabian, Introduction to the critical edition of Alexander Gerard, *An Essay on Genius, 1774* (Munich, 1966), the most stimulating recent study on the problem of genius; P. Kaufman, "Heralds of Original Genius," *Essays in Memory of Barrett Wendell* (Cambridge, Mass., 1926); L. Pearsall Smith, "Four Words: Romantic, Originality, Creative, Genius," *S.P.E.* (Society for Pure English), Tract No. **17** (Oxford, 1924), last reprinted as: "Four Romantic Words," *Words and Idioms Studies in the English Language* (London, 1957), 95–114; both Smith's and Kaufman's are pioneering papers; they have been extensively used here; H. Thüme, *Beiträge zur Geschichte des Geniebegriffs in England* (Halle, 1927), a Hamburg dissertation, still important even though the categories used are no longer satisfactory; H. Wolf, *Versuch einer Geschichte des Geniebegriffs in der deutschen Ästhetik des 18. Jahrhunderts* (Heidelberg, 1923), with chapters on the conception of genius in French and English aesthetics; E. Zilsel, *Die Entstehung des Geniebegriffs* (Tübingen, 1926), still the basic study, but scarcely goes beyond the sixteenth century.

The following bibliography in alphabetic sequence contains a few items to which no reference is made in the text, but which have proved useful in writing the article.

M. H. Abrams, see above. L. B. Alberti, *On Painting*, trans. with Introduction and Notes by J. R. Spencer (London, 1956). P. Aretino, *Lettere sull'arte*, ed. Camesasca (Milan, 1957), II, 180. L. Babb, *The Elizabethan Malady* (East Lansing, Mich., 1951). K. Badt, *Kunsttheoretische Versuche* (Cologne, 1968), with papers on "Artifex vates and artifex rhetor" and "God and Artist." P. Barocchi, *Giorgio Vasari, La Vita di Michelangelo*, 5 vols. (Milan and Naples, 1962), IV, 1645–70. J. Bialostocki, "Terribilità," in *Stil und Überlieferung in der Kunst des Abendlandes* (Berlin, 1967), III, 222–25, discusses the changing meaning of the term. W. Blake, *Poetry and Prose*, ed. Geoffrey Keynes (London, 1941), pp. 660, 770ff. A. Blunt, *The Art of William Blake* (New York, 1959), Ch. 3. D. F. Bond, "The Neo-Classical Psychology of the Imagination," *ELH* (A Journal of English Literary History), 4 (1937), 245–64, on the term in English seventeenth-century writing. P. Booz, *Der Baumeister der Gotik* (Munich and Berlin, 1956), p. 10. E. Cassirer, *The Philosophy of the Enlightenment* (first German ed., 1932; Boston, 1955), pp. 316ff., Shaftesbury on genius. Cennino D'Andrea Cennini, *Il libro dell'arte*, ed. D. V. Thompson, Jr. (New Haven, 1932). E. R. Curtius, *Europäische Literatur und lateinisches Mittelalter* (Bern, 1954), pp. 400–04, Imitation and Creation; 467–69, Divine Madness in Middle Ages; 527–29, Deus Artifex; trans. W. R. Trask as *European Literature and the Latin Middle Ages* (Princeton, 1953). A. Dresdner, *Die Enstehung der Kunstkritik* (Munich, 1915; reprint 1968), with an excellent chapter on the artists in antiquity. W. Duff, *An Essay on Original Genius* (London, 1767). M. Easton, *Artists and Writers in Paris. The Bohemian Idea, 1803–1867* (New York, 1964), of importance for Part III, 4, 5 of this article. B. Fabian, see above, par. 2. C. von Fabriczy, *Filippo Brunelleschi* (Stuttgart, 1892), p. 97. F. Flora, *Tutte le opere di Matteo Bandello*, 2 vols. (Milan, 1934–35), I, 646. C. Frey, *Die Dichtungen des Michelangiolo Buonarroti* (Berlin, 1897), lxxx, 2; lxxxi. G. Gaye, *Carteggio inedito d'artisti . . .* (Florence, 1839–40), II, 489. A. Gerard, *An Essay on Taste* (Edinburgh, 1759; 3rd ed. Edinburgh, 1780), p. 165; idem, *An Essay on Genius*, see above, par. 2, under Fabian. C. Gilbert, "The Archbishop on the Painters of Florence," *The Art Bulletin*, **41** (1959), 76. R. Goldwater and M. Treves, *Artists on Art* (New York, 1947), p. 295, from a Courbet letter of 1861. E. Gombrich, "Botticelli's Mythologies," *Journal of the Warburg and Courtauld Institutes*, **8** (1945), 59; idem, *Art and Illusion* (New York, 1960), pp. 192ff.; idem, "Style," in *International Encyclopedia of the Social Sciences* (New York, 1968), 15, 352–61. G. F. Hartlaub, "Caspar David Friedrichs Melancholie, in *Fragen an die Kunst* (Stuttgart, 1951), pp. 217–36; idem and F. Weissenfeld, *Gestalt und Gestaltung. Das Kunstwerk als Selbstdarstellung des Künstlers* (Krefeld, 1958). K. Heitmann, *Ethos des Künstlers und Ethos der Kunst. Eine problemgeschichtliche Skizze anlässlich Diderots* (Münster, 1962), most important contribution to the problem of relation between character and work. F. de Hollanda, *Vier Gespräche über die Malerei*, ed. J. de Vasconcellos (Vienna, 1899), p. 21, passim. E. G. Holt, *Literary Sources of Art History* (Princeton, 1947), pp. 86ff., English translation of Ghiberti's autobiography. J. Jahn, "Die Stellung des Künstlers im Mittelalter," *Festschrift Dr. h. c. Eduard Trautscholdt* (Hamburg, 1965), pp. 38–54, concentrates on an evaluation of early inscriptions by artists. A. Kalkmann, *Die Quellen der Kunstgeschichte des Plinius* (Berlin, 1898). P. Kaufman, see above, par. 2. R. Klibansky, E. Panofsky, F. Saxl, *Saturn and Melancholy* (London, 1964), a basic study of which Part III, Ch. 2 is particularly relevant. E. Kris, *Psychoanalytical Explorations in Art* (London, 1953), pp. 25ff., 60. E. Kris and O. Kurz, *Die Legende vom Künstler. Ein geschichtlicher Versuch* (Vienna, 1934), basic study of traditional *topoi* in anecdotes about artists; pp. 56ff., for *divino artista* and natural talent. G. P. Lomazzo, *Trattato dell'arte della pittura, scoltura ed architettura* (Milan, 1584). E. E. Lowinsky, "Musical Genius—Evolution and Origins of a Concept," *The Musical Quarterly*, 50 (1964), 321–40, 476–95. H. Ludwig, *Leonardo da Vinci. Das Buch von der Malerei*, 3 vols. (Vienna, 1882), I, 18, artist as god; 114, the solitary painter. E. L. Mann, "The Problem of Originality in English Literary Criticism 1750–1800," *Philological Quarterly*, 18 (1939), 97–118, relevant for Part IV, 3. G. Milanesi, *Le lettere di Michelangelo Buonarroti* (Florence, 1875), No. cdlxv. S. H. Monk, *The Sublime* (1935; Ann Arbor, 1960), Ch. I, pp. 10ff.; idem, "A Grace Beyond the Reach of Art," *Journal of the History of Ideas*, 5 (1944), 131ff. N. Nelson, "Individualism as a Criterion of the Renaissance," *Journal of English and Germanic Philology*, 32 (1933), 316–34, critique of Jacob Burckhardt's definition of individualism. G. Northcote, *The Life of Sir Joshua Reynolds*, 2 vols. (London, 1813–15), II, 322. W. von Oettingen, *Über das Leben und die Werke des A. Averlino Filarete* (Leipzig, 1888), p. 272. J. Overbeck, *Die antiken Schriftquellen zur Geschichte der bildenden Künste bei den Griechen* (Berlin, 1898). E. Panofsky, *Idea* (Hamburg, 1924; 2nd. ed. Berlin, 1960), pp. 68–71, for Dürer's advanced conception of talent and inspiration; idem, "Artist, Scientist, Genius: Notes on the 'Renaissance-Dämmerung'," *The Renaissance. Six Essays* (New York, 1962), pp. 173f., on the word *creare* in Leonardo's writings. W. Philips, in *Art and Psychoanalysis* (New York, 1957), XIV. Pliny, *The Elder Pliny's Chapters on the History of Art*, Commentary and Introduction by E. Sellers (London, 1896). H. Poeschel, *Kunst und Künstler im antiken Urteil* (Munich, 1925). H. Read, *Art and Alienation. The Role of the Artist in Society* (New York, 1967), p. 44. Sir Joshua Reynolds, *Discourses*, ed. R. R. Wark (San Marino, Calif., 1959), p. 17. J. P. Richter, ed., *The Literary Works of Leonardo da Vinci*, 2 vols. (London and New York, 1939), I, 35, No. 8. C. Ridolfi, *Le maraviglie dell'arte . . .* (Venice, 1648), new ed. by D. von Hadeln (Berlin, 1914–24), pp. 64f. F. Sacchetti, *Il Trecentonovelle*, ed. V. Pernicone (Florence, 1947), p. 191. M. Schapiro, "On the Aesthetic Attitude in Romanesque Art," *Art and Thought*, issued in Honor of Dr. A. K. Coomaraswamy (London, 1947), pp. 130–50. J. von Schlosser, *Beiträge zur Kunstgeschichte aus den Schriftquellen des frühen Mittelalters* (Vienna, 1891); idem, *Lorenzo Ghibertis Denkwürdigkeiten (I Commentarii)* (Berlin, 1912). B. Schweitzer, "Der bildende Künstler und der Begriff des Künstlerischen in der Antike," *Neue Heidelberger Jahrbücher* (1925), pp. 100ff., basic for Part III, l. E. Sellers, see Pliny. Anthony Ashley Cooper, Earl of Shaftesbury, *Characteristicks*, 3 vols. (1710–11), I, 51–53, on Divine Enthusiasm. L. Pearsall Smith, see above, par. 2. H. Sommer, "Génie, Beiträge zur Bedeutungsgeschichte des Wortes," Marburg thesis (1943) published by P. Sumthor, in *Zeitschrift für Romanische Philologie*, 66 (1950), 170–201, concerned with French seventeenth-century writers. H. Thüme, see above, par. 2. Ch. de Tolnay, *The Art and Thought of Michelangelo* (New York, 1964), pp. 94ff. G. Vasari, *Le vite de' più eccelenti pittori, scultori ed architetti*, ed. G. Milanesi, 9 vols. (Florence, 1878–85), II, 168, 204, 205, 217, 289; VI, 16. H. Walpole, *Anecdotes of Painting in England* (1762), ed. R. N. Wornum (London, 1876), I, xvii. O. F. Walzel, "Das Prometheussymbol von Shaftesbury zu Goethe," *Neue Jahrbücher für das klassische Altertum, Geschichte und deutsche Literatur*, 13 (25th vol., 1910), 40–71, 133–65. B. Weinberg, *A History of Literary Criticism in the Italian Renaissance* (Chicago, 1961). R. Wellek, *A History of Modern Criticism: 1750–1950*, 4 vols. (London and New Haven, 1955–65), I, 13; II, 46, 164, 299, etc., for Part IV, 4. M. L. Wiley, "Genius: A Problem in Definition," *Studies in English, No. 16*, The University of Texas Bulletin No. 3626 (July 8, 1936), 77–83, lexicographic definitions in the seventeenth and eighteenth centuries. R. Wittkower (1961), see above, par. 1; idem, "The Young Raphael," *Allen Memorial Art Museum Bulletin*, Oberlin College, 20 (1963), 163ff.; idem, and M. Wittkower (1963), see above, par. 1; R. Wittkower, "Imitation, Eclecticism, and Genius," *Aspects of the Eighteenth Century*, ed. E. R. Wasserman (Baltimore, 1965), pp. 143ff.; idem, Introduction to *Masters of the Loaded Brush. Oil Sketches from Rubens to Tiepolo*, Exhibition Catalogue (New York, 1967); idem, "The Artist," *Man Versus Society in 18th Century Britain*, ed. J. L. Clifford (Cambridge, 1968), 70–84. H. Wolf, see above, par. 2. R. Wood, *An Essay on the Original Genius and Writings of Homer* (London, 1769; 1775). E. Young, *Conjectures on Original Composition* (London, 1759). Zilsel, see above, par. 2.

Unless indicated otherwise translations are by the author of the article.

RUDOLF WITTKOWER

[See also Creation; **Genius;** Iconography; **Individualism, Types of;** Mimesis; Neo-Platonism; **Renaissance;** Romanticism; Style; **Taste;** *Ut pictura poesis.*]

MUSICAL GENIUS

THE ORIGINS and evolution of the concept of musical genius have rarely been treated in reference works. The idea of musical genius grows and changes in close association with the evolution of music itself so that the history of the idea is inseparable from the history of music and the concept of the musician as it developed from Greek antiquity.

I. CONCEPT OF MUSICIAN IN ANCIENT GREECE

The concept of the musician has changed throughout the history of Western civilization. Greek poets endowed individual musicians with the magical power of affecting men and gods—Arion, Timotheus, and above all Orpheus are archetypes of the magic musician. In all ancient civilizations music and magic are closely connected. But the Greek writers on music ignored the magical and slighted the practical aspects of music. Their customary definition of the musician is confined to his speculative, theoretical function.

Aristoxenos (ca. 354–300 B.C.) defines a musician as one who commands the "knowledge" of the science of music (Macran, pp. 95, 165). Aristides Quintilianus (probably fourth century B.C.), in Book I, Chapter 4 of his treatise on music, precedes the various definitions of music with the following statement: "Music is the science of melody (μέλος) and all elements having to do with melody" (Winnington-Ingram, p. 4)—a definition easily understandable in the light of the purely melodic and rhythmic nature of Greek music, and echoed by Bacchius Senex (probably fourth century A.D.) almost word for word (Meibomius, p. 1).

II. BOETHIUS

Boethius (ca. A.D. 480–524), transmitter of ancient Greek philosophy, aesthetics, and theory of music to the Christian West, follows Greek tradition when, in the last chapter of Book I of his *De institutione musica*, he defines a musician as he "who masters the musical art not through mechanical exercise but after theoretical investigation through the power of speculation" (Friedlein, p. 224). Boethius admits the existence of two other kinds of musicians, performers and composers. To performers he denies any competence to judge and understand music because of the merely mechanical character of their work (*quoniam famulantur*), and because they bring no rational powers to bear on music but, on the contrary, are utterly devoid of the capacity for thought; the composers share the same fate because in composing they are not motivated by philosophical speculation, but by some natural instinct: *non potius speculatione ac ratione, quam naturali quodam instinctu fertur ad carmen* (Friedlein, p. 225).

The concept of the *instinctus naturalis* as the motivating force animating the composer is used by Boethius in a pejorative sense. A philosophy that places *ratio* at the head of all human faculties, that considers sensory experience as uncertain and as the source of error and illusion, cannot give anything but a low place to natural instinct. "It is much greater and nobler to know what one does than to do what one knows," says Boethius (Friedlein, p. 224).

III. THE MEDIEVAL VIEW

The contempt for practice and the one-sided exaltation of theory flow from Boethius' treatise into the medieval philosophy of music and the arts. It is formalized in consigning the work of the practical musician, as of any other practicing artist, to the *artes mechanicae* rather than to the *artes liberales*. The mechanical arts, definable as those activities that need the human hand for their execution, were considered the province of the lower classes; the liberal arts, definable as those that need chiefly the human mind for their exercise, were the province of the free man. Farming, hunting, navigation, medicine were thrown together with painting and sculpture as mechanical arts, much to the distress of the artists. The distinction between mechanical and liberal arts goes back to classical antiquity, but the sharpness with which Boethius and, following him, most medieval writers on music downgrade the performing musician seems to express more a medieval than an ancient view. It is well conveyed in the famous jingle attributed to Guido of Arezzo (ca. 992–1050) that was quoted at least until late into the sixteenth century:

> *Musicorum et cantorum*
> *Magna est distantia.*
> *Isti dicunt, illi sciunt,*
> *Quae componit Musica,*
> *Nam qui facit, quod non sapit,*
> *Diffinitur bestia.*

("There is a vast difference between musicians and singers. The latter merely perform, whereas the former understand what makes music. For he who performs what he does not understand is a mere brute.")

Boethius seems to have been the first to use the term *quadrivium*, joining music with the mathematical arts of arithmetic, geometry, and astronomy. Without these four disciplines the philosopher cannot find the truth. The mathematical arts or sciences were considered the most noble because they contained "the greater certainties of the intellect"; the language arts of the *trivium*—grammar, dialectics, and rhetoric—were held to be of a lower order due to the implied reference to the senses and human emotions, from which spring deception and uncertainty.

Music, as taught at medieval universities, was accepted as a part of the *quadrivium* and constituted the theoretical consideration of an art whose every element—rhythm, melody, harmony—was reducible to mathematical proportions. The speculative character of the medieval concept of music is further reflected in Boethius' division of music into *musica mundana*, *musica humana*, and *musica instrumentalis*—following ancient models—music of the spheres (macrocosm), the harmonious conjunction of body and soul (microcosm), and music properly speaking, the art of sound produced on instruments, which includes the human voice, called *instrumentum naturale* (Johannes Affligemensis [Johannes Cotto], in his *De musica cum tonario* [ca.

313

1120]; Waesberghe [1950], p. 57). The distinction survived at least into the Renaissance. Pietro Aron differentiates between *stormento naturale*, the voice, and *stormento artificiale*, the instrument properly speaking (Aron, Libro II, Opp. XI).

Although medieval writers on music held with surprising tenacity to Boethius' and Guido's views, they could not suppress occasional marvel at the natural talent of untrained musicians. Aribo Scholasticus (ca. 1070), one of the most original and independent medieval thinkers on music, proves Man's inborn gift for music by pointing to jongleurs who, though devoid of all knowledge in the art of music, joyfully sing popular songs, free of error, observing accurately the position of tones and semitones, and ending correctly on the appropriate final tones. While appearing to follow Guido's definition, Aribo expands it significantly, expecting of the professional musician not only that he master the whole science of modes and intervals, but also that he know how to judge what is right, how to amend what is wrong, and how to compose perfect melodies himself (Waesberghe [1951], p. 46). Thus Aribo includes in his definition the composer, excluded in Boethius' definition of *musicus*. Moreover, in his scheme of things he creates a place even for the untutored musical talent by distinguishing between the natural and the professional musician (the chapter referred to is entitled *De naturali musico et artificiali*). The terminology is related to the distinction between *musica artificialis et naturalis* introduced by Regino of Prüm (d. 950); but *musica naturalis* was for the latter a vast concept encompassing the harmony of the spheres, the human voice, and the voices of animals, whereas *musica artificialis* was confined to the music thought out by human art and ingenuity and played on instruments (Pietzsch [1929], pp. 63–66). Aribo adds the new element of fresh and unprejudiced observation of musical performance, correct according to the canons of the art, although executed by illiterate jongleurs.

Boethius called the composer *poëta*, from the Greek ποιητής, originally meaning maker, producer, contriver, and later confined to the author of a poem. The term *poeta* for composer, revealing the unity of poem and melody, of word and tone in the medieval view, survived into the Renaissance. But as early as the twelfth century we find the term *compositor* used by Johannes Affligemensis in the combination *cantuum compositor* (Waesberghe [1950], p. 119). The esteem of the composer increased in medieval writings to the degree that the compositional process was conceived to be rational rather than, as Boethius thought, prompted by natural instinct. Adherence to rules was taken to distinguish a good composition from a poor one, a good composer

from a bad one. Odo of Cluny, tenth-century abbot, in his dialogue on music, has the master say: "A rule, certainly, is a general mandate of any art; thus things which are singular do not obey the rules of art" (Strunk, p. 115). A clearer subordination of individuality in art to rules is hard to find. "Any art," says Johannes of Garlandia, "is a collection of many rules. The term art derives from the word *arto, artas*, which is the same as *restringo, restringis*, to restrict, because it limits us and constrains us lest we do otherwise than it teaches us" (Lowinsky [1964], p. 477).

Garlandia, the thirteenth-century theorist, speaks for a polyphonic art, in which the plain chant serves as *cantus firmus*, that is, as the basis over which the other voice or voices sing their counterpoints. The thirteenth century saw the emergence of polyphonic music that emancipated itself from dependence on the Gregorian chant. The conductus, set to freshly written texts of a spiritual, moral, or political nature, is the first form of polyphony in which all parts are written by the composer himself without the aid of a *cantus firmus*. At about 1260 Franco of Cologne described the composition of a conductus as follows: "He who wishes to write a conduct ought first to invent as beautiful a melody as he can, then . . . use it as a tenor is used in writing discant" (Strunk, p. 155). Franco, in postulating invention first, then contrapuntal elaboration, doubtless follows Cicero's venerable division between invention, disposition, and elocution. His precepts are those of a craftsman, who, absorbed in producing a beautiful piece of work, is utterly unconcerned about the inner processes that lead to the work of art.

In a remarkable passage, Johannes Grocheo (ca. 1300) distinguishes between the composing of polyphony based on a *cantus firmus* and freely conceived polyphony, specifically between *organum* and motet on the one hand and the conductus on the other. The process of composing over a *cantus firmus* he calls *ordinare;* for the projection of free polyphony he reserves the term *componere:*

But I say "order," because in motets and organum the tenor comes from an old, pre-existent chant, but is subjected by the artificer to rhythmic mode and measure. And I say "compose," because in the conductus the tenor is a totally new work and is subject to mode and duration according to the artificer's will (Lowinsky [1964], p. 490).

Yet, even this fine and rare distinction does not amount to anything more than a recognition of two different procedures by one and the same craftsman. It does not mean recognition of two types of musician, or two types of creativity. But it does stress, for the first time in the theory of polyphonic music, the concept of the "new"—as yet without showing any overt preference for it.

IV. THE RENAISSANCE

It is not until the last quarter of the fifteenth century that this neutrality is abandoned. In the writings of Johannes Tinctoris, the Flemish composer and theorist who emigrated to Italy, the composer is defined as the creator of a "new" musical work: *Compositor est alicuius novi cantus aeditor* (Parrish, p. 14). Unquestionably, there were musicians and connoisseurs in the Middle Ages who enjoyed novelty in musical composition, for there was a constant, if slow-moving, stream of novelty from chant to sequence and rhymed offices, from Saint Martial's incipient polyphony to the masters of Notre Dame, from Perotinus to Machaut. But it would be hard to find a source of medieval theory stressing novelty or originality as the qualities that make a composer. Even though the fourteenth century spoke of an *ars nova*, Philippe de Vitry, in his treatise by that name, and Johannes de Muris, in his *Ars novae musicae*, deal in a matter-of-fact manner with the notational signs of the new rhythmic language of the *ars nova* without a word of appreciation of the new art itself. Yet, the violent critique of the *novus cantandi modus* by Jacobus of Liège (ca. 1330) as *cantandi lascivia curiositas*, in which "the words are lost, the harmony of consonances is diminished, the value of the notes is changed, perfection is brought low, imperfection is exalted, and measure is confounded" (Strunk, p. 190), furnishes eloquent proof that the new art was considerably more than a new notation.

This raises the question why the theorists of the *ars nova* were so reticent in their appraisal of the new art. The answer is that ideas change at a slower pace than practices—and this for two reasons: the extraordinary strength of tradition gives the stamp of approval to what is known and accepted; but the new has not only to fight for recognition, it has as yet to seek the rational and ideological basis for its existence. In the Middle Ages, where *auctoritas*—the authority of the ancients, of the Church Fathers, of tradition—was regarded as a pillar of the cultural edifice, it was doubly difficult for the new to assert itself. Interestingly enough, the *ars nova* sought to justify itself through studied alliance with the old. The new motet, even when displaying secular texts of amorous character in the vernacular in its lively upper voices, carried a Gregorian melody in the slow-moving tenor. The new many-voiced chansons adhered to the formal patterns of the old troubadour and trouvère songs.

In a situation where the artist himself does not dare to make a clean break with tradition, the theorist cannot be expected to come forward with a clear position and rationale of the "new." This explains why it is the fifteenth and sixteenth centuries rather than the thirteenth and fourteenth that emphasize the importance of novelty, of newness in art. For it is this great period, the "Renaissance," that witnesses the creation of a music new in most of its fundamental aspects—expansion of the tonal system, both external (increase of the tonal space) and internal (complete chromaticization of the scale), tuning, simultaneous instead of successive composition of parts in a harmonic complex, liberation of the composer's imagination by freeing the polyphonic work of art from ties to *cantus-firmus* construction, expression of human affects replacing decoration of the divine service as the chief goal of music.

It takes an innovative epoch to develop an aesthetics in which innovation is made the touchstone of creativity. When Tinctoris, in the *proemium* to his *Proportionale musices*, extols the Franco-Flemish composers and disparages the English, he uses the concept of innovation as a yardstick: "The French freshly invent new songs every day, whereas the English keep writing in one and the same style—surely a sign of a wretched talent" (*quod miserrimi signum est ingenii*; Lowinsky [1966], p. 133).

Even two generations later, while commenting on the preceding statement of Tinctoris, Sebald Heyden, writing in Germany—the pace of innovation being slower in the North than in Italy—felt he had to defend the new music against the reproach of novelty:

The fact that it is a new art and quite unknown to ancient Greeks does not render it less worthy of praise and admiration than any other arts, however ancient they may be. . . . What is that invention of the ancients with which the art of printing, thought out in our times, and by us Germans, could not contend in fame? Equally far be it that the novelty of our music be a reason to hold it in contempt rather than to praise it (Heyden, Dedication).

With much greater confidence, and considerably deeper insight, Othmar Luscinius (Latinization of the German "Nachtigall") confronts the question of the new and the old in his *Musurgia* (1536). A humanist, a friend of Conrad Peutinger, Erasmus, and Glareanus, expert in Greek and writing a polished Latin, but also a brilliant organist, Luscinius looks back at the music of 200 years earlier, examples of which he had studied. He exclaims:

O God, how cold these compositions are when compared to those of our day! Each epoch has its own laws, its own taste. And how strange that we find in matters of music a situation entirely different from that of the general state of the arts and letters: in the latter whatever comes closest to venerable antiquity receives most praise; in music, he who does not excel the past becomes the laughing stock of all (Luscinius, pp. 97–98).

Luscinius cites a four-part setting of lines from the Song of Songs, *Tota pulchra es amica mea*, by a contemporaneous Dutch musician, Nicolaus Craen, "by Jove, a man of outstanding genius" (*vir me Hercle praestantis ingenij*). The work (printed in Petrucci's *Motetti C* of 1504 and not published since) breathes the air of freedom that characterizes more and more the music of the Renaissance. Instead of choosing the liturgical text *Tota pulchra es, Maria, et macula originalis non est in te*, Craen goes back to the original text of the Bible, *Tota pulchra es amica mea et macula non est in te*. Instead of taking the continuation of this verse, he assembles his text freely from the lines of various chapters. The old technique of building a musical edifice on the ground plan of a *cantus firmus* is abandoned. All four voices are freely invented by the composer with the manifest intent to echo the enthusiastic voices of the lovers and to bring to life the emotional tone of the poem. Luscinius remarks with what felicity Craen neglected the precepts of the older generation, and how much praise he deserves for sidestepping the rules of the past. Indeed, no one ought to be censured for so doing, provided that it be done properly in every respect (*si modo decenter ex omni parte fiet*), that is, provided there is a sense of wholeness, a sense of "style" to his enterprise.

Nothing characterizes more sharply the new respect for the artist and his work than the Renaissance theorist's habit of referring to a specific work by a specific composer. Glareanus, who printed in his *Dodekachordon* (1547) no fewer than 121 polyphonic compositions, exceeded all of his colleagues in this regard. Medieval theorists, on the other hand, rarely name composers or refer to specific works, save for the demonstration of notational practice. They seem hardly interested in a composition as a work of art marked by individual aesthetic traits. The new rank accorded to the creative artist in the scheme of things musical is also expressed in other ways. Tinctoris dedicated a treatise to the two composers he admired most, Ockeghem and Busnois (Coussemaker, IV, 16). In one of his tracts he called the former *optimi ingenii compositor* (Coussemaker, IV, 152). Even the musical performers, relegated before to the realm of *artes mechanicae*, now receive a new appreciation. Their virtuoso feats and their appeal to the emotions cause them to be listed by name and to have their art described in critical detail. Again, Tinctoris leads the way by dedicating one of his writings to a singer of the Papal Chapel (Coussemaker, IV, 41).

But one of the most interesting developments is the emergence of music critics from the ranks of the noble amateurs or the intellectual elite. Their critiques of the great performers of their time were often published in book form. Luigi Dentice, a Neapolitan nobleman

(*Dialoghi*, 1553), and the Florentine mathematician Cosimo Bartoli (*Ragionamenti accademici*, 1567) have left us delightful samples of the beginnings of concert reviews—concerts, to be sure, given in the private circles of princes, popes, and academies (Lowinsky [1966], pp. 140–41).

The significance of these and other reports lies in the growing kinship between the composer and the performer of the Renaissance. The latter, following the example of the former, places his art more and more into the service of the expression of human affects. Many are the stories of the miraculous emotional effect made by great lutenists and clavecinists of the sixteenth century—stories that recall the ancient myths of Orpheus and Timotheus and that place the performer, held in contempt in the Middle Ages, closer and closer to the creative sphere by virtue of his personal, passionate involvement and the resulting original interpretation of the music performed.

The art of singing and playing itself becomes the subject of theoretical interest; whole books appear on the singer's and player's art of improvising embellishments. Here is an area where the newly won freedom of the performer clashes with that of the composer, for few were the composers who enjoyed having their works "embellished."

The emphasis on composer and performer indicates that the Renaissance returned music to the sense of the ear. Music, in the Middle Ages, was like a window through which the philosophical mind gazed at the universe to perceive its harmonious order. In the Renaissance it was in the first place an object of aesthetic enjoyment. "The ear is the true teacher," wrote Adrian Petit Coclico in 1552 (Bukofzer, fol. B2^v). But Tinctoris already had taken the decisive step from the medieval emphasis on music as number to the new stress on music as sound when in one of his famous eight rules of counterpoint he said: "This, however, is in my opinion to be left entirely to the judgment of the ears" (Lowinsky [1965a], p. 365).

The realization of the individuality and originality of a composer leads quite logically to the downgrading of the rules and to a new appreciation of talent and inspiration. The Bolognese composer, choir director, and theorist Giovanni Spataro wrote to a Venetian musician in a letter of 5 April 1529:

The written rules can well teach the first rudiments of counterpoint, but they will not make the good composer, inasmuch as good composers are born just as are the poets. Therefore, one needs almost more divine help than the written rule; and this is apparent every day, because the good composers (through natural instinct and a certain manner of grace which can hardly be taught) bring at times such turns and figures in counterpoint and harmony as are not demonstrated in any rule or precept of counterpoint (Lowinsky [1964], p. 481).

Spataro transferred the aphorism "The poet is born, not made" (*Poeta nascitur non fit*), which became so popular in the poetic theory of the Renaissance, to the composer. Characteristically, he uses the term *instinto naturale* to designate the irrational power in a great composer that guides him in the regions uncharted by rules. Whereas Boethius conceived of natural instinct as of a lower form of consciousness, Spataro opposes it to rational learning as a higher, and almost divine, form of awareness. In this he was preceded by Baldassare Castiglione, who in his *Il Cortegiano* (published 1528, completed 1514) has the Count uphold the independence of a great artist against Signor Federico's insistence on imitation of the great masters. The Count asks Federico, "Who should have been Homer's model, and whom did Boccaccio and Petrarch imitate?" and he goes on to say that the true master of these great writers was their genius and their own inborn judgment (*Ma il lor vero maestro cred'io che fosse l'ingegno ed il lor proprio giudicio naturale*). And he persuades Signor Federico to the point where the latter is willing to admit that, in the choice of genre, and the display of style and temperament, every artist should follow his own instinct (*s'accommodi allo instinto suo proprio;* Lowinsky [1964], p. 482 n. 74).

In the same vein, the Florentine music theorist Pietro Aron, a friend of Spataro who figures in the latter's correspondence, writes in his *Lucidario* (1545):

Experience teaches that some who have practiced the art of composition for a good part of their lives are surpassed by others who have been composing for a short time only. Wherefore one may believe that good composers are born and cannot be made through study and long practice but rather through heavenly influence and inclination: graces, to be sure, that heaven grants to few in large measure. . . . As we see that one and the same figure and form treated by different sculptors in marble or in other material has much more perfection in the one than in the other as their creators differ from one another in excellence, likewise, I say, it happens in this our harmonic faculty, which many of our composers possess. Each one of them knows the material, i.e. the musical intervals, and gives them a fitting harmonic form which differs in excellence, in sweetness and loveliness according to the composer's individual skill and natural grace (Lowinsky [1964], p. 483).

Pietro Aron almost anticipates the brilliant formulation in which Giordano Bruno, in his *Eroici furori* (1585), condemns the pedantic makers and watchers of rules: "There are as many kinds of poetic rules as there are kinds of poets" (Thüme, p. 26). Bruno in turn comes

close to Kant's definition of genius, which will be discussed below.

"Invention" and "originality" now become so essential that Glareanus, in his *Dodekachordon* (1547), can pose the question: "Shall we not consider him who invented the melody of the *Te Deum* or the *Pange lingua* a greater genius than him who later composed a whole Mass on it?" (Lowinsky [1964], p. 479). Pursuing this question, Glareanus says:

In both [the melodic inventor and the contrapuntist] this is to be ascribed more to the energies of genius, and to some natural and inborn talent than to craftsmanship. And this can be proved through those who never studied music, and nevertheless show a miraculous ability in inventing melodies, as is apparent in our vernacular [folk song], the Celtic [French] or the German; but also through those who are masters of counterpoint although they were often poorly taught—to say nothing of the other disciplines. From this it appears certain that neither is possible for a man unless he is born for it, or, as the people say, unless his mother gave it to him—which is just as true for the painters, the sculptors, and the preachers of the Divine Word (for about the poets there can be no doubt) and for all works dedicated to Minerva (Lowinsky [1964], p. 479).

The word translated here as "genius" is the Latin *ingenium*. Edgar Zilsel has pointed out that the term *ingenium* as characterizing extraordinary inborn talent was unknown in the Middle Ages (Zilsel, pp. 251ff.). The word was used in many senses ranging from art and intrigues (see the Italian *inganno*) to legal document and instrument of war ("engineer"). Only in the Renaissance did it assume the meaning of outstanding talent; it was so used by Alberti, Leonardo, Aretino, and countless other writers of the period. However, the weight of Glareanus' statement rests not on the interpretation of *ingenium*, but on his distinction between extraordinary natural talent and craftsmanship, and on his insistence that the former far exceeds the latter in importance.

Glareanus' statement recalls Aribo's admiration for the *musicus naturalis;* it anticipates the romantic idea of the genius of folk song and folk singer as well as the modern system of the arts. It antedates by fifty odd years Jacobus Pontanus' poetics (1600) that contains "the most explicit comparison between poetry, painting, and music that I have been able to discover in Renaissance literature" (Kristeller, p. 517). In fact, Glareanus adds to painting, poetry, and music, discussed by Pontanus, sculpture and eloquence. Glareanus' source of inspiration—considering that he, like Luscinius, knew Greek—was probably Plato's *Ion* in which Socrates is presented as speaking of precisely the same combination of arts: painting, sculpture, music, poetry, all of which are related to Ion's profession, the recitation of Homer, for which Glareanus substitutes eloquence in the divine service.

The stress on originality brings with it the appreciation of individuality. A German publisher, Hieronymus Formschneider, in a print of three-part compositions of 1538, excuses the lack of author attributions with the remark that each of the composers has his own outstanding style easily recognized by the connoisseur. Theorists discuss the individual style of composers—again Glareanus leads his contemporaries in the sharpness of his critical judgment—and poets sing the praises of composers as creators of a recognizable personal idiom of expression.

One hears an echo of Glareanus' ideas in the dialogue on music, *Solitaire second ou prose de la musique* (1552), by the French poet and humanist, Pontus de Tyard:

. . . as poetry takes its source from natural talent and the inspiration of the sacred choir [of Muses] of Parnassus, so Music, too, requires natural gift, impelled by the same enthusiasm. It may take more talent to invent a single melodic turn of phrase for the expression of a conceit to write the "air" or the "theme" of a chanson, than to place two, three, or more counterpoints against a *cantus firmus* and to write what one calls figured music, or a finished composition (*chose faite*), though the latter requires more learning (Tyard, p. 132).

As the sixteenth century progresses, the irrational aspect of the compositional process gains increasing attention. Spataro used the term *instinctus naturalis* to account for the marvelous inventiveness and originality of great composers. Other writers change this term to *inclinatio naturalis*. Hermann Finck, in a treatise published in 1556, which, significantly, stresses the importance of an expressive rendering of the text, reserves the title of *musicus* for the composer:

But only composers deserve that title. I consider those as composers who, as the learned agree, were carried to that field of study by natural inclination, and who cultivated their natural talent from tender youth on through art, practice, and varied and frequent exercises. . . . And if it is of importance in the other disciplines who your first teacher and mentor is, certainly in this art it is of greatest significance that he who by nature burns with a love of music use an experienced teacher and devote himself totally to imitating him (Lowinsky [1964], pp. 487–88).

To early and rigorous training Finck adds three irrational elements in his characterization of the composer: natural talent, natural inclination, and enthusiasm, for this is surely what he intends to convey with his expression, "by nature burning with a love of music." And all three elements—talent, inclination,

enthusiasm—carry the adjective *naturalis* or *a natura*. Not training and practice alone make the composer, but an inborn quality that cannot be rationally accounted for except as a gift of Nature.

What is translated here as enthusiasm is not what Plato had in mind when he spoke of the *furor poeticus*, a concept that has played a significant role in the literary criticism of the sixteenth century (Weinberg, I, Ch. VII). Finck's "enthusiasm" shares with Plato's *furor poeticus* the element of emotional intensity with which poet or musician embraces his chosen art, but what separates the two concepts of Finck and Plato is the element of rationality. Plato believes that once the poet is inspired—and without inspiration he has no invention—he is out of his senses and out of his mind. "For not by art does the poet sing, but by power divine" (Lowinsky [1964], p. 488). But the Renaissance theorist, however strongly he may stress irrational elements, never abandons the idea of a rational and practical mastery of the musical craft as an indispensable basis for the work of genius. Indeed, Finck stresses the necessity for the young genius to grow up in the workshop of an older master, whose compositions he should take as models for his own.

This is apparent even in those formulations in which, finally, the *instinctus naturalis* and the *inclinatio naturalis* are elevated to the *impetus naturalis*. Lampadius, Protestant cantor in Lüneburg and author of a textbook on music published in 1537 (*Compendium musices*), describes the process of composition in these words:

As poets are stirred by a certain natural impulse to write their verses, holding in their minds the things that are to be described, so the composer must first contrive in his mind the best melodies and must weigh these judiciously, lest one single note vitiate the whole melody and tire his listeners. Then he must proceed to the working-out—that is, he must distribute the contrived melodies in a certain order, using those that seem most suitable (Lowinsky [1964], p. 489).

We have here one of the earliest descriptions of the process of composition as we conceive it today. Lampadius distinguishes three phases: melodic invention (the musician is stirred by some inward power), careful evaluation (the aesthetic judgment passes on the work of inspiration), and finally elaboration (the composer proceeds to work out the purified melodic ideas—he selects, he rejects, and he organizes). This is much the same working process as we will find described by Roger North and, more articulately, by Friedrich Nietzsche.

Dedications and prefaces to sixteenth-century prints of music reflect the change of ideas. When the Parisian music publishers, Adrian Le Roy and Robert Ballard, in the dedication of a print of motets by Orlando di Lasso of 1564, wished to pay tribute to the genius of the youthful composer, they called him *a natura factus magis, quam disciplina institutus,* "more a product of nature, than of professional training" (Van den Borren, p. 836).

Medieval theory does not admit that a composer may at times disregard rules with impunity, indeed that this may make him a better composer. This idea begins to take shape in Renaissance writings. We saw how Luscinius praised Nicolaus Craen for sidestepping the traditional rules. Zarlino, too, in his celebrated *Istitutioni harmoniche* of 1558 (p. 235), states that poetic license is allowed to the composer as well as to the poet. "Poetic license" becomes an integral part of the concept of genius. It is not by chance that the most advanced definition of genius should occur in the treatise of a man claiming to have been a pupil of Josquin des Prez and to report the master's method of teaching, Adrian Petit Coclico's *Compendium musices* (1552). Josquin des Prez was to the Renaissance musician the very incarnation of musical genius. Here is what Coclico reports on Josquin's method:

Josquin did not consider everybody cut out for the study of composition; he decided that only those should be taught who were carried by a singular natural impetus to that most beautiful art, for he used to say that there exist so many lovely compositions that hardly one in a thousand could compose anything as good or better (Lowinsky [1964], p. 491).

And again, when enumerating the requirements for the student of composition, Coclico lists in the first place the ability to improvise a counterpoint and in the second place

that he be led to composing by a . . . certain natural impetus so that neither food nor drink can please him before he has finished his musical work. For when the inner impetus urges in this way one can achieve more in one hour than otherwise in a whole month. Useless are composers who lack these singular raptures (Lowinsky [1964], p. 492).

Coclico's ideas are formulated in a framework of decided opposition to the whole philosophy of medieval theory. In a complete reversal of the medieval hierarchy of musicians Coclico pronounces as "kings of music" not the theorists but those who combine theory with practice, who understand thoroughly the art of composing, who know how to embellish a composition and how to express all emotions in music.

The two ideas of music as expression and of musical genius go together historically and conceptually. The Renaissance theorists who come closest to the modern concept of genius are the same ones who stress the idea that music serves to express human emotions. Not only do these two concepts go hand in hand, they converge in their attitude towards "the rules."

In transcending the rules, genius opens new vistas and music gains new dimensions of expressiveness. Any musical device, to reach the sphere of emphatic expression, must verge on the limits of the permissible or, indeed, pass beyond them. Any work of genius will, of course, transcend all ordinary limitations. Yet, the extraordinary and the impermissible need the ordinary and the permissible as background without which they lose their significance and their effect. This is why Zarlino advises the composer not to persist too long in the use of *licenze,* for he understands that a series of breaches of rules will never amount to a work of art. Genius knows how to endow the breaking of a rule with that same sense of necessity that the rule itself embodied; the disregard of convention is not the goal, but a by-product of his work.

The Renaissance is the first epoch in European intellectual history that recognized that neither observation of rules nor practice and experience suffice to make the good composer, that great composers will find felicitous turns and figures not demonstrated in any textbook, that there are artistic elements of manner and grace that defy definition, and that rules, teaching, practice, and experience are all superseded by the inborn talent, the *ingenium* of the individual, who is driven to his art by a natural impetus so strong that it overcomes hunger and thirst, so powerful that it may put the composer into a state of ecstasy, and that in such a state of heightened awareness and activity the composer's mind can achieve more than in long periods of ordinary work. For all this the composer, according to some writers, must enjoy divine help and heavenly inspiration.

The Renaissance drew a clear line of demarcation between craftsman and genius. Glareanus even goes so far as to elevate the nature of genius above that of talent—a question that occupied the attention of later thinkers a great deal. He already suggests the classical definition found in eighteenth-century writings by attributing greater *ingenium* to the inventor of new melodies than to the contrapuntal elaborator of a given melody. Invention and originality distinguish genius from talent. Talent imitates; genius assimilates and creates.

The Renaissance replaces the medieval definition of creation as making something out of nothing with the concept of creation as making something new, something that the world had not seen or heard before, something fresh, original, personal. Nothing illuminates more sharply the heightened confidence of the Renaissance writer in man's unlimited abilities than the belief that the artistic genius reaches up to God Himself,

GENIUS, MUSICAL

sharing with Him in the joy of creation. Had not Julius Caesar Scaliger, in the opening chapter of his *Poetices libri septem* (1561), called the poet "another God" (*alter Deus*), and Shaftesbury later a "second maker"? No wonder, then, that the epithet *divus*, applied in the Middle Ages only to saints, was transferred by the secular urban society of the Renaissance to secular celebrities. Aretino appears to have been the first to use the term in a letter to "the divine Michelangelo" (Zilsel, pp. 276ff.). It is precisely in the same period that the term *divinus* enters into writings on music. In 1542 the Venetian Sylvestro Ganassi del Fontego speaks of the Flemish composer Nicolas Gombert, master of the choirboys in the Emperor's chapel, as *huomo divino in tal professione* (Lowinsky [1964], p. 484). And in the second part of the same work published one year later, he calls the chapel-master of San Marco in Venice, Adrian Willaert, *nuovo Prometheo della celeste Armonia*. The same Aretino who had called Michelangelo "divine" speaks in his *Marescalco* of Willaert as *sforzo di natura*, "miracle of nature" (Lowinsky [1964], p. 484). All of these expressions point to a concept of creativity based on the new ideas of originality and inventiveness. Insofar as Man is creative in this new sense he partakes of God's nature and may therefore properly be addressed as "divine."

To the medieval mind such thought was blasphemous. "God alone creates," pronounced Saint Thomas Aquinas; "no mortal being can create" (*Summa Theologica*)—a position that followed logically from his definition of creation as *creare ex nihilo*: "To create means to produce something out of nothing." Earlier, Saint Augustine in his *De Trinitate* had maintained: *Creatura non potest creare*, "the creature cannot create" (Lowinsky [1964], p. 477).

The Renaissance is the first period in the history of music in which composers are viewed as individuals endowed with an extraordinary personal and psychological constitution. The same agent who, in writing to Ercole of Ferrara about Isaac and Josquin, conceded that Josquin was the better composer, also remarked that as a person he was difficult, both in his relations with other musicians and with his patron, that he composed only when it pleased him and not when commanded. From Serafino dall'Aquila's sonnet of 1503 addressed to Josquin we know of the master's fits of melancholy and despair. We hear from Manlius not only of his outbursts of temper during rehearsals, from Glareanus the anecdotes of his witty musical responses to forgetful or demanding patrons, but also of his unending search for perfection that made him go over his compositions again and again, changing, polishing, refining (Osthoff, I). A picture emerges of an altogether original character, endowed with a strong temperament and a deep sense of obligation to his genius, an individual utterly unwilling and unable to compromise in matters of his art.

The anecdotes concerning Josquin and his noble patrons also suggest that a new relationship between artist and patron is in the making: here are the beginnings of parity between the aristocracy of talent and the aristocracy of blood and rank. The incredibly familiar tone of Orlando di Lasso's letters to his patron, Duke Wilhelm V of Bavaria, with whom he drank, played, and joked, is an illustration of this new relationship between an artist and a prince in the latter part of the century.

Carlo Gesualdo, finally, is a representative of the free artist. Born a prince, and hence economically and socially independent, he was in his own employ, as it were, accountable only to himself. The freedom of his style is a reflection of his independence as well as of the fierce and uncontrolled temperament that led to the well-known tragic events of his life.

Josquin, Lasso, Gesualdo, however different they were in character and as artists, share one essential quality: they are musical geniuses whose extraordinary gifts are matched by extraordinary personality; they exhibit immense strength of feeling, spontaneity, originality, independence as personalities and in their social relationships; they are great individuals, and each one of them was hailed in his time as the foremost representative of an expressive style of music. At the same time Josquin, Lasso, and Gesualdo conformed to the psychological image of the Renaissance concept of genius. The famous Problem XXX,1 of Aristotle—or Pseudo-Aristotle—begins with the question: "Why is it that all those who have become eminent in philosophy or politics or poetry or the arts are clearly melancholics?" (Klibansky, Panofsky, and Saxl, p. 18). Problem XXX,1 was well known in the Renaissance. It was taken up by Marsilio Ficino, celebrated for his attempt to reconcile Plato and Christianity. It was he who "gave shape to the idea of the melancholy man of genius and revealed it to the rest of Europe" (in his three books *De vita triplici*, 1482–89; Klibansky, Panofsky, and Saxl, pp. 255ff.). And indeed, our three great composers fit surprisingly well into this picture: Josquin, the loner, the temperamental conductor, the ceaseless refiner of his works, writing when his inner voice compels him, a deep melancholic in life, and in his music a "specialist" in melancholy; Lasso and Gesualdo, preoccupied with the idea of Death in their work as no composers before them, the former suffering from a mental collapse two years before his death, the latter involved in the double murder of his wife and her lover, an event that cast an ineradicable shadow over his whole creative life (the murder took place

320

in 1590; the first publication of Gesualdo's music occurred in 1594).

A new personal style in music and a new image of the musician as a person different from the common run of people seem to emerge more or less simultaneously. This appears from censures as well as from anecdotes about musicians that begin to circulate in the sixteenth century. Joachim Vadian, poet and humanist at the court of Maximilian I, in a eulogy (1517) of the composer and organist Paul Hofhaimer, criticized the musicians who "believe themselves to be lacking in genius, unless their demeanor is frivolous and dubious, and who act as if seized by Platonic madness" (Moser, p. 44). Antonfrancesco Doni, in his entertaining and witty dialogue on music (1544), expressed a view of the artistic personality that must have been current for some time in the literary circles of Italy: "Musicians, poets, painters, sculptors, and their like are all real people, attractive, and often cheerful, though at times eccentric when the fancy strikes them" (Lowinsky [1964], p. 486). Doni proceeds to tell humorous stories about the clash between artists and ignorant and presumptuous Philistines—*plebei*, as he calls them—stories that prove that the Renaissance created not only the image of the "artist," but also its foil, that of the "Philistine."

V. THE BAROQUE

The Renaissance created the concept of genius and determined the basic outlines of its evolution through baroque and classicism to romanticism. We have been told by a well-known music historian and Bach scholar:

It is characteristic of baroque mentality not to make the slightest fuss about a great artist's genius. . . . Nowhere . . . is there a hint of the select nature of the great artist or of the divine origin of his creative gifts. These are concepts created by romanticism. In Bach's time we find no talk of "depth of feeling," "originality," or "personal approach," and certainly not of a composition expressing an attitude towards life and the world. These ideas lay outside the baroque world of thought (Schering, pp. 85–86).

In reality, the first theoretician of opera, Giovanni Battista Doni (1594–1647), had already coined the classical formulation of the contrast between counterpoint as a craft and dramatic music as the creation of genius:

Counterpoint requires art and exercise rather than natural inclination, since it consists of many rules and observations and is based on practice acquired by long use. But in dramatic music he who is wanting in natural disposition should not even try to undertake it. Never will he achieve perfection, even though he may arrive at mediocrity through long study and knowledge acquired thereby, things equally needed by those singularly privileged by Nature. The composer of dramatic music, therefore, must be very inventive and versatile, he must have a quick mind and a strong imagination: qualities that he has in common with the poet, wherefore it is said *Poetae nascuntur, Oratores fiunt*, poets are born, orators are made. Thus we may compare to orators those composers who ordinarily take the *cantus firmus* or subject from others and, weaving over it an artful counterpoint, draw various melodic lines from it, which often have something dry or labored, in that they lack a certain grace and naturalness, which is the true spice of melody. This is what today's musicians have noted in Soriano, who, while most experienced in counterpoint, never had talent to write beautiful and graceful melodies, wherefore he devoted himself to the writing of canons and similar laborious compositions. . . . Gesualdo, Prince of Venosa, on the other hand, who was truly born for music, and with a gift for musical expression, and who could clothe with his musical gifts any poetic subject, never attended, as far as one knows, to canons and similar labored exercises. Such should be, then, the genius of the good composer, particularly for that genre of musical compositions which should bring to life all inner affects of the soul with vivid expression (Lowinsky [1964], pp. 338–39).

Doni could not have chosen apter personifications for his concepts of craftsman and genius than Palestrina's disciple, Soriano—famous for his 110 canons over a Marian hymn—and the princely composer, Gesualdo, who, for the sake of truth of sentiment, broke every rule in the book.

In another passage Doni comments on the dilemma in which "modern" composers find themselves with regard to tradition:

One will think it was not permissible to depart from the rules left behind by the predecessors, another will be more daring and follow these modern composers like the Prince of Venosa, indeed he will spontaneously invent new things. This is why Monteverdi seeks more the dissonances, whereas Peri hardly departs from the conventional rules (Lowinsky [1964], p. 340).

The stylistic separation between counterpoint and expressive music goes back to Monteverdi's famous distinction between the old and the new style or, as he phrased it, the *prima* and *seconda prattica* of the beginning of the seventeenth century. But Monteverdi had not yet said—perhaps he implied it—that it took less genius to write in the old style. He merely postulated greater liberty for the *seconda prattica*, the new expressive style of music.

If testimony is needed that concepts such as "depth of feeling," or "composition as expressing an attitude towards life and the world" or the "divine origin of creative gifts" are indeed part of baroque mentality, a reading of Thomas Mace's *Musick's Monument* (1676) should provide it. Mace, a clerk at Trinity College in Cambridge, although no more than a fine craftsman and mediocre composer, entertained the most sublime ideas of music, its power and origin:

Musick speaks so transcendently, and Communicates Its Notions so Intelligibly to the Internal, Intellectual, and Incomprehensible Faculties of the Soul; so far beyond all *Language of Words*, that I confess, and most solemnly affirm, I have been more *Sensibly, Fervently*, and *Zealously Captivated*, and drawn into *Divine Raptures*, and *Contemplations*, by Those *Unexpressible Rhetorical, Uncontroulable Perswasions*, and *Instructions of Musicks Divine Language*, than ever yet I have been, by the best *Verbal Rhetorick*, that came from any Mans Mouth, either in *Pulpit*, or elsewhere.

Those Influences, which come along with It, may aptly be compar'd, to *Emanations, Communications*, or *Distillations*, of some *Sweet*, and *Heavenly Genius*, or *Spirit; Mystically*, and *Unapprehensibly* (yet *Effectually*) *Dispossessing* the *Soul*, and *Mind*, of *All Irregular Disturbing*, and *Unquiet Motions; and Stills*, and *Fills It*, with *Quietness, Joy*, and *Peace; Absolute Tranquility*, and *Unexpressible Satisfaction* (Lowinsky [1964], pp. 333–34).

Such raptures are not confined to the peculiar temperament of an eccentric musician, as one might think Mace to have been. One of the sturdiest, worldliest gentlemen of seventeenth-century England, a man of wealth, power, and fame, Samuel Pepys, discourses in a surprisingly similar vein about his musical experience. Having heard a concert of wind music for *The Virgin Martyr*, he wrote in his diary:

. . . [it] is so sweet that it ravished me, and indeed, in a word, did wrap up my soul so that it made me really sick, just as I have formerly been when in love with my wife; that neither then, nor all the evening going home, and at home, I was able to think of any thing, but remained all night transported (Weiss, p. 64).

Another Englishman, Roger North (1653–1734), Attorney-General to James II, and one of a lengthy series of English amateur musicians and writers on music, insisted that

good musick must come from one by nature as well as art compleately made, who is arrived at a pitch to throw away the lumber of his rules and examples, and act upon the strength of his judgment, and knowledge of the subject matter itself, as if it had bin bred and born in him *ab origine* (Lowinsky [1964], p. 332).

Anticipating Rousseau and later romantic writers, North saw music's finest jewel in melody, or as the English were wont to call it, "ayre," of the invention of which he said:

But as for securing an Ayre, if it must be above the indifferent, it is like securing witt in poetry, not to be done; and after all will be found to flow from a genius, and not without some accidents or rather felicitys of fancy, as well as sound judgment, to make it sublime (Lowinsky [1964], p. 332).

The term *génie* is also part of the vocabulary of French musical theory of the baroque. De la Voye, in his *Traité de musique* (1656), after having dealt with elementary theory, counterpoint, and fugue, concludes his treatise with these words:

The other artifices of music, such as recitatives, echoes, the variety of movements, the order of cadences, the beauty of the melodies, the mixture of modes, the natural expression of the words and passions, they depend on the genius and the invention of the composer (Lowinsky [1964], p. 332).

The greatest French theorist of music in the age of the baroque, Jean Philippe Rameau, was accused by the partisans of Jean Jacques Rousseau of nurturing the belief that the composer needed not genius but only the science of harmony. However, in his *Traité de l'harmonie*, published in Paris in 1722 when Rousseau was a boy of ten, Rameau speaks constantly of *le génie et le goût*. "There is a world of difference," he observes, "between a music without fault and a perfect music" (Lowinsky [1964], pp. 329–30), and with this remark Rameau demolishes the notion of the artist as a craftsman whose excellence can be measured by his success in following the rules of his craft. In speaking of melody he remarks:

It is well-nigh impossible to give rules concerning it [melody], inasmuch as good taste has a greater part in it than anything else; thus we leave it to the happy geniuses to distinguish themselves in this genre on which the whole strength of sentiment depends (Lowinsky [1964], p. 330).

As happens so often, the critics had not read what they criticized. Rameau defends the composer against the pedantic guardians of the rules who, he says, become deaf if you want to show them the good effect of freedom, license, and exception in a music composed apparently against the rules.

Nothing shows Rameau's appreciation of imagination in the composer's work better than his plea for freedom in the writing of what is usually thought of as one of the strictest and most rational forms of music, the fugue, which he called

. . . an ornament of music which has only one principle, good taste; the very general rules governing it [the fugue] that we just outlined do not suffice in themselves to insure perfect success in it. The various feelings and events that one can express in music constantly produce novelties that cannot be reduced to rules (Lowinsky [1964], p. 330, n. 29).

Aside from genius, a composer, according to Rameau, also needs good taste. With *le goût* another irrational element enters our discussion, one that cannot be measured, prescribed, or fixed in rules. Yet it is to some extent rational—and in that regard typically French—in that it resides in aesthetic judgment rather than in emotion, an essential attribute of genius in German and Italian writings. The irrational concept of empathy, the dramatic composer's ability to put himself in the place of his characters and re-create them in tones by the sheer force of sympathetic imagination—and Rameau was a composer of opera himself—is already a part of Rameau's aesthetics. At the end of Chapter 20, Book Two, on the propriety of harmony, he says:

For the rest, a good musician must surrender himself to all the characters that he wishes to depict, and, like a skilful comedian, put himself in the place of the speaker, imagine himself in the localities where the events to be represented occur, and take part in them as much as those most involved in them, be a good orator, at least within himself, feel when the voice should rise or fall more or less, so as to shape his melody, harmony, modulation, and motion accordingly (Lowinsky [1964], p. 331).

VI. THE EIGHTEENTH CENTURY AND THE BEGINNINGS OF ROMANTICISM

No statement on musical genius had a more profound impact on the world of art and letters than the article on *génie* by Jean Jacques Rousseau in his *Dictionnaire de musique* (1768)—the first dictionary of music to deal with the concept. Because of its seminal significance, the entire article follows in translation:

Don't ask, young artist, "what is genius?" Either you have it—then you feel it yourself, or you don't—then you will never know it. The genius of the musician subjects the entire Universe to his art. He paints all pictures through tones; he lends eloquence even to silence. He renders the ideas through sentiments, sentiments through accents, and the passions he expresses he awakens [also] in his listener's heart. Pleasure, through him, takes on new charms; pain rendered in musical sighs wrests cries [from the listener]. He burns incessantly, but never consumes himself. He expresses with warmth frost and ice. Even when he paints the horrors of Death, he carries in his soul this feeling for Life that never abandons him, and that he communicates to hearts made to feel it. But alas, he does not speak to those who don't carry his seed within themselves and his miracles escape those who cannot imitate them. Do you wish to know whether a spark of this devouring fire animates you? Hasten then, fly to Naples, listen there to the masterworks of Leo, of Durante, of Jommelli, of Pergolesi. If your eyes fill with tears, if you feel your heart beat, if shivers run down your spine, if breath-taking raptures choke you, then take [a libretto by] Metastasio and go to work: his genius will kindle yours; you will create at his example. That is what makes the genius—and the tears of others will soon repay you for the tears that your masters elicited from you. But should the charms of this great artist leave you cold, should you experience neither delirium nor delight, should you find that which transports only "nice," do you then dare ask what is genius? Vulgar man, don't profane this sublime word.

What would it matter to you if you knew it? You would not know how to feel it. Go home and write—French music (Lowinsky [1964], pp. 326–27).

It is easy to see why poets, musicians, and aestheticians were stirred by Rousseau's concept of genius. This was not an ordinary dictionary article; this was a dithyrambic ode, every word of which echoed Rousseau's own intense musical experiences in the Venetian opera houses during his days as secretary to the French Embassy in Venice.

Creative activity engendered by enthusiasm, fire, imagination, and above all, by the ability to feel, and feel passionately—all of these essential elements in the romantic concept of genius hail from Rousseau. Rameau's careful balance between craft and inspiration, rules and good taste, technical mastery and genius, is scornfully thrown aside by Rousseau in exchange for a one-sided emphasis on emotion and empathy. Being himself the very model of an untutored genius given to passionate outbursts of tears, he would never have dared to set his own hand to composing libretto and music of his operetta, *Le Devin du village* (1752), without the profound conviction that feeling, more than anything else, is needed to create music that goes to the heart. "A student of three months could write the 'Devin'"—Rousseau said later—"whereas a learned composer would find it hard to embark upon a course of such decided simplicity" (Lowinsky [1965b], p. 201).

One element is conspicuously absent in Rousseau's definition of genius: musical originality. Rousseau was primarily a man of letters; as a musician he was decidedly an amateur. Music was for him a means to enhance the emotional appeal of the spoken word, of the drama. This agreed with his belief (*Essai sur l'origine des langues*, 1753) that in the beginning word and tone, speech and melody, were one. Nor were his democratic convictions that led him to espouse a style of folk song-like simplicity designed to foster appreciation of musical originality.

Thus we find ourselves facing the paradox that the eighteenth-century apostle of feeling could think of genius without the attribute of originality—indeed, it is in "imitating" Metastasio that a musician becomes a genius—whereas the century's most detached and rational thinker, Kant, conceived of originality as the chief attribute of genius.

Immanuel Kant, in his *Critique of Judgment* (*Kritik der Urtheilskraft*), calls genius "the talent (natural gift) that gives the rules to art" (Lowinsky [1964], p. 328). This is an ingenious, indeed, an elegant definition in its studied avoidance of opposition between rule and inspiration, talent and genius. Kant succeeds, nevertheless, in making a sound distinction between them, especially as he goes on to say that genius "is a talent to create that which escapes all definite rules: it is not natural skill for what can be learned according to any rule; hence, originality must be its first attribute. . . . Everyone agrees that genius must be opposed completely to the spirit of imitation" (Lowinsky [1964], p. 328). Thus Kant manages to avoid the emphasis on emotion that was contrary to the nature of his analytical mind, and yet to stay basically within the framework of thought of his time. It has been remarked (Serauky, p. 162) that there is an irreconcilable contradiction between Kant's definition of genius as rejecting "the spirit of imitation" and his belief that music is the art of imitation of human emotion—an idea current throughout the eighteenth century and developed particularly by Charles Batteux in his *Traité des beaux arts, réduits à un même principe* (1746). Kant uses the term in two meanings: imitation of one artist by another in a specific artistic medium, and imitation as a re-creation of human emotions in tones. There is no contradiction between these two ideas. Notwithstanding his emphasis on originality, Kant did not escape the criticism of the emerging romantic movement led by Herder, who printed excerpts from Kant's definition of genius together with devastatingly sarcastic glosses.

The eighteenth-century literary movement of *Sturm und Drang* was keenly interested in the nature of genius in general and of musical genius in particular. All of its exponents were fired by Rousseau's ideas. Christian Friedrich Schubart, poet, musician, keyboard player, famous for his improvisations, philosopher, imprisoned for his ideas as a free thinker, wrote in his essay *Vom musikalischen Genie* words reminiscent of Rousseau's:

Musical genius is rooted in the heart and receives its impressions through the ear. . . . All musical geniuses are self-taught, for the fire that animates them carries them away irresistibly to seek their own flight orbit [*Flugbahn*].
The Bachs, a Galuppi, Jommelli, Gluck, and Mozart excelled already in childhood through the most significant products of their spirit. Musical harmony lay in their soul and they soon threw away the crutch of art (Lowinsky [1964], p. 326).

But unlike Rousseau, Schubart added: "Nevertheless, no musical genius can reach perfection without cultivation and training. Art must perfect what Nature sketched in the raw" (Lowinsky [1964], p. 326).

Schubart, in his *Ideen zu einer Aesthetik der Tonkunst* (1784–85), eulogizes Rousseau, his ideas on music, and his *Dictionnaire de musique*. Rousseau's inspiration also hovers over Johann Gottfried von Herder's essay "Von Musik" in which Fontenelle's

"*Que me veux-tu, Sonate?*"—the opera composer's defiance of "mere" instrumental music, of "academic" art—made famous by Rousseau's enthusiastic approval, is quoted without indication of its source.

Rousseau is also the indubitable inspiration for the romantic poet, composer, pianist, conductor, and music critic E. T. A. Hoffmann and his conception of the nature of musical creation:

To touch us, to move us mightily, the artist himself must be deeply affected in his own heart. Effective composition is nothing but the art of capturing with a higher strength, and fixing in the hieroglyphs of tones [the notes], what was received in the mind's unconscious *ecstasis*. If a young artist asks how to write an effective opera, we can answer only: read the poem, concentrate on it with all the power of your spirit, enter with all the might of your fancy into all phases of the action. You live in its personages; you yourself are the tyrant, the hero, the beloved; you feel the pain and the raptures of love, the shame, the fear, the horror, yes, Death's nameless agony, the transfiguration of blissful joy. You rage, you storm, you hope, you despair; the blood flows through your veins, your pulse beats more violently. In the fire of enthusiasm that inflames your heart, tones, melodies, harmonies ignite, and the poem pours out of your soul in the wonderful language of music. . . . Technical training, through study of harmony in the works of the great masters, and your own writing bring it about that you perceive your inner music more and more clearly; no melody, no modulation, no instrument escapes you, and thus you receive, together with the effect, also the means which you now, like spirits subject to your power, detain in the magic lines of your score. To be sure, all this amounts to saying: take care, my good friend, to be a very musical genius. The rest will come by itself. But thus it is, and not otherwise (Lowinsky [1964], pp. 323–24).

Musical creation as the volcanic eruption of a glowing soul in the grip of ecstatic revelation, technical study as the magical means to summon the spirits of the art: this indeed is a truly romantic concept.

Whereas one will have difficulty finding an entry on "genius" in modern musical dictionaries, it occurs in nineteenth-century dictionaries such as Peter Lichtenthal's *Dizionario e bibliografia della musica* (1826) or in August Gathy's *Musikalisches Conversations-Lexikon* (2nd ed., 1840). Neither offers a history of the concept, but both define it in terms derived from Rousseau. Gathy, in addition, shows the influence of the romantic writer Jean Paul, in whose writings we come to the final inversion of the medieval hierarchy of values. Boethius saw the highest human faculty in *ratio*, the lowest in *instinctus naturalis*, with which he credited the composer. In Jean Paul's *Vorschule der Aesthetik* (1804; 2nd ed., 1813) the "unconscious" is the great motivating power of the creative artist (*Das Mächtigste im Dichter . . . ist gerade das Unbewusste*).

Genius is guided by "divine instinct"—a term picked up by Gathy. Each artist has his own specific "organ," the painter the eye, the musician the ear; "the supremacy of one organ and one force, for example in Mozart, operates with the blindness and assurance of the instinct" (Miller, pp. 55–67). The divine instinct speaks more clearly, more forcefully in the genius; it is he who gives us the view of the whole—talent can provide only views of details.

Jean Paul defines the limits of talent versus genius; it remained for Richard Wagner, in *Die Meistersinger von Nürnberg* (1867), to create the immortal double image of genius and craftsman: Walter is an idealization of genius, Beckmesser a caricature of the craftsman. Walter personifies the artist whose creativity rests on inspiration, and whose inspiration springs from an imaginative mind and a generous and sensitive heart, open to love and enthusiasm. Beckmesser's art rests on the pedantic observation of timeworn rules. His pedantry is at home in a small, petty, scheming mind, equally incapable of noble emotions and of the flight of fancy. Between these two extremes stands Hans Sachs, his roots in the world of the mastersingers, but his heart and mind open to Walter's freely inspired art, in which, he confessed,

> No rule would fit, and yet
> no error could I find
> (*Kein Regel wollte da passen,*
> *und war doch kein Fehler drin,* Act II).

The opposition between conventional rule and fresh inspiration, the idea that the genius, unlike the mere craftsman, can transcend rules without committing errors and that in so doing he can make new revelations, is a leitmotif in the history of the concept of musical genius.

Friedrich Nietzsche, who had turned from an ardent admirer to a bitter critic of Wagner, restored the balance between inspiration and rational judgment when he wrote the ironic words (*Menschliches Allzumenschliches,* 1878):

The artists have a vested interest in our believing in the flash of revelation, the so-called inspiration, as if the idea of the work of art, of poetry, the fundamental idea of a philosophy shone down from heaven as a ray of grace. In reality, the imagination of the good artist or thinker produces continuously good, mediocre, and bad things, but his judgment, trained and sharpened to a fine point, rejects, selects, connects as one can see now from Beethoven's sketchbooks where he appears to have slowly developed the most beautiful melodies and to have selected them, as it were, from many diverse starts. . . . All great artists and thinkers were great workers, indefatigable not only in inventing, but also in rejecting, sifting, transforming, ordering (Gast, p. 163).

Nietzsche wrote these words only a few years after Gustave Nottebohm had published his *Beethoveniana* (1872), the first thorough presentation and discussion of Beethoven's sketches. No wonder they impressed Nietzsche. For if ever there was a representative of musical genius, it was Beethoven, both as a man and as an artist. As a man he was strong and sensitive, gentle and irascible, generous and passionate, proud, suspicious, love-seeking, frankly eccentric, and without compromise in matters of art and of honor; as an artist, he was creator of a new world of spirit and form, in which passionate utterance was contained by the most severe discipline of form, a novel dynamic form that derived its inner laws from the new spirit of untrammeled freedom of artistic expression. "There is no rule that may not be broken for the sake of greater beauty," he once wrote.

Yet, the sketches revealed the titanic struggle that this great master fought for the ultimate realization of his ideas, which often began in a conventional, if not banal, form to grow by degrees—at times it took as many as thirty sketches—into exquisite original thoughts. It was Nietzsche who, following Beethoven's example, discovered an element of musical genius often overlooked by writers from the Renaissance through romanticism: endless patience and infinite striving (*Streben*) or effort. One of the few writers remarking upon this was Glareanus, when he spoke about Josquin des Prez. And, indeed, there is a peculiar affinity between the personalities and the creative characteristics of the great genius of the fifteenth century who came out of the Middle Ages and moved toward the new world of the Renaissance, and the composer of the eighteenth century who moved from classicism to romanticism, creating in the process a musical amalgam of an utterly unique character (Grout, p. 183).

It remained for our own time not only to make light of the whole idea of genius, both past and present (Ricci, pp. 80 and 83), but also to replace feeling, imagination, planning, and aesthetic principle with mathematical formulas, computers, and "chance." The inherent paradox of this modern approach to composition lies in this: whereas aesthetic principles have been abandoned in the process of composition, the results are presented to modern audiences having no other possible approach to the understanding of music than one based on aesthetic perception. This unresolved contradiction of modern music contains in itself the seeds of its own necessary destruction. Either music is to be heard, and then it must proceed from principles of perception and aesthetics; or it proceeds from merely intellectual and mathematical principles or chance, and then it makes no sense to present as sounding form what was not experienced as sound and form. Once this dilemma has been resolved, musical genius will return to the artistic scene and move from its present underground to the center of the stage in an affirmation of faith in the possibility of choice, decision, and creation. The musician alone cannot do it. The whole age will have to reconquer faith in the humanity of Man and in the individuality of his art.

BIBLIOGRAPHY

Pietro Aron, *Lucidario in musica* (Venice, 1545). Heinrich Besseler, "Johannes de Muris," *Die Musik in Geschichte und Gegenwart*, Vol. VII, cols. 105–15. Manfred F. Bukofzer, ed., *Adrian Petit Coclico, Compendium Musices*, Documenta Musicologica, Vol. IX (Kassel, 1954). E. de Coussemaker, *Scriptorum de musica medii aevi*, Vol. IV (Paris, 1874): Johannes Tinctoris, "Liber de arte contrapuncti," pp. 76–153, and "Proportionale musices," pp. 153–77. Hans Heinrich Eggebrecht, "Ars musica: Musikanschauung des Mittelalters und ihre Nachwirkungen," *Die Sammlung, Zeitschrift für Kultur und Erziehung*, **12** (1957), 306–22; idem, "Der Begriff des 'Neuen' in der Musik von der Ars Nova bis zur Gegenwart," *International Musicological Society, Report of the Eighth Congress, New York, 1961* (Kassel, 1961), pp. 195–202; idem, *Studien zur musikalischen Terminologie*, Akademie der Wissenschaften und der Literatur, Abhandlungen der geistes- und sozialwissenschaftlichen Klasse (Jahrgang 1955), No. 10. Ernest T. Ferand, "Komposition," *Die Musik in Geschichte und Gegenwart*, Vol. VII, cols. 1423–44. G. Friedlein, ed., *Anicii Manlii Torquati Severini Boetii De institutione musica* (Leipzig, 1867). Peter Gast, ed., *Nietzsches Werke, Erste Abtheilung*, Vol. II (Leipzig, 1923). D. J. Grout, *A History of Western Music* (New York, 1960). Sebald Heyden, *De arte canendi* (Nuremberg, 1537). Raymond Klibansky, Erwin Panofsky, and Fritz Saxl, *Saturn and Melancholy* (London, 1964). Paul O. Kristeller, "The Modern System of the Arts: A Study in the History of Aesthetics," *Journal of the History of Ideas*, **12** (1951), 496–527, **13** (1952), 17–46. Edward E. Lowinsky, "Music in the Culture of the Renaissance," *Journal of the History of Ideas*, **15** (1954), 509–53; reprinted in *Renaissance Essays from the Journal of the History of Ideas*, ed. Paul Oskar Kristeller and Philip P. Wiener (New York, 1968); idem, "Music of the Renaissance as Viewed by Renaissance Musicians," *The Renaissance Image of Man and the World*, ed. Bernard O'Kelly (Columbus, Ohio, 1966), pp. 129–77; idem, "Musical Genius—Evolution and Origins of a Concept," *The Musical Quarterly*, **50** (1964), 321–40, 476–95; idem, "Renaissance Writings on Music Theory (1964)," *Renaissance News*, **18** (1965a), 358–70; idem, "Taste, Style, and Ideology in Eighteenth-Century Music," *Aspects of the Eighteenth Century*, ed. Earl R. Wasserman (Baltimore, 1965b), pp. 163–205. Othmar Luscinius, *Musurgia* (Strasbourg, 1536). Henry S. Macran, ed., *The Harmonics of Aristoxenus* (Oxford, 1902). Marcus Meibomius, *Antiquae musicae auctores septem* (Amsterdam, 1652), chapter on "Bacchii Senioris Introductio artis musicae." Norbert Miller, ed., *Jean Paul, Werke*, Vol. V (Munich, 1963). Hans Joachim Moser, *Paul Hofhaimer* (Stuttgart and Berlin, 1929). Helmuth Osthoff, *Josquin Desprez* (Tutzing, 1962–65). Carl Parrish, ed., *Dictionary of Musical Terms by Johannes Tinctoris* (London, 1963). Gerhard Pietzsch, *Die Klassifikation der Musik von Boethius bis Ugolino von Orvieto* (Halle, 1929); idem, *Die Musik im Erziehungs- und Bildungsideal des ausgehenden Altertums und frühen Mittelalters* (Halle, 1932). Leonardo Ricci, *Anonymous (20th Century)* (New York, 1962). Arnold Schering, *Das Symbol in der Musik* (Leipzig, 1941). Walter Serauky, *Die musikalische Nachahmungsästhetik im Zeitraum von 1700 bis 1850* (Muenster, 1929). Oliver Strunk, *Source Readings in Music History* (New York, 1950). Hans Thüme, *Beiträge zur Geschichte des Geniebegriffs in England*, Studien zur englischen Philologie, 71 (Halle, 1927). Pontus de Tyard, *Solitaire second ou prose de la musique*, 2nd ed. (Lyons, 1555). Charles van den Borren, "Deux Recueils peu connus d'Orlande de Lassus," *Actes du Congrès d'histoire de l'art, Paris, 1921* (Paris, 1924), III, 833–45. J. Smits van Waesberghe, ed., *Aribonis De musica* (Rome, 1951); idem, *Johannis Affligemensis De musica cum tonario* (Rome, 1950). D. P. Walker, *Der musikalische Humanismus im 16. und frühen 17. Jahrhundert* (Kassel, 1949). Bernard Weinberg, *A History of Literary Criticism in the Italian Renaissance* (Chicago, 1961). David G. Weiss, *Samuel Pepys, Curioso* (Pittsburgh, 1957). R. P. Winnington-Ingram, ed., *Aristidis Quintiliani De musica libri tres* (Leipzig, 1963). Edgar Zilsel, *Die Entstehung des Geniebegriffes* (Tübingen, 1926).

Translations, unless otherwise indicated, are by the author of the article.

EDWARD E. LOWINSKY

[See also **Creativity in Art;** Empathy; **Genius;** Music as a **Divine Art;** Pythagorean Harmony.]

GNOSTICISM

GNOSTICISM was a religious movement which flourished alongside and, to some extent, within Christianity and Judaism during the first three centuries of the Christian era. In it, great emphasis was laid on knowledge (*gnōsis*) derived from secret revelations and capable of bestowing salvation on the knower. The term should be differentiated from "Gnosis," which refers to any kind of knowledge of divine mysteries reserved for an elite. In Gnosticism there is a particular kind of Gnosis, usually involving the notion of a divine spark in man which needs to be awakened and reintegrated with its divine source. The awakening and the movement toward reintegration are provided by a revealer-redeemer who brings knowledge of the way to return to the divine source, usually through the heavenly spheres above.

The modern usage of these terms does not precisely coincide with that found in ancient sources, where only a few sects are specifically called "Gnostic" and the term "Gnosticism" does not appear. The various groups actually derived their names from their founders or from localities, activities, doctrines, or objects of worship. The modern usage is intended to point toward the basic similarities among the groups, for in general all agreed in rejecting the world of material phenomena as created by an evil demiurge, inferior and hostile to the supreme deity known only to the Gnostic. The Gnostic, like the Platonist, regarded his body as a tomb and longed to escape from the body and the world, returning to the "unknown god" (i.e., unknown to others) who dwells beyond the regions ruled by the hostile planetary deities and (or including) the demiurge.

During the late third century and afterwards, Gnosticism was in decline. Its adherents, driven out of the Christian church and soon proscribed by the state, may have turned to Manichaeism, similar to Gnosticism but more vigorous and better organized. Still later, there were definite Gnostic tendencies among such groups as the Bogomils and the Cathari, some of whom made use of old Gnostic books. In modern times Gnosis, if not ideas derived from Gnosticism as such, is sometimes encountered in theosophical teaching.

I. SOURCES OF KNOWLEDGE ABOUT GNOSTICISM

For many centuries Gnosticism was known almost exclusively from the writings of Christian opponents. By the middle of the second century the Roman apologist Justin had composed a treatise, now lost, in which he argued that Gnostic movements, inspired by demons, first arose after Christ's ascension. The first Gnostic teacher was Simon Magus (who in Acts 8 is not depicted as a Gnostic); he was followed by his disciple Menander and, later on, by Marcion of Pontus. Justin's argument is not convincing, for Menander held himself to be the revealer and can hardly have been Simon's disciple, while Marcion's doctrines had little to do with either Simon or Menander. Justin was trying to show the generic development of Gnosticism from a single, demon-inspired source, and he was uncritically followed by later antiheretical writers. Different explanations of Gnosticism were sometimes provided. Thus, Hegesippus (ca. 180) argued that the church, originally a "pure virgin," was corrupted by varieties of sectarian Judaism which led to the major Gnostic schools of the second century. About the same time Saint Irenaeus (Church Father, second century) claimed that Gnostic teaching was due to vanity, immorality, skill in magic, or love of mythology for

its own sake. These explanations can be called psychological. Other anti-Gnostic writers argued that Gnostic ideas were derived from Greek philosophers, though, actually, they provided little proof for the point.

Modern discoveries made in Egypt have revealed the existence of many documents used by the Gnostics themselves, occasionally in Greek but usually in Coptic translations. The most important works published before 1956 were the third- or fourth-century *Pistis Sophia* and the Berlin versions of the *Gospel of Mary* (Magdalene), the *Apocryphon* (secret book) of John, and the *Sophia* (wisdom) of *Jesus Christ*. In 1956 the situation began to change, for in that year the first of 51 treatises, bound in 13 leather volumes and found near Nag-Hammadi (Chenoboskion) in upper Egypt, was published; this was the so-called *Gospel of Truth*—possibly, but by no means certainly, identified with a Valentinian *Evangelium veritatis* mentioned by Irenaeus. The whole collection of Gnostic documents was later described by H.-C. Puech, J. Doresse, and (most reliably) M. Krause (see Bibliography). By the end of 1967 only a few of these documents—discovered as early as 1945—had been published. These include the *Gospel of Truth*, the *Gospel of Thomas*, the *Gospel of Philip*, three versions of the *Apocryphon of John*, an *Epistle to Rheginus on the Resurrection*, a treatise without a title, and a collection of apocalypses ascribed to Saint Paul and Saint James, and to Adam. The writings in this Gnostic library seem to date from the fourth century, but in at least one instance it can be shown that the original was two centuries older. Proof of this point was given when H.-C. Puech identified two Oxyrhynchus papyri, written in Greek in the early third century and previously called the "sayings of Jesus," with the newly discovered *Gospel of Thomas*. In addition, something like the *Apocryphon of John* was known to Irenaeus and used in his *Adversus haereses* (i. 29)—though this Gnostic work was evidently subject to a good deal of modification. Two of the Nag-Hammadi versions are longer than the other one, which in turn corresponds fairly closely with the Berlin version; and Irenaeus' source is different from all of them.

The picture of Gnosticism emerging from the Nag-Hammadi texts is like that given by the church writers in that a great deal of variety was present; some documents are Valentinian, others Sethian, some even consisting of the non-Christian Hermetic writings. A complete assessment can be provided only when all are published. For the moment it can be said that the only document thus far clearly non-Christian (apart from the Hermetica) is the Apocalypse of Adam, apparently a synthesis of Jewish and Iranian motifs.

II. SOME GNOSTIC SYSTEMS

Ethics. It is important to begin with ethics because, while Gnostic systems vary greatly, the ethical outlook of the Gnostics seems to reflect a basic alienation from the world which is expressed in two extreme forms. (1) In the system ascribed to Simon Magus there is the view that the spark within the Gnostic needs to be freed from the repressions of conventional morality. The Old Testament law is the epitome of such morality; it was ordained by rebellious angels who imprisoned their mother, Simon's "first thought," in various human bodies including those of Helen of Troy and, later, a Tyrian prostitute. Simon's descent to rescue his "first thought" is thus a model for the coming of Gnosis to rescue all Gnostics. His reputed use of magic, especially love-magic, symbolizes the Gnostic's control over his environment, from which he is now free. Other Gnostics vigorously attacked the Old Testament law; Epiphanes, for example, argued that the repressive injunctions against theft and against coveting a neighbor's wife were ridiculous, for in the natural and original state of mankind there was neither property nor monogamy. Other schools insisted upon the positive necessity of breaking conventional laws. According to the Valentinians, it was the Gnostic's duty to imitate the unions of the angelic powers above. "Whoever is *in* the world and does not love a woman so as to possess her does not belong to the truth and will not attain to the truth; but he who is *from* the world and does not possess a woman will not attain to the truth, because he has not possessed a woman with desire." (In part this language is based on the Gospel of John, but the conclusion the Gnostics drew was that continence and good works were necessary for ordinary Christians, not for themselves.) Several groups claimed that sexual morality was not the only kind of morality that had to be transcended. They argued that the Gnostic had to experience "everything" so that the spark could be saved. For this reason they held that the great sinners of the Old Testament were the real saints, and that Judas Iscariot was the author of Man's salvation. In some respects these doctrines remind us of Greco-Roman Cynicism, but the Gnostic found them sanctioned by divine revelation. (2) At the other extreme there lies a pessimistic and repressive view which led to extreme asceticism (there is no trace of magic in these systems). Saturninus, for example, held that the savior (Jesus) came to destroy evil men and demons and to save the good; the good were those who rejected marriage and reproduction as instituted by Satan.

Both kinds of ethical outlook were derived from a common alienation from convention and from ordinary human existence, to be transcended either by compulsive promiscuity or by compulsive asceticism. Although in both Judaism and Christianity freedom could lead to license and self-discipline to asceticism, the Gnostic ethical outlook was different because it was related to the conviction that the world lay permanently under the control of evil creators from whom only the Gnostic could escape.

Theology. Four second-century systems serve to illustrate common themes and variations on the themes. The first two can be regarded as close to mythology and to syncretistic reinterpretation of the Old Testament; the second two will show how the myths were developed, somewhat more systematically, in the direction of the New Testament. (1) The Coptic versions of the *Apocryphon of John* begin and end with a framework relating the Gnostic revelation to Christian tradition. At the beginning, John, the son of Zebedee, sees a vision on a mountain top; at the end, he tells his fellow disciples what the savior said to him. In the middle, however, there is the revelation itself, which clearly reflects the Old Testament narrative but reinterprets it drastically. The revealer appears in "a unity of many forms" and declares himself to be the Father, the Mother, and the Son; but the ultimate reality is a spirit of immeasurable light, transcending all gods. From this spirit proceeded a series of emanations, the lowest of which, Wisdom, produced from herself an ugly son named Ialdabaoth (presumably a parody of some form of the name Yahweh). In turn Ialdabaoth produced twelve angels, each accompanied by seven more; each of the seven had three "powers." Then he made twelve more "authorities" or "principalities," seven to rule over the seven heavens, five over the underworld. The total is thus 360 and corresponds with the days in a lunar year. In various lists the seven world-rulers are assigned slightly different names, but in essence all are based on names of Yahweh in the Old Testament (Yahweh, Adonai, Elohim, Sabaoth). Thus far, only the names suggest any relation to the Old Testament.

At this point, however, the *Apocryphon* begins to correct the Old Testament narrative. It was Ialdabaoth who said, "I am a jealous god; there is no other god beside me"—thus proving that other gods really exist. What was "borne about" (Genesis 1:2 in Greek) was not the wind or the spirit of Elohim but Ialdabaoth's mother, who had just realized that he had emanated from her. This took place "not as Moses said, Above the waters." The seven authorities saw an image reflected from the Holy Perfect Father above and said to one another, "Let us make a man after the image and after the appearance of God." They were unable to give him life, and therefore some of Wisdom's power had to be breathed into him before he could stand upright. The whole story of paradise, largely "not as

Moses said," tells of how Ialdabaoth and the others tried to maintain control over the man.

(2) Another mythological system, that of a certain Justin as set forth in his book entitled *Baruch*, shows how some Gnostics fused Greek, Jewish, and Christian elements. At the beginning, Justin states that the supreme deity, called "the Good," is to be identified with the Greco-Roman fertility god Priapus, though the story of the universe is not concerned with him (presumably because he plays no role in mythology). This story tells of two inferior principles named Elohim and Eden. The connection with the Old Testament is obvious. Elohim loved Eden, for Eden was also the Old Testament Israel; he "planted a garden in Eden" (Genesis 2:8), and this garden consisted of twelve angels who resembled their father, twelve who resembled their mother. "The angels of this paradise are allegorically called trees"; thus the tree of life is Baruch ("blessed"), while the tree of the knowledge of good and evil is Naas ("serpent"). When Elohim later abandoned Eden as his love for her cooled, she tried to torment him, especially through the activities of her angel Naas. Elohim's angel Baruch tried to summon men to follow Elohim and leave the world, but his efforts, made not only through Moses and the other Hebrew prophets but also through Hercules (twelve labors!), were not successful. Jesus, unlike his predecessors, remained faithful to Baruch and, in spirit, ascended to the Good. This story is supposed to provide a key to Greek mythology as well as to the Bible. Thus Elohim really equals Zeus, who appeared to Leda-Eden as a swan and to Danae-Eden as a shower of gold.

Justin's system was not only mythological but also liturgical; at baptism an initiate took the following oath: "I swear by the One above all, the Good, to keep these mysteries and to tell them to no one and not to return from the Good to the creation." At baptism, then, he obviously entered into the spiritual world above, following the example of Elohim himself. Such oaths, found among other Gnostic groups as well, remind us that the mythology was produced in the context of religious cult.

(3) A somewhat more philosophical form of Gnosticism, at least in expression, is to be found in the system of Basilides of Alexandria (ca. 117–38). Originally there was absolutely nothing; then the nonexistent god made the nonexistent cosmos (= pure potentiality) out of the nonexistent, "establishing" the seed of the universe which contained a "triple sonship." (It has been suggested that Basilides may have come in contact with Indian ideas at Alexandria, and that they explain his emphasis on nonexistence.) The first of these sonships returned to the nonexistent god, while the second tried to do so but could not come close until "winged with

the Holy Spirit"; the third remained in "the mixture of seeds." After this a great archon (ruler) arose and with his son created the universe; in turn the second ruler generated a third. (This part of the system is probably based on Christian ideas.) The function of all three rulers was to reveal the nature of existence to the beings beneath them and to assist the third sonship to move upward. Jesus, the son of Mary, was their agent. He himself ascended above and thus provided a model for other souls to imitate. When the whole third sonship has returned above, cosmic ignorance will come upon every being left below, and even upon the archons. They will remain in ignorance of what is above and "will not be tormented by the desire of what is impossible." Various expressions used by Basilides find parallels in Middle Platonism and in the Aristotelian language sometimes employed therein. As a whole, however, the system is not philosophical, as Wolfson has pointed out. Basilides himself claimed, rather unconvincingly, that his doctrine came from the apostle Peter.

(4) Probably the most important system or group of systems in the second century was Valentinianism, surviving to be denounced with other heresies by the emperor Theodosius in 428. Its founder was a certain Valentinus, at Rome about 140, but it was systematically developed in various directions by Ptolemaeus (toward philosophy; refuted by Irenaeus), Theodotus (toward mythology), and Marcus (toward magic and numerology). The basic system involved either one or two first principles from which emanated thirty "aeons", also called the "pleroma" or totality of the spiritual beings above the cosmos. The cosmos originated when the thirtieth aeon, Wisdom, fell into outer darkness, became pregnant, and gave birth to the demiurge. He in turn made the seven heavens (angels) out of his mother's emotions and their expressions (e.g., water from tears, light from laughter). Much of the story thus far is obviously close to that in the *Apocryphon of John*, but we know that the Valentinians went on to describe the process of salvation. The Savior descended from the pleroma to redeem fallen Wisdom and the spirits which she had breathed into men. There are three classes of men: material, with bodies controlled by soul; psychic, with body and soul but capable of obtaining spirit; and spiritual, with body and soul entirely controlled by spirit. Spirit is to be rescued from spiritual men, and this rescue has already taken place for those whose spirits the Savior presented as brides to the angels in the pleroma.

The Valentinians usually proved the truth of their statements by exegesis of isolated New Testament texts, although Ptolemaeus was able to find the pleroma in the whole prologue to John, and a little later, 329

Heracleon produced the first commentary on John in order to prove his case.

Expressions paralleled in Jewish mysticism often occur in Valentinian writings, especially in the *Gospel of Truth* (though it may not be fully Valentinian). It would appear, however, that the essence of the system lies in a Judaized and Christianized version of a myth like that in the *Apocryphon of John*. Conceivably it arose in a heterodox Jewish-Christian environment.

III. GNOSTIC ORIGINS

The problem of Gnostic origins has not been solved, and it sometimes looks as if presumed sources depend primarily on the concerns of those who find them. Generally speaking, five kinds of treatment are current. (1) Some have found the seeds of Gnostic thought in Jewish heterodoxy, especially apocalyptic and/or mystical. It is difficult, however, to view the common idea of a hostile creator-god as Jewish in any sense, and the suggestion that some Gnostic teachers were ex-Jews lacks any evidence to support it. (2) It has been held that Gnosticism was basically a Christian heresy, but while some evidence points in this direction, the notion of heresy itself requires explanation (see below). (3) Some have urged that Gnostic ideas primarily reflect Greek religious philosophy, especially Middle Platonism with its emphasis on divine transcendence. If so, it seems odd that among the most militant opponents of Gnosticism were Plotinus and his disciples. The Gnostics were not philosophers (Wolfson). (4) Others have sought for Gnostic origins in Greco-Roman, Syrian, Egyptian, Mesopotamian, Iranian, and/or Indian religion, i.e., in the syncretistic religious environment of the early empire. Some evidence points in this direction. The heavenly world of the Ophites, as Celsus noted, was like that of the Mithraists. It is not clear, however, that syncretism provided the starting point for Gnosticism rather than an environment in which it flourished. (5) Some (especially Hans Jonas) have endeavored to treat Gnosticism as a phenomenon essentially unique but susceptible of interpretation in existentialist categories. Jonas has also gone on to combine this approach with historical analysis (see Biblio.).

It would appear that none of the five approaches can be completely neglected and that the most adequate explanation of Gnostic origins will have to take all into account. Some are obviously more important than others. Thus, one might begin with Jonas by delineating Gnosticism as a specific phenomenon and then inquire what concrete historical circumstances might have provided an occasion for its rise. It seems significant that the earliest known Gnostic teacher lived in Samaria during the time of turbulence just before the Jewish revolt of 66–70, when Christianity was beginning to spread. According to the church fathers, Simon was related to paganism, to Judaism, and to Christianity. It may also be significant that the Gnostic teacher Basilides taught at Alexandria just after a Jewish revolt in the time of Trajan. Similarly, Marcion brought his Gnostic message to Rome, where Jewish Christianity was flourishing, just after the war of 132–35. To be sure, not everything in Gnostic "history" was related solely to Jewish revolts; the *Apocalypse of Adam* briefly describes no fewer than thirteen "kingdoms" which arose before the true revelation was given.

Most of the Gnostic systems were closely related to Christianity, and Harnack defined Gnosticism as "the acute secularizing or Hellenizing of Christianity," while Wolfson has preferred to speak of "the verbal Christianizing of paganism," since in his view the Gnostic angels and aeons are derived from polytheistic sources, and Gnostic contacts with philosophy (implied by "Hellenizing") were extremely limited. Certainly, the doctrine of the Simonians reflects little derived from Judaism, much from Christianity and, indeed, from pagan thought. For most of the later Gnostics the only savior was "the Christ," usually differentiated from the human Jesus. The doctrine that either Jesus or the Christ merely seemed to suffer ("docetism") was not specifically Gnostic but was held by many Gnostic teachers.

The major Gnostic systems of the second century are undeniably Christian in intention. The question as to whether or not they are somehow Jewish in origin has been much debated, as already indicated. E. Peterson and G. Quispel have inferred the existence of a pre-Christian Jewish Gnosis, and G. G. Scholem has supported their conclusions from esoteric Jewish literature, especially the Hekhaloth (see Bibliography). In spite of the importance of these studies for Gnosis in general, it remains difficult to see how, at least in the first and second centuries of the Christian era, Jews could become Gnostics without ceasing to be Jews. In addition, Gnosticism probably cannot be derived from a single origin.

IV. INFLUENCE ON EARLY CHRISTIANITY

It is often claimed that Gnostic teachers and teachings flourished in the primitive Christian communities; traces of Gnostic thought have been found in some of the letters written by Paul or later ascribed to him, as well as in the Johannine literature and the letters of Saint Ignatius of Antioch (ca. 110). Probably, however, what is being opposed by the early Christian writers should be called "Gnosis," for no developed Gnostic system has been convincingly recovered. One cannot read Valentinian exegesis of Paul, for example, back into the first century and assume that either he or his opponents meant what the Valentinians said they meant.

On the other hand, it is clear that Christian theology owed much to the Gnostics. At first the borderline between "orthodoxy" and "heresy" was by no means as clear as it later seemed to be; in addition, without the impetus proved by the Gnostic systems as such, Christians would probably not have turned to philosophical theology as, for good or ill, they did. They would not so soon have tried to develop systematic teaching in theology and ethics. The syncretistic aspects of Gnosticism also probably provoked Christian teachers to insist upon the exclusively apostolic origins of their faith and practice.

The basic difference between both Christianity and Judaism, on the one hand, and Gnosticism, on the other, seems to lie in their contrasting views of human nature and history. For the Gnostic, man was essentially a spiritual being whose goal was reunion with his divine source. For Jews and Christians, man was composed of body and soul together, and his goal was both worldly and otherworldly. Insofar as there was an elite, it was not constituted "by nature" but by adherence to a community in this world, a community which would ultimately be raised from the dead and vindicated by the God who made the world.

Gnosticism as a phenomenon of the early centuries of the common era no longer exists, although it is sometimes used by modern theologians as a term of opprobrium for the ideas of their opponents. Gnosis, on the other hand, is present in almost every kind of theosophical movement, and ideas related to it seem to flourish in esoteric or "underground" groups today. It remains possible that out of such Gnosis new expressions analogous to Gnosticism can arise.

BIBLIOGRAPHY

The most important older studies of Gnosticism are W. Bousset, *Hauptprobleme der Gnosis* (Göttingen, 1907) and E. de Faye, *Gnostiques et Gnosticisme*, 2nd ed. (Paris, 1925). Criticisms and reinterpretations are provided by A.-J. Festugière, *La révélation d'Hermès Trismégiste*, 4 vols. (Paris, 1945–54); H. J. Schoeps, *Urgemeinde—Judenchristentum—Gnosis* (Tübingen, 1956); H. Jonas, *The Gnostic Religion* (Boston, 1958); R. McL. Wilson, *The Gnostic Problem* (London, 1958); and C. Colpe, *Die religionsgeschichtliche Schule* (Göttingen, 1961); see also K. Wegenast, "Gnosis, Gnostiker," in K. Ziegler and W. Sontheimer, *Der Kleine Pauly: Lexikon der Antike* (Stuttgart, 1967), II, 830–39. The newer discoveries are discussed by J. Doresse, *The Secret Books of the Egyptian Gnostics* (New York, 1960), and accurately listed by M. Krause, "Die koptische Handschriftenfund bei Nag Hammadi," *Mitteilungen des Deutschen Archäologischen Instituts, Abteilung Kairo*, 18 (1962), 121–32; 19 (1963), 106–13. On special points see also H. A. Wolfson, *The Philosophy of the Church Fathers* (Cambridge, Mass., 1956), I, 495–574; G. G. Scholem, *Jewish Gnosticism, Merkabah Mysticism, and Talmudic Tradition* (New York, 1960); and R. M. Grant, *Gnosticism: an Anthology* (New York, 1961), and *Gnosticism and Early Christianity*, 2nd ed. (New York, 1966). For the important Messina conference see U. Bianchi, ed., *Le origini dello gnosticismo: Colloquio di Messina* (Leiden, 1967) and *Studi di storia religiosa della tarda antichità* (Messina, 1968).

ROBERT M. GRANT

[See also **Dualism;** God; Heresy; Hierarchy; Myth; Neo-Platonism; Prophecy; Sin.]

IDEA OF GOD FROM PREHISTORY TO THE MIDDLE AGES

I. PREHISTORY

IT IS IMPORTANT to bear in mind that man's ability to conceive of deity antedates his ability to record his conceptions in writing. The religions of the so-called primitive peoples of the modern world attest to the fact that a rich complex of belief in supernatural beings, and ritual practices connected with their service, can flourish without the support of a sacred literature. That such a situation existed before the invention of writing in Mesopotamia and Egypt, in the early part of the fourth millennium B.C., is evident from prehistoric archeology. Although the interpretation of archeological data concerning human thought and belief, unsupported by written texts, must necessarily be speculative, artifacts nonetheless are documents of man's mental activity. The making of a stone axe, for example, can tell much, if carefully interpreted, of its prehistoric maker's social and economic needs and his skill in meeting them.

Paleolithic culture has left behind some notable evidence of what might reasonably be considered as mankind's earliest known essays in the conception of deity. The most striking instance of this evidence is the so-called "Venus of Laussel" (Figure 1). This is the image of a woman carved on a block of stone, which was found at Laussel, in the Dordogne district of France. When found, the figure occupied the central position among a series of other carvings, so arranged as to suggest that the place of their location was a rock sanctuary. The "Venus" figure represents a nude woman with the maternal attributes grossly exaggerated, while the facial features are undepicted; the figure holds a bison's horn in the right hand. Similar

FIGURE 1. The "Venus" of Laussel, probably the oldest representation of deity, in the form of the Mother Goddess. *Les Éditions d'art et histoire*

of Laussel, the earliest known evidence of man's deification of the female principle. "Deification" in this Paleolithic context must, of course, be carefully qualified; for our knowledge of the ability of the human mind at so remote a period necessarily rests on deduction from archeological data only.

The original location of the Venus of Laussel suggests that it was an object of worship, in other words, that those who made and reverenced the image sought thereby not only to portray the female principle, but also to establish a special relationship between themselves and what they conceived to be the source or creatrix of new life. How they made the mental transition from the phenomenon of birth, as observed in individual women of the community, to the conception of a transcendental Woman or Great Mother as the source of fertility and new life is beyond our present comprehension. But, as we shall see, these Venus figures constitute Paleolithic prototypes of the Mother Goddess or Great Goddess, whose cult is well attested in the Neolithic period, and finds subsequent expression in many of the famous goddesses of the ancient Near East.

The Venus of Laussel may, therefore, be reasonably regarded as the earliest known depiction of the idea of deity for the purpose of worship. It is important to note that the idea probably stemmed from the concern of Paleolithic man with the phenomenon of birth as the operation of a mysterious power that replaced the deceased members of his community by others newly-born. The depiction of pregnant animals in Paleolithic cave-art provides evidence of similar import; namely, that these primitive hunting peoples were deeply concerned with the reproduction of the animals upon which they lived. Thus the original conception of deity was intimately related to a basic human need.

The deification of the female principle in Paleolithic culture is more certainly attested than that of the male principle. The most likely instance of the latter is provided by the figure of the so-called "Sorcerer" of the Trois Frères Cave in the department of Ariège, France. This designation for the figure does, in fact, represent an interpretation of it which negates the alternative interpretation that it depicts a god. The figure is a strange composition. In form it is generally anthropomorphic; but the body is shown as covered with a hairy pelt, and with an animal's tail and genitals. The head, moreover, which is surmounted by the antlers of a stag, has furry ears, owl-like eyes, and a long tongue or beard. The posture of the figure is suggestive of the action of dancing, though other equally reasonable explanations could be offered.

In view of the evidence that exists of a Paleolithic

figures, of much smaller scale and carved in the round, which have also been found on various Paleolithic sites, would seem to indicate that a common motive inspired their making. A clue to this motive is possibly to be found in the strange fact that the faces of the figures are invariably blank, whereas the maternal features are carefully depicted. This difference of treatment is surely significant. It would seem to show that the carvings were not designed as portraits of individual women, but rather to symbolize "woman" as the "mother" or source of new life. The context of their relevance, if this was their meaning, is clear. The phenomenon of biological birth provided the Paleolithic peoples, who made the images, with ocular evidence of the emergence from the female body of new beings of their own kind. The phenomenon, moreover, was probably the more impressive since it is unlikely that the process of procreation was properly understood at the time. There is reason, accordingly, for seeing in these figures, and particularly in the Venus hunting-ritual in which men disguised as animals performed mimetic dances, many prehistorians have interpreted the figure as representing a sorcerer performing such a magical dance (Figure 2). But this interpretation encounters the difficulty of explaining why such a figure should be depicted in a cave which appears to have been used as a sanctuary. The problem involved here, though interesting and important, is outside the scope of this article. The alternative interpretation, which some eminent specialists in prehistory have advanced, is that the figure represents a supernatural "Lord of the beasts," whom the Paleolithic hunters conceived of as the owner of the animals, and who had to be propitiated by those who hunted and killed them. This interpretation is reasonable; but it has to be regarded as less certain than that which presents the Venus of Laussel as the earliest depiction of the idea of deity.

The intimation given by Paleolithic culture that the earliest conception of deity was inspired by man's concern with the production of new life finds remarkable confirmation in Neolithic culture: the most notable instance will be briefly described here. Excavation of the Neolithic town at Çatal Hüyük in Anatolia, which dates from the seventh millennium B.C., has revealed a flourishing cult of a Great Goddess, who was concerned with both birth and death. This ambivalence of concept is evidenced in a strange way. The sanctuaries of the Goddess were adorned by friezes of plaster models of the female human breast. These objects were found to contain the skulls of vultures and foxes and the jawbones of boars. No written texts, unfortunately, exist to explain this strange symbolism. However, the union of symbols of maternal nourishment and care with symbols of death is profoundly suggestive, and this significance is reinforced by other symbols found in the sanctuaries: human skulls, the horns of bulls, and mural paintings of great vultures menacing headless human corpses. The interpretation of these symbols is necessarily speculative; but the idea of a Great Goddess, who is the source of life, and to whom all return at death, is known in other later religions, for example, in Crete and the Greek Eleusinian Mysteries. In such an ambivalent context, the Great Goddess is identified or associated with the earth as Mother Earth, whose womb is conceived as both the source of life and the place of repose, and possibly of the revivification, of the dead.

The tradition of the deification of the female principle, which can thus be traced from the Paleolithic on through the Neolithic period, found expression in the early literary cultures of the ancient Near East and the Indus Valley. The tradition is embodied, with certain variant features, in such famous goddesses as the

FIGURE 2. Dancing Sorcerer. DRAWING BY MISS E. A. LOWCOCK

Mesopotamian Innina-Ishtar, the Syrian Astarte, the Egyptian Isis and Hathor, the Anatolian Cybele, the Cretan Great Goddess, and the Cyprian Aphrodite. Many of these goddesses combined the roles of Virgin and Mother, and they were often intimately associated with a young god who, alternatively as their son or lover, was the deified spirit of vegetation.

II. THE ANCIENT NEAR EAST, GREECE, AND ROME

The earliest written records, dating in Egypt and Mesopotamia from the fourth millennium B.C., reveal in both places a polytheistic form of religion which had evidently been long established. The Egyptian form, since it is generally the better documented and certainly more graphically presented, will be considered first.

In the great corpus of religious texts, known as the *Pyramid Texts*, which were inscribed on the interior walls of the pyramids of certain pharaohs of the Fifth and Sixth Dynasties, a great number of divinities, male and female, are named. Their divine nature is denoted by a hieroglyph (*ntr*), resembling an axe or a flag unfurled horizontally from its pole. The symbol indicates that already the ancient Egyptians had conceived of deity or divinity in an abstract form. Unfortunately the essential meaning of the hieroglyph *ntr* remains an enigma, despite many attempts to interpret it. It looks like an axe; but there is some evidence that in its more primitive form it showed two streamers projecting horizontally from a pole, which might represent the standard that stood before primitive shrines. But, whatever be the origin of the symbol, it is significant that in their earliest texts the Egyptians were already able to envisage divinity as a distinctive quality or character that could be attributed to certain specific entities regarded as deities.

333

Although they were thus able to conceive of divinity, the Egyptians evidently believed that the virtue found expression or was embodied in a variety of personified beings, who were distinguished by individual names or titles. These deities ranged in nature and status from cosmic beings such as the sun to strange animals and insects, such as the ibis (a wading bird related to the heron) and the scorpion, which were worshipped at various local centers for reasons unknown to modern scholarship. Some deities were personifications of abstractions such as Shu ("air"), Maat ("truth"), or Atum (*itmw*), a designation which seems to have meant "the not-yet-Completed-One, who will attain (completion)."

The iconography of the Egyptians shows that they envisaged their gods in concrete forms of varying kinds: as men and women in Egyptian attire; or as having human bodies and animal heads; or as wholly animal (i.e., mammals, birds, reptiles, and insects). Some of these conceptions were evidently of primitive origin; but some derived from a complex transformation of imagery. The most notable instance of the latter was the representation of the sun-god Rē by a scarab-beetle. The ancient Egyptian word for the scarab-beetle was *kheprer* which was akin to *kheper*, "come into being" or "exist." Since the sun-god was regarded as self-existent, and consequently called Khepri, the relevance of the scarab-beetle as a symbol is intelligible. But for the Egyptians the symbol had a further meaning. Scarab-beetles were believed to be of male sex only, and they have the curious habit of pushing about balls of dung, on which they feed. Since ancient Egyptian cosmogonic myth was structured on the imagery of biological procreation, the sun-god, being self-existent, was pictured as commencing the creation of the universe by masturbation, while he was also thought of as rolling the sun across the heavens each day.

It has been well to analyze this scarab symbol, in view of its curious compound of metaphysical thought and esoteric imagery concerning the concept of divine self-existence inherent in the word *kheprer*. The scarab symbol may thus serve to show how behind the strange iconography of Egyptian religion there may often reside ideas that are remarkable for their metaphysical content.

So far as it is possible to define the quintessence of divinity as it finds expression in the many deities of ancient Egypt, it would seem that it inheres in the idea of power. But it was power to do particular things: to give life, fertility, prosperity, maintain cosmic order, to have supernatural knowledge, generally of a magical kind. In the Egyptian pantheon, several deities had special functions or abilities; and there was a tendency to associate local deities with the great state or cosmic deities so as to give the appearance of a kind of henotheism. There is much evidence, too, of the use of the expression *ntr ʿ* (the "Great God"), without a personal name; generally the reference is to Rē, the sun-god, but sometimes it denotes Osiris.

The chief characteristics of the Egyptian idea of deity were expressed in three gods: Rē, Osiris, and Set (Figure 3). The first, as the sun-god, was the state-god par excellence. The pharaoh was regarded as the "Son of Rē," and his representative on earth. Rē was the creator of the universe and the source of all life and power. He sustained the order (*maat*) of the cosmos, and Maat, the personification of truth, justice, and order was regarded as both his daughter and his food. Consequently, Rē was often thought of as the judge of mankind. This association with the moral law has a unique significance. It first appears in Egyptian texts about 2400 B.C., and thus constitutes the earliest evidence of the involvement of the concept of deity with ethics. Such involvement is not inevitable, and the history of religions affords numerous examples of amoral and unmoral deities. The Egyptian records fortunately permit us to see how Rē became associated with the moral order. The idea of *maat* was basically that of cosmic order as opposed to chaos. For example, the Egyptians conceived of a monster of darkness,

FIGURE 3. Egyptian Deities. HIRMER VERLAG MÜNCHEN AND S. G. F. BRANDON

Apophis, which threatened to destroy the sun each day as it rose and set. The social order in Egypt, which was maintained by the pharaoh, the son of Rē, was part of the cosmic *maat*. Consequently, anyone whose conduct was not in accord with the accepted mores abused *maat*, the good order of things, of which Rē was the upholder, and so incurred his vengeance in this world or the next.

Osiris was a deity of a wholly different kind, and one of peculiar significance for the history of religions. For whereas Rē and all the other deities were by nature immortal, Osiris was a god who had died and been raised to life again. There has been much specialist discussion about the origin of this extraordinary conception, but no agreed conclusion has emerged. What is certain is that in the *Pyramid Texts* Osiris first appears as an ancient divine king, who had been resurrected after being murdered by his evil brother Set. The *Texts* show that a ritual technique of embalmment and magical revivification was performed on the dead pharaoh, following the pattern of what had once been done for Osiris. On the principle of sympathetic magic, it was believed that the repetition of the rites would raise the king to a new life as Osiris had been raised. This mortuary ritual was gradually democratized until all Egyptians, who could afford it, looked forward to obtaining resurrection after death through Osiris.

Osiris, by reason of his legend and soteriological significance, had a deep human appeal, and became the most popular of Egyptian deities, and his cult spread far outside Egypt. He increasingly acquired cosmic attributes, and was associated with the fructifying flood of the river Nile and with the annual life-cycle of vegetation, especially grain. But, he also assumed another role. Already in the *Pyramid Texts* Osiris was venerated as the ruler of the dead, and by the New Kingdom period (1580–1085 B.C.) he had become the dread judge before whom the dead were tried by the weighing of their hearts against the symbol of *maat* ("truth").

The idea of a "dying-rising god," who saves those who are ritually assimilated to him, is a truly remarkable notion, and it is not easily explained in terms of those basic human needs and intuitions to which the idea of deity generally relates. Osiris is the most notable example of such a category of deity before the emergence of the conception of Christ as the divine savior who dies and rises again to life. Some other religions of the ancient Near East provided similar, but less well-constituted examples, namely, the Mesopotamian god Tammuz, and the better known figures of the Phrygian Attis and Adonis of Syria. Each of these deities was connected in some way with the life-cycle of vegetation: their deaths and resurrections being related ritually to the dying and reviving of vegetation each year. However, in the *mythoi* of both Osiris and Christ, although the imagery of the death and resurrection of the grain does occur, their deaths and resurrections are regarded as historical events. The origin of the Christian idea of a god who saves mankind by his death and resurrection will be discussed later. Here it must suffice to note that in the earliest documents, i.e., the *Pyramid Texts*, Osiris appears as the key figure in a mortuary ritual practiced to achieve immortality by reenacting his legendary embalmment and resurrection.

The third deity who embodies a distinctive aspect of the Egyptian concept of deity is Set. Originally this god was associated with the desert and storms, which doubtless invested him with an austere character. In the *Pyramid Texts*, he appears most notably as the murderer of Osiris. This sinister role meant that, with the growing popularity of the cult of Osiris, Set was gradually transformed into a god of evil. In later religious thought he became the personification of cosmic disorder, being identified with Apophis, the monstrous serpent of chaos who unceasingly threatened to extinguish the sun. Thus Egyptian theology progressively assumed a dualistic character, although its dualism never became so radical as in the Zoroastrianism of ancient Iran.

The Mesopotamian concept of deity differed in some striking ways from the Egyptian. Although the religion of the Mesopotamian peoples (the Sumerians, Babylonians, and Assyrians) was polytheistic like that of Egypt, their gods formed a hierarchy that was carefully related to the constitutive parts of the universe. According to ancient Mesopotamian cosmology, the universe was made up of four parts: heaven, earth, the waters that surrounded the earth, and the underworld of the dead. Each part was governed by a god: Anu, who ruled the heavens, was the first in status; he was followed by Enlil, presiding over the earth, Enki (or Ea), the god of the waters, and Nergal, lord of the underworld. Below this cosmic hierarchy were three deities connected with the chief celestial bodies: Sin (the moon-god), Shamash (the sun-god), and Ishtar (the planet Venus). Vegetation was deified under the Sumerian name of Dumuzi. The deity is generally known by the Hebrew name of Tammuz, and Ezekiel 8:14 refers to the annual rites of lamentation for his death. In mythology, Tammuz was associated with Ishtar (who was also the goddess of fertility) as her lover, by whom he was rescued from the underworld.

The Mesopotamian pantheon contained many other gods of lesser significance, including national gods such as Marduk of Babylon and Assur of Assyria who were accorded leadership over the other gods by their own peoples. Despite this multitude of deities with varying functions, there was a distinctive concept of deity in Mesopotamia which finds expression in various myths and legends concerning the relations of the gods to mankind. Thus it is related that the gods created men as servants who would relieve them of the task of feeding and housing themselves: hence the building of temples and the offering of sacrifices within them. But from these human servants the gods withheld the immortality which they themselves enjoyed. This belief that man could not hope to survive death profoundly affected the Mesopotamian *Weltanschauung;* it provided the main theme of the celebrated *Epic of Gilgamesh.* Associated with the belief was a corresponding concept of destiny. It was held that in the divine economy each person had a "destiny," i.e., a part or purpose to fulfil. When the gods no longer had use for an individual, he had no "destiny" and so died. The gods were generally regarded as benign towards their human servants, and as protecting them from demonic attack so long as they continued punctilious in their service.

In effect, the Mesopotamian conception of deity was a realistic evaluation of the world as understood in terms of contemporary thought. The hierarchy of the gods represented cosmic order as opposed to the demonic forces of chaos (the idea is mythologically portrayed in the conflict between the gods and Ti'âmat, the personification of primeval chaos, in the Babylonian Creation Epic, known as the *Enûma elish*). Mankind's purpose and welfare lay in its integration with and the support of the divine order.

Of the religions of the other ancient Near Eastern cultures that of the Hebrews was destined to have a profound influence upon later Western thought and culture. Its conception of deity was essentially linked with the cult of the god Yahweh, and, in its development, reflected the transformation which the character of this deity underwent in process of time, owing to a variety of causes.

The origin of the cult of Yahweh has been the subject of much specialist discussion. It seems to be generally agreed that Hebrew tradition reflects an awareness that the cult had been specifically adopted by the ancestors of Israel on some notable occasion in the past. Thus, in Hebrew literature constant reference is made to the idea that a covenant had once been made between Yahweh and Israel. The transaction is dramatically described in the account of the giving of the Law to Moses on Mount Sinai (Exodus 19:1ff.). Various explanations have also been offered of the original location of the cult of Yahweh before its adoption by Israel, but none has won general acceptance. The most that can safely be said is that Yahweh appears to have been a desert god, closely connected with war.

A passage in Exodus (3:13–14) reveals that the Hebrews were curious about the name "Yahweh," and attempted to explain it etymologically. Thus, in answer to Moses' question about the name of the god who had appeared to him in the burning bush and commissioned him to go to the Israelites who were then in bondage in Egypt, the deity is represented as replying: "'I AM WHO I AM.' And he said, 'Say this to the people of Israel, I AM has sent me to you.'" (R. S. V.) This mystifying statement is due to an attempt to derive the name "Yahweh" (traditionally rendered "Jehovah" in English) from the Hebrew root *hayah* or *hāwāh,* meaning "to be." Modern scholars have concentrated on the problem here, and a variety of interpretations has been suggested: according to the opinion recently expressed by a specialist of great standing, the explanation in Exodus 3:14 derived from an original formula, "It Is He Who Creates What Comes into Existence" (W. F. Albright, p. 148). This formula might be compared with the title *Khepri* of the Egyptian sun-god, mentioned above.

Whatever may have been the original meaning of the name "Yahweh," there is no doubt that it took some centuries before the deity was firmly established as the sole god of Israel. During the complex process, which is documented by the pre-Exilic writings of the Hebrew Bible, it is probable that the original conception of Yahweh was adjusted to the needs of the agrarian culture that the Israelite tribes had adopted on their settlement in Canaan. Thus there is some evidence of the assumption by Yahweh of some of the attributes of El, the chief Canaanite god.

During the pre-Exilic period, the Yahwist prophets were chiefly concerned to present Yahweh as the god who had delivered the Israelites from their Egyptian bondage and given them Canaan as their homeland. They represented him as a "jealous god," who commanded his chosen people: "You shall have no other gods before me" (Exodus 20:3). It is difficult to be certain whether, at the earlier stage of Israel's religious development, Yahweh was regarded as the only god of the universe, or as being more powerful than the gods of other peoples. However that may be, the Yahwist prophets laid such emphasis upon the supremacy and omnipotence of their deity that the religion which they promoted was virtually monotheistic. Thus in the Yahwist creation-story in Genesis 2:4ff., Yahweh is represented as the creator of the universe and of mankind. And so absolute was the emphasis upon Yahweh's omnipotence that he is actually depicted as the author of both good and evil. (For example, it is "an evil spirit from Yahweh" that torments Saul in I Samuel 16:14, and Yahweh causes David to number Israel and then punishes him for doing so by decimating the people with a pestilence in II Samuel 24:1ff.)

The Yahwist prophets, besides stressing the omnipotence of their god, also presented him as a just god, who demanded a high standard of moral conduct from his people. The incompatibility of these two aspects of Yahweh soon became apparent on both the communal and personal planes.

Yahwism was essentially an ethnic religion: it was primarily concerned with the relationship of Yahweh and his chosen people Israel. The logic of the Sinai Covenant was that Yahweh would protect and prosper his people, if they were faithful to him. In the period preceding the Babylonian Exile (586 B.C.), the various disasters that Israel suffered at the hands of neighboring nations were explained by the prophets as Yahweh's just punishment for acts of apostasy. But from the Exile onwards a new attitude begins to appear. Since the misfortunes of Israel vis-à-vis the other nations were such as could not reasonably be explained in terms of Israel's greater iniquity, another message had to be found. This finds expression in the apocalyptic literature of the period (ca. 200 B.C.–A.D. 100). The prophets now proclaimed that Yahweh would eventually vindicate his suffering people, and punish their Gentile oppressors.

Since Yahweh was now firmly regarded as the only God and Ruler of the universe, this apocalyptic faith tended to take on a transcendental character. It was, moreover, conditioned by the influence of Iranian dualism, which Israel had probably first encountered through its incorporation into the Persian empire of the Achaemenides after the Exile (538 B.C.). This meant that Yahweh's eventual vindication of Israel became identified with his ultimate overthrow of the demonic powers with whom the gods of Israel's Gentile oppressors were associated. These ideas were set forth in an eschatological imagery that represented the "day of Yahweh" as the catastrophic overthrow of the existing world-order and its replacement by a new supernatural order, described as the "Kingdom of God" or "Kingdom of Heaven." In some forms of this apocalyptic eschatology a supernatural minister of Yahweh, the Messiah ("Anointed"), was expected to overthrow the forces of evil and judge the nations (cf. Brandon, *Judgment*, pp. 70ff.). This intense nationalistic view of Yahweh logically stemmed from the Covenant idea, and, with various modifications, it has characterized the Jewish conception of deity. Even when a more universalist estimate of Yahweh's providence has occasionally found expression, it has been in terms of the peculiar spiritual status of Israel. The irenic vision of Zechariah 8:23 significantly illustrates this: "Thus says the Lord [i.e., Yahweh] of hosts: In those days ten men from the nations of every tongue shall take hold of the robe of a Jew, saying, 'Let us go with you, for we have heard that God is with you.'"

The discrepancy between the idea of Israel's god as being both omnipotent and just, and the unhappy fortune of Israel itself, was accordingly explained in terms of apocalyptic eschatology. The problem of Yahweh's dealings with the individual similarly found its solution. This problem arose from the original Yahwist doctrine of human nature, which precluded any hope of a significant post-mortem life for the individual. Instead, it was taught that Yahweh rewarded the pious with long life and prosperity in this world, and punished the impious by misfortune and early death. At death the shade of the individual descended to a wretched existence in the gloomy depths of Sheol, which was the Hebrew counterpart of the Mesopotamian *kur-nu-gi-a*, "the land of no-return." But since experience proved that often it was the pious that were afflicted with misfortune and early death, while the impious flourished like the proverbial green bay-tree, an emerging sense of individuality in Israel brought a questioning of Yahweh's justice.

The problem was discussed in the Book of Job, one of the finest products of Hebrew literature. Job's misfortunes are presented therein as a test case. For Job is an upright and pious man, so that the sufferings that befall him are demonstrably undeserved. The drama turns on Job's belief that God is both omnipotent and just, and the conflicting evidence of his own undeserved sufferings. Job's agony of faith is made the more poignant by his acceptance of the orthodox view that death was virtual extinction. Although the problem is acutely discussed, no adequate solution within these terms was found by the author of the book. Indeed, no such solution was found elsewhere in Israel, until the second century B.C., when finally belief in a resurrection of the dead was accepted into Judaism. With this belief went also a belief in a personal post-mortem judgment, so that Yahweh's justice was vindicated after death, if it had not been in this life. The description of the Last Judgment in II(IV) Esdras 7:32–38, however, graphically shows how powerful the ethnic factor still was in the Jewish conception of God in the first century A.D.; for therein the post-mortem fate of individuals is insensibly merged in the divine judgment of the nations.

In the history of religions the Jewish conception of God is remarkable for its embodiment of the profound conviction that God, under his ineffable name of Yahweh, had specially chosen the descendants of Abraham for a unique destiny: namely, to be his holy people, and be settled by him in the land of Canaan, where they should worship him in the great Temple of Jerusalem, built on the spot which he had signified. This belief was presented in a superb literature which set the distinctive pattern of the Jewish conception, namely, of God as the "Lord of History." This title

337

FIGURE 4. The central figure on this eighth-century B.C. silver strip from Luristan may represent Zurvān, the ancient Iranian god of Time. CINCINNATI ART MUSEUM

has been used by scholars to describe the way in which the Bible shows how Yahweh's providence for Israel was progressively revealed in historical events, or what is presented as historical events. The revelation involves a linear view of time, which was unusual; for most ancient peoples envisaged the temporal process as cyclic in movement. To Jews, history has ever been *Heilsgeschichte*, i.e., "Salvation-History," or, in other words, a teleological process in which the purpose of Yahweh for Israel has progressively been revealed and fulfilled. This teleological conception was, in process of time, transmitted to Western thought and culture by Christianity. However, before the Christian idea of God can be properly considered, it is necessary to evaluate the conceptions of deity in ancient Iran and Greece; for each of these contributed to the religious situation of the Greco-Roman world into which Christianity was born, and by which it was influenced.

The concept of deity in ancient Iran before the sixth century B.C. is fundamentally obscure, since the earliest written evidence is provided by Zarathustra or Zoroaster (born ca. 570 B.C.). His *Gāthās* document the reform of Iranian religion which he initiated, and which profoundly affected the subsequent religious tradition of Iran. Much attention has been given by specialists in Iranian studies to the obvious problem of pre-Zoroastrian religion. Since it is known that the early Aryan settlers in Iran shared a common cultural tradition with the Aryans who settled in the north-western area of the continent of India, the literature of the latter (especially the *Rig-Veda*) has been studied as relevant to the situation in Iran. Evidence has also been sought in some post-Zoroastrian traditions of Iran. From this research not only is it certain that primitive Iranian religion was polytheistic and akin to that represented in the *Rig-Veda*, but it appears that there was a disposition to conceive of deities of ambivalent form. Thus there are indications of the worship of sky-gods named Mithra and Vayu, who each represented both the good and sinister aspects of reality. Another such deity was Zurvān, who assumed an important role in later Persian religion (Figure 4). The name of this mysterious deity meant Time, and a form of the name occurs as early as the twelfth millennium B.C. on tablets found at Nuzi.

Zarathustra seems to have rejected this Iranian propensity to an ambivalent conception of deity by proclaiming the God whom he calls Ahura Mazdā, the Wise Lord, as the only true God, and by identifying him exclusively with *Arta* ("Righteous Order"). There has been much speculation as to the origin of Ahura Mazdā, and some specialists think that the conception was derived by Zarathustra from an Iranian counterpart of the Vedic god Varuna (see below).

Whatever the origin of his Wise Lord, Zarathustra was concerned to trace the dualistic nature of the universe to a supernatural source. This he does in the *Gāthās* by positing two primordial spirits: the *Spenista Mainyu* ("Bounteous Spirit"), and the *Angra Mainyu* ("Evil" or "Destructive Spirit"). These spirits represent the opposing aspects or forces of the universe: light and darkness, life and death, good and evil. However, despite Zarathustra's emphatic identification of Ahura Mazdā with the principle of good order (*Arta*) and his radical condemnation of the *Druj* ("Lie"), some vestige of the earlier ambivalence of deity appears in the *Gāthās*. For Zarathustra regarded Ahura Mazdā as the sole cosmic creator, to whom the origin of both light and darkness are attributed (*Yasna*, 14:5.). This is a segment of the Avesta. This indication of an earlier tradition, which derived the two contrasting aspects of cosmic phenomena from a single divine source, is

338

significant in view of later developments in the Iranian conception of deity.

In the classic form of Zoroastrianism, Ahura Mazdā, under the name of Ohrmazd, was virtually equated with the *Spenista Mainyu*, and represented the principle of Good; the opposing principle of Evil was called Ahriman. The equation had the effect of making Good and Evil coeval; and, although Zoroastrian eschatology foretold the ultimate victory of Good (Ohrmazd) over Evil (Ahriman), logically the two principles were equal in status, each having always existed uncreated. This implicit equality provided no ground for the belief that Good should ultimately triumph over Evil; in fact, their mutual opposition was usually described as eternal. During the Sassanian period (A.D. 208–651), it would appear that an attempt was made to resolve the metaphysical problem involved in this orthodox form of Zoroastrianism by representing Ohrmazd and Ahriman as being both derived from Zurvān (Time) in such a manner as to establish the inferior status of the latter, and thus justify his ultimate elimination. Unfortunately the true nature of this Zurvanism is fundamentally obscure, owing to the unsatisfactory character of the extant documentation. What seems reasonably certain, on the authority of Eudemus of Rhodes, a disciple of Aristotle, is that the Persians were known to derive "a good god and an evil daemon" from Space (*topos*) and Time (*chronos*). In the later *Persian Rivâyat* it is categorically stated: "with the exception of Time, all other things have been created. . . . Then it [Time] created fire and water, and, when these had intermixed, came forth Ohrmazd. Time is both Creator and the Lord of creation which it created" (Spiegel, pp. 161ff.).

There seems, accordingly, to have been some tradition in Iran of Zurvān as an ambivalent creator-deity, and that this was utilized in Sassanian times by certain thinkers who were dissatisfied with the metaphysical basis of orthodox Zoroastrianism. Orthodox reaction to this Zurvanite heresy found expression in the *Bundahishn*, where Ohrmazd is identified with Time: "Thus it is revealed in the Good Religion. Ohrmazd was on high in omniscience and goodness; for infinite Time he was ever in the Light" (XV, 1ff.).

There is evidence that the Persians conceived of two forms of Time: Zurvān *akarana* ("Infinite Time"), and Zurvān *dareghō-chvadhāta* ("Time of long Dominion"). With the former Ohrmazd was identified as Infinite Time. Zurvān *dareghō-chvadhāta* signified the destructive aspect of Time, which brings decay, old age, and death to all living things. This form of Time was associated with Ahriman, and the conception was incorporated into Mithraism, where it found striking iconographic expression. Many Mithraic sanctuaries contained images of a monstrous being, having a man's body, wings, and a lion's head. Around the monster's body a large serpent is entwined, and upon the nude body the signs of the zodiac are depicted; the monster stands upon a sphere and holds a long staff and keys. The image and its symbols were evidently designed to represent Time that rules and destroys all. Its presence in Mithraic sanctuaries as an image of Ahriman probably indicates that the temporal sovereignty of Ahriman in this world was recognized in Mithraic theology.

The influence of the Iranian dualistic conception of deity was very considerable. It can be traced in Gnosticism and Manichaeism, in Judaism and the beliefs of the Qumrân sectaries, and in Christianity. This influence was doubtless due to the fact that it helped to explain the origin and nature of Evil, which constitutes a basic problem for all monotheistic faiths. It has been noted that Iranian dualism was not a logically absolute dualistic interpretation of reality; it looked forward to the ultimate triumph of Ohrmazd over Ahriman. In this sense it was an ethical eschatology; for it summoned mankind to align itself on the side of Good (Ohrmazd) against Evil (Ahriman), because Ohrmazd would finally win and Ahriman would be exterminated. In other words, the Iranian conception of God, which seems in its original form to have reflected the ambivalence of man's experience of reality, became in its Zoroastrian form an expression of his hope that what he identified as the principle of Good would ultimately prevail over that which he evaluated as Evil. The dualistic *Weltanschauungen* of those other religions and cults, which were influenced by Zoroastrianism, were inspired by a like optimism.

The Greek conception of deity comprises two different traditions: the religious and the philosophical. Although the philosophical conception naturally commands the attention of historians of thought, for Greek philosophy has long been regarded as one of the greatest products of Greek culture, it was the idea of deity implicit in religious faith and practice that really reflected the outlook of the Greek people. Philosophical conceptions of the divine, such as Plato and Aristotle expounded, were destined to have a great influence upon medieval Christian and Muslim theology; but they had little effect upon contemporary Greek life and thought; indeed, most of the philosophers themselves conformed to the prescriptions and usages of the traditional religion.

The Greek view of deity first finds expression in the *Iliad* and *Odyssey* of Homer, and since these epics enjoyed a unique place in the Greek scheme of education, the Homeric view became the established evaluation. According to it, the universe was governed by a hierarchy of gods, presided over by Zeus. The majority of these gods were probably of Indo-European origin, being akin to those of the Aryan invaders of India and Iran. They were brought into Greece by the Hellenic tribes who conquered the Aegean peoples who lived there, and whose religion seems to have been based on the cult of the Great Goddess. The religion that finds expression in the Homeric literature probably represents a fusion of Indo-European and Aegean traditions; but with the former predominating, for Zeus is essentially the Aryan sky-god.

The essence of divinity in Homer is supernatural power, generally associated with the more violent or deadly aspects of cosmic phenomena: Zeus wields thunderbolts; Poseidon is associated with the sea and earthquakes; Apollo's arrows are equated with pestilence. But it is controlled power; a divine government that makes the universe a cosmos, not a chaos. This aspect finds graphic expression in the Homeric poems in anthropomorphic terms, for the Greeks instinctively conceived of their gods as "men writ large."

A very significant instance occurs in the *Iliad* XVI, 431–61, which describes the reaction of Zeus to an incident in the struggle between the Greeks and Trojans. Patroclus, a Greek hero, is fated to kill Sarpedon, the human offspring of one of Zeus's many liaisons with mortal women. The Homeric writer pictures Zeus as earnestly desirous to save his son. He communicates his intention to the goddess Hera, who, in reply, warns him that if he interferes with what is fated, the other gods will follow his example. Zeus sorrowfully recognizes the truth of what she says, and allows Sarpedon to go to his fate. The episode reveals that the Greeks believed that there was a proper order (*moira*) of things that maintained the balance of forces in the universe. Zeus was the embodiment of this order, as the Egyptian sun-god was of *maat* and the Iranian Ahura Mazdā was of *arta*. Zeus was omnipotent; but if he acted ὑπὲρ μόρον ("beyond what is fated") he would disrupt the order of the universe and induce the other gods (being deifications of power), whom he ruled, to act in like manner, so that chaos would replace cosmos. Greek mythology was very conscious of the forces of chaos in the universe, which it personified under the image of Giants and Titans, whom the Olympian gods had once subdued after a truly titanic struggle.

In the Homeric poems Zeus is described as "the father of gods and men." This title did not signify that he was regarded as the Creator of the universe; it connoted his sovereign supremacy. In these poems, also, the classic pattern of the Greek estimate of man's situation vis-à-vis the gods first emerges. The gods, and preeminently Zeus, are represented as being capricious in their dealings with men. This presentation undoubtedly derived from the fact that the Greek conception

of deity was inspired by experience of the forces operative in the natural world. The general harmony of cosmic phenomena suggested an orderly divine government; but the irrational variety of human fortune indicated divine caprice. In the *Iliad* XXIV, 527–33, this impression is illustrated by a vivid imagery: Zeus is portrayed as arbitrarily giving out good and ill fortune to mankind from two urns, set on the floor of Olympus. Generally the assignments are balanced mixtures of good and ill; but sometimes, without apparent cause, an unfortunate is given only of the bad.

Homeric religion allowed no hope that the inequalities of this life would be divinely adjusted after death. In the *Odyssey* the belief is graphically presented that death irreparably shattered the psychophysical constitution of the individual person, and that only a wraith-like replica, without consciousness, survived to descend into the gloomy depths of Hades, which was ruled over by Pluto and his queen Persephone.

Except for certain minor variations, the Homeric conception of deity formed the main tradition of Greek theology into the age of Greco-Roman culture. It finds expression in poetry and drama; and negatively in sepulchral art, where the sad scenes of farewell make no reference to Zeus and the other gods. Religious iconography, although it produced some superb depictions of deity in the idealized perfection of the human form, portrays only a calm dignity, aloof from human emotions, and remote from concern with the aspirations and fears of mortal beings.

It was in Stoicism, which appealed to many as a philosophy of life, that an attempt was made to set forth the traditional view of deity in a carefully articulated scheme that rationally accounted for the universe and man's place in it. As Cicero succinctly defined Stoic theology: "Zeno and the Stoics generally maintain that God is *aether*, endowed with Mind, by which the universe is ruled" (J. von Arnim, *Stoicorum Veterum Fragmenta*, I, frag. 154). Man could not, therefore, have a personal relation with God; but he was counselled to live "according to Nature," which meant integrating himself with the cosmic process and not aspiring to a destiny outside that process. The Stoics assumed that the cosmic process was rational, being the expression of the divine providence (πρόνοια). The difficulty of preserving this belief, however, against the logic of experience is significantly reflected in the *Meditations* of Marcus Aurelius, who nobly strove to live according to Stoic precepts: "Either all things come from a single rational source, and combine together in a coherent whole (ἐνὶ σώματι) . . . or there are only atoms (ἄτομοι), a formless disintegrating mass" (ix, 39). Marcus desired that the former be true; but his reason warned him of the equal probability of the latter.

That the gods of classical Greece, and the Roman gods who were later identified with them, continued to be worshipped until paganism was suppressed by the Christian emperors in the fourth century was due primarily to their political importance. In the Greek city-states and in Rome the gods represented the divine guardians of social order and prosperity, and all citizens were expected to participate in their public worship as evidence of their integrity and loyalty. The power of this political faith is not to be underestimated: it found, significantly, bitter expression against Christianity in 410, when Rome was sacked by Alaric the Goth, shortly after the abolition of the old Roman gods in favor of Christ.

The idea of deity in these state-cults did not represent or satisfy the spiritual needs of many people. Hence they turned to the mystery-religions, which promised their initiates salvation of some kind, usually in the form of rebirth from death. The gods of these mystery-cults were not remote cosmic deities; a *mythos* usually told how they had died and risen to life again. Osiris provides the classic example, although the original form of the rites associated with him were of a mortuary character as described above. Other notable mystery-gods were Attis, Adonis, and Dionysus-Zagreus. The significance of the mystery-cults of the Greco-Roman world, in the present context, lies in the attraction of a deity, conceived as having undergone suffering and death and then rising triumphantly to a new eternal life.

The conception of deity in Greek philosophy, despite the various terminology and imagery used by individual thinkers, expressed a common aim from the time of the first speculations of the Ionian philosophers. This was to define a source of existence in terms of metaphysical attributes considered to connote perfection of being. Thus Plato saw God as the essence or idea of the Good, eternal, unchanging, and unmoved. To Aristotle, God was essentially the Prime Mover, Himself unmoved, who is the first and the final Cause of all things. Of greater metaphysical complexity was the conception of Plotinus (A.D. 204–70), the founder of Neo-Platonism. He distinguished a kind of divine trinity. The One, equated with God and the Good, was both transcendent and immanent: "while it is nowhere, nowhere is it not"; the *Nous* ("Mind" or "Spirit"), being the image of the One; and the Soul, the offspring of the *Nous*, which is the cosmic creator.

In Greco-Roman society there was a deep concern about religious issues, and many attempts were made to remove the difficulties of the traditional mythology and accommodate the deities of other religions. For example, Plutarch (ca. A.D. 46–120) utilized Plato's idea of *daimones*, as beings intermediate between gods and men, to effect a reconciliation between polytheism and monotheism; and Sallustius (fl. A.D. 350) distinguished between mundane and supramundane gods. Syncretism was also fashionable; it produced the noble presentation of the Egyptian goddess Isis as the "mistress of all the elements," "queen of the dead," "the principle of all in heaven," "manifested alone and under one form of all the gods and goddesses" (Apuleius, *Metamorphoseon*, XI, 3ff.).

III. CHRISTIANITY

The Christian conception of deity derived from two traditions: Hebrew and Greek. The factors that molded it after the fusion of these traditions, and that gave to it its peculiar distinction, were various, and were related to certain historical situations. An appreciation of these factors is essential for understanding the complex theology in which the Christian doctrine of God was eventually embodied.

The original Christian movement, centered on Jesus of Nazareth, was one of a number of Messianic movements that took place in Palestine during the first six decades of the first century (Figure 5). These movements resulted from the reaction of the Jews, who believed that Israel should be a theocracy, to the imposition of Roman rule in A.D. 6. So far as the purpose of Jesus can be made out from the problematic evidence of the Gospels, it would appear that he sought to prepare his fellow Jews for the establishment of the Kingdom of God. This aim was inspired by current Jewish apocalyptic hopes which have already been described. The achievement of his aim would have involved the abolition of Roman rule. The execution of Jesus by the Romans was, therefore, the inevitable penalty inflicted by them on one whom they thus adjudged to be guilty of sedition. After his crucifixion, the disciples of Jesus continued to believe that he was the Messiah, and that he would soon return with supernatural power "to restore the kingdom to Israel" (Acts of the Apostles 1:6). His death at the hands of the Romans was regarded as a martyrdom for Israel, and it was interpreted in terms of the Suffering Servant of Yahweh, described in Isaiah 53:1ff. The background of this belief was Judaism, with its strong monotheistic tradition. Hence, although he was recognized as the Messiah, Jesus was regarded as being essentially human in origin and nature.

The Apostle Paul was responsible for introducing a fundamentally different evaluation of Jesus and his crucifixion. Paul had not been an original disciple of Jesus; and although he was a Jew, he was of the Diaspora and familiar with Greco-Roman culture. For reasons too complicated to describe here (cf. Brandon [1962], pp. 211–16), Paul believed that God had com-

FIGURE 5. Christ in Majesty. Royal Porch of Chartres Cathedral. THE MANSELL COLLECTION, LONDON

missioned him to preach a "gospel" specially designed for the Gentiles, and one which radically differed from the gospel of the original disciples of Jesus. In his gospel Paul presented Jesus as a preexistent, divine being, whom God had sent into the world for the salvation of mankind. Paul envisaged the human race as enslaved by the demonic powers that controlled the planets (Galatians 4:3–4). To rescue its members from their state of perdition, this preexistent "Lord of glory" had been incarnated in the person of the human Jesus. The demonic powers (*archontes*), not recognizing his true nature, crucified him (I Corinthians 2:7–8). Their error cost them their dominion over mankind; for they could not hold their divine victim, who rose to life again. Through ritual assimilation to Christ, in his death Paul taught that Christians shared, at baptism, in Christ's resurrection to a new immortal life (Romans 6:3ff.).

Paul, accordingly, presented Jesus Christ as the divine Savior of mankind, who had provided the means of salvation by his incarnation, vicarious death, and resurrection. This interpretation became the established form of Christianity owing to the disappearance of the original Jewish Christian community in the Roman destruction of Jerusalem in A.D. 70. Paul, however, had not defined the relationship between God and Christ, but had referred to the latter by various titles, the implications of which he did not discuss. A title of frequent use was that of "Son of God," which implied a unique filial relationship.

Christian thinkers soon became aware of the problem involved in the divinization of Christ, if the basic principle of monotheism, which Christianity had inherited from Judaism, were to be maintained. The problem was, in effect, twofold. If Christ were divine in an absolute sense, yet distinct from God, there were thus two gods, and Christianity was a form of ditheism, not monotheism. On the other hand, if the filial relationship were literally interpreted, then God the Father would be the progenitor of God the Son. But the logic of this relationship meant that Christ would not be fully God, since there must have been a time when he "was not" and God the Father alone existed.

The problems thus involved in the divinization of Christ led to the great Arian controversy, which convulsed the Church in the fourth century. A solution was found, and imposed by imperial decree, at the Council of Nicaea in 325. Christ was proclaimed as coequal and coeternal with God the Father; and the Greek term *homoousios* ("of like substance") was used to define his relationship to the Father in a manner such as was thought to describe his essential and unqualified divinity, while preserving his distinction as the Son. In the definition of orthodox belief at Nicaea, brief mention was also made of belief in the Holy Spirit. This belief stemmed from certain passages in the New Testament which presented the Holy Spirit as a divine entity distinct from the Father and the Son. In the so-called Constantinopolitan Creed (ca. 381), the belief received official definition, thus making the orthodox conception of the Godhead a Trinity comprising God the Father, God the Son, and God the Holy Spirit. The doctrine is carefully stated in the Athanasian Creed or the *Quicunque Vult*, which dates between 381 and 428: "And the Catholic faith is this: That we worship one God in Trinity, Trinity in Unity; neither confounding the Persons: nor dividing the Substance."

This Trinitarian conception of the Deity was essentially the product of Christian soteriology. Paul's interpretation of Christ's death as a divinely planned means to save mankind from spiritual perdition necessitated the deification of Jesus, and hence the problem of his relation to God. The hypostatization of the Holy Spirit, which in many scriptural contexts seems to be an attribute or aspect of God, completed the process. It is to be noted in this connection that since Christianity developed in the world of Greco-Roman culture, its doctrine of God was thought out by men educated in Greek metaphysics, and officially defined in terms drawn from the categories of Greek philosophical thought.

The establishment of the Trinitarian conception of the Deity as Christian orthodoxy has endured to the present day. During the Middle Ages much effort was devoted to the philosophical justification and statement of the doctrine of God. Most notable was Anselm's ontological argument in his *Monologion* and Abelard's exposition of the Trinity in the *Theologia summi boni* (ca. 1120). Thomas Aquinas (ca. 1225–74), the most renowned exponent of medieval theology, whose thought was influenced by Aristotle, significantly defined God *inter alia*, as *primum movens immobile* ("First Unmoved Mover"), and *actus purus* ("Pure Act"). But such metaphysical definitions were not understood by ordinary Christians, and the popular idea of God is to be found concretely depicted in medieval iconography. Thus, in statues and pictures, God the Father was shown as a venerable old man, crowned with a kind of papal tiara: he holds God the Son, represented crucified, while God the Holy Spirit in the form of a dove radiating light, emanates from Him. But though reference to the Trinity has always been frequent, Christian liturgy, art, and literature attest to a preoccupation with God the Son, whose incarnated form could be more easily visualized and had the greater emotional appeal.

The soteriological character of Christianity has also provided an abiding problem for its conception of God. It finds expression in the basic tension between the doctrine of divine predestination and human free will. It is significant that the Church has never officially defined how Christ's death is accepted by God as an atonement or propitiation for human sin.

IV. HINDUISM, BUDDHISM, CHINESE RELIGION, AND ISLAM

The Hindu conception of deity combines, or rather comprises, two distinctive traditions, which might be conveniently designated the "popular" and the "philosophic." The former reaches back to the Indus Valley civilization of the third and second millennium B.C., and to the Aryan tribes that entered the northwestern areas of the continent about 1400 B.C. The religion of the Indus Valley peoples is known only by archeological data, which is of uncertain significance; but it may be reasonably inferred that several deities were worshipped, and that some may have been prototypes of the later Hindu deities. The religious beliefs of the Aryans are documented by the hymns of the *Rig-Veda*, which are addressed to a variety of divinities. The gods concerned were chiefly deifications of cosmic phenomena. The most prominent is Indra, a storm-god conceived as a victorious warrior-king. Other important gods were Varuna, a sky-god, associated with cosmic order (*rta*); Agni, the fire-god, identified with the ritual fire that consumed sacrificial victims; Rudra, a terrible god who brought disease; Yama, the death-god and ruler of the underworld. These deities were often of ambivalent character: for example, Rudra not only inflicted suffering, he also healed.

How some of the Vedic deities and those of the Indus Valley peoples became the gods of Hinduism presents many problems that are yet unsolved. Of the complex multitude of Hindu gods two are of outstanding importance and distinction, namely, Vishnu and Śiva. Each has an ambivalent nature, and typifies the creative and destructive aspects of the empirical world. Thus in the *Bhagavad-Gītā*, one of the foundational documents of Hinduism, Vishnu is first revealed, in all the multiplicity and complexity of his being, as the creator and sustainer of the universe. Then follows another vision. The god appears as an awful monstrous being, with many mouths set with dreadful fangs, into which all living things pass to their doom. The terrible deity announces in explanation: "Know I am Time, that makes the worlds to perish, and come to bring on them destruction" (*Bhagavad-Gītā*, XI:32). This equation with Time is significant and recalls the Iranian Time-god Zurvān. The equation relates to the Hindu interpretation of reality: that all existence in the phenomenal world involves an unceasing process of life and death; for Time governs this world and all implicated in it, and its process is cyclic. However, despite this revelation of the awful aspect of Vishnu, the *Bhagavad-Gītā* teaches that the deity was benign to those who worship him with a deep personal devotion (*bhakti*).

Śiva, the other great deity of Hinduism who commands the allegiance of millions, similarly represents the creative and destructive aspects of the phenomenal world. His creative power is symbolized by the *lingam* or phallus. In iconography he is portrayed as Natarāja ("King of Dancers"), who performs the cosmic dance, symbolizing the energy of the universe, perpetually creating, sustaining, and destroying the forms in which it manifests itself. As Bhairava, the terrible destroyer, Śiva is imagined as haunting places of cremation, entwined by serpents and wearing a necklace of skulls. He is also called Kāla-Rudra (all-devouring Time). By a strange transformation of imagery, the *śakti* or activating energy of Śiva, has been hypostatized as a goddess. This process has resulted in the conception of the goddess Kālī, who personifies Time. She is often represented as trampling on the corpse-like body of Śiva, from whom she has emanated. Iconographically, she portrays the unceasing cycle of life and death manifest in the natural world.

The philosophical conception of deity, which finds expression in the *Upanishads*, is difficult to define because it is basically imprecise, being presented in an imagery and terminology that is both subtle and complex. "Brahman" signifies the Ultimate Reality, with which the "*Ātman*" (the "Self") is identified; in turn the self (*ātman*) of the individual person is identical with the transcendent *Ātman*. The subtlety of the equation is seen in this passage from the *Śatapatha Brahmana* (X.6.3): "One should venerate Brahman as the True. . . . One should venerate the Self (*ātman*) who consists of mind . . . greater than the sky, greater than space, greater than this earth, greater than all existing things. He is the self of breath (life), he is my own self" (Zaehner [1962], p. 66). From the concept of Brahman, the idea of a personal creator-god Brahmā was derived, and an attempt was made to relate the other two great deities of Hinduism, Śiva and Vishnu, in a *Trimūrti* or "One God in three forms": Brahmā (the creator), Vishnu (the preserver), and Śiva (the destroyer). However, the conception has never established itself in popular Hinduism.

Buddhism has often been described as atheistic. Such an evaluation, without further qualification, is misleading, since it is generally based upon some tacit assumption of what constitutes deity. So far as the original and essential nature of Buddhism can be determined, it may be said that it was not concerned with the idea of God as the Creator of the universe. The Buddha sought to emancipate people from regarding this world as reality and involving themselves in it. However, since the Buddhist concept of Nirvāna is described as Truth, Reality, the Good, and by such adjectives as the "unbecome," "deathless," "unchanging," it may reasonably be regarded as constituting the essence of deity. In its popular forms, Buddhism is theistic in two ways. Thus, many of the gods of Hinduism have been recognized as superhuman entities; though, like mankind, they are held to be subject to decay and death and the laws of *samsāra* ("rebirth") and *karma*. But

more important has been the deification of the Buddha himself. His image in temples is treated as a holy object and is the focus of worship. And what are conceived to have been, or will be, other forms of the Buddha-nature such as *Adibuddha* and *Amitabha* (*Amida*), and Bodhisattvas such as Avalokitesvara, have also been deified and worshipped. In this latter Buddhist conception of deity, however, the operative factor is soteriological significance; little concern is shown about the cosmological or metaphysical attributes that characterize the conceptions of other religions.

In China, about 1000 B.C., the kings of the Chou dynasty effected a religious change which had a long-lasting influence. Seeking to avoid the worship of *Ti*, the divine founder-ancestor of the Shang dynasty which they had supplanted, they called this ancient deity *Shang Ti*, i.e., the *Ti* above, or the supreme *Ti*, and equated it with *T'ien*, the deification of Heaven. This new deity was presented as the supreme God, who was concerned with the prosperity and well-being of the Chinese people. To this end it was conceived as demanding good government, and ready to remove rulers who failed to provide this—as it had removed the Shang dynasty. The worship of *Shang Ti* became the state-cult, with the emperor as its charismatic high-priest, he being the Son of Heaven. The supreme act of national worship was the annual sacrifice to *Shang Ti*, at the time of the winter solstice, offered by the emperor at the Altar of Heaven in Pekin. Although thus the god of the official cult, this deification of Heaven could be the object of personal devotion, as the teaching of the great philosopher Mo-tzŭ (fl. 400 B.C.) shows. Mo-tzŭ also spoke of the "Way" (*Tao*) of Heaven as a kind of divine providential ordering of the world. The term *Tao* was also used by the early Taoists to describe the eternal principle of being, underlying and sustaining the universe. According to the important *Tao-tê-ching*, the *Tao* is "formless yet complete," it preexisted heaven and earth, it is "as the mother of all beneath heaven," and the sage seeks to be in perfect harmony with it. This naturalism, which characterized ancient Chinese thought, also found expression in the concepts of Yin and Yang, regarded as alternating principles manifest in every aspect of life. The tendency to monism or dualism did not, however, rule out recognition of lesser forms of deity; and Chinese religion included both ancestor worship and belief in a multitudinous variety of minor gods and spirits.

The Arabic word *Allah* is a shortened form of *alilāh* ("The God"), and it expresses the quintessence of the Muslim conception of God. Supreme emphasis is laid in the Koran on the unique unity of Allah, often with reference to the Christian deification of Jesus and Mary.

Muhammad thus proclaims his deity: "Allah—there is no god but He, the Living, the Self-subsistent. . . . He is the High, the Mighty One" (Sūrah 2:256). Elsewhere in the Koran, Allah is presented as the Creator, and the implacable Judge of mankind at the end of the world. In stressing the omnipotence and omniscience of Allah, Muhammad found himself involved in the inevitable problems of divine predestination and human free will with which Jewish and Christian theologians have wrestled. Inconsistently he represents Allah as predestinating men severally to salvation or damnation, while he also describes him as "the Compassionate One, the Merciful." Much of this inconsistency probably stemmed from his own spiritual experience, and because he was by nature a prophet, not a thinker. In subsequent Muslim thought the conception of Allah was greatly developed. The traditional ninety-nine names of Allah constituted a widely diversified list of qualities attributed to him, and attempts were made to explain away the anthropomorphic ideas and terminology used in the Koran. But despite such sophistications, the Muslim conception of Allah has remained fundamentally that which Muhammad proclaimed, under the impulse of his own peculiar inspiration, and in reaction to the crude polytheism of his fellow-Arabs and his contacts with Judaism and with Christianity.

It may be observed, in concluding this survey, that in a subtle but very significant way which has not yet been properly investigated, the idea of deity reflects the character of the people or culture that has produced it. Whereas certain attributes such as power, immortality, and eternity, represent commonly held notions of what constitutes divinity, the forms in which deities have been conceived are curiously varied. It will suffice, for illustration, to mention only the depiction of deity in ancient Egypt, in Hinduism, and in Christianity.

BIBLIOGRAPHY

General: S. G. F. Brandon, *Man and his Destiny in the Great Religions* (Manchester, 1962); idem, *Creation Legends of the Ancient Near East* (London, 1963); idem, *History, Time and Deity* (Manchester and New York, 1965); idem, *The Judgment of the Dead* (New York and London, 1968); idem, *Religion in Ancient History* (New York, 1970); idem, editor, *Dictionary of Comparative Religion* (London and New York, 1970). *Encyclopaedia of Religion and Ethics*, ed. J. Hastings, 12 vols. (Edinburgh and New York, 1913), 6, 243–306; *Die Religion in Geschichte und Gegenwart* (Tübingen, 1958), II, 1701–25. C. J. Gadd, *Ideas of Divine Rule in the Ancient East* (London, 1948). E. O. James, *The Concept of Deity* (London, 1950); idem, *The Worship of the Sky God* (London, 1963). R. Pettazzoni, *The All-Knowing God* (London, 1956). G. van der Leeuw, *La religion dans son essence et ses manifestations* (Paris, 1948).

Prehistory: H. Breuil and R. Lantier, *Les hommes de la Pierre Ancienne* (Paris, 1951). J. Maringer, *The Gods of Prehistoric Man* (London and New York, 1960). P. J. Ucko and A. Rosenfeld, *Palaeolithic Cave Art* (London and New York, 1967).

Egypt: H. Bonnet, *Reallexikon der ägyptischen Religionsgeschichte* (Berlin, 1952). J. G. Griffiths, *The Origins of Osiris* (Berlin, 1966). H. Kees, *Der Götterglaube im alten Aegypten*, 2nd ed. (Berlin, 1956). S. A. B. Mercer, *The Religion of Ancient Egypt* (London, 1949).

Mesopotamia: M. David, *Les Dieux et le destin en Babylonie* (Paris, 1949). E. Dhorme, *Les religions de Babylonie et d'Assyrie* (Paris, 1945). S. N. Kramer, *Sumerian Mythology* (Philadelphia, 1944).

Israel: W. F. Albright, *Yahweh and the Gods of Canaan* (London, 1968). A. Lods, *Israël: des origines au milieu du viiie siècle* (Paris, 1932); idem, *Les prophètes d'Israël et les débuts du Judaïsme* (Paris, 1935). G. F. Moore, *Judaism . . .*, 2 vols. (Cambridge, Mass., 1927). S. Mowinckel, *He That Cometh* (Oxford, 1956). W. O. E. Oesterley and T. H. Robinson, *Hebrew Religion* (London, 1930). J. Pedersen, *Israel*, Vols. 3 and 4 (London and Copenhagen, 1940). H. H. Rowley, *The Faith of Israel* (London, 1956). H. Wildeberger, *Jahwes Eigentumsvolk* (Zurich, 1960).

Iran: J. Duchesne-Guillemin, *Zoroastre* (Paris, 1948). G. Dumézil, *Les dieux des Indo-Européens* (Paris, 1952). F. Spiegel, *Die Traditionelle Literatur der Parsen* (Vienna, 1860). G. Widengren, *Hoch gottglauben im alten Iran* (Lund, 1938). R. C. Zaehner, *Zurvān: A Zoroastrian Dilemma* (Oxford, 1955); idem, *The Dawn and Twilight of Zoroastrianism* (London, 1961).

Greece and Rome: L. A. Campbell, *Mithraic Iconography and Ideology* (Leiden, 1968). Franz Cumont, *Les religions orientales dans le paganisme romain* (Paris, 1929). W. K. C. Guthrie, *The Greeks and their Gods* (London, 1950). W. Jaeger, *The Theology of the Early Greek Philosophers* (Oxford, 1948). M. P. Nilsson, *Geschichte der griechischen Religion*, 2 vols. (Munich, 1950; 1955).

Christianity: S. G. F. Brandon, *Jesus and the Zealots* (New York, 1968). E. Bréhier, *La philosophie du Moyen Age* (Paris, 1949). F. C. Copleston, *Aquinas* (Harmondsworth, 1955). A. Grillmeier, *Christ in Christian Tradition* (London, 1965). A. Harnack, *History of Dogma*, 7 vols. (London, 1894–99; reprint New York, 1961). M. Werner, *Die Entstehung des christlichen Dogmas* (Bern and Tübingen, 1957).

Hinduism and Buddhism: E. Conze, *Buddhism* (Oxford, 1957). S. A. Dasgupta, *A History of Indian Philosophy*, Vol. I (Cambridge, 1922), Vol. II (Cambridge, 1932). C. Eliot, *Hinduism and Buddhism*, 3 vols. (London, 1954). J. Gonda, *Die Religionen Indiens*, Vol. I (Stüttgart, 1960). E. J. Thomas, *The History of Buddhist Thought* (London, 1949). R. C. Zaehner, *Hinduism* (London, 1962).

China: Fung Yu-Lan, *A History of Chinese Philosophy*, Vol. I (London, 1937). M. Granet, *La pensée chinoise* (Paris, 1950); idem, *La religion des Chinois* (Paris, 1951). D. H. Smith, *Chinese Religions* (London, 1968).

Islam: M. Gaudefroy-Demonbynes, *Mahomet* (Paris, 1957).

345

D. B. MacDonald, *The Development of Muslim Theology, Jurisprudence and Constitutional Theory* (London, 1903). A. J. Wensinck, *The Muslim Creed* (Cambridge, 1932).

S. G. F. BRANDON

[See also Buddhism; **Christianity in History;** Cycles; Determinism in Theology; Dualism; Gnosticism; Hierarchy; Islamic Conception; Neo-Platonism; **Religion, Ritual in.**]

IDEA OF GOD, 1400–1800

WE WILL now take a conspectus of the period 1400–1800, since these centuries not only mark the formation of the modern mind but also the time of emergence for modern conceptions of God. The early stirrings are described in the first three sections: (1) God in the Mathematical Analogy, (2) The Renaissance Spectrum on God, and (3) The God of Reformers and Skeptics. Then the concluding three sections analyze the fully matured positions: (4) God as a Function in Rationalist Systems, (5) God Neutralized by British Empiricism, and (6) God in the Crucible of the Enlightenment and Kant.

1. God in the Mathematical Analogy. Cardinal Nicholas Cusanus (also "of Cusa") in the fifteenth century already presages, by his treatment of God, that fresh formulations are underway. For he seeks guidance from the mathematical model of cognition and its method of limits rather than from played-out metaphysical arguments, mounted around causal demonstration and theories of essence as related to existence. Although accepting several sources for our meaning of God—faith, mystical experience, reflection on the universe—he does not regard their claim to knowledge as indisputable, but seeks to justify that meaning by allying it with the mathematical way of knowing.

Five aspects of mathematical thinking furnish a symbolic basis for learning how the human mind approaches God. (1) It starts somehow with aspects of the perceivable world. For all his stress on the interiority of our path to God, Cusanus requires that this journey begin humbly with a pondering of everyday experience. (2) Mathematics induces the mind to withdraw somewhat from physical immediacy into the sphere of reflective meanings, thus preparing for our further move toward God's invisible reality. (3) In epistemological terms, we get reoriented from the uncertainties of sense perception to the clear and certain concepts and theorems in mathematics. Although not reducing God's reality to a mathematically proportionate expression, Cusanus does seek to render the theory of God more determinate and patterned.

(4) His chosen model for reforming the approach to God comes from the mathematical way of dealing with infinites, such as the geometrical study of the infinite line and of the parabolic curve's approach to its limit. Reflecting upon this analogy, Cusanus suggests five distinctive names of God which will reconstitute the entire tradition of the naming of God. The linguistic sensitivity underlying his theological reform stands forth in this declaration of purpose: "I will endeavor, by the power of language, to lead you to God in the simplest and truest way I know" (*De sapientia* [1450], 2).

First, we can call God *the absolute maximum.* He is infinitely simple and actual unity, which totally includes the being of all things and is formatively active within them all. To appreciate the sense of Cusanus' next and most famous name—God as *coincidentia oppositorum,* or the reconciling unity of all opposites—we must conceive of God's relationship to the many different entities in the universe as one of active containment and generation, analogous to the manner in which the infinite line contains and generates the determinate lines, triangles, circles, and other geometrical figures. God also surpasses all things, since he includes them without their finitude, restrictive otherness, and oppositions.

To show that we can affirm this unifying divine transcendence, without apprehending how it exists, Cusanus offers as the third primary name of God: *the incomprehensible.* This warns that although the mathematical analogy elucidates, it does not violate the divine mystery and does not penetrate rationalistically into the divine essence itself. We can attain only to a dark knowing, to use language familiar to Dionysius and Eckhart and soon to be thematized by John of the Cross. Yet Cusanus adds that it is a *docta ignorantia,* a well-instructed unknowing which combines a firm awareness of our noetic limits and of the divine mystery with a sturdy effort to know still more.

The human mind's effort to plumb deeper gets embodied in the fourth and fifth divine names: *the not-other* and *the can-be* of all that is (as announced by Cusanus' treatises *De non aliud* and *De possest*). Although God is unknowable in his own substantial being, we can name him relationally. Our world is the realm of differences or the other-than; God is that reality whereby the world achieves its plurality and differences; hence God can be named negatively, yet significantly, as being not-other-than-the-not-other. To show that this signifies the intelligent powerful source of all things, we must add that God is the can-be, the internal patterning and shaping principle of all forms of being. Using more prosaic terms, Galileo and Leibniz will signify this same ordering activity by calling God the divine geometer of the universe, the mathematizing source and goal of all relationships.

(5) The final use of the mathematical comparison is to suggest that, corresponding to technological applications of mathematical physics, there are important practical consequences of a well conducted study of God. Cusanus the social reformer treats his studies on the vision of God, the nature of wisdom, and the peace of faith as helpful tools for overcoming religious divisions and social antagonisms among men. To conceive of God as the generative source and reconciling unity of all human ideals is to foster religious ecumenism and the social unification of humanity. In the measured words of *De pace fidei* (1453), xvi: "The voice of God speaks forth in all of us, urging that we love him from whom we have received our very being, and urging that golden rule, that we do not do unto others what we would not wish them to do to us."

2. *The Renaissance Spectrum on God.* The Renaissance contribution to the theory of God consisted not so much in specific doctrines as in two general insights. First, the recovery of many classical philosophies and their different methods led to explicit and vivid recognition of the very broad range of alternate conceptions of God open to us and worthy of exploration. Second, the modern mind was made aware of the strict correlativity between the meaning of man and that of God, between various forms of humanism and proportionate variations in the theory of God. Just as options were developed on the significance of human life, so were they developed in corresponding manner about God's significance for us.

Marsilio Ficino and Pietro Pomponazzi represent a contrast between the Neo-Platonic and Aristotelian views of man and immortality, but do so in harmony with their contrasting ways of stating the God-and-man relationship. Ficino's God closely harmonizes the paths of faith and philosophical reasoning, so that man's dignity will correspond with God's free creativity, personal providence, and purposive unifying of our moral life. What makes the claim of human immortality intelligible is not just our love for eternal life but, more specifically, our love for sharing such life with a personal God who can respond with acts of knowing and loving directed toward men.

But from Pomponazzi, we learn the consequences of muting the faith view of man and God, and rethinking their relationship in terms of philosophic naturalism. A God who is caught up in the toils and determining laws of nature does not function as the direct liberating goal of men. Hence in the closing pages of *De immortalitate animae* (1516), Pomponazzi ordains men morally toward this-worldly virtue. His synthesis of Aristotelian naturalism and Stoic moral values is philosophically coordinated with an assimilation of God's reality to the workings of an impersonal cosmic order, devoid of miracle and the special ordinations of a caring God.

A striking instance of the delicate mutual adjustment between the themes of man and God is furnished by Giovanni Pico della Mirandola's two main works. The central thesis of his *Oratio de hominis dignitate* (published posthumously, 1496) is that human dignity does not rest upon what man is already or what place he statically occupies in the universe, but rather upon what he can freely become and make of himself. This is not a Promethean autonomizing of human freedom, however, since the latter both originates from the divine creative intent and achieves value by orienting man and the universe jointly toward God. God serves here as the measure of human dignity, and not as its devaluing rival.

When Pico tries to revitalize metaphysics in *De Ente et Uno* (1491), his strategy is simultaneously to humanize the transcendental notes of being and to "theize" their significant reference. Thus in its humane basis, unity of being signifies the human spirit's constant search for the good and powerful spiritual reality of God. Conversely, to call God the One is not to render him remote from us, but to affirm him as our creative source and beckoning homeland. "In the being of things, we can admire the power of God working; in truth, we can venerate the wisdom of the artisan; in goodness, we can love in return the liberality of the lover; in unity, we can receive the unique (as I may say) simplicity of the founder" (*De Ente et Uno*, 8). Christian Platonism and the hermetic tradition lead Pico to temper the One's exaltedness by the reciprocal love binding men with the creative personal God.

The highpoint of Renaissance philosophizing on God is reached in Giordano Bruno, who interweaves many classical and medieval sources with his own original complementarity of the universe with God. His dialogue *De la causa, principio e uno* (1584) furthers man's highest destiny of contemplating and loving the infi-. nite, by regarding the universe itself as infinite and divine. To sustain this vision, he amends the Christian God along noetic, metaphysical, and ethical lines.

(1) Epistemologically, Bruno uses the Copernican reversal of everyday perspectives in order to criticize sense perception and every theory of God based on sense-reliant reason. Only after we overcome the separatist and substantializing tendencies of sensuous reason, can we reach the plane of spiritual understanding and its comprehension of the universe as being one, infinite, and truly divine. Our mind learns to seek God in and as the immanent center of the ever active cosmic process. Like Cusanus, Bruno makes a reform

of knowledge the key to every reform in philosophical theology.

(2) His metaphysico-cosmological aim is both negative and positive. The critical side looms large in *De l'infinito universo e mondi* (1584), where Bruno argues against the reality of substantial change and the plurality of substances in the many world-systems constituting the one universe. After establishing the monism of substance, he identifies God with the sole substantial reality at the heart of the universe. What we experience are not distinct substantial existents but aspects, affections, or relative patterns of change within the all-embracing substantial being of God himself. Bruno thus removes the transcendent remoteness of God with a vengeance, since all forms of reality are configurations and active expressions of the divine nature, are its modular and temporary actuations.

Since some tension still remains between the unicity of the divine basis and the many changing things of experience, Bruno attempts a positive reconstruction in *De la causa* (1584). He absolutizes the root metaphor of matter and form, so that it is a tool of theological as well as physical explanation. God is the absolute identity of universal matter and form, the infinite ground in which they are indifferently one, and out of which they can emerge to structure the modal entities and events of experience. By divinizing the material principle, Bruno prepares for Spinoza's attribution of infinite extension to God, as well as for a religious interpretation of the scientist's study of the universe. And by applying universal form to God, he achieves the double effect of rendering the divine world-soul totally immanent to the universe and also filling every cosmic event with the spark of divine life and minded activity.

Yet in order to account for our human sense of estrangement and striving for a divine union, Bruno also maintains some distinction between God and modal phenomena. God is both the transcendent *cause* and the immanent formal *principle* of the universe. As its intelligent cause, God retains some distinction from the world of modal expressions and affections; but as internal formative principle, God enjoys a basic identity with the totality of things in their patterns of order and active change. Bruno restates this relationship in language adapted from Cusanus. God transcends things insofar as he is *omnia complicans* or their base of containment; and yet he is essentially one with them insofar as he is *omnia explicans* or taken in the aspect of active unfolding and differentiation. Just as the universe receives a divine quality from this correlativity, so does the Brunonian God receive a germ of finitude and change from being one with the striving totality of modal things and happenings.

(3) An ethico-religious dimension must be added to this relationship, both because Bruno's dialectic of identity remains speculatively unexplicated and because of his own drive toward practical realization. He reinterprets the schema of substance and modal aspects in moral terms as man's recall from illusion, as the return of our fragmentary finite mind to the infinite whole of spiritual life (a theme to be developed by Hegel), and in some definite sense as a soaring of the human lover to his beloved. In *De gli eroici furori* (1585) and other ethico-religious dialogues, Bruno makes room in this necessarily unfolding universe for heroic human efforts at purging vices and sharing in eternal life. Just as moral man becomes aware of his condition as a free and loving mind, so does the cosmic term of his searching manifest itself as a divine principle able to meet man's act of love and surrender. Bruno best expresses this belief in the poem contained in his Prefatory Epistle to *De la causa, principio e uno* (1584), trans. Jack Lindsay, as *Cause, Principle and Unity* (1964):

> Through you, O Love, I see the high truth plain.
> You open the doors of diamond and deep night.
> Through eyes the godhead enters; and from sight
> Is born and lives, is fed, holds endless reign.

That the humanization of the divine and the divinization of the human spirit are perspectives upon the same cosmic process, is Bruno's deepest conviction.

3. The God of Reformers and Skeptics. It would be misleading to concentrate solely on the constructive speculations on God reaching from Cusanus to Bruno. For there is a strong concurrent note of distrust for our capacity to make any cognitive headway in the study of God, and this note also characterizes the modern attitude. The no-confidence verdict has several roots: the very diversity of philosophical theologies and the threat of naturalism; theological strictures of the reformers, anxious to reserve a saving knowledge of God for the economy of grace; and the application of skeptical tropes to the theory of God.

Erasmus prefaces his Greek and Latin edition of the New Testament with the *Paraclesis*, his exhortation to shift one's guides on God and religion from pagan sources and contentious schoolmen to the Bible and the Fathers. As spokesman for the *devotio moderna* and biblical humanism, he distinguishes sharply between conflicting human opinions on God and the real certitude found in the philosophy of Christ. The latter is a discipline of the heart, rather than still another speculative theological school.

Although Erasmus and Luther clash on many issues, they agree that all human philosophies of God are both noncertitudinal and deforming of the divine reality.

Luther does concede that men of every era are natively equipped with some basic notions about God. But this is a nonsaving knowledge, which only fitfully illuminates its object and inevitably leads to self-serving idolatry. As Martin Luther's Lectures on Romans 1:21–23 (1516) puts it: "People even today come to commit spiritual idolatry of a more subtle kind [than that of pagan thinkers], and it is quite frequent: they worship God not as he is but as they imagine and desire him to be." For a true and liberating understanding of God, we must turn from the philosophers to Scripture and spiritual life.

Although basically accepting this dichotomy, John Calvin reflects his own classical training and sensitivity to skepticism by assigning considerable (if nonsalvific) work to human reason inquiring about God. In his early commentary on Seneca's *De clementia* ([1532], I, 1), he commends Plato for making "God a sort of commander of the human race, assigning to each his station and military rank." And there are many sound points in the Stoics. They ". . . attribute the superintendence of human affairs to the gods, assert providence, and leave nothing to mere chance."

The Calvin of the *Institutio Christianae Religionis* is much more reserved about philosophical doctrines on God and morality, lest they corrupt or render superfluous the revealed word of God. Yet he does admit that, even in that ruin of the divine image which is fallen man, there remains a basic instinct or sense of the reality of God. And on the objective side, God continually manifests himself in the natural world as being good and powerful. Still, as far as the human interpreter of nature is concerned, Calvin requires him to use the light of faith to discern God's presence in experience and history. On similar theological grounds, Francis Bacon reduces natural theology to a faint glimmer, reserves any elaborate treatment of God and the spiritual side of man for Christian theology, and supposes that the pious scientist will study nature through the lenses of faith for its religious significance.

The problem of God undergoes radical modification with the recovery of Sextus Empiricus' report of skeptical argumentation and its persuasive rephrasing in modern terms. In his *Examen vanitatis doctrinae gentium* (1520), Gianfrancesco Pico della Mirandola (nephew of Pico) rejects the ideal of harmonizing all philosophies and religions into one ecumenical wisdom, and finds in skepticism a potent weapon for disintegrating all human certitudes, especially those about God. Whether it be a philosophy or a reasoned theology of God, whether it be based on sense experience or on an intellectual criterion, every human doctrine on God is infected by incertitude and can rise no higher than to a restricted personal opinion. Gianfrancesco

Pico is a Savonarola among the philosophers of God, herding them all away from the truth found exclusively in Christian faith and discipline.

Much more humane in its general atmosphere, but just as separatist in treating human theories of God as alien to Christian faith, is the skeptical fideism of Michel de Montaigne and Pierre Charron. It is no accident that the former's *Essais* devotes a long analysis to the incoherencies, absurdities, and equivocations which mark all human talk about God.

We say indeed "power," "truth," "justice"; they are words that mean something great; but that something we neither see nor conceive at all. We say that God fears, that God is angry, that God loves—"Marking in mortal words immortal things." Lucretius—These are all feelings and emotions that cannot be lodged in God in our sense, nor can we imagine them according to his. It is for God alone to know himself and to interpret his works (*Essais* [1580; 1588], II, 12, trans. Donald Frame).

This saying sinks deeply into the mind of Blaise Pascal and the Christian skeptics of the seventeenth century, who attune our heart to the Scriptural self-revealing of God rather than to the rationalist philosophical concepts of him. But they cannot fend off the objection of freethinking skeptics that there is no human means left for checking on such faith-centered assertions about God, and that in any case such separatist assertions are unrelatable to our lives.

4. God as a Function in Rationalist Systems. The reintegration of the God-inquiry into its human context of thought and practice is a prime objective of the great seventeenth-century rationalists. However widely Descartes, Spinoza, and Leibniz may differ, they concur on the need for a fully employed God in their philosophies. What they develop is a completely functionalized meaning for God, one that has important tasks to perform within their systems. We can observe how the concept of God gets transformed, by examining its instrumental relation to these new systematic aims in method and knowledge, in theory of nature and man, and in the ethical order.

(1) One major point in methodology concerns the proper starting point of philosophy. God is intimately involved in this question, since it concerns whether or not to begin our philosophizing with God. Descartes is reluctant to do so, since as a safeguard against skepticism he seeks to found philosophy upon the directly experienced reality of the thinking self. The specific quality of Cartesian thought comes from ordering every inquiry about God from some basis and implication found in the *Cogito*. In this way, Descartes seeks to communicate a new rigor to the theory of God, so that it will share in the resistance of the *Cogito* to skeptical doubt and in its evidenced truth. Because the

Cartesian God is approached across the horizon of the reflective human self, he remains personal in nature and intimately present in human concerns. Moreover, this God is functionally fitted to guarantee the veracity of our memory and the reliability of our belief in the external world. A God who performs this epistemological work earns a central place in the Cartesian reconstruction.

Why, then, does Spinoza trace all of Descartes' shortcomings to his treatment of God as having human desires (final causes)? In methodic terms, philosophy must either begin with God or not really begin at all as a full discovery of truth. As Spinoza explains in his *Tractatus de intellectus emendatione* (1660–65; 1677), philosophical method

. . . will be absolutely perfect when the mind gains a knowledge of the absolutely perfect being or becomes conscious thereof. . . . In order to reproduce in every respect the faithful image of nature, our mind must deduce all its ideas from the idea which represents the origin and source of the whole of nature, so that it may itself become the source of other ideas.

Unless philosophy founds itself upon the idea of God, it lacks the fertile and powerful principle whereby the order and linkage of things can be expressed through the order and linkage of philosophical truths. Hence Spinoza must replace the Cartesian thinking self with God, as the originative truth from which the rest of the *Ethica* flows forth. Furthermore, a God which is charged with these systemic responsibilities must express its power necessarily and entirely in the production of the universe, lest the gap made by divine transcendence and freedom be translated into a gap in the philosophical argument itself. God cannot function fruitfully in Spinoza's thought and still retain the image of a free, personal creator.

Ever the diplomat, Leibniz seeks to retain that religious image and still find enough necessity in God to anchor his noetic principles and inferences. Hence Leibniz begins with the composite substances of our experience rather than with God, but soon invokes God as the ground for holding that our first principles of knowledge are also universal principles of the real universe. God's own reality and action are subjected to the sway of the principles of identity, continuity, and sufficient reason, so that we can confidently apply them everywhere else as well. Thus the Leibnizian God functions as universal enforcer of those intelligible laws which underlie the reality reference of all our ideas and reasons.

(2) The remarkable thing about the rationalist proofs of God's existence and nature is that they are directed ultimately less to the understanding of God than to the interpretation of man and nature. Their highly functional reshaping is plainly visible in Descartes' *Meditationes de prima philosophia* (1641). Here, the number of proofs of divine existence is drastically reduced, not only to increase their rigor but also to restate them as aids in the study of the human thinking self and the general structure of the world.

We miss the point of theistic functionalism, if we think that Descartes is only reciting a pious litany when he remarks: "By the word 'God' I mean an infinite substance, [eternal, immutable,] independent, omniscient, omnipotent, and that by which I myself and all other existent things, if it is true that there are other existent things, have been created and produced" (*Meditationes de prima philosophia*, 3). Descartes is interested in proving, not the bare existence of God, but the determinate existence of a God precisely so qualified by these attributes bearing upon cosmic and human problems. Divine omnipotence meets the price by insuring the universal effectiveness of the primary laws of mechanics. Immutability pays its way by keeping these laws constantly operative and intelligible for scientists. Most significant is Descartes' conditional statement about existent things other than myself. God's perfection and veracity are affirmed so as to convert this conditional assertion into an apodictic truth, as well as to go bond for the existential import of the criterion of other clear and distinct ideas about the existing universe.

Our modern piety toward everliving nature owes much to Spinoza's great emendation of the God-nature relationship. He renders this relationship fully convertible and functional, naturalizing the divine reality in such fashion as to give a divine glow to the entire modal world of natural processes. An advance is made beyond Bruno precisely because Spinoza's position is built on careful argumentation and conceptual development, not only on enthusiastic vision. The theory of divine causality is revised to assure its necessary immanence rather than its witness to a free, transcendent creator. Divine substantiality is analyzed to the point of showing its eternally necessary reality and unique predication of God-or-nature as a totality. And the problem of whether to admit unbounded extension as well as thought among God's attributes gains human significance and urgency, when Spinoza makes it the foundation of man's striving for unity with God and the active whole of nature. Herder, Goethe, and the romantic pantheists may not be able to follow the rigorous Spinozistic analysis of modal things. But they do release for wider appreciation the key theme of *natura naturans:* the living and divinely significant reality of nature, of which men constitute both an integral part and a unique base of evaluation.

(3) The ethical stress in rationalist philosophies of God differentiates them both from previous theological moralities (which adapt moral concepts to the idea of God, rather than the converse) and from subsequent naturalistic divorcement of moral norms entirely from reference to God. Descartes cannot dispense with God in the practical order, where he has manifold usefulness. Without God, there would be no real unifying term to the human pursuit of wisdom, no reasonable ground for advocating self-discipline and a hopeful attitude toward eternal life, and no religious sanction for man's technological penetration of nature. Cartesian humanism is a blending of scientific-moral-religious motivations, based on a theistic conviction that the scientific study and control of our world is a vocation from God and a means of leading mankind together toward God.

Spinoza's deliberate removal of personal traits of mind and will from God is not made in a despoiling spirit, but as a step toward assuring man's ultimate practical unification with his divine center. Every step in our self-understanding as active modal expressions of the divine is also a liberating move toward our virtuous (knowledgeable and powerful) union with Spinoza's redefined God. There are religious and mystical overtones in the great cry which fills the final part of the *Ethica* ([1677], V, 36, scholium): "Our salvation, or blessedness, or liberty consists in a constant and eternal love towards God, or in the love of God towards men." Although every term in this statement has metaphysico-ethical import as freeing us from the illusions of Cartesian theism, it also signifies that the God which is one with the incessantly active whole of nature achieves the values of love through our human response to its infinite power and necessity.

Perhaps the last word in the rationalist dialogue on God can be reserved for Leibniz. For he steers a mediating course between the Cartesian self-to-God relationship, with its danger of individualistic isolation, and the Spinozistic model of a mode-acknowledging-its-substantial-ground, which remains too abstruse for most moral agents. Leibniz finds balance in the interpersonal community of men and God. Metaphysically, community is co-constituted by all active centers of existence; morally, it expresses the joint effort of men and God to secure just relationships in practical life; and religiously, it uses the image of the City of God to symbolize the reflective communion of all finite minds with the father of persons. "We must not therefore doubt that God has so ordained everything that spirits not only shall live forever, because this is unavoidable, but that they shall also preserve forever their moral quality, so that his city may never lose a person." This closing affirmation of the *Discours de*

métaphysique ([1685–86], 36) captures Leibniz' communitarian theism better than do the tortuous justifications of God against evil made in his theodicy.

5. *God Neutralized by British Empiricism.* The modern wars of religion deeply scarred the European conscience, compelling it to find safeguards against using differences over God as a basis for social conflicts. The impact of the ideal of toleration and the deistic minimum of belief was not only to remove the cause of God from the social arena but also to lessen the role of God in philosophical thought. Especially the British philosophers found the topic of God less and less essential for resolving their theoretical and practical issues. Thus there was a correlation between the minimalizing and neutralizing of God as a philosophical theme and the growth of some modern forms of humanism and political life which permit no disturbing influence from the idea of God.

Hobbes surrounds the theory of God with a formidable, three-tiered wall. First, the human inclination to reach God as first cause of motion is dampened by the caution that the causal principle cannot be used with strict existential necessity, and that a scientifically attuned philosophy is bound to interpret God in corporeal and mechanical categories. Next, Hobbes discourages any appeal to God's spiritual attributes, since these divine names refer to their human passional source rather than to God's own being. Hence the *Leviathan* ([1651], I, 12) concludes dryly: "In these four things: opinion of ghosts, ignorance of second causes, devotion towards what men fear, and taking of things casual for prognostics, consists the natural seed of *religion.*"

Lastly, if one nurtures this fear-sown seed into a religious institution, Hobbes appeals to the ancient notion of civil religion. Whether a theory of God belongs to the human or the divine politics of religion, its social significance is not a matter of truth but of the disposition of power within the commonwealth. Paradoxically, Hobbes and Spinoza politicize the religious meaning of God to the extreme point of divorcing it from any claim to truth and hence robbing it of its strong practical allure.

Although John Locke grants some demonstrative knowledge of God, his way of ideas notably advances the process of defunctionalizing God. His critique of innatism deprives philosophers and religious enthusiasts alike of the sanction of a divinely implanted set of truths and a pre-given meaning for God. Not having any innatist status in the *Essay concerning Human Understanding* (1690), the idea of God accepts a much reduced role and submits to the common rule of developing its meaning out of the elements of human experience. Locke's quite shaky derivation of the ideas of

351

power, incorporeality, and infinity from our experience affects the slender basis for a theory of God. Epistemologically, the idea of God is almost put out of play. For Locke requires it to serve neither as a Cartesian guarantor of memory and objective truth nor as a Spinozistic basis of continuity and liberation, nor yet as a Leibnizian mediator among monads and between philosophical constructions and cosmic realities. What attracts deists and Enlightenment thinkers to the *Essay* is its pared-back approach to God. Breathing room is found for the trials and errors indispensable for reaching probable judgments in physical, moral, and political questions. Yet Locke does maintain that God's existence is demonstrable.

Eighteenth-century British discussion of God has three main pivots: scientific theism, George Berkeley's personalistic theism, and David Hume's critique of theology and empirical reduction of religion. Under new forms, the respective questions underlying these positions are still facing us. Can we extrapolate from some current scientific view of nature to its divine source and goal? Can we take the interior journey to God as correlate of the personal self and the interpersonal community? And yet does not our intellectual and moral integrity depend upon keeping the idea of God at the bare theoretical minimum and without practical influence?

(1) The scientific theism of Newton, Clarke, and the physicotheologians delivering Boyle's Lectures, is multiply instructive. It illustrates the tendency to ally a study of God with the prevailing tendencies in science, whether Newtonian or evolutionist. It also spells out the price of such alliance to be a shrinking of the viable meaning of God to a reflection of the current scientific categories. Thus the God of Galileo is a divine geometer, that of Newton is a very powerful mechanic, that of Derham and Paley is a skilled designer or watchmaker, and that of Teilhard in the post-Darwinian age is a center of convergence for evolutionary tendencies.

But Berkeley and Hume are already making two criticisms of scientific theism, despite their own wide differences on the leeway for a theory of God in empiricist philosophy. First, it is epistemologically naive to use the causal principle without determining its meaning, range, and probative capacity. Berkeley's point is that the mechanistic and physical-design approaches never attain to genuine causation, which resides in the spiritual agency of persons rather than in the sequence of bodies. Hume's reduction of every mode of causal belief to immanent habituations of our mind shrinks, still further, the capacity of causal inference to reach God. The second empiricist criticism of God the mechanic and designer is that such designa-

tions concern only his natural attributes (speculative traits of intellect, will, and power). From this divine artisan we cannot infer those moral attributes of goodness, justice, and mercy toward men which are the core traits required for making religious response to God.

(2) Berkeley suggests that nevertheless we have an alternative route leading to the God of theism and religious belief. We do experience genuine causation in our personal spiritual agency. This furnishes an experiential analogate whence we can develop a personalistic conception of God as the infinite spiritual agent, working both through physical events and through human relationships. Berkeley construes the physical processes in nature symbolically as the language of God, as the manifestation of his presence and care for men. "This visual language proves, not a creator merely, but a provident governor, actually and intimately present, and attentive to all our interests and motions" (*Alciphron, or The Minute Philosopher* [1732], IV, 14). Thus on theistic grounds, Berkeley advocates exchanging the metaphor of nature as a machine for that of nature as a symbolic language process. And to deepen the meaning of a morally worthy and responsive nature in God, he seeks an analogy in our personal moral ideals and the interpersonal relations which can be enlarged to include the bond with God.

(3) But Hume is skeptical about making any quite determinate theistic inference from the natural and moral worlds of human experience. His most radical move in *Dialogues concerning Natural Religion* ([1779], XII) is not that against the *a priori* and design arguments for God's existence, but rather that against making any moral attributions whatsoever about God. Provided that the inferences to God's existence are deprived of all demonstrative pretensions, Hume will concede this standing for philosophical theology: It ". . . resolves itself into one simple, though somewhat ambiguous, at least undefined proposition, *that the cause or causes of order in the universe probably bear some remote analogy to human intelligence.*" But this meaning is so indeterminate that it is compatible with either a monotheistic or a polytheistic view of the divine principle. And most importantly, it tells us nothing at all about the moral quality of the divinity which is inferred with such tenuous probability and analogy.

The evils in nature and human life stand athwart every effort to expand this minimalist surmise into a moral-religious recognition of God. Hence Hume completes the neutralization of God by divorcing moral principles and motives entirely from theistic assent. The clear Humean lesson for subsequent thinkers is that they must base morality upon the active tendencies of human nature, and must newly relate the idea of God to our moral experience or let it shrivel up as useless.

6. God in the Crucible of the Enlightenment and Kant. Immanuel Kant hailed the Enlightenment men for daring to think for themselves, and on no subject did they display this freedom with more verve than on God. Despite continued political scrutiny, they extended the logic of toleration from ecclesiastical differences to those arising from conflicting theories on God. With the Bible undergoing nascent criticism through the cross-reference system in Bayle and D'Alembert, with data on non-Christian religions and deities flooding the reading public, and with the genetic approach being taken to mankind's religions, the climate was ripe for loosening and pluralizing the meanings of God.

In this situation, no one view of God taken alone represents "the" Enlightenment conception, since that conception consists precisely in the interworkings among the many diverse theories of God. At least the opposing extremes are well marked by the rationalistic theism of Christian Wolff on the one border and the dogmatic materialism of Holbach on the other.

Wolff's *Theologia naturalis* (1736–37) is the grand repository for *a priori* and *a posteriori* demonstrations of God, conducted by abstract analysis of the meaning of the most perfect being. But for all his deductive certainties, Wolff stops short of dispelling the mystery of the divine creative will. Hence he founds moral obligation upon the intrinsic structure of human nature rather than upon the elusive will of God. As a dovetailed opposite, Holbach's *Système de la nature* (1770) treats the natural world as the proper subject for the divine attributes of necessity, perfection, and essential relationships. Since nature, or the active totality of matter in motion, contains its own eternal energies, repair operations, and peak achievements (especially man), there is no need for the God of Newton and Wolff. Our moral destiny is to seek happiness within this natural scene, thus depriving theists of any moral proof of God.

In between these extremes, there is room for considerable variation among Enlightenment inquirers about God. Voltaire restates the case for a revised scientific theism, one that will admit greater limits in our study of God's nature and even some limits intrinsic to God's own knowledge and power, in the face of evil. The *Dictionnaire philosophique* (1764–69, "Théiste") sketches this minimal moral theism: "The theist does not know how God punishes, how he protects, how he forgives; for he is not rash enough to flatter himself that he knows how God acts; but he knows that God does act and that he is just." Denis Diderot is dissatis-

fied with even this modest assertion. He oscillates between a vitalistic version of Holbach's naturalism and an occasional flight of imagination in favor of some unorthodox images of the divine nature. Perhaps we are entangled in the web of some spider deity (as Hume also surmised), engaged in blindly and remorselessly spinning out this tangled heap of luck-pleasure-injustice. Diderot faces up to the possibility (raised in *Le Rêve de D'Alembert*, 1769; 1782) of a literal death of God. "Since it would be a material God—part of the universe and subject to its processes—it might grow old and even die eventually."

Yet Rousseau presses the heart's search for a personal God, having some reserved being of his own and responding to our moral loyalty and religious affection. The Savoyard vicar depicts a just and merciful God correlated with the springs of morality in man's self-love and conscience, even though infinitely beyond our conceptualizations. "I worship his almighty power and my heart acknowledges his mercies. Is it not a natural consequence of our self-love to honor our protector and to love our benefactor?" (*Émile*, IV, "Profession de foi du vicaire savoyard," 1762). With this question, Rousseau tries to synthesize egoistic values and openness to a moral God, rather than set the two principles in opposition.

Kant weighs all these diverse currents on God, subjects the whole topic to critical reconsideration, and offers his own view of personal theism. In each of his *Critiques* he studies a distinct facet of the question, and in his theory of religion he presents a moralized and religionized conception of God.

(1) Kant achieves three goals with his analysis of speculative proofs of God's existence in the *Kritik der reinen Vernunft* (1781; 2nd ed., 1787). First, he shows the impropriety of claiming to have demonstrative knowledge of God, since "to know" concerns only existents which are finitely present and connected in a space-time context. Next, a morally and religiously relevant meaning of God cannot be obtained from either the ontological and cosmological routes (since a necessary and ontically perfect being may not be morally responsive) or from the study of physical design (which need not yield an infinite and morally purposive agent). Thirdly, we can make a fruitful regulative use of the idea of God even in the theoretical order. The idea of a wise and unifying God can give the researcher confidence in seeking ever more comprehensive principles of explanation.

(2) In the *Kritik der praktischen Vernunft* ([1788], Part I, Book II, ii, 5), Kant wholeheartedly accepts the Enlightenment's refusal to base moral duty upon the divine will and law, but adds that rejection of such a "theological morality" tells only half the tale of moral

analysis. There is still need for a moral theism, which anchors our belief in God upon certain aspects of the human moral situation integrally considered. When our moral will is considered, not in its autonomous law-giving function but in that of seeking its realization in a highest good, then a meaningful distinction develops between the derived and the underived good for man. "The postulate of the possibility of a highest derived good (the best world) is at the same time the postulate of the reality of a highest original good, namely, the existence of God." Such a postulate is not a fictional device but an interpretation of the full requirements for responsible moral action in the world. Kant's *Kritik der Urteilskraft* (1790) adds that the idea of God also has interpretive use in the study of organic structures. It enables us to conceive of nature in terms of living unified purposiveness, even though we cannot convert the symbol from analogical to literal significance.

(3) Finally, in *Die Religion innerhalb der Grenzen der blossen Vernunft* (1792; 1793), Kant shows how the moral concept of God involves a religious meaning related to our world of personal and social evils. In this context, we think of a God of personal hope and historical fidelity to the people of God. Kant makes a crucial reorientation of the theory of God's moral attributes. No longer can they be regarded as prolongations of a speculative ontology of the divine essence: instead, they correspond with our basic moral-religious interpretation of existence. Thus God's justice correlates with moral conscience and religious fear; his goodness with our search for happiness and our religious love; and his holiness with our moral experience of lawgiving and religious reverence. Thus the Kantian idea of God rests upon a thoroughly moralized and religionized foundation.

As the story of the idea of God passes now into the post-Kantian era of strenuous systematic reformulation in idealistic, positivistic, and evolutionistic contexts, it may be well to bear in mind a remark made by Kant's fellow Königsberger and critic, J. G. Hamann. "Here on earth we live on crumbs. Our thoughts are fragments. Our knowledge itself is patchwork" (*Brocken,* 1758). This consequence of the human condition applies to our inquiries about God with full force. We have been given some fragmentary glimpses into the meaning of God by the modern thinkers through Kant, and we may reasonably expect that the prospects now about to be opened up will also share this patchwork and perspectival character.

BIBLIOGRAPHY

1. General Studies. J. Collins, *God in Modern Philosophy* (Chicago, 1959); idem, *The Emergence of Philosophy of Religion* (New Haven, 1967). J. Dillenberger, *Protestant Thought and Natural Science* (New York, 1960). C. Fabro, *Introduzione all'ateismo moderno* (Rome, 1964), trans. A. Gibson as *God in Exile: Modern Atheism* (Westminster, Md., 1968). R. Kroner, *Speculation and Revelation in Modern Philosophy* (Philadelphia, 1961). W. Schulz, *Der Gott der neuzeitlichen Metaphysik* (Pfullingen, 1957).

2. Renaissance Studies. S. Dangelmayr, *Gotteserkenntnis und Gottesbegriff in den philosophischen Schriften des Nikolaus von Kues* (Meisenheim, 1969). S. Greenberg, *The Infinite in Giordano Bruno* (New York, 1950). P. O. Kristeller, *Eight Philosophers of the Italian Renaissance* (Stanford, 1964). J. Nelson, *Renaissance Theory of Love* (New York, 1958). R. Popkin, *The History of Scepticism from Erasmus to Descartes* (New York, 1960; rev. reprint 1968). F. Wendel, *Calvin: Sources et évolution de sa pensée religieuse* (Paris, 1950), trans. as *Calvin: The Origins and Development of His Religious Thought* (London, 1963).

3. Modern Studies. J.-L. Bruch, *La Philosophie religieuse de Kant* (Paris, 1968). F. England, *Kant's Conception of God* (London, 1929). H. Gouhier, *La Pensée métaphysique de Descartes* (Paris, 1962); idem, *La Pensée religieuse de Descartes* (Paris, 1924). T. Greene and J. Silber, "Introductions" to the Greene-Hudson translation of I. Kant, *Religion within the Limits of Reason Alone* (New York, 1960), pp. ix–cxxxiv. R. Grimsley, *Rousseau and the Religious Quest* (New York, 1968). R. Hurlbutt, *Hume, Newton, and the Design Argument* (Lincoln, Nebraska, 1965). J. Jalabert, *Le Dieu de Leibniz* (Paris, 1960). R. Lauer, *The Mind of Voltaire* (Westminster, Md., 1961). A. Leroy, *La Critique et la religion chez David Hume* (Paris, 1930). F. Manuel, *The Eighteenth Century Confronts the Gods* (Cambridge, 1959). J. Orr, *English Deism: Its Roots and Fruits* (Grand Rapids, 1934). B. Rousset, *La Perspective finale de "L'Éthique" et le problème de la cohérence du spinozisme* (Paris, 1968). E. Sillem, *George Berkeley and the Proofs for the Existence of God* (New York, 1957). N. Smith, "Introduction" to his edition of D. Hume, *Dialogues concerning Natural Religion* (New York, 1947; reprint 1963), pp. 1–123. J. Yolton, *John Locke and the Way of Ideas* (Oxford, 1956).

JAMES COLLINS

[See also Deism; **God;** Holy (The Sacred); Neo-Platonism; **Religion;** Renaissance Humanism; Theodicy.]

IDEA OF GOD SINCE 1800

THERE IS little question that since the eighteenth century the traditional theistic idea of God inherited from medieval and Reformation developments has increasingly found itself in grave difficulties. Subject to accelerating criticism from various quarters, it has been progressively refashioned and reworked. The result is that, on the one hand, few theologians today defend such a traditional view of God, and on the other hand, other contemporary theological voices are declaring that as an idea, "God" is useless and meaningless. Our article on the idea of God will deal with this long-term process of change or refashioning on the right, and this present-day rejection on the left, primarily amongst theologians because they provide the clearest index to this development.

It should be remembered, however, that roughly the same process has in a prior and an even more radical form occurred in philosophy. Whereas in the seventeenth century most philosophers made "God" the pivot of their systems, increasingly this concept has been pushed aside, appearing in our century at best only rarely among philosophers, and most frequently rejected out of hand as philosophically superfluous, invalid, or unintelligible. Clearly, therefore, the development in theology which we shall trace reflects a deeper tendency in the culture as a whole, a development of spirit most helpfully called a "secularizing" of our culture's life and thought, and therefore one which increasingly removes the idea of God from men's habitual and significant modes of thought and action. Whether or not this secular trend reflects the closer approximation to the *truth* about what is, is a matter with which a descriptive article cannot easily deal. Let us say that what a culture tends to think true or significant is, even when it is our culture, not necessarily so; and that an undeniably secular trend in cultural history may as easily reflect a *misunderstanding* of reality as it does a more accurate grasp of what is really the case.

At the end of the seventeenth century the idea of God seemed on the one hand intelligible and secure, and on the other generally agreed upon with regard to its content. Had not nearly all of the century's great scientists, such as Newton, Boyle, Dalton, and Ray, been convinced that their vast advances in science only showed more clearly the wonder of the Creator? Had not nearly all of the century's greatest philosophers: Descartes, Leibniz, Locke, and Spinoza, made "God" the center of their systems, often the first certainty as well as the first cause of being and of intelligibility? Were not almost all the greatest social thinkers: Bodin, Grotius, and Lipsius, devout Christians, albeit now influenced by liberal Stoic ideas? And finally, Spinoza excepted, was there any real question about what this culture, Catholic or Protestant, lay or clerical, *meant* by the concept "God," namely a transcendent, self-sufficient, all-powerful, changeless, perfect, and therefore supernatural being, endowed with intelligence and will, and characterized by moral rectitude and benevolence towards his creatures? The intellectual bases of this traditional theism were, to be sure, differ-

ent: Catholics still sought to prove his existence as the necessary first cause of finite creatures; modernizing Protestants tended to prefer the proof from the natural order newly uncovered by science; and some, such as Pascal and Bayle, preferred a "wager" or fideism to such coldly intellectual proofs. Nevertheless, in the seventeenth century virtually all agreed that such a being exists, that He could be known with certainty, and that He was ultimately the source and ground of all being, order, and hope. The seeds of a speedy disintegration were there, partially evident in the exclusivist empiricism of Bacon and the materialism of Hobbes, but they had not yet flowered. The seventeenth century was, as Peter Gay rightly remarks, the era of "pagan Christianity" (Gay, Ch. V), secular in many of its modes of thought, but still deeply religious and Christian in its ultimate vision of things.

To trace briefly the ways in which eighteenth-century thought and life challenged and virtually overcame the certainty, the centrality, and even the character of this traditional theistic notion of God is impossible except in summary form. Although only a number of French *philosophes* were blatantly atheistic, almost any eighteenth-century thinker in tune with his time was radically critical of traditional Christianity and not least of this, its inherited conception of God. That idea, as we have noted previously, had enjoyed a multiple base: in science, in metaphysics, in morals, in scriptural authority, and finally, through the social and historical establishment of religious institutions in European life. On every one of these fronts the spirit of the Enlightenment challenged these bases for "God"—and the continuation of that multi-faceted challenge into our own day represents the main character of our own developing secularity.

In general this attack may be characterized as the effort, through radical criticism of all untested notions, to strip life down to the simplest, most immediate, and most "natural" base, to disenchant the world of all supernatural, mythical elements, and to leave there only what is directly experienced, what is immanent within the natural order, and what can help immediately in the present life of man. The result was an almost frantic wish to dispense with all inherited or traditional beliefs which could not be so validated or which had no immediate, this-worldly, utility. Thus the science of the eighteenth century tended to limit scientific hypotheses to the natural, material order, and to eschew the seventeenth-century relation of science to metaphysics, to natural theology, and so to proofs of God. Philosophy correspondingly lost its speculative, metaphysical urges, and in Hume, Kant, and many others became increasingly skeptical of metaphysical systems and so of any cognitive certainty of God.

Morals and social thought in their turn became more and more "secular" in character, finding their base first in natural laws, and then successively in our natural affections and needs, in prudence or utility, and in the autonomous laws of practical reason—but in no case were Enlightenment morals founded directly on a religious basis. In this way, in becoming thus radically "secular," eighteenth-century science, philosophy, and morals alike ceased to provide bases for the traditional concept of God.

Finally, the whole brunt of Enlightenment attitudes militated against traditional authorities or untested faiths as a basis of religious certainty and conviction. The age's hatred of all forms of unquestioned authority and unexamined superstition, its scorn of prejudice and parochial passion, and its bitter experience of confessional intolerance and wars, and of clerical privilege and conservatism made appeals to divine revelation, to ecclesiastical authority, or to inner religious experiences abhorrent to many thinkers of the Enlightenment. It was an age that emphasized, above all, immediate experience, personal and human autonomy, this-worldly values, and a critical or skeptical attitude towards all social, historical, and cosmological beliefs. And in less than one hundred years, that combination of attitudes exploded the metaphysical, fideistic, moral, and historical-social bases of the traditional concept of God. The debris remaining was well described by Schleiermacher in 1799 when he remarked that for the cultured of his age, religion was merely "an instinct craving for a mess of metaphysical and moral crumbs" (Schleiermacher, p. 31).

Despite its shattering effects on traditional dogmas and concepts, the result of the eighteenth-century Enlightenment on its descendants in the nineteenth century was by no means the total eradication from theology, philosophy, or culture of the idea of God. To be sure, there was an increasing spread of atheism as the century developed through the thought of such men as Feuerbach, Marx, Nietzsche, Comte, and Darwin; still, God remained a central concept in most nineteenth-century thought. The dominant reaction of this century was to modernize or even to "secularize" this religious concept, to refashion traditional theism in terms intelligible to the contemporary man. And the reason was that there still remained, for most nineteenth-century minds, a deep sense of a divine dimension of things, manifesting itself for them in the eternal and so divine law of orderly development or Progress. What the eighteenth-century Enlightenment seems, therefore, to have accomplished was the permanent shattering of that inherited union of ontological and religious categories which had formed the concept of a transcendent, omnipotent,

changeless, and yet all-wise and all-loving being, what we have called traditional or classical theism. Except for a lingering Thomistic tradition, since mid-twentieth century under fire in Roman Catholicism itself, this traditional theistic concept has not reappeared importantly in theology in either the nineteenth or the twentieth centuries. Whatever may be the case with God as he is in himself, there is little historical question that, in non-Roman circles at least, this inherited concept of God "died" circa 1800. Let us now see how this concept was transformed.

The Enlightenment bequeathed to its descendants in the nineteenth century many presuppositions which helped to direct the course of this reformulation. First was an emphasis on immediate experience and on human autonomy, and a consequent conviction that whatever is meaningful, real, and of value must be in continuity with ordinary experience and with human powers. Second, in both the eighteenth and the nineteenth centuries reality was seen as a harmonious whole. Increasingly during the nineteenth, however, the idea that this whole represents a developing process towards perfection comes to dominance. And third, because of the belief in the continuity of man's development with the ultimate purposes of process, man, in his higher capacities as a rational and moral being was felt legitimately to claim to be the measure of reality and truth. Thus for the nineteenth century the immanence of the divine in the unfolding process of nature and of human history becomes the key theological motif. Consequently, many a thinker, who was influenced by the eighteenth-century background repudiated—but for slightly different reasons—the traditional notion of a God who was completely transcendent, who was hidden from a fallen and lost world incapable of relating itself to him, and who consequently could be known only by metaphysical inference or by ecclesiastical or scriptural religious authority. Such a being, separated from ordinary experience and appearing only in miracle, seemed to the confident, scientific mind of the nineteenth century, to be unknowable, unreal, irrelevant at best, and superstitious and repressive at worst. While, however, typical minds of the preceding eighteenth century had sought either to rescue this traditional deity in an intellectually purified deism—for example, that of Voltaire or Rousseau—or to excoriate him in the scientific materialism of Holbach, the typical nineteenth-century reaction was radically to refashion the idea of God according to its own "romantic" emphases on moral passion, wholeness, and feeling. Again we can only summarize briefly these reformulations which flowered into what is usually called religious and theological liberalism.

First there was the reformulation effected by Kant

and his followers. Kant at the end of the eighteenth century had expressed vividly the Enlightenment's antipathy to metaphysics, and thus had called a halt to a speculative foundation for the concept of God. We cannot, he said, *know* God, for knowledge is confined to the sensible, phenomenal world and to *a priori* mathematics and logic, that is, to empirical and formal sciences. Thus with the demise of a metaphysical base for theology, the ontological functions and attributes of the traditional idea of God were removed from post-Kantian religious thought. According to Kant, however, the moral if not the cognitive capacities of man, although self-grounded in man's own autonomous practical reason, cannot fulfill themselves without a theistic framework: as a moral being, man must postulate, even if he cannot demonstrate, the reality of God and of immortality. God is here no longer, as in the seventeenth century, the experienceable and knowable *ground* of finite being, human autonomy, moral experience, and future hope; for Kant, the idea of God is rather (in part) the implication of an unknowable ideal of pure reason, supplementing an autonomously studied nature, and (much more surely) the consequence and so the postulate of autonomously acting moral reason.

The theological implications of this radically transformed status for the idea of God were worked out by Albrecht Ritschl and his school in the second half of the nineteenth century. For Ritschlian liberalism metaphysical or ontological categories were quite irrelevant to religious interests; such concepts, said they, are a "Greek" inheritance alien to the purely moral and historical concerns of the religion of the prophets and of Jesus. Thus God, while appropriately called Creator and Ruler by religious faith, should not be identified with the cosmological First Cause, a speculative Absolute, or even a divine spiritual Force within nature. He is known and experienced by us only in our moral life, as providing the framework within which human moral personality can fulfill itself. Thus for Ritschl God as Creator guarantees our "moral supremacy over nature"; as the Ruler of history he guarantees the moral development of history towards the kingdom of God; and, above all, as the loving Father of Jesus, who founded the kingdom of love, he calls us in personal communion to fulfill ourselves morally in a spiritual worship of him which is selfless service to the growth in history of his moral kingdom. The anti-metaphysical bias of Kant (making easy union with Luther's historical antipathy to scholasticism) removed from much of subsequent Protestant thought the ontological characteristics of the traditional God; the optimism of the nineteenth century about man's moral possibilities removed his historic judgmental or "wrathful" characteristics; the belief in historical

progress dissipated the eschatological or otherworldly element primary to orthodoxy; and so all that was left in most of Ritschlian theology was the loving, personal God of moral idealism and of historical progress.

German theology of the twentieth century, however divergent in its religious emphases from Ritschlian moralism, has after this inheritance never been able to contemplate a metaphysical conception of God with anything but horror, or be concerned in theology with such categories as self-sufficiency, necessity, being, substance, changelessness, or eternity. To contemporary continental theologians, as to Ritschl and Harnack, these are "Greek" concepts alien to the moral, personal, and historical genius of the Christian notion of God.

A quite different reformulation appeared in Hegel. For Hegel, as for Kant, there was no possibility of knowing a *transcendent* God by inference, and there was for him even less desirability in worshipping such a God on the basis of authority. The divine must be immanent to experience if it is to be real, relevant, and at all creative. But God cannot be in continuity with only a *part* of experience, for comprehensiveness and universality are surely characteristics of both deity and truth. Thus God must be both immanent and universal, that which grounds and so unites every facet of experience: logical and cognitive, natural and cultural, social and historical, emotional and moral. In other words, when truly understood by philosophy instead of merely pictured by religion, God is the immanent Absolute, as concrete as are the immediate facts of experience that are his modes, and as universal as a total system enveloping everything. If, moreover, God as immanent is not separate from the concrete particulars of which he is the ground and the unity, then, while to be sure he is self-sufficient and so absolute, producer and not produced, still he cannot be changeless and static. Becoming and development are the essential characteristics of logic, of life, and of social history, and so, as the ground and unity of these, God shares in dialectical movement. Once again mediation was achieved, this time between the logical relations of ideas, now dynamically interpreted, and matters of fact—a pair formerly sundered by the speculative timidity of the Enlightenment. Finally, since all post-Kantians agreed that creative production of particulars according to logical structures is the essence of rational spirit, the Absolute is rational; and thus reality—natural, historical, and personal—in all its bewildering variety and apparent confusion, is to the unifying philosophical gaze the creation of rational Spirit.

If one asks how such a global vision of the all-comprehensive rational unity of actual things is possi-

357

ble for finite intellects, Hegel answered that such a suprahuman philosophical synthesis was possible only because the divine spirit, the Absolute, had *already* become incarnate in history, had united itself with mankind in the historical development of autonomy and intelligence, and had finally realized itself as self-consciousness in the understanding of the philosopher. The union achieved in speculative philosophy between the secular and the religious, between the manifold of individual and historical life and the ultimate or the Absolute, is possible only because the divine has already united them by its action of incarnation in humanity and so in history. Thus did Hegel, by rendering God radically immanent and dynamic rather than transcendent and changeless, produce possibly the last religious or theological expression of Western culture as a whole. For in his view the trinitarian God of traditional faith has descended from his separateness into actuality and has become the unfolding Absolute whose inner life of rational spirit has expressed itself through the process of social history in the story of the development of human autonomy.

Hegel's magnificent synthesis of philosophy and theology, culture and religion, the profane and the sacred—being too intellectualistic in that it tended to "raise or transform religion into philosophy"—never became the basis for a widespread "church theology," as did Ritschlianism. Nevertheless overtones of Hegel's idealistic conception of God, in which God is the symbol for the Whole of experience, appear prominently in philosophical and religious thought throughout the nineteenth and into the early twentieth centuries: in Bernard Bosanquet, F. H. Bradley, Borden Parker Bowne, A. S. Pringle-Pattison, W. T. Harris and the St. Louis School, Josiah Royce, W. E. Hocking, and Brand Blanshard.

A third mode of reformulation far more pervasive in liberal religion than Hegelianism and so a balancing motif to Ritschlian moralism was that of Friedrich Schleiermacher. Agreeing with other post-Enlightenment figures that metaphysical inference could not establish a transcendent deity, and that for modern men neither ecclesiastical nor biblical authority could alone provide a sufficient base for religion and its doctrines, Schleiermacher denied nevertheless the Kantian base of religion in morality and the Hegelian tendency to transform religion into philosophical speculation. Rather, he regarded religion as founded autonomously on feeling, a pre-rational and pre-moral awareness, a sense or "taste for the Whole" or the Infinite, or, as he put it later, the self-consciousness of being absolutely dependent as opposed to the "secular" self-consciousness of relative dependence and relative freedom with respect to the things of the world. On this ground of feeling, or, as we might put it, of existential

self-awareness as absolutely dependent, Schleiermacher reinterpreted religion in general, Christian faith and experience, and, of course, the symbol God. God is now conceived as the Whence of this unique feeling, and so all talk about God is really talk about our religious feelings with regard to their source and ground.

Several important new characteristics of God follow from Schleiermacher's starting point. First of all, only that which is immediately derivable from present religious experience can be said of God; nothing merely on the basis of rational speculation or traditional authority can be stated of him as he is in himself. Secondly, while this feeling is "religious" in that it is not a feeling of the world around us, still it is "secular" in the sense that once developed it accompanies, as a part of our basic self-consciousness, all of our life. It is not one special, "churchy" feeling or experience among others, but the ground tone of our total everyday existence. Correspondingly, God, as the Whence of this feeling, is not one cause (albeit supernatural) among others, but God is Absolute Causality as the cause of all finite causes. It is not the case that he is in church but not in nature, in *Heilsgeschichte* but not in ordinary experience, "here" and not "there." He is rather omnipresent and everlasting, as the ground of our existence and all that occurs. And finally, God is quite beyond the relative reciprocity and freedom of finite things in their mutual relations. In this way Schleiermacher refashioned the notion of God, as had Kant and Hegel, so as to place it in continuity with the nineteenth-century confidence in life and experience generally, and especially so as not to run counter to the world order of Enlightenment science. God here is not a transcendent supernatural being who intervenes into a fallen world from the outside; he is the ground, rather, of all causal order as the timeless, absolute cause of all causes.

What Schleiermacher contributed to nineteenth-century liberal religion was the emphasis on immediate religious experience as the basis of piety and so of all faith and doctrine, the sense of the immanence of God in all life and culture, and a magnificently worked out modern reinterpretation of all major Christian doctrines, which did not conflict with an acceptance of science in all its forms. Where his notion of God has seemed insufficient was its latent pantheism, his weakened sense of alienation from God and so of sin (a fault shared by most other liberal theologies), and especially the apparent lack of "personal being" in God because God as Absolute Causality lacked freedom among alternatives, and therefore intentionality. Nevertheless, since almost every major theologian since Schleiermacher's time has spoken of God on the basis of some aspect of present experience—be that experience conceived romantically, pietistically, or existentially—and no longer (whatever his protestations) defines God on the basis exclusively either of speculation or of external ecclesiastical or scriptural authority, it is not hard to see why, even in the very different atmosphere of the twentieth century, Schleiermacher continues to be called "the father of modern theology," at least in Western culture.

Finally, one other important reformulation of the idea of God begins to appear in the later nineteenth century. The conception that reality is a developing, evolving, or progressing Process had been latent in Enlightenment thought about history, had appeared in dramatic, albeit idealistic, form in Hegel, and seemed to receive final approbation in the developing cosmology, geology, and finally biology of the nineteenth century. It is fair to say that well nigh every aspect of inquiry at the end of the nineteenth century was dominated by this evolutionary presupposition, and correspondingly religious thought as well found itself using the concept of evolving process as its most fundamental clue to the character of reality and so of God. In opposition to Hegel's absolutistic use of the concept, however, most forms of evolutionary or process thought at the end of the nineteenth century conceived of God as finite, the spiritual or intentional force within natural and historical process which accounts for the "facts" of evolutionary development and of historical progress. Insofar, therefore, as such forms of progressive development were regarded as "empirical," God as their source or cause was believed to be "empirically derived"; insofar as this development had evidenced manifest evil and so had clearly involved a struggle, God could be neither absolute nor omnipotent; and finally, insofar as he is a "struggling God," in reciprocal relations with natural and historical events, God is surely neither self-sufficient nor changeless.

God is thus regarded as "becoming" or "changing" as process unfolds, and as the process as a whole achieves over time its own perfection, so God fulfills his own being, as well as his purposes, in and through the perfecting of a recalcitrant world. A wide variety of such concepts of God or of deity as an immanent, finite, developing force for progress appeared in the latter nineteenth and early twentieth centuries: in John Stuart Mill, William James, and Henri Bergson; in Lloyd Morgan and Samuel Alexander; in F. R. Tennant, H. N. Wieman, Edgar Brightman, and E. S. Ames. The most influential significant form of this view of God as a developing factor within process appears, however, in the first third of the twentieth century in the thought of A. N. Whitehead, regarded by many as perhaps the greatest speculative philosopher the present century has yet produced—and so with his thought we move beyond the nineteenth-century liberal reformulations of God into the twentieth century.

In theology, as in so much of its life, the twentieth century has been in sharp revolt against its predecessor—as the nineteenth was against the eighteenth. Its first half—from 1918 to roughly 1960—was almost totally dominated by theological and religious views explicitly and directly antithetical to the liberal reformulations pictured above. Consequently, in the "neo-orthodox," "neo-Reformation," dialectical, or crisis theology characteristic of that half-century, a quite new understanding of God appears in Western history. The theological situation of the 1960's is in turn pervaded by the rather sudden collapse of this view of God, and by the consequent question, raised for really the first time within theology itself, whether there be a God for theology to talk about at all.

The causes of the rise of the neo-orthodox view of God were· multiple. Most prominent of all was the breakdown of the confidence of the nineteenth century in the *religious* significance of "process," that is, in the progress of history and the goodness and perfectibility of man, a confidence which, as we noted, had led to the dominant liberal themes of the immanence of God and so to the continuity of the divine and the human. Social experience in the first half of the twentieth century was characterized by the sudden eruption of vast human evils; of paralyzing and debilitating wars; of impersonal, technological, and industrial cultures that seemed to smother personal and moral life alike; and by the threat of the imminent collapse of the very culture the endless development of whose values had in the first place led to the idea of social process as Historical Progress. Instead of manifesting in its secular life the divine spirit, man's history appeared to express nothing but estrangement, injustice, cruelty, and pride. Man's truth, in the physical and social sciences alike, opened as many possibilities for the exploitation as for the fulfillment of man. If, therefore, there was to be hope either for history as a whole or for the meaningfulness of an individual life, it must come from beyond man; the divine which saves must be transcendent rather than immanent, and the man who is saved must be "reborn" rather than merely "matured." Transcendence reentered Western experience as the only possible alternative to twentieth-century despair. Ironically, our century's cultural experience was providing a kind of "prolegomenon" (if not a natural theology!) to what Karl Barth called the strange, new world of the Bible, or "biblical faith," insofar as the latter was characterized by such traditional categories as transcendence and mystery, crisis and redemption, sin and lostness, judgment and damnation, revelation and grace, justification and salvation.

A complementary philosophical development must be mentioned if we are to understand the idea of God in the twentieth century. With the breakdown early

359

in the century of the nineteenth-century sense of progressive development and so of rational order, there appeared in philosophy as well a rather violent swing away from speculative metaphysics. With World War I the dominance of idealism evaporated, leaving only the organismic philosophy of Whitehead as a powerful speculative metaphysical influence. Almost all Anglo-Saxon philosophy took a radically naturalistic and even a positivistic turn, insisting with Dewey, Santayana, Morris R. Cohen, et al. that philosophy like science can only describe the immanent and generic traits of the plural, changing world of immediate experience, or with the Vienna school and linguistic philosophy that philosophy's sole task is not at all that of knowing "the real," but merely the analysis of language. In neither case, obviously, was there the possibility of the kind of systematic metaphysical speculation that might establish or even undergird a philosophical conception of God. The other major philosophical movement was existentialism, which emphasized on the one hand man's despairing situation in a meaningless world, and on the other the radical distinction between objective scientific talk about things, and personal, involved awareness of one's own being, freedom, anxieties, and dilemmas.

Although much of secular existentialism was atheistic, this form of philosophy, whose origin after all lay in the religious writings of Kierkegaard, could be translated for theological purposes, which quickly happened. In this role, existential philosophy implied that theological language about God was exclusively personal, involved, and subjective, the language of the inward, personal experience of guilt and despair, of faith and commitment, and not at all a language suited to objective philosophical reasoning. Consequently, existentialist theologians insisted that metaphysical language about God, like scientific language about nature, inevitably distorted and obscured God by making him into a thing or an object to be manipulated. Both these developments in philosophy, therefore—the naturalistic, positivistic, and linguistic development and the existential development—implied unequivocally that philosophy could give no help to theology in its quest to understand and describe the nature of God. For most of the first half of the twentieth century, therefore, if God was to be known and conceived at all, it had to be by other means than by philosophical inquiry.

We can now understand the rather peculiar character of the neo-orthodox God. Our description seeks to bring together (if possible) the important and generic elements in the theologies of Karl Barth, Emil Brunner, Gustaf Aulen, Anders Nygren, Rudolf Bultmann, the Niebuhrs, and many others. For this whole circle of theologians, since estranged man bound in sin and unable to rise by himself beyond immediate experience either knows nothing of the transcendent at all or else distorts the hints he does receive, all true knowledge of God is based on revelation alone. Only through the Word of God, communicated to men through the "mighty acts" of God in Israel's history and in Jesus Christ, witnessed to in the scriptures and acknowledged and known by living faith, can God be known at all. No proofs of God are possible or relevant to faith, and no metaphysical speculation can discover his attributes; thus all philosophical categories are alien to a true understanding of God. The God of Christian faith is, consequently, solely the God of the Bible, and all we can validly say of him must have this biblical base. Thus are the "Greek" categories of being, pure actuality, necessity, changelessness, self-sufficiency, and absoluteness quite irrelevant to theology and distorting to faith.

Correspondingly, the blindness of the nineteenth-century liberal to the reality of our sin and so his antipathy to the judgmental and "wrathful" sides of God must be equally rejected as both unempirical and unbiblical. The biblical God is primarily one who as a personal being acts and speaks; one who is not in the first instance a God of nature but one involved in the events of man's history, manifesting his will and his nature there; and what He manifests there are his personal judgments on man's sin, his unmerited acts of redemption, and his promises of salvation for the future. Thus God is fundamentally characterized by the personal attributes of dynamic activity, freedom, self-manifestation, righteous will, moral intentionality, and *agapē* or outgoing love. He is a God who is transcendent in the epistemological sense that he is hidden or veiled to man's ordinary gaze, but he is also the God who "comes" and who "speaks"—that is, who is related to the events of history and to ourselves, who reveals himself within time and space, and who above all confronts us in personal encounter as the divine Thou. To be sure, as a free and transcendent *Lord* of all, God is implicitly also the self-sufficient creator, the source of all being, and transcendent to temporal passage.

Most neo-orthodox theologians, however, became nervous about speaking of these obviously ontological and potentially static and separatist characteristics, and contented themselves with emphasizing God's personal and living character as the transcendent Lord related to history. In sum, the neo-orthodox or biblical God took over some of the *religious* and so *personal* characteristics of the traditional Protestant God: intentionality and freedom, intelligence and will, righteous judgment on sin, and merciful love. But in place of the classical ontological attributes expressing self-sufficiency and changeless eternity of being, they substituted an emphasis on the dynamic, active, related character of God as the sovereign actor and ruler in history.

In many respects, however, even religiously this view did not represent the traditional Reformation God. Although the liberal God of immanent love was excoriated, many liberal principles were quietly accepted. First of all, although for the neo-orthodox God "spoke" to men in revelation and "acted" in historical events, no neo-orthodox theologians thought that the sentences of the Bible represented God's infallible words, nor did they understand his acts in terms of miracles. The liberal sense of the relativity of the words of Scripture and of the creeds of theological tradition, and the liberal assumption that the manifold of nature and of history manifest immanent causes to be investigated by science and not by theological inquiry, were alike assumed. Also, the liberal antipathy to the classical doctrines of particular Providence (God wills and causes *all* events, sickness, plagues, and wars), to the doctrine of double or even single predestination (God wills some men to enter eternal damnation and some to salvation), and to the doctrine of eternal condemnation (some will be condemned, for their sins, to eternal damnation), were either rejected outright by the neo-orthodox or transformed almost out of recognition. The God of neo-orthodoxy "spoke," but no concrete divine words resulted; he "acted," but not in miraculous or otherwise identifiable or even specific ways; he "ruled," but not by omnipotently willing any particular and certainly no evil events; and he "judged," but not in terms of divine punishment either presently evident or even to be expected eternally.

Since these theologians also repudiated a metaphysical understanding of what they said about the activities of God, it was not surprising that the second generation neo-orthodox experienced later difficulties in saying just *what* they meant by the crucial verbs that they applied to God concerning his speaking, his acting, his sovereign willing and ruling, and his judging and saving work. Finally, in Rudolf Bultmann (who believed thoroughly in this neo-orthodox view of God) the tendency to regard God solely as the subject of his own revelation instead of as the object of our thought went so far that almost no *theological* doctrine of God becomes possible. God can speak to us through the kerygma (preaching of the Gospel), said Bultmann, but all of our speech about God objectifies him, is in danger of "mythologizing the transcendent," and so should be shunned. Thus did one of the century's great theologians and believers himself make it almost impossible for subsequent theologians to speak of God.

While this neo-biblical view of God dominated European and most of Anglo-Saxon Protestant theology, two other traditions continued in a somewhat quiescent if not defensive mode: that of Thomism and that of process theology. In both Roman and high Anglican circles the Thomist conception of God was reformulated and defended by a series of scholarly and sophisticated minds (R. Garrigou-Lagrange, Henri de Lubac, É. Gilson, and J. Maritain in Roman Catholicism, and E. L. Mascall, Austin Farrer, and Eugene Fairweather, et al. in Anglicanism). While this group agreed, of course, with neo-orthodoxy that Revelation was necessary for a full Christian understanding of God's nature, nevertheless they diverged sharply from the dominant Protestant group on two counts. (1) A philosophical, "natural" theology, they said, is necessary for two reasons: (a) it alone can establish rationally and objectively the existence of God—though this group tended to regard natural theology less as a purely intellectual "proof" prior to all religious experience or commitment, than as a rational, and so universally intelligible, formulation of what is known by a metaphysical intuition or even received from Revelation. (b) Since natural theology is a branch of secular philosophy, it can become the base for a language about God intelligible in terms of ordinary experience. It thus provides the possibility of further meaningful theological elaboration based on revelation in a language in essential relation to the language we use in other areas of ordinary life. Without this relation of theological discourse through philosophy to ordinary experience, said these men, we cannot know what we *mean* when we use theological words; as subsequent events have shown, there is no question that they were right on this point.

(2) They maintained also that while such categories as, for example, personal freedom or "Thouness" are applicable to God, the *essential* way to speak of God is in terms of Being, to be understood as the pure act of existing; and correspondingly, the most basic relation of God to the world for theology is not that of a personal manifestation of himself through his Word, but the relation of God as creative cause of being to his finite creatures. Thus God is here understood essentially in the traditional terms of Thomistic philosophical theology: as self-sufficient, perfect, and changeless actuality, as the transcendent though intentional cause of finite being, and as the redeeming source of saving grace in Incarnation, Ecclesia, and Sacrament. Here is the one place where both in its dogmatic form and in its philosophical and theological content, the traditional or classical idea of God has appeared in important twentieth-century theology. It was surely its consequent anachronistic character, both philo-

sophical and theological, that proved the abiding weakness of this view, for interested students had almost to become medieval men in order to find its theological arguments convincing or its philosophical categories meaningful. And in recent days few in either form of Catholicism felt themselves willing or able thus to step back in time.

The other important tradition during this period was represented by the continuation of the process theology developed at the end of the nineteenth and the beginning of the twentieth century. The most important leaders of this Whiteheadian philosophy were the philosopher Charles Hartshorne and the theologian H. N. Wieman. Like their Thomistic rivals, this group emphasized, over against the neo-orthodox, the absolute need of a philosophical or metaphysical base for a valid concept of God. In order, they said, to make religious language intelligible to modern minds, in order to know what we mean when we speak of God's "person" or his "acts," and in order to validate religious belief's claim to truth in its statements, religious language must be translated into the terms of an appropriate modern philosophical system. While not disputing the reality of some form of revelation, this group tended, more than either neo-orthodoxy or Catholicism, to base its idea of God solely on natural experience and on philosophical reason; its theology was therefore almost all natural theology.

Despite their agreement with the Thomists on the need for philosophy, however, the *content* of their idea of God was radically opposed to the traditional theistic view. As with James and Whitehead, the God they found metaphysically intelligible and "religiously worthy" was a finite God, one who has reciprocal, even internal (i.e., affecting *both* parties), relations with his creatures, and therefore one who is himself in the process of change and becoming as time unfolds. God here is both "creator" as the finite source of order, novelty, and therefore of value to the developing process, and also "redeemer" as the one everlasting and all-inclusive reality that feels, empathizes with, and so "loves" all creatures, and thus preserves their experience of value in his own. At two major points this view significantly departed from the traditional view: (1) God is not self-sufficient, changeless, omnipotent, or omniscient, nor is he the source of all aspects or factors in existence. On the contrary, he is *one* factor among others in an all-inclusive process, and thus his becoming itself is dependent on the free development of other entities in process over whom he has no essential or final control. (2) God has little if any judgmental role against sin, nor any role in redeeming the world from it. To be sure, he rescues his creatures from disorder, mediocrity, sameness, and above all from the fragmentariness of their being and the transcience of their values. But since no serious break with God in sin enters these predominantly metaphysical theologies, the God here pictured lacks the capacities either of radical judgment or of unmerited forgiveness and justification. In this sense this immanent, dynamic, finite, "loving" God is a legitimate heir of the liberal tradition of the nineteenth century, which repudiated God's wrath and emphasized only his positive relation to our values.

Finally, a brief word should be said about another vision of God in the twentieth century, partly because it was substantially different from the other three and attacked by all of them, and because like them it promises to have its own influence on future theology. This is the idea of God in the work of Paul Tillich. A spiritual descendant of Schelling, Hegel, and Schleiermacher (rather than of Kant and the Ritschlians, as were the neo-orthodox), Tillich emphasized the immanence of God as the ground of finite being in all its aspects, as the unconditioned depth in which man's reason, his morals, his aesthetics, and his social and historical existence, as well as his personal life, have their origin and fulfillment. This God is not transcendent in the sense of being separate from or over against finite life; rather, as in Hegel, God is the dynamic, self-developing ground of natural and historical process, and of man's history as the microcosm and agent of that process. However, unlike his nineteenth-century romantic forebears, Tillich also was vividly aware of the estrangement and distortion of man's life. Consequently he held that man's being, his thinking, his morals, and his social and historical existence cannot fulfill themselves as they normally function but must find reintegration with the divine depths through revelation, the gift of faith, and the creation of a new spiritual community. Religion based on revelation, rather than being a lower stage than philosophy, is thus here the *answer* to the *questions* which secular human existence and so philosophy raise in their finitude and their distortion. Through this method of "correlation" this system united the secular and the transcendent, the profane and the sacred, but on a new basis more congenial to theology.

Tillich combined, therefore, several elements characteristic of the other competing twentieth-century schools. Like the process thinkers, he understood God philosophically in terms of ontological categories as well as biblically, for a philosophical understanding of the problems or questions of human existence for him paved the way to and so provided the categories for the religious answers of revelation. Like the neo-orthodox, he believed in an existentialist method in theology and in man's estrangement and separation from God, and thus in the relevance of revelation and grace if man is to be whole. And like the Thomists he understood God fundamentally as Being itself, which is the source and ground both of our own being and of its fulfillment. God to Tillich was thus the unconditioned dynamic power of being, positing creatures in and through his unfolding (and trinitarian) divine life, reuniting them to himself in the New Being (in Jesus as the Christ) in spiritual unity through the divine love. As in Schleiermacher, God here is only barely intentional and so hardly personal; nor, as the immanent ground of all we are and do, do we "encounter" him as judge over against us and as forgiveness towards us in quite the same way as in neo-orthodoxy. Nevertheless, Tillich expressed as fully as do any other modern theologies the dynamic, related, active character of deity; and yet at the same time he achieved a remarkably fruitful union of secular interests with a surprisingly faithful reformulation of traditional Christian symbols.

Insofar as they carried on debate with one another during the forty years or so from 1920 to 1960, these various groups—neo-orthodox, Thomist, and process—were involved in a strange sort of three-cornered war, for all alike attacked Tillich, who was part of no school. Although in fact they were all about equally diverse, each of these three groups tended to emphasize one or two aspects which the other two held in common, and thus to regard both of the others as similarly deluded. For example, neo-orthodoxy, emphasizing a revelational method in theology above all else, regarded the Thomists and the process thinkers as essentially alike because both were *philosophical* theologies, based on metaphysical inquiry and so on what revelationists called a purely human wisdom. And it criticized both accordingly as producing speculative, uninvolved, impersonal, and therefore idolatrous concepts of God quite unrelated to the transcendent, self-manifesting Thou of the Bible who is known only through his Word in history and encountered only in personal commitment, faith, and obedience. The Thomists on the other hand tended to see in the other two only the rejection of traditional "Greek" elements and their common affirmation of strange, modern, and so dynamic and related attributes of God. Consequently Thomists bemoaned in their rivals the lack of the classical Aristotelian epistemology and the ontological notions of being, aseity, necessity, and changelessness. After all, Oscar Cullman's denial on biblical grounds of the divine eternity and his affirmation of exclusively temporal traits in God was not all *that* dissimilar from Whitehead's philosophical temporalizing of God into an entity who "becomes" as do all other entities! Finally, the process theologians, interested primarily

in the ontological problems of the finitude of God and his reciprocal relations to other creatures, saw only what they called the "absolutistic" characteristics of, say, Barth's free God and Gilson's pure Being, and so regarded Protestant neo-orthodoxy and Catholic Thomism alike as repetitions of a classical theism whose God is transcendent, self-sufficient, and essentially independent of his creatures. With regard to the difficulties raised by the secular vision of things and so of atheism, with which the theological fraternity as a whole was increasingly faced in the twentieth century, each group proclaimed the other two vulnerable (and itself invulnerable) because of that particular characteristic which the others shared in common. The neo-orthodox blamed theology's woes on the injection of speculation and so of secular philosophy (the word of man) into theology on the part of the other two; the Thomists blamed the same woes on those modernizing tendencies that had weakened the true and strong concepts of traditional theism; and the process theologians blamed our problems on anachronistic characteristics of traditional, "absolutistic" concepts of God which, said they, had no meaning for the modern man. As recent events have shown, each was right in asserting that the other two were in deep trouble, but each was quite wrong in believing that his own view alone was secure against the acids of modernity.

This debate about the way we should talk of God (whether by revelation or by philosophical inquiry) and the character of this object of theological discourse (whether God be a transcendent, personal, free, dynamically active Thou; a transcendent, changeless, pure Actuality; or an immanent, finite, related, and developing process) went on somewhat serenely until relatively recently, about 1960. Then almost without warning a change occurred. Each of the three groups found itself radically questioning its own presuppositions about God, and then suddenly each of these groups appeared to lose its sustaining power and seemed almost to evaporate before our eyes. Briefly what happened was that instead of asking about *how* we are to speak of God, theologians suddenly found themselves wondering *whether* they could speak of him at all in a secular age—and this, as they discovered, was a much more radical and explosive question to ponder.

The symbol, if not the precipitating cause, of this sudden change was the appearance of the "God-is-dead" or "radical" theologies. These were "theologies"—of William Hamilton, T. J. Altizer, Paul Van Buren, and the Rabbi Richard Rubenstein—which sought in quite varied ways to give an interpretation of authentic Christianity (or Judaism in the case of Rubenstein) which did not use, and so clearly rejected,

363

the idea of God. It now seems that on its positive side this effort did not succeed; any interpretation of Christianity or of Judaism without God is in all probability neither systematically intelligible nor religiously viable. However, the reasons given by these men for their rejection of the idea of God remain immensely important, for they reflect the final entrance of the fully developed secularity of modern cultural life—whose first steps we noted in our discussion of the Enlightenment—into the ecclesiastical and so into the theological and clerical life of the mid-twentieth century. The problems that led these men to disbelieve in God and to abjure him from their Christianity are the same problems that are felt by all modern Christians and which in turn provide contemporary theologians with their major difficulties.

Briefly, the difficulties or crises that led these theologians to proclaim the "death of God" were four: (1) for Hamilton, the presence and certitude of inner faith were too unsure to allow him as a contemporary man to say on the *basis* of his faith either that God is or what he is; faith seemed no longer free enough of doubt to provide a basis for knowledge of God. (2) For Altizer, modern culture and so any contemporary man who expresses its mood, finds the transcendent God both unreal and repressive, a threat to our human creativity, authenticity, and freedom; only, said he, if we dare to declare this transcendent God dead and cease to depend on him, can we appropriate the divine that is immanent in us in the Living Word that always changes its forms. (3) For Van Buren, a secular culture finds only those words which relate to and can be verified in actual, daily experience to be intelligible, or, technically put, only empirical propositions are meaningful and therefore have the capacity of being true. God, as understood either theologically or metaphysically, is not a possible subject of such empirical propositions, and therefore in our age "God" (as anything more than a word for our ideals) is no longer a meaningful symbol. (4) For Rubenstein, the horrors of the twentieth century, especially the murder of six million Jews, make it impossible and immoral to believe that the covenant God, the God of Israel and the benign Ruler of history, exists. To hold that he *willed* this carnage is impossible—the Jews were not *that* guilty; to believe on the other hand that he did *not* will it is to make a mockery both of his rule in history and of his interest in the Jews. Far better to hold with Albert Camus that men suffer because existence and history are inherently absurd (i.e., godless) than because they themselves are guilty. Whether or not these various caveats *should* have had argumentative power in theology is perhaps a question; but that they did in fact strike home with many clergymen,

laymen, and theologians is not to be doubted, and indicates how widely shared was the secular mood which they expressed.

These "radical" theologians have been raising the question whether God can be intelligibly and meaningfully conceived or spoken of by contemporary men, and, while each wishes to retain his relation to his own religious community, all feel that "no" is the only honest answer to this basic theologial question. If we ask why theologians today are for the first time in Judeo-Christian history raising *this* question and giving *this* answer, we must reply that it is the secular spirit permeating our culture—and so ourselves—that forces this question on all of us, and that expresses itself in each of the objections these radicals have uttered. This "spirit," which practically defines the most fundamental attitudes of our present culture, may be described as follows: (1) only the contingent, temporal, natural world of relative creatures is real; only finite natural causes are effective; and only empirical propositions are indicative. (2) As a consequence, if contingency is all there is, there is in the wider cosmic environment of man neither an eternal order nor a benevolent purpose: things *are* merely because they are, and for no other reason or purpose. (3) Therefore, the only grounds for hope and meaning in life lie in human autonomy, in man's intelligence and moral will. The suddenly current phrase, "God is dead," means in effect that the cosmos is blind and empty of meaning; the complementary phrase, "Man is on his own," means that whatever meanings history is to manifest must be created by man himself. Almost every major form of modern philosophy—naturalism, positivism, most ordinary language analysis, and existentialism—reflects this disenchanted, critical, or "secular" view of man's wider environment and this corresponding belief in man's autonomy.

It is this cluster of views, permeating religious as well as secular minds, that has challenged so pointedly not only the traditional idea of God characteristic of the seventeenth century, but also those reformulations of that idea which, as we have traced, have appeared in the nineteenth and twentieth centuries. For inevitably in such a secularly apprehended world, talk in the Catholic mode of a transcendent, changeless, timeless, perfect Being, in the neo-orthodox mode of a transcendent, active, yet hidden Ruler of history, or in the process mode of an everlasting Orderer of things, creative and then retentive of value, will seem problematic and difficult at best, and empty and irrelevant at worst. Speaking methodologically, as current forms of philosophy show, such a mood has made metaphysical speculation virtually impossible; metaphysics "died" among the dominant philosophies of the West over fifty years before the death of God was widely reported in theology. Consequently the metaphysical bases for the notion of God, championed by Thomist and by process theologians alike, have largely evaporated. Correspondingly, to the secular minds of modern churchmen, faith as a response to scriptural revelation cannot help but seem infinitely precarious and subject to doubt; especially is this so if that "faith" is related to none of the other empirical and secular modes of thought characteristic of our daily life. Consequently a neo-orthodox theology based alone on the Word and on faith has seemed in the last decade unable to provide a solid ground for the idea of God.

Theology since 1960 has, therefore, been in a state of disruption about its own most basic possibilities. Much like its sister, philosophy—who shortly before had almost abdicated her ancient role of *knowing*— theology has been forced to wonder if it can do what it had always supposed that it could do, namely, to speak about God. As we have noted, this is a new and much more radical question than the one debated earlier, *how* we are to speak of God, through science, philosophy, revelation, or faith. Consequently, none of the schools trained in the early twentieth-century debate seemed immediately able to deal with this new question: Thomistic and organismic theologies had to assume the possibility of metaphysics, and neo-orthodoxy had to assume the presence of faith. If neither could be assumed, as seemed to be the case in a secular age, then how *was* theology to begin, and how were knowledge and certainty about God to be reached? The number of theologians in the late 1960's who have as a result of those questions found themselves forced basically to reexamine their views about theology and about God, and even radically to change both, is astounding.

The result is that contemporary theology, conscious of the brooding presence of radical doubt both without and within, presents a very fluid and confused picture with regard to the idea of God, a picture in which no clear constructive position has yet appeared. Clearly the most confused group, and yet that with perhaps the most creative possibilities, is the Roman Catholic. In this same half decade Roman Catholic theologians have had to deal with two severe crises, crises which had appeared in Protestant history benevolently stretched out over two hundred years. The first of these is the challenge to the traditional structure of Catholic theology. Begun, as we have noted, in the eighteenth and nineteenth centuries, this challenge has two aspects: on the formal side it questions the possibility in the modern age of the absolute ecclesiastical and scriptural authorities of classical theology; on the material side it questions the intelligibility to the modern

mind of the transcendent, changeless, necessary, perfect Being of classical speculative theology. For some twenty years, and especially since Vatican II, the effects of this long-term and very profound onslaught on traditional Catholic theology have been increasingly felt. And consequently a great deal of present Roman Catholic thought represents a radical movement away from an authoritarian dogmatic theological stance and from traditional Thomist categories, toward a modern, existential, "internal" stance and toward Hegelian, Heideggerian, Whiteheadian, even "biblical" categories: Fathers Karl Rahner and Edward Schillebeecx, Leslie Dewart, and a host of others represent this basic attack from the point of view of modern theology on the traditional forms of Catholic theology. But back of this argument, essentially one between the eighteenth and the nineteenth centuries, hovers the newer twentieth-century problem; namely, Can a modern secular man speak of God at all—whether in traditional *or* in modern ways? Thus every present Roman Catholic theological construction is forced into two battles at once: against conservative traditionalism on the one hand, and against an even more potent atheism on the other. If they are not aware of this *dual* necessity, and regard the debate as merely a new form of that between the ancients and the moderns, then their theological proposals, while possibly creative with regard to clerical *aggiornamento,* will probably fail to answer the most important questions about God which Catholic youth is raising.

Continental Protestant theology, continuing in much diluted form the tradition of biblical neo-orthodoxy, is, it seems, even more unaware than is Catholic theology of its real situation. Although it has continued to do excellent biblical and historical work, and although it has undoubtedly produced creative reinterpretations of Revelation as the Word-event resulting in faith (in Heinrich Ott, Klaus Fuchs, and Gerhard Ebeling), of Christology and the relation of salvation to history (in Wolfhart Pannenberg), and of eschatology in relation to revolutionary history (in Jürgen Moltmann), Continental theology has so far ignored the most basic twentieth-century questions about the reality of God and the possibility of meaningful talk about him. Rarely is there discussion of the grounds either for our faith in God or for any knowledge of him in terms of our ordinary experience. Theological concentration continues to focus, as it has since Bultmann, on logically subsidiary problems in theology, such as Revelation and Scripture, Jesus and his relation to Christology, and the meanings for us of biblical eschatology, and so it remains exclusively confined within the circle of traditional biblical assumptions and questions.

In an age when at its most "religious" our culture

is asking if it makes any sense to speak at all of God, these theologies proceed on the assumption that the modern churchman already acknowledges a divine Revelation, an inspired Scripture, and so possesses not painful questions but a quite undoubting faith! In such a situation, if theology cannot specify what sorts of meanings all of this language has in relation to ordinary experience—how, in other words, the divine dimension itself, represented by the symbol God, fits into our secular apprehension of existence—then theological language, however "biblical," about the divine Word, about the Christ-event, and about God's eschatological promises will remain empty and meaningless.

Probably because it has traditionally been much more aware of the moods of its secular context, current American theology presented in the 1960's the most enigmatic and fluid picture of all. The secular acids we have described have dissolved for many their certainty about the two starting points available for speaking about God: Revelation and metaphysical speculation. The result is that younger theologians have been driven to the immediacy of pre-thematic experience itself in order to see there how and on what grounds they can dare begin to use religious language. In this search, which each carries on in his own way, there are appearing a few common or shared interests. One is a usage of both linguistic and phenomenological philosophical tools for the exploration of ordinary experience, and the other is agreement that it is the "sacred" or some such category which is the object of this inquiry. Such an inquiry is not a traditional natural theology in the sense that it seeks to provide a philosophical proof of the reality of "God" as Christians know him; it is, however, a secular or neutral prolegomenon to theology, essential insofar as it reveals those contours or regions of ordinary experience to which our religious language applies and in relation to which theological words have meaning and relevance.

If it be in fact the case, that man, even in a secular age, is a religious being, in essential relation to a dimension of ultimacy and sacrality in all that he is and does, then a *purely* secular use of language, dependent on an exhaustively secular understanding of man, and a faith, however touching, solely in human autonomy, will in the end break down. The sacred dimension grounding all the aspects of ordinary life is what Christians, in their own symbolic terms and because of their own unique experiences in their historic community, term "God." A secular culture has tended to lose touch with these depths of its existence, and consequently the idea of God has, as our survey has shown, not only been radically refashioned, but has also tended to dissolve into emptiness. Our culture can be strengthened and refreshed if it learns again to make contact with these grounds of its being, its order, and its hope, and so to reappropriate in modern and relevant forms the classic symbols of religious discourse, of which the central, unifying symbol is that of God.

BIBLIOGRAPHY

Eighteenth and Nineteenth Centuries. G. W. F. Hegel, *Lectures on the Philosophy of Religion*, 3 vols. (New York, 1962; reprint, 1968). Immanuel Kant, *Religion Within the Limits of Reason Alone* (Chicago, 1934; new ed., New York, 1960). Albrecht B. Ritschl, *Die christliche Lehre von der Rechtfertigung und Versöhnung*, 3 vols. (Bonn, 1870–74), esp. Vol. III, trans. H. R. Mackintosh and A. B. Macauley as *Critical History of the Christian Doctrine of Justification and Reconciliation* (Edinburgh and New York, 1872–1900). F. Schleiermacher, *On Religion: Speeches to its Cultured Despisers*, trans. John Oman (London, 1893; New York, 1958).

Early Twentieth Century. Gustaf Aulen, *Faith of the Christian Church*, rev. ed. (Philadelphia, 1961). Karl Barth, *The Epistle to the Romans*, 6th ed., trans. Edwyn C. Hoskyns (London and New York, 1933). Emil Brunner, *Dogmatics*, Vol. I, *The Christian Doctrine of God* (Philadelphia, 1950; 1962). Austin Farrer, *Finite and Infinite*, 2nd ed. (New York, 1959). Étienne Gilson, *The Unity of Philosophical Experience* (New York, 1937; also reprint). Charles Hartshorne, *Man's Vision of God and the Logic of Theism* (Hamden, Conn., 1941). Jacques Maritain, *The Degrees of Knowledge*, Vol. II, 4th ed. (New York, 1959). Eric L. Mascall, *He Who Is* (New York, 1943). Reinhold Niebuhr, *The Nature and Destiny of Man*, Vols. I and II (New York, 1949; 1964). Paul Tillich, *Systematic Theology*, Vols. I, II, and III (Chicago, 1951; 1967). A. N. Whitehead, *Process and Reality* (Cambridge and New York, 1929; New York, 1967).

Contemporary. Thomas J. Altizer, *The Gospel of Christian Atheism* (Philadelphia, 1966). Leslie Dewart, *The Future of Belief* (New York, 1966). William Hamilton, *The New Essence of Christianity* (New York, 1961). Karl Rahner, *Hearers of the Word* (New York, 1969). Richard Rubenstein, *After Auschwitz* (Indianapolis, 1966). Paul Van Buren, *The Secular Meaning of the Gospel* (New York, 1963).

General Surveys. Karl Barth, *Protestant Thought: From Rousseau to Ritschl* (New York, 1959). James Collins, *God in Modern Philosophy* (Chicago, 1959; also reprint). Peter Gay, *The Enlightenment: An Interpretation* (New York, 1966). John Herman Randall, Jr., *The Making of the Modern Mind*, rev. ed. (Boston, 1940).

LANGDON GILKEY

[See also **Agnosticism;** Buddhism; **Christianity;** Deism; Evil; **Evolutionism; Existentialism;** Faith; Hegelian . . . ; **Holy;** Positivism; Progress; Reformation; Sin and Salvation.]

CONCEPT OF GOTHIC

IN CURRENT usage the term "Gothic" has two main applications: (1) to a Germanic tribe that played a major role in the dismemberment of the Roman Empire in the fourth and fifth centuries of our era, and (2) to the last of the great medieval styles of art and architecture, flourishing chiefly from the mid-twelfth through the fifteenth century. (Note that the use of Gothic as a term of stylistic analysis is restricted to modern times; it was not so employed during the medieval period itself.) Apart from these well-defined and seemingly unrelated current senses, scholarly and polemical writings from the fifteenth through the nineteenth century reveal a surprisingly wide range of meanings, most of them now surviving in at best shadowy form—though they once had far-reaching implications for aesthetics, political thought, and social customs. In fact the two currently accepted senses may be likened to modern towns built on very old sites, with the present urban pattern overlying successive strata of earlier development and with the roads and tracks which linked the two sites in former times just discernible.

Historically, two great trends—ethnological and critical-aesthetic—have conditioned the growth of the idea of the Gothic. The first trend is a body of ethnological and historical speculation combining the preservation of authentic traditions with fanciful embroidery based on a defective philological method. In the Middle Ages the term Goth served—as it still does today—to designate the Germanic tribal group that migrated into Spain, southwestern France, and Italy in the late phase of the Roman Empire. In addition, however, through confusion with the Getae, a historically distinct group, its scope was extended to the inhabitants of Scandinavia, which was sometimes regarded as the original home of the larger amalgam. This extension figures prominently in the sixth century in the *Gothic History* of Jordanes, who denied it from Orosius and Cassiodorus. Another source, a ninth-century vernacular rendering of Bede, was to lead seventeenth-century English students of Anglo-Saxon language and literature to a further amplification, identifying the Goths with the Jutes who had settled in southern England. Thus the Old English dictionary compiled by William Somner (*Dictionarium Saxino-Latino-Anglicum*, Oxford, 1649) defines *Gothi* as "Jutes, Getae, Gothes." Through this process of identification the scope of the term Goth expanded enormously: geographically, to the borders of the Germanic world in Scandinavia and its offshoots in Iceland and Greenland, as well as to England; and temporally, reaching early modern times so that, for example, it seemed natural to hail the seventeenth-century Swedish king Gustavus Adolphus as a paragon of the Gothic virtues.

The second main trend appearing in writings on the historical evolution of the Gothic idea is a value judgment. Gothic appears as a pejorative label for medieval traits and customs considered outworn and repugnant.

Not only were the Goths lumped together with the Vandals and Huns as destroyers of classical Mediterranean civilization, but they were also held to have played a further disastrous role in the creation of the bastard culture that took its place. Thus Gothic came to be employed to designate bad taste in general.

In the discussion that follows other factors will emerge, but the main development results from the interweaving of the ethnological and aesthetic trends. Paradoxically, Gothic is and is not equivalent to medieval *tout court*, and the connotations associated with it are complex, so much so that they seem at times to defy exact definition. In order to bring out the variety of nuances it has sometimes been necessary to depart from a strictly chronological exposition in the following account, which stresses the critical-aesthetic trend at the outset, then the ethnological.

1. The Renaissance Tradition: "Gothic Barbarism." The pejorative use of the term "Gothic," which was dominant in modern times at least until the late eighteenth century, depended on a three-stage concept of history apparently first adumbrated by Petrarch, and then elaborated and diffused by Filippo Villani, Leone Battista Alberti, and other Italian humanists of the Renaissance. According to this concept two periods of cultural excellence—classical antiquity and the nascent modern era—flank a dark chasm of ignorance and barbarism, the Middle Ages. The Italian scholars blamed the Germanic invaders for this catastrophe. In two areas of cultural development—handwriting and architecture—they specifically emphasized the pernicious role of the Goths. Lorenzo Valla, whose anti-medieval attitude is exemplified in his best-known achievement, the exposure of the "Donation of Constantine" as a forgery, condemned the "monkish" Black Letter script as Gothic, a designation which serves to distinguish late medieval script from the Carolingian and Renaissance hands that precede and follow it. (In Germany a version of Gothic script, termed *Fraktur*, survived in printed books into the twentieth century.) Valla also suggested that the Goths were responsible for the decay of the Latin language. From this usage the term could be extended, as by François Rabelais, to condemn a coarse and rustic literary style, i.e., one employed by writers insufficiently disciplined by study of good Greek and Latin models. Yet the most influential pejorative use of the Gothic idea is due to the reflections on architecture of the art historian Giorgio Vasari. In his *Lives of the Architects, Painters and Sculptors* (1550), Vasari generally follows his fifteenth-century predecessors Manetti and Filarete in designating medieval architecture as simply "German" (*tedesco*). On several occasions, however, he attributes it specifically to the Goths (though he does not use the adjectival form *gotico*, only the noun). Vasari condemns medieval architecture as disorderly, mean, overdecorated, and flimsy in appearance. The architectural style presumably introduced by the Goths was thus synonymous with a whole array of faults of taste, standing at the opposite pole from the classical style, which was held to be a universally valid model.

In the seventeenth century Vasari's polemic was echoed in transalpine Europe, not only by specialist writers on the visual arts such as Sir Henry Wotton and Joachim von Sandrart, but also by poets such as John Dryden and Molière. The last-named author, for example, in his poem "La Gloire du Val-de-Grâce," inveighs against the *fade goust des ornamens gothiques* ("outmoded taste for Gothic ornamentation"). All these writers used the adjective Gothic—first attested in 1610 in this sense—as a matter of course, discarding the older term "German," possibly because of the chance of confusion with modern Germany where cultivated taste had long since rallied to the classical ideal. Moreover, the characteristic seventeenth- and eighteenth-century doctrine of the parallel of the arts invited the extension of the pejorative connotation of Gothic to other media besides architecture. Charles Dufresnoy (1611–88), in a posthumously published tract which was to enjoy great popularity, *De arte graphica*, applied the idea to painting. In France this approach struck deep roots: in 1757 the *Encyclopédie* defined Gothic painting as *un genre de peinture aux formes grêles et raides* ("a style of painting with harsh and rigid forms"), a judgment frequently echoed down to the first decades of the nineteenth century.

Literature, however, provided the largest arena for the search for Gothic aberrations, though it is notable that the parallel with architecture is never far out of mind, witness John Dennis' disapproving remarks on the state of English literature in his day (1701): "While the French reformed the structure of their poems by the noble models of ancient architecture, . . . we resolved . . . to adhere to our Gothic and barbarous manner." The attractions of the parallel were, of course, enhanced by the vogue among the nobility of the Grand Tour, in which examples of ancient and modern classical architecture were carefully inspected with a view to the cultivation of taste in general. In literature, apart from the broad condemnation of rustic modes already found in Rabelais, more specific features, correctly or incorrectly traced to medieval sources, were exposed to pillory as Gothic faults. Poets, for example, were admonished to cast off "Gothic rhyme" and turn instead to blank verse, which was held to be more in accord with the precepts of the ancients. This admonition may be traced back as far as Roger Ascham's *Scholemaster* (1570), and Jean-Antoine de Baïf's *Étrennes de poésie* (1574). And in

England admirers of Tasso, Ariosto, Spenser, and other supposedly medievalizing epic poets had to cope with the charge that these works were hopelessly marred by fanciful and chivalrous elements redolent of lingering Gothic taste.

In the work of some critics the idea of the Gothic escaped entirely from its historical moorings so that phenomena we now would term baroque—Italian opera, the architecture of Francesco Borromini, and the complex metaphors of metaphysical poetry—are tarred with the Gothic brush. In this way the category of the Gothic could merge with that of the bizarre or grotesque. Oddly enough, even the geometric gardens of the Renaissance incurred censure as Gothic by Bishop Richard Hurd (1719–1808) and other enthusiasts for the freer and more "natural" art of English landscaping. These writers were, of course, unaware that this trend in gardening, as Arthur O. Lovejoy has shown (*Essays . . .* , pp. 136–65), was a subversive intrusion, a harbinger of a new aesthetic orientation that was, among other things, to achieve the rehabilitation and even for a time the exaltation of the Gothic.

In England such social customs as duelling and hunting were denigrated as survivals from the era of Gothic darkness. In some eighteenth-century writers the adjective is often reduced to an epithet meaning simply "old-fashioned" or "countrified," as in Oliver Goldsmith's *She Stoops to Conquer* (1773), where Mrs. Hardcastle, a self-proclaimed lady of fashion, complains ironically of the "Gothic vivacity" (i.e., dullness) of her husband, a conservative country squire.

Gradually, then, the idea of the Gothic broadened to embrace almost any fault of taste, ranging from a harmless social gaffe to the crudest barbarity. Paradoxically, Gothic aberration might stem not solely from rusticity and lack of cultivation but also from perverse overrefinement, as in the phenomena we now generally regard as baroque. Thus the sanity of the classical golden mean stood between the opposing menaces of the Gothic Scylla and the Gothic Charybdis.

2. Positive Undercurrents. In this torrent of abuse two underground trends of more positive character still emerge, one in England, the other in Spain—two countries which have always been somewhat peripheral to the main currents of European civilization, but thereby more open to innovation. It was noticed by English defenders of parliamentary rights as against the presumed monarchic encroachments of seventeenth-century Stuart absolutism that the institutions of representative government did not in fact stem from the much lauded era of classical antiquity. Even Tacitus, that haughty Roman, could be summoned to testify to the claims of the Germanic tribes to priority in the invention of this institution. Thus according to the

Parliamentarians, the Germanic peoples of northern Europe had an inbred disposition to free institutions in ineradicable opposition to tyranny and privilege.

This happy trait of the northern peoples, as contrasted with their less fortunate Mediterranean counterparts, was sometimes designated "Gothic balance," "Gothic government," or "Gothic polity." As Algernon Sidney remarks, "All the northern nations, which upon the dissolution of the Roman Empire possessed the best provinces that had composed it [sic], were under that form which is usually called the Gothic polity: They had king, lords, commons, diets, assemblies of estates, cortez and parliaments in which the sovereign power of these nations did reside, and by which they were exercised" (*Discourses concerning Government*, London, 1698). In the seventeenth century English interest in the national past was not restricted to political theory, nor was it confined to any particular group—it spread into various circles concerned with diverse realms of enquiry: royalist and parliamentarian, Puritan and Catholic, aristocratic and popular. As a result the English did great service in pioneering in the exploration of various aspects of the constellation that historically makes up the phenomenon of Gothic. This cultural nationalism stimulated enthusiasm for the Anglo-Saxon (or Old English) language, as exemplified by the production of various dictionaries and philological treatises, an activity that spread to the Continent in the first edition of the Stockholm fragment of Bishop Ulphilas' fourth-century version of the Bible in the Gothic language (Dordrecht, 1665), prepared by Franciscus Junius, who had been the Earl of Arundel's librarian. Furthermore, attention was directed to the surviving monuments in stone: the cathedrals and other buildings of medieval England. The three volumes of William Dugdale and Roger Dodsworth's *Monasticon anglicanum* (1654–73) constitute, as Paul Frankl (1960) has remarked, the "first illustrated architectural history of a medieval style," though not surprisingly they provide little hint of the various ramifications of the style.

Not long after, however, the architect Sir Christopher Wren was to evolve, despite his primary allegiance to the Renaissance tradition, a perceptive account of the style and even to practice actual building in a late Gothic mode that anticipated K. F. Schinkel, A. W. N. Pugin, and others. (It is significant that Wren's Saracenic theory of the origin of the style, while mistaken, has been revived by serious writers of the mid-twentieth century.) The English state of awareness contrasts with the fantastic approach to the Gothic style that generally (though not invariably) prevailed across the channel, where alchemical, astro-

logical, and generically hermetic explanations were in vogue, as exemplified by Gobineau de Montluisant's *Explication très curieuse des énigmes et figures hiéroglyphiques . . . de Notre-Dame de Paris* (Paris, 1640). This hermetic approach to Gothic monuments was to resurface in Victor Hugo's popular novel *Notre-Dame de Paris* (1831) and, a century later, in *Le Mystère des cathédrales* (Paris, 1925, and later editions) by an occultist who called himself Fulcanelli.

Other temptations, however, lay in wait for seventeenth- and eighteenth-century Englishmen who boldly sought to explore the Gothic *terra incognita*. Apart from the understandable temptation to exalt Gothic as a purely national achievement, it could also be viewed as a response to the salutary rigors of the northern climate, thus resembling Arnold J. Toynbee's later concept of "challenge and response." In this way the ground was laid for the later notion of "Nordic" culture traits as contrasted with outworn, indeed decadent Mediterranean values. In the earlier period of English investigation and theorizing, however, the need to defend the so-called "Gothic balance" and related phenomena greatly diminished after the Glorious Revolution of 1688 and the establishment of the Hanoverian Dynasty in 1714. In the nineteenth century, however, the notion was to enjoy a new lease on life in the work of such historians as Edward Augustus Freeman and John Richard Green, who traced the progressive institutions of Victorian England to the country's remote medieval past.

In Spain, the second exceptional country, the presumed Visigothic origin of the nobility led to much speculation, ethnic, political, and social. In his *De rebus Hispaniae* (1243) Archbishop Rodrigo of Toledo used Jordanes to prove that the Spanish Goths were related to the inhabitants of Gothia in Scandinavia. This connection was repeated and embroidered by later Spanish writers, contributing to an amusing imbroglio at the Council of Basel (1431–49), where the Scandinavian and Spanish delegates disputed over precedence on the grounds of Gothic lineage. Gradually there developed an extension of the meaning of the noun *godo* ("Goth") to signify "noble, well-born, illustrious" (attested as early as 1490). In Spanish sixteenth- and seventeenth-century authors the term acquired an ironic twist, as in the expression *hacerse de los godos* ("to claim nobility, to put on airs"). And it is significant that the art theorist Vicente Carducho in his *Diálogos de la pintura* (1633), while condemning Gothic architecture in the wake of Giorgio Vasari, takes pains to point out that this degenerate mode was created by the Ostrogoths of Italy and not by the revered Spanish Visigoths. In Spain, then, the concept of the Gothic is bound up with the emergence of a peculiar sense of national

369

distinctiveness, for which Cervantes' Don Quixote stands, in some respects, as the archetypal figure.

3. Pre-romanticism and the "Gothic Mood." The positive sub-trends just mentioned were but exceptions that proved the rule, for in the seventeenth and eighteenth centuries the general attitude to the idea of the Gothic was overwhelmingly pejorative. The true basis for a revaluation of the idea was laid in a series of far-reaching changes in taste that developed primarily in England (if present-day scholarship is correct) and then spread to the Continent. This shift in taste presupposed a loosening of the bonds of normative classicism with its insistence on qualities of clarity, regularity, and symmetry—qualities often exemplified, as has been noted, by reference to concrete architectural models. The shift was achieved by a gradual redefinition of the pivotal concept of Nature, which had hitherto been monopolized by the classicists. Partly as a result of the influence of the new fashion for English landscape gardening, writers began to emphasize that irregularity and variety were inseparable from any adequate concept of Nature. Ultimately, these aspects were subsumed under the general rubric of "the Picturesque," which was popularized by William Gilpin (1724–1804). A related aesthetic concept, that of the Sublime, assumed a pole of sensory experience, strongly tinged with emotional expectancy, that was very different from its opposite, the Beautiful. From this it was but a step (though many, because of the prestige of classical normative concepts, refused to take it) to identifying the Beautiful with the classical, the Sublime with the nonclassical. In this way the tables could be turned, and Nature in its highest sense (the Sublime) be linked to a departure from the constraint of classical rules. In another direction, an ambiguous position developed from the association of the natural with the primitive or primordial, as in the work of the French architectural critic, the Abbé Marc-Antoine Laugier (1713–69). These various trends in taste are often linked with emergent romanticism and the whole vast movement is consequently termed "pre-romanticism."

Another major factor in the improved climate of response to the Gothic constellation is the growth of the trend towards aesthetic relativism. As Bishop Hurd asserted in 1762: "The Gothic architecture has its own rules by which when it comes to be examined, is seen to have its own merit, as well as the Grecian" (*Letters on Chivalry and Romance*, Letter VIII). Gradually and uncertainly there developed the conviction, by no means universally established even today, that every cultural manifestation deserves to be evaluated in terms of the conditions prevailing in the age in which it was produced, rather than being judged in advance in accordance with some predetermined external stand-

ard. Thus the rise of aesthetic pluralism is closely linked with the emergence of an appreciation for the phenomena previously denigrated as Gothic.

It is important to note, however, that this rehabilitation of Gothic was a complex process, developing in the later eighteenth century out of the mists of an aesthetic constellation known as the "Gothic mood." Throughout the eighteenth century—and even into the nineteenth as Michelet and Victor Hugo attest—exploration of Gothic themes continued to be tinged with an aura of the forbidden, the exotic, and the supernatural. Such preoccupations were certainly to the fore in the eighteenth-century fashion for graveyard or sepulchral verse compositions, sometimes simply called Gothic poetry. Such works as David Mallet's *The Excursion* (1726) and Thomas Warton's *The Pleasures of Melancholy* (1747) present lurid images of ghosts and owls infesting desolate moonlit landscapes punctuated by tombs and ruins. Later in the century the poems of "Ossian" with their evocation of a rude but noble society localized in a quintessentially northern setting were to bring this trend closer to the sphere of aesthetic primitivism. Since the Celts of the Ossianic poems were often wrongly annexed to the Germanic stock, it was a simple matter for Klopstock and others to enshrine Ossian in their pantheon of primordial Germanic antiquities. Another feature closely connected to this general complex is the so-called Gothic novel, the fashion for this term being launched by Horace Walpole's sensational *The Castle of Otranto: A Gothic Story* (1764).

Walpole is, of course, also significant for his interest in architecture, evidenced notably by the creation of that important landmark in the early development of the Gothic revival, Strawberry Hill, his country seat near London, where the new work began in 1750. This structure was, in all frankness, a somewhat flimsy and unconvincing exercise, and the host of English garden pavilions that followed in its wake deserve little better than to be called sham Gothic. Yet the eighteenth century indubitably saw the beginnings of the first genuine efforts to grapple with the problem of giving a firm theoretical basis to the understanding of Gothic architecture.

One of the most important lines of development in this effort to achieve theoretical justification was to trace Gothic building practices to a conscious imitation of plant forms, especially trees (an idea that, incidentally, was broached as early as 1510 by an anonymous writer, the pseudo-Raphael, in a report to Pope Leo X on the antiquities of Rome, and then apparently forgotten). In 1751 Bishop Warburton developed at some length the idea that the Goths who had been accustomed to worship in sacred groves were subsequently impelled to give their permanent religious shrines the appearance of an avenue of trees. This supposed origin of Gothic architecture, actually devoid of any historical foundation, was nonetheless important for the eighteenth century because it suggested a link between Gothic and the mysterious fecundity of Nature. Apart from such explanations, Gothic might also be made more palatable by reforming it so as to bring the style at least within hailing distance of classical respectability. Thus an "improved" Gothic, suitably pruned and chastened, could be exhibited as virtually the peer of the classical orders, just as long before the Italian Tuscan order had been cleaned up to take its place among the other orders of pure Greek lineage. This reform was primarily accomplished by the brothers Batty and Thomas Langley in their *Ancient* [i.e., Gothic] *Architecture Restored and Improved by Rules and Proportions* (London, 1742). The Langleys' presentation of Gothic as a separate order had been anticipated by Hans Vredeman de Vries' *Architectura* (Antwerp, 1565). Nonetheless, as has been noted, actual Gothic revival building of the eighteenth century remained trifling and largely unserious, flourishing alongside the ephemeral fashions for chinoiserie and arabesque.

4. The Apotheosis of Gothic. The nineteenth century was to see a complete reassessment of the qualities of Gothic architecture, for building now became the central concern of those who admired Gothic. For some enthusiasts a startling reversal of values occurred, and medieval architecture, at least in its culminating phases, was seen to tower immeasurably over the aesthetic muddle of Renaissance work. In the atmosphere of widespread disillusionment with the Enlightenment tradition and the complementary fascination with medieval civilization engendered by the romantic movement, Gothic architecture came to be regarded as a quintessential embodiment of true spiritual values— and specifically as the vehicle of the highest aspirations of the Christian religion. At the same time more attention was paid to the historical variations of medieval building. Gothic was clearly differentiated from the preceding Romanesque period, and its various phases clarified. The enthusiasm for Gothic architecture paralleled the glorifying of pre-Renaissance painting— the so-called taste for the primitives—which was especially promoted by English and German collectors, artists, and critics. This interest led to a great revival movement championed initially by the group of German brethren known as the Nazarenes (founded in 1809 as the Lukas-Brüder, or Guild of Saint Luke) who in Vienna and later in Rome tried to recapture the devotional purity and innocence of late medieval painting. The Nazarenes were followed at a distance

by analogous movements elsewhere, notably the Italian *purismo* and the English Pre-Raphaelite group.

The trend toward a revaluation of the architecture and painting of the Gothic era was furthered by a powerful impulse toward a return to traditional Christianity in the early nineteenth century. In fact, many of the key figures in this movement either were or became Roman Catholics. Enthusiasm for medieval antiquities was undeniably broadly diffused among the romantics; in 1832 Heinrich Heine went so far as to claim that romanticism was "nothing but the reawakening of the poetry of the Middle Ages, as it manifested itself in songs, sculptures and architecture, in art and life (V, 217). In some respects this enthusiasm for the Middle Ages and for Gothic architecture in particular was a matter of fashion: thus Parisian letters of 1834 record as superlatives current in the salons— alongside such curiosities as *pyramidale, babylonien,* and *apocalyptique*—the epithets *gothique, ogival,* and *flamboyant.* Yet in the long run the contribution of this enthusiasm, vague and unfocussed as it sometimes was, to the understanding of medieval architecture and the culture that produced it was enormous.

It is an ironic fact that a key role in the rehabilitation of the concept of the Gothic was played by a figure who later turned his back on the style and in fact on romanticism as a whole. Goethe's *Von deutscher Baukunst* (1772), written in a highly rhapsodic style, records the impact of Strasbourg Cathedral (or more precisely the structure's west façade) during Goethe's stay in the city. Despite the obscure circumstances of its publication, this pamphlet came to be cherished by all the principal German eulogists of Gothic during the romantic era as a manifesto of prime significance. Goethe likens the cathedral to a "tree of God," its marvelous wholeness accruing from the harmonious interaction of countless tiny details. The German poet's emphasis on the organic and living quality of the building was to evoke a powerful response among his younger contemporaries. At the same time, in his explicit polemic against the Abbé Laugier, whom Goethe unfairly pilloried as a typical representative of narrow French taste, he links his admiration for the cathedral with the burgeoning German effort to escape from French tutelage by rediscovering what would appear to be one of the great landmarks of the national past (actually Strasbourg Cathedral displays strong French influence).

Moreover, Goethe, in exalting the creative genius of the cathedral's architect Erwin von Steinbach, ignored the building's character as a product of medieval Christian ethos—quite apart from its national and personal affiliations. This broader aspect of Gothic architecture was, however, singled out a little later by the novelist Wilhelm Heinse whose diary of 1780 describes Milan Cathedral as "the most glorious symbol of the Christian religion that I have seen." The Christian and mystical character of Gothic architecture was strongly emphasized by the romantic critic and theorist Friedrich Wilhelm Schlegel, who is also responsible for diffusing the concept of Gothic architecture as the tangible expression of the Infinite, a view which had been adumbrated by the Englishman John Milner in 1800. The German enthusiasm for Gothic architecture, tinged as it was by national and Christian accents, culminated in the decision to complete Cologne Cathedral according to the thirteenth-century plans (1842).

It was the English, however, with their greater economic resources, who took the lead in the actual construction of Gothic revival buildings. Neo-Gothic structures erected in the first three decades of the nineteenth century varied considerably as to archaeological accuracy. Yet the gradual diffusion of illustrated handbooks assembled by such men as John Carter, John Britton, and Thomas Rickman permitted the architects to achieve a higher standard, while at the same time helping to educate public taste.

The Gothic revival movement found an eloquent champion in Augustus Welby Northmore Pugin, like Friedrich Schlegel a convert to Roman Catholicism. Apart from his emphasis on the essentially Christian character of Gothic building, Pugin is important for his early formulation of what was later to become the functionalist credo in architecture. At the beginning of *The True Principles of Pointed or Christian Architecture* (London, 1843), he laid down two guiding rules: (1) "That there should be no features about a building which are not necessary for convenience, construction or propriety," and (2) "that all ornament should consist of enrichment of the essential construction of a building." In addition, Pugin linked the understanding of Gothic architecture with the older idea that architecture was the direct outgrowth of a society; in the effort to return to Gothic standards no mere mechanical copying of Gothic forms could suffice, for what was needed was to recapture the spirit of medieval civilization in its entirety.

Pugin was an eloquent spokesman for two important doctrines, functionalism and the ethical evaluation of architecture, both founded on his personal view of the strengths of the Gothic style. The functionalist credo, transmitted by William Morris and the English Arts and Crafts Movement, was to come to fruition in the German Bauhaus and related and widespread twentieth-century trends. The ethical approach to architecture had a shorter efflorescence, mainly in the middle years of the nineteenth century when it was championed by

a host of writers associated with the Cambridge Camden Society. Echoes of this approach, and even dogmatic reformulations of it, are nonetheless occasionally found in later writers such as Ezra Pound; cf. his well-known usury Canto of 1937 (*Canto XLV*). The veritable Lucifer of the ethical approach, however, is John Ruskin, who despite his often strident advocacy of the merits of Gothic, weakened the force of the revival by various equivocations, among which was his glorification of the bastard Venetian Gothic, an alien model which undercut the claim of Gothic to eminence as the characteristically northern (and consequently English) style.

Despite these critical confusions, an enormous amount of building was done in the revived Gothic style, and the success of such nineteenth-century English Gothicists as the prolific Sir George Gilbert Scott, the sensitive George Edmund Street, and the forceful William Butterfield greatly assisted the emergence of analogous movements on the European Continent and in North America. In the United States, alongside much work that was imitative of the English and European examples, there developed an indigenous type of skyscraper Gothic, as exemplified by Cass Gilbert's Woolworth Building (1913) in New York. Perhaps the most creative figure to develop from the matrix of the Gothic revival was the Catalan architect Antonio Gaudì, for whom Gothic forms served as the starting point for bizarre and personal experiments. Moreover, beginning in the late nineteenth century the effects of faceting and fragmentation suggested by Gothic buildings attracted progressive painters in search of new principles of visual organization. Claude Monet's series on Rouen Cathedral was succeeded by cubist and expressionist interpretations of Gothic structures, such as those of Robert Delaunay, Lyonel Feininger, and Chaim Soutine. The impress of Gothic forms is also evident in the sets of German expressionist films, notably Robert Wiene's *Das Kabinett des Dr. Caligari* (1919). Incidentally, in Germany in the troubled times after World War I the Gothic cathedral might serve as a symbol of social reconciliation, as in Fritz Lang's film *Metropolis* (1925), where the representatives of capital and labor join at the end before a huge Gothic cathedral façade.

Paralleling the various efforts to make creative use of Gothic forms, however, were serious efforts to gain a better understanding of the principles, sources, and course of development of the style. Those following this approach, which Paul Frankl (1960) terms "the scholarly trend," could draw on a considerable body of antiquarian research, especially that accumulated in England from the mid-seventeenth century onwards. Jean-François Félibien des Avaux (1658–1733) had been exceptional in France (and elsewhere in Europe) in giving a clear statement of the difference between the light and elegant mode of building we now know as Gothic and the more massive work that had preceded it (*Recueil historique de la vie et des ouvrages des plus célèbres architectes,* Paris, 1687). This necessary distinction was at best fitfully observed in the following century, and one of the urgent tasks confronting nineteenth-century scholars was still to separate clearly Gothic architecture from the preceding style, which was baptized Romanesque (a term apparently invented independently about 1819 by William Gunn and Charles de Gerville). The true principles of the Gothic structural system were first elucidated by the German scholar Johannes Wetter, in a guide to Mainz Cathedral (1835). A little later his fellow countryman, Franz Mertens, conclusively demonstrated that the style had first appeared in France, at the Abbey of Saint-Denis, and not in Germany or England, as writers in these countries had chauvinistically assumed. In France the greatest theorist and historian of Gothic architecture was the brilliant and industrious Eugène-Emmanuel Viollet-le-Duc, who, benefitting from the labors of such archaeologists as Arcisse de Caumont and Alexandre de Laborde, worked out a prodigiously detailed account of the style, embodied in his *Dictionnaire raisonné de l'architecture française du XIe au XVIe siècle* (Paris, 1854–68), and *Entretiens sur l'architecture* (Paris, 1863–72), that remains unsurpassed. Viollet-le-Duc regarded Gothic architecture primarily as a system of equilibrium, and emphasized the rationality and economy of its procedures. His theories exercised a strong influence on nineteenth-century building in iron and steel, as seen, for example, in Gustave Eiffel's famous tower in Paris and in the work of Baron Victor Horta in Brussels. Viollet-le-Duc's rational approach to the interpretation of medieval buildings was, however, to receive severe criticism from Pol Abraham in *Viollet-le-Duc et le rationalisme médiéval* (Paris, 1934). Abraham considered the earlier scholar's method to be fantastic, a *mécanique romancée.* More specifically, Abraham denied the functional value of the rib; this debate, which involved many scholars in the interwar period, has not yet been conclusively resolved.

5. Aftermath. As the nineteenth century drew to a close enthusiasm for Gothic generally slackened, while at the same time the fashion for Gothic revival building yielded to new modes derived from Renaissance and baroque exemplars. Scholarly attention began to focus increasingly on a more careful examination of individual monuments and groups of monuments so as to define their status more exactly, a course that is still being fruitfully pursued in the 1970's. In the twentieth

century, however, there were renewed efforts to understand Gothic art and architecture as the products of a single essence of the civilization, thus harking back to the broader perspective of the seventeenth and eighteenth centuries. The German art historian Wilhelm Worringer, for example, advocated a semimystical conception of Gothic as the product of an inborn racial factor, the Nordic spirit (*Formprobleme der Gotik,* Munich, 1912). A more abstract concept was set forth by Dagobert Frey in his *Gotik und Renaissance* (Augsburg, 1929), where the key to the Gothic attitude is seen in the factor of succession as against simultaneity, which was supposed to have prevailed in the Renaissance. Frey's concept, though buttressed by many ingenious observations regarding such varied topics as mapmaking and stagecraft, is essentially unverifiable, as shown by the fact that it has been possible for Marshall McLuhan to maintain just the opposite, namely, that the era dominated by the principle of succession set in only with the spread of printing, i.e., after the effective end of the Gothic age. In a more restricted fashion Erwin Panofsky attempted a demonstration of the often mooted parallel between Gothic architecture and scholastic philosophy, but without success because of faulty methodology. It is significant that historians of music and literature, though often receptive to such art-historical concepts as mannerism and baroque, have generally ignored the concept of Gothic.

The inherent difficulty of reaching conclusions about such a broad and much contested concept as Gothic civilization may be illustrated by the thinking of Paul Frankl who devoted much of his long life to a tenacious effort to clarify just this problem. While Frankl eloquently affirmed his faith in the idea of Gothic Man (concretely symbolized for him in the figure of the suffering Jesus), he was forced to admit that even in his chosen sphere of architecture most castles built during the so-called Gothic period are decidedly un-Gothic in style. Thus the Gothic cannot be defended as a universally valid period concept even in architecture, but is only applicable to ecclesiastical buildings, their decoration, and sphere of influence.

In conclusion, attention must be drawn to two important results of the centuries-long quest for the meaning of the idea of the Gothic (apart, that is, from the incidental illumination it may offer to historians in search of bypaths relating to such concepts as classicism and the sublime). The first result is an elucidation of certain essential and original traits of medieval civilization—parliaments, the feudal system, special genres of lyric and epic poetry—even though none of these is normally termed Gothic nowadays. The second result is the enhanced understanding of Gothic art and architecture and its decoration. With its various phases and manifestations, especially in cathedral building, Gothic architecture is now generally recognized as one of the greatest creations of Western civilization.

BIBLIOGRAPHY

P. Frankl's vast *The Gothic: Literary Sources and Interpretations through Eight Centuries* (Princeton, 1960), contains much valuable material and a large bibliography, but is mainly concerned with architecture. A valuable pilot project spreading a wider net in a particular area is J. Haslag, *"Gothic" im siebzehnten und achtzehnten Jahrhundert* (Cologne and Graz, 1963).

The following list gives other useful studies. E. S. de Beer, "Gothic: Origin and Diffusion of the Term," *Journal of the Warburg and Courtauld Institutes*, **11** (1948), 143–62. Jan Białostocki, "Late Gothic: Disagreements about the Concept," *Journal of the British Archaeological Association*, **29** (1966), 76–105. A. Bøe, *From Gothic Revival to Functional Form* (Oslo, 1957). K. Clark, *The Gothic Revival*, 3rd ed. (London, 1962), has valuable illustrations. C. L. Eastlake, *A History of the Gothic Revival* (London and New York, 1872). R. Haferkorn, *Gotik und Ruine in der englischen Dichtung des 18. Jahrhunderts* (Leipzig, 1924). H. Heine, *Sämtliche Werke*, ed. E. Elster, 7 vols. (Leipzig and Vienna, 1924). George Henderson, *Gothic* (Harmondsworth and Baltimore, 1967). S. Kliger, *The Goths in England* . . . (Cambridge, Mass., 1952). A. O. Lovejoy, *Essays in the History of Ideas* (Baltimore, 1948), pp. 136–65, "The First Gothic Revival and the Return to Nature." H. Messmer, *Hispania-Idee und Gotenmythos* (Zurich, 1960). E. Panofsky, "The First Page of Giorgio Vasari's Libro: A Study on the Gothic Style in the Judgment of the Italian Renaissance," in *Meaning and the Visual Arts* (Garden City, 1955), pp. 169–225. N. Pevsner, *Ruskin and Viollet-le-Duc: Englishness and Frenchness in the Appreciation of Gothic Architecture* (London, 1970). R. Menéndez Pidal, *Los Godos y la epopeya española* (Madrid, 1956). G. Previtali, *La Fortuna dei primitivi: Dal Vasari ai neoclassici* (Turin, 1964). A. W. N. Pugin, *The True Principles of Pointed or Christian Architecture* (London, 1843). W. D. Robson-Scott, *The Literary Background of the Gothic Revival in Germany* (Oxford, 1965), contains an extensive bibliography. E. Stutz, *Gotische Literaturdenkmäler* (Stuttgart, 1966). J. Svennung, *Jordanes und Scandia*, Skrifter utgivna av k. humanistiska vetenskapssamfundet i Uppsala, Vol. 44, No. 2A (Stockholm, 1967); idem, *Zur Geschichte des Goticismus*, Vol. 44, No. 2B, see above (Stockholm, 1967). L. Venturi, *Il Gusto dei primitivi* (Bologna, 1926). Otto von Simson, *The Gothic Cathedral* (New York, 1956; also reprint). N. Wagner, *Getica: Untersuchungen zum Leben des Jordanes und zur frühen Geschichte der Goten* (1967), Quellen und Forschungen zur Sprach- und Kulturgeschichte der germanischen Völker, N. F., 22. J. F. White, *The Cambridge Movement: The Ecclesiologists and the Gothic Revival* (Cambridge, 1962).

WAYNE DYNES

[See also **Baroque**; Beauty; Classicism; Culture and Civilization; Hermeticism; **Romanticism; Style**]

HAPPINESS AND PLEASURE

THE CONCEPTS of happiness and pleasure have a rich and varied history, and have functioned on diverse fronts in human life and thought. Occasionally, as in psychology, they have been made objects of direct study. More often they have been put to work. Their use in ethics has, of course, been central. In religion, they are found within conceptions of salvation and damnation. In aesthetics, the concept of aesthetic pleasure is one of the foci of the field. In medicine, pain is a major starting-point in both practical concern and the development of the concept of health. In psychology, the concepts of pleasure and pain have an important, if not always dominant, place in motivational theory. In politics, the changing place of the pursuit of happiness among the tasks of organized society is a key to basic shifts in theoretical orientation. In economics, ideas of maximizing satisfactions or preferences became tied into the formulations of major schools. In sociology, moral attitudes to pleasure and pain, as in the traditional puritan morality and its residues, impinge on the analysis of social treatment of sex, of work and play, of success and failure. In education, similar attitudes enter into the theory of discipline, of motivation, of learning, and of educational design. In conceptions of social reform generally, whether in the shape of wholesale creation of utopias, or specific workaday policies concerning poverty and welfare, or justifications in city planning and architectural mainlines, concepts of happiness often have an immediate place.

In ethics, both happiness and pleasure are early found as candidates for the good. Pleasure is sometimes, however, portrayed as a villain; pain is overwhelmingly so considered. In ethical systems in which they do not play such roles, happiness and pleasure and pain become cast in neutral fashion as psychological phenomena, to be evaluated in the ethical system itself.

When the concepts are used in an ethical way, they function with a certain value-orientation. (1) They usually impart a *this-worldly* character to the ethical view, but not always, for an otherworldly concept of blessedness may be invoked. (2) They steer ethics toward *individualism*. For happiness and pleasure are basically properties of the individual person and the individual consciousness. Even when the ethics deals with general or community happiness, there is a distributive reference to the aggregate of individuals. (3) In modern uses of the concept, there enters an element of measuring or ordering and a spur toward *maximization*. An ethics of happiness or a pleasure-pain ethics tends to be an optimizing ethics. (4) Again, happiness and pleasure, in an ethical system, are usually regarded as *intrinsic values*. Only rarely are we urged to be happy as a means—because some divine figure commands it, or (as on occasion with Kant) as insurance lest unhappiness tempt us into immorality. The analysis of these concepts is thus involved with the basic complexities that attend the difficult conception of intrinsic value itself. (5) In the ethical uses, happiness, when distinguished from pleasure, carries the notion of well-being (Aristotle's *eudaimonia*) as a more total (or sometimes totalling) phenomenon; or it is identified with a background or pervasive mood (contentment), or is more concerned with criteria for relating wholes and parts of life.

There are a number of central problems in the philosophical analysis of these concepts. (1) There is the initial methodological question of explicating the *meaning* of these notions and furnishing their *modes of identification*—for example, whether they are to be seen as phenomena of consciousness (and in the dualistic tradition, therefore, as *subjective*), or whether they can be identified in a deeper analysis of what is going on in the human being. Here occur the problems, too, of the mutual comparison of the phenomena and the inspection of the differing properties of pleasure and pain. (2) As a consequence of such distinctions and of diverse epistemological outlooks, questions arise about possible distinctions in this domain between *real* and *apparent or illusory* pleasures; and comparably for happiness and pain. These issues are sometimes formulated in metaphysical terms. (3) Questions of comparison constantly arise in terms of both qualitative differences and measurement of amounts. Here the logical investigation of the nature of measurement in the human domain impinges directly on the issues. (4) Scientific questions are perennial about the relation of these concepts to psychological and biological phenomena—for example, of pleasure to desire, or to bodily tension and organic needs. (5) It was early realized that the language of happiness and pleasure and pain is richer than these three terms alone. How far we are dealing with a whole family of concepts of which these are only a conceptual elite, whether the linguistic variety can be related to scientific differentiations, have been long-standing questions. As men became more conscious of their language as a system of practices, and studied its finer shades, the whole impact of such language study on the understanding of pleasure and pain and happiness acquired a greater philosophical importance.

The exposition of the roles which our concepts have played, the properties they have exhibited, and the problems they have involved, can best be set in a brief historical sketch in which, while ethics is the guiding thread, each concept finds its place at the points and times at which it became a matter of reflective concern.

I. EXPLORATIONS AND USES IN ANCIENT AND MEDIEVAL THOUGHT

In most ancient writings about man there is in the background a happiness-like concept of well-being, of faring well or doing well, of prospering, of things working out well, and of course the opposite. In the Old Testament or in Homer we see who prospers and who is cast down. Hesiod describes the sad condition of the peasantry, and Herodotus tells of Solon's warning that no man—so precarious is the state of well-being—should be judged happy until he has died. Such a state of well-being is just as likely to be conceptualized in terms of the good as in terms of happiness. To fashion an explicit concept of happiness for a theoretic role requires more specialized deliberation about the human good.

In ancient Greek ethics, the transition seems tied with the growth of individualism, which is already apparent among the Sophists. While Protagoras thinks chiefly of survival of the group, maintenance of justice and order, and the requisite qualities of man, more power-oriented Sophists like Thrasymachus or Callicles, as portrayed by Plato, have an explicit notion of the good as lying in the individual's satisfaction of his desires by using political power as the instrument. Into such controversies Socrates introduces the logical dimension: it now becomes important to decide whether pleasure and good mean the same thing, or whether some pleasures are good and others not. In Plato's *Protagoras*, Socrates talks as if he were a hedonist, identifying pleasure and the good, but this is in a context in which he is trying to show that no man voluntarily chooses evil, thereby rejecting the greater pleasure for the smaller pleasure. In Plato's *Gorgias*, where the uninhibited tyrant has been praised as the happiest of men, Socrates maintains that a good man is happy and an evil man unhappy; here there is an explicit refutation of hedonism.

Major opposing views were held by Socratic disciples other than Plato. Antisthenes, founder of Cynicism, took pleasure to be an evil in its upsetting of reason, exalted independence of spirit, and condemned both indulgence of appetite beyond necessity and irrational conformity to custom. Aristippus, founder of the Cyrenaic school, saw pleasure as the good which all living things naturally seek, exalted the bodily pleasures as most intense, and inclined to a view of wisdom as an ability to make the most out of the present in pleasure and avoidance of pain, though not without thought of the similar consequences of present action.

In Plato, happiness, while not yet the keystone concept of ethics, plays a major part in formulating the chief ethical questions, and in justifying the choice among alternative theories. Thus, in the *Republic*, the central problem is to show that justice and morality

375

are more advantageous and profitable than injustice and immorality, in the sense of making men happy rather than miserable; Socrates assumes his argument to be complete when he has shown that the much-admired, unscrupulous, all-powerful tyrant is the unhappiest of men. Three kinds of lives are candidates for the highest form of happiness, each with its typical goals and each related to a different part of the human makeup. The intellectual life expresses the rational part in us, and its goal is knowledge as ultimate vision of the real; the life of ambition and success expresses the spirited part, and its goal is honor or prestige; the pursuit of wealth expresses our appetites, and its goal is bodily comforts and pleasures. These three parts of the soul are symbolized by the human, the lion, and the dragon, and the happy life is to be found in the rule of justice or order in which the human, assisted by the lion, keeps the insatiable dragon in his place. (The social analogue is control exercised by the intellectual elite, assisted by the executive army, in keeping the mass of the people from participation in social policy.) Appetite thus has no inner principle of control and seeks immediate release of its tensions.

In the treatment of pleasure—chiefly in the *Republic* and the *Philebus*—Plato achieves a breadth rarely equalled before the present century. Especially striking is the variety of methods unified in his inquiry. In contrast to the later subjectivist tradition, he refuses to regard pleasure as simply a subjective phenomenon whose character and reality are wholly open to the subject in whose consciousness it occurs and to him alone. Plato's account of pleasure probes to its functioning in the parts of the human makeup, in a fashion very similar to what we should today call depth psychology. Yet so far from neglecting phenomenal analysis, he engages in a minute search for interpretive elements in the experience. And he adds attempts at physical explanation. His achievement is somewhat obscured by the dichotomy that his metaphysics of the eternal introduces into pleasure so that the experience is cut asunder and set against itself; and even more by the authoritarian strain which, in his fear of the dragon, leads him to depreciate the integrity of the individual's consciousness.

The treatment of pleasure in the *Republic* is many-sided involving both psychological analysis and moral evaluation, as well as tracing its relations to many aspects of human life. In Book IX, Plato distinguishes the three states of positive pleasure, positive pain, and a neutral restful one between them. The transition from pain to rest, as from sickness to health, is mistakenly felt as pleasure, whereas it is really removal of pain or release of tension. Plato extends this to the bodily pleasures: these, he finds, usually occur where there

has been depletion and repletion, and so they are essentially feelings of release from tension in the process of restoring a normal state. (In the *Timaeus*, he offers a supplementary physical explanation in which a violent or intense change from the natural state accounts for pain, and a similar restoration accounts for pleasure; where the dislocation is gradual there is no pain, but the restoration being rapid may bring pleasure; and conversely.) Positive pleasures do not arise from pains; Plato offers the example of a pleasant smell, but he chiefly emphasizes intellectual pleasures which have a cumulative and deepening character. He interprets bodily pleasures, as he has understood them, to be somehow less real, the additional premises to secure this degree of reality being metaphysical: the intellect is concerned with the eternal, the bodily senses with the changing; the eternal is more real than the changing; hence intellectual pleasures share more in the real than do bodily ones.

In spite of this separation of the different types of pleasure, Plato's moral evaluation of pleasure tends generally to be negative. He regards it as a lure to evil, denies that perfect beings such as gods feel pleasure, compares the life of uninhibited pleasure to the attempt to fill a sieve with water. In general, one has to conquer pleasure to be happy. In the treatment of the virtue of courage in the *Republic* he emphasizes resistance to pain, but later in the *Laws* he sees pleasure as the more formidable danger—it is not to be simply avoided, but one has to learn to take it under controlled conditions to make possible resistance to it. No phase of life with educative impact is spared his criticism; he even rejects the common view that the value of music lies in the pleasure it affords the soul, and his treatment of tragedy looks not to a particular aesthetic pleasure, but to the fear of rousing the emotions and awakening the dragon.

In the *Philebus*, which is thought to be a late work, Plato achieves a more definitive reckoning by analyzing more minutely the place of pleasure in the good of man. Pleasure is pinned down and isolated, so that to be pleased does not even involve a consciousness of being pleased, nor a recollection of having been pleased. Such awareness and memory constitute separate phenomena of the intellect. Plato reckons with pleasures and pains of anticipation, distinctions of mixed and pure types, elements of interpretation that enter into the experience and make possible judgments of truth or falsity of pleasures, and other questions in the psychology and phenomenology of pleasure. The criteria employed initially for the human good are its completeness or perfection, its adequacy or sufficiency, and the fact that it is sought by all who know about it. Pleasure by itself fails to pass these tests, but it is an ingredient to be mixed with the intellectual element. However, with pleasure so narrowed, the intellect assumes a dominant role in giving pleasure any value. Plato here regards pleasure as an indeterminate entity which, left to itself, is without form or measure or beauty or truth, but which rises to a place in the good when infused with our vision of the eternal. It is the same contrast as in his psychology of insatiable appetite bound by reason.

Aristotle's metaphysics to some degree heals the breach and enables him to give a unified account of pleasure. Also, his psychology is more naturalistic than Plato's and he conceives of the soul as the form or actuality of the organic body; hence he does not look to pleasure for metaphysically different types, and the differences among pleasures are seen as the differences among the appropriate activities they accompany. Again, Aristotle does not have a dragonian view of human nature, regarding it rather as the raw material for fashioning of human character.

Aristotle envisages all processes in nature as the actualization of specific potentialities, in which the projected goal or end guides the development. But he distinguishes sharply between changes which have a time-span and in which the goal is approached in steps, and actualities or activities in which the end is fully embodied at every moment. The rise of a building takes time for completion, but the activity of the builder when he is building is going on fully at every moment. So too, seeing and thinking and being pleased are not processes, but actualities. But pleasure is not an independent activity like sensing; it accompanies the activity of a sense organ that is in sound condition, perfecting and supervening on the activity, says Aristotle, like the bloom in those who are at the flower of their youth.

Aristotle is thus able to defend pleasure against most of the traditional attacks. It can be good, though some pleasures are not good because their activities are not. Pleasure as such does not impede noble activities; interfering activities do this, but the pleasure of the noble activity itself is of help. Yet there is no point in abstracting pleasure to see it as the good; that involves the more complex concept of happiness. Nevertheless, Aristotle traces the role of pleasure at numerous points and in many areas. In the development of virtue, the fact that good acts are done with pleasure rather than pain is the mark of an achieved good character. In the specific virtue of self-control or temperance, the very materials of the virtue are the pleasures of touch and taste. Pleasure and pain are also studied in phenomena of continence and incontinence, especially at the point of yielding to temptation to do what is wrong in spite of knowing the good. Pleasure

is distinguished from utility and love of the good, as one of three types of motivations in friendship, and the character of the sort of friendship based on pleasure is explored in detail. There are comments on the place of pleasure in the family, in aesthetic contexts, in education; and there is the assignment of a lofty status to pleasure when Aristotle insists that the gods, so far from feeling no pleasure, have continually the highest of pleasures, that of intellectual contemplation.

With respect to happiness, Aristotle builds it into a systematic concept out of the general idea of well-being referred to earlier. It emerges as the successful candidate in his identification of the good. For the good is the ultimate object of human striving, complete and self-sufficient, and happiness alone satisfies this. In the *Rhetoric*, where he is summarizing popular conceptions, he lists such characteristics of happiness as prosperity combined with virtue, secure enjoyment of maximum pleasure, good condition of body and property and the power of preserving and using them, and so on; and he itemizes constituents of happiness ranging from good birth and friends, strength and stature, children and wealth, to honor with state burial and statues! In the *Nicomachean Ethics*, he sees happiness as lying in activity, not in merely the potentiality that character furnishes; as requiring a whole life-span, not merely intense short-range feeling; as having need of external goods and other people as friends. Conceptually, happiness is then a life of activity in accordance with complete virtue (in which reason plays a large part). In this sense, the whole of the ethics is an exploration of the nature and requirements of happiness, set in a full view of the nature of man as a bio-social being. And though Aristotle concludes that supreme happiness is found in the isolated act of contemplation, still, man is a social animal; even the happiness of good men involves friends, and in any case the greater part of human life is the life of social practice.

Aristotle's *Politics* is continuous with his *Ethics*, and since happiness is the good, the great use that he makes of the good in analyzing political and institutional concepts is translatable directly into the terms of the conditions of a happy life for men. This is obvious enough when he discusses the ideal state and gives priority to basic goals of peace over war, leisure over business, or plans a healthful city or an education which will make men critical participants in politics and culture. But it enters even into his definition and classification of political forms, for example, when he uses aiming at the common welfare as a criterion of good as against bad constitutions, or at the very outset in his definition of the state itself as an association aiming at the highest good. He even declares that a city has really ceased to be a city and has become just an alliance of men who happen to be living close by when the pursuit of a common welfare is abandoned. In short, the communal pursuit of happiness is a central and integral part of Aristotle's conception of the *polis*.

In the Hellenistic shift to an individualistically oriented ethics there is an obvious retreat from the social conception of a communal welfare. The ideal of peace of mind, internal tranquillity, and individual independence, that in different forms is shared by Stoic and Epicurean, functions as a surrogate for happiness. But in the detail of the theories there are opposing attitudes to pleasure. The Stoics see it as contrary to nature, with its impulse as a disturbing movement in the soul and so basically irrational. Joy, however, is distinguished as a rational elation of the mind. Most of the objects of human desire are put into the category of indifferent things. The Epicureans see pleasure as proper to the nature of man, but pain as contrary to it. In their theory, pleasure occupies the central position of the good. But whereas Aristippus had held all pleasures to consist in motion, Epicurus distinguishes those of motion from those of rest. He also points out that though bodily pains are more acute, they are transient; while in the pleasures and pains of the mind, memory and anticipation extend the scope. Epicurus makes it clear that the pursuit of pleasure recommended is not sensuality or revelry, but that inherent in a virtuous life. It is rather by moderating desires than by multiplying and pursuing them that a happy life is maintained. The garden of Epicurus is, on the whole, a refuge from pain and turbulence, devoted to simple joys and friendships, with little place for politics or for energetic attempts to control nature.

In Lucretius' poem, *On the Nature of Things*, we see how central to the Epicurean this-worldly outlook in ethics is their general view of nature and man. Epicurus had adopted the atomic physics of Democritus and (except for a chance swerve of the atoms absent from Democritus' more complete determinism) the philosophical concepts that went with it—a reduction of large-scale phenomena to physical terms and a causal as against a teleological mode of explanation. This removed the pains that come from fears and superstitions about death and the afterlife; death is simply the separation of the organism into its particles and there are no rewards and punishments. The impact of Epicureanism among its contemporaries was thus that of a rigorous philosophical materialism.

The growing religious thought, from biblical through medieval times, added two distinctively religious elements to the shape that the concepts of happiness and pleasure were taking in the Greek tradition: the depiction of blessedness as supreme happiness, and the concept of damnation. There are also, of course, to be found purely philosophical developments in the religious thinkers, as, for example, Augustine's treatment of desire and joy as volition of consent to the things we wish, thus giving a voluntaristic core to pleasure rather than simply a reactive-affective one.

In the Old Testament, the happiness that is bestowed by God and sought by man is still what was referred to above as well-being. Job after his tribulations is rewarded with the same kind of worldly goods and relations that had characterized his pretrial prosperity. Yet there are occasional emphases moving away from the outer world and the temporal to the inner otherworldly and, if not the eternal, at least the everlasting. There is also the strong sense of being at one with God in one's intent and abiding faith, and, in the book of Ecclesiastes, there is the declaration that all life is vanity, precisely on the ground that it does not last and only the everlasting could fully satisfy the spirit. The Sermon on the Mount, steering men away from the worldly, clearly sets the path to and through inwardness, to God as the paternal source of each soul.

The chief nonworldly or otherworldly tendency among the concepts of happiness is to be found in this religious concept of blessedness. It emerges also in the Greco-Roman philosophical tradition, especially in Neo-Platonism. Thus for Plotinus, the whole world is an emanation of God or the One, who is beyond all being and all thought. The soul seeks to return to this source, and happiness is found in the perfecting of life by appropriate abstinence and pursuit of wisdom, catharsis of spirit, till at the utmost limit one stands on the verge of the mystic experience. The unity in which one is absorbed in the divine is quite literally ecstatic in that one stands outside of oneself; it is ineffable because it is true unity whereas discourse involves the duality of thought and its object. The mystic experience of blessedness colors the whole being, reinforces detachment from earthly pleasures, and bends the striving totally toward the One.

In Christian mysticism—both in the medieval Catholic form and in later Protestant forms—the same type of quest characterizes the striving of the soul for unity with God, and successful culmination is found in the experience itself, achieved only intermittently in life but remaining as a promise of blessedness in the hereafter. Various mystics differ chiefly in two respects—the attempted description of the experience and the stages of preparation for it. Some accounts present it as a beholding or illumination, a concentrated vision; some as being overcome in a kind of merging; some as an identity with rather than in; some as a blaze of intense active being; and so on. In all, there is agreement that in some sense time disappears, that the distinction of subject and object is gone, that the sense of total good is wholly present. Metaphors of union with the beloved abound. As for stages of approach, they differ widely, some stressing turning away from the sensible and achievement of deeper knowledge, some the growth of love, some the diminution of self-orientation, and there are differences in the degree to which grace is invoked. Saint Bonaventura is a good example: his *The Mind's Road to God* has six stages followed by the sabbath of perfect ecstasy.

Just as the essence of blessedness is found in the closeness to a union with God, so the essence of damnation in Christian theory is found in the separateness from God. Damnation does not lie in pain and torture alone; there is the basic distinction between pain and moral evil, physical and moral suffering. Hell is therefore not a purely external sanction. The moral evil lies in the abandonment of God by the will, manifested in disobedience, and in the whole array of sins; the gravity of their punishment, as in Dante's depiction in the *Inferno*, is almost directly proportional to the distance from God that is manifest in the act. The blessedness of salvation and the hell of damnation are thus not two separate questions but opposite extremes in the one basic relation.

II. FROM THE SECULARIZATION OF HAPPINESS TO THE GREATEST HAPPINESS OF THE GREATEST NUMBER

In the seventeenth- and eighteenth-century revolutions of life and thought, there are marked changes in the exploration and uses of the conceptions of happiness and pleasure. The end point is, of course, the utilitarian philosophy which raised these concepts to the pinnacle of ethical theory by the beginning of the nineteenth century, which identified happiness with pleasure and which made maximum surplus of pleasure over pain the human goal. To see these centuries in this light is to look for the intellectual movement which made happiness into utility, utility into pleasure, detached pleasure from other ends and relations and left it theoretically supreme—only then to find itself uncertain about its identity. In this account, what happened to happiness is the overall story; what happened to pleasure inner detail.

The concept of happiness became increasingly attached to the growing liberalism with its secular and worldly mood, its intense individualism, its scientific orientation, and its libertarian social outlook. The secular characterized especially the content of happiness, associating the concept with worldly success, pursuit of wealth, power, and prestige. The scientific orientation strengthened the critical mood in the breakdown of traditions, and made room for the hope of progress. The libertarian element released individual

energies. But it was the whole individualist foundation in the economic and social relations that had the strongest impact in political and ethical theory. The social contract theory for understanding the basis and function of government is only an extreme instance of the increasingly prevalent view that an individual is bound only by that to which he has directly or indirectly consented. Institutions thus came increasingly to be regarded as instruments for the individual's well-being as reckoned by individual judgment and determined by individual will.

Nevertheless, the nation state as it emerged was not given the task of providing for the happiness of its citizens. This goal, which Aristotle had assigned for political organization, had long receded. In the intervening centuries the conception of man as sunk in original sin put earthly happiness out of reach, and at best the laws of a society could keep human nature in check sufficiently to maintain some social order. Then the rise of the new political theory, as in Machiavelli, substituted power for the good in traditional ethics, as the characteristic aim of the state. This was indeed its impact from the point of view of the rulers. But from the perspective of the ruled, the aim is better seen in Hobbes, where emphasis falls on the need of individuals for peace and order and the necessary conditions for the pursuit of their individual aims. These conditions, including protection of life and property, guarantee of contract performance, and so on, are seen as natural laws which reason leads men to accept. Nevertheless, as states achieved greater stability and economic advance brought greater prosperity, and as the growth of scientific knowledge enhanced men's hope of greater control of their environment and their lives, the aims of organized society themselves advanced in theory from minimal conditions of order to ensuring conditions of progress and the pursuit of happiness. If Locke in the seventeenth century assumed that the protection of property was equivalent to securing the common good, Jefferson in the late eighteenth century replaced it with the pursuit of happiness as an inalienable right in the Declaration of Independence. And though it did not get into the federal constitution, it yet retained some occasional hold in legal decisions to strike down restraints and to preserve freedom of contract and freedom to labor. In general, the idea of progress itself, soon entrenched in the Western liberal outlook, carried the implication of greater instrumentalities and greater human sensitivity productive of more general happiness.

The curve of rising expectations can be traced also in the imaginative projection of the good society found in the succession of utopias—from Thomas More's *Utopia* (1516) and Francis Bacon's *New Atlantis* (1624) to the early nineteenth-century visions of Fourier, Robert Owen, and Saint-Simon. Utopias generally embody a conception of the happy life, whether it is a fixed pattern, as in the earlier forms, or whether it has internal room for change, as the later ones do. Utopias also pinpoint the miseries of the time against which they are directed, as More laments the state of the dispossessed peasantry; or they rebel against a perennial repression, as many a utopia does in depicting sexual liberation. Equally significant for the period we are considering was the general rise of the idea of progress, replacing older conceptions of decline from an original paradise into increasing corruption. Eventually, given the acceleration of social change and the recognition that reality often moves faster than dreams, the pursuit of happiness takes the form of direct political programs, such as for governmental intervention to alleviate miseries or develop educational institutions.

In ethical theory, the concept of happiness played an increasingly prominent role. In Hobbes, happiness is frankly equated with the satisfaction of appetite whose direction identifies the good; and in Locke there are the beginnings of a hedonism. Even more significant, however, is the role happiness plays in the very theories that are fighting a Hobbesian egoism by trying to show a natural basis in man for sympathy. For here too—in Shaftesbury or Butler or Hutcheson—the moral field tends to get divided between self-love and benevolence. Self-love, as Butler describes it, is admittedly concerned with the individual's well-being, the long-range harmony of his desires. And benevolence, though the moralist's eye is on justifying it to the individual, is itself a concern for other people's happiness or their rescue from misery. Even such rationalists as the Cambridge Platonists include the duty of beneficence among the moral axioms.

The moralistic objection to happiness has rarely been to making others happy, only to limiting the happiness effort to oneself. Kant, whose insight in such detail is impeccable, points out that it is our duty to seek our own perfection and others' happiness, not our happiness and others' perfection. Again, moral philosophers, having established to their own satisfaction that sympathy is a spontaneous reaction in terms of which our conception of virtue can be understood, began to look for its underlying laws of movement—analogous to the gravitational principle in the Newtonian model. Hume and Adam Smith, rendering explicit what had been emerging over the century, fixed on the notion of utility: though men did not calculate utility in making their moral judgments, the underlying principle was the general conduciveness to happiness of the action sympathized with or approved.

Utilitarian suggestions and developments had already been numerous. Cumberland had talked of the common good in a utilitarian way as the supreme law; Hutcheson used the phrase, "the greatest happiness of the greatest numbers" in treating of the goodness of actions; Gay had invoked the happiness of mankind as a criterion of God's will, itself the criterion of virtue (a path that Paley's utilitarianism was later to take). And Priestley, whom Bentham acknowledged as a source for the utility principle, in fact had a well-developed theory of individual socialization so as to identify his interest with a common good, effected by natural sanctions set in the context of an ever-improving environment including improving institutions. In France, too, there had been a rapid rise of happiness theory in ethics. Locke's hedonism had a strong and direct influence there. Helvétius accounted for moral standards by tracing their development out of experiences of pleasure and pain, and Holbach's theory of ethics started from the individual's pursuit of his own happiness, and developed into a full utilitarianism. In Italy, Beccaria's influential analysis of punishment rested squarely on utilitarian premises.

To make Bentham's utilitarianism possible, happiness had to be equated with pleasure or else to be built out of pleasant experiences in some manner; pleasure itself had also to be detached from its traditional interrelations with appetite and desire and action so as to be able to serve as an isolable goal of human striving. The first of these was readily accomplished. Since the community was treated as a sum of individuals, every statement about the common good or the general welfare was in principle translatable into statements about the happiness of individuals. Moreover, if happiness meant anything more for the individual than pleasure and the absence of pain, it would be a complex built up by pleasurable and painful associations; this psychological principle was adopted by the utilitarians from David Hartley's formulation of association. The second requirement—the detachment of pleasure so that it could serve as an isolated goal—was the outcome of a long scientific-philosophical development beginning with Descartes.

Aristotle had regarded pleasure as completing or perfecting an activity. The question facing the subsequent tradition was the more minute one of what this completing consisted in. Aristotle saw it in almost aesthetic-decorative terms, though he also gives it occasionally an enhancing effect. Augustine, as noted above, gave it the active role of the will consenting to the course of action. Hobbes, when he distinguishes pleasure from appetite as other than expected terminus, regards it as an inner motion continuing and helping vital action, and pain as frustrating or hindering it; in any case, pleasure and pain are intimately related to appetitive and aversive processes. For Leibniz and for Wolff, pleasure and pain are a direct awareness of perfection or imperfection, that is, of well-being or ill-being. In all of these, pleasure is still tied to some process in relation to which it performs a service of some kind and that service is its defining property.

Descartes started pleasure on its path to independence, because his dualism attempted to apportion experience to either the body or the soul. Some experiences in the soul arise from it, but passions, like sensible experiences, are excited from without. Although Descartes still sees a teleological role for the passions in disposing the soul to will things nature requires, this is an external relation; pleasure and pain are becoming self-contained items in the life of the soul. Thus Locke treats them as simple ideas, and Hume regards bodily pleasures and pains as original impressions arising in the soul without any antecedent perception. In Condillac, pleasure and pain are already the sole motives of action. In addition, pleasure and pain shared in the general atomicity which characterized the treatment of ideas in Locke or impressions in Hume. Each experience of pleasure or pain is a single isolated event, telling its whole story within itself. This approach is found not only in phenomenalism, where it is of course strongest, but also in materialist inquiry into motions: Hartley looks to faint vibrations left as traces by sensory experiences, and mental pleasures and pains are thus the traces of sensory pleasures and pains excited associatively by recurrent circumstances.

It is not surprising, then, that Bentham starts out with a psychological hedonism in which pleasure is both the goal of all purposive behavior and the sole good in it. Nor is it surprising that Bentham sets as a feasible project to work out a felicific calculus in which the value of a given lot of pleasure or pain would be reckoned by measuring each of its components for intensity, duration, certainty or uncertainty, propinquity or remoteness, fecundity, purity, and (where more than one person is concerned) the extent or number of persons affected. And he had the hope, at least for a long time, that subtle units would be found to make such calculation more precise. His applications of his calculus are sometimes direct, for example, in comparing the pains of punishment on offenders of different sensibility; often, they are indirect, such as the legislator's assumption that a law which increases people's wealth will increase their happiness. And large social problems such as the desirable form of property-system are worked out as pleasure-problems: property is but a name for socially supported expectations of pleasure, hence the type of system desirable is the one

that experience shows will yield the greatest happiness. Bentham at times used different formulations for his central idea—the greatest happiness, the greatest happiness of all, the greatest happiness of the greatest number. The last of these has the widest currency.

The amazing thing about Bentham's pleasure-pain theory is the vast spread of work that it is made to do: utilitarianism at the hands of Bentham and J. S. Mill drew conclusions for major social, legal, and political institutions; for most areas of personal life and human relations. A glance at the topics of Mill's writings—liberty, representative government, economics, the position of women, and so forth—is sufficiently indicative. The central critical question is therefore how far pleasure-pain theory was really doing the work, or how far it was simply a garb for more effective though more hidden working premises.

There is no unanimity among the nineteenth- and twentieth-century critics of hedonistic utilitarianism. Some stopped at the outset with the felicific calculus, argued that pleasure was an evanescent phenomenon, that it could not be added or summed up. F. H. Bradley, in a famous chapter of his *Ethical Studies* (1876), thus cleared the way for his own self-realizationist ethics. Others, more interested in what utilitarianism accomplished in spite of its pleasure orientation, thrust the latter aside; John Dewey, for example, took the pleasure language to be an historical accident, and the effective ethical thrust to lie in the empirical examination of consequences of actions and policies, for solving the problem-situations to which they were addressed. In a precisely opposite direction, Marx took the pleasure theory to be the most significant theoretical feature of Benthamism. In *The German Ideology* (written in 1846) he traces the development of the philosophy of pleasure from the language of the pleasure-loving court nobility to the official bourgeois economic category of luxury. The bourgeoisie generalized pleasure, separated it from its specific contexts, and analyzed all interpersonal relations as a process of extracting pleasure. This reduction to utility Marx sees as the ideological reflection of the bourgeois practice of exploitation, in which one aim, the increase of money, becomes the measure of all value. Benthamism is thus seen by Marx as the exaltation in ethics of a view of private exploitation of the world.

Perhaps J. S. Mill too can be seen as a critic within the utilitarian school itself of the pleasure theory. For not only does he amend the calculus by insisting on qualitative differences in pleasures, so that an intellectual or aesthetic pleasure is not just quantitatively equivalent to a large number of physical pleasures, but he also broadens the conception of happiness. His statement in Chapter II of his *Utilitarianism* (1863) is worth quoting at length:

If by happiness be meant a continuity of highly pleasurable excitement, it is evident enough that this is impossible. A state of exalted pleasure lasts only moments, or in some cases, and with some intermissions, hours or days, and is the occasional brilliant flash of enjoyment, not its permanent and steady flame. Of this the philosophers who have taught that happiness is the end of life were as fully aware as those who taunt them. The happiness which they meant was not a life of rapture; but moments of such, in an existence made up of few and transitory pains, many and various pleasures, with a decided predominance of the active over the passive, and having as the foundation of the whole, not to expect more from life than it is capable of bestowing. A life thus composed, to those who have been fortunate enough to obtain it, has always appeared worthy of the name of happiness. And such an existence is even now the lot of many, during some considerable portion of their lives. The present wretched education, and wretched social arrangements, are the only real hindrance to its being attainable by almost all.

Mill's statement shows also the dominantly reformist aims of the utilitarians, just as in other contexts his recognition that happiness can come by association to include virtuous activity as a constituent, not merely as a means, shows his basic educational orientation.

It seems most likely that if the specific theory of pleasure cannot bear the burden of all the work the utilitarians expected of it, nevertheless the major historical properties of pleasure—the secular and worldly character, the individualistic emphasis, the rational ordering tendency in the comparison of activities, the critical aspect in the demand for a reckoning of policy in terms of happiness whatever precisely it be—all together supported effectively the variety of applications. But if this be so, the concept of pleasure, precisely at its theoretical peak, loses its firm identity and dissolves into a whole family of indices going perhaps in different directions and generating different enterprises. From this point on in the nineteenth century and into the twentieth, the career of pleasure is best studied in the variety of disciplines in which it was varyingly used and interpreted.

III. THE COURSE OF NINETEENTH- AND TWENTIETH-CENTURY STUDIES

Biopsychological Disciplines. In biology, psychology, and medicine, pleasure and pain maintained their most literal sense. They were certain conscious experiences that had to be located, explored, and related to other processes. The direction taken reflected in large measure the underlying theory of body-mind relations, which went through a succession of phases in the nine-

teenth and twentieth centuries. First there was the sharp separation, heritage of dualism, in which consciousness was explored on its own, introspectively, usually in terms of its elements and their association. Here pleasure was either a separate element or a quality of sensory experiences. On the physical side, some correlation was assumed, such as the excitation of the nerve endings. As the weight of investigation inclined more heavily to the organic, and specific physiological bases were sought for the emotions and feelings, the conscious experiences were often identified as a cognitive awareness of some pinpointed physiological process. Especially when the epiphenomenalism of the end of the nineteenth century emerged, the mental side received proportionately less attention.

Differences of approach about the physiological basis centered on a number of issues. Some looked to peripheral processes of the sense-organs, others to central visceral or brain processes. As to type of process, one trend took pleasure to go with adequate or abundant expression, another with proper balance as against an overstrained or repressed exertion, another with greater systematization, another with achievement of equilibrium or stability. Distinctions emerged between unpleasantness and pain, and between pleasantness as a tonal quality and pleasure as sensory. Wilhelm Wundt worked out three necessary dimensions for feeling: pleasantness-unpleasantness, excitement-depression, tension-relaxation; and he sought specific bodily changes to correlate with each.

In some twentieth-century psychological schools, pleasure and pain as conscious experiences were almost dismissed from scientific inquiry. In the behaviorist school of J. B. Watson, while emotion was taken to be a visceral phenomenon, feelings involved primarily seeking and avoidance, and so could be bypassed in favor of such behavioral description. William McDougall, while recognizing that pleasure and pain strengthen or weaken paths of striving, saw them as themselves determined by success or failure in striving; hence the intermediate pleasure-pain phenomena could be left out in exploring motivation. Dewey, too, insisted on seeing pleasure and pain in the full context of action; as noted above, he took the utilitarian use of pleasure to be really a treatment of preference as choice in conduct. Nevertheless, in contemporary learning theory, which is a contemporary form of behaviorism, it is possible to hold that the theory of reinforcement is a pleasure-pain principle in disguise. For there being no natural tendencies postulated, there might seem to be required some vehicle by which particular experiences have negative or positive effect.

Attempts to revive a direct study of consciousness apart from the whole physiological inquiry are found in Gestalt and phenomenological approaches. They differ from the older introspectionism in concentrating on the total field of awareness and its sensitive exploration. Gestalt treatment of the visual field and its properties has served as a paradigm for extending the method to value fields. Phenomenological psychiatry has stressed trying to see the world as the patient sees it rather than directing his attention inward to probe his feelings. Accordingly, Gestalt theory has tried to broaden the concept of motivation to reach beyond the range of egoistic pleasure and pain.

Another way of studying pleasure and pain which avoids their simple physiological reduction or their behavioristic omission is to focus more explicitly on the genesis and functions of consciousness in a broader study on several levels. This approach was prompted by the evolutionary outlook in the nineteenth century, and was omitted in the narrower vista of the body-mind theories sketched above. It can be illustrated from Herbert Spencer and from Freudian depth psychology.

Spencer's treatment of pleasure and pain shows clearly the new turn that evolutionary theory had given to the understanding of consciousness, in directing attention to genetic and functional inquiry and in supplying the test of survival through natural selection. In ethics, Spencer starts out as ostensibly a utilitarian: he compares pleasure as a necessary form of moral intuition to space as a necessary form of intellectual intuition. Now since pleasure is a feeling we seek to bring into consciousness and retain there, and pain correspondingly what we seek to keep out, it follows that if pleasures were correlative to acts injurious to the organism, that organism would not survive. Hence natural selection brings about the coincidence of pleasure and what is conducive to health and survival. From here Spencer moves in many directions—to physiology, psychology, sociology. Physiologically, he relies on stimulation of the nervous system to explain elation and depression (due, respectively, to a high pressure and a low pressure). Local pleasures and pains are directly (peripherally) aroused by special stimuli. Psychologically, he is interested in showing how the development of man matures the moral feelings in the attempt to set up regulative processes in men's pursuit of satisfactions, and how the pleasures and pains originating in the moral sentiments become incentives and deterrents adjusted to human needs. And he adds the sociological view in a similar spirit, showing the lines of change to be expected in men's attitudes as evolution proceeds. Whatever the defects in Spencer's specific theories on each level, his general view of the scope of exploration required for consciousness is highly sophisticated.

Freudian treatment of pleasure and pain is only slightly more restricted, but in turn much richer in specific content. The hedonistic element is central in the Freudian notion of the pleasure principle, not in the conscious calculative sense but as the tendency of the organism toward gratification by the release of tension built up by instinctual energies. The accumulation of excitation is felt as pain and the diminution as pleasure. The "reality principle" arises as experience builds the ability to defer gratification in the light of conditions of life and familial-interpersonal relations. The contrast of pleasure and reality principles plays an almost defining role in the structural picture of the id and the ego, supplemented by the superego which involves diversion of energy from the id to set up an internalized regulatory procedure. In Freud's exploration of the operation of the principles and this structure, the scope of pleasure and pain is both extended and deepened. Pain is seen under definite conditions to beget anxiety, and anxiety again under specific conditions is differentiated into realistic or objective, neurotic, and moral or guilt forms. Similarly, pleasure, in the whole range of the uses of the Freudian apparatus in depth psychology, was tracked down in its repressed as well as overt forms, and with the specific quality it had and in its admixtures with anxiety in varieties of neurotic conditions. For example, phenomena of masochism and sadism were thus analyzed into components in relation to the internal economy of the person, in a spirit reminiscent of Plato's early depth probing, though of course with altered theory and greater scope of evidence. Unlike Plato, Freud's view does not make possible metaphysical judgments of the unreality of some pleasures, but it does have an impact on evaluation when, for example, the Don Juan is analyzed as a man fearful of his masculinity rather than as having a strongly positive pleasure in his conquests.

In his later speculations, Freud gave primacy to the death instinct as a tendency of the complex organism to move to a lower level, a reinstatement of earlier simpler conditions. Offered as an explanation of such phenomena as repetition-compulsion, it became tied with the idea that aggression had to be expressed outwardly to avoid its turning inward. The pleasure principle was reduced to serving the death instinct by lowering tension. These conceptions were carried by Freud into the social domain. Seeing the growth of civilization as demanding the increase of libidinal ties over an increasingly wider range, Freud pessimistically viewed the increased repression involved as bound to yield accumulated aggression and occasional violent breakthrough.

In general, Freud's influence invigorated the study of pleasure and pain. Even on the purely descriptive and conceptual level the impact of its depth analysis was to underscore the variety of the phenomena, encouraging thereby a greater conceptual complexity. Erich Fromm, for example, in his *Man For Himself* (1947), distinguishes: satisfaction of physiological needs, irrational pleasures as rooted in insatiable and anxiety-driven desires, joy as rooted in psychological abundance rather than psychological scarcity, happiness as an integrated experience of joy reflecting an inner productiveness, gratification as the pleasure of accomplishment, and finally pleasure as the feeling resulting from relaxation.

With the tremendous impact of twentieth-century anthropology on psychological studies of personality development, the question has arisen whether even apparently elementary reactions of pleasure and pain may not be infused with cultural content and exhibit variation. This may even extend to rudimentary physiological reactions, not merely to variations in affective response to visual and auditory experiences. Indeed, even pain itself may have varying meanings in different cultural traditions; to some it is simply something to be gotten rid of, while to others it is a sign of something wrong in the organism so that cessation of pain does not itself mean an end of concern.

The many-sided character of the study of pleasure and pain does not preclude the possibility of success in the dominant tradition of the search for simple physiological correlates. For example, in the 1960's, the work of James Olds and his associates—implanting electrodes in the limbic system of the brain and so arranging it that the electric current could be turned on by the experimental animals, who turned out to give greater preference to this self-stimulation over the usual rewards—has seemed to some to strengthen the view of a pleasure center in the brain. Such determination, if it be successfully maintained, would rather broaden the area of work to be done in establishing the systematic relations between such facts and the whole form of development on the other levels.

Insufficient attention, as a source of theoretical insight, has probably been paid to medicine, which is increasingly facing problems of pleasure and pain. Pain, together with inability to function, was doubtless the starting-point for the notion of ill-health. Medicine has by now developed a complex concrete conception of health, but at its growing points problems of forms of pain are still relevant. The justification for treating mental health as a form of health lies in the depth-psychological theory of the origins of anxiety in its pathological forms. In addition, medicine has direct problems with several contexts of pain and pain-reduction. The older issue of the use of anesthetics in birth processes, although obscured by claims of the natural role of birth pangs for the mother, raised issues

of the medical and psychological functions of pain and of the consciousness in which it occurs. Similarly, the development of tranquilizers has raised both moral issues, where they are used to avoid working through a basic situation, and psychological-medical issues concerned with the actual character of ataractic processes in the inner workings of the person. In some contexts, such as the dying patient, there is still insufficient knowledge about the fear of death to guide treatment during the process of dying. In the rapid advances of medicine we may expect fresh materials to deepen our understanding of pain and its roles in conscious experience.

Political Economy. The concern with well-being or general welfare has been in one sense indigenous to political economy. Its relations to utilitarianism and the concept of pleasure have, however, been even more direct. This is especially true of the concept of utility and the theory of welfare economics.

The hedonistic affiliation of the concept of utility in economic usage is related to the shift in the theory of value from classical economics to doctrines of marginal utility, especially in the work of W. S. Jevons. In the earlier, value was dependent on some objective quality such as embodied labor, in the second it referred to the production of pleasure or prevention of pain in an individual whose wants and demands would thus be operative in economic transactions. While for a time some shared the Benthamite faith in the cardinal measurability of pleasure and so of utility, this did not long remain. Ordinal measurability, in which an individual's needs are arranged on a scale of preference, was found to be a sufficient basis for complex theoretical constructions in economics.

A central difficulty from the outset was that of interpersonal comparison of utility. Especially with the replacement of cardinal utility by ordinal utility, the effective elements are individual preferences as ordered by the individual himself. If there is no way to compare individual preferences, there would appear to be no ready formulation of a concept of social welfare. This problem is central to welfare economics since it requires a basis for judging among alternative economic proposals, in the light of their contribution to social welfare. One possibility is to assume that competition of individuals constitutes an optimizing process, but this raises issues of differences in starting-point with respect to money and power. A theoretical formulation of optimality was offered by Pareto, according to which a situation is socially optimal if no change can be made which does not make at least one individual worse off (by his own preference scale). Subsequent modifications introduce the idea of compensation for the losers.

A quite different possibility, less committed to the existent distribution pattern, is to have a welfare conception enter economic processes from outside. This might come from a political determination of social goals by a democratic process. Or it might come from a moral conception of welfare distinct from the preference picture, and used to criticize the latter; for example, it might determine priorities such as a floor of human necessities to be first satisfied, or a set of human opportunities to be furnished to everyone (such as employment or education). Such a path would, of course, be abandoning the directly hedonistic basis—from which in any case welfare economics had moved in the use of preferences—and going back to the more general notion of happiness and its conditions noted earlier.

Sociology, Social Policy, and Practical Disciplines. Sociological analysis of contemporary society, and policy proposals both for the shape of life itself and for practical fields such as law and education, show numerous points at which the conception of happiness and theories of the role of pleasure and pain are either quite explicit or else implicit in the operations of the institution.

Most prominent is the passing of the traditional "puritan morality." With the expansion of technology and the increased productivity, the older emphasis on work as against leisure is well on the way to being reversed. Thrift is replaced by conspicuous consumption and installment buying on credit. The pursuit of happiness is held up as within the reach of all, and self-denial is increasingly seen to have been the reflex of scarcity. This permeates theory as well as attitudes and practice. Thus it is a commonplace to point to the crippling effect of undue guilt feeling upon men's capacity for happiness. Different psychological outlooks here flow into a common stream. Thus the psychological school that stresses self-actualization, as in the writings of G. W. Allport and Abraham Maslow, sets a freer and a broader range for men's development.

Again, Herbert Marcuse, in his *Eros and Civilization* (1955), argues that the prevalent repression of instincts was not really so much a necessity for accomplishment or performance in human life as it was a consequence of social domination; accordingly he looks to gradual decontrolling of instinctual development, in short, a freer operation of the pleasure principle. In practice, the signs of a growing positive concern with satisfaction have long been manifest in many ways. The psychology of sex has combined with literature to make sexual satisfaction an almost respectable goal of female as well as male striving. The fantasy world of advertising ties every incidental gadget to the promise of splendor, pleasure, and ecstasy. In revolts against the Establishment—with its traditional goals of work, postponement of gratification, competition, and success—the "hippie" philosophy counterposes enjoyment, deeper inner experience, direct affiliative relations, and doing "one's thing."

Only occasionally in the general acknowledgment of happiness do we find a note of reservation. Martha Wolfenstein, in a paper on "Fun Morality: An Analysis of Recent American Child-Training Literature" (1951), traces the transformation in the view of the child from dangerous impulses to benign inclinations and the corresponding shift from repression to encouraged expression, yet she points out the lurking puritanical quality in the feeling that it is a duty to have fun with one's child. And Moritz Schlick earlier, in his *Problems of Ethics* (1939), replaces the Kantian principle of duty with the moral principle of "Be ready for happiness," a principle which he finds much more tangible than the greatest happiness of the greatest number, since it turns concrete attention not to pleasure but to definite human capacities; yet he makes clear that much is involved in the cultivation of spirit that enables one to share in happiness when it presents itself.

To consider the use of pleasure and pain in the diverse institutions that seek to regulate or cultivate men would be here too extensive a task. A brief reference to law and education will indicate the kinds of problems involved and how their treatment responds to men's attitudes toward pleasure and pain. In law the dominant sanction has been some form of pain. The types of pain involved in punishment have been gradually reduced, and we have come to realize how limited is the accomplishment of the theory of punishment in achieving the ends toward which it is directed; thus ideas of reform and prevention have made inroads on retaliatory and even deterrent conceptions. On the whole, rewards have been little employed in the law, apart from reduction of punishment for cause.

In education, the issues have not seemed directly concerned with pleasure and pain, except in the realm of maintaining discipline. But this appearance is deceptive. In the wider sense, the whole controversy over modes of teaching, as epitomized most sharply in the contrast of traditional and progressive education, is a question of the educative role of pleasure. For the advances that stressed concern with the child's interests, with stimulating the child's abilities, are in effect pursuing those paths in which joy or satisfaction in endeavor will promote education more effectively than merely repetitive exercise or at best trusting obedience. In the same way, sanctions and motivations that underlie any significant human institution, when brought to explicit attention, will raise comparative questions about the role of pleasure, pain, and happiness.

385

HAPPINESS AND PLEASURE

Contemporary Philosophical Treatments. In the 1960's many of the traditional problems about our concepts find new form in discussions of value, both in general value theory and in such special fields as aesthetics. For the most part, the issues that have been traced above are repeated. For example, some value theorists go directly to phenomena of pleasurable experience or satisfaction, characterize value by it, and trace its different forms in art, religion, intellectual activity, social relations, and so on. Other value theorists tend rather to identify value by the context, by appetition or purpose, or by a complex problem-situation, and regard the structure of the context rather than the quality of the consummation alone to be of central relevance to theoretical formulations. In aesthetics, the issue is sometimes sharp, between the former, who look to the spectator and his enjoyment and try to pinpoint a special aesthetic pleasure, and the latter who stress the productive process of the artist and the spectator's appreciation of the problems in the production.

While considerable advances have been made in the explorations of value theory, perhaps the most striking philosophical contributions in the 1950's and 1960's to the analysis of pleasure and pain have come through the linguistic approach. Ordinary language analysis has been especially employed in dealing with pleasure, and it has brought to the task the kind of assumptions that have characterized the method generally. Essentially, of course, it consists in analyzing the use of the term "pleasure" and related terms, in the varied contexts in which we employ them; this is contrasted with locating a phenomenon and doing a scientific investigation of it. Yet it is thought that sensing the fine texture of use brings us beyond language to a kind of phenomenological awareness. Again, the contexts being quite varied, there is no assumption of any inherent unity among them. Yet for each mode of use there is taken to be in the language a definite pattern of what is permissible, and this pattern constitutes a kind of informal logic of the term. In addition, there is a respect for ordinary language as expressing the accumulation of experience under the hard conditions of communication for centuries, as contrasted with technical language which, though essential to the developed sciences, may in other fields express fairly arbitrary notions. Accordingly, confusions are taken to come from using technical terms along inappropriate models, and clarification from tracing and analyzing the pattern of ordinary language.

Even the mere suggestion that we consult the dictionary brings fruitful insights. For the synonyms and related terms for "pleasure" pile up: for example,

"contentment," "gladness," "joy," "satisfaction," "ecstasy," "rapture," as well as, of course, "happiness," and "blessedness." To round out "pain" there are "displeasure," "sorrow," "suffering," "misery," "sadness," "unhappiness," "frustration," "anxiety," and so on. Fresh uses are pointed to when we employ some of these in the plural, and speak of "pleasures" or "sorrows." Nor are we limited to nouns. There are verbs like "thrive," "prosper," "flourish," "please," "gladden," some of them transitive, some intransitive. And prepositions enter the picture when we think of the difference between being "pleased at," "pleased by," "pleased about." All this indicates but a small part of the pasture at which analysis can nibble.

The basic treatment of pleasure along these new lines was carried out by Gilbert Ryle, first in the context of a general reanalysis of mental terms, in his *The Concept of Mind* (1949; see the chapter on "Emotion"), then in an essay on "Pleasure" in his *Dilemmas* (1956). His analysis is rich in the variety of terms invoked; for example, he tells us that by "feelings" he has in mind what people may describe as thrills, twinges, pangs, throbs, wrenches, itches, prickings, and so on. In addition to "feelings" he distinguishes classes of "inclinations," "moods," "agitations." The general supposition that "pleasure" always signifies feelings is rejected as a mistaken belief in internal episodes. Instead, "pleasure" is found to have two distinct senses. In the one sense, "pleasure" simply refers to enjoying some activity; thus in a man who enjoys digging, digging is not a vehicle of his pleasure but his pleasure itself. In the other sense, "pleasure," like "delight" or "joy," signifies moods. In the essay on "Pleasure," Ryle denies that pleasure is a sensation at all, and points out the difficulties in regarding pleasure and pain as counterparts. He further traces the problems that arise when "pleasure" is made into a technical term. This represents the hope of using pleasure as a mental force in terms of which one could employ a mechanical model and find equivalents to physical notions of pressure and attraction, friction and acceleration, and establish a system of human dynamics. Rejecting this and other models as misleading, Ryle concludes that for contexts of everyday discourse we can get along very well with such verbs as "enjoy," "dislike," and "hurt."

Various aspects in the vista thus opened up have been explored subsequently in the analytic movement. There have been critical reevaluations of Ryle's arguments, but often enough ending with similar conclusions. There is an intensive probing of many related issues, which cross into familiar epistemological problems. For example, knowledge of pain has been dealt with considerably, both one's knowledge that others are in pain and one's awareness of one's own pain, with special concern about the privacy of such phenomena and the need or possibility of evidence. Questions too have been raised about the role of belief in pleasure, the extent to which pleasure generally involves some belief, and the implications of such facts as that one can be pleased by what he believes to be the case, though the belief itself is false. This raises the further issue whether we can intelligibly speak of false pleasures, or whether such modes of speech refer rather to the justification of specific pleasures, the extent to which they may be unfounded, as well as the question whether a person may deceive himself into thinking he is enjoying something he is not. A further topic of considerable concern for morality is how far the fact that one is pleased by or likes a certain action is a reasonable ground or adequate justification for doing it, and under what conditions it is or is clearly not justifiable.

It is perhaps too early to evaluate the contributions of the linguistic approach as a whole in this field, in comparison to traditional approaches. Certainly it has broadened the area of data for the study of pleasure and pain and exhibited subtle varied patterns. On the other hand, its rejection of the scientific tradition in the study of these phenomena makes a sharp cleavage between the ordinary-life concepts and the scientific concepts. One cannot help thinking of the time in the history of physics when the rich variety of phenomena was also presented in ordinary-life concepts. Thus the ancient account of motion, as in Aristotle, differentiated rolling and sliding and pushing and pulling and falling, and so on; similarly, classification into basic types was in ordinary language terms—growth and diminution, coming-into-being and passing-away, qualitative alteration, and locomotion. In physics the ordinary account came early, and the discovery that a unifying account was possible in micro-terms and laws relating those terms came much later. Perhaps the trouble in the history of pleasure and pain is that the variety of phenomena was neglected in the hope of a quick theoretical formulation. The current emphasis on the varieties of phenomena need not then be hostile, as it tends to be, to scientific theory; it may rather be preparing us for a better theory to come. In addition, the reaction has been against a dualistic (Cartesian) philosophy of mind and body; this, as noted above, also influenced scientific developments in a special way along perhaps a blind alley. The criticism has thus been of a special scientific theory, and should not entail rejecting the possibility of fruitful scientific study of pleasure and pain.

Indeed, the variety of approaches to pleasure and happiness in the historical career of the concepts makes isolation to any one perspective no longer plausible. The linguistic-analytic study brings a greater appreciation of the complexity of the phenomena, but must not stand in the way of the scientific study of the phenomena so revealed. And a full scientific study can no longer limit itself to physiological bases, but must now embrace genetic and functional aspects on all levels. These in turn are enriched by a view of the variety of applications in diverse fields of human life and social practice. Out of such investigations we may expect a more developed and more integrated conception of happiness as a guide to individual and communal well-being.

BIBLIOGRAPHY

Sources on individual philosophers referred to are to be found in the bibliography of the article on "Right and Good." See also V. J. McGill, *The Idea of Happiness* (New York, 1967). Howard Mumford Jones, *The Pursuit of Happiness* (Cambridge, Mass., 1953; Ithaca, 1966), deals with American legal and social uses of the concept of happiness. For psychological trends, see H. M. Gardner, Ruth Clark Metcalf, and John G. Beebe-Center, *Feeling and Emotion, A History of Theories* (New York, 1937); for political philosophy, George H. Sabine, *A History of Political Theory* (New York, 1937); for economics, Eric Roll, *A History of Economic Thought*, revised and enlarged ed. (New York, 1946). Recent analytical treatments of pleasure are discussed in David L. Perry, *The Concept of Pleasure* (The Hague, 1967).

For references cited and further references: David Braybrooke, *Three Tests for Democracy: Personal Rights, Human Welfare, Collective Preference* (New York, 1968). Erich Fromm, *Man for Himself* (New York, 1947), Ch. IV. Herbert Marcuse, *Eros and Civilization* (Boston, 1955). Karl Marx, *The German Ideology*, is the English title given to the work which was first printed in full in the *Marx-Engels Gesamtausgabe*, 12 vols. (Moscow, 1927–35), Abt. I, Bd. 5. A relevant excerpt of Part II appears as Appendix III in Sidney Hook, *From Hegel to Marx* (New York and London, 1936; reprint 1950). Gilbert Ryle, *The Concept of Mind* (London, 1949), Ch. IV; *Dilemmas* (Cambridge, 1956), Ch. IV. Moritz Schlick, *Problems of Ethics*, trans. David Rynin (New York, 1939), Ch. VIII. Herbert Spencer, *The Principles of Ethics*, 2 vols. (New York, 1896), Vol. I, Chs. I–VIII. G. H. von Wright, *The Varieties of Goodness* (London, 1963), Chs. III–V. Martha Wolfenstein, "Fun Morality: An Analysis of Recent American Child-Training Literature," *Journal of Social Issues*, **7**, 4 (1951), 15–25, reprinted in *Childhood in Contemporary Cultures*, ed. Margaret Mead and Martha Wolfenstein (Chicago, 1963), Part III.

ABRAHAM EDEL

[See also Cynicism; Epicureanism; **Platonism;** Progress; Right and Good; Social Welfare; Stoicism; **Utilitarianism;** Utopia.]

HARMONY OR RAPTURE
IN MUSIC

"CONCERNING the straunge opinions of the world of Musicke," wrote Stephen Batman, in addition to his famous translation of Bartholomaeus Anglicus in 1582, "I have thought good . . . somewhat to speake thereof: . . . wheras many cannot away at all with Musick, as if it were some odious skill ranged from hell, . . . some are indifferent, . . . and some do so far dote in musicke, without the which they think ther is no religion, that betweene these unindifferent judgmentes, I am in doubt . . . to frame a speech that might qualifie so foule a discord." There were, indeed, those who believed, with the reformer Philip Stubbes, that "sweet Musick, at the first delighteth the eares, but afterward corrupteth and depraveth the minde"; others who considered it "neyther Good nor Evyll" except as it was used for virtuous or wicked purposes, or who ignored it altogether as beneath the regard of "manly spirits." But not a few looked upon music as a reflection of the divine, a ladder by which man could mount to God, the Creator of all music: "Even that vulgar and Tavern-Musicke," wrote Sir Thomas Browne, in his *Religio medici* ([1635], Part II, sec. 9), "which makes one man merry, another mad, strikes in me a deep fit of devotion and a profound contemplation of the First Composer."

Music, to Browne and many another, had in it something beyond sensuous sound to please the ear—an essential harmony that appealed even to reason and that could lead the mind to contemplation or knowledge of other things. Audible music was an image of higher kinds of harmony, that of the soul and body of man or of cosmic order, "an Hieroglyphical and shadowed lesson of the whole World, and creatures of God." If the basic principles of music were discovered, it was said, all things in the universe might be understood. Here was a key to the unchanging laws that determine the ideal concordance and unity of all that exists. And here, too, was a "gift of God" to which man might respond instinctively as well as intellectually with joy and profit.

The immutable properties of music were often said to derive from mathematical proportions that were to be found in all creation. They depended, according to another reasoning, on the inevitable progression of notes of the scale from low to high, a law to be observed also in the "ordre of astates and degrees" in the well-ordered commonwealth, where, it was believed, each class had its destined place: "Take but degree away, untune that string,/ And, hark! what discord follows" (Shakespeare, *Troilus and Cressida*, I. iii. 109–10). Harmoniousness was frequently defined as a reconciliation of opposites, a fitting together of disparate elements, whether in music, universe, the body politic, or the body of man. A thoughtful person might learn many practical lessons from music and from the instruments that make it sound.

From another less analytical viewpoint, music was thought, also, to possess an inspired virtue, not easily defined, but revealed in its power to alter man's very being: there is "nought so stockish, hard, and full of rage,/ But music for the time doth change his nature" (Shakespeare, *The Merchant of Venice*, V. i. 81–82). "Yea, the inarticulate sounds have, in themselves, I know not what secret power, to move the very affections of mens soules," wrote George Wither, in *A Preparation to the Psalter* (1619, p. 81). "Some raise the spirits to that excessive height, as the soule is almost ravished, and in an extasie." Through the senses the soul could be moved or transported.

Conjectures about the universal qualities in music, their uses and effects, were most widely expressed in England during the last quarter of the sixteenth century and early decades of the seventeenth, later than on the Continent, and at a time when counterforces of Puritanism and scientific empiricism were already in play. This period saw a flowering, too, of English music. It was then that the madrigal reached its peak (later than in Italy). Instrumental music was developing; the Anglican church achieved a music of its own to replace abolished Catholic ritual. Then, too, significant changes in musical style were taking place through the influence of humanist poets and musicians in France and Italy, who, on the basis of fragmentary evidence, attempted to restore the music of the early Greeks.

Speculative writing, however, reveals little interest in technical aspects of composition or performance that were the concern of practical musicians. Indeed, in the process of evolving analogies between perceived music and that which could only be glimpsed by the mind—or reading musical qualities into the universe and universal qualities into music—music made by man was often all but forgotten, or dismissed as similar but far inferior to divine harmony. Composers, on the other hand, while they defended their art as a representation of world symmetry and proportion or as a symbol of the divine, made no application, as far as has been noted, of metaphysical ideas to the music they composed. As had been true in the past, speculative and practical ideas about music remained two distinct spheres of thought (Hollander, pp. 22–24, 43, 53).

Speculative ideas of music were more a part of philosophy and literature than of music as we think of it today, and in these areas their influence was profound. They afforded a vast storehouse of poetic imagery, but even more significantly, they provided a broad and seemingly indispensable philosophical hypothesis that was inextricably woven into the fabric of contemporary belief. Even when not accepted literally, these ideas about music were found to image uniquely and aptly Renaissance concepts of harmony in the universe and of man's relation to it. In an age when all things, from lowest stone to highest angel, were believed to be united in a "great chain of being," in which motion or defection of one part moved the whole; when (to change the figure) all levels of existence—man, his society and government, geocosm and macrocosm—were thought to function in similar ways, each level influenced by the others and all, ideally, operating as a perfect whole, parallels could easily be found in music. The inevitable order of notes of the musical scale, the similarity of intervals within consecutive octaves, the concordant sounding of different parts as they were played together, the discord that followed "when time is broke and no proportion kept," all these made music a fitting image of world harmony.

The origins of these ideas are in the remote past, in classical philosophy, especially Pythagoreanism, in Egyptian thought, and in early myth and religious rite—sources different from those used by practical musicians who were searching for hints of ancient musical style. Early ideas were adapted by Church Fathers to Christian theology, restated by medieval Arabian writers, and synthesized by Neo-Platonists of the late fifteenth and early sixteenth centuries, chiefly by Marsilio Ficino (1433–99), to become a significant part of the Renaissance world view. Of these concepts, three will be considered here: music as a mathematical key to universal order, whether in the spheres or on earth; music as an image of the soul's harmony and as a bridge between the soul and heaven; and finally, music as a vehicle of World Spirit.

1. Music of the Spheres. The place of music in the cosmic pattern goes back, first of all, to the discovery of the Pythagoreans (as reported by later writers) that while musical strings of the same length, thickness, and tension, when plucked, invariably produce the same pitch, one such string divided in half always sounds an octave higher, a segment two-thirds as long a fifth, one three-fourths as long a fourth. An octave or diapason was represented by the numerical ratio 1:2, the fifth (diapente) by 2:3, the fourth (diatesseron) by 3:4. Tones were thus measurable in space, with pitch related to frequency of vibration. It seemed, then, by a process of analogy, that these same proportions might be applicable to motions of an ordered and unchanging universe, in which planets, from moon to outermost stars were thought to move at varying speeds in fixed and concentric circles around the spherical earth as center—an astronomical system which, highly refined

and varied by Ptolemy, was still widely accepted throughout the Renaissance, despite the new heliocentric theory of Copernicus. Intervals between the spheres, it was suggested (with spheres imagined either as crystal balls or as orbital pathways of the planets), might be similar to those revealed by strings of musical instruments; the cosmic instrument could conceivably produce musical sound comparable to that of instruments made by man.

The Pythagorean myth of Er, recounted in Plato's *Republic* (X. 614B–621D), pictured the spheres as wheels turning on an adamantine spindle, on each a siren singing one tone and together forming a harmony, while the three Fates controlled the motions both of the spheres and of the lives of men. Here was the "Sirens harmony" described by Milton in the *Arcades* (lines 63–73), sung "to those that hold the vital shears, And turn the Adamantine spindle round,/ On which the fate of gods and men is wound." Philosophers after Plato changed sirens to Muses or Intelligences, while in the Christian context they were corrected to Angels, who, in hierarchical order from Angels on the moon to Seraphs on the sphere nearest to God, filled the heavens with song. The "Crystall sphears," in Milton's *Nativity Ode* (lines 125–32), made "up full consort to th'Angelike symphony."

Whether or not the spheres and planets actually produced musical sound was a question argued for centuries, as it was still in the Renaissance. Aristotle, believing spheres to be crystalline, denied the possibility on the basis that sound, if it existed, would be so loud as to shatter solid matter. On the other hand, Macrobius, in his fifth-century *Commentary on Cicero's "Dream of Scipio"* (*De re publica*, VI. xviii. 18–19), discussed seriously the "great and pleasing sound" of the spheres, unheard by man because of the limited range of his hearing (or because, others suggested, man's soul, dragged down by his body, is closed in by "muddy vesture of decay"). In the Renaissance, philosophers of the occult, led by Ficino and Cornelius Agrippa, attributed specific tones and voices to the planets, while Aristotelians restated their Master's argument. From the beginning, however, this music had been most often considered a poetic symbol of universal harmoniousness. Milton could write poetically in the *Arcades* (lines 72–73) of this music "which none can hear/ Of human mould with grosse unpurged ear," but in his prolusion "On the Music of the Spheres," he saw it as a figure to symbolize in a "wise way" the intimate "relations of the orbs and their eternally uniform revolutions according to the fixed laws of necessity." Yet, on the Continent, the astronomer Johannes Kepler (1571-1630), who accepted the Copernican theory that the sun and not the earth is

389

the center of the universe, and who, himself, replaced the circular orbit of heavenly bodies by elliptical ones, could not abandon the belief that mathematical harmony in celestial order is analogous to that of heard music; and in *Harmonices mundi* (1619), he attempted still to express planetary motions in musical notation.

Into this mathematical-musical cosmic scheme were drawn the four elements, which Empedocles made the indestructible constituents of all things, changed only by motions of harmony and discord, and which Aristotle placed in concentric shells between the spheres of the moon and the earth. Fire, air, water, and earth eventually added four strings to the cosmic lyre or made an unheard music of their own. It was not mere whimsy that led Robert Fludd, in his *Utriusque cosmi* (1617, p. 90), to picture the entire universe as a monochord that reached from earth through the elements and the spheres, each intervening space designated as a musical interval, with the hand of God reaching from outermost heaven to tune it. "Water and Air He for the Tenor chose," wrote Abraham Cowley (1618–67), in his youthful poem, *Davideis* (Book I, secs. 35–36); "Earth made the Base, the Treble Flame arose," a song accompanied by the sounding strings of the planets. Man, too, "a little world made cunningly of elements," joined in music of macrocosmic spheres and elements.

On the authority of Pythagoras, and of Plato, who had, in his *Timaeus*, envisaged a mathematically and musically ordered universe more intricately contrived than that suggested by early Pythagorean experiments, men concluded that the basis of all harmony in macrocosm and microcosm alike is mathematical; that whatever exists is based on proportion or number, the concordant relationships of which are revealed in music. For this reason music was included in the medieval quadrivium of the liberal arts—along with arithmetic, geometry, and astronomy—where it gained a standing as an intellective study not otherwise to be achieved. "How valuable a thing music is," wrote the schoolmaster Richard Mulcaster, in prefatory verses to Tallis and Byrd's *Cantiones sacrae* (1575), "is shown by those who teach that numbers constitute the foundation of everything that has form, and that music is made up of these."

Of these numerical relationships the easiest for the layman to grasp were the Pythagorean intervals of diatesseron (fourth), diapente (fifth), and diapason (octave), which by mathematical manipulation could be combined or altered to form all other concords—for "musick is but three parts vied and multiplied." As Jean Bodin remarked, in his *Commonweale* (1606, p. 457), Plato's numbers are so difficult that even Aristotle had jumped over them "as over a dich," even as Bodin, and to a large degree, his contemporaries continued

to do. Intervals of the fourth, fifth, and octave, considered most harmonious and pleasing, symbolized for many the harmoniousness of all creation. The commonwealth "decays when harmonie is broken," wrote Bodin (p. 455), "which chaunceth when . . . you depart farthest from those concords which the Musitions call diatesseron and diapente." By these intervals, the music philosopher and physician, John Case, in his *Praise of Musicke* (1586, p. 44), measured proportions of the rational, irascible, and concupiscible faculties of the soul. On the authority of the Italian architect, Leone Battista Alberti (1404–72), who had learned "from the Schoole of Pythagoras" that harmony in sight is related to harmony of sound, Sir Henry Wotton advised, in *The Elements of Architecture* (1624, pp. 42–43), that measurements of doors and windows be based on musical intervals of octave, fourth, and fifth. Music revealed the secrets of all mathematical order, in spheres, commonwealth, the soul of man, and in his artifacts.

2. Music and Soul. Metaphysical interpretations of music were vastly enriched and broadened by Platonic ideas (not all of which originated with Plato) that carried over into Christian thought. In the *Timaeus* especially, the concept of music was extended to mean harmoniousness and concord in the broadest sense. Numbers, in themselves, had significance only as they represented abstract Ideas. They took on philosophical and ethical implication. Furthermore, the whole world, Plato taught, was animated by soul.

According to the *Timaeus* (29E–42E), the Demiurge (later called God), good and rational (in the *Symposium* motivated by love), brought the conflicting elements of Chaos into a harmony, proportion, and unity modeled on His own Idea of perfection, an ever-existent Idea intelligible only to reason, of which the sensible world is an imperfect copy. Into this body, circular in form and motion, He set a Soul, also circular in motion and numerically proportioned, but invisible, partaking of reason and harmony. Stars, planets, elements, all had souls or gods to move them—beings later designated as angels or demons, which could descend to earth in order to aid mankind. A bit of World Soul passed from the stars, whose gods added lower parts to the rational, to become the souls of men. The soul of man is tripartite, Plato continued (69C–70A), and the Renaissance thinkers, on the whole, agreed. Immortal and rational soul in the brain is distinct from mortal soul, located in the thorax, which is filled with passions and dominated by irrational sensations, and which is further divided by the midriff to form still another soul that is concerned with wants of the body. Even animals were granted an inferior soul. Living man was a part of a living universe and shared its harmony.

Following this tradition, Renaissance Platonists

imagined the soul to be endowed, as was music itself, with an innate harmony derived from that of the universe, a harmony too often broken by sin or intemperance, but restorable by dominance of Reason or by withdrawal from material things to contemplation of the divine. This harmony was described with varying metaphor: concord between intellect and desire sounded music like that of angel's song; reason played on lower faculties of the soul and those of the body, as a lutenist on his instrument, to produce the "music" of Virtue; the soul's "tune" was transposed by prayer to make the "music" of Love.

Because the soul was by nature harmonious, it was thought to respond instinctively to the similar harmony in audible music. It might take intellectual delight in viewing this image of the divine, but it was moved "naturally," too, on both an infra-rational and a super-rational level. Renaissance meanings of "nature" and "natural" were varied and require a brief digression. Nature meant, first, all things made by God in contrast to those made by man; but it was also a force or energy, which, acting as an agent of God, dominated natural things. By Nature, each existing thing was endowed with an essential property that determined its behavior. By immutable Laws of Nature, order was imposed and reactions controlled. The eternal substance of number in the universe was established by a Law of Nature— that "Numb'ry Law" remarked on by Du Bartas in his *Divine Weekes and Workes* (1621, p. 301), "which did accompany/ Th'Almighty-most" in the world's creation. Another law decreed that "every kindred substance" move inevitably "toward its kind," as iron moves toward the lodestone, or move with it in sympathy, as an idle instrument sounds when one similarly tuned is struck. It seemed "natural," then, that the soul of man, to the extent that it retains its original harmony, should respond or be attracted to music even without conscious thought.

Man need not be intellectual to be so affected. The most barbarous peoples, it was said for centuries, are inevitably charmed by harmonious sound, an opinion repeated by John Case in his *Praise of Musicke* (1586, p. 42): the infant, destitute of reason, is stilled by the songs of his nurse; ploughmen and carters "are by the instinct of their harmonicall soules compelled to frame their breath into a whistle," which delights not man alone but the oxen and horses. And the cause of this "delectation," Case concluded (pp. 53–54), is "the convenience and agreement which musicke hath with our nature."

The lowliest souls, even those of animals, experienced irrational pleasure in musical sounds, but the soul could be moved on a higher instinctive level. It could, by sympathetic response to the harmonious motions of music, be brought back to its original harmony. "Music . . . in so far as it uses audible sounds," Plato had written in the *Timaeus* (47C–D), "was bestowed for the sake of harmony. And harmony, which has motions akin to the revolutions of the Soul within us, was given . . . not as an aid to irrational pleasure, . . . but as an auxiliary to the inner revolution of the Soul, when it has lost its harmony, to assist in restoring it to order and concord with itself." "The very harmony of sounds . . . carried from the ear to the spiritual faculties of our souls," echoed the Elizabethan churchman, Richard Hooker, in *Of the Laws of Ecclesiastical Polity* ([1597], Book V, sec. XXXVIII [1]), "is by a native puissance and efficacy greatly available to bring to a perfect temper whatsoever is there troubled." By sympathetic response like that of "Brethren strings," wrote Abraham Cowley in *Davideis* (Book I, secs. 39–40), "Davids lyre did Sauls wild rage controul,/ And tun'd the harsh disorders of his Soul."

Music was credited with even greater powers. By virtue of its harmoniousness, it could, by an "occult magnetism," draw the soul from body in ecstasy; the soul returned with delight to its divine origins. Poets made a commonplace of the image of soul being literally drawn from the body through the ear. "Heavenly sounds, . . . with Division (of a choice device),/ The Hearers soules out at their ears intice," Sylvester translated from Du Bartas' *Divine Weekes and Workes* (1621, p. 25). Crashaw's lutenist, in "Musick's Duell" (1646, lines 145–50), is ravished by the music he makes, his soul "snatch out at his Eares/ By a strong Extasy" to ascend "through all the sphaeares of Musicks heaven" to the "Empyraeum of pure Harmony." Shakespeare transformed oddity to magic in *The Merchant of Venice* (V. i. 67–68), when musicians are told to "pierce your mistress' ear/ And draw her home with music," or to humor in *Much Ado About Nothing* (II. iii. 60–63), when Benedick remarks on the strangeness of the fact that "sheeps' guts should hale souls out of men's bodies."

Poets described, also, a less passive inner rapture or ecstasy in which soul did not leave the body completely, but in which, through contemplation of the universal in the particular, of World Harmony revealed in audible sounds, mind could separate itself from sense and rise even above reason to an understanding or vision of the divine—an idea that has deep roots in philosophies of love as they had come down from Plato through Plotinus to Renaissance Neo-Platonists. This is the ecstasy desired by the contemplative man of Milton's "Il Penseroso" (lines 161–66), where "pealing Organ" and "full voic'd Quire . . ./ In Service high, and Anthems cleer," dissolve the listener "into extasies,/ And bring all Heav'n before . . . [his] eyes."

391

In "At a Solemn Musick," "divine sounds" of "Voice, and Vers" present to the "high-rais'd phantasie" a vision (not here called ecstasy) of heavenly singing, from which phantasy rises still higher to understanding of inaudible music made by God among men, which sounded "In perfect Diapason" until broken by "disproportion'd sin."

These ideas of the power of music to draw soul from body or to free it from earthly ties merged in an unexpected context. They became basic argument for defenders of church music, who, in answer to the opposition's denial of music's power to touch the soul, stated their belief that there is a virtue naturally in music to give spiritual joy and to elevate the soul to oneness with heaven, a power that can "knit & joyne us unto God." These men avoided outright commitment to the "fancie" that the soul is, or possesses, harmony; claims that music could create ecstasy were qualified. But no better image could be found, apparently, hyperbolic as it was, to explain the efficacy of music to move affections of the soul and to lift man's "cogitations above himself." "So pleasing" are the effects of musical harmony, wrote Richard Hooker, in *Of the Laws . . .* (op. cit.), "that some have been induced to think that the soul itself by nature is or hath in it harmony . . . there is also that carrieth as it were into ecstasies, filling the mind with an heavenly joy and for the time in a manner severing it from the body." George Wither emphasized, more than had Hooker, the soul's ascent through contemplation, when he wrote, in *A Preparation to the Psalter* (1619, p. 83), of the "divine raptures" of church music "that allure and dispose the soule unto heavenly meditations, and to the high supernaturall apprehension of spiritual things." "Spiritual song," agreed Charles Butler, in his *Principles of Musik* (1636, p. 1), "ravisheth the minde with a kinde of ecstasi, lifting it up from the regarde of earthly things, unto the desire of celestiall joyz." Champions of music in divine service returned, throughout the century, to these notions of a universal harmony in music and its power to elevate the soul.

3. Music and Spirit. Speculative ideas of music in the Renaissance also had intricate relationships with Spirit. The harmony of the universe was sometimes attributed not to World Soul but to World Spirit. By association with Spirit, it was said, music has its effects, not on the soul of man, but on his spirits.

No greater muddle faces the modern reader than the many older meanings of "Spirit" and "spirits," all of which were involved in theories of the nature and effects of music. From the early Greeks came the idea of World Spirit, a unifying element in the universe, sometimes equivalent to World Soul, sometimes an intermediary between Soul and matter. This concept

is related to Aristotle's postulation in *De caelo* (269a 30–270b 20) of a fifth element (which came to be called the quintessence), an aether, more subtle than fire or air, a substance similar to that of the stars, immortal and eternal, which pervades all things (as in the Stoic World Soul—*anima mundi*). It exists in its purest state outside of the spheres, Aristotle theorized, but with increasing impurity it spreads down through spheres and elements to lowest earthly matter. Every form or body depends on the nature of its spirit: in ascending scale, body becomes more pure and aethereal; celestial Intelligences have no material body at all but are souls clothed in pure spirit. (This pervasive fifth element explained for astrologers the pathway by which stars and planets transmit their influence. Alchemists hoped, by infusing superior spirit into lower forms, to convert base metals to gold.) Spirit might indicate, also, an astral or sidereal vehicle given to souls by the stars. Hebrew theology introduced, further, the transcendent Spirit of God, which brought order out of Chaos and breathed life into man. Spirits in the form of angels or demons, good or bad—souls with spiritual bodies— inhabited the empyreal heavens, planets, or elements.

There were also the aerial but corporeal spirits of man—natural, vital, and animal—which were expressed from the blood, refined in the heart, further subtilized in the brain, each serving a function of the tripartite soul, and linking soul to body as World Spirit mediated between World Soul and matter. They were usually discussed in a purely medical sense, but they were, even so, related to the quintessence, by which they were nourished, and occasionally to astral Spirit, whose nature they shared. However described, they were considered quite distinct from the Spirit of God, a spark of which resided only in the rational soul.

Pagan and Christian, materialistic and occult ideas, were confused or interrelated so as to baffle the most earnest scholar then as now. Every writer made his own interpretations, which varied in different works, or even in the same work. Sometimes "soul" and "spirit" were used synonymously. Any brief review, then, of the relation of music to spirit must be simplified, ignoring, as it must, historical evolution of ideas, variation in individual philosophies, and specific theological controversy.

In writing influenced by Platonic tradition, however, one view remains constant: spirit is musical. World Spirit *is* the harmony of the universe and shares that of the planets. "Th'all-quickning Spirit of God," in the imagery of Du Bartas, in *Divine Weekes and Workes* (1621, p. 301), turns the "whirling wheels" of the universe to make a music like that made by a blast of air in a great organ. In George Herbert's "Easter," the "blessèd Spirit" of God is called to "bear a part" in the music of "heart and lute." Angelic Spirits sing in heaven; "Millions of spiritual Creatures," described by Milton in *Paradise Lost* (IV. 677–82), "walk the Earth/ Unseen," raising "Celestial voices to the midnight air." Spirits in man, moving harmoniously, make a harmony of soul and body. Music itself has and breathes spirit (Finney, p. 106), which affects other spirit.

Everyone agreed that music moves human spirits. The most common explications, being basically physiological, are only indirectly related to ideas discussed in this article and need be reviewed only briefly. Since the species or forms of sense impressions were thought to be carried to the soul by spirits, and all psychological or emotional response to be reflected in predictable motion of spirits in the body—especially in the heart, the center of emotion—it could be assumed that perception of musical sound inevitably alters the spirits. Music can move spirits, also, it was believed, by physical contact. Hearing, more than any other sense, wrote Ficino (Walker [1958], pp. 7–10), has immediate effect on the spirits, because moving air, the vehicle of sound, strikes directly the innate air in the ear, which is or has in it aerial spirit, and sets up a motion that penetrates to the innermost parts. The effect of music is thus corporeal, but it is psychological, too, for harmony shapes the spirits to its own motions and moods. Francis Bacon having explained, in his *Sylva sylvarum* (Century II, exp. 114) that "the sense of hearing striketh the spirits more immediately than any other senses," continued to an accepted analysis of musical effects: "Harmony, entering easily, and mingling not at all, and coming with a manifest motion, doth by custom of often affecting the spirits and putting them into one kind of posture, alter not a little the nature of the spirits," and thus communicates the feelings of gaiety or sadness of "musical tunes and airs." Even without perception, argued Thomas Wright, in *The Passions of the Minde* (1604, p. 170), motion can be transmitted from the ear to spirits in the heart to induce a "posture" of the spirits there that produces a "semblance" of passions in the mind.

According to still another theory popularized by Neo-Platonic philosophers of love, air entering the ear carries with it not only harmonious sound or moving air, but also the spirits of the singer. That voice is caused by breath and spirit striking the windpipe, and that living spirit issues with breath, were established beliefs in the inherited physiology of the Renaissance. Song, then, is animated breath carrying with it the feelings and temperament of the singer, which are communicated to spirits of the listener, just as spirits from the eye of a beloved alter those of the lover, or as spirits from an "evil eye" infect with disease.

Occult philosophers, however, believed that music could also transmit World Spirit and thus alter the "quintessential" or astral spirits of man. As a man's spirits could be fed by those in plants or wine, or altered by spirits of the singer, so they could be affected by celestial Spirit, which carries influences of the stars and planets. From Hermetic works, early Neo-Platonic texts, and medieval writings on magic, came belief in the use of talismans, odors, lights, and music to invoke this influence—ideas especially related to music by Ficino and by the chief disseminator of his ideas, the peripatetic German philosopher, Cornelius Agrippa. Because music has the same numerical proportions as the heavenly bodies, Ficino argued, it has power to make the spirits of man similarly proportioned, so that they vibrate in sympathy with the planets and are able to breathe in more copiously the heavenly Spirit and influence (Walker [1958], p. 14). Music could, in this way, alter dispositions and manners; it was a kind of Philosopher's Stone by which the spirits of man, by spiritual alchemy, could become angelic. Music "doth wonderfully allure the Celestial influence," wrote Agrippa, in his *Occult Philosophy* (trans. 1651, p. 255), so as to "change the affections, intentions, gestures, motions, actions and dispositions of all the hearers." And again (p. 278): "Wise ancients . . . did not in vain use Musical sounds and singings, as to . . . make a man sutable [sic] to the Celestial Harmony, and make him wholly Celestial." Ficino himself, in a rare union of speculative and practical music, composed songs, adapted to the aspects of the stars and to the temperament of the person to be affected, which he supposed to resemble the Orphic Hymns, and by which he hoped to approach the magic of Orpheus, who had moved trees and stones and charmed Pluto by his singing (Walker, pp. 19–24).

The power of music to attract or infuse World Spirit, implicit in Ficino's theory, was further emphasized in his interpretation of a passage in the *Asclepius*, attributed to the ancient Egyptian theologian, Hermes Trismegistus, a work that Ficino had translated. There he found an account of the art of making gods by infusing into idols or statues the souls of demons and angels with the aid of talismans, odors, and music. This passage he assumed to be the source of one in the *Enneads* of Plotinus (IV. 3. 11), which he interpreted to mean that by music "one can attract into and retain in a material object 'something vital from the soul of the world and the souls of the spheres and stars'" (Walker, pp. 40–41). Life could be given to inanimate matter. Ficino did not envisage the invoking of Spirit in the form of demons and angels, who presumably had souls. He disclaimed use of any such "demonic magic"— "black magic"—a practice condemned by the Church.

393

He was firm in insisting that talismans and music infuse only impersonal World Spirit and that they affect only the spirits and not the soul of man (ibid., p. 45). Certain of his followers, however, were less cautious. His pupil, Francesco da Diacetto, gave serious consideration to attracting planetary demons or gods by music, as did Agrippa, more influentially, in his *Occult Philosophy* (ibid., pp. 30–35, 94–96). Through Agrippa's writing, especially, Ficino's theories were carried into the realm of forbidden magic and brought into disrepute.

Invocation of planetary gods and demons was clearly heretical, a return, contended orthodox Catholics throughout the sixteenth century, to Egyptian mysteries and medieval magic. This practice was thought to disregard the supreme power of God, who alone controlled Heavenly Spirits and alone gave life. English Protestants found even more to condemn in the use of ritualistic scents, images, or music to attract Divine Spirit. That the mind might be directed to God by contemplation of universal harmony imaged in music had defense; that the Spirit of God could be attracted by earthly music rarely did. Even the biblical parallel to be found in the account of God's Spirit descending to the accompaniment of psaltery and pipe, to inspire Elisha to prophecy (II Kings 3:51), noted by Wither in his *Preparation to the Psalter* (1619, p. 83) and by Charles Butler in *The Principles of Musik* (1636, p. 115), as proof of music's force, was usually interpreted as a miracle attributable not to music but to the "extraordinary Interposition" of God Himself.

Yet all of these esoteric Ficinian ideas contributed to English thought. Belief in the power of music to attract stellar influence and even to call down demons and angels enjoyed a vogue in occult writing, especially in the 1650's, following the translation of Agrippa's *Occult Philosophy* in 1651, but earlier, too—in writings consistently attacked as religiously unorthodox. William Ingpen, in *The Secrets of Numbers* (1624, pp. 94–95), repeated Agrippa's enthusiastic account of the force of music: "Musical harmony" has such "power and vertues . . . that shee is called the Imatatrix of the starres, . . . And when she followeth celestiall bodies so exquisitely, it is incredible to think, how shee provoketh those heavenly influxes." By means of harmonious and pervasive World Spirit, wrote the Rosicrucian, John Heydon, in *The Harmony of the World* (1662, p. 115), "man is made subject to the influence of the Stars." Through this medium, lights and sounds—which share the same "Harmonicall proportions" as the planets—can draw down souls from the moon to be "effectual in the operations of nature" (p. 75). These notions explain the imagery of Edward Benlowes' poem, "A Poetic Descant upon a Private Musick-Meeting" (1652), in which he describes each musical

instrument as a planet, possessing the same capacity to move emotions or to "Re-inspire our lumpish clay."

Occult ideas of the power of music to control Spirit or to infuse life found most subtle expression, however, in the charming imagery of earlier verse. Freed of specific explication and theological association, poetic elements remained, to add incalculable richness to the verse of Shakespeare, Milton, and many lesser men. The "Sphear-born harmonious Sisters, Voice, and Vers," of Milton's "At a Solemn Musick," "Wed . . . divine sounds" to pierce "Dead things with inbreath'd sense." Sabrina, the water spirit in *Comus* (lines 817–920), invoked by song, by song gives life to the Lady "in stony fetters fixt." Hermione, in Shakespeare's *The Winter's Tale* (V. iii. 98–111), who seems turned to a statue, is given life, as were the statues in the *Asclepius*, by music. By her voice, Chapman's Corynna, in *Ovids Banquet of Sence* (1595, stanza xi), as she bathes near statues of Niobe and her children, woos the gods to add their power to hers to "try if with her voyces vitall sounde/ She could warme life through those cold statues spread." Later poets, as did Thomas Stanley, in "Celia Singing" (1651), imagined the beloved possessed by an angel who disposed her breath to harmony that could not only draw soul from body but also infuse into "Plants and Stones," a new life "that Cherubins would choose; . . . Kill those that live, and dead things animate."

By mid-seventeenth century, however, ideas of world harmony imaged in music, and of the power of music to exert divine influence, long under attack, had, with rare exception, lost both actual and symbolic significance. With the sun made the center of the universe, with planets moving in what seemed to many, as to John Donne, a "various and perplexed course," man found himself bewildered and alone in a fragmented universe, no "commerce" left between his world and heaven. Music itself came to be judged as acoustically measured sound, its universal mathematics reduced to physics or technical practice, with no direct relationship to world harmony and no hidden power to move the soul of man. There were those, late in the century, who stood against the flood of scientific change, and who claimed still, as did Thomas Mace, in *Musick's Monument* (1676, p. 3), that music has "wonderful-powerful-efficacious Virtues and Operations . . . upon the Souls and Spirits of Men Divinely-bent," or as did Charles Hickman, in a sermon preached on St. Cecilia's Day, 1695 (1696, pp. 16–17), that musical sound "is an Inlet . . . to Divine Visions and Revelations," that it "carries such extasies, and Raptures, . . . as to elevate the Soul of man into a higher Region." But, in the main, imagery inspired by old ideas had fallen to the level of poetical conceit or subject of jest. For many years, however, it provided men with words and symbols by which to express their belief in universal harmony, order, and unity.

BIBLIOGRAPHY

For early ideas of music see Warren D. Anderson, *Ethos and Education in Greek Music* (Cambridge, Mass., 1966); Edward A. Lippman, *Musical Thought in Ancient Greece* (New York, 1964); Leo Spitzer, "Classical and Christian Ideas of World Harmony," *Traditio*, **2** (1944), 409–64 and **3** (1945), 307–64; Eric Werner and Isaiah Sonne, "The Philosophy and Theory of Music in Judaeo-Arabic Literature," *Hebrew Union College Annual*, **16** (1941), 251–319 and **17** (1942–43), 511–72. On Ficino and music see D. P. Walker, *Spiritual and Demonic Magic from Ficino to Campanella* (London, 1958). For reflection of philosophical ideas of music in Renaissance verse see Gretchen Ludke Finney, *Musical Backgrounds for English Literature 1580–1650* (New Brunswick, N.J., 1962); John Hollander, *The Untuning of the Sky* (Princeton, 1961); James Hutton, "Some English Poems in Praise of Music," *English Miscellany*, **2** (1951). Humanistic trends in music, especially on the Continent, are discussed by Edward Lowinsky, "Music in the Culture of the Renaissance," *Journal of the History of Ideas*, **15** (1954), 509–53; D. P. Walker, "Musical Humanism in the Sixteenth and Early Seventeenth Centuries," *The Music Review*, **2** (1941), 1–13, 111–21, 220–27, 288–308 and **3** (1942), 55–71. For music in England consult Morrison Comegys Boyd, *Elizabethan Music and Musical Criticism* (Philadelphia, 1940); Gustave Reese, *Music in the Renaissance* (New York, 1954), pp. 763–883; Walter L. Woodfill, *Musicians in English Society* (Princeton, N.J., 1953). Primary sources not completed in the text include: Heinrich Cornelius Agrippa von Nettesheim, *De occulta philosophia* (1631), trans. as *Three Books of Occult Philosophy* (London, 1651); Francis Bacon, *Sylva sylvarum* in *Works*, ed. James Spedding, Robert Leslie Ellis, Douglas Denon Heath (New York, 1864), IV, 231; Stephen Batman, *Batman uppon Bartholome* (London, 1582), Addition to Book XIX, fol. 424 *verso;* Edward Benlowes, "Poetic Descant," in *Minor Poets of the Caroline Period*, ed. George Saintsbury (Oxford, 1921), I, 483; Jean Bodin, *Les six livres de la République* (1576), trans. Richard Knolles as *The Six Books of a Commonweale* (London, 1606); Richard Crashaw, "Musick's Duell," *The Delights of the Muses*, in *The Poems*, ed. L. C. Martin (Oxford, 1927), pp. 149–53; Guillaume du Bartas de Salluste, *La Sepmaine; ou Création du monde* (1578), trans. Joshua Sylvester as *Du Bartas, his Divine Weekes and Workes* (London, 1621), "The Columnes. The IIII. Part of the Second Day of the II. Week"; Macrobius, *Commentary on the Dream of Scipio*, Book II, Chs. 1–5, trans. William Harris Stahl (New York, 1952), pp. 185–200; Philip Stubbes, *The Anatomie of Abuses* (London, 1583), "Of Musick."

GRETCHEN LUDKE FINNEY

[See also Alchemy; Chain of Being; Demonology; Love; Macrocosm and Microcosm; **Music as Divine Art;** Nature; Neo-Platonism; Platonism; **Pythagorean Harmony.**]

HEALTH AND DISEASE

I

HEALTH AND disease are familiar notions, commonly used in a complementary sense, viz., health as absence of disease and disease as a lack of health. But any attempt at a precise definition of these two concepts meets with considerable difficulties and throws doubt on the validity of the popular usage.

A person suffering from an ordinary cold may declare himself ill, whereas the same person laid up with a broken leg may claim to be in perfect health. These common examples indicate the complexity behind the concepts of health and disease, a complexity apparent throughout the history of mankind. Health and disease have been experienced by almost every human being, and the emotional as well as rational reactions have differed and have manifested themselves differently. The history of these two ideas must, therefore, take into account definitions and explanations by philosophers and physicians, as well as the reactions and usage of others. Within this vast history, any order can be achieved only by neglecting innumerable details, by paradigmatic use of relatively few opinions and practices, and by admitting that a different point of view may show a different panorama.

The myths of many ancient civilizations tell of a golden age, free from ills, then followed by troubled and disease-ridden times. Before Pandora's box was opened, men lived on earth "without evils, hard toil, and grievous disease." But now that the lid is off, "thousands of miseries roam among men, the land is full of evils and full is the sea. Of themselves, diseases come upon men, some by day and some by night, and they bring evils to the mortals" (Hesiod, *Works and Days*, 90–103). Sickness here is just one among the many forms of suffering to which man has been subjected at all times. When and where he began to separate illness from other kinds of suffering we do not know, and down to our own days the demarcation has remained uncertain.

In the *Atharva-Veda* of ancient India there is a prayer for a mad person, that the gods might "uncraze" him, as the translator has it. "Crazed from sin against the gods, crazed from a demon—I, knowing, made a remedy, when he shall be uncrazed." It seems impossible to tell whether the crazy person is believed "sick" or whether he falls into a different category. The *Atharva-Veda* is not a medical work; it contains prayers against many ills and sings the praise of many things. In this case it is not easy to maintain a sharp distinction between disease and other kinds of suffering.

Evidence of very early specialization in ancient Egypt suggests, on the other hand, that some groups of people learned how to remedy certain painful or incapacitating conditions and bequeathed such limited knowledge without any theories or even clear notions of disease.

The manner in which illness was approached in the archaic civilizations of Egypt and Mesopotamia shows considerable similarities. Disease is described as a complex of symptoms; often the localization in a special part of the body is stated. There are many different complexes of symptoms, of what may "befall" the person (the meaning of the Greek word *sumptoma*), and there are consequently many diseases, which may be given names or may be connected with actions of demons and deities. The disease pictures can offer indications for the outcome, for death or recovery; they also offer a basis for action.

Most of the types of disease are described as symptoms or syndromes presenting themselves at a certain moment. For instance, the surgical Edwin Smith Papyrus, whose original composition probably goes back to the Old Kingdom, tells what the physician will find when he examines injured men. The descriptions vary with the kind of injury and its location, and there is something approaching a diagnosis, and a prognosis, and there is, of course, therapy. Examination of the patient has led to a recognition of the nature of the case. The text then adds that the ailment is one "which I will treat," or "with which I will contend," or "not to be treated," verdicts connected with a forecast of the disease as curable, uncertain, or incurable. Analogy with the development of prognosis in the times of Hippocrates (ca. 400 B.C.) suggests the possibility of a social motive for such forecasts. The physician may have felt the need to protect himself against possible later reproach, especially if he undertook the cure of a patient who then died.

While an injury invited examination and an immediate decision, internal ailments also were described in both Egypt and Mesopotamia as pictures presenting themselves at the height of the illness. However, such a static view was not the only one. In Mesopotamia, where the reading of omens was developed into an art, the symptoms of the disease were understood as omens too, just as a potsherd found by the exorciser on his way to the sick man could be of ominous portent. The symptoms need not all appear at once; they could be observed over a length of time or could change. "If, at the beginning of the disease, the temples show heat and if, afterwards, heat and transpiration disappear, (it is) an affection due to dryness; after suffering from it for two or three days, he will recover" (Labat, 1951). The reference to dryness points to the realm of observation and to reasoning in terms of natural phenomena. But in a subsequent case, the demon "râbisu" is accused of having attached himself to the sick man, feeding on his food and drinking his water.

Disease in Mesopotamian medical texts often was connected with "the hand" of some deity, and "the hand" of such a god was also recognized in nonmedical contexts (Labat, 1951). Similarly, Leviticus 13 describes a skin condition diagnosed as *Zara'ath*, which is usually translated as leprosy. Not only is this identification medically doubtful, but *Zara'ath* was more than a human disease; it could be found in houses and garments as well. It was a term denoting ritual impurity, sometimes inflicted as punishment by God, as in the case of Miriam (Numbers 12:10) and of Gehazi, the servant of Elisha (II Kings 5:27).

Disease receives meaning when placed in man's moral universe when its occurrence within a scheme of creation and right and wrong actions is accounted for. In the archaic civilizations of Egypt, India, Israel, and Mesopotamia, this universe was comprised of everyday life, as well as of magic and religion. Disease was punishment for trespass or sin, ranging from involuntary infraction of some taboo to wilful crime against gods or men. Disease could also be due to the evil machinations of sorcery. Gods or demons could cause disease without taking possession, or they could represent the disease within the body. The magic and religious interpretations of disease did not necessarily exclude naturalistic explanations. Archaic civilizations were not logical systems rejecting what did not fit into the dominant scheme of things. Mesopotamian medical works have been characterized as mere literary fixation of old medical lore (Oppenheim, 1962). For ancient Egypt it has been contended (Grapow, 1956) that no single concept could be found to cover the different approaches to disease. Yet there were beginnings toward a speculative rather than magical view of disease. The connection of heart beat with pulse beat was recognized, and systems of blood vessels were invented, thought to carry disease to various parts of the body. Possibly a noxious agent (*Whdw*) was assumed, which spread putrefaction and indeed forced the body or its parts to undergo the very process against which embalming was to protect the corpse (Steuer, 1948). *Whdw* could also be a demon, and this has suggested the transfer from an originally demonistic to a more physiological principle. If this interpretation (Steuer, 1948) is correct, we see here the beginning of the metamorphosis of archaic into the rationalized and systematic thought of the medical and philosophical works of classical India, China, and Greece. But no arbitrary end can be assigned to the archaic ways of looking upon health and disease; many features even survive in the superstitions and the unconscious motivations of modern man.

II

In the Indian *Caraka Samhitā* the emergence of diseases prompts the great sages, compassionate doers of good, to acknowledge that "Health is the supreme foundation of virtue, wealth and enjoyment, and salvation," and that "diseases are the destroyers of health, of the good of life, and even of life itself." They send a messenger to Indra to ask him how to remedy diseases, whereupon the god teaches the messenger the science of life, which begins with general speculations on the world, on causality, on man and his components, viz., mind, spirit, and body. Body and mind are the dwelling places of health, as well as of disease. Wind, bile, and phlegm are the three "dosa" responsible for disease in the body, while passion and delusion cause disease of the mind. Somatic and spiritual remedies help in the former, whereas the latter must be approached through "religion, philosophy, fortitude, remembrance and concentration" (Sutrasthana, Ch. I). Both health and disease thus have their place in a religious, philosophical, and medical sphere. Diseases originate from a wide range of external or internal causes of a somatic or psychological nature; but demons are still one of the possibilities.

In India, medicine, *ayurveda*, is the veda of longevity. Similarly, in China, health and disease are incorporated into the philosophy of the Tao and the two polar principles, the yin and the yang. Health and disease are now states of the human microcosm, which has its parallel in the macrocosm. In accordance with the role played in Tao philosophy and practice by the notion of prolonging life, health and longevity tend to be identified. However, there is a gulf between the natural association of good health and long life on the one hand, and the association of health and potential immortality on the other. Western religions and, until the eighteenth century at least, prevailing Western philosophy too, thought of death as man's unavoidable fate (Gruman, 1966). The same is true of Buddhism. "So this is life! Youth into old age, health into disease" (*Dhammapada*). This was the insight that started Prince Siddhartha on the long journey leading to his illumination as Buddha. His four noble truths have been compared with the questions an Indian physician would ask himself when confronted with a patient: Is he ill, what is the nature and cause of his illness, is the disease curable, what treatment is indicated? (Zimmer, 1948). But Buddha's goal of treatment was not immortality; it was Nirvana, eventual extinction.

For the Greeks, too, health was one of the greatest goods. To be healthy, said Theognis (frag. 255), is the "most desirable" thing. The high level of Greek medicine is, in itself, a sign that disease was abhorred. Hygiene, the maintenance of health, played a very great role, above all for the well-to-do, who were expected to devote much of their time to it. For the philosopher, health had its value as the necessary basis for the practice of virtue. But since health does not altogether depend on man's actions, the Stoic philosophers did not declare health an absolute value. The sage was superior to all disease, of body as well as of soul (Cicero, *Tusculan Disputations*, III, xxxiv, 82), but this did not prevent Stoic philosophers from taking great interest in the minute classification and subdivisions of disturbances (*perturbationes;* ibid., IV, x, 23ff.). They thought of disturbances of the mind, discussing them in analogy to bodily diseases. For since early times, disease, to the Greeks, was a somatic disturbance with manifestations that could be somatic or psychic. The causes of disease could be many; gods, too, could send diseases and could cure them, as they could cause or alleviate any disaster. But Greek physicians and philosophers agreed that disease was a natural process, so that the secularization of the concept of disease was limited only by the divinity of nature herself. A Greek physician of about 400 B.C. could, therefore, say that all diseases were divine and all were human (Hippocrates, *On the Sacred Disease*, Ch. XXI), thereby meaning that all diseases had their roots in the body and in human actions and were influenced by external agencies which, like cold, sun, and winds, were divine. Epidemic diseases were attributed to pollutions (*miasmata*) in the air inhaled by all the people of an afflicted region. The *miasmata* might be caused by the action of the sun, which replaced the sun god Apollo, who, according to the myth, had inflicted a plague upon Thebes which was polluted by the deeds of Oedipus (Sophocles, *Oedipus the King*, 96–98).

Medical speculations on the origin of disease paid little attention to divine or magic interference, but all the more to mistakes in the way of life, above all in diet (Hippocrates, *On Ancient Medicine*, Ch. III). Some four hundred years later, the Latin author Celsus believed that in Homeric times health had been generally good. Indolence and luxury had later spoiled man and led to much disease. Therapy fell into the hands of physicians who treated by means of diet, and who became interested in natural philosophy (*De medicina*, prooemium, 1–5 and 9).

On the practical side, dietetic treatment paralleled practices of the athletic trainers. On the theoretical side, it went together with a view of health as balance, harmony, symmetry, and of disease as their disturbance. Using political metaphors, Alcmaeon of Croton (fifth century B.C.) taught that health was maintained by the balance (*isonomia*) of such powers as moist, dry, cold, hot, bitter, sweet, whereas disease was caused by single rule (*monarchia*) (frag. 4). Other explanations were

397

offered in terms of elements, body fluids (humors), or atoms. In the second century A.D. Galen, in the tradition of Hippocratic, Platonic, Aristotelian, and Stoic ideas, elaborated a doctrine which was schematically systematized in late antiquity and then remained dominant till the seventeenth century. Four basic qualities in binary combinations characterized four elements which had their analogues in the four principal humors of the body. Hot and dry corresponded to fire and yellow bile, hot and moist to air and blood, cold and dry to earth and black bile, cold and moist to water and phlegm. These analogues could be extended to the ages of man, the seasons, and winds, so that man in health and disease was explicable in terms of natural philosophy. The humors were products of digested food and of metabolism, and man's functions were regulated from the anatomical centers of liver, heart, and brain, from which veins, arteries, and nerves originated, and in which the natural soul, the vital soul, and the rational soul, respectively, had their seats. The soul had somatic, as well as psychological, functions: the natural soul represented man's appetites and regulated his nutrition; the vital soul represented the passions, especially anger, and regulated the body heat through the *pneuma* of the arteries; the rational soul accounted for thinking, feeling, and willing, receiving messages and imparting its commands via the nerves.

Man was in good health if his body, its parts and humors, had the temperament proper to them, and when the structure and functions of the organs were intact. Otherwise there was disease, as a consequence of which all possible symptoms could befall the patient. In view of the labile condition of the body, ideal health was rarely attained. But only when there was pain, and when a man was impeded in the functions of his personal and civic life, was actual disease considered to be present. There existed a borderland of relative health between perfection and actual disease.

Such a concept of health and disease rests on a teleologically conceived biology. All parts of the body are built and function so as to allow man to lead a good life and to preserve his kind. Health is a state according to Nature; disease is contrary to Nature. It is thus possible to speak of disease as a disturbance, and of health as good, as deteriorating, or as improving.

In its medical aspect the Galenic doctrine grew out of a particular set of ideas found in the works of Hippocrates, whose name was given to some seventy Greek medical writings of about 400 B.C. Many of these writings, allegedly associated with the island of Cos, the birthplace of Hippocrates, reveal a strongly individualizing approach to disease. It is left to the physician to combine the many physical and mental symptoms into a diagnosis of the particular case.

But that did not exclude recognition of diseases as entities. The Hippocratics spoke of consumption, pneumonia, pleurisy, the sacred disease, i.e., epilepsy. On the last there even exists a monograph which discusses causes, development, course, and major symptoms; it illustrates that a disease was thought of as a process developing in time. On the other hand, rather than arrange symptoms into disease pictures, Hippocratic physicians often associated symptoms with the constitution of their patients, usually expressed in humoral terms. The four temperaments, phlegmatic, sanguine, choleric, and melancholic, still spoken of today, echo a psychosomatic classification of human constitutions according to the Hippocratic-Galenic tradition.

In some books of the Hippocratic collection, ascribed to the medical center of Cnidos, disease entities stand in the foreground. Four "diseases" are connected with the kidneys; there is a dropsy coming from the spleen; the disease "hepatitis" is attributed to the black bile flowing into the liver. In short, diseases are classified, ascribed to organs, and, together with their symptoms, explained in humoral terms. After the advances made in anatomy from the early third century B.C., anatomical considerations were given increased space, for instance in Galen, Rufus of Ephesus, and Aretaeus.

Not all ancient physicians thought it necessary to give anatomical and physiological explanations for disease. The "empiricist" sect, relying on experience only, tried to assemble the syndromes of diseases but refrained from dealing with any causes other than such evident ones as cold, hunger, fatigue. The "methodist" sect, though it had developed from the atomistic speculations of Asclepiades (first century B.C.), according to which the pores of the body could become too wide or too narrow, was satisfied with acknowledging the existence of three conditions: constriction, relaxation, and a mixture of both, conditions recognizable from the symptoms without recourse to speculation (Edelstein, 1967).

At the end of antiquity, these sects all but disappeared in the Greek-speaking East. The Galenic system predominated and was inherited by Syrians, Arabs, Persians, and Jews, to make its entrance into the West from the eleventh century on. The biological basis of the Galenic system was little changed. But it was transferred into a world that looked upon health and disease otherwise than did the pagans.

III

To the Greeks, the preservation of health through temperance in eating, drinking, and other activities was a model for healthy thinking (Snell, 1953), *sōphrosynē*, soundness of mind. With it were connected well-being and deliverance from ills, as the etymological roots of the allied Greek words *sōs, sōtēria,* "suggest." For Aeschylus (*Eumenides,* 535–37) "much desired happiness, beloved by all, [comes] from a healthy mind." To the Stoic philosopher, happiness lay in virtue; a person was healthy if his contentment relied on the things in his power (Seneca, *Epistulae morales,* lxxii, 7). The wisdom of the sage thus coincided with his attainment of true health.

Here was a transition from the classical ideal of health as symmetry and beauty (Plato, *Timaeus* 87E–88A) to the ideal of spiritual beauty and spiritual health, acquired, if necessary, at the expense of the body, "the flesh," as the Gospel has it.

Suffering in general and disease in particular had long been seen as consequences of sin. With the spread of Christianity, they could appear as chastisement of those whom the Lord loved. Disease could be a portal through which man acquired eternal salvation. Jesus told the sufferer from a palsy that his sins were forgiven. To show "that the Son of man hath power on earth to forgive sins," he bade the sick man: "Arise, take up thy bed, and go unto thine house" (Matthew 9:2–7). Again, Jesus justified his eating "with publicans and sinners" by saying that "They that be whole need not a physician, but they that are sick" (ibid., 10–13). Thus sickness was not only a consequence of sin, sin itself was a disease which needed healing. This has found expression in endless allegories from Origen to authors of modern times. When Matthew (17:14ff.) speaks of a lunatic boy whom Mark (9:14ff.) describes as deaf and dumb, Bede interprets this as a reference to persons waxing and waning in sundry vices as the moon changes, deaf to the sermon of faith and dumb because not expressing faith.

The ascetic life regarded disease not only with indifference but even with pride, as mortification of the flesh. To care for the lepers and thereby to expose oneself to infection was a sign of sanctity. It has to be admitted that the positive evaluation of disease had also another, secular, root. In the pseudo-Aristotelian *Problems* (xxx,i) the question was raised why all men outstanding in philosophy, politics, poetry, or the arts appeared to be of a melancholic temperament, even to the extent of being afflicted with the sicknesses arising from the black bile. This was to lead to the notion of melancholy as a disease of superior intellects, a notion that achieved its best-known artistic expression in Dürer's engraving *Melencolia I* (Klibansky et al., 1964) and its most learned treatment in Burton's *Anatomy of Melancholy* (1621).

The concept of disease at a given period is not altogether independent of the nature of the prevailing ailments. The Middle Ages and the Renaissance suffered much from infections that appeared in massive epidemic waves or were endemic, i.e., native to the population. Arabic and Latin authors of the time elaborated the ancient concept of infections and contagious disease. As a dye or a poison (*virus*) could stain a large amount of water or kill a large animal; as putrescent material, marked by an evil smell, corrupted what had been sound, so an infection polluted the body and could spread among a population. Virus, stain, evil smell, putrescence, and miasma were the notions associated with infection and contagion.

The concept of infection was broad and unclear: infection could develop in the body with the disease, it could be due to the influence of the stars (hence "influenza"), and it could take on different forms (the word "pestilence" designated any severe epidemic). If the disease spread by personal contact, it was contagious. Of all epidemics, the plague, which manifested itself in bubonic and pulmonary forms, was the most severe. It appeared during the reign of the emperor Justinian (A.D. 527–65), then in the fourteenth century ("the black death"), and in many subsequent outbreaks, of which those of London (1665) and Marseilles (1720) were among the last in Western Europe. The plague, dreaded as contagious, provoked public health measures, quarantine and isolation, to counteract the danger. In *Romeo and Juliet* (Act V, Scene ii) the searchers of the town, suspecting that Friar Laurence and his brother monk ". . . both were in a house/ where the infectious pestilence did reign/ seal'd up the doors. . ." and did not let them leave.

The most serious endemic contagion was leprosy; then from about 1495, syphilis assumed first place. Whether syphilis was imported from the new world by the crew of Columbus or had existed in Europe before is a moot question. The disease became widely known as the French disease (the French, in turn, calling it *mal de Naples*). The name syphilis was given to the disease in a Latin poem *Syphilis sive morbus gallicus* (1530), by Girolamo Fracastoro, who also elaborated a theory of contagious disease which in its fundamentals survived till the mid-nineteenth century. Imperceptibly small particles, *seminaria,* capable of propagating themselves, transferred contagious diseases by direct contact, through an object (*fomes*), or at a short distance. It is not likely that he thought of the *seminaria* as microorganisms; rather he anticipated something of the notion of a leaven (Greek: *zumē*). A contagious disease was specific: it retained its character in the transmission from man to man. The ontological view of diseases, i.e., thinking of them as real, distinct entities, was nothing new. Even the comparison of a disease with an animal was old—Plato (*Timaeus* 89B)

399

had used it, and Varro (116–27 B.C.) had actually spoken of animals, too small to be seen by the eye, "which by mouth and nose through the air enter the body and cause severe diseases" (*Rerum rusticarum* 1, 2). But in the sixteenth to seventeenth centuries the ontological concept of disease was considerably strengthened. The Paracelsists, including their master Paracelsus (1493–1541) and their rebellious member van Helmont (1577–1644), contributed by endowing disease with a body, thinking of it as a parasite, attributing its causes to external factors independent of man. Van Helmont, in particular, opposed the old theory of diseases as catarrhs, as fluxes from the brain to which vapors had ascended. He spoke of the *spina*, the thorn, i.e. irritations, the form in which diseases acted in the body. Outside the circle of Paracelsists, William Harvey (1578–1657) in his embryological work (Exercise 27) thought of tumors as leading a life of their own, and of diseases from poison or contagion as having their own vitality (Pagel, 1968).

The most impressive presentation of the ontological point of view came from Thomas Sydenham (1624–89). He took up the Hippocratic notion of the "constitution" of a year, associated with the diseases prevalent during the period. According to Sydenham, epidemics had different constitutions depending upon "an occult and inexplicable alteration in the very bowels of the earth, whence the air becomes contaminated by the kind of effluvia which deliver and determine the human bodies to this or that disease" (*Opera*, 1844). Diseases should be observed and their species studied as plants were studied by the botanists, and though he could not explain the formation of the species, Sydenham, nevertheless, hinted at their origin. When the humors of the body could not be concocted, or when they contracted "a morbific blemish from this or that atmospheric constitution" (ibid.), or when they turned poisonous because of a contagion, then they were "exalted into a substantial form of species" (*Works*, 1848). The disease itself was Nature's struggle to restore health by elimination of the morbific matter. With great praise, Sydenham quoted the Hippocratic saying, "Nature is the healer of disease." Nature needed simple help from the physician; sometimes not even that.

Sydenham was one of the founders of nosology, the science of classifying diseases, which came into its own at the time of the great systematist Linné (1707–78). Boissier de Sauvages (1706–67), Cullen (1710–90), Pinel (1745–1826), and Schoenlein (1793–1864) created nosological systems which, on the basis of clinical symptoms, classified diseases into orders, families, genera, and species. This was the practitioner's science: if, by its symptoms, he could diagnose the disease and find its place in the scheme, he could then also prescribe the remedies recommended for it. If he wished, he could go further and instruct himself about the scientific explanation of the disease, but he need not do so if he distrusted the various theories offered.

IV

With the decline of Aristotelian science, the challenge to the Galenic doctrines by the revolutionary Paracelsus, the reform of anatomy by Vesalius, and the discovery of the circulation of the blood by William Harvey, pathology had undergone decisive changes. The humors did not disappear at once, but the new physics and chemistry replaced the Galenic doctrine of health and disease as a balance or imbalance, respectively, of the qualities. Descartes thought of the animal body as a soulless machine; even in man only the conscious mental processes involved the soul. To overcome the difficulty regarding acts which were seemingly purposeful yet independent of, or even contrary to, man's will, Descartes introduced the idea of reflex action. The Cartesian philosophy favored a physiology and pathology on strictly mechanical principles with the help of a corpuscular theory which permitted the inclusion of chemical explanations.

If the body is a machine, health will be represented by a well-functioning machine, disease by a defective one. A machine can have some self-regulatory mechanisms built in, but it does not create new ones when the situation so demands. It was, therefore, logical for Robert Boyle to refuse to see all diseases as healing processes. His theological bias was against the pagan view of nature as a benevolent being. Natural processes were blind and could be destructive. A dropsical person might be plagued by thirst, yet drinking would aggravate the disease (Boyle, 1725). The radical Cartesian dichotomy of body and soul also entailed a basic difficulty concerning mental diseases. It was logically absurd to think of the soul, a *res cogitans*, as being prone to sickness in the manner of the body; this could only be done metaphorically in the manner in which crime, sin, heresy had long been called diseases of the soul.

Revolutionary as the new mechanical orientation was, it did not sweep everything before it. Even those physicians who were inclined towards mechanistic theories admitted their ineffectiveness at the bedside. They recommended a Hippocratic attitude and patient observation of the disease. Many physicians were unwilling to follow the new mechanistic trend, and to some of them theories altogether meant little.

Generally speaking, in the seventeenth century mechanization was less successful in biology than in the world of physics. Harvey himself, van Helmont,

Glisson, Wepfer, Stahl are outstanding among those who, in one form or another, did not believe that life, health, and disease could be understood without assuming the participation of the soul or of vital principles immanent in the body. They spoke of *anima*, of the Archeus, of a "president," or they endowed all fibres with irritability. It all meant that the human organism was actively engaged in preserving or restoring health.

Before the middle of the eighteenth century, discussions about the respective roles of mechanism and vitalism were mainly carried on by doctors of medicine, who devoted their attention and practice to internal diseases. Apothecaries were interested in chemical medicine, and it fell to them to prepare the chemical drugs that had come into vogue with Paracelsus. In England they gradually assumed the role of general practitioners. Here the apothecary, who sold the medicine, dispensed medical advice together with his medicines. For this kind of practice nosological orientation was particularly valuable. Another class of medical man, the surgeon, also looked upon disease differently from the doctor of medicine. In the Middle Ages the surgeons had become separated from the physicians and were organized in guilds, usually together with the barbers. They looked after wounds, ulcers, abscesses, fractures, dislocations, diseases of the skin and venereal diseases, tumors, possibly also cataracts, herniae, and stones of the bladder. Moreover, they bled patients if the doctor so prescribed. Their domain was external disorders in contrast to internal illness. In most cases, these disorders were localized, and in judging them and treating them the surgeon had to know something of the anatomy of the human body. Anatomy became the surgeon's preferred science, as chemistry was that of the apothecary.

With the exception of relatively few well-trained men, the guild surgeon was not educated enough and his social status was too low to allow him a decisive influence on medical thought. Nevertheless, it is not by chance that, though a doctor of medicine, Vesalius, the reformer of human anatomy, was professor of surgery at the University of Padua. With the appearance of his *Fabrica*, in 1543, normal human anatomy became firmly based on dissections of human cadavers. Pathological anatomy, which studied morbid changes, developed more slowly, in spite of the fact that postmortem dissections to establish the cause of death had been performed prior to anatomies intended to teach the structure of man's body. Postmortem dissections concerned cases where the disease showed unusual features or where legal questions arose. With G. B. Morgagni's *De sedibus et causis morborum* ("On the Seats and Causes of Diseases," 1761) pathological anatomy became a science in its own right. Its practical aim was to correlate the course of the disease and its symptoms with the changes noticed after death.

As the title of his book indicates, Morgagni traced the symptoms back to lesions in the organs, something surgeons had usually done. But in surgical disorders, the lesions were mostly visible or palpable, which in internal diseases they were not. Pathological anatomy, therefore, was of little use to the physician as long as it was not possible to explore the condition of internal organs during life. Two steps helped realize this goal. Auenbrugger taught (1761) that changes in sound elicited by percussion of the chest yielded information about changes in the consistency of the organs of the chest. Auenbrugger's work was popularized by Napoleon's physician, Corvisart, after the French Revolution had led to a union of medicine and surgery. The second step, made by Laennec, consisted in the introduction of the stethoscope (1819). With its aid Laennec was able to compare more effectively than before the sounds heard over the heart and the lungs under normal conditions with sounds heard when these organs were ill. Percussion and auscultation helped the physician to obtain an objective view of the patient's illness; he was less dependent on subjective complaints. The Paris school, leading in the new anatomical concept of disease, found followers in London, Dublin, Vienna, and elsewhere. The new insight into disease through the combination of clinical and anatomical pictures led to the elimination of old disease entities and the solid establishment of others, like typhoid fever, gastric ulcer, multiple sclerosis, and diphtheria.

The new objectivity found its place in the hospitals, which housed a large number of patients, many of them suffering from the same disease. Apart from wards, hospitals also included dissection rooms and then laboratories. Down to the later nineteenth century, the hospital was predominantly a place for indigent patients, who were not under the personal care of a particular physician but became "material" for observation and charitable treatment. Thereby the large hospitals invited a statistical approach to sickness and to therapy. In the eighteen-twenties Louis, in Paris, investigated the influence of bleeding in the early stages of pneumonia upon the course of the disease. Some patients were bled early, as was the custom, others were not. The results showed that early bleeding did not improve the chances for recovery. A very important insight into the unreliability of time-hallowed therapeutics had been gained, and the numerical method had been well illustrated.

The objective view of illness found in the large hospitals had not originated there alone. The rise of the modern state developed statistical methods which covered the nation's health. In England, bills of mortality stating the number of deaths from various causes had come into use sometime in the sixteenth century. Originally designed as intelligence about the spread of epidemic disease, these bills, in the seventeenth century, were used by John Graunt as a basis for vital statistics. Mercantilism, with its advocacy of national industries in the interest of a positive balance of trade, calculated the economic advantages of health and the loss incurred to the national economy through sickness and untimely death. Bellers, in 1714, suggested that Parliament make provisions for the improvement of medicine so that the population

. . . may, once in Sixty or Seventy Years, be Reprieved from Destruction; and consequently, the Number of the People in the Kingdom, in that time, may be doubled, and many Millions of the Sick may be recovered from their *Beds* and *Couches,* in Half the time that they usually are now.

Every Able Industrious Labourer, that is capable to have Children, who so Untimely Dies, may be accounted Two Hundred Pound Loss to the *Kingdom* (p. 3).

The lack of sentimentality which permitted estimating human life and suffering in terms of shillings and pence presupposed the existence of a large anonymous population in urban centers. It expressed the development of a rationalized way of life.

With beginnings less clearly defined, the medical application of scales, clocks, and thermometers also promoted objective study of disease. These instruments and a few simple chemical reactions were the forerunners of the powerful array of the diagnostic laboratory. Greek physicians had already used clocks to measure the pulse rate and had proposed scales to determine metabolic processes. Moreover, both these instruments, and the thermometer for measuring the temperature of the body, had been explored for medical use by Santorio Santorio (1561–1636). But their widespread acceptance was very slow. As late as 1860 Wunderlich found it necessary to argue that the use of the clinical thermometer was neither too expensive, neither too time consuming for the practitioner, nor too bothersome nor altogether superfluous (Ebstein, 1928). A common principle underlying these instruments and their much more complicated successors is the need to establish numerical data. In the Galenic tradition, normalcy had been viewed as an optimal natural state. Vesalius described the human body in its theoretical perfection. But the numerical limits of normal pulse rate or body temperature must be based on measurements in many individuals. The elaboration of tables of numerical values gave health and disease a statistical aspect, and the physiognomy of diseases could be expressed on graphs. The typical fever curves of many

infectious diseases, worked out by Wunderlich, enabled the physician to make a tentative diagnosis from the chart.

To be sure, all these aspects of modern "laboratory medicine" (Ackerknecht, 1955) were far ahead of the eighteenth century, when even scales, clocks, and thermometers were used only by a few relatively audacious minds. Yet it is not without significance that De Haen (1704–76), whose hospital reports were a major contribution to the practical medical literature of the century, also urged the use of the thermometer and tried to establish the normal temperatures for various age groups (Ebstein, 1928). Essentially, the use of numerical data in the diagnosis of disease presupposes that the latter is a physiological process. The activities of the body can increase and diminish and still remain within the range of the "normal." There is a transition from undoubted health to manifest disease.

This notion was elaborated in the system of John Brown (1735–88). He assumed that the interaction between the excitability with which the body was endowed and the stimuli, external and internal, which it encountered during life determined health and the contrasting conditions of asthenia and sthenia. Health was the territory between these two conditions. In a few countries the direct impact of this system was dramatic, in others it was slight. But its indirect influence on the development of physiological medicine in the nineteenth century was very great. Both health and disease represented life, and disease differed only in representing life under changed circumstances.

V

To look upon disease as detrimental to the national interest, as a natural process under changed but yet natural conditions, as a process to be studied objectively at the bedside, in the dissecting room, and in the laboratory, was part of the "Enlightenment" of the Western world after about 1700. But the Enlightenment, notably in the teachings of Jean Jacques Rousseau, had its own sentimentality, which it also bequeathed to the nineteenth century.

Rousseau and his followers looked upon health as a gift of man's natural state, which luxury and civilization had spoiled. Mothers should breast-feed their babies, children should wear clothes that do not restrict their bodies as fashionable dress does. It was bad to expose the mind, especially the feminine mind, to the incessant reading of novels. In the eyes of middle-class society vices led to disease, and some diseases, notably alcoholism and venereal disease, were shameful because rooted in an immoral life. The fight which Tissot (1728–97) and generations of physicians after him led against masturbation, warning against its alleged baneful effects upon health, was a secular version of a biblical taboo (onanism). On the other hand, Tissot gave advice in matters of health to the people who had no access to medical help, and Johann Peter Frank's great work, *System einer vollständigen medicinischen Polizey* (1779ff.), was to serve the absolute, yet enlightened authorities in ruling their subjects for the latter's own good.

That health was seen as such a good was in itself significant. The more the promises of another world receded, the more desirable health appeared, not only as a state to which all people at all times had aspired, but as an ideal toward which society might actively work. The practice of variolation was a step in this direction. Paradoxically enough, in the United States it found an early advocate in Cotton Mather, who had played so notorious a role in the Salem witchcraft trials of 1692. Variolation, since it transferred real smallpox, though by means of dried matter from a light case, still was a risky procedure. The risk was eliminated by Edward Jenner's introduction of vaccination with cowpox in 1798. In this case at least it was now proven that man need not be helpless but could remove the very threat of epidemics.

Vaccination was introduced during the English industrial revolution, which created health problems of its own and, like wars, illustrated the dependence of health not only on nature but on social conditions as well. Enlightenment and, to some extent, the industrial revolution brought about a revaluation of the significance of disease. Epidemics and the appearance of new diseases had often been viewed as signs of the wrath of God punishing sinful mankind. The 1495 mandate of Emperor Maximilian, which mentioned syphilis as the punishment for man's blasphemous life, was as typical of this concept as were the sermons preached in New York in 1832, when Asiatic cholera made its appearance (Rosenberg, 1962). But medical disasters could be averted. Edwin Chadwick, a pupil of Jeremy Bentham and secretary of the Poor Law Commission, was responsible for the report on *The Sanitary Condition of the Labouring Population of Great Britain* (1842). The report urged the prevention of illness to save expense and pointed out the sanitary factors responsible for widespread sickness and early death. Moreover, industrialization had led to new hazards in the occupational life of the workers, and these should be prevented.

The attention of the student of public health was forcibly drawn to the social conditions of the times. It was against this background that Virchow, in 1848, claimed for the history of epidemics a place in the cultural history of mankind: "Epidemics resemble large

warning tables in which the statesman of great style can read that a disturbance has appeared in the development of his people which even indifferent politics must no longer be allowed to overlook." This meant that social factors superimposed themselves upon biological ones to the extent that certain diseases really were social phenomena (Ackerknecht, 1953). Such ideas, evoked in the revolutionary period of 1848, were largely dormant in the following decades, only to reappear in the twentieth century.

Few movements might be expected to show less affinity than industrial revolution and romanticism. Yet while pulmonary tuberculosis was predominant among industrial workers, it also numbered among its victims John Keats, Novalis, Chopin, Schiller, and two of the great medical explorers of tuberculosis, Gaspard Bayle and Laennec. If periods have diseases fitting their style (Sigerist, 1928), pulmonary consumption was a romantic disease just as syphilis had belonged to the late Renaissance, gout and melancholia or love-sickness to the baroque. But apart from the high incidence of tuberculosis during the time (1760–1850) covering both the industrial revolution and the romantic movement, disease, somatic as well as mental, received almost loving care by romantically inclined authors and opera librettists. This is not only true of tuberculosis, but also of chlorosis, the anemia of the young girl, and of morbid mentality ranging from madness in the gothic novels to somnambulism and the bizarre characters of E. T. A. Hoffmann and Edgar Allan Poe. The neurotic character as hero made its debut with Goethe's Werther (Feise, 1926). The romantic movement thus reaccentuated the concept of disease as a contributor to cultural life.

Equally romantic, however, was the frequent glorification of healthy primitive life. "Beneath the rustic garb of the plowman and not beneath the gildings of the courtier will strength and vigor of the body be found," exclaimed Rousseau (*Discours . . .* , p. 104), and "Healthy as a Shepherd-boy," sang Wordsworth. Nature, the country, the wilderness were the antidotes to the cities, the foci of human degeneracy. Disease was caused by an infringement of the laws of nature, and these laws, so the phrenologists claimed, included mental life too, since the mind had its organs in areas of the cerebral cortex. An infringement of Nature's laws was an infringement of God's laws. Health was not only desirable; in Anglo-Saxon countries its preservation was propagated as something like a moral duty, a glorification of God. This combination of enlightened thought and romantic mood gave a religious overtone to the sanitary movement in its broadest sense.

The medical profession was strongly represented among the phrenologists and various kinds of sanitary reformers. Skepticism of traditional curative methods led many physicians to believe that the healing power of nature was superior to any medication, especially since the homeopaths with their unbelievably weak solutions of drugs showed at least as good results as did regular practitioners. Some expected progress from prevention rather than from therapy. The so-called therapeutic nihilists, e.g., Josef Dietl, thought that medicine should exert all its efforts towards becoming a science; until then, it would be best to abstain from all healing and merely help nature by providing hygienic conditions for the sick. There was, moreover, no uniform understanding of disease and its causes. The anatomico-clinical trend, which led to the recognition of new disease entities, seemed to favor an ontological concept of disease. But upon reflection, this appeared doubtful. It could be argued that while an ulcer of the stomach explained some of the concomitant symptoms, the presence of the ulcer itself remained unexplained. Anatomy did not provide an understanding of the causes of disease, which could only be obtained from physiology, an experimental science.

It was the stress on experiment that distinguished the new physiological concept of health and disease from the earlier one of John Brown and Broussais. Claude Bernard's *Introduction à l'étude de la médecine expérimentale* (1865; *Introduction to the Study of Experimental Medicine*, 1926) became the classical philosophical exposition of the new concept. "The words, life, death, health, disease, have no objective reality," wrote Claude Bernard. Life referred to a number of functions which could proceed normally or abnormally. The task of physiology was to find out how the body worked, and this could only be done experimentally. The supremacy of the physiological concept of disease had been recognized by Claude Bernard's teacher Magendie and by the German school of physiologists, pathologists, and clinicians, who, in the 1840's, were aligning German medicine with the progress made abroad. It was also recognized by Virchow, though his epoch-making contribution, *Die Cellularpathologie in ihrer Begründung auf physiologische und pathologische Gewebelehre* (1858), was in some respects a culmination of older trends.

After Morgagni had looked to the organs as the seat of diseases, after Bichat (1771–1802) had pointed to the tissues, Virchow declared the cells responsible for the body's health and disease. To Virchow, the body was a social organism dependent on the functioning of its elements, just as the state depended on the activities of its elements, the citizens. Virchow tried to explain changes visible in the cells physiologically, by recourse to the concepts of irritation (for active processes) and degeneration (for passive ones). But

these physiological explanations were not the direct outcome of experimental work, and cellular pathology impressed the medical world as anatomical in character. Nor was it free from vitalistic features displeasing to a group of physiologists around Carl Ludwig, Du Bois-Reymond, Brücke, Helmholtz. They, too, had their own revolutionary program, which Du Bois-Reymond proclaimed in 1848: eventually physiology would be dissolved into biophysics and biochemistry, with analytical mechanics as the ideal form of all science. This was radical reductionism in its classical form.

The physiological concept of disease, whether reductionist or not, did not well agree with ontological systems. There was no reason why nature should be bound to rigid types. Since every individual differed from another, and since life could be subjected to an infinite variety of changed conditions, every sick person really represented his own disease. Claude Bernard did not overlook this. Ordinary causes, such as cold, hunger, thirst, fatigue, and mental suffering, were modified by idiosyncrasy, which was partly congenital and partly accidental. The pathological predispositions were nothing but special physiological conditions: a starved and a satiated organism reacted differently.

In disease, nature played the role of the experimenter; the observable changes could be viewed as experiments of nature and analyzed accordingly. Nosology, it was argued, was no more than a practical makeshift to be disregarded by the medical scientist. The existence of a clear demarcation between health and disease was altogether doubtful. Virchow, who had followed Henle in defining disease as life under changed circumstances, later came to realize the inadequacy of this definition. Circumstances might change drastically; a man could find himself in jail and yet remain healthy. Disease began at the moment when the regulatory equipment of the body no longer sufficed to remove the disturbances. "Not life under abnormal conditions, not the disturbance as such, engenders a disease, rather disease begins with the insufficiency of the regulatory apparatuses" (Virchow [1869], p. 93).

In this respect, Virchow and Claude Bernard were not very far apart. The latter placed increasing emphasis upon the internal milieu, i.e., blood and tissue fluids, which provided a steady environment for the cells composing the body and made it independent of the vagaries of the external environment. The constancy of the internal milieu was largely maintained through the regulatory functions of the nervous system. Later (1928) Walter Cannon introduced the term "homeostasis" to designate the condition of actively sustained equilibrium prevailing in the organism. By then, the significance of endocrine glands in the regulatory mechanisms of the body had been recognized.

VI

Both Claude Bernard and Virchow had expressed their respective ideas before Robert Koch's discovery of the tubercle bacillus in 1882 won the decisive victory for the germ theory of disease. Many reasons militated against easy acceptance, one of these being the clash with the anti-ontological tendencies of many medical scientists. Louis Pasteur, Koch, and their followers had demonstrated that specific microorganisms were responsible for specific diseases. Diseases could even be defined bacteriologically. Thus the argument about the relationship of pulmonary consumption and the disease in which tubercles appeared was now solved: tuberculosis was a disease characterized by the presence of the tubercle bacillus, just as diphtheria was "caused" by the diphtheria bacillus; the formation of a membrane which originally had given its name to the disease was no more than an anatomical symptom.

Although bacteriology concerned infectious diseases only, its influence on the general concept of disease was great. Presumably, diseases could be bound to definite causes; hence the knowledge of the cause was needed to elevate a clinical entity or a syndrome to the rank of a disease. Moreover, an infection had a beginning and it ended after the annihilation of the invading microbe. Between these two points in time the person in question was sick; before and afterwards he was healthy; consequently, health was absence of disease. What really mattered was the invasion by the microbe, hence the study of the microbes and of the circumstances of their transmission appeared of primary importance. The consideration of social and nonscientific environmental factors, which were so important to the older sanitarians, receded into the background (Galdston, 1940). Bacteriology and the science of immunology, which developed in its wake, had their home in the laboratory, where experiments were performed on animals, sera obtained from them, and vaccines produced out of attenuated or dead cultures of bacteria and out of sera obtained from animals. To the die-hard sanitarian this was the negation of the holy campaign against filth; the new science did not lead to real health, which was to be freedom from suffering for man and beast alike (Stevenson, 1955).

Actually, of course, bacteriology was far from proving so simple in its concepts of health and disease as at first appeared. The microorganism was not just a demon which possessed man once it had entered. It remained true that during epidemics some people became ill, others did not. Cases became known of persons harboring pathogenic microorganisms without

themselves falling ill. Obviously then, the microorganism was not the sole cause; generally speaking, bacteria were just one form of external cause of disease. Traditionally, antecedent, predisposing causes of disease were distinguished from proximate causes, which, under the name of *aitiai prokatarktikai*, the Greeks had identified with external causes. Julius Cohnheim, an early sponsor of Robert Koch, declared in his famous lectures on general pathology (1877) "that the causes of disease are not and cannot be anything else but conditions of life or, expressed differently, they are *outside the organism* itself" (p. 8). In the general field of pathology, this paralleled what Pasteur and other early bacteriologists claimed for infectious diseases. At the same time, Cohnheim's argument was a logical extension of the view of disease as life under changed circumstances. The body's regulatory mechanisms enabled it to function normally, i.e., as observed in the majority of people. Disease was a deviation from the normal process of life caused by a reciprocal action between external conditions and the internal regulatory abilities of the organism. It seemed logical to argue that "the normal process of life" could be "disturbed" only by an overpowering change in external conditions.

Cohnheim, like many others before and after him, believed that the concept of health and disease could be derived from a statistical definition of what was "normal." But statistical deviations only separate the frequent from the rare. If disease was to be defined as deviation from the regular, i.e., the healthy process of life, then deviation must imply a more than statistical evaluation.

Cohnheim and many physicians, then and now, unconsciously adhered to the old biological idea of "normal" as successfully self-preserving and self-propagating, and of "abnormal" or morbid as an impediment of, or danger to, these potentialities. Thus Virchow, in 1885, could even go so far as to say that disease was "life under dangerous conditions" (p. 221). From the reductionist point of view such a definition was hardly tenable, for what does "dangerous" mean in physical and chemical terms? Indeed, Ricker (1951), a German pathologist of the twentieth century, denied that health and disease were truly scientific concepts. They belonged to the realms of applied sciences, "health and its preservation to that of theoretical *hygiene*, disease to that of medicine as the doctrine of the healing of diseases."

VII

Modern concepts of disease are the result of a linking of scientific thought, practical achievements, and social factors. Bacteriology developed at a time when Western countries were entering a new phase of the indus-

405

trial revolution, marked by the association of technology and science. Antiseptic surgery offered an immediate practical application of the germ theory. From the mid-seventies an increasing number of diseases were made accessible to surgical treatment; more important perhaps, surgical treatment could increasingly count on a successful outcome. Here was one branch of medicine where medical help promised results rather than mere hope. Health began to take on the nature of a purchasable good, but at the same time, the purchase of health began to become more costly. Major surgical operations now were more easily performed in the hospital than at home, and the replacement of antiseptic surgery by aseptic methods reinforced this trend. The pattern that surgery established by utilizing scientific methods was followed by internal medicine, which also relied more and more on the laboratory and on hospital facilities. Application of the principles of bacteriological sterilization led to obvious results in decreasing infant mortality. Bacteriology and immunology offered scientific tools for the sanitation of disease-ridden districts and the prevention of many infectious diseases. DDT proved a successful contact poison against the insect vectors of pathogenic microbes. The sulfonamides (1935) and, by the end of World War II, the antibiotics, presented "miracle drugs" in the treatment of infectious diseases.

Helped by these scientific achievements, the disease picture since the middle of the twentieth century differs from that of around 1900. The infectious diseases have yielded their place in the table of mortality to degenerative diseases, to tumors, and to accidents, and life expectancy (particularly at birth) in Western nations has continued to rise. The more possible it has become to avoid diseases, or to be cured of them and to enjoy health, the more health appears as a desirable good to which everybody has a "right." Such a right did not extend to other purchasable goods, but the special status that Christianity once granted to the sick prepared the way for this special claim. Social developments during the nineteenth century moved the matter from the realm of religion and philanthropy to that of politics. Compulsory sickness insurance was introduced in Germany in 1883 as a strategic measure in Bismarck's fight against the social democrats. In the twentieth century, other countries followed. In the United States, voluntary insurance and medicare and medicaid programs all serve the idea of making medical care available to an increasing number of people. Western achievements look no less desirable elsewhere, including the so-called underdeveloped countries. Even in the League of Nations the health activities continued after the decay of the political body. Its UN successor, the World Health Organization, has accepted a program geared to the definition of health as "a state of complete physical, mental, and social well-being and not merely the absence of disease or infirmity."

The history of the ideas of health and disease begins with the crystallization of these ideas out of human suffering. Of the stages through which these ideas have gone, some belong to the past, others have merely seen a metamorphosis. Disease as a physiological process and disease as an entity are recurrent themes which have been likened to the struggle between nominalism and realism. Disease has been seen as nothing but a form of misery, and health as part of man's salvation. But there are also those, like Thomas Mann (*The Magic Mountain*), who see a positive value in disease as the price at which a higher form of health must be bought. The prevailing tendency at the present moment seems to merge disease once more with much that formerly was considered distinct from it and to take so broad a view of health as to make it all but indistinguishable from happiness.

The history of the ideas of health and disease cannot decide these issues; it can only present them. In doing so it can, however, point out that health and disease have not shown themselves to be immutable objects of natural history. Health and disease are medical concepts in the broadest sense. This means that man's life in its inseparable union of body and mind is seen under the aspects of possible preservation and cure. Thus they are distinguished from purely scientific concepts on the one hand and from purely social ones on the other.

BIBLIOGRAPHY

The literature on the history of the concept of disease is very great, and the items listed below are but a very small selection. The books of Berghoff, Riese, Sigerist, Edelstein (for Greco-Roman antiquity) deserve particular attention.

Erwin H. Ackerknecht, *Rudolf Virchow: Doctor, Statesman, Anthropologist* (Madison, 1953), p. 127; idem, *A Short History of Medicine* (New York, 1955). *Atharva-Veda Samhitā*, trans. William Dwight Whitney, rev. ed. Charles Rockwell Lanman, Harvard Oriental Series, Vols. VII, VIII (Cambridge, 1905), VII, 361. John Bellers, *An Essay Towards the Improvement of Physick. In Twelve Proposals. By which the Lives of many Thousands of the Rich, as well as of the Poor, may be Saved Yearly* (London, 1714), p. 3. Emanuel Berghoff, *Entwicklungsgeschichte des Krankheitsbegriffes*, 2nd ed. (Vienna, 1947). Claude Bernard, *An Introduction to the Study of Experimental Medicine*, trans. Henry Copley Greene (New York, 1927), p. 67. Robert Boyle, "A Free Inquiry into the Vulgar Notion of Nature," *The Philosophical Works*, 3 vols. abridged, ed. Peter Shaw (London, 1725), II, 106–49, esp. 143. *The Caraka Samhitā* (Jamnagar, India, 1949), II, 4, 13. Julius Cohnheim, *Vorlesungen über all-*

gemeine Pathologie (Berlin, 1877), I, 8, 12. Erich Ebstein, "Die Entwicklung der klinischen Thermometrie," *Ergebnisse der inneren Medizin und Kinderheilkunde*, **33** (1928), 407–505, esp. 462, 482. Ludwig Edelstein, *Ancient Medicine: Selected Essays*, ed. Owsei Temkin and C. Lilian Temkin (Baltimore, 1967). *The Edwin Smith Surgical Papyrus*, with translation and commentary by James Henry Breasted, 2 vols. (Chicago, 1930). Ernst Feise, "Goethes Werther als nervöser Charakter" (1926), reprinted in *Xenion: Themes, Forms, and Ideas in German Literature* (Baltimore, 1950), pp. 1–65. Iago Galdston, "Humanism and Public Health," *Bulletin of the History of Medicine*, **8** (1940), 1032–39. Hermann Grapow, *Kranker, Krankheiten und Arzt. Grundriss der Medizin der alten Ägypter*, III (Berlin, 1956). Gerald J. Gruman, *A History of Ideas About the Prolongation of Life*, Transactions of the American Philosophical Society, **56**, 9, new series (Philadelphia, 1966). Raymond Klibansky, Fritz Saxl, and Erwin Panofsky, *Saturn and Melancholy* (London, 1964). *The Dhammapada*, translated from the Pali by P. Lal (New York, 1967). René Labat, *Traité akkadien de diagnostics et pronostics médicaux* (Paris and Leiden, 1951), pp. 157, xxiii. Claudius Mayer, "Metaphysical Trends in Modern Pathology," *Bulletin of the History of Medicine*, **26** (1952), 71–81. A. Leo Oppenheim, "Mesopotamian Medicine," *Bulletin of the History of Medicine*, **36** (1962), 97–108. Walter Pagel and Marianne Winder, "Harvey and the 'Modern' Concept of Disease," *Bulletin of the History of Medicine*, **42** (1968), 496–509; this article contains references to Dr. Pagel's important works on Paracelsus and van Helmont. Gustav Ricker, *Wissenschaftstheoretische Aufsätze für Ärzte*, 2nd ed. (Stuttgart, 1951), p. 48. Walther Riese, *The Conception of Disease, its History, its Versions and its Nature* (New York, 1953). George Rosen, *A History of Public Health* (New York, 1958). Charles E. Rosenberg, *The Cholera Years* (Chicago, 1962). Jean Jacques Rousseau, *Discours sur les sciences et les arts*, ed. George R. Havens (New York, 1946), p. 104. Henry E. Sigerist, *Civilization and Disease* (Ithaca, N.Y., 1943); idem, *A History of Medicine*, 2 vols. (New York, 1951–61); idem, "Kultur und Krankheit," *Kyklos*, **1** (1928), 60–63; idem, *On the Sociology of Medicine*, ed. Milton I. Roemer (New York, 1960). Bruno Snell, *The Discovery of the Mind*, trans. T. G. Rosenmeyer (Cambridge, Mass., 1953), p. 162. Robert O. Steuer, "Whdw, Aetiological Principle of Pyaemia in Ancient Egyptian Medicine," *Supplements to the Bulletin of the History of Medicine*, No. 10 (Baltimore, 1948). Lloyd G. Stevenson, "Science Down the Drain," *Bulletin of the History of Medicine*, **29** (1955), 1–26. Edward A. Suchman, *Sociology and the Field of Public Health* (New York, 1963). M. W. Susser and W. Watson, *Sociology in Medicine* (London, 1962). Thomas Sydenham, *Opera omnia*, ed. G. A. Greenhill, Sydenham Society (London, 1844), pp. 30, 16; idem, *The Works*, trans. R. G. Latham, 2 vols. (London, 1848), I, 19. Owsei Temkin, "The Scientific Approach to Disease: Specific Entity and Individual Sickness," *Scientific Change*, ed. A. C. Crombie (New York, 1963), pp. 629–47. Rudolf Virchow, in *Medicinische Reform*, No. 8 (25 August 1848), reprinted in *Gesammelte Abhandlungen aus dem Gebiete der öffentlichen Medicin und der Seuchenlehre* (Berlin, 1879), I, 22. Rudolf Virchow, "Über Akklimatisation," (1885) and "Über die heutige Stellung der Pathologie," (1869), in Karl Sudhoff, *Rudolf Virchow und die deutschen Naturforscherversammlungen* (Leipzig, 1922), pp. 221, 93. Henry R. Zimmer, *Hindu Medicine* (Baltimore, 1948), pp. 33f.

OWSEI TEMKIN

[See also Behaviorism; **Death;** Demonology; Enlightenment; **Genetic Continuity;** Macrocosm and Microcosm; Primitivism; Romanticism, Stoicism.]

HEGELIAN POLITICAL AND RELIGIOUS IDEAS

1. Hegelian Idealism. Hegel's philosophy is generally described as Absolute Idealism. Carl Michelet, one of Hegel's leading nineteenth-century followers, said that in Absolute Idealism, Subjective and Objective Idealism are united. It is characteristic of Idealism, he wrote, to regard thought as fundamental in the world, but in the Subjective Idealism of Kant and Fichte the objective world is neglected in favor of merely subjective mind, and in the Objective Idealism of Schelling subjectivity is lost in an impersonal cosmic order. Hegel, according to Michelet, reinstated Aristotle's teaching that thought and its object are identical in what is free from matter: "theoretical knowledge and its object are the same" (*De anima* III. 4). According to Michelet, Hegel combined Idealism with Realism by means of his dialectical method in which the thought of the philosopher becomes identical with the objective development of reality (*Geschichte der letzten Systeme der Philosophie in Deutschland*, I, Berlin [1837], 34 and II, Berlin [1838], 602–11).

The central feature of the German Idealist philosophy which began with Kant's *Critique of Pure Reason* (Riga, 1781) and culminated in Hegelianism, is its defense of spontaneity and freedom against the empiricism and materialism that flourished during the Enlightenment. Like Kant and Fichte, Hegel thought that freedom is of the very essence of mind, but he developed this idea in a more systematic way than they had done. Thought, he held, cannot be limited by fixed and ready-made categories, and in the first part of his system, the *Logic*, he tried to show that each limited category gave rise to contradictions which can only be resolved by advancing towards progressively less limited ones until the Absolute Idea, the most comprehensive category of all, is reached. Using language like that applied by Rousseau to the laws of the state and by Kant to the moral law, Hegel wrote that thought is "a self-developing totality of determinations and laws which it gives to itself and does not find already formed within itself" (*Encyclopedia*, 3rd ed. [1830], §19).

The second part of his system, the *Philosophy of Nature*, is concerned with what is not free, with what occurs as it must and yet might have been other than it is. Even the wickedness of men, he says, "is infinitely superior to the law-like turning of the stars or to the innocence of the plants; something that goes astray is nevertheless mind" (*Encyclopedia*, §248).

The third part of Hegel's system is called by him the *Philosophy of Mind*. Mind (*Geist*), he says, is essentially freedom, but is manifested at various levels. There is first the level, which Hegel calls "subjective mind," at which mind turns from the natural world and finds freedom in itself. Then there is an opposite stage where a world of artifacts and institutions has been produced in which particular minds can recognize both their own achievements and the constraints they impose. This, says Hegel, is the world of "objective mind" in which "freedom lies before it as necessity" (*Encyclopedia*, §385). The third and highest stage of mind Hegel calls "absolute mind." This is the sphere of art, religion, and philosophy, in which man is taken beyond his particular social milieu, and even beyond the international order and the course of human history. In art the Absolute is manifested in sense-objects, in religion it is revealed in forms of consciousness that need no philosophical training, and in philosophy it becomes thought aware of itself, and, as Aristotle put it (*Metaphysics*, XII. 7), on the occasions when men think philosophically they are fitfully enjoying what God enjoys eternally.

We can now understand the philosophical context within which Hegel's views on politics and religion are presented. It is within the context of a philosophy in which mind is fundamental to the world, in which freedom is of the essence of mind, and in which freedom shows itself in thought as self-development by contrast with mere conformity to fixed and uncriticized categories. Men, as thinking beings, do not submit to natural necessity but transform nature and create institutions which do not merely constrain individuals but also give expression to their thoughts. Political activity has its place in this sphere of objective mind. Art and religion, however, elevate man to the sphere of Absolute Mind where religion is the stage that prefigures the highest achievement of mind, which is that of self-conscious philosophical thought.

2. Hegel's Political Philosophy. Hegel's philosophy of politics and law is set out in detail in his *Grundlinien der Philosophie des Rechts* (Berlin, 1821), although a briefer account of it is contained in his *Encyclopädie*

der Philosophischen Wissenschaften im Grundrisse (1st, 2nd, and 3rd eds., Heidelberg, 1817, 1827, 1830)— referred to here as the *Encyclopedia*. Like the rest of Hegel's systematic writings the *Philosophie des Rechts* is divided into three main parts in dialectical progression. The first part, "Abstract Right," is concerned with property, its transfer, and the means of dealing with fraud and coercive crime. The second part, "Morality," deals with human conduct insofar as its propriety is thought to depend upon intentions and conscientious motives. The third part, "Ethical Life" (*Sittlichkeit*), deals first with the family, then with "civil society," i.e., the economic world and the legal, administrative, and penal arrangements it makes necessary, and culminates with the state, which Hegel considers to be the supreme and most effective embodiment of reason in the social sphere.

We cannot here describe the dialectical transitions through which Hegel passes in developing his system of social philosophy. He starts with the notion of persons, as creatures who transcend nature by being aware of themselves and each other, and he concludes with a sketch of world history in which the succession of predominating states is taken to be the evolution of human freedom from its first emergence from the natural world towards the highly complex, self-conscious form it exhibited in the Christian Europe of his day.

Hegel argued that property is essential to the exercise of the free will of persons. By taking possession of natural objects, by forming, and even by marking them, persons emerge from their isolation and enter into social, as distinct from biological, relations with one another. Hegel rejected slavery on the ground that owning a person involves treating him as if he were a natural object. For slavery to be possible, however, the slave himself must allow it, and to that extent he shares with his master responsibility for his condition. The institution of slavery has some point during the transition from the animal condition to that of self-consciousness, but it is eradicated by the modern state. Hegel argued that ownership is in essence free and complete, and he therefore thought that feudal forms of property, insofar as they placed limits on this, ought to be eliminated. He also held that, since ownership implies the will to use the property, it ceases when that will decays, as with bequests for purposes that have ceased with the passage of time. He intended this argument to justify such policies as the Dissolution of the Monasteries by Henry VIII.

Property is handed down within families and is produced and exchanged in the course of business transactions. In the family, what began as a merely biological relationship is rendered human and self-conscious by being deliberately entered into by persons who respect one another. In "civil society" the wants of individuals are supplied, not by the unpaid devotion that is called for in families, but by each individual's pursuit of his own particular interests. Out of this bargaining and trafficking arises the spontaneously ordered system which Adam Smith, Say, and Ricardo described and explained in the new science of Political Economy. Family or tribal organization has *esprit de corps* but is incompatible with developed economic activity. Civil society, through the division of labor, money, and market activities, supplies individual wants, but lacks *esprit de corps*. According to Hegel, it is in the modern state that the loyalty characteristic of families is united with the spontaneous progress of market enterprise. The state, he writes, is "the self-conscious ethical substance, the union of the principles of the family and of civil society; the unity which is in the family the feeling of love, is the essence of the state, but this essence also receives the form of conscious universality through the second principle of intelligent and spontaneously active will . . ." (*Encyclopedia*, §535).

Hegel was appointed to the chair of philosophy at Berlin in 1818, at a time when the Prussian government, although modernized as a result of the Napoleonic invasion and the Wars of Liberation, was still an absolute monarchy. There were elected local assemblies but no parliament for the country as a whole. In his *Philosophie des Rechts*, published soon after his arrival in Berlin, Hegel makes a detailed defense of *constitutional* monarchy. He advocated elected upper and lower chambers and an administration by civil servants, the chief of whom would be appointed by the Crown for their expertise, and others who would be elected by the business community in order to ensure realistic execution of the government's policy. In publishing this at a time when liberals throughout Europe were calling upon reluctant monarchies to grant constitutions to their subjects, Hegel might seem to have aligned himself with the liberals. His arguments, however, were very different from those used by the liberals. He considered that reason played such a large part in the modern world, that the family and historical tradition were no longer capable of sustaining men's highest allegiance. The French Revolution, that "glorious sunrise," as he called it in his *Lectures on the Philosophy of History* (given every two years from 1822–23 until his death in 1831) was an attempt to gain freedom and to enthrone reason, but the freedom was anarchic and destructive, and the conception of reason was too limited. The French revolutionaries first subordinated everything to the legislature and then, having abolished the monarchy, they fell under the tyranny of men who, regarding themselves as virtuous

and their opponents as sinful, concentrated all power in the executive which they controlled. Hegel concluded that mind, at the level it had reached in his day, required a legislature to establish laws, an executive to bring particular cases under the universal prescribed in the laws, and a monarch "as the will with the power of ultimate decision" (*Philosophie des Rechts*, §273).

Hegel did not, however, support this view with the current utilitarian argument that this sort of constitution would lead to the general happiness. For in his opinion, to use such arguments was to assume that the state exists to satisfy particular wants and desires, and hence to confuse civil society with the state. In an era when Protestant Christianity fostered freedom of conscience, and when paternalism and traditionalism had given way before freely thinking intellect, any political arrangements would be defective which failed both to distinguish and to unite the three "moments" we have just listed. Hegel preferred hereditary monarchy both to elective monarchy and to republicanism, but although he accepts such arguments as that elective monarchy and republicanism are likely to be unstable, he said that empirical arguments are not decisive in such matters. What is decisive is that in a society in which men can think freely and wish to do so, there must be an ultimate authority with unquestioned "majesty," as well as free public discussion in a legislature where laws are rationally framed and rationally executed by those with executive authority. Hegel even compares this form of constitution with the necessary existence of the Perfect Being of the Ontological Argument for the existence of God, and compares the monarch within it with the self-moved mover in Aristotle's *Metaphysics* (*Philosophie des Rechts* §281—and see Knox's note to this on p. 370 of his translation). Hegel thought that this majestic constitutional monarch must be hereditary because his position would be arbitrary if subjected to the chances of voting rather than to the impersonal processes of nature.

Arguing in this *a priori* manner we have just called attention to—he himself would have said that it is the proper philosophical method—Hegel maintained that states are by their very essence a plurality, so that a world state is not rationally thinkable. Given the complexities of things and the willfulness of men, states are bound to conflict with one another and to engage in wars. War brings suffering and evil but is also a means of breaking deadlocks and of preventing a torpid acceptance of the *status quo*. As the various potentialities of mind are developed, various levels of freedom are achieved in the institutions which states foster and protect. Mind—Hegel often speaks of "the Idea"—finds increasingly subtle means of realizing itself in the history of mankind. One by one the civilizations develop some one-sided aspect of free mind and, one by one they reach their peak, exhaust themselves, and sink from lack of conviction or will to continue. Hegel thought that the European Protestant civilization of his day was the highest achievement of independent individual mind, as it combined freedom of thought and conscience with rational control over events that would become anarchic if left to themselves.

Throughout his life Hegel was deeply interested in political events. He read English and French as well as German newspapers, and wrote, and sometimes published detailed comments on constitutional problems. In 1817 there appeared in the *Heidelbergische Jahrbücher* a long article by Hegel entitled *Verhandlungen der Landstände des Königreichs Württemberg im Jahre 1815 und 1816*. This contains a detailed discussion of a dispute in which the King of Württemberg wished the Estates to accept a new constitution, while the Estates, which had not met since before the French Revolution, wished to go back to the pre-Revolutionary constitution. Hegel here expressed his opposition to the legalistic attitude of the Estates in standing on antiquated rights when they had the opportunity of extending the popular influence in the government of the country. A large part of Hegel's *Der Englische Reformbill* appeared in the *Preussische Staatszeitung* in 1831, but the King of Prussia prohibited publication of the last part, apparently on the ground that it was too critical of the British constitution. In this article Hegel criticizes the irrational traditional elements of the British constitution, comparing them to their disadvantage with the reformed codes of law and systems of administration that had arisen in Prussia and elsewhere in Europe as a result of the French Revolution. He thought that the proposed reforms did not go far enough, even though he was apprehensive lest the passage of the Bill would intensify conflicts between the aristocracy and the people. Both of these essays show that, cautious as he was, Hegel was no advocate of traditionalism.

3. Hegel's Philosophy of Religion. Hegel's philosophy as a whole has been described as "contemplative theology" (I. 1lj, in *Die Philosophie Hegels als kontemplative Gotteslehre*, Bern, 1946), and this is an apt description in that Hegel equated the ultimate reality, which in philosophical language he called the Infinite and the Absolute, with the God of the Christian religion. The philosopher, he held, comprehends in thought what religious believers represent to themselves in less purified intellectual terms. Religious thinking is said by Hegel to belong to the realm of "representation" (*Vorstellung*). In his *Encyclopedia* (§§451ff.) Hegel describes *Vorstellung* as a form of

thinking between perception, on the one hand, and fully developed thought, on the other. It involves the use of memory-images and of both reproductive and productive imagination. This last is the point at which the power of thinking in terms of generalizations from experience begins to acquire the freedom of independent thought. In his *Lectures on the Philosophy of Religion* (given in Berlin four times from 1821 to 1831) Hegel says that *Vorstellung* must not be confused with imaging or picturing, even though it makes use of them. It is less bound with particulars than imaging is, and adumbrates or prefigures completely rational thought. It falls short of this by failing to elicit the rational connections between its elements. For example, when God is said to be "all-wise," "good," or "righteous," no image of him is presented, nor is he described as something that could be sensed or directly encountered in history. Nevertheless, these three predicates are not shown to have any necessary connection with one another as would be the case if they were grasped philosophically. In the part of his *Lectures* (Part One, B, II, 3) in which he discusses *Vorstellung*, Hegel compares the Gospel story with the myths of Plato. Plato's myths allegorically express philosophical truths. The deeds and actions of men and states express moral truths "which are the essential moral powers" which operate in history. People may be dimly aware of them without fully understanding them, and this, says Hegel, is the position of the unphilosophical Christian towards the historical elements of Christian doctrine. The story of Jesus, he says, holds (*gilt*) not only as a myth, in the manner of pictures, but as something perfectly historical. This is its "representational" side (*Das ist denn für die Vorstellung*), but it has another side, "it has the divine for its content, divine doing, divine, timeless happening, absolutely divine action, and this is what is internal, true, substantial in this story and is the very thing that is the object of reason." Hegel here raises the question of how the historical elements of Christian doctrine are related to the moral and philosophical truths they exhibit. He here says that there are moral truths in *all* historical events without saying precisely what differentiates the Gospel history from the rest. He discusses this in a later section of the Lectures.

Hegel, like Spinoza, believed that the Infinite must exist, that the ultimately real must appear, must manifest itself. He argued, too, that to regard the Infinite as merely not finite, was to regard it as limited and hence as not infinite. He concluded that the true infinite must somehow include the finite. Kant, therefore, was wrong in abstracting the world of appearances from the real world, and theologians are wrong to regard the Perfect Being as hidden or remote. According to Hegel, the great philosophical importance of Christianity resides in the doctrine of the Incarnation, according to which God became man and suffered as a man. Furthermore the doctrine of the Trinity exhibits the dialectic of opposites and reconciliation. God the Father is said to be the Absolute grasped in thought, God the Son the Absolute believed in representative thinking, and God the Holy Spirit the Absolute reconciling man and God by love and worship in the Church.

That "God does not exist apart from the Son and has sent the Son into the world" is, according to Hegel, philosophically incontestable. A distinct question, he holds, is: "Was *this particular individual*, Jesus of Nazareth, the carpenter's son, the Son of God, the Christ?" What is different between Socrates and Jesus such that Jesus is the Son of God and Socrates is not? Part of Hegel's answer (*Lectures*, Part Three, C, II, 3 and C, III, 1), seems to be that Jesus rose from the dead by continuing to live in the Church. Hegel warns against regarding the Resurrection and the Ascension as empirically verifiable events. They belong, he says, to the faith of Christian believers. Furthermore, the Incarnation and the Ascension could be believed by ordinary men only if the history or story (*Geschichte*) is "perceived" (*angeschaut*). "It is not the story of a particular individual, but it is God who carries it through, that is, it is the perception that this is the story that is universal and ultimate" (*für sich Seiende*).

Hegel seems to argue, then, that Jesus, by continuing to live in his Church, has provided the only possible means by which ordinary men, as distinct from Hegelian philosophers, can, through faith, participate in the divine life and love. But at the very end of the published lectures he expresses doubts about the power of the Church to continue in existence. There is a split, he says, between the unself-conscious faith of ordinary Christians and the reasonings of critics and philosophers. These reasonings cannot be ignored, and these are not times in which religion can be upheld by commands and the power of the state.

When the Gospel is no longer preached to the poor; when the salt has lost its savour and all foundations are tacitly removed, then the people, whose solid reason can only grasp the truth in the form of representation, no longer know how to direct the pressures that build up within them. . . . they seem to themselves to have been deserted by their teachers; for these have managed to help themselves by means of reflective thought and to find satisfaction in what is finite, in the sophistication and ultimate frivolity of subjective experience.

Hegel goes on to say that the philosophical understanding of religion is "a sanctuary apart," that those who serve it form "an isolated priestly order," and that it is not the business of philosophy to predict what

will emerge from this division between the religion of the people and the ratiocinations of philosophical critics.

4. Hegel and His School. Hegel was well known when he went to Berlin in 1818. He was invited there by von Altenstein, head of the recently formed "Ministry of Spiritual, Educational and Medical Affairs," who admired Hegel's writings and was ready to grant him special privileges. Hegel's arrival and the official support he received were of particular concern to two leading Berlin professors, Friedrich Schleiermacher, the theologian and philosopher, and Friedrich von Savigny, the most eminent member of the so-called "Historical School" of law. Hegel came into conflict with both of them. Schleiermacher's view that religion is man's feeling of dependence is not compatible with Hegel's view that religion is philosophy or reason in representational form, and Hegel did not try to smooth over the differences. In a preface he wrote for a book by a former pupil (H. F. W. Hinrichs, *Die Religion im inneren Verhältnisse zur Wissenschaft*, Heidelberg 1822) Hegel said that if religion were the feeling of one's dependence, dogs would be the best Christians. According to Schleiermacher, Hegel used to criticize him in his lectures. As we have seen, Hegel was no supporter of traditions as such, and favored a rationally constructed system of legislation. He did not himself directly criticize Savigny, but in the Introduction to the *Philosophie des Rechts* he criticized the work of G. von Hugo (*Lehrbuch* . . . , p. 20) who, like Savigny, had regarded Roman law as eminently rational, and in §211 he said it was "an insult" to a civilized people to question their ability (as Savigny had done) to codify their legal system.

Not long after his arrival in Berlin in 1818, Hegel wrote to the Minister of Education suggesting that a journal be founded under official auspices in Berlin for the publication of signed reviews of new publications both from abroad and in Germany. This was not agreed to. In 1825 the Stuttgart publisher Cotta and Hegel's friend and disciple Eduard Gans, a Professor of Law at Berlin, endeavored to come to an agreement with Victor Cousin in Paris, to publish a journal that would appear simultaneously in both capitals. This fell through. Then Cotta and Gans, with Hegel's support, arranged for the publication of a journal that was to be controlled by a newly formed body, the *Societät für wissenschaftliche Kritik*. This journal was called the *Jahrbücher für wissenschaftliche Kritik* and began to appear in January, 1827. Schleiermacher was deliberately excluded from it, and the evangelical leader Hengstenberg wrote: "à bas la philosophie. Alongside the Word of God philosophy is a pleonasm" (Fritz Schlawe, "Die Berliner Jahrbücher für Wissenschaftliche Kritik," *Zeitschrift für Religion und Geistesgeschichte*, Cologne [1959], 11, 240–58, 343–56).

The Jahrbücher soon came to be known as the "Hegelzeitung," but it was not as exclusively Hegelian as Hegel himself wished it to be. There were contributions by the diplomat, literary critic, and historian Varnhagen von Ense, whose reviews of historical works are still of interest. He wrote of Sir Walter Scott's *Life of Napoleon*, that Scott ". . . regards the French Revolution exclusively from the shores and ships of Great Britain." Ranke contributed too. Nevertheless, it was primarily an organ of the Hegelian School. In the first volume, for example, E. Gans reviewed the fourth volume of Savigny's *Geschichte des Römischen Rechts im Mittelalter* (Heidelberg, 1826), in which, while praising his erudition, he said that Savigny made no attempt at an historical and rational assessment of the place of the Roman law in the history of Europe, so that the book as a whole "lacks thought." An important document in the history of Hegelianism is Hegel's review in 1829 of Friedrich Göschel's *Aphorismen über Nichtwissen und Absolutes Wissen im Verhältnis zur Christlichen Glaubenserkenntnis* (Berlin, 1829). This book, the work of a lawyer and civil servant with whom Hegel was not then acquainted, began with a dialectical criticism of Jacobi's view that God is beyond the sphere of human knowledge, passed on to a discussion of man's knowledge of God and relationship to Him, and concluded with an account of the importance of faith as well as knowledge. The author's general position was that the categories in terms of which both fideists like Jacobi and their rationalist critics thought were inadequate for their subject matter. Hegel agrees with Göschel that by means of speculative philosophy a "self-alienation of man's natural existence and knowledge" and "a spiritual rebirth" are achieved. He quotes with approval Göschel's words: "The being and knowledge of God in me contains, therefore, not only the knowledge that God has of me, but the knowledge that I have of Him . . . ," and goes on to say that those who accuse the holders of this view of deifying man fail to notice that to say that man is *in* God is not to say that he *is* God. In discussing Göschel's account of faith and knowledge Hegel remarks that "a philosophy without a heart and a faith without understanding are abstractions," and goes on to say that since no one can "understand the Holy Writ except through the Holy Spirit," it is philosophically inappropriate to try to interpret the Bible merely on the basis of the texts or to "spare oneself the trouble of examining the feeling, the understanding, the logic which is conducting the exegesis."

It has been said that in these passages, and in a passage of the *Encyclopedia* (§564), Hegel was influenced not only by Göschel but by the thirteenth-century German mystic Meister Eckhart. Hegel mentions Eckhart once in his *Lectures on the Philosophy of Religion* (Part One, C, I, *On Faith*) where he quotes the famous passage: "The eye with which God sees me is the eye with which I see him; my eye and his eye are one. . . ." Hegel's distinguished follower, Karl Rosenkranz, says (*Hegels Leben*, Berlin [1844], p. 102) that as a young man Hegel copied from various literary periodicals extracts from Eckhart and Tauler, and in his *Hegel als Deutsche Nationalphilosoph* (Leipzig, 1870) Rosenkranz devotes a chapter to the German mystics, and his chapter on Hegel's philosophy of religion interprets him as believing that man ". . . in faith knows himself to be one with God. What is all this virtuosity of culture, what are all his failures in the ascetic struggle, what is all the happiness and unhappiness of his existence, in comparison with this reconciliation?" (p. 205). It is interesting to note that Henry Crabb Robinson reports in his diary (Dec. 10, 1825), a meeting he had with the poet William Blake: ". . . on my asking in what light he viewed the great question concerning the divinity of Jesus Christ, he said: 'He is the only God'; but then he added: 'and so am I and so are you'." Like Hegel, Blake rejected the empiricist thinkers of the seventeenth century. According to Robinson, Blake said on the same occasion: "Bacon, Locke and Newton are the three great teachers of atheism or of Satan's doctrine." Hegel would have said that they remain ensnared in the categories of the finite.

5. *David Strauss*. David Strauss came to Berlin from Tübingen in 1831 in order to study under Hegel, who died, however, when Strauss had been able to hear only a few lectures. Strauss had studied biblical scholarship and church history under F. C. Baur at Tübingen, and during his first years at Berlin he acquired a knowledge of Hegel's philosophy of history and went to lectures by Schleiermacher, Michelet, and Philipp Marheineke, a theologian of Hegelian views who preached at Hegel's funeral and edited his *Lectures on the Philosophy of Religion*. In 1832 Strauss reviewed in the *Jahrbücher* Karl Rosenkranz's *Encyclopädie der theologischen Wissenschaften* (Bonn, 1832), and maintained that Rosenkranz was wrong to argue that the absolute activity of God was bound to manifest itself in miracles when exercised in the human sphere. He also thought that some of Rosenkranz's interpretations of Hegel "went straight over into mysticism." His *Leben Jesu* (Tübingen, I [1835]; II [1836]) is a detailed examination of the Gospel narratives within a Hegelian framework of ideas. The central theme is that the facts of the birth, career, and death of Jesus were occasions around which myths were formed which gave expression to the longings and aspirations of the early Christian community. The myths were not deliberately invented, but developed because of the expectations of a Messiah learned from the Old Testament. But Strauss emphasizes that the central myths of Christianity represent important truths that are not affected by the rejection of false historical beliefs. In the Preface he writes: "The supernatural birth of Christ, his miracles, his resurrection and ascension, remain eternal truths, whatever doubts may be cast upon their reality as historical facts," and at the end of the book, after summarizing Hegel's interpretation of Christian doctrine, he says that Christian clergy should continue "to adhere to the forms of the popular conceptions" but should take every opportunity "to exhibit their spiritual significance." In general, this significance is that "it is humanity that dies, rises and ascends to heaven. . . . by the kindling in him of the idea of humanity, the individual man participates in the divinely human life of the species." Strauss differs from Hegel in rejecting mysticism and in regarding the human race rather than the Church as the body in which Christ continues to live.

Strauss's justifications in the controversy that ensued are contained in his *Streitschriften zur Verteidigung meiner Schrift über das Leben Jesu* (Tübingen, 1838; new ed., 1841). Strauss remarks that Hegel was unhappy about historical criticism because, like Goethe, he was unwilling for great heroes to be depreciated. But Strauss shows that his account of the dwelling of the Holy Spirit in the Church is the same as Hegel's. Strauss says, too, that whereas Fichte was a revolutionary philosopher, Hegel was the philosopher of the Restoration—"Hegel's term 'objective mind' describes the transformation." Fichte emphasized the struggle with things as they are, Hegel the mind that is already in them. It is here that Strauss began the practice of characterizing religious and philosophical outlooks in terms of politics. Göschel, he says, was on the Right, and he himself on the Left, even though he is not welcome there. A new note is struck when he writes: ". . . the victory which man achieves over the natural forces within him by education and self-mastery, and over the natural forces outside him by inventions and machines, is of more value than controlling nature by the word of a thaumaturge" (1841 ed., III, 116). Here there is the suggestion that moral control and mastery over nature through science and industry is an improved substitute for religion.

6. Contemplation and Action. In 1838 there was founded at Halle, under the editorship of Arnold Ruge and T. Echtermeyer, the *Hallische Jahrbücher für deutsche Wissenschaft und Kunst.* In an early issue there is a review by Rosenkranz—on Strauss's scale a Hegelian of the Right or Right-Center—of Hegel's

Lectures on the Philosophy of History which had been published in 1837. Rosenkranz points out that Hegel himself had believed that philosophy could only elicit the reason in the events of the past, but that people had asked him for "a history of the future." Rosenkranz argues that since, according to Hegel, the essence of mind is "reason and freedom," we can expect them to spread in the future. Later that year, a pupil of Michelet, the Polish Count August von Cieszkowski, published a book entitled *Prolegomena zur Historiosophie* (Berlin, 1838) in which it was argued that since philosophy is concerned with the eternal essence of mind it cannot be confined to the past and present but must extend to the future too. The end of history is the rational freedom and eventual divinity of mankind. As long as men are unaware of their place in history they cannot be free, but as they sweep away brute facts and substitute conscious deeds for them they transform the natural, secular community into a universal church. Control of social circumstances by conscious action (called by Cieszkowski "Praxis") will make the world divine. The radical implications of these views were explored by Moses Hess in *Die Europäische Triarchie* (Leipzig, 1841), with acknowledgments to Cieszkowski's "philosophy of the deed." Hess called for an alliance between France, Prussia, and England to oppose Austria and Russia, and to make possible the establishment of a completely free society in Europe. In 1841 Hess met Karl Marx when the *Rheinische Zeitung*—to which both Marx and Hess later contributed until it was closed down at the behest of the Russian Government—was being founded, and he claims, too, that he converted Engels to communism during a discussion at Cologne that same year.

In the *Hallische Jahrbücher* of 1842 Ruge published a remarkable discussion of Hegel's political philosophy. According to Ruge, Hegel's constitutional proposals in his *Philosophie des Rechts* are presented as if they were "eternal truths" instead of what was suitable at a particular period of Prussian history. Ruge noticed in Hegel a "split" between his "theory and his practice." The philosopher, Ruge wrote, "should throw the whole truth as a ferment into the world." When what exists is unreasonable, there is "the demand for 'Praxis,' and the strong duty to engage in it." This, in turn, requires the reforming "Pathos of religion" which must emerge in "fanaticism." "As long as there are batteries to be taken or positions to defend, there is no history without fanaticism." Ruge soon came into association with Marx and Engels, who published their earliest theoretical writings in his *Deutsch-Französische Jahrbücher* (Paris, 1844).

Hegelians of the Left, then, claimed that Hegel had failed to recognize the implications of his own basic

413

ideas. Ignoring Hegel's interest in mysticism, they developed his views about the "myths" of Christianity, and moved towards the idea that God and humanity are one. They used Hegelian arguments, too, to undermine Hegel's view that philosophy can only understand the reason embodied in the past and cannot predict the future. His linkage between reason and freedom was their justification for advocating the forcible realization of freedom in the existing irrational social order. "Orthodox" Hegelians were ill prepared to oppose this development because of their hostility to the Historical School of Law. Hegel's insistence that the divine is in *this* world and not beyond it, led some Hegelians (e.g., Feuerbach) to become empiricists and nonreductive materialists and hence to abandon Hegelianism altogether.

In his magnificent *Hegel und seine Zeit* (Berlin, 1857) Rudolf Haym took the view that Hegel was a political time-server, who supported Napoleon when he was on top and Prussian absolutism when he had his chair at Berlin. The last part of this charge is questionable, but Haym was correct in noticing a certain passivity in Hegel's views. "Will and freedom," Haym wrote, "evaporated away in Hegel into thought and knowledge." He wrote of "the whole duplicity of the system," and said that in it the notion of freedom was "devalued." According to Haym, Hegel's philosophy of religion is "archaistic," exhibits "apologetic, reactionary (*restaurative*) tendencies," and is an attempt, like that of the Neo-Platonists, to refurbish the myths of a dying religion. Haym concluded that, just as the metaphysics of Leibniz and Wolff were followed by Kant's Critical Philosophy, so Hegel's metaphysics would be followed by a critical philosophy which would ask: "How is the synthesis possible of language, art, religion, and of legal, moral, scientific activity?"

7. The Revival of Hegelianism. In 1860 a new Hegelian periodical, *Der Gedanke* (Berlin, 1860–84) was founded under the editorship of Carl L. Michelet. Among its German subscribers were Göschel and David Strauss, Ferdinand Lassalle and Rosenkranz, Moses Hess, Lasson, and Zeller. When subscriptions were asked for in 1870 for a bust to commemorate Hegel, subscriptions came (among others) from J. H. Stirling, T. H. Green, Caird, Wallace, and Benjamin Jowett, and Ruge responded from his home in Brighton. There were members in France, Great Britain, Italy, Holland, Scandinavia, and the U.S.A. In Germany Michelet and Rosenkranz continued to be the leading Hegelian writers. Michelet contributed to *Der Gedanke* a series of "world-historical surveys" (in which he castigated Napoleon III) and defended the "philosophy of the deed of our friend and member Count von Cieszkowski" (*Der Gedanke*, 1861). He published *Naturrecht*

oder *Rechts-Philosophie als die praktische Philosophie*, 2 vols. (Berlin, 1866). The influence of Hegel's *Philosophie des Rechts* on this book is considerable, as to both form and content. But Michelet objected to Hegel's defence of hereditary monarchy, arguing that "in our times the Idea has become more stable than nature," that "the vote has become more stable than legitimacy," and that as mind masters the world "what is the most rational becomes also the most useful." (We may note the Hegelian, nonempiricist distinction between rationality and the satisfaction of wants, and the idea that since voting is established it is right.) Michelet also argued, following Hegel, that freedom of persons necessitates freedom of contract, and, going beyond Hegel, that this necessitates universal free trade. He also held that the incorporation of one people by another can never be justified, but that what is unjust from the standpoint of the Law of Nations can be just from the standpoint of world history. (The idea of a constantly rationalized and developing world history is a theme of many Hegelians.) A state can be defeated by others who become "the bearers of civilization" (*Träger der Bildung*), but this should not prevent the losers from continuing their internal life "so that the natural limitations of their spirit still give expression to a side of the universal human spirit" (II, 215).

J. H. Stirling's *The Secret of Hegel*, 2 vols. (London, 1865) helped to introduce Hegel to the English-speaking world. Although he makes a defense of Hegel against Haym's political aspersions, Stirling is mainly concerned with the Hegelian logic and epistemology, and to some extent with Hegelian religion. He refers to Strauss and Feuerbach as the "Atheistico-Materialistic set," and makes a good attempt to expound the outlines of Hegel's Christology: "Hegel ascribes to Christ the revelation that God is man or that man is God. . . . Before Christ, God was external to man, and worship or obedience to him consisted in external ceremonies. But since Christ, God is inward to man: he is our conscience. We no longer ask the will of God from external oracles, but from our own selves: that is, we are now a law unto ourselves, we are to our own selves in the place of God, we are ourselves God, God and man are identified" (I, 149).

Stirling was the first of a number of Scottish Hegelians, of whom Edward Caird and William Wallace are the best known, and a number of Scottish ministers contributed to Hegel's bust. T. H. Green, F. H. Bradley, and Bernard Bosanquet, however, partly because of their connections with Oxford, exerted a greater influence. All three thought that Hegel had refuted the empiricist and atomic (or pluralist) metaphysics they attributed to J. S. Mill and the utilitarians, and all three held that individual men are essentially related to the community to which they belong. Green argued that the state should, by social legislation, enable individuals to make the best of themselves, Bosanquet that the state was necessary to make ultimate decisions—Hegel's "majesty," perhaps, in nonmonarchical form. Bosanquet lived into the period when socialism was being publicly discussed in England, and in a lecture given to the Fabian Society in 1890 he quoted Hegel's justification of private property in the *Philosophie des Rechts*, and gave no comfort to his state-socialist listeners ("Individualism and Socialism" in *The Civilisation of Christendom*, London, 1899). Bradley employed Hegelian concepts (e.g., the concrete universal) to show that patriotism and retribution are not superseded. At the end of *Ethical Studies* (Oxford, 1876) he writes of religious faith as the belief "that you too are really one with the divine," and quotes Böhme to this effect. He also discusses the notion of worshipping "Humanity," as advocated by the positivist Frederick Harrison. Bradley, quoting Trendelenburg in his support, questions whether all human beings, past and present, make a single being, and argues that even if they did, it would not be worthy of worship unless it were more than human. Green, in an early paper, "An Essay on Christian Dogma" (*Works*, ed. Nettleship, Vol. III, London, 1888), argues on Hegelian-Straussian lines that the central Christian doctrines represent profound philosophical truths, but in his review in 1880 of a book in which J. Caird defended Hegel's philosophy of religion he objects that it is not credible that the individual could be identified with God. Bosanquet (*What Religion Is*, London, 1920) says that "religion just *is* the weld of finite and infinite," but although this is Hegelian, Bosanquet does not link it with Christian doctrine even to the extent that Strauss had done.

The influence of Hegelianism in the United States can be seen in *The Journal of Speculative Philosophy* (St. Louis, 1867–93), edited by William T. Harris. In the first issue there is a preface by the editor who announces that there will be discussions of positivism, articles on *Faust* and Beethoven, and a defense of Speculative Philosophy. "The day of simple experience," he writes, "is past." Harris thought that hitherto "national unity seemed an external mechanism," but now people were reaching "a consciousness of the other essential phase, and each individual recognizes his substantial side to be the State as such." This was Hegelian political philosophy much as Bradley understood it nine years later, but the journal was more concerned with literature, metaphysics, aesthetics, and the philosophy of religion than with politics. Harris contributed a great deal himself, including translations from Hegel's *Logic*, sympathetic criticisms of Herbert Spencer, and a defense of the immortality of the soul:

"But if anything is, then there must exist the Absolute and its reflection; and its reflection implies immortal beings" (*Journal . . .* , **4,** 2 [1870], III). Hegel himself had not been explicit on this subject, but Göschel had been, and chapters from his *Von den Beweisen für die Unsterblichkeit der menschlichen Seele im Lichte der spekulative Philosophie* (Berlin, 1835) were published in English in the *Journal* in 1877 and 1883–85. Josiah Royce, influenced though he was by German Idealism as a whole, can hardly be called a thoroughgoing Hegelian in his political or moral philosophy. For although his *Philosophy of Loyalty* (New York, 1908) stresses the need for the individual to find his station in society and identify himself with a community, his admiration for loyalty to lost causes is contrary to the main tendency of Hegelianism whether of the Right or of the Left. For according to Hegelianism, reason now or in the future must master the world. It is interesting to note that in *The Philosophy of Loyalty* (p. 238) Royce uses Hegel's phrase "the self-estrangement of the spirit" to express the loss of individuality suffered when people become mere units in some over-large community.

8. Concluding Comments. Not all Hegelians have opposed liberal forms of enterprise economy, for they believe that the Whole is at work in every finite particular, and that the total Unity comes from struggle. But all Hegelians have regarded the State as ultimate and rational, as "mind on earth" (Hegel, *Philosophie des Rechts*, §270), or as more real than individual men (Bosanquet, *The Philosophical Theory of the State*, London, 1899). Hegel and Bosanquet, however, were more impressed by the mind *already* at work in the world, whereas Hegelians of the Left were anxious to *put it there*, to realize the Idea by the force of a revolutionary ardor or fanaticism that Hegel would have regarded as abstract and destructive, "the fanaticism of destruction," and "the fury of disturbance" as marks of "negative freedom" (*Philosophie des Rechts*, §5). Revolutionary transformation went well with the Hegelian thesis that man and God are somehow identical. Hegel and his orthodox followers interpreted this in Protestant or possibly mystical terms, but the step from the unity of man and God to the positivist thesis of Comte that mankind is God and should be worshipped as such is easy to take, as Bradley pointed out (*Ethical Studies*, last footnote).

Hegelianism has been regarded as a glorification of the state and of militarism. Hegel said (*Philosophie des Rechts*, §338) that "in war, war itself is characterized as something that ought to pass away," but that civilized peoples (e.g., agriculturalists) are justified in regarding the rights of barbarians (e.g., pastoral peoples) as inferior to their own, and the autonomy of barbarians "as only a formality" (§351). To proceed thus, Hegel held, is to secure the victory, not of force but of reason (§342). This can be interpreted as a plea to defend civilization by force or as an excuse on behalf of existing and successful might. There is some ambiguity, too, between saying that it is wrong for barbarians to destroy the civilized world and saying that in the long run it is impossible. The Hegelian scholar, Georg Lasson, writing, in his introduction to Hegel's *Lectures on the Philosophy of History* (*Werke*, VIII, Leipzig [1920], 172) referred to the First World War in these words: ". . . it will not come to an end until the nation to which Providence has given the task of making the principle of the true cultivation of the state at home in humanity throughout the world, has been so physically strengthened and spiritually matured that those powers which today fancy themselves to be justified in subjecting the planet to their inferior principles can no longer resist it."

BIBLIOGRAPHY

On Hegel's political writings the basic works in English are T. M. Knox's translation, *Hegel's Philosophy of Right* (Oxford, 1942), and T. M. Knox (translator) and Z. A. Pelczynski, *Hegel's Political Writings* (Oxford, 1964). Knox's notes to the first and Pelczynski's introduction to the second provide detailed commentaries. There is an excellent discussion in E. Weil, *Hegel et l'état* (Paris, 1950), in which important earlier works are mentioned. See also: John Plamenatz, *Man and Society*, Vol. 2 (London and New York, 1963), Chs. 3, 4. On Hegel's philosophy of religion, J. McT. E. McTaggart's *Studies in Hegelian Cosmology* (Cambridge, 1901) covers the main topics, but for more recent discussions, see G. R. G. Mure, "Hegel, Luther and the Owl of Minerva," *Philosophy*, **41**, 156 (April, 1966), and F. C. Copleston, "Hegel and the Rationalisation of Mysticism," *Talk of God*, ed., G. N. A. Vesey, Royal Institute of Philosophy Lectures, **2** (London, 1969). For G. von Hugo, see his *Lehrbuch der Geschichte des römischen Rechts*, 5th ed. (1815).

Extracts from writers of the Hegelian School are contained in the following: K. Löwith, ed., *Die Hegelsche Linke* (Stuttgart and Bad Cannstatt, 1962), with extracts from Ruge, Hess, Feuerbach, Marx, and others. H. Lübbe, ed., *Die Hegelsche Rechte* (Stuttgart and Bad Cannstatt, 1962), contains extracts from Rosenkranz, Gans, Michelet, and others. Sidney Hook's *From Hegel to Marx*, new ed. (New York, 1962), deals with the movement away from Hegel of the Hegelian Left, and K. Löwith's *From Hegel to Nietzsche* (London, 1964; first German edition, Zürich, 1941), covers a wider field that is not exclusively Hegelian. J. Gebhardt, *Politik und Eschatologie: Studien zur Geschichte der Hegelschen Schule in den Jahren 1830–1840* (Munich, 1963) should not be missed. See also: David McLellan, *The Young Hegelians and Karl Marx* (London, 1969). The references to Hegel's *Lectures on the Philosophy of Religion*, found in section 3 of this article, can also be found, successively, in Hegel's *Werke*, ed. P. Marheineke, 2nd ed. (1840), XI, 137ff.; XII, 286ff. and 308ff.; XII, 354–56; XI, 212. These passages are translated by the author of the article.

H. B. ACTON

[See also **Authority**; Christianity in History; Church as an Institution; Constitutionalism; **God**; Liberalism; **Marxism**; Property; **State**.]

HERESY IN THE MIDDLE AGES

HERESY IS a deviation from orthodoxy. It is therefore defined in relation to orthodoxy. In the Middle Ages this was done by the Church, as the arbiter of Christian faith; and its decrees were binding upon all members of society, who were regarded by definition as Christian. However it might arise, then, heresy was the outcome of official condemnation by the Church.

Intellectually, the Middle Ages were distinguished by the existence of a prevailing orthodoxy and a universal authority to enforce it. On the one hand there was a divinely inspired book—the Bible—as the source of all truth, and a divinely ordained institution—the Church—to mediate it. On the other hand the unparalleled unity that resulted offered no outlet for the tensions between precept and practice. For that reason heresy was endemic in medieval society. If it did not become significant until the twelfth century, there was nevertheless no independent terrain from which any aspect of reality could be considered. Whether the issues were theoretical or practical, metaphysical or physical, moral or social, they had to remain within a recognized Christian framework. To move beyond it was to be opposed to authority. There could be no neutrality. To reject the teaching of the Church was to reject God's communion.

Heresy was not, however, the automatic accompaniment of error, nor were its penalties inflexibly applied. Error was of varying degrees which were far from uniformly heretical. For the most part heresy took generations, occasionally—as in the case of the doctrine of Christ's absolute poverty—centuries, to define. Above all, heresy was ultimately a moral issue: pertinacious error. The heretic was condemned as such for obduracy in refusing to abjure after his fault had been shown to him. Correspondingly, conviction for heresy was a defeat for the Church; it meant failure to save a soul, which was its mission on earth. There was thus an ambivalence towards the heretic. Unlike the infidel, he was the direct responsibility of the Church; only if he could not be reformed must he be punished.

Heresy was one of the preoccupations of medieval, as of any closed, society. The efforts to overcome it, by coercion and persuasion, were for the most part disproportionate to the numbers involved; but they cannot be measured quantitatively. From the later twelfth century the issues raised by dissent increasingly impinged upon the outlook of the epoch, inspiring numerous treatises as well as the creation of a permanent repressive machinery in the inquisition.

Although Christian heresy goes back to the early centuries of the Church it only began to emerge in its characteristically medieval form in the eleventh century. This heresy differed from earlier ones in being the almost invariable outcome of a search for reform and/or spiritual renewal. Many of the heresies of the third, fourth, and fifth centuries, in contrast, had been directly doctrinal, concerned with the conceptions of the Trinity, the divinity of Christ, free will, grace, predestination, original sin, the sacraments, and so on; although these questions recurred throughout the Middle Ages, they arose initially from the attempts to establish a coherent Christian doctrine. In that sense they were the product of a still inchoate theology. Moreover, they took place in a yet largely inchoate church as an institution. Until well into the seventh century the Church was far from being the universal arbiter of faith; whole kingdoms and regions in the fourth and fifth centuries were under the influence of rival versions of Christianity, such as Arianism and Donatism, while many remained pagan until long after. Opposition to the early church did not therefore have the same doctrinal or institutional implications as it did later. Only as orthodoxy became defined and the authority of Roman church established did that which was contrary to either become by implication and definition heretical. Accordingly where most of the early heresies became such only in retrospect, through failure to become orthodoxy, heresy by the eleventh century—although definitions remained fluid—represented from the outset a direct challenge to the Church.

This difference, in turn, directly affected the nature of medieval heresy. However it originated its existence was a challenge to the Church as an institution; the claim by an individual or a sect to its own version of Christian truth was a denial of the role of the Church as the arbiter of God's will on earth, and thus the spiritual power to which all believers had to submit. To be heretical was therefore inevitably to be anti-sacerdotal; for, no matter what the circumstances, heresy was branded as such by the Church. A group

or doctrine could only continue in opposition, either openly or clandestinely; this inevitably made it subversive. Whether or not heresy led to the formation of independent churches, in every case it meant the rejection of the Roman church.

Now it was as a response to the Church that the main heresies developed. With the exception of the Cathars—whom we shall consider later—heresy was an outcrop from commonly held Christian beliefs. Its impulse was invariably the search for a fuller spiritual life, and it drew above all upon the truth revealed in the Bible to realize an essentially Christian aspiration. There was a regular progression from initially nonheretical belief to open heresy. All the main sects started from the accepted Christian tenets; only subsequently, through growing hostility between them and the Church, did their ideals take on a more extreme and debased form culminating in a group's exclusion from the Church. Even so its adherents continued to believe that they were the true faithful and that the hierarchy which persecuted them was heretical.

No one of the main medieval sects, the Cathars apart, was non-Christian in outlook; nor, with the exception of John Wycliffe's followers, did they begin by embracing doctrines which had already been condemned as heretical. It is at first sight paradoxical that the important movements sprang not from the teachings of an original heresiarch or from overtly anti-Christian ideas but from the common stock of accepted belief. This can be seen in the main themes around which heresy revolved; poverty, prophetic belief in a new order, insistence upon a true apostolic church, and the mystical search for God in the soul. These were, at different times, among the major doctrinal and spiritual preoccupations of the period from the eleventh century onwards. What marked off their heretical from their nonheretical expression were the conclusions drawn from them. It was the significance given to the notion of poverty as in itself sacrosanct that led the extreme wing of the Franciscan order—the Spirituals—to defy first its own superiors and then the papacy; similarly members of the sect of the Free Spirit in the later thirteenth and the fourteenth centuries identified a mystical awareness of God with self-deification. In both cases as in nearly all others heresy arose from pressing accepted notions too far.

To that extent heresy was the outcome of heterodoxy, either through giving an unorthodox meaning to existing beliefs, such as poverty or the example of Christ's life, or by introducing new ones such as Joachim of Floris' belief in three world ages or Meister Eckhart's mystical teaching on the birth of God's word in the soul. Since, moreover, such ideas were initially formed by the literate and intellectually articulate, the

417

sequence tended to be from learned to popular. What begins as a new concept or interpretation takes on an independent significance as the program of a group. In the process it becomes distorted and more extreme so that its original meaning changes. This occurred with all the major heretical issues of poverty, prophecy, the Church, the search for God, and so on. The reason is that heterodoxy was not in itself the cause of heresy but rather the middle term between heresy and orthodoxy. Throughout the Middle Ages many ideas were censured as heterodox or heretical—Gottschalk in the ninth century on predestination, Berengarius on the eucharist and Roscelin on the Trinity in the eleventh century, Abelard and Gilbert de la Porrée on the Trinity in the twelfth century, the exponents of a naturalistic Aristotelianism in the thirteenth century, Ockham, Marsilius of Padua, Eckhart, and Wycliffe in the fourteenth century, to mention only a few of the more outstanding examples. Yet apart from Wycliffe and perhaps Eckhart none of these doctrinal errors directly inspired a new heresy. Conversely, the great sources of heresy were among the most universally venerated—the Bible, Saint Francis, Joachim of Floris. The discrepancy lies in the application they were given. Where it led to the formation of dissenting groups heresy was the invariable result. In that sense heterodoxy became heresy when branded as dissent. To be so, it did not suffice to exist as an idea; it had to be upheld by adherents in opposition to the Church.

The ways in which this occurred were diverse; but we may distinguish the main heresies according to the themes which we have already mentioned. That does not imply that to each of them there corresponded a specific heretical sect or that each was always to be found separately. Rather these were the foci around which the main movements gathered. The heresies also shared certain common traits that came from being a movement of protest. To begin with, there was the sense, produced by persecution, of being an elect group. Most heretics saw themselves as the true defenders of Christ's law; they identified their sufferings with Christ's in the same cause of evangelical truth against Antichrist. They had an assurance in their final triumph which gave them a righteous acceptance of their tribulations. Again, they were prepared to take God's law into their own hands and reject that of the Church. This led to treating the Bible as supreme truth, to be understood according to their own interpretation. It put the emphasis upon preaching and individual experience of God's word as the source of all religious understanding. This in turn depreciated the outward forms of the sacraments and ceremonial. The return to Christ was seen as renunciation of the ways of the present church for the simplicity of Christ's apostolic life. It was accompanied by an insistence upon the quality of life as the test of individual probity. Only those who lived in accordance with Christ's precepts could claim to be his disciples. Many sects, above all, the Waldensians, the Lollards, and the Taborites, declared that a sinful priest could not administer the sacraments, and thus resurrected the Donatist heresy of the third century. It was now, however, directed against the very existence of the Church as a privileged corporation with its own wealth, hierarchy, coercive authority, and the vices of worldliness—above all simony—which they bred. This made the criterion of spiritual power moral not sacramental, and transferred it from the Roman church to those outside it.

Within this framework the most universal of all notions was poverty. It was venerated by religious and heretical movements alike, whether in the absolute form of the Arnoldists, Waldensians, and Franciscans or as a necessary part of a religious vocation, with its demands of poverty, chastity, and obedience. Poverty together with chastity expressed one facet of the inherent Christian dualism between the flesh and the spirit, acceptance of the world and withdrawal from it. Poverty had always been a powerful element in the Christian outlook from the time of the Fathers, and was inseparable from the notion of personal holiness. It received a new impetus in the eleventh century from the spread of monasticism and the demands for religious reform. On the one hand reformers like Peter Damian, himself a monk and hermit, and Humbert, condemned as sinful all clergy who took money (simony) or lived in concubinage; they demanded a return to apostolic purity and the refusal of spiritual ministrations from priests who did not live virtuously—later decreed by the First Lateran Council in 1139. On the other hand religious life was becoming increasingly ascetic. The new monastic foundations of the Grande Chartreuse in 1086 and Citeaux in 1098 were both set in the wilderness with the stress upon austerity and the rejection of all superfluity. The ideals of Citeaux, under Saint Bernard (d. 1153) were the focus of monasticism in the first half of the twelfth century. But it was also the age of the hermit and the wandering preacher; and around the latter many of the heretical groups of the eleventh and twelfth centuries formed. Such men as Tanchelm, Henry of Lausanne, Peter of Bruys, and Arnold of Brescia attracted a mainly lay following. Although they preached a similar doctrine of ascetic and moral reform they differed from their orthodox counterparts in directing it to the populace of towns and ultimately to attacking the very existence of the Church in its present visible form. They reached these more extreme positions through coming into conflict with the Church. Either through personal aberration in the case of Tanchelm and Henry of Lausanne or through refusal to accept the present state of the Church, as seems to have been the case with Peter of Bruys and Arnold of Brescia, such men ended by acting outside the Church. It was then that the impulse to reform became revolution.

In the second half of the twelfth century, however, poverty, after having been predominantly a moral attitude, became also a *Weltanschauung* in its own right. The change was expressed in the Peter Valdes' group—the Waldensians or Poor Men of Lyons founded in about 1170—and later the Franciscans, and was of the first importance for the outlook of the subsequent Middle Ages. It was bound up with a new conception of Christ conceived as a man, and the desire to emulate his human example. Peter Damian had been the first to stress the humanity of Christ. With the Waldensians it came to be identified with a life of mendicant poverty and preaching, which was taken as the model of the apostolic church and those true to it. This introduced a new historical dimension into the conceptions of Christ, the Church, and the Bible.

So far as Christ was concerned it is one of the paradoxes of the period from the later twelfth century that the figure of Christ as a man became the most potent challenge to the Church as a divine institution. The historical events of Christ's life became the touchstone by which to judge the Church's authority. Christ and the apostles, possessionless and humble, should mean a church without wealth or privileges. Loyalty to Christ was shown by living as he had lived, and this was the condition of belonging to his communion.

The effects of this attitude upon the Church were revolutionary. Those who held it no longer regarded the Church as the timeless and unchanging instrument of God's will. Instead of a direct continuity with the age of the apostles, there had been a break and subsequent decline. By the early thirteenth century, the Waldensians saw the change as having come with the so-called Donation of Constantine, a document—subsequently discovered to have been forged, but accepted as genuine in the Middle Ages—in which the emperor made over control of the Western Empire to the papacy. Such a view was not confined to the Waldensians; it became current among diverse thinkers, including Dante, Marsilius of Padua, and later Wycliffe and Hus, while the Franciscan dissidents and other sects saw the Church hierarchy as Antichrist. It at once provided an explanation for the present ills of the Church and a justification for their remedy in opposition to its hierarchy—and in the case of a sect like the Waldensians, for the rejection of the authority of the Church altogether.

This rejection was, in turn, accomplished largely by invoking the Bible. It thereby took on a new role. As the source of Christ's life and teaching, the Bible was not only revealed truth but historical testimony to events which had happened on earth. Always the criterion of truth it now provided the norm for judging the Church. In the hands of the latter's opponents, both within and outside the Church, the Bible as God's law was repeatedly contraposed to the human laws and false claims of the present hierarchy. It became the most destructive weapon in the outlook of the later Middle Ages; for it turned God's word and Christ's example against the Church to deny the latter divine sanction and to make the Church's abandonment of its wealth and privileges the condition of its return to Christ. To have done so would have led to the Church's dismemberment.

These implications, which only become fully apparent by the later thirteenth century, were the outcome of the ideas first given currency a hundred years earlier in the search for an apostolic life. The Waldensians and the Franciscans were the two greatest exponents of these ideas. Nowhere is the convergence between heresy and orthodoxy more striking. Each group owed its inspiration to a similar apostolic ideal and veneration of Christ's poverty. The founders of both—Valdes ca. 1176 at Lyons, Saint Francis in 1206 at Assisi—renounced the wealth and the conventions of a mercantile life for one of wandering poverty and preaching, because they had received a vision of their true vocation. Each soon attracted a band of followers pledged to the same ideal. But whereas Valdes and his group were condemned by the bishop of Lyons in 1181 and then by Pope Lucius III in 1184, Saint Francis' band was recognized by Pope Innocent III in 1210 and was established as a new order. The Waldensians thus became heretical, developing into a universal counterchurch; the Franciscans, having been accepted, became one of the two great religious forces of the thirteenth century and one of the main bulwarks of the Church. What began from a common aspiration diverged through circumstances. The differences between the groups lay not in ends but in largely fortuitous external factors, which could have operated the other way. Although it is inconceivable that Saint Francis could ever have been a heretic, it is more than possible that in different circumstances Valdes might have remained within the Church, as his profession of faith shows. Conversely without the insight of Innocent III, Saint Francis' and Saint Dominic's bands might never have been formed into new orders.

Even so, the boundaries from one to the other were crossed by their followers: a group of Waldensians, under Durandus of Huesca, was constituted by Innocent III into a separate order of the Catholic Poor, while Saint Francis' more zealot followers—the Spirituals—were persecuted as heretics within fifty years of their founder's death in 1226, and their doctrine of the absolute poverty of Christ on earth, of which Saint Francis was the apostle, was condemned by Pope John XXII in 1323. In the process poverty took on a new meaning for all those involved, including the papacy.

To begin with the Waldensians, their excommunication changed their character as a movement. Although they did not immediately evolve into a full-fledged heretical sect, they henceforth developed in opposition to the Church. What had been a group of pious unlettered laymen had by 1215 become an intransigeant sect claiming to be the one true apostolic church and denouncing the Roman church in the language of the Apocalypse as the body of the damned (*congregatio malignantium*) and the Whore of Babylon. They nevertheless remained the one exclusively indigenous popular movement which survived the Middle Ages and spread to most parts of Western and Central Europe. Their strength lay in the consonance of their practice with their apostolic beliefs. Although they set themselves up as an independent church with their own priests and sacramental forms, they consciously modelled themselves on the practices of Christ and his disciples, regarding themselves as their direct successors. Their priests (*perfecti*) were pledged to a distinctive life of austerity and spiritual ministration; they lived on alms and devoted themselves to preaching in the vernacular from the New Testament and the Fathers; for this they were excused from manual labor. They alone had the power of the keys (hearing confession and granting absolution) which they received direct from God because they alone were free from sin: the inefficacy of sinful priests—which included all those in the Church of Rome—was one of the Waldensians' main tenets. The Waldensian priests, in contrast, were believed to return periodically to heaven to renew their faith.

The power of the Waldensian church was matched by the universality of its appeal; it required not initiation into a new cult but a heightening of Christian faith. The Christian believer in joining the Waldensians was becoming a full apostle of Christ, bringing practice into conformity with precept. He could continue as a believer in his present way of life, as peasant, artisan, or weaver, even showing outward obedience to the Roman church, as was the case with the Waldensian congregations scattered over central Europe. But he gave his allegiance to the *perfecti;* by following them he entered into Christ's true communion, where alone salvation lay. He listened clandestinely to their preaching, supported them with alms, and confessed to them. In such circumstances the discovery of

Waldensian groups was difficult enough; the elimination of Waldensian beliefs was virtually impossible, and they continually recurred in the same areas generation after generation.

The foundation of Waldensian belief was, therefore, in its claim to direct apostolic succession, which was justified historically as we have said in the Donation of Constantine, and practically in the apostolic lives of the *perfecti*. It licensed them to oppose the Roman church and to reject virtually the whole of its laws and ritual—all forms of ecclesiastical coercion (such as excommunication and interdict), the taking of life, the passing of sentences and swearing of oaths, saints' days, feast days, vigils, pilgrimages, offices, benedictions, all prayers save the Lord's Prayer—all on the same grounds: that Christ had forbidden them, and neither Christ nor his disciples had practiced them. Even churches were at best merely stone buildings, and cemeteries pieces of open ground, and more often the work of priestly avarice. Thus the Waldensians drew strength from what they took to be the historical image of the true church. Their success is to be seen not only in their survival but in the spread of their ideas to the English Lollards and the Hussites in the later fourteenth and fifteenth centuries. Their conviction that they were the true church already constituted explains the almost complete absence of apocalyptic tendencies; they had no call to invoke a new era or Christ's imminent return to vindicate their claims. Christ had already done that by handing to them his powers which the Roman church had forfeited after the Donation of Constantine.

In the case of the Franciscans, the issue of poverty dominated their history for over 150 years and led not only to schism within it but to heresy, the combating of which became of a major preoccupation of the papacy. The conflict arose from the absoluteness of Saint Francis' belief in poverty as the badge of an evangelical life; in treating his conception of poverty as a direct revelation from God, Francis' outlook was at once more personal and inflexible than that of the founders of the other main religious orders. To have followed Saint Francis' rule in its full rigor, without buildings, books, or amenities of any kind, was incompatible with the organization which its numbers and role demanded. In that sense the struggles which grew up within the order were between the conflicting demands of an ideal and its institutionalization. On the one hand, there were the Spirituals who adhered to the example of Saint Francis and the letter of his rule. On the other, there was the main body of the order, the Community or Conventuals, who were prepared to modify the practice of absolute poverty to the corporate needs of the order as an arm of the

Church—in preaching, learning, spiritual ministration. The distance between them grew as the order evolved. It was exacerbated by the legal fiction, first formulated by Gregory IX in 1229 in his bull *Quo elongati*, that the order possessed nothing in its own right; it merely used goods of which the papacy was the owner. This distinction between use and possession enabled the order to lead a life indistinguishable from that of any other while remaining formally pledged to absolute poverty. For the Spirituals it meant being implicated in all the paraphernalia which Saint Francis had shunned. The contradiction between theoretical poverty and actual wealth led from the 1250's to a growing insistence by the Spirituals upon a life based on the practice of poverty (*usus pauper*), as opposed to the pursuit of wealth. The conflict reached a climax from the last two decades of the thirteenth century until 1318 when the Spirituals were effectively crushed as a movement by Pope John XXII in conjunction with the leaders of the order under Michael of Cesena. By then the Spirituals had joined in open revolt not only against the Conventual party but against the hierarchy of the Church which had sanctioned Franciscan privileges and a departure from Saint Francis' teachings.

In the course of their struggle the Spirituals, as a persecuted minority, evolved an apocalyptic outlook which they adopted from Joachim of Floris (d. 1202). Their fusion of poverty with prophecy was not fortuitous. Joachim's teaching on the coming of a new order of spiritual men who, barefooted, would renew the life of Church in the thirteenth century had soon found a response among both the Dominicans and the Franciscans. It appealed especially to the latter just because Saint Francis was the apostle of poverty, and its observance, in obedience and chastity, the basis of Franciscan life.

To the Spirituals suffering in the cause of poverty, Joachism appeared as their vindication. Not that—as interpreted by them—it bore any direct relation to Joachim's own teachings. On the contrary, in transposing Joachim's essentially symbolic scheme of the world's history into the history of the Franciscan order during the thirteenth century, they betrayed Joachim. They turned Joachim's speculations and parallels into justification for their own revolt, making tangible and specific what for Joachim had been a spiritual and often poetic conception. Names, dates, and events in the Franciscan calendar provided the dramatis personae for which there was no place in Joachim's thinking; his notion of a new spiritual order became invested with meanings which were not his: Joachim's spiritual church became for the Spirituals and their offshoots that of the Franciscan dissidents, and the carnal church which opposed them that of the pope at Rome; the

eternal gospel, which for Joachim signalized a new spiritual understanding of the Bible, came for the zealots to signify Saint Francis' rule and the writings of leading Spirituals, above all Peter John Olivi. Antichrist came to signalize either popes like Boniface VIII and John XXII or kings and emperors, including the mythical future Frederick III, descendent of the Emperor Frederick II, the leading opponent of the papacy in the thirteenth century.

Above all, the Spirituals and their followers regarded the belief in absolute poverty as the touchstone of discipleship of Christ. They took over the imagery of the Apocalypse, which Joachim had employed, to depict the denouement between themselves and their opponents as that between the forces of Christ and Antichrist. In that cosmic setting the doctrine of poverty became transformed into the guiding thread of mankind's history which would receive its consummation with the triumph of the bearers of Saint Francis' ideals. When John XXII finally condemned the doctrine of absolute poverty in 1323 he was thus seeking to destroy one of the most potent myths of the epoch. His action only led to driving those affected by his ban into open revolt which lasted for another century before it finally disappeared. Numerically neither the Spirituals nor the later groups of the Fraticelli were of comparable significance with the Waldensians. But, together, the doctrine of poverty led them—although by different routes—to condemn the Church in its existing form.

For that reason it had a direct bearing upon the very notion of the Church and the ideas of church reform; thus the separation of one from the other is largely artificial. They can be distinguished in the degree to which other elements were significant. For the Franciscan Spirituals and other groups, poverty remained the supreme criterion, acceptance or rejection of which defined the membership of the spiritual and carnal churches; since the full realization of the true church was conceived apocalyptically, as an event still in the future, it remained imaginary. The Waldensians, on the other hand, had a clearly defined notion of the Church which they identified with themselves and their own practices. They appealed to history to justify what had already come into being.

Between these two extremes came the doctrines of Wycliffe and the Hussites who distinguished between the visible church under the present hierarchy and the invisible church of the saved. This was also a development of Saint Augustine's division between the two cities of the damned and the saved, and of the apostolic ideal. Where Saint Augustine's earthly and heavenly cities were eschatological, constituting men's final separation in the next world, Wycliffe applied them to this world. The saved alone were members of the Church, and for all eternity. Conversely the damned were eternally of the devil's congregation. Hence they could never meet, even temporally. Since, moreover, no one knew whether he was saved or damned it was impossible to identify those of the true church; there was no ascertainable relation between the visible priesthood and the true priesthood of Christ. The Church was no longer the communion of all the faithful, embracing the damned and the saved in this world, and so, in its outward form, it lost any raison d'être. This was the new element in Wycliffe's church doctrine.

He did not, however, rest there; he harnessed the apostolic idea as it had been developed by Marsilius of Padua to deny scriptural support to the powers and practices of the hierarchy. Here, like Marsilius, he drew upon the ideas given currency by the Waldensians and the Franciscan disputes, to contrast Christ's precept and example with the condition of the Church. By taking the Bible as his criterion he was able to show that there was no scriptural foundation for the pope's headship or for the existence of cardinals, or ecclesiastical possessions and powers of coercion. His remedy, like that of Marsilius, was the forcible disendowment of the Church by the king and lay lords in order to restore it to its exclusively spiritual role.

These ideas with modifications, especially as to the means of achieving them, were common to much of the church doctrine of the fourteenth and fifteenth centuries, and were not confined to Wycliffe or the Hussites. They shared a critical attitude towards the Church as an institution, from treating it historically. Whether conceived as a counter-church, a future church, or as the reform of the present church, they all posited a prototype in Christ's life on earth.

The third main area of heresy, that of mysticism, had no immediate affinities with the other two. It was a comparatively late development only becoming significant in the fourteenth century. Although mysticism as a withdrawal from the experience of the everyday world often had poverty as its accompaniment, its concern was with spiritual rather than material states. Where the pursuit of evangelical poverty was the attempt to return to Christ by literally following his word in scripture, mysticism was the search for God in the soul. It came to permeate the spiritual life of the later Middle Ages as the apostolic ideal did its ecclesiastical beliefs. In the same way much of it became heretical. To seek direct contact with God within oneself was to tend to look away from the mediation of the Church; it could mean denying its truths and sacraments in the name of inner truth.

This is what occurred with the heresy of the Free Spirit. Although its origins cannot be firmly attached to any particular group or place, the Free Spirit sprang essentially from the pantheism latent in Neo-Platonism. The progressive disengagement of the soul from awareness of the senses could lead to reunion with its spiritual source standing above the material world. In the early years of the fourteenth century Meister Eckhart formulated this notion of spiritual detachment, and leading to the soul's rediscovery of God, into a new outlook. It became widely diffused through the Rhineland not least by Eckhart's own powers as a preacher in the vernacular. Eckhart was a man of deep and genuine spirituality; but in his efforts to reach his hearers, mostly nuns or laymen untutored in theology, he resorted to paradoxes which taken out of context could appear dubious or heretical. In particular he ceaselessly stressed that mystical experience culminated in man's reunion with God in the depths of and in a special region of the soul. He called its attainment the birth of the word or the son in the soul; the soul was reunited with God to become one with him again. The language which Eckhart used to describe this state often came near to both pantheism and a depreciation of the accepted forms of sacramental life. It was too easy to misinterpret his sayings on the oneness of man with God (in which man became God's son just like Christ and in which the birth of the word in the soul was more important than the Virgin birth), or the divinity of the spark in the soul, or the eternity of the place where it dwelt, or the subsidiary role of works and prayer. Taken out of context they appeared dangerous to faith. In the last years of his life Eckhart had to answer for a series of propositions which were abstracted from his writings and sermons by the ecclesiastical authorities at Cologne. In 1329, two years after his death, twenty-eight articles attributed to him were condemned by a papal bull at Avignon.

Eckhart remained a devout member of the Church throughout his life, and had no connection with the heresy of the Free Spirit. Nevertheless there can be little doubt that he indirectly contributed to its dissemination by the vogue that his teaching—possibly misunderstood and out of context—gave to this form of mysticism. Where Eckhart, however, made union with God the culmination of spiritual experience, for the Free Spirit it became the starting point for indulgence of the senses, above all, sex freed from any limitations. On the pretext that a man who had found God in the soul himself became divine, the exponents of the heresy claimed that he was now also free in spirit and released from all the constraints imposed by the Church: he could have sexual intercourse when and where he wished; he had no need to venerate Christ or attend masses, or fast before communion or obey the commandments of the Church or perform virtuous actions. These were all obligations which applied only to those still unfree and in a state of imperfection.

The blasphemy of this outlook marks it off from all the other heresies. Although its full extent remains obscure it was found mainly in the Rhineland and Central Europe among the semi-religious lay communities of the Beguines and Beghards, and propagated by individuals travelling from city to city, and claiming to be divine. There are also several instances of whole Beguine and Beghard houses being under the control of the adepts of the Free Spirit, with their inmates, mostly unlettered and theologically untrained, revering them as their spiritual superiors in the place of priests. Although such an outlook entailed anti-sacerdotalism this was rather a by-product of what was essentially a quietism. The heretics of the Free Spirit sought to withdraw from the jurisdiction of the Church rather than attack it; they challenged it not as a rival congregation but as representing a different plane of experience which no longer had need of the Church's mediation. How seriously the Church treated the danger can be seen from the succession of condemnations and inquisitorial operations which it launched from the first decade of the fourteenth century to its close, after which little is heard of the heresy.

Finally there were the Cathars. They were distinguished from all the other principal heresies in having a strong non-Christian element. They also came closest to taking control of an entire region—in Provence—enjoying the support of the nobles as well as the populace. Although not confined to southern France, it was there that the Cathars were entrenched, receiving the name of Albigensians from their association with the city of Albi. It was also against them in southern France that the war known as the Albigensian crusade was proclaimed by Pope Innocent III in 1210, after all other previous efforts at conversion, including preaching missions by the Cistercians and the future Dominicans, and coercion had failed. The ensuing war, conducted by the northern French nobles ended in the ultimate destruction of the distinctive culture of Provence and the annexation of the area to the French king. But it was not until the capture of Montségur and the burning of 200 heretics in 1244 that the Cathars' destruction was virtually complete. A remnant continued in existence until the 1320's; but it was of no significance.

It is generally accepted that Catharism came to the West through the Bogomils in Bulgaria, but whether in the eleventh or twelfth centuries is disputed. The central tenet of the doctrine was that all being was a dualism between spirit which was good and matter which was evil. As developed by the Bogomils this was conceived as a conflict between the soul which was from God and creation which came from the devil. Man's true spirit was not engendered in this world and was alien to it; he was a fallen spirit imprisoned in an evil body and circumscribed by an evil world. The problem he faced was of extricating himself from these surroundings and so returning to his true source. To do so man had to renounce the whole material order; this meant denying the satisfaction of all physical needs which perpetuated it.

The opposition of such an outlook to the Christian belief in creation as the work of God, and so essentially good, hardly needs stressing. Nevertheless in its practical and moral aspects there was a resonance between Catharism and Christianity in stressing the antinomy between the flesh and the spirit. As found among the Cathars of southern France it was expressed in the division into the elect (*perfecti*) and ordinary believers (*credentes*). The elect lived a life of self-abnegation as the path away from the devil's work. They were celibate; they abstained from eating flesh and practiced the austerities of asceticism. The faithful, who were not capable of such demands, were permitted the ordinary indulgences, provided they received, before death, special absolution (the *consolamentum*). This raised the recipient into the elect and was therefore administered only when he seemed beyond recovery. Should he survive, however, he was saved from the perils of relapsing into his imperfect state either by fasting to death or voluntary asphyxiation (the *endura*).

Despite their non-Christian inspiration the practical effect of these beliefs was an asceticism among the *perfecti* far more in accord with Christian precepts than the laxity of many of the Roman clergy. Moreover, Cathar doctrine itself became modified by its new Christian milieu. During the later twelfth century a mitigated form of Catharism grew up which confined the work of the devil to only existing material beings. God was responsible for the elements and the species; only in their actual physical state were they evil. This came closer to the widespread Christian distinction between an intelligible order of archetypes or forms and their created embodiment. Similarly in the thirteenth century Christ came to be recognized by the moderate Cathars as the son of God.

Despite these changes, however, Catharism both as a body of belief and as an independent church constituted a direct challenge to the Roman church and Christian faith, which ultimately was met by the Cathars' forcible destruction. If they were eliminated as a sect, some of their ideas—especially of their own priesthood and sacraments—were taken up by the Waldensians, who were frequently the object of the same repressive activity, especially in southern France and Lombardy. In that sense Cathar tenets became incorporated into an essentially Christian piety which survived them as an independent sect and extended to most parts of Western Christendom.

Heresy, then, for all its diverse forms had a common thread in the desire to come nearer to God. Whether expressed by poverty, reform, or mystical union, its danger lay in circumventing the mediation of the Church.

BIBLIOGRAPHY

An extensive bibliography of medieval heresy from the twelfth century is contained in G. Leff, *Heresy in the Later Middle Ages*, Vol. 2 (Manchester, 1967). Other important studies are: A. Borst, *Die Katherer* (Stuttgart, 1963); H. Grundmann, *Religiöse Bewegungen im Mittelalter* (Hildesheim, 1961); J. B. Russell, *Dissent and Reform in the Early Middle Ages* (Berkeley, 1965); C. Thouzellier, *Catharisme et Valdéisme en Languedoc à la fin du XIIe siècle et au début du XIIIe siècle* (Paris, 1966).

GORDON LEFF

[See also Analogy in Patristic and Medieval Thought; **Christianity in History;** Double Truth; Gnosticism; God; **Heresy, Renaissance;** Impiety; Pietism; **Prophecy; Religious Toleration;** Sin and Salvation.]

HERESY, RENAISSANCE
AND LATER

THE ROMAN Catholic Church defines a heretic as "any baptized person who, retaining the name Christian, pertinaciously denies or doubts one or another truth believed by divine and catholic faith" (*Corpus iuris canonici*, c. 1325, §2). Historically most Protestants have not demurred from that fundamental delineation, and, as the sixteenth century often noted, Protestant churches holding mutually contradictory doctrines exemplified attitudes toward heresy which were identical to the Catholic's. In practice, however, the formal conditions have not always obtained, and those views have been regarded as heretical which the Church or its leaders, Catholic or Protestant, have judged to be so. This has meant that orthodoxy and heresy have not been uniformly specified from age to age and from group to group.

The implications of such a definition of heresy are several. First, norms for judgment must be specifiable. Second, not every sect or each instance of dissent can be regarded as heretical. Theoretically, neither Jew nor Turk is a heretic since neither claims the Christian faith, although the distinction between the heretic and the infidel was not always honored. It has thus always been possible to differ, within certain bounds. Third, the alleged heretic must hold to his deviant view and to his claim to the name Christian obstinately. Fourth, the label "heresy" has acquired an exclusively pejorative meaning.

The term "heretic" is applicable to individuals or groups, to laymen or clergymen. There are several distinctions within the general category: objective heresy indicates an overt statement contradicting a dogma. Subjective heresy is the acceptance of such a statement. Formal heresy denotes the actual articulation of a heretical statement and requires fitting punishment. Material heresy circumscribes an inarticulate error in belief held in ignorance.

I. THE RENAISSANCE, THE REFORMATION AND THE PROBLEM OF HERESY

The Problem. One of the most important aspects of the history of heresy before the middle of the sixteenth century was the notion that heresy was disruptive of the structures of society and hence destructive of society, the *corpus christianum*, itself. Thus the heretic was an offender against the State as well. Both Roman Catholics and Protestants adhered to this view. It was the basis of the attack by a combined Catholic and Lutheran army against Münster in 1534–35. The "New Jerusalem" which had been set up in that city by religious dissidents was regarded as sufficiently threatening to surrounding society that confessional differences could be overlooked in suppressing it. And this theory was the buttress of Theodore Beza's defense of the burning of Michael Servetus in Geneva in 1553: to allow men with views like Servetus' to go unhindered was not only offensive to God but disintegrative of the social order. The concern thus was not exclusively for dogma. Assumed social ramifications were almost always associated with the repression of heretical dissent.

However, the significance of this idea began to dwindle when the Huguenots in France managed to introduce the principle of religious pluralism in the midst of political monism and obtained the Edict of Nantes in 1598. For almost a century thereafter a religious and political stalemate between Calvinists and Catholics was recognized, and the liberty of conscience and territorial coexistence implicit in the Edict did not destroy the French kingdom.

The churches' responses to heresy in the Renaissance and Reformation were in the form of punishment and repression. The theory underlying their attitude stems ultimately from Saint Augustine who held that force short of death may be used in love to recall men from error. Its more proximate source in this period, however, was in Saint Thomas Aquinas (*Summa theologica* II-II, q. 11, §§3–4). Thomas held that the Church's action against the heretic actually shows great mercy. As advocated in Titus 3:10, she does not immediately condemn the erring one, but first admonishes him twice. The aim is to retrieve the lost soul to the fold through penance. Forgiveness is the goal, not punishment. If the heretic remains obdurate, however, or if he relapses into his error after penance and rehabilitation, he must be punished. It is right, Thomas suggests, for such persons to suffer, for the contagion of their views jeopardizes the welfare of all. The goal then becomes the salvation of the community. Thomas construed heresy as the worst possible offense, and if the counterfeiter of coin is executed, how much more should the heretic, the counterfeiter of divine truth be put to death. Since God is regarded as the supreme sovereign, a feudalization of the idea has taken place: the severity of the crime is determined by the status of him against whom it is perpetrated. John 15:6, which states that a withered branch is to be burned, though not used by Thomas, seems to be the scriptural basis for the Church's position.

The Inquisition and the *Index librorum prohibitorum* were primary weapons of Roman Catholicism for dealing with heresy in the late Middle Ages. The former was systematized by Gregory IX and the Synod of Toulouse in 1229. Its legal and coercive powers were independent of local ecclesiastical and political controls, and it was much feared. The Index of prohibited books comes to the fore especially with the Council of Trent, 1545–63.

The operative legal principle in the churches' oppression of heresy was borrowed from criminal law. There, in the words of Andreas of Isernia (d. 1316), "the offense is in the will, and unless it be voluntary, it is not a crime." In the hands of the churchmen, this was construed to fit all heretics by definition. Theodore Beza, successor of Calvin in Geneva, assumed hypocrisy in all his opponents and regarded any activity against the Church as based on *dolus* ("deceit"). Every heretic "wills to ignore the truth." Beza's Protestant position was not unique, and it can be viewed as simply the logical extension of the position of Thomas (ibid., I–II, q. 76, §§2–3), who, by distinguishing between nescience (absence of knowledge) and ignorance (privation of knowledge), was able to deny the validity of a plea for clemency on the basis of ignorance. Not to know what one ought to know involves the sin of omission. Moreover, provisions of the Roman law, formulated in the Code of Justinian, which called for the death penalty for those who repeat baptism or deny the Trinity were revived.

There was no great formal difference between the confessions on this point when seen in toto. Luther in 1521 declared that heresy should be subject to no physical penalty, but ten years later he assented to the death penalty for blasphemy, which consisted in a public proclamation of heresy, and for sedition, when heresy subverted the State. Calvin openly regarded heresy itself as punishable by death, not that error as such was being punished, but offense against God, the Church, and society. Zwingli, although he could find room for certain pagans in paradise, approved Zurich's edict of 1526 which prescribed death by drowning for Anabaptists. Roman Catholicism had long since come to terms with the need to execute the heretic.

The State responded to dissent by treating heresy as a civil as well as a religious offense, for both Church and State were seeking the same supernatural end. The ends of salvation and the realization of God's kingdom were regarded to be supernatural ends. The Church was instrumental in securing this judgment. The Church, forbidden herself to shed blood, invoked the arm of the State to inflict the penalty. Recalcitrance by a civil ruler was countered with threats to relieve the ruler's subjects of their oath of allegiance, to excommunicate the ruler or impose the interdict upon him, or to cause the forfeiture of his lands and goods. Perhaps the most powerful statement on this matter is the bull of Innocent IV, *Ad extirpanda*, in 1252, which caps the decision of the Fourth Lateran Council (1215) to excommunicate any ruler who did not implement the will of the Church.

The interpretation of heresy as a civil offense punishable by death had been given legal basis by Emperor Frederick II (Constitutions of Melfi, 1231), and Innocent IV, in his bull, *Cum adversus haereticam pravitatem*, of 1245, sanctioned the Emperor's view with papal approval. Charles V developed an imperial heresy law for the Holy Roman Empire in 1523 which remained valid for more than a century. The absolute need for political and religious unity in the interest of the whole community is clearly presupposed. The magistrate thus serves the whole community in eliminating heretics. The right to determine the doctrinal boundaries of orthodox faith therefore became exceedingly important. Catholics and Protestants were alike in agreeing that right belief is necessary for salvation. Renaissance thinkers, however, saw an ever increasing disagreement on what constituted "right" belief.

There was opposition both within and without the churches to their treatment of heresy, and the Renaissance produced literature advocating the toleration of dissent. The literary debate came largely at the hands of the humanists. Some of these men were no longer content to seek solutions to religious and ethical questions within the elaborate dogmatic and legal structures of the Scholastic Roman church. Inner conviction came to the fore. Theology should be simplified and virtually reduced to ethics, and only the very minimum of dogma essential to salvation ought to be required of any man. These men were anti-traditional, anti-Scholastic, and, in some senses, anti-theological in inclination. In consequence, they were incensed at the viciousness with which the churches persecuted the heretics.

In their writings of opposition, various humanists differed from each other with respect to approaches and goals. The burning of Servetus at Geneva on October 27, 1553, evoked numerous protests. Sebastian Castellio wrote a strong complaint in his *De haereticis* (1554). His argument was for religious toleration and liberty of thought. He was quite prepared to see the Church's truth relativized. Minus Celsus wrote a similar treatise some years later, *In haereticis coercendis* . . . (1577). Celsus was not sympathetic with Castellio's relativizing Christian truth and argued simply that the death penalty for heresy ought to be abolished. If the magistrate wishes to imitate Christ, he must show mercy, not the iron fist. Religion is spiritual, and the *miles christianus* is restricted to spiritual weapons. "We have as little right to burn 'Arians' (anti-Trinitarians) and Anabaptists," he wrote, "as the Pope has to punish us with death" (ibid., II 85; cited Fimpel, p. 55). His argument is not for freedom for heretical activity, but only against the death penalty. Erasmus of Rotterdam, on the other hand, equivocated. He was a theological reductionist with an aversion to dogma. Faith is inward and simple and should consist in assent to minimal propositions. Correct belief about complex theological questions is unessential to salvation, and as little definition should be made as possible. In any case sincere faith cannot be induced by coercion. An utterly contumacious heretic may, however, be punished, not so much because of his error as of his attitude.

Some humanists responded to church persecution by emigrating to safer territory. The Italian humanists often fled to Geneva, Basel, and Poland. The Protestants fled England under Catholic Queen Mary as the so-called "Marian Exiles" and went to Germany (especially Frankfurt) and Switzerland. Anabaptists also participated in this reaction, and many fled to Eastern Europe and, eventually, to America.

The Heresies. Late medieval thought bequeathed to the Renaissance many emphases which, as synecdoches, easily created problems and even heresy. Voluntarism, emphasis upon God's will rather than his intellect, appeared in John Duns Scotus, William of Ockham, and others. On this view one cannot predict or demonstrate theological principles by *a priori* reasoning, and one is led into a kind of positivism and fideism wherein one believes a dogma solely on the authority of the Church's authentication. A stringent notion of predestination found articulation in the fourteenth century in John Wycliffe and Jan Hus. The subversive element here was the lurking possibility that God's eternal predestination of one to salvation eliminated the need for Jesus Christ as Mediator and the need for the Church's sacramental system. And mysticism which required neither dogma nor sacrament for mystical union with God was present in the *Devotio moderna* and in the speculative mysticism in Germany, e.g., Meister Eckhart.

Moreover, Ockhamite nominalism combined with other voluntaristic and atomistic elements to erode the monolithic concept of the Church and dogma. The Thomistic understanding of the Church as a feudal hierarchic structure with its essence filtering down from the papacy at the top was rejected in favor of a view which located the essence of the Church in its members. Nominalism flourished during the Renaissance and furnished a direct line into its skepticism about the Trinity and immortality. Ockham, for example, treated the former as philosophically incomprehensible and religiously believable only on the basis of a special mode of knowing; the great Arab thinkers in Spain, especially the Averroists, raised doubts about personal immortality which were not without influence in the Christian West. Thus there was fertile ground for intellectual heresies at the opening of the Renaissance.

Not all of the medieval movements which continued as heresies in the Renaissance were intellectual, however. Many of the sects the Church labeled heretical were originally reform movements. They advocated reform of the Church, apostolic simplicity in demeanor, and renewed concentration on the Bible with a literal understanding of its injunctions. They generally opposed sacramentalism, clericalism, and intellectualism. Since they were not ordinarily made up of learned men, the Church's intellectual elite often thought of them as anachronistic. Alienated from the Church, some of them moved into superstition and witchcraft, but most of the disenchanted remained much closer to a traditional faith. The Cathars were fairly well under control by the outset of the Renaissance. They had been unique in the West: having begun outside the Christian tradition, they became heretics by adopting and adapting that tradition. The Waldenses continued to inhabit the high valleys of northern Italy, secure in their faith but separated from Roman Catholicism.

Witchcraft was another element with medieval roots which penetrated the Renaissance. It is not clear that those regarded as witches and warlocks were technically heretics—claiming to be Christian—but the Church exercised itself against them on scriptural grounds (Exodus 22:18 and Deuteronomy 18:10). The year 1374 marks the first documented use of the Inquisition against witches, but the records of the inquisitors reveal witchcraft to have been a major concern thereafter. The bull of Innocent VIII, *Summis desiderantes* (1485), is a notable example of papal concern.

Witchcraft seems clearly reflected in some notable art of the Renaissance. Hieronymus Bosch's *Temptation of St. Anthony* portrays a black mass scene which may have been inspired by sabbat rites alleged to have been common among witches. A similar influence seems present in Matthias Grünewald's Isenheim altar paintings. Not until the Counter-Reformation had done its work and Europe had entered upon the period of the Enlightenment was art to lose interest in magic, witchcraft, and the black arts.

Moreover, a number of other factors contributed to the social unrest and changes which began with the fourteenth century. The middle of that century witnessed successive waves of the deadly plague decimate Western Europe's population. Many (e.g., the Flagellants) responded to that disaster by becoming preoccupied with the problem of death. There were social uprisings like the Wat Tyler rebellion in England in 1381. The nascent universities were fomenting new ideas. The whole of Western culture seemed ripe for change.

There were also other highly varied streams of thought pulsing through the Renaissance, many of which could not help affecting religious life and thought—often, in the eyes of official Christendom, adversely. Classical learning and letters experienced a rebirth, and many elements of it were both mutually antagonistic and uncongenial to traditional theology, especially Scholasticism. Stoicism, with its natural law teachings, its notions of the rationality of the universe and the cosmic community, and, in a man like Machiavelli, ideas of the State not unlike those of the ancient Sophists, were present.

Neo-Platonism was clearly the most important strand of thought retrieved from the ancients during the Renaissance. The thought of Plato and Plotinus was revived against the regnant Aristotelianism. Under its aegis man was seen as in the center of a great chain of being with freedom to rise to union with God or to descend away from him without the mediation of a savior. Moreover, various other oriental factors came into view again in association with Neo-Platonism: the Sybillines, the allegedly Christian Hermetic literature, and the Kabbala traditions. The effect of this orientation on Christian thinkers was to heighten interest in other religions and to foster syncretistic approaches.

Giovanni Pico della Mirandola sought to demonstrate the basic harmony among the doctrines of all religions and philosophies. Attempts were made to uncover the doctrine of the Trinity in other, non-Christian religions. The most important representative of this Neo-Platonic revival was the Platonic Academy at Florence, which, however, remained basically Christian in tendency.

Few Renaissance humanists intended to repristinate the thought forms of antiquity, and fewer still can be said seriously to have adhered in any religious sense to the pagan mythologies so ubiquitous in their works. Rather this material served them as foils for wrestling with Christian themes. Though generally antagonistic to ecclesiastical and theological authority, these men were not necessarily irreligious or even anti-Christian. They thought Scholastic theology unimpressive and brittle. And their thought often lent itself to relativism in dogma, tolerance of different ideas, and syncretism.

While the Protestant Reformers did not lack concern for traditional theology and could have agreed with their Roman Catholic opponents on a formal definition of heresy, both sides drew up quite different lists of heresies. Catholics considered Lutherans, Calvinists, Zwinglians, Anabaptists, and some of the humanists as heretics; Protestants included the Anabaptists, the Schwenckfelder, and some radical humanists. The general agreement on the Anabaptists derived from the common fear that they would destroy the *corpus christianum*. All of these groups, however, stood over against those humanists and other dissidents who found all churches and creeds too restrictive. Guillaume Farel (1489–1565), for instance, could castigate Erasmus as a "pestilent adversary of the Gospel," for his theological reductionism.

All of the Protestants rejected the appellation "heretic" for themselves. They thought of themselves as representing the truth against apostasy. Curiously, however, the major Reformation groups did not label Roman Catholicism per se heretical. Luther regarded the pope as the apostate of the New Israel and spoke of "the swarm of vermin in Rome," but he did not designate Catholicism as heresy. He was pessimistic about the outcome, but he did not yield his hope for peace with a reformed Rome. For Calvin there was no Church of Christ at Rome because the signs of the true church—the Word rightly preached and the sacraments rightly celebrated—were missing (*Institutes* IV. vii. 23).

In the eyes of Rome, the whole Protestant movement was heretical. This view was especially characteristic of the early years of the sixteenth-century Reformation. It is true that the Council of Trent did not designate Protestantism or even particular Protestants as heretics. The formula is *si quis . . . anathema sit* ("If anyone believes such and such let him be anathema"). However, such polemical writings as Johannes Cochlaeus' *Commentaria de actis et scriptis Martini Lutheri Saxonis* (1549) expressly call Luther a heretic, and the Index of prohibited books makes the judgment official. This interpretation has been perpetuated into the present century by works like Dominican Heinrich Denifle's *Luther und Luthertum in der ersten Entwicklung* (1904–06), and Jesuit Hartman Grisar's *Luther* (1911–12).

Other learned men also presented crises of orthodoxy to the Church. Bacon, Copernicus, Kepler, Galileo, Gassendi, and Newton were among them. These men refused to regard reason as ancillary to theology and set themselves vigorously to its use in science with inductive methodologies. They challenged the notion of miracle. They developed principles of critical historical study. With respect to heresy, they raised the question of what could be accepted as individualistic adiaphora in the Christian confession. Was geocentrism essential? Catholicism ruled that it was, although the Protestant Osiander's preface to Copernicus' work tried to make it optional (1543).

The Huguenots in France effectively introduced a tolerant pluralism to Europe. Not everyone in the same political geography had to adhere to the same religion. Protestants and Catholics could inhabit the same land, and the principle *cuius regio, eius religio* articulated at the Peace of Augsburg (1555), was no longer widely observed. The Edict of Nantes lasted only until Louis XIV revoked it in 1685, but it was importantly strengthened in the Peace of Westphalia (1648), which ended the Thirty Years War. The major thrust of that treaty was not toward pluralism, but pluralism was to prevail under certain conditions. The Puritan Civil War under Oliver Cromwell introduced this idea to seventeenth-century England. Pluralism succeeded in these important experiments no better than it had in the earlier attempts to establish a *pax dissidentium* in Poland (1573) among Lutherans, Calvinists, and Hussites, and in Antwerp (1578) between Calvinists and Catholics, but the principle presented a striking option to religious strife. Not until the nineteenth century was pluralism to become dominant in the Western world, however.

II. THE MODERN WORLD

Until toward the mid-eighteenth century, a kind of unity permeated the history of Christian thought. Despite the polarization of Protestant and Catholic confessional views, the bases from which theologians operated, the methods which they employed, and even many of their conclusions were not essentially dissimilar. Their principles of reasoning, their concepts of revelation and their views of authority as such they held in common. The later eighteenth and the nineteenth centuries, however, mark important shifts away from the older views. Not disjunction from the past, but reorientation in view of various challenges emerged.

The eighteenth century experienced an increasing exasperation with the dictum of Vincent of Lérins (ca. A.D. 434), *quod ubique, quod semper, quod ab omnibus creditum est* ("what is believed everywhere, always, by everyone") with respect to the doctrinal content of the faith. J. B. Bossuet, representing the epitome of Gallicanism, had written in 1688 to the effect that tradition is absolutely unchangeable, that Christian doctrine came from Christ true and complete. But even as he wrote, critical principles of historical study were rendering his judgments indefensible. Both Roman Catholics and Protestants were beginning to engage in critical historical studies which were making them impatient with attempts to describe and adduce in support of a polemical position a supposed patristic consensus. Catholic opponents of Jansenism were having to oppose Augustine, and Catholic biblical scholars were wondering about the historical reliability of some details of the Gospel narratives. Protestants, in contesting Gallicanism, were, especially among English Latitudinarians, more than prepared to espouse the view that theology had changed and improved since the early Fathers. The Enlightenment taught them that doctrine does not remain static simply because formulae remain unchanged. Words change meanings as time passes, and our understanding of terms and ideas changes also. Some sort of development was inherent in the situation. And as this spirit entered the nineteenth century, the breach between propositional theological certitude and the relativity of the results of historical investigation became clear.

Various components of the nineteenth century only exacerbated that problem and brought additional challenges to traditional modes of Christian thought. Extremely influential were romanticism, nationalism, and pluralism. Critical religious studies, including biblical criticism, historical studies involving views of doctrinal development and historical change, and the History of Religions School (*Religionsgeschichtliche Schule*) of German scholarship, were highlighting fundamental questions about traditional views of Christianity. Historical relativism in the guise of so-called "historicism" occupied the foreground. Scientific method in the Enlightenment recovered the rationalistic emphasis of the Renaissance which both Protestantism and Catholicism had feared so intensely. The growth of science passed on to the nineteenth century not only great confidence in natural theology, but also the

Newtonian revolution, the dispute about evolutionary geology and Genesis, the Darwinian controversy, Social Darwinism, environmental sociology, and a positivistic empirical approach to all reality.

The churches reacted variously. Some Protestants took refuge in Pietism. Some embraced the rationalism of the Enlightenment and adopted an indifferentist, common sense attitude toward these problems and accepted easily the notions of natural law and of Christianity as merely an example of a universal natural religion. Still others concentrated on feeling in religion. Liberal Protestantism in general emphasized subjective experience and, relatedly, a philosophical idealism which, in some quarters, came virtually to replace theology. The doctrine of man was revised in man's favor and to the disadvantage of Augustinian ideas of original sin. Men like Albrecht Ritschl (1822–89) viewed history with great optimism about the destiny of man. History for some virtually became the agent of salvation, the Christ. Moreover, ethics and social concerns were strongly emphasized and evoked responses like America's Social Gospel movement. Positivism and realism were victorious.

Friedrich Schleiermacher, a German theologian working at the beginning of the nineteenth century, illustrates the liberal response in terms of subjectivism and antipathy to propositional theology. John Locke, in his *The Reasonableness of Christianity* (1695), had wanted to reduce the essential Christian confession to the proposition "Jesus is the Messiah." His position was similar to the theological reductionism of Erasmus. Schleiermacher's position was quite different. He shifted the fundamental basis of the problem. In his *Der Christliche Glaube* (1821, §§21–22), he brings his view to bear on the problem of heresy. Heresy is described as a sickness of the whole organism of the Church. It must, for the good of the whole, be healed. Every dogmatic system, he held, will have a principle which serves as a criterion of judgment for that which is acceptable and that which is unacceptable. That principle will be the essence of Christianity. Schleiermacher's principle was the redemption wrought in Jesus Christ. He then proceeded to interpret that principle subjectively. What is essential (§24) is the relation of the individual to Christ, his savior, and this relationship determines his relationship to the Church. He saw this view as opposite to that of Roman Catholicism which he understood to hold that one's relation to Christ was determined by his relationship to the Church. The result of his position was to render uncertain each delineation of heresy and to deny the absolute validity of the formal decisions of the Church respecting heresy. Not right belief, but a relationship to Christ saves. Doctrinal heresy is thus virtually obsolete.

Disapprobation of dogma is also present in Ralph Waldo Emerson's "Divinity School Address" at Harvard in 1838. Contempt for propositional theology also appears in Horace Bushnell. Bushnell's essay on "Language" in his *God in Christ* (1849) denies the validity of rationalism and dogmatism. The logical method is rebuffed: religious language is always ambiguous and always partly false. Bushnell would prefer to affirm logical contradictions when speaking of God rather than accept the dictates of logic and rationalism as absolutes.

There were also reactions to the challenge of the nineteenth century by tenaciously conservative Protestants. Various confessionalist movements emphasized radically the differences between theology and contemporary philosophy. John Henry Newman's emphases on the historical Church and its creeds exemplify such a mood in England. Lutheranism in Germany experienced a similar confessionalist revival, and in America, Charles Hodge at Princeton illustrates the conservative response.

Finally, the so-called Fundamentalist movement in America represented the height of the retreat from the modern world, and looked at "modernism" as heretical. These people were basically alienated from the newer currents of intellectual life at the end of the nineteenth century. Ordinarily they regarded acceptance of such doctrines as the following as essential for true Christian faith: inerrancy of the scriptures, the deity of Christ, his virgin birth, the substitutionary atonement, and Christ's physical resurrection and visible second coming. Challenge to any of these points was heretical, and most contemporary intellectual movements were ruled out of bounds for the Christian.

Roman Catholicism's official response was one of almost exclusively negative impulse. Three events connected with Pope Pius IX illustrate this reaction: the promulgation of the doctrine of the Immaculate Conception of Mary on 8 December 1854, the publication of the Syllabus of Errors on 8 December 1864, and the calling of the First Vatican Council, largely to formulate the doctrine of papal infallibility, on 8 December 1869. The Syllabus of Errors designated most contemporary philosophical, intellectual, and social currents heretical. Similarly, Pius X felt it necessary to condemn the so-called "Modernist" heresy for its willingness to accommodate new thought.

As a result of these conflicting strands of eighteenth- and nineteenth-century history, the notion of heresy and its place in Christian history was altered. The dominant stress within Protestantism was away from propositional theology and toward an emphasis on feeling and subjectivity. Inductive sciences were gaining credence at the expense of traditional views of theology. Despite occasional conservative revivals, the prevailing mood of the period was not in that direction.

The historiography of heresy has also made significant contributions toward a change in attitude concerning heresy. Much of the recent literature on the topic—both historical and systematic—reflects this important shift. Until the monumental effort of Gottfried Arnold in his *Unparteyische Kirchen- und Ketzer-Historie von Anfang des Neuen Testaments biss auff das Jahr Christi 1688* (1699–1700), polemical interests had never been far from each consideration of the problem of heresy. The heretic was an enemy who was to be held in disgrace. Arnold and, following him, Johann Lorenz von Mosheim (*Versuch einer unparteiischen und gründlichen Ketzergeschichte*, 1746) attempted to write fair and objective histories of heresy. Party loyalties were consciously subordinated to faithful recitation of the facts.

More recently several studies have been published which build upon the spirit of fairness, the development of critical historical methodologies, and the destruction of such myths as the patristic consensus. Walter Bauer, in his *Rechtgläubigkeit und Ketzerei im ältesten Christentum* (1934; 2nd ed., 1963), has demonstrated the historical untenability of the view of the early Church that orthodoxy and heresy were distinguishable from apostolic times and has proposed that, until well into the second century, there were no clear-cut ways of distinguishing the status of one position from the other. What was later to be regarded as orthodox Catholic Christianity was a minority view in the Church in some parts of the early Christian world. A more radical departure from prior views of heresy is hard to imagine, but, though not undisputed, Bauer's position is widely accepted.

Many current Roman Catholic scholars are also treating the question of heresy differently from their predecessors. Karl Rahner has suggested that adherence to unmodified formulae from the past may involve one in heresy in the present. Hans Küng has called for a change in attitude toward the heretic. Not only is the punitive power of the Inquisition rejected, but its spirit also, and the heretic is to be treated with love and understanding. Heresy is seen as a call to self-criticism by the Church, for the heretic normally becomes so by overemphasizing one aspect of Christian truth respecting which the Church has been lax. Thus an *interpretatio benigna* is required.

Moreover, contemporary Roman Catholic scholars are engaged in critical historical studies of major Protestant thinkers (especially Luther) and theology. This scholarly work derives from basic research in the Protestant sources and is making important contributions to Protestant self-understanding. It has also brought the older polemical works of men like Denifle and Grisar (early twentieth century) into disrepute and has created a basis for theological discussion with Protestants as fellow Christians rather than as heretics.

Finally, the important role of pluralism in the disruption of the traditional views of heresy for the contemporary world must be noted. The basic principle of pluralism removes the question of heresy from the area of truth and places it in the area of discipline. Each church can work out its own confessional stance, regard it as true, and demand that its members subordinate themselves to it. Each church may also choose to regard all others who claim to be Christian as heretical. But those so accused can either leave that particular church or, if they are not members of it, simply ignore the charge. Neither punitive action against person or property nor social stigma attaches to such a "heretic" in the larger pluralistic society. This also means that not every "heresy" will affect every church; e.g., the confessional Protestant churches were little touched by the excesses of liberal theology. It has also tended to mean, historically, that the relativizing of dogma begun, in a sense, by the humanists (e.g., Castellio) and given impetus by the nineteenth century's great theologians (e.g., Schleiermacher) has rendered many churches less sensitive about doctrinal dissent and deviation.

Although the early part of the twentieth century witnessed some major heresy trials among Protestants—e.g., the attacks by conservatives on Charles Briggs and by Fundamentalists on Harry Emerson Fosdick; cf. also the Scopes trial on evolution—the last four decades (1930–70) have not been congenial to the heresy-hunter. There is a mood of impatience with preoccupation in doctrinal concerns and a disinclination to regard any formulae as propositional absolutes. Claims to absolute truth are not widely accepted. Nevertheless, heresy is not a completely anachronistic notion, and it remains of particular concern for those churches which are marked by a tight confessional stance.

BIBLIOGRAPHY

On heresy in the Renaissance, see Roland H. Bainton, *Hunted Heretic: The Life and Death of Michael Servetus* (Boston, 1953); idem, "The Parable of the Tares as the Prooftext for Religious Liberty," *Church History*, 1 (1932), 67–89; idem, *Sebastian Castellio: Concerning Heretics* (New York, 1935); Delio Cantimori, *Italienische Haeretiker der Spätrenaissance* (Basel, 1949); Ludwig Fimpel, *Mino Celsis Traktat gegen die Ketzertötung. Ein Beitrag zum Toleranzproblem des 16. Jahrhunderts* (Basel and Stuttgart, 1967); Joseph Lecler, *Histoire de la tolérance au siècle de la Réforme*, 2 vols. (Paris, 1955), trans. as *Toleration and the*

Reformation, 2 vols. (New York, 1960); Ulrich Mauser, *Der junge Luther und die Häresie* (Gütersloh, 1968). On the bequest of the Middle Ages to the Renaissance, see Heiko A. Oberman, *The Harvest of Medieval Theology. Gabriel Biel and Late Medieval Nominalism* (Cambridge, Mass., 1963). On the eighteenth-century developments, see Owen Chadwick, *From Bossuet to Newman. The Idea of Doctrinal Development* (Cambridge, 1957); Aimé Georges Martimort, *Le gallicanisme de Bossuet* (Paris, 1953). On Schleiermacher, see Klaus-Martin Beckmann, *Der Begriff der Häresie bei Schleiermacher* (Munich, 1959). On later nineteenth-century developments, see Reinhold Niebuhr, *Faith and History* (New York, 1949). On Fundamentalism, see Ernest R. Sandeen, "Towards a Historical Interpretation of the Origins of Fundamentalism," *Church History*, **36** (1967), 66–83. On the modern Roman Catholic developments, see, e.g., Karl Rahner, *On Heresy* (New York, 1964); Hans Küng, *Die Kirche* (Freiburg, Basel, and Vienna, 1967), pp. 288–310.

DAVID LARRIMORE HOLLAND

[See also **Christianity in History;** Enlightenment; **Heresy in the Middle Ages;** Hierarchy; Historicism; Neo-Platonism; **Reformation; Religious Toleration;** Renaissance Humanism; **Sin and Salvation; Witchcraft.**]

HERMETICISM

THE *Hermetica* is the body of writings supposedly given by God to Egypt's Hermes-Mercurius-Trismegistus, also thrice-great Thoth, to disseminate among the wise of all lands. In essence, it adopts the Platonic-Christian idea that man must strive to transcend matter and rise to heavenly purity. At the same time, the *Hermetica* affirms a number of nonclassical, non-Christian ideas about chaos and darkness as sources of life and about man as divinely creative. Merging with similar ideas of the ancient Near East to form, as it were, a "chaos syndrome," it has exerted a profound influence during times of upheaval, serving as inspiration for innovators of the Renaissance, as well as of the romantic and modern periods.

The unorthodoxy of Hermetic thought is often overlooked by scholars who detour the dark esotery of pre-twentieth-century thought by insisting that symbols of darkness and chaos, serpents, monsters, and the like, were readily Christianized (Walker, 1953). If this were so, Renaissance art, for example, would differ little from medieval art. Evidence indicates, however, that in a number of Renaissance works the powers of darkness frequently suggest, not destruction, but fruitfulness, joy, and energy. One may say, in fact, that the bloodstream of art, paling at the close of the medieval and then the neo-classical and Victorian periods, is

revitalized by a transfusion from sources of the ancient Near East.

We can study this process of cultural transfusion by focusing on one of the more effective systems of esotery used by Western writers, the *Hermetica*. Made up of the *Corpus Hermeticum*, the *Asclepius* (wisdom imparted by Trismegistus to his son, Tat), and *The Emerald Table*, it was compiled by a number of unknown authors of Hellenistic Egypt during the second or third century A.D. Until the seventeenth century, Neo-Platonists and alchemists encouraged the belief that its wisdom was given by God to Trismegistus instead of to Moses because the arcane had to be preserved for certain wise men of Egypt, Phoenicia, and then of Greece, Italy, and England. Kristeller and Yates (1960, 1964) have documented the numerous translations from the original Greek as well as the references and commentaries on them. All quotations in this article are taken from the simple but complete translation into English by J. Everard, *The Divine Pymander of Hermes Trismegistus* (1650). It contains the basic text, the "Divine Pymander" or creation story, and the *Asclepius*.

In substance, the *Hermetica* shares a number of unorthodox features with ancient cosmogonies of Egypt, Babylonia or Chaldea, Persia, and the early gnostic sects. Compiled from the ancient cosmogonies, a list of nine such unorthodox features can be used now to show the nature of the "chaos syndrome":

(1) Creation is the result of a cataclysmic or sexual encounter between at least two major forces. The world is created from preexisting chaos.

(2) Creation includes elements of the grotesque and the irrational.

(3) Mutability, darkness, mud are life-producing.

(4) Serpent and hybrid creatures, symbols of energy, are often deified.

(5) Eternal Recurrence: Creation is an ever-renewing process. As a living body, the world is perpetually renewing itself.

(6) "As above, so below": the doctrine of correspondence: the divine descends to participate in human affairs, alternating with humans as civilizing agents, involved in wandering, lamentation, and suffering as part of the creative process.

(7) *Superbia:* Man is exalted to the level of divinity.

(8) The Valuable Descent: a descent into the depths, an encounter with monsters, provides the revitalizing experience sought by men and gods.

(9) Stylistically, "chaos" writings are lavish as well as confusing.

In contrast, the orthodox view sees chaos as a force of evil only. Its God, without partner or helper, creates from absolutely nothing, in a smooth and orderly man-

431

ner. Energy symbols are discredited, and the world, created just once, is headed for ultimate dissolution. Separated from God, man is essentially worthless, limited as an artist to imitating what he sees, and warned to strive for rhetorical bareness. Such ideas predominate, not only in church fathers like Tertullian and Augustine, and in Renaissance poets like Drayton, Thomas Heywood, and Jonson, but in modern religious leaders and non-Christian thinkers as well. For, despite the decline of Christianity today, a negative attitude towards chaos continues to dismiss disorder and mystery as evil and, in the name of order and truth, encourages a chronic dread of dissenting groups and strange ways of thought.

Unlike orthodox writings, the *Hermetica*, affirming chaos and change, retains a singular importance for the adventurous mind. It is true that it retains at least two orthodox tenets: the all powerful God precedes chaos, and love of body can be an "Error of Love" (Everard, pp. 11, 17). In other respects, however, the *Hermetica* belongs to the "chaos syndrome." It derides the idea of creating from nothing: "And all things are made of things that are, and not of things that are not" (p. 75); the chaos from which its world is created is powerful and essential to the creative process: "infinite darkness . . . abyss . . . bottomless depth" (p. 24) recall the coeval chaos of pagan mythology as well as the *materia prima* of alchemy (Jung, 1953, 1963).

In the opening of *The Divine Pymander*, Trismegistus asks for understanding. Poemander, Mind of God, begins the education, not with an explanation of rationally ordered principles, but with a plunge, instead, into the experience of creativity, a plunge as sudden as the mystical twinkling of an eye in which all things can happen. There is a darkness "fearful and hideous," then a moisture "unspeakably troubled," then a voice of the Son of God, ". . . unutterable . . . mournful . . . inarticulate" (p. 10). From here on, the idea is reiterated: the web of life consists of good and evil, order and chaos, light and darkness. Unity cannot exist without contrariety, ". . . for, of contraposition, That is Setting One against Another, and Contrariety, all Things must Consist" (p. 32).

Continuing to mirror the human experience, the Hermetic cosmos lives and breathes: "The whole universe is material. . . . The whole is a living wight . . ." (p. 33). Unlike the asexual Creator of the world by word alone, the Hermetic God is male and female, ". . . it is his Essence to be pregnant, or great with all things . . ." (p. 46). The world is his womb of creation: Fire weds Moisture, Air and Water copulate out of desire (pp. 15–16), and new things are generated not mechanically or revengefully, as in the classical cosmogony of Hesiod, but from love and desire.

Hermetic man is created with love (p. 13), but when, restless and searching, he wishes to separate from God and fall to work on his own, he is not punished. When he breaks through the Circles "to understand the Power of him that sits upon the Fire" (p. 14), the Seven Governors of the world share their divine natures with him, and he finds, beyond the known, another form of God in the beautiful shape of Nature, ". . . the massive, elusive being" who is also in Plotinus and in Spenser (Holmes, 1932). Himself a mystery, hermaphroditic, mortal and immortal, loved by God and the Governors, falling freely without guilt or terror, and loved by Nature as a man is loved by a woman, Hermetic man loves the mystery and excitement of life. Writers of titanic energy—Blake, for example—have been fascinated by passages like the following:

. . . consider, O Son, how Man is made and framed in the Womb; and examine diligently the skill and cunning of the Workman, and learn who it was that wrought and fashioned the beautiful and Divine shape of Man; who circumscribed and marked out his eyes? who bored his nostrils and ears? who opened his mouth? who stretched out and tied together his sinews? . . . (p. 45).

In contrast to the orthodox view, which posits a world moving inexorably toward dissolution, the *Hermetica* expresses the idea of Eternal Recurrence. The energy of a world created from chaos is repeatedly renewed. Change exists to provide a means of continuing purification. Death is not destruction, but the dissolving of a union that is endlessly renewable (pp. 26, 32, 87).

From a theory of creation that reflects man's experience with sexuality, darkness, and change, comes the Hermetic theory of Eternal Connectedness between God and man. The divine descends to participate in the world and is called variously workman, painter, carver (p. 46). In this connection, it is interesting to note that writings sharing a view of the humanized God tend to favor the messenger deity, Hermes or Mercury. In contrast to the unsympathetic treatment of Hermes as trickster and thief (Frothingham, 1916; Brown, 1947), or as the first evil deity who must be destroyed by Christ (Pico, 1507), Hermetically influenced works present him instead as divine messenger, worshipped in silence, praised for his understanding and invention (Iamblichus, Cartari, Valeriano). Spenser's Mercury saves the world from destruction; Shakespeare expresses eloquence and fancifulness in the beloved Mercutio and the alchemical vision of the living statue in Hermione (*The Faerie Queene*, VII, vi, 14–17; *Romeo and Juliet*, I, iv, and *The Winter's Tale*).

The idea of Connectedness is crystallized in the Doctrine of Correspondence, as it appears in the "Emerald Tablet of Hermes":

What is below is like that which is above, and what is above is like that which is below. . . . Ascend with the greatest sagacity from the earth to heaven, and then again descend to the earth, and unite together the powers of things superior and things inferior. Thus you will obtain the glory of the whole world, and obscurity will fly far away from you (Read, p. 54).

In *The Divine Pymander*, too, earth corresponds to cosmos, the microcosm of man to the macrocosm of the universe. Like the figure of Hermes, the derivative symbols of chain and ladder between heaven and earth suggest that man is neither separated from God as in the medieval view nor chained to his link as in the neo-classical. Instead, he is linked to God; divinely creative, he ascends, ". . . he leaveth not the Earth, and yet is above; So great is the greatness of his Nature" (p. 40). The ladder he ascends is the same that God descends, ". . . an Earthly Man is a Mortal God, and . . . the Heavenly God is an Immortal Man" (pp. 40–41).

Such ideas are far removed from the traditional identification of macrocosm and microcosm as a solely Platonic or Christian metaphor for the belief in an otherworldly sphere, and a separation between man and nature (Lovejoy, 1936; Tillyard, 1959). The Hermetic philosophy suggests instead that God, matter, and man are linked by an understanding of the life-principle that inspired both the religious and artistic impulses of man (Taylor, 1962). This, and not the traditional idea of separation, would have inspired that quality of *superbia* with which we associate Renaissance man. In the *Hermetica* he found the authority he needed for his breakthroughs as well as for his orthodoxy.

Well documented as the primary source for alchemical speculation and authors like Bruno and Vaughan, the *Hermetica* has influenced also writers as varied as Bernardus Silvestris, Spenser, Shakespeare, Boehme, Milton, Sterne, Blake, and Longfellow. Ideas about the primacy of chaos, the eternal presence of order and disorder, the eternal renewability of the world, the connectedness of God and man appear in Alberti, Goethe, Wordsworth, Nietzsche, G. M. Hopkins, D. H. Lawrence. One may go so far as to say that the first significant treatment of Hermetic thought by Bernardus Silvestris in the twelfth century, and then a renewed application by Spenser in the sixteenth century mark the inception and the development of the European Renaissance. Silvestris (ca. 1150) incorporates a number of ideas that are antithetical to Christian theories of creation, but remarkably close to those of the "chaos syndrome." He writes about the two principles of all things, unity and diversity. The primeval forest of *De mundi universitate* exists in an ambiguous state of good and evil, fertile with plurality. Since the world evolves by perpetual activity, it can never weaken or be undone. During creation, spinning whirlpools confound the forest, a fiery force emerges from what was confused and turbid, earth settles down, fire darts up, air and water take middle positions. Physis, dreaming of the construction of man through the power of nature, sees the radiance of Urania reflected much as Nature sees the reflection of man in the *Hermetica*.

Four centuries later, Spenser was using both orthodox and unorthodox materials to create a new mythology and a Renaissance in English poetry (Feinstein, 1968). *The Faerie Queene* (the first three books appeared in 1590) is filled with Egyptian imagery; the hideous storm, stench of smoke and sulphur, and fearful noise are examples in Book III. Sexual analogies for creation and images of an eternal chaos that guarantees renewal appear in the "Garden of Adonis" passages:

> . . . in the wide wombe of the world there lyes,
> In hatefull darknes and in deepe horrore,
> An huge eternal chaos, which supplyes
> The substaunces of Natures fruitfull progenyes.
> (III, vi, 36).

Substance is eternal so that when life decays, form does not fade or return to nothing, "But chaunged is, and often altred to and froe" (III, vi, 37).

Hermetic ideas spurred Giordano Bruno to move still further from medieval restriction. Like Spenser's *Faerie Queene*, Bruno's *Expulsion of the Triumphant Beast* (1584) repudiates the idea of Creation from Nothing and exalts Nature and the eternally renewing capacity that enjoys mutability and discordance as well as the opposites:

> . . . if in bodies, matter, and entity there were not mutation, variety, and vicissitude, there would be nothing agreeable, nothing good, nothing pleasurable.

Another innovator to find affirmation in mystical writings, William Blake, in 1794, describes the God who creates the tiger in terms very close to the Hermetic God who creates man. Compare "who circumscribed and marked out his eyes? . . . who stretched out and tied his sinews?" to Blake's "In what distant deeps or skies/ Burnt the fire of thine eyes?. . . . what shoulder, & what art,/ Could twist the sinews of thy heart?" A terrible God, yet human; a powerful God, yet a workman.

We can mention only a few of the many who have used the ideas of *Hermetica*: the fire and wheel imagery of the seventeenth-century mystic Jacob Boehme (1620); the observation by Alberti (1433–34) that there is no light without darkness. Milton in "Il Penseroso" (line 88) refers to "thrice great Hermes"; Longfellow in "Hermes Trismegistus" captures the spirit of the immortal man and the mortal God; the name of Sterne's hero, Tristram, is a distortion of Trismegistus. Nietzsche's belief in eternal recurrence is well known, but the idea is in G. M. Hopkins as well ("Generations have trod, have trod, have trod. . . ./ And for all this, nature is never spent"). D. H. Lawrence's apostrophe to chaos (1928) is a central part of his philosophy.

But more important than listing citations, we need to understand why writers of so many different countries and ages have borrowed from a complex of ideas that move outside the mainstream of Western thought. Perhaps we can say that innovators searching for a sense of balance in their conceptions of life and creativity found in the esotery of the Near East, the *Hermetica* in particular, an affirmation that was lacking in orthodox doctrine. As a result, their writings broke with tradition to embrace ideas of chaos as well as order, and so came to show that this mutable world, with all its chaos and change, is as meaningful as the immutable realm of Heaven.

BIBLIOGRAPHY

Leon Battista Alberti, "Libri della famiglia," *Opere volgari*, ed. Cecil Grayson (Bari, 1960), I, 31. Jacob Boehme, *Six Theosophic Points* (Ann Arbor, 1958), pp. 12, 16, 27. Norman O. Brown, *Hermes the Thief* (Madison, 1947), pp. 6–21, 53. Giordano Bruno, *The Expulsion of the Triumphant Beast*, trans. Arthur D. Imerti (New Brunswick, N.J., 1964), p. 89. J. Everard, trans., *The Divine Pymander of Hermes Trismegistus*, 1650 (New York, 1953) by Rosicrucian Society. Blossom Feinstein, "*The Faerie Queene* and Cosmogonies of the Near East," *Journal of the History of Ideas*, **29** (1968). A. L. Frothingham, "Babylonian Origin of Hermes the Snake-God, and of the Caduceus," *Archaeological Institute of America*, **20** (1916), 175. Paul O. Kristeller, ed. *Catalogus translationum . . .* (Washington, D.C., 1960), I, 137–56. D. H. Lawrence, "Chaos in Poetry" (1928), in *Selected Literary Criticism*, ed. Anthony Beal (New York, 1932). Arthur O. Lovejoy, *The Great Chain of Being* (Cambridge, Mass., 1936). Gian Francesco Pico, "Hymn to Christ" (*Hymnus ad Christum*, Milan, 1507), English trans. Eve Adler from the Latin. Bernard Silvestris, *De mundi universitate*, eds. Carl S. Barach and Johann Wrobel, (Frankfurt am Main, 1964 reprint), Book I, iv, 25–29; II, xiii, 1–2. F. Sherwood Taylor, *The Alchemists* (New York, 1962), p. 175. E. M. W. Tillyard, *The Elizabethan World Picture* (New York, 1959). D. P. Walker, "Orpheus the Theologian and Renaissance Platonists," *Journal of the Warburg Institute*, **16** (1953), 105–07. Frances A. Yates, *The Art of Memory* (Chicago, 1966), p. 146.

The most penetrating studies of Bruno and Vaughan are Frances A. Yates, *Giordano Bruno and the Hermetic Tradition* (Chicago, 1964), Ch. 1, and passim; Elizabeth Holmes, *Henry Vaughan and the Hermetic Philosophy* (London, 1932); of alchemy in general, C. G. Jung, *Psychology and Alchemy* and *Mysterium coniunctionis, Collected Works*, trans. R. F. C. Hull, Vols. 12 and 14 (New York, 1953 and 1963); and John Read, *Prelude to Chemistry, An Outline of Alchemy* (Cambridge, Mass., 1966), pp. 51–55; and of English alchemy in particular, Allen G. Debus, *The English Paracelsians* (New York, 1966).

BLOSSOM FEINSTEIN

[See also **Alchemy; Creation in Religion;** Hierarchy; Macrocosm and Microcosm; Neo-Platonism; **Renaissance Humanism.**]

HIERARCHY AND ORDER

HIERARCHY denotes that Occidental mode of thought which transmuted man's persistent inclination to assert Order into a particular conception of the universe in terms of precisely-arranged levels of existence commonly termed "degrees." While this mode of thought may well appear to remain static, even to terminate in itself, in fact, however, it underwent dramatic changes—each stage of its development marked by a dynamic adjustment to contemporary views. In effect, the history of Hierarchy is the history of Occidental thought. But it is also a testimony to the ever-present craving for—and indeed obsession with—Order. Donne's remark in 1627 reverberates across the centuries: "The roote of all is Order."

The connection between Order and Hierarchy was made explicit by numerous writers during the Renaissance, among them Zacheus Mountague in *The Jus Divinum of Government* (1652). In his words, "What else is order, but unity, brancht out into all the parts of Consociate bodies, to keep them intire and perfect" (pp. 7–8). The usual Renaissance arrangement of these "parts of Consociate bodies" into one comprehensive scheme is so well-known that here we need only survey its most fundamental assumptions, all repeatedly emphasized by a number of scholars (see Craig, Tillyard, Wilson, Winny, et al.). The first assumption was that the created order is tightly knit through an elaborate system of interdependent "degrees" which extend vertically—as Samuel Ward said in *The Life of Faith* (1622)—"from the Mushrome to the Angels" (p. 2). A generation earlier Spenser had visualized the system as "linkt with adamantine chaines," while earlier still Sir Thomas Elyot in *Of the Knowledge whiche maketh a Wise Man* (1533) had seen it as an all-pervasive order which "lyke a streyghte lyne issueth oute of prouydence, and passethe directely throughe all thynges" (folio 44). It was not difficult for imaginative writers to lapse into rhapsodies, and many did. According to

Peter Sterry in *A Discourse of the Freedome of the Will* (1675, p. 30):

Being it self, in its universal Nature, from its purest heighth, by beautiful, harmonious, just degrees and steps, *descendeth* into every Being, even to the lowest shades. All ranks and degrees of Being, so become like the mystical steps in that scale of Divine Harmony and Proportions, *Jacobs Ladder*. Every form of Being to the lowest step, seen and understood according to its order and proportions in its descent upon this Ladder, seemeth as an *Angel*, or as a Troop of Angels in one, full of all Angelick Musick and Beauty.

The Scale of Nature—to use Adam's phrase in *Paradise Lost* (V, 509)—was said to have a number of rungs which at times, for the sake of lucidity, was reduced to four. As Gabriel Powel contended in *The Resolved Christian* (1616, p. 2):

There are foure sorts of Creatures in the world. . . . The first have essence or being onely, as the earth, the water, the fire, the aire, the Sun and the Moone. The second have essence and life, which are called vegetative, as hearbs, trees, and all plants. The third have essence, life, and sence, or feeling, as fishes, foules, and all beasts. The fourth have essence, life, sence, and reason, as Man.

The members of each of these four levels of existence were themselves thought to observe "degree, priority and place," more or less in the manner argued by Henry Peacham in *The Compleat Gentleman* (1622, pp. 1–2):

If we consider arightly the Frame of the whole Vniuerse and Method of the all-creating Wisedome in her worke; as creating the formes of things infinitely diuers, so according to Dignity of Essence or Vertue in effect, wee must acknowledge the same to hold a Soueraigntie, and transcendent prædominance, as well of Rule as Place each ouer either. Among the heauenly bodies we see the Nobler Orbes, and of greatest influence to be raised aloft, the lesse effectuall, depressed. Of Elements, the *Fire* the most pure and operatiue to hold the highest place; in compound bodies, of things as well sensible as insensible, there runneth a veine of Excellence proceeding from the Forme, ennobling (in the same kind) some other aboue the rest.

The Lyon we say is King of Beasts, the Eagle chiefe of Birds; the Whale and Whirle-poole among Fishes, *Jupiters* Oake the *Forrests King*. Among Flowers, wee most admire and esteeme the Rose: Among Fruite, the Pom-roy and Queene-apple; among Stones, we value aboue all the Diamond. . . .

Finally, within the rung occupied by Man are a number of interlocking orders reducible—as in Johann Gerhard's detailed exposition—to three: "The Ecclesiasticall, Politicall, and Oeconomicall: The First, of the Church; the Second, of the Common-wealth; the Third of the private familie" (*Divine Aphorisms*, trans. R. Winterton [1632], Chs. XX–XXIII).

The "foure sorts of Creatures" by no means exhausted the levels of existence within the Scale of Nature. The scheme was also thought to extend upwards to include the angels, and often downwards to include the devils. The angels were themselves arranged in hierarchies, traditionally said to number nine in accordance with the system first devised by pseudo-Dionysius the Areopagite in *De coelesti hierarchia* (VII–IX) but expanded to an indeterminate number once his authenticity was questioned and the absence of biblical support for any precise scheme became apparent (see Patrides). The devils, on the other hand, were not always thought to form part of the Scale. But the existence of "degrees" in Hell was generally upheld, and many writers were even prepared to accept a ninefold infernal hierarchy "contrary to the nine degrees of angels" (Sigmund Feyerabend, *Theatrum diabolorum* [1569], fols. 57ff.; Heinrich Cornelius Agrippa, *Three Bookes of Occult Philosophy*, trans. J. French [1651], pp. 397ff.).

The one aspect of the Scale of Nature which its expositors constantly emphasized was the conviction they all shared with the Polish alchemist Michael Sendivogius in *Novum lumen chymicum* (1604) that there is "no *vacuum*, or vacuity in the world" (trans. J. French [1650], p. 88). What this belief involved was made repeatedly clear. When Bishop Godfrey Goodman declared in *The Fall of Man* (1616) that all creatures are "linckt and tyed together" (p. 427), he had in mind nothing less than the sort of detailed "explanation" which Sir Richard Barckley had already borrowed from others and incorporated into *A Discourse of the Felicitie of Man* (1598, pp. 532–33):

The great God of nature hath tyed together all his creations, with some meane things that agree and participate with the extremities, and hath composed the intelligible, ethereall, and elementarie world, by indissoluble meanes and boundes; as betweene plantes and liuing creatures, hee hath made sponges and oysters, that in part resemble liuing things, and in part plants; betweene the creatures of the earth, and those of the water, Otters, Tortoyses, and such like; betweene those of the water and birds of the aire, flying fishes; betweene brute beastes, and those of a spirituall essence and vnderstanding, which are the Angels, he hath placed man, which combineth heauen and this elementarie world.

Barckley's reference to Man falls within the circumference of the generalization by Guillaume de la Perrière in *Les considérations des quatres mondes* (1552): *Or est en l'hôme (par la resolution de tous bons autheurs) le vray & merueilleux lien de deux Natures, spirituelles & corporelles* (signature M3ᵛ). Man was accordingly described by Oswald Crollius as "the bond and buckle of the world" (*Mysteries of Nature*, trans. H. Pinell

435

FIGURE 1. The Scale of Nature in the form of a chain, one of the many variations of the theme of cosmic hierarchy, from Didacus Valades, *Rhetorica christiana*, 1579. BY COURTESY OF THE TRUSTEES OF THE BRITISH MUSEUM

[1657], p. 54), by William Drummond of Hawthornden as "that Hymen of eternall and mortall things" (*Flowers of Sion* [1623], p. 66), and by Sir Thomas Browne as the "amphibious piece betweene a corporall and spirituall essence" (*Religio medici* [1643], I, 34). But even more persistently Man was hailed as a microcosm, a "little world" whose very constitution was said to be analogous to the hierarchical structure of the universe. Dr. Helkiah Crooke in Μικροκοσμογραφία. *A Description of the Body of Man* (1615) endeavored to explain in precisely what sense Man may be called "a Little world, and the paterne and epitome of the whole universe." The head, he wrote, resembles "that supreme and Angelicall part of the world," even as the heart corresponds to the second division of the universe, "the Middle and Cælestiall part." The third

division, "the sublunarie part of the world," is even more strikingly reflected in Man, for

> The terrible lightning fierce flashes and impressions, are shewed in the bloody suffusions of our eyes when we are in a heat and furie. . . . The violent and gathering rage of blustering winds, tempestuous stormes and gusts, are not onely exhibited, but also fore-shewed by exhaled crudities and by the hissing, singing and ringing noyses of the eares. The humor and moistnesse that fals like a current or streame into the emptie spaces of the throat, the throtle and the chest, resembleth raine and showers . . . (2nd rev. ed. [1631], pp. 6–8).

Crooke's statement may strike us as absurd, yet it differs only in degree from countless similar affirmations, among them Sir Walter Ralegh's in *The History of the World* ([1614], I, ii, 5), William Jackson's in *The Celestiall Husbandrie* (1616, p. 7), and Samuel Purchas' in *Purchas his Pilgrim* (1619, pp. 30ff.). Moreover, the same conviction underlies Renaissance psychological theory (see Bamborough, Campbell) even as it informs Renaissance painting (see Benesch). Indeed, pictorial representations of the Scale of Nature like that in Didacus Valades' *Rhetorica christiana* (Figure 1) indicate the extent to which the scheme was frequently conceived in explicitly literal terms. The same conclusion emerges from a consideration of the structure of the Elizabethan theater, in itself a microcosmic representation of the macrocosm, and—in one celebrated instance at least—significantly named *The Globe*. Equally relevant is the valiant effort of the "more divine than human" Giulio Camillo to construct for Francis I a model theater of the world, the Scale of Nature presented as a circular structure rising in seven tiers connected through a mass of intricate correspondences (see Cirillo).

Camillo's vision of the world as a hierarchy enclosed within a circular pattern was by no means singular. The circle was widely venerated as the most perfect figure and therefore as "a clear embleme of eternity" (Fulk Bellers, *Jesus Christ* [1652], p. 10). Ever-present in conceptions of the universe, it can be seen in every schematic presentation of both the Ptolemaic cosmos and the new-fangled world of Copernicus, witness the diagrams in Petrus Apianus' *Cosmographia* (Figure 2) and Thomas Digges' *A Perfit Description of the Cælestial Orbes* (Figure 3), in turn related to the persistent visual attempts to set out the connection between the circular universe and the microcosm of man (Figures 4 and 5). As scholars have often assured us, the "haunting spell of circularity" (Koyré; Panofsky, p. 25) was so much a part of traditional modes of thought that it penetrated the innermost recesses of the "new philosophy," especially the writings of both Copernicus and Galileo, and continued to affect the minds of men

FIGURE 2. The Ptolemaic universe according to Petrus Apianus' *Cosmographia*, 1524. BY COURTESY OF THE TRUSTEES OF THE BRITISH MUSEUM

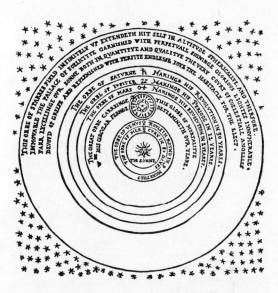

FIGURE 3. The Copernican universe according to Thomas Digges' *A Perfit Description of the Caelestiall Orbes*, 1576. The circle persists but the stars intimate the advent of cosmic infinity. From F. R. Johnson, *Astronomical Thought in Renaissance England*, Baltimore, 1937

FIGURE 4. The microcosm of man in relation to the macrocosm of the universe according to Robert Fludd's *Utriusque cosmi maioris et minoris historia*, 1617. BY COURTESY OF THE TRUSTEES OF THE BRITISH MUSEUM

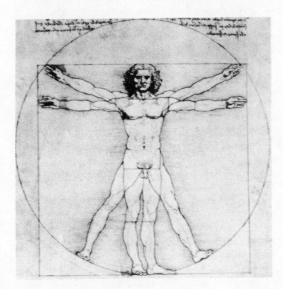

FIGURE 5. The proportions of man according to Leonardo da Vinci (ca. 1490?), based on Vitruvius' *De architectura* (III, i. 3). ACCADEMIA, VENICE. PHOTO ALINARI-ART REFERENCE BUREAU

437

long after the Renaissance (see Mahnke, Nicolson, Panofsky, Poulet).

Renaissance expositions of Hierarchy include the well-known affirmations by Shakespeare in *Troilus and Cressida*, I, iii, 83ff. (see Phillips, Spencer, Tillyard, et al.) and Milton in *Paradise Lost*, V, 469ff. (see Curry, Lewis, Patrides, et al.).

Hierarchy was also upheld in a host of other works which at first sight do not appear to be relevant. Treatises on numerology, for instance, may only seem concerned with what John Selden in his *Table-Talk* (1696, pp. 109f.) dismissed as "those mysterious things they observe in Numbers," but in reality aimed to strengthen further the structure of the universe through a multitude of numerical correspondences. Some writers were accordingly partial to Four, "the roote and beginning of all numbers" (see Heninger); others preferred either Three or Seven (e.g., Thomas Tymme in *A Dialogue Philosophicall* [1612], Part I, Chs. 4–6, and Robert Pont in *The Right Reckoning of Years* [1599]), or indeed both Three and Seven (e.g., David Person in *Varieties* [1635], Book V)—while an encyclopedic work, William Ingpen's *The Secrets of Numbers* (1624), sweepingly maintained the validity of One through Ten since "there is no knowledge, either rationall, morall, physicall, or metaphysicall, which hath not some cognation or participation with Numbers." Cabbalists like Guillaume Postel were particularly obsessed with numerology (see Bouwsma) but even talented mathematicians favored the reconstruction of the Scale of Nature in terms of "Numbryng."

Order was even more frequently asserted in terms of the Christian view of history which posited a linear progress through time from the Creation to the Last Judgment (see Patrides). Formulated in the main by Saint Augustine in *De civitate Dei* and Paulus Orosius in *Historia adversus paganos*, this view was developed further by Saint Bede and Otto of Freising, consolidated during the Middle Ages in the colossal *Speculum historiale* of Vincent of Beauvais, and accepted by the Protestant Reformers with marked enthusiasm, witness the extremely popular *Chronica* (1532) of Johann Carion and *De quatuor summis imperiis* (1556) of Johann Philippson surnamed Sleidanus. Whether the scheme was ordered by means of the Four Monarchies or the Seven Ages (see Laneau, Rowley), it testified alike to the existence of a horizontal unity throughout history, precisely as the Scale of Nature upheld a vertical unity "from the Mushrome to the Angels."

The Christian view of history during the Renaissance was grounded on the speculations of patristic and medieval authorities. The concept of the Scale of Nature also leaned on these authorities but depended in addition on ideas adapted from Plato and Aristotle

(Lovejoy, Ch. II). It is instructive to observe the extent to which one idea in particular, from Aristotle's *Historia animalium* (VIII, 1; trans. D. W. Thompson) was misunderstood. According to Aristotle,

Nature proceeds little by little from things lifeless to animal life in such a way that it is impossible to determine the exact line of demarcation, nor on which side thereof an intermediate form should lie. Thus, next after lifeless things in the upward scale comes the plant [μετὰ γὰρ τὸ τῶν ἀψύχων γένος τὸ τῶν φυτῶν πρῶτόν ἐστιν], and of plants one will differ from another as to its amount of apparent vitality; and, in a word, the whole genus of plants, whilst it is devoid of life as compared with an animal, is endowed with life as compared with other corporeal entities. Indeed, . . . there is observed in plants a continuous scale of ascent [μετάβασις, *literally 'change' or 'transition'*] towards the animal.

The generalization informs the entire *Historia animalium* as it does *De partibus animalium* and, to a lesser extent, *De generatione animalium*. Its burden is clearly the description of things as they are; no attempt is made to propound a theory concerning either the origins or the future development of organic forms, much less to extend the "scale" beyond the material world or indeed to interpret it metaphysically. Yet it is this very passage which in time became the *locus classicus* for all expositions of the Scale of Nature, further strengthened by Aristotle's conception of the universe as geocentric, finite, "closed," and sharply divided into two realms—the terrestrial which is changeable, and the celestial which is "eternal and not subject to increase or diminution, but unageing and unalterable and unmodified" (*De caelo* I, 3; trans. J. L. Stocks [1930]). The "haunting spell of circularity," moreover, was justified philosophically through the argument that in a finite universe the movement of the spheres must necessarily be circular since the alternative—rectilinear movement—would require infinite space (*Physica* VIII, 9; cf. *De caelo* I, 2–4; II, 4). Plato, in the meantime, had provided the basis for what has been called "the principle of plenitude," which is to say that the various levels of existence are interlocked so as to yield a "full" universe. But while "plenitude" afforded endless opportunities for meditation on the "fullness" of the universe, it also contained the seeds of an idea which would eventually undermine the entire Scale of Nature and bring Plato into direct conflict with Aristotle. We mean, of course, the idea of infinity.

Before the advent of Neo-Platonism in the third century A.D., Hierarchy was rather suggested than affirmed categorically. Cicero, for instance, argued the existence of God by positing a gradual ascent "from the first rudimentary orders of being to the last and most perfect" (*De natura deorum* II, 33f.; trans. H. Rackam [1933]), while the legendary Hermes Trismegistus claimed that the various parts of the universe are arranged in a "straight line" extending from the top of the natural order to its very bottom (*Hermetica*, ed. W. Scott [1924], I, 512). When we reach Plotinus, however, we sense at once that vagueness has given way to certainty, to a distinct assurance (see Armstrong). The sum total of the universe, visible and intelligible both, is now argued to be "a life, as it were, of huge extension, a total in which each several part differs from its next, all making a self-continuous whole" (V, ii, 2; trans. S. McKenna [1962]). Its origin, by a process of "emanation," is a movement from the unity of the One toward the multiplicity of the many; and its ultimate destiny, the eventual return of the many into the One. The interim history of the universe is the history of an "unbroken whole" which is comprised of sharply-distinguished levels of existence "for ever linked" (IV, viii, 6) and which depends for its sustenance on ἔρως, "love" (III, v). As Proclus was to maintain two centuries after Plotinus, "love" constitutes a chain, an ἐρωτικὴ σειρὰ which links heaven and earth (see Nygren, II, 352ff.), even as the universe is a hierarchy of power if not of existence (see Rosán). But it is in the light of other developments as well, notably the emphasis placed by Porphyry and Iamblichus on the triadic patterns pervading the universe, that we can best appreciate the influential synthesis achieved near the turn of the fifth century into the sixth by pseudo-Dionysius the Areopagite.

The Areopagite is of fundamental importance to the history of Hierarchy (see Roques). Under cover of the authoritative name of Saint Paul's convert in Athens, he merged manifold strains of Neo-Platonism into an imaginative scheme which affected the thought of Christians everywhere for well over a thousand years. In a language elevated to the height of his great argument, he did not so much dispense revelations as celebrate the mysteries of cosmic hierarchy in a sustained hymn of thanksgiving like that of the order of priests who in *De ecclesiastica hierarchia* appear "collected together in hierarchical order" (III, 3:15). His insistence that Hierarchy is "a kind of symbol adapted to our condition," a faint image of the archetypal truth (ibid., I, 5; V, 2), was in time displaced by the widespread belief that his vision was an exact description of the universe under the "law of well-ordered regularity." But he had been rather too precise. He defined Hierarchy in *De coelesti hierarchia* as "a sacred order and science and operation, assimilated, as far as attainable, to the likeness of God, and conducted to the illuminations granted it by God, according to capacity, with a view to the Divine imitation" (III, 1). But

thereafter, with a marked fondness for details, he went on to describe the threefold hierarchy of angels, each hierarchy further subdivided into three orders—an arrangement which in *De ecclesiastica hierarchia* is said to be the prototype for the orders within the visible church. The Areopagite's purpose had in any case been accomplished: the Christian God manifest in history was merged with the impersonal One of Plotinus to yield a Deity at once immanent and transcendent, and a universe whose multiple triadic levels connected into a unified structure through myriad correspondences.

The hierarchical structure of the universe proclaimed by the leading Neo-Platonists and codified by the Areopagite was bequeathed to the Middle Ages to be "methodized" into a scheme which affected every single aspect of the period's life and thought. Diverse ideas, borrowed freely from a variety of sources, were pressed into the service of Hierarchy with a breathtaking disregard for their frequent incompatibility. Yet the scheme did not crumble into its atomies because the Middle Ages succeeded in cultivating a fondness for analogical thinking which made it possible to draw within the compass of one comprehensive scheme the factual and the fictional, and to accept as reality what was but an image of the ultimate verities. Thus the analogy involving music, we have been told by many scholars (see Abert, Gérold, Hollander, Spitzer), yielded belief in the act of creation as a musical performance but also certainty that the heavenly bodies emit in their revolutions a pattern of sounds, indeed a melody,

> the melodye . . .
> That cometh of thilke speres thryes thre,
> That welle is of musik and melodye
> In this world here, and cause of armonye.
> (*The Parliament of Fowls*, lines 60–63)

This particular myth, already sanctified by time when adopted by the Middle Ages, continued to exercise a profound influence on diverse thinkers as late as the eighteenth century. But two other products of analogical thinking are even more relevant to our purposes. One—already encountered in the formulation ventured by Dr. Helkiah Crooke in 1615—was the idea of the microcosm of man; the other was the idea that the cosmic structure is analogous to a Scale, indeed *is* a Scale. Both ideas reached the Middle Ages with impressive credentials and were alike bequeathed to the future. In the case of man's microcosmic nature it is almost easier to enumerate the authorities who did not uphold it than those who did (see Allers, Conger; for visual representations: Saxl, Seznec; and for later developments, Hirst). In the case of the Scale it is hardly possible even to detect a dissenting minority: the weight of tradition appears to have crushed all opposi-

439

FIGURE 6. The Pantocrator in the cupola of the church at Daphni near Athens (usually dated ca. 1100) occupies the center of the interior's hierarchically-oriented decoration. The mosaics surrounding the cupola descend gradually to the terrestrial world of the spectators. FOTO MARBURG-ART REFERENCE BUREAU

tion. The "sources" of this concept are ultimately two: Jacob's vision of a Ladder which reached from heaven to earth (Genesis 28:10–15), and the Homeric σειρὴ χρυσείη (freely translated as *aurea catena*, "golden chain") which Zeus bade hang down from his abode (*Iliad* VIII, 19–27).

Jacob's Ladder was not only accepted as biblical endorsement of the Scale of Nature; in time it fathered the multitude of other ladders which also populated the medieval mind (see Nygren, II, 378ff., 403ff.). The Homeric "chain" has had an even more spectacular history (see Edelstein, "Eirionnach," Wolff, esp. Lévêque), but our interest in it must necessarily be limited to one of its manifold applications in particular, its use as an affirmation of the hierarchical structure of the universe. The most famous relevant statement was supplied by Macrobius. As he wrote in the *Com-*

mentariorum in somnium Scipionis (I, xiv, 15), with typical disregard of Homer's context and meaning,

Since all follow on in continuous succession, degenerating step by step in their downward course, the close observer will find that from the Supreme God even to the bottommost dregs of the universe there is one tie, binding at every link and never broken. This is the golden chain of Homer which, he tells us, God ordered to hang down from the sky to the earth (trans. W. H. Stahl, 1952).

It was to prove the most influential single statement of the "Chain of Being." But the celebrated phrase itself did not gain wide currency until the eighteenth century.

During the Middle Ages belief in Hierarchy inevitably affected theology, especially the work of Saint Thomas Aquinas (see Wright). In addition, Hierarchy dictated the structure of the *Summae*, themselves the product of the mental habit which constructed the Gothic cathedral and would later create Renaissance architecture (see Panofsky, Simson; and on the Renaissance, Wittkower). In literature the definitive manifestation of Hierarchy is of course Dante's journey through the manifold levels of the cosmic structure (see esp. Mazzeo). Beatrice's statement in the *Paradiso* (I, 103–05) echoes across the length of the Middle Ages:

> Le cose tutte a quante
> hann'ordine tra loro; e questo è forma
> che l'universo a Dio fa simigliante.

"All things whatsoever observe a mutual order; and this is the form that maketh the universe like unto God" (trans. P. H. Wicksteed [1899]).

Eastern Christendom had in the meantime developed a scheme which was even more hierarchically-oriented than the one in the West. History's linear progress ever since the world's creation was seen to focus ultimately on the Byzantine Empire, presently said to constitute the final stage in God's promises to mankind. At the same time the Empire was thought to be patterned after the hierarchy of Heaven, the Emperor placed at the apex of the political and ecclesiastical structure as the icon or image of God on earth. The pattern itself is visibly set out in all Byzantine churches (see Demus, Michelis). The decoration in each instance begins with the Pantocrator who is allotted the position of central importance either in the cupola—as in the church at Daphni (Figure 6)—or in the apse—as in the Monreale Cathedral (Figure 7). The Theotokos is presented next, either beneath the Pantocrator or in a secondary apse. Thereafter the decoration descends to angels and saints who represent Heaven, then to prophets and other biblical personalities who intimate the Holy Land or Paradise, and finally to the terrestrial world, merging at last with the actual spectator within the microcosmic representation of the universe which is the Byzantine church.

The Byzantines may on occasion appear wrapped in the mantle of Plato but were in fact (as Coleridge was to say of the Cambridge Platonists) "more truly Plotinists." It is not so much Plato as Plotinus and his successors who loom behind any espousal of Hierarchy, whether by Christians like John Scotus Erigena, Muhammadans like Avicenna and Averroës, or Jewish philosophers like Avicebron. Later, other traditions were to maintain Hierarchy independently of Plotinus, as when cabbalism asserted with Moses de Leon in the thirteenth century that "everything is linked with everything else down to the lowest ring on the chain" (see Scholem, p. 223). Plato, in any case, remained on the periphery of medieval reflections on Hierarchy, the implications of his "full" universe not comprehended until the fifteenth century when the first discordant note in the medieval paean to Hierarchy was struck by Nicholas of Cusa.

Nicholas of Cusa was no less obsessed with order than were his contemporaries. Not only did he insist that the universe functions according to strict mathematical laws; he also extended the preoccupation of Saint Augustine, Proclus, and the Pseudo-Dionysius with the host of triadic patterns in the universe (see Sigmund). Accordingly, the celebration of Hierarchy in *De concordantia catholica* is not necessarily "original." Neither is the reiteration of the commonplace view that God is both center and circumference (*De docta ignorantia*, II, 11–12, etc.), nor even the impressive ascription to God of a "coincidence of opposites"—"that coincidence where later is one with earlier, where the end is one with the beginning, where Alpha and Omega are the same" (*De visione Dei*, X; trans. E. G. Salter, 1960). The novelty in the Cusan's vision consists rather in his bold transfer of traditional ideas into another realm altogether, the realm of the infinite. The doctrine of *coincidentia oppositorum* is not significant in itself; entirely subordinate to the doctrine of divine infinity, it palpitates with life only when seen in direct relation to the infinite God. It is indeed the vision of an uncircumscribed and centerless God which also permitted Nicholas of Cusa to consider—in one spectacular leap of the human imagination—that the created order's center and circumference "coincide," that the sum total of reality is likewise infinite (*De docta ignorantia* II, 1–2, 4, 12, etc.; see esp. Cassirer). At this point Hierarchy ceases to be of importance. It has no place in the final vision of Nicholas of Cusa because it has no place in a "full" and therefore infinite universe.

Nicholas of Cusa like a colossus bestrides every account of the transition from the closed world to the

FIGURE 7. The Pantocrator in basilical structures like the Monreale Cathedral (last quarter of the twelfth century) is placed in the apse. But Hierarchy is retained, here seen to begin with the first level which depicts the Theotokos with angels. PHOTO ANDERSON-ART REFERENCE BUREAU

infinite universe (see Burtt, Kuhn, but esp. Koyré). However, though his theological ideas enabled him to advocate the infinity of the universe, he was not immediately instrumental in the reorientation of Occidental philosophy. Only in retrospect, and close upon the heels of other developments, did his originality become apparent.

To consider every factor that paved the way for the newly manifest world view is not necessary for our purposes, nor indeed possible. But some of the most important signposts pointing to the future should be consulted, even as others should be enumerated in passing in order to appreciate the multiplicity of byways which connect with the central concept. Four developments are apparent immediately: the socially- and religiously-oriented revolutions of the sixteenth and seventeenth centuries; the ever-increasing disposition to question traditional assumptions; the tendency

441

toward diversification in every field; and the gradual secularization of every aspect of life and thought. The first involves the Reformation which, like the Puritan revolution a century later, effectively undermined the theory of the divinely-sanctioned hierarchical society by removing its practice. Representative of the second was the eventual rejection of any number of time-honored traditions, among them the Areopagite's nine-fold celestial hierarchy (noted earlier) and the manifold Ladders of the Middle Ages which Luther sweepingly brushed aside (see Nygren, II, 483ff.). Representative of the third—the tendency toward diversification—was the compartmentalization of society as dictated by economic interests, and the consequent displacement of the myth of unity by the reality of heterogeneity. Representative of the fourth—the gradual secularization—was the advent of secular theories of history as well as of new schemes of periodization which no longer placed the Incarnation at the center of world history (see Mommsen, Spangenberg)—a development which in time shattered the horizontal unity heretofore said to have existed throughout history. But even as these developments were taking place, several individuals ventured contributions which in one way or another affected the fortunes of Hierarchy decisively. They were Marsilio Ficino and the Count Pico della Mirandola, Copernicus and his variegated followers, and the improbable Giordano Bruno.

The Neo-Platonists of Florence were so far from being opposed to Hierarchy that they upheld it with an enthusiasm which often verged on hysteria. Only fitfully brilliant, they bent with the mighty wind of tradition more often than they managed or even wished to divert its path. Ficino, for instance, recast the Plotinian universe into a new mold (see Kristeller). Collecting "all Being into five degrees," he placed "God and Angel in nature's highest place, Body and Quality in the lowest, and Soul right in the middle between these highest and lowest degrees," so that Soul became "the mirror of divine things, the life of mortal things, and the connection between the two" (*Theologia platonica* III, 2). The sum total of existence, moreover, was said to pulsate with Love. Pico agreed, however further afield he looked for support of his own scheme. His *Heptaplus* distinguishes the "regular series of ranks" into three levels of hierarchy: the elemental world, the celestial world, and the invisible world. Man could be said to constitute a fourth world were it not that "he is the bond and union of the three already described" (V, 6; trans. D. Carmichael, 1965). On the other hand, as Pico makes clear in his celebrated oration *De hominis dignitate,* Man might also be looked upon as a world entirely unto himself, independent of the rest of creation.

Pico's panegyric on Man is not in itself unique. It had been preceded by several eulogies from other pens, notably Giannozzo Manetti's *De dignitate et excellentia hominis* (see Gentile); moreover, Pico's subject had been anticipated by patristic writers, especially the Greek Fathers who so insistently celebrated the deification of Man (see Garin, Lot-Borodine). Ficino, too, was no less favorably inclined. His universe is decidedly anthropocentric, for Soul is expressly designated "the center of nature, the middle point of all that is, the chain of the world, the face of all, and the knot and bond of the universe" (*Theologia platonica* III, 2). Ficino's Man is already beginning to soar aloft: *homo quidem terrena est circumfusa nube* (*Opera* [1576], I, 659). But only Pico's Man is "confined by no bounds," being rather detached from the Scale of Nature altogether (see Kristeller). Significantly, Pico even eschewed the traditional designation of man as a microcosm; for a microcosm is necessarily earthbound, while Pico's Man has potentiality of attaining infinity.

Copernicus is in some respects less important than his enthusiastic disciples. He argued the theory of a heliocentric universe in an attempt to emphasize cosmic order, not to deny it; and he retained, we observe, both the finitude and the circularity of the traditional world view. His disciples, on the other hand, promptly seized on several implications latent in his theory and developed them in directions which Copernicus would not have endorsed. His emphasis on the mathematical order of the universe led in time to the displacement of the concrete older world-scheme by the abstract spatio-mathematical scheme of the "new philosophy." His removal of the fixed stars to an enormous distance from the center of the universe raised the problem of the interim "empty" space and started an avalanche which overwhelmed the "principle of plenitude" once Tycho Brahe rejected the material shells of the planets and Kepler their circular orbits (see Rosen). Above all, Copernicus' disciples burst through the bounds of his "closed" universe. The first sign of this development appeared in England in 1576 (see Johnson, Kocher). A diagram of the Copernican universe in Thomas Digges' *A Perfit Description of the Cælestiall Orbes* (Figure 3) places several stars outside the traditionally circular world, and as simply heralds the advent of cosmic infinity.

Thomas Digges as a scientist was content to intimate cosmic infinity; Giordano Bruno as an undisciplined thinker proclaimed it with all the emotional fervor at his disposal. Never more respected than after he was burned at the stake for refusing to retract his speculations, he has rightly emerged as the foremost Renaissance exponent of the infinite universe (see Greenberg, Michel). His vision depends on the equation of finitude with imperfection and of infinity with perfection. A finite universe, he thought, argues the absurd notion that God himself is finite, imperfect. As Bruno repeatedly insisted in *De l'infinito universo et mondi* (1584), "infinite perfection is far better presented in innumerable individuals than in those which are numbered and finite"; indeed, he went on, "as [God's] active power is infinite, so also as a necessary result, the subject thereof is infinite" (I, II). This "subject" is nothing less than the universe unfolding to infinity in terms of an infinite number of worlds. Divine fecundity obliges us to reach no other conclusion: "Why should infinite amplitude be frustrated, the possibility of an infinity of worlds be defrauded? Why should the excellency of the divine image be prejudiced, which ought rather to glow in an unrestricted mirror, infinite, immense, according to the law of its being?" (ibid., I). Bruno in further exercising his fertile imagination decided also that the universe constitutes a "monad," one "substance" which is manifested in a plurality of forms inclusive of God and nature: *eadem materia, eadem potentia, idem spacium, idem efficiens æqué ubique potens Deus & natura* (*De immenso et innumerabilis* IX; in *De monade* . . . [1591], p. 181). Bruno was in consequence propelled toward a scheme which has been rather grandly termed "pantheistic immanentism." He was at any rate inclined to merge God with nature, and especially the celestial with the sublunar.

Hierarchy suffered. In *De immenso* man is invited to raise himself to the contemplation of universal beauty *"per scalam pro specierū gradibus"* (*De monade* [1591], p. 149), but in *De l'infinito* (III) the "lovely scale of nature" is dismissed without hesitation:

The famous and received order of the elements and of the heavenly bodies is a dream and vainest fantasy [*un sogno, et una vanissima phantasia*], since it can neither be verified by observation of nature nor proved by reason or argued, nor is it either convenient or possible to conceive that it exists in such fashion. But we know that there is an infinite field, a containing space which doth embrace and interpenetrate the whole. It is an infinity of bodies similar to our own. . . . Thus there is not merely one world, one earth, one sun, but as many worlds as we see bright lights around us, which are neither more nor less in one heaven, one space, one containing sphere than is this our world in one containing universe, one space or one heaven; trans. D. W. Singer, 1950.

Bruno's world view was not calculated to appeal to theologians, whatever their affiliation. But it did not even attract the "new philosophers": Kepler looked on Bruno's infinite universe with "horror" (*De stella nova serpentarii* [1606], p. 105; see Koyré, Ch. III). On the other hand, the activities of Bruno and the astronomers converge in at least one significant point, their joint enthusiasm for Plato at the expense of Aristotle; Kepler's geometrical universe was also inspired by a Being who in the *Harmonice mundi* is said to be "Geometriæ fons ipsissimus, et, ut PLATO scripsit, æternam exercens Geometriam" (*Werke*, ed. M. Caspar [1940], VI, 299). Aristotle, once "the Philosopher," was now mentioned only to be dismissed, as in John Wilkins' militant statement of 1638, that "'tis not *Aristotle*, but truth that should be the rule of our opinions" (*The Discovery of a World in the Moone*, p. 30). The nature of this "truth" had been defined over six decades earlier on the appearance of the great nova of 1572. John Stow accurately reported that the nova appeared "Northward very bright and cleare in the constellation of *Cassiopeia*," remaining visible for almost sixteen months. But as he added (*Annales*, rev. ed. [1631], p. 673): ". . . it was found to have been in place celestiall farre above the Moone,"—in the very region, that is to say, which Aristotle had claimed was "unageing and unalterable and unmodified." The Creator was not, apparently, disciple of Aristotle after all.

The seventeenth century marked the total eclipse of Aristotle's "closed" world. Individuals like Donne may have initially hovered on the brink of despair, but others were soon able to accommodate themselves to the emerging infinite universe, even to glory in it. Thomas Traherne, for instance, was ecstatic before a world "surrounded with infinit and Eternal Space" because it proclaimed the boundless goodness of the Creator: "Infinit Lov cannot be Expressed in finit Room: but must hav infinit Places wherin to utter and shew it self" (*Centuries of Meditation*, I, 19; II, 80).

But even while Plato was influencing the thesis concerning the potentialities of "Infinit Lov," he was dictating the marked partiality to mathematics already shown by Nicholas of Cusa and Copernicus and even more fully demonstrated during the seventeenth century by Kepler, Galileo, and Newton (see Burtt, Koyré). Hierarchy was affected most adversely by the precision of mathematics as well as by the resultant conception of the universe in terms of a vast machine. Kepler's view of the cosmic machine was much qualified by an almost mystical belief in "harmony" which again terminated in Hierarchy (see Pauli). But Descartes, unable to bridge the gap between matter and spirit, lapsed into dualism and thereby severed the universe asunder. Hobbes even more alarmingly rejected the spiritual dimension altogether and posited a universe permeated by matter (*Leviathan* [1651], Chapter XLVI):

The World (I mean not the Earth onely . . . but the *Universe*, that is, the whole masse of all things that are) is Corporeall, that is to say, Body; and hath the dimensions of Magnitude, namely, Length, Bredth, and Depth: also every part of Body, is likewise Body, and hath the like dimensions; and consequently every part of the Universe, is Body; and that which is not Body, is no part of the Universe.

The orthodox were of course scandalized. In the hunting of "Leviathan" which ensued (see Mintz) perhaps only the Cambridge Platonists managed to shun scurrility. In opposition to the materialism of Hobbes no less than to the dualism of Descartes, they reiterated the ethical legacy of Greece and Rome even as they reasserted the Scale of Nature. Belief in what Cudworth described as "a *Scale* or *Ladder of Perfections* in Nature, one above the other, as of *Living* and *Animate Things*, above *Senseless* and *Inanimate; of Rational* things above *Sensitive*" (*The True Intellectual System of the Universe* [1678], p. 648), afforded opportunities to emphasize cosmic unity by means of an all-pervasive "plastic nature" (Cudworth, ibid., I, iii, 37) or "spirit of nature" (Henry More, *The Immortality of the Soul* [1659], I, iii). The Cambridge Platonists were to this extent "more truly Plotinists," yet they also partook of that traditional disposition toward analogical thinking so evident in affirmations such as Cudworth's that

there is [an] Interiour Symmetry and Harmony in the Relations, Proportions, Aptitudes and Correspondencies of Things to one another in the Great *Mundane* System, or Vital Machine of the Universe, which is all Musically and Harmonically composed (*A Treatise concerning Eternal and Immutable Morality*, posthumous ed. [1731], pp. 183–84).

The Cambridge Platonists notwithstanding, the "new philosophers," even when not under the spell of Cartesianism, were increasingly obliged to separate spirit from matter and finally to reduce God to the level of an impersonal First Cause. Descartes himself, as Pascal sagely noted, "would gladly have left God out of his whole philosophy. But he could not help making Him give one flip to set the world in motion. After that he had no more use for God" (*Pensées*, §194; trans. J. M. Cohen, 1961). Scientists like Newton did not ostracize God quite to the same extent. They hoped that somehow the study of "the Mechanism of the World" would lead them to "the very first Cause" which—Newton rather anxiously remarked—"certainly is not mechanical" (*Opticks*, 3rd rev. ed. [1721], p. 344). In fact, however, not only did Newton reduce the Scale of Nature to a hierarchical system of particles within matter (see Vavilov; cf. Gregory) but argued that the First Cause intervenes only when required to mend the clock-like machine of the universe. The implications of this argument did not escape Leibniz:

Sir Isaac Newton, and his followers, have also a very odd opinion concerning the work of God. According to their doctrine, God Almighty wants to wind up his watch from time to time: otherwise it would cease to move. He had not, it seems, sufficient foresight to make it a perpetual motion. Nay, the machine of God's making is so imperfect, according to these gentlemen, that he is obliged to clean it now and then by an extraordinary concourse, and even to mend it, as a clockmaker mends his work (*The Leibniz-Clarke Correspondence*, ed. H. G. Alexander [1956], pp. 11–12).

Leibniz' statement constitutes a warning of the perils inherent in any halfhearted attempt to "save appearances." What then were the alternatives? To agree with Hobbes that the universe is "Body"? But this would be extreme, unwarranted by experience. To insist with the Cambridge Platonists that the Scale of Nature in its traditional form is a reality after all? But this would be equally impossible, especially because analogical thinking declined once the "new philosophy" demanded that "all the amplifications, digressions, and swellings of style" be replaced by "a close, naked, natural way of speaking, . . . bringing all things as near the Mathematical plainness as they can" (Thomas Sprat, *The History of the Royal-Society* [1667], I, §20). In the event, the concept of Hierarchy was retained during the eighteenth century in name if not in substance until dissenting voices undermined its foundations and necessitated its reconstruction in line with other developments. In advance, however, Spinoza and Leibniz endeavored to impose order on the threatening chaos by erecting edifices which remain formidable landmarks in the history of Hierarchy.

Spinoza's contemporaries would have been surprised to find him mentioned in connection with Hierarchy, and amazed to discover that he was anything more than what Henry More described him as being, "a Jew first, after a Cartesian, and now an atheist." But this judgment was wild and can no longer be sustained (see Colie, Hampshire, Roth). Spinoza was indeed excommunicated by his co-religionists of Amsterdam but he did not deviate from the uncompromising emphasis of the great prophets on holiness. Moreover, though he was favorably inclined toward Cartesianism at the outset, he soon inverted it by deploying an equally relentless logic which bridged Descartes' dichotomy between body and spirit. Nor can the charge of "atheism" be entertained, unless we believe with his contemporaries that the celebrated phrase *Deus sive natura* ("God or nature") undermines the imperative distinction between God and nature, confounding both. Spinoza certainly did reject the distinction as in itself pernicious, no less pernicious indeed than the Cartesian distinction between thought and extension. He maintained instead that the world, the sum total of existence including God, constitutes a unity, one infinite and all-inclusive "Substance" which at the outset of his *Ethica* (1667) is defined as "that which is in itself and is conceived through itself: I mean that, the conception of which does not depend on the conception of another thing from which it must be formed." God and nature, the entities traditionally distinguished as *natura naturans* (nature "naturing" or creative) and *natura naturata* (nature "natured" or created), are accordingly merged (*Eth.*, I, Prop. 29, Note; cf. I, Prop. 8 and 14, Proof). Even terms like "Creator" and "creation," or "Spirit" and "matter," are consistently eschewed, since both import a division in the universe which Spinoza found unacceptable in the light of his vision of a cosmic unity which is "always the same and one everywhere" (*Eth.*, III, Pref.). Hence the appropriateness of proposing as an alternative to the term Substance the controversial phrase "God or nature." The studied indifference of "or" is itself significant, for it too argued the coherence of "all being," as when Spinoza in *De intellectus emendatione* (1677) formally asserted that *Deus sive natura* is "a being unique, infinite, that is, all being, and that beyond which nothing can be granted" (§76; trans. A. Boyle [1959]).

One fundamental consequence of this scheme went totally unobserved by Spinoza's contemporaries, else they would have been obliged to welcome their "atheist" with open arms. "God *or* nature" appears to intimate pantheism; in effect, however, it is a proclamation that the phenomenal world is not so much under God as *in* God, totally divine. This conviction, sustained by belief in God as "the indwelling and not the transient cause of all things" (*Eth.*, I, Prop. 18), was never more forcefully phrased by Spinoza than in the remarkable statement, "Whatever is, is in God" (*Eth.*, I, Prop. 15). Spinoza's universe is more, not less, spiritual than its counterpart in the thought of the Cambridge Platonists. The Scale of Nature was not retained, largely because Spinoza's mathematically-oriented methodology directed him away from metaphorical thinking toward "the essence and properties of things" (*Eth.*, I, App.), but also because the aggregate he terms "God or nature" could not accommodate a scheme rising by distinct steps from the material to the immaterial. On the other hand, Spinoza was so disinclined to eschew Hierarchy that he envisaged "all things from the highest grade to the the lowest" in a definite line of order (*Eth.*, I, App.; see Hampshire, Ch. II; Lasbax; Roth, Ch. II, sec. ii). The infinite and all-inclusive Substance—"God or nature"—is differentiated to infinity, "varies in infinite modes, yet remains always the same" (Letter to G. H. Schuller, 29 July 1675). Basically, then, we have Substance: "A substance is prior in its nature to its modifications" (*Eth.*, I, Prop. 1). Thereafter we obtain "infinite things in infinite modes" (*Eth.*, I, Prop. 16) which range from the Attributes of God—"infinite attributes, each of which expresses eternal and infinite essence" (*Eth.*, I, Def. 6)—to the infinity of "particular things" which are said to

be "nothing else than modifications of attributes of God, or modes by which attributes of God are expressed in a certain and determined manner" (*Eth.*, I, Prop. 25, Coroll.).

It is of course obvious that Spinoza's Hierarchy of Modes cannot possibly be severed from his overriding concern to assert cosmic unity in terms of One Substance. Priority belongs to the latter, not the former; for it is the latter which so effectively dispenses with Cartesian dualism in that it enables us to see that "extension and thought are either attributes of God or modifications of attributes of God" (*Eth.*, I, Prop. 15, Coroll. 2)—or, better still, that "thinking substance and extended substance are one and the same substance" (*Eth.*, II, Prop. 7, Note). Was Spinoza's "Substance" anticipated by Bruno? It is doubtful. For what possible relationship can be said to exist between a term which in the maelstrom of Bruno's ideas surfaces almost accidentally, and that which in the severely ordered thought of Spinoza forms the groundwork of one of the greatest philosophical systems ever constructed? Suffice it that Bruno can rarely be understood without the assistance of his imaginative commentators. But the only commentary required to understand Spinoza's *Ethics* is Spinoza's *Ethics*.

The occasional claim that Bruno influenced Spinoza is no less improbable than the claim that he influenced Leibniz. Here the crucial term is the "monad," its basic meaning clearly defined by Leibniz in the opening section of his *Principes de la nature et de la grâce fondés en raison* (1718): "*Monas* is a Greek word which signifies unity or that which is one." Thus far at least Bruno might have agreed. But was he likely to have recognized the term within the context of Leibniz' eminently rational philosophy? For Leibniz the "monad" represented something quite specific which he repeatedly elucidated in several treatises but especially in *La Monadologie* (German trans., 1720; Latin trans., 1721; 1st ed. of the French original, 1840). The "monad," he tells us, is "a simple substance which enters into compounds; *simple*, that is to say, without parts" (*Monad.*, trans. Mary Morris [1934], §1). Indestructible and indivisible, it is unaffected by external factors yet subject to continual "natural changes [which] come from an *internal principle*" so that "the present state of it is big with the future" (ibid., §§11, 22). Moreover, each monad varies in quality and perfection from the next to such an extent that their confluence to form various pluralities—"compounds"—has resulted in an infinitely varied universe, a unity-in-diversity which is ever augmented as new monads are produced, "born, so to speak, by continual fulgurations of the Divinity from moment to moment" (ibid., §47). There are consequently no vacuities in the uni-

445

verse. "All nature is a plenum" "which means that the whole of matter is connected"—a connection "of all created things with each, and of each with all the rest" (*Princ.*, §3; *Monad.*, §§61, 56). In the phrase so often quoted by Leibniz—as in the Preface to his answer to Locke, the *Nouveaux essais sur l'entendement humain* (1765)—"all things conspire" (σύμπνοια πάντα), as Hippocrates said. They conspire, moreover, in strict obedience to the Law of Continuity, so that the infinite monads which constitute the universe are arranged hierarchically in a sequence which reaches up to God, "the dominant Unity of the universe," the *monas monadum* or "original simple substance," expressly set "outside the series" (*De rerum originatione radicali*, 1st ed. [1840]; *Monad.*, §47; and letter of 6 Feb. 1706 to the Electress Sophia of Hanover). Given this "gradual connection of species," Leibniz remarked (*N. Ess.*, IV, xvi, 12; cf. Preface, and III, vi, 13), it must be thought that

Everything goes by degrees in nature, and nothing by leaps, and this rule regarding changes is part of my law of continuity. But the beauty of nature, which requires distinct perceptions, demands the appearance of leaps, and so to speak musical cadences in phenomena, and takes pleasure in mixing the species (trans. A. G. Langley, 1949).

Leibniz' Hierarchy of Monads is best set forth in another treatise, the *Essais de Théodicée sur la bonté de Dieu, la liberté de l'homme, et l'origine du mal* (1710). Appropriately enough, the concept is "accommodated" to our understanding in a dream within a fable. A dazzled Theodorus is enabled by the Goddess Pallas to see the universe in the form of "a pyramid, becoming ever more beautiful as one mounted towards the apex, and representing more beautiful worlds" (*Théod.*, trans. E. M. Huggard [1951], §§413–17). Leibniz' argument is not that the universe is beautiful and therefore perfect but that it is perfect and therefore beautiful. The "continual fulgurations of the Divinity," he thought, are never divorced from harmony, "the harmony pre-established from all time" (*Princ.*, §15). The idea is so basic to Leibniz' philosophy that he often described himself as "the author of the system of pre-established harmony." This system, he argued time and again, is a logical deduction from the fundamental truth which is the existence of God. A perfect God must necessarily have formed a perfect world; to deny the latter is to deny the former, since "one acts imperfectly if he acts with less perfection than he is capable of" (*Discours de métaphysique* [1st ed., 1846], trans. G. Montgomery, 1960). Hence Leibniz' constant reference of all his arguments to the nature of God—"the first reason of things" (*Théod.*, §7)—as in the typical assertion that "everything is regulated in things

once for all in as much order and agreement as possible, since supreme wisdom and goodness cannot act without perfect harmony" (*Princ.*, §13).

Leibniz did not hesitate to draw the conclusion which later was to be so ferociously attacked by Voltaire:

It follows from the supreme perfection of God that in producing the universe He chose the best possible plan, containing the greatest variety together with the greatest order; the best arranged situation, place, and time; the greatest effect produced by the simplest means; the most power, the most knowledge, the most happiness and goodness in created things of which the universe admitted. For as all possible things have a claim to existence in the understanding of God in proportion to their perfections, the result of all these claims must be the most perfect actual world which is possible (Leibniz, *Princ.*, §10; cf. esp. *Théod.*, §8, and *Monad.*, §§53–55).

Optimistic to the end, he remained convinced that "in things which are eternal, though there may be no cause, nevertheless there must be known a reason" (*De rerum originatione radicali*). Impressed, the Age of Reason welcomed Leibniz as one of its principal spokesmen. No one observed, and possibly no one cared, that Leibniz had dramatically transformed the traditional Scale of Nature by propounding a scheme which was, all too lucidly, a-Christian.

Hierarchy entered the eighteenth century deprived of its Christianized context, its mystery, and even—it could be said—its poetry. The entry was by way of Locke's indifferent assertion of the infinite "links" in nature which by "gentle degrees," he wrote, "ascend upward from us toward [God's] infinite perfection, as we see they gradually descend from us downwards" (*An Essay concerning Human Understanding* [1690], III, vi, 12). The "Chain of Being"—now the most common designation of cosmic Hierarchy—moved outwardly from Locke to be asserted repeatedly with a minimum of variation. Addison expounded "the little transitions and deviations from one species to another" which merge to form "the chain of Beings" (*The Spectator*, No. 519, 25 Oct. 1712); Henry Brooke celebrated the "grand Machine" of the universe with its "endless Links," not to mention "Earth's prolific Entrails" (*Universal Beauty*, 1735); John Wesley endorsed the "chain of beings" which he saw mounting by degrees "from an atom of disorganised matter, to the highest of the archangels" (see Southey); James Thomson wrote of

The mighty Chain of Beings, lessening down
From infinite Perfection to the Brink
Of dreary Nothing, desolate Abyss!
(*Summer* [1727], lines 284–86; 2nd version 334–36)

Edward Young was dazzled by the vision of

The chain unbroken upward, to the realms
Of incorporeal life . . . .
(*Night-Thoughts* [1744], VI)

—and of course Pope exclaimed with equal fervor:

Vast chain of being, which from God began,
Natures æthereal, human angel, man,
Beast, bird, fish, insect! what no eye can see,
No glass can reach! from Infinite to thee,
From thee to Nothing! . . .
(*An Essay on Man* [1733], I, 237ff.)

But Dr. Johnson was not impressed. He thought the *Essay on Man* was "certainly not the happiest of Pope's performances"; "the poet was not sufficiently master of his subject: metaphysical morality was to him a new study; he was proud of his acquisitions, and, supposing himself master of great secrets, was in haste to teach what he had not learned." "He tells us," added Johnson drily, "that there is a chain of subordinate beings 'from infinite to nothing,' of which himself and his readers are equally ignorant" (*Works*, ed. R. Lynam [1825], IV, 265–66). But Johnson's impatience was in the end directed particularly against Soame Jenyns who in *A Free Inquiry into the Nature and Origin of Evil* (1757) attempted still another exposition of Hierarchy "from infinite perfection to absolute nothing" (see Sachs, Willey). Johnson's review of Jenyns' work commences on a note of skepticism: "This doctrine of the regular subordination of beings, the scale of existence, and the chain of nature, I have often considered, but always left the inquiry in doubt and uncertainty." But no longer (*Works* [1825], V, 675–76):

The scale of existence from infinity to nothing, cannot possibly have any being. The highest being not infinite must be, as has been often observed, at an infinite distance below infinity. . . . Nor is this all. In the scale, wherever it begins or ends, are infinite vacuities. At whatever distance we suppose the next order of beings to be above man, there is room for an intermediate order of beings between them; and if for one order, then for infinite orders: since every thing that admits of more or less, and consequently all the parts of that which admits them, may be infinitely divided.

Johnson's assault on the assumptions supporting the Chain of Being was matched within a few years by Voltaire's. Voltaire, ever bent on arresting the widespread optimism generated by Leibniz (see Besterman, Brooks), correctly judged that the Chain of Being appeared to support the notion that the universe is "the most perfect actual world which is possible." Initially "filled with admiration" for the traditional concept, he soon found that "this great phantom could not bear the light of careful examination."

The imagination is at first pleased with the imperceptible transition from brute matter to organized substance, from plants to zoophytes, from zoophytes to animals, from animals to men, from men to genii, from genii with light, immaterial bodies to immaterial substances, and finally to a thousand orders of these substances which spanning the gap between beauty and perfection, ascend to God Himself. . . . But there is a greater distance between God and his most perfect creatures than between the Holy Father and the dean of the Sacred College. The dean may become a pope, but the most perfect genii created by the Supreme Being cannot become God. Between him and God lies infinity (*Dictionnaire philosophique* [1764], "Chaîne des êtres créés," trans. W. Baskin [1961]).

Johnson and Voltaire encountered no violent disapprobation because their contemporaries were themselves aware that the static Chain of Being did not always correspond to reality. Was not Pope's enthusiastic exposition of Hierarchy followed by that apocalypse of imminent cataclysm, *The Dunciad*? Was not Addison as convinced of "the little transitions and deviations from one species to another," as he was of the cessation of the melody "that cometh of thilke speres thryes thre"? The eloquence of Reason may not necessarily compensate for the silence of the stars:

What though, in solemn Silence, all
Move round the dark terrestrial Ball?
What tho' nor real Voice nor Sound
Amid their radiant Orbs be found?
In Reason's Ear they all rejoice,
And utter forth a glorious Voice,
For ever singing, as they shine,
'The Hand that made us is Divine'.
(*Ode*, "The Spacious Firmament" [1712],
lines 17–24).

Yet the Chain of Being was still not dismantled. It was instead adjusted to another emerging idea, cosmic evolution. Leibniz pointed the way when he maintained in *De rerum originatione radicali* that "there is a perpetual and a most free progress of the whole universe in fulfilment of the universal beauty and perfection of the works of God, so that it is always advancing towards a greater development." Kant in *Allgemeine Naturgeschichte und Theorie des Himmels* (1755) even more expansively asserted cosmic progress in terms of a universe infinite in both time and space (Ch. VII; trans. W. Hastie, 1900):

Creation is not the work of a moment. When it has once made a beginning with the production of an infinity of substances and matter, it continues in operation through the whole succession of eternity with ever increasing degrees of perfection. Millions and whole myriads of millions of centuries will flow on, during which always new worlds and systems of worlds will be formed after each other in the distant regions away from the centre of nature, and will attain to perfection.

447

The Chain, which once extended vertically "from the Mushrome to the Angels," was now seen as emblematic of the evolution of the universe toward "perfection."

The next development was the gradual extrication of the past from its narrow confines in biblical chronology (see esp. Haber). The apex was reached in 1859 upon the publication of Darwin's *Origin of Species*.

Darwin's theory of evolution may have been an extension of formulations already advanced by others (see Glass, et al.; Greene), but his thesis that evolution progresses by "natural selection" was entirely original. It raised a storm of protests. "Natural selection" appeared to endorse chance: "it is the law," said the astronomer J. F. W. Herschel, "of higgledy-piggledy." Moreover, Darwin converted the traditional Scale of Nature into a hierarchical system which could be said to exist only for purposes of classification, not as a reflection of reality. His "hierarchy," in any case, terminated in man—not in emulation of Aristotle's Scale indeed, but in accordance with a dynamic form of evolution which should in time progress beyond its present apex in man. Darwin's contemporaries understandably sped to the conclusion that the descent of man had been placed within a thoroughly materialistic framework. What then of the mention of "the Creator" in the final paragraph of *The Origin of Species?*

Thus, from the war of nature, from famine and death, the most exalted object which we are capable of conceiving, namely, the production of the higher animals, directly follows. There is a grandeur in this view of life, with its several powers, having been originally breathed by the Creator into a few forms or into one; and that, whilst this planet has gone cycling on according to the fixed law of gravity, from so simple a beginning endless forms most beautiful and most wonderful have been, and are being, evolved.

But the phrase "by the Creator" was in fact an afterthought. Not present in the first edition of 1859, it is quoted here from the third revised edition of 1861.

H. G. Wells, in updating the story of Job, arranged for Sir Eliphaz Burrows to invite a distressed Job Huss to

think of the stately procession of life upon the earth, through a myriad of forms the glorious crescendo of evolution, up to its climax, man. What a work is man! The paragon of creation, the microcosm of the cosmos, the ultimate birth of time . . . (*The Undying Fire* [1919], p. 113).

A misunderstanding of Darwin, further undercut by the distorted echo of Hamlet's words, is not secure foundation for optimism. Worse, it would appear that as the Darwinian theory is now being revised in the light of genetics, hierarchy is declining into a merely artificial scheme, to vanish at last within the infinite space-time continuum of our ever-expanding universe.

But not quite. For Hierarchy is only a brief sentence within the larger paragraph which is man's constant search for Order, indeed his refusal to concede that he resides within a universe of chance. Science may have destroyed Hierarchy but refuses to reject Harmony. "Without the belief in the inner harmony of our world," said Einstein, "there could be no science" (see Schneer, p. 368). Hierarchy has passed but Order lingers. Still "the roote of all," it has of late appeared in a number of guises, notably the attempt of Teilhard de Chardin to argue that the universe evolves from cosmogenesis through anthropogenesis to Christogenesis. His ultimate aim was to look beyond "the incoherent multiplicity of things" toward Unity—"the vision of a universe structurally unified in its main lines and energies." Nor is it surprising that he also favored the "monad"—"a Greek word," as Leibniz said, "which signifies unity or that which is one."

BIBLIOGRAPHY

Hermann Abert, *Die Musikanschauung des Mittelalters* (Halle, 1905). Rudolf Allers, "Microcosmus: From Anaximandrus to Paracelsus," *Traditio*, **2** (1944), 319–407. A. H. Armstrong, *The Architecture of the Intelligible Universe in the Philosophy of Plotinus* (Cambridge, 1940). J. B. Bamborough, *The Little World of Man* (London, 1952). W. H. Barber, *Leibniz in France* . . . (Oxford, 1955), Part III. Otto Benesch, *The Art of the Renaissance in Northern Europe* (Cambridge, Mass., 1945), esp. Ch. III. Theodore Besterman, *Voltaire Essays* (London, 1962), Ch. III. William J. Bouwsma, *Concordia mundi* (Cambridge, Mass., 1957), esp. Ch. IV. Richard A. Brooks, *Voltaire and Leibniz* (Geneva, 1964). Edwin A. Burtt, *The Metaphysical Foundations of Modern Physical Science* (London, 1925). Lily B. Campbell, *Shakespeare's Tragic Heroes: Slaves of Passion* (Cambridge, 1930), esp. Ch. V. Ernst Cassirer, *The Individual and the Cosmos in Renaissance Philosophy*, trans. M. Domandi (New York, 1963), esp. Chs. I–II. Albert R. Cirillo, "Giulio Camillo's *Idea of the Theater:* The Enigma of the Renaissance," *Comparative Drama*, **1** (1967), 19–27. Rosalie L. Colie, *Light and Enlightenment: A Study of the Cambridge Platonists and the Dutch Arminians* (Cambridge, 1957), Chs. V–VI. George P. Conger, *Theories of Macrocosms and Microcosms in the History of Philosophy* (New York, 1922). Hardin Craig, *The Enchanted Glass: The Elizabethan Mind in Literature* (New York, 1936), Ch. I. Walter C. Curry, *Milton's Ontology, Cosmogony and Physics* (Lexington, Ky., 1957), Ch. VIII. Otto Demus, *Byzantine Mosaic Decoration* (London, 1947), Part I. Ludwig Edelstein, "The Golden Chain of Homer," in *Studies in Intellectual History*, eds. G. Boas, et al. (Baltimore, 1953), pp. 48–66. Eirionnach, "Aurea Catena Homeri," *Notes and Queries*, 2nd Series, **3** (1857), 63–65, 81–84, 104–07, and **12** (1861), 161–63, 181–83. Eugenio Garin, "La 'Dignitas homini' e la letteratura patristica," *La Rinascita*, **1** (1938), §4, 102–46. Giovanni Gentile, *Il* *pensiero italiano del Rinascimento*, 3rd ed. (Florence, 1940), Ch. III. Théodore Gérold, *Les Pères de l'Église et la musique* (Strasbourg, 1931). Bentley Glass, O. Temkin, and W. L. Straus, eds., *Forerunners of Darwin: 1745–1859* (Baltimore, 1959). Sidney Greenberg, *The Infinite in Giordano Bruno* (New York, 1950). John C. Greene, *The Death of Adam: Evolution and its Impact on Western Thought* (Ames, Iowa, 1959). Joshua C. Gregory, "The Newtonian Hierarchic System of Particles," *Archives internationales d'histoire des sciences*, **33** (1954), 243–47. Francis C. Haber, *The Age of the World: Moses to Darwin* (Baltimore, 1959). Stuart Hampshire, *Spinoza* (Harmondsworth, 1951). S. K. Heninger, Jr., "Some Renaissance Versions of the Pythagorean Tetrad," *Studies in the Renaissance*, **8** (1961), 7–35. Désirée Hirst, *Hidden Riches: Traditional Symbolism from the Renaissance to Blake* (London, 1964). John Hollander, *The Untuning of the Sky: Ideas of Music in English Poetry, 1500–1700* (Princeton, 1961). Francis R. Johnson, *Astronomical Thought in Renaissance England* (Baltimore, 1937), Ch. VI. Paul H. Kocher, *Science and Religion in Elizabethan England* (San Marino, Calif., 1953), esp. Chs. VII–IX. Arthur Koestler, *The Sleepwalkers: A History of Man's Changing Vision of the Universe* (London, 1959). Alexandre Koyré, *From the Closed World to the Infinite Universe* (Baltimore, 1957). Paul O. Kristeller, *The Philosophy of Marsilio Ficino*, trans. V. Conant (New York, 1943), esp. Ch. VI; idem, "Ficino and Pomponazzi on the Place of Man in the Universe," *Renaissance Thought II* (New York, 1965), Ch. V. Thomas S. Kuhn, *The Copernican Revolution* (Cambridge, Mass., 1957). Auguste Laneau, *L'Histoire du Salut chez les Pères de l'Église: La doctrine des âges du monde* (Paris, 1964). Émile Lasbax, *La Hiérarchie dans l'univers chez Spinoza*, rev. ed. (Paris, 1926). Pierre Lévêque, *Aurea catena Homeri: . . .* (Paris, 1959). C. S. Lewis, *A Preface to 'Paradise Lost'* (London, 1942), Ch. XI. M. Lot-Borodine, "La doctrine de la 'déification' dans l'Église grecque jusqu'au XIᵉ siècle," *Revue de l'histoire des religions*, **106** (1932), 5–43, 525–74, and **107** (1933), 8–55. Arthur O. Lovejoy, *The Great Chain of Being: A Study of the History of an Idea* (Cambridge, Mass., 1936). Dietrich Mahnke, *Unendliche Sphäre und Allmittelpunkt* (Halle, 1937). Joseph A. Mazzeo, *Medieval Cultural Tradition in Dante's 'Comedy'* (Ithaca, N.Y., 1960), esp. Ch. I. Paul-Henri Michel, *La cosmologie de Giordano Bruno* (Paris, 1962). P. A. Michelis, *An Aesthetic Approach to Byzantine Art*, trans. S. Xydis and M. Moschona (London, 1955). Samuel I. Mintz, *The Hunting of Leviathan* (Cambridge, 1962). Theodor E. Mommsen, "Petrarch's Conception of the 'Dark Ages'," *Speculum*, **17** (1942), 226–42. Marjorie H. Nicolson, *The Breaking of the Circle*, rev. ed. (New York, 1960). Anders Nygren, *Agape and Eros*, trans. P. S. Watson (London, 1938–39), esp. Part II. Erwin Panofsky, *Galileo as a Critic of the Arts* (The Hague, 1954), esp. pp. 22–31; idem, *Gothic Architecture and Scholasticism* (Latrobe, Pa., 1951). C. A. Patrides, *Milton and the Christian Tradition* (Oxford, 1966), Ch. III; idem, "Renaissance Thought on the Celestial Hierarchy: The Decline of a Tradition," *Journal of the History of Ideas*, **20** (1959), 155–66, and **23** (1962), 265–67; idem, *The Phoenix and the Ladder: The Rise and Decline of the Christian View of History*

(Berkeley, 1964); idem, *The Cambridge Platonists* (London and Cambridge, Mass., 1969). W. Pauli, "The Influence of Archetypal Ideas on the Scientific Theories of Kepler," trans. Priscilla Silz, in *The Interpretation of Nature and the Psyche* (London, 1955), pp. 147–240. James E. Phillips, Jr., *The State in Shakespeare's Greek and Roman Plays* (New York, 1940). Georges Poulet, *Les Métamorphoses du cercle* (Paris, 1961). René Roques, *L'Univers dionysien: structure hiérarchique du monde selon le Pseudo-Denys* (Paris, 1954). Laurence J. Rosán, *The Philosophy of Proclus* (New York, 1949). Edward Rosen, "A Full Universe," *Scientific Monthly*, **63** (1946), 213–17. Leon Roth, *Spinoza* (London, 1929). H. H. Rowley, *Darius the Mede and the Four World Empires in the Book of Daniel* (Cardiff, 1959). Arieh Sachs, "Samuel Johnson and the Cosmic Hierarchy," in *Scripta Hierosolymitana*, Vol. XVII: *Studies in English Language and Literature*, ed. A. Shalvi and A. A. Mendilow (Jerusalem, 1966), 137–54. Fritz Saxl, *Verzeichnis astrologischer und mythologischer illustrierter Handschriften des lateinischen Mittelalters*, Vol. II: *Die Handschriften der National-Bibliothek in Wien* (Heidelberg, 1927), Ch. IV. Cecil J. Schneer, *The Search for Order* (London, 1960). Gershom G. Scholem, *Major Trends in Jewish Mysticism*, 2nd rev. ed. (New York, repr. 1961). Jean Seznec, *The Survival of the Pagan Gods*, trans. B. F. Sessions (New York, 1953), pp. 64–69. Paul E. Sigmund, *Nicholas of Cusa and Medieval Political Thought* (Cambridge, Mass., 1963), esp. Chs. III, V. Otto von Simson, *The Gothic Cathedral: . . .* (London, 1956). Robert Southey, *The Life of Wesley*, 3rd ed. (London, 1846), II, 88. H. Spangenberg, "Die Perioden der Weltgeschichte," *Historische Zeitschrift*, **127** (1923), 1–49. Theodore Spencer, *Shakespeare and the Nature of Man*, 2nd ed. (New York, 1951). Leo Spitzer, *Classical and Christian Ideas of World Harmony*, ed. A. G. Hatcher (Baltimore, 1963). E. M. W. Tillyard, *The Elizabethan World Picture* (London, 1943). S. I. Vavilov, "Newton and the Atomic Theory," in *The Royal Society Newton Tercentenary Celebrations* (Cambridge, 1947), pp. 43–55. C. F. von Weizsäcker, *The History of Nature*, trans. F. D. Wieck (London, 1951); idem, *The World View of Physics*, trans. M. Greene (London, 1952). Basil Willey, *The Eighteenth Century Background* (London, 1940), Ch. III. F. P. Wilson, *Elizabethan and Jacobean* (Oxford, 1945), Ch. I. James Winny, ed., *The Frame of Order: . . .* (London, 1957). Rudolf Wittkower, *Architectural Principles in the Age of Humanism* (London, 1949). Emil Wolff, *Die goldene Kette: . . .* (Hamburg, 1947). John H. Wright, *The Order of the Universe in the Theology of St. Thomas Aquinas* (Rome, 1957).

A number of relevant texts have been brought together by Milton K. Munitz in *Theories of the Universe* (Glencoe, Ill., 1957). The most comprehensive study of the background is Pierre Duhem, *Le système du monde: histoire des doctrines cosmologiques de Platon à Copernic*, 10 vols. (Paris, 1913–59).

C. A. PATRIDES

[See also **Chain of Being; Infinity;** Macrocosm . . . ; **Nature; Neo-Platonism;** Perfectibility; Platonism; Renaissance.]

449

HISTORICAL AND
DIALECTICAL MATERIALISM

HISTORICAL AND dialectical materialism are terms conventionally employed to describe two aspects of the theoretical structure known as Marxism. Although logically independent of each other, the two concepts are historically linked by virtue of the fact that they evolved from a common intellectual stem. For practical purposes it is also relevant that Marx and Engels are widely regarded as joint creators of a unified system of thought encompassing nature and history. The fact that this interpretation is erroneous does not render it less significant. Insofar as the term "Marxism" has come to stand for a systematic doctrine elaborated by Engels and others after the death of Marx, the latter's original intentions may be said to have been "developed" or "misinterpreted," depending upon one's viewpoint. Irrespective of where one stands on this issue, it is a comparatively simple matter to distinguish the historical materialism of Marx from the dialectical materialism of Engels. In tracing this distinction, we begin with Marx's writings on history, and then proceed to a consideration of the materialist ontology outlined by Engels and subsequently institutionalized in the dogmatic system of Marxism-Leninism. This approach inverts the familiar procedure wherein historical materialism is treated as the application to history of the general doctrine of dialectical materialism. Since no such view was at any time entertained by Marx, we are on safe grounds in disregarding it.

1. Marx's Historical Materialism. A consideration of this topic can usefully start out from an early work, *The Holy Family* (1845), in which Marx draws a distinction between two divergent currents stemming from the rationalist philosophy of the French eighteenth-century Enlightenment. On the one hand, the *philosophes* had opposed what Marx called "mechanical materialism" to the metaphysics of Descartes, Spinoza, and Leibniz, thereby preparing the way for the emancipation of natural science from Cartesian metaphysics. Having successfully divorced Descartes' physics from his metaphysics, this "Cartesian materialism" eventually merged with "French natural science." The heritage of Descartes—who in his lifetime had already encountered opponents in Gassendi ("the restorer of Epicurean materialism") and in Hobbes—was, however, gradually dislodged by doctrines rooted in Locke and was eventually given a new form by Condillac and Helvétius. According to Marx, "As Cartesian materialism merges into natural science proper, the other branch of French materialism leads direct to socialism and communism" (Marx, *Holy Family* [1845], p. 175). Its ultimate source was an anthro-

pological doctrine which emphasized the goodness of man:

There is no need of any great penetration to realize that the teaching of materialism on the original goodness and equal intellectual endowment of men, the omnipotence of experience, habit and education, and the influence of environment . . . is necessarily connected with communism and socialism. If man draws all his knowledge, sensation, etc., from the world of the senses and the experience gained in it, the empirical world must be arranged so that in it man experiences . . . what is really human and . . . becomes aware of himself as man (ibid., p. 175, slightly revised).

This Marxian humanism, as formulated in the *Holy Family,* the *Theses on Feuerbach* (1845), and the *German Ideology* (1845–46), was a development of eighteenth-century French materialism, minus its Cartesian physics and the related epistemological problem, in which he took no interest. The basic orientation of this materialism was practical, and its application to social life was seen by Marx to follow inevitably from insight into the human condition. "If man is shaped by his surroundings, his surroundings must be made human" (*Holy Family*, p. 176). This conclusion followed without question for anyone who had incorporated the ethics of the French Enlightenment in his own assumptions about the world. Marx was never conscious of a moral problem in this respect, because his values formed part of a commitment to the belief that the humanization of nature (including that part of "human" nature which was in fact pre-human, i.e., a heritage of man's animal past) was both possible and desirable. In this sense, historical materialism from the start incorporated a particular value-system: that of the Enlightenment. At the same time the doctrine had a specific theoretical content which differentiated it from contemporary liberalism: it rejected the then fashionable disjunction between society and the individual. When he wrote in his sixth *Thesis on Feuerbach* that "The essence of man is no abstraction inherent in each separate individual. In its reality it is the *ensemble* of social relations," Marx reemphasized a notion already stressed in the passage from *The Holy Family* cited earlier: "If man is social by nature, he will develop his true nature only in society, and the power of his nature must be measured not by the power of separate individuals, but by the power of society" (*Holy Family*, p. 176).

The difference between the liberal and the socialist position then, as Marx perceived it in the 1840's, reduced itself to this: the socialists (or communists), having taken seriously the proposition that man *is* the sum total of his social relations, were concerned to remake society, whereas liberal rationalism postulated a fixed and stable individual human essence which could be relied upon to find adequate expression in appropriate social institutions—always supposing that no artificial barriers were placed in the way. In practice, liberalism identified human rationality with enlightened self-interest, and the desirable social order with one in which private initiative was permitted free play. In this respect the liberals went back to the philosophers of the eighteenth century, but then so did Marx, with the difference that he rejected the individualism of the Scottish moralists and of Adam Smith, in favor of the collectivism inherent in the French materialists. It is important to realize that in its origins "historical materialism" was an anthropological doctrine before it became a sociological one. Its significance for Marx lay in the fact that it enabled him to treat socialism (or communism) as the consistent application *to society* of general principles extracted from the philosophical study of human *nature*. Once this nature was perceived as "social," in the sense that it always and everywhere refracted the character of the cultural environment which men had constructed, the "socialist" conclusion followed from the "materialist" assumption. Or rather, it followed for Marx because he took for granted the value-system of writers like Holbach and Helvétius, for whom true self-love was inconceivable in abstraction from human solidarity.

The notion that this anthropological naturalism is anchored in a general theory of the universe, which represents the world as a process of "dialectical" movement from one stage to another, finds no support in Marx's writings. For him, the only "nature" that enters into practical consideration is man's own nature. The external world, as it exists in and for itself, is irrelevant to a thinker who approaches history with a view to establishing what men have made of themselves and are still capable of becoming. It is the more irrelevant because on Marx's assumptions about the active role of consciousness in constituting our picture of reality, the world is never simply "given," any more than that man is the passive receptacle of sense-impressions. An external environment, true knowledge of which is possible in abstraction from man's role in shaping the world, is a fantasy, at any rate so far as society is concerned. The only world we know is the one we have constituted: that which appears in our individual and collective experience. Man is indeed part of nature, so that the distinction between natural and historical science can only be relative, not absolute. But "historical materialism" has to do with "anthropological nature," not with nature in the abstract. At the same time, the emphasis upon the "historical" aspect of the new viewpoint served to distinguish it from the naturalistic approach of the eighteenth-

century French *philosophes* (and of Feuerbach), which virtually ignored the historical process. A materialist critique of the prevailing social and political conditions presupposed an understanding of the manner in which they had come into being, the forces which upheld them, and the tendencies pointing beyond them. The *Theses on Feuerbach* in particular represent a break with "contemplative" materialism, and the adoption of a "practical" standpoint which is revolutionary by its very nature.

Historical materialism in this sense had a "dialectical" element built into its conceptual structure from the very first. It was at one and the same time an analysis of the historical process, and the theoretical underpinning of a particular viewpoint (the socialist one) which implied a critique of liberal individualism and its objective correlative: civil (or bourgeois) society. This introduction of an activist element into a doctrine of society proved baffling to most of Marx's critics who accepted the positivist interpretation of history as an ongoing process analyzable in strictly factual terms. Historical events, on this view, were analogous to the facts of natural science. They were simply there to be studied in as dispassionate a manner as possible, and the task of the historian (in Ranke's words) was to explain "what really happened" (*wie es eigentlich gewesen*).

Marx by the later 1840's was sufficiently close to positivism to reject Hegel's philosophy of history, and by implication the entire notion of a *philosophy* (as distinct from a theory) of history: an enterprise whose theological purpose had become evident to him, once he had emancipated himself from Hegel and absorbed the impact of Anglo-French materialism. At the same time he differed from Comte (whose principal work he first read in 1866, and then dismissed as rubbish) in refusing to treat history as an accretion of data which could be studied on the model of the natural sciences. History to Marx was a self-activating totality ultimately rooted in the "production and reproduction of material life." Its objectivity was not of the kind that could be discerned by the study of "facts," and for the same reason it did not lend itself to the framing of general laws analogous to Newtonian physics: the model of Comte's "social physics." The materialist approach was outlined by Marx in the *German Ideology* of 1845–46, and subsequently confirmed in the well-known Preface to the *Critique of Political Economy* (1859):

The mode of production of material life conditions the social, political and intellectual life-process in general. It is not the consciousness of men that determines their being, but on the contrary their social being that determines their consciousness.

It has for its counterpart the activist note struck in the *Communist Manifesto* (1848):

The history of all hitherto existing society is a history of class struggles.

These two modes of perception are held in balance by the notion that the "materialist conception of history" is both a theory of the historical process and a means towards its mastery. Men become masters of their fate in the measure in which they become conscious of the mechanism whereby history is set in motion and kept going. In turning their insight to practical account, they do not for this reason abandon the scientific standpoint. Rather, they employ their insight into the antagonistic character of the historical process—specifically of its ultimate stage: contemporary bourgeois society—for the purpose of overcoming the antagonism. Marx's historical materialism differs from Comte's positivism in that it incorporates practical (political or ethical) postulates within its very conceptual structure. He does not formulate general laws on the basis of a dispassionate study of "objective" data; he conceptualizes the historical process, and in this very act unifies (critical) theory and (revolutionary) practice.

Although Marx never employed the term "sociology" (possibly because he held Comte's work in low esteem), it has become customary to treat the approach briefly sketched out in the 1859 Preface, and extensively developed in *Capital* (1867), as a sociological doctrine analogous to that of Comte. Within the Marxist school itself this fashion was inaugurated by Engels, who in his *Anti-Dühring* (1878) attributed to Marx "two great discoveries," one of them being "the materialist conception of history." This was described by Engels as the doctrine "that the production (of the means to support human life) and, next to production, the exchange of things produced, is the basis of all social structure; that in every society that has appeared in history, the manner in which wealth is distributed and society divided into classes or orders is dependent upon what is produced, how it is produced, and how the products are exchanged." Marx, who had read the *Anti-Dühring* in manuscript, did not bother to correct this simplified exposition of his very complex approach, presumably because he regarded the book as a popular tract destined for a semi-literate public. In consequence it came to be widely believed that "scientific socialism" (another term coined by Engels) had for its theoretical foundation a species of economic determinism valid for all stages of recorded history. In the light of this quite unfounded assumption, the relationship of the so-called "economic base" to the "political" or "ideological" superstructure assumed the status of a major theoretical difficulty whose solution kept a small army of exegetes ceaselessly employed. The "materialist" standpoint was understood in terms of Engels' statement (in the passage already cited) as signifying that "the final causes of all social changes and political revolutions are to be sought . . . not in the *philosophy,* but in the *economics* of each particular epoch" (Engels, 1878).

In point of fact, the problem of relating the "political superstructure" to its "material foundation" had originally (in 1842–44) presented itself to Marx as an aspect of his critique of Hegel's political philosophy, notably as formulated in the latter's *Philosophy of Right* (1821). While already conscious of the distinction between "state" and "society," Hegel had assigned a subordinate role to the latter. Marx's "materialism," by contrast, took for its starting point the autonomy of a society which had manifestly developed a dynamic of its own: Western European bourgeois society, itself propelled forward by the mechanism of what he termed the "capitalist mode of production." To this extent his approach was in tune with the procedure common among the classical economists, notably the founders of that discipline of "Political Economy" which had grown up in Western Europe between 1770 and 1830. The novelty he introduced lay in the fusion of what was later termed "economics" with "sociology" and "history." An introduction to some bulky 1857–58 manuscripts (first published in 1939–41) defines the subject of his investigations as the sphere of "material production." He goes on to suggest that, within the totality of production-distribution-consumption, one element—namely production—predominates. "From it, the process continually recommences. . . . There is interaction between the various elements. This is the case in every organic whole." Nowhere does Marx assert that production is "in the last analysis" the causal factor "determining" the shape of society, still less that "economics"—in the vulgar sense of economic interest—"determines" the political process. These notions were introduced by his interpreters, beginning with Engels (1878), in an attempt to generalize a principle of investigation into an all-embracing causal explanation.

It is equally worth noting that Marx does not speak of a "materialist conception of history," contenting himself with the more modest term "materialistic and thus scientific method." The conversion of his critical *method* into a determinist social *philosophy* was primarily the work of Engels, who after the death of Marx in 1883 assumed the role of exegete. The next step consisted in transforming the Marxian critique of society into a comprehensive doctrine embracing both nature and history. This process too was set in motion by Engels, and continued (after his death in 1895) by the orthodox school, primarily represented by Karl Kautsky, G. V. Plekhanov, and Antonio Labriola. It will be considered in the following section. Here it remains to be noted that in its original Marxian form the "materialist conception of history" had a twofold character: (1) As a general principle of historical investigation, or conceptualization, it remained a mere sketch, although of great potential fertility for the social sciences, a circumstance clearly recognized by Max Weber, whose own work bore the imprint of his lifelong preoccupation with the problems raised by Marx. (2) As a finished theory of the actual historical process, the new method had originally been employed for the critical analysis of one particular social formation only: bourgeois society. *Capital* (1867–94) contained an historical sketch of the rise of capitalism in Western Europe, but did not attempt to answer the question why no corresponding development had occurred elsewhere. As for the pre-capitalist formations briefly considered in the *Grundrisse* of 1857–58, the analysis, while "materialist" enough, did not point to "internal contradictions" similar to those which (in Marx's view) were at work in contemporary bourgeois society.

In fairness to all concerned, it may be said that Marx's theoretical approach in the crucially important Preface of the 1859 *Critique*, as well as in his earlier and later writings, lent itself to an equivocation. On the one hand, he had inherited from his predecessors—notably Adam Smith and David Ricardo—the notion of an autonomous economic sphere interacting with the remainder of society (including the political and cultural "superstructure"). On the other hand, he had taken over from Hegel the conception of history as a self-activating totality within which all the seemingly independent elements were "organically" linked. By fusing these two modes of thought, he arrived at a vision of modern society as a uniquely determined totality of social relations, dynamically propelled by an equally unique and unprecedented mode of production. The "historical" element in this "historical materialism" lay in the fact that he described as "bourgeois" the social relations (or production relations) which Smith and Ricardo had treated as "natural." The "materialism" lay in his ascription to the "relations of production" of a higher degree of reality than had been accorded to them by Hegel and the other "idealist" German philosophers. But if the "relations of production" were virtually synonymous with "society," there was no specificity of the economic sphere, and the distinction between base and superstructure broke down. It cannot be said that Marx ever quite managed to solve the problem, or even to state it in an entirely unambiguous manner. Had he done so, both his followers and his critics would doubtless have been saved a great deal of trouble.

2. *The Dialectical Materialism of Engels.* In contrast to the "historical materialism" of Marx which, whatever its inadequacies, represents a momentous intellectual achievement, the "dialectical materialism" of Engels cannot be regarded as an important contribution to philosophy. Its significance lies in the fact that, for historical reasons, it has become the keystone of an institutionalized system of thought binding upon the adherents of what is officially known as Marxism-Leninism. This philosophy having obtained official status in the USSR and in Eastern Europe (not to mention China, where it has undergone a further process of barbarization and banalization), every discussion of the subject necessarily assumes an unwelcome quasi-political character. In what follows, these circumstances are disregarded as much as possible, and attention is centered upon the intellectual substance of the doctrine. The topical importance of what for convenience may be termed "Soviet Marxism," or "Marxism-Leninism," makes it necessary to direct the reader's attention to the existence of an indigenous literature on the subject; but it needs to be emphasized that this literature holds little interest for anyone concerned with the basic philosophical issues (Jordan, 1967).

Unlike Marx, who had undergone a rigorous academic training and possessed a comprehensive knowledge of both ancient and modern philosophy, Engels was self-taught in philosophic matters, a circumstance which weighed heavily upon his subsequent attempts to effect a synthesis of Hegelian logic and natural science. A man of great talent, enormous versatility, and inexhaustible capacity for work, he nonetheless lacked the intellectual power which enabled Marx to unify history, sociology, and economics into a coherent system of thought. At the same time, the example set by his senior associate, and his own profound attachment to the Hegelian tradition—of which in a sense he remained a lifelong prisoner—activated a dormant ambition which he shared with other German writers of his time: the desire to bring about a reconciliation between the "natural philosophy" of the romantic school and the positive sciences which had developed under the quite different impact of Cartesian and Hobbesian "mechanical materialism." The resultant synthesis—sketched in outline by Engels in his writings of the 1870's and 1880's, and eventually termed "dialectical materialism" by Plekhanov—became the philosophical foundation of what from the 1890's onwards was very generally described as "Marxism"; the term encompassing at one and the same time the

453

historical materialism of Marx (as interpreted by Engels), and the pseudo-ontological doctrine constructed by Engels from the debris of the Hegelian system.

While it has been noted that Marx's naturalistic approach from the start contained a "dialectical" element, in that it left room for the interaction of human consciousness and a nonhuman environment, the materialism of Engels could be described as "dialectical" for reasons much more closely connected with the enduring legacy of Hegel's system. Hegel had seen in nature and history the unfolding of a metaphysical substance which he termed "Spirit"; ultimately a theological conception, although Hegel for the most part stayed closer to Aristotelianism than to Neo-Platonism. For Marx there was no such universal principle of motion. What he inherited from Hegel was rather a species of holism which placed the idea of totality at the center of all theoretical conceptualizations. From this he deduced the methodological rule that the elements of a social structure could not be dissociated from each other: they had to be regarded as parts forming an organic, interconnected whole. While in principle there was no reason why this rule should not be extended to the domain of nature, Marx did not in fact attempt to outline a general logic applicable to nature and history alike. His doctrines relating to societal evolution were not deduced from a general principle, nor did he infer from his reading of Hegel's *Logic* (cf. *Wissenschaft der Logik*, 1812–16) that particular changes in society were traceable to the operation of a universal law of motion. Least of all was he concerned with the concept of an eternal material substance underlying the phenomena. "The anthropological realism of Marx precluded the adherence to absolute materialism of any sort, including dialectical materialism" (Jordan, p. 93).

In contrast to Marx, who had genuinely abandoned the Hegelian search for an all-embracing logic of (material or spiritual) development, Engels revived the notion that an objective process of this kind was actually discoverable. Moreover, he undertook to show that the dialectical principle—self-transcendence by way of internal conflict to higher levels of development—was operative in human history, conceived as a singularity within the domain of nature. The basic assumption of the dialectical method, on his reading, was that:

The world is not to be understood as a complex of ready-made *things*, but as a complex of *processes*, in which the things apparently stable, no less than their mental images in our heads (*Gedankenabbilder*), the concepts, go through an uninterrupted change of coming into being and passing away, in which despite all seeming accidentality and tem-

porary retrogression, a progressive development asserts itself in the end (*Ludwig Feuerbach*, in *Selected Works*, II, 351).

This speculative hypothesis in turn became the foundation of an evolutionary doctrine applicable to nature and history alike. In contrast to the prevailing positivist evolutionism which was popular among liberals because it specified an uninterrupted forward movement from "barbarism" to "civilization," Engels' quasi-Hegelian approach emphasized the self-contradictory nature of the process; dialectical motion implied progress through conflict between opposing forces. In its application to society this principle was invoked by Engels' followers to account both for the necessity of class conflict and for the inevitability of socialism as the resolution of one particular conflict between classes. This presentation of the subject was not understood as an imaginative metaphor—as such it might have had some limited usefulness—but as the "scientific" description of an ongoing process, one that possessed a logic quite indifferent to the subjective volition of its human representatives. As in Hegel's philosophy of history, the Idea (the hidden rationality of the Whole) triumphed at the expense of its own agents, who might include entire classes, nations, or generations. This reversion to Hegel's metaphysical construction of world history was dubbed "dialectical materialism" for no better reason than that Engels substituted "matter" for "spirit" as the ontological substance underlying the motion of the phenomena. In practice his approach represented an abandonment of Marx's revolutionary humanism and a return to the Hegelian standpoint.

While Engels' partiality to the romantic *Naturphilosophie* inaugurated by Schelling, Carus, and other German writers of Hegel's time had no practical consequences, his adoption of a determinist approach in the field of history opened the door to the subsequent introduction by Kautsky of an evolutionism virtually indistinguishable from that of Auguste Comte and Herbert Spencer. The irony lay in the circumstance that this mode of thought was positivist rather than speculative. But having once introduced a determinist monism in the name of "dialectical materialism," it proved comparatively easy to extrude the Hegelian element while retaining the determinism. This became the distinguishing mark of the Social-Democratic variant of "orthodox Marxism." In contrast to this evolutionism, which went with democratic optimism in politics, Lenin from about 1914 onwards systematically reintroduced the Hegelian emphasis upon conflict and contradiction as the motivating force. Before that date he had been content to expand Engels' hints into a "materialist" philosophy of science which was not particularly "dialectical," but rather concerned to defend the "objective" reality of the external world against the "subjectivism" of Kant and his followers (Jordan, pp. 208ff.).

In purely philosophical terms, the difference between Engels' ontological, or metaphysical, materialism, and the doctrine of Plekhanov and Lenin is not without interest. Plekhanov, and following him Lenin, eliminated from the concept of "dialectical materialism" the ontological notion of "matter" as an absolute substance or constituent element of the universe. In its place they introduced the rather more common sensible use of "matter" as a logical concept signifying little more than the externality of the world for the reflective consciousness. In other words, they substituted for Engels' metaphysical monism an ordinary epistemological realism which at least had the advantage of being compatible with the procedure of the natural sciences. The *locus classicus* of this transformation (which was never described as such) is Lenin's *Materialism and Empirio-Criticism* (1909), a work which after 1917 obtained canonical status in the USSR and for the Marxist-Leninist school generally. Unfortunately, the philosophers of this school have simultaneously had to cope with Engels' own quite different (because fundamentally metaphysical) understanding of the term "materialism," as well as with Lenin's quasi-Hegelian logical speculations in his *Notebooks* of 1915–16. The resulting conflicts and contradictions have furnished material for exhaustive logical tournaments among philosophers in Eastern Europe, without for that reason bringing any nearer that fusion of dialectical logic with positive science which remains the stated aim of the Marxist-Leninist school. Insofar as the gradual change in the intellectual atmosphere since the late 1950's has encouraged greater independence of thought in the Soviet sphere, there has been a tendency for two "revisionist" trends to crystallize outside the official orthodoxy: existentialist humanism, oriented on the writings of the young Marx, on the one hand, positivist scientism and empiricism on the other. In countering these trends, the official dogmatism of the Leninist school, while retaining its function as an integrative ideology or *Weltanschauung* for the benefit of the Communist party, appears to have been placed on the defensive; a position from which it is unlikely to emerge.

BIBLIOGRAPHY

K. Marx, and F. Engels, *The Holy Family* (Moscow, 1956), pp. 168–76. For the original text see *Die Heilige Familie* (1845) in Marx-Engels *Werke*, (Berlin, 1959), 2, 132ff. T. B. Bottomore and M. Rubel, *Karl Marx—Selected Writings in Sociology and Social Philosophy* (London, 1956; New York, 1964), gives a selection of relevant passages on various aspects of historical materialism. Although conventionally attributed to both Marx and Engels, *The Holy Family* was almost entirely composed by Marx, and the remarks cited in the text represent a "materialist" and post-Hegelian view on the subject of French naturalism as the ultimate source of "socialism and communism": the latter term carrying more specific implications concerning the abolition of private property. See also *Karl Marx—Early Writings*, trans. and ed. T. B. Bottomore, with a foreword by E. Fromm (New York, 1964), passim. The rather overworked theme of Marx's views on human "alienation" is best approached by consulting the *Economic & Philosophic Manuscripts of 1844* in the edition prepared and introduced by Dirk J. Struik (New York, 1964) on the basis of Martin Milligan's translation from the German text, as first published in Marx-Engels, *Gesamtausgabe* (hereafter MEGA), Abt. I, Band 3 (Berlin, 1932). An excellent analytical and critical introduction to the topic of historical materialism in general, and Marxian sociology in particular, is to be found in Karl Korsch, *Karl Marx* (New York, 1963), passim.

Marx, *Theses on Feuerbach* (1845), posthumously published by Engels as an Appendix to his own *Ludwig Feuerbach* (1888), now in *Werke*, Vol. 21 (Berlin, 1962), 263ff. (without the Appendix); see MEGA, I, 5, 533ff., for the original German text of the *Theses*. For an English-language edition of Engels' essay and of the *Theses*, see Marx-Engels *Selected Works* (Moscow, 1951), II, 324ff. For Marx's critique of Feuerbachian materialism see *The German Ideology*, in MEGA, I, 5, and the various translations. See also Marx's letter to Engels of 24 April 1867 (MEGA, III, 3, 383), where he observes that "the cult of Feuerbach" notable in the *Holy Family* now seems rather out of date. It is fair to say that Feuerbach's critique of religion was of greater importance for Engels than for Marx, who took his materialism straight from the British and French philosophers of the eighteenth century. On this subject see Korsch, op. cit., pp. 172ff.; Sidney Hook, *From Hegel to Marx* (New York, 1950), pp. 220ff.

Marx, Preface to *A Contribution to the Critique of Political Economy* (Berlin, 1859); see Marx-Engels, *Selected Works* (Moscow, 1958), 1, 361ff. The subject is discussed from a Marxist standpoint in Korsch, op. cit., pp. 183ff., and from a positivist one in Z. A. Jordan, *The Evolution of Dialectical Materialism* (London and New York, 1967), pp. 111ff. It is undisputed that in the 1840's Marx received his decisive intellectual stimulus towards what was later called the materialist conception of history from Henri de Saint-Simon and his pupils. The latter had once included A. Comte, whose *Cours de philosophie positive* (1830–42) was then unknown to Marx and made no impression on him when he finally read it, many years later, in Littré's edition of 1864. Jordan (op. cit., pp. 125ff.) suggests that the Comtean notion of social physics has its counterpart in the Marxian approach, and that for Marx—as for Comte—"society is the true reality, and the individual the abstraction" (p. 132). The present writer is unable to accept these conclusions. Neither does it seem to him that the 1859 *Preface* constitutes a retreat from the sociological realism of Marx's earlier writings in favor of a neo-Hegelian philosophy of history (Jordan, op. cit., p. 299).

F. Engels, *Anti-Dühring. Herr Eugen Dühring's Revolution in Science* (Moscow, 1954), p. 369. For the original German text see *Werke* (Berlin, 1962), 20, 248ff. For an account of what Marx intended by his "materialist" method of investigation see Korsch, op. cit., pp. 167ff.; Bottomore, *Karl Marx—Selected Writings . . .* , op cit., pp. 14ff. For an extensive specimen of Marx's actual historical investigations, see *Karl Marx: Pre-Capitalist Economic Formations*, trans. Jack Cohen, edited and introduced by E. J. Hobsbawm (London, 1964). This presents a brief extract from the bulky manuscript composed by Marx in 1857–58 in preparation for *Capital* (1867–94). While part of this material was used by him for his *Critique of Political Economy* (1859), and some minor excerpts appeared in Kautsky's *Neue Zeit* in 1903–04), the entire manuscript saw the light only in 1939–41, when it was published in Moscow under the title *Grundrisse der Kritik der Politischen Ökonomie*. Virtually ignored at the time, it was republished in its entirety in Berlin in 1953 (in a volume running to over 1,000 printed pages) and translated into Italian in 1956. Its importance for the concept of historical materialism lies in the fact that in it Marx, for the first and last time, dealt at some length with the structure of non-European societies. He thus supplied a basis for some of the startling generalizations of the 1859 *Preface*. Antedating *Capital* by a few years, the *Grundrisse* already belong to his mature period, and their study is essential for an understanding of his peculiar fusion of history, sociology, and economics. They also cast some light on the concept of the "Asiatic mode of production" briefly adumbrated in the 1859 *Preface*, and subsequently ignored in Soviet literature for reasons apparent to anyone conversant with the circumstances of the Stalinist era. For a dispassionate critique of the Marxian approach from an empiricist standpoint, strongly marked by the influence of Max Weber, see J. A. Schumpeter, *Capitalism, Socialism, and Democracy* (New York, 1942), passim. This work, however, antedates the publication of the *Grundrisse* in an edition available to Westerners, and thus does not entirely come to grips with the problems raised by Marx's investigations.

Z. A. Jordan, *The Evolution of Dialectical Materialism: A Philosophical and Sociological Analysis* (London, 1967) is the best introduction to this subject. Starting from the now generally accepted distinction between the original approach of Engels and that of Marx, the author traces in considerable detail the exfoliation of Engels' unsystematic essays into the fully developed system of "dialectical materialism" first outlined by G. V. Plekhanov and subsequently codified by Lenin and his successors, down to and including Stalin. Gustav A. Wetter, *Dialectical Materialism: A Historical And Systematic Survey of Philosophy in the Soviet Union* (London, 1958), offers an equally learned, but differently organized, account of the topic, the author giving little space to Marx and Engels, while centering attention upon the evolution of Soviet philosophy since 1917. Unlike Jordan, he deals at some length with Bukharin, Deborin, and some lesser figures. For a critique of Engels' philo-

sophical writings see Sidney Hook, "Dialectic and Nature," in his *Reason, Social Myths and Democracy* (New York, 1950), pp. 183ff. For the impact of Leninism on the philosophical and scientific discussions in the USSR before the full rigor mortis of Stalinism set in, see David Joravsky, *Soviet Marxism and Natural Science 1917–32* (London, 1961). For a more recent and less technical discussion of Marxism-Leninism as a pseudo-ontological system of speculation about nature and history see A. James Gregor, *A Survey of Marxism* (New York, 1965). The brief reading list appended to this work provides a guide to official Soviet literature on the subject, as well as to works by Western authors and a few "revisionist" critics of Leninism who have retained the Hegelian-Marxist approach antedating the formulation of Soviet orthodoxy in the 1930's. For a brief but pregnant discussion of this latter theme, see Eugene Kamenka, "Philosophy in the Soviet Union," *Philosophy* (Journal of the Royal Institute of Philosophy), **38**, No. 143 (Jan., 1963).

GEORGE LICHTHEIM

[See also Determinism; Economic History; Enlightenment; Evolutionism; **Ideology; Marxism;** Positivism; **Revolution;** Romanticism, Post-Kantian; **Social Democracy.**]

HISTORICISM

"Historicism" as a Term. It is difficult to give a concise meaning to the term "historicism" (German, *Historismus*). Meinecke, Heussi, and Antoni in their studies of historicism assumed that the term originated in the late nineteenth century and became well known only in the twentieth century in connection with the "crisis of historicism," the deep uncertainty regarding the value of Western historical traditions and the possibility of objective historical knowledge. In fact the term is considerably older and was well established in Germany by the middle of the nineteenth century. Until 1918, the term often, but not always, had a negative meaning. Friedrich Schlegel in 1797 speaks of historicism as a "kind of philosophy" which places the main stress on history. Beginning in the 1830's, Ludwig Feuerbach uses the term extensively in a critical sense, coupled with "empiricism" and "positivism," to denote historical relativism and the uncritical acceptance of the world as it presents itself. In a neutral sense, Braniss in 1848 sharply distinguishes between "naturism" which seeks to understand all phenomena, including historical ones, in terms of nature and "historicism" which seeks to comprehend all reality, including natural reality, historically. Historicism, he suggests, rejects the idea of static "Being" as the essence of reality and views "Being" itself as resting

upon action (*That, Act*). Carl Prantl in 1852 speaks of a "true historicism" which recognizes individuality in its "concrete temporal-spatiality" (*concrete Zeitlich-Räumlichkeit*) and differs both from a shallow empiricism or realism for which nothing exists except "tangible concreteness" and from a system-building idealism in the Hegelian manner which ignores "factuality." By the middle of the nineteenth century, historicism is identified with the methodological approach of the Historical School of law (Savigny, Eichhorn) and of economics. I. H. Fichte, the son of the philosopher, in 1850 criticizes the Historical School of law for its exclusive concern with Roman and Germanic law and calls for a "true historicism" which through a "comparative history of law according to ethnographic and world historical standards" would investigate how "the practical ideas which operate everywhere in human consciousness" find their expression "in every people, but according to its spiritual individuality and its external conditions of life." Historicism in the bad sense is identified with the abandonment of theory, particularly in economics and law. Thus Eugen Dühring in 1866 accuses the Historical School of economics of a purely "descriptive" and "false historicism" having a different logic for every age; it therefore in the end seems to want to have no logic and "renounces convictions and principles." Carl Menger in 1884 attacks Gustav Schmoller, the most important economist of the Historical School, in a polemical work, *Die Irrtümer des Historismus in der deutschen Nationalökonomie* (1884; "The Errors of Historicism in German Political Economy"), and Adolf Wagner subsequently identifies these errors as the confusion of economic theory with economic history (cf. Heussi, 1932).

With the approaching World War I, the emphasis shifts. Ernst Troeltsch in 1913 (*Aufsätze . . .* , p. 628), sees in "historicism" the dominant attitude of the nineteenth and the twentieth centuries. The core of historicism consists in the recognition that all human ideas and ideals are subject to change. This attitude, Karl Mannheim suggests about ten years later, has led to the rejection of the stable, transcendent norms to which medieval Christianity had clung and which in a secularized form the rationalist philosophers of the Enlightenment had maintained. Historicism is now identified with cultural relativism. In the course of the nineteenth century, Troeltsch observes, historical scholarship showed how all institutions and ideas were historically related and thus destroyed all points of reference. Nevertheless, for Troeltsch, historicism constituted a tremendous advance in man's understanding of himself. There was no escape from man's historical character. The task to which Troeltsch now devoted himself, after the war, in his massive, uncompleted

work *Der Historismus und seine Probleme,* was to find new norms for a modern world through the study of history. In his *Die Enstehung des Historismus* ("The Origins of Historicism") Friedrich Meinecke now hailed historicism as the "highest attained stage in the understanding of things human" (*Entstehung . . .* , p. 4) and the most important intellectual development in Europe since the Reformation. He saw the core of historicism in the replacement of a "generalizing" by an "individualizing" approach. Through its focus on individuality and on development, historicism had liberated modern man from the rigid unhistorical naturalistic conception of man and of ethics which had dominated Western thought since Roman antiquity, and which, Meinecke maintained, still dominated Western European thought and practice. Although Meinecke saw the beginnings of an historicist attitude in the renewed general interest in history in eighteenth-century Europe, he saw the fulfillment of historicism in Germany in Goethe and Ranke, and identified historicism with the classical tradition of German historical thought. Meinecke's book thus became a reaffirmation of his faith in the superiority of the German intellectual and cultural heritage over the Western European heritage at a time when his confidence in Germany's political development had already been deeply shaken.

Outside of Germany, the term had little of an indigenous history. In Italy, Benedetto Croce used the term *istorismo* in 1902 in his *Estetica* to contrast an historical against a rationalistic or formal approach to art. He later identified historicism (*istorismo*) with the German tradition of historical thought (cf. Antoni, *Storicismo,* 1969) and coined a variation of the term (*storicismo*) to describe his own philosophic position, which we shall briefly discuss later. In the English-speaking countries, the terms "historism" and "historicism" began to be used after 1900, the former to describe German thought, the latter as a translation of Croce's use of *istorismo* and *storicismo.* By the 1940's, the term "historicism" had replaced "historism" almost entirely. Karl Popper gave the term "historicism" a meaning, which has not been generally accepted, as a theory of historical predictability and determinism in contrast with the usual meaning of the term which denotes the opposite, individuality, spontaneity, and the avoidance of generalizations. But when Popper wrote the manuscript of *The Poverty of Historicism,* the term "historism" was still often used to denote the German tradition and Popper explicitly distinguished his use of the term "historicism" from the conventional use of "historism."

Particularly in Germany, but also elsewhere, historicism has come to be understood essentially in the sense in which Troeltsch and Meinecke understood it as an outlook on the world (*Weltanschauung*) which recognizes the historical character of all human existence but views history not as an integrated system but as a scene in which a diversity of human wills express themselves. Historicism has come to be understood not only as an idea but also as an intellectual and scholarly movement which dominated historical, social, and humanistic studies in nineteenth-century Germany, and which recognized that "the special quality of history does not consist in the statement of general laws or principles," but in the grasp, so far as possible, of the "infinite variety of particular historical forms immersed in the passage of time" (Meyerhoff, 1959). The term as used by Meinecke, Troeltsch, Antoni, and others denoted a scholarly and intellectual movement many of whose exponents in the eighteenth and nineteenth centuries, e.g., Vico, Herder, Ranke, Savigny, Droysen, never used the term to describe their own outlook although it was applied to them in the nineteenth century by some of their critics. As a scholarly movement, historicism rejected positivistic attempts to explain social behavior by theoretical models applicable to various societies; as a movement of political thought it rejected not only natural law theory but any attempt to formulate norms of political behavior or rights of men.

The Development of Historicism as an Intellectual Movement. Historicism as an intellectual movement arose in the eighteenth century in a concrete institutional and intellectual setting. A prerequisite of historicism as described above is a sense of history, an awareness that the past is fundamentally different from the present. This awareness seems to have been absent in medieval and in non-Western culture, even in ancient China which possesses a long tradition of historical writing, and to have existed only in a very limited sense in classical antiquity (Burke, 1969). A sense of history is, however, not quite identical with an historicist attitude. A new critical approach to historical evidence began to emerge during the Renaissance. The seventeenth and eighteenth centuries, which were considered "unhistorical" by their romantic critics, had in fact already become periods of intense historical interest and scholarship. But neither the antiquarian interest of the seventeenth-century erudites nor the philosophic concerns of the great eighteenth-century historians, such as Montesquieu, Voltaire, Gibbon, Schlözer, were historicist. The former, such as Jean Mabillon, were most concerned with establishing the authenticity of texts, the latter with asking questions of history which sought to establish typical or recurrent normal human phenomena in diverse human societies. Historicism was concerned with the comprehension of

the past in its uniqueness and rejected the attempts by the philosophic historians to measure the past by the norms of the Enlightenment.

The nineteenth century saw a remarkable development of critical historical study in France, Great Britain, and elsewhere. The study of politics became an historical discipline in Western Europe as well as in Germany. Not only Edmund Burke, in his critique of the French Revolution, but also other, explicitly liberal and democratic, thinkers increasingly based their arguments on history rather than on abstract conceptions of political justice. Yet for historians such as Guizot, Macaulay, or Michelet the historical development of their own country embodied values of general human concern. They thus maintained the Enlightenment belief that institutions must be judged by standards of a common human rationality although they believed that these norms must be apprehended through historical study. The more narrow historicism which predominated in Germany stressed that every institution and idea was an inseparable part of a specific, integrated national culture and was therefore incapable of being transplanted. This form of historicism reflected circumstances of which some were unique to Germany, such as the political division of the country, the uneven and belated development of modern economic institutions after the sixteenth century, and, as Troeltsch suggested (in his *Social Teachings*, 1931), the unique intellectual and religious heritage of Lutheran Germany with its stress on individual culture (*Bildung*) and its de-emphasis of political liberty. While not in itself a political ideology, historicism from the beginning had implications for politics. Historicist arguments were used in the eighteenth century to defend local institutions against the encroachment of the modern, centralized bureaucratic state, and used in the nineteenth century against the extension of Western European models of parliamentary government and democracy to Germany. During World War I, Troeltsch and others saw in the historicist outlook the roots of the basic distinction between the German and the Western European conceptions of freedom (*Deutscher Geist und Westeuropa*).

Two early formulations of historicist ideas were contained in Giambattista Vico's *Scienza nuova* (1725) and Johann Gottfried Herder's *Auch eine Philosophie der Geschichte* ("Also a Philosophy of History," 1774). Vico suggested that the history of man was to be distinguished from the history of nature by the fact that man makes his history but does not make nature, and that the study of history dealing with human volitions and actions thus requires different methods from those of the study of nature concerned with the insensible motion of bodies. But Vico was relatively little known or understood outside of Italy until Michelet translated the *Scienza nuova* into French in 1827. Herder in his philosophy of history presented the first extensive formulation of historicist principles, and rejected the Enlightenment conception of a uni-linear development of human civilization. Mankind was indeed one but, he maintained, this mankind can only be understood in its historical manifestations in diverse national cultures. Religion, philosophy, science, and art thus do not exist in any absolute sense; there are only the religions, philosophies, sciences, and arts of specific cultures at specific stages in their develop-ment. All cultures, Herder held, European and non-European, primitive and civilized are thus equally worthy of study, in a sense the primitive more so insofar as they are closer to the original genius of a people. Any attempts to use abstract tools of analysis to understand national cultures were mechanistic and unhistorical. History as life can only be grasped through empathy (*Mitfühlen*).

The first two significant historical works which reflect an historicist spirit are probably Justus Möser's *History of Osnabrück* (1768) and Johann Joachim Winkelmann's *History of the Art of Antiquity* (1764).

Möser sought to study the "liberties" or privileges of the Osnabrück patriciate as interwoven with the peculiar history of Osnabrück within the peculiar his-tory of the Holy Roman Empire. Winckelmann, while sharing the Renaissance reverence for Greek art as the most sublime aesthetic expression attained by man and hence a part of the common heritage of man, never-theless recognized that the art of the Greeks was inimitable because it was interwoven with a total cul-ture which occupied a unique point in history and was incapable of being recreated. For him the spirit of Greek culture could be understood only by immersion into the primary evidence, in this case the remnants of Greek works of art, which reflected this spirit.

Winckelmann's approach foreshadowed the critical philological method which emerged among German classicists and Biblicists in the late eighteenth century and which laid the foundation for the critical historical method of nineteenth-century historical scholarship (Niebuhr, Ranke). This method has often been confused with the critical examination of evidence. The criteria for such examination had already been systematically formulated by Jean Mabillon in 1681 in his *De re diplomatica*. For F. A. Wolf, in his *Prolegomena to Homer* (1795), scholarship did not end with the critical analysis of documents but proceeded to view these documents in their historical context. Greek philology for him concerned itself with the totality of Greek life as reflected in the remnants of the Greek past, particu-larly its literature. Immersed in his evidence, the

scholar then by inference and intuition had to proceed to the comprehension of the spirit of the culture in which the evidence originated. The documents thus had a very different meaning for Niebuhr and Ranke and the scholarship which followed them than for Mabillon or the erudites. The critical use of the docu-ments required more than the establishment of a cor-rect and authentic text, although the latter was the prerequisite of all scholarship. To be understood the documents had to be examined within the historical and cultural framework of the age and nation of which they formed a part.

In the early nineteenth century almost all social and humanistic studies in Germany were placed on histori-cist foundations. Historical study replaced systematic analysis. The Historical School of law (Savigny, Eich-horn) opposed any codification of the law and held that law is an expression of the spirit of a people, develops with it, and that jurisprudence is therefore not con-cerned with the formulation or critique of law on rational foundations but with the study of the positive law of concrete historical societies. The new science of linguistics (Bopp, Lachmann, the Grimms) neglected structural considerations for studies of the evolution of specific languages and language families within specific national cultures. The new Historical School of economics (Roscher, Knies, Schmoller) rejected the conception of classical political economy that abstract, quantifiable laws govern the economy, and viewed economic behavior as deeply influenced by non-economic considerations, including political ones, which reflect the ethos of a people. All these disciplines thus replaced a theoretical approach by a preeminently descriptive one.

The theoretical foundations upon which the new methodologies rested were well formulated by Leopold von Ranke (1795–1886). Ranke insisted on a history based on a rigorous examination of primary evidence. Yet his prescription that the historian not judge the past but merely describe it *wie es eigentlich gewesen* has often been misunderstood as an exhortation to factualism. The term *eigentlich* as understood by Ranke should not be translated as "actually," as it often has been, but as "really," "properly," or "essentially," so that it becomes the task of the historian not merely to narrate the events of the past as they occurred but to go beyond these events to the reconstruction of the past "as it essentially was." Far from calling on the historian to restrict himself to the bare factual account, Ranke called upon him "to rise . . . from the investi-gation and contemplation of the particular to a general view of events and to the recognition of their objec-tively existing relatedness" (Ranke, p. 23). In the last analysis, all history was therefore to be world history. **459**

For Ranke, history alone, not abstract philosophy, could provide a guide to the ultimate questions of human concern. Ranke's optimism regarding the philosophic function of history rested on certain metaphysical assumptions which Wilhelm von Humboldt had already formulated in the famous essay "On The Historian's Task" (1821), asserting that "every human individuality is an idea rooted in actuality" (p. 21). For Humboldt, as for Ranke, nations and states possessed the characteristics of individuality, and to an even higher degree than persons. The study of the particular thus made it possible for the historian to attain the general. The task of the historian, Humboldt had written in words similar to those used four years later by Ranke, is "to present what actually happened." But, he continued, "an event is only partially visible in the world of the senses; the rest has to be added by intuition, inference, and guesswork" (p. 5). Ranke similarly maintained that "history can never have the unity of a philosophical system" but is not "without inner connection"; still this connection—Ranke spoke of "tendencies" in history and the "leading ideas" of an age—"cannot be defined or put in abstract terms but one can behold them and observe them" (Ranke, pp. 57, 55, 100). Thus despite Ranke's rejection of factualism he restricted critical scholarly study to the establishment of concrete reality. The understanding of social movements as well as of social norms was thus left to intuition and inference governed by no logic of inquiry. To the detached observer, the forces at work in history would reveal themselves. No theory was necessary. Theory indeed distorted. What was needed was total immersion in the facts.

Ranke and much of German scholarship in the historicist tradition drew certain consequences for politics and ethics from the above assumptions. Ranke was undoubtedly right in seeing the state itself as a product of historical forces, and not (as had the rationalists) as an unhistorical mechanism standing apart from the popular culture. But this did not justify Ranke's assertion that states were integrated personalities towering above the conflicting interests of society. Such a conception of the state in fact separated the state from the total historical development. It viewed the primary activity of the state as the extension of its power. In practice it led to a narrowing of historical perspective from the broad cultural and comparative concern of the philosophic historians of the eighteenth century to a narrow emphasis on national history and international relations. History became a narrative centering largely on the acts of a small number of statesmen as reconstructed from official documents. Such a history was necessarily a truncated one. That the recognition that each age must be viewed through its own values could be reconciled with a broader cultural approach was demonstrated by Ranke's Swiss disciple, Jakob Burckhardt. Burckhardt escaped an event-oriented, narrative approach and sought to reconstruct the spirit and the structure of an age. But the scope of his cultural history was also focused on an aristocratic elite and separated the culture of this elite from the broader social framework within which it existed.

The Rankean school prided itself on its objectivity. Ranke rightly insisted that the historian not project his own value conceptions into his historical subjects but seek to understand his subjects as they understood themselves. But he uncritically assumed that the persons and institutions found in history represented positive values. Ranke demanded impartiality on the part of the historian because he firmly believed that "moral energies" or "spiritual substances" manifested themselves in history to the detached observer. All states, he maintained, represented "thoughts of God" (Ranke, pp. 117, 119). At this point the profound difference between the historicism of Ranke, including the Historical School, and that of Hegel becomes apparent. The core of Hegel's philosophy was that all existence as well as logic itself was immersed in historical change but that history itself was a rational process. For Hegel, as for Ranke, the state was an expression of spirituality; but for Hegel the spirituality of the state rested on its rational structure and the course of history itself was the test of its rationality. For Ranke the test of its spirituality and the justification of its power-political striving was its uniqueness which defied all rational inquiry or judgment. As the young Marx, steeped in Hegel, suggested in 1842, the Historical School of law in holding with Ranke that historical institutions, no matter how oppressive must be accepted uncritically as they manifest themselves in history, in fact, sought to prove that "what is positive is not rational," that "the pimple is as positive as the skin" (*Writings of the Young Marx*, pp. 98, 99). Ranke uncritically assumed that all power rests on spiritual foundations, that the state in extending its military power strengthens the foundations of freedom and culture. Nevertheless, such a view introduced metaphysical assumptions as well as an ideological bias into historical writing. It subordinated all considerations of domestic policy and social concern to the strivings of the established political order to maintain its power.

Within Germany, the historicist outlook was firmly established in the social and cultural sciences until the late nineteenth century. As scholarship became increasingly professionalized and university-centered also outside of Germany, historicist assumptions and methods entered scholarly practice there too. In practice the broad historical perspective of Herder gave way in the course of the nineteenth century to a parochial, nationalistic, and event-oriented history, leading often to pedantic factualism and narrow specialization. The "crisis of historicism" came in two stages: first, before World War I as a result of the decline of idealistic assumptions upon which this scholarship rested and the inability of this scholarship to deal adequately with the complex processes of a technological, mass society; but, secondly, only after World War I in the face of the German national defeat. For historicism despite its explicit rejection of the idea of progress had been deeply optimistic about the course of history. The deep currents of pessimism in European philosophy and literature at the turn of the century found few echoes in historicist scholarship. Classical historicism had, however, assumed the soundness of the social, economic, and political order of pre-1914 Germany. The political, social, and cultural dislocations which followed Germany's defeat in World War I thus dramatically intensified the "crisis of historicism."

The extensive Neo-Kantian philosophic discussion of the nature of historical knowledge (Wilhelm Dilthey, Wilhelm Windelband, Heinrich Rickert) before World War I has too often been misunderstood outside of Germany as an expression of the "crisis of historicism" and disillusionment with German historical traditions. This was not the case. In part, this literature was directed at the attempts of Karl Lamprecht to introduce generalizations and social analysis into historical writing. It represented for the most part a reiteration of the faith—expressed by Ranke, J. G. Droysen, and others earlier in the century—in the autonomy of historical knowledge and, in Dilthey's case, an attempt to develop further a logic of historical inquiry in the sense of classical historicism. The vehemence with which German historians, including Meinecke, combatted Lamprecht was related to the fact that they believed they saw in Lamprecht's work not only a challenge to German idealistic notions but also a threat to German political traditions.

Yet only after World War I did the recognition of the historicity of all human life and thought lead to a radical skepticism regarding the possibility of objective historical knowledge and the meaning of the historical process. Troeltsch had in 1902 recognized that once the theological presuppositions of historicism were abandoned the idea of a unified human history would become untenable. The logical conclusion, which Troeltsch recognized but was unwilling to accept, was that there is no history but only histories and that we can only know the history of our culture. Moreover, whatever is historical is also relative, for historical and relative are identical (Troeltsch [1902], pp. 48–49). Hence Christianity loses its claim to be

the absolute religion and Western Civilization its claim to being the one civilization. This thesis was, of course, close to anticipating Oswald Spengler's position in the *Decline of the West* (1918). Carried even further the recognition of the historicity of all knowledge led to the recognition that there is no objective historical cognition but that all historical knowledge is relative to the standpoint of the historian. The crisis of historicism, as understood by Troeltsch in *Der Historismus und seine Probleme* (1922), derived from the fact that in the course of the nineteenth century all ideas and ideals had come to be viewed in their historical setting with the result that all stable norms had been destroyed. History, Troeltsch reiterated, leads to relativism. For a host of German thinkers of the 1920's, the study of history also reveals the absurdity of history and the irrationality of the traditional humanistic values of the West.

Nevertheless within the academic intellectual community in Germany and in Italy the attempt was made to overcome the dilemmas of historicism within the framework of an historicist outlook and thus to save not only the idealistic heritage of the nineteenth century but also the political and social values of the German and Italian educated bourgeoisie which had been a part of this heritage. Convinced that the problems of historicism could be overcome only through the study of history, Troeltsch argued that a critical selection of the ideas and values of Western Civilization could yet create a cultural synthesis meaningful to modern man.

Meinecke, who earlier, in *Weltbürgertum und Nationalstaat* ("Cosmopolitanism and the National State," 1908), had maintained that political values were also to be found in history and that German political development in the nineteenth century represented the highest symbiosis of culture and power, now after World War I recognized the irrationality of power. But if historicist concepts were no longer applicable to political history, they were relevant to intellectual and cultural history, the realms which ultimately mattered. In its highest formulations, in Goethe and Ranke, historicism succeeded in overcoming historical relativism, in discovering the elements of transcendent truth contained in "historical life in its temporal, individual form" (Meinecke, p. 221).

Benedetto Croce's "absolute historicism" represented a third attempt to overcome historical relativity through history. More radically than Troeltsch or Meinecke, Croce stressed that all "history is contemporary history" reflecting the interests and perspectives of the present. In the final analysis "history is principally an act of thought" (Croce [1921], p. 19). In a very similar manner Collingwood argued that written history is the reenactment of past thought in the mind of the historian (Collingwood, p. 282). What preserved Croce, as it did Collingwood who proceeded along similar lines, from the radical subjectivism implicit in the German historicist concept of *Verstehen* was the belief that thought itself had a rational structure and that "historicism is a logical principle" (Croce [1955], p. 74). Yet in identifying history with thought, Croce and Collingwood assumed that history consisted of the conscious acts of men. Such a history was unable to take into account those factors, subconscious or collective, which did not enter directly into the awareness of the agents of history. Croce then, in fact, wrote history which in the idealistic manner of classical historicism understood politics largely as a function of ideas abstracted from their broader social context.

The Decline of Historicist Attitudes. The impact of historicism on contemporary thought was lessened considerably in recent decades, particularly since the end of World War II. In a sense the modern outlook continues to be historicist, if by historicism is meant merely the recognition that all human ideals and institutions are subject to historical change. But the implications which classical historicism drew for scholarly method as well as for ethics and politics have been questioned by many contemporary scholars. This has occurred as the intellectual, social, and political conditions of the pre-industrial, pre-democratic, and in many ways still Christian setting within which classical historicism arose gave way to a complex, technological society in which politics was much more broadly based and the relative importance of the European nation state on the world scene had declined.

We have mentioned, above, the skepticism regarding the possibility of objective historical knowledge which followed the collapse of the idealistic presuppositions of classical historicism. This skepticism led in two directions. Theodor Lessing immediately after World War I asserted that history has no objective meaning and that all historical writing is myth-building. Similarly Carl Becker, Charles Beard, and Karl Popper held that since subjectivistic and perspectivistic factors always enter into historical knowledge no science of history is possible. But the main currents of historiographical thought went in other directions. Historians sought new methods which took into account that the historian is not a detached passive observer but an active investigator, that historical inquiry like other forms of scientific inquiry requires hypotheses and generalizations, in short, that history is inseparable from theory.

Nevertheless there have been few attempts to construct an historical science seeking historical laws such as historians in the nineteenth century, e.g., Henry Thomas Buckle, had proposed. But historians and cultural scientists very often have concerns different from those of their predecessors. Scholarship has become much more concerned with the study of complex social processes, not merely with comprehending unique processes but with explaining typical recurrences and defining trends of development. The questions asked by philosophic historians in the eighteenth century have thus become relevant again. The attempt has, however, been made to devise methods by which these questions can be approached empirically and analytically. The positivistic tradition has reasserted itself in political science and economics—particularly outside of Germany—which have moved increasingly in the direction of the quantitative behavioral sciences. But within disciplines less oriented by behavioral science, and also in linguistics, literary and aesthetic criticism, and law, once dominated by an historicist approach, there has been a growing movement away from a descriptive to an analytic, structural approach.

In historical writing, methods and concepts derived from Max Weber, Karl Marx, the French *Annales* circle, and the American social sciences have had an increasing influence. Weber, Marx, and to a lesser extent *Annales* historians (Bloch, Febvre, Braudel) all had roots in German historicism and in basic ways they both preserved and modified historicist concerns. Max Weber was closest to the historicist tradition in his insistence that "knowledge of cultural processes is inconceivable except on the basis of the meaning which the reality of life, which always takes on individualized forms, has for us in specific, individual relationships" ("Objectivity," p. 80). But he also stressed that knowledge requires concepts and that human behavior is not unpredictable in the sense in which Ranke and the Historical School had held it to be. The task of the social scientist for Weber is to formulate concepts specifically suited to the meaning and value-laden phenomena with which the social sciences deal, to work out the patterns of behavior and development which follow ideally from the central value and thought structures of the social unit, and then to study empirically the approximation of the historical phenomena to the theoretically constructed types. It was thus possible to combine the historicist search for the comprehension of the "uniquely individual character of cultural phenomena" (ibid., p. 101) with rigorous methods of social inquiry.

In a sense Marx had undertaken something very similar in Volume I of *Capital*. Moreover, Marx and Weber had each provided in their work important methodological suggestions for the application of historical methods to comparative intersocietal and intercultural studies of social and civilizational development. The Marxism which has been an influence on contemporary historical scholarship has often been relatively free from the mechanistic, unilinear views of history attributed to Marx after his death. Modern interpreters of Marx—Gramsci, Lukács, Korsch, and the Frankfurt School—have pointed out that Marx almost consistently rejected natural law models. Throughout the body of Volume I of *Capital*—although perhaps not in the prefaces—Marx insists that social phenomena, even the apparently biological ones such as population trends (cf. Marx [1967], I, 632), cannot be explained in terms of abstract laws but must be studied historically. The differences with classical historicism are, of course, clear in Marx's insistence that theory is inseparable from practice and that the task of the scholar does not consist so much in contemplating the world as in analyzing its social contradictions and changing it.

Finally the structuralism of the French *Annales* circle needs to be mentioned as a serious attempt to combine important elements of the positivistic and historicist traditions. For the *Annales* group, history was concerned not only with the narrative recreation of unique chains of events but even more so with the analysis and comprehension of long enduring historical structures. More radically than either Weber or the Marxists, the *Annales* historians sought to broaden the concern of the historian to all aspects of human life, including the material and biological aspects in their cultural context, and to study comparatively all societies and cultures, primitive as well as civilized, European as well as non-Western. History was once more to become the key to all knowledge, but a history which in integrating the methods of all the sciences dealing with man—physiology, cultural anthropology, depth psychology, linguistics as well as economics and sociology—sought to create the foundation of a new historical "science of man."

The historicist stress on the neutrality of values has, however, survived relatively intact, and has been shared by many scholars close to the classical positivist tradition as well. On the other hand, the idealistic assumptions upon which the precept of value neutrality had rested in classical historicism were seriously shattered by Max Weber. Weber agreed that all cultural phenomena are value-laden and that any study of society involves the comprehension of its value outlook. But he rejected the historicist notion that the values of historical societies represent unique expressions of divine will or historical logic. In any ultimate sense all values are irrational and history appears as the perennial conflict between irreconcilable systems of value (Weber [1946], p. 147). The rationality of value systems can be judged only in a purely instrumental

sense, by their efficacy as means toward ends, and logically by their inner consistency. Weber thus intensified the positivism about values which is inherent in the historicist position. This positivism of values has been challenged in recent years, most notably by the Frankfurt School—H. Marcuse, Max Horkheimer, T. Adorno, J. Habermas—who have emphasized the elements of historicism in Marx's thought, a historicism rooted, however, in Hegelian philosophy which rejects the value neutrality of both classical historicism and classical positivism. The Frankfurt group have called for a "critical theory" which does not content itself with observing the world as it appears empirically but, in the manner of the Marx of the early writings or of the *Capital*, proceeds to examine the rationality of social institutions in terms of a conception of human needs and human freedom. Yet they, like Marx, have rejected the concept of a fixed human nature and have argued that the norms themselves must be created from human "practice" within objective historical situations. The question remains whether a dialectical method without rational norms which have intrinsic validity beyond the historical situation can overcome the dilemmas of historicism.

BIBLIOGRAPHY

Louis Althusser and Étienne Balibar, *Reading Capital* (London, 1970); in Part II, Chapter V, "Marxism is not a Historicism," Althusser argues against modern Marxist interpretations of Marxism as a form of historicism. Carlo Antoni, *From History to Sociology. The Transition in German Historical Thinking* (Detroit, 1959), chapters on Dilthey, Troeltsch, Meinecke, Weber, and Wölfflin; idem, *La lotta contro la ragione* (Florence, 1942), German trans., *Der Kampf wider die Vernunft* (Stuttgart, 1951); discussion of the origins of historicism in Switzerland and Germany in eighteenth-century political context; idem, *Lo Storicismo* (1957; 2nd ed. Turin, 1968), French trans., *L'Historisme* (Geneva, 1963); a discussion of varieties of European historicisms since the eighteenth century. Chr. J. Braniss, *Die wissenschaftliche Aufgabe der Gegenwart* (Breslau, 1848), pp. 113–38, 195, 200, 248. Peter Burke, *The Renaissance Sense of the Past* (New York, 1969). R. G. Collingwood, *The Idea of History* (Oxford and New York, 1946). Benedetto Croce, *Aesthetic*, trans. D. Ainslie (London and New York, 1909), pp. 32–38; cf. *Estetica . . .* (1902; Bari, 1958), pp. 37–44; idem, *La storia come pensiero e come azione* (Bari, 1938), trans. as *History as the Story of Liberty* (New York, 1955); idem, *Teoria e storia della storiographia* (Bari, 1917), trans. D. Ainslie as *History—Its Theory and Practice* (New York, 1921). E. Dühring, *Kritische Grundlegung der Volkswirtschaftslehre* (Berlin, 1866), p. 47. Friedrich Engel-Janosi, *The Growth of German Historicism* (Baltimore, 1944). Ludwig Feuerbach, Review of "Kritik des Idealismus von F. Dorguth" (1838) in *Sämtliche Werke* (Leipzig, 1846–66), II, 143–44. I. H. Fichte, *Die philosophischen Lehren von*

Recht, Staat und Sitte in Deutschland, Frankreich und England von der Mitte des achtzehnten Jahrhunderts bis zur Gegenwart (Leipzig, 1850), pp. 469–70. Karl Heussi, *Die Krisis des Historismus* (Tübingen, 1932). Wilhelm von Humboldt, "On the Historian's Task," in Leopold von Ranke, *The Theory and Practice of History* (Indianapolis, 1971), pp. 5–23. Georg G. Iggers, *The German Conception of History. The National Tradition of History* (Middletown, Conn., 1968). I. S. Kon, *Geschichtsphilosophie des 20. Jahrhunderts*, 2 vols. (Berlin, 1964), a Soviet critique of historicism. Dwight E. Lee and Robert N. Beck, "The Meaning of 'Historicism'," *American Historical Review,* **59** (1953–54), 568–77; an examination of major uses of the term. Karl Mannheim, "Historismus," *Archiv für Sozialwissenschaft und Sozialpolitik,* **52** (1924), 1–60. Karl Marx, *Capital,* Vol. I (1867; New York, 1967); idem, *Writings of the Young Marx on Philosophy and Society,* ed. Loyd D. Easton and Kurt H. Guddat (Garden City, N.Y., 1967); see particularly Marx's editorial on "The Philosophical Manifesto of the Historical School of Law," pp. 96–105. Karl Marx and Frederick Engels, *Selected Correspondence* (Moscow, 1956); on the uniqueness of historical phenomena and of European capitalism, see Marx's letter to the Editorial Board of the *Otechestvenniye Zapiski* (November 1877), pp. 376–79. Hans Meyerhoff, ed., *The Philosophy of History in Our Time* (Garden City, N.Y., 1959); on historicism, see particularly pp. 9–18. Friedrich Meinecke, *Die Entstehung des Historismus* (Munich, 1936; 1965). Karl Popper, *The Poverty of Historicism* (Boston, 1957). Carl Prantl, *Die gegenwärtige Aufgabe der Philosophie* (Munich, 1852), passim. Leopold von Ranke, *The Theory and Practice of History,* ed. Georg G. Iggers and Konrad von Moltke (Indianapolis, 1971). Pietro Rossi, *Lo Storicismo contemporaneo* (Turin, 1968); a discussion of German and Italian historicism since Dilthey and Croce and of neo-positivism. Erich Rothacker, "Das Wort 'Historismus'," *Zeitschrift für deutsche Wortforschung,* **16** (1960), 3–6; early uses of the term. Friedrich Schlegel, *Kritische Ausgabe,* Vol. XVIII (Munich, 1963), p. 91. Schlegel here speaks of different "types of philosophy" (*philosophische Arten*)—"systems," he comments, would be "a bad expression"—among which he includes "ethicism," "politicism," "logicism," "poeticism," and "historicism" depending on the emphasis within the philosophy. For a different use of the term, see his notes of December 1802, ibid., p. 481. Ernst Troeltsch, *Die Absolutheit des Christentums und die Religionsgeschichte* (Tübingen, 1902), pp. 48–49; idem, *Aufsätze zur Geistesgeschichte und Religionssoziologie* in *Gesammelte Schriften* (Tübingen, 1912–25), IV, 628; idem, *Deutscher Geist und Westeuropa* (Tübingen, 1925); idem, *Der Historismus und seine Probleme* (1923), Vol. III of *Gesammelte Schriften;* idem, *Der Historismus und seine Überwindung* (Berlin, 1924), trans. as *Christian Thought. Its History and Application* (London, 1923); idem, *The Social Teachings of the Christian Churches,* 2 vols. (London, 1931). Max Weber, "Objectivity in Social Science and Social Policy" (1904), in *Max Weber on the Methodology of the Social Sciences,* trans. and ed. E. A. Shils and H. A. Finch (Glencoe, Ill., 1949), pp. 80, 101; idem, "Science as a Vocation" (1919), in *From Max Weber. Essays in Sociology,* trans. and ed. Hans Gerth and C. Wright Mills (New York, 1946).

GEORG G. IGGERS

[See also Enlightenment; **Historiography;** Marxism; **Nationalism; Positivism in Europe to 1900;** Relativism in Ethics; State.]

HISTORIOGRAPHY

History of Historiography. The history of historical writing; initially tending to deal with a succession of books, authors and schools; but later extending itself to include the evolution of the ideas and techniques associated with the writing of history and the changing attitudes to the question of the nature of history itself. Ultimately it comprises the study of the development of man's sense for the past, and the manifold relationships between living generations and their predecessors.

I. THE ANCIENT WORLD

1. Pre-classical Times. We may look around for the past, but it is nowhere to be seen. Only after immensely long periods, and under the pressure of strange compulsions, did it come to be realized that a past once forgotten could be recovered to a considerable degree by research.

Men may remember the things that have happened within their own experience, and they have tended to treasure what we call the "tales of a grandfather." These latter have often been regional in character, and in England and elsewhere have been turned into local ballads even in the nineteenth and twentieth centuries. Handed down within a tribe from generation to generation they would be rapidly altered in ancient days through the very processes of oral transmission—the accretion of legendary matter, for example. Some of them—perhaps after being captured into a great theme by a mastermind—would be organized into the epic, which might be associated with a combination of tribes. For the people concerned, the epic, which might achieve great artistry and would be transmitted through professional storytellers, represented their actual history—sometimes the only history they knew beyond the time of their grandfathers. But, on internal analysis alone—that is to say, in the absence of independent evidence—the modern student cannot disentangle the historical truth from the element of fiction. In some ways the epic seems to have assisted the transition to what we regard as "genuine" history, stimulating an interest in the past and providing a narrative technique. Occasionally it may have been so satisfying that it checked the desire for anything better. There was a period when in Egypt it seems to have had even a damaging effect on the style of the campaign-annals.

The earliest historical writing of a more authentic kind is nearer to earth, and the impulse both to enquiry and to the production of a record seems to arise out of some necessity. It is possible that owing to the character and the needs of society men had an urgent concern to secure accurate genealogies before they became interested in historical enquiry, or aware of its possibilities. Perhaps the earliest and simplest form of a more authenticated kind of history consists of dynastic lists, which come to be strung together—some of them strung in succession, when in reality the families ruled simultaneously. In the tremendous list from ancient Sumer, one or two of the kings are identified by a brief note referring to an episode in an epic, and it does not appear that a name was identified except where it was one that had occurred in an epic. In another list from ancient Egypt, "events" are included in the case of a number of monarchs, but though, towards the end, their number reaches a dozen or more in the year, they are copied from the monarch's annual reports which seem to be announcements of duties done—many of them ceremonial obligations, but including an annual measurement of the flooding of the Nile. In early times, the years were not numbered, but in the first Babylonian empire they would be named after some event, and official lists of them had to be kept, so that the dates on business documents, etc., could be identified. The result was a lengthy list, with one event for each year; but, here again, the events were sometimes ceremonial—not the ones that an historian would have chosen. It has been conjectured that these "date-lists" are the things that led to the idea of the "chronicle."

Some of the earliest pieces of narration that survive are on ancient Mesopotamian boundary stones, where the story is told as a way of establishing the rights of the case and rehearsing the precedents. Some descriptive pieces from the same region—with vivid accounts of the sacking of cities—turn out to have been prayers or songs of lamentation. Again, in ancient Mesopotamia, one monarch who had carried out a reform provided a splendid description of the state of things which had existed before he had taken action. And here, after Babylon had first established an empire, there appeared the first interpretation of history, based on the very ancient view that disaster fell on any state which neglected its gods. A Hittite monarch, explaining a policy-decision, provided a retrospective survey that

ran through a number of reigns; and Hittite treaties are remarkable for the very considerable account they give of the origin of wars. From a much older date—and for a long period—in ancient Egypt a distinguished man who needed food and libations to secure his happiness after death, would on his monument implore the passerby to take pity on him; and, in order to support his case, he would present an account of his life—not so much a series of events, but a list of honors enjoyed, a proof that he had been esteemed by the pharaoh while he actually lived. In all these cases, the recording of events is connected with something that one might almost call a "utilitarian" purpose. In Mesopotamia men asked interesting questions about the early history of the human race and seem to have seen that things might be explained by a study of origins. But in this connection they produced, rather, myths, which appeared in epic form.

For over a thousand years there existed what has always been recognized as an historical literature of remarkable extent and importance. It consisted of the annals produced for the rulers of great empires—the Egyptian, the Hittite, the Assyrian, in particular —beginning in almost the form of notes, but developing into long and pretentious narratives, disappearing whenever the empire declined. These were engraved on the walls of palaces and temples, each monarch recording now his building feats, now his prowess in the hunt, but chiefly his military successes. The ruler's purpose may have been to overawe his subjects or impress his neighbors or secure his future fame, but he may have been reporting to a god on the carrying out of a commission (since warfare was conducted on behalf of a god) or he may have been expressing his thanksgiving on the walls of a commemorative temple. The disproportionate space often occupied by the itemization of the booty (of which the temple had a great share) suggests a religious origin on many occasions; and it has even been conjectured that the Assyrian annals may have developed from letters in which a monarch reported to the god on his execution of his commission. But the curses on anybody who should ever tamper with the monument, show that, though these writings give no sign of any interest in the past, the rulers concerned had great solicitude for their future fame. All this represented history of the type of the commemorative monument, and though it was produced over so long a period, it could not develop beyond a certain point, and came to a dead end. Its most remarkable feature was the literary elaboration that it received. The Hittite annals would seem to have been the most distinguished, whether as history or as historical explanation; and, though deeply religious, coming close in this respect to the ancient

Hebrews, they bring us surprisingly near to ancient Greece as well. The handsome and impressive reliefs from ancient Assyria provide excellent examples of illustrated history.

Before the Assyrian annals had reached their peak, however, the ancient Hebrews had come on to the stage of history. They had been semi-nomads, yearning for settlement in cultivated territory, and expecting from their god that he would provide them with it—almost testing his authenticity by his ability to keep his promise. Perhaps because the fulfillment of the promise was so long-delayed, they made a great deal of it when it actually came, connecting it with an exodus from slavery in Egypt which could only have been experienced by a section of the combined tribes. Henceforward, the gratitude for release from Egypt and for the entry into the Promised Land became the tradition of the whole people and stood as the ground for religious obedience, the reason for submission to the divine commandments. The Children of Israel worshipped the God who had brought them up out of the land of Egypt more than the God who had created the world. They were able to make a great contribution to religion, partly because they had their eye on the God of History rather than on the gods of nature, and this had important ethical consequences. Even when they became cultivators of the soil they did not transfer their allegiance to the gods of fertility; and even when they borrowed from their neighbors ceremonies based on the cycle of the seasons, they transformed these (as they transformed circumcision itself) into the celebration of an historical event. Their religious ideas, covenant, judgment, the Promise, the Messiah, are connected with history. If they took over from their neighbors in Western Asia the idea that a national disaster is a punishment for neglect of the god or gods, they added the notion of history as characterized by the continuing Promise—a conditional Promise, subject to terrible acts of judgment, but renewed after the judgment had been suffered, and even developing, so that it became something higher every time.

No country—not even England with its Magna Carta—has ever been so obsessed with history, and it is not strange that the ancient Hebrews showed powerful narrative gifts, and were the first to produce anything like a national history—the first to sketch out the history of mankind from the time of the Creation. They reached high quality in the construction of sheer narrative, especially in the recording of fairly recent events, as in the case of the death of David and the succession to his throne. After the Exile they concentrated more on the Law than on history, and they turned their attention to speculation about the future and in particular about the end of the mundane order. In a sense they lost touch with the hard earth. But they did not quickly lose their gift for historical narrating, as is seen in I Maccabees before the Christian era and the writings of Josephus in the first century A.D.

2. Greece. The classical Greeks began with a remarkable handicap. They had behind them—behind Homer—a brilliant civilization, the records of which have recently become comprehensible to scholars. But they knew scarcely anything about this earlier world and could not have deciphered its texts; for after a hiatus more complete than the Dark Ages in Europe, they had learned a different art of writing which came to them from a different source. Only a little oral evidence, some of it difficult to disentangle from the fictional material in Homer, had filtered down to them, to give them a hint of that earlier age which we call Mycenaean. And they, like the modern world, could not even be sure that its language had been Greek, though they were leaning to this view in the first century A.D. For a long time they believed that only a few centuries of history lay behind them, and in the fifth century A.D. some of them were surprised when the Egyptians produced the evidence that the past went back for thousands of years. Even of their own history as they emerged from their Dark Ages—indeed, of the whole of Greek history since the Trojan war—they knew hardly anything; for they did not have monarchs who glorified themselves in annals, and they were astonishingly late in producing documents at all. It is difficult to see how the states that existed before the fifth century can have been governed with so few records. The earliest to appear were lists of officials and priests. The Jewish writer, Josephus, in the first century A.D. taunted the Greeks for these defects and for the period before the fifth century B.C. it would seem that even modern scholarship will never be able to make good the loss. Athens appears to have been particularly defective in this respect.

They had Homer, and the *Iliad* appears to have taken shape in the Ionian region about the ninth century B.C. There was an epic tradition in Ionia, and in later centuries there were poets who filled in the narrative of the Trojan war, and also carried the story back to the supposed origins of the Greeks, and the legends of warfare between the gods. They attempted to deal with problems that Homer had failed to answer and tried, for example, to straighten out the chronologies and genealogies, and to show what happened to the heroes in later periods—perhaps to satisfy the needs of families that wanted to clarify their connection with such distinguished ancestors.

Ionia produced the earliest Greek prose, developed what we should call philosophy and science, and saw the beginnings of Greek historical writing. The stimulus to this last would seem to have been given by great events; and Hecataeus, overlapping the sixth century and the fifth, like Herodotus later in the fifth century, would seem to have been stirred by Greco-Persian conflicts. Thucydides, later again in the century, was moved by the Peloponnesian war. At the same time the city-states of the Greeks had so developed that the age was propitious for the awakening of the historical consciousness in the effective general public. Down to this time, and even much later still—even in the twentieth century—war has been the most powerful stimulus to the awakening of an interest in history; Hecataeus and Herodotus were impelled to take a great interest in neighboring peoples; and the situation of Ionia was important partly because the interesting Lydians, and later the Persians, were so near, partly because it was almost the meeting-place of eastern Mediterranean civilizations.

Greek historical writing developed to a considerable degree out of the description of neighboring peoples and the attempt to understand them. It emerged in association with geography and ethnography; and this in itself tended to give it a scientific bent, especially as, before Herodotus, men had been writing about the influence of climate and landscape on human nature. In any case history emerged in Ionia at a time when something of the scientific mentality had already been developing there; and here (as in China) a civilization distinguished by science also applied itself to history. It is difficult to know how much the Greeks owed not merely to the science but also to the historical writing that had developed so greatly in Mesopotamia and Asia; but it would appear that a genuine stimulus came from Egypt; and to Egypt the Greeks went in the fifth century B.C. to see if they could find answers to questions about the Trojan war.

In the absence of written sources, oral tradition became particularly important in Greek historiography from the start. Herodotus is dependent on it for the history of the Persian war, which took place not long before his time. Thucydides seems to have been skeptical about the reconstruction of earlier Greek history, though his opening pages contain inferences from what we should call archaeology. It is easy to understand, therefore, why the Greeks in general failed to feel assured about the recovery of a remoter past, once that past had been forgotten. Their great achievements were in fields more nearly contemporary.

What they learned from Egypt, and the little they knew about the Mycenaean age, seems to have given them a powerful impression of history as involving great progress up to a certain point and then decline or collapse. They easily ran to the notion that there

had been a lot of these ups-and-downs, so that civilization repeatedly had to start over again from almost the beginning, without even the memory of former achievements. We hear of the Egyptians taking special pride in the advantages they had over the Greeks through the continuity of their history and particularly their immunity from damage by fire and flood, which were sometimes regarded as the cause of the greatest catastrophes. All this became part of the Greek way of experiencing history—part of man's very feeling for the time-process. And perhaps it was really for this reason that Greek philosophy so easily ran to cyclic views of history, contemplating on occasion the notion of a cosmos and a world which—at colossal intervals of time—go on forever repeating their history in the minutest detail. Greek philosophy has been held to be "antihistorical" therefore, and in a sense responsible for the limitations of Greek historiography. Certainly the Greeks lacked the Jewish feeling that the whole of creation is moving to some great end, as well as the modern feeling that time itself is a generative thing.

Yet our debt to the Greeks is immense; for they opened the way to a deeper kind of history and to a host of modern sciences by their determination to subject historical data (once these were established) to quasi-scientific procedures. They were not content, like the Mesopotamians or the Chinese, to narrate history as though everything were the result of acts of will on the part of men or gods who could easily have willed something else. They attempted to move to analysis, and get behind the acts of volition, examining causes, connections, and the operation of conditioning circumstance. They opened the way to a political science which could examine the cause of the decline of a state or the rise of a tyrant. And their cyclic views reinforced their belief that, by the collation of instances, one could arrive at maxims of statecraft, likely to be useful because history sufficiently repeats itself. All this entered into the very texture of historical writing. The most masterly example of this was Polybius (see below), a Greek slave of the Romans, who set out to describe the expansion of Rome in a book which was largely a history of his own times. To the Greeks we owe the view that history can be a political education.

It did not take them long to apply the canons of rhetoric to the writing of history, and this was not so indifferent a matter as we today might think. On the Isocratean system the historian should interpret and elucidate the story, discussing the plans of a leader, describing the way in which he put them into effect and explaining the results. But there is an alternative method—simply to allow the reader to have the story taking place before his eyes. It has been described as "peripatetic" because it seemed to be connected with Aristotle's theory of tragedy. The scenes are reproduced and one watches the action in the way that one watches a play; and this is sufficient, without a discussion of causes—the action itself producing the required pity and terror. Attention may come to be concentrated too much on these issues of presentation as well as on the style and the techniques which are appropriate to particular occasions. The result is liable to be a decline in the quality of the history that has to be presented—a decline evident at times in both Greece and Rome.

The earliest of the great Greek historians whose work has come down to us is Herodotus, who was born in the 480's and seems to have died soon after 430 B.C. He wrote history partly in order that great deeds (whether of Greeks or non-Greeks) should be placed on record, and partly because he wished to lay out the causes of the Greco-Persian War. He was interested in the way in which things came to happen and would look for rational explanations, showing the influence of climate and geographical factors and presenting excellent portrayals of character, though he was liable to impute important events to trivial incidental causes, the influence of women and purely personal factors. At the same time he had a disturbing sense of supernatural influences, showed the inadequacy of human calculations, the retribution that Heaven would inflict on great misdeeds, and introduced dreams, oracles, visions, and divine warnings of approaching evil. He seemed to make a point of repeating whatever versions of a story had been reported and letting the reader decide between them. He had a great admiration for Athens which was connected with his love of democratic freedom and his feeling for the role of the city in the Persian War.

Thucydides (who died early in the fourth century B.C.) intended his history of the Peloponnesian War to be useful to the future; for, since in his view human nature and human behavior would be forever the same, he held that similar situations and problems recurred, so that the lessons of one period would be serviceable in another period. He was influenced by the science of the time and tried to apply the principles and methods of Hippocratic medicine to politics, so that everything could be covered by rational explanation. He could separate the immediate occasion from the deeper causes of an event, and was able to proceed to general conclusions, as when he analyzed the relationship between wealth and power, or the remorseless logic behind the development of Athenian imperialism. He envisaged the characters of men as the result of circumstances. He was compelled to leave a role for chance, but his attitude to chance may not have been very different from that of the twentieth century. He saw that, with the resources and techniques then available, only something like "contemporary" history was really feasible; and he made use of speeches to communicate what we should regard as the historian's explanations of facts or situations, or of the motives and ideas behind human actions.

Polybius (who was born in the decade or so after 198 B.C. and reached the age of 78) achieved a wide form of general history in a work which examined the rise of Rome and particularly its development to world-empire within a period of less than fifty-three years down to 167 B.C. He ostentatiously stresses the didactic and pragmatic character of history, the fact that it would be better if written by statesmen, and the importance of the subject for people in public life; and both in this and in his remarks about the critical treatment of sources, he is in reaction against the "dramatizing" methods that had become popular amongst historical writers. Though he traces causes and effects, he fails to see the interconnections in the whole network of events, or to discern general tendencies, and he shows the operation of chance, the role of the unexpected, as part of the very constitution of history. He did not originate the idea of cyclic succession in history or the predilection for a "mixed" form of government, but in the latter case it was his formulation of the idea that influenced the modern world. He came to the conclusion that even Rome would not escape the tendency to fall into decline, a tendency which he attributed to moral reasons.

3. Rome. At a time when events carried or acquired religious associations, the chief of the priests in Rome would note them (as well as omens, prodigies, etc.) on a white board which recorded the names of the officials of the year and then served as a kind of calendar. The boards were kept available for future reference (though they were liable to be destroyed by fire, as when the Gauls sacked Rome in 390 B.C.), and the people of the city came to have a sentimental attachment to them. Such records were curiously typical of the character of Roman historiography in general, which was governmental in a sense (written by and for members of the senatorial class), annalistic in form (beginning each year with the names of the officials, and including the omens, prodigies, etc.) but also flavored by religion, by a certain piety towards the past, and by a deep regard for public morality. The sense for history was also—and perhaps primarily—promoted by the traditional devotion of the aristocratic families to their ancestors, the religious observances connected with these, the care taken over the preservation of domestic archives, and the regular recital of old funeral orations. All this intensified, if it did not generate in the first place, the special feeling of piety towards the past, and it helped to bring biography into favor in Rome. It ensured also, however, that historical writers—more than usually dependent on private archives—would produce narrative distortions based on family prejudices or interests.

In a sense the Romans took to history more fervently than the Greeks, who had their "antihistorical" side; and at least their genius was more adapted to history than to philosophy. They produced historical writing that had a character of its own. Yet they contributed nothing essential to the development of scholarship or technique. They came to appreciate the finished product but they learned historical writing from the Greeks, and they met Greek historiography when it was overripe. The result was that, from a comparatively early stage, they saw it as really a species of rhetoric, and gave their minds to the problem of presentation. They knew that history ought to be true, of course; but they never realized (as Thucydides realized) the amount of thought and labor and science which is needed for the establishment of the truth over and above the ordinary requirement of honesty. They never really gave themselves to the task of investigation.

It was the Greeks who began the writing of Roman history; for, just as Herodotus had interested himself in the peoples further east, his successors came to be interested in their neighbors to the west of them, especially when warfare in Sicily brought home to them the expansion of Roman power. The Greeks in any case were inclined to enquire and speculate about the origin of other people's cities and from them came some of the legends concerning the foundation of Rome. The first history produced by the Romans themselves was written in Greek; and this is not so paradoxical as it might seem, for, after the conquests of Alexander the Great, a number of peoples—the Babylonians and Egyptians, for example—showed a desire to present their history in the language of what had become the prevailing culture. The earliest Roman example of this, Fabius Pictor, emerges in connection with the Second Punic War, towards the end of the third century B.C.—an important stage in the development of something like a national consciousness—a moment, too, when it might have been felt that the Greeks were seeing things too much from the Carthaginian point of view.

The first historical work in Latin was in verse, and the first prose work in this field was written towards the end of his life by Cato (d. 149 B.C.), who was influenced by the Greeks and was exceptional in his desire to escape the annalistic form. In the subsequent decades Greek culture exercised an increasing influence on aristocratic circles in Rome that were interested in public service, in literature, in philosophy, and in the work of Polybius. They developed Latin prose, sought to promote history rather than annals, and picked up Stoic ideas of morality which were to help still further to give Roman historiography its special character. They produced historical writing of no special distinction, however, and towards the middle of the first century B.C., Cicero, in whom Latin prose reached the stage of maturity, was clearly dissatisfied with the general condition of Roman historiography. But though he drew from Polybius some notions about the objectives of historical writing, he called attention mainly to questions of form—the need to follow the rhetorical rules which had been developed under Greek influence.

By this time there had begun to appear monographs on limited themes (such as the Second Punic War) and works which had the character of memoirs or autobiographies—works which statesmen and soldiers produced for the purpose of self-justification. The *Commentaries* of Julius Caesar (d. 44 B.C.) are particularly important representatives of this latter class; partly because they are so precise and sober, so rich in their incidental information and so skillful in their concealment of their propagandist purpose. To the class of monographs, however, belong *The Conspiracy of Catiline* and *The Jugurthine War* by Sallust who, during the few years after the assassination of his patron, Caesar, withdrew from public life to produce history of remarkable quality. Behind everything he was preoccupied with the decline and fall of the Roman Republic, which he attributed to a moral collapse; and he emphasized the Stoic teaching which regarded the evils as the result of luxury and ambition. He supported with his intellect and fame a notion of ancient Roman virtue which was already current and which came to be of crucial importance, though it looks like a legend produced and regularly transmitted by Roman historiography. Though he had no love for the populace and hankered after older aristocratic ideals, he wrote history with an antisenatorial bias, so that some people have seen in it a propagandist purpose. It was history in which *Fortuna* played an important part, and religion made perhaps only a conventional appearance, the passions of men occupying the central place, with the result that situations are dramatically developed, and characters are presented with power. Sallust owed much of his fame to his style, which was suited to his subject; tense, rugged and dynamic, but with studied archaisms—itself a creative achievement, owing much to Thucydides and Cato, but a challenge to Ciceronian ideals.

Livy (59 B.C.–A.D. 17) produced 142 books of Roman **469**

history which carried the narrative from the foundation of the city to A.D. 9, though only about thirty-five of these books survive. He conforms to the Roman ideal of a historian—the ideal which Cicero did so much to create—not the discoverer of new facts, not the scientific analyst, but the narrator who looks for motives, discusses results, portrays character, supports the cause of virtue and moves the reader by literary artistry. The past inspires him with a mood of *pietas* and he tells us that, when he is dealing with the early history, he feels that he has been captured by the spirit of those times. In this mood he seems unable to allow even the legendary to be forgotten and in so far as he did not create it, he expresses Rome's tradition about herself, including an element of the mythical which even the modern European has found it difficult to sweep out of his mind. Livy presents—not without a vein of poetry and a sense for drama—the whole tremendous procession of the centuries, Rome being chosen for greatness by the gods, who remain not inattentive to her story throughout the generations. Above all, the rise of Rome was a reward for a certain virtue and greatness of heart which seemed to survive only here and there in the present, but belonged to earlier generations, comprising the things which the Stoics loved—the simple life, *gravitas*, due deference to authority, and some regard to religious observances. But, although the discussion of authorities may add plausibility to the narrative, it is evident that the author does not realize the need to come to grips with the problem of sources. And in spite of his general honesty, Livy can distort the narrative in favor of Rome.

Tacitus (ca. A.D. 55–120) expressed the view that the deeds of good men ought not to be forgotten and that evil men ought to be made to fear the judgment of posterity. It is not clear, however, that he believed in the possibility of altering things in his degenerate age; and, as he realized that the moral decay reached back to republican times, he seems to have felt that there was no point in attacking the imperial system as such. In his *Histories* and *Annals* he directed his hostility against the individual emperors who ran the system, and whom he described from the point of view of that senatorial aristocracy which was the chief sufferer from their misdoings. In his bitterness, he painted some of these emperors as worse than modern scholars would regard them, worse than would be suggested by the facts that he himself adduced; and sometimes where he recognized their good deeds he connected even these with malignant motives. His narrative communicates, therefore, something of the anguish of his soul, and he speaks so much in terms of the way in which he experienced the system that he fails to produce what

we should regard as the larger history of the empire and of imperial policy. Even where he suggests something like supernatural action, he is sometimes tempted to feel this (and the operation of Fortune itself) as actively malignant. He was careful in his researches, skillful in the production of dramatic effects, most distinguished of all perhaps in his pithy style, characterized by epigram and irony. His eulogies of the Teutonic tribes, whose virtues appeared as an oblique criticism of Roman decadence, seem to anticipate the methods of French writers in the eighteenth century. He emerges as the most remarkable historian that Rome produced.

4. Early Christianity. The earliest Christians seemed to have little place for mundane history; in a sense they were too otherworldly, too intent on the spiritual life. They thought that the end of the world was near; and, even when the end did not come, they felt that Christ had won the decisive battle—nothing else that might happen in history could really matter. They held to what we call the Old Testament, however, and, though the gospel was preached to the Gentiles, the continuity with the ancient Hebrew religion was maintained. The Old Testament committed them to history in a sense; however, they did not attach themselves to the mundane side of the narrative—they abstracted from the Scriptures a skeleton of supranatural "salvation-history," a story that culminated in the Crucifixion and the Resurrection. This could easily be an obstruction to any interest in what we ordinarily mean by history; especially as the mundane events in the Old Testament narrative could be given a figurative or symbolic significance.

It would have been difficult to maintain this situation for a long period, especially as people were bound to enquire about the life of Jesus in the world. As time went on, it became important to assert his humanity as well as his divinity, and the fact that Christianity did not involve mythical figures or demiurges, but one who had been a real historical personage, became no doubt part of its strength. With the passage of time, there were decisions of the Church in Jerusalem to be remembered, martyrs to be commemorated, stories to be told about the missionary work in the Roman Empire. In the controversies with the pagans it became necessary to answer the charge that Christianity was only a recent innovation—it had to be explained why it maintained the continuity with historical Judaism and, this being the case, why it broke with contemporary Judaism. It came to be held that Christianity was a return to the religion of primitive humanity and that this latter had everywhere fallen into corruption, Moses himself securing later only a partial restoration. Moses had preserved the worship of Yahweh, but the

Jews were still recalcitrant and needed the straitjacket of the Law. When the Church had to answer the noble pagans, and some of its own converts were unable to forsake their devotion to Plato, it came to be held that the Greeks—though more corrupted by polytheism than the Jews—had themselves possessed gleams of light. The total result was that Christianity was henceforth regarded as the heir of both Greek philosophy and the Old Testament. The wisdom of the ancient Hebrews was older, Homer not so early as Moses, while Plato and Pythagoras were younger than some of the prophets, and Plato himself even being indebted in certain ways to the earlier prophets. Furthermore, the language of the ancient Hebrews was taken to be the oldest of all, anterior to the confusion of tongues, indeed the language of God himself.

In this way a Christian interpretation of large-scale mundane history was gradually developed; but, before these ideas had been reached, churchmen had had to tackle the elaborate enterprise of comparing the widely differing chronological systems of the ancient world, synchronizing events in one region with events in another. Some time not far from A.D. 221 Julius Africanus produced an important pioneering work in this field, which had the further effect of involving the scholar in universal history. The book of Genesis, with its account of the primitive state of the human race, the division into nations and languages, and the origin of the arts and crafts, encouraged the whole notion of a history of mankind. Till the early eighteenth century, it still provided the material for the opening chapter of such a work. Political history is generally the narrative, of one's own state and people; but religious and quasi-religious ideas encourage meditation upon the destiny of mankind as a whole, and Christianity was to give a great impetus to universal history, though this had already emerged, particularly in a Stoic context, amongst the Greeks and Romans. Jewish apocalyptic literature had begun to periodize history, and had seen the rise of colossal empires as in a way a judgment of God—in a way the beginning of the end. It had caught from abroad the theory of the Four Monarchies or World Empires; and this, as formulated in the book of Daniel, governed the periodizing of universal history until the seventeenth and even the eighteenth century. But for a time, while the Church was settling down for a more protracted life in the world, millenarian speculation was more interesting to believers than the story of what had happened in the past. In the Epistle of Barnabas, which may have appeared between 70 and 130 A.D., it was suggested that since the Creation took six days, a day was as a thousand years to God, and the world was likely to have a life of 6000 years, Christ was regarded as having been born between 5000 and 5500 years after the Creation so that the end of the world still seemed reasonably near.

The world was then envisaged as remarkably small, and the stars as forming part of the scenic background. Amongst the Jews there existed the belief that Jerusalem stood at the very center of the map. In Aristotelian physics, the noblest things of all—fire and air—tended to rise above everything else, and the heavenly bodies were made of an especially ethereal kind of matter. For both Christians and non-Christians, the air was full of active spirits, some of them wicked demons. There were converts who held their Christianity rather as they had previously held their pagan beliefs, regarding God as the successful worker of magic.

The historical consciousness as it emerges in Eusebius, who wrote before and after 300 A.D., was adapted to this toy-universe that still expected only a short life-span. This consciousness was stimulated by the stirring events of the time, and the feeling that things were now coming to a climax. For Eusebius, Christ appears in "the fulness of time" (itself an interesting historical concept); also he arrives appropriately when the Jews happen to have no king of their own line. In addition to this, both the Mosaic dispensation and the philosophy of Greece had been provisional in character, only a "preparation" for the gospel; and since the days of Irenaeus, ca. A.D. 180, it had been realized that time had a part to play in God's plan, an "educational" function perhaps. The junction of these two strands of Hebrew and Greek history, and, in addition to these, the Incarnation itself, coincided with the establishment of the Roman Empire, divinely ordained to bring the peace, and the easy communications which were required for the spread of the Gospel. Christ by his victory thwarted the evil demons who were henceforward doomed to fight a hopeless rearguard action. Indeed, from this time, the very pagans were regarded as having softened their manners. From this point in his historical work, Eusebius stands as virtually the founder of what we call ecclesiastical history—trying to trace the successors of bishops in their sees, to commemorate the martyrs and describe the various heresies, though even he can use strong language about the evils in the Church. The culmination of everything is the conversion of Constantine, who achieves supreme worldly success through miracles, and appears as something like a wonder-child himself.

A century later, Saint Augustine has seen the evils that can flourish even after the empire has become Christian. He has to meet the charge that the desertion of the ancient gods has been punished by barbarian

471

invasions and disaster in Rome. He surveys the whole human drama and asks fundamental questions: How did the world begin? What is the nature of time? He also asks questions which are closer to earth, closer to history: Where did civilization begin and why were the early Romans so successful? He says that God bestows empire and military success—like the sunshine and the rain—on the good and the wicked indifferently. Otherwise men might be induced to become Christian for the purpose of achieving worldly success. Furthermore, it was the Christian God—not at all the pagan deities—who had brought Rome to greatness, giving mundane virtues their appropriate mundane reward, though in the eyes of eternity these virtues could be analyzed into something else and would appear also as terrible sins. Augustine not only recognizes the existence of profane history but comes near to treating it as an autonomous realm. The despoiling of Rome was the result of the customs of war. The destruction of Carthage robbed Rome of its great fear, and this led to a moral relaxation. The Roman conquests had become too vast—her empire was beginning to break under its own weight. Even the peace which the empire established did not cancel the wickedness of the wars that had made it possible; and Rome, in spite of all that is owed to it, is only a second Babylon. Augustine seems to prefer small states, if only they could be turned into a family of states; but in his heart he knows how difficult this is—he realizes that it was the turbulence of the neighboring peoples which had provoked the Roman attacks upon them. In regard to sacred history, salvation-history—in regard to the Incarnation, for example—he sees events as conforming to a divine plan; but, in respect of mundane history, he has more flexible ideas than Eusebius—a greater readiness to study ordinary causation—and he does not envisage Providence as working mechanically to a blueprint.

In the *City of God* we see him arguing his way out of a cyclic view of history, for he cannot allow that everything that happens will go on repeating itself throughout endless time—this would turn the Incarnation into a puppet-show. Yet he had previously been tempted by a cyclic view of history, and perhaps it was really the pull of the Old Testament that saved him from it.

He confided to his disciple Orosius the task of demonstrating in detail that Rome and the world had suffered great evils before the appearance of the Christian religion. And Orosius achieved a certain degree of relativity, showing that the rise of Rome had involved disasters for many peoples, and wondering why the greatest miseries of past ages do not seem to produce in us anything like the pain that we suffer

from being stung by a fly at the present day. Coming from Spain, he asked the Romans to imagine what they would have felt like if they had been the defeated Carthaginians. He was prepared to think that the barbarians of his time might someday establish an order and a culture that would become as acceptable to the people involved as the Roman empire had been. He differed from Augustine in his excessive providentialism and he was too content to think that God rewarded piety with worldly success. He imagined that not only the barbarities of the pagans, but the cataclysms in nature—the ferocity of Mount Etna—had been mitigated by the very fact that the Incarnation had occurred. His treatise became one of the most influential books in world-history; and the Middle Ages, when they thought they were following Saint Augustine, were really following Orosius' view of Providence, which was more easy for them to understand. It was Orosius who provided the model for an interpretation of world-history that lasted well into early modern times.

II. THE MIDDLE AGES

1. Europe. The downfall of the Roman Empire, the migration of the barbarians, the attacks from outside Europe, and those centuries of war and upheaval which refashioned the map of Europe, had the effect of reducing society to comparatively primitive forms and led to a hiatus in the history of civilization. In some respects historiography seemed to go back to the beginning again and, in semi-barbarian conditions, we see the emergence once more of the epic. We find also the chronicle evolving afresh from notes that had been inserted in calendars. For men who in that kind of world had a simpler faith, the past was relevant and interesting chiefly in the form of *Heilsgeschichte*, the unfolding story of God's plan of salvation. A slightly greater degree of sophistication seemed to produce a love of pattern-making, an attachment to symmetries, parallelisms, symbols—great pleasure at the thought that the Annunciation occurred at the place where Adam was born, the Crucifixion at the place where he died. Even when it has limited materials to work upon, the human mind does not cease its questioning or its ingenuity. Men asked how the carnivorous animals fared in the Ark and wondered whether perhaps all of them had not once been vegetarian—for, if so, a reversion to this would not have been impossible for them for a time. At a higher level the scholars even now had to engage in serious controversy about the date of Easter.

In the sixth century, when darkness had fallen upon Italy, Gregory of Tours produced fine chronicle work amongst the Franks, but after that, historiography, which had become humdrum, seemed to be disappearing altogether. The great surprise is the emergence of Bede (ca. 673–735), whose *Ecclesiastical History of the English People* remains so important, so charming and readable even at the present day. He was greatly interested in recording the history that was nearly contemporary, but he showed also the intellectual transformation that could be produced in those days when a man made use of what was available in the Christian and pagan heritage. He possessed what was then an unusual amount of classical knowledge and brought a surprising number of sources to support his wider work on universal history. He applied labor and ingenuity to problems of chronology, worked out that the world was created on 18 March, rejected the view that the six ages of history must last 6000 years, and allotted much of his space to the controversy over the date of Easter. His work on universal history was widely disseminated, and, along with Jerome's version of the *Chronicle* of Eusebius, lay at the base of much of the historical writing of the subsequent period. Anglo-Saxon missionaries carried it to Germany, and it was prefaced to various Frankish annals; and Bede had a stimulating effect on the continent. Since the Anglo-Saxon system of dating events by the regnal years in the various monarchies proved cumbrous when applied, e.g., to synods of the English Church at which a number of these kingdoms were represented, he originated in his *Ecclesiastical History* the practice of dating events from the *Incarnation*—a system introduced two hundred years before in the compilation of Easter Tables.

After a short classical revival under Charlemagne around the beginning of the ninth century (when Einhard, following a classical model, wrote a life of the Emperor) the return of violence and disorder produced a further decline of historiography, particularly in Germany. Only after the middle of the tenth century did Otto the Great secure stability again, so that a long-term cultural development became possible. Then, in the eleventh century there is a distinct awakening of historical consciousness and the conquests of the Normans in England and Sicily, the religious reforms, and the advance of the papacy, and above all the beginning of the Crusades—in other words all the large-scale history-making that was going on— undoubtedly contributed to this broader vision of things, especially as it drew attention to a wider world, including Byzantium and the Near Eastern lands. If there was a livelier concern for contemporary affairs there was also a revival of interest in ancient history. At the same time the writing of Latin became more easy and fluent—less like a school exercise—and in the general realm of scholarship a rapid development took place. In the twelfth century—a really creative period—medieval historiography came to its climax.

For men who envisaged a small world, with a comparatively limited time-span, universal history was perhaps more practicable than it became at later periods; and those who knew something of the Bible and the surviving traditions of Rome had both the incentive and the basis for such an undertaking. Sigibert of Gembloux (ca. 1030–1112) carried this form of writing to a height never previously attained. He wrote a world-history based on wide reading and extensive in its political range—including the first attempt to understand the history of Byzantium. Secular history was balanced against ecclesiastical history, and, though he lived in the crusading period, he gave bygone centuries their due proportion of space. Hugh of Saint Victor, slightly later, brought out a world-history which was intended to help biblical exegesis. He suggested a division into three periods: an age that lived under natural law; another that was represented by the Mosaic system; then the present age that was under Grace.

In the first half of the twelfth century medieval English historiography blossoms out in the work of William of Malmesbury who does not merely narrate but embarks on historical disquisition. For a considerable period both before and after this, the Benedictines are making an important contribution to history, as we can see in the chronicles of some of their great English houses. On the continent, a number of famous writers, such as Guibert of Nogent, Foulcher of Chartres, Raoul of Caen, and Ordericus Vitalis seem to show the stimulating character of the early crusading era. Historical writing had now become a serious matter, and some of the writings of this time took decades to produce.

The whole medieval view of history was brought to its climax by Otto of Freising, an important bishop and member of a princely family, who had both practical experience in the work of government and a profound knowledge of theology and philosophy. He produced in 1143–46 a universal history which he entitled *The Two Cities* in token of the fact that he was combining Saint Augustine and Orosius; and indeed there was a still wider sense in which he was attempting a synthesis of *Heilsgeschichte* and profane history. Lacking modern historical analysis, Otto was chiefly impressed by the spectacle of the mutability of things and he felt that pagan historians, describing the actions of great men, had failed to do justice to the miseries of mankind. In this respect, he meant to continue the work of Orosius, and he wrote out of the bitterness of his soul, he says, for the miseries seemed at their worst when he was writing, and they opened his eyes to what mankind had suffered in the past. His

473

narrative is most detailed and impressive when it approaches his own time; and in 1156–57, after the accession of his nephew, Frederick Barbarossa, he worked over his treatise again for presentation to him, having in mind the utility that history might have for an emperor. He accepted the theory of the four world-monarchies and tried to work out its implications in secular history, taking Babylon as the starting-point of civilization. If he saw culture moving from east to west, he found that now, when it had established its seat in France and Spain, there was nowhere further for it to go. This was a further proof that the end of the world was at hand. The profane history dovetailed into the salvation-history, and the work concluded with a full exposition of the end of the world. Otto writes movingly on occasion—for example when he wonders whether the Church was not better when it was in humble circumstances—whether its power and wealth were really the will of God. Above all, he was concerned to expound the deeper meaning of history. Only he, in the Middle Ages, understood Augustine, and (in spite of the wide circulation of his work) there seems to have been nobody who could rise to the level of Otto's own thought.

A little later, William of Tyre, the historian of the Crusades, had sufficient objectivity to be able to commend even Arab and Turk, and to give a not unfavorable picture of Nureddin and Saladin. He recognized the importance of commerce, analyzed personal motives and human factors, was prepared to discuss alternative possible policies and showed a breadth of view that was unusual in Europe at the time.

Decadence was already beginning, however. Literary preoccupations were becoming detrimental to scholarship. Henceforward, the finest work came from what we should call the contemporary historians, including in England the monks of Saint Albans, especially Roger of Wendover and Matthew Paris who wrote on a very considerable scale. World-history came into decline, suffering from superficiality and over-schematization, and becoming a rigid curriculum for schools. Research into bygone ages went out of fashion—the English writers were ready to take the story of the remoter past ready-made from the chroniclers of the twelfth century.

More of the religious houses produced annals and these were kept more continuously than before. Archives and charters were consulted for contemporary affairs rather than for the study of the past. Local history became important, especially the history of abbeys and the chronicles of cities. The chief contribution of the Middle Ages in general was in the field of local and contemporary history. By the thirteenth century, one meets the idea that history is valuable as an education in politics.

2. Islam. Islam had drawn upon Jewish and Christian sources, and continued to have contact with such sources (with the culture of the Byzantine empire for example) all of which contributed to its consciousness of being an "historical religion." Its students learned much from ancient philosophy and science, but did not discover the historians of classical Greece, though, in Aristotle or elsewhere, they learned how history could contribute to a science of politics. They were aware of early Christian historiography, however, and were acquainted with the writings of Eusebius and Orosius. For them it was the life of Muhammad that made the great dividing-line in history. Even if the prophet himself had not attached great importance to history, they would have wanted to know more about the men around him or to discuss the difficult historical references in the Koran. It generally appears that an unusually large section of the literature of Islamic peoples is connected with history, and the works produced were sometimes very substantial in size. In some countries, like India, a serious interest in the past (as we understand it) and a considerable literary production in this field, did not really emerge until the coming of Islam. Yet the Muslim theologians were jealous of history, which was a minor branch of study, without a place in higher education; it never provided the stimulus for an important intellectual movement. The West in the Middle Ages seized upon the science of the Arabs but seems to have ignored their historical work. It is doubtful whether in any case the Muslims would have contributed very much to European historiography from the time of the Renaissance.

It seems that in pre-Islamic Arabia there had existed a feeling for the past, and this expressed itself in forms which are typical of primitive societies in that part of the world. It issued in "battle-day" narratives of the kind which survive from earlier times in parts of the Old Testament—a Semitic product, describing the events and adding a song, like the Song of Deborah in Judges 5. As Islamic historiography emerges in the eighth century, such things have developed into literary pieces, dealing with a single person or event. Influences from the Byzantine empire seem to have stimulated annalistic writing, extending to points of cultural history and to notes about unusual occurrences in nature, as in the work of al-Tabari at the beginning of the tenth century. The same writer produced an influential treatise, the most important of a number of world-histories which appeared in that century. The Muslim writers did not devote themselves greatly to the remoter past, or learn much about the pre-Islamic world, or establish a chronology for ancient times. They did not go to archives for a more effective recovery of a previous age, but would engage in documentary work if they were producing histories of their own period. And what the annalist wrote about his own day carried a special authority; it would be reproduced without change by the writers of subsequent generations. Much of the writing was the work of official historians, commissioned to produce the life of a ruler, and possessing authority because they had held high office or had inside knowledge. Partly perhaps because of the interest in Muhammad and his associates, numberless biographies were produced, and they formed an important part of history itself, while the course of politics was regarded as determined by human wills, personal motivation, and the character of individuals. Historical novels abounded, but there were also histories on special topics, like plagues; and one learns of treatises on subjects such as "those rulers of Islam who received the oath of allegiance before they reached puberty." These latter developments came to their peak in the fourteenth and fifteenth centuries.

The one writer who might have influenced the West was Ibn Khaldūn (1332–1406), for a considerable early section of his *History* was a quasi-scientific treatise on the formation of states, the rise and fall of dynasties, the maintenance of a civilization, and the relations between urban and desert societies. From the Greek geographers he had learned to relate peoples to their environment, and he seems to stand alone amongst Islamic writers in his attempt to connect history with political science and forms of sociological enquiry. He believed in the possibility of divine intervention in human affairs, but allowed it only an exceptional role, and was not deterred from a study of processes. He held a cyclic view of the destiny of dynasties and states. When the Westerns discovered him at a late date they were astonished that Islam should have produced anything that came so close to Vico and Montesquieu.

3. Historical Methods before the Renaissance. In the days of the pre-classical empires, history was very much under the command of those monarchs who produced narratives written in the first person singular. In Egypt, by the time of Thutmose III (ca. 1490–1436 B.C.) the ruler made use of a recorder who accompanied the army and noted the events of a campaign. Amongst the Hittites one has the impression that for a contemporary story, there has been a resort to the archives—the occasional use of a political or military letter. In the case of the Assyrian annals, the ruler may contradict in a later narrative what he has said in an earlier one. But the situation was such that the outsider—and particularly the reader of the future—would have little chance of getting behind the imperial record in order to test its accuracy; and in any case it would hardly occur to him to attempt such a thing. Later generations would feel it a miracle that so much as this had been salvaged.

The implications of all this were far-reaching, and,

at this initial stage in the development, we have to abandon (or even reverse) some of our present-day assumptions. The historian of a future generation hardly expected to be able to improve on the record that had been handed down, and could do little more than copy or paraphrase or abridge the original story. There was no point in advertising the names of the writers of history, who would suffer rather than gain from a reputation for originality. They acquired authenticity by convincing people that they had had the narrative straight from the horse's mouth; and we are told that signatures in Assyrian writings are intended really to attest the accuracy of transcriptions. In the first century A.D., the Jewish historian, Josephus, is quite sure of himself when he taunts the Greeks for their lack of this really genuine thing—this story straight from the age in which the events actually happened. The Greeks had to reconstruct their past by investigation, by detective work; and so there were differences of opinion—the past seemed to have no firm ground to rest upon. His own people, said Josephus, could glory in a narrative which had been handed down for so many centuries without suffering alteration.

We must remember that Thucydides himself had doubts about the possibility of discovering by investigation a past which had once been lost; and even the modern scholar will say on occasion that we shall never recapture the decades immediately prior to the Peloponnesian War because no Thucydides has transmitted the firsthand story. The Greeks in general appear to have felt that the natural field for an historical writer was the period which, if not actually contemporary, was nearly so. Indeed, the notion that the past is to be recovered and reconstructed by detective work is more modern than is usually realized; and, in spite of exceptions that will emerge, it might be said that for two or three thousand years—and indeed down to recent centuries—the favored basis for the narration of events that were at all remote was the work of some writer who had produced the "history of his own times." It was principally with the purpose of undermining this system that Ranke published his famous critical exercise of 1824.

It may have been useful for history when, even in the ancient countries of Western Asia, the priests were able to take the writing of it out of the hands of the egotistical rulers. This happened amongst the worshippers of Marduk in Babylonia and in the Hebrew Scriptures; and at least it meant the production of a record that might criticize the government. But where the priestly narrative possessed a virtual monopoly, the technical situation would remain exactly as before. There are occasions where priests or religious men may have taken an accepted narrative or followed a palace-chronicle, merely infusing into this an interpretation of their own. The priests would seem in any case to have been the first "interpreters" of history, and a prevailing (though not unquestioned) view would regard the writer who is called the "Yahwist" as having performed upon ancient materials a highly creative work of this kind, the result becoming a main constituent of the early books of the Bible. On the other hand, behind many of the technical problems with which Old Testament history must always confront us lies the fact that, in a certain sense, Josephus was wrong. The ancient Hebrews refused to allow the original record to sleep or the story to become fixed. Precisely because history was such a living thing amongst them, they would not let it alone; what we possess has been so altered by editing and re-editing that it is we of the twentieth century who would give our eyes for a glance at the record in its original state. It may still be possible for us to do less than justice to the superstitiousness with which ancient peoples clung to things that had been handed down from the past. When the editors of the Old Testament allowed two versions of an event or an episode to remain in the text, they may have imagined that the accounts referred to two separate things; but, like some historians elsewhere, they may have felt that the transmission of the two versions was the best way of doing justice to the past.

The historiography of the pre-Greek period enables us to see why the world was so slow in learning that "criticism" could be more important than even trust in documents or fidelity to an original text. And the world was slower still in coming to the realization that "criticism" could be a creative thing. The delay is almost incredibly long; for, from the beginning of the story, it had been amply realized that human beings could be both mistaken and dishonest. Even the ancient emperors had been so aware of this that they would add to their campaign-annals a lengthy chapter of curses against any descendant of theirs who altered their record. On repeated occasions later, a world that was capable of philosophical profundity and mathematical subtlety would go on treating historical evidence with remarkable crudity. Clearly, this was not because man's intelligence was then incapable of rising to the necessary procedures but because of the limitation of the available resources, the fact that the mind was not alerted to the needs and the possibilities; also the existence of the feeling that there was nothing to be done if one failed to believe what had been handed down. Nor did men conceive that the connected events of the past could be established in an almost "scientific" manner, or a bygone century reconstituted once it had been forgotten—i.e., unless a fairly contemporary record had been handed down. One might almost say that, as yet, history was not even supposed to be a science—it was more like a collection of stories, of which the best were those that could claim to have come straight from the horse's mouth. We are often surprised, but we ought not to be surprised that, even at the Renaissance, history was treated as a branch of belles lettres.

Even before the emergence of Greek historiography there had been an occasional particular enquiry into the past, but these seem to have been prompted by a utilitarian purpose rather than an antiquarian interest. From Egypt we have an account of a hunt in the archives for the correct way of representing a god who was to be honored by the creation of a new statue. We hear of archaeological "digs" in the later Babylon, but it turns out that these were necessary because, when a temple was to be restored, one had to recover from the ruins of the old one the inscription in which the god had prescribed the form of the original building. It would appear that such an enquiry would bring to light also the name of the monarch who had erected the older building; and then somebody would consult the king-list (which settled the date) and occasionally he would note with amazement the great number of years which had intervened. Greek historians seem to have made some use of inscriptions from the very first—when they were curiously rare—and in the early pages of Thucydides there are some interesting inferences from what we should call archaeological evidence. It is perhaps surprising that this people did not advance further in the archaeological field, especially as they had the intelligence and the instruments for the task, and they came to appear as fervent collectors of "antiquities." But it takes a long accumulation of knowledge and thought—tremendous procedures of trial and error—to turn archaeology into a system in which items can be recognized and dated and properly related to one another. Only after two thousand years do the collectors of "antiquities" make the effective union with history.

We have seen that amongst the Greeks, history had to be a form of "investigation" from the very start; and, by the necessities of the case, criticism itself seems to have been more remarkable amongst them in the early stages of the story than the later. At the beginning, it was the epic that was examined—subjected to a kind of historical criticism—this being exercised at first by those poets who hoped to supplement Homer or clear up the things he had left in doubt. Since there was a lack not only of annals but also of literary records, the early Greek historians had to make much use of oral evidence or local tradition, which proved impracticable for remoter periods and, even in respect of recent events, must have presented obvious challenges to criticism. The chief contribution of the

Greeks to historical criticism emerged by necessity at a very early stage, and is to be seen in both Herodotus and Thucydides. It involved the realization that live informants need to be not only heard but harried, that even the eyewitness needs to be closely cross-questioned, so that his evidence can be made to square with that of other people—to square even with itself. Thucydides used official records, but even his successors amongst his own people failed to maintain his critical standards. For a long time, the progress of history was slowed down by the fact that, even while recognizing the criterion of truth, men so often thought that an easy honesty was sufficient. It took a long time to realize the need for training and technical equipment, the need also for deep self-examination, if bias were to be removed.

As time went on, the original paucity of sources was no longer the same problem, and the writing of history could in any case become an easier matter. For even those authors who were writing about remoter periods might normally use previous narrators, inscriptions, official lists and registers, public documents and private letters. They could also travel in order to settle topographical points, or talk to eyewitnesses, or examine local traditions. This is a pattern that endures for nearly two thousand years; but in ancient Greece and Rome, where the literary presentation had become so important, the sources would be buried into the running political narrative. A matter of notorious controversy might be discussed or a clash between earlier narrative authorities might be alluded to (sometimes vaguely, as though rather to make a show of criticism). But only at the high spots did there appear to be a real wrestling with the evidence, and sometimes an author would be satisfied to use a single earlier narrative source for a considerable stretch of history. Where two previous narrative authorities contradict one another the need for criticism would seem inescapable; yet, in spite of some exceptions, it is amazing to see the enormous period during which even this problem was for the most part weakly handled all over the world, partly, no doubt because of the lack of crucial material, but partly because of the superficiality of the detective work. Rome added nothing essential on the technical side and a modern scholar leaves us with the question whether Livy, who followed now Polybius, now some alternative source, was able to recognize that Polybius was better in quality than the alternatives. This weakness was possibly peculiar to political history (i.e., to history as ordinarily understood). Hellenistic scholarship in neighboring fields shows the activity of more alert and penetrating criticism—e.g., in the handling of problems in ancient literature.

In respect of the earliest stages of Christianity, the narratives that have come down to us raise some curious points concerning the use of evidence. The disciples of Jesus could not have foreseen—and would not have been interested to know—what scholarship in the far future would regard as necessary for establishing the historicity of an event or the authenticity of a piece of evidence. For the purpose of dealing with doubters in their own day they evidently referred on occasion to other "witnesses"; but, in the records that have come down to us, the point is mentioned only in general terms. There must have been an early attempt to lay out one section of the history of Jesus in proper narrative form, and with a more than usual degree of order, precision, and detail—namely the course of events that led to the Crucifixion. Here there exists what some people have thought may be a pointer to specific outside witnesses (Mark 15:21; Luke 23:26). But, in general, for the life of Jesus, we are dependent on Gospels which come short of proper chronological and narrative form and which—whatever literary compilations may have intervened—must go back to oral material, much of it of a special kind because adapted and shaped (if not originally presented) to serve the purposes of the preacher. The Church must quickly have decided that its organization should be primarily directed to securing that the evidence of the original disciples should be properly preserved; and, later, it excluded much obviously apocryphal matter, testing in the light of its main tradition the host of pretended "Gospels" that emerged. But evidence which has gone—or which even may have gone—through such a process as this will not suffice to "establish historically" for a skeptical mind the details of a biography, or the conviction that the ecclesiastical tradition itself went back to the very beginning. The fact that the evidence as it reaches us has suffered this processing, and is so difficult to reduce to an assured original form—also that the early Christian narratives are not produced with what we today should regard as an unmixed historical intent—help to account for the modern debate concerning the very feasibility of "the quest for the historical Jesus." The epistles of Saint Paul carry us back directly to the first generation of the Church, though even they were neither produced nor preserved to serve the purposes of the historian. The Acts of the Apostles, which arise out of an interest in the early Church and the missionary journeys of Saint Paul, have the advantage of including diary material by a man who accompanied Paul for a time.

A further anomaly may throw light on the mentality of men who would be attached to the truth but without the modern feeling for what we call historical evidence. When Jesus was recognized as being in important respects the fulfillment of Old Testament prophecy, there seemed to occur a large-scale hunt for further "anticipations" until scriptural history itself seemed to be transformed into a great collection of prophetic prefigurings. Clearly the matter came to have a dominating place in the mind; and the issue is raised as to whether the original process of thought may not have been put into reverse on occasion. In quite good faith, and in conformity with the whole general outlook, one could come to feel that what had been predicted *must actually have happened* in the time of Christ, when all the prophecies were being fulfilled at once. In the first centuries of our era there are Christian writings in which one gets the impression that the author is going to provide an historical introduction, a discussion of antecedents. In reality one finds that over great numbers of heavily loaded pages, everything has been transmuted into prophecies and prefigurings. For a time men are prevented from realizing other, more mundane kinds of connection between the Jewish past and the Christian present.

The Christian Church developed, however, in a Greco-Roman world in which civilization was highly advanced. The Fathers of the Church took over the scholarly traditions of Hellenistic Greece, and some of them were more at ease in the realm of criticism than their successors during a long course of centuries. Such criticism, however, would tend to be textual rather than historical. Some of them realized for example that the Scriptures had suffered from the errors of transcribers and that chapters or verses were out of order because scrolls had not been properly attached to one another. One encounters in these early Christian centuries the view that the narrative in the Pentateuch was indebted to earlier historical writings. The task of correlating and unifying the immensely varied and difficult chronological systems of the ancient world came to involve Christian scholars in serious work of a fairly technical kind. In his *Ecclesiastical History*, however, Eusebius, in the early decades of the fourth century, made a contribution that was to be curiously significant in the history of historiography. Though he may not have been quite without precursors, he had to reconstruct the earlier centuries of Church history and so had to be to a considerable degree an "original" historian, a pioneer who actually investigates. Also he had in mind certain things which had long been making history important for Christians—the need to refer to older ecclesiastical decisions, the importance of recording the succession of bishops, the commemoration of the feats and sufferings of the martyrs, and the description of the rise of heresies. Much of his material was local in character and he needed to travel, though he concentrated with some justice on his own Eastern half of the Church, and seemed to learn surprisingly little about Western regions. He was not uncritical, and easily ignored a lot of popular miracle stories and apochryphal narratives, though he seems to have been better able to detect the spurious literary work than the unreliable evidence; and he lacked whatever it was that was necessary to prevent his being deceived by the supposed literary correspondence between Jesus and King Agbar of Edessa.

Eusebius is especially interesting, however, because of the general character and form of his *Ecclesiastical History*. He was so greatly concerned with church debates and intellectual issues that it was perhaps natural for him to imitate from ancient Greece the biographies of philosophers and historians of philosophical controversy rather than the pattern of the political historians. It has been suggested that he may have been influenced too by Jewish-Hellenic historiography (Josephus, for example) where the religious aspects of the story were so important. He adopts the method of reproducing considerable extracts from literary works—a method he himself abundantly follows in other large works of his which are more specifically connected with the history of thought; and he reproduces in the same way other kinds of literary evidence (including letters of Origen, of which he had a hundred available). Something of the same can be seen in Bede's work on the English Church, and in the revival of ecclesiastical history in the epoch of the Reformation controversies.

It has been alleged that Eusebius wrote history by stringing masses of long extracts together. But he set the example of not allowing the evidence, the documentary materials, to be lost (i.e., to be dissolved away in the narrative text). And so ecclesiastical history emerged as a more erudite affair than political history. It has been suggested, therefore, that we may have learned from Eusebius to check our references. We are told also that the first writer to present Roman history in a similar documentary way was Louis-Sébastien le Nain de Tillemont (1637–98), originally an ecclesiastical historian.

When, after the emergence from the Dark Ages, medieval historiography makes its interesting development, it does not lead to anything that is scientifically novel. It has perhaps the rarer distinction of producing a number of people who really bring home to themselves the need for criticism—a need which in century after century may be conventionally recognized while nobody realizes the effort, the originality, that it calls for. In the twelfth century William of Malmesbury goes beyond the humdrum in that, while carrying his enquiry back for centuries, he transcends the scissors-and-paste methods in his handling of earlier chronicles. He uses them rather as materials for constructions which were his own; so that he achieves something by just being genuine in a further sense. Glastonbury was to acquire considerable prestige for itself through its claim to have been founded only a few decades after the Crucifixion. But William, for his part, did not flatter this presumption; he confined himself to the cautious statement that there were "annals of good authority" which reported the sending of missionaries to England in the second century. A little later, Ordericus Vitalis, on the continent, went to archives, bewailed the manuscripts that had been destroyed in Viking raids, and complained that monasteries treated their papers so carelessly. He studied burial inscriptions, visited monasteries abroad in order to examine local chronicles, and consulted the great men of his time. He enquired also into oral tradition, and would talk to the peasants, who have a way of keeping things in memory. As a writer of fairly contemporary history, he may have found these procedures imposed upon him—he was committed to being a pioneer. It still remained true—as in the ancient world—that those who worked in very recent fields had the greater need for research. Ordericus is impressive in the ample way in which he conceives the task.

But if we wish to find in the Middle Ages an anticipation of the mood and vigor of Renaissance criticism, we must go to the Muhammadan, Ibn Khaldūn working in the latter half of the fourteenth century. This man— one of the greatest of all the students of the past—urged that the historian should study conditions, states of society and the march of civilization. A knowledge of the conditioning circumstances of an age was the means of weeding out the legends and untruths which encumbered the history handed down from bygone times, he said; it enabled one to discover that the supposed event could not have happened—one eliminated a whole class of errors because one could show that the alleged happening was impossible in the nature of things. The prime example of his method was his treatment of the story, based on Numbers 26, that Moses had over 600,000 men in the Israelite army. He set out to show that there could have been no sufficient basis—no adequate political organization—for such an army, and that in any case no military leader could ever have maneuvered such a body. He pointed out that the descendants of Jacob (Israel), who was regarded as having lived only four generations before Moses, could not have multiplied at the speed required. He recalled that Persia—a vast empire compared with the people of Israel at their best—only had 120,000 men at the time of the greatest concentration of its forces; while King Solomon, who saw the Israelite state at its maximum, was described on Israelite evidence as having only 12,000 troops. He drew a conclusion which might

usefully have been hammered home to Western historians down to comparatively recent times:

Whenever contemporaries speak about the dynastic armies of their own or recent times, and whenever they engage in discussion about Muslim or Christian soldiers, or when they come to figuring tax revenues and the money spent by government, the outlays of extravagant spenders, and the goods that rich and prosperous men have in stock, they are quite generally found to exaggerate, to go beyond the bounds of the ordinary and to succumb to the temptation of sensationalism (Ibn Khaldūn, I, 19).

Ibn Khaldūn had a prejudice against "Israelite stories." But his critical approach was more than the mere effect of this.

4. *China.* In China, the beginnings of history were very remote and independent of outside influences; the achieved tradition was unparalleled in its length and its internal consistency, the prestige of the subject exceptional, and the literary output of incredible bulk. Most imposing of all was the way in which the classical values, the established techniques, and the organization of the profession were able to maintain themselves for century after century, and almost down to the present.

From the very first the importance of the individual historian is a significant factor in the story. He descends from the "temple-archivist" who, in the place where sacrifices were made to ancestors, looked after the documents—the registers, inventories, family trees, records of contracts, and decisions of the oracles. In the case of princely houses, he would draw up treaties, record edicts, and draft the documents which granted feudal enfeoffment. But also he had charge of divination and would decide the day for making a journey, holding a ceremony, beginning a war. From an early date this archivist-astrologer recorded events, and in this he was perhaps regarded as making a report to ancestral spirits. He would also look after the calendar, record eclipses of the sun and moon, and deal with the timetable generally. Even at a later date the account of events, anomalies, or catastrophes in nature would sometimes have a disproportionate place in historical writing, and some have suggested that, for the Chinese, there existed an intrinsic relationship or a special sympathy between the workings of nature and the workings of history. A certain mystique always attached to writing itself and it seems to have been regarded as a way of communicating with the divine order. The recording of an historical event was important therefore; in a sense it was necessary in order to catch and clinch the event—like the case of a run in any game, which is unachieved unless it gets into the score-book. At the imperial court the archivist-astrologer-recorder sometimes acquired great influence, and acted as secretary to the ruler or went on diplomatic missions.

The cataclysms of Chinese history seem to have spared little of the historical writings of the pre-Confucian days, and from early times there was controversy over the genuineness and the textual accuracy of the things that did survive. This did not prevent the establishment of a small group of Chinese classics, which everybody was required to study; and amongst these was the *Shoo King,* known as the "Book of History" or the "Book of Documents." It is a collection of royal speeches, edicts, memorials, feudal documents, etc., some of which purport to go back to very ancient times. There are sections which anticipate the later treatises on governmental institutions, but the importance of the work lay in its political and moral teaching. Another classic was the *Spring and Autumn Annals,* an example of a type of literature which the princes of various states were apparently producing from at least 753 B.C. It consists of the crude annals of the principality of Loo, the country of Confucius, whose connection with the work is so difficult to understand that even in ancient days there were conjectures that it must have been written in a kind of code, or valued in view of some oral tradition attached to it.

The Chou dynasty had already been ruling in China for six hundred years when, in the fifth century B.C. it entered its final stage, which lasted till the third century and is known as the period of Warring (or Contending) States. It coincided with a tremendous flowering of culture, bringing philosophical thought to its climax (almost synchronizing with the rise of philosophy in Greece) and producing in thought and literature an originality and freshness never acquired again. For a long time before this there had been a movement towards what we should call rationalism—one which brought incidental support to history by insisting on the "immortality" that men might secure in the memory of future ages. But history was still more greatly helped because philosophy at this place and time did not mean either cosmological theory or metaphysical speculation; it meant the kind of wisdom that is necessary for the conduct of life, and particularly the conduct of government. Philosophy came down to street-level and greatly affected the general mentality; but also it sought to exercise its persuasive power on princes, and it resorted, not to deductive reasoning, but to the exploitation of historical examples. Confucius in particular (born probably 551, died in 479 B.C.) stressed the importance of history, and seems to have been afraid that, in those times of confusion and war, the records of the past would be destroyed. A reverence for the past and respect for the example set by one's ancestors were an important part of his teach-

ing. In this period, converging forces were in fact doing much to shape the Chinese mentality and to dispose it for a great development in the study and writing of history. And history which had once been almost a ritual art, was turned into a secular moralizing affair, greatly addicted to "praise and blame."

In 213 B.C. the famous "burning of the books," decreed by an Emperor who had united the country and was hostile to the Confucians, combined with a change in both the forms and the materials of writing to produce a serious cultural hiatus. But in 206 B.C. the victory of the Han dynasty led to the reversal of the ban on books and now the Confucians came under imperial patronage. The recovery of the ancient writings became a great objective, but clearly proved more difficult than a Westerner can easily understand, so that these ancient writings emerged in a state of confusion. The followers of Confucius took charge of the restoration of the classics, the reestablishment of the tradition and the revival of history. Confucianism, in fact, secured the whip hand in China at this moment, and men were taught to see the past with Confucian eyes, but also to treat the ancient texts with superstitious care. As a result of the vicissitudes that had been suffered by these texts there emerged a subtle technique of textual criticism, which was later to develop greatly and became one of the remarkable features of Chinese scholarship.

Then the famous Ssŭ-ma Ch'ien (ca. 145–87 B.C.) inherited from his father the undertaking to narrate the course of history from the very beginning. The work that he produced is mythical in its early parts, but, from the middle of the third century B.C., it becomes more detailed, more personal—a more precise piece of connected narrative. When it comes to the fuller story of the Han dynasty (down to the Emperor Wu) it uses official records, but supplements these by personal experience and the cross-questioning of eyewitnesses. Sometimes the narrative is strange and difficult for the Western reader, because different aspects of it emerge as it is repeatedly retold in successive studies of leading people. The reader who wants the overall story is left to look after the dovetailing himself. The author does not see the need for connections, developments, underlying movements of causation—all the things which enable a Western narration to become more organic. The whole texture is governed by the fact that the author sees history as the product of men's wills and does not seek to get behind the wills. It is as though we had stories from eyewitnesses who reported what they had actually seen in a battle but never envisaged the affair as a whole, or looked for any policies behind it. If Ssŭ-ma Ch'ien sees things in the large—the collapse of an empire for example—it is for the purpose of moralizing. The result is most impressive as literature, and it achieves real beauty, standing as perhaps the best thing in Chinese historiography. Besides recording imperial history, Ssŭ-ma Ch'ien produces chronological tables, monographs, annals of vassal princes, and biographies, e.g., of scholars. The monographs include studies of music, the state of the calendar, hydrography, and political economy, for Chinese historical writing was intended to be of particular use to public officials. Ssŭ-ma Ch'ien's influence on the future was to be very great.

Henceforward the specialized role of the historian becomes recognized as part of the civil service, and one can trace the early stage in the development of the examination system which was to make the entry into the bureaucracy so conditional on scholarship. Under the T'ung dynasty (from the seventh century A.D.) there emerged a History Office which was an organ of government, and history became an important subject in the civil-service examination, which now achieved its permanent form as a competitive affair. The Chinese bureaucracy always produced a great amount of writing—reports from officials, financial accounts, memoranda concerning government, criticisms of contemporary conditions. A high proportion of government officials would spend part of their careers in the History Bureau, and historical narratives came to be produced on the committee method. The *Diaries of Activity and Repose* reproduced the utterances of the Emperor and the business that he conducted, day by day. These were abridged so that when the Emperor died there emerged the *Veritable Record*, a survey of his whole reign. When a dynasty came to an end, a comprehensive account would be written under the succeeding dynasty; and this, the *Standard History*, was an important thing, produced for nearly two thousand years on a pattern set initially in the first century A.D. by Pan Ku in his *History of the Former Han Dynasty.* The succession of *Standard Histories,* if translated into English, is calculated to require 450 volumes and 500 pages each; and this is only a small proportion of the vast historical production of China. No other nation possesses such voluminous, continuous, and (within their own terms) accurate records of so long a past. One of these dynastic histories, begun in the year 1679, took forty-six years of labor though fifty-three historians had been set to work upon it.

It was all official history, written by civil servants for civil servants and not intended to form reading matter for a wider public. Even those who wrote history privately would themselves belong to the official class and would need government records—they might even be aspiring to enter the civil service. The historian had to register discrete facts, not to produce generalizations, or describe the background or examine processes. He was not supposed to be an interpreter, but if his words could coincide with the text of actual documents, it was imagined that his objectivity was complete. It was really in essays and monographs that he was able to discuss institutions, economic conditions, the state of the arts, etc. As time went on, everything tended to become conventionalized, and in any case there would sometimes exist a conspiracy of silence— the refusal to take note of the important influence of Buddhism during a number of centuries, for example.

The Chinese were remarkable in their textual criticism. They could seize on the anachronism that exposed a forgery or an interpolation. They learned a great deal about the transmission and the vicissitudes of ancient texts, and were helped by masses of bibliographical material that had been handed down from very early times. As successive historians so often copied one another verbatim, they could check the authenticity of ancient texts by comparing what had been reproduced by previous writers at various times. It naturally followed that an important aspect of Chinese criticism was the detection of forgeries. On the other hand they seem to have assumed that if a statement in a chronicle or a document had not been contradicted anywhere, this alone would justify their accepting it as true. Where there were two contradictory accounts of an event, their first impulse would be to try to reconcile them with one another, or to produce a story that would embrace both. At worst, they would have to opt for one of the two and they would not say why—they might simply leave the rejected source unmentioned. When they were satisfied about the genuineness of a document, it did not occur to them to interpret it—construing it in terms of the people or the situation behind it. They would not ask whether a witness might be insincere, or prejudiced or moved by vested interest; and—in their reverence for the written word—they did not see that a document ought to be treated rather as a detective would use a clue.

III. MODERN TIMES

1. Renaissance and Reformation. The custom of producing annalistic notes about the chief events in Florence has been traced to the early part of the twelfth century. At this time, lists of officers would be kept, and, as they served to mark the chronology, the principal happenings would be recorded under the successive names. At the same time there emerged the story that Florence had been founded by Caesar after Fiesole had rebelled and been destroyed. Florence could claim to have been "Roman" therefore, while her rival, Fiesole, had been "anti-Roman." At a time of

patriotic awakening and emergent political consciousness, the municipality remembered its tradition or
created one for itself. Giovanni Villani (ca. 1273–1348)
produced a chronicle still medieval in many ways and
going back to a legendary epoch but rich in information about recent times. It acquired a lasting popularity
and influence.

At the opening of the fifteenth century, the city was
in conflict with the Visconti of Milan, and was beginning to conceive itself as defending democratic liberty
against a tyrant. Its citizens now turned from their
admiration of the Roman Empire, and from their former interpretation of history, though this latter had
been supported by the authority of Dante. They also
began to look for an origin earlier than the supposed
foundation by Caesar, and they discovered it in the
world of free city-states which had preceded the expansion of Rome. From this time, they construed their
whole history as a story of liberty and took to themselves the eulogies once bestowed on Athens, interpreting their political life in terms of the ancient Greek
city-state. Humanist scholars, no longer preferring the
contemplative life, became preachers of civic pride and
civic virtues. Leonardo Bruni, the influential writer,
who has been called "the first modern historian," was
at the heart of this movement. And the revival of
historiography at the Renaissance is connected with
the development of the modern political consciousness.

The long task of recovering the thought and learning
of antiquity was coming now to a climax, and producing perhaps a general change in man's attitude to the
past. Its objective transcended that of the historian for
it sought not merely to recapture out of antiquarian
zeal but to reinstate for working purposes in a living
world all the higher aspects of a culture that had been
at its peak in classical times. For the new age, antiquity
was beginning to emerge as a world that had an identity of its own. A modern lay intelligentsia found in
ancient literature something that answered to its own
secular outlook; and the historical narrator began to
dispense with the more obvious machinery of the supernatural—began, indeed, to envisage his task in
something of the ancient spirit. Under the stimulus of
Leonardo Bruni, and primarily in Florence, there
developed a humanist historiography which went too
far in its subservience to antiquity, breaking up the
continuities of narrative and theme by its "annalistic"
method, encouraging artifice by its restriction of vocabulary, and allowing rhetorical affectations to carry
it to a conventional kind of theatricality which prevented either the proper portrayal of men or the genuine interpretation of what had happened. The new
historiography performed a political service, however,
for its function in the first place had been partly to

celebrate the glories of Florence and partly to communicate the desired image of the city to the outside
world. And all this was a thing that any city-state might
covet, so that other governments in Italy, wishing to
produce the same result, employed humanists as official
historians for the purpose in the fifteenth century.
Indeed, between 1450 and the 1530's, Italian humanists
served as something like court historiographers to an
emperor in Germany and to kings in France, England,
Spain, Poland, and Hungary. One of the significant
features of the new historiography was the closeness
of its identification with the new kind of territorial state
that was emerging; and, since this relationship was to
endure, here was a significant moment in the development of modern nationalist historiography. At the same
time there had been awakened an interest in the sheer
pastness of things past, a genuine sentiment for the
remnants that had happened to survive. While the ruins
of Rome were still being plundered to provide material
for builders there emerged a great fervor for "antiquities" which began to show itself in societies, museums,
and imposing publications. In a tremendous drive to
discover new manuscripts, further ancient historical
writings came to light, e.g., in 1455 the *Agricola* and
Germania of Tacitus, and in 1506 part of the same
writer's *Annals*. Better manuscripts were secured,
sometimes from Constantinople; and it became particularly important to have translations into Latin, a great
part of Polybius, for example, in 1473. The invention
of printing and the wider circulation of both ancient
and modern books meant that history henceforward
was to play a much more important part in the development of political consciousness and the shaping
of public opinion. At the same time the greater speed
in intercommunications enabled scholarship to develop on a broader international scale.

The whole movement came to its finest blossoming
in a number of cultivated men who in the early decades
of the sixteenth century talked about politics in
Florence and produced historical work of considerable
quality in the vernacular. The troubles of the city had
led to constitutional speculation and to debate about
both the present and the past, which brought history
and politics into a more intimate relationship with one
another. The French invasion of Italy in 1494, the
political downfall of the peninsula during the subsequent conflicts, and the defeat of Florentine republicanism in 1512 provoked serious thought about the
ups-and-downs of nations, and historians were stimulated somewhat as Thucydides had been by the
Peloponnesian War. The influence of classical Greece
was now most apparent in the attempt to approach
both history and politics in a semi-scientific manner,
to meditate on the processes that take place in states,

and to produce political maxims for the man of action—indeed to produce narratives that were tingling with the practical man's concern for policy problems and the work of decision-making. Now, more definitely than before, the case for both reading and writing history was based on its importance in the education of a statesman.

Niccolò Machiavelli went further than others in his belief that laws of political action could be elicited from history and that, for any given contingency, the ancient Romans were likely to have discovered the right policy. Though his *History of Florence* in 1525 escaped some of the limitations of humanist historiography, and in places showed a real ability to see things in the large—to grasp connections between events—it makes clear that his interest was not in research or the establishment of facts.

Francesco Guicciardini had had a longer and more successful career in politics, and insisted that Machiavelli was not sufficiently flexible in his attempts to apply to modern situations the lessons drawn from the past. In the last few years of his life both the tragedy of Italy and his own disillusionments and disappointments brought Guicciardini to a great confrontation with the whole epoch, and his *History of Italy* (from 1492 to 1534) is the most impressive Renaissance achievement in this kind of literature. It is not limited to Florence but deals with a complicated general field—a system of interacting states. It set a standard for sophisticated narrative in what we call political history. It can almost be regarded as the beginning of study of diplomatics. Perhaps it sees events a little too much as the result of contrivance and intrigue on the part of unscrupulous men. But Guicciardini has turned out to be more scholarly, more interesting and authentic in his historical methods, than was realized until the mid-twentieth century.

In the north of Europe, a tremendous zeal for the past was awakened, and the humanists had an important part to play; but here the development started from a lower cultural level than in Italy. Those who were now stirred into some consciousness of history tended to ask the old, universal "stock questions"—How did nations begin, how did our own nation acquire its name?—and there emerged the kind of spirit which had been significant in Florence, the patriotism which, as it turns to the past, hunts for things to commemorate. The various countries liked to claim their origin from the sons of Noah, and sometimes seemed unwilling to leave a gap in the subsequent succession of generations. There was a desire to go one better than the Greeks and Romans in the matter of antiquity, and show that one's ancestry could be traced through some leader of the defeated Trojans. All this was particularly strong

in Germany and was accentuated there by the jealousies which the brilliant Italians of the Renaissance had provoked; it was manifested also in the determination to assert, against the French, the German character of Alsace. The Germans thought to outdo the Greeks and Romans, claiming an empire more ancient still, and a prior cultural supremacy.

The fact that it is easy to exaggerate the modernity of the sixteenth century is illustrated in the case of England, where the infatuation for King Arthur reached unprecedented heights and proved enduring. The accession of the Tudors, the resulting glorification of Wales, and the acceptance of Henry VII as being of King Arthur's line—the naming of a Prince of Wales after this monarch—helped to multiply the manifestations of the myth in pageantry, in social life, in antiquarian speculation and in literature. And this was a King Arthur who was supposed to have defeated the Roman Empire, conquered most of Europe, and acquired Norway, Iceland, and Greenland—the King Arthur described in the twelfth century by Geoffrey of Monmouth in a work that had not always been credited even in the Middle Ages. In England the antiquarian enthusiasts themselves could not forgive the Italian humanist Polydore Vergil for his reservations on this subject; and it is remarkable to see how, down to the end of the century, the more scholarly historians (including William Camden) hesitated to attack the prevailing myths. On the contrary, in the work of Sir John Price in 1573, the skill and the knowledge of the antiquarian operated powerfully in favor of the myths which still kept their currency in the seventeenth century. Eyes were fixed, therefore, on the ancient Britons, and there were some people who said that they saw no point in studying the Anglo-Saxons. Some were prepared to insist that Christianity had been brought to England by Joseph of Arimathea not long after the Crucifixion. Before the end of the century it was coming to be held that the English constitution, the liberties of Englishmen, and the House of Commons itself went back to the ancient Britons.

In the meantime, the Reformation had led to the resurgence of religious preoccupations even in regions where, during the Renaissance, historiography had become secularized. The upheaval in the Church was bound to give a stimulus to the study and writing of history, and the emphasis now placed on the Bible—the special importance which the Old Testament came to have—resuscitated in the modern world some of those things which historiography owed to the ancient Hebrews. The challenge presented by Martin Luther to the papacy and to other branches of ecclesiastical government—indeed to the whole notion of authority as hitherto understood in the Church—directed attention to the opinions held in earlier ages, the controversies of the past, the precedents, the traditions of fifteen hundred years. Such a debate could only lead sooner or later to the development of ecclesiastical history and to a closer analysis of actual official documents. Apart from this, there emerged also a need for a history of the Reformation itself and the Protestant, Johannes Sleidanus (1506–56), produced in Germany in 1555 a documented study of the religious events of the reign of the Emperor Charles V. He showed in both his attitude and method the temperament of a contemporary historian, not a mere polemical writer. In 1563 John Foxe, greatly developing previous work, produced what became famous as *The Book of Martyrs*—a study not merely of Protestant sufferings (involving the use of bishops' registers), but the englobing of this within a framework of Church history —the whole highly polemical, even dishonest in its use of the sources.

The ecclesiastical issues of the Reformation were dealt with in a more imposing manner through a cooperative work directed by Matthias Flacius between 1559 and 1574—the famous *Magdeburg Centuries*, a highly documented production, but crude in its partisanship. The real answer to it from the Catholic side appeared in twelve volumes of *Ecclesiastical Annals* (1588–1607) by Cesare Baronius, a cardinal, who used documents from the Vatican. Gradually these controversies came to serve the cause of criticism, as each party answered the arguments of the other, and each came to realize that a vigilant enemy was ready to expose its mistakes.

But the Reformation affected wider areas of historiography. In England the "historical revisions" of the sixteenth century produced a remarkable reaction against Thomas Becket because he had sided with the pope against his own country. It led to a still more remarkable adulation of King John, because he was held to have been victimized by a pope. On all sides, Protestants were ready to suspect Catholic perversions and they made a point of attacking the kind of history that monkish chroniclers had produced. In England, again, the desire to find a historical basis for the conception of a national church gave a stimulus to Anglo-Saxon studies, especially in Elizabeth's reign. The attachment of Luther (and, still more, of Philipp Melanchthon) to the general study of the past was to have significant and enduring ecclesiastical effects in Germany. Once again, the call for "universal history" came from the side of religion, and this branch of study—both stimulated and influenced by the reading of the Old Testament—gained a firm foothold in the German universities, ancient history forming an important part of the program. There was a revival of

the system of periodization according to the four World-Empires—a system abandoned by the humanists, but accepted now by the Catholics, so that in the eighteenth and nineteenth centuries men were able to regard it as having been invented by Melanchthon's friend, John Carion (1499–1537).

2. Historical Criticism in the Fifteenth and Sixteenth Centuries. In the humanist writing of fifteenth-century Italy there seems to be something like a general advance in historical criticism, so that amongst the Italian cities there is less credulity about implausible "myths of origin" than one finds in the rest of Europe. Italian humanists abroad—Polydore Vergil in England, for example, as we have seen—showed a certain distrust of such legends in other countries, though it was no doubt more easy to deprecate the cherished fables of another nation. While the natives of the country concerned were inclined to attribute the criticisms to the jealousy of the foreigner, it would seem that at this extreme point the Italians had reached a higher degree of critical awareness. On the other hand, though there existed a fervor for ancient history, the scholars of the Renaissance did not attempt to reconstruct for themselves the narrative that had been handed down from classical times. They believed—and, in general they were right, as yet, in believing—that they could not improve upon what a distant generation had reported about itself. At this point in the development—when, in any case, one tended to compile the story of the past from previous narrators, whether ancient historians or medieval chroniclers—there existed, in a harder form than we should accept, the assumption that the older source was always the better authority. Amongst other things, it was normally taken for granted, and one finds it explicitly stated, that a medieval source called for criticism while a classical one did not. The reliability of Herodotus came to be questioned, but even this was a further example of the subservience to antiquity; for the doubts about this writer were taken over from the scholarship of the ancient Greeks, the resulting controversies becoming a factor in the development of early modern criticism.

Flavio Biondo completed in 1453 a work chiefly on Southern Europe since the decline of the Roman Empire, which, owing to its disregard of the rhetorical canons, failed to qualify as a piece of humanist literature, though it could be used as a quarry and was both important and influential. It drew attention to the medieval period as a whole and tried to vindicate it in the face of current prejudices. It set out to present the best of the source material, and then to produce from this evidence an account of the period from about 410 to 1442 A.D. Biondo used not only chronicles but documents—letters for example; and he was able to keep closer to earth because he based himself on the evidence that came earliest, though he lost a point sometimes by dismissing a later tradition. In other works on Roman topography and antiquities, he contributed to the development of classical archaeology.

In fifteenth-century Italy, however, there appeared a kind of critical endeavor of which there had been some traces in Ibn Khaldūn—a full-dress affair, exhilarating and clever—a case of calling up the troops and marshalling all the arguments to dispose of a widely-accepted legend. This kind of work brings us closer to the genuine technical issues but it suggests—what many other things confirm—that there is nothing like violent partisanship for setting criticism alight and driving it to ingenuity. The case is illustrated by the famous work of Laurentius Valla who in 1440 set out to prove that—as some had previously believed—the Donation of Constantine had been a forgery. The work appeared at a time when Valla was secretary to a king who was at war with a pope. It was avowedly part of a bitter publicistic campaign.

His treatise presents first of all a whole series of arguments that might be said to rest on common sense or ordinary experience—that no emperor would disinherit his children so shabbily, for example, and the Roman Senate would never have agreed to the alienation of the western lands of the empire. Secondly, there is a wide range of arguments to show that the Donation cannot be squared with what is otherwise known of the history of that time. Thirdly, Valla examines the status of the document itself, the contradictions and absurdities in the text, the barbarity of its Latin and the mistakes in terminology. Bernardo Giustiniani, whose career was spent in public service in Venice, brought his practical knowledge of affairs to the criticism of source-material even in early Venetian history, showing, for example, what was militarily impossible, and doing this in a manner that was remarkable at the time. Over a century later, and at a date when the massing of big guns was perhaps no longer necessary for the purpose in France, L. V. de la Popelinière produced with great humor and ingenuity a large-scale attack on the legend that the Franks were descended from the Trojans. He followed something like the pattern of Valla: firstly, arguments from common sense and from his own military experience; secondly, objections arising from the fact that the story could not be squared with other things that were known about the history of the relevant periods; and thirdly a destructive analysis of the supposed evidence for the belief. More clearly than Valla, however, he dealt with a point that is of some importance, if the critical task is to be completed and the argument clinched. Granted that

the Trojan story was untrue, he made a point of enquiring how the legend could have arisen.

But, though the humanists did something to alter the general outlook in Italy for a time, it cannot be said that either Laurentius Valla or Bernardo Giustiniani or La Popelinière established a standard or brought new methods into general currency. It cannot be asserted that, now, at last, this much ground had been gained for scholarship or science. As yet, at least, there could be no organic story of the development of historical technique, and the battles that had been won for a moment would have to be fought over again in the future. Even during the Renaissance, the attempt of the writers in Northern Europe to answer the questions that preoccupied them—questions about the origins of nations, place-names, institutions, arts and crafts, etc.—was often based on wild inferences from flimsy evidence or from etymological speculations, where it was not due to the easy acceptance of forgeries. It is perhaps curious that one of the most disastrous and influential of literary forgeries—a compilation associated with Annius of Viterbo, which was soon detected in Italy, but almost dominated German writing—should have been so closely associated with the Renaissance.

It is possible that, in spite of the nascent criticism, the weight of fabulous matter in the world was actually increased in the sixteenth century. The great exception in Germany is Beatus Rhenanus (1486–1547), who travelled widely in search of inscriptions and antiquities, rejected the Annius forgery, and set himself to work critically at the sources of early German history. In this and in his further unfulfilled ambition for an adequate treatment of German antiquities, he was a follower of Flavio Biondo.

Amongst those who wrote "contemporary history" Guicciardini has come to have a special interest because of what came to be learned later about his sources and method. His working papers have shown the wide range of his primary materials, and particularly of the official documents, including archives of the Council of Ten which he had taken into his possession a few years before. It has also been possible to see how he worked over these papers, abridging and copying, and then redrafting, until he had turned them into narrative. It transpires that even a Ranke had been unable to detect how much was behind this *History of Italy*, for sources have been found for one or two speeches, as well as for statements and events, which Ranke had accused Guicciardini of inventing. A proper system of footnoting would have made the position clear from the first.

A significant impulse was given to history on the technical side by the work on Roman Law conducted

485

on the part of humanist writers, particularly in France. The law that they studied threw light on the institutions and conditions of the ancient world, and in order to recover the exact meaning of the texts it was necessary to examine many aspects of Roman life and activity, interpreting the legal terminology in the light of the social arrangements that then existed. This led—as in the case of Guillaume Budé—not merely to an attempt to recover the realities of ordinary life in ancient times but also to a study of the transition to feudal times, an enquiry and then a controversy as to the role of Roman Law in the transition to the medieval order of things. At a much later date, as will be seen, this interest in the feudal order of society passed to England, where it had an important influence on historiography.

John Bodin produced in 1566 his *Method for the Easy Comprehension of History.* His ideas on criticism were vague. He ratified Aristotle's view that authorities were likely to be unreliable if they were either too ancient or too recent; yet, when they clashed with one another, he preferred the more recent, provided it supplied effective proofs of its assertions. He thought it better, where possible, to follow a writer who was intermediate, i.e., neither a hostile nor a friendly witness. He considered geographical factors in history and said that people who lived under extreme climates were prone to vice; but he allowed also for the influence of the heavenly bodies. In his chapter on chronology he gave a lengthy proof that the world had had a beginning. One of his ideas was to study the beginnings, the flourishing, and the downfall of empires—comparing the ancient with the modern and confronting the views of philosophers with those of historians in order to get a better grasp of universal history. Here we see that modernism of the sixteenth century which is so often still mixed with medievalism.

3. *Scholarship, 1600-1750.* In the seventeenth century, historiography comes to be more scholarly, more technical, and this is due not only to the ecclesiastics but also to the lawyers who deal with constitutional rights and historical precedents, with charters, laws, and other documents. In England the common lawyers, with their theory of the "immemorial constitution" and their interpretation of Magna Carta, provided an historical basis for the ideology of the antiroyalists, and the controversy brought out great masses of documentary material. Sir Henry Spelman, however, (under the influence of continental scholarship) called attention to the feudal system and the danger of arguing from a past that was assumed to have been like the present; and his ideas helped to produce after 1660 an important reaction against lawyers' history. Particular emphasis was now placed on the fact that words still in

currency might, when used in a medieval text, carry a different meaning, and that a document like Magna Carta must be interpreted with reference to the kind of society from which it had emanated. The revolution of 1688, however, swept away for a century these ideas which were tending to a more historical view. They were the kind of ideas that emerge but drop out again, so that in the history of historiography they have to be repeatedly rediscovered, as well as being repeatedly brought home at different levels.

The Reformation controversy, which in the *Magdeburg Centuries* and in Baronius had covered vast ranges of Church history, produced more permanently interesting results when in 1619 there appeared the famous history of the Council of Trent by Paolo Sarpi. Working as a pioneer in a fairly contemporary field, Sarpi could use knowledge that he had acquired from men who had been present at the Council, as well as archival sources, private correspondence, etc. His antipapal narrative was answered in 1656 by Sforza Pallavicino who had secured access to great quantities of material in Rome. The transition to a more scholarly type of historiography, however, goes back to a cooperative endeavor, particularly amongst the Jesuits— the *Acta Sanctorum* (the first volumes appeared in 1643) associated with John Bolland and then with the famous Daniel Papebroch. Almost contemporary with this was the attempt of the Congregation of Saint Maur to recover for the Benedictine order the distinction that it had had in medieval historiography. From 1668 the *Acts of the Saints of the Benedictine Order* began to appear, and from 1703 the *Annals of the Benedictine Order*—works in which Jean Mabillon played a leading part. It was to be of the greatest importance for scholarship that the men concerned in these enterprises had no doubts about their religion—they believed that they could pursue their enquiries and criticisms without any fear that the result would be detrimental to the faith.

Daniel Papebrochin found himself in the position of having to assert the important truth that the oldest authority might not necessarily be the best—that the quality of the source had to be considered. On the other hand, an error of his provoked Dom Jean Mabillon to defend his order in a treatise of 1681—itself a momentous demonstration of the fact that matters relating to distant centuries could be established with something like moral certainty—without dependence on mere "reporting." He dealt with old charters which might still be essential as evidence for proprietary rights or constitutional claims or monastic privileges, but were easy to forge, so that the lawyers had long been interested in discovering how to test their authenticity. He showed how these documents could be properly assessed through detective work on the parchment, the writing materials, the form of the seals, the technical terms employed, the kind of Latin used; he investigated also the way of describing dignitaries, of stating dates, of introducing and concluding the main text. In other words, he is the real founder of the auxiliary science of diplomacy. Many of his criteria would not have been feasible if a great deal of knowledge had not been accumulated about the history and geographical distribution of materials, formulas, language peculiarities, and so forth. In this sense there was a certain analogy with the work of the archaeologists on nonliterary material, and Mabillon's technique could have been established only after many other matters had been settled.

The period from 1660 to 1720 has been described as the grand age of scholarly research, and the "second Alexandrian period of scholarship." At a time when there was also great interest in the assembly of specimens in the natural sciences, the collection and study of the actual remains of the past—archaeological survivals, inscriptions, coins, etc.—had become large-scale. The general study of these "antiquities" led to important developments in what historians call the "auxiliary sciences," but it still stood apart from the work of the ordinary writers and narrators. In a similar way, and partly through cooperative enterprise, there occurred in this period massive publications of documents—more than could be properly digested as yet into the narrative-writing, though sometimes vast quantities would be shovelled into the rambling texts that were now being produced.

In the realm of ancient history an important crisis had arisen. Laurentius Valla had expressed doubts about Livy, and in 1685 Jakob Perizonius challenged the reliability of the sources of early Roman history. There followed a period that is associated with "historical Pyrrhonism," that is to say, with skepticism about the very possibility of history. These doubts were not removed and Levesque de Pouilly made a more trenchant attack in 1722, while Louis de Beaufort, in his *Dissertation sur l'incertitude des cinq premiers siècles de l'histoire romaine* (1733 and 1750), declared that, down to the third century B.C., the history of Rome had been built up out of material that was really legendary. The controversies over this issue reveal the fact that, in this field, Western Europe did not yet greatly differ from China in its criteria. It relied on previous historians who had been contemporary or nearly contemporary, unless there seemed special cause for distrust; and men argued that a Livy would not have survived if he had not secured acceptance in his own day, when people were better equipped to judge him (and he better equipped to judge his own sources) than modern scholars could be. One even meets the assertion that

if two ancient historians provided different versions of a story, it was preferable to construct a narrative which would embrace both; also, that for a great simple event like the Flood, a mere tradition might be a sufficient authority, provided it were old enough, and not contradicted by known facts, and not the kind of thing that somebody might have had an interest in inventing.

Owing to the limitations of existing resources, the insistence on criteria more strict than these would have left no alternative but skepticism and would have led—indeed, sometimes did actually lead—to the feeling that history was impossible. The disciples of the natural sciences, led by Descartes, sometimes doubted the bases of historical knowledge. Some of the students of "antiquities" declared on the other hand that it was only the nonliterary sources that could be trusted.

For the rest, religious and political partisanship was often the powerful motor behind a new critical endeavor. In the early eighteenth century a circle of scholars in England made an interesting and significant attempt to rescue ecclesiastical history from the Protestant and nationalistic prejudices which had constricted it down to the time of Bishop Burnet's *History of the Reformation* which began to appear in 1679. This movement was connected, however, with a High Church and nonjuring party, that was unable to reconcile itself with the Revolution of 1688. Voltaire and his successors did some service by raising the issue—by talking about criticism—but their own constricted outlook would have prevented their solving the problem even if they had had the patience to carry out the detailed work that was required. Like the Protestants of the sixteenth century they thought that the proper target for the critic was ecclesiastical tradition and that it was sufficient to reverse what the Catholics had said. And, as in the case of the Protestants, the procedure was sometimes right, but it was capable of carrying them further than ever from the truth. Their determination to see history as the transition from savagery to culture and to condemn the past in the light of the present, makes it not improper to describe them as in a certain sense "unhistorical." Yet they did a great service to historiography by the kind of questions they asked, by their determination to give the past a kind of structure, and by their attempts to draw laws from historical data. Voltaire in his *Age of Louis XIV* (1751) introduced a wider conception of general history, to include art, learning, science, and many varied aspects of life. In his *Essai sur les moeurs* (1754) he rose above the older kind of compiling and used reasoning and thought to give meaning to a universal history that was conceived in the same generous manner. The elimination of the supernatural factor was

487

used to clear the way for deeper mundane reflections about the processes of time.

4. The Impact of New Ideas. In the sixteenth century, the upholders of the "moderns" against the "ancients" claimed for the benefit of their side the compass, gunpowder, and printing, as though these were recent Western achievements. Giordano Bruno saw the "moderns" enjoying the advantage of the astronomical observations of ancient Greece, together with all that had been recorded since, and concluded that the Greeks really had belonged to the childhood of the world. When towards the end of the seventeenth century, the feud of "ancients" and "moderns" broke out again, those who argued that the literature of Louis XIV's reign excelled that of antiquity, still did not necessarily believe in the idea of progress, for some of them thought it possible that a relapse would take place sooner or later.

It was perhaps more important that the victory of the "scientific revolution," the achievement of Sir Isaac Newton and the overthrow of Aristotelian physics destroyed the authority of both the Middle Ages and classical antiquity. Technical advances and the perception that society was ceasing to be static—also the reports of travellers about men in a more primitive state—tended to supersede the picture of an ideal world long ago, and the belief that in society there was a natural tendency to decline. Gradually men carried their conclusions beyond their observations, and swallowed some of the misgivings that they had at times; and, as theorists and manufacturers of broad historical surveys, they would advance ideas of general and indefinite progress. In a sense just as the notion that the Jews were God's "chosen people" became transmuted, and the English themselves claimed the benefit of it, so the Jewish belief that history was based on "the Promise" became in a certain sense secularized. In other words, the transition to the idea of progress was assisted by faith and a forward-looking spirit. The Greeks had been able to conceive of progress from primitive conditions up to a certain point. The early Christians had come near it when they saw both the Old Testament and Greek philosophy as a "preparation" for the Gospel. Henceforward the idea helped to provide the structure for a new world view.

History was bound in the long run to be greatly influenced by this idea of progress; for it was no longer a case of one generation succeeding another on the same virtually unchanging stage, countries merely having their ups-and-downs—all the centuries still forming only a rope of sand. Here was something which made it possible to give shape and structure to the course of ages. In a way it contributed a meaning to history, and gave point to the temporal succession, making change more than kaleidoscopic, and turning time itself into a generative thing. In spite of a certain pessimism about human beings in the eighteenth century, it gradually came to appear that world-history had something like an objective—one which lay within history itself. Paradoxically, a world that now began to turn its eyes to the future rather than the past did not desert the study of what had gone before, but became more interested in history than ever, as though the subject had acquired a new relevance. Men became exceptionally interested in lengthy surveys—in studying the way in which mankind, from a primitive beginning had come to its present civilized state.

In 1681 Bishop Bossuet had produced his *Discourse on Universal History,* which followed Saint Augustine rather than the cruder views of Eusebius and Orosius, while avoiding the danger that the conflict between good and evil might be interpreted as a conflict between religious and secular organizations in the world. He saw the divine ends often achieved through identifiable secondary causes, the turns of the story being repeatedly decided by the fact that men and nations are what they are. God achieves his objects often by the control of the human heart or by just leaving men to their passions; the key to human history is *l'esprit des hommes,* though God has something to do with the character of this *esprit.* It was easy to eliminate the last stage of this argument, to get rid of the supernatural and move to the Voltairean view that history depends on the spirit of men.

The universal histories of the eighteenth and early nineteenth centuries followed the pattern of the Christian ones in the sense that they were intended to explain the meaning of things and to show an analogy to the Providential plan, a purposeful history-making that goes on over men's heads. Even the pattern of the book of Genesis leaves its mark on these works, though the chapter on the Creation comes now to be replaced by a scientific account of the globe itself. Instead of theologies of history, we now have works which, from the time of Voltaire, call themselves "philosophies of history." They brought into their survey the whole social and cultural history of the world, not concentrating on politics, not confining themselves to courts and kings. They extended the horizon of the historians, including India and China in their survey of world-history, and thinking it a feather in their cap when they could add Tibet. They begin with Voltaire and then, through Herder, Condorcet, et al., run in a series which culminates in Hegel. When "academic history" emerged, it took up arms against such philosophers of history, at least until the time of Ranke, because they inferred so much of their generalizing from their theories about life, instead of allowing it to emerge more slowly from careful researches. Yet even Ranke said repeatedly that his ultimate object was "universal history."

In 1725, however, Giambattista Vico published his *Scienza nuova,* and in certain respects he represents a reaction against the tendencies of his age. He set out to vindicate historical knowledge, in a world that had doubts about it; and he asserted that man can know history—events and institutions or mental achievements—for the simple reason that one can know the things that one actually makes. Only God (not the scientist) can know Nature with equal intimacy—know it as the creator of it. While believing in Providence, he identified its influence with the workings of history, and regarded it as securing its objects through human beings, using even their passions to serve its purposes. Contemplating the whole development of civilization, he divided the story into three stages, representing respectively the ages of gods, heroes, and men— themselves corresponding to the mental development of the human race, from feeling to imagination, and then to thought. He differed from the eighteenth century in general in that he was so sympathetically preoccupied to recover the mood, the notions, and the animating forces of primitive man, in whom he saw wisdom of a poetic kind. Early myths and legends were not merely fictions to him, but embodiments of a kind of truth. He traced Homer back to folk-poetry and regarded the leading "Legislators" of early history as mythical, for he conceived of law as having rather a spontaneous origin, emerging out of society as a whole. He is a precursor of modern historicism, yet he does not seem to have influenced the eighteenth century, and, though he was rediscovered in the nineteenth, the influence attributed to him during the romantic period may rather have been due to Herder. In fact, the twentieth century may have found more in him than did any preceding age.

Montesquieu influenced historians, though he never came to grips with primary sources except when he studied Merovingian Gaul. In his *Considérations sur les causes de la grandeur des Romains et de leur décadence* (1738) he broached the questions which have most engaged the minds of historians for nearly two thousand years, but he intended only to ponder on the knowledge that had long been current, and behind all other factors he imputed the real cause to the fact that Rome had extended too rapidly and too much, while he assigned great importance in history to *l'esprit général.* In his *L'esprit des lois* (1748) he became interesting to historians because he applied the comparative method, and sought to explain causation in the historical realm, showing the influence of climate and other physical conditions, as well as the importance of the economic factor. For the rest, his influence also reinforced that of Voltaire (see above) whose main historical contribution takes place in the 1750's.

Two writers of history were important for the influence that they had in the development of a more organic conception of the whole subject. Johann Joachim Winckelmann, in his *Geschichte der Kunst des Altertums* (1764, *History of Ancient Art*), was unhistorical in that he treated one Greek standard of beauty as absolute, and saw development too schematically; but he broke away from the practice of treating literature and the arts by the study of individuals or separate schools, and set out to achieve a genuine history— including the things which happen over the heads of individuals and are not consciously willed—the whole being related to the entire life and culture of the Greeks, to the spirit of a people, and even to climatic and economic conditions. Justin Möser, in his *Osnabrückische Geschichte* (*History of Osnabrück*), in 1768 was concerned with a small territorial unit, but was distinguished in the period of the *Aufklärung* by his attitude to the Middle Ages—an admiration without romantic sentiment. He used original sources and brought an intensely practical mind to the analysis of them. Above all, in a constitutional and administrative history, he found a place for all the needs of a people, including geographical, economic and social factors, working these into connection with one another.

Johann Gottfried von Herder, the effective founder of the philosophy of history in Germany, is in some respects analogous to Vico, and stands as partly the product of eighteenth-century rationalism, partly a pioneer in the reaction against it. He had an undoubted influence on practicing historians and is one of the people who, through their interest in the Bible, in Homer, and in earlier states of society as presented in Ossian, learned to understand a little more about the "historical sense"—the gift of "feeling" oneself into the past—the thing the *philosophes* had lacked. He saw nations and ages as organic unities, in which all things were fused into something like a unique "personality" by the governing influence of a spirit—morals, laws, and artistic production so interrelated in a given culture that they could not be transplanted from one nation to another. They all sprang from their own central spiritual source, which was unlike anything else in the world, and all required to be judged in their own context. To a great degree it was through Herder that the romantic movement became so influential amongst historians.

In many respects the influence of the romantic movement in Europe in the late eighteenth century and the first half of the nineteenth came to be regarded as unfortunate. This is illustrated in some of the extravagances of "romantic nationalism," including the excessive adoration of the primitive culture of one's own people. In some respects the ideas of the romantic movement were beneficial, however, and this has remained as a final deposit, becoming a constituent part of the historical outlook. This was the case with that particular aspect of the revolt against the *philosophes* which involved the rejection of the policy of treating previous generations as though they were only links in a chain leading to the present day. History was only too easy if one seized on what a bygone age had contributed to one's own time, and assessed its ideas by their analogy with those of the present, or judged personalities by the standards of a later period. The romantic movement showed the importance of being interested in the past for its own sake, seeing things or people or ideas in their own context, and even judging men in terms of their own age. Realizing that for each generation life has its aspect as an end in itself, exactly in the way that it has for those living today, the historian contributes something of himself to achieve understanding—the past having one claim on us, and one only: namely the right to be understood. The sympathetic imagination plays its part in the effort of understanding; and, in a sense, this means that the historian should really be drawn to the past and deeply interested in it—not simply anxious to use it, not merely concerned with it as it throws light on the present day. Something of all this was brought to its climax in Leopold von Ranke's famous dictum: that all generations are immediate to God. Even this had its dangers, for the romantic historians sometimes excused too many things on the ground that they had been tolerated in a given period; and it would have been better if they had learned that history (particularly their kind of history) had the function of explaining rather than either judging or exonerating. Also, though the romantic historian loved detail and sought a concrete visualization of the past, something in his sentimental equipment seems to have made him soft, where he ought to have been hard, in historical criticism.

5. New Developments in Criticism. Even in the eighteenth century the effects of criticism might be limited if the work was governed by the concealed assumption that only the evidence of the "other party"—now, perhaps, the Catholic, now the Tory, now the foreigner—called for the critical endeavor. And this limitation could be overcome only as the passion for historical understanding became all-consuming—a thing which was happening in the eighteenth century, and still more in the nineteenth, as this branch of scholarship became more autonomous. Even today it is always possible for a man's view of

the past to be distorted through his prejudices in respect of the present. On the other hand, in the middle of the eighteenth century the world still needed in any case a form of criticism that went further than a blind dependence on a witness or an early historian who was deemed reliable, or an equally blind rejection of one who was regarded as unsafe. This would be a "positive" form of criticism, constructive (and not merely destructive) in its results, like the kind which had enabled Mabillon to show that certain things can in fact be established with moral certainty. It might also be a creative kind of criticism, bringing the historian to something new, something not contained in the sources themselves. In this respect historiography made a great stride in the eighteenth century.

At this point, the study of the ancient world and even biblical scholarship made a remarkable contribution to the development of history; for, owing to the priority of these branches of study since the Renaissance, owing to the amount of ingenuity which they devoted to a limited number of sources, and owing to the importance attached to the results, these fields had made the greatest technical advances. A point of particular importance in modern historiography can be best illustrated perhaps by work that was done on the earliest books of the Bible. In 1685 a French writer, Richard Simon, picked up the problem, saying that he was only continuing a work of criticism already begun by the Fathers of the Church. He held that Moses—still regarded as the author of the Pentateuch—must have used detailed chronicles of an earlier date. In the middle of the eighteenth century, Jean Astruc claimed that one could identify some of these sources, particularly the main two which were distinguished by their different ways of naming the deity. He showed further that when these were disentangled—the patches and fragments of each extracted from the present text and properly arranged—they formed a better narrative than Genesis, where the interweavings have produced repetitions, contradictions and passages that appear in the wrong order. The result was a pattern of what could be achieved by getting behind a piece of historical writing, detecting the earlier sources that had been used, and then even reconstituting them after they had been lost. It was to become an important matter that the historian should discover "the source of the source."

In Göttingen, where a similar analysis of Genesis was produced, a great development was made in historical study in the later decades of the eighteenth century, so that the University acquired a reputation in this field which lasted through the early decades of the nineteenth century. Here were created the first seminar and the first learned journal in the subject, and much attention was given to the auxiliary sciences, such as diplomatics and numismatics. Here Professor August L. von Schlözer transported the various techniques of the classical and biblical scholars into the medieval field in his edition of the Russian "Chronicle of Nestor," for which he, too, reconstituted a lost source. And here men first dreamed of what was to be the *Monumenta Germaniae historica* (a vast critical edition of sources, discussed below), besides carrying the development of historiography to the point from which Ranke began. It was virtually the birth of "academic history," for the University was able to improve its standards, and hand them down in a teaching tradition, so that henceforward there could be a continuity of development. Rejecting some things from the *philosophes* but accepting others, choosing sometimes rather the principles that were associated with the romantic movement, but insisting at the same time on scholarship, they brought the "antiquarians" and the narrators or generalizers closer together for the final synthesis, a synthesis more adequately achieved for the time being, however, in the work of Edward Gibbon.

Gibbon found a magnificent theme in *The Decline and Fall of the Roman Empire* (6 vols., 1766–88) and his work is the greatest monument of eighteenth-century historiography. He showed great enterprise in dealing with a thousand years of Byzantine history after the downfall of the empire in the West, though this later section of the work, running to 1453, shows his hand less sure and his command of the sources less firm. He distinguished himself by combining some of the virtues of the Enlightenment with the assiduity of the *érudits;* and he mastered the original historians and primary sources of the classical period, though it was noted at the time in Germany that he was not quite up to the stricter standards of criticism which were becoming current. Otherwise the work made maximum use of the resources then available, and it provided (perhaps in a more provocative manner than its author really intended) an interesting attempt to deal on a considerable scale with the rise of Christianity from the point of view of the profane historian. Standing as an end in itself it ranks as a masterpiece, but it lacks that sense of the importance of, e.g., economic factors, which some writers were beginning to have, and it was not calculated to influence the course of things so much as were certain Scottish historians of the time, who were moving to the wider view.

A further achievement, stimulated this time by classical scholarship, is illustrated by the "Prolegomena ad Homerum" in an edition of the *Iliad* published in 1794–95 by Friedrich August Wolf, who was himself not without antecedents and was even accused of plagiarism. He traced the development of the Homeric poem back to sources no longer extant, and declared that the epics were a later construction, compounded out of heroic songs and primitive folk-poetry. This field of scholarship became particularly relevant because the historian learned how light could be extracted even from legendary material, even from scraps and survivals once rejected as simply untrue.

Barthold Georg Niebuhr, in his *Römische Geschichte* (which first appeared in 1811) was responsible for the transmission of these techniques to the ordinary field of history; he applied the method to the early part of Livy's *History of Rome*, the unreliability of which had created so much uneasiness at the beginning of the century. Niebuhr began with the assumption that the early part of Livy had ultimately arisen out of primitive nationalist poetry. As a romanticist, he was interested in origins, myths, and folk-art—anxious not to wipe out this material as merely untruthful, but to do detective-work on it and use it as evidence. He knew how to distinguish the different kinds of source—the original from the secondhand, the newer from the older—but also how to compare societies that were similar in pattern though distant from one another in time and place. He used his romantic sympathy to give him a grasp of the relations between early Roman society and the North Friesland agrarian life which he knew at firsthand. Neither his results nor Wolf's would be accepted today, and the former himself revised so many of his conclusions that his second edition was almost a different book. Niebuhr is important because he transplanted into historiography a dynamic contribution to the "positive" type of criticism.

In Germany the awakened spirit of nationality, the pride in an imperial tradition and the romantic love of the Middle Ages reinforced the demand of various Göttingen professors for a critical edition of the sources of German medieval history. In 1819 there was founded the society which inaugurated the *Monumenta Germaniae historica;* all the auxiliary sciences were invoked to locate the original texts, to discover the best traditions, to follow the fate of the various manuscripts, to test the genuineness and value of the sources, to examine their relationship with other sources, to trace earlier documents that had been embodied in later ones, and to discover where a writer had contributed original matter. Until this time the French and Italians had been ahead of the Germans in producing these critical editions of their national sources. Gibbon had called for the publication of the chroniclers of medieval England, but it was not until 1863 that William Stubbs began his great work on the Rolls Series.

In 1824, Ranke produced his first book—the *Geschichten der Romantischen und Germanischen Volkes von 1494 bis 1535*, and appended to it an essay which was later regarded as a landmark in the history of criticism. He was anxious that the new methods in ancient history—translated into the medieval realm by one of his teachers, G. A. H. Stenzel—should be introduced into the modern field, and he exposed the uncertainty of the ground on which modern history had hitherto been largely based. Of late modern history had been in the hands of men like Robertson and Roscoe, Coxe and Sismondi, good easy men whose merit consisted chiefly in making things more accessible which were quite well known already. In a criticism of Guicciardini which in some respects later proved to have been unfair, Ranke at least insisted that the writers of "histories of their own times" could no longer be regarded as first-class sources. The insufficiencies of "memoirs" in particular were now widely recognized.

4. The Nineteenth and Twentieth Centuries. In the long previous history of the subject, nothing had equalled the surge of historiography in the nineteenth century, and the accompanying leap of Western Europe into historical consciousness. This has sometimes been attributed to the reaction against the French Revolution, which had represented an unusually defiant break with the past. In the period after 1800 the world was in a position to remember chiefly the atrocities and failures of the Revolution, and its culmination in dictatorship and war. It was as though the human race had gone through a tremendous new experience, and even in the political realm one had learned the danger of flying in the face of history. Edmund Burke had been the chief representative of this point of view. It is clear that his particular fusion of politics and history and his views about tradition—about maintaining the continuity between past and present—had existed before 1789, but it was through his opposition to the French Revolution that he became an important European influence.

But, visible also before 1789, the romantic movement in general literature had its part in the story—particularly that side of the movement which hankered after the past and ran something of man's emotional life into the sympathetic appreciation of bygone ages, now studied for their own sake. Furthermore, if the *philosophe* movement had been unhistorical, particularly in its way of judging early periods by the standards of the present and seeing them only as the stepping-stones to the present, it had made a great contribution to the understanding and analysis of the whole course of general history, including man's cultural development. In spite of a certain reaction against the thought of Enlightenment, which was regarded as responsible for the evils of the French Revolution, it proved possible for students to combine the best of the romantic movement with the best of the *philosophes;* and, as the nineteenth century proceeded, more of the thought of these latter re-entered historiography. It was as though the *philosophes* had been right in many of their hunches, but had been deficient in the researches necessary for working them out.

Amongst the factors which came together and gave a tremendous impetus to historiography, was that course of technical development in scholarship which had led to the emergence of "academic history" in Göttingen. In the 1820's this achieves more definite self-consciousness as Ranke emerges, and the *Monumenta Germaniae historica* is inaugurated. Great importance must be attached also to the fact that, in a number of countries, a wide range of population had come to be concerned with politics, and therefore with issues of a historical nature.

It might almost be said that, if the present day is under the dominion of science and technology, it was really history that held the presidency in the nineteenth century. This was a period of remarkable progress in the subject itself; the world has still to learn whether the tendencies of the twentieth century will turn out to have been equally beneficial to history, regarded as a sheer study of the past—a study very much at the mercy of the winds that play upon it. In the early decades of the nineteenth century, Hegel is a demonstration of the way in which philosophy itself had come to crown its endeavor with a survey of the universe in its historical dimension. The theologians now became engrossed in history, and a great feature of their work was to be "the quest for the historical Jesus."

Already in the eighteenth century the natural scientists had become interested in the history of animal species, of the earth itself and of the solar system. Now, however, the interest in the time-process is heightened —the great scientific idea of the nineteenth century is that of evolution; and even before Charles Darwin had produced the *Origin of Species*, the notion of development was coming to be important in various fields of thought and scholarship. It may have seemed natural that history should provide an intellectual basis for a new kind of conservatism in politics after the French Revolutionary period, but in the 1830's a new kind of liberalism emerged in Mazzini against a background of schematized general history. In the 1840's, Karl Marx was developing a doctrine of revolution and a general outlook on life which were based on a study and interpretation of history. Henceforward, we meet the paradoxical truth that, in the world of politics, it was the revolutionaries who most had the mania for history, and the determination to make use of history.

The development in historiography, and the wider emergence of the historical consciousness, were most remarkable of all in Germany, which led the technical advance in scholarship, as well as the development in the theory of the subject. Largely through its historical achievements, that country marched forward to a general cultural leadership. In the early decades of the century Göttingen enjoyed international distinction as a school for historians, where George Bancroft and John L. Motley, for example, went for training. Initially through the work of Protestant writers, the German Middle Ages were rediscovered and the epic of the Holy Roman Empire—the reminder that the country had had its glories in the past—assisted that awakening of national feeling which had been produced in the War of Liberation against Napoleon. But a better understanding of the work of the medieval Church stimulated the German Catholics in their turn, and helped to produce an intellectual Renaissance amongst them. In Europe as a whole, from this time, the interest in history played an important part in the development of the idea of nationality. Countries acquired a pride in the past, an affection for the primitive stages of their own culture, a veneration for their traditional languages, and a better awareness of the territory which had once been theirs but had been lost at one time or another. Perhaps to an unreasonable degree, history—now more closely connected with the life of men and states—was used to provide the basis for political claims.

But Germany also had Ranke, whose stature and influence would in any case have given her the primacy in the historical field. He developed along with the nineteenth century itself, but at the same time he was the pioneer who planned and led much of the development. An important stage in the evolution of his manuscript work was his use of the famous *relazioni*—the long descriptive accounts produced by Venetian ambassadors after their period of residence abroad. This procedure still had its limitations, and it was still a case of using the finished pieces produced by what were almost "contemporary historians." Also it involved the employment of diplomatic documents for the recovery of the internal history of various countries. Soon Ranke came to the conclusion that the whole of modern history needed to be torn to pieces and reassembled with the help of all available manuscript sources. He held a privileged position and was able to secure early access to archival sources at a time when the scholar who had the first glimpse of the official documents could be certain of rich returns. His famous seminar helped the development of research on the new methods and the establishment of recognized standards and techniques.

The opening of government archives to scholars, first partially in the 1830's, and then on a more generous scale in the 1860's, came as the crown of the whole development, providing it with its most essential instrument, and enabling men to feel that history had now come into its own. Its importance lay not merely in the fact that things were now revealed which governments had hitherto kept hidden, or even the fact that vast ranges of documents now available had been produced by men who could not have dreamed that their productions would ever be exposed to the outside world. Most significant of all was the fact that, now, more than ever before, the historian could base himself on something that was not mere "reporting," whether on the part of contemporary historians or memoir-writers, or Venetian ambassadors in their *relazioni*. Henceforward he could study the papers in which (and by means of which) the business of government had actually been transacted. To a great degree he could study official papers in their continuity and, following events day by day, could reconstruct the framework of an entire narrative.

The new history, arising from the archives in various European capitals, concentrated itself largely on the work of government and tended to see events from the point of view of government. Political history was now triumphant, and, possibly because diplomatic documents were so accessible, so nicely arranged and so easy to use—so capable moreover of presenting the reader with their own story, in all its continuity—there was an emphasis on the external relations of states, and on that states-system which had already been a great subject of study at Göttingen. Ranke himself has sometimes been held to have been responsible for this, but, insofar as a certain bias of the mind was involved, something is due to his predecessors; his own outlook was so broad that the "cultural historians" were nearer the truth when, later in the century, they claimed his support in their criticism of the prevailing system. For a very short period in his younger days Ranke had a connection with a conservative political journal, but quickly found the situation unsatisfactory. For the rest, he held that the historian should be primarily a scholar, aloof from the movements of his time. He received moral reprobation for this, and even his pupils (who tended to grasp only parts of his teaching) proved unwilling to follow his austere example.

The historical movement of the nineteenth century came into alliance therefore with the powerful German national movement that culminated in 1870-71; the result was shown in what came to be the classical school of German historiography, which from 1861 was dominated by supporters of Prussia and entrenched itself in the universities, putting history at the service of the national cause, and even insisting on this as a point of ethics. As the work of Frederick the Great and Bismarck acquired such a central place in the story of modern Germany, it became easy for any student to draw conclusions about the nature of history and politics very different from those which would be drawn by Germans taking their bearings at the present day. Even in 1870 Gervinus vainly tried to point out that a wider view of Germany's past would have produced a better understanding of the real tradition of the country, enabling historiography to do greater service in its role as the discoverer or creator of a nation's tradition about itself.

In the middle of the century the great works were appearing which showed that, over a wide area, historiography had been carried to a new stage. Ranke himself had completed between 1839 and 1847 his massive treatise on *German History in the Age of the Reformation:* and, after dealing with Prussia, he moved in the 1850's to large-scale work first on French history in the early modern period, and then on England in the seventeenth century. The most formidable scholar amongst his pupils, Georg Waitz (1813–86), was publishing from 1844 a tremendous work on *Deutsche Verfassungsgeschichte*, which went back to the customs and institutions of the early tribes and showed his mastery of medieval sources. After Waitz moved to Göttingen in 1849 he made that University the most distinguished school of medieval history in Europe. Macaulay published the four completed volumes of his History of England between 1848 and 1856; and, though limited by the excessive positivism of his judgments, by the smallness of the area of history that he really mastered, and by the extraordinary insularity of his whole outlook, he took some pains in the collection of his materials; nor was his Whiggism more prejudiced—more detrimental to his work—than the partisanship of some of the Prussian giants of the period.

A powerful pupil of Ranke who came to diverge from his master because he so strongly believed that history should be put at the service of what was regarded as a great public cause, was Heinrich von Sybel. From 1853 he was producing his most imposing work, his *History of the Revolutionary Period*, which, in its use of sources, represented a significant advance in its own field. It had been intended from the start to show up the evils of political radicalism, though in the course of execution it came to be still more dominated by the idea of demonstrating the effect of external relations on internal development, the primacy of foreign policy, and the influence of the French Revolution on other countries. Johann Gustav Droysen was not a pupil of Ranke and was influenced rather by Hegel, but must be regarded as perhaps the chief of the founders of the Prussian school. In the thirty years or so from 1855 there appeared the successive volumes of

his *History of Prussian Policy*, a work based to an almost unprecedented degree on manuscript sources, and packed with new material. It has been described as one of the most important of the achievements of the new historiography and, by G. P. Gooch, as "the most exhaustive study of the foreign policy of a great power ever written"; yet, by the constant anachronistic attribution to Prussia of a national German policy, it showed how tremendous learning can be piloted to produce a false result. The work was dominated by Droysen's view of the state as a vast power-organization.

One of the most distinguished of the pupils of Ranke was Wilhelm von Giesebrecht, and his great work, the *History of the Period of the Empire* began to appear in 1855. It was inspired by the idea of awakening the Germans to the glory of their medieval history—the romanticism and the achievements of their famous emperors—and Giesebrecht proved to be a wonderful narrator, the evidence of his immense scholarship being relegated to the footnotes. Giesebrecht had the distinction of reconstructing an old chronicler from later writers who had made use of him, and then having his scholarship confirmed when the work itself came to light a generation later. It was his history of the *Kaiserzeit* which provoked the great controversy over the effects of medieval imperialism on the cause of German nationalism.

In 1856 Alexis de Tocqueville published *L'ancien régime et la révolution*, a treatise based on the study of provincial and other local archives, and devoted to an examination of the roots of the Revolution—the effective opening of analytical work on the character and structure of ancient France.

Other forms of history were developing, however, principally in Germany itself; their challenge to the prevailing system built up the pressures which in the 1890's produced controversies on the very nature of a history—controversies that mark another stage in the story, since the position and state of the whole subject could never be quite the same again (though the classical school maintained its hold through the universities).

In various countries there had long been antecedents of what we should call economic history; in the eighteenth century these are to be found in Adam Smith's *Wealth of Nations* and in histories of commerce, some of which covered a considerable area of economic life. Descriptive works—regional studies and accounts of particular industries, for example—went on appearing in the nineteenth century; and, partly perhaps through the influence of Montesquieu, possibly also as a result of influences from the Scottish Enlightenment, examples were to be found in Göttingen at the very beginning of the century, particularly in the work of

A. H. L. Heeren. The main nineteenth-century movement owes its rise, however, to Wilhelm Roscher, who had been influenced by Heeren; and, for some decades, the real purpose of the movement—a purpose already made clear in Roscher's famous "manifesto" of 1843—was to establish a new kind of economics, which should attain a wider kind of generalization based on the study of the past as well as the present, and particularly a comparative study of the development of the various nations. William Ashley, who held at Harvard the first chair of economic history ever created, took his start from this position, and it was only in his Inaugural Lecture in 1893 that he began to depart from it. By the late 1870's books had begun to appear in Germany which claimed to be "economic histories," and some were proposing to cover the whole economic history of the country, for, here as elsewhere, what was particularly required was the full-length account of a nation's development. By the late 1870's, however, Gustav Schmoller, who became the dominating figure in Germany (and greatly influenced Ashley, for example) was concentrating on the economic policy of Frederick the Great; and, whether because of the analogy with political history or because of the existence of etatist views, or because the sources were governmental, or because economists hoped that they might be advisers on policy, economic history at this stage in its development tended to be preoccupied with the work of government, or to see events from the point of view of government. It was in the nature of the subject to envisage, however, a life and activity that sprang from society in all its length and breadth, and the transition to this wider survey of a nation's material development was continually assisted by the appearance of regional studies and descriptive accounts of particular industries. The depiction of an economic life which rises autonomously out of the whole landscape would seem to have depended somewhat, also, on the availability of a larger range of nongovernmental sources.

In the meantime, Jakob Burckhardt's *Civilisation of the Renaissance in Italy,* published in 1860, had given a fresh stimulus to that cultural history which had been quickened by the work of Voltaire and the interest of the eighteenth century in the history of the arts and sciences. In the late 1880's there was a foretaste of the larger controversy that was due to appear shortly afterwards. Dietrich Shäfer's insistence that the state must be the central point in historical reconstruction was answered by Eberhard Gothein, who held that *Kulturgeschichte* was necessary for the achievement of the essential synthesis. In various countries the kind of history which concerned itself with the processes of society rather than the narrative of political events

had already begun to raise important issues. The influence of Auguste Comte had encouraged a tendency to believe that the study of the past could be regarded as analogous to the natural sciences, aspiring to achieve generalizations and laws. This had shown itself in H. T. Buckle's *History of Civilisation in England,* which had appeared in 1857 and was receiving renewed attention in the 1890's; and a brilliant and imposing illustration of it was Hippolyte Taine's *Origines de la France contemporaine,* published between 1876 and 1894. By the end of the 1870's, furthermore, some economic historians were insisting that, in any comprehensive history of culture and society, the economic factor must have the determining role and in reality provides the clue to the processes of historical change. It is not clear that this view owed anything to the influence of Marx in academic circles, though the first volume of *Das Kapital* had been published in 1867. At the same time the system that Marx produced—however much it owed to antecedent writers—must be regarded as one of the most remarkable and powerful contributions ever made to the interpretation of the past, and in the period after 1917 it came to have an important influence even on historians who were not themselves Marxists.

It was the publication (from 1891 to 1913) of Karl Lamprecht's large-scale *German History* which, by provoking a considerable controversy, led to the discussion of some of these larger issues, and to heated debates amongst historians themselves on the subject: "What is history?" Lamprecht's conception of his work as a comprehensive study of society and culture, his views about the importance of the economic factor in the synthesis, his insistence that history should be regarded as a science—and the interest which he also had in social psychology—made him militant against the prevailing school in Germany. And ideas which, though not necessarily new, were thrown out in this controversy—and so gained a general hearing—have remained in currency during the controversies of the twentieth century. The battle in the 1890's was a very bitter one and Lamprecht attempted on one occasion to gain control of the *Historische Zeitschrift,* which was the chief instrument of his opponents. Lamprecht was vulnerable himself in many ways, but, though he failed to dislodge his opponents, he could not be repressed and he preached his doctrines in the United States. For historiography, a new period had in fact opened.

In the meantime the development of historiography had produced problems still more profound—problems that were calculated to tax the mind of the philosopher—and the discussion of these reached great intensity in the 1890's, though its influence amongst practicing historians tended to come later. Funda-

495

mental issues affecting the emergence of "historicism" had been raised by the writings of Friedrich Karl von Savigny from the year 1814. He had taught that law was not to be manufactured rationalistically from a blueprint, but grew naturally out of the *Volksgeist*, like a country's language or its manners or its constitution—an attitude that tended to lead to historical relativism. Later still, what had begun as a conflict with positivism became in Dilthey, Wilhelm Windelband, and Heinrich Rickert an enquiry as to the basis (and the very possibility) of historical knowledge—a discussion which, this time, stressed the differences between history and the natural sciences, probed into the problem of the historical consciousness itself, and posed the question whether the universe has any ethical meaning. Instead of the old "philosophy of history" there now emerged a primary concern with methodological and epistemological issues in the historical realm; and (through Max Weber, Ernst Troeltsch and Friedrich Meinecke, for example) these discussions carried their influence into the realm of the actual historian, particularly in the twentieth century. In the 1890's, furthermore, there emerged some imposing criticisms of Marx.

By the last two decades of the nineteenth century, academic history had come to have an imposing character in books both massive in form and intricate in texture. The intensity of research, the accumulated results of government support in the publication of great amounts of archival sources in various countries, and the vast range of manuscript material to which historians had now found their way, were transforming the whole landscape and giving scholarship its modern appearance. The adoption of the new methods and the new standards by universities—the palpable effects of all this during the last two decades of the century in the United States and at Oxford and Cambridge—secured that a regular progress should take place on all sides; and the fruits of the movement were apparent even in Russia.

The establishment of learned journals in one country after another encouraged the natural tendency of research to become more microscopic, and, in 1900, the inauguration of the International Congress of the Historical Sciences turned historians into a cosmopolitan fraternity, though it failed to eliminate the constrictive effects of nationalism. The whole study made solid advances irrespective of the theoretical controversies that seemed in the 1890's to be shaking its very basis. There were interesting developments in historical thinking, characterized in the case of Great Britain by the revision of anachronistic and excessively Whiggish interpretations in the writings of William Stubbs and in the modern history field. Still more important were

the problems raised in Germany by writers like Max Weber and Ernst Troeltsch. As a result of many decades of work and a long accumulation of documentary materials, certain fields of sixteenth-century history—particularly the Revolt of the Netherlands, the French Wars of Religion and the period of Philip II of Spain—were due for a considerable reshaping by the end of the century; French Revolutionary studies had achieved a great development, the emergence of François V. A. Aulard marking a new era; and similarly the intensified researches into Frederick the Great and Napoleon now brought scholarship to a new stage.

From the time of the ancient campaign annals, historical writing repeatedly had a curious relationship with war. The historical consciousness was sometimes awakened (or spread more widely) as the result of a conflict that had come as a great human experience. War would also seem to have been the point at which men of all classes were compelled to feel the impact of historical events. All this has been illustrated afresh in the twentieth century, when two world wars (and the revolutions more or less connected with them) have greatly altered the position of history. Immediately after 1919 the consequences came in a flood—the host of memoirs from political and military leaders, the controversies over the question of "war-guilt," and the interest of governments in the production of the record.

The flood itself went on mounting in every subsequent decade. Massive selections, particularly of diplomatic documents, were published. Archives were opened to a more recent date, especially in the case of defeated or revolutionized governments. There emerged avowedly "official histories" and sometimes the most recent documents would be made available to such scholars as were deemed reliable. The special concern which the general public had for issues that were still in a sense alive brought a revival of the tremendous importance which had so often been attached to the writing of "contemporary history." In a world in which democracies have a special claim to information and the journalists have a special skill in exposing the underside of events, the production of "instant" history, and the attempt to achieve scholarly accounts of episodes still very recent, have altered the center of gravity in historiography.

The situation has its dangers, especially where a wider general public can act as the arbiter, and its voice may have an effect on scholarship itself. Men are more completely locked within the framework of their age than they ever realize, and history can easily lose what Lord Acton once specified as its important function: to release men from the tyranny of the present. Even for the purpose of writing "contemporary history," it may be best that a student should have received his training in a past sufficiently remote to allow of a certain degree of detachment, and should have had exercise in the mental transpositions which are required for an understanding of more distant ages—an understanding of men not like-minded with himself.

The pursuit of immediately "utilitarian" objects, and the assumption that the past is interesting only as the preparation for the present can be unfortunate for both students and writers, who may never learn that further dimension which historical thinking acquires when its roots go back to more distant times. Even the European (and still more the global) scene is altered by the fact that young democracies, young nationalities, find it so difficult to combine their necessary sympathies with the due degree of detachment in respect of their own history. The powerful position of communism has made it hard for men of both Left and Right to be judicious about Marxist history, though, particularly in the economic history field, a genuine dialogue between the West and Russia has been more possible in recent years. It would be unfortunate if historians, anxious to secure special privileges (special access to documents, for example) should compete with one another for the favor of government.

On the other hand, the "contemporary historian" has an advantage, for the passage of time, which in some respects makes it possible to produce a fairer record, is attended by losses as well as gains. So much of the atmosphere of a period—or of a given circle, a given episode—may disappear; and the future may fail to recover that host of thoughts and assumptions which never needed to be expressed because they were part of the atmosphere—the future may even forget the delicate connotations of words. It has become evident that those sensitive aspects of an age which disappear from sight once direct contact with that age has been lost are the ones that require for their ultimate resurrection the most penetrating and laborious kind of research. The "contemporary historian" may fail to realize that, by "taking sides," even perhaps unconsciously, or by otherwise accepting a framework of a story already current, he has made the task of mounting and organizing the narrative too easy for himself. But if he possesses judgment and training he may pass down to the future a record of permanent and unique importance.

Another important feature of twentieth-century historiography is the relationship with the social sciences, which themselves had reached a new stage (and had come into closer contact with history) in the work of men like Émile Durkheim and Max Weber. That work arose out of lively intellectual movements of the 1890's, and was paralleled in the United States, where

Frederick Jackson Turner's paper on "The Significance of the Frontier in American History" appeared in 1894. Turner's "frontier" hypothesis and his insistence on the importance of sectionalism in American life sprang from a more comprehensive view of the whole past and had great influence on historical study in the United States. After a period of intense discussion and rapid progress, his paper on "Social Forces in American History" appeared in 1910 and along with it, James Harvey Robinson, writing on "The Relation of History to the Newer Sciences of Man," prepared the way for his volume, *The New History*, which came out two years later and launched a further controversy.

So far as historical scholarship is concerned, it is particularly since the Second World War that the whole landscape has been transformed as a result of the developments in the social sciences. The application of social science procedures to various problems and periods of the past has tended to change the direction of historical enquiry itself, and to alter the notion of what might be needed to achieve satisfactory forms of historical explanation. The historian himself now has a different view of what must be done to produce, for example, a "reconstruction of the ordinary working world of the politician" in a bygone period. At the same time, he enters upon forms of analysis which would hardly have been possible if masses of further source material had not become available and research-work had not been organized so as to make a cooperative endeavor more feasible.

The historian, also, is now more ready to envisage society as a whole and movements in the mass, and to turn his mind to population problems, the sociology of religion, and so forth. For a long time, even during the twentieth century, the historian and the social scientist were in conflict with one another, and seemed unable to agree about their respective roles in the recovery or the explanation of the human story. Today when the historians (though so many of them continue to work as before) are more prepared to use the results and the methods of the social scientists, and even to move further afield, to psychology, for example, the controversy has not been brought to an end. The claim has arisen that history should itself be regarded as a social science—no more and no less—and this is construed as though it meant relegating into the realm of mere useless antiquarianism that work which historians throughout the ages (and still largely even at the present day) have been accustomed to producing: namely, the sheer recovery of the past and the narration of what actually happened.

History is enriched by the developments that have taken place, but those who build up their outlook only from the social sciences will have only a sectionalized

497

view of the overall process of historical change, a process in which the genius of a single leader who sees and uses existing conditions can secure an enormous leverage, and a handful of men who have faith can move mountains, as the twentieth century itself has shown. It is possible that democracy will also radically turn its back on what was for so long a main objective of historical writing—the communication of what the art of statesmanship requires. When help has been recruited from all available sciences, there is something left for the mind of the historian who, surveying the whole, can make the presidential contribution that is itself something like an act of statesmanship. Sometimes the subject has been reduced almost to a study of conditions, but Camille Ernest Labrousse and Georges Lefebvre, students of conditions, came to admit that the French Revolution cannot be explained without the political narrative, and that a man like Henri IV on the throne of France, instead of Louis XVI, might have given a different turn to the whole story. It is still going to be true that when a people has been involved in a war, it will want to know how that war came about and how its leaders behaved; and perhaps this basic human demand for narrative will secure the survival of what has always been regarded as history, and will tend to keep the subject on the rails. Indeed, there is something absolutely essential in history and in the processes of time to which justice cannot be done save in the form of a narrative in which one does not know in advance what is going to happen next.

BIBLIOGRAPHY

Acton, John Emerich Edward Dalberg (Lord Acton), "German Schools of History," *Historical Essays and Studies* (London, 1919), pp. 344–92. H. Baron, *The Crisis of the Early Renaissance*, 2 vols. (Princeton, N.J., 1955). B. C. Brundage, "The Birth of Clio," *Teachers of History: Essays in Honor of Laurence Bradford Packard*, ed. H. S. Hughes (Ithaca, N.Y., 1954), pp. 199–230. J. B. Bury, *The Ancient Greek Historians* (London, 1909; reprint New York, 1957). H. Butterfield, *Man on his Past* (Cambridge, 1955; reprint Boston, 1960). R. G. Collingwood, *The Idea of History* (Oxford and New York, 1946). B. Croce, *Storia della storiografia italiana nel secolo decimonono* (Bari, 1921). H. C. Dent, ed., *The Idea of History in the Ancient Near East* (New Haven, 1955). M. A. Fitzsimons, et al., *The Development of Historiography* (Harrisburg, Penna., 1954). Robert Flint, *Historical Philosophy in France and French Belgium and Switzerland* (London, 1893). E. Fueter, *Geschichte der neueren Historiographie*, 3rd ed. (Munich, 1936). F. S. Fussner, *The Historical Revolution . . . 1580–1640* (London and New York, 1962). V. H. Galbraith, *Historical Research in Medieval England* (London, 1951). C. S. Gardner, *Chinese Traditional Historiography* (Cambridge, Mass., 1938). G. P. Gooch, *History and Historians in the Nineteenth Century*, 2nd ed. (London and New York, 1952). J. Higham, et al., *History*, Princeton Studies of Humanistic Scholarship in America (Princeton, N.J., 1965). E. Hoemsel, "Das Ethos der chinesischen Geschichtsschreibung," *Saeculum*, 1 (1950), 111–28. G. Hölscher, *Die Anfänge der hebräischen Geschichtesschreibung* (Heidelberg, 1942). H. S. Hughes, *Consciousness and Society: The Reorientation of European Social Thought, 1890–1930* (New York, 1958; London, 1959). Ibn Khaldūn, The *Muqaddimah*, trans. F. Rosenthal (New York, 1958). G. G. Iggers, *The German Conception of History, The National Tradition of Historical Thought from Herder to the Present* (Middletown, Conn., 1968). P. Joachimsen, *Geschichtsauffassung und Geschichtsschreibung in Deutschland unter dem Einfluss des Humanismus*, Teil 1 (Leipzig and Berlin, 1910). D. Knowles, *Great Historical Enterprises* (London, 1963). B. Lasch, *Das Erwachen und die Entwickelung der historischen Kritik im Mittelalter, VI–XIII Jahrhundert* (Breslau, 1887). B. Mazlish, *The Riddle of History: The Great Speculators from Vico to Freud* (New York, 1966). F. Meinecke, *Die Entstehung des Historismus*, 2 vols. (Munich, 1936). S. Mellon, *The Political Uses of History: A Study of Historians in the French Revolution* (Stanford, 1958). R. L. P. Milburn, *Early Christian Interpretations of History* (London, 1954; reprint New York). L. Pearson, *Early Ionian Historians* (Oxford, 1939). C. H. Philips, ed., *Historical Writing on the Peoples of Asia*, 4 vols. (London, 1961–62). J. G. A. Pocock, *The Ancient Constitution and the Feudal Law: A Study of English Historical Thought in the Seventeenth Century* (Cambridge and New York, 1957). F. Rosenthal, *A History of Muslim Historiography* (Leiden, 1952). *Saeculum*, 8 (1957), and 9 (1958), essays on Hittite oriental historiography. H. R. von Srbik, *Geist und Geschichte vom deutscher Humanismus bis zur Gegenwart*, 2 vols. (Munich and Salzburg, 1950). Social Science Research Council (Committee on Historiography), Bulletin 54, *Theory and Practice in Historical Study* (1946); idem, Bulletin 64, *The Social Sciences in Historical Study* (1954). P. Stadler, *Geschichtsschreibung und historischen Denken in Frankreich, 1789–1871* (Zurich, 1958). J. W. Thompson, et al., *A History of Historical Writing*, 2 vols. (New York, 1940). H. Vyverberg, *Historical Pessimism in the French Enlightenment* (Cambridge, Mass., 1958). F. X. von Wegele, *Geschichte der deutschen Historiographie seit dem Auftreten des Humanismus* (Munich, 1885). E. Weis, *Geschichtsschreibung und Staatsauffassung in der französische Enzyklopädie* (Wiesbaden, 1956).

HERBERT BUTTERFIELD

[See also Ancients and Moderns; **Causation in History; Christianity in History;** Historical; **Historicism; Historiography, Influence of Ideas on Greek;** Islamic Conception; **Nationalism;** Periodization in History; Progress; **Renaissance Literature and Historiography;** Romanticism; Theodicy.]

THE INFLUENCE OF IDEAS ON ANCIENT GREEK HISTORIOGRAPHY

ARE IDEAS the product of events, or do ideas influence events? This question has been discussed since the mid-twentieth century, both in general and with regard to whether or not ancient Greek historiography has been influenced by ideas and theories not originating from the historians themselves (*Histoire et historiens dans l'antiquité*, pp. 129ff.). The question is, however, rather pointless, since it appears obvious that ideas frequently come into being in response to events, but receive their specific form from individual thinkers and then in turn may exercise a very strong influence on future events, including literary works. Marxism, for instance, was a product of modern industrialism. The social conditions created by early industrialism almost inevitably gave rise to socialist ideas. But the form in which they exercised the greatest influence both on future political events and on a considerable section of historiographical literature was given to them by one man: Karl Marx. A study of the influence of ideas on ancient Greek historiography, therefore, should be a study of this interplay of events, ideas, and historiographical works. Furthermore, the concept of idea should be taken in a rather wide sense, to include not only ideas that have been precisely formulated but also "ideas" that at certain periods can be said to have "been in the air," i.e., ideas that in one way or another appear to have entered into or to have formed the background of the thinking of outstanding men in various fields of intellectual activity without having been expressly and clearly formulated by anyone.

Critical historiography in the modern sense first came into being in Greece in the beginning of the fifth century B.C. It came into being through ideas which in turn were, in a way, the product of events or of a situation produced by preceding events. The immigration into Asia Minor of Greeks from the mainland during the preceding centuries had produced a multitude of more or less scattered Greek settlements on the fringe of more highly developed civilizations with traditions greatly differing from one another, as well as from those of the Greeks. The Jews of the Old Testament who were in a similar situation—which differed however from that of the Greeks in that they were not scattered over a long shoreline but concentrated in one area, "Palestine"—defended themselves against the overwhelming foreign influences by strengthening their own traditions. The Greeks, on the contrary, or at least their intellectually most gifted representatives, tried to find a way in these bewildering surroundings by taking an entirely new and fresh look at the world and by trying to create a new picture of the world by means of observation and speculation.

The first Greek thinker to create an entirely new cosmology and cosmogony was Anaximander of Miletus, who lived in the first half of the sixth century B.C. His theory included not only an explanation of the way in which our cosmos, with its stars and their revolutions, came into being, but also a theory of the gradual evolution of living beings—a theory that, although in a very primitive form, has remarkable similarities to Darwin's theory of evolution. After Anaximander's attempt to elaborate a history of the development of life and living things on earth, it was natural for his successor, Hecataeus, to supplement his history by a history of man as the latest product of the evolution of living beings. Hecataeus of Miletus (ca. 550–480 B.C.) may not have been born early enough to have known Anaximander personally, but he is said to have considered himself Anaximander's pupil.

But the history of human beings in general, or of the Greeks in particular, cannot be reconstructed solely by present-day observation and speculation. By necessity it has to make use of tradition. But tradition is just what had become doubtful in the face of so many conflicting traditions. Besides, existing accounts concerning past Greek history consisted, at least for the more remote past, nearly exclusively of legends elaborated by poets. These legends contained much that appeared miraculous, i.e., in conflict with what could be observed in the philosopher's or would-be historian's own time. Thus Hecataeus conceived the idea of purifying tradition of its miraculous elements and of doing so, so to speak, on a psychological basis. Men in general, he seems to have reasoned, are inclined to exaggerate, to take literally what is meant metaphorically, and to take as absolute what is only relative. Thus when, according to legend, King Aegyptus had fifty sons and Danaos had fifty daughters, Hecataeus said that there were probably about twenty on either side; when legend told of the hell-hound Cerberus (whom Hercules was said to have bound and brought to King Eurystheus), Hecataeus responded that the hell-hound was probably an extraordinarily big snake that had bitten many people so that they went straight to Hades. So people called it "hell-hound," and later the legend of a real hell-hound originated from this. For the legend that Hercules had brought the cattle of Geryon from the end of the world to Sparta, Hecataeus said that he probably brought them from the bay of Ambracia. Ancient people would have thought that the world reached no farther at this point because they could not see any land westward beyond it.

It is obvious that Hecataeus was mistaken when he believed that a true reconstruction of history could be achieved by taking the miraculous element out of

499

legend. Both the objects had to be changed and subtler methods had to be found if what Hecataeus had in mind was to be attained. Nevertheless, Hecataeus' idea that tradition has to be purified by rational criticism has remained the foundation of critical historiography in the twentieth century.

In the following generation political events decisively influenced the development of ideas, which in turn had a great influence on Greek historiography. Hecataeus had acted as adviser in the so-called Ionian rebellion, when in 500 B.C. the Greeks of Asia Minor rose up against the Persians, who, about half a century earlier, had subjected them to their rule. In the following two decades the Persians had tried to extend their domination to the Greeks of the Greek motherland, but were finally defeated in the battles of Salamis and Plataeae (480–79), after which the Greeks of Asia Minor were also delivered from the Persian yoke. As a result of this violent conflict, the attention of the Greeks naturally focused on the differences between the two nations, specifically on the differences in political organization.

It was then that the race theory first raised its head: not in the form of Gobineau's *Essai sur l'inégalité des races humaines,* (1853–55), in which the attempt is made to show that the Nordic race is superior to all other races and destined to rule over them, but in a form which can be found in Montesquieu's *De l'esprit des lois:* a form in which racial differences are derived from climatic differences. In a treatise attributed to the famous physician Hippocrates, but in fact composed by an unknown author (in modern translations usually published under the title "Hippocrates on Climate"), the theory is advanced that not only the general character of the inhabitants, but also the political institutions prevailing in different parts of the world are ultimately products of the climate. The climate of Asia Minor is very temperate; the differences of temperature in the different seasons are not very great. In consequence, the people who have lived there for generations usually have well-proportioned bodies, but are soft and not very energetic. They therefore easily submit to the rule of one hereditary ruler, which is why despotic forms of government appear to prevail in oriental countries. The climate of northern Europe, in contrast, has extreme variations of temperature. This makes the people there savage, violent of temperament, and unruly, lacking self-control. They too need rulers and have kings, but for the opposite reason. Monarchy in northern Europe differs from that of the oriental countries in that members of the former would not meekly submit to the whims of a hereditary despot. Rather, they choose their kings according to qualities of leadership.

The climate of the Greek mainland has temperature variations which are greater than in the Orient, but less great than in northern Europe. The climate, therefore, is invigorating; it makes the inhabitants energetic, but not savage and violent. On the contrary, Greeks are self-reliant and composed; they are the only people who can govern themselves by submitting to laws that have been self-imposed. Their native form of government is autonomy. Even where, as in Sparta, there are kings, these are constitutional rulers subject to the laws of the land. Greeks are the only free men (ἐλεύθεροι).

This race theory is not mentioned or even alluded to in the work of the first great Greek historian, Herodotus, but he appears to have derived from it, or from its antecedents, the guiding idea of his description of the great conflict between the Persians and the Greeks in the beginning of the fifth century B.C. namely, the contrast between Greek liberty and oriental despotism. With Herodotus, however, this idea has entered into combinations with other ideas, some of them very old. From Homer to Greek tragedy the relation of human beings to the gods played a central role. What this relation should be is expressed with unsurpassable conciseness in the famous inscription of the temple of Apollo at Delphi, γνῶθι σεαυτόν ("know yourself"). This does not mean that man should try to inquire into the innermost recesses of his soul, but that he should know his place, know that he is a human being and not a god, and should not try to rise above his station and condition.

This is another aspect of that self-control and self-restraint that is an indispensable element in Herodotus' notion of Greek liberty. Herodotus has further enlarged this idea through the notion of the "envy" of the gods, who do not permit man to rise above the limits of a human being, and who strike man down when he least expects it if he tries to exceed those limits. The combination of these ideas forms the background of Herodotus' story of Solon and Croesus; of the great Athenian statesman who knows the limits of a man's achievement or aspiration, and the great oriental king who is in no way a cruel despot, but a most magnanimous and fair-minded ruler. Croesus, nevertheless, is struck down by the gods with one terrible blow after another for no other reason than that he believed himself to be the happiest of all men, and had tried to live in superhuman splendor.

But it is most interesting to observe how Herodotus, having taken as his guide this idea of the contrast between Greek liberty and simplicity and Oriental despotism and luxury, is gradually led on to meditate further about the implications of the Greek concept of liberty. He recognizes that there are several possible variations of this concept of liberty and that all these variations, when applied in practice, also have their inherent dangers. There is a story in Herodotus about Deioces, the founder of the Median dynasty, who rose from a private station to the position of an absolute ruler, because the Medes, after freeing themselves from the foreign domination of the Assyrians, found the state of anarchy that prevailed in their country so intolerable that they preferred to submit to the rule of a despot—Deioces—rather than continue as they were. This is, of course, a very good illustration and confirmation of the idea expressed elsewhere in Herodotus that liberty can subsist only on the basis of strict adherence to self-imposed law and that "liberty" in the sense of anarchy and lawlessness inevitably leads to tyranny or despotism. But in the last books of *The Persian Wars* (in all likelihood the latest written and in which he has to describe the defense of Greek liberty against the extension of ·oriental despotism), Herodotus is forced to take a closer look at the Greek concept of liberty and to make somewhat more subtle distinctions. In a grandiose dialogue between the exiled Spartan king, Demaratus, and the Persian king, Xerxes, the former says: "The Spartans, being free, are not entirely free but have a master, the law, whom they obey more than your subjects obey you, and this master does not (like a despot) say one day this and another day something else but it says always the same" (VII, 104).

But as the narrative proceeds other anecdotes show that this Spartan concept of liberty also has its deficiencies. First, it applies in its full sense only to Spartan citizens and is not even extended to the rest of the population of Lacedaemonia. As a consequence the Spartans felt no obligation to defend liberty everywhere, not even in Greece, except where this was indispensable for the defense of liberty at home. Second, the law is too rigid, so that (1) it impairs the flexibility of action necessary to defend it, and (2) it is always in danger of becoming intolerable to the most outstanding men of the country, so that they are tempted to break away from it. The most important example of this in the time of the Persian Wars was King Pausanias, but a good many examples appear later. Thus Herodotus finds it necessary to distinguish the Athenian concept of liberty, which is both more comprehensive and more flexible, from the Spartan concept. But the distinction is not further elaborated in detail within the work of Herodotus.

A very penetrating analysis of the difference between the Athenian and the Spartan concept of liberty, however, is given in the famous funeral speech of the Athenian statesman Pericles in Thucydides' *History of the Peloponnesian Wars*. It can be proved that some of the ideas expressed in this speech are taken from a speech actually made by Pericles. But its elaboration in detail is indubitably the work of this second great Greek historian. In this speech also the concept of liberty is positively connected with the concept of law, not primarily with the special laws of Athens, though these are also included, but "with those unwritten laws which exist for the protection of those who are wronged and whose transgression brings shame (not legal sanctions) on the transgressor" (II, 37, 3). For the rest, he says, the life of the Athenians is not rigidly regulated and subjected to severe discipline (like that of the Spartans). In ordinary times we let everybody live according to his whims and pleasure. Yet when the good of the community requires it, we are no less ready to do our share and to obey those in command whom we ourselves have chosen. This is a much idealized picture of Athenian society; reality corresponded to it only most imperfectly. But it is interesting to see how ideas which, if we include the opposition to Athenian tyranny in the name of equality before the law (ἰσονομία), came into being a full century earlier, continued to influence historical writing and, reflecting the change of time, were further elaborated.

In this case the nature of the influence of earlier ideas on the work of Thucydides is easy to see. But most of the ideas that made his work so different from that of Herodotus were the kind that "are in the air," but are not exactly formulated. Thus it is by no means easy to define with precision their influence on his work. The period of Thucydides' early youth, as well as of his adult life, was a period of rationalism, of "enlightenment," and of "science awakening." While Herodotus often explains the course of events on the basis of either laws established by the gods or direct actions of divine powers, Thucydides speaks of the gods or divine powers only to show how the actions of *men* on various occasions were influenced by belief in divine powers; Herodotus himself never speaks in a way which indicates clearly that he believes in such powers.

Herodotus had been interested in the causes of events. The first sentence of his work says that one of his purposes in writing it is to record the cause or reason for the Greek-Oriental wars. These causes appeared to be rather on the surface, visible for all who had knowledge of the external events. In the meantime, with post-Eleatic philosophers in general and with the atomists in particular, the notion had become prevalent that the true causes of things are hidden. Hence the famous utterance of Democritus that it would be a greater pleasure for him "to find out one cause or reason" (μίαν αἰτίαν εὑρεῖν) than to come into possession of all the riches of the king of Persia. This notion of hidden causes is, in a way, also at the bottom of Thucydides' famous distinction between those "causes" of a war that are, on the one hand, spoken of openly 501 and bandied about in the feuding powers' accusations against one another, and, on the other hand, those "causes" that are real motives about which nobody dares to speak openly.

Because of this distinction it has often been said that Thucydides introduced a "scientific spirit" into historiography by transferring to historiography the categories and methods of natural science. This is a great oversimplification. Nor would Thucydides be praiseworthy if he had done what is imputed to him. In the atomistic philosophy of Democritus the notion of "necessity" (ἀνάγκη), i.e., of the unbreakable law of causality that governs everything, plays a dominating role. Yet even in Democritus' system, necessity appears not only in the form of mechanical compulsion, but also in the form of compulsive motivation, as when the rise of material civilization is explained by the "needs" (χρεῖαι) which compelled human beings to make inventions and to work with newly invented instruments in order to meet these needs. In this field of human motivation Democritus appears even to have left a certain area of free decision. Obviously assuming a state of civilization where the needs are no longer absolutely compelling, he says that virtue consists in doing what is needed (τὰ χρὴ ἐόντα), lack of virtue in not doing what is needed ("needed" in order to keep up a life worthy of a human being).

In the work of Thucydides, "necessity" in the form of psychological compulsion plays a similarly dominating role. The truest motive (which was not mentioned publicly) that brought about the Peloponnesian War was that the fear of the Athenians' increasing power compelled (ἀναγκάσαι) the Spartans to wage war upon them in order to stop this increase. But when Pericles advises the Athenians not to give in to the demands of the Spartans, he is also motivated by a compelling fear: that, by giving in to the Spartans' demands in order to avoid the war, the Athenians would so weaken their own power, that the Spartans could destroy the Athenian power altogether whenever they wished to do so. At the bottom of all this there appears to be the notion that there are historical forces which, though psychological in nature, are so compelling that it is useless to struggle against them.

On the other hand, Thucydides in his work stresses again and again the important role played by the genius of great statesmen, their insight and foresight that enable them to influence events favorably (from the point of view of the country they represent). Thus he expresses the opinion that Athens would not have been defeated in the Peloponnesian War but would have come out of it victorious, if Pericles' successors had followed the principles of general strategy that he had laid down at the beginning of the war. There

is perhaps a possibility of reconciling the notion of absolutely compelling historical forces, against which it would be in vain to struggle, with the notion of the capability of great statesmen to exert a decisive influence on the course of events. But no attempt to arrive at a clear resolution of the problem posed by these seemingly conflicting notions can be found in the work of Thucydides.

The age of Thucydides was not only an age of "enlightening" and of awakening science, but also of the rise of moral philosophy with its initiator and representative, Socrates, who was approximately ten years older than the historian. It has often been said that, in contrast to many other ancient historians, the moral element is completely lacking in the work of Thucydides and that it is, in fact, from the beginning excluded by his "realism" that refuses to contemplate anything but the play and counterplay of power politics. It is perfectly true that Thucydides throughout his work carefully avoids all direct moralizing concerning the events and the actions of the actors on the political scene. But he was by no means blind to the moral implications of the events. This is shown clearly by his violent aversion to Cleon (who in many ways adhered to the strategy of Pericles, as described by Thucydides, but who initiated terroristic methods against the "allies" of the Athenians who in the course of time had become their subjects), the Melian dialogue, and above all, the famous chapters in his third book which describe the depravation and reversal of all moral concepts as a result of the hatreds aroused by the war and the accompanying civil wars.

However, Thucydides was not a Socratic. His personal attitude is perhaps best illustrated by what he says about Nicias. Nicias seems to have been impressed by Socrates. But Plato, in his dialogue *Laches*, accuses Nicias, though indirectly, of not living up to Socratic principles. It was Socrates' opinion that one should be more afraid of doing wrong than of having to face material loss or even death as a consequence of having done right. Nicias, as a leader of the Sicilian expedition, appears to have been more afraid of being condemned to death by the Athenians for breaking off the Sicilian enterprise prematurely (as it seemed to them) than of causing the destruction of the whole Athenian army by delaying the necessary retreat. Thucydides must have been aware of this. But he says that Nicias was, according to all accepted and traditional standards, a most honorable, decent, and conscientious man, and that this was no slight thing. He adds that Nicias deserved in no way the fate that befell him. This seems to indicate that Thucydides was not quite unaware that there is something higher than accepted and traditional morality, but that he thought it was not quite common among men to try hard and successfully all through one's life to live up to the standards of accepted morality. He, therefore, was unwilling to condemn a man who in his opinion, had fully lived up to the standards of morality, and this not in a private station, where observing conventions is perhaps not too difficult, but under the most trying circumstances.

In a way, one may say that the work of Thucydides is not only the description of the political and military battles of a great war, but is also itself the battleground of partly conflicting ideas. For the most part, these ideas are not directly expressed, but make their influence felt in the description of the events. But this influence is very strong and contributes greatly to the intensity of the narrative as a whole.

An influence of conflicting ideas can also be found in the *Greek History* (*Hellenica*) of Xenophon (second quarter of the fourth century). Xenophon was a pious man who believed in the gods as guardians of justice and morality. He was an admirer of Socrates, but, like some other Socratics, mingled Socratic principles with his own ideas of practical wisdom. His ideas of practical wisdom in turn were influenced by Spartan notions concerning the way in which political problems ought to be handled. In parts of his historical work, especially the third and fourth books, one finds a considerable number of anecdotes, many of them in the form of dialogues modeled on the Socratic dialogues, that could be grouped under the phrase "how to win friends and to influence people." But only the way in which the leaders of these conversations address their questions to their interlocutors, not the content of the questions, is Socratic. However, most of them are at least not in direct conflict with Socratic principles or ideas, although there is an interesting example of conflicting principles in the later books of *Hellenica*.

The story concerns the occupation of the so-called Kadmeia, the fortress of Thebes, by the Spartan general, Phoibidas, contrary to a solemn promise made by the Spartans to respect the liberty of the Greek cities. Xenophon first reports how, upon a complaint of the Thebans with the Spartan government, it was discussed whether or not the forces should be withdrawn and Phoibidas punished for his action. He then tells, without a word of criticism or disapproval, how King Agesilaus (for whom Xenophon felt great admiration) rose up and said that it was an old political principle with the Spartans in such cases to ask whether or not the illegal action had been to the advantage of the Spartan state. If it was not advantageous to Sparta, then, of course, the man in question should be punished, but if what he had done was clearly to the advantage of Sparta, a general should be permitted "to improvise a little," upon which Phoibidas went un-

punished. But when a little later Xenophon has to tell the story of the battle of Leuctra, in which the Spartans suffered a crushing defeat at the hands of the Thebans, the Socratic and the pious believer in divine justice speaks up and says that in his (Xenophon's) opinion this defeat was the just punishment meted out to the Spartans by the gods for the illegal and unpunished action of Phoibidas.

As far back as the middle of the fifth century Athenian statesmen and speakers in the Athenian popular assembly began to use examples and illustrations from past history to support their political arguments. This was done to a much greater extent in the fourth century by the "rhetor" Isocrates. He did not speak in assemblies but published—largely in the form of fictitious speeches—political pamphlets by which he tried to influence the policy not only of the Athenians but also of other countries or governments, including various foreign monarchies. On the basis of this practice Isocrates' disciple, Ephorus of Cumae, conceived the idea that it was the main task and purpose of historiography to provide examples by which statesmen and politicians could guide their actions. The advice, he said, of an old man is rightly considered much more valuable than that of a young man because the former has a much longer experience of human life. But the life-span of even a very old man is not very long. Hence it is necessary to extend our experience beyond the life of an individual. This is what historiography can do for us. In practical application of this idea, he wrote an introduction to every section of his Greek history in which he pointed out what lessons could be learned from the history of the period that he was going to describe.

Only summaries of a very small part of these introductions have come down to us. The wisdom which Ephorus tries to impart to his readers in this way is on the whole not very profound, but of a kind which, if it could be easily applied in practice (which, as history shows, is not the case), would be very useful. Thus, for instance, he says historical events are not good or bad in themselves, but whether they are good or bad depends on what we make of them. The attack of the Persians on Greece in the beginning of the fifth century appeared to be a terrible thing for the Greeks. But when the Greeks collected all their forces and were victorious, a period of undreamt-of expansion of power and prosperity began. A great victory, on the other hand, seems to be a very good thing, but if it leads to illusions of grandeur in the victors, as often happens, it may become the cause of a catastrophe much worse than simple defeat. On another occasion Ephorus says that democracies cannot be overthrown except by persons or groups of persons who have had a long time in which to gather adherents and to make preparations. It is therefore easy to stop such a process when it is still in its early stages. But if a democracy waits too long to cope energetically with its opponents it may be too late, and the democracy will be replaced by an oligarchy or a tyranny.

Another disciple of Isocrates, Theopompus of Chios, took a quite different direction. Many conservatives of the fourth century regretted what they considered the overdemocratization of political and social life in some Greek cities, especially Athens. It was not good, they thought, for all political decisions to be made by a popular assembly in which the majority inevitably consisted of people with no insight into the intricacies of diplomacy or into the financial requirements of an energetic foreign policy. They were also of the conviction that good manners, which can be developed only over a longer period of time in a selected society, as well as certain aristocratic principles of honor, were destroyed by the application of democratic principles of equality. But the times in which the remnants of the old aristocracies could have set up oligarchic governments by their own strength appeared to have ended with the downfall of the so-called thirty tyrants in Athens. Not unlike the many German conservatives in the period of the Weimar republic, they began to be on the lookout for a "strong man" who, they thought, might be able to bring back something of the good old times and to reestablish some kind of hierarchic political system and society.

Isocrates, to a certain extent, can be counted among them. But the idea was, above all, embraced with violent passion by his most gifted disciple, Theopompus. In one way or another it dominates a very large part of his historical works. In his *Greek History* (*Hellenica*, ca. 394 B.C.) various candidates for the role of the strong man and reformer of Greek institutions appear on the horizon, including the Spartan Lysander and the Thessalian Iason of Pherai. But after Philip, the father of Alexander the Great, had ascended the Macedonian throne and had proved himself a most energetic ruler whose policy more and more affected the whole of Greece, Theopompus broke off his earlier work which had been a continuation of that of Thucydides, and made a new start with the year of Philip's accession.

Though this new work, like the old one, dealt with the whole of Greek history, he gave it the title *Philippica*, which might be translated *Greek History in the Philippan era*. Yet here, too, there arose a conflict, if not between different ideas and ideals, then between ideas and their actualization in reality. In Macedon the hereditary aristocracy of big landowners, in addition to the king, still played a large role. This political

and social order theoretically corresponded exactly to Theopompus' ideals. But while the king personally was deeply steeped in Hellenic culture and a man of refined manners, many of the lords and dynasts of half-barbarian Macedon were certainly anything but cultured gentlemen after the heart of an old Greek aristocrat like Theopompus. Thus, while he sets his greatest hopes upon King Philip, he sometimes speaks in the most disparaging terms of the barbarous and "swinish" behavior of some of the Macedonian war lords, though what he is really interested in is not monarchy but the restoration of an aristocratic political and social order.

A large section of one of the books of the *Philippica* was devoted to a description of the wickedness of the Athenian demagogues, his pet hatred. But he did not approve of Plato either. Plato, in his opinion, was quite right insofar as his ideal state was one governed by an aristocracy. But he disapproved of Plato's Socratic method of discussing with young people what was right and what was wrong. This, he thought, could only have the effect of putting wrong ideas in their heads. To tell them in no uncertain terms what was good and what was bad behavior—that, in his opinion, was the right way to educate young people.

With Alexander's conquest of Greece and of Persia, monarchic ideas and ideals quite different from those of Theopompus naturally emerged. An interesting example is Aristotle's nephew, Callisthenes. He had written historical works of considerable size before Alexander set out to conquer Persia. In these works a kind of hero worship for great men of the past, like Pelopidas and Epaminondas, had played a great role. Thus, when Alexander showed himself superior even to these men as a military leader, it was quite natural that Callisthenes, who knew how to write in a most inspiring fashion, considered it his task to become the herald of the great deeds of the king. But he was very far from abject flattery. He renewed the race theory of the superiority of the Greeks over the Orientals: the former born to be free, even if led by a great hero king, the latter destined to be subjects of a despot. Above all, however, he had a very high opinion of his station as a great writer. It had often been said that the glory of the deeds of Achilles would have vanished but for Homer's poems. Historiography, in the meantime, according to Callisthenes' opinion, had taken the place of epic poetry. The hero and the poet or writer were dependent upon each other. The poet could not become a great poet without a worthy object. But the glory of the hero could not be handed down to posterity in a worthy fashion without the help of the great poet or historian. Callisthenes therefore claimed a rank or station almost equal to that of the king. When in 328 Alexander introduced the oriental custom of προσκύνησις ("prostration before the king"), not only for Orientals but also for Greeks and Macedonians, Callisthenes refused to comply. At that time he got away with it. But when soon after, as an educator of the Macedonian cadets, he stirred up in his students a spirit of rebellion against the introduction of oriental customs which led to a conspiracy (in which Callisthenes does not seem to have been involved directly), he was taken into custody and somewhat later executed. This is a rather peculiar example of the influence of ideas not only on historiography but also on the life of an interesting historian.

In the historical work of Ptolemy I, the founder of the Ptolemaic dynasty in Egypt, the monarchic idea and ideal appears again in an entirely different shape. Having been one of Alexander's generals, but by far not the most outstanding among them, he immediately made, after the death of Alexander, every effort to secure for himself the governorship of Egypt, obviously from the beginning with the idea that here, within a limited area but with easily defendable boundaries, a kingdom and a dynasty could be created that could be made to last. And, in fact, though in later periods the country had for quite a time the most incapable rulers, it lasted longer than any of the other Hellenistic kingdoms founded by Alexander's successors. Ptolemy's history of Alexander bears witness that at an early time he had not only dreamt of acquiring a kingdom for himself, but had also done a good deal of serious thinking on the tasks, duties, and the correct attitude and behavior of a good monarch.

He always speaks of King Alexander with great respect. He praises Alexander's chivalry and gentlemanly behavior towards the captive Persian princesses who approached him in fear and trembling. He defends the king against what appears to him the petty criticisms of Nearchus who had already written about Alexander and who had blamed the king for having frequently exposed himself to great personal danger. Yes, Ptolemy says, but nothing great is ever achieved without taking great risks. But Ptolemy also censures Alexander severely where it appears to him that he had not acted as a king should: a king should not participate in drinking bouts with his friends and drink so much that he loses control over himself. Above all, he expresses his strongest disapproval of the destruction of Persepolis, the residence of the early Persian kings. He calls it a senseless action; it was insane to try to take revenge on men long dead. On many occasions criticism of Alexander's action causes Ptolemy to formulate general maxims for rulers. For example, a king should most of all be on his guard against flatterers, since they are apt to induce him to do foolish things; it is one of the most important tasks of a king to see

to it that the inferiors among his subjects are not mistreated by their superiors; a king should never try to deceive his subjects; he should always be most careful to keep his promises.

The historical work of Ptolemy I has often been criticized in recent times. Primarily, it has been said that he distorts the true perspective of events by putting his own person too much in the foreground. It is quite true that he tells much more about events in which he participated or at which he was present, and that there is a tendency to relate everything in some way to himself. But in another way this makes his work all the more interesting, because everything is pervaded by his meditations and his ideas on true monarchy.

It is not possible here to analyze the host of historians who wrote about Alexander the Great. But it may just be mentioned that among the historians of Alexander there was also a Macedonian aristocrat, Marsyas of Pella, scion of one of the oldest and most noble families, who wrote about the king from an entirely different viewpoint. Apart from his history of Alexander, he also wrote a history of Macedon, beginning with the mythical period. We do not have much of his work, but what we do have shows that Marsyas attributed the astounding accomplishments of the king not so much to the king's personal genius as to the old virtues of the Macedonian people. His work seems to have been the most thoroughly "patriotic" history up to that time.

The historiography of the following two centuries was influenced in various ways by ideas and theories of the philosopher, Aristotle. Foremost among these ideas was his theory of evolution, which was derived from his biological studies. This concept of evolution is quite different from the modern concept of evolution which, on the basis of Darwin's discoveries, was elaborated most importantly by Herbert Spencer. The modern concept is of an evolution starting in a very remote past and continuing more or less in a straight line into an equally remote future, in the meantime producing ever more complicated and differentiated but at the same time ever more perfect forms of life. Furthermore, it is an evolution about whose beginning and possible end nothing is known, except for a vague idea that it may finally end either in a universal catastrophe or in a slower process of dissolution.

Aristotle's concept of evolution, on the contrary, presupposes the eternity of the world as we know it. It is the concept of an evolution that, like the evolution of living beings, begins with a comparatively simple and primitive state, and then develops gradually to a state of ever greater differentiation and perfection. But when the evolving form has reached a certain degree of comparative perfection which we call maturity, it

505

continues in that state for a limited period of time, then begins to decay, and finally dies. In the meantime, however, other living beings have started the same process. In other words, according to this concept of evolution, the world does not develop as a whole, but remains the same, while *within the world* living beings and certain products of human civilization develop, that is unfold, and after some time decay and die, in an everlasting circle. It is a biological concept of evolution which, however, by Aristotle and his disciples was transferred and applied to the field of cultural phenomena.

A most interesting example of this is Aristotle's own discussion of the development of Greek tragedy in his treatise on the art of poetry. Here he tries to show how the Attic drama, starting from very primitive beginnings, gradually developed into the two forms of tragedy and comedy: he follows the development of the former down to the great tragedies of the first of the three great Attic tragedians and then remarks: "after it had gone through a great many changes it ceased [to change], since it had achieved its nature" (*Poetics* 1449a 14–15). The implication is obviously that tragedy continued to flourish as a type of great art until, after the death of Euripides, it began to decay; then by the time of Aristotle, for all practical purposes, it was already dead. This is at least indirectly indicated by the fact that Aristotle does not mention any Greek tragedians living in his own time. The same is true of the old type of Greek comedy. But in the meantime, tragedy and comedy together had produced a new offspring, the so-called new comedy, which, while more similar to Euripides' tragedy than to Aristophanes' comedy, may claim both as its parents, and which, soon after Aristotle, reached its own maturity.

The same idea of evolution was applied by a number of Aristotle's disciples to various sciences which had not yet reached their maturity at the time of Aristotle, but did so in later times and then decayed, withered away, and nearly died. These sciences did not produce new offspring until centuries later, first to some extent with the Arabs, and then in the Western countries at the time of the so-called Renaissance. It is a rather remarkable fact that the Greeks, who believed in continued cycles of birth, evolution to maturity, death, and rebirth (of something new but similar), in eternal succession, actually produced or experienced within their civilization exactly such cycles, some longer, some shorter, within their arts and sciences. By contrast, modern man, who believes (or who until recently believed) in unending or almost unending evolution and progress has thus far actually produced, at least in his sciences, the product most characteristic of our age, an apparently unceasing and in fact ever accelerated

progress. However, with the works of Spengler and Toynbee, there has also been a return to the idea of cycles of civilization, and in recent years the symptoms of possible decay and dissolution of modern civilization have become ever more visible.

Within Greek civilization at the time of Aristotle, the idea of evolution in the biological sense seemed to work well when applied to special arts and sciences. But it was much more difficult to apply it to civilization or even to Greek civilization as a whole. Thus the work of the man who made the attempt, Aristotle's disciple, Dicaearchus of Messene, became a battlefield of conflicting ideas. The idea of a development of human civilization as a whole is, of course, very old. It is found as far back as the *Theogony* and the *Works and Days* of Hesiod (eighth century B.C.). Here already we encounter conflicting ideas. For example, it was the Olympic gods who taught mankind the arts of both material and moral civilization; it was Prometheus who brought fire and the technical arts dependent on fire to mankind against the will of the Olympic gods; in the time of Kronos, before the rule of Zeus and the Olympic gods, mankind lived in a golden age of bliss, but afterward—interrupted only by the age of the Homeric heroes—almost steadily deteriorated.

A similar conflict of ideas can be observed in Dicaearchus' work entitled Βίος Ἑλλάδος (*The Life of Greece*) in which, as the surviving fragments show, he tried to sketch a history of human civilization from its beginnings, culminating in Greek civilization. In this work he used a concept of evolution that has a certain affinity to the evolutionary theory of Spencer and the nineteenth century. Dicaearchus taught that human beings first lived on what they collected without instruments, then invented weapons by which they could kill larger animals and became hunters, then domesticated animals and became cattle raisers, then invented agriculture and used it to replace or supplement those earlier methods of procuring a livelihood for themselves and for their offspring, and finally developed ever more complicated methods of distributing different tasks and functions among themselves—thus creating what we call higher civilization. Since Dicaearchus believed in the eternity of the world, he also introduced the idea of the biological cycle, though he appears to have also considered the possibility that civilizations might not always die a natural death by gradual decay after a period of maturity, but might be destroyed by natural catastrophes so that the survivors would have to start on the same cycle again.

Generally speaking, however, the evolution described seems to imply the idea of progress. Some fragments of the work, on the other hand, indicate that Dicaearchus regarded the youth of mankind, rather than the period of its maturity, as a kind of natural paradise from which, with the evolution of material civilization, man had moved farther and farther away. Traces of the somewhat sentimental view that childhood is the most happy period in the life both of the human invididual and of mankind can also be found elsewhere in Hellenistic literature and sculpture. While this view seems rather characteristic of the age in which Dicaearchus lived, it is far removed from the views of Dicaearchus' teacher, Aristotle. Since we have only fragments of Dicaearchus, it is unfortunately not possible for us to see in detail how Dicaearchus managed to combine all these conflicting viewpoints in attempting a historical reconstruction of a remote past.

In a totally different way, a considerable section of Hellenistic historiography was influenced by a famous sentence in Aristotle's *Poetics* which says that poetry is more philosophical than history. His reasons are: (1) poetry (he has especially dramatic poetry in mind) is more καθόλου (more "general"), and (2) history tells what has actually happened, while poetry represents what might have happened according to necessity or probability. To say that (dramatic) poetry is more general than history may seem strange at first, since ancient tragedy usually stages in great detail what is supposed to have happened in one day or less, while historiography is quite unable to go into so much detail, and to tell what every actor on the political scene has said or done within the compass of one day.

What Aristotle means is that in actual life much happens that is purely accidental, having no deeper significance, while poetry, especially tragic poetry, places the extreme possibilities of what can happen to a human being in a most concentrated form before the eyes of the spectators. In other words, poetry provides within the narrow compass of a play a deep insight into fundamental aspects of what has been called *la condition humaine*. Aristotle called this kind of representation of human life, in the concentrated form of dramatic action (or epic narrative), *mimesis*.

It may seem strange, but it is proved by rather incontestable evidence, that a certain school of Hellenistic historians was induced to mix the principles of historiography and dramatic poetry by the very statement with which Aristotle tried to distinguish the two. The movement, so far as we can see, was led by Duris of Samos, a tyrant of his homeland, who had been a disciple of Theophrastus, and who, in the time left from his governmental duties, developed a rather extensive literary activity. Duris wrote not only several historical works, but also various treatises on poetry, especially dramatic poetry. In the introduction to one of his historical works he blamed the historians Ephorus and Theopompus because there was no *mimesis* in their

works; that is, he blamed them because their historical works lacked what Aristotle had considered the essence of poetry in contrast to historiography. It looks as if Duris had been irked by Aristotle's statement that poetry was more philosophical than historiography, and had tried to raise historiography to the highest possible level by making it more poetical.

That this was actually his intention is shown by the surviving fragments of his historical works, many of which show a strong tendency towards dramatization of the events. An especially good illustration of his method is provided by a fragment from his history of Samos. In this fragment Duris relates a most dramatic incident that is supposed to have occurred in the war between Athens and Aegina at the beginning of the fifth century. A whole detachment of Athenians that had made an inroad on the island are captured on their way back, and all of them are killed except one man who is sent to Athens in order to tell the story of what has happened to his comrades. When he arrives at Athens with the terrible news he is surrounded by the wives, mothers, and sisters of his dead comrades, who ask him angrily where he has left their husbands, sons, and brothers and why he is the only one who has escaped. Then they unfasten the buckles with which their clothes are held together and use the tongues to pierce his eyes, and finally kill him. This story might be considered factual, but Herodotus tells the same story at a different occasion. Both authors, Herodotus and Duris, add that henceforth the Athenians forbade their women to wear buckles or brooches with sharp, long tongues so that the incident could not be repeated.

It appears, therefore, that Duris—who can hardly have failed to know the work of Herodotus, but who had no occasion in his histories to tell the story in the connection in which it is told in Herodotus' work—used it in order to make his history more dramatic and thereby in his opinion also more philosophical, by giving an example of the extreme situations which can arise in human life. As this use of the Aristotelian *mimesis* shows, Duris derived the idea from Aristotle; in this form it is not truly Aristotelian, but Duris obviously found followers. For in the next two generations, many historians wrote highly dramatized histories. Phylarchus, who was about two generations younger than Duris, is the most outstanding example.

There was also, however, a strong reaction against this idea of dramatizing history. The most well-known representative of this critical attitude is Polybius of Megalopolis. He criticized the dramatizing type of historiography on two grounds: (1) that it induced the historians to tamper with the facts (for which the Duris-fragment, though not mentioned by Polybius, is a good example), and (2) that it was the main task of historiography to provide material for the enlightenment of statesmen. In this latter respect Polybius agreed in principle with Ephorus. But he had little regard for historians who had never played an active role in politics. History, in his opinion, should be written by active or retired statesmen for active statesmen, because only they could have a real understanding of political life and history. He coined for this kind of historiography the new term πραγματικὴ ἱστορία ("pragmatic history"), by which he meant a history written by men of practice for men of practice. He met the requirement inasmuch as his father, Lycortas, had been one of the leading statesmen of the so-called Achaean League. Also Polybius himself had grown up amidst the most intense political activity, in which he began to participate at a very early age until, in 169 B.C., with a great number of other Achaean politicians, he was brought to Italy as a hostage. There he had the good fortune to become attached to the family of Aemilius Paullus and soon after became the mentor of Paullus' son, P. Cornelius Scipio Aemilianus, the later conqueror of Carthage. This, after his active experience in Greek politics, enabled Polybius to acquire a deeper insight into the machinery of Roman government than any other non-Roman had ever had.

More specifically then, in his opinion, it was the main task of the historian to enable future statesmen to foresee future events and thus to make it possible for them to influence the events on the basis of this foresight. Theoretically, this concept appears to involve a certain contradiction. For if foresight enables a statesman to give the events a turn desired by him, it is *not* foreseeable whether and in what way he will have this foresight, which impairs the foreseeability of events. This apparent contradiction is obviously also at the bottom of Polybius' concept of τύχη ("fortune"), which has created great difficulties for those who tried to interpret his work. In some passages he inveighs against those who speak of τύχη in regard to events which were clearly caused by the folly or the lack of foresight on the part of the actors on the political stage. At other times he appears to regard τύχη as an irresistible force that pervades everything and against which human wisdom is of no avail. But the apparent contradiction can be resolved. One should not, in Polybius' opinion, attribute to luck or fortune what is the foreseeable result of human actions, whether wise or foolish.

But there remains much that is unforeseeable and beyond human control. The very same event can then be contemplated from opposite viewpoints. The expansion of Macedonian power in the second half of the fourth century and of Roman power in the third and second centuries was certainly not due to fortune or good luck. The former was due to the superior skill and wisdom of Alexander the Great and his father Philip; the latter was primarily due to the excellence of the Roman constitution. But the fact that in the fourth century the Macedonian kings possessed great skill and wisdom, and that in the fourth and third centuries the Romans, of all people, should be wise enough to create a constitution that would be largely responsible for their later successes, could not have been foreseen by anyone and may therefore be attributed to τύχη.

In the theory that the enormous expansive power of the Romans was due to the excellence of their constitution, Polybius has combined the idea of the foreseeability of future events on the basis of historical knowledge with two other ideas which he elaborated on the basis of earlier theories. One of these was in fact a kind of combination of two correlated ideas, the idea of the cycle of constitutions and the idea of the "mixed constitution." As far back as Herodotus we find the notion that certain political constitutions, because of their inherent deficiencies or weaknesses, are unstable and therefore, after some time, naturally are replaced by different constitutions. In Herodotus' story the process always ends with monarchy (which does not represent Herodotus' opinion, but is the result of the function of the story within its context, i.e., the reestablishment of Persian monarchy after the overthrow of the "false Smerdis"). By later authors, including Plato, Aristotle, and Dicaearchus, the notion was developed that all "simple" constitutions, i.e., absolute monarchy, pure oligarchy, and unrestricted democracy, are unstable, and that in order to have stability a good constitution must be something between the three or a mixture of all three.

From these earlier notions Polybius derived the idea of a rather mechanical cycle: the earliest form of human government was monarchy instituted by the rule of the strongest, analogous to the rule of the strongest among gregarious animals. This form of rule deteriorated when it became hereditary. This leads to a revolt which results in the rule of an elite, called aristocracy. When this, through heredity, has deteriorated to oligarchy, there is another revolt which results in democracy. But democracy in due time deteriorates to ochlocracy, or the rule of the rabble, and anarchy. This finally results in tyranny, and the cycle begins anew. On the basis of the observation of this cycle a statesman can foresee how a given state will next develop when it has reached a certain stage within the cycle. But the vicious cycle can be stopped if a wise man or wise men succeed in establishing a mixed constitution (which is of course not quite foreseeable). This has happened several times in different places.

The two outstanding examples, in Polybius' opinion, are Sparta and Rome.

But there was, in his view, a very essential difference between the two. The Spartan constitution was the construction of one man: Lycurgus. The Roman one was the result of a gradual development; when the monarchy was overthrown, it was not replaced by a pure oligarchy, but by a government which retained a monarchic element in the consuls with their nearly monarchic but divided power, which was also restricted in time. When a revolution was brewing against the oligarchic government with its monarchic element, a compromise was reached by which monarchic and oligarchic elements were retained side by side with the newly acquired powers of the democratic elements of the assemblies of the plebs and the plebean tribunes. But the Spartan constitution, though more stable than those of most other Greek states, had not lasted forever. It had broken up, partly from within, partly through the onslaught of foreign forces—as Polybius believed, because of certain faults in the constitution's construction. Of the Roman constitution Polybius, at one time, seems to have believed that it would remain stable, if not forever, at least for an unforeseeable future. But in his later years he became doubtful. He then applied to it the Aristotelian idea of biological growth, maturity, and decay. For, in contrast to the Spartan constitution, mechanically constructed by one man, the Roman constitution appeared to have "grown" (though one might think that it had not grown in the strict sense of the word, but had been the result of the actions of succeeding statesmen, concluding "constructive compromises"). Thus here again we have an example of two, to some extent conflicting, ideas which an historian had taken over from earlier writers and which in turn had been developed on the basis of the observation of historical events.

Since the first half of the fourth century, when three historians (Xenophon, Theopompus, and Cratippus) had begun historical works with the events with which the unfinished work of Thucydides closes, the idea had gradually spread that in each generation a great historian should take up the task of continuing the history of Greece or of the world as then known at the point where death had compelled his greatest predecessor to relinquish it. In this way the work of Polybius was continued by Posidonius of Apamea, who gave his most important historical work the title τὰ μετὰ Πολύβιον (*What Happened After Polybius*). Yet this work represents an entirely different type of historiography, influenced by totally different ideas. It is also characterized by extending historical analysis to a field which had been almost totally neglected by nearly all earlier Greek historians. Posidonius was, however, to some extent preceded in this respect by one man, Agatharchides of Cnidus, whose many historical works have been almost completely lost. But Agatharchides' famous geographical work on "The Red Sea" (the Indian Ocean and its shores) did survive, and extensive fragments contain most vivid descriptions of social conditions prevailing among various sections of the populations of those regions. It was this kind of material that played a very large part in Posidonius' historiography and of which he made an entirely new use.

Posidonius was a Stoic philosopher who, however, broke away from some of the most fundamental doctrines of early Stoicism, especially its intellectualistic ethical doctrines, according to which all vices and evil deeds were ultimately due to intellectual errors: nobody who had real ethical insight could consciously act unethically. In opposition to this intellectualistic concept, Posidonius acknowledged the independent power of irrational forces in the human soul. Emotions, in his opinion, were just as fundamental as the intellect and not, as the earlier Stoics had believed, simply the result of intellectual error. Consequently, all human actions arise from conflicts between the rational and the irrational elements in the human soul. On the basis of this conviction Posidonius developed a psychology that tried to penetrate the depth of mechanisms of human motivation, explaining the behavior and the actions of human beings on the basis of their insights and errors, prejudices and emotions, vanities and ambitions, hopes and fears, resentments and illusions. He also applied this psychology to the interpretation of historical events.

Like many of his great predecessors, Posidonius was intensely interested in the causes of historical events. But his idea of the essence of historical causation was quite different from the ideas of Thucydides or Polybius. Thucydides had distinguished between, on the one hand, the public accusations made by governments and nations in order to win the approval of the neutrals, and, on the other hand, the true motives which the parties never admit openly. Polybius had made a threefold distinction between (1) the real underlying causes, for, e.g., starting a war, (2) the pretexts used by the politicians to justify their decisions, and (3) the events immediately leading to the outbreak of a war (that had long been in the offing). No such distinctions can be found in the fragments of the works of Posidonius. He seems not to have attributed great importance to them. In his opinion all events were the result of a coming together of many causes, all of them equally important.

In a way, Posidonius renewed the race theory, but made an entirely new application of it. In his opinion, not only the populations of different continents constituted different races, but every tribe or nation had its racial characteristics which were the product of hereditary factors, climate, diet, training, and traditions. Because of the interaction of these factors there was also a correlation between their bodily constitutions, their temperaments, and their habits. How individuals acted in a given situation, then, was due to a combination of their racial and their individual character, the social conditions in which they lived, the degree of their insight and foresight, but above all, to the effect of the situation on their emotions.

It is a recurring motive with Posidonius to show how a man who tries hard and honestly to work for the common good and for necessary reforms, but meets with resistance, is carried by his resentment far beyond what would serve his aims, through the increasing use of violence becomes a destructive force, and finally ends in a catastrophe. Examples of this are the Gracchi and Marius.

Posidonius' description of the causes, the outbreak, the course, and the outcome of the great slave war in Sicily goes into much more detail. He first describes the intolerable conditions on the big estates in Sicily caused by the absentee ownership of rich men in Rome and Italy, who took no interest in their property other than to draw from it as much money as possible. This attitude was also adopted by some estate owners living in Sicily. One owner whose slaves complained that they had to dress in rags and needed clothes told them to get them from the travelers on the roads. Thus, on the instigation of their master, they became highway robbers. Being sturdy men and having in this way become accustomed to lawless violence, they naturally began to think of turning against their masters. But in order to start a rebellion with any chance of success they needed a leader. On one of the estates owned by a Sicilian there was a slave who was an expert in various branches of what is now called show business, especially in the tricks of "magicians." He was favored by his master, who enjoyed his performances. But he also made a great impression on his superstitious fellow slaves. A woman had prophesied that one day he would be king, and this turned his head. He won adherents among the slaves and became their leader in an uprising against the estate owners and the Roman government. He received succor from all sides and, in the beginning, had some spectacular successes even against regular troops. But in the end his loosely organized army was no match for the power of the Roman state. His troops were scattered. With his bodyguard of 1000 men he fled into a cave. When they were surrounded, nearly all of them committed suicide. But he, not having the courage to follow their example, was captured and met a miserable death in a prison.

There is a similar description of an uprising against Roman rule in Athens, led by a demagogue named Athenion, who had been at the court of King Mithridates of Pontus and who appeared dressed in gold and silver before the Athenian populace to stir them up against the Romans. The emphasis with Posidonius everywhere is not, as with Thucydides, on high policy and the decisions of statesmen and leading politicians, but on social forces and the psychology of individuals and of the masses.

It is also interesting to compare Posidonius with Thucydides in regard to their attitudes towards the moral aspects of historical actions. Thucydides, with very rare and slight exceptions (as in the case of Nicias), carefully refrains from passing moral judgments on historical figures or on their individual actions. Nevertheless one feels Thucydides' passionate engagement in what has happened and his approval or disapproval, even though it is not directly expressed. Posidonius never hesitates to say what he considers morally good or morally bad. But he is a true Stoic in that he remains personally aloof and unengaged. He is convinced that a divine spirit pervades and rules everything. Unhappiness is the inevitable consequence of wickedness and unjust actions, regardless of external success or failure. Likewise, material losses and misfortune or even ill health and bodily pains cannot make a good and wise man essentially unhappy. The wickedness and folly of men cannot affect the divine order of the world. Thus history is a spectacle that the philosopher follows with interest, but it cannot affect him personally.

Most interesting also is Posidonius' attempt to reconstruct the origin and early rise of human civilization, and his application of the ideas used in this reconstruction to the history of his own time. We find in his reconstruction the same contrast, as in Dicaearchus, between an optimistic and a pessimistic view of the development of the human race: optimistic in regard to the development of material civilization, where a certain progress is undeniable; pessimistic in regard to the development as a whole. Posidonius appears also to have adopted to some extent the Democritean notion of χρεία ("need") as a stimulus in the progress of material civilization. But he has added a new idea, which makes everything appear in a different light. This is the Stoic notion, stated above, that a divine spirit pervades and guides everything. All human inventions have been anticipated by nature. The wise men and inventors of old may have received the stimulus for their inventions from need, but they made them by learning from nature. The net, by which fish or birds are caught, was invented by imitating the spider. The rudder, by which a ship is steered, was invented by observing how a fish propels himself in the direction it wishes by using its tail as a rudder.

It is also a law of nature that what is of lower rank (in regard to insight and wisdom) should be ruled by and freely submit to what is of higher rank. In earlier periods, men voluntarily submitted to wise kings who governed everything according to their insight, so that there was no need of laws, which are always general and therefore can never completely fit the varying circumstances of human life. But because of the imperfection of man, who is the only living being capable of deviating to some extent from the divine law (though when he does so, he always does it to his own detriment and cannot disturb the divine order as a whole), some kings became tyrants and governed according to their whims instead of according to true insight and for the benefit of their subjects. Thus to prevent this, laws had to be invented, by which everyone, including the rulers, was bound and restrained. These laws again were invented and imposed by wise men like Solon and Lycurgus. But there remained a rift. The original harmony was not restored. From this point of view the whole of history becomes a process in which alternately the baser natures revolt against the divine law and the rule of the better and wiser, but then again are more or less forcefully brought back into submission by the consequences of the harm which they do to themselves by their lack of insight.

Naturally the so-called Roman Revolution, starting with the Gracchi, appeared to Posidonius as a revolt of this kind against the divine order. But he was far from putting the main blame on what we call the socially lower classes or on the slaves. Just as in his reconstruction of the early history of civilization, when he had the first deviation from the original harmony begin with the folly and wickedness of kings, his history of the slave wars shows very clearly that he found the first cause of the revolt of the lower classes in the depravity of and the faults committed by the majority of the members of the ruling class.

Posidonius is the last of the great Greek historians before the Byzantine age. Perhaps the necessarily sketchy survey attempted in this article may give the reader at least an inkling of the great variety of ideas that have influenced historiography in this period and of the very different types of historiography that have resulted from these influences.

BIBLIOGRAPHY

Translations, if not otherwise identified, are by the author of this article.

Entretiens sur l'Antiquité Classique, Foundation Hardt pour l'Étude de l'Antiquité Classique, Vol. IV: *Histoire et historiens dans l'antiquité* (Vandoeuvres, 1956). *L'Histoire et ses interprétations*, Entretiens autour de Arnold Toynbee sous la direction de Raymond Aron, École Pratique des Hautes Études, Sorbonne, sixième section: Sciences économiques et sociales. Congrès et Colloques III (Paris, 1961). Karl Reinhardt, *Poseidonios* (Munich, 1921). Kurt Riezler, "The Historian and Truth," *The Journal of Philosophy*, **45** (1948), 345–88. James T. Shotwell, *Introduction to the History of History* (New York, 1939; rev. ed. 1950). Hermann Strasburger, *Die Wesensbestimmung der Geschichte durch die antike Geschichtsschreibung* (Wiesbaden, 1966). Kurt von Fritz, *Die griechische Geschichtsschreibung*, Vol. I: *Von den Anfängen bis Thukydides* (Berlin, 1967); idem, "Conservative Reaction and One Man Rule in Ancient Greece," *Political Science Quarterly*, **56** (1941), 51–83; idem, "The Historian Theopompus. His Political Convictions and his Conception of Historiography," *American Historical Review*, **46** (1941), 765–85; idem, "Aristotle's Contribution to the Practice and Theory of Historiography," *University of California Publications in Philosophy*, **28** (1958), 113–38.

KURT VON FRITZ

[See also Causation in History; Cycles; Environment; **Historiography; Poetry and Poetics; Progress in Antiquity.**]

HOLY (THE SACRED)

BY "THE HOLY" and "the sacred" we in the twentieth century denote what partakes of qualities ascribed to the divine. In some current contexts the two terms appear virtually interchangeable, especially if they set God or religion over against the profane or secular. In other contexts, the meanings differ. This article attempts a description of the relationship of the words "holy" and "sacred" in common adjectival usage, followed by a discussion of their role as key terms in the organization of explicit discourse about an idea.

The Terms as Words. Perusal of the wealth of dated entries under "holy" and "sacred" in the *Oxford English Dictionary* will demonstrate that in the language the Anglo-Saxon term "holy" is older than the Latin "sacred," and at one time covered all that was divinely hallowed or was associated with such by men. Following the appearance of the word "sacred," a partial separation of functions between the two took place. This separation, it may be argued, amounts to a difference in the degree to which the user of these words is willing to imply participation in the religious tradition under discussion.

To refer to something as holy implies, in the overwhelming majority of the cases cited, a commitment to the proposition that the thing in question is in fact holy, that it has been hallowed by God. To call something sacred, on the other hand, may or may not imply a commitment to its sacredness on the part of the speaker, for the term is descriptive of the veneration accorded by men; in fact, though the verbal force of the word is no longer felt, it has in the past meant "consecrated." The general contrast between the semantic fields of the two words is obvious if one pairs the *Holy Bible* with the *Sacred Books of the East;* in the first case, one's own tradition affirms the writings' holiness, while in the latter the title is descriptive of others' reverence for them. Thus music, man's creation, may be sacred but is not called holy; man's affections, such as one's honor or the memory of one's beloved, are spoken of as sacred; and a "sacred cow" is something in others' veneration of which the speaker manifestly does not share.

To test this general evaluation one looks about for instances which do not fit. The Christian speaks of the saint, the man whose conduct or experience he understands to conform to holiness, and yet whose counterpart in another community he will call a "holy man" rather than a "sacred man." Such an example, however, alerts one to the fact that in English "holy" covers a range of morality or discipline which "sacred" does not: to distinguish holiness and goodness would be a complex ethical point, but to distinguish sacredness and goodness seems less so.

The semantic contrast between holy and sacred may be discerned to a certain extent in European languages derived from Latin, where medieval usage held *sanctum* in higher esteem than *sacrum* (though the two have a common etymological origin, and a rich and subtle set of contexts in pre-Christian classical usage): French *saint/sacré,* Italian *santo/sacro,* etc. The distinction is, however, largely absent from German: as verbs, *heiligen/weihen* correspond to "sanctify"/ "consecrate," but "sacred" and "holy" fall together as *heilig.* The implications of this are fascinating. In the Middle Ages, the domain of authority claimed in Latin by the *sacrum imperium Romanum* became semantically extended when rendered through German as the Holy Roman Empire. And in twentieth-century study of religion, our topic was shaped by Rudolf Otto, who wrote in German and for whom therefore *heilig* was, as we shall see, usefully ambiguous.

Holiness as a Religious Goal. Through much of the history of religion in the West, the word holy has been not so much a key term for independent reflection as it has been an attribute of the divine. A history of the adjectival force of the term thus approximates a history of those qualities of inaccessibility, power, authority, and goodness which have attended the idea of God.

In a sense Western traditions have not classically regarded the idea of God's holiness to have *developed* but have seen it as present in the earliest revelations. God's holiness was his presence, as when Moses trem-

bled in awe before its radiance, or when Isaiah exclaimed, "Holy, holy, holy is [the Lord] of hosts." Various precincts were the localization of that presence: the land of promise, but within that the holy hill of Zion and especially the inmost courts of the Temple; or the nation as God's people but within that the priesthood; the institutions of Hebrew society and warfare but especially the cultus, with particular special acts and moments. In all of this the holy was God's domain, in contrast to the profane, which was only more ambiguously so.

An increase in the specifically moral implications of holiness in ancient Israel developed in the course of time, in part through the teachings of some of the eighth- through sixth-century (B.C.) prophets and in part as a result of the destruction of some of the more tangible Israelite political and cultic institutions by foreign conquest in the prophets' day and again in the first and second centuries A.D. Nonetheless Jewish tradition has clung to its emphasis on purity of life and thought as a people holy to God through very specific cultic and communal acts, and holiness in Talmudic usage has been interpreted largely in such terms. It has been in modern times beginning with the Enlightenment that there has been within Judaism significant questioning of the sacredness of traditional ritual or locality and a discussion of the extent to which being a holy people entails separateness from the surrounding society.

On the subject of God's essential holiness Christendom likewise has from the start held it to be majesty and power, with the area of contention what institutions or forms of conduct reflect it. Under persecution, holiness implied steadfastness for the early *ecclesia,* the community called apart from the world; but from Constantine onwards, that community came to have more of the world, including emperors, within it. The collapse of the Roman Empire in the West gave the church much secular as well as sacred authority, and while in principle a distinction existed between the church's spiritual holiness and the sacredness it conferred on kings and princes, in practice even the idea of holiness was intimately linked with the struggle for authority in the high Middle Ages.

With the secularization of the European social order, the selfless moral purity and devotional perfection of the saint remained as the principal content of holiness. In the Catholic tradition the saint, besides being the model for the individual, has been seen as interceding on his behalf with God. Protestantism has stressed the element of law and judgment in God's holiness, with wrath awaiting the wicked, but it too asserted that his redeeming grace can sanctify the lives and wills of men; of this grace the pietists and "holiness churches" especially claim a vivid awareness. Holiness, in the internal theological writings of Western Christendom, remains in part the domain of the transcendent God, in part an ethical and devotional aspiration.

The Sacred as a Comparative Observation. Just as "holy" can be seen principally as an aspect of the idea of God, so "sacred" has been through most of Western intellectual history a description of the objects of *religion* rather than an integrating idea in its own right. While, in one's own piety, to hold something sacred is to affirm that holiness is mediated through it, the interplay of civilizations and traditions has repeatedly brought men into contact with the sacred things of others, reverence for which they did not share, and posed the opportunity to describe religiousness from without. We must leave aside here the details of how Hesiod, Herodotus, Philo, and many others dealt with situations where gods were many but truth presumed to be one, but must observe at least that an awareness of religious diversity is as old as Western culture itself.

For centuries in Christian Europe, the principal religious horizons included the Muslims as an alien world without, the Jews as an alien world within, and classical pagans as an alien world in the past; while the piety of these was seen as religion and its objects as sacred, comparisons of them with Christian "truth" remained odious. Interest in the religiousness of others gained momentum gradually during the sixteenth and seventeenth centuries, with the secularization and humanism of the Renaissance, the fragmenting of ecclesiastical authority in the Reformation, and Europe's voyages of discovery and trade. Now a genre of literature describing the religious customs of the world would appear, and the word "religion" would be used for the first time in the plural as denoting various communities of piety rather than piety itself. A Christian attempt to baptize Chinese customs as appropriate to the church in seventeenth-century China was made there by Jesuits, but evoked strong opposition from the Franciscans and Rome in the so-called Rites Controversy.

In the eighteenth century there were those outside the church who held it to be benighted along with the rest. David Hume and Immanuel Kant argued that one could not have valid knowledge of such a thing as the sacred. Friedrich Schleiermacher, working from Kantian premises, was at least able to ground religion in the feelings. The romantics argued from the universality of myths to their appropriateness in human emotion and feeling. But from the sixteenth through the early nineteenth century such arguments were logical rather than chronological: at bottom, they were philosophical rather than historical speculations on the nature of religion.

Modern use of "the holy" and "the sacred" as key terms for analysis we owe, however, to the emergence of the comparative study of religion which began in the mid-nineteenth century. Increased historical and archaeological discovery, coupled with the intellectual excitement generated by Charles Darwin's idea of biological evolution, turned many minds toward the construction of developmental theories of human cultural institutions and, among them, religion. The period from Darwin to the First World War saw a wealth of major theories of the origin (and, thereby, the nature) of religion. Noteworthy among them, to mention only three, were the attempts to see religion as belief in animate spirits (Edward Tylor), or as stemming from interpersonal conflict (Sigmund Freud), or as symbolizing communal solidarity (Émile Durkheim). Most of the theories held that the prehistoric origin and present essence of religion could be tested by observation of contemporary primitive cultures. In addition, these theories can be described as reductionistic, in that they explained religion as an adaptation to psychological or other human needs. Such functions of religion have remained the content of behavioral-scientific study of religion to the present.

Two terms in particular came into wide use in European languages in the description of primitive religion: *mana* and *tabu* ("taboo"). *Mana*, a Melanesian word, refers to an aura of potency and mystery, and came into use as a generic term for the primitive "holy." Taboo, also a term from the Pacific islands, denoted, like "sacred," that which is set apart from common use or contact.

Thus it was that Nathan Söderblom, writing the general article on "Holiness" in the *Encyclopaedia of Religion and Ethics* in 1912, would find it appropriate to introduce the subject through a recapitulation of primitive equivalents of *mana* and taboo, bringing the Western sense of the divine into explicit parallel with ethnographic data. Thus it was, also, that W. Robertson Smith would in 1889 treat the early traditions of the Old Testament as of a piece with primitive Semitic religion. It became common especially in liberal Protestant scholarship to portray as primitive sacerdotalism the background from which the prophets and Jesus rescued the faith of Israel through an ethical conception of holiness.

On the eve of World War I, the net effect of these themes was to present Christianity as one of the fruits of religious evolution, and religion as the function of man's social or psychic needs. While for Protestants Karl Barth was to reassert the incomparability of Christianity, another Protestant theologian was to reassert the irreducibility of religion.

Religious Theories of Religion. A synthesis between 513 participation in the Western traditional valuation of holiness and behavioral description of it was the most notable accomplishment of Rudolf Otto, a German Protestant theologian who had, among other things, traveled in Asia. His book *The Idea of the Holy*, published in German in 1917, was widely influential. Indebted to Schleiermacher's analysis of religion as feeling, Otto termed the object of such feeling "the holy." The word implied, as all Christendom knew, goodness; but there was more to holiness than goodness, in the realm of power so recently explored as *mana*, taboo, and the like. For this realm Otto coined the word "the numinous," describing this aspect of the holy as an overwhelming yet fascinating mystery. Otto's effort was to show that the central object of all religion was *sui generis*, reducible neither to philosophical nor psychological nor any other components. With Otto "the holy" as a noun became at last a prime term for analysis, combining what we have reviewed as the participant's perception of God with the observer's perception of religion, in that language where the holy and the sacred are one.

While Christian theologians after Barth were eager to argue that the Christian revelation is *sui generis* as against religions, certain comparativists after Otto were to state, notably in what was termed the phenomenology of religion, a similar claim for religion in general as over against other aspects of culture, at times drawing on Otto for support. Holding that each religious experience must be understood on its own terms, the school has sought to chart the variety of man's religiousness in general patterns as a response to the sacred, according the sacred the status which Otto gave the holy. Whereas Otto had argued the ultimacy of the holy largely in terms familiar within European religion and philosophy, Gerardus van der Leeuw and other phenomenologists of religion were arguing its ultimacy from non-Western practices, myths, and texts as well.

Thus although many behavioral scientists have regarded such endorsement of the sacred as highly suspect, there has emerged an explicitly comparative sense of "the holy" or "the sacred" in theological and literary circles. Such usage is fraught with ambiguity as to the objective status of a power such as "the holy" correlated with man's religious concern. Like Paul Tillich, a theologian reminiscent of and indebted to Otto, many who employ "the holy" or "the sacred" as nouns to denote a transcendent power argue from man's religiousness as the best accessible evidence.

A use of "the holy" where once one might have used "God" has developed as a result of the information and the attitudes of recent cultural and religious pluralism. Christendom's long-standing tradition of the holy and Western culture's long history of description of diverse sacreds have interacted and to some extent fused in modern times. The tendency to include other cultures' sacred as well as one's own is not likely soon to be reversed.

BIBLIOGRAPHY

Encyclopedia articles: *Encyclopaedia of Religion and Ethics; Lexikon für Theologie und Kirche; Die Religion in Geschichte und Gegenwart; Theological Dictionary of the New Testament.*

On biblical and Christian usage: William Robertson Smith, *Lectures on the Religion of the Semites* (Edinburgh, 1889; also reprint); Johannes Pedersen, *Israel* (Copenhagen, 1940), Vols. III, IV; Helmer Ringgren, *The Prophetical Conception of Holiness* (Uppsala, 1948); Eduard Williger, *Hagios* (Giessen, 1922); André M. J. Festugière, *La sainteté* (Paris, 1952); John M. Mecklin, *The Passing of the Saint* (Chicago, 1941); Alexander M. Harváth, *Heiligkeit und Sünde im Lichten der thomistischen Theologie* (Freiburg in Switzerland, 1943); J. Baines Atkinson, *The Beauty of Holiness* (London, 1953); Owen R. Jones, *The Concept of Holiness* (London, 1961).

On comparative theories: Henry Pinard de la Boullaye, *L'étude critique des religions*, 3rd ed. (Paris, 1929–31); Jan de Vries, *Godsdienstgeschiedenis in vogelvlucht* (Utrecht, 1961), trans. Kees W. Bolle as *The Study of Religion* (New York, 1967; also reprint); Wilfred C. Smith, *The Meaning and End of Religion* (New York, 1963; also reprint); William A. Lessa and Evon Z. Vogt, *Reader in Comparative Religion*, 2nd ed. (New York, 1965); Hutton Webster, *Taboo* (Stanford, 1942); Robert A. Nisbet, *The Sociological Tradition* (New York, 1966), Ch. 6.

The Holy and the Sacred: Wilhelm Windelband, "Das Heilige," in his *Präludien*, 2nd ed. (Tübingen, 1903); Rudolf Otto, *Das Heilige* (Breslau, 1917), trans. John W. Harvey as *The Idea of the Holy* (London, 1923; also reprint); Gerardus van der Leeuw, *Phänomenologie der Religion* (Tübingen, 1933), trans. John E. Turner as *Religion in Essence and Manifestation* (London, 1938; also reprint); W. Brede Kristensen, *The Meaning of Religion*, trans. John B. Carman (The Hague, 1960); Mircea Eliade, *Traité d'histoire des religions* (Paris, 1949), trans. Rosemary Sheed as *Patterns in Comparative Religion* (London, 1958; also reprint); Mircea Eliade, *Das Heilige und das Profane* (Hamburg, 1957), trans. Willard R. Trask as *The Sacred and the Profane* (New York, 1959; also reprint).

Topical applications: Roger Caillois, *L'homme et le sacré* (Paris, 1939), trans. Meyer Barash as *Man and the Sacred* (Glencoe, Illinois, 1959); Bernhard Häring, *Das Heilige und das Gute* (Krailling, 1950); Jacques Grand'maison, *Le monde et le sacré*, 2 vols. (Paris, 1966, 1968); Gerardus van der Leeuw, *Wegen en granzen* (Amsterdam, 1932), trans. David E. Green as *Sacred and Profane Beauty* (New York, 1963; also reprint); Vincent Buckley, *Poetry and the Sacred* (London, 1968).

WILLARD GURDON OXTOBY

[See also **Church as Institution**; Evolutionism; **God**; Myth; Primitivism; **Sin and Salvation**; Theodicy.]

HUMANISM IN ITALY

HUMANISM enjoys a very high prestige among modern intellectual currents; it is connected with a great number of basic philosophical ideas, and is usually considered as having had its source in Italy. What actually was Italian humanism?

Humanism is best defined as the rise of classical scholarship, of the *studia humanitatis* (a term used in the general sense of literary education by ancient Roman authors like Cicero and taken up by Italian scholars of the late fourteenth century), during the Renaissance. There had been several revivals of classical studies during the Middle Ages—notably by scholars of Charlemagne's court—and then especially in the twelfth century, when the works of ancient Latin writers served as models for contemporary authors. These "Protorenaissances," as they are generally called, did not, however, survive very long, nor did they penetrate so deeply into the consciousness of the time as did the Renaissance humanism of the fifteenth and sixteenth centuries.

The humanism of the twelfth century, i.e., the grammatical and classical studies which formed part of the curriculum of French cathedral schools, was overshadowed and replaced by scholastic philosophy and theology and by the study of Roman and canon law (which had originally been part of twelfth-century humanism) in the universities of the thirteenth and fourteenth centuries, and it is hardly admissible to call scholastic philosophers, such as Thomas Aquinas, humanists, simply because they were indebted in their work to Greek philosophy. It was in Italy that classical studies started to blossom again about 1300, and finally witnessed their lasting revival in the fifteenth century. Prior to the thirteenth century, Italy had been lagging behind in the cultural development of Europe. In classical studies, it had little that could match the highlights of twelfth-century French humanism. Yet Italy had a tangible and persistent tradition that connected her Middle Ages with ancient Rome, mainly in the practice and study of Roman law and of grammar and rhetoric—which were not limited to clerics, but were also widespread among laymen. Furthermore, the geographical position of Italy exposed her to the Greek tradition of Byzantium.

Italian humanism was largely rooted in the field of Italian classical tradition proper—in grammar and rhetoric, in epistolography and oratory. The study of these subjects, the so-called *ars dictaminis*, had begun at Montecassino or Bologna about 1100 and had spread from there to other regions, reaching a new climax in Capua at the time of the Emperor Frederick II (1215–50). It was then continued by the rising humanism of the fourteenth and early fifteenth centuries. Here the path from the medieval tradition into Renaissance humanism is most evident. Yet the early Italian humanists were eager to apply classical standards in their grammar, rhetoric, and oratory. Thus the art of letter-writing and of oratory underwent a slow but considerable change in the course of the fourteenth century. The style of Cicero and of other classical authors became more influential than before (as could be seen in the letters of Geri of Arezzo shortly after 1300), although neither the characteristics of technical medieval Latin nor those of twelfth-century Italian and French rhetorical tradition disappeared. Even as late as about 1400, a humanist like Coluccio Salutati combined, in his numerous letters, stylistic elements of medieval chanceries, twelfth-century French epistolography, and the letters of Cicero.

It was most important that the Italian humanists, from the fourteenth century onwards, attained a notable influence in elementary and university education, where they soon held the professorships of grammar, rhetoric, and poetry. Thus, during the first half of the century, the *studia humanitatis*, the "humanities," became a well-defined cycle of scholarly disciplines that included the study of grammar, rhetoric, poetry, history, and moral philosophy, i.e., a broad spectrum of secular learning independent of—but not necessarily irreconcilable with—other scholarly disciplines of the university curriculum, such as theology, metaphysics, natural philosophy, medicine, and mathematics. It was among the scholars of Italian universities that the word *umanista* (in the vernacular, whence it was taken over into Latin as *humanista*) was first applied to the professors and students of rhetoric. The earliest examples that have so far come to light appear, however, as late as the end of the fifteenth century (Campana). Soon afterwards the word was also applied to the students of classical learning. (The abstract noun "humanism" is of even later origin; it was first used by German scholars of the early nineteenth century.)

Characteristic of the Renaissance humanists was a familiarity with classical Latin and Greek (later also with Hebrew) language and literature, from which they derived their stylistic ideals; there was also a certain degree of philological and historical criticism related to their widespread contempt for medieval culture, and showing a serious concern with moral problems. They were convinced that they were living in an age of a rebirth of learning and literature.

According to the traditional opinion (Voigt and others), Italian humanism started with Petrarch. However, recent studies (Weiss, 1969; Kristeller, *Eight . . . Philosophers . . .*) have ventured to include the so-called pre-humanists, i.e., the Paduan circle with Albertino Mussato, Geri of Arezzo, and others, in the discussion of early humanism. As far as its terminal

515

time limit is concerned, many modern students of Italy tend to restrict the period of humanism to the fourteenth and fifteenth centuries, reserving the Renaissance to the sixteenth, and thus distinguishing humanism and Renaissance as two different intellectual movements. Other modern scholars are inclined to restrict Italian humanism to the first half of the fifteenth century. If, however, the definition of humanism as the revival of classical scholarship during the Renaissance is accepted, Italian humanism survived far into the sixteenth century, although it passed its peak around 1500. After the middle of the sixteenth century, scholars became increasingly aware that they had not only matched but in most fields surpassed the example of the ancients, and that progress was no longer dependent on an imitation of classical models, but on their own originality. The seventeenth century saw the beginning of a new period in philosophy and science, as humanist traditions gave way to more modern conceptions. The revivals of classical thought in the eighteenth and nineteenth centuries were limited to literature, the visual arts, moral philosophy, and education, but did not involve science, where the ancients could no longer be considered as masters.

The basis for the spread of the knowledge of ancient Roman literature was the discovery and diffusion by the humanists of manuscripts of classical authors (Sabbadini). Many Roman authors, like Vergil, Ovid, and Seneca, were well-known and widely read during the Middle Ages, while others, such as Lucretius, Tacitus, and Manilius, although extant in a few but neglected medieval manuscripts, had to be rediscovered by the humanists. Of others, like Cicero, a number of works were widely diffused during the Middle Ages, while the rest were relatively unknown. In the case of Cicero, for example, his *Brutus*, his letters, and many orations were rediscovered, and the humanists became familiar with certain trends in his thought that had been little known before. One of the foremost achievements of the Italian humanists in the field of classical scholarship was that they not only rediscovered forgotten ancient Latin literature, but also did extensive work first as copyists, editors, and later as printers (e.g., Aldus Manutius in Venice) of Roman classics, thus ensuring their wide diffusion. This activity was combined with an effort to perfect the techniques of textual criticism and of historical interpretation by an intense study of classical Latin spelling, grammar, rhetoric, history, mythology, epigraphy, archeology, and similar subjects. In this way, the humanists soon far surpassed the medieval knowledge of ancient Rome and of classical literature.

Italian humanism reached its maturity during the fifteenth century with the study of Greek. There was

still at this time some knowledge of Greek in parts of Calabria and the Salentino (Terra d'Otranto), where a Greek population, clergy, and liturgy had survived the Norman occupation and lingered on until the sixteenth century. But the medieval Byzantine remnants in southern Italy were too meager to give a decisive impulse to the Renaissance revival of Greek learning—despite the fact that it was from a Calabrian monk, Barlaam (who had probably been partly educated in Constantinople), that Petrarch acquired some very elementary knowledge of Greek. There had been some sporadic knowledge of Greek in the early Middle Ages and some translating from the Greek in the West, mainly of Aristotle, since the twelfth century. The translators had acquired their knowledge of the Greek language and literature either in the East or in southern Italy. Their translations were mainly a word-by-word rendering of the Greek text into Latin without a firm understanding of grammar and syntax. In typical scholastic fashion they showed little genuine interest in literary style. Efforts to teach Greek, Hebrew, and Arabic at the universities were mostly futile. The decisive impetus to Greek studies came with the first arrival of Greek scholars (like Manuel Chrysoloras), with the participants (e.g., Bessarion) of the Ecumenical Council of Florence (1438–39), and then with the Greek scholars who fled to Italy after the downfall of the Byzantine Empire (1453).

At this time and even after the Turkish occupation, many Italians such as Aurispa, Tortelli, Filelfo, Ciriaco of Ancona, and others went to Constantinople and Greece (which remained partly under Venetian domination for a long time to come) to study Greek language and literature, and to acquire manuscripts of the classical authors. After 1450, there was a rapid increase in exact Latin translations of classical Greek literature (which had been studied almost uninterruptedly in the Byzantine East during the preceding centuries, but was relatively unknown in the West) such as the works of Homer, Plato, Herodotus, Thucydides, Xenophon, Isocrates, and others. Furthermore, the humanists provided new and better versions of the earlier translations. This marked the beginning of Greek philology in the West, and it entailed a growing interest, not only in Greek and Byzantine philosophy and theology, but also in Greek grammar, rhetoric, mythology, and history.

Greek scholars in the West were to a great extent responsible for the preservation of classical texts that might otherwise have been lost after the occupation of the Byzantine East by the Turks. Many Greek manuscripts were brought to Italy, copied there, and later issued in printed editions. A considerable part of the literary production of the humanists consists of letters.

As chancellors or secretaries to popes, princes, and republics, it was their official duty to draft letters and manifestos furthering the interests of their employers, and the Florentine state letters are especially interesting sources for the history of political thought and propaganda. The greater part of this correspondence is still unpublished. They are mostly preserved in the registers of the chanceries and in the widely diffused humanistic letter collections, which served mainly literary and stylistic purposes as examples for other writers. The transmission of such letters was very similar to the transmission of medieval letters (some manuscripts even contain collections of medieval and humanistic letters together). Beside such official correspondence, the humanists wrote many private letters of literary significance, but in many cases it is difficult to draw a distinction between private and official letters. Some of the private letters grew into short treatises or essays of scholarly or literary content.

The humanists also drafted numerous speeches (or orations), of which a great number have been preserved. Most of them were inspired by specific occasions, such as weddings, funerals, university ceremonies, visits of princes, etc., and the rhetorical elements are dominant. Examples of political and forensic speeches are rarer. The individualistic and propagandistic aspects of humanistic literature also became evident in the many invectives the humanists used to defame either their rivals, or the political opponents of princes and republics in whose service they stood. They are part of the rhetorical tradition and their content should not be taken too seriously, as the humanists themselves often considered them to be merely pieces of literary exercise rather than of personal engagement. The same is true of the numerous eulogies of princes and communes, arts and sciences. Humanist prose literature, besides imitating classical models, also borrowed from the vernacular literature. Thus the *novella* became popular among the humanists who translated such short stories into Latin and also composed original pieces. Even more popular were collections of anecdotes and of facetious stories.

To the humanists, poetry was an art that, to a great extent, could be taught and learned. It consisted mainly of the study of poetics and verse-making and of the interpretation and imitation of ancient poets. The coronation of poets—which began at Padua with the honoring of Albertino Mussato in 1314 and is best known from Petrarch's coronation by the Roman Senate in 1341—was little more than an academic degree granted less for pieces of original poetry than for versatility in verse-making, composition, and interpretation of ancient poetical works (Kristeller). As the art of verse-making was less developed in Italy than in France before the second half of the thirteenth century, the Paduan group of pre-humanists, Albertino Mussato, Lovato Lovati, Geremia of Montagnone, and Rolando of Piazzola (all of them professional lawyers) may have been stimulated by French examples. Nevertheless, humanist Latin drama played an important role in the rise of vernacular dramatic literature during the sixteenth century. Latin eclogues, satires, and pastoral poems exerted a strong influence on vernacular lyrical poetry.

Examples of the more demanding kinds of classical poems, such as odes, were less frequent among humanists because of their metrical difficulties. Epic poems were widespread, including verse translations of Homer, as well as Dante's *Divine Comedy*. Many of them, beginning with Petrarch's *Africa*, deal with subjects of ancient history and ancient mythology. Others are epic versions of biblical and theological subjects, such as the life of Christ and the lives of the saints. Still others are didactic poems on natural history, astrology, and other arts and sciences. This kind of epic poetry was in no way an invention of the humanists. It was widespread during the Middle Ages, and the humanists mainly improved the style and the meter by imitating classical examples more closely than medieval authors had done. The largest part of humanist poetry, however, consisted of elegies and epigrams. Elegies composed after the models of Ovid, Tibullus, and Propertius are among the best specimens of poetry that the humanists have left. Although to a great extent conventional in their contents, the elegies of Poliziano, Pontano, and others sometimes show a poetical perfection and a beauty of imagery that is rare in other kinds of humanistic poetry.

In the long run, Italian humanists showed no aversion to the vernacular in principle (Kristeller, in *Renaissance Thought* II, 119ff., 130ff.; Migliorini; Dionisotti). They certainly preferred Latin during the fourteenth century and also later in the fifteenth and sixteenth centuries, when they wished to give their works a wide diffusion among an international audience of scholars and educated people. The vernacular (*Volgare*), however, was used for works and especially letters that were intended for an Italian public, and the more so if the recipients were poorly educated and not able to read or understand Latin. The state letters of the Florentine chancery, which was dominated by humanist chancellors like Salutati, Bruni, and Poggio, may serve as an example to demonstrate this. As they were addressed to recipients with different educational backgrounds, one may expect that the humanist chancellors took this into consideration when choosing the language in which their respective letters were written. But Salutati used the vernacular in only a few instances, the bulk of his state letters being in Latin regardless of their recipients. Under Bruni and later the situation underwent a complete change. An ever increasing part of the letters (up to one half and more), especially those addressed to uneducated condottieri and statesmen like Francesco Sforza, were now written in *Volgare*, while those addressed to communes were written either in Latin or in the vernacular—with no obvious reasons for the choice in many cases except, perhaps, that it was easier to express one's thoughts more frankly and directly in the vernacular than in rhetorical Latin. On the whole, the development of vernacular literature in the fifteenth century was not seriously hampered by the humanists, and some of them even had a considerable share in this development.

The contribution of the Italian humanists to the reform of handwriting is still evident today. During the thirteenth century, Gothic script, characterized by compression, angularity, and the fusion of letters, had prevailed almost everywhere in Europe. Its characteristics had not become as extreme in Italy as elsewhere. In Bologna especially a more rounded type was used. The early humanists, such as Petrarch and Salutati, preferred manuscripts in a clear, legible writing, in *littera antiqua*, which was the script of the ninth to the twelfth centuries, the Caroline minuscule. Petrarch, Boccaccio, and others, in their personal handwriting, tried to avoid the extremes of Gothic script. The decisive initiative towards a more radical reform of book script was undertaken by Salutati when around 1400 he started imitating the earlier Caroline minuscule. His initiative was soon taken up by his pupil Poggio, the actual inventor of humanistic book minuscule. The result was an imitation of Caroline minuscule.

The most common form of humanistic cursive was invented by Niccolò Niccoli about two decades later. Further research is necessary regarding the genesis of humanistic cursive and the diffusion of humanistic script in general—research which should take into account the material preserved in archives. Both kinds of humanistic script, the book hand invented by Poggio and the cursive of Niccoli, were preferred by the Medici and by the early Italian printers (Niccoli's cursive developed into the italic type of Aldus Manutius) and eventually developed into the present-day antiqua and italic types. Handwriting and print are thus a living heritage of the human striving for clarity through calligraphy.

A moral aspect is clearly evident in humanistic historiography. The humanists shared the belief that one of the most important tasks of historical writing was to teach moral lessons by means of examples from many classical and medieval authors. Great person-

alities of the past were to be presented to the reader as models worthy of imitation. This basic intention gave rise to an extensive biographical literature dealing with the lives of famous ancient and contemporary personalities, princes, saints, scholars, poets, artists, and other distinguished citizens. The underlying belief was that human nature was basically the same at all times and that it was therefore possible to study the ancients as models of human conduct, to learn from their mistakes, and to imitate their achievements. Humanist historians thus lacked all understanding of the genetic and evolutionary aspects of history. Their opinion that history teaches by example is basically the same (even if presented in a more secularized form) as that held by many medieval historians. Compared with medieval historiography, humanist historical writing, however, lost its universal aspects. History was no longer embedded in the divine plan of salvation; it centered around limited and well-defined subjects—cities or states. Little thought was given to the theory of history, except that some humanists took over the cyclical theory of history from ancient authors, i.e., the conception that the historical process is characterized by endless repetition, always leading back to its starting point.

The limitation of historical writing to circumscribed subjects, such as principalities and city-states, eventually brought about a closer contact between history and politics, although the beginnings of this development, in Florence and Milan for example, are to be found in the preceding medieval centuries. The humanist device of placing the founding dates of important Italian cities in Roman times is also a continuation of medieval myths. A great amount of humanist historiography was connected with the professional activities of their authors as chancellors and secretaries to princes and cities for which they had acted as official historians. Their style is often highly rhetorical, the contents impaired by errors, eulogy, and deliberate bias and by the introduction of fictitious speeches. On the other hand, the humanists (as did medieval authors before them) used original documents from the archives, and their philological approach resulted in some historical criticism, especially as far as ancient history was concerned. On the whole, however, their contribution to the development of historical writing was limited, their works often vague, superficial and sometimes even inferior to medieval historiography, if we take modern historical criteria of concreteness and objectivity. Real progress in historiography began with Francesco Guicciardini.

The diffusion of Italian humanism from the fourteenth to the sixteenth centuries took place mainly through personal contact and, later on, through the press. Hundreds of students from north of the Alps attended Italian universities, where they became acquainted with the *studia humanitatis* while studying law or medicine, these being subjects for which Italian universities were famous. During this period the humanistic movement and the Renaissance civilization secured Italy a position of cultural predominance that it had never possessed during the Middle Ages and was never to possess again.

Italians, on the other hand, visited the regions north of the Alps, mainly in the retinue of the Papal Curia or of cardinals, secular princes, and princesses, and as participants of the church councils. Many of them entered, at least temporarily, the service of foreign princes. Others went abroad to teach or study at French, German, and English universities, while native scholars who had studied the humanistic disciplines in Italy received professorships of grammar and rhetoric, and thus introduced the *studia humanitatis* into universities like Basel, Erfurt, Louvain, Vienna, Paris, Oxford, and Cambridge. Not only the classical authors, but also works of Italian humanists became part of the curriculum and thus became well-known. The contacts were further intensified by widespread correspondence and a diffusion of manuscripts and books between Italian humanists and their counterparts in countries abroad. In this way, entire libraries consisting of manuscripts and books of Italian origin were brought together, such as the libraries of Humphrey, Duke of Gloucester, in England, and of King Matthias Corvinus of Hungary. Humanism in other European countries reached its climax at the end of the fifteenth and during the sixteenth century, when Italian humanism was already in decline.

Humanism is often believed to have been a predominantly philosophical movement, but the prerequisite for an understanding of humanistic phenomena seems to be the common background that all humanists shared, namely the literary and scholarly ideal of the study of classical antiquity. Asserting that humanism was primarily a literary movement does not, however, imply that it lacked philosophical implications. The humanists undoubtedly exerted an indirect influence on philosophical thought in general through their methodological and philological contributions. But most of them showed little interest in logic (except Valla, Agricola, and a few others), metaphysics, or natural philosophy; their preoccupation with questions of moral and political philosophy was more personal than systematic, their foremost aim being the education and moral perfection of man—the combination of eloquence and wisdom, of intellectual and practical abilities. In this sense humanists like Guarino of Verona and Vittorino da Feltre became very successful teachers in the fifteenth century. Most of the humanists' philosophical writing (in the proper sense) was either derived from classical sources (which thus became better known) or served educational, literary, and even rhetorical purposes, where stylistic elegance was often more important than philosophical depth or logical accuracy. Treatises like those of Salutati, Bruni, Poggio, Valla, Filelfo, and others served limited purposes and appear rather void of coherence and substance if compared with works of ancient or scholastic philosophers.

In many cases, the humanists were more eager to discuss several opinions on a given philosophical, moral, or political issue than to betray their personal convictions. It has justly been pointed out that even Machiavelli's *Discorsi* and his *Principe*, with their apparently irreconcilable differences of political attitudes, must still be viewed as part of the humanistic tradition (Gilbert). Most of the subjects were conventional, including such topics as happiness and the supreme good, the power of fortune in relation to human reason, the educational value of classical authors, the comparison between republican and monarchical governments and between elective and hereditary monarchy (on this point humanists like Salutati could simultaneously arrive at entirely opposite conclusions), the question of nobility (the humanists usually appeared to prefer nobility by merit to nobility by birth), the advantages of the active or the contemplative life, of married rather than single life (and vice versa), of laymen over clerics or monks, and the merits of certain arts and sciences. Concerning all of these subjects the humanists expressed so many different views—the same author often arriving at completely contrasting conclusions—that it is hardly permissible to regard any of the pertinent opinions as characteristic of Italian humanism in general or even of an individual humanist. On the whole there were no specific philosophical doctrines characteristic of the humanist movement, but rather numerous philosophical ideas expressed by individual humanists.

Furthermore, there were many philosophers and scientists in this period whose basic education was undoubtedly humanist, but whose works were influenced by other traditions and ideas and thus cannot be satisfactorily explained by their humanistic starting point alone. The negative attitude of many humanists towards scholasticism ought to be seen against the background of the emphasis they placed on rhetorical, literary, and moral subjects. In a way it was thus a continuation of the medieval battle of the arts. Medieval philosophy of the thirteenth and fourteenth centuries was based mainly on Aristotle and some Neo-Platonic sources. The humanists effectively enlarged this basis by making accessible the works of Plato,

Plotinus, Diogenes Laërtius, Lucretius and the Epicureans, Epictetus and the Stoics, the Skeptics, and many others. These new sources consequently brought a new stream of ideas into Western philosophy. The overriding authority of Aristotle was no longer generally recognized, but the humanists even contributed to the better understanding of Aristotle himself by replacing the insufficient medieval translations with new ones that showed a better understanding of the Greek text, and also by making accessible the Greek commentators of Aristotle that now replaced the medieval Arabic and Latin commentaries. The Stoics had a considerable influence on Renaissance scholars. Besides, Marsilio Ficino, Giovanni Pico della Mirandola, and Francesco Patrizi became adherents of Plato; Lorenzo Valla was a follower of Epicurus. In this way, a great variety of philosophical schools developed as a result of humanistic studies. The further history of these schools should, however, be separated from the cultural contribution of humanism, insofar as they included many studies, such as metaphysics and cosmology, that were alien to the humanist tradition. Strictly speaking, the Platonists, the later Aristotelians, and the natural philosophers of the sixteenth century do not fall into the mainstream of the humanist movement.

On the other hand, the contents of humanistic writing were not limited to moral and philosophical thought, for we also find a great variety of attitudes towards Christian religion among the humanists. There was certainly much talk about the pagan gods and heroes within the framework of allegory and astrology, but hardly any of the Italian humanists seriously intended to revive ancient pagan cults. Humanism was neither Christian nor anti-Christian. The philological and literary orientation of the movement simply gave rise to different religious attitudes expressed by individual humanists, extending from piety and devotion to pantheism, skepticism, indifference, agnosticism, and even atheism, although many of the characteristic views were cloaked in rhetorical fashion or in allegories, and do not betray the innermost conviction of their authors. Accusations of secret or overt atheism often resulted from literary feuds among humanists and should not be taken too seriously.

Modern scholars, and some politicians, have added complications by applying aprioristic conceptions —Christian, liberal, or atheist—in their evaluation of humanism. For example, there has been a widespread tendency among Anglo-Saxon and German Protestant historians to regard not only Erasmus (because he did not become a partisan of Luther) but even more the Italian humanists as pagan, irreligious, and immoral. But not even the most skeptical humanists undertook a general critique of Christianity, as was done by eighteenth-century philosophers. Those humanists—from Petrarch and the Florentine Augustinians to Ambrogio Traversari, Erasmus, and Thomas More—who took a genuine interest in theology, showed an approach to this subject similar to that of others condemning scholastic theology, i.e., the application of logic and dialectics to theology, and advocating the return to the original sources of Christian doctrine, the Bible, and the Church Fathers (especially Saint Augustine). Their intention was to harmonize humanist learning with the essentials of Christian religion based on these sources. To this end, Italian humanists like Valla and Manetti applied their newly developed method of textual criticism to the study of the Bible and the Latin Church Fathers, later to be followed by Erasmus and others. They translated the Greek Fathers, such as Basil, John Chrysostom, Gregory of Nazianzus, and others. Furthermore, they applied textual and historical criticism to the study of church history; Valla's attack on the Donation of Constantine serving as a famous example.

Thus the humanists had their share in the rise of Protestant and Catholic church reforms during the sixteenth century, in which personalities with a humanist background, such as Melanchthon, Calvin, many Italian heretics, and Jesuits played an important role, while many others preferred an attitude of religious toleration and reconciliation that soon came under attack from the Protestant as well as from the Catholic side. But there were other humanists who emphasized certain elements of natural religion and theology without directly interfering with specific doctrines of the Church. Still other humanists were adherents of (in their theology) of the medieval doctrines of realism and nominalism. Yet it seems hardly admissible to derive humanism from medieval religious schools (like Thomism) or from the medieval tradition, as it seems equally mistaken to divide humanism and Reformation into two different periods. Generally speaking, one can say that the humanists north of the Alps—especially in Germany and England, and partly also in Spain—were more deeply concerned with theology and religion than were the Italian humanists of the fifteenth and sixteenth centuries, among whom secular elements prevailed. These humanists supported the further growth of nonreligious interests and attitudes in contrast to the religious ideas of Italian humanists like Petrarch and the Augustinians a century earlier.

Humanism provided the cultural soil and classical background for the growth of science or natural philosophy, by making available new or better texts and translations of pertinent classical authors. Of course scientific progress was not primarily dependent on humanistic studies. To some degree, the importance attributed to certain classical authors was an obstacle rather than a contributing factor to scientific research. On the other hand, the "medieval" Parisian and Paduan Aristotelians of the fourteenth and fifteenth centuries had, to a certain extent, paved the way for modern science, and even Galileo was still under the influence of the Paduan school.

Progress in science during the fifteenth century was not spectacular; the real turning point did not occur before the sixteenth and advanced most rapidly in the seventeenth century. The knowledge of Greek and Arabic authors sometimes helped to overcome erroneous conceptions of the Middle Ages (as the medieval tradition could help to overcome errors diffused by ancient scientific literature). Knowledge of Greek and Arabic science served mainly as a point of departure for independent mathematical reasoning and empirical observation. Thus, for example, Nicolaus Copernicus, who had acquired humanist learning in Italy, came to his revolutionary views concerning the nature of the solar system by analyzing, mainly by theoretic reasoning, the different cosmologies of the ancient "mathematicians" (i.e., astronomers) and by replacing the Ptolemaic system with a heliocentric system that he defended as Pythagorean. On the other hand, the occult tradition with its precedents in late antiquity (e.g., astrology) or in Arabic scientific writing (e.g., in alchemy and magic) found a fertile soil in Renaissance society. It was a serious obstacle to scientific progress and was not finally overcome before the seventeenth century. The rapid increase in scientific knowledge and technology in the following centuries was mainly due to the close cooperation, and even identity, of scholars, craftsmen, and artisans characteristic of Western civilization of this period. Many of the newly discovered ancient scientific conceptions had to be singled out and appropriated, and the natural philosophy of the Aristotelians had to be successfully attacked by Galileo before the final breakthrough of physical science occurred in the seventeenth century.

Here the Platonist tradition with its mathematical conception of the universe and its notion of cosmic harmony was especially strong, but not always in a positive way, because of the preference given to number symbolism and astrology. While Kepler's relationship with Platonism is beyond dispute, Galileo's adherence to it is a controversial matter—although it is generally admitted that his claim for the certainty of mathematical knowledge is Platonic, while other essential experimental aspects of his thought are not. It was Galileo who took a decisive step forward by applying mathematical and experimental methods to the solution of problems of physics.

Renaissance medicine was still influenced by Aristotelians like Galen and Avicenna, but freed itself, through observation and experiment in anatomy and surgery, from outdated medical theories. The humanists' main contribution lay in the fact that they translated into Latin several writings of Hippocrates and Galen that had not been translated in the eleventh and twelfth centuries. In biology, progress was made within the Aristotelian tradition during the sixteenth century. In geography, the humanists for the first time translated two most valuable Greek sources, Strabo and Ptolemy.

In the field of art, humanist learning profoundly influenced Renaissance architecture and the iconography and the style of Renaissance painting. Little was known of ancient music, but ancient musical theories were used as a justification of new developments in Renaissance music that lay outside the proper realm of humanist scholarship. The reading of the relevant passages in Plato's *Timaeus* may have influenced Marsilio Ficino, an enthusiastic amateur in music and author of several treatises on musical theory.

In law, the traditions of the canonists and legists developed at Bologna and other universities continued through the Renaissance period. Their method was dialectical and systematic; the authorities collected in the *Decretum Gratiani*, the *Decretals*, and the *Corpus iuris civilis* were quoted and harmonized with little regard to their historical development. This legal tradition, often referred to as *mos Italicus*, as it was most widely spread at the Italian universities, now came under the attack of the humanists. The new method which they propagated, and which did not reach its full development before the sixteenth century, became known under the name of *mos Gallicus*. The method of dialectical reconciliation of legal authorities, "harmony from dissonance" (Kuttner), without regard for their historical background, was replaced by a philological and historical interpretation of Roman law. This tendency, although it weakened the actual influence of Roman law on legal practice, resulted in a deeper though still limited historical understanding of it. But on the whole, the medieval traditions of the canon and civil lawyers and the notaries with their glosses, commentaries, formularies, questions, and opinions remained very strong throughout the entire period of Italian humanism. Many of those lawyers who had a humanistic education did not abandon the traditional legal method, as can be clearly seen in Florence and elsewhere.

From the sociological point of view, humanism was not restricted to any one class. Yet, on the whole, as one might expect in the surroundings of Italian urban civilization, the bourgeois element prevailed. Many humanists were of humble origin and yet worked their way up to become members of the upper classes (as was also true of other scholars) and part of the *noblesse de robe*. Many of them collected large incomes as lawyers, secretaries, notaries, and chancellors. Others, like Niccolò Niccoli in Florence, were born as members of the oligarchy and later squandered their rich inheritance by investing their money, as dead capital, in large libraries. Generally speaking, the picture of the poor humanist scholar living on his idealism and on the favor of princes sprang from a generalization of some individual occurrences, and can be considered as largely mythical—although there were instances of (at least temporary) poverty and dire need.

Social considerations may serve better to explain certain elements of Italian humanism, such as the propagandistic-rhetorical attitude of the "republican" circle around Salutati and Bruni in Florence, or certain phenomena of Italian humanism at the courts of Italian princes, but there is no general sociological criterion that can explain the great variety of Italian humanists. As teachers the humanists were often successfully engaged in educating the children of princes and of the urban patriciate, many of whom became convinced that their social status required a humanist education. But the diffusion and the depth of such education should not be exaggerated. The reading public of the humanists consisted of fellow scholars, students, a minority of educated businessmen, and some learned princes and noblemen. It was not until the sixteenth century that an increasing number of people of the middle class became interested in humanistic literature.

In Florence, where a republican form of government had been preserved during the fourteenth and fifteenth centuries, humanists like Salutati, Bruni, Palmieri, Alberti, Niccoli, and Poggio—many of them as chancellors to the republic—became especially involved in the *vita activa* (the active life of city politics), and championed the ideal of man taking a responsible part in public affairs.

An individualist outlook prevailed in this regard also, and different humanists held different views. While the Florentines praised the ideal of active life, others favored a life of contemplation. While the Florentine humanists subordinated their lives to the interests of the republic, others emphasized the uniqueness of the individual and the resulting strife for personal honor and glory. Since the Florentine humanists had worked their way up to become members of the upper class of society, or belonged to that class by birth, they naturally supported the policy of the ruling oligarchy and its struggle for communal independence, the more so as many of them had been born outside Florence (such as Bruni in Arezzo, whose loyalty to Florence was never beyond doubt) and had to overcome, by pronounced and unceasing support of the Florentine cause, the natural suspicion of the native patriciate. Salutati, chancellor from 1375 to 1406, still propagated the ideology of Guelfism, i.e., communal liberty and cooperation with the papacy and France, at a time when the ideology had long lost its political foundations (adding, however, reminiscences of classical political thought). Bruni, however developed the ideal of republican liberty, which was originally an old Guelf concept but which now received a fresh inspiration from the study of Republican Rome. Ideas like these were spread during the struggle between Florence and Giangaleazzo Visconti of Milan (died 1402), but their rhetorical and propagandistic purposes were too evident, and they apparently had little influence on the political conceptions of the governing oligarchy, as the unpublished minutes of the consultations of the Signoria show. Bruni did not even apply the political ideas of his literary works in his official correspondence, and on the whole Florentine politics in the fifteenth century was little affected by humanistic ideologies.

The realistic attitude that we observe in the policy of the commune was largely due to a political experience that went back to the thirteenth century. Classical models played a certain, but not a decisive role in overcoming the medieval outlook and in strengthening the determination to preserve communal liberty. This largely coincided with the political interests of the ruling oligarchy and showed little regard for the "liberty" of other communes such as Pisa and Arezzo. Appeals for popular government did not result in the participation of a larger section of the city's population in the government of Florence. Florentine "civic" humanism, though it sometimes strengthened "republican" tendencies, was to some extent a literary fashion, and its actual impact on Florentine politics is proved, by a mass of unpublished material, to have been rather weak. Salutati, for example, expressly stated that he did not take most of his rhetorical outbursts against "tyrannical" Milan too seriously; he and others rather considered themselves to be part of the entire humanistic movement with its mainly literary and scholarly interests. Besides, there was a great variety of humanistic writing in Florence, much of it unaffected by the political issues of the Salutati-Bruni circle.

The defense of monarchy was taken up by other humanists under Milanese rule, such as Antonio Loschi and Pier Candido Decembrio, and it became a literary fashion with some humanists. The question of whether Caesar was to be preferred to Scipio and Brutus was an interesting subject for comparing the relative merits of monarchical and republican government. Political theory had long been a part of moral philosophy, and the humanists' interests in this field has to be viewed in this light. Beside "republicanism," there was a strong component of monarchical thought in humanistic political theory. This is especially true of the sixteenth century, but even Salutati toyed with similar ideas when he wrote two treatises on hereditary and elective monarchy proving simultaneously the advantages of each of them over the other respectively. Italian humanism as a whole, because of its literary and philological starting point, was politically neutral; it could serve the purposes of "despotic" rulers as well as those of "republican" communes. Even in Florence, where humanists continued to defend the republican form of government during the fifteenth century, champions of "republicanism" like Bruni later acquiesced with the increasing manipulation of republican government by the Medici.

In most of the subjects discussed here, Italian humanism changed the intellectual climate, gradually overcame medieval traditions, and paved the way for the future. It survived the Protestant and Catholic Reformations of the sixteenth century. In philosophy and science, both subjects that have held key positions in the evolution of the modern mind, humanism was superseded, during the seventeenth century, by new developments started by Descartes and Galileo, but at least partly prepared by Renaissance humanism. In other fields, such as literature, arts, and education, humanistic ideas survived or were revived during the following centuries. Thus the contribution of Italian humanism to the development of Western civilization is an important one. Humanistic ideas have proved to be of great educational value in the formation of civilized and responsible personalities, and they are still a counterweight against anti-intellectual tendencies today.

BIBLIOGRAPHY

The most comprehensive view of Italian humanism with which the author agrees on most points may be found (with excellent bibliographies) in P. O. Kristeller, *Studies in Renaissance Thought and Letters* (Rome, 1956; reprint 1969); idem, *Renaissance Thought*, 2 vols. (New York, 1961–65).

Other major studies are: F. Chabod, *Machiavelli and the Renaissance* (London, 1958). W. F. Ferguson, *The Renaissance in Historical Thought* (Boston, 1948). E. Garin, *L'umanesimo italiano*, 2nd ed. (Bari, 1965), trans. P. Munz as *Italian Humanism* (Oxford, 1967). F. Gilbert, *Niccolò Machiavelli e la vita culturale del suo tempo* (Bologna, 1964). B. L. Ullman, *Studies in the Italian Renaissance* (Rome, 1955).

All discussions of Italian Renaissance humanism still have to start with two nineteenth-century works: J. Burckhardt, *Die Kultur der Renaissance in Italien*, 2nd ed. (Basel, 1869); critical edition by W. Kaegi (Berlin and Leipzig, 1930);

several English editions; and G. Voight, *Die Wiederbelebung des classischen Alterthums oder das erste Jahrhundert des Humanismus*, 3rd ed. by M. Lehnerdt, 2 vols. (Berlin, 1893; reprint 1960).

Other relevant works include: H. Baron, *The Crisis of the Early Italian Renaissance*, rev. ed. (Princeton, 1966); idem, *Humanistic and Political Literature in Florence and Venice at the Beginning of the Quattrocento . . .* (Cambridge, Mass., 1955; reprint New York, 1968); idem, *From Petrarch to Leonardo Bruni* (Chicago and London, 1968). G. Billanovich, *Petrarca letterato*, Vol. I (Rome, 1947). M. F. Bukofzer, *Studies in Medieval and Renaissance Music* (New York, 1950). K. Burdach, *Vom Mittelalter zur Reformation*, 9 vols. (Berlin 1912–39); idem, *Reformation, Renaissance, Humanismus*, 2nd ed. (Berlin and Leipzig, 1926; reprint Darmstadt, 1963). G. Cammelli, *I dotti bizantini e le origini dell'umanesimo*, 3 vols. (Florence, 1941–54). A. Campana, "The Origin of the Word 'Humanist'," *Journal of the Warburg and Courtauld Institutes*, **9** (1946), 60–73. E. Cassirer, P. O. Kristeller, J. H. Randall, Jr., eds., *The Renaissance Philosophy of Man* (Chicago, 1948). E. Cassirer, *Individuum und Kosmos in der Philosophie der Renaissance* (Leipzig and Berlin, 1927), trans. M. Domandi as *The Individual and the Cosmos in Renaissance Philosophy* (New York, 1964). A. Chastel, *Art et humanisme à Florence au temps de Laurent le Magnifique* (Paris, 1959). C. Dionisotti, *Gli umanisti e il volgare fra Quattro e Cinquecento* (Florence, 1968). P. Duhem, *Études sur Léonard de Vinci*, 3 vols. (Paris, 1906–13). E. Garin, *La cultura filosofica del Rinascimento italiano* (Florence, 1961). D. J. Geanakoplos, *Greek Scholars in Venice* (Cambridge, Mass., 1962). F. Gilbert, "The Renaissance Interest in History," *Art, Science and History in the Renaissance*, ed. C. S. Singleton (Baltimore, 1968), pp. 373–87; idem, *Machiavelli and Guicciardini* (Princeton, 1965). M. P. Gilmore, *Humanists and Jurists* (Cambridge, Mass., 1963). E. H. Harbison, *The Christian Scholar in the Age of the Reformation* (New York, 1956). C. H. Haskins, *The Renaissance of the Twelfth Century* (Cambridge, Mass., 1927). H. Haydn, *The Counter-Renaissance* (New York, 1950). P. Herde, "Politik und Rhetorik in Florenz am Vorabend der Renaissance," *Archiv für Kulturgeschichte*, **47** (1965), 141–220. A. Hyma, *The Christian Renaissance* (New York, 1924). G. Kisch, *Humanismus und Jurisprudenz* (Basel, 1955). A. Koyré, *Études Galiléennes*, 3 vols. (Paris, 1939). P. O. Kristeller, *Iter Italicum: A Finding List of Uncatalogued or Incompletely Catalogued Humanistic Manuscripts of the Renaissance in Italian and other Libraries*, 2 vols. (London and Leyden, 1963–67; to be completed); idem, *Renaissance Philosophy and the Medieval Tradition* (Latrobe, Pa., 1966); idem, "The European Diffusion of Italian Humanism," *Italica*, **39** (1962), 1–26; is also found in *Renaissance Thought*, Vol. II (New York, 1965; also reprint); idem, *Eight Philosophers of the Italian Renaissance* (Stanford, 1964). S. Kuttner, *Harmony from Dissonance: An Interpretation of Medieval Canon Law* (Latrobe, Pa., 1956). D. Maffei, *Gli inizi dell'umanesimo giuridico* (Milan, 1956). A. Maier, *Die Vorläufer Galileis im 14. Jahrhundert* (Rome, 1949); idem, *An der Grenze von Scholastik und Naturwissenschaft*, 2nd ed. (Rome, 1952). L. Martines, *The Social*

World of the Florentine Humanists, 1390–1460 (Princeton, 1963). B. Migliorini, *Storia della lingua italiana*, 2nd ed. (Florence, 1960). E. Panofsky, *Renaissance and Renascences in Western Art* (Uppsala, 1965). A. Pertusi, *Storiografia umanista e mondo bizantino* (Palermo, 1967). J. H. Randall, *The School of Padua and the Emergence of Modern Science* (Padua, 1961). G. Reese, *Music in the Renaissance*, rev. ed. (New York, 1959). V. Rossi, *Il Quattrocento*, 5th ed. (Milan, 1953). R. Sabbadini, *Le scoperte dei codici latini e greci nei secoli XIV e XV*, 2 vols. (Florence, 1905–14). F. Saxl, *Lectures*, 2 vols. (London, 1957). E. Seidlmayer, *Wege und Wandlungen des Humanismus* (Göttingen, 1965). J. E. Seigel, *Rhetoric and Philosophy in Renaissance Humanism: . . .* (Princeton, 1968). K. M. Setton, "The Byzantine Background to the Italian Renaissance," *Proceedings of the American Philosophical Society*, **100** (1956), 1–76. J. Seznec, *The Survival of the Pagan Gods*, trans. B. F. Sessions (New York, 1953). M. Tafuri, *L'architettura dell'umanesimo* (Bari, 1969). L. Thorndike, *A History of Magic and Experimental Science*, 8 vols. (New York, 1923–58). G. Toffanin, *Storia dell'umanesimo*, 3 vols. (Bologna, 1950); idem, *La religione degli umanisti* (Bologna, 1950). C. Trinkaus, "Humanism," in *Encyclopedia of World Art* (New York, 1959–64); idem, *In Our Image and Likeness: Humanity and Divinity in Italian Humanist Thought*, 2 vols. (London, 1970). B. L. Ullman, *The Origin and Development of Humanistic Script* (Rome, 1960). A. von Martin, *Sociology of the Renaissance* (London, 1944; reprint New York, 1963). D. P. Walker, *Der musikalische Humanismus* (Kassel and Basel, 1949). A. Warburg, *Gesammelte Schriften*, ed. G. Bing, 2 vols. (Leipzig, 1932). B. Weinberg, *A History of Literary Criticism in the Italian Renaissance*, 2 vols. (Chicago, 1961). R. Weiss, *The Dawn of Humanism in Italy* (London, 1947); idem, *Il primo secolo dell'umanesimo, Studi e Testi* (Rome, 1949); idem, *The Spread of Italian Humanism* (London, 1964); *The Renaissance Discovery of Classical Antiquity* (Oxford, 1969). E. H. Wilkins, *Studies in the Life and Works of Petrarch* (Cambridge, Mass., 1955); idem, *Life of Petrarch* (Chicago, 1961). E. Wind, *Pagan Mysteries in the Renaissance* (New Haven, 1958). R. Wittkower, *Architectural Principles in the Age of Humanism* (London, 1952).

PETER HERDE

[See also **Classicism in Literature;** Cosmology; Myth; Periodization; Platonism; **Renaissance Humanism; Renaissance Literature;** Universal Man; *Virtù*.]

ICONOGRAPHY

THE WORD iconography comes from the Greek word εἰκονογραφία; in modern usage iconography is a description and/or interpretation of the content of works of art and therefore its history belongs to the history of human ideas. We propose, however, to distinguish between what one could call "the intended (or implied)

iconography" and "interpretative iconography." By the first we understand the attitude of the artist, the patron, or the contemporary observer toward the function and the meaning of visual symbols and images. Sometimes it was formulated in writing in documents like contracts (for example, "Contract for Painting an Altarpiece of the Coronation of the Virgin for Dominus Jean de Montagnac by Enguerrand Quarton," 1453); in programs (known for several late-baroque ceiling paintings); in iconographical treatises (for example, Joannes Molanus, *De picturis et imaginibus sacris*, 1570); in utterances of the artists (for example, Giorgio Vasari's *Ragionamenti*, written 1567, published 1588), or of the patrons (for example, Abbot Suger's *De consecratione ecclesiae S. Dionysii*). Sometimes we can reconstruct it only by historical methods, by adducing philosophical, theological, or literary ideas contemporary with or current at the time. By "interpretative iconography" may be understood precisely that branch of historical study of art which aims at the identification and description of representations, and at the interpretation of the content of the works of art (this last function now preferably called "iconology"). Whereas "interpretative iconography" is a historical discipline of the study of art, the "intended or implied iconography" is an element of the general outlook and aesthetic attitude of the period. The degree of consciousness in approaching the problem of content in art varied at different times and places.

In order to outline the changing relations of images and ideas, we shall in the present article discuss first the development of "intended iconography," i.e., the attitude toward images and visual symbols as manifested in art and art literature in western Europe; the formation of what may be called "systems of iconography": the medieval religious system, the Renaissance, and baroque humanistic system; the dissolution of systems around 1800, and finally, the new developments in the last hundred and fifty years. In the second part of the article we shall be discussing the development of "interpretative iconography," i.e., of art historical studies concerning problems of iconography, with a special stress on recent developments in that field.

I

1. The origins of art are closely connected with religion and myth. The works of art of early civilizations were religious symbols, idols, expressions of fears and desires. An interpretation of meaning connected with these works of art is however uncertain due to a lack of reliable records. It is often impossible to say to what extent an idol or a religious symbol was considered as a representation of some divine power and to what extent it was considered as embodying that power. The meaning of concepts like that of image (*eikon*) and of the corresponding Latin concept (*imago*) as well as of *figura* varied greatly; in general it evolved from that of substitution to that of representation (Auerbach, 1959; Bauch, 1967).

In classical antiquity, due to the Greek tendency to anthropomorphic depiction of mythical divinities, an art world was created which was divine and human at the same time. Far from producing only representative statues of gods, suitable for cult worship, and adoration, or for the narration of mythical events, classical art soon proceeded to create an allegorical interpretation of myth (Hinks, 1939).

The primitive mind is aware only of a generalized daemonic force outside itself, to which it is subject and which it must propitiate; and as it grows, the mythical presentation of its experience progresses from the undifferentiated daemonic power to the personal god, and from the personal god to the impersonal abstraction which is merely for convenience imagined in a human shape. . . (Hinks, p. 107).

Just as the myth was provided with an aetiological explanation when it had ceased at length to be self-explanatory, so the image came to be interpreted allegorically when it had lost its self-evident character. . . . As soon as philosophic reflection became self-conscious, the habit of furnishing straightforward mythical representations with allegorical explanations made its appearance in iconographical as in literary criticism (Hinks, pp. 11f.).

Hinks devoted a penetrating study to this problem. For the Greeks poetry and myth were more serious, more philosophical than history, since myth and poetry concern general truths whereas history concerns particular ones (Aristotle, *Poetics* IX. 3). Hence, there appeared a tendency to make mythical events express allegorically particular historical events; mythical wars of Greeks with Amazons, or of Lapiths against Centaurs, were represented instead of the historical struggle of the Athenians against the Persians. Mythical symbols were always preferred to historical images. This is a particular case of a general polarization which can be observed in iconography between the general and the particular, the mythical and the secular, the timeless and the historical, between the symbol and the story. The symbol corresponds to the mythical frame of mind, the image to the historical:

. . . even when, during the sixth and fifth centuries before Christ, the Greek mind succeeded in detaching itself from the object of its contemplation, and the mythical and logical forms of comprehension were theoretically distinguished, this immense intellectual advance did not disintegrate the plastic vision of the ancient artist, in the same way as the enlargement of the scientific horizon in the nineteenth century destroyed the coherence of the modern artistic vision (Hinks, p. 62).

In this way forms of iconography originated which were to have a long life in European art, viz., those of personification and allegory. The classical gods received new, allegorical functions denoting natural phenomena or abstract concepts. On the other hand, abstract notions received personified form.

There also appeared in classical art mixed, transitional forms, for example, what Hinks calls *"mythistorical"* representations, in which heroes and/or gods participated beside mortal humans and allegorical representations (Pánainos' *Battle of Marathon*). Since for the Greeks the essential meaning of an event was its moral sense, the only way to bring this out in art was to represent it in an allegorical way: "the moral situation must be personalized: the dramatic conflict of ethical principles must be represented by the concerted action of their symbols" (ibid., p. 66). The greatness of the Greeks consisted in that they knew how "to construct a mythical framework within which the movements of the planets and the passions of the heart are converted into symbols not merely comparable but actually to some extent interchangeable" (ibid., p. 94).

In the later periods of antiquity when irrational Orphic and Dionysiac religious movements prevailed over the reasonably organized world of Olympian gods, and when the Imperial Roman form of the state prevailed over the tradition of small democratic Greek states, there appeared new forms of iconography, which were to remain influential in the Christian period. Tomb decoration began to flourish, based on the allegorical interpretation of mythical imagery: Seasons, Bacchic myths, Venus Anadyomene, Sea-Thiasos (Cumont, 1942); imperial ceremonies gave form to elaborate triumphal iconography and they decisively influenced Christian symbolism. Late classical art elaborated also the representation of the internal dialogue of a man with his soul or conscience in the form of an external dialogue with an allegorical person, often acting in an inspiring way: a Muse, a Genius, an Angel, thus giving shape to a long-lived representation of inspiration, or of conversation with superhuman powers, current in art until modern times (Saxl, 1923; Hinks, 1939).

2. The history of iconographical attitudes in postclassical times is to a considerable degree a history of accepting or rejecting the classical tradition. Everything which recalled a heathenish idol-cult was rejected, and the meaning of *imago* was limited mainly to painted images, which being flat and therefore not similar materially to what they represented, suggested only the shape of divine figures. Nevertheless Christian art adopted various images and functions of images from the pagan tradition, developing, as it did, an allegorical imagery of its own, a historical narration, and icon-portraits of Christ, of the Virgin, and of the Saints. The cult of the images seems to go back to a pagan tradition (images of the emperors, portraits of the deceased) and most probably existed among the first generations of Christians (Grabar, 1968). That cult, which rose to greater importance in the fifth and sixth centuries, and the belief in the part of the holiness of their saintly prototypes being inherent in these images, became the object of a long theological quarrel, as a result of which attitudes towards religious iconography were differentiated in the West and in the East.

In the Byzantine Empire the problem of religious images acquired an exceptional importance as the object of violent theological and political discussions and of decisions of the Church Councils (Grabar, 1957). At the Councils of 730, 754, and 815 images were prohibited, but at those of 787 (Nicaea) and of 843 they were again allowed. Although the partisans of the images triumphed, a very strict iconographic doctrine was established, which provided extremely precise regulations concerning religious imagery in the decoration of East-Christian churches. These regulations have been followed in the Eastern Church ever since. The traditional character of Byzantine iconography is demonstrated by the fact that the iconographic handbook by Dionysius of Fourna, *Hermeneia tes zographikes technes*, published by A. N. Didron (1845) was for a long time considered as a document of an early period of Byzantine art, and it was only in 1909 that A. Papadopoulos Kerameus proved it to be a work of the eighteenth century, obviously reflecting a very old tradition. In this static world of iconographical thinking little change is noticeable, although Eastern Christian art had its important artistic evolution and often absorbed Western influences, sometimes even in iconographic respects (e.g., the influence of German prints on the wall paintings in the Athos monasteries).

3. For medieval Christian thought everything in the world was a symbol. Things, persons, and events actual and historical, were considered as symbols of other things, persons, and events, or as symbols of concepts and ideas. The doctrine of "universal symbolism" originated in Saint Augustine (*De Trinitate*) and first of all in the Neo-Platonic philosophy of Pseudo-Dionysius the Areopagite, for whom "visible things are images of invisible beauty." Thanks to John Scotus Erigena's translation, the ideas of Pseudo-Dionysius spread widely and it was Hugh of St. Victor who presented the complete theory of universal symbolism: "all nature expresses God" (*omnis natura Deum loquitur*). For Hugh the universe is "a book written by the hand of God." Alain de Lille has given a popular, compact, poetic formula of universal symbolism:

Omnis mundi creatura
quasi liber et pictura
nobis est et speculum

("Every creature of the world is for us like a book and a picture of the world, and it is like a mirror"). Saint Bonaventure finds that created beauty, being a sign of the eternal, leads men to God. Theologians discerned mainly two kinds of symbolism under different names but signifying two more or less basically similar divisions: (1) existing things endowed with meaning (*res et signa*) and (2) conventional signs (Chydenius, 1960). In the practical use of symbolism in art one can discern another diversity: an Aristotelian, rational trend and a Neo-Platonic, irrational, and mystical one (Gombrich, 1948; 1965). In the first case, the images were not considered as including any more content than their verbal equivalents; they constituted a code, a conventional language of signs used to communicate religious messages. In the second case, experience of symbolical images was believed to give the observer another, higher knowledge than that transmitted by words; it was meant to give a direct ecstatic, and enthusiastic contact with abstract ideas incorporated, as it were, in images. Medieval art used generally symbolic images conceived as a code transmitting its messages to everybody, also to those who were not able to read. The other attitude to symbols appeared in the Middle Ages in the mystical trends. The image which can be grasped in a sensual way was a means of transgressing the limits of the corporeal world, and of reaching the spiritual one. Such a function of images was formulated by various theologians. Jean Gerson, in the fifteenth century, put it in the following words: "And we ought thus to learn to transcend with our minds from these visible things to the invisible, from the corporeal to the spiritual. For this is the purpose of the image" (Ringbom [1969], p. 165).

The didactic doctrine had been formulated already in the early period of the Church; according to that doctrine, images were considered as a form of writing accessible to those unable to read (Paulinus of Nola, Gregory the Great; also Thomas Aquinas considered images to be useful, *ad instructionem rudium*). This attitude lasted until the very end of the Middle Ages (later it was revived in the period of the Counter-Reformation), and it found expression as late as the fourteenth and fifteenth centuries in the early graphic imagery of such typological compendia as *Biblia pauperum* and *Speculum humanae salvationis*. The didactic aims encompassed not only the direct moral lessons which were transmitted through the imagery of "prohibition" and "dissuasion," of the Last Judgment and of the Virtues and Vices, but also the visual representation of sometimes complicated links among the events of sacred history, considered as prefigurations and fulfillments which were established between the figures and events of the Old and the New Dispensation. Thus typological thinking connected images into symbolic relations. Visual unity was established in the religious imagery through the large encyclopedic compendia, e.g., *Glossa ordinaria* (the large body of Commentaries to the Bible, until recently held to be a compilation by Walafrid Strabo), and Gulielmus Durandus' system of liturgy *Rationale divinorum officiorum*, or Vincent of Beauvais's *Speculum maius*, an image of the world seen in the symbolistic mirror. These books contributed to the realization of the tremendous iconographical programs of the great cathedrals of the high Middle Ages, where God, nature, and man were united into an exceptionally elaborated system of symbolic images, mirroring the model of the world current in the period of Gothic art. Art at that time followed the symbolistic way of thinking which prevailed in theology as well as in liturgy, in profane ceremonials, and in the other fields of life. Art gave artistic form to the abstract structure of the cosmos as seen by medieval theologians and brought it close to the understanding or to the imagination of every man. This does not at all mean that medieval symbolism was always understandable to everybody and everywhere. Very specific theological problems and controversies found their way into iconography, and when deciphered by modern iconographers they disclose often complicated religious and/or political situations (for example, the imagery of the Ruthwell Cross, which reflects the conflicting ideologies of Northern versus Roman Christianity in England, as revealed in an analysis by Meyer Schapiro, 1944).

Neo-Platonic symbolism was developed especially under the impact of writings by Pseudo-Dionysius the Areopagite. His influence promoted to a great extent medieval ideas about the symbolism of light. The symbolism of light found its highest achievement in the creation of Gothic architecture, dominated by the mysticism of light (von Simson, 1956). Abbot Suger, the *auctor intellectualis* of Gothic architecture, presented in his writings an excellent record of that attitude toward symbolism. In his *De rebus in administratione sua gestis* (XVII) he writes about the doors with gilt bronze reliefs: "Bright is the noble work; but being nobly bright, the work / should brighten the minds, so that they may travel through the true lights, / to the true light where Christ is the true door / . . . . The dull mind rises to truth through that which is material . . ." (Panofsky [1946], pp. 46–49). Contemplating precious stones transports Suger's mind to a contemplation of the supernatural:

When—out of my delight in the beauty of the house of God—the loveliness of the many-colored stones has called me away from external cares, and worthy meditation has induced me to reflect, transferring that which is material to that which is immaterial, on the diversity of the sacred virtues: then it seems to me that I see myself dwelling, as it were, in some strange region of the universe which neither exists entirely in the slime of the earth nor entirely in the purity of Heaven; and that, by the Grace of God, I can be transported from this inferior to that higher world in an anagogical manner" (ibid., pp. 63–65).

To a similar sphere of mystical symbols the specific symbolism of numbers also belongs. Numbers in the Bible and those referring to quantitative relations in architecture were considered as having a mystical meaning: "the Divine Wisdom is reflected in the numbers impressed on all things" (Saint Augustine, *De libero arbitrio* II, XVI). The belief in the mystical significance of numbers, which originated in Pythagoreanism and was revived by Neo-Platonism, was transmitted to the Middle Ages by the Fathers of the Church (Mâle [1898]; English ed. [1958], p. 10). Complicated ramifications of this numerical symbolism in the field of medieval architectural iconography are studied by J. Sauer (1924) as well as by E. Mâle (ibid., p. 10). The number eight, for example, connected with the idea of new life by the Fathers (since it comes after seven, the terminal number of human life and of the world), expresses the concept of resurrection and therefore that of the Baptism; because of that early belief baptisteries and baptismal fonts are octagonal (Mâle, ibid., p. 14). One may trace in such use of numerical symbolism a mystical rather than a didactic attitude.

The general adoption of a symbolic attitude does not mean that in the Middle Ages no actual events were represented in art. However, since medieval art was very much traditional and remained faithful to *exempla* or compositional visual patterns, the actual events, when they were sometimes taken as subjects of representation, used to be transformed to fit preconceived traditional patterns. The written lives of the saints have been composed according to literary and mythical *topoi*. The same may be observed in art. When a new subject had to be represented it used to be molded according to existing patterns. As an example we may adduce the story of Saint Adalbert represented on the bronze doors of the twelfth century at Gniezno, Poland. The formerly executed European bronze church doors represented Christological narrative or allegorical figures or ornaments. The fairly recent hagiographic story had to be given visual shape. It is not surprising that the representations in most cases follow the patterns of Christological iconography (Kalinowski, 1959). Secular subjects, as for example,

527

the conquest of England by William the Conqueror and its circumstances, represented on the so-called Bayeux Tapestry, followed in the general idea the classical tradition. It seems that perhaps more of a direct experience of the actual medieval life found its way into art than is usually admitted, but the relative share of symbolism and realism, of system and freedom is still a matter of discussion among medievalists (Berliner, 1945; 1956).

In the late Middle Ages the general system of iconography persisted, but new subjects, especially the representations of the most human episodes and relationships in Christ's life, namely of His infancy and His emotional connections (with the Virgin and Saint John) as well as His Passion and the episodes of Our Lady's life come to the fore. Although symbolical and didactic thinking maintained its importance, the means to communicate with the faithful changed: most subjects popular in the late Middle Ages appeal to the beholder's emotions rather than to his reason. Scholars have selected a group of so-called devotional pictures as opposed to dogmatic and to historical representations, but the precise delimitation of such a group is still a matter of discussion, as is also the question of how much this art was influenced by literature and especially by pious poetry. With the development of the graphic arts new cheap pictures spread widely the typological imagery systematized in the *Biblia pauperum*, and in the *Speculum humanae salvationis*. Great collections of religious meditations, compiled in monasteries, like *Meditations on the Life of Christ* by Pseudo-Bonaventure (ed. I. Ragusa and R. B. Green, 1961), spread widely a new emotional approach to iconography. Also the religious theater had some influence on the way stories in art were told.

4. In the iconography of the Renaissance art "history" was shifted to the fore at the expense of symbolism. It does not mean that symbols ceased to exist. Pictorial allegory and symbolism played a very important part in the conception of humanistic art. But what was placed in the center of the new art theory was the concept of *istoria*. The first and the most important task of the work of art, according to L. B. Alberti (*De pictura*, 1435; *Della pittura*, 1436), is to present a story. This story had to be selected from authoritative literary sources, either sacred or profane; it should represent, in a possibly convincing and expressive way, an episode from the Holy Scriptures, from sacred or classical history, from mythology or legend. This new concept of *istoria*, which was to dominate iconographic considerations for more than three hundred years (the meaning of the term *istoria* or *storia* changed of course in that period) was one of the consequences of the Renaissance idea of the priority of literature over the visual

arts. There were several reasons for that priority, one being a complete lack of known classical theory of art. In its stead the theories of poetry and rhetoric were adopted as guiding principles for the visual arts. Hence the dominating Horatian principle *ut pictura poesis,* which subordinated the visual arts to the rules of literary theory. This identification of literature and art lasted until G. E. Lessing in 1766 revolted against it in his *Laokoön* (R. W. Lee, 1940). In the humanistic theory of visual arts the concept of *istoria* took the central place. *Istoria* had to be chosen for its moral value (Alberti chose as his examples the subjects showing stoic moral firmness, as the "Death of Meleager," the "Immolation of Iphigenia," or the "Calumny" of Apelles), it had to be represented according to the principle of *decorum* and *costume*, i.e., with regard to its dignity, and most truthfully to the literary prototype. Everything should be suitable in "size, function, kind, color, and other similar things": Alberti stressed the necessity of varied and convincing expressions of emotions by suitable gestures.

The dependence of post-medieval iconography on literature increased with time, and in the seventeenth century the truthfulness of the pictorial formulation of literary subjects became one of the most valued qualities of a work of visual arts. "Read the story and the picture at the same time," Nicolas Poussin wrote to M. de Chantelou, one of his customers. In the French Royal Academy of Painting and Sculpture lengthy discussions were going on concerning the relation of pictures to literary sources. To be able to represent well subjects taken from poetry, the artist had to be a *doctus artifex*, well-informed in various fields. G. P. Bellori (1695) stressed, however, the fact that not everything good in writing comes out well in painting. Therefore, the painter, to be able to transform the story, had to acquire "an universal knowledge of things and he should contemplate precisely nature and realities." Some freedom was given to the artist from the beginning: Alberti was far from limiting the painter too much by this dependence on literature. He stressed the specific requirements of the visual arts, as for example, the necessity to limit the number of represented figures in order to keep a balance between "copiousness" and "solitude in painting." This made it, of course, necessary to reduce crowded scenes to an easily graspable number of figures in order to avoid "dissolute confusion" (Spencer [1956], pp. 23–28).

The interest of early Renaissance art theorists in iconography was not great. They concentrated their attention chiefly on the discussion of the means needed to achieve a convincing and beautiful representation of the *istoria*, and on the specific problems of representation—correct (by adoption of the rules of perspective), and beautiful (by adoption of the rules of proportion). Leonardo da Vinci does not show a specific interest in iconography, but in some passages of his incompleted *Treatise on Painting* he gives literary programs of pictures; remarkably, however, the pictures are not of stories, but of representations of powerful natural or human happenings, such as storms and battles. Here the naturalistic interests of the Renaissance come to the fore.

An important achievement of the Renaissance, partly affecting iconography, was the reunion—as noticed and described by E. Panofsky and F. Saxl (1932) and Panofsky (1960)—of the literary and visual traditions of classical antiquity during the fifteenth century. During the Middle Ages the literary tradition of classical subject matter was separated from the visual tradition of classical artistic motifs, so that there was no awareness of their belonging together. The classical subjects, for example those taken from Ovid, used to be represented in contemporary medieval stylistic forms; classical artistic motifs, on the other hand, for example the forms of garment folds, human types, gestures, compositional patterns, and so on were used to represent Christian subject matter, as in the western portals of the Reims cathedral or in the pulpits of Nicola or Giovanni Pisano. It was only in the High Renaissance, e.g., in the works of Raphael, Titian, Michelangelo, and Correggio, that forms and iconography, themes and motifs became reintegrated. In this way the classical vision of classical subjects became sometimes so perfect that some works created around 1500 could have been taken for classical originals (for example, *Bacchus* by Michelangelo). The growing understanding of classical ideas and forms led to another specific Renaissance phenomenon, called by Panofsky "pseudomorphosis":

Certain Renaissance figures became invested with a meaning which, for all their classicizing appearance, had not been present in their classical prototypes, though it had frequently been foreshadowed in classical literature. Owing to its medieval antecedents, Renaissance art was often able to translate into images what classical art had deemed inexpressible (Panofsky [1939], pp. 70f.).

In the north of Italy, beside the concept of *istoria, poesia* appears, a fact which also points to a dependence on poetry; this was understood mainly as referring to lyrical poetry, and not to epic or heroic. Mythological pictures by Titian were described in such a way (Keller [1969], pp. 24f.). The stress was on the poetical mood more than on an important human action; a lyrical tonality was preferred to a heroic one. The archaeological interests then current in Padua and Venice, visible, for instance, in the works by Andrea Mantegna, were moderated by an elegiac poetic mood

in reconstructing the classical world. Pictures by Giorgione, who worked for exclusive circles of humanists, were so hermetic in meaning that several of them, like the *Three Philosophers* (Vienna), or the *Storm* (Venice) are iconographic riddles up to our own day. The same is true of the enigmatic and poetic iconography of some pictures by Titian (*Sacred and Profane Love*, in the Borghese Gallery in Rome) by Lorenzo Lotto, or by the Ferrarese Dosso Dossi.

The most important document of this romantic archaeological vision, which strongly influenced iconographical invention in Italy and outside of Italy, was a fantastic romance *Hypnerotomachia Poliphili*, attributed in the most plausible way to a Franciscan monk Francescó Colonna, and published, with beautiful woodcuts, by Aldus Manutius in Venice in 1499. Poetic visions of a dreamy classical landscape, full of ruins, in which the lovers Poliphilo and Polia wander, influenced the imagination of artists not less than the excellent woodcuts; their impact can be found as far and as late as in the gardens at Versailles. The illustrations to *Hypnerotomachia* also popularized hieroglyphic signs which make their appearance in iconography as a specific phenomenon of the Renaissance.

5. Art conceived as a language may be addressed to large or to small groups. It depends on the scope of communication. It can be intended as a message to a possibly large audience, but it can also be limited in its appeal to a small selected group of observers. In an extreme case the polarization could be that between a didactic art appealing to everybody and an elitarian cryptic message understandable only to the initiated few. Medieval art belonged by far to the first category; the art of the Renaissance to the second. Even in the monumental wall-paintings, decorating the most celebrated places of Christianity such as the *Sistine Chapel*, or the official rooms of the Popes, like the *Stanza della Segnatura*; even in the sepulchral chapels of the most important families like the Sassetti and the Medici, the iconographic programs and symbolism are extremely complicated. The meaning of the decoration of the great Gallery of François I at Fontainebleau is so cryptic that it was hypothetically explained only recently by the best specialists in iconography (D. and E. Panofsky, 1958). Few works of medieval art have provoked such a number of interpretations as the well-known, and at first glance seemingly easy to understand, pictures like Botticelli's mythologies (*Birth of Venus, Spring;* The Uffizi, Florence), like Titian's *Sacred and Profane Love,* or like sculptures such as Michelangelo's Medici tombs. The same is true of works by Dürer, Holbein, and Bruegel in the North. A deep symbolism, a complicated iconography—especially current in the circles influenced by Neo-Platonism—belonged to the perfection of the work.

This idea had a long life: it recurs in 1604 in Carel van Mander's *Book of the Painter*, as well as in Bernini's utterances on the beauty of the concept which adorns the work. The more refined the concept, the more difficult the symbolism, the narrower the circle of those who can really understand the work.

Art was considered, especially in the exclusive, court social groups, or among the humanists, as a secret language, accessible to the initiated. The visual sign was connected with words into a specific union of literature and art, which flourished at the time of the Renaissance, of mannerism, and of the baroque in the form of *impresa*, of *hieroglyph*, and of *emblem*. The roots of the *impresa*—the personal sign and motto—are to be found in chivalrous devices and signs, popular in the late Middle Ages; it was brought to Italy from France and connected with Neo-Platonic speculation (Klein, 1957). *Hieroglyphs* became popular thanks to the discovery in 1419 of the *Hieroglyphica* by Horapollo Niliacus (of the second or fourth century A.D.), published in 1505. The humanists believed that this enigmatic image-script disguised a profound wisdom of the Egyptians: "they supposed that the great minds of Greece had been initiated into these Egyptian 'mysteries'—which in their turn, were of course one more prefiguration of the teachings of Christ" (Seznec [1953], p. 100). *Emblems* originated from an erudite, intellectual play among the humanists, aiming however at a moral lesson and sometimes considered, in a Neo-Platonic way, as symbols revealing to those who contemplate them a higher knowledge of divine mysteries. Emblem included a motto, called *lemma*, an image, and an epigram. Only the whole of the emblem can be understood, each element of it giving only one part of the meaning. All those cryptic codes of expression, connecting words and images, originated as secret and elitarian. The problem of the degree of obscurity was one of the main points discussed by the theorists of the emblematics (Clements [1964], pp. 191–95). Erasmus of Rotterdam stressed that one of the virtues of the *impresa* is that its meaning can be grasped only with an intellectual effort. Cesare Ripa (*Iconologia*, 1593) demands that symbolic images be composed "in the form of enigma." Sambucus (1564) required *"obscuritas"* and *"novitas"* from the emblems. Paolo Giovio represented a reasonable middle: "The device should not be so obscure as to require the Sybil to interpret it, nor yet so obvious that any literal-minded person can understand it." Later however, the cryptograms of hieroglyphics and emblem books began to be popularized and explained. Collections of emblems became widely known. New systematization of icon-

ography, now of a humanistic one, was inaugurated.

In 1556 Vincenzo Cartari published the first modern handbook of mythological imagery: *Le imagini colla sposizione degli dei degli antichi* (Venice, 1556). In the same year Pierio Valeriano produced a rich collection of *Hieroglyphica* (Basel, 1556). Earlier in 1531, Andrea Alciati had compiled the first emblem book (*Emblematum liber*, Augsburg, 1531). The influence of such books, which went through many translations and editions and which were imitated and continued all over Europe, grew at the close of the sixteenth and in the seventeenth century. In exclusive groups it happened much earlier that hieroglyphic, astrological, and emblematic imagery influenced the iconography of important works of art, as, for example, at the court of Maximilian I (M. Giehlow, 1915); sometimes this concerned works done by the most distinguished artists, like Dürer's *Melencolia I* (Klibansky, et al., 1964). Emblematic principle of composition, uniting as it did the image with the verbal formulations, found great popularity in northern Europe, perhaps because, the importance of the word, so prominent in Protestantism, was stressed (Luther required "fragments from the Holy Writ" to be included in the Epitaph-pictures). Epitaphs and other religious pictures of the Protestant North connect words and images in the harmonious indivisible whole (Białostocki, 1968).

In the Netherlands emblems played an important part in the development of realistic painting in the seventeenth century, since they furnished a rich repertory of imagery, charged with allegorical meaning (de Jongh, von Monroy). However, the meaning of those images, obvious to the viewer who remembered the original emblematic context, eluded for a long time later interpreters who were no longer conversant with the emblems.

After Cartari and his followers furnished artists and patrons with images of classical gods, there was a need felt for another handbook, which would enable the artist to represent, and the patron to understand, the abstract, moral, philosophical, scientific, and other ideas symbolized. Only then was art able to express complex thoughts. This task was fulfilled by Cesare Ripa of Perugia, who in 1593 published his *Iconologia*, a handbook explaining how to represent all the incorporeal concepts. In 1603 *Iconologia* was republished with illustrations and became one of the most popular and influential art books. With Ripa in hand art historians—initially Émile Mâle (1932)—were able to decipher hundreds of allegorical statements in paint and stone, guided by this alphabet of personifications. Ripa's basic entity was a human figure, female more often than male, whose costumes, attributes, gestures, and other particulars express specific qualities of the idea represented. With the publication of Ripa's work—translated soon into many languages and frequently republished and revised—the humanistic system of allegorical iconography was established: classical gods and personifications, hieroglyphic signs and emblems connecting words and images: this was the material used by the artists of mannerism and the baroque when they did not choose to keep to the "historical" world, i.e., to borrow their subjects directly from literature. When they did so, when they painted stories, they used to select them not only from Ovid and Vergil, but also from the more recent poems by Ariosto and Tasso, and also from the works of less known writers, ancient and modern. Valerius Maximus furnished them with examples of virtuous behavior. These historical examples were in general either connected with allegorical generalizations (in the big decorations of the late baroque the central fresco was often an allegory and the accompanying canvas-pictures presented historical examples of virtues; Garas, pp. 280–83) or conceived in an allegorical way. *Ovide moralisé* was popular already in the late Middle Ages. Its influence persisted also in the time of the baroque. Myths and stories underwent allegorical interpretations along the lines of that moralizing commentary.

What was considered necessary for an artist around 1600 can be seen from Carel van Mander's *Book of the Painter* (1604). It included a long, theoretical poem, a history of classical and modern Italian and Netherlandish artists, a translation and a moral interpretation of Ovid's *Metamorphoses,* and finally a description of personifications. There is no specific section on religious iconography, since artists were well furnished with books giving them rules in this respect.

Against the humanistic conception of art the Council of Trent proclaimed rules, constituting a new system of religious iconography, which put an end to the live tradition of medieval art. These rules were published officially by the Church and they have been commented upon and elaborated in books by Joannes Molanus (1570), Saint Carlo Borromeo (1577), Gabriele Paleotti (1581), Federico Borromeo (1624), and several others. The rules of the Council governed the decoration of churches and other sacred buildings, and the character of pictures representing sacred subjects. A break between the religious and the secular iconography became obvious in theoretical literature, although there existed many emblem books of a very distinct religious character (G. de Montenay, 1571; B. Arias Montanus, 1571; H. Hugo, 1624). A new strictly formulated system of religious iconography coexisted in the seventeenth century with humanistic subject matter, symbolism, and allegory. The classical nude, introduced by the Renaissance into art, was strictly forbidden now in religious art, but found a free field of development in secular mythological and allegorical works. Many artists exercised their imagination in both fields; in some specific fields such as sepulchral iconography, cooperation between religious and humanistic symbolism was common. In the work of P. P. Rubens the various aspects of the new iconography found perhaps their best expression. In his art allegorical concepts, classical gods and heroes, triumphs of mythical beings as well as of secular rulers accompany martyrdoms of Catholic saints and the triumphs of the Eucharist. What began to be separated in theory could yet coexist in harmony in the work of a great artist.

6. In northern European art (before Rubens) the renewal of the arts during the Renaissance took the form of the new study of nature and the elaboration of the most convincing means of representing the material world in an illusionistic way; traditional medieval symbolism was transformed in a specific way, producing what E. Panofsky called in 1953 "disguised symbolism." The symbolic meaning connected with objects and qualities persisted, but a new mastery reproduced these symbolical objects with such a degree of realism that they did not differ any longer from other objects not charged with any metaphorical meaning. Sometimes the symbolical meaning of represented objects results from the traditional iconography in an unmistakable way, sometimes the meaning is hinted at by the inscriptions placed in the picture or on its frame. But in many cases the modern viewer remains perplexed without any sufficient clue to decide whether, in the picture he observes, he has to do with the beginnings of the representation of reality for its own sake, or whether the search for specific metaphorical meaning is justified. It is still always a matter of discussion to decide at which moment the representation of some objects or some scene in life without any symbolical (or "historical") implications became possible (Gilbert, 1952). Observers of the eighteenth and nineteenth centuries to whom the meaning of old symbols was wholly forgotten took many images of the fifteenth and sixteenth centuries for simple representations of life: Bruegel, for example, was considered as simply a painter of joking or working peasants. Recent studies in iconography have shown that these pictures are saturated with disguised meaning and that it is extremely rare before about 1550 to meet simple representations of nature in painting. In graphic arts the direct depiction of life and landscape began earlier, as in the works of Lombard draughtsmen or in the incredibly fresh, convincing drawings and prints by the Master of the Housebook. There are also early exceptions in painting like Albrecht Altdorfer's landscape without any human figures. But in general it was only during the second half of the sixteenth century that landscape, genre, and still-life painting began to acquire equal rights with religious and humanistic history and allegory, predominantly in Venice and in Antwerp. Even then, however, the representations of people working in fields (Jacopo or Francesco Bassano) followed the old traditions of Calendar-pictures and in the background of genre scenes, as in Pieter Aertsen's pictures, a biblical motif may be found, which transforms the whole composition into a *storia*, however unorthodox.

With the development of realistic painting in the seventeenth century there appeared specific iconographic problems. New subjects slowly found convenient form. They entered the scene patterned after the venerable stories of sacred or of profane iconography. H. van de Waal described (1952) the process of the formation of national historical iconography in Holland. Scenes depicting recent happenings from a long struggle for national independence appeared first in forms assimilated to well-known religious or mythical scenes. This was not only an expedient facilitating their composition, for by this means the new subjects gained the *decorum* inherent in the adopted patterns formed to express traditional stories. Similar procedures may be seen in the eighteenth and nineteenth centuries, when more and more sections of reality became interesting enough to be represented in art.

The transfer of *decorum* from the sacred or allegorical figures to the humans represented is a means used in what modern iconographers call "allegorical portraiture." Renaissance painters had represented real people under mythological or even sacred disguise; they gave actual faces of living people to the figures represented with all the attributes and characteristics of their mythical, sacred, or even allegorical qualities. Later it was only the pattern which remained: still in the eighteenth century English portraitists patterned the effigies of contemporary aristocrats after Michelangelo's Sybils or after allegories like the Caritas (Wind, 1937). J. B. Oudry represented the Polish King in exile, Stanisław Leszczyński, with all the attributes of the allegory of exile, taken from Ripa, identifying him in this way with personification of his most prominent quality (Białostocki, 1969).

Dutch realistic painting of the seventeenth century is a document of an important iconographic conquest. Landscapes, seascapes, moonlit night scenes, snapshots of people skating in winter landscapes, views of market places, church interiors, backyards, fishermen, old women preparing food, fashionable dishes ready for lunch, merchants and artisans, elegant gentlemen paying visits and folk-surgeons performing sensational street-operations: all this became subject matter for

representation and continued to be considered worthy of depiction until the end of the nineteenth century. It was first considered as such in Holland only, then slowly everyday subject matter was recognized also by art-theorists in other countries, although it was regarded as much less dignified than religious, mythological, or allegorical subjects. Only in the nineteenth century did the vogue of realistic representation of everyday subjects become widespread. In Dutch pictures of the seventeenth century we are often confronted with nothing else than representations of picturesque reality. Sometimes however these genre pictures appear to be illustrations of proverbs, expressing moralistic folk-wisdom; sometimes they recall scenes from the popular threater of the *rederijkers* or rhetoricians, especially pictures by Jan Steen (Gudlaugsson, 1945); they contain allusions to emblems. Sometimes the elegant scenes from bourgeois life include quite indecent erotic allusions (de Jongh, 1967; 1969). The ambiguity of these pictures was certainly a source of specific pleasure for those who knew the key to their true meaning.

7. In Catholic countries allegorical art, sacred as well as profane, flourished. The twofold character of symbolic representations, mentioned above, persisted in the seventeenth century. Aristotelian rational symbolism, which used images as words, was widespread in the orthodox Catholic iconography of the Counter-Reformation, as well as in the humanistic visual language codified by Ripa and others. A mystical Neo-Platonic symbolism transcending reason reappeared too. Its outspoken document is the treatise by Christoforo Giarda, *Bibliothecae alexandrinae icones symbolicae* of 1626 (Gombrich, 1948). For Giarda symbolic images give the beholder a direct insight into the mysteries of religion, which are not accessible to reason.

Thanks to symbolic images, the mind which is banished from heaven into this dark cave of the body, its actions held in bondage by the senses, can behold the beauty and form of the Virtues and Sciences divorced from all matter and yet adumbrated if not perfectly expressed in colours, and is thus roused to an even more fervent love and desire for them. . . . Who, then, can sufficiently estimate the magnitude of the debt we owe to those who expressed the Arts and Sciences themselves in images, and so brought it about that we could not only know them, but look at them as it were with our eyes, that we can meet them and almost converse with them . . . (Gombrich [1948], pp. 188f.).

Great allegorical compositions covering the ceilings of baroque churches are often realizations of this principle. For those however, who conceived allegory as a rational operation, as a language used for didactic aims, the main problem remained the clarity of the allegorical message. The larger the audience to whom allegory was addressed, the simpler, more obvious its symbolism should have been. The banality of allegorical language provoked criticism in the eighteenth century. Francesco Algarotti (1762) prefers without any doubt historical representations to the "empty allegories and complicated mythological allusions" (Garas [1967], p. 280). Especially criticized was the obscurity of these allegories in which completely original, unknown symbols were used. Roger de Piles praises his favorite master Rubens, who "introduced only such allegories, elements of which were already known from ancient art" and opposes him to Charles Lebrun, who "instead of taking symbols from some known source as the ancient fable and medals, has invented almost all of them and thus the pictures of this kind became riddles, which the beholder does not want to take the task to solve." To keep the balance between platitudinous redundancy and utter incomprehensibility was the crucial problem of late baroque allegorism. What is interesting, however, is that the idea of the picture as a riddle was not foreign to the seventeenth century. It appears in France as well as in Sweden, where David Klöcker Ehrenstrahl (1694) proposed that pictures present riddles that could not be solved by everyone. In France, however, the "painted enigma," fostered by the Jesuits in their schools, flourished especially well in the seventeenth century (Montagu, 1968). These "painted enigmas" lent themselves to various interpretations and gave interpreters an opportunity to show their ingenuity. These pictures and their interpretations seem to prove that a considerable flexibility of meaning was intended.

We might rather accept that a work of art was regarded in the seventeenth century as, in a certain sense, an open symbol, raw material like the myth or sacred story which it illustrates, on which the interpreter might exercise the power of his ingenuity, turning it into an allegory of Christian doctrine or a panegyric in honour of his patron (Montagu [1968], p. 334).

Such a situation probably existed only in some specific circles. It was a limiting case. The other extreme was to use in an uninteresting, routine way Ripa's symbolic images, or those of other popular symbolic handbooks. Such practice continued well into the eighteenth century. The general trend, fed by ideas of the Enlightenment was to make allegories more and more obvious. It is understandable that some theorists, like the Count de Caylus, looked for new subject matter, presenting as he did *Tableaux tirés de l'Iliade* (1755), or that J. J. Winckelmann tried to revive allegory and to give it a new force. It was, however, too late. In the eighteenth century, together with the whole system of humanistic tradition, the systems of iconography began to disintegrate. The great break in the tradition concerned not only style but also iconography. Emblematic roots may be discovered in Goya's symbolism as well as in the reasonable allegories of the Enlightenment, but generally speaking, there was a search for new, not known, or not used sources—as in William Blake's biblical individualistic imagery—or the new staging of the old ones, as in Jacques Louis David's classical subjects.

The art of romanticism was a definite break with the past, much more in the field of ideas and iconography than in a stylistic respect, where romanticists retrospectively looked back either to medieval and pre-Raphaelite, or to baroque sources. Symbols and allegories yielded to an all-pervading mood, and the traditional repertory of religious, allegorical, mythological, and historical iconography gave way to a new iconography. Although several encompassing images of Christian and humanistic art survived, they received new content and essentially changed their character. New attitudes of the individual to the world of nature and history, to society and destiny, to time and death, and new problems resulting from the striving after freedom (which was a new, perhaps most important principle of human behavior in all fields of human activity), found expression in new thematic fields and in new particular themes such as "Storm-tossed Boat," "Lonely Wanderer in the Mountains," "A Death of the Hero" (Eitner, 1955; Hofmann, 1960; Białostocki, 1966).

Romanticism has not formed and could not have formed an iconographic system, for, since they strived first of all for originality of individual conception, the romantics interpreted images in a subjective way as expressions of mood. Romanticism has, on the other hand, introduced new heroes and martyrs into art, instead of religious ones: the national, social, and artistic ones. It created a new image of history, seen now as a set of political and moral examples—as in baroque—but often put together now according to a very individualistic principle of choice. A correlative to pathetic and heroic romanticism was a bourgeois and intimate romanticism; its expression was, for example, the new imagery of the open window, which shows to the viewer wide perspectives, but shelters him at the same time from the dangers of the unknown (Eitner, 1955).

When the world of ideas and images, created at the moment of the flowering of romanticism, began to be popularized for the use of the large bourgeois masses, the content—ideological and iconographical—of romanticism lost its original authenticity and left behind not a new system of original images, but a dispo-

533

sition to melodramatic experiences and an inflation of a theatrical gesture (Hofmann, 1960; Białostocki, 1966).

The nineteenth century developed a realistic portraiture of man and nature and took over worn out clichés of the Renaissance and baroque allegories. It introduced new subject matter, taken partly from tradition, partly from observation of reality, tinted with vague symbolism, such as "Forge" or the "Funeral of the Peasant," but it did not create a new system of iconography, in spite of short-lived revivals of symbolistic attitudes in such movements—incidentally not limited to, and not initiated in, the visual arts—as "symbolism."

New, ephemeral artistic movements, which constituted the history of European art in the last hundred years, show an interesting bracketing of style and iconography, in spite of a preponderant lack of iconographic interest. Their representatives chose subjects suitable to specific artistic aims and means which they developed and were interested in. Impressionists painted seaside scenes, landscapes, and genre pictures showing the life of artistic and intellectual milieus. Cubists introduced a specific repertory of still-life motifs, symbols of the artist's atelier and of the life of the bohème: bottles, musical instruments, books, fruits, flowers, newspapers. How much these motifs were connected with specific cubist style appears when one looks at works of artists foreign to the original cubist group, but imitating its style, as for instance several Czech artists like Emil Filla. They adopted cubist iconography together with cubist style. Abstract movements in general lacked iconography, although they were not foreign to symbolic tendencies, especially in sculpture (Brancusi, Moore). Only in the decades of 1950–70 can a revival of more articulated and programmatic symbolism be observed. One may suppose that this revival is at least in part brought about by the development of research in iconography and symbolism, which took place in the second and third quarters of our century.

II

1. The origins of "interpretative iconography" may be seen in the descriptions (*ekphrasis*) of works of art known in classical literature. But these descriptions, like those by Philostratus the Elder or Lucian, are limited simply to description and lack in general any interpretation. Moreover, it is not certain whether they are descriptions of actual or fictitious works of art; at least opinions in this respect vary. Brief medieval *tituli,* which formulated in words the content of religious images were, to be sure, interpretative sometimes, but they were short and cannot be connected with the tradition of artistic erudition. We have to look to

modern times to indicate the beginnings of iconographic interpretation and research. From Vasari's *Ragionamenti,* in which interpretations of the paintings decorating the Palazzo Vecchio in Florence are given, we learn how complicated and how undecipherable iconographic concepts might have been, even to people living in buildings decorated by paintings expressing these concepts. But perhaps the first really to be considered as interested in iconographic research was the seventeenth-century archaeologist and art theorist Giovanni Pietro Bellori. In the introduction to his *Lives of Artists* (1672) Bellori stressed that he paid special attention to the content of the works of art he was talking about, and he even credited the painter Nicolas Poussin with having directed his attention to iconography. In his *Lives* Bellori presented short interpretative descriptions of pictures, and he sometimes developed these interpretations further in small iconographic essays; the influence of classical *ekphrasis* on him is a possibility. Sometimes his errors took deep roots in the subsequent history of art, as when he explained Poussin's *Triumph of Flora* (Dresden) by designating Ovid's *Metamorphoses* as its source. The true source, Marino's *Adona,* was finally found by R. E. Spear in 1965.

What is interesting in Bellori's procedure is that he first identifies the motifs, tries to connect them with classical or modern literary sources, and then proceeds to find out the deep meaning, the general symbolic idea of the work. Therefore he may be considered as one of the pioneers not only of iconography as a discipline of research, but also of iconology, as formulated by its recent partisans. That even in the second half of the sixteenth century some observers were inclined to look for hidden meaning in each element of the work of art, we learn from Joannes Molanus (1570), who in *De picturis et imaginibus sacris* states reasonably that "it is not necessary to ask for meaning of everything that can be observed in a picture: in such cases a lot of absurd things may result." But the consciousness of the importance of iconography increased and at the end of the seventeenth century André Félibien stressed that in order to attribute a picture to a painter it is not enough to know the way he uses his brush; one needs also to know his *esprit,* to learn his *génie,* and to be able to foresee in which way he is able to form his conceptions. Thus iconographic analysis was considered necessary even for the purpose of attribution.

Descriptive interpretations of the works of ancient art appeared in the big archaeological publications of the seventeenth and eighteenth centuries, such as Jacques Spon's *Miscellanea eruditae antiquitatis* (1679), G. P. Bellori's *Admiranda romanarum antiquitatum ac veteris sculpturae vestigia* (1693), P. de Caylus' *Recueil d'antiquités égyptiennes, étrusques, grecques et romaines* (1752–67), and in an interesting endeavor (although very much criticized by Lessing) of Joseph Spence to explain classical poets through works of art and vice versa (*Polymetis*, 1747). Classical archaeology, however, has not been especially interested in iconography, and the use of the term itself by archaeologists was limited to portraiture. The first great development of iconographic studies was connected with the romantic movement, although an important prelude for it was hagiographical collections of sources such as *Acta sanctorum* published by the Bollandists (1643–1794, resumed later). Among the pre-romantic scholars in iconography the eminent German poet G. E. Lessing is to be noted. His study of the representation of death in classical times can be considered as one of the first essays in interpretative iconography, which is now called iconology. In *Wie die Alten den Tod gebildet* (1769) Lessing tries to interpret the classical iconographic type of Amor with the inverted torch and to find its "intrinsic meaning" by taking into account the religion, customs, and philosophy of the classical world. The work of art is interpreted by Lessing as "a symptom of something else." While Lessing's predecessors (like B. de Montfaucon) "explained the classical past by monuments" he, for the first time, did the opposite: "he explained the monuments by Antiquity" (Maurin Białostocka [1969], pp. 92–100).

Pre-romantic and romantic interests in myth and symbol found their expression in publications and discussions by German philosophers and scholars like F. Schlegel, J. Herder, J. J. von Görres, and F. Creuzer. Creuzer's work, *Symbolik und Mythologie der alten Völker* (1810), which shows the influence of mystical Neo-Platonic ideas on symbols (Gombrich, 1965), was the most influential in the romantic period in Germany. Under the impact of Chateaubriand's *Le Génie du christianisme* (1802), research in medieval iconography developed mainly in France. Works by French scholars, mostly clergymen, which were indeed concerned with Christian medieval art, dominated iconographical study in the nineteenth century. Since most of these writers were not professional scholars, their work was often amateurish in character, but it is undeniable that books by A. N. Didron, *Histoire de Dieu* (Paris, 1843), the first part of a comprehensive, projected, but not completed iconography of Christian art; A. Crosnier, *Iconographie chrétienne* (Caen, 1848); C. Cahier, *Caractéristiques des saints* (Paris, 1867); C. Rohault de Fleury, *Archéologie chrétienne: les saints de la messe et leurs monuments*, 12 vols. (Paris, 1893–1900); L. Bréhier, *L'art chrétien: son développement iconographique des origines à nos jours* (Paris, 1918); P. Perdrizet, V. Leroquais, and G. de Jerphanion

have built up a solid body of iconographical knowledge, on which scholars of the twentieth century were able to erect a modern, comprehensive structure. In the field of Byzantine iconography, it was Gabriel Millet's *Recherches sur l'iconographie de l'évangile aux XIVe, XVe, et XVIe siècles . . .* (Paris, 1916; reprint 1960) that was basic for any further study. For Western, chiefly French art, a well-written and learned work, appealing to the general reader as well as to the scholar, was produced by Émile Mâle, who in his four volumes of the history of religious art (1898–1932) has presented a well-composed, synthetic image of iconographical development. A lexicographic summary of these studies of generations of French scholars is presented in the *Dictionnaire d'archéologie chrétienne et de liturgie*, published from 1907 to 1953, and edited by F. Cabrol and H. Leclerq. A recent reference work is that by L. Réau, *Iconographie de l'art chrétien* (Paris, 1955–59). Russian scholars have done important work in the field of Byzantine and Orthodox iconography of religious art. The most prominent are: N. P. Kondakov, *Ikonografia Bogomatieri* (St. Petersburg, 1911; 2nd ed. 1914–15); D. V. Ainalov, *Mosaiki IV i V vekov* (St. Petersburg, 1895); and N. Pokrovski, *Otcherki pamyatnikov christianskogo isskusstva i ikonografii* (St. Petersburg, 1894; 3rd ed. 1910). V. Lasarev and M. Alpatov, belonging to the mid-twentieth-century generation of Russian scholars, discuss iconography in several works on religious art. German scholarship produced, in the nineteenth century, works by F. Piper, A. Springer, and H. Detzel. Useful compendia were produced in the early twentieth century by J. Sauer, W. Molsdorf, K. Künstle, and J. Braun. Dutch scholars C. Smits, J. B. Knipping, and J. J. M. Timmers contributed to iconographic studies in recent times; Knipping's book (1939–40) being the most important work on the iconography of the Counter-Reformation and supplementing Mâle's volume of 1932. In the twentieth century, on C. R. Morey's initiative, iconographic studies were inaugurated in North America. Focused on earlier medieval art, these studies developed at Princeton University.

A new direction, characteristic of iconographic studies in the twentieth century, has been given to them by the international school of art historical research inaugurated by the Hamburg scholar Aby Warburg. At the International Congress for the History of Art at Rome in 1912 he presented a sensational astrological interpretation of the frescoes painted by Francesco Cossa and his collaborators in Palazzo Schifanoja at Ferrara. Warburg solved the secret of those representations which had puzzled the ingenuity of several former students, interpreting them as images of zodiacal signs and their decans. But he did not limit his contribution to the presentation of his results. He wanted to stress the importance of his approach and of the method of study, which later became connected with his name. He said:

I hope that through the method used by me for explication of the frescoes at the Palazzo Schifanoja of Ferrara, I have proved, that an iconological analysis, which does not allow itself to be diverted by the rules of frontier police from considering antiquity, Middle Ages, and modern times as interconnected periods, nor from analyzing the most liberal and the most applied works of art as equally important documents of expression, that this method, endeavoring, as it does, to throw light upon one dark spot, clears up at the same time great interconnected developments (Warburg, 1912; Heckscher, 1967).

Warburg's influence on the history of art was very great, although he himself did not write much. It was mainly the posthumous impact of his ideas, promulgated, as they were, by Fritz Saxl, which contributed to the specific direction of studies, concentrated in the library Warburg founded in Hamburg, and which Saxl succeeded in transplanting during the Nazi era to London, where it became the Warburg Institute of the University of London. While the object of study of the nineteenth-century iconographers was mainly religious art in its relation to religious literary sources and liturgy, for Warburg, the study of images was a study of their relations to religion, to poetry, to myth, to science, and to social and political life. Art was for him closely connected with the polyphonic structure of historical life.

Warburg's ideas had a great importance for the most influential theory of iconographic interpretation in our century, that elaborated by Erwin Panofsky. In Hamburg, where Warburg, Saxl, and Panofsky were active in the twenties, Ernst Cassirer built up his philosophy of symbolic forms, which constituted an additional background for Panofsky's system, being derived, as his own methodology was, from the traditions of Kantian philosophy. Around 1930 Panofsky's ideas ripened into a system, which found formulation in his book *Herkules am Scheidewege* (1930) and later in a theoretical article of 1932. G. J. Hoogewerff was, however, the first to propose the word "iconology" as a name for the method of an analysis of content in a work of art (Warburg spoke of iconological analysis). In 1931 he proposed distinguishing between iconography, as a descriptive science aiming at the identification of themes, and "iconology," aiming at the understanding "of symbolic, dogmatic or mystical meaning which is expressed (or hidden) in figurative forms." He stressed that "iconology" deals with works of art without classifying them according to the technique used or to the achieved perfection, taking into account only

their meaning. Hoogewerff saw the last aim of iconology in finding out the cultural and ideological background expressed by works of art, and the cultural and social significance which can be attributed to certain forms and to means of expression in the same time. Hoogewerff's part in the expansion of iconology was limited, because he did not endorse his methodical proposals with examples of historical interpretations.

Erwin Panofsky, with whose name iconology has been connected ever since, not only developed its theoretical foundations, but contributed by his practical work in art history to the main triumph of iconology after the Second World War. The most influential book by Panofsky has been *Studies in Iconology* (1939), in which his masterly presentation of the method was connected with its equally excellent exemplification.

2. Panofsky considers the interpretation of a work of art as falling on three levels. On the first level, the object of interpretation is the primary or natural subject matter. The function of interpretation is called "pre-iconographical description." In order to be able to arrive at a correct interpretation on that level the interpreter must have a practical experience ("familiarity with objects and events") common to everybody, at least in one cultural sphere. However, he has to control his observations by a "corrective knowledge of the history of style" ("insight into the manner in which, under varying historical conditions, objects and events were expressed by forms"). On the second level, the function of interpretation is called "iconographical analysis"; its object is the "secondary or conventional subject matter," constituting the world of images, histories, and allegories. The interpreter's equipment in this case is obviously the knowledge of literary sources, giving him a "familiarity with specific themes and concepts." The interpreter has to control his observations by "the insight into the manner in which, under varying historical conditions, specific themes or concepts were expressed by objects and events." On the third level, the function of interpreting is called "iconographical analysis in a deeper sense" (1939), or "iconological analysis" (1955). Its object is the "intrinsic meaning or content" of a work of art. The interpreter's equipment on that level should be a "familiarity with the essential tendencies of the human mind," and he has to control his interpretation by the "insight into the manner in which, under varying historical conditions, essential tendencies of the human mind were expressed by specific themes and concepts." Thus, taking all the time into account what Panofsky calls the history of tradition, the interpreter has to aim at understanding the work of art, its "primary" as well as "secondary subject matter," as symptoms of some fundamental tendency of the human mind, typical of

a place, a time, a civilization, and of an individual responsible for the creation of the work. "Iconology"— for Panofsky—"is a method of interpretation which arises from synthesis rather than analysis." Trying to find the intrinsic meaning of a work of art,

The art historian will have to check what he thinks is the intrinsic meaning of the work, or group of works . . . against what he thinks is the intrinsic meaning of as many other documents of civilization historically related to that work or group of works, as he can master. . . . It is in the search for intrinsic meaning or content that the various humanistic disciplines meet on a common plane instead of serving as handmaidens to each other (Panofsky [1955], p. 39).

The concept of *intrinsic meaning* of a work of art was elaborated by Panofsky much earlier (1925), when he interpreted in his own way the concept of *Kunst-wollen*, introduced by A. Riegl to research in art. Panofsky understood this "artistic volition" as an immanent, ultimate meaning of a work of art, which is manifested in the way basic artistic problems are solved in that work. He used the same concept further to bring art closer to the other fields of human activity. Since the "immanent ultimate sense" of the work of art is nothing else than uniformity in the way of solving basic artistic problems, it is possible to compare that immanent sense with immanent senses of the other human works in various fields. Panofsky did it, for instance, when in one of his later works he compared the structural principles of Gothic architecture with those of scholastic thinking (1951).

The system elaborated by Panofsky and exemplified by his own work in art history was the first consistent system of an integral interpretation of a work of visual arts, based on the analysis of content. In principle Panofsky's system takes into account all the elements of the work of art, since it takes as the point of departure the sensual, exterior shape of the work. It is, however, clear, that its main scope is not the interpretation of form as a bearer of meaning, but the understanding and interpretation of conventional allegories, literary themes, and symbols as symptoms of the history of the human mind. It was that method in the history of art which programmatically fostered a collaboration with all the other disciplines of historical studies. It was therefore one of the most influential methods, not only among art historians, but also among representatives of the other branches of humanistic studies. Although there were art historians who expressed a critical attitude toward "iconology," as the new method was soon baptized, its influence was overwhelming.

3. It is not only, but mainly, due to Panofsky, that one can venture to call "iconographical" that period of art history as a historical discipline, which followed the Second World War, and to oppose it to the "stylistic" one which preceded it. It does not mean, of course, that no iconographic research took place in the twenties or thirties: the works of Mâle, Knipping, van Marle, Wilpert, Saxl, and of Panofsky himself would contradict such a statement. Neither is it true that purely formal research aiming at stylistic classification and analysis discontinued after World War II. It is evident that in the last decades (from 1940 on) iconographic interests came to the fore and became dominant in many countries. Iconographical studies grew so much in number and importance, that they made it possible to undertake and to publish new reference works of iconographic character, like dictionaries written by one scholar (Guy de Tervarent, Aurenhammer) as well as larger works based on a collaboration of several scholars (Encyclopedias of German art, of Antiquity and Christian civilization, of Byzantine art).

Interest in meaning and iconography has appeared also among historians of political, social, and religious institutions. The symbolism of signs, ceremonies, costumes, and arms was studied by such scholars as A. Alföldi, "Insignien und Tracht der römischen Kaiser," *Mitteilungen des deutschen Archäologischen Instituts, Römische Abteilung* (1935), 1ff.; "Die Geburt der kaiserlichen Bildsymbolik," *Museum Helveticum*, **9** (1952), 204ff.; also by A. Grabar, *Martyrium* (Paris, 1943–46); by E. H. Kantorowicz, *Laudes Regiae* . . . (Berkeley and Los Angeles, 1946); *The King's Two Bodies* (Princeton, 1957); by H. P. L' Orange, *Studies in the Iconography of Cosmic Kingship in the Ancient World* (Oslo, 1953); *Art Forms and Civic Life in the Late Roman Empire* (Princeton, 1965); and by P. E. Schramm, *Herrschaftszeichen und Staatssymbolik* (Stuttgart, 1954–56). In their studies iconography far transcends the borders of art, and it helps to build up a history of ideas by following their various visual expressions.

Pioneering studies by K. Giehlow, F. Saxl, and E. Panofsky enlarged iconographical interests above all to encompass the large field of secular art, whereas they had been mainly limited to religious iconography in the work of preceding generations of scholars. The whole, complicated, and hardly known large body of meanings, disguised by the cryptic language of hieroglyphs, emblems, and iconologies, became one of the main topics of study.

This established a collaboration between historians of art and literature. Mario Praz's admirable study of emblems and his bibliography of emblem books (1939–47) belongs now to the foundations of studies in that field. Publications by W. S. Heckscher and A. K. Wirth, by R. S. Clements, E. F. von Monroy, and

H. M. von Erffa, E. de Jongh, and H. Miedema, and several other scholars, have elucidated the structure and meaning of emblems and have shown their tremendous influence on art, even in its most monumental and dignified forms. An uninterrupted flow of reprints of emblem books, which brought within the reach of modern students inaccessible volumes of sixteenth- and seventeenth-century emblem writers, were crowned by the monumental undertaking of Arthur Henkel and Albrecht Schöne, who compiled an excellent volume including almost all the texts and images needed for the study of emblems—*Emblemata, Handbuch zur Sinnbildkunst des XVI. und XVII. Jahrhunderts* (Stuttgart, 1967). Research was under way on hieroglyphs (Erik Iversen), and on the *imprese* (the late Robert Klein), as well as on iconologies and allegories. These studies have disclosed meanings of the art of the Renaissance, of mannerism, and of the baroque not understood by nineteenth-century scholars.

E. Panofsky deciphered extremely farfetched and individualistic programs of decoration of such famous ensembles as the Camera di San Paolo by Correggio in Parma, the Gallery of François I at Fontainebleau. Edgar Wind, André Chastel, and other scholars interpreted Raphael's decorations in the Pope's apartments. Michelangelo's art furnished material to detailed comprehensive studies by Panofsky, Ch. de Tolnay, H. von Einem, and Pope-Hennessy, in which the share of Neo-Platonic thinking in the ideological background of the celebrated works of Michelangelo was discussed. Innumerable studies have been devoted to Titian's mythological paintings. J. R. Martin presented explanations of the Carracci frescoes in the Camerino Farnese and in the great gallery of the Palazzo Farnese. Bruegel, considered in the nineteenth century as a *drôle* painter of peasant life, has been shown by de Tolnay, Stridbeck, and others to be an allegorist expressing a skeptical, humanistic outlook. J. S. Held and W. Stechow contributed several articles to the understanding of mythological and allegorical contents in Flemish and Dutch art of the sixteenth and seventeenth centuries. Rembrandt's iconography was put into new light by the two above-mentioned scholars as well as by H. M. Rotermund, H. van de Waal, J. G. van Gelder, H. von Einem and Ch. Tümpel. The intricate symbolism and subject matter of historical and mythological pictures by Nicolas Poussin were elucidated by such masters of iconographic research as E. H. Gombrich, W. Friedländer, E. Panofsky, and above all by A. Blunt, who in his monograph on Poussin presented a new, deep, synthetic view of the ideas expressed by that artist's works. Goya's individualistic, secret symbolism was also studied with the help of emblems and the allegorical tradition. Bernini's works received iconolo-gical treatment by R. Wittkower and H. Kauffmann. All of this research does not mean that there was a lack of interest in religious iconography. M. Schapiro, A. Katzenellenbogen, H. Bober, F. Wormald, and V. Elbern, among others, have contributed considerably to deepen our understanding of the not completely explained motifs and prominent works of medieval art. Panofsky has also shed a new light on several problems of sepulchral iconography; studies by such scholars as R. Berliner, G. von der Osten, L. Kalinowski, S. Ringbom, and T. Dobrzeniecki contributed to late medieval iconography in a new way; Berliner stressed the autonomous invention of visual artists or their patrons, while according to the traditional view, popularized by Mâle, late medieval art should have followed strictly literary sources.

The religious content of modern art, especially its allegorical form in the late baroque period, has been examined, and thanks to studies by such scholars as W. Mrazek and H. Bauer, has become better known, and understandable. A great change was introduced by "iconology" into architectural history. Buildings which were formerly interpreted from aesthetic and functional points of view only, have been shown to present allegorical, symbolical, or even emblematic ideas. Publications by leading art historians (R. Wittkower, B. Smith, G. Bandmann, O. von Simson, and G. C. Argan) have presented medieval and modern architecture as a bearer of meaning and have essentially changed the character of architectural history.

The iconography of classicism and romanticism received a thorough treatment in books by W. Hofmann and R. Rosenblum, as well as in several studies devoted to individual themes and pictures. G. Hersey has, for example, shown how much Delacroix's decoration of the library in the Palais Bourbon owed to Giambattista Vico's ideas about history. More recently, studies on "Symbolism" have been undertaken. Vincent van Gogh's symbolic language and iconography were the object of studies by J. Seznec, C. Nordenfalk, and other scholars. On Cézanne's iconography interesting remarks have been published by M. Schapiro.

Along with the development of iconographic studies the establishment of centers of documentation has advanced. The "French" stage in the development of iconography has not left any marked trace in this respect. It was in America, thanks to C. R. Morey, that the famous *Index of Christian Art* at the Department of Art and Archaeology of Princeton University was founded, at first limited to the early Middle Ages, then enlarged so as to include art up to the end of the medieval period. Copies of the Princeton Index are to be found also at the Istituto Pontificio d'Archeologia in Rome, and in the Dumbarton Oaks Library and

Collection in Washington, D.C. But that Index ends "where art begins"—as Panofsky used to say jokingly. The need for systematic iconographic files for modern art was strongly felt. In 1956, A. Pigler published a very useful book, *Barockthemen*, in which he listed thousands of works of art of the baroque period, according to their subjects. It was, however, far from being a systematic work. The first essay in establishing a systematic iconographic index for art of any time was done by The Netherlands Institute for Art History at the Hague, then directed by H. Gerson, which took the initiative around 1950 of publishing a postcard-size photographic index of its rich collection of photographs of Netherlandish art, ordered according to an iconographic principle. Once such an idea was formulated, the need for a comprehensive, consistent, and clear iconographic classification was urgent. H. van de Waal of Leiden University devised such a system of classification, based on decimal divisions, consistent and easy to read. He based his system on experiences of ethnology and on such elaborated systems of classification as that devised by Stith Thompson in his *Motif-Index of Folk Literature*, Vols. I-VI (Bloomington, Ind., 1932–36; rev. ed., 1955–58). Van de Waal has elaborated a system in which the first five main sections classify five fundamental groups of portrayable things, namely: (1) The Supernatural, (2) Nature, (3) Man, (4) Society, (5) Abstracts. The last four classify specific subjects, such as: (6) History, (7) The Bible, (8) Myths, Legends, and Tales (with the exception of classical antiquity), (9) Myths and Legends of Classical Antiquity. Van de Waal combines the classification in the first and in the second group in order to classify general as well as specific subjects. Christ, in his system, is described with the sign "11 D" ("1" standing for Supernatural, "11" for Christianity, "D" for Christ); the adult Christ = 11 D 3; since "shepherd" on the other hand bears the signature 47 I 22.1, the adult Christ as a shepherd can be described in this system by the following formula: 11 D 3 = 47 I 22.1. Van de Waal has also provided means to describe more complex images, which he expresses by adding elements between brackets. The Annunciation with God the Father and a winged Angel is expressed by the following formula: 73 A 5 (+1+41), "1" standing for God the Father and "41" for a winged Angel (van de Waal, 1952). This system elaborated for many years by its inventor, and prepared for publication in many volumes, has proved most useful in the practical arrangement of the Iconographical Index of the Netherlandish Art and, as the only one until now in existence, it became used more and more, in spite of some ambiguities and difficulties. As an endeavor to classify "all portrayable" things, persons, events, and ideas, and to create a consistent

method to describe every possible image, van de Waal's system may be considered as one of the important achievements of the "iconographical stage" in the development of art history. Iconographic files exist of course in many institutions, as for example in the Ikonologisch Instituut of Utrecht University, one of the main centers of study in emblematics, and of course in the most venerable institution of iconographic research, the Warburg Institute of the London University and in other places.

4. What was the result of this "iconographic" turn in the development of the history of art? One thing is certain: that this discipline by necessity has come closer to other humanistic disciplines. Since the "intrinsic" meaning—in Panofsky's terminology—of a work of art cannot be described in terms used by the history of art, but only in terms borrowed from the history of philosophy, of religion, of social structures, of science, and so on, the "iconological method" took for granted and provoked such a collaboration. Art history was perhaps the first, or one of the first to show new interest in investigation of meaning. It was followed by similar developments in ethnology and in linguistics.

We have mentioned above a parallel development in Byzantine and classical studies. Panofsky's influence has been considerable in the other fields of humanistic research. Since "iconology" aimed at discovering ideas expressed by a work of art, it awoke in art historians an interest in the history of ideas. This general shift of emphasis and of the direction of studies from mainly formal ones to studies aiming at ideas underlying art, was perhaps responsible, among others, for the fact that several contributions to the *Journal of the History of Ideas* have been written by historians of art.

It is not difficult to see that such a development should have provoked criticism on the side of those who care about the purity and autonomy of methods. Iconology was criticized as far as its internal coherence, and also as far as its claim to be the integral method of the study of art are concerned (Białostocki, 1962). Studies by R. Klein, E. Forssman, G. Previtali, G. Kubler, B. Teyssèdre, C. Ginzburg, and G. Hermeren expressed critical opinions in one or the other respect. Iconology linked art with the rest of history, but it disrupted the links between the work of art and other things (Kubler, 1962). Concentrating on meaning, iconology neglected art as form, as individual expression. Iconology implied a rational relationship between intellectual content and artistic form. On the one hand, one spoke of "iconological diminutions" (Kubler, 1962)—limitations of research to meaning only. But on the other hand, the overstatements of iconology were criticized: its representatives sometimes seemed

539

to assume everything symbolized something. And some iconologists seemed to consider important in art not that which makes art a different field of human activity, but that which connects art with other fields—with the history of ideas.

There were of course critics who had the opposite opinion. Since the end of the eighteenth century, a direct experience of art was more and more valued, and its symbolical function considered as a burden. J. G. von Herder said: *Ein Kunstwerk ist der Kunst wegen da; aber bei einem Symbole ist die Kunst dienend* ("A work of art is there because of art; but with a symbol art is a service"). Similar opinions were expressed by nineteenth-century art writers, and in this century they have been voiced by Benedetto Croce and by other Italian opponents of *contenutismo*, by which they meant interest in content. For such critics to put stress on iconography was to miss the essential in art and to focus attention on a subordinate function of art.

Also among scholars who considered the function of representation and of communication as a legitimate and important function of art, criticism was expressed, not against the principle of an iconographical or iconological investigation, but against overstatements in their application. The introduction of the idea of "disguised symbolism" has created a danger, of course, of opening the way to fanciful interpretations. The allegorical and symbolical function of mythological imagery in classical art is also difficult to interpret precisely. Since no literary sources give a key to an interpretation of the iconography of the sarcophagi, very divergent theories have been expressed concerning their meaning. Some archaeologists, like F. Cumont (1942), believe that mythological and allegorical imagery (Anadyomene, Sea-Thiasos, Personifications of the Seasons) is to be read symbolically. The Sea-Thiasos, for instance, is to be interpreted as a symbol of the journey of the souls of the deceased to the islands of the blessed. Others, like A. D. Nock (1946), do not find enough evidence to accept other than a decorative function in such imagery.

The intrusion of some representatives of psychology, e.g., C. G. Jung, into iconographic studies, giving them an unhistorical turn in their search for "archetypal images," has complicated the situation, although art historians in general understandably have not accepted that kind of approach to symbolism (Frankfort, 1958; Gombrich, 1965).

The fact that iconographic interpretations sometimes lack satisfactory proofs does not detract from the importance of such investigations, so long as they are conducted according to the requirements of historical methods, and take into account the corrective principles established by Panofsky. A correct acquaintance with the way of thinking of the artist, the patron, or the viewer based on a satisfactory knowledge of documentary, visual, and literary sources, an awareness of the choice situations produced by historical developments, may enable art historians to discover the secondary meaning of a work of art as well as its intrinsic meaning. It is, of course, possible that the art historian will meet some works for which it will not be possible to reconstruct in a satisfactory way the world of ideas that would account for the meaning of those works. In such cases a reliable interpretation is simply not possible.

R. Berliner (1945; 1966) criticized the widespread opinion according to which content of the works of visual arts in the Middle Ages had to be checked against the literary sources, considered as the only medium in which ideological innovations were permitted. Berliner pleaded for assuming a considerable "freedom" in the medieval artist and he considered iconographic innovation possible, even when no written evidence could be found. Meyer Schapiro (1947) presented proofs that sometimes purely aesthetic reasons decided the character of the work of art even as early as the Romanesque period.

We can only touch on some specific discussions going on in the field of iconographic research. But iconographic research is far from being a closed system and the relative share of iconographic and stylistic criticism in the work of art historians is always a matter of discussion. It is certain that the "iconographic" period in the study of art has enlarged in a considerable way the understanding of the art of the past and that it has connected art history, in a way unknown before, with the other historical disciplines, and above all others with the history of ideas.

BIBLIOGRAPHY

L. B. Alberti, *On Painting*, ed. J. Spencer (New Haven, 1956; revised ed. 1966). E. Auerbach, "Figura" (1944); trans. and published in *Scenes From the Drama of European Literature* (New York, 1959), pp. 11–76. K. Bauch, "Imago" (1960), *Studien zur Kunstgeschichte* (Berlin, 1967), pp. 1–20. G. P. Bellori, *Descrizione delle imagini dipinte da Raffaello . . .* (Rome, 1695; ed. used is 1751). R. Berliner, "The Freedom of Medieval Art," *Gazette des Beaux-Arts*, 6/**28** (1945), 263–88; idem, "Bemerkungen zu einigen Darstellungen des Erlösers als Schmerzensmann," *Das Münster*, **9** (1956), 97–117x. J. Białostocki, "Iconografia e Iconologia," *Enciclopedia Universale dell'Arte* (1962), Vol. VII, cols. 163–75; trans. as *Encyclopedia of World Art* (1966), Vol. VII, cols. 769–85, lists almost all important older contributions to this field; idem, "Romantische Ikonographie," *Stil und Ikonographie* (Dresden, 1966), pp. 156–81; idem, "Kompozycja emblematyczna epitafiów śląskich XVI wieku" ("Emblematic Composition of Silesian Epitaphs of the Sixteenth Century"), *Ze studiów nad Sztuka XVI wieku na Ślasku* (Wrocław, 1968) pp. 77–93; idem, "Esilio Privato," *Bulletin du Musée National de Varsovie*, **10** (1969), 95–101. J.

Chydenius, *The Theory of Medieval Symbolism* (Helsingfors, 1960), Series of the Societas Scientiarum Fennica: Commentationes Humanarum Litterarum, **27**, 2. R. J. Clements, *Picta Poesis: . . .* (Rome, 1960). F. Creuzer, *Symbolik und Mythologie der Alten Völker* (Leipzig and Darmstadt, 1810; revised ed. 1819). F. Cumont, *Recherches sur le symbolisme funéraire des Romains* (Paris, 1942). L. Eitner, "The Open Window and the Storm-Tossed Boat," *Art Bulletin*, **37** (1955), 281–90. H. Frankfort, "The Archetype in Analytical Psychology and the History of Religion," *Journal of the Warburg and Courtauld Institutes*, **21** (1958), 166–78. K. Garas, "Allegorie und Geschichte in der Venezianischen Malerei des 18. Jahrhunderts," in proceedings of the XXI International Congress of the History of Art, Bonn: *Stil und Überlieferung in der Kunst des Abendlandes* (Berlin, 1967), 3, 280–83. K. Giehlow, "Die Hieroglyphenkunde des Humanismus in der Allegorie der Renaissance," *Jahrbuch der Kunsthistorischen Sammlungen des Allerhochsten Kaiserhauses*, **32** (1915), 1–232. C. Gilbert, "On Subject and Not-Subject in Italian Renaissance Pictures," *Art Bulletin*, **34** (1952), 202–16. C. Ginzburg, "Da A. Warburg a E. H. Gombrich: Note su un problema di metodo," *Studi medievali*, series 3, **7** (1966), 1015–65. E. H. Gombrich, "Icones Symbolicae. The Visual Image in Neo-Platonic Thought," *Journal of the Warburg and Courtauld Institutes*, **11** (1948), 163–92; idem, "The Use of Art for the Study of Symbols," *American Psychologist*, **20** (1965). A. Grabar, *L'iconoclasme byzantin. Dossier archéologique* (Paris, 1957); idem, *Christian Iconography. A Study of Its Origins* (Princeton, 1969). S. J. Gudlaugsson, *De Comedianten bij Jan Steen en zijn tijdgenooten* ('s-Gravenhage, 1945). W. S. Heckscher, "The Genesis of Iconology," *Stil und Überlieferung in der Kunst des Abendlandes*, Akten des XXI. Internationalen Kongresses für Kunstgeschichte (Berlin, 1967), 3, 239–62. G. Hermerén, *Representation and Meaning in the Visual Arts. A Study in the Methodology of Iconography and Iconology*, Lund Studies in Philosophy, Vol. I (Lund, 1969). R. Hinks, *Myth and Allegory in Ancient Art* (London, 1939). W. Hofmann, *Das Irdische Paradies* (Munich, 1960). G. J. Hoogewerff, "L'Iconologie et son importance pour l'étude systématique de l'art chrétien," *Rivista d'Archeologia Cristiana*, **8** (1931), 53–82. E. de Jongh, *Zinne- en minnebeelden in de schilderkunst van de zeventiende eeuw* (—1967); idem, "Erotica in Vogelperspectief. De dubbelzinnigheid van een reeks 17de eeuwse genrevoorstellingen," *Simiolus*, **3** (1968–69), 22–72. L. Kalinowski, "Treści ideowe i estetyczne Drzwi Gnieźnieńskich" ("Ideological and Aesthetic Content of the Gniezno Bronze Doors"), in *Drzwi Gnieźnieńskie*, ed. M. Walicki (Wrocław, 1959), 2, 7–160. H. Keller, *Tizians Poesie für König Philip II. von Spanien* (Wiesbaden, 1969). R. Klein, "La théorie de l'expression figurée dans les traités italiens sur les *imprese*, 1555–1612," *Bibliothèque d'Humanisme et Renaissance*, **19** (1957), 320–41, republished with the other relevant studies in *La forme et l'intelligible* (Paris, 1969). R. Klibansky, E. Panofsky, F. Saxl, *Saturn and Melancholy* (London, 1964). J. B. Knipping, *Ikonografie van de Contra-Reformatie in de Nederlanden* (Hilversum, 1939–40). G. Kubler, *The Shape of Time* (New Haven and London, 1962). R. W. Lee, "Ut pictura poesis," *Art Bulletin*, **22** (1940), 197–269. E. Mâle, *L'art religieux du XIIIe siècle en France* (Paris, 1898), English ed. used (New York, 1958); idem, *L'art religieux de la fin du Moyen-Age en France* (Paris, 1908); idem, *L'art religieux du XIIe siècle en France* (Paris, 1922); idem, *L'art religieux après le Concile de Trente* (Paris, 1932). J. Maurin Białostocka, *Lessing i sztuki plastyczne* ("Lessing and the visual arts"), (Wrocław, Warszawa, Kraków, 1969). E. F. von Monroy, *Embleme und Emblembücher in den Niederlanden: 1560–1630*, ed. H. M. von Erffa (Utrecht, 1964). J. Montagu, "The Painted Enigma and French Seventeenth Century Art," *Journal of the Warburg and Courtauld Institutes*, **31** (1968), 307–35. W. Mrazek, *Ikonologie der barocken Deckenmalerei* (Vienna, 1953), Österreichische Akademie der Wissenschaften, Philosophisch-historische Klasse, Sitzungsberichte, **228**/3. A. D. Nock, "Sarcophagi and Symbolism," *American Journal of Archaeology*, **50** (1946), 166ff. D. Panofsky and E. Panofsky, "The Iconography of the Galérie François Ier at Fontainebleau," *Gazette des Beaux-Arts*, 6/**52** (1958), 113–90 E. Panofsky, "Über das Verhältnis der Kunstgeschichte zur Kunsttheorie," *Zeitschrift für Aesthetik und allgemeine Kunstwissenschaft*, **18** (1925), 129–61; idem, *Studies in Iconology* (New York, 1939); idem, ed. *Abbot Suger* (Princeton, 1946); idem, *Gothic Architecture and Scholasticism* (Latrobe, Pa., 1951); idem, *Early Netherlandish Painting* (Cambridge, Mass., 1953); idem, *Meaning in the Visual Arts* (Garden City, N. Y., 1955); idem, *Renaissance and Renascences in Western Art* (Stockholm, 1960); idem, *Tomb Sculpture* (New York, 1964). E. Panofsky and F. Saxl, "Classical Mythology in Medieval Art," *Metropolitan Museum Studies*, **4** (1932–33), 228–80. M. Praz, *Studies in Seventeenth Century Imagery* (London, 1939–47; 2nd ed., Rome, 1964). S. Ringbom, "Devotional Images and Imaginative Devotions. Notes on the Place of Art in Late Medieval Private Piety," *Gazette des Beaux-Arts*, 6, **73** (1969), 159–70. Joseph Sauer, *Symbolik des Kirchengebäudes und seiner Ausstattung in der Auffassung des Mittelalters*, 2nd ed. (Freiburg i. B., 1924). F. Saxl, "Frühes Christentum und spätes Heidentum in ihren künstlerischen Ausdrucksformen," *Wiener Jahrbuch für Kunstgeschichte*, **2** (1923), 63–121. M. Schapiro, "The Ruthwell Cross," *Art Bulletin*, **26** (1944), 232–45; idem, "On the Aesthetic Attitude in Romanesque Art," in *Art and Thought, issued in Honour of Ananda Coomaraswamy* (London, 1947), 139–50. J. Seznec, *The Survival of the Pagan Gods* (New York, 1953). O. G. von Simson, *The Gothic Cathedral* (New York, 1956). R. E. Spear, "The Literary Source of Poussin's Realm of Flora," *The Burlington Magazine*, **107** (1965), 563–69. L. Volkmann, *Bilderschriften der Renaissance* (Leipzig, 1923). Hans van de Waal, *Drie eeuwen vaderlandsche geschieduitbeelding: 1500–1800* ('s-Gravenhage, 1952); idem, "Some Principles of a General Iconographical Classification," in *Actes du XVIIe Congrès International d'Histoire de l'Art, Amsterdam, 1952* (La Haye, 1955), 601–06. E. Wind, "Charity: the Case History of a Pattern," *Journal of the Warburg Institute*, **1** (1937), 322ff.

JAN BIAŁOSTOCKI

[See also Allegory; Baroque; Classicism; Criticism; Enlightenment; Motif; **Myth;** Naturalism in Art; **Neo-Platonism; Renaissance Humanism;** Romanticism; **Symbolism;** Temperance; *Ut pictura poesis*.]

IDEA

ETYMOLOGICALLY the Greek word "Idea" is related to the verbs "to see" and "to know," and it is not fanciful to conclude that its primitive denotation was "that which is seen" or "that which is known." So in modern English one says, "I see what you mean," when "I see" is equivalent to "I understand." Thus Pindar (*Olympians* 10, 123) could write of a beautiful idea and mean by it a beautiful sight or form without any implication that knowledge in the derivative sense of the word is involved.

The notion that ideas can be apprehended by a kind of vision or intuition, by looking and seeing them, has never been lost in Occidental philosophy, for knowing as a kind of insight, illumination, revelation, has almost always been retained. The clearest example of this is the belief that knowledge is of two sorts: one immediate, sensory, direct grasping of that which is known, and the other mediated, "intellectual," inferential. These two sorts have sometimes been correlated respectively with the Latin *cognoscere* and *scire*, the French *connaitre* and *savoir*, and the German *kennen* and *wissen*. In English both members of the pairs have to be translated by the one verb, "to know." One knows one's friends and one knows geometry, though the two experiences are very dissimilar.

1. Plato. Ideas enter philosophy in the dialogues of Plato. They are an answer to the question, "What do common nouns signify?" though that is not Plato's way of putting it. A common noun is obviously peculiar, as it groups a number of things together instead of differentiating an individual from all other individuals. One uses the adjectives which correspond to these nouns in much the same way. One speaks of a picture as "beautiful," of an act as "kind," of hypocrisy as "evil," of apples as "red," and in doing so one classifies the objects and acts referred to. But the moment this is done it is admitted that some properties or qualities are common to a number of things. Several pictures may be "beautiful" and things other than apples may be "red." The common property therefore is not restricted to any place or date and hence is entirely different from a material object.

We learn as children that spatiotemporal location is an essential characteristic of material things. We say that two material objects cannot occupy the same space at the same time and that a single material object cannot be in two places at the same time, a bit of information which is the basis of an alibi in court. But a large number of common properties may be present in a single object and a single common property may characterize a large number of objects at the same time. We learn the consequences of this when we study

geometry in school and are warned not to argue from the looks of the figures that we draw. The triangle on paper, we are taught, is not the triangle we are discussing; it is an imperfect representation of the geometrical triangle.

It is possible that Plato's theory of ideas was suggested by these geometrical forms. If we are not studying the triangle drawn on paper, what one are we studying? The answer usually is: "Something defined by abstract rules," or "A plane figure bounded by three straight lines." But there are no real planes or straight lines in human perception and hence we resort to saying that such things are intellectual constructs, abstract concepts, creations of the mind. Yet we also insist that they are not imaginary beings like mermaids or unicorns, for once defined they follow certain laws, imply certain consequences, and actually control our thoughts rather than obey them. The sum of the angles of a plane triangle has to be 180 degrees, neither more nor less, and we cannot by an act of will or of fantasy change it. This, however, is true of all common properties. Once we know what we mean by "beautiful," "evil," "red," "kind," we are committed to certain other assertions which those adjectives presumably entail.

Plato then is first convinced that ideas cannot be spatiotemporal like material objects. If they are not material, some other term must be found for them. "Mental" will not do since, as we have said, that would put them in a class with volitions, fantasies, feelings, and so on. The term used was "eternal" or "timeless." The idea of a triangle may be discovered at a certain date and in a certain place, but it did not come into being at that place and date. This seems to be true of all common properties and if so, they may be said to form a realm of their own existing apart from the material world. Their interrelations are not causal but logical. The nature of a plane surface does not cause three straight lines to be the smallest number to enclose a plane figure, but it implies that the smallest number of straight lines that may bound a figure is three.

This being so, no ideas can be known by our sense-organs. Just as we do not see real triangles, we do not see real kindness, evil, beauty, or redness. We see kind acts but know that they are kind; we see evil deeds but know that they are evil, and so on. We ask ourselves whether a certain deed which we observe is really good or not and it is reflective thought, not perception, that gives us the answer. The process of reflection is exhibited in the Platonic dialogues. A question is asked, an answer given, the answer is analyzed to find out if it is logically consistent, and if it is not, it is rejected. Many of the dialogues, called by the ancient editors "dialogues of search," end at this point.

The ideas then determine what the particular objects are. It is, for instance, the presence of evil in an act that makes it evil, the presence of beauty that makes a picture beautiful. This is a cardinal point in Plato's theory of ideas and the relationship of the particular thing to the ideas that characterize it was called "participation." The picture participates in beauty. But how a spatiotemporal object can participate in an eternal being was left unclarified. When the matter is discussed in *The Sophist*, participation is named and the limitations of participation defined, but it is clear that the gap between what was later—by Philo Judaeus—called the Intelligible World and the Sensible World was simply accepted by Plato as a fact.

If we cannot perceive the presence of an idea in our ordinary experience, how do we know what we are experiencing? The answer was given in the form of a myth in the dialogue *Meno*. Since we cannot apprehend an idea through our sense-organs, we must come into the world with a stock of them. These are the innate ideas. They are probably of a mathematical nature for the most part—ideas of equality, identity, difference, and similar relations. In the myth it is said that the soul before birth was in the world of ideas and that it retained a dim memory of some of them after birth. As we grow up, the myth continues, on certain occasions we are reminded of what we knew in our prenatal life, and we are able to light upon the idea that fits the case before us. The mythical details of this need not detain us, though much was made of them in the Renaissance by the Florentine Platonists, and they survived to be incorporated in Wordsworth's *Ode on Intimations of Immortality* (1806). What is of greater importance is the suggestion that the human mind is limited to certain ways of thinking, to certain logical rules, certain categories of existence, and that it awakens to these as its education progresses.

This appears in our own day in that theory of teaching known as the "Socratic Method," according to which the teacher serves to bring out of the pupil's mind that which lies hidden in it. In Aristotle these categories were to be named and in the nineteenth century they were "deduced" by Kant and his followers. But as far as Plato is concerned, they are traits of all ideas and are utilized whenever a person reasons. Thus all ideas are differentiated from some others; some are harmonious with some others; some are implied by some others and naturally imply others. These traits are known instinctively. Anyone knows that if something is good, it cannot also be bad at the same time and in the same respect. But only dialectical training will teach a person to apply such information in actual cases of reasoning.

The ideas, since material things participate in them, are models by means of which we can judge the adequacy or perfection of things. If we know, for instance, what justice is, we can discover how closely a given state approaches justice in its constitution. What such a state would be like is described twice by Plato, once in *The Republic* and once in *The Laws*, his last work. What is relevant here is the technique by which the idea of justice is defined. After disposing of a popular and false definition, Plato begins afresh and comes up first with the statement that whatever justice may be, it has terminal value, i.e., it is good in itself and its by-products, such as happiness, need not be considered. Hence if just men suffer at the hands of their fellows, this is of no more importance to the nature of justice than are the imperfections in the drawings of circles made in the sand. An idea is always to be discovered by the dialectical method of question and answer, and Plato is convinced that a false definition will reveal its falsity by its inner inconsistencies. We must try to approximate an idea's perfection as closely as possible, though knowing that the task is hopeless in real life.

At this point one sees that the idea has become what we would call the "ideal," and that the dualism between the ideal and the existent has widened. This was to lead to attempts in post-Platonic philosophy to reduce the duality. And since the ideas or ideals were accessible only to the reason, two kinds of cognition were established, perception which grasped the temporal, changing, multiple things in the material world without knowing what it was grasping, and reason which knew the eternal, immutable, unified things of the ideal world. It was the latter world that was "really real," the former being a dim reflection of it. Since only a few human beings, the philosophers, were capable of reasoning, they would be in charge of the state if the state were just and perfect. The majority of men are either led by their appetites or their passions, but both should be controlled by the reason. The trouble with society as it exists is that appetitive and passionate men, who confuse opinion with knowledge, are at its helm. *The Republic* and *The Laws* discuss what must be done to put them in their proper places.

The ideas then have at least the following properties: they are universals, class-characters, analogous to mathematical figures; they are timeless and unchanging; they are ideals, not existent objects in space-time; they are known only to the reason.

2. Aristotle. At times Plato substitutes the word *eidos* for "idea." Both words are synonymous in his writings and both are derived from the Greek word meaning "to see." But what is seen is a shape or form, and Plato's pupil, Aristotle, preferred the term *eidos*, probably because he could not accept his master's theory of ideas. *Eidos* ($\varepsilon\tilde{\iota}\delta o\varsigma$) was translated into Latin 543 either as *species* or *forma* and in English it is usually called "form." In order to fill the gap between the world of ideas and that of things, Aristotle assumed that the forms were always incorporated in things. That is, there is no such thing as justice in the abstract; there are only just people or just acts and we derive our ideas of justice from the people and acts in which it is embodied. Thus an idea, though a common property, might be a form in the sense of the pattern that processes exemplify; or it might be the shape of finished works of art.

And, indeed, in reading Aristotle one has the impression that his basic metaphors had a twofold origin, one in biology and one in the visual arts. A seed or an egg as it develops always moves to a determined end, the plant or the chicken, unless it is killed on the way. This constantly repeated pattern of development, beginning and ending in the same way, combined Plato's notion of the idea as the invariable character of classes of things with the temporal dimension of growth or of process. The idea or form was "realized" or actualized in the end-product; but it must have been somehow present in the origin, the seed or egg, in order for its realization to be fulfilled. Aristotle named this kind of presence "potentiality." The form then was potentially present in the egg and actually present in the chicken.

This much was largely explanation by terminology. But the terminology was made concrete by the example of artistry. When a sculptor sets out to carve a statue or a painter to paint a portrait, they have in their minds an idea of what the finished work of art will look like. It should be noted in passing that this would not apply to the so-called romantic artist who does not know how his work is to terminate until it is finished. We must assume that the Greek artist was a planner. If Aristotle's notion of artistry is correct, the finished statue exists as an idea in the sculptor's mind before he sets to work, as a potential form in the marble, and as a realized form in the finished statue. Just as Nature, so to speak, guides the egg in its development towards the chicken, so the sculptor guides the marble towards the statue.

The form has now taken on the additional character of being an end or purpose, the "final cause" of a process. But it may be the purpose of a human being or a natural purpose—i.e., the end term of a natural process. It was an easy matter to confuse the two and think of them as identical, to speak of Nature's purposes or ends when referring to the constancy of physical law. Or reciprocally to urge men not to modify their purposes once formed, to be consistent, never to waver. In fact even by Sir Isaac Newton natural law was thought of as the decrees of a divine lawgiver, though Newton was not a believer in final causes.

Aristotle's theory of forms would not have had such extraordinary influence, if he had not carefully distinguished between those processes which are natural and those which are unnatural. It could not be denied that sometimes things went awry, that eggs were eaten before they turned into chickens. A distinction therefore was imperative between those ends which were realized on the whole and those which were only occasionally realized. The latter were accidental, brought about by chance; and the former were essential, brought about by nature. It was clear that things had a number of properties which were of no scientific interest. When a physicist is talking of the mass of the earth, he is not interested in how many continents there are, who inhabits them, what languages the inhabitants speak. Mass can be measured without regard to such things. All science feeds on abstractions and the making of an abstraction demands the discarding of a number of differences. If one is discussing humanity as a whole, one need not bring in skin color, intelligence quotients, arts and crafts, and kinship tables.

These matters may be of great importance historically; but they do not distinguish human beings from the nonhuman, and furthermore they vary from group to group and in some details from individual to individual. They are what Aristotle would have called accidental traits as contrasted with essential ones. Natural processes are always the realization of the essential traits. The realization of accidental traits is no concern of science.

The identification of the idea or ideal with the form or essence had certain practical consequences. It meant that when one was discussing ethics, politics, or art one had first to discover the essences of the activities involved and then set up ways of realizing them. In ethics one had to define the essence of humanity, which was rational animality, and then investigate what had to be done to perfect it. The end of human life is happiness, but all men do not reach that end. Why not? The end of politics is to make the ethical end possible. But tyranny, oligarchy, and mob rule stand in the way. What would have been the end of art was not stated by Aristotle, for his *Poetics* is only a fragment, and what it has to say is far from clear. But in his consideration of tragedy he first tells us what the essence of tragedy is and then suggests the prerequisites for realizing it. This would be standard Aristotelian procedure. It is easy to see that for it to work required an intellectualistic psychology. It was assumed by him, as by Plato, that at least some men could act in accordance with intellectual motives. This assumption ran through the writings on normative sciences up to very recent times when, due to Marx and Freud probably, action was thought of in terms of stimuli that were not intellectual.

How did one know what the essences were? In natural processes they could be determined by that which occurred always or on the whole. But in human activities, they were largely determined by tradition. Aristotle thought, for instance, that his definition of "tragedy" was based on the actual tragedies written before his time, which he apparently thought of as eternal patterns. And though his definition does not fit all of them, it does well enough for an understanding of Greek tragedy. But even if he had discovered the essence of the plays of Aeschylus, Sophocles, Euripides, and their fellows, that did not imply that later dramatists were obligated to imitate their Greek predecessors. Yet aesthetic theorists and literary critics insisted that the idea of tragedy as expounded by Aristotle was not only a generalized description of certain Greek dramas, but also a rule to be followed by all dramatists for all time. The idea now became a genetic trait, a form, an ideal, and a rule.

3. Neo-Platonism. By the third century A.D. a fusion of Platonic and Aristotelian doctrines had been formulated (also in Greek) by Plotinus, an Alexandrian philosopher teaching in Rome. He accepted the doctrine that the Platonic ideas formed a world of their own, that they were universals rather than particulars, and that they were more real than the particulars for which they were the models. But he added certain details which lingered on and which can be found as late as the end of the eighteenth century, at least in England. These details, which are neither in Plato nor in Aristotle, were foreshadowed in the works of Philo Judaeus (who was active in the early part of the first Christian century) and in those of Numenius, a second-century figure, and probably in others now forgotten. Plotinus' innovations in the history of the meanings of idea may be summarized as follows.

(1) The world of ideas in Plotinus forms a hierarchy at the apex of which were the most real, most general, best, and most beautiful and at the base of which were the least real, most particular (individual), worst, and ugliest. At the very top of the hierarchy is that Idea which is so general that it can only be called The One. Immediately below it—or him—is the Intelligence (*Nous*) and the Soul of the World. The Intelligence gives rise to another scale of beings, the Ideas. The Soul of the World is the source of all the other souls, of men, beasts, and plants. Reality thus becomes something which has degrees, matter being the least real and hence the most evil and the ugliest. It is the complete absence of reality.

(2) By a process called emanation the beings on the lower levels flow out of those above them like, to use Plotinus' own metaphor, light from a candle which disappears finally into darkness. The process of emanation has no source in either Plato or Aristotle; it is distinctive of Neo-Platonism. It comes to a terminus in the darkness of the material world, at which level beings strive to move upward and gain the greater reality from which they descended. They strive, in short, to realize the potentialities that are in them. Men do this by turning away from the bodily life, practicing asceticism so as to deny their animal and vegetable nature, engaging in the contemplation of ideas, and finally merging into the One in a mystic vision. The process of emanation follows the pattern of a logical hierarchy, exemplified in biology when varieties are collected into species, species into genera, genera into families, families into orders, orders into classes, classes into phyla, and phyla into kingdoms.

Plotinus' pupil Porphyry bequeathed to posterity a logical hierarchy which became standard in the teaching of philosophy to beginners. It is called the Tree of Porphyry.

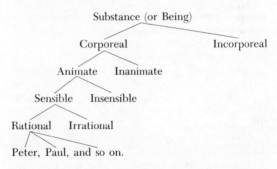

Substance (or Being)
Corporeal   Incorporeal
Animate   Inanimate
Sensible   Insensible
Rational   Irrational
Peter, Paul, and so on.

The classes were subdivided by a technique known as dichotomy, but neither Porphyry nor anyone else ever explained where one was to cut a class in two. When ascending the scale one drops off those characteristics which differentiate and thus one becomes absorbed into a more inclusive but simpler class. That is, there are more sensible beings than rational animals but the latter group has more traits than the former.

(3) The ideas in Plotinus are known by a special process sometimes called "intellectual intuition." They are not expandible into declarative sentences but are apprehended as visual objects are apprehended, as units. Plotinus thought—wrongly—that the Egyptian hieroglyphs were perceptual presentations of ideas; later, in the Italian Renaissance, much was made of this. In fact it was the hint that in all probability developed into that great mass of writings and drawings known as emblem literature.

(4) The ideas apparently could be present to the mind of an individual without the stimulation of an object. Plotinus held that an artist desiring to make a statue of Zeus beheld in a sort of vision the idea of the god and put that into stone. Beauty was in fact the visual presence of the ideal or form and since the

soul was the Aristotelian form of the body, the two forms responded sympathetically to each other. This application of the theory of ideas also became important in the Renaissance and later, and the doctrine that painters should paint the ideal rather than the physical lasted through Ingres into the nineteenth century.

4. Saint Augustine. In Saint Augustine the Platonic ideas became ideas in the mind of God, ideas in accordance with which He had created the world. In the Wisdom of Solomon (11:20) one reads, ". . . Thou hast ordered all things by measure and number and weight," a verse which during the Middle Ages was understood to be the basis of all physical science. But measure and number and weight were mathematical ideas and since Neo-Platonism was highly colored with Pythagoreanism, it became almost a rule to identify the ideas in the mind of God with the mathematical ideas. The identification was the easier in that numbers were often associated with geometrical figures, being at times squares and at other times cubes; the former symbolizing surfaces, the latter solids. The ideas now took on qualities that were almost magical: number symbolism was dilated upon with the greatest enthusiasm and it is next to impossible to differentiate the Neo-Platonic from the Neo-Pythagorean. In Augustine the symbolism of numbers is dwelt upon at great length and the numbers which he discusses stand for ideas. Hence the ideas in the mind of God are really those mathematical ideas in terms of which He ordered all things.

This version of what might be called Christian Neo-Platonism is the foundation of much that we know of medieval aesthetic theory. It appears in the musical theories of Boethius (A.D. 480–524) and even, as Otto von Simson has shown (1956), in the shapes and proportions of Gothic cathedrals. Wisdom 11:20 was to be illustrated whenever Wisdom (*Sapientia*) herself was pictured. And the notion that God created the world after His archetypal ideas could be used to prove its perfection and rationality. In short, if science was possible, that was because Nature was an embodiment of the divine wisdom.

5. Realism and Nominalism. Plotinus' pupil Porphyry, to whom we have already referred, had raised three questions about the nature of ideas in his *Introduction to the Categories of Aristotle.*

(1) Are they beings with independent existence or do they exist only as human concepts?
(2) If they are independent, are they material or immaterial beings?
(3) Do they always exist in sensible objects or not?

These questions were not merely of technical philosophic interest. Church dogma included some statements that seemed to be based on the reality of the universals. For instance, according to Augustine, we all sinned in Adam because we were in Adam, presumably as particulars participating in a universal. Christ again, "the second Adam," could atone for the sins of mankind, for He was God-made-Man. The Church Invisible was present in all churches just as God was entirely present in all three Persons of the Holy Trinity. These and other dogmas seemed explicable if the ideas, universals, were real beings, independent of anyone's mind, and not tied to their incorporation in sensible objects. As has been pointed out, mathematicians do not believe that they are talking psychology. Their subject matter behaves in a manner which no one can make subservient to his desires or fantasies. How are other universal ideas different?

The earliest answer to this question, which Father Copleston, in his *Medieval Philosophy* (1950), has called "exaggerated realism," maintained that universal ideas were not different in any way. Whenever an idea is predicated of a subject (e.g., "This is a man"), what is asserted is the presence of a universal. The theological difficulties of this doctrine need not concern us here. It is of more interest to point out that it turned the world into an imperfect picture of an ideal design. The man of the early Middle Ages was to direct his eyes upward and to think of this world as useful only as an incentive towards the ideal. In fact it led one of its proponents, Saint Anselm (1033–1109), to argue from the reality of an idea to the existence of that of which it was the idea.

But logical realism was vigorously opposed by a contemporary of Saint Anselm, Roscellinus. He is said to have maintained that universals were only names, a doctrine called "nominalism." This seemed to some to imply that when we are discussing ideas we are talking about words. Mathematics does not appear to be lexicography nor do any of the natural sciences. When a physicist talks about gravitation, he may exemplify his point by citing the relation between the masses of the moon and the earth, but his real subject matter is much more extensive. Hence the eleventh-century clash in opinion has not been definitely settled even today. The Middle Ages, however, were more fortunate than we. They were given a compromise solution by Saint Thomas Aquinas. He said that the ideas have a being independent of things (*ante rem*) in the mind of God; they have a being in things (*in rebus*) as common characters; they exist in our minds (*post rem*) as concepts formed by us through the powers of abstraction. Like all compromises this raised an additional problem: how can a single being, justice for instance, be all three of these things and yet be one and the same?

6. Empirical Science. During the fourteenth and fifteenth centuries men's attention was increasingly directed towards this earth. Their interest seems to have switched from the contemplation of eternal truths to the control and prediction of the future. Whether this was astrological or magical or alchemical, whether it eventuated in exploration and discovery or in experimentation, step by step men reoriented their researches, and the individual, the curious, the novel, seem to have been of more interest than the traditional, the authoritative, and the proven. In fact one of the favorite words for "heresy" was *novitas*, "novelty." In the late fifteenth century Platonism was revived in Florence in the work of Marsilio Ficino, and after its revival had a career lasting to the present in one form or another. But except in the fine arts, it had a recessive character. The dominant theme was anti-Platonic.

One of the tenets of nominalism was that only individual things are real. If this was true, then some intellectual technique of handling individuals was needed and that technique did not develop to any great extent until the seventeenth century when statistics and the theory of probability became the framework, although a weak one at that time, of scientific thought. The statistical collection took the place of the Platonic-Aristotelian class. The idea now became the range of more or less similar responses to a method of investigation. But that result took four centuries to come to maturity, and meanwhile the scientifically minded were satisfied either to call traditional investigators by bad names or to speak of experience as if its nature were self-evident.

An Italian "philosopher of nature" like Telesio (1509–88) might properly be chosen as one of the initiators of the new science since he selected an easily identifiable source of change as primordial. Heat and cold, expansion and contraction, hark back to the pre-Socratic philosophers, but after centuries of talk about what exists in terms of what ought to exist, the naturalism of Telesio was refreshing. And when Francis Bacon cleared the air by indicating the obstacles to discovery in his Four Idols, it was possible to raise the basic question of the origin of knowledge. To the Neo-Platonist that origin was inborn in us. To Lord Herbert of Cherbury (1583–1648) the fundamental principles of knowledge, both religious and scientific, were innate. But his opponents argued that if this were so, then all men ought to agree more than they disagree. And yet, as John Locke insisted, there is no evidence that men lacking experience know anything whatsoever. Ideas emerge not from our untaught minds but from experience.

Experience now became one of those "sacred words," like Nature or Art or Democracy, which everyone was in favor of and few could define. In Locke and his successors it came to denote the immediate apprehension of sensory qualities, colors, sounds, tastes, for instance, plus the ideas of pain and pleasure or of anything known only to oneself. Locke himself said that he was using "ideas" to express "whatever it is which the mind can be employed about in thinking" (*Essay Concerning Human Understanding*, Book I, Ch. I, Sec. 8). But thinking he identified with awareness. And hence the ideas which in Plato could be known only after long dialectical analysis now became something which lay open to the eyes of anyone willing to look. This was a dramatic reversal of meaning. The matter was complicated by Locke's conclusion that some ideas were purely subjective, a conclusion that dates from the atomism of Democritus in the fifth century B.C., some copy qualities of the objective and physical world, and some are known by "bare intuition" (Book IV, Ch. II). But these last do not appear in Locke's *Essay Concerning Human Understanding* until the fourth book is reached, the whole work taking twenty years (1670–90) for completion. The ideas known by bare intuition are logical rules, mainly those derived from the Law of Contradiction.

The development of the theory of ideas in Great Britain lay in the direction of simplification, passing through Bishop George Berkeley and David Hume. By the time Hume had completed his investigations, ideas had become faint copies of sensory impressions, whereas in Plato, it will be recalled, they had been that of which sensory impressions were faint copies. This was not merely a difference of terminology. For the Platonic ideas were standards of truth, whereas in Hume it was the impressions that had become the standards. The result was that in Condillac and his successors in the eighteenth century, in Auguste Comte and the nineteenth-century Positivists, in Ernst Mach (1838–1916), and in the Viennese Circle in the twentieth century, attempts were made to break down all ideas into those perceptual data of which they were presumably composed. One of the difficulties of these attempts was the admitted existence of Locke's objects of bare intuition, the logical rules, in short the schemata of methodology.

7. The Kantian School. These rules and schemata, the forms of knowledge, were believed by Immanuel Kant to be unanalyzable into perceptual data. We may perceive colors and sounds but we cannot perceive the spatial matrix in which they are located. For if we empty space of all perceptual content, nothing is left. Similar arguments apply to time. Hence both space and time in Kant became the forms of perception, ideas by which the mind organizes its perceptions but which have no perceptual correspondence whatsoever. Similarly when we make scientific judgments of causality, quantity, quality, or necessity, there are no sensory data which could possibly compose them. These categories are the means by which we think, and they have no sources beyond our minds. It had been pointed out in the seventeenth century by Géraud de Cordemoy and Nicolas Malebranche that one could see, for instance, a rolling ball touch another, but one could not see it cause the other to move.

Causation, then, is an idea of ours which we project into the world of observation. Similarly Hume had pointed out that we could observe the regularity of events but not their necessity. Necessity was one of our feelings induced by the sight of regularity. Kant's categories of the understanding were in an analogous situation. They were the mind's way of making experience intelligible. They were regulatory principles which gave structure to our knowledge, knowledge whose content might be perceptual but whose form was entirely subjective.

Hume had shown to the satisfaction of most philosophers the impossibility of penetrating the perceptual screen of impressions and reaching some material cause which might explain its presence. In Kant the question of such a cause does not arise, for perceptual ideas exist as if they were the experiences of a single over-individual mind. They take the place of an objective world. But besides these ideas there are the two types of forms (space, time) and categories through which all men are bound to order their knowledge. Hence, as was evident to Kant's immediate successor, Fichte, any talk about unknowable things-in-themselves is nonsense. For as soon as we begin to talk, we inescapably use the categories. And the categories are relevant only to our ideas.

There is moreover another set of ideas in Kant and these have no ground whatsoever in perception or science. He recognized that we have religious and moral ideas, ideas of God, freedom, and immortality. These ideas cannot be correlated with any perceptions for the simple reason that we admittedly do not see (i.e., perceive) what they stand for. Moreover they are not categories of the understanding, for science not only can get along very well without them, but actually contradicts one of them, the idea of freedom, and gives no evidence for the truth of the other two.

One might conclude that they were false and should be abandoned. But Kant introduced a new function for an idea at this point. These three ideas, though antiscientific, were necessary postulates for ethics. Doing one's duty would be unjustifiable if there were no God, if the will were not free, and if life ended in the grave. Kant did not entertain the possibility that life is a tragedy and duty an illusion. On the contrary,

he assumed that the world must be so made that doing one's duty was imperative. Thus a new criterion for the truth of an idea was introduced, its necessity for the justification of moral values.

From then on it was possible to think of the world as essentially a stage for human life and for the solution of human problems, which was a reversion oddly enough to the medieval point of view. Philosophy, to be sure, was no longer the handmaiden of theology but of ethics. The innovation as it was made by Kant and developed by Fichte may not have been radical, but it became so as the nineteenth and twentieth centuries evolved. For if an idea could be a postulate for the religious and moral life, why could it not be a postulate for the aesthetic, the political, the economic life? An idea could easily become an instrument by means of which a man could substantiate any of his ends, ends which could be chosen rationally by reasons which were more useful than true. In such a case the true would turn into the useful.

Schopenhauer had maintained that reasoning was at the service of the will-to-live, as Nietzsche was to put it at the service of the will-to-power. Ideas were a mask for desires, a doctrine which was developed by Sigmund Freud, substituting the *libido* for the will. The great Kantian scholar, Hans Vaihinger (1852–1933) made all ideas fictions of various types which we set up to make the world intelligible. These and similar views seemed to dethrone the ideas and to become not the guideposts to impersonal truth, completely detached from human desires, forming the matrix of reality, but rather signs of what we would like to believe, conventions by means of which we can confer plausibility upon our thoughts and aspirations. Seldom has the history of an idea manifested such a reversal of meaning.

BIBLIOGRAPHY

The literature on the Platonic theory of ideas is very extensive. Almost anything that has been said about it has been, and will be, contested. For the most complete list of articles and books on the subject, see Harold Cherniss, *Lustrum*, 1959, No. 4 and 1960, No. 5 (Goettingen, 1960, 1961), pp. 278ff. The most authoritative account of the entire Platonic philosophy is Paul Shorey, *What Plato Said* (Chicago, 1933). For Aristotle's writings as a whole the best translation is that usually referred to as the Oxford Translation, by a variety of scholars, in twelve volumes (1910–52). A single work on Aristotle that is frequently cited is W. D. Ross, *Aristotle*, 5th ed. (London and New York, 1955). But, as is true of Platonism, anything said about Aristotelianism will be contested. There is no satisfactory translation into English at present of Plotinus but one is promised for the Loeb Classical Library. For the modern philosophers, see J. H. Randall, Jr., *The Career of Philosophy*, to be three volumes (New York, 1962, 1965, 19—); G. Boas, *Dominant Themes of Modern Philosophy* (New York, 1957); and the various volumes of Frederick Copleston, S.J., *A History of Philosophy* (Westminster, Md., 1946–63). Each of these histories is written from a special point of view which must be kept in mind when they are consulted. For the influence of Platonism and Neo-Platonism on art and aesthetics, see Katharine Gilbert and Helmut Kuhn, *A History of Esthetics*, rev. ed. (Bloomington, Ind., 1953). For number symbolism in the Gothic cathedral, see Otto von Simson, *The Gothic Cathedral*, 2nd ed. (New York, 1956).

GEORGE BOAS

[See also Causation; Freedom; Naturalism; Neo-Platonism; Number; Pragmatism; **Primitivism**; Pythagorean . . . .]

IDEAL IN PHILOSOPHY FROM THE RENAISSANCE TO 1780

I

"THE IDEAL," as a substantive, does not appear in French or in German earlier than the eighteenth century, and appears in Italian, in Spanish, and in English still later (probably not before the late eighteenth century). The adjective, "ideal," is of course much more ancient (Latin: *idealis*); "the Ideal" derives, as a substantivized adjective, from some of its uses.

The history of the notion of *ideal* as an adjective mainly belongs to that of the substantive it derives from, "Idea"; among its various meanings, as "phenomenal" (versus "real": ideal space or time) or as "imaginary" (versus "true"), "intelligible" (versus "sensitive") is important in this context as the origin of *The Ideal*.

This meaning derives from the Platonic tradition in general, sponsoring the view that an exemplar or archetype of the world is thought by God, and may, on certain conditions, be partly apprehended by man, although not empirically. This exemplar reveals part of the true structure of the existing world, as opposed to the distorted representation of it which man gains through the senses; and in another aspect (as a *normative* exemplar) it represents a maximum of perfection which should be pursued, but can hardly ever be reached within the existing world.

In the first sense it is used in metaphysics (e.g., Norris, 1701–04), in the second chiefly in aesthetics (particularly in art theory) and in ethics. It is in this second (normative) sense that "ideal," as ideal beauty or goodness, gave birth to a substantive, the Ideal of beauty or of goodness, as a more specific synonym of

that Idea lying at the foundation of that beauty or goodness (in order to distinguish it from empirical ideas). As such, the term "ideal" at first was used indiscriminately as synonymous with the "Idea of Beauty," and later tended to supplant it; in a few cases both were used, but a more sophisticated distinction was introduced between them. The doctrine of ideal beauty leading to the ideal of beauty is a late development of aesthetic Neo-Platonism, advanced in Italy chiefly by G. P. Bellori in 1664. Reacting against both mannerism and Caravaggio's naturalism in painting, Bellori asserts that true beauty can be reached neither by abstract intuition nor by illumination (as most of the earlier Platonists assumed), nor through the simple imitation of natural objects. Beauty requires a perfection which cannot be found in nature, but which can be reached through the study of nature only: beauties perceived in different natural objects should be selected according to a mental standard of perfection, and combined into an imaginary representation or Idea more perfect than any natural thing, as an exemplar for the work of art. The tale of Zeuxis, combining the charms of five different real virgins in order to create his image of Helen of Troy becomes again, as of old, the symbol of an artistic theory. Thus, ideal beauty is considered to have, against the older Platonic tradition, a kind of empirical foundation; nevertheless, the mind creates on this foundation something supranatural, according to an interior (nonempirical) standard of perfection. Similar *natural-selective* doctrines were propagated by Bernini, Félibien, Du Fresnoy, Fréart de Chambray (Panofsky, 1926; Bredvold, 1934).

The Idea of goodness, again, is part and parcel of the Platonic tradition as a nonempirical representation of perfect goodness; with this generic meaning, this term was used also by other philosophical schools (Micraelius, 1662). Bayle mentioned a *bonté idéale* intended as sovereign goodness—in God (Bayle, 1720 ed.); the expression, however, was rather ambiguous, so that Crousaz, criticizing Bayle, could misinterpret it as "imaginary" goodness (Crousaz, 1733).

II

However, aesthetics had a prominent part in the evolution of the idea in question. The Dutch critic ten Kate seems to have been the first to use *Ideal* as a substantive (also *Idéalité*), in a sense still very close to that of Bellori; but for him the peak (*partie sublime*) of the Ideal is à *je ne sais quoi*, being an *harmonieuse Propriété*, a *touchante Unité*, a *convenance pathétique* (ten Kate, 1728). This doctrine played a leading role in Diderot's aesthetics, where it underwent some important transformations: the Idea or the ideal model, far from being extra-empirical, is conceived almost as

549

of experimental origin, and understood as representing the perfect "type" of a certain kind of objects. The Idea is animated through imagination and feeling, and is strictly connected with moral values: every great Idea is a moral maxim, and is, at the same time, the unity of the work of art (Belaval, 1950). The influence of Diderot's doctrine of the ideal model was limited by the fact that his most significant works in this connection were published posthumously. The Ideal, as a substantive, is used by Diderot only occasionally, and probably not before 1765 (Diderot, 1875–77 ed.).

Otherwise, eighteenth-century French authors are not very receptive to "ideal" aesthetics. Batteux, among the few, gives attention (1746) to the *beau idéal* (Batteux, 1764); and Louis Racine distinguishes, in art, between *le vrai simple* and *le vrai idéal*, which "embellishes" (*embellit*) (Racine, 1747). The Dutch philosopher and critic Hemsterhuis at times mentions (1769) ideal beauty (Hemsterhuis, 1846). Ideal, as a substantive, is not listed in Diderot's *Encyclopédie;* it appears for the first time in 1777 in the Supplement to this work, in an article influenced by Winckelmann, Mengs, and probably by Sulzer (*Nouveau Dictionnaire,* 1776–77). British aesthetics, although permeated in some of its principal trends by Platonism, makes little use of the terms in question. In his original elaboration of the notion we are studying, Shaftesbury (*Characteristicks,* 1711) uses, for example, such expressions as "forming forms," "interior numbers," etc. (Shaftesbury, 1790). But Webb discusses "ideal" or "inventive" (versus imitative) painting (Webb, 1740); and Sir Joshua Reynolds (writing in the 1770's) fully revives Bellori's doctrine of the "Idea of Beauty" (Reynolds, 1884).

III

In Germany only the Ideal has had, as a term and as a doctrine, an early and large diffusion, and becomes very fashionable especially after 1770, in spite of the unsympathetic attitude of the *Sturm und Drang* ("Storm and Stress") group. This is chiefly due to Winckelmann's influence: he had been permeated first by French, then by Italian seventeenth-century art theory. His original development of the doctrine of the Ideal, being the center of his aesthetic theory, attracted his contemporaries' attention to this notion, and urged them to organize around it many Platonic suggestions drawn from British aesthetics. In Winckelmann's earlier works (1754f.) two different theories of ideal beauty (*idealische Schönheit*) can be found: (1) the natural-selective, deriving from Bellori and (2) the more originally Platonic theory, whereby the Idea of beauty completely derives from the mind, without any connection with experience—as for Lomazzo and others. Universal ideal beauty reaching beyond the

individuality of natural beauty makes matter "spiritual" (*geistig*); the artist is considered as a creator. In his *History of Art in Antiquity* (1764), Winckelmann tries to unify both theories: the Ideal of beauty is composed by natural elements selected by a supranatural standard of beauty, but other nonmaterial elements are superadded to them, deriving from the intuition of divine beauty; in the statue of *Laokoön* natural elements are prevalent, in the *Apollo del Belvedere* they are minimal. A kind of beauty merely deriving from the natural-selective process is still mentioned but it is not called "ideal" any more. In ideal beauty, according to the Greek καλοκἀγαθία ("beauty and goodness") a strong ethical element is present (Zeller, 1955; Will, 1958; Winckelmann, 1825–29). The term "the Ideal" makes its appearance comparatively late, not before 1759 (e.g., Winckelmann, 1825–29, "Torso"); previously, "Idea" (*die Idee*, also *die Idea*) and "Concept" (*der Begriff*) have been used instead, and still appear later. Wieland had used "the Ideal" as a substantive in 1755: he mentions the Ideal of beauty and of goodness as the highest perfection of the human mind, corresponding to the notion of the universe as a whole, and states that the term "the Ideal" is growing fashionable (Wieland, 1824; *Teutscher Merkur,* 1755). Moses Mendelssohn seems to accept as early as 1757 the doctrine of ideal beauty (*Idealschönheit*), but in its natural-selective aspect only; he stresses its character as an artificial *whole* of natural beautiful parts, as God would have created, if his aim in creating every object had been beauty alone. But Mendelssohn carefully distinguishes ideal beauty from virtue: perfect virtue, represented in art, does not correspond to the highest beauty. For Mendelssohn, as for later authors, ideal beauty does not apply to visual art only, but to art in general (Mendelssohn, 1968; Goldstein, 1904). Some time later he also uses "the Ideal" as a substantive, and as "moral Ideal" too (Briefe, 1760–61).

Klopstock, on the contrary, discussing in 1760 a work of Winckelmann, criticizes ideal beauty insofar as it is claimed to be above nature (Klopstock, 1830). The painter Mengs, a friend of Winckelmann, supported a version of the natural-selective theory as a means for reaching beauty, i.e., visible perfection; this is achieved in a complete unity of the *determined concept* of a thing with its representation, viz., of the Spiritual with the Material; now, the Spiritual is also called the Ideal (Mengs, 1762). Hagedorn accepts the doctrine of ideal beauty, but he makes it almost subservient to the more traditional theory of imitation (Hagedorn, 1762). Riedel seems to have noticed the different aspects of Winckelmann's theory: he distinguishes three kinds of Ideals in art: (1) real nature, (2) imaginary ideal nature, and (3) original creation with very few natural elements. Some "ideal" works of art are not only "imaginative" but "intellectual," i.e., they summon "higher Ideas" into the mind of the observer. In 1768 Riedel extended this doctrine to morality ("the moral Ideal," *das sittliche Ideal*) (Riedel, 1767; 1768).

The notion of Ideal reaches at this time a considerable diffusion. Herder discusses the ideal perfection and beauty of the German language (Herder, 1767; 1877–1913). Lessing discusses the Ideal in dramatic theory, and tries to retrace the origin of this term as a noun to the Italian philosopher Lana Terzi, who in fact had used it as an adjective only (Lessing, 1886–1924; von Stein, 1886; Lana, 1670). The discussion becomes so lively that it attracts the attention of academic philosophers such as Feder and Ferber, who try to forestall possible interpretations of the doctrine of the Ideal leading to the acceptance of some form of nonempirical knowledge (as certainly Winckelmann had meant). In fact, they reshape this theory within the traditional frame of the psychology of their time: Ideals originate from the senses, and are elaborated by the imagination (Feder, 1770a; Ferber, 1770). In the same spirit, Feder and Frömmichen try to identify the Ideal with the traditional notion of universal concept (Feder, 1770b; Frömmichen, 1771).

The term penetrates also into poetry, as shown by Wieland (Wieland, 1771). In 1771, Sulzer devotes an article of his famous aesthetical dictionary to the Ideal. The "ideal form" is created by the genius of the artist using empirical elements; still, Sulzer rejects the natural-selective theory: the Ideal cannot result from an assembly of singular traits, or it would represent an individual only; on the contrary, the Ideal is the sensuous representation of the abstract concept (or Idea) of a genus or of a species as such (and therefore it is superior to natural objects). Thus, a difference is made between Idea (intellectual) and Ideal (sensitive); and an Ideal represents not a single thing, but a kind or type of things *sub specie sensibilitatis*, e.g., a virtue, a temper, etc. (Sulzer, 1771–74). Sulzer's article, translated into French, was republished in the *Encyclopédie d'Yverdon* (Felice, 1770–75): thus, the term "the Ideal" appeared for the first time as a substantive in a general dictionary. Shortly thereafter, the art theorist Scheyb devotes a long eclectic discussion to the Ideal (or Idea), quoting many ancient and modern authorities (Scheyb, 1774).

The term Ideal appears in Kant's reflections between 1764 and 1768, both in aesthetics and in ethics, but it is widely used by him only after 1770; between 1770 and 1780, the doctrine of the Ideal becomes an important element in his philosophy. Ideals are basically distinguished from Ideas (although occasionally they may be called Ideas). Both Ideas and Ideals are principles of unity and ordinance of the empirical multiplicity, as totalities preceding their parts; and they are not of empirical origin (although a certain kind of Ideal is called "empirical"). But an Idea (properly) cannot be intuited *in concreto* (can only be thought abstractly), while an Ideal is an Idea as intuited *in concreto* (or is the sensible representation of an Idea). Ideals are either empirical or spiritual. In the first case they are universal principles underlying every empirical object, as the transcendental unity (completion of the synthesis) of the unlimited sensible world. In the second case, they are original creations of the mind, representing an example of perfection, which cannot be found in the empirical world, relating an object to its essential end; this perfection is in some cases a maximum (something in its totality), in other cases an average (the Ideal of a certain species of things, being an average of the things belonging to that species). According to another division, Ideals are either speculative, or aesthetical, or pragmatic (Kant, 1910f.; Schlapp, 1901; Schmucker, 1961; Tonelli, 1966). As in many other cases, Kant has accepted and incorporated into his system a notion current in his time, after having submitted it to adequate changes.

In the meantime, the doctrine of the Ideal was attacked from different quarters. The *Sturm und Drang* group in its opposition sponsored a different aesthetic theory; Lenz, for example (1774), opposed the "abstract" ideal of beauty by offering instead the notion of "characteristic" beauty (Lenz, 1949; R. Pascal, 1953). On the other hand, Lavater tried to rescue natural from ideal beauty, stressing the natural-selective theory of the Ideal, and contending that ideal beauty is not supra-natural: on the contrary, it always imitates some natural beauty without equalling it (Lavater, 1777). Wieland responded immediately, contending that there are several kinds of ideal works of art: some originate from a process of natural selection, but some others derive from an Ideal which is superior to nature, generated in the artist's soul by a mysterious process, as if inspired by a god; some others are a mixture of both kinds (Wieland, 1777). But the merely empiricist view finds another supporter in Lossius (Lossius, 1777). The doctrine of the Ideal grew so popular, that in 1780 this term appears even in the title of a tragedy ("The Ideal of Unfortunate Love, or Kleodon, A Tragedy," by F. Prinner, 1780).

BIBLIOGRAPHY

C. Batteux, *Traité des beaux arts réduits à un seul principe* (1747), in *Principes de la littérature* (Paris, 1764), I, 122. P. Bayle, *Dictionnaire historique et critique* (Amsterdam, 1734), art. "Origène," n. E. Y. Belaval, *L'esthétique sans paradoxe de Diderot* (Paris, 1950), pp. 96–121. L. I. Bredvold, "The

Tendency towards Platonism in Neoclassical Esthetics," in *English Literary History*, 1 (1934). *Briefe, die neueste Literatur betreffend* (1760), V, 124; IX, 56. J.-P. de Crousaz, *Examen du Pyrrhonisme ancien & moderne* (The Hague, 1733), p. 560a. D. Diderot, *Oeuvres complètes*, ed. J. Assézat and M. Tourneux, 20 vols. (Paris, 1875–77), X, iii; XI, 206, 238 (*Salons of 1765 and 1767*). J. G. Feder, *Lehrbuch der praktischen Philosophie* (Göttingen and Gotha, 1770a), p. 97; idem, *Logik und Metaphysik* (Göttingen and Gotha, 1770b), p. 148. F. B. de Felice, *Encyclopédie, ou dictionnaire universel raisonné des connaissances humaines* (Yverdon, 1770–75), Vol. XXIV(1773), art. "Idéal." J. C. C. Ferber, *Vernunftlehre* (Helmstädt and Magdeburg, 1770), p. 67. K. H. Frömmichen, *Briefe philosophischen Inhalts* (Göttingen, 1771), p. 58. L. Goldstein, *M. Mendelssohn und die deutsche Aesthetik* (Königsberg, 1904), pp. 45f. C. L. von Hagedorn, *Betrachtungen über die Mahlerei*, 2 vols. (Leipzig, 1762), *Von den Grenzen der Nachahmung*, pp. 85–89. F. Hemsterhuis, *Lettre sur la sculpture* (1769), in *Oeuvres philosophiques* (Leeuwarden, 1846), I, 38, 41. J. G. Herder, *Fragmente über die neuere deutsche Literatur* (1767), Samml. I, 3, Beschluss, in *Sämtliche Werke*, ed. B. Suphan, 33 vols. (Berlin, 1877–1913), I, 50. I. Kant, *Gesammelte Schriften*, ed. Die Preuss. Akademie der Wissenschaften (Berlin and Leipzig, 1910f.), XIX, 95–96, n. 6584, 108, n. 6611; II, 395–96; XV, 330, n. 757, 342, n. 782, 390, n. 892, 393, n. 900, 403, n. 918; XXVIII, 308–09. F. H. Klopstock, *Sämtliche Werke* (Leipzig, 1823–30), XVI, 129. F. Lana Terzi, *Prodromo, ovvero saggio di alcune inventioni nuove* (Brescia, 1670), Ch. II. J. C. Lavater, *Physiognomische Fragmente zur Beförderung der Menschen-Kenntniss und Menschenliebe*, 3 vols. (Leipzig and Winterthur, 1775–78), III, 41f. J. M. R. Lenz, "Anmerkungen übers Theater" (1774), in *Sturm und Drang. Kritische Schriften*, ed. E. Loewenthal (Heidelberg, 1949), p. 728. G. E. Lessing, *Gesammelte Werke*, eds. Lachmann and Muncker, 23 vols. (Stuttgart and Leipzig, 1886–1924), IX, 281; XV, 288. J. C. Lossius, *Unterricht der gesunden Vernunft* (Gotha, 1777), p. 243. M. Mendelssohn, *Ueber die Hauptgrundsätze* (1757), in *Schriften zur Philosophie, Aesthetik und Apologetik*, ed. Brasch (Hildesheim, 1968), II, 151f.; idem, *Die Idealschönheit* (1759), ibid., II, 283f. R. Mengs, *Gedanken über die Schönheit und über den Geschmack in der Mahlerei* (Zurich, 1762), Ch. I, sec. 5. J. Micraelius, *Lexicon philosophicum terminorum philosophis usitatorum* (Stettin, 1662), col. 219. J. Norris, *An Essay towards the Theory of the Ideal or Intelligible World* (London, 1702–04). *Nouveau Dictionnaire pour servir de Supplément au Dictionnaire des Sciences . . .* (Paris and Amsterdam, 1776–77), art. "Idéal." E. Panofsky, *Idea, Ein Beitrag zur Begriffsgeschichte der älteren Kunsttheorie* (Leipzig and Berlin, 1924), Ch. V. R. Pascal, *The German Sturm und Drang* (Manchester, 1953), Ch. VIII. F. Prinner, *Das Ideal unglücklicher Liebe, oder Kleodon, Ein Trauerspiel* (Salzburg, 1780). L. Racine, *Réflexions sur la poésie*, in *Oeuvres* (Paris, 1747), III, 253. J. Reynolds, *Discourses*, ed. E. Gosse (London, 1884), Discourses III and IV (1770–71). F. J. Riedel, *Theorie der schönen Künste und Wissenschaften* (Jena, 1767), pp. 23, 26, 29, 345; idem, *Ueber das Publicum. Briefe an einige Glieder desselben* (Jena, 1768), p. 72. F. C. von Scheyb, *Orestrio von den drey Künsten der Zeichnung* (Vienna, 1774), pp. 22f. O. Schlapp, *Kants Lehre vom Genie und die Entstehung der "Kritik der Urtheilskraft"* (Göttingen, 1901), pp. 102, 137, 142, 165, 172, 201–02. J. Schmucker, *Die Ursprünge der Ethik Kants* (Meisenheim am Glan, 1961), pp. 308–14. Anthony Ashley Cooper, Third Earl of Shaftesbury, *Characteristicks of men, manners, opinions, times* (1711; Basel, 1790), I, 117, 286; II, 327, 333–39, 343, 351; III, 150–52. K. H. von Stein, *Die Entstehung der neueren Aesthetik* (Stuttgart, 1886), p. 389. J. G. Sulzer, *Allgemeine Theorie der schönen Künste* (Leipzig, 1771–74), Vol. I, art. "Ideal." L. H. ten Kate, *Discours préliminaire sur le beau idéal*, in J. Richardson and J. Richardson, Jr., *Traité de la peinture et de la sculpture*, trans. L. H. ten Kate (Amsterdam, 1728), III, vi f. *Der teutsche Merkur*, 4 (1755), 62. G. Tonelli, "Kant's Early Theory of Genius (1770–1779)," in *The Journal of the History of Philosophy*, 4 (1966), 117f., 126f., 129f. D. Webb, *An Inquiry into the Beauties of Painting* (London, 1740), p. 4. C. M. Wieland, *Der neue Amadis* (Leipzig, 1771), 7, 30f.; 9, 31; 11, 29; idem, "Gedanken über die Ideale der Alten," *Der teutsche Merkur*, 2 and 4 (1777); idem, *Sämtliche Werke*, ed. J. G. Gruber, 56 vols. (Leipzig, 1824–28), XLIV, 85. F. Will, *Intelligible Beauty in Aesthetic Thought. From Winckelmann to Victor Cousin* (Tübingen, 1958), pp. 92f. J. J. Winckelmann, *Sämtliche Werke*, ed. J. Eiselein (Donaueschingen, 1825–29), Vol. I, *Beschreibung des Torso*, secs. 1, 14; Vols. III–VI, *Geschichte der Kunst des Altertums*, Book IV, Ch. II, secs. 20, 22, 25, 33, 35; Book V, Ch. I, secs. 1, 39, 40; Book XI, Ch. III, secs. 11, 12. H. Zeller, *Winckelmanns Beschreibung des Apollo im Belvedere* (Zurich, 1955), pp. 130f., 140f.

GIORGIO TONELLI

[See also Art and Play; **Beauty; Idea;** Neo-Classicism; Neo-Platonism; **Taste.**]

IDEOLOGY

ONE OF the most controversial concepts in the history of social thought has been the concept of ideology. Some scholars have emphasized the epistemological aspects of ideology, others its sociological components, and still others its psychological or cultural features. An examination of these approaches will provide the components of ideology on which most scholars appear to agree.

At the outset it is necessary to distinguish between ideology as concept and ideology as political doctrine. The analysis of ideology as a generic concept (e.g., its nature and function) constitutes an intellectual activity of quite different order than the analysis of ideology as a body of political beliefs (e.g., conservatism, liberalism, socialism). Similarly, it is quite impermissible to confuse someone's (e.g., Marx's) analysis of the concept of ideology with *his* own ideology or political doctrine (i.e., Marxism). It is of course true that one's analysis of the concept of ideology may be conditioned "ideologically" (in the second sense)—as indeed Marx's was—but these questions are analytically distinct. We are concerned in this article only with the analysis of ideology as a concept in social thought.

Epistemological Approaches. Historically this is the earliest approach to ideology, and its chief exponents were the French Ideologues of the latter part of the eighteenth century, mainly Étienne Bonnet de Condillac, Pierre J. G. Cabanis, Antoine Louis Claude Destutt de Tracy and Claude Adrien Helvétius. One of the earliest uses of the term "ideology" was in Destutt de Tracy's *Élémens d'idéologie*, 4 vols. (1801–15).

In this approach ideology is based upon a sensationalist theory of knowledge. The basic assumption is that all ideas, all knowledge, and all the faculties of human understanding—perception, memory, judgment—rest on sensory data. The validity of an idea can be ascertained only in terms of its congruence with sense impressions. The study of the origin and development of ideas in terms of sensations is the only guarantee against errors in cognition and judgment.

In expounding the sensationalist point of view, and in seeking to extend scientific methodology to the study of ideas and knowledge, the Ideologues posed a sharp challenge to the rationalistic tradition of the eighteenth century, especially Cartesianism. For them, knowledge was a process of inductive generalization from particular sensations.

In developing their philosophy the Ideologues relied heavily on Francis Bacon and John Locke. Condillac, widely acknowledged as the founder of the school of ideology, praised Bacon for having developed the scientific method which in turn had proved so essential in the study of physical nature; Bacon, he thought, was the first to understand the truth that all knowledge comes from the senses.

Condillac similarly praised Locke for having revolutionized philosophy by launching a systematic attack upon rationalism. He was particularly impressed with Locke's concept of *tabula rasa* and the concomitant rejection of innate ideas. However, Condillac argued, Locke had not gone far enough in locating the source of ideas in experience and observation—which, themselves, according to Condillac, could be reduced to sensations.

Condillac's central objective was to do for philosophy what Bacon had done for science. He was interested in a scientific approach to the study of man and ideas. He was particularly impressed with Bacon's warning against *idola* ("idols, phantoms, or misconceptions") as sources of error in knowledge. (This has led some scholars to trace the genesis of "ideology" to Bacon's *idola;* for example, Karl Mannheim, p. 61.) Condillac wished to reconstruct philosophy into an analytical method for the study of the nature, sources, and implications of ideas.

Condillac's philosophy was further developed and formally systematized by Cabanis and de Tracy. Cabanis based ideas on sensations, but he approached the study of the mind from a physiological rather than an epistemological point of view. Knowledge of the physical nature of man, he held, was the basis of all philosophy. Physiology, moral philosophy, and the analysis of ideas constitute "three branches of a single science: the science of man" (Van Duzer, p. 43).

Physical sensibility, according to Cabanis, is the basic factor in knowledge, as also in the intellectual and moral life of man. Just as physical life is a series of movements originating in impressions received by the various organs, so psychological phenomena result from movements initiated by the brain. These movements are received and transmitted by the nerve endings of the various organs. It is sensibility that makes us aware of the external world; sensations bring the outside world within the mind, as it were. Sensations differ in intensity, duration, and so on, depending on the physiological functioning of the individual (his age, sex, physical constitution) and environmental conditions.

In his *Élémens d'idéologie*, Destutt de Tracy set out to systematize the philosophy of sensationalism and to put it into textbook form. While crediting Condillac with the creation of ideology, and Cabanis with its further development, Destutt de Tracy proceeded to introduce his own variation upon it. The importance attached to sensation and physiology had inclined Condillac and Cabanis toward a materialistic interpretation of the mind. Destutt de Tracy went further by directly viewing ideology as a part of zoology. Human psychology—"the science of ideas"—should be analyzed in biological terms, without attention to moral or religious dimensions. Only in this way could an objective science of the mind be realized. According to Destutt de Tracy, "One has only an incomplete knowledge of an animal if one does not know its intellectual faculties. Ideology is a part of zoology, and it is above all with reference to the study of man that this science has importance" (Germino, p. 48). There is thus no qualitative distinction between man and lower animals; metaphysical, philosophical, and religious conceptions must be discarded because they are not subject to scientific investigation.

The political and moral implications of sensationalism were developed largely by Helvétius. Helvétius relied on early utilitarianism in emphasizing a principle that the later utilitarians were to label "the greatest happiness of the greatest numbers." Morality, politics, and legislation were to be directed toward maximizing pleasant sensations and minimizing unpleasant sensations. Helvétius believed in ethical and political relativism, in limited government, in the need for harmonizing public and private interests, and in the possibility of human progress through education (this a residue of the Enlightenment). In other words, the political implications of sensationalism could be called "democratic."

It is not surprising, then, that the Ideologues should have vigorously opposed Napoleon and his imperialistic dictatorial policies. Nor is it surprising that Napoleon should have reciprocated with intense hostility, and should have pejoratively labeled the group *Idéologues*, denoting "visionaries" or "daydreamers." That is where the term "ideologue" originated and that is how it came to take on a derogatory connotation, which it has retained to the present day.

The Ideologues' treatment of the ideology concept entailed some difficulties. Despite their appeal to science, a great deal of their analysis was strikingly speculative and intuitive. Moreover, there was considerable confusion, especially found in Cabanis and de Tracy, concerning physiology, psychology, and epistemology. Finally, their approach to ideology is not directly relevant to twentieth-century understandings and concerns.

Sociological Approaches. A watershed in the study of the ideology concept was reached in the works of Karl Marx and Friedrich Engels, who viewed ideology as a system of false ideas, a statement of class position, and a justification for class rule. Ideologies are secondary and unreal, since they are part of the "superstructure" and as such a reflection of the more fundamental material economic "base."

One's thought and belief patterns, Marxist theory holds, are conditioned by one's socioeconomic existence. Socioeconomic relationships, particularly property relationships, set the stage for man's bondage and "alienation." They dehumanize man by thwarting his creative impulses. They separate man from himself, his productivity, and the society to which he belongs.

Socioeconomic relationships are institutionalized in social classes. One's ideology is therefore a function of the class to which one belongs. More specifically, ideologies are deliberate creations of false images by the dominant class to manipulate and control the masses, and to perpetuate its own rule. "The ideas of the ruling class," wrote Marx and Engels, "are in every epoch the ruling ideas: i.e. the class, which is the ruling material force of society, is at the same time its ruling intellectual force" (*The German Ideology*, p. 39).

Marx and Engels attached a derogatory connotation to ideology, since they viewed all ideological thought as the dishonest use of reasoning, as the conscious or unconscious distortion of facts in order to justify the position of the ruling class. Ideology represents, in Engels' memorable phrase, "false consciousness."

The proposition that false consciousness may provide a basis for action suggests, as many have pointed out, that ideas and ideologies enjoy a measure of autonomy —a realization that runs counter to Marx's earlier assertion about the dependence of ideas on the economic system. Engels was to explain, after Marx's death, that Marx had indeed overemphasized the economic factor, and for a good reason. He wrote: "Marx and I are ourselves partly to blame for the fact that younger writers sometimes lay more stress on the economic side than is due to it. We had to emphasize this main principle in opposition to our adversaries, who denied it, and we had not always the time, the place or the opportunity to allow the other elements involved in the interaction to come into their own rights" (*Selected Correspondence*, p. 477). However, Engels maintained, although there is no inflexible one-way relationship between idea systems and economic systems, sooner or later the two will coincide.

Marx and Engels, by basing ideas on the socioeconomic system, raised an issue that, at the hand of Karl Mannheim, came to be known as the "sociology of knowledge": the study of social bases, conditions, varieties, and distortions of ideas. To this extent, sociology of knowledge is reminiscent of the epistemological approach to ideology, except that Mannheim proposed to elevate the enterprise to a truly scientific status devoted to the unmasking of the ideological biases in thought.

Mannheim's approach differed from Marx's in important respects. Influenced by Max Weber, Mannheim abandoned Marx's primarily class approach and based ideology on the total social structure, particularly political parties. (This prompted some scholars like R. K. Merton in his *Social Theory and Social Structure* [New York, 1957, p. 490] to call Mannheim a "bourgeois Marx," a label that was applied earlier to Weber.) Moreover, Mannheim argued, Marx's approach had inappropriately fused two distinctive types of ideology: the "particular" and the "total."

The particular conception of ideology denotes that "we are skeptical of the ideas and representations advanced by our opponent," because "they are regarded as more or less conscious disguises of the real nature of a situation, the true recognition of which would not be in accord with his interests." It includes "all those utterances the 'falsity' of which is due to intentional or unintentional, conscious, semiconscious, or unconscious, deluding of one's self or of others, taking place on a psychological level and structurally resembling lies." This conception is "particular" because "it always refers only to specific assertions which may be regarded as concealments, falsifications, or lies without attacking the integrity of the total mental structure of the asserting subject" (Mannheim, pp. 55–56, 265–66).

Mannheim contrasts the particular conception of ideology to the total conception: "Here we refer to the ideology of an age or of a concrete historico-social group, e.g. of a class, when we are concerned with the characteristics and composition of the total structure of the mind of this epoch or of this group" (ibid., p. 56). The total conception, in other words, refers to the *Weltanschauung* of an age or of a historical group.

The two conceptions of ideology have in common the fact that they are determined by one's social circumstances. Beyond this they differ in some important respects: (1) the particular conception calls into question only a portion of the opponent's assertions, whereas the total conception challenges the opponent's entire world-outlook and admits of no nonideological thought; (2) the particular conception rests on a psychological analysis of ideas, whereas the total conception operates at an epistemological-ontological level wherein the entire "thought-system" is analyzed as socially-historically determined; (3) the particular conception is associated largely with individuals, the total conception with collectivities; (4) the particular conception historically precedes the total conception.

Mannheim draws a further distinction between "ideology" and "utopia." Ideology, according to this formulation, is an idea system congruent with, and supportive of, the status quo. Utopia, by contrast, is an idea system opposed to the status quo and supportive of an alternative social order. Only those mental orientations are utopian, Mannheim holds, "which, when they pass over into conduct, tend to shatter, either partially or wholly, the order of things prevailing at the time" (ibid., p. 192). The ideology-utopia distinction is rather farfetched, however, since either concept may be simultaneously opposed to (or supportive of) a given status quo and supportive of (or opposed to) a rival one.

Conclusions strikingly similar to those of Marx were reached via an entirely different route by two early European sociologists, Gaetano Mosca and Vilfredo Pareto, who were in some respects the intellectual nemesis of Marx. Mosca and Pareto believe in a scientific approach to social analysis. To be fruitful, they maintain, social science must be objective; to be objective, it must rest on observable and verifiable grounds. The most fundamental fact of social existence is that human society at all times has been characterized by a fundamental division between a minority that rules and a majority that is ruled, between elite and mass.

According to Mosca, the most decisive feature of any society is its ruling class. A society's art, culture, politics, religion, etc., are all determined by the dominant social stratum. As such, social analysis must begin and end with the ruling class—its origin, development, composition, and change. Politics consists of violent struggles among contending groups for power, for the ruling positions in society. The leaders maintain, perpetuate, rationalize, and justify their own rule through the skillful manipulation of "political formulas" or ideologies.

Pareto stresses the prevalence of the irrational in human conduct. He insists, under the influence of Freudian psychology, that significant portions of human behavior are motivated and sustained by nonlogical drives lying well below the level of consciousness. Man's conduct is governed as much by unconscious habit as by deliberate choice.

Pareto's approach is also influenced by a conception of "myth" developed by Georges Sorel. All society, according to Sorel, is guided and directed by myth; the myth is the most important factor in social life. A myth consists of a body of symbols and images capable of evoking sentiment and propelling men to action. More specifically, a myth has two components: a statement of goals or objectives, and a commitment to a line of action toward the materialization of the objectives. A myth, in other words, is an "expression of a determination to act" (Sorel, p. 50); it binds a group of people together, taps their sentiment and emotion, and directs their energy toward specific objectives. The most important function of any leadership group is to provide the appropriate myth for a society.

Pareto divides all human conduct into two categories—logical and nonlogical—in terms of whether it employs suitable means in pursuit of attainable objectives. He contends that most human action is nonlogical, and that nonlogical action is especially pervasive in the sociopolitical realm. All societies, he points out, are filled with taboos, magic, and myths. In the political realm, codes, constitutions, platforms, and programs fail to meet the criteria of logical action, since, among other things, they are stated in the vaguest, most rhetorical, most meaningless terms.

Pareto distinguishes two types of nonlogical action: "residues" and "derivations." Residues refer to a fairly small number of constant factors—"nuclei"—in human behavior that change little from age to age, culture to culture. Derivations consist of the large number of factors that change rapidly with time and place; they are manifestations and expressions of residues. Derivations are the verbal expressions—including "ideologies"—that seek to explain, rationalize, and justify the residues through appeal to sentiment, emotion, custom, and tradition. Residues and derivations are interdependent; they are motive forces of social conduct. (It is interesting to note Krishna P. Mukerji's comment that Pareto's theory of residues and derivations is a variation on Marx's theory of base and superstructure; Mukerji, p. 17.)

The concept of ideology, then, is a major variable in these writers' analyses of society. Used synonymously with "myth," "political formula," or "derivation," ideology is viewed as the matrix of social behavior, the guiding force in human society, and the principal means for attaining social solidarity. It is approached as an instrument for leadership manipulation and control of the masses, a means for rationalizing, legitimizing, and perpetuating a given state of affairs.

Among contemporary sociologists, Talcott Parsons and Daniel Bell deserve special attention. In general, Parsons defines ideology as "an empirical belief system held in common by the members of *any* collectivity." More specifically:

An ideology . . . is a system of beliefs, held in common by the members of a collectivity, i.e., a society, or a sub-collectivity of one—including a movement deviant from the main culture of the society—a system of ideas which is oriented to the evaluative integration of the collectivity, by interpretation of the empirical nature of the collectivity and of the situation in which it is placed, the processes by which it has developed to its given state, the goals to which its members are collectively oriented, and their relation to the future course of events (Parsons [1951], pp. 354, 349).

The phrase "a sub-collectivity of one" suggests that ideology may be a purely personal phenomenon. Parsons states in the same work, however, that ideology refers "primarily" to the belief system of collectivities, and he proposes to call the belief system of individuals "personal ideology" (ibid., p. 331).

Moreover, it is clear from the larger definition, ideology involves goal-directed behavior; it serves as a basis for action toward improving the welfare of the collectivity. It binds the community together, and it legitimizes its value orientations. Finally, ideology involves an element of distortion: "the strongly evaluative reference of ideologies tends to link in with the 'wishful' or romantic-utopian element of motivation which is present in every social system. There will generally . . . be a tendency to ideological distortion of the reality in the direction of giving reign to the wishful element" (ibid., p. 357).

Elaborating on this point elsewhere, Parsons identifies the "essential criteria of an ideology" as "deviations

from [social] scientific objectivity." He identifies two types of deviations: one associated with the selectivity with which ideologies approach problems and treat issues; the other with the positive distortions of those problems and issues that ideologies do choose to treat. He writes: "The criterion of distortion is that statements are made about the society which by social-scientific methods can be shown to be positively in error, whereas selectivity is involved where the statements are, at the proper level, 'true,' but do not constitute a balanced account of the available truth" (Parsons [1959], p. 38).

The "functional" approach to ideology—its action-orientation, its ability to promote or undermine legitimacy, its potential for attaining social solidarity and value integration—has been emphasized by Daniel Bell. According to Bell:

Ideology is the conversion of ideas into social levers. Without irony, Max Lerner once entitled a book *Ideas Are Weapons.* This is the language of ideology. It is more. It is the commitment to the consequences of ideas. . . . For the ideologue, truth arises in action, and meaning is given to experience by the "transforming moment." He comes alive not in contemplation, but in "the deed" (Bell [1960], pp. 370–71).

Elsewhere, Bell defines ideology as

. . . an interpretative system of political ideas embodying and concretizing the more abstract values of a polity (or social movement) which, because of its claim to justification by some transcendent morality (for example, history), demands a legitimacy for its belief system and a commitment to action in the effort to realize those beliefs (Bell [1965], p. 595, n. 6).

To sum up, the sociological approaches are centrally concerned with ideology as a system of socially determined ideas, without necessary truth-value but with great potential for social solidarity as well as for social control, mobilization, and manipulation. In addition, ideologies may serve to justify (or reject) a particular set of goals and values and to legitimize (or denounce) political authority. Some writers attach a derogatory connotation to ideology, whereas others see it in a neutral light.

Psychological Approaches. The psychological theories see ideology primarily as a means of managing personal strain and anxiety, whether socially or psychologically induced. Among the most important of the psychological theories are those of Sigmund Freud, and of Francis X. Sutton and colleagues.

We may associate with Sigmund Freud a unique approach to the concept of ideology, although to our knowledge he nowhere undertakes an explicit analysis of the subject. He does give a fairly extensive treat-

556

ment of religion, and he does suggest that religion and ideology have much in common—indeed, that they may belong to identical species of thought. Consider the following statement, for example: "Having recognized religious doctrines to be illusions, we are at once confronted with the further question: may not all cultural possessions, which we esteem highly and by which we let our life be ruled, be of a similar nature? Should not the assumptions that regulate our political institutions likewise be called illusions?" (Freud [1957], p. 59). In a word, we would be well justified in substituting "ideology" wherever Freud uses "religion."

Freud's starting point is that man's life is governed by instinctual drives, many of which are subconscious or unconscious. These instincts are primarily of two types: life instincts (Eros) and death instincts (Thanatos). The demands of man's instinctual behavior are in conflict with those of society, culture, and civilization. (The distinctions among these three concepts are not crucial for our present purposes.) Indeed, the very possibility of civilization lies in man's ability—voluntarily or otherwise—to divert, rechannel, and sublimate his instinctual energies into more conventional behavior. Culture and civilization demand sacrifices and instinctual renunciations from the individual. This in turn intensifies man's natural aggressiveness toward society, so that "every individual is virtually an enemy of culture" (ibid., p. 4). It also intensifies man's aggressiveness toward his fellow man, so that "civilized society is perpetually menaced with disintegration through this primary hostility of men toward one another" (Freud [1958], p. 61). The ultimate consequence is war.

At the same time, aggressiveness creates a pervasive sense of guilt under the pressure of the superego. If culture and civilization are to exist, their prohibitions must be internalized by the individual as an integral part of his moral code. The individual must internalize not only the prohibitions of culture but also "its heritage of ideals and artistic creations," for these ideals offer "substitute gratifications for the oldest cultural renunciations" (Freud [1957], pp. 71, 19; [1958], p. 15). And now we come to the heart of Freud's argument: ". . . the most important part of the psychical inventory of a culture . . . is . . . its . . . religious ideas" (Freud [1957], p. 20; cf. [1958], p. 38).

Religious conceptions are illusions. They are falsehoods created to control man, restrain instinctual behavior, and perpetuate culture. Freud writes: ". . . religious doctrines . . . are all illusions, they do not admit of proof, and no one can be compelled to consider them as true or to believe in them. . . . [The] reality value of most of them we cannot judge; just as they cannot be proved, neither can they be refuted." The strength of religious ideas lies in the fact that they are "fulfillments

of the oldest, strongest and most insistent wishes of mankind; the secret of their strength is the strength of these wishes" (Freud [1957], pp. 54, 51).

Religion (ideology), then, performs the function of wish-fulfillment. It affords protection and security to the individual; it controls instinctual behavior and relieves man of his sense of guilt; it counteracts man's alienation from society. (The concept of alienation is implicit in Freud's argument that the undue demands of civilization create a disjunction between man and society, but he does not actually use the term.) Religious ideas "allay our anxiety in the face of life's dangers, the establishment of a moral world order ensures the fulfillment of the demands of justice, which within human culture have so often remained unfulfilled, and the prolongation of earthly existence by a future life provides in addition the local and temporal setting for these wish-fulfillments" (ibid., pp. 51–52).

Religion (ideology) is essential to man's psychological well-being as well as to the continuity of culture.

Sutton and his colleagues offer a conception of ideology as a response to strain generated by social roles. Modern life, they argue, engenders a host of problems and stress situations with which each man has to cope. Individuals daily confront conflicting demands and anxiety situations in the course of performing their roles. Since human behavior is patterned in systems of roles, so are the strains that these roles inescapably generate.

Since man's reaction to strain is patterned rather than random, individuals need some "guiding principles" in the light of which to react. Ideology is a system of ideas that enables man to cope with strain. "Ideology is a patterned reaction to the patterned strains of a social role. . . . Where a role involves patterns of conflicting demands, the occupants of that role may respond by elaborating a system of ideas and symbols, which in part may serve as a guide to action, but chiefly has broader and more direct functions as a response to strain" (Sutton et al., pp. 307–08).

Although there is a basic relationship between ideology and strain, the actual linkages are by no means clear or simple, for the individual may react to strain in a variety of ways, including pathological behavior, Ideology is merely one way of responding to stress. It is "a symbolic outlet" for emotional disturbances generated by social and personal disequilibrium. This includes release of emotional tension by displacing it into symbolic enemies (e.g., scapegoatism). Ideology performs the function of tension management and sustains the individual in the face of continued stress.

The psychological approaches, then, focus on ideology primarily in terms of its relation to the individual and its consequences for social conduct. They are par-

557

ticularly interested in ideology as a means of stabilizing the psychological makeup of the individual, equipping him with an appropriate set of psychological reactions, reconciling him to the conflicting demands of social life, and providing relief from anxiety and strain.

Psychocultural Approaches. Among the psychocultural approaches to ideology, the work of Léon Dion and of Clifford Geertz may be examined. Dion refers to ideology as "a more or less integrated cultural and mental structure." By this he means a pattern of norms and values that is both objective (cultural) and subjective (mental). More specifically:

Our hypothesis is that political ideology is a cultural and mental complex which mediates between the norms associated with given social attitudes and conduct and the norms which the political institutions and mechanisms tend to crystallize and propagate. In other terms, political ideology is a more or less integrated system of values and norms, rooted in society, which individuals and groups project on the political plane in order to promote the aspirations and ideals they have come to value in social life (Dion, p. 49).

Expressing dissatisfaction with the existing approaches to ideology, Clifford Geertz sets out to provide a more adequate nonvaluational theoretical framework for its analysis. He approaches ideology in terms of symbols and symbolic action, for he seeks to show, at least in part, "how symbols symbolize, how they function to mediate meanings" (Geertz, p. 57).

Geertz's initial assumption is that thought consists of the construction and manipulation of symbol systems. Symbol systems, whether cognitive or expressive, are extrinsic sources of information in terms of which man's life is patterned (since intrinsic or genetic sources of information are so few). Symbol systems are extrapersonal mechanisms for perception, judgment, and manipulation of the world. Culture patterns—whether religious, scientific, or ideological—are "programs" that provide a blueprint for the organization of social and psychological processes. More specifically, states Geertz, "it is through the construction of ideologies, schematic images of social order, that man makes himself for better or worse a political animal" (ibid., p. 63).

Ideology, in other words, is more than a mere psychological response to strain; it embodies social and cultural elements as well. Broadly understood, ideology is a cultural symbol-system that aims to guide man in his political life. The attempt of an ideology to render confusing social situations meaningful accounts for its highly symbolic form and for the intensity with which it may be held. As such: "whatever else ideologies may be . . . they are, most distinctively, maps of problematic social reality and matrices for the creation of collective conscience" (ibid., p. 64).

The psychocultural approaches, then, attempt to unify the mental and the environmental elements in ideology. In this view ideology requires both a psychological outlook and a cultural context. Its primary function is to enable the individual to make sense of the cultural symbol-system.

Summary. We have identified several approaches to the concept of ideology and we have examined each at some length. Each approach throws light on a different dimension of the concept; together they reveal its extraordinarily rich and variegated intellectual heritage. We may extrapolate from these approaches a synthetic conception of ideology along the following lines. Ideology is an emotion-laden, myth-saturated, action-related system of beliefs and values about man and society, legitimacy and authority, acquired as a matter of routine and habitual reinforcement. The myths and values of ideology are communicated through symbols in simplified, economical, and efficient manner. Ideological beliefs are more or less coherent, more or less articulate, more or less open to new evidence and information. Ideologies have a high potential for mass mobilization, manipulation, and control; in that sense, they are mobilized belief systems.

BIBLIOGRAPHY

David E. Apter, ed., *Ideology and Discontent* (New York, 1964). Daniel Bell, *The End of Ideology* (New York, 1960); idem, "Ideology and Soviet Politics," *Slavic Review,* **24** (December 1965), 591–603. Gustav Bergmann, "Ideology," *Ethics,* **61** (April 1951), 205–18. Norman Birnbaum, "The Sociological Study of Ideology (1940–60)," *Current Sociology,* 9 (1960), 91–117. Richard H. Cox, ed., *Ideology, Politics, and Political Theory* (Belmont, Calif., 1969), Ch. 1. Léon Dion, "Political Ideology as a Tool of Functional Analysis in Socio-Political Dynamics: An Hypothesis," *Canadian Journal of Economics and Political Science,* **25** (February 1959), 47–59. Sigmund Freud, *Civilization and Its Discontents* (1930; New York, 1958); idem, *The Future of an Illusion* (1928; New York, 1957). Clifford Geertz, "Ideology as a Cultural System," in David E. Apter (cited above). Dante Germino, *Beyond Ideology: The Revival of Political Theory* (New York, 1967), Ch. 3. Robert E. Lane, *Political Ideology* (New York, 1962). George Lichtheim, "The Concept of Ideology," in *The Concept of Ideology and Other Essays* (New York, 1967). Karl Mannheim, *Ideology and Utopia* (London and New York, 1936). Karl Marx and Friedrich Engels, *The German Ideology* (1845–46; New York, 1947); idem, *Selected Correspondence, 1846–1895* (New York, 1942). Gaetano Mosca, *The Ruling Class* (New York, 1939); idem, "The Final Version of the Theory of the Ruling Class," in James H. Meisel, *The Myth of the Ruling Class* (Ann Arbor, 1958). Krishna P. Mukerji, *Implications of the Ideology Concept* (Bombay, 1955). Vilfredo Pareto, *The Mind and Society,* 4 vols. (London, 1935). Talcott Parsons, "An Approach to the Sociology of Knowledge," *Transactions of the*

Fourth World Congress of Sociology (Louvain, 1959), 25–49; idem, *The Social System* (New York, 1951). Mostafa Rejai, ed., *Decline of Ideology?* (New York, 1971). Giovanni Sartori, "Politics, Ideology, and Belief Systems," *American Political Science Review*, **63** (June 1969), 398–411. Edward Shils, "Ideology: The Concept and Function of Ideology," *International Encyclopedia of the Social Sciences* (New York, 1968), 7, 66–76. Georges Sorel, *Reflections on Violence* (1906; New York, 1961). Francis X. Sutton, Seymour E. Harris, Carl Kaysen, and James Tobin, *The American Business Creed* (Cambridge, Mass., 1956). Charles H. Van Duzer, *Contribution of the Ideologues to French Revolutionary Thought* (Baltimore, Md., 1935).

MOSTAFA REJAI

[See also Alienation; Baconianism, **Idea; Ideology of Soviet Communism; Marxism;** Perfectibility.]

IDEOLOGY OF SOVIET COMMUNISM

THE IDEOLOGY of Soviet communism is that of the party which seized power in the former Russian Empire, a party with monolithic authority and influence which reaches beyond the borders of the Soviet Union and imposes on several European countries. Its history, or rather its prehistory, goes back to 1903, when the Second Congress of the Russian Social Democratic Workers Party adopted its doctrinal program.

This program, or statement of principles was drawn up by G. V. Plekhanov and was amended and presented to the Congress by the editorial staff of the journal *Iskra* (while Lenin was on its staff). It was very similar to the French Workers Party program (written by J. Guesde and P. Lafargue, and adopted at Roanne in 1882) and to the German Social Democratic Party program (composed by K. Kautsky and adopted at Erfurt in 1891, inspired by the ideas of Karl Marx and Friedrich Engels). The Russian program of 1903 proclaimed its identity of purpose with the aim of social democrats in all countries. It formulated the universal ideas of Marxian socialism as it was understood up to the World War of 1914–18.

According to these general ideas capitalist society consists of a small privileged class, which owns the means of production and exchange, and a huge majority of proletarians or semiproletarians exploited by the dominant minority. The inevitable evolution of this society through technological advances, economic crises, and imperialist wars only accentuates the antagonistic interests and conflicts between the diminishing minority and the growing majority, thus creating conditions which bring about the replacement of capitalist production by the relations of socialist production; in short, the achievement of a "social revolution." After replacing the private ownership of the means of production by collectivist ownership, this revolution would finally abolish the division of society into classes, and would liberate all of oppressed mankind by putting an end to the various forms of exploitation of labor, manual or intellectual.

Besides the expression of these general principles, the Russian program of 1903 departed nevertheless on one point from the French and German programs:

The necessary condition of this social revolution is the dictatorship of the proletariat, that is, the seizure by the proletariat of the political power which will enable it to crush all resistance by the exploiters.

The source of this idea was the French socialist Louis Auguste Blanqui, and its formula, if not the idea itself, reappears very briefly in certain writings of Marx and Engels; but they thought that the dictatorship of the proletariat would be exercised democratically as a transitional stage by the great majority of people through universal suffrage. This dictatorship was, however, understood differently in Russia when the Social Democratic Party there became divided and broke up into two factions, Bolshevik and Menshivik, in conflict with each other during the internal party struggles preceding the Russian Revolution of 1917.

The rest of the 1903 program conformed to the aspirations of all the socialist parties of the time, but with certain features pertaining to the Tsarist autocracy. It advocated the instauration of a democratic regime with a single Parliament, elected by direct universal suffrage and secret ballot available to all citizens; the inviolability of person and home; freedom of conscience, of speech, of the press, of assembly, of unions and their right to strike; the equality of all before the law without discrimination of sex, religion, race, or nationality; the autonomous right of nations to govern themselves; the replacement of a standing conscripted army by a volunteer army of the people; the separation of church and state; universal free education; the elimination of indirect taxes; an eight hour workday and a day of rest each week; and finally, a set of social laws and measures to cover improved working conditions for city workers and peasants, all of which was to be brought about by a Constituent Assembly fully elected by the people.

Such was the ideology of the Bolshevik Social Democrats who seized power in 1917, eight months after the first World War had caused the fall of Tsarism. But between the former regime (March 1917) and the

Bolshevik coup (November 1917) a new sort of social reality appeared, which the Party had not anticipated, namely, the spontaneous creation of the "Soviets," that is, not well defined "councils" of delegates consisting of laborers, peasants, soldiers. They assumed different prerogatives, depending on the situations and circumstances, in the absence of representative legal and established institutions. The two factions of social democracy, Bolsheviks and Mensheviks, though claiming the same program and proclaiming the necessity of a sovereign "Constituent Assembly," were bitterly opposed to each other on the granting of power to the Soviets, in which the Bolsheviks finally won a substantial majority.

After November 1917 the more radical social democratic ideology soon became the Soviets' specific ideology, and because of its wish to maintain power, the politically victorious party gradually relinquished the essential features of its previous program. It idealized the worst circumstances after making a virtue of necessity, and set up as lasting models the temporary measures of expediency that were enforced contrary to principles previously announced. It was to be the new ideology decreed by the so-called dictatorship of the proletariat, actually effected by the party which monopolized the totality of power.

A rapid transformation was achieved in the course of the civil war which broke loose after the military coup had proclaimed "power to the Soviets." All the freedoms inscribed in the Party's program, the rights of man and the rights of the people, universal suffrage, democracy, and a parliament, and *a fortiori*, the end of the army and the police, etc. became nothing more than historical and literary memories. The Constituent Assembly met on January 5, 1918 with the Bolsheviks in a minority, and was dissolved the next morning by force. The single party in power assumed the label "Communist Party" in 1918 and decided on a new program to be drawn up by Bukharin and Lenin; it was adopted by the Eighth Congress of the Party in 1919. Approximately from that time on, the terms "Communist" and "Soviet" became synonymous, and the official ideology of the regime consists in justifying by code and propaganda all the practices contrary to the Party's theories but dictated by circumstances in order to support and perpetuate the new power.

While Lenin was alive, the ideology of Soviet communism flowed chiefly from his personal views with various changes at times, from his new articles, his speeches, and his books. However, an ever deepening abyss occurs between theory and practice; ideas more or less well argued remain academic, whereas actions constitute reality whose expression becomes in effect the actual Soviet ideology. Lenin's Marxism, already adapted to specifically Russian conditions, takes on an original character by underscoring certain disputable or challenged ideas, or by accentuating in any case, nonessential ones borrowed from Marx and Engels.

More particularly, between the two Russian revolutions of 1917, Lenin developed and formulated theories of the State considered simply as the instrument of domination by the propertied classes. He maintained that the advent of the proletariat to power, in reality, the dictatorship of his party, which he identified as the "conscious avant-garde" of the proletariat, would determine by itself the withering away of the State, that is to say, the progressive extinction of the bureaucracy, of the police, and of the army, supplanted by the benevolent, direct administration of the people. All public offices being elective and all office holders being subject to recall at any moment by their electors, what would follow would be the disappearance of all class superiority, of all privilege, of all parasitism, and the realization of this masterpiece of Lenin's plan, as the supplement to the Party's program, would finally attain the realization of the anarchistic ideal.

However, during the course of a half century or more, reality has continued to belie the fiction; the Soviet State far from withering away has continued to grow in power, attaining an omnipotence never before known in history; the professional bureaucracy, the secret police, and the army as a vocation compose the strongest apparatus of coercion the world has ever seen. Distinctly separate from the people, a stranger to the nation, the single Party retains exclusively all the political and economic privileges, controlling the State as its private property while the utopia on its books remains inseparable from the communist ideology (cf. Lenin, *The State and Revolution*, Petrograd [1918]; countless editions in all languages).

The government defines itself as being the "dictatorship of the proletariat," contradicting the theory of the withering away of the State until its extinction, and Lenin did not fear declaring that the dictatorship signifies "unlimited power depending on violence and not on law." He repeated time and again that "the scientific acceptance of the dictatorship is nothing more than a power which can provide no limits, that no law nor absolute rule can restrain, and which is based specifically on violence" (*On the History of the Dictatorship*, in Lenin's *Works*, 3rd ed., Moscow [1937], Vol. 25).

Moreover Lenin was to recognize that his Party, once it was in complete command of the State and of the means of production, was in the hands of a real "oligarchy," namely, the Central Committee and its Politburo, with the power to decide everything and to subordinate the many organizations called "soviets"

(Lenin, *Infantile Malady of Leftism in Communism*, St. Petersburg [1920], in numerous editions in all languages). The official ideology registers this remark of Lenin's on "the oligarchy," even while it persists in asserting that the power of the Soviets belongs to the city workers and to the peasants organized spontaneously in Soviets, but which have lost their original character and are appointed by authority from above, i.e., through the corresponding echelons of the Party.

Even after the Civil War (1917–21), while conflicts resolved by sheer force were stamped in his memory, Lenin specifically prescribed in the Penal Code (1922) the use of terror, asserting its "justification or legitimacy" in "the broadest possible" manner; the application of capital punishment was left to the decision of judges recruited at random (cf. Lenin's *Complete Works*, 5th ed., Moscow [1964], 45, 190). Apologies for the use of terror, paralleling its growing intensive application, increased in proportion as the original causes invoked to motivate such terror kept losing any basis in reality, to the point of becoming nonexistent.

In this regard, Soviet ideology admitted that methods of repression and oppression in the service of a despotic "oligarchy" were turned over to the secret police; growing in numbers soon beyond count, ubiquitous, skilled in jailing, tormenting, judging, deporting, and executing millions of defenseless victims in disregard of all legal forms, of all guarantees of justice, this unprecedented body of police became an actual State within the State.

Nevertheless the old socialist program of the Party had remained unchanged, held in common by the Menshevik social democrats and the new Bolshevik communists, but when a new program was adopted in 1919, with its first part largely reproducing the 1903 program, the term "social democracy" was replaced by "Communist Party." There was added to the old text a thesis dear to Lenin, namely imperialism as the "supreme stage of capitalism," corresponding to the evolution of capitalism in "putrefaction" and opening up, it seemed, "the era of the universal socialist revolution." This thesis, dating back to 1916, was obviously shown to be false by tangible historical facts but it remained an integral part of communist ideology, for it subsists in the third program of the Party elaborated during a period of about thirty years and ratified by the twenty-second Communist Congress in 1961. While Lenin was alive the theory inherited from the socialist past remained unchanged, but thereafter it was augmented by new ideas that were inspired by the improvised practices of the bolshevism that came into power.

The Soviet ideology, as received from its creator, rests first on the dogma of absolute materialism, which presupposes that matter exists independently of human consciousness or sensations, and implies that material conditions determine all historical phenomena, social and spiritual. Lenin and his intellectual disciples think, as did J. J. Rousseau, that man was innocent in the beginning, but lost his innocence through his contact with a corrupt society, more precisely with the capitalist world. By abolishing private ownership of the means of production and by forbidding the exploitation of labor by a minority of property owners, the Soviet regime was gradually to suppress class differences; it would allow workers to blossom out in complete freedom while giving the best of themselves to society. The idea then was to undertake the establishing of socialism by stages, developing to its logical goal along the lines stated by the principle: "From each according to his abilities, to each according to his needs," the goal of communism.

However, Lenin, contrary to his explicit doctrine, employed the terms "socialism" and "communism" indifferently during the first years of his regime. If by "ideology" we mean the cluster of principles and ideas professed by a given group of people, then the Soviet ideology appears to be more and more elusive in proportion to the ways in which the march of events and succession of historical facts impose on this group's thinkers (especially on its leading thinker) variations of language, terminology, and opinion which belie the initial intentions and diminish the chances of rendering a coherent translation. Lenin's successive trenchant declarations intermingling strategy and tactics, marked by a realism belatedly contradicting academic utopianism, continue to be corrected, superseded, and refuted to such an extent that Soviet ideology is becoming unrecognizable from one year to the next.

In his commentary on the new program of 1919, Lenin expounded the view that "the program of a Marxist party should be founded on facts established with absolute certainty" ("Marxist," "socialist," and "communist" were synonyms for Lenin). The specifically Soviet ideology was thus the reflection of the Leninist union of "practice" with the "theory" of the former social-democratic party. By "absolute certainty" he meant the "fact" that the decay of capitalism leads to imperialism and that "the era of social revolution on a worldwide scale" begins with the seizure of power by the Bolshevik party in Russia, the prelude to the institution of socialism in the whole world. But, Lenin remarks, "as to stating what the achieved socialism will look like, we simply do not know." For he emphasizes the fact that "we do not have enough material to enable us to define socialism. The bricks to be used in the building of socialism are not yet made."

What Lenin believed he did know with scientific certainty was that socialism meant "the suppression

561

of class distinctions"; now, "so long as there will continue to be urban workers and peasants, there will be different classes, and consequently there will be no integral socialism." At the same time he judged that "the dictatorship of the proletariat is the extension of the proletarian class's struggle in new forms." On another occasion he would say that socialism is "bookkeeping." But he would agree that "our attempt to pass immediately to communism has rewarded us with defeat. . . ." He confessed that "we have thought it possible . . . to pass directly to the construction of socialism," and he stated elsewhere that "we have been vanquished in our attempt to bring about socialism by assault." Thus communism and socialism, at this stage of his reflection, were interchangeable ideas. And at the end of an ill considered policy, which tended to ruin the stages of social evolution, he proposed "abandoning the immediate construction of socialism in order to fall back on state capitalism in many economic matters." Thus socialism, communism, and state capitalism coexist intermingled with a problematic ideology.

In speaking of state capitalism as defining the "new economic policy" (abbreviated as NEP), Lenin in 1921 put an end to the preceding economic policy which he called "war communism." But among the leading ideologists of the Party an obscure debate and controversy arose as to whether the NEP was to be considered a form of state capitalism or state socialism, with no conclusive result. For the soviet "intelligentsia," after Lenin's death in 1924, the terms socialism, war communism, and state capitalism amounted to an uncertain and very confused doctrine.

The disturbed period which followed brought no clarification; on the contrary, when the leaders of the Party became increasingly and actively hostile to traditional religions, taunting, repressing, and persecuting them mercilessly, they soon saw to it that an atheistic substitute for religion was systematically instituted, namely, the cult of Lenin's personality; they are both the officiating priests and beneficiaries of that materialistic cult. After various crises, in the course of which the major ideas imposed on the population were those selected from the works of Lenin, complicated by contradictions and uncertainties, a new order of ideas was framed and steadily imposed under the banner of "Leninism," namely, the views of a new leader, Stalin. The verbal similarities remain deceptive.

The term "Leninism" was not in use in Soviet Russia under Lenin, who would not tolerate it, for he claimed that his doctrine was simply "Marxism." By "Marxism," of course, he meant his particular interpretation of it, which was sharply disputed by socialists of other tendencies. The two main factions of the Party, struggling with each other for the succession to Lenin, elaborated Leninism in contradictory ways, each claiming to be the true continuators of Lenin. This system implies the myth of Lenin's infallibility and developed into a sort of complex theology with its dogma, mystique, and scholasticism; as a new ideology, it was not only soviet but ecumenical, since it was propagated in all countries by the Communist International (Comintern) and by many auxiliary public and secret organizations with branches throughout the world.

Stalin first formulated the Leninist creed (after Lenin's burial), then the first catechism, *Principles of Leninism* (Moscow, 1926), and the articles of faith, *Questions on Leninism* (Moscow, 1926). Subsequently, having decreed that Leninism was "the Marxism of the age of imperialism," Stalin deemed it necessary to establish a link with Karl Marx. The expression "Marxism-Leninism" was adopted to stand for the body of Stalin's judgments and aphorisms; it is known outside the Soviet Union as "Stalinism."

The ideology of Marxism-Leninism, that is to say, Stalinism, reflects the mass of empirical measures decreed by Stalin in order to maintain and perpetuate himself in power as long as possible. From the verbal heritage of Marxism and Leninism the ideology retains the outer husk of the words in defiance of the kernel; it invokes the word which kills at the expense of the spirit which gives life. The socialist phraseology persisted while the exploitation of man by man increased even to a greater degree than in any Western capitalist country. The international revolutionary preaching continued; in 1924 Stalin predicted worldwide revolution, whereas in 1925 he was compelled to recognize the facts when he definitely admitted the "stabilization of capitalism." Lenin, who understood the necessity of the *NEP*, had stressed that it should be enforced "seriously and for a long time"; Stalin suppressed it at short notice remarking that Lenin had not said "forever." The right of nationalities to self-determination, to settle their own affairs (*disposer d'eux-mêmes*), including the right to break away from Russia, a right about which Lenin had theorized for many years, was definitely denied to ethnic groups who were subjected to increasing national oppression, much worse than the relentless political oppression and social and economic exploitation from which all people under the communist oligarchy suffer.

Stalin's "Marxist-Leninist" ideology assumed the contrary of the thesis of Marx and Lenin in Stalin's claim that socialism could be attained in one country, more exactly, Russia. In vain did Lenin write in 1918 that socialism is inconceivable for only one country, "even less backward than Russia." On this point he really did not vary, even though he had earlier, in 1915, seen the victory of socialism possible in only one country, but in the sense in which one party, called socialist, acceded to power; and even in 1923 when he believed it possible to hope for a transformation of the commercial economy by means of widespread "cooperation," freely agreed to, and which would take "a whole era of cultural development of the masses." Basically he says unequivocally: "It is very doubtful whether the next generation will be able to realize socialism in all its spheres." The following year he repeats: "We cannot actually introduce a socialist regime here; God wills that it should be installed by our children, perhaps even by our grandchildren." And finally, in his last article in 1923: "We are not sufficiently civilized to proceed directly to socialism, although we have the political premises." However, in 1932 Stalin decided that the basis of socialism was established in his country, and in 1936 he would celebrate "the total victory of the socialist system in all spheres of the national economy." The word, socialism, had changed its meaning.

Lenin had developed many times the theme which Stalin disregarded while pretending to respect it: "Socialism is impossible without democracy"; but Stalinism was the antithesis of democracy and of socialism, even while it proclaimed to the whole world that the Soviet Constitution was "the most democratic in the world." In fact Stalin's regime turned out to be more "totalitarian" than fascism, a term which Mussolini invented. But Soviet totalitarianism through its chauvinism, militarism, and anti-Semitism shows its kinship chiefly with German "national-socialism." It surpasses all previous and contemporary regimes of terrorism by carrying out on the reverse side of its ideology and with unbridled violence the forced "collectivization" of the countryside, which involved a hecatomb of cattle, and sacrifice of millions of human lives.

Here again we have evidence of the flagrant antinomy in the repeated prescriptions of Lenin favoring the overwhelming majority of peasants, although the prescriptions were camouflaged in a slogan which became classical: "the alliance of the proletariat and the peasants." The height of the repudiation of socialist ideology, or of genuine communism, was reached when Stalin concluded a pact with Hitler in order to throw the second World War out of gear; with a stroke of the pen Stalin soon suppressed the Communist International, the creation of Lenin who had assigned to the Comintern a role of fundamental importance in his dream of world revolution.

Whereas Stalinism made unrelenting use of the same terminology to justify everything and the oppo-site of everything during climactic crises and turning points of history, circumstances compelled the Soviet Union to draw closer to the really democratic nations when it needed temporary alliances to carry out its great "patriotic war against the Berlin-Rome axis." Stalin then changed his language in order to praise England and the United States, who contributed an enormous amount of material aid and saved the Soviet regime; ideology was adapted to the circumstances. Once the danger was over, Stalin returned to his position of systematic hostility to the Western democracies, and modified the ideology again in order to bring it into conformity with his politics, strategy, and tactics; he kept on denouncing an undefined "imperialism," and in particular the United States. At the same time he proclaimed a doctrine of "peaceful coexistence" to cover subversive activities operating underground and undermining the free world. He supported and stirred up social disturbances everywhere and encouraged local wars. He used the rostrum and lobbies of the United Nations to sow dissension, poison relations, and provoke discord. After his death the epigons persevered in the same Marxist-Leninism dissociating themselves to some extent from the homicidal practices which had horrified public opinion all over the world. These followers persist in preserving the heritage of an ideology fabricated of fiction and myth. Such is the ideology of Soviet communism, an ideology which does no more than make one aware of the realities it conceals.

BIBLIOGRAPHY

Everything concerning Lenin is in the collections of his works of which there exist (in Russian) five editions, each more complete than the last, though not quite complete yet; they are augmented by copious annotations presenting a great many variants and contradictions. Cf. Lenin, *Works*, first edition in 20 vols. (Moscow, 1924–27); third edition in 30 vols. (Moscow, 1927–35); *Complete Works*, fifth edition in 55 vols. (Moscow, 1958–65). The second and third editions are similar; the fourth is to be avoided.

Stalin's texts up to January 1934 are found in the collection called *Works* in 13 vols. (Moscow, 1946–51), the publication of which was held up after the death of the author. A supplement of three volumes covering the years 1934–53, edited by Robert H. McNeal, was published by the Hoover Institution (Stanford, 1967).

All matters pertaining to the ideology and life in the Soviet Union, except those that are state secrets, are treated in the encyclopedias and dictionaries the successive editions of which reveal the official versions and reflect the changes between editions. Cf. *The Great Soviet Encyclopedia* in 65 vols. (Moscow, 1931–47); 2nd ed. in 51 vols. (Moscow, 1949–58); *The Small Soviet Encyclopedia*, 10 vols. (Moscow, 1930–31); 2nd ed., 11 vols. (Moscow, 1933–47); 3rd ed., 11 vols. (Moscow, 1958–61). *Small Philosophical Dictionary*

(Moscow, 1952); 4th ed., (Moscow, 1954). *Political-Dictionary* (Moscow, 1940; 1958). *Diplomatic Dictionary*, 2 vols. (Moscow, 1948–50); 3 vols. (Moscow, 1960–64).

BORIS SOUVARINE

[See also **Historical and Dialectical Materialism; Marxism;** Marxist Revisionism; Social Democracy; **Socialism;** State; Totalitarianism.]

IMPIETY IN THE CLASSICAL WORLD

I. INTRODUCTION:
SOME ORIENTAL NOTIONS

THE ENGLISH word "impiety" derives of course from the Latin *impietas.* Our notion of *impiety* (if we still have one) is, however, the result of complicated cross-influences in which we can isolate at least four components: the old notion of *impietas;* the Greek classical notion of *asebeia* (which in its turn affected the notion of *impietas* from the times of the Roman Republic), the Greek (mainly Septuagint) rendering of various Hebrew words indicating "evil"-doers and "evil" doings, and finally the early Christian transformation—partly with Jewish precedents—of the classical notion of *asebeia.*

No doubt the story of impiety begins much earlier. The Hebrew notions which contributed to the formation of the Christian notion of impiety have to be compared with Egyptian and Akkadian notions. The question has to be asked whether this comparison points to Egyptian and Akkadian models for Hebrew ideas. This question is legitimate because Egyptian and Akkadian religious hymns and didactic literature, in which such notions are deeply embedded, have long been known for their similarities in other respects to Hebrew texts. But unfortunately Egyptologists and Assyriologists have not yet made available to other scholars a clear analysis of the Egyptian and Assyrian vocabularies referring to the transgression of the approved order of things. We are left uncertain even about the existence of a "secular" zone in these civilizations, though we have repeatedly been told that Mesopotamian law is strictly "secular." The fact that leading Egyptologists apply the term "heresy" (a purely Christian notion) to the religious reform of Akhnaton is evidence of this confused state of affairs.

We shall only note in passing that the Egyptians had various words to indicate the fool, the ignorant, the senseless, the man who does not want to be educated, in situations which recall the actions of the impious in Jewish-Christian terminology. There is also in Egyptian a word, usually translated as "abomination" (*bwt*), which indicates the religious interdiction of certain acts; the prohibition affects not only cultual acts, but rules of behavior, such as lying and displaying a lack of solidarity with one's fellow citizens (see for instance the list of interdictions for nome XVIII collected in the Ptolemaic period in the Jumilhac Papyrus).

Similarly, Mesopotamian texts provide an abundant terminology for the godless, the wicked, the impure, the blasphemous, etc. A word which is translated by "abomination" (*ik-kibu*) can apply both to human actions and to the presence of a pig in a temple. From these texts it is possible to fabricate a composite image of a Mesopotamian anomic man who superficially is not very different from his apposite number in Egypt. But confessions of sins and purifications, not to speak of divination, played a far greater part in the life of Mesopotamian man (at least in the second and first millennia B.C.) than in Egypt. The techniques of evoking or re-establishing the protection of the gods in this life were both more necessary and more developed in Mesopotamia than in Egypt. The Mesopotamians had what the Egyptians seem to have lacked—a comprehensive idea of sin. The Egyptian was taught how to proclaim his innocence in the afterlife, but seldom confessed his transgressions in this life. The confessions of sins found at Deir-el-Medina, a village west of Thebes, are those of workers for the kings of the XIXth dynasty (thirteenth century B.C.) and may be due to foreign influence. As the Mesopotamian king was normally not considered to be a god, he was capable of sins and had to proclaim his innocence every year at the festival of Marduk. The faults of an Egyptian king, who *was* a god, were a far more delicate question. Only the successor of Akhnaton was in a position to deal with the religious vagaries of his predecessor.

Two features immediately strike the observer when he passes from Mesopotamia to Israel. The Hebrews practiced a collective confession of sins (apart from the individual one); they never seem to have singled out the sins of the king as the only sins relevant to the welfare of the community as a whole. Their religious life was based on a unique relation to Yahweh, and this affected everyone. At different times and in different writers the transgression against Yahweh might be idolatry (the main theme of the Deuteronomic writer) or an offense against the rules of justice (one of the main themes of prophetic preaching). There was also a progression from the emphasis on the collective solidarity of Israel to the notion of the individual responsibility of each Jew. The offense of the sinners might (or might not) be presented in juridical terms as a violation of the Covenant between Yahweh and Israel. All these (and many other) aspects of the Hebrew understanding of the state of *anomia* are represented in the Old Testament with very little effort to harmonize and unify them. What emerges, however, is the insistence on a proper relationship between Yahweh and the Jew which is based on the justice of both. Yahweh *is* just, and the Jew *may* be just: in some writers justice is indeed extended to the non-Jew. But Yahweh can never be unjust, though questions about his justice are asked—and seldom rhetorically. Man can be, and very often is, unjust; there is, however, no precise suggestion that he is irretrievably unjust by nature. The Hebrew words we translate by "just" (*zaddik*) and "unjust" (*rasa*ᶜ) are some of the most common and central terms of the Old Testament (*rasa*ᶜ 261 times). But there are other terms such as "pious" (*hasid*) and "rebellious" which complete the picture. All these terms were often translated rather indiscriminately into Greek by *eusebes* and *asebes* (significantly, the Septuagint writers do not use the word *atheos*), and thus contributed to the Jewish-Christian connotation of *asebes* and *asebeia* as impiety involving idolatry and/or violation of the moral rules imposed by the true god. The classical notion of *asebeia* was differently oriented and, on the whole, more limited in scope.

Post-biblical Hebrew had new words to indicate the Jewish unbeliever, an indication of a new situation in which outright skepticism, on the one hand, and sectarian distinctions within Judaism, on the other hand, became prominent. One word has a familiar Greek ring, *apikuros*, meaning the individual skeptic or unbeliever (to be found, for instance, in a saying by Rabbi Eleazar ben Arach which is quoted in the "Sayings of the Fathers"). The other word is *min* (literally "species," "sect"), indicating the man (plural *minim*) who holds opinions at variance with the Jewish orthodox faith, for instance, the Judeo-Christian or the Gnostic. Rabbi Samuel the Little, a pupil of Rabbi Gamliel II, wrote a prayer for the extirpation of the *minim* about the end of the first century A.D., which was inserted in the "Eighteen Benedictions." This is also approximately the time in which we meet the prototype of the Jewish "heretics," Elisha ben Abujah. Judaism was engaged in fighting both the spread of Christianity and internal dissolution. The notion of *min* is certainly parallel to the notion of heretic which Saint Paul found among the Christians of his time. It may have been provoked by it.

There is a further question about the connection of these two notions (*min*, heretic) with the notion of *zandik* which appears in Middle Persian to indicate those who interpret the *Zand* or commentary of the Avesta in an unorthodox way and more generally the unbeliever, the dissident—sometimes the Manichean.

The Iranian evidence seems to be later than the Christian and Jewish (third century A.D.).

II. ASEBEIA: IMPIETY IN GREECE

The Greeks did not know heresy: they knew *asebeia*, as opposed to *eusebeia*, which is the proper behavior towards the gods, the parents (and the native land), and the dead. The word *asebeia* first appears in a line of Theognis (line 1180). Theognis tells his friend Kyrnos that fear of the gods prevents the doing and the saying of "impiety." Thus, in the sixth century B.C., the Greeks knew that man can either do or say something *asebes*, impious, but the term is not explained more precisely. A fragment of Pindar (132, Schroeder) would be much more interesting: it says that the souls of the impious hover between earth and sky. Unfortunately this fragment is almost certainly spurious (late Hellenistic?). Fifth- and fourth-century evidence about *asebeia* is much fuller. It confirms that *asebeia* was not confined to offenses against gods. One might be *asebes*, impious, in relation to the dead, to one's own parents, to ambassadors of foreign countries, etc. In the criminal law of Athens *asebeia* was a technical term. Felling of sacred trees was probably treated as *asebeia* just as much as parody of mysteries. The wrong type of sacrifice for a given occasion might be *asebes*. We also have evidence that the introduction of new gods into the *polis* was, at least in certain cases, considered a crime. On the whole one gathers the impression that *asebeia* was an offense against established religious customs rather than a denial of accepted dogmas.

About 430 B.C. a law was passed that extended the scope of the crime of *asebeia* and penalized opinion in religious matters as such. The decree of Diopithes which was directed against Anaxagoras penalized both atheism and the introduction of new doctrines about celestial phenomena (Plutarch, *Pericles* 32; cf. [Pseudo-] Lysias, 6, 10). This was, no doubt, the law that made possible the prosecution, and in certain cases the condemnation, of philosophers living in Athens during the late fifth century and the fourth century B.C. The list of names includes Protagoras, Socrates, Stilpo, Theodorus of Cyrene, Aristotle, and Theophrastus. Aspasia, too, was probably accused of impiety under this law.

Doubts about the existence of the gods had become fashionable among the Sophists, and this law tried to cope with the new situation. It is, however, worth noticing that there are political reasons for all these accusations. Anaxagoras and Protagoras (not to mention Aspasia) were accused because they were friends of Pericles; Socrates was accused because he was a friend of the oligarchs; the later philosophers were all pro-Macedonian. Furthermore, it must be observed that we have no evidence of persecution of philosophers

565

in Athens after the fourth century B.C. In the Greek world outside Athens, evidence of persecution for impiety is limited, as far as we know, to some obscure allusions. They refer to the persecution of the pessimist Hegesias in Alexandria; to the expulsion of one or more philosophers from Thrace under Lysimachus, and to the expulsion of philosophers in general from Syria, possibly under Antiochus VI, and from Messene. The reasons for the persecutions are never given, except in the case of Hegesias, whose pessimistic lectures increased the rate of suicides in Egypt (Cicero, *Tusculan Disputations* I, 83). The goddess Asebeia, to whom the notorious admiral of Philip V, Dicaearchus, is said to have built an altar about 200 B.C., was not the goddess of freethinkers, but of pirates.

Thus our evidence suggests that the incrimination of persons for their religious opinions as such was a peculiarity of Athens. Even there it was used as a political weapon not earlier than about 430 B.C. and not later than the end of the fourth century B.C. It is, however, possible that some of the persecutions of philosophers during the Hellenistic age were due to genuine religious motives.

The Athenian prosecutions of the philosophers are the historical precedent for the penalization of religious opinions advocated by Plato in his *Laws*. Plato proposes to punish a man who believes that the gods do not exist or that the gods exist but are indifferent to mankind or that they are to be easily won over by the cajolings of offerings and prayers. Plato's opinion—altogether remarkable for a pupil of the persecuted Socrates—is made even more remarkable by the fact that he does not uphold the traditional city-state religion, with its Olympian gods, but his own theological tenets. Furthermore, Plato elaborates a system of moral pressure before actual punishment that reminds us of later ecclesiastical practices. Even in this case we cannot speak of repression of heresy because the notions of revelation and apostolic tradition are absent. Yet there is no doubt that Plato helped to keep alive the notion that opinion on theological matters can and must be penalized. Though it would be difficult to indicate the channels through which Platonic thought percolated—and it would be unjust to make Plato alone the fountainhead of intolerance—it is certain that he encouraged uniformity of opinions in religious matters. Plato contributed to the notion of heresy insofar as he contributed to the idea of intolerance.

On the other hand, the evidence makes it very difficult to assume a direct influence of the notion of *asebeia*, as defined by Diopithes, on the origins of heresy. Intolerance in religious matters was not widespread in the Hellenistic age. The difficulties are increased by an internal analysis of the notion of *asebeia*.

There are certainly analogies between the accusations against philosophers in Athens and the accusations against heretics in Christianity. The city claimed an authority comparable to that of the Christian Church insofar as it decided who were the people with the right kind of opinion. But the differences are obvious. In Athens a man was not incriminated because he disagreed with the majority about the nature of god, but because he denied the existence of the gods of the polis or offended them by introducing competitors or behaved improperly towards them. The punishment of unorthodox opinions about heavenly bodies was in fact the condemnation of doctrines that denied their divine nature. Furthermore, as the Greeks had no sacred books—Homer was not one—the problem of deciding who were their authorized interpreters did not exist. While the essential feature of heresy is opposition to the official interpretation of a religious doctrine by a Church, the essential feature of impiety as described by Diopithes' decree is either denial of the existence of the gods of the polis or offense given to the gods of the polis. It follows that the corporate body primarily concerned with the repression of impiety is not that of priests or theologians, but that of ordinary citizens.

III. LATIN IMPIETAS

The oldest meaning of *pius, pietas* seems to have been "what is acceptable to the gods." The archaic formula about just war—*puro pioque bello* (Livy I, 32)—reflects this way of thinking, which has parallels in other languages of ancient Italy. Hence *piaculum, piare* in sacral language. In the ordinary Latin of republican and imperial times, *pius* characterizes proper behavior towards gods, parents and other relatives, and the Roman state, as well as respect for treaties. "Pius Aeneas" and "Antoninus Pius" got their nickname from their behavior towards their respective fathers. *Impius, impietas* indicated of course the opposite, and normally expressed strong disapproval, though there are strange exceptions in inscriptions which seem to use *impius* in the sense of "unhappy." The influence of *eusebes* and *asebes* accentuated the subjective, personal aspects rather than the ritualistic connotations of *pietas* and *impietas*. Vergil, more than anybody else, made *pius* an attribute of the ideal Roman, and thus rendered *impius* an un-Roman qualification. Propaganda in coins and inscriptions broadcasted *pietas*. Augustus claimed *pietas* as one of his qualities (with *virtus, clementia, iustitia*). But *impius, impietas* never became important words of Roman political ideology. They primarily remained words of the domestic and religious life. There was never a crime of *impietas* in Roman law (notwithstanding some texts to the contrary, such as Tacitus, *Annales* 6, 47); religious persecution was based on other grounds. Latin-speaking Christians had no difficulty in using *impius* and *impietas* with the new meanings which Greek-speaking Christians had attributed to *asebes* and *asebeia:* disregard of god, idolatry, and even heresy.

BIBLIOGRAPHY

For Egypt see A. Erman, *Die Religion der Ägypter* (Berlin, 1934); H. Frankfort, *Ancient Egyptian Religion* (New York, 1948); S. Morenz, *Ägyptische Religion* (Stuttgart, 1960). For Mesopotamia: Ch. F. Jean, *Le péché chez les Babyloniens et les Assyriens* (Paris, 1925); J. Morgenstern, *The Doctrine of Sin in the Babylonian Religion* (Berlin, 1905); A. L. Oppenheim, *Ancient Mesopotamia* (Chicago, 1964); A. van Selms, *De Babylonische Termini voor Zonde*, dissertation (Utrecht, 1933). For both Egypt and Mesopotamia in relation to Judaism: *Les sagesses du Proche-Orient, colloque de Strasbourg* (Paris, 1963), with bibliography; H. H. Schmid, *Wesen und Geschichte der Weisheit* (Berlin, 1966). For the Jews and early Christians: M. Avi-Yonah, *Geschichte der Juden im Zeitalter des Talmud* (Berlin, 1962), pp. 136–45; W. Eichrodt, *Theologie des Alten Testaments*, 5 ed., Vol. II (Stuttgart, 1964); L. Köhler, *Theologie des Alten Testaments* (Tübingen, 1936); J. Neusner, *A History of the Jews in Babylonia* (Leiden, 1968), III, 12–16; G. von Rad, *Theologie des Alten Testaments*, Vol. II (Munich, 1962); H. L. Strack, *Jesus, Die Häretiker und die Christen* (Leipzig, 1910); *Theologisches Wörterbuch zum Neuen Testament* (Stuttgart, 1964), VII, 168–95; G. Vermes, *In Memoriam Paul Kahle* (Berlin, 1968), pp. 232–40. For Iran: U. Bianchi, *Zaman i Ohrmazd* (Turin, 1958), p. 160; H. H. Schaeder, *Iranische Beiträge*, Vol. I (Halle, 1930); G. Widengren, *Iranisch-Semitische Kulturbegegnung in parthischer Zeit* (Opladen, 1960), p. 104; R. C. Zaehner, *Zurvan* (Oxford, 1955). For the Greeks: J. C. Bolkestein, *Hosios en Eusebes* (Amsterdam, 1936); P. Décharme, *La critique des traditions religieuses chez les Grecs* (Paris, 1904); E. Derenne, *Les procès d'impiété* (Paris, 1930); W. Fahr, *Theous nomizein* (Hildesheim, 1969); D. Loenen, "Eusebia en de cardinale deugden," *Med. Kon. Nederlandse Akad.*, N.R. **23**, 4 (1960); J. Rudhart, *Notions fondamentales de la pensée religieuse et actes constitutifs du culte dans la Grèce classique* (Geneva, 1958); idem, *Museum Helveticum*, **17** (1960), 87–105; W. J. Tergesten, *Eusebes en Hosios in het grieksch taalgebruik na de IV Eeuw* (Utrecht, 1941). For the Romans: M. P. Charlesworth, *Journal of Roman Studies*, **33** (1943), 1–10; H. Fugier, *Recherches sur l'expression du sacré dans la langue latine* (Paris, 1963); K. Latte, *Römische Religionsgeschichte* (Munich, 1960), pp. 39–40; Th. Mommsen, *Römisches Strafrecht* (Leipzig, 1899), pp. 540, 583; *Thesaurus Linguae Latinae*, Vol. VII (Leipzig, 1934–61), see *impietas*; S. C. Tromp, *De Romanorum piaculis* (Utrecht, 1921); Th. Ulrich, *Pietas(pius) als politischer Begriff* (Breslau, 1930). In general: R. Pettazzoni, *La confessione dei peccati* (Bologna, 1929–35).

ARNALDO MOMIGLIANO

[See also **Heresy**; Platonism; Prophecy in Hebrew Scripture; **Religious Toleration**.]

IMPRESSIONISM IN ART

1. The Impressionist Revolt against Academic Painting. The word "impressionism" is applied to a style of painting which flourished, especially in France, during the eighteen-seventies. Most of the impressionists emphasized effects of sunlight and color in landscape, as produced by a technique of painting in perceptible, contrasting brush-strokes and dabs of relatively unmixed colors. The concept of impressionism was later extended to somewhat analogous styles in other arts, including sculpture, music, and literature.

Impressionist painting spread to England, the United States of America, and other countries. During the eighteen-eighties it developed along divergent lines which led to post-impressionism and various twentieth-century styles. It is still practiced to a lesser extent by conservative painters, sometimes in combination with other techniques.

This article will deal mainly with impressionism in painting, but will touch also on some of its historical and cultural relationships, including analogous styles in other arts.

The following are usually classed as impressionists: Édouard Manet, Claude Monet, Camille Pissarro, Paul Cézanne, Edgar Degas, James A. McNeill Whistler, Alfred Sisley, Auguste Renoir, and Berthe Morisot. Georges Seurat is sometimes classed as an impressionist; more often as a post-impressionist or pointillist.

The leaders of impressionism in the eighteen-seventies differed considerably as individuals. They produced several new styles, which can be regarded as variants of impressionism. Some of them painted in the impressionist manner at times and differently at other times. They were united for a while by a spirit of revolt against the official Paris Salon. This led some of them to exhibit as a group in the *Salon des Refusés,* beginning in 1874. Their aim was to show the public experimental works of the kind which they had been exhibiting separately, and which had been rejected by the ultraconservative juries of the official Salon. As a group and as individual artists, they made a lasting contribution to art in helping to free the painter from outworn, academic rules, and in calling his attention to the wealth of color and light in the world about him. The impetus they gave to a progressive, experimental attitude in all the arts has lasted up to the present day, even though the attention of style leaders has moved on to other tasks and methods.

The nature of this contribution can be most clearly understood by contrasting it with the academic tradition of the official Paris Salon, which exercised great power by appointing juries to decide which contemporary works could be exhibited under its favorable

FIGURE 1, OPPOSITE TOP. Édouard Manet, *Boating*. 1874. THE METROPOLITAN MUSEUM OF ART, BEQUEST OF MRS. H. O. HAVEMEYER, 1929. THE H. O. HAVEMEYER COLLECTION. NEW YORK

FIGURE 2, OPPOSITE BOTTOM. Claude Monet, *La Gare St. Lazare*. 1877. FOGG ART MUSEUM, HARVARD UNIVERSITY. BEQUEST—COLLECTION OF MAURICE WERTHEIM

FIGURE 3, RIGHT. J. A. McN. Whistler, *Nocturne in Black and Gold: The Falling Rocket*. ca. 1874. COURTESY OF THE DETROIT INSTITUTE OF ARTS. PURCHASE, THE DEXTER M. FERRY, JR. FUND

FIGURE 4, BELOW. Pierre Auguste Renoir, *Le Moulin de la Galette*. 1876. LOUVRE, PARIS. AGRACI–ART REFERENCE BUREAU

auspices. Year after year, the Salon favored dramatic, religious, historical, and mythological scenes, often in a rather tightly formal, monumental style of composition, symmetrical or firmly balanced, and self-contained. It favored smooth, gracefully neo-classical forms, emphasizing line and solid shape rather than color and light, and modeled in a weak version of the sculptural style of Raphael and the Florentine Renaissance. As in the paintings of Nicolas Poussin (1594–1665) and J. A. D. Ingres (1780–1867), color was secondary to line, mass, and perspective. It was usually added after the composition, highlights, and dark shadows had been sketched in without it. Usual subjects were the parks, palaces, wars, and amusements of the rich and the noble in all their luxury, in addition to trivial genre scenes, pretty nudes, and sentimental conversation pieces. Academic art often tended to flatter the government and the wealthy bourgeoisie, as well as the hereditary aristocracy and the higher clergy. Typical academic painters of the eighteen-fifties were Thomas Couture and William Adolphe Bouguereau.

Most academic or Salon painting was done in the studio; most impressionist painting out of doors. The latter was based more on direct observation of nature. The Salon pictures tended to make all figures and objects almost equally sharp and clear, except in the misty, aerial perspective of distant horizons. Impressionists saw that even under the clearest weather conditions, only those parts of the field of vision on which attention is focused have maximum sharpness; others seem somewhat vague, blurred, or shadowy. So it was, in a sense, realistic to represent them so. Likewise, according to the impressionists, the eyes tend to see some reflected color in shadows. To represent them so is realistic and also enriches the texture of the whole picture.

The impressionists favored a direct, painterly approach to the canvas in terms of pure colors, with little or no mixture on the palette. Instead of beginning with a dark surface for the shadows and gradually building up the highlights through a succession of lighter glazes, they followed from the start various methods for achieving a lighter, brighter surface. One method (sometimes practiced by Manet) was to begin with a very light surface and gradually to fill in the darker areas, putting shadows where they would help produce a luminous design, full of contrasts (Figure 1).

The characteristics most commonly associated with the name "impressionism" are those of Claude Monet. They are found to some extent in the work of others of the group, but not all of them, and even Monet did not always use this method. These characteristics (called *stylistic traits*) consist (1) in representing scenes in such a way as to emphasize the reflections of sunlight on colored objects out of doors, including the vibrating or shimmering effect which sunlight often produces; (2) as a means to this end, the technique of juxtaposing small strokes or dabs of different unmixed colors closely together. This method has been called "broken color" or "divided color" and also, "vibrism" or "divisionism." In such painting, color and light tend to dominate over line and solid shape. These remain, but the contours of objects are often somewhat blurred and their relative distances obscured by the brilliance of the colored surfaces. Extremely bright, shimmering tonalities are often achieved by this method, but not always. Dimmer effects of winter, mist, or evening half-lights are also sought; in each case with a definite tonality approximating one observable in the everyday world (Figure 2).

Degas sometimes used divided color in his ballet scenes, not to represent sunlight, but for a general effect of rich color and artificial luminosity, as under a theater spotlight.

2. Types of Pictorial Impressionism. The two stylistic traits just mentioned have at times been practiced separately, producing individual variants. These will be called in the present article Types One and Two of pictorial impressionism. While many of the impressionists dealt with bright sunlight reflections at various times of day and seasons of the year, one of them, Whistler, worked out a variant of Type One in showing moonlight, twilight, the glow of lamps as seen through fog or reflected on moving water, and the flashing, short-lived brilliance of fireworks (Figure 3). Whistler, born in America but living in England, was in close touch with the French group. He preferred the darker, more subtle and delicate lights and atmospheres near dawn or darkness, to the often glaring, obvious effects of full sunshine. He liked the momentary burst of soaring rockets against a black sky, and the wispy streaks of lamplight on distant strollers in a park. He used the butterfly as part of his signature, to symbolize the lightly poised, ephemeral nature of the phenomena he chose to represent.

One of the outstanding characteristics of sunlight reflection is the rapid change and evanescence of each particular aspect, as in a sunrise or sunset. As one looks and tries to set it down in paint, it is fast changing into something different. Its beauty is fleeting, and for that very reason even a partial success in arresting it on canvas can be welcome. This was an ever-present interest of Monet and of others in the group. But sunlight is not the only kind of transitory, quickly vanishing phenomenon. In many of Degas' works there is little or no vivid sunlight. The emphasis is not on color, but on momentary configurations of line and solid shape, such as those formed by the prancing legs of racehorses or the graceful movements of ballet dancers. These he represented again and again, often with rich color but without the sunlight radiance which Monet sought. To heighten the effect of rapid change, he often showed part of a figure at the edge of the canvas, overlapped by the frame, as if just entering or leaving the picture. A group of persons in a café corner could be shown as if arranged by accident and about to move (Figure 4). This was foreign to the posed and self-contained, monumental type of composition which the Salon favored. Conservatives referred to it as "bleeding off." Degas' bathing women, maids, laundresses, and shopgirls lacked the academic types of statuesque beauty admired by academic taste, but they presented unconventional, unposed, naturalistic designs, formed by living bodies in the course of ordinary activities.

This emphasis on transitory visual phenomena, other than light reflections, produced a third type of pictorial impressionism. If one had to choose a single, very comprehensive term to characterize impressionism in general, it might well be that of representing transitory phenomena. But this would ignore some other important variants and oversimplify the account.

The quality of transitoriness is sometimes attributed to the scene or object depicted, sometimes to the artist's perception of a still or moving object, and sometimes to both. In any case, the artist tries to communicate that quality to the observer. It is not implied that the artist worked quickly or sketchily. He may have done so, or he may have labored long to produce that appearance. Said Degas: "No art was ever less spontaneous than mine. . . . Of inspiration, spontaneity, temperament I know nothing" (Rewald, p. 177). "The study of nature," he said, "is of no significance." It was more important, he thought, to learn to draw as Holbein did.

Although Degas is now commonly classed as an impressionist, because of his association with the group and his interest in transitory phenomena, he did not like this designation for himself. He preferred to be called a naturalist or realist, and these terms fit him equally well. Like Courbet, he represented many aspects of life and the world, including some which are commonly regarded as ugly. He depicted scenes of city life as well as the countryside, and did not avoid subjects possessing dramatic, human interest. In choosing city scenes and human activities, both he and Courbet stepped outside what is commonly called "nature" in a narrow sense of that word. In a broader sense man and all his works, as well as dancers and racehorses, are all parts of nature. Artists who classed themselves as naturalists, in the mid-nineteenth century, stressed the ideal of truth in art, as opposed to the specious,

FIGURE 5. Edgar Degas, *Danseuse sur Scène*. ca. 1876. LOUVRE, PARIS. AGRACI–ART REFERENCE BUREAU

artificial beauties of the classic and romantic schools. Many of the characters whom Courbet and Degas represented were from the working class, and these artists showed them objectively, without emotional partisanship. Most of the impressionists showed a more specialized interest in the purely visual aspects of country landscape.

Degas' trait of letting human figures, horses, and other objects emerge from the edge of the picture, so that parts of them are cut off, makes some of his pictures look like modern photographic snapshots (Figure 5). In amateur photography, this may be a result of careless failure to organize the picture within the rectangular frame. With Degas, it is intended for the sake of heightening the transitory, momentary aspect of the scene.

The similarity has caused some writers to suppose that Degas was influenced by photography. The extent of this influence, if any, is controversial. Baudelaire denounced photography as impoverishing French art

571

(Rewald, p. 33). The Daguerrotype process had been invented by Daguerre and Niepce in 1839, and photography had had a generation of development since then. As men of the world, living much in Paris, the impressionists must have noticed this development and wondered about its future possibilities. James Clerk Maxwell, physicist, demonstrated a kind of color photography in the eighteen-sixties, but a practicable method was not invented until 1904. This was done by the Lumière brothers in France. (C. G. and M. R. Mueller, p. 72). In the eighteen-seventies photography was still rather slow and laborious. The age of fast snapshots, of the candid camera indoors and out, was still far off. Still more remote was the motion-picture film. Degas had little to learn from the actual photographs of his day, most of which were very static portraits. But there can be no doubt of the opposite influence: that of Degas' action-drawing on photography and the cinema.

It was not until near the end of the century that the possibilities of photography as a medium for serious art were commonly recognized. The possibility of representing moving bodies by that means, and stationary bodies as if from a moving point of view, was actively demonstrated in the last decade of the century. Still photography and painting could not carry it far enough to satisfy the demand for movement, which eventually led to the motion picture. The interest in realistic light and color, stimulated and satisfied to a large extent by the impressionists, led eventually to the color film of the twentieth century. Still photography was a democratic medium, requiring little expenditure or technical training for the amateur, although such training and equipment brought additional rewards.

The recent high development of color photography, especially in the film, has led some critics to disparage impressionist painting as limited in scope and superseded by these mechanical devices. It is certainly true that some of the things landscape painting tried to do, and did with much difficulty in the nineteenth century, are now done in a flash by color photography without the aid of laborious techniques. The same sort of claim can be made for color photography as replacing all realistic painting, of human figures, animals, still life, and every other subject. But one should not, of course, minimize the personal touch which is still vitally important in art. In spite of the great advances which it has made, photography is still much less flexible than painting, and less capable of expressing the subtleties of individual style. This may not always be the case, and the ways in which the film can excel painting are already numerous.

In the meantime, it is well to remember that many of the effects now most admired in color film and photography were derived from previous paintings, impressionist and other. In the best color films, one is often struck by the number of shots adapted from paintings. In the cinema, the term "impressionism" has come to mean a series of shots which build up a mood or atmosphere, or the quality of a scene, without any definite story or logical connection. The representation of change and motion, which could not be fully achieved in still painting, is raised by the film to a level of infinite power and scope. But, fascinating as it can be in a theater, or for occasional showings at home, it does not fulfill the functions of a motionless picture which can be hung on a wall or painted on a wall, to be studied carefully at will, or seen "out of the corner of one's eye," as an ever-present source of enjoyment.

3. Beginnings of and Changing Attitudes toward Impressionism. The word "impression" as applied to a painting, and "impressionism" as applied to the style developed by Monet and his friends, were used at first as terms of ridicule. At the time, they implied something hasty and superficial, perhaps unfinished, crude, and therefore inferior to the academic product. European taste, elite and popular, had for centuries favored works of art and other products which were finely finished, like a smoothly polished piece of furniture, as a sign that the workman was master of his craft. True, Michelangelo and a few other great artists had left some apparently unfinished surfaces, but this method had not been widely followed. The influence of Ingres, Corot, J. L. David, Boucher, and Chardin had been on the side of smooth finish. That of Delacroix had not, but he had been bitterly attacked by Ingres and others for his emphasis on color.

To call one's picture an "impression," as Monet modestly did in 1874, suggested that it was not thoroughly worked out; that it was rather incomplete and unimportant as a picture, though perhaps worth keeping as a souvenir of a brief experience. To call a picture by someone else a "mere impression" was definitely belittling. These ambivalent meanings helped to make the painters themselves rather doubtful about it, until the movement acquired substantial prestige.

Later on, their friendly critics insisted that a picture was not necessarily bad or trivial, merely because it recorded a quick impression. It could even be, in a sense, superficial; that is, concerned with surfaces and with directly visible aspects, rather than with inner structures. It could seem unfinished by ordinary standards, and yet have reached the point in its development at which the painter wished to stop; at which he had said all he wished to say in this particular work, and at which he would defeat its purpose if he said more. In its own way, the picture is completely finished. The practice of omitting some visible details, which might not be noticed in a quick glance, was not only excusable, but a positive means to the desired effect of evanescence, as in a landscape with setting sun. In addition, it might be a means to bringing out a design.

The steps which led to the acceptance of impressionism by influential critics can be summarized as follows (Rewald, p. 19). The Academy of Fine Arts in Paris, a part of the *Institut de France,* had long ruled the world of art through its power to select the jury for choosing pictures to be shown at the biennial Salon. The prestige to be gained by exhibiting there could bring fame and fortune to a young artist, especially by recommending his work to wealthy and official patrons. Students who followed the academic rules and the tastes of their teachers were likely to profit by it. Individual protests against the situation had not been lacking, but had produced little effect.

As the time for opening the Salon of 1863 drew near, rumors circulated that the jury was to be more severe than ever. In April the official results showed that three-fifths of the five thousand paintings submitted had been rejected (Rewald, p. 79). A storm of protests broke out, some of which reached the ears of Emperor Napoleon III. He proposed that the rejected works be shown elsewhere in the same building as the Salon proper. This was done, much to the satisfaction of the young radicals. The new exhibition was entitled the *Salon des Refusés.* Manet, Whistler, Pissarro, Cézanne, and Jongkind were among those exhibiting (Rewald, p. 80). The crowds are said to have mingled surprise with laughter. Most of the comments were negative, but a few critics ventured to praise the *Refusés,* notably Fernand Desnoyers and Jules Antoine Castagnary. Émile Zola was hesitant, but on the whole friendly, especially to Manet. Zacharie Astruc praised Manet with enthusiasm, but the Emperor considered his *Déjeuner sur l'herbe* "immodest." (This painting, of a nude outdoors in the company of two clothed men, was not impressionist but a naturalistic version of a Raphael engraving.) In 1863 Charles Baudelaire, a discerning critic and important poet, in praising the sketches of contemporary life by Constantin Guys, put his finger on an essential feature of impressionism. It was the artist's role, he declared, "to disengage the eternal factors from the transitory ones." He coined the word "modernité," which he defined as "the transitory, the fugitive, the contingent, one-half of art of which the other half is the eternal and the immutable" (Rewald, p. 127).

In the late sixties, many appeals were sent to officials for a new *Salon des Refusés,* but without success. Courbet and Manet built their own pavilions in the World's Fair of 1867. Meanwhile, the loosely assembled group of radicals (as yet unnamed) drew closer together and engaged in active, café discussions, especially about the merits of open-air painting, which most of them favored. Individually, they exhibited in shops and galleries. Some of them were extremely poor, especially Monet. Only Manet was really wealthy. Degas and Sisley were moderately affluent. Year after year, paintings in the new style attracted more attention from the critics, pro and con.

In 1873 the group organized as a joint stock company, under a vague title (*Société des artistes, peintres,* etc.) which did not commit the members to any particular style of art. Degas cooperated with it, but called it a "realist" movement. Manet refrained from exhibiting with them.

When the pictures were being hung in 1874, Renoir's brother Edmond (in charge of editing the catalogue) objected to the monotonous titles Monet had given to his works. They were, for example, *Entrance of a Village, Leaving the Village, Morning in a Village,* and the like. Monet then replied: "Why don't you just put Impression!" The picture he selected, a view of Le Havre from his window with the sun appearing through vapors, painted in 1872, was catalogued as *Impression, Sunrise* (Rewald, pp. 315–17).

Shortly after the show opened, under the title "Exhibition of the Impressionists," an article ridiculing it appeared in the magazine *Charivari.* It was signed by Louis Leroy (Rewald, pp. 318, 608). The article consisted of an imaginary conversation between himself and an academic landscape painter during a visit to the exhibition. Paintings by Renoir, Monet, Pissarro, Sisley, and others were appraised in such terms as "palette-scrapings," "dirty canvas," "black tongue-lickings," "mud-splashes," "hair-raising," "slap-dash," and "noxious." Sarcastic remarks were made about the term "impression." "Leave me alone, now, with your impression . . . it's neither here nor there."

This magazine, says Mr. Rewald, is the first publication in which the painters were called "impressionists," and it is typical of the countless attacks made on the successive group exhibitions. The first publication devoted to the impressionist group avoided the term "impressionist." It was by Edmond Duranty, *La nouvelle peinture* (1876), and dealt with "the group of artists who exhibit at the Durand-Ruel Galleries." An English critic, P. S. Hamerton, charged them with "neglect of details, their lack of drawing, their indifference to the charm of composition." An anonymous American critic called two pictures by Monet "two of the most absurd daubs in that laughable collection of absurdities." But the young poet, Stéphane Mallarmé, defended the group, while J. A. Castagnary praised them as making a step in the right direction.

573

"They are impressionists," he said, "in the sense that they render not a landscape but the sensation produced by a landscape" (Rewald, p. 330). H. Garland, in *Crumbling Idols* (1894), published what Mr. Rewald calls "the first all-out defense of the movement to be written in English." The first definition of the term "impressionists," says Mr. Rewald, came from a friend of Renoir who wrote: "Treating a subject in terms of the tone and not of the subject itself, that is what distinguishes the impressionists from other painters" (p. 338). This was hardly an adequate definition of the style.

Mr. Rewald's own descriptive summary of impressionism in painting mentions several aims or effects and several technical means to them. The impressionists, he writes, "selected one element from reality—light—to interpret all of nature." They sought "to retain the fluid play of light" and to enrich the color effects. "The multitude of obvious touches and the contrasts among them had helped to express or suggest the activity, the scintillation of light." The painter sought, through a technique of vivid strokes, "to retain

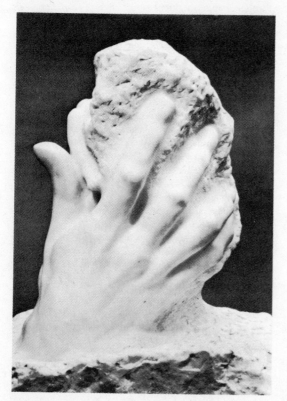

FIGURE 6. Auguste Rodin, *The Hand of God*. Before 1898. THE METROPOLITAN MUSEUM OF ART, NEW YORK. GIFT OF EDWARD D. ADAMS, 1908

rapidly changing aspects" and to work rapidly in choosing some of the aspects presented by nature, "in order to translate the miracles of light into a language of pigment and two dimensions" (p. 338). This list of characteristics applies, obviously, to pictorial impressionism but not to the analogous styles in music and literature. Within the impressionist group, it applies more to the individual style of Monet than to that of Degas.

4. Sculptural Impressionism. In the very different art of sculpture, a tendency arose which is somewhat analogous to impressionist painting. Sculptural impressionism is most highly developed in the work of Auguste Rodin (Figure 6). As if to ignore and overcome the inherently static, rigid quality of marble and bronze, he represented in them the most fluid, melting, and evanescent of forms, such as clouds and water. Human or human-like figures in his work seem to be in the process of breathing, awakening, moving, or expiring; of being created by the hand of God. Rough, uneven, deliberately unfinished parts abound in his statues, as if to show the finished parts emerging from them. (In this he shows the influence of Michelangelo.) In portrait sculpture, Rodin's surfaces are sensitive and expressive, while he often seems to care little for building a strong inner structure.

In *The Age of Bronze* (also called *The Awakening of Man*), Rodin expressed his early interest in evolution and primitive man. Rodin's sculptural style can be linked with Degas as a kind of visual impressionism. It relies, not on color, but on surface and solid shape, together with light reflections, to suggest the moving, changing aspects of living flesh and human feeling.

5. Musical and Literary Impressionism. Musical and literary impressionism constitute a fifth and sixth manifestation of the style. They consist in representing the transitory nature of phenomena other than visual ones, especially in music and poetry. As often happens in the history of a style, the name "impressionist" was applied more and more broadly in the late nineteenth and early twentieth centuries. It was differently understood by artists working in different media. Artists and critics discerned analogous effects in various arts and in those aspects of the outside world perceptible through different senses. Baudelaire had pointed out what he called *Correspondances* between the various senses. Some composers felt that certain keys in music resembled certain colors. Individuals differed on just what these associations were, but the discussion stimulated active efforts to produce in music and poetry effects like those of impressionist painting. For these they used rich, dissonant chords and unusual rhythmic and harmonic effects, as well as exotic instrumental timbres.

There was a real psychological ground for these efforts in that music and literature, being time arts, are inherently adapted for suggesting change and movement. This is not a question of any fixed limits for *pictura* and *poesis*, or of what they ought to do, but of what is relatively easy and natural for them. Music, moreover, is usually hampered by its own self-imposed limitations which are derived from trying to imitate natural sounds exactly, but it can and does try to suggest in its own way moods, actions, and ideas analogous to those conveyed in other arts. Impressionist music broke up the traditional "correct" harmonic and melodic progressions and reorganized the elements into more free, impulsive, irregular forms.

In the late nineteenth century, program music was much in vogue, partly through the influence of Richard Wagner. Afterwards, Richard Strauss, Claude Debussy, and Maurice Ravel continued to compose in this way, often with explicit hints of impressionist painting. Debussy gave to several of his compositions titles suggesting visual imagery, such as *Reflections in the Water*, *Goldfish*, *Fireworks*, and *Gardens in the Rain*. The impressionist painters had used musical titles, such as *Nocturne*. As if to reinforce this connection between various arts and various senses, Debussy sometimes quoted a line or two of poetry in a musical score, so that a similar mood or image was conveyed: for example, *Les sons et les parfums tournent dans l'air du soir* ("Sounds and perfumes turn in the evening air"). Tastes and odors are, of course, among the most evanescent of phenomena, and poetry of the time is full of references to them. It was Joris-Karl Huysmans, in his novel *A Rebours*, who imagined symphonies of tastes and perfumes.

Poetry has advantages and limitations, unlike those of other arts, and these affected its attempts to emulate impressionist painting. But Verlaine, Rimbaud, and Mallarmé in France, and later the "imagist" poets such as Amy Lowell in America, all showed the influence of impressionist painting and music. In prose, Henry James in America, Marcel Proust in France, and James Joyce in Ireland and England, developed this approach at length. To be sure, the use of words to describe fleeting images and to call up vague hints of their emotional overtones, was not a new creation of modern French or English poetry. Nature poetry and prose had helped to show the impressionist painters where to look. But the close personal association of leaders in all these arts, in café and studio conversations, resulted in much cross-fertilization of the arts themselves. Active friendship with painters of the avant-garde helped to enrich the content of poetry and music. Even where definite imitation was prevented by the nature of the medium, each pioneer experiment in one art was a challenge for those in other arts.

One way in which poetry showed this influence was in the heightened emphasis on sensory images with vague emotional associations, at the expense of clear-cut, rationalistic thinking. Some poets, notably Mallarmé, specialized on the obscure "symbolic" associations of rare words and exotic images; also on composing by the free association of words, without advance planning of the work as a whole. Such reliance on impulse and subrational association is a late stage in the romantic movement. "Symbolism," in this sense, does not imply a systematic use of established religious or metaphysical meanings, as in medieval art. Some of these poets were mystics and supernaturalists, but they were also strongly individualistic and determined to preserve their artistic independence. As the century drew near its close, both poetry and visual art took on an air of conscious decadence, dwelling on strange sins, perversions, neuroses, and insanity, along with expressions of satiety and world-weariness, often accompanied by thoughts of suicide or of return to the Church. These trends drew the symbolists away from the pictorial naturalism of Courbet and the impressionists, and from the literary naturalism of Émile Zola, which aspired toward scientific truth.

Literary impressionism in general involves a tendency of the writer to report his observations and his feelings toward outer objects in detail but rather casually; without any definite, prearranged plan or system. At times it leads to a series of miscellaneous memoirs and away from any definite plot or conceptual framework.

6. Impressionistic Criticism. *Criticism* is usually regarded as a distinct branch of literature, and from that point of view one can speak of critical impressionism as a kind of literary style. In accordance with the mentality of the critic and his aims at the time of writing, criticism verges toward prose narrative or philosophic exposition, science or lyrical verse. The kind of criticism now classed as impressionistic is exemplified by Anatole France and Walter Pater. The former discussed what he called "the unsubstantiality of aesthetics" in the Preface to his *Life and Letters*. "The good critic," says France, "is he who relates the adventures of his soul among masterpieces." (But surely the good critic is not limited to studying masterpieces.)

Pater defended hedonism in his "Conclusion" to *Studies in the History of the Renaissance*. His skeptical hedonism places him close to the French naturalists, but in other respects he differs, being more subjective than they and less interested in the scientific observation of nature. Anatole France's genial skepticism extends to aesthetics and criticism as well as to theology and metaphysics. From his point of view there are no firm grounds for objectively evaluating works of art. All the critic can justifiably do is to give his impressions of each work of art that he encounters, together with his emotional responses to it. He can describe the work as it appears to him and say whether he likes it or not, but he cannot prove how others should feel about it. However, his own impressions may help others to enjoy it or to make up their minds about it.

Like pictorial impressionism, the critical type emphasizes the direct, immediate experience of particular phenomena, whether of nature or of art. Its approach is unsystematic in that it follows no preconceived plan or general theory. As in early impressionist painting, this approach tends to avoid the conventional ways of unifying criticism, and may produce only miscellaneous anecdotes. In the works of discerning and discriminating writers like France and Pater, who know how to communicate their experiences, some unity is imparted by the consistent expression of a definite personality and point of view. A particular work of art may impress the critic very differently on different occasions, or even while he is observing it.

The tendency of modern thought, says Pater in the "Conclusion," is to regard all things and principles as inconstant fashions. Each object is detached into a group of impressions—color, odor, texture—in the mind of the observer. What is real in life reduces itself to a series of momentary, sharp impressions. What we have to do is to be forever curiously testing new opinions and courting new impressions. Art professes to give "nothing but the highest quality to your moments as they pass, and simply for those moments' sake." In spite of his antipathy toward theories, Pater is here advancing an ethical and aesthetic theory of his own, based on Epicurean naturalism, and applicable to the criticism of painting as well as other arts.

7. Impressionism in the Historical Process. To appreciate the human associations of impressionism, one must think back to the centuries when painting and sculpture were servants of church and state and devoted largely to idealizing their dignitaries, to dreams of Heaven and Hell, or to glorifying scenes of slaughter and bloody martyrdoms. One must also think back to the styles which followed impressionism, each with its own contribution to man's artistic heritage, but mostly disdaining to represent the simple, peaceful, fleeting beauty of the countryside. Wars and revolutions, the mechanization of life by large-scale industry, the crowding of roads by endless lines of automobiles and trucks, anxieties about the future—these and other ills are sometimes regarded as the only realities. They lead to the belief that it is somehow naïve and reprehensible to "escape" for a while into the serenity of impressionism. True, that style did not tell the whole truth about Europe in the nineteenth century; there was an ugly side, and darker forces were gathering power

behind the scenes. No doubt the owners of some of these pleasant gardens acquired them by exploiting the workers. The Paris Commune foreshadowed rising class struggles, and the war with Prussia foreshadowed 1914. To most of the impressionists these facts would have seemed irrelevant; they had their own jobs to do.

As far as it went, impressionism showed one set of values: the brighter side, emotionally and visually. Some of these values were fast disappearing from the world; perhaps never to return. In any case, it is worthwhile to record them with some permanence, and to hope that similar ones can sometime be provided more widely, whatever the social order may be.

In another sense of "realism," it is almost the antithesis of "naturalism." It involves a different conception of reality as well as of nature, based on the philosophy of medieval Neo-Platonism. Conceiving nature as the world of phenomena, observable by human senses, this school of philosophy declares that nature is not the whole of reality. Naturalistic art is not realistic in the deepest sense, according to this view. There is a higher level of reality, the spiritual plane, and on it there are spiritual beings who cannot be ordinarily seen by human senses. Truly realistic art would not be limited to representing things as they appear to the senses; it would give some idea of spiritual reality.

From this point of view, religious art which people commonly regard as fantastic, untrue, and unrealistic may be profoundly realistic. Medieval and Oriental artists made no claim to showing gods, angels, devils, or scenes from Heaven and Hell exactly as they would look to human eyes. The picture or statue could be expected to give only a vague, symbolic idea of a kind of reality which was essentially invisible, except when the supernatural power intentionally manifested itself in visible form. Realism in this medieval sense is opposed to nominalism and empiricism. From the standpoint of this theory, impressionist art is comparatively naturalistic but not deeply realistic. In this it is said to be like all Western art since the Renaissance. In spite of its limitation to a superficial level of reality, say the Neo-Platonists, it may occasionally hint at deeper truths, through the symbolic meaning of the sensory images which the naturalistic artist portrays.

Philosophic naturalism takes an opposite stand on this issue. Its conception of reality is based on natural science, and it doubts or denies the existence of a distinct, supernatural realm. It regards any representation of supernatural beings as lacking in both realism and naturalism.

In describing a single style in one art, the historian runs the risk of making it seem a static, frozen pattern, as in a collection of pictures in a single museum gallery. In fact, styles in every art are in constant, evolutionary change, especially in modern Western culture. Primitive styles were, on the whole, more long-lived. Today, stylistic change accelerates more and more rapidly, to satisfy the popular demand for novelty. Artists are under constant pressure to devise new styles in every medium; to "break with the past" and produce revolutionary innovations.

Change in art was fairly rapid, even in the late nineteenth century. It was stimulated in part by far-reaching social changes, many of them consequences of the French Revolution and the fall of the old régime, followed by a succession of smaller wars and revolutions, putting power and wealth in the hands of different social groups. Some artists, notably Jacques Louis David, lived through several régimes. Not only were different styles officially approved; new patrons emerged, able and willing to pay for the latest thing in art. But changes of style are not due entirely to social factors. There is also an internal line of cultural descent within each art, descending from teacher to pupil and from one generation of artists and critics to the next. Sometimes imported styles, such as that of Chinese decoration in the eighteenth century, merge with indigenous ones to form new hybrids.

Any particular style, such as impressionism, is a temporary stage, a partial equilibrium in a long historical process. It is a small but often influential pattern of thought and action within a larger culture-pattern, interacting with patterns old and new in the same and other arts. It is never entirely original; in every modern style, however revolutionary it may claim to be, there are vestiges of older styles, combined with new features through the creative power of individual artists and the requirements of new modes of life. Old styles divide as certain features of one are abandoned, while other features are preserved in different combinations.

The conscious revolt of artists from the current fashion seldom turns out to be as complete as it promised to be; reactions soon occur, and even at the height of revolt important features from the rejected style may survive. Thus the impressionists retained in some degree certain features of academic painting, such as perspective, anatomy, scale, and modeling with darker shadows. But they modified these considerably, as by blurring perspective with surface hues, and by changing shadows from brown or gray to complementary hues. They often used the traditional palette with tubes of oil paints, but refrained from mixing their colors on the palette as was usually done.

Again and again, a movement in art which is hailed by its leaders and friendly critics as a break with tradition is only a break with one tradition and a revival of another. The one revived may be a remote and foreign one, radically unlike previous styles in the group. This happened around 1906, when primitive Negro sculpture began to influence Picasso, Braque, and others in Paris. The one revived may be a familiar one, temporarily *démodé* but easily reestablished in the taste of elite connoisseurs. This happened around 1865 when the venerable tradition of coloristic painting, long practiced by the followers of Rubens but recently out of fashion through the hostility of David and Ingres, was revived by a new generation of colorists.

The importance of any style, and the greatness of any artist practicing it, are judged to a large extent in terms of originality. This raises questions of chronological priority and of influence, in view of the fact that greater credit goes to the originator and the one who influences others, rather than to the imitator. Judgments of chronological order in Western art can now be made with considerable reliability, because of the many documentary records available and the interest in objective historiography on the part of modern scholars. It is possible to date with considerable reliability the main events in the rise and acceptance of impressionism and the chief contributions of its various leaders. This provides one basis for evaluating them in terms of originality, as in the case of Monet's study for the *Déjeuner sur l'herbe*, done three years later than Manet's picture with the same name, but much more impressionistic in style (Rewald, pp. 84, 119). Monet's degree of originality, which was not complete, can also be estimated by comparing his works with those of Daubigny, as in the latter's *Spring Landscape*, done in 1862 (Rewald, p. 100). When two similar works are produced by artists living in the same milieu at or near the same time, one can risk the hypothesis that the later artist saw and learned something from the earlier work, or at least heard it discussed. It is a problem for comparative analysis, not necessarily involving relative value, to decide how much of Monet's style (if any) is already present in the earlier works of Daubigny and Manet.

Going farther, one can try to chart the main sequence of steps leading up to impressionism in the history of Western art as a whole. Since impressionism involves an emphasis on landscape as a subject and on luminous color as the main component, one can think of it as a recent stage in two pictorial traditions. Giovanni Bellini (1431–1516) can be taken as a somewhat arbitrary starting point for both traditions. Landscape painting appears then in the Italian Renaissance, and for some time thereafter, mainly as a background for figure-compositions. This includes its development in the works of Giorgione, Titian, and Tintoretto in Italy; in those of Velázquez and El Greco in Spain (excepting the latter's *View of Toledo*), and in those of Nicolas Poussin and Claude Lorrain (1600–82) in

France. In these last two, we see the human figures and architecture (largely classical in form) increasingly subordinated to the parklike, landscape background. In the north (Flanders and Holland) this occurs also in Patinir and in some works by Pieter Bruegel the Elder, Peter Paul Rubens, and Rembrandt. In the Dutch painters Cuyp, Van Goyen, Hobbema, and Jacob van Ruysdael, landscape is definitely dominant, although some human figures or human products, such as houses, often remain for the sake of scale and human interest. Landscapes become more naturalistic and more the home of peasants and small farmers; less parklike. The same can be said of most landscape painting thereafter, including the impressionist phase. In France and England during the early nineteenth century, the classical landscape tradition of Claude Lorrain and Poussin survives in Corot, Turner, and sometimes in Constable, but naturalism gains ground.

In eighteenth-century England, there is mutual influence between the nature poets and the landscape painters. It is highly romantic in flavor. Constable occasionally shows a grander scene, as in his English noble estates and cathedrals, while Turner definitely prefers the romantic grandeur of Venice, storms at sea, great conflagrations, and the conflict of sunshine with mist and smoke. In France, the naturalistic tradition survives in landscape through the work of Corot, whom Baudelaire praised on the eve of impressionism; also in Millet and the Barbizon group, Daubigny, and Courbet. Throughout the first half of the century in France, the darker greens and browns predominate except for lighter tones in Corot's pastoral idylls.

These great traditions of European classic, romantic, and naturalistic landscape show how strong and varied a foundation the impressionists had to build upon. In addition, they had the equally great tradition of coloristic painting in general, which was likewise derived to a large extent from the Venetians. Though often applied to landscape, it also flourished in the painting of human, superhuman, and animal figures, with or without landscape backgrounds. It reached a climax of magnificence and vivid realism in Rubens' grandiose portrayals of divine and noble personages. In an aristocratic society such as that surrounding Rubens, neither purely natural landscape nor modest suburban gardens had sufficient appeal to inspire the impressionist type of landscape. But the mastery of color which he displayed was afterward transferred to other subjects, including a bright and varied palette and the use of varicolored shadows.

The high level of painterly colorism in Rubens, Velázquez, Tiepolo, Vermeer, and Chardin during the seventeenth and eighteenth centuries was ably maintained by Delacroix in the early nineteenth. The romantic movement of his generation found this tradition far more congenial than that of coldly linear neoclassicism, and included the important ability to make reflected light and color areas seem, not like paint on canvas, but like integral parts of solid objects in deep space.

FIGURE 7, OPPOSITE. John Constable, *The White Horse.* 1819. COPYRIGHT THE FRICK COLLECTION, NEW YORK

FIGURE 8, RIGHT. J. M. W. Turner, *Burning of the Houses of Parliament.* 1834. THE CLEVELAND MUSEUM OF ART. JOHN L. SEVERANCE COLLECTION, 1936

The debt of French landscape painting to England, especially Constable (Figure 7) and Turner (Figure 8) has been much debated. Certainly a close inspection of their mature works, such as Constable's *The Hay Wain* and Turner's *The Fighting Téméraire* anticipate some of the principal features of impressionism. Constable frequently uses small dabs of contrasting colors close together. This enriches the texture and adds to its realism, but the main tonality usually stays in the browns and greens, and in local colors rather than momentary reflections. Turner deals more with the transitory aspects of sunshine and tempest, as in his *Rain, Steam, and Speed* (1844). He paints the vague and melting forms of mist and water as seen in different lights and shadows, with striking iridescence and prismatic brilliance. If he had painted in Paris twenty years later, there would be little trouble in admitting him as an impressionist, but he was a lone, reserved figure with few friends or admirers.

Pissarro and Monet recognized some influence from the watercolors of Constable, Turner, and Old Crome. They visited London museums and painted in the suburbs in various seasons. But Monet remarked that Turner's work "was antipathetic to him because of the exuberant romanticism of his fancy." Pissarro stated that "Turner and Constable, while they taught us something, showed us in their works that they had no understanding of shadows" (Rewald, p. 258). Turner, he said, did not apply tone division correctly and naturally. Both Sisley and Whistler spent some years

in England, and both were interested in the work of Turner and Constable.

It must be remembered that artists are not always correct in saying who has or has not influenced them, especially those whose works resemble their own and were done only a little earlier. There is a very human tendency to deny such influence. Nationalistic sentiments may cause one to deny any foreign influence.

Certainly it should not be assumed that resemblance and priority alone are enough to prove influence. Coincidence and parallel innovation are often possible. The French impressionists would have found it easier to learn from Delacroix at home than to go abroad for lessons in color. Facilities for seeing other artists' works were much less available a hundred years ago than now. Travel abroad was expensive; there were no accurate color-print reproductions. (In America, Currier and Ives were selling their reproductions by the thousand at this time; many of them landscapes.) The difficulty of inferring causal influence is often great in the case of individuals, but less in that of a whole style or movement in which many participated. There can be little doubt that French impressionism was much indebted to all the great traditions just mentioned. The main problem is to decide exactly how and how much.

In 1865 these traditions lay ready at hand for the impressionists to use in their own way, to satisfy their more specialized naturalism. Only the great prestige and hostility of Ingres, supported by the Academy and official Salon under government auspices, could have kept the coloristic tradition so long in subjection. With Ingres' death in 1867 at the age of eighty-seven, this obstacle to the full employment of color and to unconventional types of drawing (as by Degas) was removed. The importance of Delacroix was more fully realized and his influence on the techniques of painting grew, while his romanticism had less appeal to the rising generation.

Several other kinds of influence, some from outside the arts, helped to determine the course of painting in the seventies. One was the rising level of wealth in the French middle class, due to increasing industry and trade. The unsuccessful war with Prussia did not long impede this growth. Increasing numbers of the bourgeoisie developed a taste for art and the means of buying it, thus providing more patronage for art, independent of church and state. Many of the newly rich preferred the obviously pretty and sentimental, as in the nudes of Bouguereau and Cabanel, but an elite in matters of taste was also developing. This elite was ready to be convinced that the new experiments were worthwhile, and that frequent changes in style were normal and progressive in the history of art. A few discerning dealers in Paris, such as Martinet and Durand-Ruel, took the risk of exhibiting impressionist paintings and sold them at prices which seem infinitesimal today. Impressionist landscape appealed to some by providing pleasant fantasies of suburban, rustic, and seaside life, such as dwellers on the crowded streets of Paris might enjoy. Men of the middle class with money to spare enjoyed the entertainment of cafés, boating, horse-racing, concerts, theater, ballet, and circus, all of which provided subjects for Manet and Degas. Women of the upper bourgeoisie spent much time at elaborate toilettes, shopping, sewing, and caring for children. Lounging and dancing out-of-doors were possible in summer. All these subjects were easily available, close at hand, while in winter or summer the muddy roads and village squares provided interesting effects of color and light. Tired of both classic and romantic idealization, discerning critics and collectors came to like the stimulating shock of almost unembellished realism.

Another influence was that of science and the naturalistic attitude associated with it. Some recent experiments in the physics of light and color bore directly on the problems of impressionist technique. As early as 1839, Michel-Eugène Chevreul had published a book on "the law of the simultaneous contrast of colors," in which both Delacroix and later Seurat expressed an interest. Another of his books, on the application of colors to industrial arts, was published in 1864. Pissarro, in a letter to Durand-Ruel dated 1886, gives credit to

Seurat and Signac for applying the modern theory of colors. When asked about his theory, Pissarro replied, "Seek the modern synthesis through scientific means, which will be based on the theory of colors discovered by M. Chevreul, and according to the experiments of Maxwell and the measurements of O. N. Rood." (Ogden N. Rood, an American physicist, made quantitative analyses of color contrasts and used a color wheel, as he reported in his book *Modern Chromatics*, 1881.) "Substitute the optic mixture for the pigmentary mixture," Pissarro continues. "In other words, the breaking up of a color tone into its component elements, for the optic mixture creates much more intense luminosities than the pigmentary mixture" (Gauss, p. 24).

The question of the nature of light and the relations between white and colored light had long interested physicists such as Isaac Newton, and poets such as Goethe. H. L. F. von Helmholtz (1821–94) studied the prismatic components of white light, showing that the eye combines the different hues on the moving color wheel into a third hue. Sensations of color, he showed, depended more on responses in the retina of the eye than on inherent properties of the object. He also wrote on *The Sensation of Tone as a Physiological Basis for the Theory of Music*, and thereby stimulated Debussy to speculate on the nature of the overtones, consonances, and dissonances (Fleming, pp. 683, 712).

In general, the effect of such trends in science was to strengthen the positivistic or empirical world-view. "Beauty," the empiricists had long declared, "is in the eye of the beholder." These trends encouraged a naturalistic approach to art, based on observing and representing facts of nature as opposed to artificial designs and fantasies of the unreal and supernatural. Among the facts of nature, they realized, were the psychological processes of sense-perception.

8. Philosophical Associations of Impressionism. Styles of art often have philosophical and other cultural associations which are not obvious to the senses, and are not clearly realized or consciously intended by the artist. Types of image used in a certain style may function as symbols of general concepts, beliefs, and emotional attitudes. In the Christian Middle Ages, the images of art were persistently interpreted in terms of mystical, theological, metaphysical, and moral symbolism. In medieval art the lamb was used as a symbol of the Incarnation and the Vicarious Atonement; also of the gentleness of Christ.

In modern times, the symbolic interpretation of art has declined, but the images used in it may still be intended or understood in that way, because of the obvious analogy between a certain image and a certain abstract meaning or meanings. This is common in poetry, where the artist can, if he likes, give in words a clear or partial explanation of the meaning. Thus to address the Deity as "Rock of Ages" is an obvious symbol of strength, stability, endurance, and protection. By contrast, Shelley uses the "wild West Wind" as a symbol of autumn, destruction, and confusion.

. . . the leaves dead
Are driven, like ghosts from an enchanter fleeing,

Yellow, and black, and pale, and hectic red,
Pestilence-stricken multitudes: . . .

Mid the steep sky's commotion,
Loose clouds like earth's decaying leaves are shed, . . .

In painting, it is less easy to convey a deeper meaning, and in any case, the impressionists were not much interested in doing so. Nevertheless, the associations in human life of such images as sunshine and gloomy skies, flowers and dead leaves, or transitory things in general, are too obvious to be ignored entirely. Even if the artist does not consciously intend them or the observer consciously think of them, such associations may be in the back of their minds, especially in contrast with the symbols of monumental stability used in academic Christian art. Philosophically minded critics are apt to be more aware of these opposing meanings than painters are. This is true of Baudelaire, Castagnary, and Zola. But we have seen that, with or without explanations, impressionist art often emphasizes images of evanescence and the transitory aspects of life. By painting examples of images which are commonly used as emotive symbols, the artist can convey their associated meanings to sensitive persons, whether he intends to do so or not.

The theme of mutability, or universal change and decay, has long been a favorite one of poets, composers, and painters, especially at the height of the romantic movement in the early nineteenth century. They lamented the death of Adonis, of Balder, Siegfried, and other folk heroes, as well as the passing of youth and beauty everywhere. Keats wrote of "Beauty that must die;/ and Joy, whose hand is ever at his lips/ Bidding adieu; . . ." Since the revival of Epicureanism in the seventeenth century, this mood of melancholy has often been followed by the admonition to "seize the day," enjoy the present while it lasts, and "Gather ye rosebuds while ye may."

The impressionists of the eighteen-seventies were somewhat indebted to romanticism for this awareness of mutability as an ever-present reality, and of the need to enjoy natural beauty while it lasted. But most of the emotional fervor of romanticism had been replaced, in their minds, by a practical disposition to preserve, with the aid of science, a little of the visual wealth which nature was offering. They did not, as a rule, associate visual change with decay or destruction, but rather with light and animation.

Clusters of images and concepts descend through centuries in cultural evolution. They are variously systematized into religious, political, and philosophical symbolism, but loosely, and in many inconsistent ways. Some reinforce each other, and some are antithetical. When a group of these ways of thinking, feeling, and acting descends from one generation to another in fairly recognizable form, historians often call it a "tradition."

In that sense, we have noticed the opposition in mid-nineteenth-century painting between the classic and romantic traditions, with naturalism as proposed by Courbet and Zola as a third possibility. Naturalism was not new in the nineteenth century, however. As a style of painting, it was practiced in the Hellenistic period and in the early Roman empire. As a philosophic theory and world view, it was a tradition descending from ancient Epicureanism, and opposed to mysticism, Platonism, and metaphysical dualism. The naturalism of impressionist painting was limited in scope and lacking in philosophical explanation. Nevertheless, it played an historical role as one manifestation of the naturalistic and empiricist traditions in Western thought.

It was mentioned above that most serious art in Europe has emphasized, not the transitory aspects of life and the world, but the eternal, stable, or long-enduring ones. These are exemplified in much religious and official art, including that of the Paris Salons, from the Gothic period to the twentieth century. The difference depends only partly on the subject matter, which in the Salons was religious and serious at times and at other times secular, playful, anecdotal, or even comic. It depends also on the form and technique, in which the academic establishment favored balanced, monumental, tightly integrated compositions with firm, hard modeling of line and mass, realistic highlights, and dark shadows. Such a style was appropriate to the representation of an hierarchical, authoritarian conception of reality on earth and in heaven; also to an aristocratic type of social order. Democratic as well as naturalistic trends, on the other hand, called for looser, more irregular patterns without persistently exalting any one type of individual, group, class, or occupation. The early impressionists, instead of revolting only against a tradition in painting, were symbolically rejecting also the authoritarian, hierarchical conception of life and the world, which the French Revolution had only partially destroyed. This rejection was far from explicit, even as a symbol; it contained **581** no anticlerical propaganda; its symbolism was vague and ambiguous, consisting only in the choice of one type of common imagery instead of another.

The symbolic conflict extended even to the word "impression." This and related words were used in philosophy and ordinary language long before the movement in French painting to which they were applied in 1874. They are derived from the Latin word *imprimere*, to press, as in making an imprint on paper. More broadly, people spoke of being mentally impressed by some outside event, person, scene, or experience. An impression was a direct perceptual effect of a sensory stimulation. Accordingly, David Hume's empiricist theory of the origin of knowledge in sense perception was sometimes called "impressionism."

In philosophy, the term "impression" usually carried a suggestion of superficiality, vagueness, and passiveness, as of something imprinted on the mind by outer influences, the mind being at birth a "blank sheet of paper." From this point of view, sense perception seemed to Platonists and Cartesians an inferior mental process, by contrast with the "clear and distinct ideas" obtained through reason. Lalande (p. 468) defines "impression" as a "combined state of consciousness, presenting a characteristic affective tone, responding to an external action; opposite to reflection and to judgment founded on analysis." Several influential philosophers of the seventeenth and eighteenth centuries belittled art as concerned with sensation, fantasy, and deception, rather than with true knowledge. Through the writings of Diderot, Comte, and others in the next two centuries, beside the slowly reviving influence of Epicurean naturalism, liberal French thought gradually became more receptive toward naturalistic empiricism. This tended indirectly to strengthen those types of visual and literary art which used and respected sensory observation, including impressionism. The conquest was far from complete, however, and a mystical element remained in French symbolism, Satanism, and *décadence* at the end of the nineteenth century.

Another element in the ideology of impressionism can be traced back even farther in history. It was Heraclitus, among the early Greek philosophers, who was credited with the idea that everything flows; that the universe is in a state of constant change. "One cannot step twice in the same river." Later philosophers developed the antithesis between change and permanence, chaos and order, the many and the one, as opposing tendencies in an endless process of cyclical alternation. Much of Greek philosophy is concerned with the problem of what (if anything) can be eternal and changeless in a universe wherein everything seems to be subject to decay and death. Democritus and Epicurus proposed the theory that atoms were eternal

and indestructible. Plato substituted the theory of Ideas or universal concepts as the principle of permanence. The Christian philosophers, in their turn, substituted the concept of God as an eternal, spiritual being, as contrasted with the inferior world of natural phenomena. Plato disparaged the arts of sensory imitation, along with the whole phenomenal world, as inferior to the knowledge of absolute truth. However, both Platonists and Christians agreed that true art could symbolize eternal truths. Art which did so was superior to that providing only sensuous pleasure.

Much religious and official art, even as far back as the Egyptians, had expressed the idea of eternal changelessness, as in the Pyramids and rigid, frontal, monumental statues of the Pharoahs. These were aimed, in part, at insuring the immortality of deceased monarchs. For millennia thereafter, a large share of officially controlled art, both sacred and secular, had tried to convey the idea of the indestructible strength of government; the survival of the ruling dynasty and the perpetuation of the status quo. Representations of change in human nature, as in the marks of old age, sickness, injuries, death, and similar "accidents" of experience, were comparatively rare. Universal types of person were represented, rather than individual peculiarities. The latter appeared in Hellenistic art in a time of actual change and insecurity. During the Renaissance and baroque eras, official art reinforced the belief in an eternal, double hierarchy on earth, spiritual and temporal. The heavenly hierarchy was represented in terms of a supreme Trinity ruling over graded ranks of archangels, angels, and saints. The representation of transitory, accidental phenomena continued in the popular arts and folklore, with inferior status.

On the other hand, the rise of science and middle-class culture, in the Renaissance and later, tended to oppose the hierarchical conception and to substitute realistic views of things as they would appear in nature and ordinary experience. This included increasingly realistic anatomy, perspective, coloring, and irregular compositions.

Surviving faith in the eternal stability of the "Great Design" on earth and in heaven received rude political shocks in the wars and revolutions which deposed a succession of French monarchs and weakened the power of the Church. Intellectually, it was undermined by Rousseau's attack on the belief in divine right of kings. The philosophy of naturalism grew in influence among French intellectuals through the *Encyclopédie* and the writings of Diderot, who criticized contemporary painting from the standpoint of a middle-class morality.

Intellectually, belief in the universality of change

was strengthened by the discovery of evolution. Later evolutionists emphasized the idea that everything changes in the moral and aesthetic world, as well as in that of organic and social structure. There are no eternal, transcendental laws of morality, art, or beauty, they insisted. Styles of art evolve as everything else does; they compete for survival as do organic species (Munro, pp. 251–88). By implication, this opened the door to new styles and methods such as those of impressionism.

In France, Auguste Comte had already advanced the theory that all civilization passes through three stages: theological, metaphysical, and positive or empirical. This theory reinforced and developed the English tradition of political liberalism. Hippolyte Taine, in the eighteen-sixties, argued that environment as well as race and historical epoch influenced the growth and decline of styles. Hegel, in Germany, had previously advanced a theory of evolution based on metaphysical idealism, with cosmic mind as the determining principle. Karl Marx and his followers proposed instead a naturalistic theory of cultural evolution, in which the arts were shown as socially determined and as weapons in the struggle between classes. Ideas such as these were prevalent in the eighteen-fifties, and the visual naturalism of Courbet (himself a political radical, once imprisoned for his activities) fitted in with them. They were fundamentally opposed to the basic ideology of the French Academy and the official Salons, even though the philosophic issues were not clearly stated at the time.

The direct contribution of impressionism to the arts was specialized and limited in scope, but indirectly its influence was far-reaching and constructive. It did much to free the artist in every style and every medium from the tyranny of powerful academies, and to encourage him in pursuing his own creative line, however unpromising it might seem at first. This tended to strengthen the forces of democracy in culture, society, and education in general.

Another contribution, as we have seen, was to open the eyes of artists and the public to the wealth of luminous color and animated movement which, though seldom noticed, lay before them everywhere. The special techniques of impressionism, such as broken color, enlarged the painter's resources even though they were not to be preferred for all purposes. The strength and richness of impressionist painting at its best stimulated workers in other arts to try analogous experiments.

The emphasis which impressionism placed on careful, analytical observation of nature helped to strengthen the work of empirical scientists along related lines, especially in the psychology of perception and color vision. The world of the senses was treated with increasing respect by philosophers. It was not, they realized, a mere source of deception, temptation, and inferior types of knowledge, but a source of inexhaustible values, aesthetic and intellectual.

BIBLIOGRAPHY

C. Baudelaire, *The Mirror of Art* (London, 1955), pp. 29, 230, 275. C. Debussy, *Préludes for Piano*, First Book, No. 4 (Paris, 1910), 15. *Reflets dans l'eau* is one of the series called *Images*. E. Duranty, *La nouvelle peinture* (Paris, 1876). W. Fleming, *Arts and Ideas* (New York, 1955), pp. 683, 712. There are also later editions. A. France, *Life and Letters*, trans. A. W. Evans, first series (London, 1911), Preface. C. E. Gauss, *The Aesthetic Theories of French Artists* (Baltimore, 1966), pp. 24–25. A. Hauser, *The Social History of Art* (London, 1951), Ch. 4. H. W. Janson, *History of Art* (New York, 1962), pp. 489–502. S. E. Lee, *History of Far Eastern Art* (New York, 1964), pp. 387, 509. A. Lalande, *Vocabulaire technique et critique de la philosophie* (Paris, 1947), p. 468. P. H. Lang, *Music in Western Civilization* (New York, 1941), pp. 1014–23. B. Maiuri, *The National Museum, Naples* (Novara, Italy, 1959), pp. 106–11. C. G. Mueller and M. Rudolph, *Light and Vision* (New York, 1966), p. 72. T. Munro, *Evolution in the Arts and Other Theories of Culture History* (Cleveland, 1963), pp. 251–88. B. S. Myers, *Art and Civilization* (New York, 1958), pp. 348–51. W. Pater, *Studies in the History of the Renaissance* (London, 1873), Conclusion. J. Rewald, *The History of Impressionism* (New York, 1961), a comprehensive, detailed, and excellent work; cited frequently in this article, it has many illustrations, some in color. Vitruvius, *De architectura*, Vol. I, trans. T. Granger (London, 1931), 203–04. E. Weber, *Paths to the Present* (New York, 1960), translations of writings by Baudelaire, Courbet, Zola, Blémont, and contributions by Pater and others. É. Zola, *Mon Salon* (Paris, 1866). P. Zucker, *Styles in Painting* (New York, 1950), p. 322.

THOMAS MUNRO

[See also Art and Play; Classicism; Classification of the Arts; Criticism; Evolutionism; Expressionism; Form; Genius; Hierarchy; **Iconography;** Romanticism; **Style;** Taste.]

IMPRINTING AND LEARNING EARLY IN LIFE

THE TERM, imprinting, as used by modern comparative psychologists, refers mainly, although not exclusively, to certain learning situations which occur very early in the lives of ground-nesting birds. But the word is also increasingly used more loosely, implying a particular aetiology (causal explanation) of adult modes of behavior in both animals and human beings. Although

583

the notion of imprinting derives directly from European zoological ethology (now defined as the scientific study of animal behavior, especially in relation to habitat—not to be confused with ethology as meaning "the science of character," as used by J. S. Mill, or with ethology, meaning environmentalism, as used by Julian Huxley), its roots are deep in the history of thought. It is especially related to the idea of "indelible impressions on young minds," long current in philosophical writings. Thus, the old concept of mental imprinting was a precursor of the later one of behavioral imprinting.

1. Tabula Rasa. The idea that the child's mind is initially a tabula rasa, a clean slate, was put forward by John Locke, but it would appear that in this matter Locke's thinking was influenced by that of the French philosopher Gassendi. Both these writers were engaged in a polemic against Descartes' notion of innate ideas, and argued that all ideas derive ultimately from sensory experience. Locke in his *Essay concerning Human Understanding* (1689, Book I) held that, to start with, the mind is a blank and that with time impressions are formed upon it so that a basis is steadily created for the whole of the individual's mental life. Some suggestion of an initial tabula rasa may be traced back at least to Saint Thomas Aquinas (in his dictum "nothing is in the mind which was not first in the senses," *De Trinitate*, I, 3), but it was Locke who developed the so-called empiricist view, viz., that the mind is passive in learning, and that ideas gradually become imprinted upon it, whereby it becomes "stocked" with experience. The child's early experience is sensory, and reflection (thinking) develops with maturation out of such sensory learning. However, Locke's own interest lay primarily in the character of the mature mind rather than in the processes of mental development.

In contrast, the topic of early learning was the main theme of the essay, *Émile, or On Education*, by Jean Jacques Rousseau (1712–78). Like Locke, Rousseau argued that the human infant, though born with the ability to learn, has initially no innate ideas. Experience, according to him, could account for all knowledge; and since animals have senses, they, too, could acquire knowledge. One of the first things that the human infant learns is that he is powerless and dependent upon the adult who cares for him. While the notion of tabula rasa focused on the impressionability of, and "exposure learning" by, the child, the emphasis on the infant's dependency pointed to what very much later came to be called instrumental learning. Rousseau believed that early training could mold the child completely; in his belief in the efficacy of early education he went too far, but he was quite right to emphasize the initial pliability of the infant.

2. Instinct and Early Learning. We must note the relevance of the writings of Charles Darwin to our topic, even though the idea of imprinting played no special part in his thinking. It is noteworthy that Darwin (in *Mind*, 1877) showed great interest in child development, including also infancy learning. Moreover, he was interested in linking together child psychology and animal behavior; and this has contributed to the subsequent development of modern comparative psychology. And in concerning himself with instinctive behavior, Darwin helped to prepare the ground for the study of the interplay of instinct and early learning, soon to be taken up by Spalding, and later, in different ways, by both Freud and the zoological ethologists.

D. A. Spalding published in 1873, in *Macmillan's Magazine*, a paper entitled "Instinct, with Original Observations on Young Animals." In it he described the behavior of young domestic fowl, and concluded that newly hatched chicks will follow almost *any* moving figure. Spalding regarded such behavior as "unacquired," that is, instinctive rather than learned. He saw that these animals' ability to recognize parents, as distinct from their approach and following behavior, is not instinctive, but is, in fact, learned. He might have concluded that early learning takes over at some stage from instinct; for there is little doubt that chicks which at first follow instinctively, then learn who their mother or mother-substitute is, and are eventually able to discriminate between her and other figures. This was later more clearly recognized by William James in *The Principles of Psychology* (Vol. II, Ch. 24).

Spalding drew attention to a remarkable feature of such early behavior, namely that the chick would follow its mother, only if it had the opportunity to do so *early enough* in life. If faced with her for the very first time after the opportune or sensitive period has passed, the chick would fail to follow her and would show no affinity whatever to her; furthermore, it would not subsequently be able to develop any attachment to its mother. We now say that a chick becomes imprinted to the mother-figure when it learns her characteristics, and forms a tie to her. Spalding reported that this development was confined to a short period soon after hatching; and this has since become known, with some degree of justification, as the critical period for imprinting.

William James considered that many modes of instinctive behavior, including approach and following responses, "ripen" at some particular stage in the organism's life, and then wane again. He also thought—and this is significant—that at the time of the instinct's "vivacity," a *habit* instigated by the instinct, but specifically determined by the environmental circumstances encountered, is acquired. Such habit-formation was regarded by James as consisting of the superimposition of early learning upon instinct. Furthermore, James suggested that "in the chickens and calves . . . the instinct to follow and become attached fades out after a few days, and that the instinct of flight then takes its place" (ibid., p. 398). This idea was later taken up by experimentalists such as W. H. Thorpe, R. A. Hinde and others, but, as research progressed, serious doubts about it began to be entertained. However, there is no doubt about the importance of the interaction between "built-in" and learned behavior early in the life of many avian and mammalian species, including man.

3. The Contribution of Ethology. The term, if not the idea, of imprinting derives from Oskar Heinroth and from Konrad Lorenz. Heinroth, a German zoologist and ethologist, read a paper in 1910 in which he described the behavior of incubator-hatched graylag goslings ("Beiträge zur Biologie, nahmentlich Ethologie und Psychologie der Anatiden," *Verh. 5 int. orn. Kongr. Berlin* [1910], 589–702). These newly hatched birds showed no fear, and attached themselves readily to human beings. Such man-attached goslings do not show any inclination to approach and stay with parent-geese; they behave as if they treated people as their parents. This kind of attachment-behavior was described by Heinroth by the verb *einzuprägen*, corresponding to the English "to stamp in" or "to imprint"; and the word "stamped in" had earlier been used, among others, by Spalding, and above all, by Thorndike ("Animal Intelligence," *Psychol. Monogr.*, 1898) in relation to firmly acquired modes of behavior.

The pioneer ethologist, Lorenz, used the noun *Prägung*, or imprinting, in his seminal paper in 1935, to refer to the process of rapid bond-formation early in the life of the so-called nidifugous birds (the fowl, ducks, geese, and the like). Lorenz went further than Spalding or James in that he specified the characteristics of imprinting, and thereby generated much interest in it, which, in turn, has resulted in further systematic observations and much controlled experimentation in this area of animal behavior. It could be said that Lorenz rather "stuck out his neck" in saying initially that imprinting differed fundamentally from, what he called, ordinary learning. First—he held—it could take place only during a brief critical period in the individual's life; and second, once it had taken place, it could not be reversed. Furthermore, imprinting was reported to occur very rapidly, without any trial and error; and, above all, imprinting would show itself, at maturity, in a courtship directed towards the original mother-figure or figures similar to her.

It was later questioned whether these features, even if true, would separate imprinting sharply from other forms of learning. Indeed, Lorenz himself, some twenty years after the appearance of his early papers, expressed the view that imprinting might be a type of conditioning. Whether it is, or is not, would depend partly on how narrowly or broadly conditioning is defined. But even if imprinting were to be shown to be continuous with, or to be a form of, conditioning, there is no doubt that it is a phenomenon deserving special attention, not only because it is of great interest to ontogenetic studies of animal behavior but also because of its implications for human developmental psychology and psychopathology.

4. The Modern View of Imprinting. Numerous post-Lorenz laboratory studies of imprinting have shown that its characteristics are not as clear-cut as was at first thought. Nevertheless, the growth of specific attachments in very young animals (attachments which are acquired through exposure to sensory stimulation rather than resulting from reward training) is a common occurrence, and a very influential one, in the development of behavior. Furthermore, there is some evidence that imprinting is an important aspect of early learning not only in birds but also in precocial mammals (that is, those born in a relatively mature state, such as guinea-pigs, sheep, horses, etc.). It may well be—but this is still somewhat controversial—that imprinting also plays an important part in the socialization of altricial species (that is, those that are rather immature when born, e.g., dogs or monkeys). If so, then it is not impossible that the human infant's tie to its mother, and later the child's social behavior, depend in some measure on the development of attachments attained in an imprinting-like manner rather than conditioned by association with physiological rewards.

In his 1935 paper in German, "The Companion in the Bird's World," Lorenz drew attention to certain analogies in human behavior to the occurrence of imprinting to, or with, inappropriate objects; he had in mind human ways of acting which, as he put it, "appear in the form of pathological fixations on the object of an instinct." This view fits in with, if it does not actually refer to, Freud's conception of the aetiology of many neurotic symptoms; and it ties up with Freud's account of psychosexual phases of child development, whereby in certain circumstances, emotional development is said to be arrested and fixated at one or another of the early psychosexual stages. Such developmental fixations could possibly include inappropriate object-attachments; and these could perhaps account for some of the well-known sexual deviations.

Learning early in life has always been of great interest to all concerned with child-rearing methods, with training, with indoctrination, and education in every sense. More recently, early learning has become the object of systematic research by students of animal behavior and by child-development psychologists. The idea of imprinting, as a special type of early learning, was inherent—in an embryonic form—in the philosophy of mind represented by the empiricist school of thought. Later, as a result of observations of the behavior of young animals, the idea has reappeared in a new guise. The study of animals has given fresh vigor to the concept of imprinting; so much so, that this idea is making a considerable impact upon modern human psychology. Thus, the interest in sensory impressions on the mind has largely given way to one in specific imprinted attachments and in fixated modes of behavior. The idea of imprinting needs now to be further developed and refined to take full account of the new experimental findings which are being continually reported. Even so, the reborn idea of imprinting has been useful in providing a mental picture of certain learning situations and, above all, in giving a new direction and purpose to current research efforts in the field and laboratory.

BIBLIOGRAPHY

More information on Gassendi and Locke may be found in R. I. Aaron, *John Locke* (London, 1937). Some original sources to be consulted are J. J. Rousseau, *Émile, or On Education* (English edition, London, 1763), and Charles Darwin, "A Biographical Sketch of an Infant," *Mind,* **11** (1877), 286–94. Spalding's paper, "Instinct, with Original Observations on Young Animals," published originally in 1873, was reprinted in *Animal Behavior,* **2** (1954), 2–11. Other references are: William James, *Principles of Psychology,* 2 vols. (New York, 1890); Robert Thomson, *The Pelican History of Psychology* (London, 1968); Konrad Lorenz, "The Companion in the Bird's World" (in English), *Auk,* **54** (1937), 245–73; W. Kessen, *The Child* (New York, 1965); W. Sluckin, *Imprinting & Early Learning* (London, 1964; Chicago, 1965).

W. SLUCKIN

[See also Behaviorism; Education; Evolutionism.]

INDETERMINACY IN PHYSICS

1. Introduction. The idea of "indeterminacy"—often also called loosely "uncertainty"—is widely used in physics and is of particular importance for quantum mechanics, but has rarely, if ever, been given a strict explicit definition. As a consequence it is used in at least three different, though related, meanings which will be sharply distinguished in the present article. (a) It may denote any type of *acausal* (accidental, contingent, indeterministic) behavior of physical processes,

usually in the realm of microphenomena, implying thereby a total or partial breakdown of the principle of causality; (b) it may denote any type of *unpredictable* behavior of such processes without necessarily involving a renunciation of metaphysical causality; (c) it may denote an essential limitation or *imprecision* of measurement procedures for reasons to be specified by a concomitant theory of measurement.

To avoid ambiguities we shall in what follows call indeterminacy if used in the sense (a), acausal indeterminacy or briefly a-indeterminacy; if used in the sense (b), u-indeterminacy; and if used in the sense (c), i-indeterminacy. Clearly, a-indeterminacy implies, but is not implied by, u-indeterminacy, and does not imply, nor is implied by, i-indeterminacy; neither do the other two imply their partners. If however predictability is understood to refer exclusively to sharp values of measurement results, i-indeterminacy implies u-indeterminacy. Furthermore, the validity of these concepts may depend on the domain in which they are applied. Thus a- or u-indeterminacies may be valid in microphysics but not in macrophysics.

2. Ancient Conceptions. In fact, the earliest known thesis of indeterminacy restricted this notion to a definite realm of applicability. According to Plato's *Timaeus* (28D–29B) the Demiurge created the material world after an eternal pattern; while the latter can be spoken of with certainty, the created copy can be described only in the language of uncertainties. In other words, while the intelligible world, the realm of ideas, is subject to strict laws, rigorous determinations and complete predictability, the physical or material world is not. However, even disregarding this dichotomy of being, Plato's atomic theory admitted an a-indeterminacy in the subatomic realm, whereas in the world of atoms and their configurations to higher orders determinacy was reinstated. "However strictly the principle of mathematical order is carried through in Plato's physics in the cosmos of the fixed stars as well as in that of the primary elements," writes an eminent Plato scholar, "everything is indeterminate in the realm below the order of the elementary atoms. . . . What resists strict order in nature is due to the indeterminate and uneven forces in the Receptacle" (Friedländer, 1958). Indeed, for P. Friedländer Plato's doctrine of the unintelligible subatomic substratum is "an ancient anticipation of a most recent development," to wit: W. Heisenberg's uncertainty principle. Still, whether such a comparison is fully justified may be called into question.

An undisputable early example of indeterminacy, in any case, is Epicurus' theory of the atomic "swerve" (*clinamen*). Elaborating on Democritus' atomic theory and his strict determinism of elementary processes,

Epicurus contended that "through the undisturbed void all bodies must travel at equal speed though impelled by unequal weights" (Lucretius II, lines 238–39), anticipating thereby Galileo's conclusion that light and heavy objects fall in the vacuum with the same speed. Since consequently the idea that compounds are formed by heavy atoms impinging upon light ones had to be given up, "nature would never have created anything." To avoid this impasse, Epicurus resorted to a device, the theory of the swerve, which some critics, such as Cicero and Plutarch, regarded as "childish"; others, like Guyau or Masson, as "ingenious." "When the atoms are travelling straight down through empty space by their own weight, at quite unpredictable times and place (*incerto tempore incertisque locis*), they swerve ever so little from their course, just so much that you can call it a change of direction" (Lucretius II, lines 217–20). To account for change in the physical world Epicurus thus saw it necessary to break up the infinite chain of causality in violation of Leucippus' maxim that "nothing occurs by chance, but there is a reason and a necessity for everything." This indeterminacy which, as the quotation shows, is both an a-indeterminacy and a u-indeterminacy, made it possible for Epicurus to imbed a doctrine of free will within the framework of an atomic theory.

In the extensive medieval discussions (Maier, 1949) on necessity and contingency which were based, so far as physical problems were concerned, on Aristotle's *Physics* (Book II, Chs. 4–6, 195b 30–198a 13), the existence of chance is recognized, but not as a breach in necessary causation; it is regarded as a sequence of events in which an action or movement, due to some concomitant factor, produces exceptionally a result which is of a kind that might have been naturally, but was not factually, aimed at (Weiss, 1942). The essence of chance or contingency is not the absence of a necessary connection between antecedents and results, but the absence of *final* causation. Absolute indeterminacy in the sense of independence of antecedent causation was exclusively ascribed to volitional decisions.

3. Indeterminacy as Contingency. With the rise of Newtonian physics and its development, Laplacian determinism gained undisputed supremacy. Only in the middle of the nineteenth century did it wane to some extent. One of the earliest to regard contingent events in physics—an event being contingent if its opposite involves no contradiction—as physically possible was A. A. Cournot (Cournot, 1851; 1861). Charles Renouvier, following Cournot, questioned the strict validity of the causality principle as a regulative determinant of physical processes (Renouvier, 1864). A philosophy of nature based on contingency was proposed by Émile Boutroux, who regarded rigorous

determinsim as expressed in scientific laws as an inadequate manifestation of a reality which in his opinion is subject to radical contingency (Boutroux, 1874). The rejection of classical determinism at the atomic level played an important role also in Charles Sanders Peirce's theory of tychism (Greek: *tyche* = chance) according to which "chance is a basic factor in the universe." Deterministic or "necessitarian" philosophy of nature, argued Peirce, cannot explain the undeniable phenomena of growth and evolution. Another incontestable argument against deterministic mechanics was, in his view, the incapability of the necessitarians to prove their contention empirically by observation or measurement. For how can experiment ever determine an exact value of a continuous quantity, he asked, "with a probable error absolutely *nil?*" Analyzing the process of experimental observation, and anticipating thereby an idea similar to Heisenberg's uncertainty principle, Peirce arrived at the conclusion that absolute chance, and not an indeterminacy originating merely from our ignorance, is an irreducible factor in physical processes: "Try to verify any law of nature, and you will find that the more precise your observations, the more certain they will be to show irregular departures from the law. We are accustomed to ascribe these, and I do not say wrongly, to errors of observation; yet we cannot usually account for such errors in any antecedently probable way. Trace their causes back far enough and you will be forced to admit they are always due to arbitrary determination, or chance" (Peirce, 1892). The objection raised for instance by F. H. Bradley, that the idea of chance events is an unintelligible conception, was rebutted by Peirce on the grounds that the notion as such has nothing illogical in it; it becomes unintelligible only on the assumption of a universal determinism; but to assume such a determinism and to deduce from it the nonexistence of chance would be begging the question.

4. Classical Physics and Indeterminacy. The various theses of indeterminacies in physics mentioned so far have been advanced by philosophers and not by physicists, the reason being, of course, that classical physics, since the days of Newton and Laplace, was the paradigm of a deterministic and predictable science. It was also taken for granted that the precision attainable in measurement is theoretically unlimited; for although it was admitted that measurements are always accompanied by statistical errors, it was claimed that these errors could be made smaller and smaller with progressive techniques.

The first physicist in modern times to question the strict determinism of physical laws was probably Ludwig Boltzmann. In his lectures on gas theory he declared in 1895: "Since today it is popular to look forward to the time when our view of nature will have been completely changed, I will mention the possibility that the fundamental equations for the motion of individual molecules will turn out to be only approximate formulas which give average values, resulting according to the probability calculus from the interactions of many independent moving entities forming the surrounding medium" (Boltzmann, 1895). Boltzmann's successor at the University of Vienna, Franz Exner, proposed in 1919 a statistical interpretation of the apparent deterministic behavior of macroscopic phenomena which he regarded as resulting from a great number of probabilistic processes at the submicroscopic level.

From a multitude of events . . . laws can be inferred which are valid for the average state [*Durchschnittszustand*] of this multitude whereas the individual event may remain undetermined. In this sense the principle of causality holds for all macroscopic occurrences without being necessarily valid for the microcosm. It also follows that the laws of the macrocosm are not absolute laws but rather laws of probability; whether they hold always and everywhere remains to be questioned; to predict in physics the outcome of an individual process is impossible (Exner, 1919).

In the same year Charles Galton Darwin, influenced by Henri Poincaré's allusion toward a probabilistic reformulation of physical laws and his doubts about the validity of differential equations as reflecting the true nature of physical laws (H. Poincaré, *Dernières pensées*), made the bold statement that it may "prove necessary to make fundamental changes in our ideas of time and space, or to abandon the conservation of matter and electricity, or even in the last resort to endow electrons with free will" (Charles Galton Darwin, 1919). The ascription of free will to electrons— clearly an anthropomorphic metaphorism for a- and u-indeterminacies—was suggested by certain results in quantum theory such as the unpredictable and apparently acausal emission of electrons from a radioactive element or their unpredictable transitions from one energy level to another in the atom. In the early twenties questions concerning the limitations of the sensitivity of measuring instruments came to the forefront of physical interest when, with no direct connection with quantum effects, the disturbing effects of the Brownian fluctuations were studied in detail (W. Einthoven, G. Ising, F. Zernike). It became increasingly clear that Brownian motion, or "noise" as it was called in the terminology of electronics, puts a definite limit to the sensitivity of electronic measuring devices and hence to measurements in general. Classical physics, it seemed, has to abandon its principle of unlimited precision and to admit, instead, unavoidable i-indeterminacies. It can be shown that this development did

not elicit the establishment of Heisenberg's uncertainty relations in quantum mechanics (Jammer [1966], p. 331).

5. Indeterminacies in Quantum Mechanics. The necessity of introducing indeterminacy considerations into quantum mechanics became apparent as soon as the mathematical formalism of the theory was established (in the spring of 1927). When Ernst Schrödinger, in 1926, laid the foundations of wave mechanics he interpreted atomic phenomena as continuous, causal undulatory processes, in contrast to Heisenberg's matrix mechanics in which these processes were interpreted as discontinuous and ruled by probability laws. When in September 1926 Schrödinger visited Niels Bohr and Heisenberg in Copenhagen, the conflict between these opposing interpretations reached its climax and no compromise seemed possible. As a result of this controversy Heisenberg felt it necessary to examine more closely the precise meaning of the role of dynamical variables in quantum mechanics, such as position, momentum, or energy, and to find out how far they were operationally warranted.

First he derived from the mathematical formalism of quantum mechanics (Dirac-Jordan transformation theory) the following result. If a wave packet with a Gaussian distribution in the position coordinate q, to wit $\psi(q) = \text{const. } \exp\left[-q^2/2(\Delta q)^2\right]$, Δq being the half-width and consequently proportional to the standard deviation, is transformed by a Fourier transformation into a momentum distribution, the latter turns out to be $\varphi(p) = \text{const. } \exp\left[-p^2/2(\hbar/\Delta q)^2\right]$. Since the corresponding half-width Δp is now given by $\hbar/\Delta q$, Heisenberg concluded that $\Delta q \, \Delta p \approx \hbar$ or more generally, if other distributions are used,

$$\Delta q \, \Delta p \gtrsim \hbar \tag{1}$$

This inequality shows that the uncertainties (or *dispersions*) in position and momentum are reciprocal: if one approaches zero the other approaches infinity. The meaning of relation (1), which was soon called the "Heisenberg position-momentum uncertainty relation," can also be expressed as follows: *it is impossible to measure simultaneously both the position and the momentum of a quantum-mechanical system with arbitrary accuracy; the more precise the measurement of one of these two variables is, the less precise is that of the other.*

Asking himself whether a close analysis of actual measuring procedures does not lead to a result in contradiction to (1), Heisenberg studied what has since become known as the "gamma-ray microscopic experiment." Adopting the operational view that a physical concept is meaningful only if a definite procedure is indicated for how to measure its value, Heisenberg declared that if we speak of the position of an electron we have to define a method of measuring it. The electron's position, he continued, may be found by illuminating it and observing the scattered light under a microscope. The shorter the wavelength of the light, the more precise, according to the diffraction laws of optics, will be the determination of the position—but the more noticeable will also be the Compton effect and the resulting change in the momentum of the electron. By calculating the uncertainties resulting from the Compton effect and the finite aperture of the microscope, the importance of which for the whole consideration was pointed out by Bohr, Heisenberg showed that the obtainable precision does not surpass the restrictions imposed by the inequality (1). Similarly, by analyzing closely a Stern-Gerlach experiment of measuring the magnetic moment of particles, Heisenberg showed that the dispersion ΔE in the energy of these particles is smaller the longer the time Δt spent by them in crossing the deviating field (or measuring device):

$$\Delta E \, \Delta t \gtrsim \hbar \qquad (2)$$

It has been claimed that this "energy-time uncertainty relation" had been implicitly applied by A. Sommerfeld in 1911, O. Sackur in 1912, and K. Eisenmann in 1912 (Kudrjawzew, 1965). Bohr, as we know from documentary evidence (Archive for the History of Quantum Physics, Interview with Heisenberg, February 25, 1963), accepted the uncertainty relations (1) and (2), but not their interpretation as proposed by Heisenberg. For Heisenberg they expressed the limitation of the applicability of classical notions to microphysics, whether these notions are those of particle language or wave language, one language being replaceable by the other and equivalent to it. For Bohr, on the other hand, they were an indication that both modes of expression, though conjointly necessary for an exhaustive description of physical phenomena, cannot be used at the same time. As a result of this debate Heisenberg added to the paper in which he published the uncertainty relations (Heisenberg, 1927) a "Postscript" in which he acknowledged that an as yet unpublished investigation by Bohr would lead to a deeper understanding of the significance of the uncertainty relations and "to an important refinement of the results obtained in the paper." It was the first allusion to Bohr's complementarity interpretation, often also loosely called the "Copenhagen interpretation" of quantum mechanics (Jammer [1966], pp. 345–61). Bohr regarded the uncertainty relations whose derivations (by thought-experiments) are still based on the de Broglie-Einstein equations $E = h\nu$ and $p = h/\lambda$, that is, relations between particulate (energy E, momentum p) and undulatory conceptions (frequency ν, wavelength λ), merely as a confirmation of the wave-particle duality and hence of the complementarity interpretation (Schiff, 1968).

6. Philosophical Implications of the Uncertainty Relations. In their original interpretation, as we have seen, the Heisenberg uncertainty relations express first of all a principle of limited measurability of dynamical variables (position, momentum, energy, etc.) of individual microsystems (particles, photons), though according to the complementarity interpretation their significance is not restricted merely to such a principle (Grünbaum, 1957). But even *qua* such a principle their epistemological implications were soon recognized and the relations became an issue of extensive discussions. Heisenberg himself saw their philosophical import in the fact that they imply a renunciation of the causality principle in its "strong formulation," viz., "If we know exactly the present, we can predict the future." Since, now, in view of these relations the present can never be known exactly, Heisenberg argued, the causality principle as formulated, though logically and not refuted, must necessarily remain an "empty" statement; for it is not the conclusion, but rather the premiss which is false.

In view of the intimate connection between the statistical character of the quantum theory and the imprecision of all perception, it may be suggested that behind the statistical universe of perception there lies hidden a "real" world ruled by causality. Such speculation seems to us—and this we stress with emphasis—useless and meaningless. For physics has to confine itself to the formal description of the relations among perceptions (Heisenberg [1927], p. 197).

Using the terminology of the introductory section of this article, we may say that Heisenberg interpreted the uncertainties appearing in the relations carrying his name not only as i-indeterminacies, but also as a-indeterminacies, provided the causality principle is understood in its strong formulation, and *a fortiori* also as u-indeterminacies. His idea that the unascertainability of exact initial values obstructs predictability and hence deprives causality of any operational meaning was soon hailed, particularly by M. Schlick, as a "surprising" solution of the age-old problem of causality, a solution which had never been anticipated in spite of the many discussions on this issue (Schlick, 1931).

Heisenberg's uncertainty relations were also regarded as a possible resolution of the long-standing conflict between determinism and the doctrine of free will. "If the atom has indeterminacy, surely the human mind will have an equal indeterminacy; for we can scarcely accept a theory which makes out the mind to be more mechanistic than the atom" (Eddington,

1932). The Epicurean-Lucretian theory of the "minute swerving of the elements" enjoyed an unexpected revival in the twentieth century.

The philosophical impact of the uncertainty relations on the development of the subject-object problem, one of the crucial stages of the interaction between problems of physics and of epistemology, problems which still persist, was discussed in great detail by Ernst Cassirer (Cassirer, 1936, 1937).

Heisenberg's interpretation of the uncertainty relations, however, became soon the target also of other serious criticisms. In a lecture delivered in 1932 Schrödinger, who only two years earlier gave a general, and compared with Heisenberg's formula still more restrictive, derivation of the relations for any pair of noncommuting operators, challenged Heisenberg's view as inconsistent; Schrödinger claimed that a denial of sharp values for position and momentum amounts to renouncing the very concept of a particle (mass-point) (Schrödinger, 1930; 1932). Max von Laue charged Heisenberg's conclusions as unwarranted and hasty (von Laue, 1932). Karl Popper challenged Heisenberg with having given "a causal explanation why causal explanations are impossible" (Popper, 1935). The main attack, however, was launched within physics itself—by Albert Einstein in his debate with Niels Bohr.

7. *The Einstein-Bohr Controversy about Indeterminacy.* Although having decidedly furthered the development of the probabilistic interpretation of quantum phenomena through his early contributions to the photo-electric effect and through his statistical derivation of Planck's formula for black-body radiation, Einstein never agreed to abandon the principles of causality and continuity or, equivalently, to renounce the need of a causal account in space and time, in favor of a statistical theory; and he saw in the latter only an incomplete description of physical reality which has to be supplanted sooner or later by a fully deterministic theory. To prove that the Bohr-Heisenberg theory of quantum phenomena does not exhaust the possibilities of accounting for observable phenomena, and is consequently only an incomplete description, it would suffice, argued Einstein correctly, to show that a close analysis of fundamental measuring procedures leads to results in contradiction to the uncertainty relations. It was clear that disproving these relations means disproving the whole theory of quantum mechanics.

Thus, during the Fifth Solvay Congress in Brussels (October 24 to 29, 1927) Einstein challenged the correctness of the uncertainty relations by scrutinizing a number of thought-experiments, but Bohr succeeded in rebutting all attacks (Bohr, 1949). The most dramatic phase of this controversy occurred at the Sixth Solvay

Congress (Brussels, October 20 to 25, 1930) where these discussions were resumed when Einstein challenged the energy-time uncertainty relation $\Delta E \, \Delta t \gtrsim \hbar$ with the famous photon-box thought-experiment (Jammer [1966], pp. 359–60). Considering a box with a shutter, operated by a clockwork in the box so as to be opened at a moment known with arbitrary accuracy, and releasing thereby a single photon, Einstein claimed that by weighing the box before and after the photon-emission and resorting to the equivalence between energy and mass, $E = mc^2$, both ΔE and Δt can be made as small as desired, in blatant violation of the relation (2). Bohr, however (after a sleepless night!), refuted Einstein's challenge with Einstein's own weaponry; referring to the red-shift formula of general relativity according to which the rate of a clock depends on its position in a gravitational field Bohr showed that, if this factor is correctly taken into account, Heisenberg's energy-time uncertainty relation is fully obeyed. Einstein's photon-box, if used as a means for accurately measuring the energy of the photon, cannot be used for controlling accurately the moment of its release. If closely examined, Bohr's refutation of Einstein's argument was erroneous, but so was Einstein's argument (Jammer, 1972). In any case, Einstein was defeated but not convinced, as Bohr himself admitted. In fact, in a paper written five years later in collaboration with B. Podolsky and N. Rosen, Einstein showed that in the case of a two-particle system whose two components separate after their interaction, it is possible to predict with certainty either the exact value of the position or of the momentum of one of the components without interfering with it at all, but merely performing the appropriate measurement on its partner. Clearly, such a result would violate the uncertainty relation (1) and condemn the quantum-mechanical description as incomplete (Einstein, 1935). Although the majority of quantum-theoreticians are of the opinion that Bohr refuted this challenge also (Bohr, 1935), there are some physicists who consider the Einstein-Podolsky-Rosen argument as a fatal blow to the Copenhagen interpretation.

Criticisms of a more technical nature were leveled against the energy-time uncertainty relation (2). It was early recognized that the rigorous derivation of the position-momentum relation from the quantum-mechanical formalism as a calculus of Hermitian operators in Hilbert space has no analogue for the energy-time relation; for while the dynamical variables q and p are representable in the formalism as Hermitian (noncommutative) operators, satisfying the relation $qp - pq = i\hbar$, and although the energy of a system is likewise represented as a Hermitian operator, the Hamiltonian, the time variable cannot be represented by such an operator (Pauli, 1933). In fact, it can be shown that the position and momentum coordinates, q and p, and their linear combinations are the only canonical conjugates for which uncertainty relations in the Heisenberg sense can be derived from the operator formalism. This circumstance gave rise to the fact that the exact meaning of the indeterminacy Δt in the energy-time uncertainty relation was never unambiguously defined. Thus in recent discussions of this uncertainty relation at least three different meanings of Δt can be distinguished (duration of the opening time of a slit; the uncertainty of this time-period; the duration of a concomitant measuring process c.f., Chyliński, 1965; Halpern, 1966; 1968). Such ambiguities led L. I. Mandelstam and I. Tamm, in 1945, to interpret Δt in this uncertainty relation as the time during which the temporal mean value of the standard deviation of an observable R becomes equal to the change of its standard deviation: $\overline{\Delta R} = <R_{t+\Delta t}> - <R_t>$. If ΔE, now, denotes the energy standard deviation of the system under discussion during the R-measurement, then the energy-time uncertainty relation acquires the same logical status within the formalism of quantum mechanics as that possessed by the position-momentum relation.

A different approach to reach an unambiguous interpretation of the energy-time uncertainty relation had been proposed as early as 1931 by L. D. Landau and R. Peierls on the basis of the quantum-mechanical perturbation theory (Landau and Peierls, 1931; Landau and Lifshitz [1958], pp. 150–53), and was subsequently elaborated by N. S. Krylov and V. A. Fock (Krylov and Fock, 1947). This approach was later severely criticized by Y. Aharonov and D. Bohm (Aharonov and Bohm, 1961) which led to an extended discussion on this issue without reaching consensus (Fock, 1962; Aharonov and Bohm, 1964; Fock, 1965). Recently attempts have been made to extend the formalism of quantum mechanics, as for instance by generalizing the Hilbert space to a super-Hilbert space (Rosenbaum, 1969), so that it admits the definition of a quantum-mechanical time-operator and puts the energy-time uncertainty relation on the same footing as that of position and momentum (Engelmann and Fick, 1959, 1964; Paul, 1962; Allcock, 1969).

8. The Statistical Interpretation of Quantum-mechanical Indeterminacy. If the ψ-function characterizes the behavior not of an individual particle but of a statistical ensemble of particles, as contended in the "statistical interpretation" of the quantum-mechanical formalism, then obviously the uncertainty relations, at least as far they derive from this formalism, refer likewise not to individual particles but to statistical ensembles of these. In other words, relation (1)

denotes, in this view, a correlation between the dispersion or "spread" of measurements of position, and the dispersion or "spread" of measurements of momentum, if carried out on a large ensemble of identically prepared systems. Under these circumstances the idea that noncommuting variables are not necessarily incompatible but can be measured simultaneously on individual systems would not violate the statistical interpretation.

Such an interpretation of quantum-mechanical indeterminacy was suggested relatively early by Popper (Popper, 1935). His reformulation of the uncertainty principle reads as follows: given an ensemble (aggregate of particles or sequence of experiments performed on *one* particle which after each experiment is brought back to its original state) from which, at a certain moment and with a given precision Δq, those particles having a certain position q are selected; the momenta p of the latter will then show a random scattering with a range of scatter Δp where $\Delta q\,\Delta p \gtrsim \hbar$, and vice versa. Popper even thought, though erroneously as he himself soon realized, to have proved his contention by the construction of a thought-experiment for the determination of the sharp values of position and momentum (Popper, 1934).

The ensemble interpretation of indeterminacy found an eloquent advocate in Henry Margenau. Distinguishing sharply between subjective or *a priori* and empirical or *a posteriori* probability, Margenau pointed out that the indeterminacy associated with a single measurement such as referred to in Heisenberg's gamma-ray experiment is nothing more than a qualitative subjective estimate, incapable of scientific verification; every other interpretation would at once revert to envisaging the single measurement as the constituent of a statistical ensemble; but as soon as the empirical view on probability is adopted which, grounded in frequencies, is the only one that is scientifically sound, the uncertainty principle, now asserting a relation between the dispersions of measurement results, becomes amenable to empirical verification. To vindicate this interpretation Margenau pointed out that, contrary to conventional ideas, canonical conjugates may well be measured with arbitrary accuracy at one and the same time; thus two microscopes, one using gamma rays and the other infra-red rays for a Doppler-experiment, may simultaneously locate the electron and determine its momentum and no law of quantum mechanics prohibits such a double measurement from succeeding (Margenau, 1937; 1950). This view does not abnegate the principle, for on repeating such measurements many times with identically prepared systems the product of the standard deviations of the values obtained will have a definite lower limit.

Although Margenau and R. N. Hill (Margenau and

Hill, 1961) found that the usual Hilbert space formalism of quantum mechanics does not admit probability distributions for simultaneous measurements of non-commuting variables, E. Prugovečki has suggested that by introducing complex probability distributions the existing formalism of mathematical statistics can be generalized so as to overcome this difficulty. For other approaches to the same purpose we refer the reader to an important paper by Margenau and Leon Cohen, and the bibliography listed therein (Margenau and Cohen, 1967), and also to the analyses of simultaneous measurements of conjugate variables carried out by E. Arthurs and J. L. Kelly (Arthurs and Kelly, 1965), C. Y. She and H. Heffner (She and Heffner, 1966), James L. Park and Margenau (J. L. Park and Margenau, 1968), William T. Scott (Scott, 1968), and Dick H. Holze and William T. Scott (Holze and Scott, 1968). These investigations suggest the result that neither single quantum-mechanical measurements nor even combined simultaneous measurements of canonically conjugate variables are, in the terminology of the introduction, subject to i-indeterminacy, even though they are subject to u-indeterminacy.

9. Indeterminacy in Classical Physics. Popper questioned the absence, in principle, of indeterminacies, and in particular of u-indeterminacies, in classical physics. Calling a theory indeterministic if it asserts that at least *one* event is not completely determined in the sense of being not predictable in all its details, Popper attempted to prove on logical grounds that classical physics is indeterministic since it contains u-indeterminacies (Popper, 1950). He derived this conclusion by showing that no "predictor," i.e., a calculating and predicting machine (today we would say simply "computer"), constructed and working on classical principles, is capable of fully predicting every one of its own future states; nor can it fully predict, or be predicted by, any other predictor with which it interacts. Popper's reasoning has been challenged by G. F. Dear on the grounds that the sense in which "self-prediction" was used by Popper to show its impossibility is not the sense in which this notion has to be used in order to allow for the effects of interference (Dear, 1961). Dear's criticism, in turn, has recently been shown to be untenable by W. Hoering (Hoering, 1969) who argued on the basis of Leon Brillouin's penetrating investigations (Brillouin, 1964) that "although Popper's reasoning is open to criticism he arrives at the right conclusion."

That classical physics is not free of u-indeterminacies was also contended by Max Born (Born, 1955a; 1955b) who based his claim on the observation that even in classical physics the assumption of knowing precise initial values of observables is an unjustified idealization and that, rather, small errors must always be assigned to such values. As soon as this is admitted, however, it is easy to show that within the course of time these errors accumulate immensely and evoke serious indeterminacies. To illustrate this idea Born applied Einstein's model of a one-dimensional gas with one atom which is assumed to be confined to an interval of length L, being elastically reflected at the endpoints of this interval. If it is assumed that at time $t = 0$ the atom is at $x = x_0$ and its velocity has a value between v_0 and $v_0 + \Delta v_0$, it follows that at time $t = L/\Delta v_0$, the position-indeterminacy equals L itself, and our initial knowledge has been converted into complete ignorance. In fact, even if the initial error in the position of every air molecule in a row is only one millionth of a percent, after less than one micro-second (under standard conditions) all knowledge about the air will be effaced. Thus, according to Born, not only quantum physics, but already classical physics is replete with u-indeterminacies which derive from unavoidable i-indeterminacies.

The mathematical situation underlying Born's reasoning had been the subject of detailed investigations in connection with problems about the stability of motion at the end of the last century (Liapunov, Poincaré), but its relevancy for the indeterminacy of classical physics was pointed out only quite recently (Brillouin, 1956).

Born's argumentation was challenged by von Laue (von Laue, 1955), and more recently also by Margenau and Cohen (Margenau and Cohen, 1967). As Laue pointed out, the indeterminacy referred to by Born is essentially merely a technical limitation of measurement which in principle can be refined as much as desired. If the state of the system is represented by a point P in phase-space, observation at time $t = 0$ will assign to P a phase-space volume V_0 which is larger the greater the error in measurement. In accordance with the theory it is then known that at time $t = t_1$ the representative point P is located in a volume V_1 which, according to the Liouville theorem of statistical mechanics, equals V_0. If, now, at $t = t_1$ a measurement is performed, P will be found in a volume V_1' which, if theory and measurement are correct, must have a nonzero intersection D_1 with V_1. D_1 is smaller than V_1 and hence also smaller than V_0. To D_1, as a subset of V_1, corresponds a subset of V_0 so that the initial indeterminacy, even without a refinement of the immediate measurement technique, has been reduced. Since this corrective procedure can be iterated *ad libidum* and thus the "orbit" of the system defined with arbitrary accuracy, classical mechanics has no un-eliminable indeterminacies. In quantum mechanics, on the other hand, due to the unavoidable interference of the measuring device upon the object of measurement, such a corrective procedure does not work; in other words, the volume V_0 in phase-space cannot be made smaller than h^n, where n is the number of the degrees of freedom of the system, and quantum-mechanical indeterminacy is an irreducible fact. This fundamental difference between classical and quantum physics has its ultimate source in the different conceptions of an objective (observation-independent) physical reality.

BIBLIOGRAPHY

Y. Aharonov and D. Bohm, "Time in the Quantum Theory and the Uncertainty Relation for Time and Energy," *Physical Review*, **122** (1961), 1649–58; idem, "Answer to Fock Concerning the Time Energy Indeterminacy Relation," *Physical Review*, **134** (1964), B 1417–18. G. R. Allcock, "The Time of Arrival in Quantum Mechanics," *Annals of Physics*, **53** (1969), 253–85, 286–310, 311–48. *Archive for the History of Quantum Physics* (Philadelphia, Berkeley, Copenhagen, 1961–64). E. Arthurs and J. L. Kelly, "On the Simultaneous Measurement of a Pair of Conjugate Observables," *The Bell System Technical Journal*, **44** (1965), 725–29. N. Bohr, "Can Quantum Mechanical Description of Physical Reality be Considered Complete?," *Physical Review*, **48** (1935), 696–702; idem, "Discussion with Einstein," in *Albert Einstein: Philosopher-Scientist*, ed. P. A. Schilpp (Evanston, Ill., 1949), pp. 199–241. L. Boltzmann, *Lectures on Gas Theory* (1895), trans. Stephen G. Brush (Berkeley, 1964). M. Born, "Continuity, Determinism and Reality," *Kgl. Danske Videnskarb. Selskab. Math.-Fys. Medd.*, **30** (1955a), 1–26; idem, "Ist die klassische Mechanik tatsächlich deterministisch?" *Physikalische Blätter*, **11** (1955b), 49–54. E. Boutroux, *De la contingence des lois de la nature* (Paris, 1874). L. Brillouin, *Science and Information Theory* (New York, 1956; 1962); idem, *Scientific Uncertainty and Information* (New York, 1964). E. Cassirer, *Determinism and Indeterminism in Modern Physcis*, trans. O. T. Benfey (1936, 1937; New Haven, 1956). Z. Chyliński, "Uncertainty Relation between Time and Energy," *Acta Physica Polonica*, **28** (1965), 631–38. A. A. Cournot, *Essai sur les fondements de nos connaisances* (Paris, 1851); idem, *Traité de l'enchaînement des idées fondamentales dans les sciences et dans l'histoire* (Paris, 1861). C. G. Darwin, "Critique of the Foundations of Physics," unpublished (1919); manuscript in the Library of the American Philosophical Society, Philadelphia, Pa. G. F. Dear, "Determinism in Classical Physics," *British Journal for the Philosophy of Science*, **11** (1961), 289–304. A. S. Eddington, "The Decline of Determinism," *Mathematical Gazette*, **16** (1932), 66–80. A. Einstein, B. Podolsky, and N. Rosen, "Can Quantum-mechanical Description of Physical Reality be Considered Complete?" *Physical Review*, **47** (1935), 777–80. F. Engelmann and E. Fick, "Die Zeit in der Quantenmechanik," *Il Nuovo Cimento* (*Suppl.*), **12** (1959), 63–72; idem, "Quantentheorie der Zeitmessung," *Zeitschrift für Physik*, **175** (1964), 271–82. F. Exner, *Vorlesungen über die physikalischen Grundlagen der Naturwissenschaften* (Vienna, 1919), pp. 705–06. V. A. Fock, "Criticism of an Attempt to Disprove the Uncertainty Relation between Time and Energy," *Soviet Physics JETP*, **15** (1962), 784–86; idem, "More about the Energy-time Uncertainty Relation," *Soviet Physics Uspekhi*, **8** (1965), 628–29. P. Friedländer, *Plato: An Introduction* (New York, 1958), p. 251. A. Grünbaum, "Determinism in the Light of Recent Physics," *The Journal of Philosophy*, **54** (1957), 713–27. O. Halpern, "On the Einstein-Bohr Ideal Experiment," *Acta Physica Austriaca*, **24** (1966), 274–79; idem, "On the Einstein-Bohr Ideal Experiment, II, ibid., **28** (1968), 356–58. W. Heisenberg, "Über den anschaulichen Inhalt der quanten-theoretischen Kinematik und Mechanik," *Zeitschrift für Physik*, **43** (1927), 172–98. W. Hoering, "Indeterminism in Classical Physics," *British Journal for the Philosophy of Science*, **20** (1969), 247–55. D. H. Holze and W. T. Scott, "The Consequences of Measurement in Quantum Mechanics. II. A Detailed Position Measurement Thought Experiment," *Annals of Physics*, **47** (1968), 489–515. M. Jammer, *The Conceptual Development of Quantum Mechanics* (New York, 1966); idem, *The Interpretations of Quantum Mechanics* (New York, 1972). N. S. Krylov and V. A. Fock, "On the Uncertainty Relation between Time and Energy," *Journal of Physics* (*USSR*), **11** (1947), 112–20. P. S. Kudrjawzew, "Aus der Geschichte der Unschärferelation," *NTM: Schriftenreihe für Geschichte der Naturwissenschaften, Technik und Medizin*, **2** (1965), 20–22. L. D. Landau and E. M. Lifschitz, *Quantum Mechanics* (Reading, Mass., 1958). L. D. Landau and R. Peierls, "Erweiterung des Unbestimmtheitsprinzips für die relativistische Quantentheorie," *Zeitschrift für Physik*, **69** (1931), 56–69. M. von Laue, "Zu den Erörterungen über Kausalität," *Die Naturwissenschaften*, **20** (1932), 915–16; idem, "Ist die klassische Physik wirklich deterministisch?," *Physikalische Blätter*, **11** (1955), 269–70. A. Maier, *Die Vorläufer Galileis im 14. Jahrhundert* (Rome, 1949), pp. 219–50. L. I. Mandelstam and I. Tamm, "The Uncertainty Relation between Energy and Time in Non-relativistic Quantum Mechanics," *Journal of Physics* (*USSR*), **9** (1945), 249–54. H. Margenau, "Critical Points in Modern Physical Theory," *Philosophy of Science*, **4** (1937), 337–70; idem, *The Nature of Physical Reality* (New York, 1950), pp. 375–77. H. Margenau and L. Cohen, "Probabilities in Quantum Mechanics," in *Quantum Theory and Reality*, ed. M. Bunge (New York, 1967), pp. 71–89. H. Margenau and R. N. Hill, "Correlation between Measurements in Quantum Theory," *Progress of Theoretical Physics*, **26** (1961), 722–38. J. L. Park and H. Margenau, "Simultaneous Measurement in Quantum Theory," *International Journal of Theoretical Physics*, **1** (1968), 211–83. H. Paul, "Über quantenmechanische Zeitoperatoren," *Annalen der Physik*, **9** (1962), 252–61. W. Pauli, "Die allgemeinen Prinzipien der Wellenmechanik," in *Handbuch der Physik*, ed. H. Geiger and K. Scheel (Berlin, 1930), Vol. 24. C. S. Peirce, *Collected Papers*, 8 vols. (Cambridge, Mass., 1935), Vol. 6, paragraph 46. Henri Poincaré, *Dernières pensées* (Paris, 1913). K. R. Popper, "Zur Kritik der Ungenauigkeitsrelationen," *Die Naturwissenschaften*, **22** (1934), 807–08; idem, *Logik der Forschung* (Vienna, 1935), p. 184; *The Logic of Scientific Discovery* (New York, 1959), p. 249; idem,

"Indeterminism in Quantum Physics and in Classical Physics," *British Journal for the Philosophy of Science,* **1** (1950), 117–33, 173–95. E. Prugovečki, "On a Theory of Measurement of Incompatible Observables in Quantum Mechanics," *Canadian Journal of Physics,* **45** (1967), 2173–2219. Ch. Renouvier, *Les principes de la nature* (Paris, 1864). D. M. Rosenbaum, "Super Hilbert Space and the Quantum Mechanical Time Operator," *Journal of Mathematical Physics,* **10** (1969), 1127–44. L. I. Schiff, *Quantum Mechanics* (New York, 1968), pp. 7–14. M. Schlick, "Die Kausalität in der gegenwärtigen Physik," *Die Naturwissenschaften,* **19** (1931), 145–62. W. T. Scott, "The Consequences of Measurement in Quantum Mechanics; I. An Idealized Trajectory Determination," *Annals of Physics,* **46** (1968), 577–92. E. Schrödinger, "Zum Heisenbergschen Unschärfeprinzip," *Berliner Sitzungsberichte* (1930), pp. 296–303; idem, *Uber Indeterminismus in der Physik—2 Vorträge* (Leipzig, 1932). C. Y. She and H. Heffner, "Simultaneous Measurement of Noncommuting Observables," *Physical Review,* **152** (1966), 1103–10. H. Weiss, *Kausalität und Zufall in der Philosophie des Aristoteles* (Basel, 1942).

MAX JAMMER

[See also Atomism; Causation; Determinism; Entropy; **Probability.**]

TYPES OF INDIVIDUALISM

"Individualism" is a term ranging over a wide variety of attitudes, doctrines, and theories, and this diversity of meaning is only increased when one takes account of historical shifts in the connotations of the very word "individual" and its synonyms (Mauss, 1937; Ullmann, 1966). The relation of these various meanings to one another is largely one of family resemblance, though "individualism" has usually been understood as expressing some cluster of such meanings, which usually are either not distinguished from one another or else assumed to be logically or conceptually related.

I. HISTORY OF THE TERM
"INDIVIDUALISM"

The first uses of the term, in its French form *individualisme,* grew out of the context of the counterrevolutionary critique of the Enlightenment. Conservative thought of the early nineteenth century was virtually unanimous in condemning the appeal to individual reason, interests, and rights, sharing Burke's scorn for the individual's "private stock of reason" and his fear that the commonwealth would "crumble away, be disconnected into the dust and powder of individuality" (*Reflections on the Revolution in France,* 1790). These attitudes were especially marked among the

French theocrats: in the earliest known use of the word, Joseph de Maistre spoke in 1820 of "this deep and frightening division of minds, this infinite fragmentation of all doctrines, political protestantism carried to the most absolute individualism," a passage found in an *Extrait d'une conversation,* in *Oeuvres complètes* (Lyon [1886], XIV, 286), while Lamennais wrote that "the same doctrine which produces anarchy among minds produces in addition an irremediable political anarchy, and overturns the very bases of human society," and after asking: "What is power without obedience? What is law without duty?" his answer was *individualism* (*Des Progrès de la révolution et de la guerre contre l'église* [1829], Ch. I). The Saint-Simonians, themselves influenced by the theocrats, were the first to use the term systematically in the mid-1820's, to refer to a complex of related elements which they held to characterize the modern "critical epoch" originating with the Reformation. Such elements were the narrow and negative eighteenth-century philosophy glorifying self-interest and the individual's conscience and rights; liberalism in politics; anarchy and exploitation in the economic sphere; and unbounded egoism everywhere. They saw the eighteenth-century philosophers as "defenders of individualism," reviving the egoism of Epicurus and the Stoics, and they held the inevitable political result of individualism to be "opposition to any attempt at organisation from a centre of direction for the moral interests of mankind . . ." (*Doctrine de Saint-Simon: exposition—première année, 1829,* 1830, twelfth session).

Partly because of the extraordinarily pervasive influence of Saint-Simonian ideas, "individualism" came to be very widely used during the nineteenth century. Among the French it mostly carried, and indeed continues to carry, a negative evaluation, though there was a short-lived "Société d'Individualistes" of French *Carbonari* in the 1820's, and various individual thinkers adopted the label, among them Proudhon—though even Proudhon wrote that "outside the group there are only abstractions and phantoms" (*Lettres sur la philosophie du progrès* [1853], Letter 1, Part IV). It is possible to fit a variety of French thinkers into a history of individualist ideas (Schatz, 1907, but note the defensive tone), yet few have welcomed the epithet, and many stressed the opposition (first formulated by the Swiss theologian Alexandre Vinet) between *individualisme* (implying anarchy and social atomization) and *individualité* (implying personal liberty and self-development). In French thought *individualisme* has almost always pointed to the sources of social dissolution, though there have been wide divergences concerning the nature of those sources and of the social order they are held to threaten, as well as in the historical frameworks in which they are conceptualized.

For some, individualism resides in dangerous ideas, for others it is social or economic anarchy, a lack of the requisite institutions and norms, for yet others it is the prevalence of self-interested attitudes among individuals. Men of the right, from de Maistre through Veuillot and Brunetière to Maurras, have seen it as all that undermines a traditionalist, hierarchical order. Socialists, including Leroux, Pecqueur, Cabet, Blanc, and Blanqui, contrasted it with "association" and "associationism," "philanthropy," "altruism," "socialism," and "communism," though Blanc also stressed its progressive aspect as a rejection of authority and a "necessary transition" to a future age of fraternity, while the followers of Fourier denied any basic opposition between individualism and socialism, and Jaurès saw socialism as the logical completion of individualism. Liberals such as Tocqueville condemned it as inimical to liberty. For Tocqueville it was the natural product of democracy ("Individualism is of democratic origin and threatens to develop insofar as conditions are equalised"), involving the apathetic withdrawal of individuals from public life and their isolation from one another, with a consequent weakening of society and the growth of the unchecked political power of the state. "Individualism" ("a recent expression to which a new idea has given birth") was "a deliberate and peaceful sentiment which disposes each citizen to isolate himself from the mass of his fellows and to draw apart with his family and friends" which "at first saps only the virtues of public life, but, in the long run, . . . attacks and destroys all the others and is eventually absorbed into pure egoism" (*De la démocratie en Amérique* [1835], Book II, Part II, Ch. II). The Americans, Tocqueville thought, only avoided this consequence because of their free institutions and tradition of active citizenship: they conquered individualism (implying privacy and born of equality) by means of liberty (implying that liberty is a public virtue born of enlightened self-interest).

No less diverse have been the historical perspectives within which French thinkers have conceived individualism. It is variously traced to the Reformation, the Renaissance, the Enlightenment, the Revolution, to the decline of the aristocracy or of the Church or of traditional religion, to the Industrial Revolution or the growth of capitalism, but there is wide agreement in seeing it as an evil and a threat to social order. (The latest edition of the *Dictionnaire de l'Académie Française*, 1932–35, defines it simply as "subordination of the general interest to the individual's interest.") Perhaps the role of *individualisme* in French thought is partly due to the practical success of "individualist" legislation at the time of the Revolution (Palmer, 1948)

together with its social, administrative, and political consequences. However that may be, the mainstream of French thought, especially in the nineteenth century, has expressed by *individualisme* the social, moral, and political isolation of rootless, self-interested, and acquisitive individuals unconcerned with social ideals and unamenable to social control. As Tocqueville wrote, "Our fathers did not have the word *individualisme*, which we have coined for our own use, because in their time there was indeed no individual who did not belong to a group and who could be considered as absolutely alone" (*L'ancien régime et la révolution* [1856], Book II, Ch. II).

Quite distinct from the French use of the term is another whose characteristic reference is German, namely, the romantic idea of individuality (*Individualität*), reacting against the abstract, uniform standards of the Enlightenment and glorifying individual uniqueness, originality, and self-development. The romantics themselves did not use the term *Individualismus*, but it came to be used in this sense from the 1840's, when a German Liberal, Karl Brüggemann, contrasted with its Saint-Simonian meaning that of a characteristically German "infinite" (*unendlichen*) and "whole-souled" (*innigen*) individualism, signifying "the infinite self-confidence of the individual aiming to be personally free in morals and in truth" (K. H. Brüggemann, *Dr. Lists nationales System der politischen Ökonomie*, 1842; see Koebner, p. 282). Thereafter the term became, in this, chiefly German, use, virtually synonymous with the early romantic conception of individuality, as found in the writings of Wilhelm von Humboldt, Schlegel, and Schleiermacher. Thus in 1917 Simmel could write:

The new individualism might be called qualitative, in contrast with the quantitative individualism of the eighteenth century. Or it might be labeled the individualism of uniqueness [*Einzigkeit*] as against that of singleness [*Einzelheit*]. At any rate, Romanticism perhaps was the broadest channel through which it reached the consciousness of the nineteenth century. Goethe had created its artistic, and Schleiermacher its metaphysical basis: Romanticism supplied its sentimental, experiential foundation (1950, p. 81).

A synthesis of the French and German meanings of the term is to be found in Jacob Burckhardt's *Die Kultur der Renaissance in Italien* (1860), where "individualism" combines the notion of the aggressive self-assertion of individuals freed from an externally-given framework of authority (as found in Louis Blanc) and that of the individual's withdrawal from society into a private existence (as in Tocqueville) with the idea, most clearly expressed by Humboldt, of the full and harmonious development of the individual personality, seen as representing humanity and pointing towards

595

its highest cultural development (Koebner, 1934). The Italian of the Renaissance was for Burckhardt the firstborn of the sons of modern Europe in virtue of the autonomy of his morality, his cultivation of privacy, and the individuality of his character.

It was in America that "individualism" came to specify a whole set of social ideals and acquired immense ideological significance: it expressed the operative ideals of late nineteenth- and early twentieth-century America (and indeed continues to play a major ideological role), advancing a set of universal claims seen as incompatible with the parallel claims of the socialism and communism of the Old World. It referred, not to the sources of social dissolution or the painful transition to a future harmonious social order, but to the actual or imminent realization of the final stage of human progress, an order of equal individual rights, limited government, laissez-faire, natural justice, and equality of opportunity, and individual freedom, self-development, and dignity. Naturally, interpretations of it varied widely.

Imported with negative connotations via the writings of various Europeans, among them the socialists and the Saint-Simonian Michel Chevalier, the economist Friedrich List, and Tocqueville, "individualism" acquired a positive meaning and expressed an evolving reinterpretation of American ideology. In 1839, an article in the *United States Magazine and Democratic Review* (VI, 208–09) already described the "course of civilization" as "the progress of man from a state of savage individualism to that of an individualism more elevated, moral, and refined." Conceptions of individualism developed under the successive influences of New England Puritanism, the Jeffersonian tradition, and the natural rights philosophy; Unitarianism, Transcendentalism, and evangelicalism; the need to elaborate an ideological defense of the North's social system against the challenge of the South; and the immensely popular ideas of Herbert Spencer (forerunner of "rugged individualism"); together with the continuing impetus of alternative European-born ideologies (Arieli, 1964). For Emerson, individualism, which he endowed with moral and religious significance, had not yet been tried; it was the route to perfection, a spontaneous social order of self-reliant and independent individuals. "The Union," he wrote, "must be ideal in actual individualism" ("New England Reformers," 1844). For Walt Whitman, the progressive force of modern history was the concept "of the singleness of man, individualism" (*Democratic Vistas*, 1871), though in the hands of such Social Darwinists as William Graham Sumner, the term acquired a harsher and altogether less idealistic significance. Eventually, it came to fuse the doctrine of laissez-faire with a business

ideology and was thus used by Andrew Carnegie and Henry Clews, author of *The Wall Street Point of View* (1900), who spoke of "that system of Individualism which guards, protects and encourages competition," whose spirit was "the American Spirit—the love of freedom,—of free industry,—free and unfettered opportunity . . ." (*Individualism versus Socialism* [1907], Ch. I). In 1928, Herbert Hoover gave his famous campaign speech on the "American system of rugged individualism," yet even such radical critics of capitalism as the Single Taxers and the Populists argued in the name of individualism. As James Bryce observed, throughout their history, "individualism, the love of enterprise, and the pride in personal freedom, have been deemed by Americans not only their choicest, but their peculiar and exclusive possession" (*The American Commonwealth* [1888], III, Part V, Ch. XCII).

In England the term has played a smaller role. Robert Owen and John Stuart Mill used it pejoratively in the French-influenced sense to refer to the evils of capitalist competition. As a favorable epithet for English liberalism, though scarcely used by the laissez-faire economists and the Benthamites, it came to be more widely used in the latter half of the nineteenth century. The Unitarian minister William McCall preached the "Principle of Individualism"; Spencer adopted the term, as did the ultra-Spencerian Auberon Herbert, author of *The Voluntaryist Creed* (1908) and editor of *The Free Life* (where he described his creed as "thorough-going individualism"). T. H. Green used it favorably, while Dicey, in an influential use, equated it with Benthamism and utilitarian liberalism (see below). It has, following Dicey, been widely used to mean the absence or minimum of state intervention in the economic and other spheres (in contrast with "collectivism"), and has usually been associated, both by its adherents and its opponents, with classical, or negative, liberalism. L. T. Hobhouse shows this meaning clearly when he writes that "individualism, when it grapples with the facts, is driven no small distance along Socialist lines" (*Liberalism* [1911], Ch. IV). Finally, "individualism" has been applied to the sterling qualities of free and self-reliant Englishmen, as when Samuel Smiles wrote of that "energetic individualism which . . . constitutes the best practical education" (*Self-Help* [1859], Ch. I).

Historians and sociologists have come to use the term in a variety of contexts. Some, such as Ernst Troeltsch, associate it with primitive Christianity and the Gospel ethic; others, like Burckhardt, with the Italian Renaissance; others, following Max Weber and R. H. Tawney, with Protestantism, especially Calvinism, and the rise of capitalism (Weber, 1904–05; Tawney, 1926), or with the growth of a "possessive market society" in seventeenth-century England (Macpherson, 1962). Others, such as Otto Gierke, associate individualism with modern Natural Law theory, from the mid-seventeenth to the early nineteenth century (Gierke, 1913), and yet others, like Simmel and Friedrich Meinecke, with the rise of romanticism. Finally, economists of a doctrinaire liberal kind, such as the Austro-liberals Ludwig von Mises and F. A. Hayek, and Milton Friedman, as well as laissez-faire ideologists like Ayn Rand, adhere to "individualism": in this sense, it is an ideological trend of the right, of comparatively minor significance in most contemporary industrial societies.

II. COMPONENT IDEAS OF INDIVIDUALISM

Almost all these uses of "individualism" combine a number of different meanings or unit-ideas, and it is therefore worth trying to analyze these elements. In attempting this, the aim is to indicate broad conceptual outlines, partly by definition (positive and negative) and partly by historical allusion, but with no suggestion that the items in the following list are either mutually exclusive or jointly exhaustive.

1. First, there is the ultimate moral principle of *the supreme and intrinsic value of the individual human being,* an idea which A. D. Lindsay describes as "the great contribution to individualism" of the New Testament and all Christianity (1930–35, p. 676); though it is also found in the religious, if not the social, ethics of Hinduism. Absent from earlier Judaism (in which God's concern was with Israel, the nation), it is adumbrated in the prophets and clearly set forth in the Gospels, as in such sayings as: "Inasmuch as ye have done it unto one of the least of these my brethren, ye have done it unto me" (Matthew 25:40). In its Christian form, centered on God and implying the supreme value of the soul, this idea was reaffirmed at the time of the reformation, with Luther's and Calvin's preoccupation with the individual's salvation, and the sectarian principle that all men are alike children of God, each with his own unique purpose. It had, on the other hand, been de-emphasized in the medieval thesis of the corporational structure of society (itself rooted in Roman conceptions), which was expressed by the principle *Utilitas publica prefertur utilitati privatae* ("Public utility is preferable to private utility"). According to that thesis, "what mattered was the well-being of society and not the well-being of the individual parts constituting it"; the "individual did not exist for his own sake but for the sake of the whole society" (Ullmann [1966], pp. 36, 42).

The idea of the individual's supreme worth was eloquently expressed in a different form by the Renaissance humanists, for whom the dignity of man was a favorite theme, above all in the writings of Giannozzo Manetti, Marsilio Ficino, and Pico della Mirandola. Indeed, this idea has come to pervade modern ethical and social theory in the West. Few modern thinkers (except some theocrats, late romantics, Neo-Hegelians, fascists, and others on the far right) have explicitly rejected it, though it has, to say the least, been treated with differing degrees of seriousness. Some are prepared to ignore it in the short run, or to qualify it by balancing it against other principles; others, from the early sects to the anarchists, have derived from it the most immediate and egalitarian conclusions. Moreover, there is room for infinite dispute concerning its practical implications.

It underlies the Benthamite principle that every man is to count for one and no man for more than one, it is enshrined in the Declaration of the Rights of Man, and it is central to the thought of Rousseau, who wrote: "Man is too noble a being to serve simply as the instrument for others . . ." (*Julie, ou La Nouvelle Héloïse* [1761], V, letter 2). It achieved its most impressive and systematic expression in the writings of Kant, who asserted that "man, and in general every rational being, exists as an end in himself, *not merely as a means . . .*" (*Grundlegung zur Metaphysik der Sitten* [1785], Ch. II). Kant saw this as an "*objective* principle" from which "it must be possible to derive all laws for the will," and as entailing the practical imperative: "*Act in such a way that you always treat humanity, whether in your own person or in the person of any other, never simply as a means, but always at the same time as an end*" (ibid., trans. H. J. Paton). In his pre-critical writings Kant sought to ground it in an innate, universal natural sentiment, while in his critical writings he offered an (unsuccessful) transcendental proof. More recently, the philosopher J. McT. E. McTaggart argued for it in a brilliant paper entitled "The Individualism of Value" (in his *Philosophical Studies*, 1934), whose thesis is that "only conscious beings and their states have value" and that, in particular, "the individual is an end, the society is only a means." In general, it has the logical status of a religious or moral postulate which is ultimate in offering a general justifying principle in moral argument.

2. Distinct from this first idea is a second: the notion of *individual self-development.* This idea, and the phenomenon of self-cultivation to which it refers, may be traced back to the Italian Renaissance (as by Burckhardt), but it was most fully worked out among the early romantics. Thus Schleiermacher in his *Monolog* of 1800 describes how

. . . it became clear to me that each man ought to represent humanity in himself in his own different way, by his own special blending of its elements, so that it should reveal itself in each special manner, and, in the fullness of space and time, should become everything that can emerge as something individual out of the depths of itself.

The same idea is found in Wilhelm von Humboldt, for whom the "true end of Man" was "the highest and most harmonious development of his powers to a complete and consistent whole," whose "highest ideal . . . of the co-existence of human beings" consisted in "a union in which each strives to develop himself from his own inmost nature, and for his own sake," and who concluded that

. . . reason cannot desire for man any other condition than that in which each individual not only enjoys the most absolute freedom of developing himself by his own energies, in his perfect individuality, but in which external nature even is left unfashioned by any human agency, but only receives the impress given to it by each individual of himself and his own free will, according to the measure of his wants and instincts, and restricted only by the limits of his powers and his rights (Ideen zu einem Versuch, die Gränzen der Wirksamkeit des Staats zu bestimmen [1852], Ch. II; trans. J. Coulthard).

The history of this idea is well known: it soon developed into a theory of organic community, the term *Individuelle* shifted its reference from persons to suprapersonal forces, and individuality came to be predicated of the *Volk* or the State. Apart from this, it entered into the liberal tradition, especially through John Stuart Mill's *On Liberty* (1859, Ch. III: "Of Individuality . . ."), and it entered as a crucial element into the ethical basis of Marx's thought, as in *Die deutsche Ideologie* ([1845–46], Part I, Sec. C, where Marx writes of the individual under communism "cultivating his gifts in all directions"), while it has remained attractive to artists of all kinds ever since Byron and Goethe. In general, it specifies an ideal for the lives of individuals—an ideal that is either anti-social (as with some of the early romantics), extra-social (as with Mill), or highly social (as with Marx, or Kropotkin, or the English Idealists).

3. The third element of individualism might be called the idea of *self-direction*, or *autonomy*, according to which the individual subjects the norms with which he is confronted to critical evaluation and reaches practical decisions as the result of independent and rational reflection.

It could be argued that this idea was first clearly expressed (since Aristotle) by Saint Thomas Aquinas. According to the traditional medieval doctrine, the order of a superior, whether just or unjust, had to be obeyed; for Thomas it need not, if conscience forbade its execution. His argument was that "everyone is bound to examine his own actions in the light of the knowledge which he has from God" (*Quaestiones disputatae de Veritate*, qu. 17, art. 4). As Ullmann has

commented: "The general principle he advocated was that 'every man must act in consonance with reason' . . . a principle which persuasively demonstrates the advance in individual ethics and a principle which began to assert the autonomy of the individual in the moral sphere" (1966, p. 127).

In the religious sphere that autonomy was clearly evident in Luther's argument: ". . . each and all of us are priests because we all have the one faith, the one gospel, one and the same sacrament; why then should we not be entitled to taste or test, and to judge what is right or wrong in the faith?" (*An den christlichen Adel deutscher Nation von des christlichen Standes Besserung* [1520], I, ii), and in Calvin's teaching (at least with respect to the Roman church) that "Our consciences have to do, not with men, but with God alone" (*Institutio religionis Christianae* [1536], IV, x, 5). In the social, and especially political, sphere, it was one of the cardinal values of the Enlightenment and the main target of the latter's critics, who were terrified by this exaltation of the individual's private judgment: hence de Maistre's "political protestantism. . . ."

The most systematic expositions of the idea of autonomy are in Spinoza's *Ethics* (1677) and, above all, in Kant. Kant's third practical principle for the will was ". . . the Idea *of the will of every rational being as a will which makes universal law*," according to which "all maxims are repudiated which cannot accord with the will's own enactment of universal law. The will is not therefore merely subject to the law, but is so subject that it must be considered as also *making the law* for itself and precisely on this account as first of all subject to the law (of which it can regard itself as the author)" (*Grundlegung . . .*, Ch. II; trans. H. J. Paton). Kant argued that "To the Idea of freedom there is inseparably attached the concept of *autonomy*, and to this in turn the universal principle of morality," and that ". . . when we think of ourselves as free, we transfer ourselves into the intelligible world as members and recognize the autonomy of the will together with its consequence—morality" (ibid.).

In itself, this idea is neutral with regard to the problem of the relativity of values (and for Kant it was evidently compatible with objective moral certainty; but see below: II, 10), though it has often been regarded as incompatible with most versions of determinism. As Kant put it: ". . . To be independent of determination by causes in the sensible world (and this is what reason must always attribute to itself) is to be free" (ibid.). It can have the logical status either of a universal proposition (*a priori* or empirical) concerning the conditions of human (or moral) action; a first-order moral principle; or a sociological ideal-type, as in David Riesman's *The Lonely Crowd* (1950).

4. The fourth unit-idea is the notion of *privacy,* of a private existence within a public world, an area within which the individual is free from interference and able to do and think whatever he chooses. This is an essentially modern idea, largely absent from ancient civilizations and medieval Europe. It constitutes perhaps the central idea of liberalism, whose history has largely been an argument about where the boundaries lie, according to what principles they are to be justified, whence interference derives, and how it is to be checked. It presupposes a picture of man to whom privacy is essential, even sacred, with a life of his own to live. Sir Isaiah Berlin has characterized this idea as "negative liberty," involving a "sense of privacy, . . . of the area of personal relationships as something sacred in its own right . . . ," arguing that

This is liberty as it has been conceived by liberals in the modern world from the days of Erasmus (some would say of Occam) to our own. Every plea for civil liberties, every protest against exploitation and humiliation, against the encroachment of public authority, or the mass hypnosis of custom or organised propaganda, springs from this individualistic, and much disputed, conception of man (1958, pp. 14, 12).

We have already met this idea in Tocqueville who, though alarmed by the social and political consequences of the excessive retreat into privacy under democracy, nonetheless held "negative liberty" as a preeminent value. It is found (with different conceptions of the private area of noninterference) in Locke, Paine, Burke, Jefferson, and Acton. It is found, above all, in the writings of John Stuart Mill and Benjamin Constant, which contain the classic liberal justifications for preserving private liberty. For Mill, the "only part of the conduct of anyone, for which he is amenable to society, is that which concerns others. In the part which merely concerns himself, his independence is, of right, absolute. Over himself, over his own body and mind, the individual is sovereign" (*On Liberty,* Ch. I). For Constant,

. . . everything which does not interfere with order; everything which belongs only to the inward nature of man, such as opinion; everything which, in the expression of opinion, does not harm others . . . everything which, in regard to industry, allows the free exercise of rival industry—is individual and cannot legitimately be subjected to the power of society (*Mélanges de littérature et de politique* [1829], Preface).

Constant further remarked on the essentially modern character of this notion of liberty as "the peaceful enjoyment of personal independence": the ancients, "to preserve their political importance and their part in the administration of the State, were ready to renounce their private independence," whereas "Nearly all the enjoyments of the moderns are in their private lives: the immense majority, forever excluded from power, necessarily take only a very passing interest in their public lives" (*De l'esprit de conquête* [1814], Part II, Ch. VI).

This idea is to be seen as contrasting not only with various types of authoritarianism, but also with that powerful tradition of thought (reaching back through Elton Mayo to Rousseau) which stresses "community" and "groupism," aiming to cure psychological and social ills, or to achieve political and social purposes, through attachment to groups, whether these are primary groups, work groups, professional associations, classes, parties, religious orders, corporations, city-states, or nations. It is this tradition which David Riesman attacks in his essay "Individualism Reconsidered," in which he concludes that "to hold that conformity with society is not only a necessity but also a duty" is to "destroy that margin of freedom which gives life its savor and its endless possibility for advance" (*Individualism Reconsidered* [1954], Ch. 2).

Perhaps the most striking, and certainly the most influential contemporary expression of "groupism" is in the thought of Mao Tse-Tung. According to Mao, liberalism "is extremely harmful in a revolutionary collective . . . a corrosive which eats away unity, undermines cohesion, causes apathy and creates dissension"; it "stems from petty-bourgeois selfishness, it places personal interests first and the interests of the revolution second. . . ." A Communist should "be more concerned about the Party and the masses than about any private person, and more concerned about others than about himself" ("Combat Liberalism," September 7, 1937).

In general, the idea of privacy refers to a relation between the individual, on the one hand, and society or the state, on the other—a relation characteristically held by liberals to be desirable, either as an ultimate value, or (as with Mill) as a means to the realization of other values.

5. The fifth unit-idea of individualism, the notion of the *abstract individual,* needs to be carefully specified, for it has so often been misdescribed, especially by its nineteenth-century opponents. It implies a conception of society according to which actual or possible social arrangements are seen as responding to the requirements of individuals with given capacities, wants, and needs. Society's rules and institutions are, on this view, regarded collectively as an artifice, a modifiable instrument, a means of fulfilling given individual objectives; the means and the ends are distinct. The crucial point about this conception is that the relevant features of individuals determining the ends which social arrangements are held (actually or ideally) to fulfil—whether these features are called instincts, faculties, needs, desires, or rights—are assumed as given, independently of any social context.

Morris Ginsberg calls this view "sociological individualism," defining it as "the theory that society is to be conceived as an aggregate of individuals whose relations to each other are purely external" (1956, p. 151). It is what Gierke meant when he observed that "the guiding thread of all speculation in the area of Natural Law was always, from first to last, individualism—an individualism steadily carried to its logical conclusions," so that, for all modern natural law theorists, from Hobbes to Kant, "a previous sovereignty of the individual was the ultimate and only source of Group-authority" and "the community was only an aggregate—a mere union, whether close or loose—of the wills and powers of individual persons"; they all agreed that "all forms of common life were the creation of individuals" and "could only be regarded as *means to individual objects*" (1934, pp. 96, 106, 111).

Gierke was right to locate the ascendancy of this idea between the middle of the seventeenth and the beginning of the nineteenth centuries. It was, obviously, intimately related to the "social contract" mode of argument and, in general, to arguments concerning society based on the conception of man in the state of nature, though it can also be seen in a different form—an abstract notion of man in general—in the early utilitarians and the classical economists. Needless to say the (pre-social, trans-social or non-social) "individuals" involved here—whether natural, or utilitarian, or economic men—always turn out on inspection to be social, and indeed historically specific (e.g., Macpherson, 1962, passim). "Human nature" always in reality belongs to a particular kind of social man.

For Hobbes, the archetypal abstract individualist, Leviathan was an artificial contrivance constructed to satisfy the requirements of the component elements of society—"men as if but even now sprung out of the earth, and suddenly, like mushrooms, come to full maturity, without all kind of engagement to each other" (*De cive* [1642], VIII, 1). Locke argued similarly, as did very many eighteenth-century thinkers, especially in France and Germany. Even Rousseau, insofar as he used the social contract idea, toyed with this conception, though the central thrust of his thought was incompatible with it. Perhaps the most explicit (and most characteristic eighteenth-century) expression of it occurs in an article in Diderot's *Encyclopédie* (1752–72) by Turgot, who wrote: "The citizens have rights, rights that are sacred for the very body of society; the citizens exist independently of society; they form its necessary elements; and they only enter it in order to put themselves, with all their rights, under the protection of those very laws to which they sacrifice their liberty" (article on "Fondation (Politique et Droit Naturel)" in Vol. VII).

The idea of the abstract individual formed a principal target for many nineteenth-century thinkers, many of whom held it to be a typically narrow and superficial dogma of the Enlightenment. It was attacked by counterrevolutionary and romantic conservatives in France, England, and Germany, by Hegel and Marx and their respective followers, by Saint-Simon and his disciples, by Comte and the positivists, by sociologists, especially in France, by German historicists, and by English Idealists. It is what de Bonald had in mind when he wrote: "Not only does man not constitute society, but it is society that constitutes man, that is, it forms him by social education . . ." (*Théorie du pouvoir* [1796], Preface); and it is what F. H. Bradley meant when he wrote that "the 'individual' apart from the community is an abstraction." Man, for Bradley, "is a social being; he is real only because he is social . . ." and if we abstract from him all those features which result from his social context, he becomes "a theoretical attempt to isolate what can not be isolated" (*Ethical Studies* [1876], essay V, "My Station and its Duties").

6. Distinct from this idea (though on certain interpretations an application of it) is a doctrine which has come to be known as *methodological individualism*. This asserts that all attempts to explain social phenomena are to be rejected (or, according to a current, more sophisticated version, rejected as "rock-bottom" explanations) unless they are couched wholly in terms of facts about individuals. Thus, according to its chief contemporary exponent, Sir Karl Popper: ". . . all social phenomena, and especially the functioning of all social institutions, should always be understood as resulting from the decisions, actions, attitudes, etc., of human individuals, and . . . we should never be satisfied by an explanation in terms of so-called 'collectives' . . ." (*The Open Society and its Enemies* [1945], Vol. II, Ch. XIV).

It was first clearly articulated by Hobbes, for whom "everything is best understood by its constitutive causes" (*De cive*, Preface), the causes of the social compound being Hobbesian men. It was taken up by the thinkers of the Enlightenment, among whom, with a few important exceptions (such as Vico and Montesquieu), an individualist mode of explanation became preeminent, though with wide divergences as to what was included, and how much was included, in the characterization of the explanatory elements. Man was seen by some as egoistic, by others as cooperative; some presupposed the minimum about social conditions, others (such as Diderot) employed a genuine social psychology. As we have seen, many reasoned as though the "individuals" in question were "prior" to society, that is, undetermined by features of their social context.

Methodological individualism was confronted, from the early nineteenth century onwards, by a wide range of thinkers who brought to the understanding of social life a perspective according to which collective phenomena were accorded priority over individuals in explanation. In Germany this was a pervasive trend, encompassing all the social sciences, such as history, economics, law, psychology, and philology (from, say, Adam Müller onwards). In France, this tradition passed from Saint-Simon and Comte through Alfred Espinas to Émile Durkheim, whose whole sociology was founded on the denial of methodological individualism. Marxists and Hegelians have likewise always been committed to such a denial, as is the mainstream of modern American sociology. Many, however, have continued to uphold it. The utilitarians were at one with John Stuart Mill in maintaining that the "laws of the phenomena of society are, and can be, nothing but the actions and passions of human beings," namely, "the laws of individual human nature" (*A System of Logic* [1843], Book VI, Ch. VII, 1). Similarly, many social scientists have been methodological individualists, most obviously all those who have appealed to fixed psychological elements as ultimately explanatory factors—such as Pareto ("residues"), McDougall ("instincts"), Sumner ("drives"), and Malinowski ("needs").

The debate over methodological individualism has recurred in many different guises—in the dispute between the German "historical" school in economics and the "abstract" theory of classical and neo-classical economics (especially as expounded by Carl Menger and the Austrian School), in endless disputes among philosophers of history and between sociologists and psychologists, and above all in the prolonged controversy between Durkheim and Gabriel Tarde (in which most of the issues were most clearly brought out). Among others, Georg Simmel and Charles Horton Cooley tried to resolve the issue, as did Georges Gurvitch and Morris Ginsberg (Ginsberg, 1954), but it constantly reappears, for example in reactions to the macroscopic theorizing of Talcott Parsons and his followers, and in the debate provoked by the wide-ranging methodological polemics of Popper and Hayek on behalf of methodological individualism.

Briefly, it may be said that methodological individualism acquires a range of different meanings in accordance with how much of "society" is built into the explanatory "individuals." At one extreme stand thinkers such as La Mettrie and H. J. Eysenck, who seek

an ultimately physiological, even physical explanation of social phenomena; then there are those, such as Pareto and Freud, who ultimately appeal to psychological variables, but with no social reference; next, there are those, from Tarde to George Homans, who seek explanations in terms of general and "elementary" forms of social behavior, but with the minimum social reference; and finally, there are those who appeal to concrete, unabstracted individuals who incorporate all the relevant features of the social context. (For further elaboration and discussion of the above, see Lukes, 1968.)

7. Next, there is a set of familiar ideas, which collectively may be labelled *political individualism*. This may be defined generically as a prescriptive doctrine which finds the source and grounds of political authority in individuals' purposes and the limits to such authority in the minimum required to achieve those purposes. Somewhat artificially, one may say that the differing varieties of political individualism have arisen from different assumptions about how the relevant individual purposes are to be identified and about the amount of authority needed to achieve them. (Insofar as the former are abstracted from a social context, political individualism becomes an application of the idea of the abstract individual.)

Hobbes is again of central historical importance here. For him, political authority derived from human purposes, not from divine or natural law (in the ancient and medieval sense), or from immemorial tradition; he wrote: "The *people* rules in all governments. For even in *monarchies* the *people* commands" (*De cive*, XII, 8). As Hegel justly observed, Hobbes, unlike his predecessors, "sought to derive the bond which holds the state together, that which gives the state its power, from principles which lie within us, which we recognise as our own" (*Vorlesungen über die Geschichte der Philosophie*, 2nd ed. [1840], Vol. III, Part III, Sec. ii, Ch. I, B [3]). Locke developed this idea, but without giving it operational significance; it was Rousseau who carried to its logical conclusion the view that "conventions form the basis of all legitimate authority among men," seeing the Sovereign as "formed wholly of the individuals who compose it" (*Contrat social* [1762], Book I, Chs. IV, VII). Political individualism became a commonplace in the eighteenth century, with its predilection for contract and consent. The article on "Autorité" by Diderot in the *Encyclopédie* put it very clearly:

The prince derives from his subjects the authority he holds over them; and this authority is limited by the laws of nature and of the state. The laws of nature and of the state are the conditions under which they have or are supposed to have submitted themselves to his rule. One of these conditions is that, having no power or authority over them except by their choice and their consent, he can never use this authority to break the act or contract by which it has been conferred on him . . . (Vol. I).

It will be seen that, as we have defined it, the limits of political individualism are in principle wide, encompassing theorists of popular sovereignty at one extreme and, at the other, those "totalitarian democrats" who have claimed to know men's "real" purposes and used them as a justification for tyranny. In practice, the term has usually been restricted to that type of political liberalism which aims to confine the functions and the authority of the state within fixed limits. Here what counts as "individuals' purposes" has often amounted to the (primarily economic) claims of the individuals of particular classes. It was in this sense that Dicey characterized legislative utilitarianism as "systematised individualism," observing that "Benthamism meant nothing more than the attempt to realize by means of effective legislation the political and social ideals set before himself by every intelligent merchant, tradesman or artisan" (*Lectures on the Relation between Law and Public Opinion in England during the Nineteenth Century* [1905], Lecture VI, Part [B]). As Macpherson's work suggests (Macpherson, 1962) within a certain range, political individualism becomes the political theory entailed by the eighth unit-idea, to be considered next.

8. This is *economic individualism*. At its simplest, this is a belief in economic liberty; it amounts to the justification of certain culturally specific patterns of behavior and a consequent presumption against economic regulation, whether by Church or State. Ever since Weber and Sombart, economic historians and others have argued about when and how these patterns of behavior emerged in the West, and in particular about their relation to the various forms of Protestantism, which often provided their early justification (Weber, 1904–05; Tawney, 1926; Robertson, 1933). It was, however, not until the mid-eighteenth century that their justification could make use of a coherent economic theory, with the work of Adam Smith in Britain and of the Marquis d'Argenson, the physiocrats, and Turgot in France. Henceforth, economic individualism became both an economic theory and a normative doctrine, asserting (if so complex a tradition or set of traditions can be reduced to a formula) that a spontaneous economic system based on private property, the market and freedom of production, contract and exchange, and on the unfettered self-interest of individuals, tends to be more or less self-adjusting; and that it conduces to the maximum satisfaction of individuals and to progress.

The nineteenth-century liberal economists carried the theory and the doctrine further. The whole subsequent history of (non-Marxist) economic analysis can be seen as an ever-more sophisticated elaboration of the model of this system, with all political and social factors removed. Léon Walras and Alfred Marshall provided the fullest nineteenth-century versions of that model, but thereafter some, though not all, economists sought to distinguish theory from doctrine, and did not necessarily wish to make reality conform to the model. Only those who do are to be counted as adherents of economic individualism, which is essentially the view that universal economic liberty is both efficient and desirable. Its rejection is, perhaps, a generic negative definition of "socialism"—a term coined in the 1820's in explicit opposition to its assumptions (Swart [1962], p. 81).

The most systematic and clearcut contemporary defender of economic individualism is F. A. Hayek, who sees it as a matter of preserving those "spontaneous formations which are the indispensable bases of a free civilisation," in particular an "effectively competitive market" ([1949], pp. 25, 21, and passim for a somewhat tendentious survey of this position's intellectual ancestry). Throughout its history there have been disagreements about the best political means for achieving this result: at one extreme there is doctrinal laissez-faire (from Frédéric Bastiat to Ludwig von Mises), at the other, various forms of selective interventionism (from Adam Smith himself to J. M. Keynes).

9. Next, there is *religious individualism*, which is conceptually closely related to the notions of autonomy and of privacy (see above: II, Secs. 3, 4). This may be defined as the view that the individual believer does not need intermediaries, that he has the right, and sometimes the duty, to come to his own relationship with his God in his own way and by his own effort. It is thus both a religious doctrine and, by implication, a view of the nature of religion; and it points to two further and important ideas: spiritual equality and religious self-scrutiny. The former was stressed in the early Church and the latter found its supreme expression in the thought of Saint Augustine. Indeed religious individualism could be traced back at least to Jeremiah, but its modern forms characteristically date from the Reformation, when it was expressed in terms of the doctrine of the "inner light" and of the universal priesthood of the believers.

It evidently embraces a wide range, from the most communal forms of Protestantism to cults of private mysticism, but it has usually been associated with Calvinism. Here spiritual self-scrutiny and the "internalization of conscience" were carried to their extremes. As Max Weber wrote: "In spite of the necessity of membership in the true Church for salvation, the Calvinist's intercourse with his God was carried on in deep spiritual isolation" (Weber, 1904–05 [1930], pp. 106–07; see Watt, 1957 for an examination of the literary consequences of Puritanism's introspective tendency). Weber stressed the connection between the doctrine of predestination and "a feeling of unprecedented loneliness of the single individual," given "the complete elimination of salvation through the Church and the sacraments (which was in Lutheranism by no means developed to its final conclusion) . . .":

In what was for the man of the age of the Reformation the most important thing in life, his eternal salvation, he was forced to follow his path alone to meet a destiny which had been decreed for him from eternity (ibid., pp. 104–05).

This "inner isolation of the individual," Weber argued, "forms one of the roots of that disillusioned and pessimistically inclined individualism which can even today be identified in the national characters and the institutions of the peoples with a Puritan past . . ." (ibid., p. 105).

10. The next and last two unit-ideas to be singled out are philosophical (moral and epistemological) theories whose conceptual and historical relations with the ideas discussed above are complex and worthy of exploration. The first of these, which may be called *ethical individualism*, is a view of the nature of morality. According to this view, the source of moral values and principles, the creator of the very criteria of moral evaluation, is the individual: he becomes the supreme arbiter of moral (and, by implication, other) values, the final moral authority in the most fundamental sense. In a sense, this view can be seen as the philosophical consequence of carrying the idea of autonomy to its extreme logical conclusion. Moreover, it is intimately linked with the logical dissociation of fact and value (and can only be expressed within a vocabulary which embodies this disjunction). It can thus be seen to have been latent in the thought of Kant and of Hume, but both avoided its implications, the former by postulating an impersonal moral law, the latter by appealing to the moral uniformity of mankind.

The dilemmas of ethical individualism have only become acute in this century, though they are clearly revealed in the thought of Nietzsche and Weber; the latter argued that when faced with conflicting moral positions, "the individual has to decide which is God for him and which is the devil" ("Wissenschaft als Beruf," 1919). Most species of existentialism, emotivism, and prescriptivism—all three denying objective universal moral principles—are forms of ethical individualism. Its most coherent contemporary expressions are in the early writings of Jean-Paul Sartre, e.g., *L'exis-*

tentialisme est un humanisme (1948), and in the work of the contemporary Oxford philosopher R. M. Hare, e.g., *The Language of Morals* (1951).

11. Finally, there is *epistemological individualism* a theory about the nature of knowledge, which asserts that the source of knowledge lies within the individual. Leaving aside certain varieties of solipsism and pragmatism, the true epistemological individualist is the empiricist (though the metaphysics of Leibniz may be said to imply an individualist epistemology). The traditional empiricist holds that we know nothing beyond our own purely subjective experience, enclosed within the circle of the mind and the sensations it receives, whether these are Locke's ideas, Hume's impressions and ideas, or the "sensa" and sense data of more recent theorists. Often he holds a psychological atomism, the problem being to reconstruct knowledge out of its simplest elements; as Hume said: "Complex ideas may, perhaps, be well known by . . . an enumeration of those parts or simple ideas that compose them," themselves copies of "impressions or original sentiments" (*Enquiry concerning Human Understanding* [1748], VII, Part I). The French disciples of Locke and Hume in the eighteenth century took this sensationalism very seriously. It is, in general, obviously closely related to the attempt to explain wholes, including social and political structures, by breaking them down into their simplest elements (see above: II, Sec. 6).

Individualistic empiricism has experienced a revival in the twentieth century, though less in the form of a psychological than a logical doctrine, a theory about meaning and understanding. The crucial objection to it, and to epistemological individualism generally, has taken two related forms: first, an appeal to a shared public world and, second, to a shared "intersubjective" language, as preconditions of knowledge. The latter objection has become a commonplace of sociological and anthropological theory (receiving a classical statement in Durkheim's studies of primitive thought and religion) and of contemporary post-Wittgensteinian philosophy. Generally, epistemological individualism is to be contrasted with all those theories which hold that knowledge is, in part at least, the product of what Wittgenstein called "forms of life" and is to be tested as genuine by reference to a public world.

BIBLIOGRAPHY

Y. Arieli, *Individualism and Nationalism in American Ideology* (Cambridge, Mass., 1964). I. Berlin, *Two Concepts of Liberty* (Oxford, 1958). G. Burckhardt, *Was ist Individualismus?* (Leipzig, 1913). H. Dietzel, "Individualismus," *Handwörterbuch der Staatswissenschaften*, 4th rev. ed. (Jena, 1923), V, 408–24. L. Dumont, "The Modern Conception of the Individual: Notes on its Genesis and that of

Concomitant Institutions," *Contributions to Indian Sociology,* **8** (1965), 13–61. O. Gierke, *Das deutsche Genossenschaft* (Berlin, 1913) IV, §§14–18, trans. E. Barker as *Natural Law and the Theory of Society: 1500 to 1800,* 2 vols. (Cambridge, 1934). M. Ginsberg, "The Individual and Society," *International Social Science Bulletin,* **6** (1954), 146–54, repr. in M. Ginsberg, *On the Diversity of Morals* (London, 1956). F. A. Hayek, *Individualism: True and False* (Dublin and Oxford, 1946), repr. as Ch. I of F. A. Hayek, *Individualism and Economic Order* (London, 1949). R. Koebner, "Zur Begriffsbildung der Kulturgeschichte, II: Zur Geschichte des Begriffs 'Individualismus' (Jacob Burckhardt, Wilhelm von Humboldt und die französische Soziologie)," *Historische Zeitschrift,* **149** (1934), 253–93. F. Koehler, *Wesen und Bedeutung des Individualismus, Eine Studie* (Munich, 1922). A. D. Lindsay, "Individualism," *Encyclopedia of the Social Sciences* (New York, 1930–35), VII, 674–80. S. Lukes, "Methodological Individualism Reconsidered," *British Journal of Sociology,* **19** (1968), 119–29; idem, "The Meanings of 'Individualism,'" *Journal of the History of Ideas,* **32** (1971), 45–66. C. B. Macpherson, *The Political Theory of Possessive Individualism: Hobbes to Locke* (Oxford, 1962). M. Mauss, "Une catégorie de l'esprit humaine: la notion de personne, celle de 'Moi,' un plan de travail," *Journal of the Royal Anthropological Institute,* **68** (1938), 263–81, repub. in M. Mauss, *Sociologie et anthropologie,* intro. C. Lévi-Strauss (Paris, 1950), Part V. L. Moulin, "On the Evolution of the Meaning of the Word 'Individualism,'" *International Social Science Bulletin,* **7** (1955), 181–85. R. R. Palmer, "Man and Citizen: Applications of Individualism in the French Revolution," *Essays in Political Theory presented to G. H. Sabine* (Ithaca, 1948). H. M. Robertson, *Aspects of the Rise of Economic Individualism* (Cambridge, 1933). A. Schatz, *L'individualisme économique et sociale* (Paris, 1907). G. Simmel, *Grundfragen der Soziologie* (*Individuum und Gesellschaft*) (Berlin and Leipzig, 1917), Ch. IV: "Individuum und Gesellschaft in Lebensanschauungen des 18. und 19. Jahrhunderts (Beispiel der Philosophischen Soziologie)," in *The Sociology of Georg Simmel,* trans. and ed. K. H. Wolff (Glencoe, Ill., 1950), pp. 58–84. K. W. Swart, "'Individualism' in the Mid-Nineteenth Century (1826–1860)," *Journal of the History of Ideas,* **23** (1962), 77–90. R. H. Tawney, *Religion and the Rise of Capitalism* (London, 1926), esp. Ch. III, III: "The Growth of Individualism." W. Ullmann, *The Individual and Society in the Middle Ages* (Baltimore, 1966; London, 1967). I. Watt, *The Rise of the Novel: Studies in Defoe, Richardson and Fielding* (London, 1957), esp. Ch. III: "Robinson Crusoe, Individualism and the Novel." M. Weber, *Die protestantische Ethik und der "Geist" des Kapitalismus* in *Archiv für Sozialwissenschaft und Sozialpolitik,* **20–21** (1904–05), trans. T. Parsons as *The Protestant Ethic and the Spirit of Capitalism* (London, 1930), esp. Part II, Ch. IV(A).

The author provided the translations of Tocqueville, Schleiermacher, Constant, and Diderot.

STEVEN LUKES

[See also Anarchism; Authority; Economic History; **Genius; Liberalism;** Progress; Reformation; Renaissance Humanism; Socialism; Universal Man.]

INFINITY

I. A SURVEY

THE OLD TESTAMENT exulted in the omnipotence of the Creator, but it did not initiate problems about the unboundedness of His power or the infinity of His creation. The Hebrew of the Bible did not have a word for "infinity" in general. It only had words about particular aspects of infinity, and leading among these was the word *'olam.* It designated eternity, that is infinity in time, without reference to spatiality. Post-biblically, however, the word began to acquire traits of spatiality, ever more so, and it may have given to the present-day Arabic word *'alam* its meaning of "world," "cosmos," "universe" (*Encyclopedia of Islam,* New Ed. [1960], 1, 349).

Greek literary works, in poetry and prose, were less theocratic than the Old Testament. But from the first there was in them an awareness of immensity and even unboundedness in the cosmos, and Greek rationality showed very early a disposition to examine the meaning of infinity in its complexity.

The standard Greek word for infinity was *apeiron* (ἄπειρον; probable etymology: *a* = non, *peiras* or *peras* = limit, bound). Close cognates to it occurred in Homer, and the word itself had a considerable literary cachet, in poetry and prose, letters and science. The word occurs in Hesiod and Pindar, in literal fragments of most pre-Socratic philosophers, and in reports about Pythagorean statements which seem verbally proximate to original utterances of theirs (Bochner, "The Size of the Universe . . . ," sec. II).

Thales of Miletus, the father of Greek rational philosophy, is not yet credited with memorable pronouncements about *apeiron,* not even indirectly; but Thales is the only pre-Socratic who is not so credited, whereas his younger compatriot Anaximander already is, even emphatically so (ibid., sec. III). After Anaximander, and up to and including Aristotle, each and every philosopher dealt with infinity, openly or disguisedly; and many of them had a good deal to say about it. This in itself sets off Thales from all other philosophers, and it justifies the shrewd observation in Diogenes Laërtius that it was Anaximander, and not Thales, with whom (Greek) speculative philosophy truly began (Diogenes Laërtius, Book 1, Ch. 13).

It seems likely that Anaximander composed a book which Anaximander himself, or others after him, called "On Nature," and that it included a chapter on *apeiron,* perhaps at the head of the book. Apparently because of this, late classical antiquity (many centuries after Anaximander) formed a consensus that Anaximander had been a one-man creator of the problem of infinity in classical Greek thought, and that this had been his central achievement. This however is a doubtful thesis.

There is nothing in Plato and Aristotle to suggest that the problem, or problems, of infinity arose at a fixed stage of the philosophical past at the initiative of a specific philosopher. Plato never mentions Anaximander or ever alludes to him. Aristotle does mention him, but relatively rarely, and somehow very guardedly (Kirk and Raven, p. 108), and without singling him out for a special link with the problem of infinity. In fact, *apeiron* occurs in all eight books of Aristotle's *Physica;* and, by Aristotle's express design, the major part of Book 3, namely chapters 4 through 9, is a concise systematic essay about *apeiron.* Yet, within this essay, Anaximander is mentioned only once, along with other pre-Socratics, and, within the essay, the total reference to him is as follows:

Further, they identify it [the infinite] with the Divine, for it is "deathless and imperishable", as Anaximander says with the majority of physicists (*Physica,* 203b 12–14, Oxford translation).

Whatever late antiquity may have thought or said, from reading Aristotle one gains the impression that the study of infinity, in its various facets, had been from the first an all-Hellenic enterprise, in which virtually everybody had participated; and so indeed it had been.

Oswald Spengler, in his ambitious work *The Decline of the West,* which was published in German in 1918, made much of the thesis, to which, in the end, even professional historians such as P. Kucharski and B. Rochot subscribed, that unlike the Middle Ages and the Renaissance, classical antiquity, before the onset and diffusion of Hellenism, did not find it congenial to abandon itself to the mystique of infinity, but was aspiring to control and suppress infinity rather than to contemplate and savor it. To this we wish to point out that even during the Renaissance and after, leading scientists like Copernicus, Kepler, Newton, and others, were approaching problems of infinity with caution and reserve, and in no wise abandoned themselves to a mystique of the infinite. Furthermore, cosmology in the twentieth century is also circumspect when admitting infinity into its context.

It is true that since the Renaissance many philosophers—as distinct from philosophizing scientists—were disposed to opt for untrammeled infinity in their findings, and Giordano Bruno (1548–1600) was a leader among them. But even this disposition may have been a stage of a development that reached back into classical antiquity, into Hellenism at any rate. Long before Bruno infinity of space was vigorously advocated, from an anti-Aristotelian stance *à la* Bruno, by the Jewish philosopher Hasdai Crescas (1340–1411) and this apparently created a fashion (Wolfson, *Crescas' . . . ,* pp. 35–36). Crescas was apparently a late product of Judeo-Arabic scholasticism, which in its turn was de-

rived from Islamic philosophy that had been in bloom in the tenth and eleventh centuries A.D.; there are historical appraisals that Islamic philosophy in its turn had been an off-shoot of general Hellenism (R. Walzer, passim).

If Greek natural philosophers of the Hellenic period were indeed wary of infinity, then this was due largely to the fact that they had precociously discovered how difficult it is to comprehend infinity in its conceptual ramifications and not because they had an innate hesitancy to be intimate with it. As is evident from various works of Aristotle (*Physica, De caelo, De generatione et corruptione,* etc.), the Greeks had by then created a host of problems about infinity that are familiar to us from cosmology, physics, and natural philosophy; then as today significant problems about infinity were correlated with problems about continuity, motion, matter, genesis of the universe, etc.

For instance, on one occasion Aristotle suggests that the belief in infinity is derived from five sources: (i) from the infinity of time, (ii) from the divisibility of magnitude, (iii) from the fact that the perpetuity of generation and destruction in nature can be maintained only if there is an infinite source to draw on, (iv) from the fact that anything limited has to be limited by something else, and finally, (v) from the fact that there is no limit to our power of thinking that would inhibit the mental attribution of infinity to numbers, to magnitudes, or to what is outside the heavens. (*Physica,* 203b 15–25; our paraphrase is adapted from W. D. Ross, *Aristotle's Physics,* p. 363.) These aspects of infinity are timeless; they might have been envisioned, spontaneously, by Aquinas, Descartes, Leibniz, Kant, or Herbart. There is most certainly nothing "ancient" or "antiquarian" about them, and there is nothing in them to suggest that Aristotle had any kind of innate hesitancy to face infinity when meeting it.

Furthermore, certain special problems about infinity which are generally presumed to be "typically medieval" were formulated in later antiquity and had roots in the classical period itself. Thus, Philo of Alexandria (first century A.D.) and Plotinus (third century A.D.) have fashioned lasting problems about infinity which are theological, in the sense that the infinity involved is a leading attribute of divinity. The Middle Ages themselves knew that problems of this kind reached back at least to Plato, and they may have reached back even to Xenophanes (late sixth century B.C.); except that only later antiquity loosened them out of the matrix of "natural philosophy" within which they had come into being first.

After the Middle Ages this theologically oriented infinity of Hellenistic provenance gave rise to a "secular" infinity in general philosophy, notably so in the many philosophical systems that were burgeoning during the scientific revolution which extended over the sixteenth, seventeenth, and eighteenth centuries and centered in the seventeenth century. We note that the transition from theological to ontological infinity was a natural development which was not "revolutionary" in itself. Logically it does not matter much whether an infinity is a leading attribute of a theologically conceived divinity, or of some secular absolute with a commanding standing in the realm of cognition and morals, and being and belief. Paradigmatically it was the same infinity, whether the absolute, of which it was an attribute, was the rationality of Descartes, the logicality of Leibniz, the morality of Spinoza, the sensuality of Hobbes, the empiricism of Locke, or the idealism of Berkeley.

In the second half of the eighteenth century Immanuel Kant made a very curious use of infinity in his *Critique of Pure Reason*. The fame of the work rests on its early chapters, in which Kant posits and expounds his celebrated thesis that space and time are *a priori* absolutes of a certain kind, namely that they are not objectively real, but only subjectively ideal in a peculiarly Kantian sense, which Kant himself calls, "aesthetical." After expounding this thesis Kant dwells at length on other matters, but in the second half of the treatise, namely in the long section called "The Antinomy of Pure Reason" (trans. N. K. Smith, pp. 384–484), he returns to the thesis and undertakes to fully demonstrate that neither space nor time can be objectively real. Kant reasons after the manner of a medieval schoolman, namely by having resort to old-fashioned antinomies. On the presumption that space (or time) is objectively real, Kant presents a thesis that it then would have to be finite, and an antithesis that it then would have to be infinite; from which it follows, according to Kant, that space (or time) cannot be objectively real but must be aesthetically ideal.

The nineteenth century was crowded with eminent representatives of general philosophy—idealists, positivists, historicists, early existentialists—and, in large works, there was much discourse on absolutes, and on their attributes, with infinity among them. But nothing that was said about infinity in works other than scientific ones struck a new note and need be remembered.

In contrast to this, in the twentieth century, and starting in the last decades of the nineteenth century, the topic of infinity has become alive with innovations; but these innovations, even when adopted and exploited by philosophers, came about primarily in mathematics and fundamental physics and only secondarily in philosophy of any kind. Yet there continue to be those philosophers who from an intellectual devotion to religion, theology, or "non-scientific" philosophy seek refuge in perennial problems about the infinity of God and of "secular" absolutes; and there continue to be books and discussions in which seemingly timeless problems about infinity are thought about, talked about, and written about almost as much in the restless hours of today as they used to be in the leisurely days of yesteryear (J. A. Bernardete; B. Welte; H. Heimsoeth).

In present-day mathematics, infinity is an everyday concept, widespread, matter-of-fact, operational, indispensable. There is no mystique, uncertainty, or ambiguity about it, except that certain foundational verities about infinity are not demonstrable, but have to be posited axiomatically, and thus taken "on faith." This organic assimilation of infinity to the general body of mathematics has been a part of the total development of analysis since the early nineteenth century. Outstanding within the total development was Georg Cantor's creation of the theory of sets and transfinite numbers, between 1870 and 1890. It was a catalytic event, and more. But a complete account has to name a string of predecessors, like Cauchy, Abel, Bolzano, Hankel, Weierstrass, and others.

Furthermore, the nineteenth century began and the twentieth century completed a separation between infinity in mathematics and infinity in physics, in spite of the fact that, since the nineteenth century, physics, more than ever, explains and interprets what mathematics expresses and exposes (Bochner, *The Role of Mathematics . . .* , especially the Introduction and Ch. 5). While infinity of mathematics has ceased to be syllogistically different from other concepts, and operationally suspect, interpretative infinity of physics is more problematic and intriguing than ever.

In fact, in rational physics and also cosmology, whether in ancient or modern times, the infinite has always been inseparable from the indefinite and even the undetermined. Physics of the twentieth century has greatly compounded the situation by creating stirring hypotheses which may be viewed as novel conceptions of the role of the indefinitely small and the indefinitely large in the interpretation of physical events and phenomena from the laboratory and the cosmos (W. K. Heisenberg; W. Pauli). Thus, the law of Werner Heisenberg (the uncertainty principle), which states that for an elementary particle its position and momentum cannot be sharply determined simultaneously, is a statement of unprecedented novelty, about the indefinitely small in physics. Next, the law of Max Born (statistical distribution of particles), which states that for large assemblages of matter the density of distribution is a probability and not a certainty, straddles the indefinitely small and indefinitely large. Finally, the unsettling principle of de Broglie (duality of waves and corpuscles), which states that every elementary particle has, ambivalently, two realizations, a corpuscular and an undulatory, can be interpreted to mean that even the undifferentiated cannot be separated from the indefinite and the infinite; in this interpretation it reaches back to an uncanny insight of the Greeks, which was perceived by them dimly but discernibly.

The indefinitely large also occurs in present-day cosmology (J. H. Coleman; G. Gamow; H. Bondi). Among cosmological models of the universe that are presently under active study there are hardly any that are as completely infinite as was the universe of Giordano Bruno, which played a considerable role in philosophy between 1700 and 1900. The models with "continual creation" are nonfinite, but they are indefinitely large rather than infinitely large (Bondi). Even the "universe of telescopic depth," which is presumed to reach as far out into the galactic vastness as the most powerful telescopes will at any time reach, is indefinitely large, inasmuch as there is a "rim of the universe" at which "galaxies fade into nothingness" (Coleman, p. 63).

In sum, in our days, the philosophical conception of infinity is back again in the matrix of "scientism" (philosophy of nature) in which it was first set, molded, and shaped in the sixth and fifth centuries B.C., in small Greek communities of inexhaustible vistas.

In the sections to follow we will enlarge upon some of the topics raised in this survey.

II. NATURAL PHILOSOPHY

When the Greeks started out to take stock of the physical and cosmological phenomena around them—whether they were Ionians, poet philosophers, Pythagoreans, Eleatics, or pluralists—they quickly perceived, in their own patterns of discernment, the difficulty of separating the infinite and the indefinite. But the Greeks did not allow themselves to become frustrated over this. During the formative stages of their rationality, even still in Plato, the Greeks reacted to this difficulty by investing the word *apeiron* with both meanings in one, and they added a range of intermediate and proximate meanings too. Thus, in the context of a pre-Socratic philosopheme, and even still in Plato, *apeiron*, when translated into a modern idiom, may have to be rendered variously by: infinite, illimited, unbounded; immense, vast; indefinite, undetermined; even by: undefinable, undifferentiated. Furthermore, in the meaning of: infinite, illimited, unbounded, *apeiron* may refer to both bigness and smallness of size; and—what is important—in its meaning of indefinite, undetermined, undifferentiated, etc., *apeiron* may refer not only to quantity but also to quality (in our sense), even indistinguishably (Bochner, *The Role of Mathematics*, Ch. 2).

A prominent ambiguity, to which we have referred before (ibid.) occurs in a verbatim fragment of Xenophanes (frag. B 28). In an excellent translation of W. K. C. Guthrie it runs (emphasis added):

> At our feet
> We see this upper limit of the Earth
> coterminous with air, but underneath
> it stretches *without limit* [*es apeiron*].

The *apeiron* in this fragment clearly refers only to what is under the surface, and not also to what is above the horizon; but what this *apeiron* actually means cannot be stated. Commentators since the nineteenth century have been debating whether it should be translated by "infinite" or "indefinite." We think that the point is undecidable, and we have previously adduced testimony from latest antiquity in support of this conclusion.

We are not asserting that a Greek of the sixth or fifth centuries B.C., when encountering the word *apeiron*, had to go through a mental process of deciding which of the various meanings, in our vocabulary, is intended. The shade of meaning in our sense was usually manifest from the context; whatever ambiguities presented themselves, were inherent in the objective situation, rather than in the subjective verbalization.

Aristotle, in his usage and thinking, tends to take *apeiron* in the meaning of "infinite in a quantitative sense," and in the second half of his *Physica* (Books 5–8), which deals with locomotion, terrestrial or orbital, *apeiron* is taken almost exclusively in this sense. At any rate, the second half of the *Physica* becomes as intelligible as it can be made, if *apeiron* is taken in this sense exclusively. But in the first half of the *Physica*, which is a magnificent discourse on principles of physics in their diversity, Aristotle is unable to keep vestiges of the indefinite out of his *apeiron*, and even tints of quality are shading the hue of quantity. In keeping with this, Aristotle's report on the "puzzles" of Zeno (see next section, III), in which *apeiron* has to be quantitative, is presented by him in the second half of the *Physica*, and only there; in the first half of the *Physica* there is no mention of the puzzles at all, not even in the connected essay about *apeiron* (see section I, above), in which all aspects of the notion are presumed to be mentioned.

All told the Greeks created a permanent theme of cognition when, in their own thought patterns, they interpreted the disparity between *perception* and *conception* as an imprecision between the indefinite and the infinite. Also, our present-day polarity between the nuclear indefinite of quantum theory and the operational infinite of mathematics proper is only the latest in a succession of variations on this Greek motif.

A remarkable confirmation of this Greek insight came in the twilight period between Middle Ages and Renaissance. In fact, in the first half of the fifteenth century Nicholas of Cusa broke a medieval stalemate when he made bold to proclaim that the universe, in its mathematical structure, is, in one sense, neither finite nor infinite, and, in another sense, both finite and infinite, that is, indefinite. A century later, in the first half of the sixteenth century, Nicholas Copernicus took upon himself to rearrange the architectonics of our solar system, but about the size of the universe he would only say, guardedly, that it is *immense*, whatever that means (A. Koyré, Ch. III). It is true that in the second half of the sixteenth century Giordano Bruno, a much applauded philosopher, made the universe as wide-open and all-infinite as it could conceivably be; but Johannes Kepler, a scientists' scientist, countered, with patience and cogency, and incomparably deeper philosophical wisdom, that this would be an astrophysical incongruity, and in the question of the overall size of the universe Kepler ranged himself alongside Aristotle (A. Koyré, Ch. IV).

In the first half of the seventeenth century, René Descartes, the modern paragon of right reason and clear thinking, insisted that his *extension* (*étendue*), which was his space of physical events, is by size *indefinite* and *not* infinite; although in some of his *Méditations*, when dealing with the existence of God in general terms, Descartes imparts to God the attribute of infinity in the common (philosophical) sense (B. Rochot).

The Platonist Henry More, an intolerant follower of Giordano Bruno, put Descartes under severe pressure, philosophically and theologically, to change the verdict into *indefinite*, but Descartes, to his immeasurable credit, would not surrender (Koyré, Ch. V and VI). And, in the second half of the seventeenth century and afterwards, Isaac Newton, in all three editions of his incomparable *Principles of Natural Philosophy* (1687, 1713, 1726), when speaking of cosmic distances, uses the Copernican term "immense" (for instance, F. Cajori, ed., *Principia*, p. 596), but avoids saying whether the size of the universe is finite or infinite, or perhaps indefinite; although between the first and second editions, in a written reply to a query from the equally intolerant divine Robert Bentley, Newton made some kind of "admission" that the universe might be infinite (A. Koyré, pp. 178–89).

Even the aether of electrodynamics in the nineteenth century, although it filled a Euclidean substratum of infinite dimensions, had, by quality, a feature of indefiniteness, or rather of indeterminacy, adhering to it. By pedigree, this aether was a descendant of the "subtle matter" (*matière subtile*) of Descartes, which

had been as indefinite as the *étendue* which it filled, and it is possible that, by a long evolution, both had inherited their indeterminacy from the original *apeiron* of Anaximander, which may have been the first "subtle matter" there ever was.

Finally we note that an imprecision between the indefinitely small and the infinitely small intervenes whenever a substance which is physically known to be distributed discontinuously (granularly, molecularly, atomistically, nuclearly) is mathematically assumed, for the sake of manipulations, to be distributed continuously. Without such simplifying assumptions there would be no physics today, in any of its parts. It was the forte of nineteenth-century physics that it excelled in field theories, which are theories of continuous distribution of matter or energy, and that at the same time, and in the same contexts, it was pioneering in the search of "particles" like atoms, molecules, and electrons (B. Schonland).

III. MATHEMATICS

A famous Greek encounter with infinity is the "puzzles" (*logoi*) about motion by Zeno of Elea, about the middle of the fifth century B.C. Best known is the conundrum about "Achilles and the Turtle." It maintains, against all experience, that in a race between a quick-footed Achilles and a slow-moving Turtle, if the Turtle has any head start at all then Achilles cannot overtake him, ever. In fact, by the time Achilles has reached the Turtle's starting point the latter has moved on by a certain distance; when Achilles has covered that distance, the Turtle has again gained a novel distance, etc. This gives rise to an unending sequence of distances; and the puzzle maintains that Achilles cannot exhaust the sum of the distances and come abreast with the Turtle (Ross, *Aristotle's Physics*, Introduction; also A. Edel, *Aristotle's Theory . . .*).

The puzzles have an enduring appeal; but their role in stimulating Greek rationality cannot be easily gauged, because the Greek documentation of them is very sparse and hesitant. The puzzles were transmitted only by Aristotle, not in his *Metaphysica*, which is Aristotle's work in basic philosophy, but only in the *Physica*, and only in the second half of the latter, which deals with problems of motion, and not with conceptions and principles of physics in their generality as does the first half. Furthermore, in classical antiquity the puzzles are never alluded to in mathematical contexts, and there is no kind of evidence or even allusion that would link professional mathematicians with them.

In a broad sense, in classical antiquity the conception of infinity belonged to physics and natural philosophy, but not to mathematics proper; that is, to the area of knowledge with which a department of mathematics is entrusted today. Nobody in antiquity would have expected Archimedes to give a lecture "On Infinity" to an academic audience, or to his engineering staff at the Syracuse Ministry of Defence. Also, no ancient commentator would have said that Anaxagoras (fifth century B.C.) had introduced a mathematical aspect of infinity, as is sometimes asserted today (e.g., in *Revue de Synthèse*, pp. 18–19).

Furthermore, such Greek efforts by mathematics proper as, from our retrospect, did bear on infinity, were—again from our retrospect—greatly hampered in their eventual outcome by a congenital limitation of Greek mathematics at its root (Bochner, *The Role of Mathematics . . .* , pp. 48–58). As evidenced by developments since around A.D. 1600, mathematics, if it is to be truly successful, has to be basically operational. Greek constructive thinking however, in mathematics and also in general, was basically only ideational. By this we mean that, on the whole, the Greeks only formed abstractions of the first order, that is idealizations, whereas mathematics demands also abstractions of higher order, that is abstractions from abstractions, abstractions from abstractions from abstractions, etc. We are not underestimating Greek ideations as such. Some of them are among the choicest Greek achievements ever. For instance, Aristotle's distinction between potential infinity and actual infinity was a pure ideation, yet unsurpassed in originality and imperishable in its importance. However, as Aristotle conceived it, and generations of followers knew it, this distinction was not fitted into operational syllogisms, and was therefore unexploitable. Because of this even front-rank philosophers, especially after the Renaissance, mistook this distinction for a tiresome scholasticism, until, at last, late Victorian mathematics began to assimilate it into its operational texture.

In the seventeenth and eighteenth centuries, mathematics was so fascinated with its newly developing raw operational skills, that, in its ebullience, it hid from itself the necessity of attending to some basic conceptual (ideative) subtleties, mostly involving infinity, the discovery and pursuit of which had been a hallmark of the mathematics of the Greeks. Only in the nineteenth century did mathematics sober down, and finally turn its attention to certain conceptualizations and delicate ideations towards which the Greeks, in their precociousness, were oriented from the first. But even with its vastly superior operational skills, modern mathematics had to spend the whole nineteenth century to really overtake the Greeks in these matters.

This raises the problem, a very difficult one, of determining the role of the Middle Ages as an intermediary between Greek precociousness and modern expertise. In the realm of mathematical infinity the thirteenth and fourteenth centuries were rather active. But studies thus far have not determined whether, as maintained in the voluminous work of Pierre Duhem (ibid., p. 117), a spark from the late Middle Ages leapt across the Renaissance to ignite the scientific revolution which centered in the seventeenth century, or whether this revolution was self-igniting, as implied in wellreasoned books of Anneliese Maier. And they also have not determined what, in this area of knowledge, the contribution of the Arabic tributary to the Western mainstream actually was.

IV. THE INFINITELY SMALL

Relative to the infinitely small, Greek mathematics attained two summit achievements: the theory of proportions, as presented by Book 5 of Euclid's *Elements*, and the method of exhaustion for the computation of areas and volumes, as presented by the essay "On Sphere and Cylinder" of Archimedes. Eudoxus of Cnidos (408–355 B.C.), the greatest Greek mathematician before Archimedes—and a star member of Plato's Academy, who was even an expert on "Hedonism and Ethical Purity"—had a share in both achievements. But not a line of his writings, if any, survives, and he is, in historical truth, only a name.

The durable outcome of these efforts was a syllogistic procedure for the validation of mathematical limiting processes. On the face of it, such a process requires an infinity of steps, but the Greeks devised a procedure by which the express introduction of infinity was circumvented. The Greeks never bestowed mathematical legitimacy on an avowed conception of infinity, but they created a circumlocution by which to avoid any direct mention of it. Thus the word *apeiron* occurs in Archimedes only nontechnically, and very rarely too. In the nineteenth century, Georg Cantor and others, but mainly Cantor, legitimized infinity directly, and the world of thought has not been the same since. But the Greek method of circumvention lives on too, as vigorously and indispensably as ever; except that a symbol for infinity—namely the symbol "∞" which was introduced by John Wallis in 1656—has been injected into the context, with remarkable consequences. The symbol occurs, for instance, in the limit relation

$$\lim_{n \to \infty} \frac{1}{n} = 0,$$

which, notwithstanding its un-Archimedian appearance, is purely Archimedian by its true meaning. In fact, since $1/n$ decreases as n increases, the Cauchy definition of this relation states that corresponding to any positive number ε, however small, there exists an integer n such that $1/n < \varepsilon$. Now, this is equivalent to

609

$1 < n\varepsilon$, or, to $n\varepsilon > 1$, and the last relation can be verbalized thus:

If ε is any positive real number, then on adding it to itself sufficiently often, the resulting number will exceed the number 1.

The Greeks did not have our real numbers; but if we nevertheless superimpose them on the mathematics of Archimedes, then the statement just verbalized becomes a particular case of the so-called "Postulate of Archimedes," which, for our purposes, may be stated thus:

If a and b are any two magnitudes of the same kind (that is if both are, say, lengths, areas, or volumes), then on adding a to itself sufficiently often, the resulting magnitude will exceed b; that is $na > b$, for some n. (E. J. Dijksterhuis, *Archimedes*, pp. 146–47 has the wording of the postulate in original Greek, an English translation of his own, and a comparison of this translation with various others).

The Greek theory of proportion was a "substitute" for our present-day theory of the linear continuum for real numbers, and the infinitely small is involved in interlocking properties of denseness and completeness of this continuum (see Appendix to this section). Our real numbers are a universal quantitative "yardstick" by which to measure any scalar physical magnitude, like length, area, volume, time, energy, temperature, etc. The Greeks, most regrettably, did not introduce real numbers; that is they did not operationally abstract the idea of a real number from the idea of a general magnitude. Instead, Euclid's Book 5 laboriously establishes properties of a linear continuum for a magnitude ($\mu\acute{\varepsilon}\gamma\varepsilon\theta os$, *megethos*) in general. If the Greeks had been inspired to introduce our field of real numbers and to give to the positive numbers the status of magnitudes, then their theory of proportions would have applied to the latter too, and their theory of proportions thus completed would have resembled an avant-garde theory of twentieth-century mathematics.

Within the context of Zeno's puzzles, Aristotle was also analyzing the infinitely small as a constituent of the linear continuum which "measures" length and time. He did so not by the method of circumvention, which the professional mathematicians of his time were developing into an expert procedure, but by a reasoned confrontation *à la* Georg Cantor, which may have been characteristic of philosophers of his time. In logical detail Aristotle's reasoning is not always satisfactory, but he was right in his overall thesis that if length and time are quantitatively determined by a suitable common linear continuum, then the puzzles lose their force. In fact, in present-day mathematical mechanics, locomotion is operationally represented by a mathematical function $x = \varphi(t)$ from the time variable t to the length variable x, as defined in working mathematics; in such a setup Zeno's paradoxes do not even arise. It is not at all a part of a physicist's professional knowledge, or even of his background equipment, to be aware of the fact that such puzzles were ever conceived.

The "method of exhaustion" is a Greek anticipation of the integral calculus. In the works of Archimedes, the syllogistic maturity of the method is equal to that of the Riemann-Darboux integral in a present-day graduate text, but in operational efficiency the method was made obsolete by the first textbook on the integral calculus from around A.D. 1700 (C. B. Boyer, p. 278). However the method also embodied the postulate of Archimedes, and this postulate has an enhanced standing today. An innovation came about in the late nineteenth century when G. Veronese (*Grundzüge*, 1894) and D. Hilbert (*Grundlagen*, 1899) transformed the "postulate" into an "axiom," that is into an axiomatic hypothesis which may or may not be adjoined to suitable sets of axioms, in geometry, analysis, or algebra. This gives rise to various non-Archimedian possibilities and settings, some of which are of interest and even of importance.

Aristotle made the major pronouncement (*Physica*, Book 3, Ch. 7) that a magnitude (*megethos*) may become infinitely small only potentially, but not actually. This is an insight in depth, and there are various possibilities for translating this ideational pronouncement from natural philosophy into a present-day statement in operational mathematics. We adduce one such statement: although every real number can be represented by a nonterminating decimal expansion, it is generally not possible to find an actual formula for the entire infinite expansion; but *potentially*, for any prescribed real number, by virtue of knowing it, any desired finite part of its decimal expansion can be obtained.

Appendix. A linearly ordered set is termed *dense* if between any two elements there is a third. It is termed *complete* if for any "Dedekind Cut," that is for any division of the set into a lower and upper subset, (i) either the lower subset has a maximal element, (ii) or the upper subset has a minimal element, (iii) or both.

If the set is both dense and complete, possibility (iii) cannot arise, so that either the lower subset has a maximum, or the upper subset has a minimum. This single element is then said to lie on the cut, or to be determined by the cut.

V. THE INFINITELY LARGE

A true departure from Greek precedents was the manner in which mathematics of the nineteenth century set out, in earnest, to deal with infinity—especially with the infinitely large—by confrontation and actualization. One such development, which we will briefly sketch in the next section, was inaugurated in geometry, that is in the theory of space structure; so-called "open" spaces were boldly "closed off" by addition of ideally conceived "infinitely distant" points that were operationally created for such purposes. Internally these were important events which affected the course of mathematics profoundly, even if philosophers did not become aware of them; but externally the dominant and spectacular development was Georg Cantor's creation of the theory of sets and of transfinite numbers. It had a wide appeal, and an enduring effect, outside of professional mathematics too. Cantor's work was not only a creation, it was a movement. As of a sudden, infinity ceased to be an object of frequently aimless and barren ideational speculations, and it became a datum of refreshingly efficient operational manipulations and syllogizations. The movement brought to the fore novel thought patterns in and out of mathematics, and it helped to create the tautness of syntax in and out of analytical philosophy. Also our present-day "New Mathematics," which—at any rate in the United States—is being introduced on all levels of pre-college schooling, is a delayed response to a permanent challenge which has been emanating from Cantor's theory from the first.

But before these Victorian achievements, that is, in the overlong stretch of time from the early Church Fathers to the early nineteenth century, and even during the ages of the scientific revolution and of the Enlightenment, mathematical developments regarding infinity were, on the whole, excruciatingly slow. Newton, Leibniz, Euler, Lagrange, or even Carl Friedrich Gauss, would not have been able to express satisfactorily, in words of theirs, when an infinite series is convergent and when not. As we have already stated, John Wallis introduced in 1656 our present-day symbol "∞" for infinitely large, and he began to operate with it as if it were one more mathematical symbol. This can be done, to an extent. But, from our retrospect, for about 150 years the operations with the symbol were amateurishly and scandalously unrigorous. However, long before that, in the great mathematical works of Euclid, Archimedes, and Apollonius, of the third century B.C., there were well-conceived convergence processes, which, within their own settings, were handled competently and maturely. It must be quickly added however, that this mature Greek mathematics did not have the internal strength to survive, but was lost from sight in the obscurity of a general decline of Hellenism, whereas the mathematics of the seventeenth and eighteenth centuries, however beset with shortcomings of rigor, has been marching from strength to greater strength without a break.

It had been a tenet of Aristotle that there cannot be anything that is infinite *in actuality*, meaning "that

no form of infinite exists, as a given simultaneously existing whole" (Ross, *Aristotle*, p. 87). But 22 centuries later, Georg Cantor retorted, boastfully, that his findings clearly controverted the tenet. Cantor also adduced illustrious predecessors of his, notably Saint Augustine, who had anticipated the actual infinity of his, even as it applies to natural numbers (Cantor, *Gesammelte . . .*, pp. 401–04 and other passages). These statements of Cantor are misleading, and we will briefly state in what way.

On the face of it, Cantor was right in affirming that there is an anticipation of the first transfinite cardinal number in Saint Augustine's *De civitate Dei*, especially in the chapter entitled "Against those who assert that things that are infinite cannot be comprehended by the knowledge of God" (Book 12, Ch. 18). However, this anticipation and the others which Cantor adduces, were ideations only, and were made and remained at a considerable distance from mathematics proper. But Cantor's theory of sets was produced in a spirit of truly "abstract" mathematics; it quickly moved into the central area of operational mathematics and has remained there ever since. Within theological and philosophical contexts, actual infinity, however exalted, is hierarchically subordinate to a supreme absolute of which it is an attribute. But in set theory, infinity, although a property of an aggregate, is nevertheless mathematically autonomous and hierarchically supreme; like all primary mathematical data it is self-created and self-creating within the realm of mathematical imagery and modality.

In some of his writings Cantor reflects on the nature, mission, and intellectual foundation of his theories, and these reflections create the impression that Cantor's prime intellectual motivation was an urge to examine searchingly Aristotle's contention that infinity can exist at best only potentially, and never actually. But Cantor's mathematical work itself, if one omits his self-reflections, suggests a different kind of motivation, a much more prosaic one. It suggests that Cantor's theory evolved out of his preoccupation with an everyday problem of working mathematics, namely with Riemann's uniqueness problem for trigonometric series. Some of Riemann's work, for instance his momentous study of space structure, is clearly allied to philosophy. But the problem of technical mathematics which attracted Cantor's attention was not at all of this kind. There was nothing in it to stimulate an Ernst Cassirer, Bertrand Russell, A. N. Whitehead, or even Charles S. Peirce or Gottlob Frege. Also, the nature of the mathematical problem was such, that Cantor was led to conceive ordinal numbers first, cardinal numbers next, and general aggregates last (Cantor, *Gesammelte . . .*, p. 102, editor's note 2). But in a later systematic recapitulation (ibid., pp. 282–356), which is "philosophically" arranged, the order of concepts is reversed.

We have dwelt on this, because, in our view, the actual infinity as conceived by Cantor, is entirely different from the actual infinity as conceived by Aristotle, so that there is no conflict between Aristotle's denial and Cantor's affirmation of its existence. In support of this view we observe as follows: according to Cantor (*Gesammelte . . .*, pp. 174–75), Aristotle had to deny the existence of an actual infinity, simply because Aristotle was not intellectually equipped to countenance the fact that if n is a finite number and α a transfinite number, then α "annihilates" n, in the sense that

$$n + \alpha = \alpha.$$

Cantor observes that, contrary to what Aristotle may have thought, this is a true and important fact, and he derides Aristotle for not grasping it but finding something incongruous in it. Cantor elaborates on this fact by further noting that if α is a number of ordinal type, and if the order of the addends n and α is inverted, then n is not annihilated, because, in fact

$$\alpha + n > \alpha.$$

Also, Cantor interprets all this to imply—in all seriousness—that if a finite number has the temerity of placing itself in front of an infinite ordinal number α then it suffers annihilation, but if it has the prudence of ranging itself in the rear of an infinite ordinal α then its existence is mercifully spared.

This bizarre interpretation, however alluring for its boldness, must not be allowed to detract from the fact that Aristotle himself, in the given context (*Physica*, Book 3, Ch. 5; 204b 12–20), to which Cantor refers (he actually refers not to this passage in the *Physica*, but to a less "authoritative" near-duplication of it in *Metaphysica*, Book II, Ch. 10), speaks not of number (*arithmos*), or even magnitude (*megethos*), but of "body" (*soma*, σῶμα), which he expressly specifies to be an elementary constituent of matter, like fire or air. Aristotle asserts that such a body cannot be infinite, because if it were, then the addition (or subtraction) of a finite amount would not affect the sum total. This assertion, whatever its merit, is a statement about physics or natural philosophy, and not, as Cantor misleadingly presents it, a statement about technical mathematics. One can easily formulate a statement which would sound very similar to the assertion of Aristotle, and which a present-day physicist might accept, or, at any rate, not find unreasonable. Thus, a present-day physicist might reason that it is incongruous to assume that the total energy of the universe is infinite. In fact, if it were infinite, the addition or subtraction of a finite amount of energy would not change the total amount of energy, and the law of the conservation of energy—if our physicist generally subscribes to it—would become pointless when applied to such a universe as a whole. It is true that nowadays the law of conservation of energy, although adhered to in laboratory physics, is not always observed in cosmology. Thus in present-day cosmological models with "continual creation of matter" the total energy is nonfinite and the law of the conservation of energy is not enforced. But the infinity involved in these models leans more towards Aristotle's potentiality than Cantor's actuality, and is certainly not as fully "actual" as in Cantor.

VI. THE INFINITELY DISTANT

The standard perspective of the visual arts, which was created in the sixteenth century, features a "vanishing point." This is a concrete specific point in the total mimetic tableau, yet, in a sense, it represents an infinitely distant point in an underlying geometry (Christian Wiener, Introduction; E. Panofsky, *Albrecht Dürer*). Mathematics since then, and especially in the nineteenth century, has introduced various mathematical constructs with infinitely distant points in them, and we will briefly report on some of them.

There were no such tangible developments before the Renaissance. Aristotle, in his *Poetics* and elsewhere, speaks of the art of painting, but not of vanishing points or other infinitely distant points in geometry. In antiquity altogether, only later antiquity had some adumbrations (Panofsky, "Die Perspective" . . .). In medieval architecture, Gothic arches and spires would "vanish" into the upper reaches of the aether; but they would stay there and not converge towards concrete specific points in the total tableau.

But the Renaissance produced perspective; and it also began to create novel theories of vision (V. Ronchi). Furthermore, since around A.D. 1600 mathematics began to construct, concretely, infinitely distant points, and in the first construction, an implicit one, the Euclidean plane E_2 was "closed off" in all directions by the addition of a point at infinity on each ray emanating from a fixed point. That is, E_2 was viewed (as already in *De rerum natura* of Lucretius) as an "open" disk of infinite radius; it was made, geometrically, into a "closed" disk by the addition of a "hoop" of infinite radius around it. This construction was not performed explicitly or intentionally, but was implied in the following assumption. By Euclid's own definition, two straight lines are parallel if, being in the same plane, and being produced indefinitely in both directions, they do not meet one another in either direction (T. L. Heath, I, 190). Now, around 1600 some mathematicians began to assume, as a matter of course, that

Euclid's definition is equivalent to the description that two straight lines in the same plane are parallel, if, after being produced indefinitely, they meet at two infinitely distant points at both ends of the configuration (and only there). To assume this is, from our present retrospect, equivalent to assuming that there is around E_2 the kind of hoop that we have described.

The same mathematicians soon began to sense, in their own manner, that to close off E_2 in this fashion is neither intellectually original nor operationally profitable. They began to "experiment" with other procedures for closing off E_2. These "experiments" were a part, even a significant part, of the sustained efforts to erect the doctrines of descriptive and projective geometries, and they were satisfactorily completed in the course of the nineteenth century only.

The outcome was as follows. It is pertinent to install our hoop around E_2, but this is only a first step. The total hoop is too wide, that is, not sufficiently restrictive, and it is necessary to "reduce" it in size by "identifying" or "matching" various points of it with each other.

First and foremost, it is very appropriate to "identify" all points of the hoop with each other, that is to "constrict" the hoop to a single point. By the addition of this single point, the plane E_2 becomes "sealed off" as infinity, and the resulting two-dimensional figure is topologically a spherical surface S_2. Conversely, if one starts out with an S_2, say with an ideally smoothed-out surface of our earth, and removes one point, say the North Pole, then the remaining surface can be "spread out" topologically onto the E_2. Such a spreading out is done in cartography by means of the so-called stereographic projection. This projection of a punctured sphere S_2 on the Euclidean E_2 is not only topological, that is bi-continuous, but also conformal, that is angle-preserving; and this was already known to the astronomer and geographer Ptolemy in the second century A.D. in his *Geography* (M. R. Cohen and I. E. Drabkin, pp. 169–79).

The one-point completion which we have just described can be performed for the Euclidean (or rather Cartesian) space E_n of any dimension n, and the result is the n-dimensional sphere S_n. Topologically there is no difference between various dimensions, but algebraically there is. First, for $n = 2$, the plane E_2 can be viewed as the space of the complex numbers $z = x + iy$, and the added point at infinity can be interpreted as a complex number ∞, for which, symbolically,

$$(°) \qquad \frac{1}{\infty} = 0, \ \frac{1}{0} = \infty.$$

This interpretation is commonly attributed to C. F.

Gauss (1777–1855). Next, for $n = 4$, E_n can be interpreted as the space of quaternions $a + ib + jc + kd$, which were created by William Rowan Hamilton (1805–65), and the point at infinity can be interpreted as a quaternion ∞ for which (°) holds. This can still be done for E_8, if it be viewed as a space of so-called Cayley numbers ($=$ pairs of quaternions), but no other such cases of so-called "real division algebras" are known (N. Steenrod, pp. 105–15; M. T. Greenberg, p. 87). As regards quaternions it is worth recording, as a phenomenon in the history of ideas, that around 1900 there was an international organization of partisans who believed that quaternions were one of the most potent operational tools which the twentieth century was about to inherit from the preceding one; the organization has been long extinct.

After the spheres, the next important spaces which arise from E_n by a suitable addition of points at infinity are so-called projective spaces; we will speak only of "real" projective spaces, and denote them by P_n. (Other projective spaces are those over complex numbers, quaternions, or Cayley numbers; see Steenrod, Greenberg, loc. cit.) For each dimension n, P_n arises from E_n if one identifies each infinitely distant point of the "hoop" around E_n with its antipodal point, that is, if for each straight line through the origin of E_n the two infinite points at the opposite ends of it are identified (that is "glued together"). The resulting space is a closed manifold (without any boundary), and it is the carrier of the so-called *elliptic* non-Euclidean geometry of F. Klein (S. M. Coxeter, p. 13). Klein's purpose in devising his geometry was to remove a "blemish" from the spherical (non-Euclidean) geometry of B. Riemann. In Riemann's geometry any two "straight" (i.e., geodesic) lines intersect in precisely two points, whereas in Klein's variant on it they intersect in precisely one point only.

The P_n, that is the *real* projective spaces, have a remarkable property: for even dimensions n they are nonorientable, but for odd dimensions orientable. A space is orientable, if a tornado (or any other spinning top), when moving along *any* closed path, returns to its starting point with the same sense of gyration with which it started, and it is nonorientable if along *some* closed path the sense of gyration is reversed. In the case of a P_n with an even-dimensional n the sense of gyration is reversed each time the path "crosses" infinity. In particular, the space P_2, that is the space of two dimensional elliptic geometry, is not orientable, but P_3 is. Thus, in P_2 a fully mobile society cannot distinguish between right- and left-handed screws, but in P_3 it can.

Nineteenth-century mathematics has created many other completions of E_n which have become the substance of the theory of Riemann surfaces and of algebraic geometry. Twentieth-century mathematics has produced a one-point "compactification" (P. Alexandroff, "Über die Metrisation . . ."), which has spread into all of general topology, and a theory of prime-ends (C. Carathéodory, "Über die Begrenzung . . ."), which in one form or another is of consequence in conformal mapping, potential theory, probability theory, and even group theory.

In the nineteenth century, while mathematics was tightening the looseness-at-infinity of Euclidean structure, French painting was loosening the tightness-at-infinity of perspective structure. The French movement is already discernible in Dominique Ingres, but the acknowledged leader of it was Paul Cézanne. Cézanne was not an "anarchist," wanting only to "overthrow" classical perspective without caring what to put in its place, but analysts find it difficult to say what it was that he was aspiring to replace perspective by. We once suggested, for the comprehension of Cézanne, an analogy to developments in mechanics (Bochner, *The Role of Mathematics* . . . , pp. 191–201), and in the present context we wish to point out, in another vein, that Cézanne was trying to loosen up the traditional perspective by permitting several vanishing points instead of one (E. Loran, *Cézanne's Composition*), and by giving to lines of composition considerable freedom in their mode of convergence towards their vanishing points (M. Schapiro, *Paul Cézanne*). This particular suggestion may be off the mark, but the problem of a parallelism between nineteenth-century developments in geometry and in the arts does exist.

VII. THE COMPLETE AND THE PERFECT

Nonscientific aspects of infinity are usually broad and elusive and mottled with ambiguities and polarities. One of the worst offenders was Benedict Spinoza, however much he presumed to articulate his thoughts *more geometrico*. In fact, the term "infinite" stands in Spinoza for such terms as "unique," "incomparable," "homonymous," "indeterminate," "incomprehensible," "ineffable," "indefinable," "unknowable," and many other similar terms (Wolfson, . . . *Spinoza*, I, 138). What is worse, Spinoza justified this license of his by reference to Aristotle's dictum that "the infinite so far as infinite is unknown" (ibid., I, 139), which Aristotle certainly would not have allowed to be exploited in this way.

But even when intended to be much more coherent, the conception of infinity in a nonscientific context, especially in theology, need not refer to the magnitude of quantitative elements like space, time, matter, etc., but it may refer to the intensity of qualitative attributes like power, being, intellect, justice, goodness, grace,

etc. There are large-scale philosophical settings, in which infinity, under this or an equivalent name, does not magnify, or even emphasize, the outward extent of something quantifiable, but expresses a degree of completeness and perfection of something structurable.

Because of all that, philosopher-theologians who strive for clarity of thought and exposition are having great difficulties with them. Thus, Saint Thomas Aquinas, in a discourse on the existence and nature of God in the entering part of his *Summa theologiae*, compares and confronts the completeness and perfection in God with the infinite and limitless in Him. In a "typically Thomistic" sequence of arguments and counterarguments, completeness and infinity are alternately identified and contrasted, as if they were synonyms and antonyms in one; and, although Aquinas very much strives for clarity, it would be difficult to state in a few sharply worded declaratory statements, what the outcome of the discourse actually is (Saint Thomas Aquinas, *Summa theologiae*, Vol. II).

Completeness in philosophy is even harder to define than infinity in philosophy, and the relation between the two is recondite and elusive. The problem of this relation was already known to the Greeks. As a problem of cognition it was created by Parmenides, and then clearly formulated by Aristotle, but as a problem of "systematic" theology it came to the fore only in the second half of Hellenism, beginning recognizably with Philo of Alexandria, and coming to a first culmination in the *Enneads* of Plotinus. From our retrospect, the "One" (τὸ ἕν) of Plotinus was a fusion between a divinely intuited completeness and a metaphysically perceived infinity. Books V and VI of the *Enneads* are full of evidence for this, and we note, for instance, that a recent study of Plotinus summarizes the passage VI, 8.11, of the *Enneads* thus:

The absolute transcendence of the One as unconditioned, unlimited, Principle of all things: particular necessity of eliminating all spatial ideas from our thoughts about Him (A. H. Armstrong, *Plotinus*, p. 63).

Also, a study of Plotinus of very recent date has the following important summary:

Within recent years there has been a long and learned discussion on the infinity of the Plotinian One, and from it we learn much. The chief participants are now in basic agreement that the One is infinite in itself as well as infinite in power (J. M. Rist, p. 25).

Long before that, Aristotle devoted a chapter of his *Physica* (Book 3, Ch. 6) to an express comparison between completeness and infinity, as he saw it. Aristotle presents a thesis that infinity is directly and unmistakably opposed to "the Complete and the Whole" (τέλειον καὶ ὅλον), and his central statement runs as follows:

The infinite turns out to be the contrary of what it is said to be. It is not what has nothing outside it that is infinite, but what always has something outside it (206b 34–207a 1, Oxford translation).

His definition then is as follows:

A quantity is infinite if it is such that we can always take a part outside what has already been taken. On the other hand what has nothing outside it is complete and whole. For thus we define the whole—that from which nothing is wanting—as a whole man or a whole box (ibid., 207a 7–11).

'Whole' and 'complete' are either quite identical or closely akin. Nothing is complete (teleion) which has no end (telos); and the end is a limit (ibid., 207a 13–14).

Immediately following this passage, Aristotle makes respectful mention of Parmenides, and deservedly so. The great ontological poem of Parmenides clearly outlines a certain feature of completeness, as an attribute of something that is, ambivalently, an ontological absolute and a cosmological universe. Ontologically this universe was made of pure being and thought itself, and there has been nothing like it since then (W. K. C. Guthrie, *A History* . . . , Vol. 2; Untersteiner, *Parmenide* . . . ; L. Tarán, *Parmenides* . . .). And yet, as we have tried to demonstrate in another context, the Parmenidean completeness was so rich in allusions that it even allows a measure of mathematization in terms of today, more so than Aristotle's interpretation of this completeness would (Bochner, "The Size of the Universe . . . ," sec. V).

The Parmenidean being and thought, as constituents of the universe, were conceived very tightly. In the course of many centuries after Parmenides, they were loosened up and gradually transformed into the Hellenistic "One" and "Logos," which were conceived more diffusely, and less controversially. Also, in the course of these and later centuries, the Parmenidean universe, with its attribute of completeness, was overtly theologized, mainly Christianized.

Aristotle took it for granted that the ontological universe of Parmenides, in addition to being complete, was also finite, and Parmenides did indeed so envisage it, more or less. But what was a vision in Parmenides was turned into a compulsion by Aristotle. That is, Aristotle maintained, and made into a major proposition, that the Parmenidean universe could not be other than finite, because, for Aristotle, completeness somehow had to be anti-infinite automatically.

With this proposition Aristotle may have overreached himself. Mathematics has introduced, entirely from its own spontaneity, and under various names, several versions of completeness, any of which is reminiscent of the notion of Parmenides, and, on the whole,

finiteness is not implied automatically. On the contrary, the completeness of Parmenides can be mathematically so formalized, that a universe becomes complete if it is so very infinite that no kind of magnification of it is possible (Bochner, loc. cit.). But mathematizations of the conception of completeness are of relatively recent origin, and it would not be meaningful to pursue the comparison between mathematical and philosophical versions of the conception beyond a certain point.

BIBLIOGRAPHY

The only general history of infinity is the book of Jonas Cohen; a supplement to it, heavily oriented toward theology, is the essay of Anton Antweiler. Of considerable interest is a collection of articles in the 1954 volume of the *Revue de Synthèse*.

A comprehensive study on infinity in Greek antiquity is the work of Mondolfo. The author is a staunch defender of the thesis that Greek thought had fully the same attitude towards infinity as modern thought. About infinity in the Old Testament see the books of C. von Orelli, Thorleif Boman, and James Barr. Occasionally one encounters the view that, in a true sense, infinity was originally as much a Hebraic intuition as a Greek one, and perhaps even more so. Such a view is implied in the books just cited, and it was expressly stated in *Revue de Synthèse*, p. 53 (remark by M. Serouya).

Infinity in the pre-Socratics is competently dealt with in the recent work of Guthrie. Infinity in all of Greek philosophy, Hellenic and Hellenistic, is also fully dealt with in the great Victorian standard work of Eduard Zeller. It is still very good on infinity in Plotinus, and also in Philo, in spite of recent special studies on the two, especially on Plotinus. In the case of Philo, it is not easy to locate infinity *specifically* in his work, and even in Wolfson's detailed study of Philo there is very little *direct* reference to it.

About infinity in medieval philosophy, European and Arabic, and in subsequent philosophy up to and including Spinoza, there is a wealth of material in Wolfson's two-volume work on Spinoza. All of volume I is very pertinent, and not only the parts dealing expressly with infinity, like Chapter V, part III (Definition of the term "Infinite"), and Chapter VIII (Infinity of Extension). The latter chapter is of special interest for the genesis of Descartes' view on the nature of infinity of his *extension* (or *étendue*); see section II above.

About infinity in scientist-philosophers, or cosmologists, or astronomers from Nicholas of Cusa to Newton and Leibniz there is the informative work of Koyré, which features a judicious selection of verbatim excerpts, all in English. There are also recent books about the relevance of infinity to nonscientific general philosophy, such as the books of Bernardete, Welte, and Heimsoeth.

Infinity in mathematics is accounted for in any general history of mathematics, but especially in Boyer's *The History of the Calculus*. For the history of Zeno's paradoxes the main account, with full references, is the article in nine parts, commencing in 1915, by F. Cajori in the *American Mathematical Monthly*. The references are carried to 1936 in the lengthy introduction to Ross's edition, with commentary, of *Aristotle's Physics*. To judge by an incidental remark in Cajori's account, the first outright association of the paradoxes with mathematics is documented only from the seventeenth century A.D., in the work of Gregory of St. Vincent.

For the roots and rise of Georg Cantor's set theory there is much material in Cantor's *Collected Works* which have been edited by Ernst Zermelo. The principal memoirs of Cantor were translated into English, with introduction and notes, by P. E. B. Jourdain. There is a lack of studies on how the emergence of Cantor's set theory fits into the history of ideas; there is, for instance, no special study on how it reflects itself in the philosophical system of Charles S. Peirce (cf. *Collected Papers of Charles S. Peirce*, ed. C. Hartshorne and Paul Weiss, Cambridge, Mass. [1933], Vol. IV).

The following works are additional references for the study of infinity. Paul Alexandroff, "Über die Metrisation der im kleinen kompakten topologischen Räume," *Mathematische Annalen*, **99** (1924), 294–307. Anton Antweiler, *Unendlich, Eine Untersuchung zur metaphysischen Weisheit Gottes auf Grund der Mathematik, Philosophie, Theologie* (Freiburg im Breisgau, 1935). Saint Thomas Aquinas, *Summa theologiae*, Latin text and English trans. by Blackfriars (London and New York, 1962), Vol. II. Aristotle, *Physica*, trans. R. P. Hardie and R. K. Gaye in the Oxford translation of Aristotle's works under the general editorship of W. D. Ross, Vol. 2 (Oxford, 1930). See also W. D. Ross, below. A. H. Armstrong, *Plotinus* (New York, 1962). James Barr, *Biblical Words for Time* (London, 1961). José A. Bernardete, *Infinity, an Essay in Metaphysics* (Oxford, 1964). Salomon Bochner, *The Role of Mathematics in the Rise of Science* (Princeton, 1966); idem, "The Size of the Universe in Greek Thought," *Scientia*, **103** (1968), 510–30. Hermann Bondi, *Cosmology*, 2nd ed. (Cambridge, 1960). Thorleif Boman, *Das hebräische Denken im Vergleich mit dem Griechischen*, 4th ed. (Göttingen, 1965); 3rd ed. trans. as *Hebrew Thought Compared With Greek Thought* (Philadelphia, 1961). Carl B. Boyer, *The History of the Calculus* (New York, 1959). F. Cajori, "The History of Zeno's Arguments on Motion," *American Mathematical Monthly*, **12** (1915), 1–6, 39–47, 77–82, 109–15, 143–49, 179–86, 215–20, 253–58, 292–97; idem, *Sir Isaac Newton's Mathematical Principles of Natural Philosophy and His System of the World*, trans. Andrew Motte (1729), revised by F. Cajori (Berkeley, 1934; many reprints); cited as *Principia*. Georg Cantor, *Gesammelte Abhandlungen mathematischen und philosophischen Inhalts*, ed. Ernst Zermelo (Berlin, 1932). C. Carathéodory, "Über die Begrenzung einfach zusammenhängender Gebiete," *Mathematische Annalen*, **73** (1913), 343–70. Morris R. Cohen and I. E. Drabkin, *A Source Book in Greek Science* (New York, 1948). Jonas Cohen, *Geschichte der Unendlichkeitsproblems im abendländischen Denken bis Kant* (Leipzig, 1869). James H. Coleman, *Modern Theories of the Universe* (New York, 1963). H. S. M. Coxeter, *Non-Euclidean Geometry* (Toronto,

1957). E. J. Dijksterhuis, *Archimedes* (New York, 1957). Diogenes Laërtius, *Lives of Eminent Philosophers*, 2 vols. (London and Cambridge, Mass., 1925). Abraham Edel, *Aristotle's Theory of the Infinite* (New York, 1934). George Gamow, *The Creation of the Universe* (New York, 1952). Marvin T. Greenberg, *Lectures on Algebraic Topology* (New York, 1967). Gregory of St. Vincent, *Opus geometricum quadratura circuli et sectionum coni* (Antwerp, 1647). W. K. C. Guthrie, *A History of Greek Philosophy*, Vols. 1 and 2 (Cambridge, 1962 and 1965). T. L. Heath, *The Thirteen Books of Euclid's Elements* (Cambridge, 1908); idem, *History of Greek Mathematics*, 2 vols. (Oxford, 1921). Heinz Heimsoeth, *Die sechs grossen themen der abendländischen Metaphysik und der Ausgang des Mittelalters*, 3rd ed. (Stuttgart, 1954). Werner Heisenberg, *Physics and Philosophy, the Revolution in Modern Science* (New York, 1958). David Hilbert, *Grundlagen der Geometrie* (Leipzig, 1899), many editions and translations. P. E. B. Jourdain, *Contributions to the Founding of the Theory of Transfinite Numbers* (Chicago and London, 1915). Immanuel Kant, *Critique of Pure Reason*, trans. Norman Kemp Smith (London, 1929). G. S. Kirk and J. E. Raven, *The Presocratic Philosophers* (Cambridge, 1957). Alexandre Koyré, *From the Closed World to the Infinite Universe* (Baltimore, 1957). P. Kucharski, "L'idée de l'infini en Grèce," *Revue de Synthèse*, **34** (1954), 5–20. Earle Loran, *Cézanne's Composition*, 2nd ed. (Berkeley, 1944). Anneliese Maier, *Die Vorläufer Galileis im 14. Jahrhundert* (Rome, 1949); idem, *Zwei Grundprobleme der Scholastischen Naturphilosophie* (Rome, 1951); idem, *Zwischen Philosophie und Mechanik* (Rome, 1958); idem, *Metaphysische Hintergründe der Spätscholastischen Naturphilosophie* (Rome, 1955). Rodolfo Mondolfo, *L'infinito nel pensiero dell'Antichità classica* (Florence, 1965). Isaac Newton, see Cajori, above. C. von Orelli, *Die hebräischen Synonyma der Zeit und Ewigkeit, genetisch und sprachvergleichlich dargestellt* (Leipzig, 1871). Erwin Panofsky, *Albrecht Dürer* (Princeton, 1945); idem, "Die Perspective als 'Symbolische Form,'" in *Vorträge der Bibliothek Warburg* (1924–25); the latter is reprinted in Panofsky's *Aufsätze zu Grundfragen der Kunstwissenschaft* (Berlin, 1964). W. Pauli, ed., *Niels Bohr and the Development of Physics* (New York, 1955). Charles S. Peirce, *Collected Papers of Charles S. Peirce*, ed. C. Hartshorne and Paul Weiss, 6 vols. (Cambridge, Mass., 1933), Vol. IV. *Revue de Synthèse* (Centre international de Synthèse), **34**, New Series (1954). J. M. Rist, *Plotinus: The Road to Reality* (Cambridge, 1967). B. Rochot, "L'infini Cartésien," *Revue de Synthèse*, **34** (1954), 35–54. Vasco Ronchi, *The Science of Vision* (New York, 1957). W. D. Ross, ed., *Aristotle's Physics, A revised text with introduction and commentary* (Oxford, 1936); idem, *Aristotle, a complete exposition of his works and thought* (Cleveland, 1959). Meyer Schapiro, *Paul Cézanne* (New York, 1952). A. Schoenfliess, "Projective Geometrie," *Encyclopädie der mathematischen Wissenschaften*, Vol. III, Leipzig, 1898–), Abt. 5. Basil Schonland, *The Atomists (1830–1933)* (Oxford, 1968). Oswald Spengler, *The Decline of the West*, trans. C. F. Atkinson, 2 vols. (New York, 1926–28). Norman Steenrod, *Topology of Fibre Bundles* (Princeton, 1965). Leonardo Tarán, *Parmenides, A Text with Translation, Commentary,* and Critical Essays (Princeton, 1965). Mario Untersteiner, Parmenide, Testimonianze e Frammenti (Florence, 1958). G. Veronese, Grundzüge der Geometrie (Berlin, 1894); the original edition in Italian is almost never quoted. Richard Walzer, Greek into Arabic; Essays in Islamic Philosophy (Oxford, 1962). Bernhard Welte, Im Spielfeld von Endlichkeit und Unendlichkeit. Gedanken zur Deutung der menschlichen Daseins (Frankfurt-am-Main, 1967). Christian Wiener, Lehrbuch der darstellenden Geometrie, 2 vols. (Leipzig, 1884). Harry Austryn Wolfson, Crescas' Critique of Aristotle, Problems of Aristotle's Physics in Jewish and Arabic Philosophy (Cambridge, Mass., 1929); idem, The Philosophy of Spinoza, Unfolding the Latent Processes of His Reasoning, 2 vols. (Cambridge, Mass., 1934); idem, Philo: Foundations of Religious Philosophy in Judaism, Christianity, and Islam, 2 vols. (Cambridge, Mass., 1947). Eduard Zeller, Die Philosophie der Griechen in ihrer geschichtlichen Entwicklung, 3 vols. (1844–52); the English translation appeared in segments.

SALOMON BOCHNER

[See also **Abstraction;** Axiomatization; Continuity; Cosmology; Mathematical Rigor; Newton on Method; Number; Rationality; Space; **Time and Measurement.**]

INHERITANCE OF ACQUIRED CHARACTERISTICS (LAMARCKIAN)

THIS IDEA can be traced back to speculative philosophy and even to primitive thought, if one is willing to fuzz the difference between science and other types of mental activity. The precise words, "inheritance of acquired characters," are not found until the eighteenth century, when they appeared as part of the first efforts at a scientific understanding of heredity.

In folklore one can find many cases that we moderns would lump under this concept, such as Shylock's retelling in The Merchant of Venice (I, iii, 78ff.) of

. . . what Jacob did.

When Laban and himself were compromised
That all the eanlings which were streak'd and pied
Should fall as Jacob's hire, the ewes, being rank,
In the end of autumn turned to the rams,
And, when the work of generation was
Between these woolly breeders in the act,
The skilful shepherd peel'd me certain wands
And, in the doing of the deed of kind,
He stuck them up before the fulsome ewes,
Who then conceiving did in eaning time
Fall parti-colored lambs, and those were Jacob's.

There is a bit of rationality in bizarre stories of this sort; an effort is being made to explain the appearance of progeny surprisingly different from their parents. Similarly the Russian peasant believes (reported by Vakar, p. 274) that seeds of wheat can engender wild oats. In painful fact peasants frequently see wheat turn into weeds. Another source of such commonsense confusions about heredity and variation is the observed fact that well-fed livestock have better qualities than ill-fed, which underlies the English farmer's paradoxical aphorism, "The breed is through the mouth." On the other hand, "Like father like son" is also a common observation, sustained by such facts as the endless reappearance of tails and foreskins on the progeny of docked and circumcised sires. Shakespeare can be quoted for this too:

There's a divinity that shapes our ends,
Rough-hew them how we will (Hamlet, V, ii, 10).

In ancient and medieval philosophy one can also find occasional speculations that we moderns would lump under the concept, inheritance of acquired characters. Thomas Aquinas, for example, drawing on previous writers, analyzes human reproduction in such a way as to explain how Adam's fall could taint all his progeny with a capacity to sin. The most noteworthy feature of Thomas' speculation, and of the other pre-eighteenth-century authors quoted in Zirkle's massive compilation, is their preoccupation not with heredity but with generation (or reproduction, as we call it nowadays). This physiological process, and the associated process of development from seed to adult, drew attention to themselves long before heredity, the elusive pattern of resemblances and differences between parents and progeny, was isolated for special study. There are no obvious forms to be associated with the function of heredity, as flowers and gonads are with reproduction, or as seeds make one wonder how mighty oaks from little acorns grow. The prolonged argument over the inheritance of acquired characters, lasting from the eighteenth century to the twentieth, was part of the wakening to the problem of heredity.

Some historians date this wakening much earlier than the eighteenth century. One author, Robert S. Brumbaugh, goes so far as to say that scientific genetics originated with the Pythagoreans (Journal of Heredity, **43,** 86–88). A less extravagant modernization of ancient texts is carried out by Darlington, who reads the clash of "hard" (Mendelian) and "soft" (Lamarckian) heredity into the rival speculations of Epicurus and Aristotle. He is actually dealing with the philosophy of science rather than the study of heredity. To reduce the purposeful activity of living things to the nonpurposeful action of material particles was Epicurus' mode of reasoning as it is the modern geneticist's. From this mechanistic viewpoint Aristotle's nonevolutionary

617

entelechy shares a fatal defect with Lamarck's evolutionary inheritance of acquired characters. They are both tainted by teleology; a future end is invoked as the determinant of a present form or process. But such correlations between ancient philosophical viewpoints and modern scientific theories are a product of hindsight. To pretend that they were already apparent before the rise of genetics is to put an undeserved duncecap on a host of modern biologists, to render inexplicable the enormous labor by which they moved toward a precise understanding of heredity and variation.

The eighteenth-century effort to classify all living things was the beginning of that labor. Defining the essence or typical characters of each species, the taxonomist was obliged to explain away the accidents or nontypical characters of many individuals and entire races that he included within a given species. Thus the more complex problem of analyzing the pooled heredity of a population was recognized long before the more elemental one of analyzing individual heredity, a common reversal of horse and cart that is probably unavoidable in the opening of a major new area of inquiry. The same reversal marked pre-Mendelian experiments with plant hybridization, which derived from the eighteenth-century effort to achieve a scientific agriculture, and, on the theoretical level, focused once again on taxonomy: When hybrids are not sterile "mules," are they to be classified as new species? Such problems, aggravated by the growing fossil evidence of extinct species, led to the suggestion of a phylogenetic or evolutionary taxonomy, a dizzying proposal to substitute patterns of ceaseless change for a clear-cut classification of fixed species. In Diderot's apothegm, "Species are only tendencies" (Rostand, p. 175).

One of the first biologists to make this bold proposal was Jean Baptiste de Lamarck. To explain how new species evolve out of old he invoked the common observation that living things adapt themselves to their environment, and added the supposition that such adaptation, if repeated by many creatures over much time, is finally transmitted to the progeny as an essential character of a new species. With the benefit of hindsight we can see that the distinction between the essential and accidental characters of supposedly fixed species, and the distinction between the hereditary and acquired characters of changing species, were groping steps toward the distinction between genotype and phenotype.

Largely ignored in his own lifetime, Lamarck's theory was part of the sporadic discussion of evolution during the generation preceding Darwin's *Origin of Species* (1859). In the excited aftermath of that epochal book the inheritance of acquired characters was not immediately seen as a crucial issue, for Darwin's stroke of genius was to separate the problem of a population's pooled heredity, which is obviously shaped by natural selection, from the problem of individual heredity and variation, which was a mystery. Darwin himself soon called attention to the necessity of solving the second problem, but he perceived it in a form that was still insoluble: What is the source of the variations on which selection works?

He and other evolutionists indulged in rather Lamarckian speculations on the subject, and experimental tests were undertaken. Some had clearly negative results, as when blood transfusions between different colored rabbits produced no change in coat color. Some seem to have proved the obvious, as when Weismann docked the tails of mice through twenty-two generations without shortening the tail on any newborn mouse. (It must be remembered that he was countering many unverified reports of inherited mutilations. Darwin himself published a report that the Muslims of Celebes are born with shortened foreskins.) The few experiments that seemed to prove the inheritance of acquired characters were subject to disputed interpretation, as when white moths, fed on the salts found in soot, produced some black progeny. (This happened in the twentieth century, and geneticists argued that the original stock had melanism as a recessive trait.) The important result of these experiments was the accumulating doubt they cast on Lamarckian inheritance, as they failed to prove beyond doubt a single instance of it.

Darwin brushed aside obviously teleological versions of Lamarckian inheritance—such as giraffes getting long necks by many generations of stretching for the higher leaves—but he saw no inconsistency between other versions and the mechanistic outlook that underlay the theory of natural selection. Nor, for all we know, did Mendel, whose contemporaneous stroke of genius was also a simplifying separation of a soluble problem from a tangle of insoluble ones. He set aside not only the evolution of species, but even the adaptive variation of individual organisms. He reduced the analysis of individual heredity to a manageable level by counting a few unchanging characters as they come and go in various combinations through successive generations of hybrids. Leading biologists overlooked or brushed aside this radical suspension of their chief concerns, until continued hybrid experiments and the development of cytology pushed them toward a similarly atomistic conception of heredity.

August Weismann proclaimed this conception in the 1880's, with a clarity and vigor that forced general attention to it. He declared heredity to be the function of self-replication localized in the "germ plasm," the nucleus of the specialized cells of sexual reproduction. This was an erroneous first approximation to the modern cytogenetic view, which localizes the hereditary function in the nucleus of all cells. Partly because of his mistake Weismann was inspired to make a vigorous attack on the inheritance of acquired characters, for, he reasoned, it is the surrounding body that acquires them, not the self-replicating germ plasm. The result was a lively debate between "neo-Lamarckians," who argued that evolution was inconceivable without the inheritance of acquired characters, and "neo-Darwinians," who denied it. The debate intensified efforts to achieve a precise, experimentally founded understanding of heredity and variation, with the result that Mendelian methods were simultaneously rediscovered by three separate scientists in 1900, namely DeVries, Tschermak, and Correns.

Thus the science of genetics was born, either denying the inheritance of acquired characters (in the Weismann version) or ignoring it as a meaningless concept (in the Mendelian). Until the 1930's many biologists nevertheless clung to some form of Lamarckism, for genetics seemed too narrow, incapable of analyzing anything but the simplest patterns of segregation and recombination of unchanging hereditary characters —and rather trivial ones at that, chosen for their convenience in counting. By the 1930's geneticists demonstrated their ability to deal with complex characters as well as simple ones, to incorporate in their theory the constant appearance of new characters, and to analyze the pooled heredity of a breeding population. The overwhelming majority of biologists then abandoned any form of Lamarckism. Its mode of reasoning, based on the distinction between inherited and acquired characters, had proved to be hopelessly vague and unproductive by contrast with that of genetics, based on the distinction between genotype and phenotype.

Aside from the Lysenkoites in the Soviet Union, the only biologists who have tried to keep some version of the Lamarckist view alive since the 1930's have been a tiny minority, such as L. Bertalanffy and H. G. Cannon, who are distressed by the implacable mechanism of contemporary biology. The hopelessness of their position is indicated by their lack of original ideas. For the most part they grasp at aspects of their opponents' work, such as the discovery of extrachromosomal inheritance, or at the arguments of geneticists like C. H. Waddington, who has strained the limits of his science in an effort to explain the "unbridgeable gaps" and the grand, persistent trends of evolution. In short, Lamarckism survives only as a portion of the vitalist creed. Mechanist versions of Lamarckism, which were fairly common from the late-nineteenth century through the 1920's, have vanished, for genetics has proved itself capable of solving the problems that gave rise to mechanistic Lamarckism in the first place.

The biologists' abandonment of the inheritance of acquired characters has been widely misinterpreted. Many people think that any environmental influence on heredity has been denied. In fact geneticists have been the first to make precise analyses of such influences. They differ from the Lamarckists in denying the "adequacy" or "specificity" of environmentally induced change in the heredity of an individual organism. That is, they deny that the hereditary mechanism of a living creature can make an adaptive response to an environmental influence, except by accident. On this purely mechanistic basis they have shown how a multitude of breeding individuals, a population, can and do make finely adaptive changes of their pooled heredity in response to environmental influences. Once these basic principles were established by the usual interplay of theorizing and experimentation, the inheritance of acquired characters was seen to be either meaningless or teleological. It is meaningless if it runs together such diverse things as the effects of fertilizing plants and the effects of radiating them. It is teleological if it ascribes to an hereditary mechanism—ultimately a molecule of nucleic acid—not only the function of self-replication, but also foreknowledge of a different, improved self. Thus, it is not environmental influence on heredity but a confused or teleological view of such influence that has been abandoned.

Other widespread misunderstandings concern the relevance to social thought of the affirmation or denial of the inheritance of acquired characters. Long a minor aspect of the controversy about the social implications of biology, these misunderstandings were widely inflated as a result of the Lysenko affair in the Soviet Union. In 1936 the Soviet mass media began to denounce the study of human genetics as a reactionary pseudo-science, aristocratic, racist, or simply Nazi in its social implications. The Lysenkoites, who were then winning political support by their reputation for aid to agriculture, quickly picked up this theme, and, in the 1940's, added another: Marxism has always committed its adherents to belief in the inheritance of acquired characters. Outside the Soviet Union astonished defenders of genetics rejected the association between genetics and the right, but many accepted the linkage of Lamarckism and the left. It fit the widespread picture of Marxism as an antiquated doctrine, and it could be provided with a semblance of logic: inheritance of acquired characters supposedly appeals to the Marxist mentality by promising that revolutionary improvement of the social environment will improve the human breed. The awkward fact that the

Lysenkoites never used this logic was ignored. Their actual arguments for a linkage between Marxism and Lamarckism—a couple of quotations from Engels' posthumous reflections on evolution, and a heavy stress on the Marxist theory of "practice" exemplified in the transformation of agriculture through Lysenkoite methods—seemed too flimsy to be taken at face value. Antiquated quackery could not improve farm yields; the Soviet leaders seemed to be *sacrificing* agricultural improvement out of devotion to Lamarckian faith in human perfectibility. The awkward fact that such a faith cannot be found in the basic writings of Marxist theorists was also ignored.

Social theorists of any political persuasion have had little to say on the inheritance of acquired characters, since it has not usually seemed relevant to their main concerns. This was the case even in the nineteenth century, when many were trying to found social science on biological principles. Comte, it is true, disputed Lamarck's theory of evolution at considerable length (*Cours de philosophie positive*, Vol. III), while Spencer admired it, and continued to insist on the inheritance of acquired characters even after he became a preacher of natural selection. Other biologizing social theorists can also be quoted on the inheritance of acquired characters—Bagehot for, Kidd against, others straddling—but in every case their stand on this issue is part of their synthetic philosophizing, inessential to their social thought. Indeed the same criticism can be extended from this subsidiary issue to all their biological arguments, which were, as Robert Mackintosh said, nothing more than "parables," "metaphors," or "mere illustrations" of their social principles (Mackintosh, 1899).

This criticism may be contested, but the facts of political affiliation are indisputable. Biologizing social theorists are bunched on the center and right of the political gradient. Only a few are to be found on the left, almost none on the Marxist left. Among the major Marxist theorists Kautsky alone had a serious interest in the biological aspects of social development, most notably in population problems, and he strongly endorsed the standard Marxist separation of biology and sociology. Marxism in all its varieties has shown an overwhelming tendency to ignore or reject any derivation of sociological principles from biology. Each discipline is considered autonomous, sharing only the materialist philosophy that prompted Marx to hail Darwin's *Origin of Species* as "the mortal blow to teleology in natural science." Using this line of argument Soviet Marxist geneticists in the 1920's and early 1930's pictured their science as a triumph of dialectical materialist philosophy. Just before the rise of Lysenko this was also the view of the leading Soviet Marxist philosophers.

The argument that Marxist philosophy commits one to belief in the inheritance of acquired characters was virtually unknown until T. D. Lysenko presented it in a 1941 paper, "Engels and Some Problems of Darwinism." It was impossible to find any comment on the subject in any publication of Marx or Lenin. Two or three fleeting remarks are in the posthumous publications of Engels, and a few more in the works of some other leading Marxist theorists, such as Kautsky, Plekhanov, Bukharin, and Stalin. Some indicate acceptance of the Lamarckian view, some acceptance of the Mendelian view, but none can reasonably be interpreted as an important part of the author's social theorizing. In each case the author was simply repeating the current biological theory, as far as he understood it, and was quite far from any thought of deriving a different theory of heredity from Marxist philosophy.

Even the rise of the eugenics movement, loosely linked with the new science of genetics and heavily tainted with contempt for the lower classes and the subject races, did not provoke a Marxist reaction against the science of genetics, or even against every kind of eugenics. There was a minority of left-wing eugenicists, such as the biologist K. A. Timiriazev, who won a permanent place in the Soviet pantheon by endorsing the Bolshevik Revolution. The first Commissar of Public Health declared eugenics to be the long-run goal of the Soviet health program, and subsidized research in that field under the guidance of leading geneticists. Within a few years friction developed over a difference in values: Soviet eugenicists tended to regard the intelligentsia as the repository of the best genes, while Bolshevik officials conferred this distinction on the proletariat and peasantry. In this Soviet version of the worldwide eugenics controversy during the 1920's, science was hardly the issue, for genuine knowledge of human genetics was slight, limited in the main to rare hereditary diseases.

Eugenics was then either grossly ideological, as in the preference for certain classes and races, or simply pessimistic, postponing hopes of basic and permanent improvement of the human condition until the distant time when geneticists might know as much about breeding humans as they already did about corn. By the end of the twenties the Soviet authorities withdrew their support of eugenics research, though still granting the theoretical possibility of a socialist program of eugenics. Research in human genetics continued, oriented mainly toward medicine and psychology, until the authorities decided that it too fostered disdain for the lower classes, whose IQ's were generally below those of the intelligentsia. Toward the end of 1936 the study of human heredity was suddenly linked with Nazi ideology and virtually suppressed, not to be revived until the 1960's. In the interim no effort was made to create a Lysenkoite theory of human heredity in place of the Mendelian theory. The traditional Marxist separation of biological and social processes was simply taken to a ridiculous extreme. "Man," declared Lysenko, "thanks to his mind, ceased long ago to be an animal." Biological science, whether genuine or pseudo, has nothing to say about such a creature.

Thus, it was not Marxist social theory that engendered the Lysenkoite belief in the inheritance of acquired characters. Neither was it the Lamarckist tradition in biology. In the 1930's Lysenko indignantly rejected his critics' assertion that he was a Lamarckist, and with good reason (see *Spornye voprosy genetiki i selektsii. Raboty IV sessii VASKhNILa 19–27 dek. 1936g.*, Moscow [1937], pp. 57, 67, 327). He was almost completely ignorant of any theoretical tradition in biology. His views derived from practical sources, as he never tired of boasting. In a time of acute agricultural crisis, resulting from forced collectivization, he was an agronomist with a flair for sensationalist public relations. He achieved fame as a bold innovator of agricultural techniques that were supposed to bring great practical benefit, in striking contrast to the supposedly barren record of orthodox scientists. First he challenged plant physiologists, by claiming that he had found a quick and easy way to boost grain yields (moisten and chill the seed), and then he fell into war with geneticists by promising to breed an improved variety of wheat within three years or less. When learned breeders and geneticists cautioned that several generations of progeny testing are necessary to establish a desirable, stable hybrid, Lysenko angrily denounced their academic learning as an impediment to practical achievement. He insisted that he could choose parent plants with foreknowledge of their progeny, and that he could make a final selection from the first generation of hybrids. These claims struck at the foundation of Mendelian genetics.

Lysenko came to the inheritance of acquired characters when he appropriated to his cause the vastly inflated reputation of I. V. Michurin (1855–1935), an uneducated breeder of fruit trees who believed in graft hybrids. The inheritance of acquired characters became a central belief of Lysenko's cult, for it enhanced his picture of living matter as structureless goo, capable of instant alteration to suit the needs of socialist farmers. Gradually he and his followers disinterred other obsolete doctrines and fancies, such as the possibility of cells forming from noncellular globs of organic matter, and the sudden transformation of wheat into weeds. In 1948, when the Central Committee of the Communist Party raised his power over biological research and education to the highest level, he acknowledged his kinship with Lamarckism. It was an ex post facto decree, very unjust to many bygone scientists who had entertained Lamarckist ideas in a serious effort to solve scientific problems.

Lysenko's main problem was to maintain his reputation as a master of "agrobiology" (the term was his invention). He promoted a series of flashy agronomic recipes, which the political bosses and the press hailed as the source of great increases in yields. The fact that their value was denied by agronomists in non-Communist countries did not undermine the faith of Stalinist officials, who became extremely xenophobic in the last part of his reign. They were not, however, completely impervious to the usual empirical criteria. A turning point came in 1952, when they recognized the fiasco of "the Great Stalin Plan for the Transformation of Nature," which was based in part on Lysenko's proposal to plant huge quantities of trees and leave them to thin themselves. (He pictured the weaker seedlings as removing themselves to help the species flourish.) Public criticism of Lysenko was allowed to revive, and became intensive after Stalin's death, but Soviet officials did not withdraw all their support from him until 1965. Then Lysenko was pushed out of power into silent management of an experimental farm, and Soviet geneticists received strong support in their effort to repair the damage done by thirty years of Lysenkoite mis-education.

It is a great puzzle how Soviet leaders could believe for so long in the practical benefit of Lysenkoism. The explanation is to be found in the Stalinist policy of extracting agricultural produce by force. Since peasants were poorly motivated and yields were generally low no matter what farming methods were used, it would have been hard to make an objective choice of farming methods in any case. But Stalinist officials were opposed on principle to objective criticism of their decisions. Only protracted stagnation of yields brought them to a grudging retreat from farming by decree, and from Lysenko's "agrobiology," which cast an aura of science over the Stalinist agricultural policy. The method of determining truth by authoritarian trial and error was justified by Stalin's doctrine that "practice" is the supreme criterion of truth. In more precise language, one learns by bossing. In some measure this doctrine can be traced back to Lenin and even, though with considerable straining, to Marx's belief in revolutionary *praxis*. That is the only significant connection between Lysenkoism and Marxist theory.

It is ironic that a Lamarckist view of human heredity should be widely ascribed to the left, for it has probably figured more often in the popular ideology of the right. Aside from H. G. Wells, it is hard to think of a socialist who has dreamed of improving the human breed by transforming society. The characteristic attitude on the left has been that the breed is basically sound; it needs only a suitable environment to express its great potential. On the other hand, many apologists for ruling classes and dominant races have argued that generations of subordination and illiteracy have made the lower classes and subject races biologically inferior to their social superiors. (Marvin Harris, in his *Rise of Anthropological Theory*, recognizes this fact, yet inconsistently repeats the association of Lamarckism with the left.) Of course, it is also possible to begin by *denying* the inheritance of acquired characters and still arrive at the same upper-class master-race bias. One has only to assume that place in the social hierarchy is determined by genotypes. Either way we are obviously dealing with self-serving illogic, based on a blurring of biological and sociological concepts.

The known facts and the genuine logic of the matter can be summarized in two sentences: the Lamarckian doctrine gives no logical support to the political right or left, because it is factually wrong. Genetical science supports nothing more than a vague equalitarianism, because genuine knowledge of human heredity is inadequate for anything more precise. As Theodosius Dobzhansky and other geneticists have shown, biology does not support the zealots of any class, nation, or race. Its most important political implication so far is the new support it gives to an old observation: individual differences in hereditary capacities are far more significant than average differences between groups may prove to be.

BIBLIOGRAPHY

For an introduction to various aspects of the topic, see the relevant portions of the following works, which have rich bibliographical leads to other studies and to the sources. W. R. Coleman, "Cell, Nucleus, and Inheritance: An Historical Study," *Proceedings of the American Philosophical Society,* **109** (1965), 124–58. L. C. Dunn, *A Short History of Genetics* (New York, 1965). A. E. Gaisinovich, "U istokov sovetskoi genetiki: bor'ba s lamarkizmom (1922–27)," *Genetika,* **4,** No. 6 (1968), 158–75. Verne Grant, *The Origin of Adaptations* (New York, 1963). D. Joravsky, *Soviet Marxism and Natural Science, 1917–32* (New York, 1961); idem, *The Lysenko Affair* (Cambridge, Mass., 1970). V. L. Komarov, *Lamark* (Moscow, 1925), in idem, *Izbrannye sochineniia,* **1** (1945); idem, "Lamark i ego nauchnoe znachenie," in Lamarck, *Filosofiia zoologii* (Moscow, 1935), 1, xi–xcvii. Zh. A. Medvedev, *The Rise and Fall of T. D. Lysenko* (New York, 1969). R. C. Olby, *Origins of Mendelism* (London, 1966). Jean Rostand, *L'atomisme en biologie* (Paris, 1956). Hans Stubbe, *Kurze Geschichte der Genetik* (Jena, 1965). C. Zirkle, "Early History of the Idea of the Inheritance of Acquired Characters and of Pangenesis," *Transactions of the American Philosophical Society,* **335** (1946), 91–151.

Other works cited in this article include the following. C. D. Darlington, "Purpose and Particles in the Study of Heredity," in E. A. Underwood, ed., *Science, Medicine, and History: Essays on the Evolution of Scientific Thought* (London, 1953), II, 472–81. Th. Dobzhansky, *Mankind Evolving* (New Haven, 1962). Marvin Harris, *The Rise of Anthropological Theory* (New York, 1968). T. D. Lysenko, *Agrobiologiia,* 6th ed. (Moscow, 1952; English trans., 1954), the largest collection of his works. Robert Mackintosh, *From Comte to Benjamin Kidd: The Appeal to Biology or Evolution for Human Guidance* (New York, 1899). I. V. Michurin, *Sochineniia,* 4 vols. (Moscow, 1939–41; 2nd ed., 1948). B. A. Vakar, *Vazhneishie khlebnye zlaki* (Novosibirsk, 1929).

DAVID JORAVSKY

[See also Biological Conceptions in Antiquity; **Evolutionism; Genetic Continuity; Inheritance through Pangenesis;** Perfectibility.]

INHERITANCE THROUGH PANGENESIS

PANGENESIS is a theory of a process of hereditary transmission according to which all parts of the organism contribute to the formation of the entire organism. First propounded in ancient Greece, the hypothesis has continually reappeared (often in different and increasingly more sophisticated terms and occasionally under different names) in both popular and scientific literature up to recent times.

The main inducement leading to the original formulation of the idea of pangenesis was the ancients' recognition that many single characters of the organism can vary quite independently of the rest and can be separately transmitted to offspring. Thus it was that instances of point-to-point resemblance between parent and offspring seemed to them to necessitate a theory of transmission based on intermediary particles possessing a parallel point-to-point correspondence.

The origins of the idea can be found in the fragments of the Pre-Socratics, e.g., Anaxagoras and the atomists. However, a fairly detailed picture of the process as envisioned in sexual reproduction appears in the Hippocratic corpus (fifth century B.C.).

Vessels for the transmission of bodily fluids are found throughout the entire body. From every part of the body are produced particles which mix with the bodily fluids in the vessels and are carried by them to the testicles. . . . The precipitating cause of this process is the pre-coital and coital stimulation. The transport of the fluids from the outlying parts is due also to this state of excitation. . . . The increasing temperature is a sign of the coction of these fluids into a smaller essence represented by the semen. . . . The offspring resembles its parent because the particles of the semen come from every part of the body (Hippocrates, VII, 471–75).

Quite understandably, the ancients focussed their attention on the adult form. The alternating generation represented in the germinal link was seen as but a slight interruption in the somatic continuum of the generations constituting the human race. Under such a view, the pangenetical process was their conceptualization of how all the heritable human traits could be funnelled from one generation into the next through the vehicle of the germ (see Diagram, p. 625).

In their original considerations, two choices had lain open to the ancient speculators. First, that the constitution of the germ linking the two generations could involve only a *quantitative* change; that is, differentiated in miniature on a point-to-point correspondence with its differentiated parent. Second, that the germ represented an actual *qualitative* change wherein the fully-differentiated constitution of the parent form had somehow been translated or distilled into an undifferentiated "essence" or "anima" which nonetheless contained the potential for future differentiation.

The first upholders of pangenesis—the atomists and those whose biological speculations were based on rather strict parallels with the physico-mechanical world—could accept only quantitative change. The first opposition to pangenesis came from Aristotle, the man whose empirical studies of generation helped to liberate biology from the physical world view. Espousing epigenesis and a teleological vitalism, he insisted on qualitative change.

Aristotle's attempt to refute the pangenetical hypothesis, however, was by no means successful. His counter to the central theme requiring unit-character transmission via corresponding particles was disappointingly tangential. He could only respond weakly by asking "how could there be such particles for abstract characters as voice or temperament, or from such nongenerating sources as nails or hair?"

Even more significant to the Greeks, for whom "first principles" dictated so much to observation, Aristotle was left in the apparently untenable position of having to contradict the very basic maxim that "nothing can come from nothing" (that is, that true multiplicity cannot arise from an undifferentiated unity). Where then, was the basis for the great differentiation that must follow? Certainly, his critics felt, not in the singularly undifferentiated matter which Aristotle had seen in the egg.

Besides this purely rational argument, there were two other equally important reasons why Aristotle did not prevail against pangenesis. First, the idealized nature of contemporary theories rendered them impervious to either proof or disproof by the limited observations of their time. Second, and relatedly, the Attic philosophy which envisioned no manipulation of

nature precluded a program of controlled experimentation that might have yielded an understanding of the roles of nature and nurture upon the construction of living things. Such was to remain the case until the scientific revolution of the seventeenth century.

The revival of pangenesis was one of the biological manifestations of the physico-mechanico-reductionism which characterized seventeenth-century science. Yet again it was the object of contemporary criticism. Mechanists such as Kenelm Digby saw insurmountable difficulties surrounding the assemblage and segregation of the gemmules purported to take place in the gonads. Vitalists such as William Harvey could not accept the theory's stress on heterogeneity and its seemingly preformationist implications. Pangenesis found its supporters chiefly among those such as Antoine Le Grand who, fervent believers in the inheritance of acquired characters, saw it as the only rational mechanical process which could account for such.

Despite the rapid inroads made by biological microscopy from the last quarter of the seventeenth century, scientists had failed to identify unequivocally the actual physical sites of germ production. Consequently, the first half of the eighteenth century was rife with speculation substituting for observation. Pangenesis would have been obscured in the great debate that followed between epigenesis preformation had it not been for Maupertuis and Buffon in the second half of the century. Accepting pangenesis as a mode of germ formation, they stressed its distinction from theories of individual development. Thus, the idea remained current, though generally ignored during the general preoccupation with the processes of ontogeny which characterized contemporary research.

In 1809 there did appear an account of inheritance based on the modification of the germ via changes impressed on the parent form. It formed the basis of the evolutionary mechanism put forward by the French biologist Jean Lamarck. The finer details of process or mechanism, however, were generally omitted by him (save for occasional references to the action of bodily fluids). On the other hand, the controversy which followed upon the promulgation of Lamarck's theory does serve to underline the important twofold nature of the subject of acquired modifications. Notwithstanding the question of the heritability of such changes (assumed by Lamarck), there remained in his view, two distinct *modes of acquisition*. First, he recognized a purely passive or unconscious form of modification. Environmental conditions brought about changes without any activity or awareness on the part of the organism. Such changes are impressed strictly from without. Second (and often in addition to the first), where sentient and thinking beings are involved, Lamarck saw the envi-

623

ronment as producing heritable change through a stimulus-response interaction—with the organism itself taking on the role of active agent in effecting change. The source of such organic response for Lamarck was the *sentiment intérieur* possessed by all sentient beings. The response of this faculty to environmental stimuli was manifested by changes in behavior, or habit, or the use of organic parts. The consequent alteration of structure was thus achieved in a quite different manner from that acquired passively. Taken together with Lamarck's often ludicrous examples, the involvement of a conscious mind or will was thus only too apparent to his readers. It was rejected with a vitriolic vehemence shocking even in its time. Due in no small part to Lamarck, theories of both evolution and hereditary transmission were scientific anathema for nearly half a century.

It must be seen that the objections over Lamarck's invoking of the will as a factor in the acquisition of change were *not* directed towards his assumptions as to the mode of transmission. In fact, a belief in the inheritance of acquired characters was almost universally held throughout most of the nineteenth century. It was Darwin who, in his *Variation of Plants and Animals under Domestication* (1868), picked up this aspect of the subject and thereby resurrected pangenesis. It was the first detailed discussion in nearly a century. The *Variation* was Darwin's conscious attempt to realize two aims that had remained unfulfilled in his *Origin of Species* (1859). First, he supplied the mass of documentation supporting domestic variation which had occupied the first chapter of the *Origin*. Second (and occupying the entire second volume of the work), he directed himself to discussing the phenomena of inheritance and the causes of variation—on both of which his evolutionary theory so evidently depended. It was in the last major chapter of this volume that he put forward what he called his "Provisional Hypothesis of Pangenesis." (Darwin gave no indication whatever that he was aware of any predecessors.)

A comparison of Darwin with Hippocrates will show how little the central theme had changed in over two thousand years. Said Darwin:

. . . I venture to advance the hypothesis of Pangenesis, which implies that the whole organization, in the sense of every separate atom or unit, reproduces itself. Hence ovules and pollen grains,—the fertilised seed or egg, as well as buds,—include and consist of a multitude of germs thrown off from each separate atom of the organism (Darwin, II, 357).

. . . We see that the reproductive organs do not actually create the sexual elements; they merely determine or permit the aggregation of the gemmules in a special manner (II, 383).

Darwin goes on to give his reasons for his hypothesis, citing the state of genetical knowledge of his time: the abundance of many sets of conflicting and seemingly contradictory observations and the lack of any synthesis in the form of a theory or set of laws consistently applicable to the known facts. "I have been led, or rather forced, to form a view which to a certain extent connects these facts by a tangible method" (II, 357).

The method was simply to address himself, in the Baconian style he espoused, to all the known classes of genetic phenomena, and from there to extract the one mechanism which could account for all. The recent historiography of science has too readily dismissed this instance of Darwin's theorizing as too patently ad hoc to merit serious attention. But the strength of such criticism is undermined by closer examination. It must be seen that it was Darwin's firm conviction that no general theory of inheritance was acceptable unless it equally explained important, exceptional phenomena. These he initially listed as: instances of noninheritance; dominance simultaneous with blending; exact duplication of parent through both sexual and asexual reproduction; inheritance of the effects of use, disuse, and habit; atavism; and saltations. In other words, for Darwin the rule must be proved by way of a valid explanatory incorporation of its exceptions. That his resultant hypothesis was not as ad hoc as modern historians have suggested is further shown by its anticipation (within, of course, the limitations of an admittedly *poly*-particulate theory) of many of the results of the machinations of the present *bi*-particulate theory of inheritance. Most noteworthy of these is his anticipation of panmixis, crossing over, and position effects (II, 396–400).

It was left to a German biologist, August Weismann, working during this same period, to put an end to the long scientific vitality of the pangenetical hypothesis. Working not only from his own observations but the accumulation of observation on the physical origins of the generative elements by others, Weismann is generally credited with the hypothesis that has since replaced pangenesis in the modern view of sexual generation. Weismann's "theory of the germplasm" (1885, published 1893) was based on the first clear distinction between two fundamental types of cell, and the two distinct forms of cell division which characterize their reproduction. These were seen as the cells constituting the general bodily structure or *somatoplasm*, and those cells comprising the reproductive or generative tissues (containing the genetic constitution) or *germplasm*. Where the great mass of ordinary body cells reproduce through *mitosis* or common, fully-duplicating cell division, the germinal elements are produced through *meiosis*, or reduction-division. The latter elements fuse

DIAGRAM

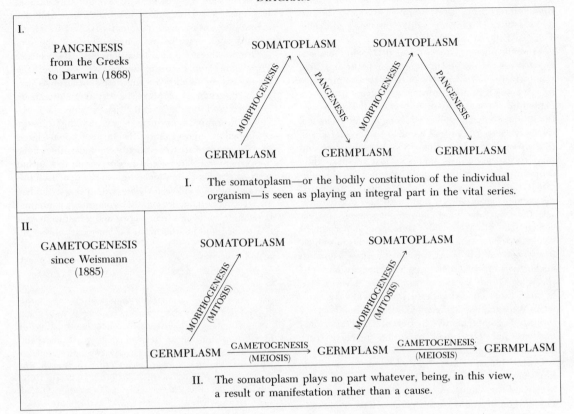

I.	
PANGENESIS from the Greeks to Darwin (1868)	SOMATOPLASM SOMATOPLASM *MORPHOGENESIS PANGENESIS MORPHOGENESIS PANGENESIS* GERMPLASM GERMPLASM GERMPLASM

I. The somatoplasm—or the bodily constitution of the individual organism—is seen as playing an integral part in the vital series.

II.	
GAMETOGENESIS since Weismann (1885)	SOMATOPLASM SOMATOPLASM *MORPHOGENESIS (MITOSIS) MORPHOGENESIS (MITOSIS)* GERMPLASM →GAMETOGENESIS (MEIOSIS)→ GERMPLASM →GAMETOGENESIS (MEIOSIS)→ GERMPLASM

II. The somatoplasm plays no part whatever, being, in this view, a result or manifestation rather than a cause.

at the inception of the new generation and upon its sexual maturity proceed to produce future germinal elements in the same way. Weismann thus demonstrated that the somatoplasm is in no way causally linked to the production of the germplasm. In such a view, ultimate biological continuity is achieved through a direct cellular continuity involving germ cells only (see Diagram).

As is so often the case in the history of ideas—particularly those emanating from scientific theories—their wider significance tends to extend well beyond the strictly literal context from which they originated. The extrapolations of interpretation have often outlived or at least outweighed their sources. This has been true whether the science upon which they are based was good or bad, the reasoning sound or fallacious, or whether the interpretations have so exceeded their bases as to bear little resemblance to the original. This has been much the case in the history of pangenesis. Thus it is necessary to discuss the major implications that have followed from it and to give some indication

of the trends of thought they have produced. These implications are: (1) The genetic constitution of organic beings can be modified from without, via changes impressed on the bodily constitution. (2) Modifications in the individual characters of one generation can be transmitted and translated into modifications in the same characters in the following generation. (3) Similar individuals exposed to similar conditions will be similarly and simultaneously modified. (4) As environmental conditions impress structural change so, in the case of sentient or thinking beings, can they effect changes through permanent alterations in habit, behavior, or—in the case of man—the direction of the mind or will. (5) As man can control his environment, so can he therefore control his genetic constitution and thus change need no longer be left to chance, but to the conscious manipulation of man. (6) As the bodily constitution of the organism lies causally prior to the genetic constitution, so it must be the principal subject for the impression of change.

It is clear that the history of the implications of

pangenesis is a longer and far more complicated one than of the concept itself. Consequently, only the two main areas of this history will be discussed here—the social and the scientific.

From the ancient Greeks through Darwin there was a general awareness and agreement upon the first three points. Darwin went part way towards accepting the fourth point but, giving primacy to structure, he excepted (or, in some cases, simply avoided discussing) the action of mind or will in effecting heritable change. (A reservation certainly not found in Lamarck!) Indeed, in the post-*Origin* years from 1868, he came more and more to rely upon these points as, first ancillary, then supporting, and finally cooperative processes of evolutionary modification of natural selection. It remained increasingly an article of faith with him that natural selection was the most important source of such change. Despite Weismann's refutation of pangenesis —and the inheritance of acquired characters for which it was the vehicle—anti-Darwinian critics chose to anchor natural selection to its mistaken assumptions regarding hereditary transmission. Thus, it was not to be until the second decade of the present century— when Weissmann's view was linked with Mendel's laws into a fully comprehensive picture of hereditary transmission—that Darwinian evolution reached truly widespread acceptance.

During this same latter third of the nineteenth century, however, a number of social thinkers (Spencer, Marx, and their followers) were just beginning to absorb the implications of the pangenetical hypothesis in its evolutionary context. Coupled with their interpretation of Darwinian evolution, it seemed to provide the very key—the ultimate biological justification—for radical change. It was their extrapolations, based on the last three of the above-mentioned implications, that provided for them the basis for a de novo establishment of revolutionary change.

Nothing runs more counter to a revolutionary philosophy than a sense of commitment to the past. The genetic constitution that identifies every living being in the world is the biological legacy from the past. It dictates the direction of our development and thus represents a commitment to a relatively fixed pattern of the future as an ineluctable continuation of the past. As such, it involves the characteristics that distinguish races and species and, from the point of view of these social thinkers, the social constructs of man based upon them. Yet in pangenesis—a doctrine as old as rational thought itself and supported by reputable scientists through to (then) recent times—lay a hope of breaking, or at least radically altering, the precedent of the past.

That Karl Marx, the first of a now-century-old line of such interpreters, should have written Darwin asking his permission to dedicate *Das Kapital* to him is at least understandable, albeit a bit ludicrous. (Darwin graciously refused on the grounds of being unable to see any connection between their subjects.)

Despite the continued scientific verification of the Weismann-Mendel theory of inheritance, and the contingent repudiation of pangenesis, Marxians and the Soviet interpreters of Marx (i.e., Lysenko, Michurin, et al.) refused to relinquish the theory which had provided the support for their dogma. Stalinist biology continued to fight against the current of accepted science in an effort to revalidate the fallen theory. In the present era, however, it is almost safe to say that with the repudiation of both Stalin and Lysenko Marxian biology enjoys no more serious support in the Soviet Union than does anti-Darwinism in America. It remains that a life-span of two and a half millennia is a record one for the history of an idea.

BIBLIOGRAPHY

C. Darwin, *The Variation of Plants and Animals under Domestication* (London, 1868). Hippocrates, "On Generation," in *Oeuvres complètes d'Hippocrate*, ed. É. Littré (Amsterdam, 1962), Vol. VII; excerpt trans. by P. Vorzimmer.

The remaining primary sources for over 2000 years of pangenetical thought are too numerous to cite here: full citations can be found below in the two best secondary sources on theories of inheritance. Both E. S. Russell, *The Interpretation of Development and Heredity* (Oxford, 1930), and F. J. Cole, *Early Theories of Sexual Generation* (Oxford, 1930) are excellent and as useful today as they have always been. For both a valuable history of the idea of the inheritance of acquired characters and for the subsequent Marxian interpretations down to recent times, see Conway Zirkle's eminently readable *Evolution, Marxian Biology, and the Social Scene* (Philadelphia, 1959).

PETER VORZIMMER

[See also Biological Conceptions in Antiquity; **Evolutionism; Genetic Continuity; Inheritance of Acquired Characteristics; Recapitulation.**]

IRONY

IRONY MAY be defined as the conflict of two meanings which has a dramatic structure peculiar to itself: initially, one meaning, the *appearance*, presents itself as the obvious truth, but when the context of this meaning unfolds, in depth or in time, it surprisingly discloses a conflicting meaning, the *reality*, measured against which the first meaning now seems false or limited and, in its self-assurance, blind to its own situation. Irony "lies," but it does so only as a dramatic means of bringing two meanings into open conflict. Some theorists assert that by encompassing this conflict in a single structure, irony resolves it into harmony or unity. The variable factors in the ironic structure are the following:

(1) The *degree* of conflict between appearance and reality ranges from the slightest of differences to diametrical opposites.

(2) The *field of observation* in which irony may be noticed ranges from the smallest semantic unit—e.g., a pun—to the cosmos. The most frequently used fields are: the relation between one meaning located in words and another meaning located either in the same words or in their context—*verbal irony;* the relation between an event or situation as interpreted from a limited point of view and that event as interpreted with a broader knowledge of the situation or of subsequent events—called *dramatic irony* in literature, in life called the *irony of fate,* God, events, things, etc.; the relation between events and an observer's state of mind—the *ironic attitude,* which may or may not externalize itself as verbal irony, dramatic irony, or the irony of fate.

(3) Irony usually has an *author,* who by analogy is a superhuman power in some fields of observation; it always has an *audience,* even if it is only the author amusing himself; and a *victim,* who is deceived by appearance and enlightened by reality, although an author may turn himself into a pseudovictim.

(4) The *aspects* of irony may be analyzed as follows. The variable factors here are the conception of reality, the degree to which author and audience sympathize or identify with the victim, and the fate of the victim—triumph or defeat. Reality may be thought of by author and (or) audience as reflecting their own values. In this context, *satiric irony* reveals the defeat of an unsympathetic victim; *comic irony* reveals the triumph of a sympathetic victim. (Throughout this article, the word *comic* refers primarily to a rise from defeat to triumph, as in Dante's *Divine Comedy.*) At the other pole, reality may be thought of as hostile to all human values. In this context, triumph is impossible, defeat inevitable. In *tragic irony,* sympathy for the victim predominates; in *nihilistic irony,* satiric detachment counterbalances or dominates sympathy, but a degree of identification always remains since author and audience necessarily share the victim's plight. *Paradoxical irony* balances these two extremes. Everything is relative: reality in part does and in part does not reflect human values; author and audience fuse, or oscillate between, identification and detachment; comic triumph and tragic defeat counterbalance each other, or the satiric norm constantly shifts.

Although the idea of irony has undoubtedly appeared under other names—e.g., Aristotle's *peripeteia,* Jean Paul's and Pirandello's *humor*—little attempt has been made to trace the idea apart from the term. The term itself, after quickly shedding most of its original meaning, has steadily extended itself from satiric and comic irony through paradoxical irony to tragic and nihilistic irony, and now encompasses all the meanings outlined above. Frequently, during this history, the use of irony has elicited intense ethical judgments, pro and con.

The most influential model in the history of irony has been the Platonic Socrates. Neither Socrates nor his contemporaries, however, would have associated the word *eironeia* with modern conceptions of Socratic irony. As Cicero put it, Socrates was always "pretending to need information and professing admiration for the wisdom of his companion"; when Socrates' interlocutors were annoyed with him for behaving in this way they called him *eiron,* a vulgar term of reproach referring generally to any kind of sly deception with overtones of mockery. The fox was the symbol of the *eiron.*

All serious discussions of *eironeia* followed upon the association of the word with Socrates. These occurred in two contexts, the ethical and the rhetorical. In ethics, the field of observation was an habitual manner of behaving, a type of human character, and here the notion of irony as actual lying persisted, narrowed however to understatement. "As generally understood," Aristotle said in the *Ethics,* "the boaster is a man who pretends to creditable qualities that he does not possess, or possesses in a lesser degree than he makes out, while conversely the self-depreciator disclaims or disparages good qualities that he does possess. Midway between them is the straightforward sort of man" (iv. 7. 1–17). Aristotle recognized that understatement (*eironeia*) might have various degrees of difference from the truth, including total denial of it. Of the two evils defined, he preferred irony because it was unostentatious. For Demosthenes and Theophrastus the *eiron* was an even less respectable liar: he understated his own powers specifically for the purpose of escaping responsibility.

Although in the *Ethics* Aristotle (ibid.) had mentioned "affected humbugs" whose "mock humility seems to be really boastfulness," a sentence that implied the full structure of irony as a lie meant to reveal the truth, it was in the rhetorical tradition that this structure came to explicit definition. Here the field of observation was narrow, limited to the brief figure of speech. As that, irony seemed ethically less censurable, and in the *Rhetoric* Aristotle spoke of it as a "gentlemanly" sort of jest. The full pattern was formulated by the fourth century B.C. *Rhetoric to Alexander:* irony is

627

blame through praise and praise through blame. This definition, by shifting attention from the logical content of an ironic statement to the implied diametrically opposed value judgments, opened the way to the later, sometimes misleading formula that irony is saying the "contrary" of what one means. Also, two aspects of irony were implied by this definition: "to blame by praise" is satiric irony; "to praise by blame" is comic irony, for undesirable characteristics attributed to a sympathetic victim draw the audience's attention to his real virtues. Ariston pointed out that Socrates' way of exalting his opponent while depreciating himself exemplified the full pattern.

In the early eighteenth century, the omnipresence of French and English satiric literature brought the idea of irony, so called, out of the classroom into the intellectual marketplace; during the intervening twenty centuries it lived in, or on the edge of, rhetorical theory, the two chief fountains of which were Cicero and Quintilian. In Cicero Socratic irony first became a completely admirable thing, which he distinguished into an isolated figure of speech and a pervasive habit of discourse. Generally speaking, these were the limits of the field during the following centuries. Quintilian, however, said that "a man's whole life may be colored with irony, as was the case with Socrates, who . . . assumed the role of an ignorant man lost in wonder at the wisdom of others" (*Institutio* ix. 2. 44–53). For Quintilian this manner was an indication and expression of goodness that was "mild" and "ingratiating."

In the early eighteenth century the third earl of Shaftesbury (d. 1713) also described a "soft irony" "spread alike through a whole character and life." Such irony was more than an indication of goodness: it was the expression of the perfect way of life to which Shaftesbury aspired. Ethically, irony here reversed the position it had held in the Aristotelian school, but Shaftesbury was seeing irony in a modern way, from the subjective angle of the individual soul rather than from Aristotle's objective social angle, with the result that Shaftesbury's emphasis fell on the mental attitude of which the ironic manner was only the external expression. The manner Shaftesbury described kept the degree of opposition between praise and blame very slight, avoiding satiric virulence or comic buffoonery: it was a fusion of modest self-abnegation, gentle gravity, and an apparent tolerance of all things behind which hid reservations about all things. The reservations were there because for the Neo-Platonic Shaftesbury the only important reality was the spirit within, which must tolerate but not be disturbed by the "immediate changes and incessant eternal conversions, revolutions of the world." He himself might often be the only audience aware of his irony and the world might find him puzzling, but he lived "disinterested and unconcerned," accommodating all appearances to his own mind and setting "everything in its due light." (See Knox, pp. 47–53, for a full discussion of Shaftesbury's conception.) Socrates was interpreted in this modern way: he had been "a perfect character; yet . . . veiled, and in a cloud . . . chiefly by reason of a certain exquisite and refined raillery which belonged to his manner, and by virtue of which he could treat the highest subjects, and those of commonest capacity . . . together, . . . both the heroic and the simple, the tragic and the comic" (*Characteristics* [1714], I, 194–95). The critical norm of this subtly satiric attitude toward the world was the absolute value contained in the ironist's own mind; all other values were limited and relative to one another.

Apart from Socrates, the rhetoricians thought of irony, in Quintilian's terms, as either "trope," a brief figure of speech embedded in a straightforward context, or "schema," an entire speech or case presented in language and a tone of voice that conflict with the true situation. Understatement, which in Aristotle had been limited to self-depreciation, spread out to include any statement whose apparent meaning falls some degree short of the reality, e.g., to say of a muscular warrior, with comic irony, that he has "a reasonably good arm." At first called *litotes* or *meiosis*, such understatement came to be called irony, at least by the end of the sixteenth century. The comic irony of praise through blame, which had also originated in Socratic self-depreciation, remained a minor figure of speech until the early eighteenth century, when in England, at least, Swift, Pope, and their friends recognized it as a delightful mode in which to write letters and converse.

The abstract definition of irony as saying the "contrary" of what one means, the most popular formula from Cicero and Quintilian on, led the rhetoricians and others occasionally to extend the opposition beyond praise and blame to logical contraries which might not involve praise or blame, such as *praeteritio* and *negatio*. Cicero had pointed out that some types of irony do not say "the exact reverse of what you mean" but only something "different." Allegory also says something "different" from what it means. Quintilian and later rhetoricians classified irony as a type of allegory, but Chambers' *Cyclopaedia* (1778–88) narrowed allegory to exclude irony: "allegory imports a similitude between the thing spoken and intended; irony a contrariety between them."

However, the dominant conception of irony socalled was satiric blame through praise. The earliest recognized strategies, derived from Socrates, were direct praise of a victim for possessing good qualities he lacks, and self-depreciation meant to imply such praise. Quintilian pointed out that the real meaning became evident to an audience "either by the delivery, the character of the speaker or the nature of the subject" (*Institutio* viii. 6. 54–58). But he also remarked that irony as trope might state both praise and blame explicitly: e.g., "it is a fine thing to be a thief"—not, "it is a fine thing to be honest." He also illustrated ironic concession, which exposes a victim's ideas by echoing them with mock approval, and ironic advice, which recommends that its victim continue to pursue those foolish or vicious courses he is already pursuing. The ironic defense was invented by Lucian.

Later rhetoricians recognized all these strategies as irony, and when in the late seventeenth century and the early eighteenth Boileau, Defoe, Swift, Pope, Voltaire, Fielding, and hosts of lesser pamphleteers and periodical writers used these strategies cheek by jowl the fallacious argument, the *reductio ad absurdum*, parody, burlesque, and the fictitious character, these other strategies also came to be called ironic. All burlesque involving people degraded them to some degree by caricature, but the author presented his characters with mock sympathy and approval, heightened in "high" burlesque by elevated language.

When such ironic strategies expanded into fictional narratives of some length—Swift's *A Tale of a Tub*, Pope's *The Dunciad*, Fielding's *Jonathan Wild* and *Joseph Andrews*—mid-century critics for the first time defined the field of irony as the totality of an imaginative work of art. Now recognizing that irony could be a literary mode of major significance, they saw Cervantes as the central model, flanked by Swift, Lucian, Erasmus. Cervantes especially had shown how to maintain an ironic manner throughout a long narrative. R. O. Cambridge in the Preface to his *Scribleriad* (1752), expressed the common view: "the author should never be seen to laugh, but constantly wear that grave irony which Cervantes alone has inviolably preserved." Talking about his own mock-heroic poem, Cambridge continued:

To complete the design of mock-gravity, the author and editors are represented full as great enthusiasts as the hero; therefore, as all things are supposed to appear to them in the same light as they do to him, there are several things which they could not explain without laying aside their assumed character. . . . Then how shall it be known whether a burlesque writer means the thing he says or the contrary? This is only to be found by attention and a comparison of passages.

And Cambridge pointed out that all of his hero's great expectations were "ironically given," "for of all of the many prophecies delivered to him, the only one fulfilled is that of his being reduced to a state of beggary in his pursuit of alchemy." Cambridge exhibits clearly how the rhetorical idea of satiric irony had been extended by the impact of fictional narrative. The mock sympathy with which ideas and opinions had been presented in ironic concession, advice, defense, and the like had become the grave presentation of character and action; the reality, which in many of the rhetorical ironies had been revealed by direct statement or burlesque exaggeration, in narrative was now revealed by the course of events: by dramatic irony.

In Germany, during the last years of the eighteenth century and the first three decades of the nineteenth, the ironies of Cervantes and Socrates collided with transcendental philosophy, and irony entered its modern phase. Friedrich Schlegel's oracular pronouncements (chiefly 1797–1800) led the way, but Friedrich's brother A. W. Schlegel, who was clearer and whose lectures *On Dramatic Art and Literature* (1808) were widely translated, may have been more immediately influential. In any case, most of literary Germany was talking about irony in a new way. It became the central principle of an aesthetic in the *Erwin* (1815) and later writings of the philosopher K. W. F. Solger, and Hegel, who before Solger's death was briefly his colleague, related irony to his own dialectical system. An admirer of Solger and student of Hegelianism, the expatriate Heine helped to make the new ironies familiar in France, and in England many of them appeared in an essay "On the Irony of Sophocles" (1833) by Bishop Connop Thirlwall, a student of German thought, and an acquaintance and translator of Ludwig Tieck. Irony finally became the subject of an academic thesis in Søren Kierkegaard's Danish *The Concept of Irony, with Constant Reference to Socrates* (1841), which added little to the complex of meanings that had developed.

Prior to the later eighteenth century, irony had always been thought of as a weapon to be used in the service of absolute human values derived from reality. For the eighteenth century, speaking very generally, this value had been "reason," supposedly reflected in the structure of the universe. Shaftesbury had found a resting place in Neo-Platonism. The German theorists of the new irony, however, found themselves in a situation that has become familiar to the modern mind. On the one hand, there seemed to be considerable evidence that human values are only subjective and sharply opposed to an external world that is chaotic, inhumanly mechanistic, or ultimately unknowable, as in the Kantian epistemology that pervaded Schlegel's Germany. On the other hand, they could not relinquish their faith that the values of the human spirit must be substantiated somewhere. No longer able to turn away from the immediate world to the certainty of a Platonic or Christian or Deistic absolute, they turned toward the flux of existence and human art, recognizing that no "limited thing" could offer a resting place, yet hoping that out of the complex interrelationships of a wide-ranging experience something might emerge.

It occurred to Friedrich Schlegel, as it had to Shaftesbury, that the best way for the mind to assert its freedom from "limited things" had been discovered by Socrates. Irony, which Schlegel sometimes called "Socratic irony," was "never-ending satire," "continual self-parody," by means of which the spirit "raises itself above all limited things," even over its "own art, virtue, or genius." On the other hand, it was in those very "things" that the spirit must now find itself. Consequently, in Schlegel the grave tolerance of Shaftesbury's ironic attitude opened outward to become "instinctive," "in earnest," "naively open." Irony was now, paradoxically, an instrument of positive engagement at the same time that it was an instrument of detachment. Behind Schlegel's new formula seem to have been Schiller's play theory of art and an analogy with the theological idea of God as both immanent and transcendent, especially in Fichte's post-Kantian, idealist version.

The new ironic attitude quickly caught on in both art and life. For Tieck, irony "saturates its work with love, yet sweeps rejoicing and unfettered over the whole" (Sedgewick, p. 16). In Shakespeare's ironic attitude A. W. Schlegel found the same combination of creative absorption and "cool indifference," though its mood was disillusioned: Shakespeare had seen "human nature through and through" yet "soars freely above it." Goethe thought irony raises the mind "above happiness or unhappiness, good or evil, death or life," from which height we may view our own "faults and errors in a playful spirit"; even the scientist should view his own discoveries ironically, for they are only provisionally true.

The external manifestation of irony Friedrich Schlegel located in an endless "tension of opposites." Satiric and comic irony had of course exhibited a *tension* of opposites at just that moment when the apparent meaning begins to give way to the real meaning. For that moment both meanings are simultaneously before the eye in a precarious balance. Such irony, however, had theoretically always resolved this tension in favor of a real meaning. So, too, would the nihilistic and tragic irony to come. But Schlegel did not wish to resolve the tension in that direction. Nothing is absolute, everything is relative. So irony became "an incessant . . . alternation of two contradictory thoughts," the contradictory thoughts usually being faith in some ideal human value on the one hand, and on the other, assent to a less ideal reality; the "subjec-

tive" versus the "objective." At times Schlegel conceived this tension as static, a fusion, as in some forms of verbal irony; more often he described it as a movement from one thought to another, as in dramatic irony. The ironic author at first appears to engage himself with one meaning—and in part really does so; he then appears to destroy that meaning by revealing and attaching himself to a contradictory meaning; this, too, however, he also destroys, either by returning to the first or moving on to a third, ad infinitum. Paradoxical irony is "self-creating alternation," "self-criticism surmounted." And since such irony does postulate appearances that are in part real, but only in part, Schlegel returned to the association of irony with allegory.

Two of Schlegel's chief models for paradoxical irony in literature were Laurence Sterne, who could both love and laugh at the creations of his imagination, and *Don Quixote*, which Schlegel saw not simply as grave satire but as an unresolved tension between satire and genuine sympathy for the Don's ideals: "a charming symmetry" produced by "rhythmical alternations between enthusiasm and irony." In such phrases as this the word *irony* retained its old force as satiric, but elsewhere it spilled over to include the "enthusiasm," a natural extension since the structure of enthusiastic commitment followed by satiric deflation paralleled on the surface the structure of satiric praise followed by blame. In this context as well, then, irony began to take on its paradoxical sense.

After the Schlegels had announced the new irony, Ludwig Tieck's early plays came to be seen as examples of it. Setting out to satirize philistine prejudices, Tieck had adopted the strategies of burlesque satire, as old as Aristophanes, especially its destruction of a primary fictional illusion by the "reality" of author, actors, even audience stepping out of their normal roles to speak as themselves, attacking each other and commenting on the primary illusion itself, a device Tieck had also been impressed by in the authorial intrusions of Cervantes and Sterne. But Tieck became lost in endless relativity. A character in *The World Turned Topsyturvy* remarks: "This is too crazy! See, friends, we sit here as spectators and see a play; in that play spectators are also sitting and seeing a play, and in that third play another play is going to be played by those third actors. . . . People often dream that sort of thing" (*Die verkehrte Welt* [1799], end of Act III; trans. Thompson, pp. 58–59).

Shakespeare too was an ironist on the new model, both Friedrich and A. W. Schlegel decided. To demonstrate this, it was necessary to find satiric elements in what most people had supposed to be a predominantly sympathetic presentation, as in *Don Quixote* enthusiasm had been found to counterbalance satire. Although A. W. Schlegel barred irony when "the proper tragic enters," which demands "the highest degree of seriousness," he found it everywhere else. In the results of Henry V's marriage to the French princess, he saw dramatic irony that cast a satiric light on Henry's ambitions. Incongruous juxtapositions might be ironic: comic scenes were often "intentional parody of the serious part." In his depiction even of "noble minds" Shakespeare had revealed "self-deception" and hypocrisy. Such irony, A. W. Schlegel said, was a defense against "overcharged one-sidedness in matters of fancy and feeling." He assumed that all intelligent people were relativists: by constant ironic qualification Shakespeare "makes a sort of secret understanding with . . . the more intelligent of his readers or spectators; he shows them that he had previously seen and admitted the validity of their tacit objections" (*Lectures on Dramatic Art and Literature* [1809–11], trans. John Black, rev. A. J. W. Morrison [1892], pp. 369–70).

Friedrich Schlegel thought that all good modern literature would be ironic. But if its irony was to be endlessly relative, where would the final values of a modern work lie? In literature, as in life, they would reside in the comprehensiveness of the author's activity: a perfected work might be "limited at every point," but in its inclusion of all contradictions it would be "without limitation and inexhaustible." (For authoritative discussions of and references to F. Schlegel's scattered pronouncements, see Immerwahr, Wellek, and Muecke.)

Hegel was not impressed. Rather unfairly, he saw the new irony of the Schlegels as entirely negative. In literature it produced "insipid" characters having "neither content nor defined position." In life itself, the Schlegelian ironist looked "down in his superior fashion on all other mortals," some of whom his ironic gravity actually deceived; he denied and destroyed all that was "noble, great, and excellent" in the interest of freedom for the self; yet, because his freedom prohibited positive action and led nowhere, he was beset by morbid feelings of emptiness and boredom. In fact, in opposing "self-will" to objective moral truth, "this type of subjectivism . . . is evil through and through and universally." (Capel's translation of Kierkegaard, Part II, Introduction, n. 7, gives a full list of references to Hegel's comments on irony.)

Actually, of course, the Schlegels' irony had also an objective side, one that was less reassuring, however, than Hegel's objective moral truth. Friedrich had found it "strikingly ironic" that *der grosse Maschinist* behind the chaos "finally discloses himself as a contemptible betrayer." In not quite so disillusioned a way, this objective source of irony moved to the foreground in

Solger's aesthetic. In Solger's view, the human artist created a beautiful work "just as the essence of God, in its non-actuality, reveals itself intact as the very core" of a human being. In both cases the idea inhabits a particular "thing." For Solger the situation was ironic, because, on the one hand, although the "thing" appeared to suggest the infinite, it was really only a thing, and on the other hand, although the "infinite" appeared to transcend the thing, it could not really do so—it must inhabit finite reality. Schlegel's tension of opposites had become the "concrete universal," the ironic symbol of a universe which intimated meanings that could not be reached in an eternal form. But at least in the artistic symbol "all contradictions annihilate themselves": irony is a unifying structure.

"Without irony," then, "there is no art." Considering the tension of opposites as moving rather than static, Solger found that irony "begins with the contemplation of the world's fate in the large": "we suffer when we see the most elevating and noble ideals dissipated through their necessary earthly existence." A. W. Schlegel had barred irony from the "proper tragic," but for Solger satiric and "tragic irony" were simply different aspects of the irony common to all art: in the first, false ideals were destroyed; in the second, admirable ones, and the audience is not detached: "we suffer." Although the dominant movement in both satiric and tragic irony was toward defeat, Solger saw an opposing comic movement arising out of destruction, as had Friedrich Schlegel in his "self-creating alteration." The very moment that breaks the brief union of idea and thing affirms both the value of the idea and the necessity of its embodiment. When Hamlet dies, Fortinbras must appear. (For discussions of and references to Solger's statements about irony, see Wellek, Mueller, pp. 225–26, Sedgewick, p. 17, and Strohschneider-Kohrs.)

Solger's version of irony Hegel accepted as a phase of his own famous dialectic, though it was only one phase: "that transition point which I call the infinite absolute negativity." For Hegel Socratic irony was negative dialectic. Socrates' humble questioning had induced his interlocutor to state a definite proposition, from which Socrates then derived in one way or another "the direct opposite of what the proposition stated." In this conception, Socrates' irony was not so much mocking praise as dramatic irony in which ideas played the roles characters and events play in fiction. "Socratic irony . . . , like all dialectic, gives force to what is taken immediately, but only in order to allow the dissolution inherent in it to come to pass." Since in the Hegelian system dialectic was deified as historical process, Hegel spoke of the negative moment in dialectic as "the universal irony of the world" (*Lec-*

tures on the History of Philosophy, trans. E. S. Haldane [1892], I, 400). And although he thought Solger's use of the phrase "tragic irony" was arbitrary, he himself called Socrates' "opposition of subjective reflection to morality as it exists" a "tragic irony," meaning, in Kierkegaard's interpretation, "the irony of the world with Socrates."

It soon became commonplace to think of the field of irony as life itself, and of mankind as the victim of a cosmic author. Heine spoke casually of the irony of God, the world, nature, fate, and even chance. The red cheeks of the elderly A. W. Schlegel, a parody of youth, were a "healthy irony of nature"; the incongruous juxtaposition of a Gothic cathedral with modern buildings was ironic. An "ironic remark" might now be, not in itself mocking, but simply the straightforward observation of an ironic fact.

Bishop Connop Thirlwall, who believed in a just god, spelled out the two movements of irony, both in life and in Sophocles. In our personal lives we eagerly pursue objects which prove worthless; but we also dread changes which fulfill our "most ardent wishes." In history "the moment of highest prosperity . . . immediately precedes the most ruinous disaster"; but the destruction of Greece spread Greek culture through the Roman world, the destruction of Rome was followed by Christianity. In Oedipus the King there is "the contrast between the appearance of good and the reality of evil"; Oedipus at Colonus "reverses that irony," for Oedipus can here say, "Now, when all's lost, I am a man indeed." Though he used only the term "tragic irony," Thirlwall, apparently following Solger, extended the conception of irony into both tragic and comic situations in which the detachment of irony was overcome by sympathy for the victim. But the satiric aspect did not totally disappear; it remained as a qualification of the dominant feeling. Clytemnestra's "vindication of her own conduct . . . assumes a tone of self-mockery," but "when we remember that, while she is pleading, her doom is sealed, and that the hand which is about to execute it is already lifted above her head," the tone becomes "deeply tragical."

In his discussion of ambiguous language in Sophocles' tragedies, Thirlwall apparently established the association of the term "Sophoclean irony" with dialogue that means one thing to the speaker, another to author and audience, whose view of the situation is wider and truer. This sort of thing had been recognized as a common form of irony in satiric narrative; Thirlwall simply extended the field to tragedy. He also pointed out a type of tragedy that contains an ironic dilemma, such as the conflict of Antigone and Creon, "in which good and evil are . . . inextricably blended on each side." The audience exhibits "a slight cast of irony in the grave, respectful attention impartially bestowed." But Thirlwall admitted that it was sometimes easier for God to preserve such an attitude than it was for humans. When "we review the mockery of fate, we can scarcely refrain from a melancholy smile" (Philological Museum, Cambridge [1832–33], II, 483–537).

Whether as the questing romantic ego, the progress of world history, or a just god of some sort, the theorists of paradoxical irony had found a hopeful movement which preserved the balance of triumph and defeat. This was seen either as a human satiric norm counterbalancing an inhuman one, or as a comic movement counterbalancing the tragic. But when even these faiths receded, as for some nineteenth- and twentieth-century minds they did, the comic movement came to seem entirely deceptive, and the norm of satire became reduced to Nothing. Human values are only illusions. One result of this loss of faith was increasing notice of tragic irony. The other was that the idea of irony as counterbalancing sympathy with detachment began to isolate from the complex of paradoxical irony what may be called nihilistic irony, that peculiar merging of the satiric and the tragic adumbrated in Thirlwall's "melancholy smile."

This view of irony became prominent in Heine, who "is repelled by the cold stars, and sinks down . . . toward our little earth." God "is sometimes a greater satirist than Tieck." In the "humoristic irony" of Don Quixote the "insane dignity" of the Don is made ridiculous by "fate," yet that ridiculous fate shows us the "tragedy of our own nothingness." Shakespeare's Troilus and Cressida "is neither comedy nor tragedy . . . there prevails in it an exultant bitterness, a world-mocking irony, such as we never met in the merriment of the comic muse. It is the tragic goddess who is very much more before us in this play, only that she here would fain be gay for once, and move to mirth. It is as if we saw Melpomene at a grisette ball, dancing the chahut, bold laughter on her pale lips and death in her heart." (See Wellek, Vol. III, for references to Heine's comments on irony.)

As the nineteenth century wore on, the new ironies gradually moved to center stage. At the turn of the century Anatole France and Thomas Hardy especially were drawing the attention of a large audience to irony. By 1908 Alexander Blok could observe, "All the most lively and sensitive children of our century are stricken by a disease"—irony (quoted in Glicksberg, p. 3). In the 1920's France's "irony and pity" became a catch phrase. H. W. Fowler (1926) announced that "the irony of fate" was hackneyed, and I. A. Richards (1924) began that preoccupation with irony among English and American academic critics which has helped to make it a central idea in literary criticism throughout the world.

Tragic irony quickly established itself as an independent aspect of irony, and G. G. Sedgewick has asserted that it does not qualify the tragic feeling: "it heightens the sense of pity and terror." *Paradoxical* and nihilistic irony have had a harder time disentangling themselves from each other, much to the confusion of criticism. The balanced relativism of paradoxical irony is clearly the core of Kierkegaard's "mastered irony," the "philosophical irony" of Renan and France, Henry James's "full irony," the "objective irony" of Thomas Mann, Richards' "balance of opposed impulses," William Empson's "double irony," Cleanth Brooks' "a very different conception of irony," and A. Zahareas' analysis (1963) of irony in Camus as nihilism counterbalanced by a stubborn determination to go on (*Texas Studies in Literature and Language*, **5**, 319–28).

As an *attitude* toward life, paradoxical irony has been both praised and attacked. F. Paulhan (1909) argued at philosophical length that all moral values are relative and only the ironic attitude can give proportional weight to the demands of both society and the ego. Nietzsche thought the ironic attitude a sign of health (*Beyond Good and Evil*, 1886). The American Randolph Bourne (1913) believed that since the ironist does not absolutely reject any experience but is constantly contrasting and criticizing and moving on to new experiences, he has an "intense feeling of aliveness" and "the broad honest sympathy of democracy" (*Atlantic Monthly*, **111**, 357–67). Attacks on this attitude have all resembled Hegel's attack on Schlegelian ethics: there is no absolute commitment to anything. So H. Chantavoine (1897) and H. Chevalier (1932) attacked Anatole France, Wayne Booth (1961) the elusive morality of modern novelists, and Jean-Paul Sartre adopted the ironic attitude as a model for analyzing self-deception or *mauvaise foi* (*L'être et le néant*, 1943).

The German romantics had tried to locate the unity and morality of paradoxical irony in its comprehensiveness, but, as J. C. Ransom (1941) observed, "opposites can never be said to be resolved or reconciled merely because they have been got into the same poem." Several American critics have attempted to solve this problem in a Hegelian way by seeing paradoxical irony not as the expression of absolute relativism, but as a dynamic learning process which produces tentative results. For Randolph Bourne irony was "the science of comparative experience" which "compares things not with an established standard but with each other": values "slowly emerge from the process." Cleanth Brooks, R. P. Warren, and Kenneth Burke have taken much the same position.

The quite different pattern of nihilistic irony has emerged elsewhere. In 1856 George Eliot commented on Heine's "strain of irony that repels our sympathy. . . . Yet what strange, deep pathos is mingled with the audacity" (*Westminster Review*, n. s. **9**, 1–33). The full pattern—a conception of reality as denying human values and the mingling of something like satiric detachment with something like tragic pathos—is evident in a number of Baudelaire's uses of the word; in turn-of-the-century criticism of Laforgue's irony by Arthur Symons, Remy de Gourmont, and James Huneker; in discussions of the "cosmic irony" of Hardy and Housman; in Georges Palante's "metaphysical principle of irony"; in Irving Babbitt's notion of "romantic irony," a term that F. Schlegel had used only in his Notebooks but which has been frequently used by German scholars since Rudolf Haym's *Romantische Schule* (1870); in Morton Gurewitch's "European romantic irony," which he traces through Byron, Heine, Grabbe, Büchner, Leopardi, Flaubert, and Baudelaire; and in notice of the irony of the Absurd, frequent since World War II.

Many critics have commented on the despair and self-pity which nihilistic irony both expresses and induces, even at its most detached extreme. Discussing *Madame Bovary*, Flaubert insisted on his absolute ironic detachment as author; nevertheless, he expected the realism of his method to produce in his audience some identification with the characters, and he himself recognized, as Kenneth Burke remarked, a "fundamental kinship with the enemy." *Waiting for Godot* was farcical vaudeville, yet Ward Hooker (1960) pointed out that the play's "irony in a vacuum" had changed the "laughter of the audience . . . to sickening doubt . . . which spreads from the addled minds of Vladimir and Estragon to engulf the audience" (*Kenyon Review*, **22**, 436–54). Few moral critics have risen to praise nihilistic irony, many to attack it: it is absolute for negation and despair.

The various types of *satiric irony* have been exhaustively analyzed by twentieth-century critics. In "The New Irony: Sicknicks and Others" (1961) Benjamin De Mott described a satiric irony based on nihilism as a positive norm, in the sense that it supplies a reason not for defeat and despair but for the ironist's arrogantly superior, ironic attack on "*all* positive assertion." *Comic irony* has apparently received almost no attention as an independent aspect of irony, and the term itself has usually meant what is here called satiric irony. What little attention it has received has been as part of an overall complex of *dramatic irony*, which has been repeatedly analyzed in tragic drama by English and American critics following Thirlwall. Henry James drew attention to a novelistic form of dramatic irony: the difference between what an un-

633

reliable narrator or center of consciousness understands in what he tells or sees and what the author and audience understand.

In the field of *verbal irony*, the analytic methods of rhetoric have been revived and intensified in the critical practice of William Empson, Cleanth Brooks, and their followers, now equipped with all the new ideas of irony as well as the old. Such criticism has found ironic incongruity in the minutest *degree* of difference between meanings. For Brooks, "every word in a good poem acknowledges to some degree the pressure of the context" and is therefore ironic. In France, Vladimir Jankélévitch (1936) had asserted much the same argument in terms of irony as allegory: all language, indeed, is more or less allegorical. R. S. Crane (1952) observed that in this sense even a mathematical equation is ironic.

In *Wit and Its Relation to the Unconscious* (1905), Freud, thinking of verbal irony as satiric, asserted that in the listener such irony produces "comic pleasure, probably by causing him to make preparations for contradiction, which are immediately found to be unnecessary." That is, the *audience* of satiric irony reacts as would the victim of comic irony. Thinking of irony as paradoxical, Richards, although not entirely satisfied with a "switchboard" psychology, located the satisfaction of the audience in a static "balance of opposed impulses." In regard to the *author*, Freud asserted that irony as saying the opposite of what one means parallels the dream, which "delights in representing a pair of opposites by means of one and the same composite image" or "changes an element from the dreamthoughts into its opposite." This notion seems to have been behind Norman Brown's "law of irony" by which it could be shown that the "partially disclaimed thought is Swift's own thought" (*Life Against Death*, 1959), and Norman Holland's definition of irony as "a defense mechanism in which the ego turns the *object* of a drive into its opposite" (*Dynamics of Literary Response*, 1968).

Irony has continued to appear in *fields of observation* outside literature. It has been analyzed in music and the visual arts, notably by Ortega y Gasset (1925), Jankélévitch, and Muecke. Goethe's observation that the truths of science should be viewed ironically has reoccurred, and Heisenberg's Principle of Indeterminacy has reinforced it for Muecke and Arthur Miller: it is "dialectical irony that the act of measurement itself changes the particle being measured" (*Collected Plays*, 1957). In the field of politics, the attitude of paradoxical irony has been recommended by Proudhon (*Confessions d'un révolutionnaire*, 1849), Palante (1906), Mann (1918), and Reinhold Niebuhr (1952): it frees the political activist from fanatical attachment to any one cause, thereby keeping the door to progress open. Both Niebuhr and Kenneth Burke have used paradoxical irony as a model for analyzing history. Niebuhr revived the Christian view of Thirlwall—God "resisteth the proud and giveth grace to the humble"; Burke took the Hegelian position that history is an ironic dialectic in which no cultural movement ever disappears—only the balance changes (*Grammar of Motives*, 1945).

The most important recent theory of irony is that of Northrop Frye, whose *Anatomy of Criticism* (1957) absorbed virtually all the available ideas of irony into a total structure of human thought and vision. Even here, however, satiric irony was not clearly distinguished from comic irony.

BIBLIOGRAPHY

G. G. Sedgewick, *Of Irony Especially in Drama* (Toronto, 1948), contains an historically oriented review of the meanings of the word *irony*, including the Greek and the Latin. N. Knox, *The Word "Irony" and Its Context, 1500–1755* (Durham, N.C., 1961), deals with developments in England. R. Wellek, *A History of Modern Criticism*, 5 vols. (New Haven, 1955–), gives consistent attention to irony as a topic in European literary criticism, with full references. D. C. Muecke, *The Compass of Irony* (London, 1969), contains an excellent bibliography. Also: W. C. Booth, *The Rhetoric of Fiction* (Chicago, 1961); C. I. Glicksberg, *The Ironic Vision in Modern Literature* (The Hague, 1969), to be used with caution; R. Immerwahr, "The Subjectivity or Objectivity of Friedrich Schlegel's Poetic Irony," *Germanic Review*, **26** (1951), 173–91; V. Jankélévitch, *L'Ironie* (Paris, 1936; rev. ed., 1950), a suggestive study; S. Kierkegaard, *The Concept of Irony*, trans. L. M. Capel (New York, 1965); G. E. Mueller, "Solger's Aesthetics—A Key to Hegel (Irony and Dialectic)," in *Corona*, ed. A. Schirokauer and W. Paulsen (Durham, N.C., 1941), pp. 212–27; I. Strohschneider-Kohrs, *Die Romantische Ironie in Theorie und Gestaltung* (Tübingen, 1960); A. R. Thompson, *The Dry Mock: A Study of Irony in Drama* (Berkeley, 1948); David Worcester, *The Art of Satire* (Cambridge, Mass., 1940).

NORMAN D. KNOX

[See also Allegory; Art and Play; **Comic Sense;** Rhetoric after Plato; **Satire;** Style; **Tragic Sense.**]

IRRATIONALISM IN THE HISTORY OF PHILOSOPHY

FOR A BIRD'S-EYE view of the history of the idea of irrationalism in philosophy, two preliminary methodological observations are in order. First, irrationalism is a retrospective concept, that is to say, its meaning is established only through contrasting it with a rationalism which has already been established. That is why the critique of rationalism could not be completely accomplished in Kant's philosophy until after the Cartesian philosophy had been formed. Nevertheless, nothing prevents us from talking about the irrationalism in Heraclitus' thoughts; it is implicit, however, and we can freely admit its positive presence in his philosophy, but only insofar as the positive element is itself implicit.

Secondly, we submit that properly speaking there is no tradition of irrationalism as there is a rationalistic tradition. What we observe are irruptions, or even, we may wish to say, eruptions of irrationalism. For irrationalism is a revolt.

In addition, we shall have the occasion to see that irrationalism perhaps comes often from too narrow a conception of rationalism. We shall have to judge to what extent rationalists are right in saying to irrationalists that they rise up against reason because they have created a false conception of reason. (See, for example, Léon Brunschwicg's criticism of Wahl's *Vers le concret*.)

From mythology to post-Nietzschean philosophy there is a long and curious road. Myths used to reveal superhuman powers ruling over the destinies of men. Destiny itself implies a certain type of irrational force; the wars of men and the genealogies of the gods are manifestations of this extraordinary and harsh force.

When a sage like Xenophanes raises his voice, he takes account of the irrationality of the gods and rejects them. But soon among the sages there appears another who proclaims that the *logos* which rules the universe and is independent of all things, is much more vast than human reason: it unites contradictory elements, day and night, silence and noise, peace and war. At times this *logos* appears like a child playing with dice, as in the thought of Heraclitus, who is great enough to be classed as both the greatest of the irrationalists and one of the greatest of rationalists. It all depends on how wide a berth is given to reason. Like Nietzsche, Heraclitus is the bard of a greater reason than man's and also the bard of the Eternal Return.

In the great classical philosophies of Plato and Aristotle reason is triumphant, but matter, as Plato represents it in the *Timaeus,* is something irrational. Elsewhere, above the Ideas and shining with the blinding resplendence of the intelligible sun, there is the Good which is inaccessible to pure reasoning. Reason is thus only an intermediary faculty between two realms of the irrational.

Aristotle's God, being Thought reflecting on itself, cannot be presented as impervious to reason; we no longer have here that higher limit of the supra-rational such as we find in Plato's Good. However, at the lower limit of being, we find prime matter which cannot be known by our reason any more than Plato's matter.

Despite all this, classical philosophy, such as Plato's and Aristotle's, appears as a triumph of reason, and emerges from the ideas and forms on which reason shines.

The Neo-Platonism of a Plotinus, a Damascius, or a Proclus offers a scheme of the world in which starting from the One, situated above reason, emanations radiate and gradually become embodied in things. If we take Hegel as our inspiration, we may say that ancient philosophy ends in skepticism, and we can see in skepticism a form of irrationalism.

However, rationalism does not assume its decisive forms until the seventeenth century with Descartes and the influence of science. But is it proper to confine thought to clear and distinct ideas? Descartes admitted clear ideas that are not distinct, for example, pain and color and everything arising from the union of the soul and body; soul and body may each be experienced distinctly but not their union which belongs to the domain of the indistinct, the indistinct being what we do not know scientifically. This also is what Malebranche meant when he regarded the human soul as an obscure domain. We cannot, however, make Malebranche an irrationalist. On the other hand, one of his contemporaries may be justifiably considered a principal representative of irrationalism, namely, Pascal. Pascal talks of the heart's reasons. He says that the heart feels that space has three dimensions. Furthermore, religious truth is not grasped by our understanding; such truth is revealed by the Incarnation and by miracles. Pascal contrasts the God of Abraham, Isaac, and Jacob with the God of the philosophers, and it is not by rational demonstrations that God's existence can be proved.

A short time before Pascal, another great writer, and like Pascal probably a reader of Montaigne, namely, Shakespeare, had said (or more exactly, had one of his characters, Hamlet, say), "There are more things in heaven and earth, Horatio, than are dreamt of in your philosophy."

At the end of the eighteenth century, the age of enlightenment or, as the Italian historians of philosophy call it, the age of *illuminismo,* irrationalism was formulated in the writings of J. G. Hamann and F. H. Jacobi. Hamann, in his *Sokratische Denkwürdigkeiten* ("Socratic Memorabilia"), inspired, he thought, by Socrates, derides human reason and seeks in numbers the symbols that will enable us to perceive the hidden Deity. Jacobi insists on the inadequacies of reason in morals.

Their great contemporary Kant writes: "I have shown the limits of knowledge in order to make room for faith." But obviously this statement scarcely covers

635

the whole of Kant's thought. What he showed is that the mind cannot grasp things in themselves; the mind can grasp only phenomena, and only because it shapes them, that is to say, because it imposes its forms and categories on the sensory manifold. Kant seeks to determine the conditions necessary for scientific knowledge to be possible. By studying these conditions we come to see clearly why a knowledge of things in themselves is impossible. There is, nevertheless, one thing in itself to a knowledge of which we can to a certain extent penetrate, namely, the self; when we have respect for others we are confronted by what is morally autonomous, and we can lay down a moral law for ourselves. Hamann and Jacobi were not mistaken in treating Kant as an enemy.

Still it is from Kant that two influential irrationalist theories were developed: F. W. J. Schelling's and Arthur Schopenhauer's. Schelling from the very first of his works stressed the role of intellectual intuition which he claimed was both a creation and an insight; that is, through intellectual intuition's creative and visionary role we can in art, as in metaphysics, come to know reality by overcoming the duality of subject and object. In Schelling's reflections there are several stages; first his thought is presented as philosophy of nature, then as philosophy of identity, and finally, the last phase, more antirationalistic than the preceding ones, as philosophy of revelation. As for Schopenhauer, the world appears to him under two aspects: as Will and as Representation. He contrasts the inescapable misfortune of the activity of our will, on the one hand, with freedom through art, on the other. We are here confronted with a double-edged irrationalism; for the will is irrational, and art, thanks to which we can escape from the irrational, surpasses reason.

From Schopenhauer we may go on to the thought of Eduard von Hartmann who presents a blind and creative unconscious, profoundly independent of all conditions (the "Unconditioned").

We cannot here go into the question of the possible influences of von Hartmann and Sigmund Freud. Going back to Schopenhauer, we can best understand him as having started from Kant. It is also to Kant's influence that we should attach the work of Hans Vaihinger. This profound commentator of Kant's philosophy established a whole theory according to which we move in a world of pure fiction (fictionalism) which can be compared to certain characteristics of Anglo-Saxon pragmatism.

While German academic philosophy was dominated by neo-Kantianism, certain philosophies of life were being developed along lines that were irrationalistic in character. However, it is rather in the writings of Georg Simmel, a penetrating thinker and remarkable writer, that we find the expression of both vitalism and

relativism. He also began to develop his ideas after reflecting on the philosophy of Kant. But the influence first of Schopenhauer and then of Friedrich Nietzsche gave a special tinge to Simmel's philosophy.

Among these thinkers Wilhelm Dilthey went farthest in expounding philosophically the difference, as he viewed it, between explanation and understanding (*Verständnis*): in the human sciences, the scientist explains more than he understands. On the basis of this assumption, we might envisage a widening of the idea of reason and a kind of compromise, necessarily provisional as all compromises are, between rationalism and irrationalism.

We must provide a special place, apart from all these groups of thinkers, for G. T. Fechner, the founder of psychophysics. He posited an earth-spirit above the souls of individuals; the earth-spirit includes individual souls and is in turn included in and absorbed by the soul of the universe. In another side of his world view, he contrasts the light of day with the nocturnal light of mechanical science. In this transmundane vision he anticipates Gaston Bachelard's views.

Is it correct to say that Bergson is an irrationalist? In a sense, yes; specifically because duration (*la durée*) for him is not something which can be understood by the intellect. *La durée* is the cumulative development of events, each moment of time unrolling from the preceding one. Of *durée* we can have what Henri Bergson later called an "intuition," and not a concept. The same is true of the *élan vital* ("life thrust"). This aspect of Bergson's thought is especially prominent in his *Introduction to Metaphysics* (*Introduction à la métaphysique*, 1903) and in the preface of his *La pensée et le mouvant* (1934). This aspect appears also in the criticism of the sciences as Edouard Le Roy conceived it. Also worthy of mention is the irrationalism of Charles Péguy and of Georges Sorel.

Clearly most of the themes of irrationalism are present in Bergsonism in which they are compressed: vitalism, criticism of science insofar as it consists of hypotheses, and general distrust of the abstract intellect. No doubt, Bergson was glad to emphasize often enough that intellect was sovereign in the realm of inert things, but that very fact shows the limitations of intelligence.

Bergson's theories were welcomed as liberating ideas by William James because they gave freedom to man and enabled the future to have an open character.

For a certain period of time Bergson's theories were overshadowed by the prevalence of existentialist ideas associated with Søren Kierkegaard, and by the phenomenological views associated with Edmund Husserl. It was only towards the end of his philosophical development that Maurice Merleau-Ponty returned to a more incisive knowledge of Bergsonian thought.

There is a Kierkegaardian irrationalism in the sense

that Kierkegaard was more effective than Kant, and in a sense as effective as Pascal, in destroying science in order to make room for faith. Kant had sought the conditions of objective knowledge, but Kierkegaard asks, of what value to us is objectivity? What matters, for him as for Pascal, is one's welfare and one's subjectivity or inner state of being insofar as it exists in an intense relation to the Absolute.

Similar ideas occur in Gabriel Marcel, who developed his theories independently of any influence by Kierkegaard. Marcel insists on the difference between being and having, between what I am, on the one hand, and the instruments or objective things in my possession, on the other hand. It is on that basis that he envisages the problem of my body which is absolutely not comparable to an instrument that I should perhaps possess: I am my body.

However, I am not isolated in my body, I am in it and through it I exist in a profound relation to others. And my soul, going towards its "invocation" (to use Gabriel Marcel's term), is constantly a call to others and finally to Thou. At this point, Marcel's thought converges on Kierkegaard's. On certain other points, for example, on the affirmation of essences, not intellectual or intelligible essence but hidden, veiled, and lived-through (*voilée-vécue*), Marcel comes close to Husserl.

By taking into account the influence of both Kierkegaard and Husserl, we can best understand the development of Jean-Paul Sartre's philosophy as well as Martin Heidegger's. These philosophies are what might be called the penultimate forms of irrationalism. Sartre gave his book *Being and Nothingness* (*L'être et le néant*, 1943), the subtitle *Essay on Phenomenological Ontology*. It is a strange view of reality which divides it into a static "thing in itself," suddenly appearing in sensation, and something "for itself" which is constantly what it is not, and is not what it is. The belief in a God or even in Platonic Ideas assumes that there can be a union of reality in itself with reality for itself. Sartre's atheism is based on the denial of such a possibility, and insists on the impossibility of such a union. Our world is henceforth mere contingency.

Nevertheless, in Sartre's thought there are mingled influences, beginning with Husserl and Heidegger, of Karl Marx, on the one hand, and of Freud, on the other. That brings us to the question of knowing in what sense it may be said that psychoanalysis and Marxism are irrationalistic. In one sense they may be said to be rationalistic and even ultra-rationalistic, but a philosopher like George Lukacs in vain entitles one of his books, the one precisely directed against irrationalism, *The Destruction of Reason* (1954). It is nonetheless true that in Freudianism, reason is relativized and consequently destroyed for the benefit of the Id and complexes; in Marxism, reason is relativized and destroyed for the benefit of the class struggle and more generally on account of economic conditions.

Heidegger places himself on quite a different plane. The fundamental question for him is the question of being, the same being of which it was said in his *Being and Time* (*Sein und Zeit*, 1927), that it could be perceived only against the horizon of time, revealing itself and hiding itself at the same time, somewhat like the hidden God of Pascal and Kierkegaard, also somewhat like Kant's "thing-in-itself"; being is revealed and is hidden in beings. Quoting a chorus in Sophocles' *Antigone*, Heidegger depicts man as the strangest and most terrible of beings. No less than man, perhaps, the things against which man's power is broken are strange and terrible. Undoubtedly man's power increases under the profound influence of technology. But who can say whether remote things, rather than what is close to us, will best reveal the presence of sky and water, of mortal and perhaps immortal things? We live in a twilight zone from which, according to J. C. F. Hölderlin, the ancient Gods have fled and into which future deities have not yet come. In this state of our existence we have to preserve the thought of being which is beyond all intelligible thought, like the Good of Plato, except that it shines in an obscure way in sensory things.

Though Plato has just been mentioned, Heidegger in fact is closer to Nietzsche. We perceive, beyond classical concepts, an essence not yet known, an eternity not belonging to concepts. We have to return, past the evolution of philosophy, which is lost in representation, to the presence of that Being which is revealed at times, but only partly in philosophical systems; but this Being came open to Nietzsche's thought as it did to Hölderlin's. A foundation for the principle of reason must hence be sought, and for Heidegger, this principle can be discovered only in the abyss of nonreason. Thus we see in Heidegger a resurgence of irrationalism.

In the contemporary world, reason is attacked on all sides. In the work, for example, of Michel Foucault, though it appears in a structured form, it is still the voice of irrationalism that speaks. Foucault thinks he can pass beyond both rationalism and humanism at the same time. What we witness in his works is an irrationalistic relativism.

It is one of the characteristics of thought in the 1960's to see beyond existence and beyond essences something that our discourse cannot reach but to which it can only point.

But just as reason has its limits, according to rationalism, irrationalism also has its own limitations which can be discerned from two viewpoints, that of science and that of common sense. In the first place, the world in which we live is one in which we perceive regularity. Secondly, the relations established by mathematical physics appear to our intellect as something certain; even the so-called uncertainty relations are valid only to a certain degree. Philosophy has always been both reflection on itself and reflection on things other than itself, in particular, reflection on science.

Meditation on science has been pursued ever since the time of the Pythagoreans and the atomists, and has continued in the great Platonic, Cartesian, and Kantian traditions. Science has grown in so complex a manner that a synthesis like that of Descartes or Leibniz is no longer conceived to be possible today. It is consequently fitting to make room in our minds for the admission of both the inexpressible and the need of knowledge. There is no contradiction between them; quite to the contrary, one calls for the other.

A study of irrationalism would not be complete if it did not turn towards the poets and towards certain romantic philosophers. William Blake, in the poem entitled "The Gates of Paradise" asks man to distrust logical truths. Later, he represents (in the guise of Urizen) the intellect insofar as it defines, describes, and encompasses the real. In the same sense, Keats can be cited for bringing a sort of curse on the legacy of Newton.

Poets, like the romantic Novalis or Hölderlin, see reality as made of contradiction. In Novalis the idea of a marriage of the seasons recalls Heraclitus as well as prefiguring the Eternal Return. From another quarter, a Max Stirner comes on the scene in pursuit of extreme individualism and is able to conceive of expressing himself in no other way than by a cry.

In the literary sphere, the surrealists form the last expression of eternal irrationalism. However, the surrealism of André Breton is not the only form of the revolt against reason or of hatred of the rational. Henri Michaux, Antoine Artaud, and Georges Bataille have each pursued from their respective standpoints this war against logical evidence. This surrealistic attitude raises the final question of knowing to what irrationalism leads us.

Glancing over the metamorphoses of irrationalism we can see that it is sometimes a revolt and sometimes a revelation. We can even distinguish the possibility of a double revelation. On the one hand, it reveals the elements below reason in which we can in turn distinguish the insights of M. Merleau-Ponty and elsewhere the disorder and chance asserted by Bataille, and, on the other hand, the revelations of a Pascal, of a Fénelon, and everything touching on that "numinous" element about which Rudolf Otto has written. Among certain thinkers irrationalism is an end in itself, and among others it is a road to religious ways; such is

the case for thinkers as different as Pascal, Blake, Novalis, and Hölderlin.

The question still remains whether above the "subrational" (meaning by that term what Merleau-Ponty and thinkers as different from him as Georges Bataille) and above the rational and "super-rational" (to take G. Bachelard's term), there is a reason broader than reason, that is, a higher reason, as Nietzsche at times thought, and as Rimbaud put it, "the rational song of the angels" (*le chant raisonnable des anges*). But at this point the philosopher can only question himself and think back on that series of transformations which goes from revolt to revelation, and who, becoming aware of the end result, returns at the same time towards Heraclitus, towards the origins.

BIBLIOGRAPHY

A. J. Ayer, "Some Aspects of Existentialism," *Rationalist Annual* (1948). William Barrett, *Irrational Man* (New York, 1958). Henri Bergson, *Essai sur les données* . . . (1887), trans. P. L. Pogson as *Time and Free Will* (London, 1910); idem, "Introduction à la métaphysique" (1903), trans. T. E. Hulme as *Introduction to Metaphysics* (New York, 1913; 1954); idem, *Les deux sources* . . . (1932), trans. R. A. Audra and C. Brereton as *The Two Sources of Morality and Religion* (London 1935; New York, 1954). Isaiah Berlin, *The Hedgehog and the Fox* (London, 1953). Albert Camus, *Le Mythe de Sisyphe* (Paris, 1942). F. Dostoevsky, *Notes From Underground* (1864), trans. Constance Garnett in *Works*, 12 vols. (New York, 1912–20). Martin Heidegger, *Sein und Zeit* (1927), trans. J. Macquarrie and E. Robinson as *Being and Time* (New York, 1962). S. Kierkegaard, *Concluding Unscientific Postscript* (1846), trans. D. F. Swenson and W. Lowrie (Princeton, 1941); idem, *Philosophical Fragments* . . . (1844), trans. D. F. Swenson (Princeton, 1962). Joseph de Maistre, *Les Soirées de Saint-Petersbourg*, 6th ed. (Paris, 1850). Richard Müller-Freienfels, *Metaphysik des Irrationalen* (Leipzig, 1927). Jean-Paul Sartre, *La Nausée* (Paris, 1938); idem, *L'Etre et le néant* (1943), trans. Hazel Barnes as *Being and Nothingness* (New York, 1956). L. H. de Wolf, *The Religious Revolt Against Reason* (New York, 1949).

JEAN WAHL

[See also **Counter-Enlightenment; Existentialism; Metaphysical Imagination; Romanticism.**]

ISLAMIC CONCEPTION OF INTELLECTUAL LIFE

ISLAM spread more rapidly than all other religions of which there exists a historical record. Only a century after its inception in Mecca (the year of the Hegira,

1 A.H., i.e., A.D. 622), the new religion dominated an area extending from the Iberian peninsula in the West to the steppes of Central Asia in the East. Moreover, to the same degree that its expansion was rapid, the consolidation of this newly conquered domain into a new world civilization was profound and permanent. Islam developed its characteristic art within a century of its birth and its own learning and arts and sciences a hundred years later. By the end of the third century A.H. (tenth century A.D.) the intellectual life of Islam had reached the peak of its activity and Islamic civilization had itself become, through the assimilation of the heritage of many previous civilizations, the new focus of intellectual life in the world.

The lands which became rapidly consolidated into the Islamic world contained centers where most of the philosophical and scientific life of previous ages had flourished. The intellectual activity of Athens had long ago been transferred to Alexandria and adjacent schools like that of Pergamum; and then through channels of eastern branches of Christianity, such as the Monophysites and Nestorians, this heritage had already become planted upon the soil of what was later to become the heart of the Islamic world, in such centers as Antioch, Edessa, and Nisibis. The more esoteric aspect of the Greco-Alexandrian tradition connected with Neo-Pythagoreanism and Hermeticism had also become established in the same region in the cult of the Sabeans of Harran, who combined in their religious and intellectual life the Hermetico-Pythagorean ideas of Alexandria with astronomical and astrological ideas drawn from late Babylonian and Chaldean sources.

Besides the intellectual heritage of the Mediterranean world, that of the Persians and Indians also became available to the Muslims. Already during the Sassanid period the Persian king, Shapur I, had established a school in Jundishapur to rival that of Antioch (fourth century A.D.). In this school Persian and Indian learning, written mostly in Pahlavi and Sanskrit, became as significant as the Greco-Alexandrian learning in Greek and Syriac. This school became important especially in medicine and astronomy and by the seventh century A.D. it was probably the most important medical center in the world, combining the scientific traditions of the Greeks, the Persians, and the Indians.

All these centers and many others became a part of the Islamic world, and their activity in fact continued in certain cases for several centuries after the Islamic conquests, in the hands of the Christians, Jews, or Zoroastrians who now became minorities with recognized rights in the new world civilization. The very fact that these minorities as "people of the book" were allowed to survive in the new order itself made the transmission of the non-Islamic sciences to Muslims much easier. When the time came for Islamic society to take cognizance of the presence of this heritage and to integrate it into its own perspective, there were translators and men of learning already present within its own borders. The scholars belonging to these minority religious communities, or those having recently embraced Islam, knew either Greek or Syriac if they were Christians or Sabeans, and Pahlavi if they were Zoroastrian. They were also masters in the sciences in question as well as being well versed in Arabic, which by now was not only the religious language of Islam but also the language of discourse and learning of Islamic civilization. When the need for non-Islamic learning was felt by Muslims, the means to acquire it was ready at hand.

But neither the presence of centers of learning nor scholars and translators would be sufficient to explain the remarkable enthusiasm and determination with which the Islamic world set out to make the knowledge of the ancients its own. This can be particularly appreciated when one realizes that the Byzantine civilization whose tongue was in fact Greek did not display the same amount of interest in the sciences of the ancient world. Islamic civilization set out deliberately and through concerted effort to master Greek, Persian, and Indian learning and science at the time when it was the most powerful nation on earth and had no military, political, or economic motive for turning attention to these sciences.

The main reason must therefore be sought in the characteristics of the Islamic revelation itself. Islam is a religion based on knowledge—and not on love as is for example Christianity—a knowledge in which the intellect (al-ʿaql) itself plays the positive role of leading man to the Divine. Islam also considers itself as the last religion of humanity and, by virtue of this very fact, a return to the primordial religion (dīn al-ḥanīf) and the synthesis of all religions that have preceded it. These two characteristics taken together made it both possible and necessary for Muslims to come to know the learning of earlier civilizations and to assimilate those elements which harmonized with its world view into Islamic civilization.

Being essentially a "way of knowledge," Islam could not remain indifferent to any form of knowledge. From the point of view of knowledge, a doctrine or idea is either true or false; it cannot be brushed aside and ignored, once its existence is known. Plato and Aristotle had expressed views about God, man, and the nature of things. Once known, their views could not be simply ignored. They were either true, in which case they should be accepted into the Islamic scheme of things considered in its universal sense, or they were false, in which case they should be refuted. But in either case they had to be studied and known.

In considering itself as the last religion of man, Islam has always believed that all that confirms its truths—which can be ultimately summarized in the axial and central doctrine of unity (al-tawḥīd)—is "Islamic" and legitimately its own. Moses and Christ are stars in the firmament of Islam irrespective of their role in Judaism and Christianity. Seen in this light, all that affirmed "unity" in both its metaphysical and cosmological senses in the non-Islamic sciences and philosophies, belonged legitimately to Muslims, and the Islamic intellectual elite did not feel any religious inhibitions in making these ideas its own. This was especially true since Muslims, like Philo before them and like certain Christian theologians in the West during the Middle Ages and the Renaissance (such as those who spoke of the "atomism of Moses"), considered philosophy and the sciences to have been derived from revelation, from "the niche of prophecy" to use the Koranic term.

The figure of Hermes is particularly significant in this connection. Already the Hermes associated with the Alexandrian school of alchemy and the Corpus Hermeticum symbolizes the synthesis of Greek and Egyptian traditions of science and cosmology. In Islam Hermes became identified with the antediluvian prophet Idrīs, mentioned in the Koran (Quran), and the Hebrew Enoch. The figure of Hermes was moreover elaborated to include three different figures each associated with an aspect of the arts and sciences. Hermes Trismegistus as known in the West comes, not from Alexandrian, but from Islamic sources. Through the three Hermes, considered as the founders of science and philosophy and the first associated with the prophet Idrīs, Islam was able to legitimize the incorporation of the intellectual heritage of previous civilizations into its own world view, to the extent that this heritage was itself compatible with the genius of the Islamic revelation.

The immediate source of the spark which ignited the fire of intellectual activity and translation of Greek, Syriac, Pahlavi, and Sanskrit texts into Arabic, more than any possible utilitarian motives to benefit from medicine and astrology, was the debates held in Damascus, Basra, Kufa, Baghdad, and other Muslim cities between Muslims and scholars and theologians of other religions. Often these debates were held in the presence of the caliphs or religious authorities, especially the Shiʿite Imams. In these debates, where open discussion was usually permitted, the Muslims found themselves on the defensive before the weapons of logic and philosophy with which their adversaries were armed. Soon the Muslims realized that in order to defend the tenets of the faith itself they had to arm themselves with the same weapons. The challenge of a theologian like John the Damascene could only be answered with a theology of similar intellectual content. Therefore, the Muslims sought to master the logic and philosophy of their religious opponents, especially those Christians who were thoroughly acquainted with Greek philosophy and logic. This movement not only led to the concerted effort to translate, leading to the founding of such vast institutions as the "House of Wisdom" (Bayt al-ḥikmah) of al-Maʾmūn in Baghdad whose specific function was translation of works into Arabic, but it was also instrumental in the particular way in which Muslim theology was formulated, as we see in the case of the Christian hypostases and the Islamic Divine Attributes.

The golden age of translation lasted for a period of nearly 150 years, from about 150 (767) to 300 (912). During this period a large number of basic Greek texts in philosophy and the sciences, in the most general sense, were rendered into Arabic, sometimes directly from the Greek, at other times through the intermediary of Syriac. Special attention was paid to the works of Aristotle and his commentators, of which there are more translations in Arabic than in European languages, and also to classical mathematical and astronomical treatises such as those of Euclid, Archimedes, and Ptolemy. Medico-philosophical treatises, especially those of Galen, were also translated extensively as were many works in the occult sciences whose original Greek or Syriac version is lost. In fact Arabic is today a valuable source of knowledge for Greek philosophy and science, especially of the later period, precisely because of the large number of texts translated and preserved as well as the high quality of many of the translations. Altogether from the point of view of quality and quantity alike the transmission of the learning of the ancient world to Muslims through the medium of Arabic is one of the most startling phenomena of cultural history; for not only was it instrumental in bringing into being Muslim sciences and philosophy but it also played indirectly a vital role in the creation of medieval and Renaissance science and philosophy in the West, and even influenced China and India.

The greatest translators belong to the Abbasid period, the most important being Ḥunayn ibn Isḥāq, who founded a school of translation known for the exactness and fluency of its renderings. Almost as significant was Ibn Muqaffaʿ, a Persian convert to Islam from Zoroastrianism, whose translations from the Pahlavi helped found the new philosophical and scientific style of prose that was being established in the Arabic language. But even before the Abbasid period translations had been made and contact established between

Islamic religious circles and non-Islamic forms of learning. The figure of Imam Ja‛far al-Ṣādiq, the sixth Shi‛ite Imam, and his interest in the non-Islamic sciences have often been taken by modern scholars as being apocryphal tales not to be accepted seriously. More recent research, however, has revealed that there is no reason whatsoever for doubting these traditional claims or for denying the link between the Imam and Jābir ibn Ḥayyān, the father of Islamic alchemy. It is most likely that the great flowering of interest in the non-Islamic sciences during the Abbasid period goes back to earlier contacts during the late Umayyad era when from the inner processes within Islam itself there grew the possibilities of contact with the non-Islamic sciences and their legitimization and integration into the Islamic tradition. It is, in fact, upon the properly Islamic basis of the first century A.H., to which was added the heritage of the ancient world through the movement of translation, that Islamic intellectual history began to elaborate and manifest itself from the second century A.H. (eighth century A.D.) onward.

The earliest intellectual activity in Islam is concerned with those Islamic sciences which are properly speaking known as "transmitted" (al-‛ulūm al-naqlīyah) such as Koranic commentary, the traditions of the Prophet (Ḥadīth), questions concerning the sacred law of Islam, theology (Kalām), as well as the sciences dealing with language, prosody, etc. This whole group of sciences is usually distinguished in the Islamic classification of the sciences from the "intellectual sciences" (al-‛ulūm al-‛aqlīyah), such as philosophy and mathematics, which in contrast to the first group need not be learned through transmission, and may be acquired through the innate intelligence possessed by man.

During the first Islamic century, while the efforts of most men of learning were concentrated in the domain of the religious sciences, particularly the Koran and Ḥadīth, in Basra and Kufa there began to develop contending schools of grammar which soon turned to different philosophies of language, the first more inclined towards Aristotelian and the second toward Stoic logic. Some of the earliest philosophical and metaphysical ideas in Islam are to be found in these early schools of grammar, and this type of philosophical analysis of language and rhetoric in fact continued throughout the Islamic period and was especially developed among some of the Andalusian Muslim thinkers like Ibn Ḥazm of Cordova. The metaphysical significance of the sounds and letters of the Arabic language, the sacred language of Islam, is also important in the esoteric and mystical aspect of Islam known as Sufism. This aspect of the Islamic tradition left its influence upon men like Raymond Lull (early four-teenth century) and others in the West who were interested in the esoteric significance of language.

Of the transmitted sciences the one that is closest to the mainstream of Islamic intellectual history as far as philosophy and the sciences are concerned is Kalām, usually translated as theology, although the significance of theology in Christianity and that of Kalām in Islam are not by any means the same. The science of Kalām has its roots in the earliest debates in the Islamic community on the questions of free will and predestination, the created or uncreated nature of the Koran, the relation of faith to works, the definition of who is a believer, etc. Concerning these basic religious questions there arose different groups during the first century A.H. such as the Murji‛ites, Qadarites, and Khawārij; each sought to answer one of these questions in such a way that it became known as a community possessing a particular and definable opinion vis-à-vis the majority of Muslims.

From these early movements there grew the first systematic theological school, named the Mu‛tazilah and founded by Wāṣil ibn ‛Atā’. This school, which gained the ascendency during the caliphate of al-Ma’mūn and continued to be influential up to the fifth (eleventh) century in Baghdad and after that for many centuries among the Zaydīs of the Yemen, sought to preserve Divine Unity from all that would blemish its transcendence. But in so doing it chose a rationalistic interpretation of the Divinity which tended to view God more as philosophical abstraction than as a Reality Who is the fountainhead and basis of revealed religion. The Mu‛tazilites proffered five main principles upon which their different followers agreed and for which they have become celebrated: the Unity of God, His Justice, promise of reward and threat of punishment for good and evil acts, belief in the possibility of a state between belief and unbelief, and finally emphasis upon ordering the good and prohibiting the evil. The main Mu‛tazilite figures such as Naẓẓām and ‛Allāf were powerful logicians and dialecticians to be reckoned with in the history of Islamic theology. It is they who for the first time developed the theory of atomism which is peculiar to Kalām and which was later developed extensively by the Ash‛arites.

The most significant influence of the Mu‛tazilites was, however, most likely in providing an atmosphere in Sunni Islam more conducive to the reception of the philosophical and scientific heritage of the pre-Islamic days. It is not accidental that their period of ascendancy in Baghdad coincides with the height of activity in the translation of works into Arabic. There are also certain similarities, although there is not in any sense identity, between the Mu‛tazilites and Shi‛ite theologians. The latter in turn were more sympathetic to the

Hermetico-Pythagorean tradition and Greco-Alexandrian philosophy in general than the Sunnis, not for any rationalistic reason but because of the more esoteric character of Shiᶜism, which permitted the integration of certain forms of Greco-Alexandrian science and philosophy into its perspective. In its support of the cause of coming to know and to understand this non-Islamic heritage, however, Shiᶜism was favorable to the climate created by the Muᶜtazilites in Baghdad, although in other fundamental questions, such as the meaning and role of the Imam, the two differ completely.

At the end of the third (ninth) century the dominance of Muᶜtazilite *Kalām* in Sunni circles was challenged by the new theological school of Ashᶜarism founded by Abuᵓl-Ḥasan al-Ashᶜarī and developed by his disciple Abū Bakr al-Bāqillānī. This school, which opposed the rationalistic tendencies of the Muᶜtazilites, sought to reestablish the concrete presence of God by charting a middle course between *"tashbīh"* and *"tanzīh,"* or by giving anthropomorphic qualities to God on the one hand, and abstracting all qualities from Him on the other. It thus depicted a conception of the Divinity much closer to the ethos of Islam and for this reason soon began to replace Muᶜtazilite *Kalām*. Of course a sizable and significant element of the Islamic community was opposed to all forms of *Kalām* as a human intrusion into the Divine order. But to the extent that *Kalām* continued to be pursued in the Sunni world, Ashᶜarism replaced Muᶜtazilism and has continued to be dominant to this day. The school of the Māturīdites, which sought a more intermediate course between the demands of reason and the dicta of revelation, was never able to gain a great deal of popularity although it was able to survive on its own. Shiᶜite theology, however, took the opposite direction from Ashᶜarism and became more and more sympathetic to gnosis (*al-ᶜirfān*) and theosophy (*al-ḥikmah*), while Ashᶜarism became the arch opponent of philosophy (*falsafah*) and all the theosophical and philosophical schools that were based on a systematic and rational—although not rationalistic—approach to knowledge.

The significance of Ashᶜarite *Kalām* in Islamic thought, besides the role it played as the opponent of philosophy and therefore the force that often caused the philosophers to take particular positions and answer particular questions, was its development of the theory of atomism already begun by the Muᶜtazilites. There is an "atomic" element in the Semitic, nomadic mentality that is clearly reflected in the Arabic language. This is the tendency of going from one truth to another by an intuitive jump and not by a continuous process. The Arabic sentence itself reflects this fact; the subject and the predicate are connected, not by a copula as in Indo-European languages, but by an invisible link which must be grasped intuitively. This "atomism" was bound to make itself manifest on the level of thought as well, even though Ashᶜarism was not exclusively Arabic by any means. Some of the greatest Ashᶜarite theologians like al-Juwaynī, al-Ghazzālī and Fakhr al-Dīn al-Rāzī were Persians. But here it became a matter of "style of thinking" that through Islam spread beyond the confines of those who were racially Arabs.

The atomism of *Kalām* divides all sensible reality into atoms or units (technically "parts that cannot be divided," *juzᵓ lā yatajazzāᵓ*) which unlike the atoms of Democritus and Epicurus possess neither length nor dimension. The atoms of *Kalām* are units without length or breadth but which combine to form bodies possessing dimensions. It is a particular form of atomism for which both Indian and Epicurean origins have been posited without any great certainty, but which in any case differs from the classical atomism of Democritus, Epicurus, and Lucretius.

The Ashᶜarites, moreover, divided time, space, and motion into atomic units as well. As a result the continuous nexus between cause and effect is denied by them. If there is no substantial continuity between things, as well as between moments of time and points of space, how can there be causality? The whole cosmic matrix was segmented and atomized. To fill this "gap," the Ashᶜarites appealed to the Divine Will. For them it is the Divine Will which relates two moments of existence together and gives homogeneity to the world about us. Fire appears to "cause" heat. It is however only the mind which, by observing the phenomenon of heat connected with fire thinks that one causes the other. Actually it is God who wills the fire to be hot; He could will that it be cold tomorrow without there being any logical contradiction whatsoever. Miracles are in fact called *khāriq al-ᶜādah*, that which breaks the habit of the mind to connect two phenomena together as cause and effect. One sees here arguments very similar to what Hume was to offer many centuries later in order to destroy the validity of the idea of necessity in causality, without, however, positing the Divine Will as the nexus between two phenomena which the mind conceives as cause and effect. In fact some of the examples of Hume are the same as those of the Ashᶜarites which makes one think that perhaps he had become acquainted with them through the Latin translations from the Hebrew translations of Averroës' *Tahāfut al-Tahāfut* and Maimonides' *Dalālat al-Ḥāᵓirīn*.

Not being bound by Aristotelian physics, the Ashᶜarites were free to develop what one might call a "philosophy of nature" of their own based on this conception of the discontinuity of things. Within this scheme they developed ideas which are of great interest in the history and methodology of science and appear as particularly attractive today when in subparticle physics a similar situation exists and causality in the classical sense is denied. Strangely enough, the Ashʿarite theologians, with a few exceptions like al-Rāzī, were not interested in the sciences of nature at all. Their aim in developing this atomism was to break the hold of reason upon the understanding of reality and open the human mind to the possibilities of understanding the verities of revelation. They were not concerned with the development of the sciences but ironically enough developed theories about time, space, motion, and causality which were fecund in the later development of physics and which appear of particular interest in retrospect.

In Islamic civilization disciplines are clearly defined and, although we can speak of the "philosophy" of *Kalām* in English, when Muslims speak of philosophy (*al-falsafah*) or theosophy (*al-ḥikmah*), they refer to particular schools with well-defined methods and ends and very distinct from *Kalām*. Islamic philosophy, properly speaking, began in the third (ninth) century after the translation of philosophical texts into Arabic and their gradual elaboration and assimilation by Muslim thinkers. Traditional Islamic sources mention Irānshahrī as the first person in Islam to have devoted himself to philosophy. He, like his successors such as al-Fārābī, believed that the original home of philosophy was the East and that in reviving interest in philosophy he had brought philosophy back to its original abode. Besides a few segments cited in later texts no writings of this mysterious figure have survived, and so we have to turn to al-Kindī, the Latin Alkindus, as the first Muslim philosopher who left behind an appreciable corpus, and who must be credited with founding the Peripatetic (*mashshāʾī*) school of Islamic philosophy, almost the only school that became known in the Latin West.

Al-Kindī in contrast to most Muslim philosophers, who were Persians, was an Arab of aristocratic descent. He was born in Basra about 185 (801), studied there and in Baghdad, where he later became famous at the court of the caliphs, and finally died in the same city about 252 (866) after having fallen from grace at court. Having received the best education of his day and having been in the current of the intellectual life of the Abbasid capital at the very moment when the great wave of translation reached its peak, al-Kindī helped more than any other figure to establish the Peripatetic school of Islamic philosophy, a school that is based on Aristotle, as seen primarily through the eye of his Alexandrian Neo-Platonic commentators and interpreted according to the unitary principle of Islam.

This Peripatic school combined Neo-Platonic and Aristotelian teachings, partly because of the unitary vision of philosophy held by Muslim thinkers and also due to the fact that Muslims considered the last parts of the *Enneads* of Plotinus to be the *Theology* of Aristotle, and took the epitome of Proclus' *Elements of Theology* to be the *Kitāb al-ʿilal* which came to be known later in the Latin world as *Liber de causis*, attributed again to the school of Aristotle. There thus developed a Neo-Platonic interpretation of Aristotelian metaphysics centered around the doctrine of the One and the emanation of the intellects and grades of being from it, a new synthesis which is not found with the same accent and color in any school of Greek philosophy. This is especially true because the Muslims emphasized being and the distinction between the Necessary Being, or God, and the possible being which comprises all things in the universe, and they stressed the contingent nature of these things.

Strangely enough in the development of this elaborate metaphysical and philosophical system al-Kindī held certain views which are particularly his own and which were not followed by the later Peripatetics. He believed in creation *ex nihilo*, more in line with Muslim theologians than philosophers, and had a conception of the classification of the sciences more akin to certain Latin scholastics than to his fellow Muslim Peripatetics. He was also profoundly impregnated with Neo-Pythagoreanism, more than were later Peripatetics, although in Islam, in contrast to the Latin West, the Aristotelian and Pythagorean-Platonic traditions did not remain completely distinct; the most famous Peripatetic philosophers were also master musicians and some were outstanding mathematicians.

In many other domains, however, al-Kindī opened avenues of thought that were followed by later Muslim thinkers. Like them, he was as much interested in the sciences as in philosophy and is therefore like the other Muslim Peripatetics a philosopher-scientist rather than just a philosopher. Also like later thinkers he was intensely interested in the harmony between philosophy and religion, although the path he trod was not pursued by his successors. He also set the tone for philosophical and scientific inquiry and is credited with a statement that characterizes the method and spirit of nearly all the members of this school: "We should not be ashamed to acknowledge truth and to assimilate it from whatever source it comes to us, even if it is brought to us by former generations and foreign peoples. For him who seeks the truth there is nothing of higher value than truth itself; it never cheapens or abases him who reaches for it, but ennobles and honours him" (Walzer [1962], p. 12).

Al-Kindī left behind an enormous corpus of nearly 270 works on practically every domain of knowledge from logic and philosophy to metallurgy, pharmacology, and the occult sciences. Most of this vast corpus has been lost, while a few of the basic works, such as *On First Philosophy* and *On the Intellect*, survive in Arabic, and a few also survive in Latin and Hebrew. Yet, al-Kindī was extremely celebrated among Muslims as well as among the Latins. His fourfold division of the intellect, based upon the commentary of Alexander of Aphrodisias (fl. A.D. 200) on Aristotle's *De anima* and contained in al-Kindī's treatise on the intellect, was not only very influential in Islamic philosophy but through the translation of this treatise into Latin as *De intellectu* came to be well known in the West. Al-Kindī was regarded throughout the Occidental Middle Ages as one of the universal authorities of astrology, and during the Renaissance Cardanus considered him to be one of the twelve most important intellectual figures of human history (Nasr, 1964a).

The new intellectual perspective of Muslim Peripatetic philosophy begun by al-Kindī was established on a firm basis by al-Fārābī (the Latin Alfarabius), whom some consider more than al-Kindī to be the real founder of Islamic philosophy. By now the center of Islamic civilization, especially its intellectual aspect, was shifting to a certain extent to Khorasan where the new Persian language and culture were also being born; and it is in this region that al-Fārābī was born about 257 (870) and where he received his earliest education. Later he came to Baghdad both to learn and teach, and finally he migrated to Aleppo where he died in 339 (950). Al-Fārābī is entitled the "Second Teacher," after Aristotle, on whom Muslims bestowed the title of the "First Teacher," to be followed in this tradition by Saint Thomas Aquinas and Dante. In this context "teacher" means more than anything else the function of clarifying the limits and boundaries of the domains of knowledge and classifying and ordering the sciences, a task that Aristotle achieved in the context of Greek civilization and al-Fārābī performed for Islam. Al-Fārābī is the author of the first influential work on the classification of the sciences, which was twice translated into Latin as *De scientiis* and played a share in determining the curricula of a "liberal arts" education in both East and West during the Middle Ages.

Al-Fārābī was also a "second Aristotle" in the sense that he commented upon the works of the Stagirite, especially the *Metaphysics* and the *Organon*, making the meaning of these works fully available to Muslim circles. Moreover he wrote himself many works on logic and must be considered as the father of this science among Muslims. Much of the exact philo-sophical and logical terminology in Arabic is due to this genius who was the master of many tongues.

Al-Fārābī must also be considered as the founder of political philosophy in Islam. In this domain he relied upon the political ideas of Plato's *Laws* and *Republic* rather than Aristotle's *Politics*, although his discussion of the virtues is akin to Aristotle's ethics. Al-Fārābī sought to harmonize the Platonic conception of the philosopher-king and divine law (*nomos*) with the Islamic idea of the prophet-ruler and divine law or *Sharīʿah*. His attempt was significant enough to have left a mark upon nearly all later speculations in this domain as we see for example in the writings of Averroës (Ibn Rushd, 1126–98) who also commented upon Plato's *Republic*. Al-Fārābī's major political work, *Treatise on the Opinions of the Citizens of the Ideal State*, remains the most popular and influential work of its kind in the history of Islamic philosophy.

In his more general and popular works al-Fārābī set out to harmonize the different philosophical schools, especially those of Plato and Aristotle, with each other and with the tenets of the Islamic religion. His *Harmonization of the Opinions of Plato and Aristotle*, in which through a Neo-Platonic interpretation of both Plato and Aristotle he sought to demonstrate the unity of their points of view, set the tone for the general vision of later Muslim philosophers who saw different schools of philosophy, not as contending and opposing philosophies, but as different expositions and aspects of the same perennial wisdom which Steuchius and Leibniz were later to identify as the *philosophia perennis*. But in his more scientific and less popular works such as *Philosophy of Plato* and *Philosophy of Aristotle* he discusses both philosophers directly and without reference to their Neo-Platonic interpretation, and seems to be fully aware of the differences in their points of view within the general harmony discussed in his better known works.

With al-Fārābī the metaphysical and philosophical doctrines characteristic of the Muslim Peripatetics and based on the "philosophy of being," the triadic emanation of the many from the One, and an elaborate cosmology and psychology based on the multiple states of being, issuing from the One and returning to It, are already found in their characteristic Muslim formulation. It remained for the great genius of Avicenna to give them their most complete elaboration and elucidation in a systematic whole.

Between al-Fārābī and Avicenna (Ibn Sīnā, 980–1037, whose medical treatise was the standard text for about 400 years, 1100–1500) there were many intellectual figures of note both in Baghdad and Khorasan. Al-Sijistānī continued the philosophical tradition in Baghdad which now became mostly devoted to logic, and al-ʿĀmirī made Khorasan the new home of Islamic philosophy by living and teaching there all his life. The latter is also of interest in that he sought to integrate the political and administrative thought of Sassanid Persia with Islam to form a political philosophy rather than turning only to Greek sources, and wrote perhaps the most passionate defense of Islam written by a Peripatetic philosopher.

Ibn Sīnā, or Avicenna as he is known in the West, crowned over two centuries of philosophical thought with an expression of Peripatetic philosophy which was so profound as to leave its effect upon all later Islamic thought. Wherever and whenever the arts and sciences have been cultivated in Islam, his spirit has hovered over them as their "guardian angel." More than that he may in many ways be considered as the founder of scholastic philosophy in its systematic formulation.

Avicenna was born near Bukhara in 370 (980) in a family devoted to learning. By the age of ten he had mastered the religious sciences, by sixteen was a well-known physician, and by eighteen had overcome all the difficulties in understanding the *Metaphysics* of Aristotle, thanks to the commentary of al-Fārābī. His precocity is proverbial in the East even today. From the age of twenty-one until his death in 428 (1037) he wandered from one court in Persia to another as physician and even vizier, spending most of this period in Ispahan and Hamadan where he finally died. During this turbulent life his intellectual activity continued unabated. Sometimes he even wrote on horseback while going to a battle. The result was over 220 works which include the *Book of Healing*, the largest encyclopedia of knowledge ever written by one man, and the *Canon of Medicine*, which became the best known medical work in East and West and gained him the title of "Prince of Physicians."

The universal genius of Avicenna, the greatest of the philosopher-scientists in Islam, hardly left any field untouched. In metaphysics he established the ontology which characterizes medieval philosophy and left a profound mark upon Saint Thomas and especially Duns Scotus. The distinction between necessary and possible being, and between existence and essence or quiddity, the identity of the act of intellection with existence in the generation of the heavenly intelligences, and the emphasis upon the role of the tenth intellect as the illuminator of the human intellect in the act of knowledge, are outstanding features of this most perfect formulation of Muslim Peripatetic philosophy elaborated by Avicenna.

Of no less significance is his study of natural philosophy. There, although continuing the Aristotelian tradition of hylomorphism, he continued the criticism begun by John Philoponus (fl. fifth century A.D.) against

Aristotle's theory of projectile motion and developed the impetus theory and the concept which later became known in the West as *inclinatio*, the father of the fundamental concept of momentum in modern physics. His geological studies contain many original features and, in fact, under the name of *De mineralibus*, the section of the *Book of Healing* on geology and mineralogy had come to be known in the West for centuries as a work of Aristotle. It is, in fact, only in the section on natural philosophy in the *Book of Healing* that the study of all the three kingdoms, carried out so brilliantly in the case of animals and plants by Aristotle and Theophrastus, was brought together for the first time. The *Canon* also contains both important medical theories and new observations on medical cases as well as studies of the pharmaceutical properties of plants.

In addition to these and many other philosophical and scientific contributions, Avicenna, toward the end of his life, wrote a series of works intended for the "elite" in which he sought to expound what he called the "Oriental Philosophy." Although some of this corpus is lost, enough survives to enable us to reconstruct the contours of this philosophy, or rather theosophy (*al-ḥikmah*), which he contrasted with the Peripatetic philosophy meant for the multitude. In this "Oriental Philosophy" the role of intellectual intuition and illumination (*ishrāq*) becomes paramount, and philosophy turns from the attempt to describe a rational system to explaining the structure of reality with the aim of providing a plan of the cosmos so that with its help man can escape from this world which is regarded as a cosmic crypt. Henceforth, in the East the primary role of philosophy became to provide the possibility of a vision of the spiritual universe. Philosophy thus became closely wedded to gnosis as we see in the Illuminationist theosophy of Suhrawardī more than a century after Avicenna.

Curiously enough this aspect of Avicenna's works did not become known in the West, and this fact is most of all the cause of the great difference existing between Islamic and Latin Avicennism. In the East Avicenna provided the first step in the journey towards illumination; even his Peripatetic philosophy became integrated by later philosophers and theosophists into a greater whole, in which the development of the rational and logical faculties itself becomes a preparation for illumination. In the West his philosophy became influential at Oxford and Paris from the twelfth century A.D. and influenced many figures like Roger Bacon, who preferred him to Averroës, or Saint Thomas, whose third argument for the proof of the existence of God is based on Avicennan sources, or Duns Scotus, who used Avicenna as the "point of departure" for the theological system that challenged Thomism in the fourteenth century. Altogether, however, in the West the influence of Avicenna was not as great as that of Averroës and it is not possible to speak with full justice of a definite "Latin Avicennism" as one speaks of "Latin Averroism." But there is, to use the term of Gilson (Gilson, 1929), definitely an "Avicennizing Augustinism" one of whose best known exponents being William of Auvergne. But the latter was especially insistent on emptying the Avicennan cosmos of the angels who play such an important role in Avicenna's ontology, cosmology, and theory of knowledge. In doing so he helped to secularize the cosmos, which was still sacred in Avicennan philosophy, and indirectly prepared the background for the Copernican revolution, which could only occur in a secularized cosmos. The difference in the interpretation of Avicenna in East and West is one of the factors that indicate the parting of ways between Islamic and Christian civilizations after the Middle Ages following centuries during which they had pursued a parallel course.

Besides the predominant Muslim Peripatetic school which reaches its culmination with Avicenna there were other philosophical and religious schools that must be considered. From the second (eighth) century Neo-Pythagorean and Hermetic philosophy were cultivated in certain circles, sometimes combined together. Followers of these schools differed from the Peripatetics in their apophatic theology, interest in immediate rather than distant causes in natural philosophy, attraction toward Stoic rather than Aristotlelian logic with its emphasis on the disjunctive syllogism, interest in Hippocratic rather than Galenic medicine, and of course their special devotion to mathematical symbolism and the occult sciences. As far as the mathematical Neo-Pythagorean philosophy is concerned, its best known exposition is found in the *Epistles* of the Brethren of Purity, a collection of fifty-two treatises which exercised a widespread influence throughout the Islamic world. Being from a general Shiᶜite background, these treatises were later adopted by the Ismāᶜīlīs, who came to develop a philosophy of their own, distinct from the Peripatetics, a philosophy which reached its peak with Nāṣir-e Khusraw who, in contrast to the early Peripatetics nearly all of whom wrote in Arabic, composed his philosophical works in Persian.

As for Hermeticism, it was naturally associated with alchemy. The first well-known Muslim alchemist, Jābir ibn Ḥayyān, wrote many treatises on Hermetic philosophy and was opposed to Aristotelian natural philosophy. Interestingly enough, his corpus, too, was adopted by the Ismāᶜīlīs who, in fact, added to it works of their own authorship but attributed to Jābir. Other famous

alchemical texts, such as the *Emerald Table* and the *Turba philosophorum*, also belong to the same Islamic Hermetical and alchemical tradition based on earlier Alexandrian, Byzantine, and Syriac sources. And the *Picatrix*, so well known in the West, is a translation of the *Aim of the Wise* of al-Majrīṭī, the Andalusian scientist and alchemist of the fourth (tenth) century, or his school. All of these texts contain an exposition of a Hermetical philosophy which was a rival to the better known Peripatetic school. In the West also the translation of these and other texts brought into being Latin alchemy and Hermeticism which throughout the Middle Ages and the Renaissance, from Lull to Paracelsus and Fludd, provided a strong rival for Aristotelianism. Of course, occasionally there was parallelism rather than opposition; Peripatetic and Hermetico-occult sciences were combined together. In fact, the first introduction of Aristotle's natural philosophy into the West came through the astrological work of Abū Maᶜshar, the Latin Albumazar, which in the translation of John of Seville was known as *Liber introductorius maior*. The earlier interest of the Latins in Islamic science had caused Adelard of Bath (fl. twelfth century) to translate a shorter work of Abū Maᶜshar into Latin which prepared the ground for the wide reception of the larger astrological work through which Aristotelian physics reached the West twenty years before any of his specific works on natural philosophy became known in Latin.

The tradition of "anti-Aristotelian" philosophy, particularly in physics, is to be found among other Muslim philosophers and scientists of the period. Among the earliest of these is Muḥammad ibn Zakariyā⁾ al-Rāzī, so well known in the West as Rhazes, who was born about 251 (865) and died in 313 (925). Al-Rāzī, who was an alchemist, physician, musician, and philosopher, was much more respected by Muslim and also Jewish philosophers for his medicine, in whose clinical aspect he was the foremost medieval authority, than for his philosophy. But his philosophical ideas, although not of great importance in the later tradition of Islamic philosophy, have recently attracted much interest because of the often unique views of al-Rāzī.

Al-Rāzī was not a follower; he considered himself as a master on equal footing with Plato and Aristotle. For this reason also he felt free to criticize them. In certain fields, especially ethics and cosmology, there are elements of pure Platonism untouched by Neo-Platonic influences evident in him. In cosmology he posited five eternal principles which present similarities to the *Timaeus* but reveal even more relations with Manichean cosmogony and cosmology. But in any case al-Rāzī was opposed to Aristotelian physics and often criticized the Stagirite on his views in natural philosophy. He had a particular love for Galen and a remarkable acquaintance with his works. He wrote specifically of his preference for Galen over Aristotle. He also opposed the general view of Muslim philosophers on the necessity of prophecy, whose existence he did not deny but whose necessity he did not accept. This was in fact the main reason why he did not have any appreciable influence upon later Islamic philosophy, which is essentially "prophetic philosophy."

Another great scientist, al-Bīrūnī, who lived 362 (973)–ca. 442 (1051), an admirer of al-Rāzī but opposed to his "anti-prophetic" philosophy, likewise wrote against Aristotelian natural philosophy. Al-Bīrūnī, whom some consider as the most outstanding Muslim scientist, was more of a mathematician, historian, and geographer than a philosopher in the usual sense, and it is through his scientific works that his philosophical views must be sought. This remarkable thinker combined the mind of a mathematician and a historian. He was the author of the first scientific work on comparative religion, the incomparable *India*, as well as the real founder of geodesy, and the author of one of the most elaborate astronomical treatises in the history of this science. It is in these works, and especially in a series of questions and answers exchanged with Avicenna, that al-Bīrūnī reveals his acute sense of observation and analysis which made him opposed to certain tenets of Aristotelian physics such as the concept of "natural place." He, in fact, wrote openly on many subjects which were against the prevalent natural philosophy, such as the possibility of elliptical motion of the planets and the movement of the earth around the sun, and remarked justly that the helio- or geocentric question was one to be solved by physics and theology and not by astronomy alone, in which parametrics could be measured the same way whether the sun or the earth was placed at the center.

Ibn al-Haytham, in Latin Alhazen, who lived ca. 354 (965)–430 (1039), was a contemporary of al-Bīrūnī, and was likewise a critic of Peripatetic philosophy in many ways. The author of the best medieval work on optics, which influenced Witelo and Kepler, Alhazen was also a remarkable experimental physicist and astronomer. He must be credited with the discovery of the principle of inertia in physics and with placing the science of optics on a new foundation. His mathematical study of the *camera obscura*, the correct explanation of the course of light in vision—as opposed to the Aristotelian view—the explanation of reflection from spherical and parabolic mirrors, study of spherical aberration, belief in the "principle of least time" in refraction, and application long before Newton of the parallelogram for resolving a velocity into its components are among his outstanding scientific accomplishments.

But even more important in the long run for the philosophy of science was Alhazen's insistence upon the crystalline nature of the spheres. In Greek science, while the Aristotelians insisted that the aim of science was to know the nature of things, the Platonic mathematicians and astronomers generally believed that their aim was to "save the phenomena." The Ptolemaic spheres were convenient mathematical inventions that aided calculation and had no physical reality. Perhaps the most important heritage that Islamic science bestowed upon the West was the insistence that the role of all science including the mathematical must be the search for knowledge of the reality and being of things. The emphasis upon the crystalline nature of the spheres by Alhazen was precisely a statement of this belief. Physics in Muslim eyes was inseparable from ontology. This quest for the real in mathematical physics and astronomy was so thoroughly adopted in the West that even during the scientific revolution no one doubted that the role of physics was to discover the nature of things. Newton was actually following a philosophy of physics that Alhazen and other Muslim thinkers had bestowed upon all sciences of nature, not only the Aristotelian but also the mathematical and geometric sciences of Euclid, Ptolemy, and their successors. The modern debate concerning the nature of modern science and whether it deals with an aspect of reality or simply with models convenient for mathematical calculation, debates which have been carried out among such men as E. Meyerson, Cassirer, and Northrop and the positivists and the analysts reveals in retrospect the significance of the realism imparted to mathematical physics by Alhazen and certain other Muslim thinkers.

During the fifth (eleventh) century, altered political and social conditions, brought about by the reunification of much of the Islamic world by the Seljuqs (or Seljuks), favored Ashʿarite theology over philosophy and the "intellectual sciences." The new university system which had come into being, and, in fact, which served as a model for the earliest medieval universities in the West, now began to emphasize the teaching of theology or *Kalām* in some places almost exclusively, and attacks began to be made by outstanding theologians against the philosophers of the Peripatetic school. In fact so many debates were held between the theologians and the philosophers that methods and arguments of *Kalām* entered into the domain of philosophy itself. Even in Latin philosophical texts reference is often made to the *loquentes* ("spokesmen") of the three revealed religions, *loquentes* being derived from its root in a manner parallel to the derivation of *mutakallim* (that is, scholar of *Kalām*) and having the same meaning.

647

Of the theologians who were most influential in determining the future intellectual life of Islam, al-Ghazzālī and Fakhr al-Dīn al-Rāzī are particularly significant. Many modern scholars have considered al-Ghazzālī as the most influential figure in Islamic intellectual history. He is certainly one of the most important. Coming at a decisive moment in the history of Islam he imparted a direction to it which has persisted ever since, especially in the Sunni world. Al-Ghazzālī was both a Sufi (a Muslim mystic) and a theologian, and he criticized rationalistic philosophy in both capacities. On the one hand he sought to curtail the power of reason and make it subservient to revelation; on the other hand he tried to revive the ethics of Islamic society by breathing into it the spirit of Sufism and by making Sufism official in the religious schools and universities. He was eminently successful on both accounts.

Al-Ghazzālī was not in any way opposed to logic or the use of reason and in fact composed treatises on logic. But what he did oppose was the claim of reason to comprehend the whole truth and to impose its partial views even in domains where it had no authority to assert itself. Therefore, while making use of reason he sought to criticize the rationalistic tendencies in Peripatetic philosophy. To this end he first summarized the views of the Peripatetics, especially Avicenna who was the foremost among them, in a work called *The Purpose of the Philosophers* (*al-Maqāṣid*), which was translated into Latin and through which Latin scholastics came to consider the author (whom they called Algazel) as a Peripatetic. Then he set out to criticize these views in his *Incoherence of the Philosophers*, a work which broke the back of rationalistic philosophy and, in fact, brought the career of philosophy, as a discipline distinct from gnosis and theology, to an end in the Arabic part of the Islamic world. The response of Averroës to al-Ghazzālī was like an Indian summer for this early Peripatetic school and did not exercise any appreciable influence upon the later course of Islamic philosophy and thought. Al-Ghazzālī also composed numerous works on Sufism of which the monumental *Iḥyāʾ ʿulūm al-din* (*Revivification of the Sciences of Religion*) is the most notable and remains to this day the outstanding work on Sufi ethics.

The second theologian, Fakhr al-Dīn al-Rāzī, who like al-Ghazzālī hailed from Persia, continued the attacks of al-Ghazzālī by selecting a single work, *al-Ishārāt waʾ l-tanbīhāt* (*Book of Directives and Remarks*) of Avicenna, and criticizing it thoroughly. This most learned of theologians applied his immense learning to criticizing and demolishing the philosophical synthesis of Avicenna of which the *Book of Directives and Remarks* is perhaps the most concise testament. But by now the *Kalām*, applied to criticizing the philosophers, had itself become philosophical and was far removed from the simple assertions of al-Ashʿarī. In fact, with al-Rāzī and later theologians like him a philosophical *Kalām* developed which along with Sufism mostly replaced philosophy in the Sunni world and especially in the Arab world, and was also of much influence among Muslims of India.

Meanwhile during the fifth (eleventh) and sixth (twelfth) centuries a great deal of intellectual activity took place in the Islamic West, that is, in Andalusia, Morocco, and the surrounding regions, a fact of particular significance for the history of European philosophy, and in the domain of Sufism for the whole later intellectual history of Islam. Both Ashʿarite theology and Peripatetic philosophy reached the Islamic West much later than their birth in the East. In fact we do not encounter any eminent representatives of either school in Andalusia until the sixth (twelfth) century. The first outstanding theologian and philosopher of Andalusia was Ibn Ḥazm, who lived 383 (993)–456 (1064), and who developed an independent school of theology, which he combined with law and the philosophy of language. This synthesis reflected all of the manifested and externalized aspects of the divine revelation combined into a unity. Ibn Ḥazm also composed the first systematic work on religious sects and heresiography, for which he has been called the first "historian of religious ideas." He is also the author of the famous *Dove's Neck-ring* which is a beautiful expression of the Platonic philosophy of love in its Islamic form.

In the sixth (twelfth) century a religious reformer, Ibn Tūmart, who was deeply influenced by al-Ghazzālī, began a movement which resulted in the establishment of the Almohads, and the flowering of philosophy in the Islamic West. Before this period there had occasionally been Sufis who had taught cosmological and metaphysical doctrines, such as Ibn Masarrah who developed a particular form of cosmology based on "pseudo-Empedoclean" fragments, a cosmology in which bodies themselves possess different degrees of existence. This cosmology was to have an influence upon the Jewish philosopher Ibn Gabirol (Latin name, Avicebron; A.D. 1021–58), who in his *Fons vitae* ("Fountain of Life") employs a similar scheme, and also upon the master of Islamic esotericism, Ibn ʿArabī.

But the regular cultivation of philosophy began with Ibn Bājjah after the Almohad conquest. Ibn Bājjah, who was well-known to the Latins as Avempace (d. A.D. 1138) is best known for his *Tadbīr al-mutawaḥḥid* (*Regime of the Solitary* or *Hermit's Rule*), a philosophical protest against worldliness which terminates with the philosopher's reaching illumination in solitude. In contrast to al-Fārābī and also Averroës, Avempace did not develop a political philosophy devoted to the creation of the ideal state, but found the role of philosophy to consist in its helping the individual to reach inner illumination. Avempace also wrote a commentary on Aristotle's *Physics* in which he continued the criticism of John Philoponus and Avicenna against the Aristotelian theory of projectile motion, but in another vein; also he proposed what can be interpreted as the first new medieval development of quantitative relations to describe this type of motion. He therefore represents, as E. A. Moody has shown (Moody, 1951), an important development in medieval dynamics and influenced late medieval physics, which was developed by such men as Bradwardine, Oresme, and Nicolas of Autrecourt. The *Pisan Dialogue* (1632) of Galileo contains the "impetus theory" coming from Avicenna through the Latin critics of Aristotle and a dynamics which has appropriately been called by modern historians of science "Avempacean."

Ibn Ṭufayl, Avempace's successor, was both a philosopher and physician, like many a Muslim philosopher before and after, and also like some of the Jewish philosophers such as Maimonides, who were so close to Muslims during this period. His *Alive Son of the Awake*, which served as a model for the *Robinson Crusoe* story and was the inspiration for some of the early Quakers as well as the source of Leibniz' *philosophus autodidactus*, is a philosophical romance whose end is mystical illumination and ecstasy. Although the title of this work is the same as that of Avicenna's, and although Ibn Ṭufayl follows the tradition established by Avicenna to write philosophical narratives in which philosophical situations are depicted in a symbolic language, the two works are not identical. Avicenna in his philosophical narratives, or "recitals" as Corbin calls them (Corbin, 1964a), was preparing the ground for his "Oriental Philosophy" where the Angel acts as the instrument of illumination; Ibn Ṭufayl was seeking to demonstrate that revealed religion and philosophy ultimately reach the same truth, if the philosopher withdraws from society to meditate by himself. Ibn Ṭufayl's emphasis upon the "inner light" shares this important element with the Avicennan cycle of narratives in that it shows the ultimate goal of true philosophy to be a knowledge that illuminates; but there is an element of "utopianism" in Ibn Ṭufayl and a tendency, within the limits of medieval Muslim philosophy, to seek to reach the divine outside the structure of revealed religion.

The last and most celebrated of the Andalusian philosophers, Ibn Rushd or Averroës, was more influential in the West than in Islam. He was born in Cordova in 520 (1126) to a distinguished family of

jurists, and received the best education possible in law, theology, philosophy, and medicine. He served as chief judge of religious courts in Seville and Cordova and court physician in Marrakesh. At the end of his life because of a change in the political climate of Andalusia he fell from grace and died a lonely figure in Marrakesh in 595 (1198).

While the earlier Muslim Peripatetics developed elaborate philosophical systems for which they are known, Averroës devoted himself most of all to commenting on the works of Aristotle. Without including small treatises on Aristotelian themes and doubtful commentaries, there are thirty-eight commentaries by Averroës on the works of Aristotle, five of which were written in three forms: long, middle, and short. In fact Averroës became known in the West as *the* commentator of Aristotle par excellence. It is by this title that Saint Thomas Aquinas refers to him, and Dante mentions him as the person who wrote the great commentary (*il gran commento*). Through his eyes the West came to know Aristotle, and the figure of Averroës was never separated from that of the Stagirite throughout the Middle Ages. Averroës also wrote certain independent philosophical works such as the *Incoherence of the Incoherence*, an answer to al-Ghazzālī's *Incoherence of the Philosophers*, and *The Harmony between Philosophy and Religion*, in which, like other Muslim philosophers but in his own way, he sought to harmonize reason and revelation by giving each its due as an independent way of reaching the truth, but not according to the "double truth" theory which is a misconception of his teachings by Latin Averroists. He also wrote on political philosophy, following upon the path of al-Fārābī, and on Plato's *Republic*.

Averroës became known to the West in two different periods. He was "twice revealed" to quote the statement of H. A. Wolfson (Wolfson, 1961). He was once translated in the twelfth century and then again during the Renaissance. The movement, begun early in the twelfth century in Toledo to translate Arabic works into Latin under the direction of the Bishop of Toledo, had incited such interest that less than twenty years after the death of Averroës his works began to be translated by such men as Hermann the German and Michael Scot, and the translations became rapidly disseminated. As the result of a misunderstanding of the Islamic background of his philosophy, Averroës became rapidly identified as a kind of anti-religious freethinker, and such works as *Errores philosophorum* of Giles of Rome devoted special sections to the refutation of his ideas. Actually the Muslim Ibn Rushd and Averroës as seen by the Latin Averroists, like Siger of Brabant (thirteenth century) or the Schoolmen, in general are very different. The Muslim Ibn Rushd, 649 while an avid disciple of Aristotle, was also a firm believer in revealed religion and its necessity. The Latin Averroës became identified with "secular learning" and around his name rallied many forces which were opposed to the official theology of Christianity but which nevertheless were instrumental in the flowering of the arts and sciences during the thirteenth century. Strangely enough Averroës was not only "twice revealed" but also twice misunderstood, for also during the Renaissance many Hellenists and humanists attacked him for not having understood Aristotle properly, although a few continued to gaze upon him as the surest guide to the understanding of Aristotle.

After Averroës, philosophy in the Islamic West and the Arab world was ended, except for one or two instances. Shortly after Averroës, Ibn Sab'īn developed a philosophy that is much more akin to the gnosis and illumination that was now dominating the intellectual life of Eastern Islam; and Ibn Khaldūn in the eighth (fourteenth) century in his *Prolegomena* developed the first thorough attempt at a philosophy of history, which has had a great influence in the West during the past century and which must be considered as the predecessor of the type of study of history and civilization developed by Vico, Spengler, and Toynbee.

The new direction which Islamic intellectual life took was determined most of all by the School of Illumination (*ishrāq*) of Suhrawardī and the intellectual and doctrinal Sufism of gnosis (*'irfān*) of Ibn 'Arabī. Moreover these currents established themselves upon the basis of a newly interpreted Avicennism rather than the "anti-Avicennan" Peripatetic philosophy developed in the Islamic West. Suhrawardī, a Persian who was born in Suhraward in 549 (1153), studied primarily in Ispahan and after travelling throughout the eastern lands of Islam, settled in Aleppo where he was killed in 587 (1191). He was able to establish during this short lifetime a new intellectual perspective which continues to this day in the Islamic world. This new school, which is called the School of Illumination, is based on both ratiocination and mystical illumination, on the intellectual training attained through formal schooling and on spiritual purification made possible through the practice of Sufism. The masterpiece of Suhrawardī, the *Theosophy of the Orient of Light*, as translated by Corbin (Corbin, 1964b), begins with a criticism of Aristotelian logic and terminates with the question of spiritual ecstasy.

Suhrawardī sought to bring together what he believed were the two authentic traditions of philosophy and wisdom in the bosom of Islamic gnosis: the tradition of Greek philosophy going back to Pythagoras and the tradition of wisdom of the ancient Persian sages. He thus had a consciousness of the presence of a universal tradition, and is perhaps the first to have employed the term "perennial philosophy." For him this integral tradition of wisdom implied the synthesis of the ways of ratiocination and intuition, and strangely enough he considered Aristotle the last of the Greek philosophers, with whom this integral philosophy, or rather theosophy in the original Greek sense of *theosophia* ("divine wisdom"), became reduced to merely discursive knowledge. Another of the biggest sign posts which indicates a parting of the ways between Islamic and Western philosophy is the fact that in the West philosophy essentially begins with Aristotle whereas for Suhrawardī and his considerable intellectual posterity it ends with him.

Suhrawardī was studied avidly in the East and his writings were translated into languages as diverse as Hebrew and Sanskrit. Through his teachings Islamic philosophy spread into India for the first time. But he was not translated into Latin and therefore was not known directly in the West. Certain Latin authors like Roger Bacon, however, seem to have come to know about his ideas indirectly, and mention themes and motifs which can be easily traced back to Suhrawardī.

A generation later than Suhrawardī, Ibn 'Arabī performed a pilgrimage in the other direction coming from Andalusia to settle in Damascus. This giant of Islamic gnosis and the authority par execellence on Islamic esoteric doctrine was born in Murcia in 560 (1165) and after spending his youth in Andalusia set out for the East as the result of a vision of the Prophet of Islam. After spending some time in Egypt and encountering difficulty from certain esoteric religious scholars, he went to Mecca to write, in this holiest of Islamic cities, the *al-Futūḥāt al-makkiyyah* ("Meccan Revelations") which is a *summa* of esoteric knowledge in Islam. Later he settled in Damascus, there to write his most celebrated work, the *Fuṣūṣ al-ḥikam* ("Bezels of Wisdom") and to die in 638 (1240). Not the least remarkable aspect of his life, which was so intertwined with visions and wonders, is the enormous corpus of several hundred works he has left behind, works which transformed the intellectual life of the Islamic world from Morocco to Indonesia.

Sufism, which is the esoteric aspect of the Islamic revelation and is completely rooted in the Koran and prophetic traditions, had not for the most part explicitly formulated its doctrinal teachings before Ibn 'Arabī. The earliest Sufis had presented the pearls of gnosis through the silence of their spiritual presence or through allusion. Rarely had they spoken openly of all aspects of Sufism even when occasionally someone like al-Ghazzālī or 'Ain al-Quḍāt Hamadānī had written on some particular aspect of Sufi doctrine. Suhrawardī also belonged to the Sufi tradition but his task was the establishment of a kind of "isthmus" between discursive philosophy and thought, and pure gnosis. It was therefore left to Ibn ʿArabī and his disciples to formulate explicitly the teachings of Sufism in vast doctrinal treatises dealing with metaphysics, cosmology, psychology, and anthropology, and of course with the spiritual significance and symbolism of various traditional sciences. These works were henceforth studied in various official centers of Muslim learning in addition to the special centers where Sufi teachings were imparted.

Ibn ʿArabī was not directly translated into Latin, but he and the Sufis in general exercised some influence through the esoteric contact that came to be made between Islam and Christianity by way of the Order of the Templars and the *fideli d'amore*. Some of the ideas of Ibn ʿArabī, such as the correspondence between the heavens and the inner state of being and certain cosmological symbols, are particularly discernible in Dante and also in Raymond Lull. The "gnostics" among Christian mystics such as Master Eckhart, Angelus Silesius, and Dante himself in fact reveal certain similarities to Ibn ʿArabī and his school, often due more to a similarity in spiritual types than to historical influences, which in this order must of necessity remain at the level of providing a means of expression or a particular language of symbolism, rather than the vision itself from which flows the truths expressed by these mystics. In the same way Sufism itself did not make any more use of Neo-Platonism or Hermeticism than finding therein an appropriate means of expression for its own verities coming from Islamic teachings that make the Sufi vision possible.

After the seventh (thirteenth) century intellectual contact between Islam and Christianity came nearly completely to an end, only revived in the twentieth century. Spain, which had been the main point of contact, ceased to play this role after its reconquest by the Christians, mostly because the Jews, who had acted as an intermediary, were dispersed or found themselves in a different cultural climate, and because the Christian mozarabs, that is, those who had adopted Arab ways, also disappeared. It is of interest to note that the Jews, who had written their theology and philosophy in Arabic until the twelfth century, began to write in Hebrew only after the destruction of Muslim power in Spain. The contacts made possible in Sicily and in the Holy Land also came to an end about the same time due to the Crusades, and two sister civilizations which had followed a similar and parallel course for centuries each began to follow its own way.

But contrary to what most Western sources have written, the intellectual life of Islam did not by any means come to an end merely because of the termination of this contact. In the seventh (thirteenth) century the philosophy of Avicenna was revived by Khwājah Naṣīr al-Dīn al-Ṭūsī, an intellectual figure of the first

magnitude who also revived the study of mathematics and astronomy. In fact it was he and his student Quṭb al-Dīn al-Shīrāzī who proposed the first new medieval model for planetary motion, as shown by the recent research of E. S. Kennedy and his collaborators, which was later employed by Copernicus and which Copernicus most likely learned through Byzantine Greek sources. It was also al-Ṭūsī who established the first astronomical observatory as a scientific institution in the modern sense, which through the observatories of Samarkand and Istanbul became the model for the earliest modern European observatories such as those of Tycho Brahe and Kepler.

Al-Ṭūsī answered the charges brought against Avicenna by al-Rāzī and other theologians, and revived his teachings and trained many outstanding philosophers himself. Henceforth Persia, which had provided most of the Islamic philosophers up to that time, became almost the exclusive home of philosophy. Gradually the teachings of Avicenna, Suhrawardī, and Ibn ʿArabī as well as the theologians became synthesized in vast metaphysical systems which reach their peak during the eleventh (seventeenth) century with Mīr Dāmād and Ṣadr al-Dīn Shīrāzī. These metaphysicians, who are the contemporaries of Descartes and Leibniz, developed a metaphysics which was no less logical and demonstrative than those of their European contemporaries and yet which included a dimension of gnosis and intuition which the European philosophy of the period lacked completely. Quite justly Corbin has called Ṣadr al-Dīn Shīrāzī, whom many Persians consider as the greatest Islamic philosopher, a combination of a Saint Thomas and a Jacob Böhme, which the context of Islam in its Persian manifestation alone could make possible (Corbin, 1964b). Moreover, these dominant intellectual figures of the Safavid period (A.D. 1502–1722) established a new school of philosophy which has survived to this day in Persia itself as well as in the Indo-Pakistan subcontinent and other surrounding regions where the influence of Persian culture has been felt.

As for its significance for the West, this philosophical tradition presents a most interesting parallel, in fact the only one that exists with which Western philosophy itself can be compared. Based in their discursive aspect upon the same Greek sources and inspired by two religions that are akin in many ways, Islamic and Western philosophy finally developed in two completely different directions. When one studies the *existenz* philosophy of the German existentialists or the nihilism of some of the French existentialists, one should also study the philosophy of Being of a man like Ṣadr al-Dīn Shīrāzī, who draw the mind to intellectual horizons very different from what has become familiar in contemporary Western philosophy.

In the same way then that Islamic intellectual life was influential for centuries in the West to the extent that the ideas in the two worlds have a nearly inseparable history, the later development of Islamic philosophy and the living tradition of philosophy and gnosis that have survived in the Islamic world to the present day can once again provide ideas that can be of great fecundity on the soil of Western intellectual life. This influence of thought appears at least among the few who through the dim glass of phenomenology, existentialism, structuralism, etc., are searching for a more penetrating vision of reality than those systems of discursive, earthly, and rationalistic philosophy which the West has been able to provide for them since the seventeenth century.

BIBLIOGRAPHY

T. Burckhardt, *Introduction to Sufi Doctrine,* trans. D. M. Matheson (Lahore, 1959); idem, *Die Maurische Kultur in Spanien* (Munich, 1970). H. Corbin, *Avicenna and the Visionary Recital,* trans. W. Trask (New York, 1960); idem, with the collaboration of S. H. Nasr and O. Yahya, *Histoire de la philosophie islamique,* Vol. I (Paris, 1964a); idem, *Le livre des pénétrations métaphysiques* of Ṣadroddīn Shīrāzī (Tehran-Paris, 1964b). P. Duhem, *Le système du monde,* Vols. II–IV (Paris, 1914–54). L. Gardet and M. M. Anawati, *Introduction à la théologie musulmane,* Vol. I (Paris, 1964). H. A. R. Gibb, *Studies on the Civilization of Islam* (Boston, 1962). É. Gilson, "Les sources gréco-arabes de l'augustinisme avicennant," *Archives d'histoire doctrinale et littéraire du Moyen Age,* 4 (1929), 5–149. Ibn Khaldūn, *The Muqaddimah,* trans. F. Rosenthal, 3 vols. (New York, 1958). M. Mahdi, *Alfarabi's Philosophy of Plato and Aristotle* (New York, 1962). L. Massignon, *La Passion d'al-Ḥallāj,* 2 vols. (Paris, 1914–21). A. Mieli, *La science arabe et son rôle dans l'évolution scientifique mondiale* (Leiden, 1966). E. A. Moody, "Galileo and Avempace," *Journal of the History of Ideas,* **12,** 2 (1951), 163–93; 3, 375–422. S. H. Nasr, *Three Muslim Sages* (Cambridge, Mass., 1964a), p. 133; idem, *An Introduction to Islamic Cosmological Doctrines* (Cambridge, Mass., 1964b); idem, *Ideals and Realities of Islam* (London, 1966); idem, *Science and Civilization in Islam* (Cambridge, Mass., 1968). S. Pines, *Beiträge zur islamischen Atomenlehre* (Berlin, 1936). G. Sarton, *Introduction to the History of Science,* 3 vols. (Baltimore, 1927–48). F. Schuon, *Understanding Islam,* trans. D. M. Matheson (London, 1963). M. M. Sharif, ed., *A History of Muslim Philosophy,* 2 vols. (Wiesbaden, 1963–66). G. von Grünebaum, *Medieval Islam* (Chicago, 1956). R. Walzer, *Greek into Arabic* (Oxford, 1962), p. 12. H. A. Wolfson, "The Twice-Revealed Averroës," *Speculum* (July 1961), 373–93, and (Jan. 1963), 88–104; idem, *Philosophy of the Kalam* (Cambridge, Mass., 1971).

SEYYED HOSSEIN NASR

[See also Alchemy; **Astrology;** Atomism; Buddhism; China; Cosmology; **Dualism;** Experimental Science; **God; Love; Neo-Platonism;** Optics; Prophecy.]

JUSTICE

JUSTICE HAS been conceived historically in two separate ways: as a supramundane eternal idea which is independent of man, and as a temporal man-made social ideal. The two meanings illustrate the difference between contemplation and action, philosophical reflection and practical conduct. Our discussion will, however, include a middle ground in which theory and practice are intermingled.

We shall, accordingly, be concerned with: (1) an idea or tradition of justice conceived to exist apart from man and stemming from a higher source, although man seeks to know its nature and draw inspiration from it in his actions; (2) a conception completely dependent upon man in its inception and practice; and (3) an intermediate ground partaking of each of the preceding two conceptions in various intermingled forms.

While each of these conceptions may be discerned in the writings of ancient and modern authors, it is in the middle ground where the tradition of justice appears currently in the forms of man's faiths, ethical beliefs, social institutions, and in those of his actions which reflect this dual nature of justice.

1. Justice as a Supramundane Idea. Justice as an idea independent of man, sans referent, and as the order of the universe, goes to a dubious extreme when it ignores or makes difficult man's knowledge and use of the idea. Historically, this independent view of justice seems first to appear in a primordial conception of the relation of man to his environment. Such a primitive concept apparently grew out of a naturalistic religion rooted in fear and need. It necessarily involved blind submission to the elements conceived as gods. In all these primitive ideas of divine justice, one discerns the supernatural envisaged as an external power, with man as the buffeted recipient of favors or punishment.

The early Homeric anthropomorphism (ca. eighth century B.C.), perhaps following Mycenaean patterns (ca. sixteenth century B.C.), created a pantheon of deities, loosely ruled by Zeus, to whom man was a plaything; and the Greek tragedies depict a universal conception of man confronting destiny. Kitto holds that "behind the gods (though sometimes identified with them) is a shadowy power that Homer calls Ananke, Necessity, an Order of things which even the gods cannot infringe" (*The Greeks,* p. 176). Such heirarchical polytheism guaranteed a justice by which man submitted to fate or destiny, although the gods themselves were not subject to such constraint in their own relations with men. Implicit in Homer's poems is the idea that the rulers on earth pronounce justice on the basis of religion and customs (although it may be argued that if these traditions are the basis for justice, then man, by adopting them, also participates in the substance of justice). Hesiod (ca. seventh century B.C.) presents a pessimistic philosophy of history, holding a degree of hope; Zeus had, for the creatures of the earth, decreed a mortality based upon mutual annihilation, but men were spared such self-destruction by means of justice, although who was to define and ultimately apply this salvational justice was not too clear.

The Greek terms for justice included *Themis* (a consort of Zeus) and *Dike* (a daughter), both permitting many and varied interpretations. For example, the former might be defined as the personification of rational thought, or as self-inherent righteousness (as in Kant and Hegel), analogous to the idea of justice; however, *Dike*, without any moral content and referring to a way of behavior, was the personification of punishment, or the decision of a judge, and was applied to relations among persons, analogous to an ideal of justice (Aristotle's subsequent distinctions of retributive and distributive justice may be referred back to these various connotations of *Dike*). Herodotus (ca. fifth century B.C.) in his *History*, and Aeschylus in his plays, later depicted man as a puppet but with some minor degree of choice, and Zeus as the punisher of overweening ambition, so that justice might now acquire a patina of man's free will; but here again man was subordinated, even though apparently elevated to a higher moral level. The ". . . immutable and unwritten laws of Heaven," to which Sophocles' Antigone appeals against Creon's decrees, offer, perhaps, the kernel of the Platonic idea of justice as well as of the ideas of natural law and natural right in the later Stoics and Romans. The Pythagoreans preached a doctrine of transmigration, along with their view that the nature of things is number, and that justice is basically equality, a notion which has remained as perhaps the most important component of the idea; an all too common application, however, of the notion of justice as "reciprocity" results in the "eye for an eye" standard of retaliation. The later Eleatic School included Parmenides whose poem "On Justice" spoke of the "All," somewhat analogous to Anaximander's Indeterminate (*apeiron*), and mentioned justice as ". . . the mighty avenger, that keepeth the keys of requital," and adds that ". . . neither production neither destruction doth Justice permit. . . ."

The most significant of the pre-Socratic philosophers for our theme are Heraclitus and the Sophists (although Plato sarcastically refers to the Sophist as "a sort of merchant or dealer in" wares, in *Protagoras* 333c). Heraclitus said that nothing is stable, that permanence is an illusion conceived by man, and that strife "is the justice of the world . . ." (Zeller, p. 46). In the next

century the Sophists compared different customs and civilizations, questioned whether the gods and institutions were really sacred and inviolable, felt these were the creatures of man and his conventions and therefore capable of change, and oriented Greek thought and ideas to a form of humanism (*vide* Rousseau, in the eighteenth century, who attacked institutions as corrupters of natural man). One of the most renowned of the Sophists was Protagoras who, in the fifth century B.C., brought the idea of justice into a humanistic framework in his famous statement "that man is the measure of all things . . ." (*Theaetetus* 152a). A further contention that change was an illusion and not a fact (illustrated by the paradoxes of Parmenides and Zeno of Elea) resulted in the ultimate *reductio ad absurdum* (by Zeno's pupil Gorgias) that if Being is infinite and eternal it cannot be located in a particular space or time and therefore cannot exist, i.e., Being and Nothing would then be the same; this argument, of course, struck at the idea that justice could vary in different places and times.

The Heraclitean-Sophist concept of justice has had and still has a considerable influence; its implications for the contrasting Eleatic and Platonic idea of the immutability of justice are significant. However, so long as man conceives of permanence as inherent in the idea of justice, then the idea of justice as eternal is necessarily a function of and inseparable from man; and since the only permanence is change, the idea of justice must be relative to man and constantly changing. While Plato was affected by Heraclitus thoughts he did not accept the latter's conclusions, and his views of eternal "higher laws" certainly did not coincide with those of the Sophists.

The following century saw the inauguration of the split in Western thought between the philosophies of Plato and Aristotle, and the idea of justice historically reflects their differing views. Both men followed old, and also created new, traditions and paths. They each also sought answers to the same questions which had burdened their predecessors. In general, they felt that a proportion and order existed from which a determinate harmony (justice) flowed, but each found this in a different manner and with different results.

For Plato the idea of justice is a transcendental and permanent harmonious unity, which while separate from man, preserves some connection or link; as an eternal object of *a priori* thought it has universal meaning (which will be defined below) and is thereby knowable, even though it may not yet have been completely embodied in man or his institutions; man therefore aspires to apply this eternal, perfect, and absolute idea to his mortal conduct in an all-embracing system of applied justice.

653

Following a hierarchical order, Plato understood the meaning of justice through its application to the three classes (philosopher-rulers, soldiers, and workers), each minding its "own business" (*Republic* 443d), ultimately in order to find out how each person could order his own life, i.e., not "be a busybody" (433b), by respecting the functions and needs of each component part of his nature (reason, will, and emotions). A proper and due harmony within the individual and within the state, regardless of any economic and political inequality which resulted, thus conformed to his idea of justice; in such ordered health of the ideal political body every part of it performs its proper task (as needed to maintain such state) in a perfect harmony (each individual in each class receives his due proportion).

Plato's theory and definition of justice is thus found in his conception of the division of the ideal state into three classes consisting of: a small body of rulers in whom wisdom is found, and who have attained a knowledge of absolute justice; the guardians (military or auxiliaries) in whom courage flows; and, lastly, the artisans or governed (slaves are excluded). Justice is the unifying and harmonizing principle which keeps all three in equilibrium, and it occurs when each individual functions properly and in harmony with the others, in compliance with his proper function according to his class and without interfering with the other two classes, whereas injustice consists of intermeddling and a refusal to give another his due. Justice is thus the only way to achieve the ideal state on earth, "for the gods have a care of anyone whose desire is to become just and to be like God," so that Plato's "counsel is that we hold fast ever to the heavenly way and follow after justice and virtue always . . ." (*Republic*, Book V, pp. 320, 329).

The idea of justice, according to the Platonic tradition, is therefore generally to be considered as being an immutable, eternally valid, and universal idea, the highest or supreme one, which is now sought to be understood and applied by man as natural justice obtained through pure reason. The idea thereby offers a formula or standard to determine the acceptance or rejection of positive rules set by legislation to govern man's conduct and actions. This is also the basis for the natural rights theory, so that in this sense justice includes such rights.

Aristotle does not disagree with Plato completely, declaring that ". . . rules of justice vary is not absolutely true, but only with qualifications"; he divides political justice into two parts, "one natural, the other conventional [legal]" (*Ethics* 1134b), and thereby supports a concept of natural justice. So Edmund Burke later wrote that human laws "may alter the mode and application, but have no power over the substance of original justice" (*Works*, Boston [1867], VI, 323). Some critics have denounced all this as a metaphysical play upon words, arguing that not only is the idea of justice unknown, but reason, as the catalyst, itself must be defined and understood; thus, they urge, there can never be a concretization of justice as a standard for man to approximate or to apply in a given situation to determine conduct, or guilt, or punishment. Hobbes, for example, denied that there could be any standard of justice apart from utility or expediency, whereas Grotius maintained that there was an essential morality as well as a natural justice governing men and nations, despite their varying customs. Hobbes's views led him to justify the state and support the imposition of justice by it, thereby providing a base for others' man-made law proposals, others who could then logically urge the irrelevance of morality or even justice in the enforcement of the laws. A parallel criticism had been urged by Epicurus who saw no sign of justice or morality in the universe, and therefore rejected any theological basis for conduct; he regarded perception and feeling as sole criteria for ethics. In Epicurus there is thus no fear of gods or death, and man is the aim of all action so that intellectual pleasure and freedom from pain are good, for they produce peace of mind, and the converse is evil; it is therefore the purpose of law to secure man against injustice, i.e., the wise abstain from unjust conduct and the others are deterred so that justice results in this negative fashion.

Another form of criticism concentrated upon the human factor, arguing that all men differ in every significant aspect of time, place, etc., and therefore each has a different mentality and reason; thus whatever is defined as natural law and applied to a given situation, is really no reflection of the universal idea but is only man's personal and distorted effort. This criticism is illustrated by Sir Frederick Pollock's statement that "Natural justice has no means . . . of choosing one practical solution out of two or more" equally plausible ones, so that "Positive law, whether enacted or customary, must come to our aid" (*Expansion of the Common Law*, London [1904], p. 128). This criticism is illustrated also by the disagreement among the Justices of the Supreme Court of the United States over the definition and application of the constitutional term "due process of law." As to this constitutional term, as early as 1898 a majority of the Justices subscribed to the view that "there are certain immutable principles of justice which inhere in the very idea of free government," so that such due process language implies "a conformity with natural and inherent principles of justice. . . ." Strong minorities later opposed this construction as it left the application of the concept "to the Court, with no guide but the Court's own discretion"; and a current minority likewise denounces the majority's ability to "roam at will in the limitless area of their own beliefs as to [due process] reasonableness" and thereby to "appropriate for this Court a broad power. . . ."

2. *Justice as Dependent upon Man.* Plato's "doctrine of ideas" was severely "criticized" by Aristotle in his *Metaphysics* (1078b–1080a); and while Aristotle does not devote the time or space to justice that Plato does, he makes known his views in several places. In his *Politics* he writes that "all men cling to justice of some kind" (1280a), and in the *Nicomachean Ethics* he concludes "that there is more than one kind of justice" (1130b), for example, that involving "the rightly-framed law" which "is complete virtue, but not absolutely, but in relation to our neighbor" (1129b). Aristotle thus believed that man was a political and social animal, who "alone has any sense . . . of just and unjust" (*Politics* 1253a), and he sought to reconcile justice with the conflicts he observed about him. In his *Politics* he states that "justice is the bond of men in states" (1253a), and in the *Rhetoric* he gives it some content by saying that justice "is a virtue which assigns to each man his due in conformity with the law," while injustice is a vice whereby man "claims what belongs to others, in opposition to the law" (1366b).

In the *Ethics* Aristotle initially divides "the just [into] the lawful and the equal or fair" (1130b); these are, respectively, his universal or general, i.e., legislative, and particular, i.e., judge-made decisions in individual cases. The legislative type of justice requires obedience to the law, and therefore comprehends a civic virtue. Judicial decisions are distinguished from morality and are now divided into distributive and corrective, that is "the distribution of honour, wealth, and the other divisible assets of the community . . . [and] that which supplies a corrective principle in private transactions." This corrective principle is still further subdivided into "those [acts and relations] which are voluntary and those which are involuntary" (1131a), examples of which he gives by referring respectively to commercial dealings, and then to personal crimes or torts upon one involuntarily made a participant (ibid.; see also his similar divisions in *Rhetoric* 1373b).

Aristotle's main concern is with the particular and corrective or remedial type of justice in which the judge's task is to redress and not to punish (Aquinas later also uses such terms and divisions but in a slightly different sense, especially in going above and beyond the Aristotelian view of nature). Aristotle further regards justice (*dike*) as embracing many if not all the other virtues, including a relation to persons as well as to things, involving a just distribution of the latter, and a fair meting out of punishment. In his *Ethics*

(1132b) he rejects the "simple" Pythagorean formula for justice as equal reciprocity, since this does not apply to either distributive or retributive justice, and then tentatively suggests a third kind of exchange or commercial justice.

There are three types of persons whom Aristotle describes as acting justly, namely: (a) the legislator or statesman who rewards; (b) the judge who decides; and (c) the farmer or entrepeneur who exchanges goods and services, although this last one does not include a moral virtue and is therefore only an economic type of justice, i.e., entitled to a just price (1132a–1133b). Equals, continues Aristotle in his *Politics*, should be treated alike, but unequals proportionally to their relevant differences, and all with impartiality, whereby justice now would be understood and served. As Muller put it, "Plato and Aristotle would [a millennium] later state the logic of [Hammurabi's] code by arguing that justice consists not in giving equal rights to men naturally unequal, but in giving every man his due" (*Ancient World*, p. 59). Almost all thinkers throughout the whole history of philosophy, down to our own century, have agreed with Aristotle's definition. However, Aristotle points out that the problem of what constitutes equals and what constitutes unequals cannot be solved easily as, e.g., those who are superior in wealth feel they are superior in everything, (although no problems exist in assigning some, e.g., slaves, to an inferior position, so long as they are given their due within this group).

Anatole France's caustic version is that "Justice is made to give everyone his due; to the rich his richness, to the poor his poverty."

Aristotle's solution is that equality must be judged on the basis of goodness (shown by noble actions), and anything short of such virtue is only a part of justice. While Plato and Aristotle therefore agree in several respects, for example, they both regard ethics and morals as basic to a philosophy of law which is subsumed under a theory of justice, their ideas and applications of the nature of justice do not coincide. Aristotle ties at least one form of justice to man. Bodenheimer feels that Plato's "realization" of justice in his *Laws* depends on the police power of the state, whereas Aristotle considers various types of law with at least one relating man and justice (*Jurisprudence* [1962], p. 47).

It is Aristotle's tying of justice to diverse human situations which may be termed the most distinguishing feature of his disagreement with Plato's central idea of justice as harmony. Aristotle's four illustrative types of voluntary acts therefore disclose that only in the last type, where man acts by a deliberate choice, are the act and doer unjust (1135a–1136a). In his *Rhetoric* 655

Aristotle further links justice to the human condition by saying that "equity is justice that goes beyond the written law" (1374a), is left by the legislators to permit a margin of fairness to soften the rigors of the statutes, and therefore provides judges with a degree of discretion (1374b). This may be Aristotle's greatest practical contribution to "justice," for the preliminary title of the Code Napoléon of 1804 restates this doctrine, the Austrian and Italian Civil Codes mandate it in the absence of express rules, and the English and American common law division into law and equity follow it, as do all nations in one fashion or another.

Legal positivists such as Kelsen nevertheless object to any extra-legal criteria and reject any effort to include such a conception of justice in the field of law.

After the Greeks, we must consider three historically important versions of justice in the Hebraic, the Roman, and the Thomistic teachings, with the latter two exercising a more direct and broader position.

The Hebraic requirement of the individual's freedom of the will paralleled his religious commandments to lead a moral life, and the idea of justice was necessarily broadened to include these. Here the idea of justice concurs somewhat with Plato's, and there is also a certain parallelism with an Aristotelian base, for the idea cannot be altered by man and yet arises out of man's needs. It was these needs which determined the concept of the idea as a moral contract between nation and God. The Covenant is a commitment which justice obligates God (voluntarily) to honor so long as man does; here justice, right, and contract are somewhat interchangeable, but only if freely-willing participants are found, i.e., a consenting partnership of presumed equals in which obligations and rights are stressed on the basis of divine commandments. While Mosaic law and justice (promulgated ca. 1250 B.C.) borrowed little from Egypt, they were later influenced by the Assyrians during the "Babylonian Captivity" (ca. 586 B.C.); thus prior to the exodus from Egypt the Jews conceived of justice as deliverance, thereafter when in exile as benevolence, and during the Roman era as strict observance; in all these it was God whose justice would be so reflected, but it was man who was required to act, as the Covenant decreed. Religion, morals, righteous conduct, and strict application to duty thus went into the Hebrew concept of justice; so long as man obeyed the Commandments he would receive justice through divine deliverance.

This "give and take" type of justice may be compared with that of the "reciprocity" or "equality" of the Pythagoreans, above; however, it is to be distinguished from the pagan notion whereby the gods would dispense with justice as a matter of favoritism, not of right. The concept of such a *quid pro quo* was expressed in the Covenant on a high level, and on a lower one by statements such as an "eye for an eye." Against this primitive idea of retaliation toward a family, clan, or a tribe for the actions of the members (as in Helen's abduction and the siege of Troy), there stood the Hebrew concept of individual moral responsibility which carried over into the later Christian teachings. This elicited the need for a corresponding doctrine of the freedom of the will and the focus upon man as a political and social animal was reinforced, as in Aristotle's view.

The Roman conquest of Greece brought, by the first century A.D., an interchange of ideas, but not any change of the aristocratic character of Greek political ideas to any form of democracy. Nor did the Roman dependence upon Greek ideas and civilization extend to an uncritical adoption of their superstitions and beliefs. Roman mythology described customs or laws promulgated by Romulus (ca. 753–16 B.C.), and thereafter by other kings, which, for example, created various classes, assigned powers, and implicitly ordered the lives of the people. The Roman Epicurean Lucretius, a contemporary of Julius Caesar, conceived of order and law in nature as free from the caprice of gods, thereby gaining security for the individual. The Epicurean could rise above his passions and bear the evil afflicting him by freeing himself from their grip through knowledge and reason, and by becoming resigned to the universal law of change and death.

This Roman wisdom, borrowed from Epicurus, was also in the chronological stream of the moral philosophy of Plato and Aristotle, for now man's first concern was to know and obey the laws of his being; the substitution of nature for deities also brought Lucretius closer to the moral philosophy of the Stoics. Stoic philosophy, however, was the main inspiration in the further development of Roman jurisprudence, which became oriented to the world rather than to the gods; and Rome's great expansion into a world power, with a consequent "Pax Romana," required a *jus gentium* ("law of nations") founded upon the concept of a universal and uniform idea of justice, equally accessible to all through reason. The term justice was, for Rome, given legal content first by Ulpian (ca. A.D. 170–228) and later by Justinian (483–565) who, in the opening pages of his *Institutes,* repeated it almost verbatim (as later did Aquinas) as "the set [fixed] and constant purpose which gives to every man his due."

Aquinas formulated the natural law from man's enjoyment "of a certain share in the divine reason," but this share could thus be limited to such law itself and therefore not partake of justice. There is, also, an uncompromising position taken by Aquinas with respect to "divine" reason which is made the touchstone for his conclusions. His formulation of the idea of justice follows both a Platonic and Aristotelian tradition; like Aristotle, Aquinas proposes the secularization of the idea, and the logical extension of his thoughts only eventually reaches an extremely religious form. The Christian ethic to that time had stressed love, e.g., of God and neighbor to achieve justice, so that baptism redeemed one from sin, the most fundamental injustice, and "it becomes us to fulfill all justice" (Matthew 3:15, Douay version); but there was a corresponding love of God for man, e.g., as through the giving of Christ (suggesting, perhaps remotely, the aspect of justice as reciprocity in the Protagorean and Hebraic approach).

Both Plotinus and Augustine had constituted the church as the only fount of justice for man, who so obtained it through his love of the highest good, i.e., God, although the state could and did exist separately and did properly dispense its own brand of justice while linked with the church as its secular arm, e.g., do unto others. Aquinas did not disagree in this division of justice but advanced the view (in greatly disputed passages) that the state, for one, could independently so dispense justice even though ultimately there was the divine idea; commutative justice therefore could, in practical effect, stand alone. He disagreed with the idea that justice was simply what was "due to each man" (e.g., as in the Pythagorean, Hebraic, and Augustinian views), for God could not properly be held to be a debtor; this severance between God and man could now also be found, and here again he did not follow Augustine's attribution of justice solely to God or its identification with His essence.

It is in Grotius that this tentative ideological severance is given rationality, and acquires a significant independence from God with a resulting dependence (solely) upon nature (or man). Grotius argues as follows: first, he agrees with Aristotle that man is a naturally social creature (and so utilizes the social contract doctrine), necessarily requiring some minimum form of law (and justice), even if God did not exist—though surely He exists; second, this minimum is a resultant of man's reason; ergo, this universal or natural law "is unchangeable—even in the sense that it cannot be changed by God. . . . He cannot cause that which is intrinsically evil be not evil" (*De Jure Belli ac Pacis*, trans. F. W. Kelsey, 2 vols., Oxford [1925], II, 40), or, conversely, tamper with the intrinsic concept of justice.

In the seventeenth century Hobbes's man warred in a "state of nature" in which notions of justice and injustice had no place, but his third law of nature required the performance of covenants, for in this "consisteth the fountain and Originall of Justice. . . . And for the definition of Injustice, is no other than the not performance of Covenant. And whatsoever is

not Unjust, is Just" (*Leviathan*, ed. Waller, Cambridge [1904], p. 109).

3. Justice as a Fluctuating Mean between Independence and Dependence on Man. The duality of the independence or dependence of the idea of justice on man would thus require that man steer by an existing star or else create one. Or, perhaps, both these could occur and be used singly, or as checks. For example, in the field of jurisprudence, used singly as where a person receives particular justice when his rights and obligations are determined, Justices W. J. Brennan and B. N. Cardozo respectively objected because, wrote the former, this is not "my sense of justice" (dissenting in *State v. Tune*, 13 N.J. 203 [1953]) to which, continued the latter, decisional law itself "should conform. Justice in this sense is a concept by far more subtle and indefinite than any that is yielded by mere obedience to a rule. It remains to some extent, when all is said and done, the synonym of an aspiration, a mood of exaltation, a yearning for what is fine or high" (*The Growth of the Law*, New Haven [1927], p. 87). Or, where the idea of justice is to be used as a check, the latter jurist also comments that "What we are seeking is not merely the justice that one receives when his rights and duties are determined by the law as it is; what we are seeking is the justice to which the law in its making should conform."

Stammler (1856–1938) seeks "to find merely a universally valid formal method" to determine whether "the necessarily changing material or empirically conditioned legal rules . . . have the quality of objective justice" (*Theory of Justice*, pp. 89f.). Here, of course, the objections earlier made against the personalization of the idea (of natural law and rights) are likewise available, but this does not necessarily mean that they do not represent the collective feelings and aspirations of men, politically, theologically, or otherwise. For example, the basic documents of the United States, France, and the United Nations, as well as England's Magna Carta, specifically and literally set forth and emphasize their yearnings for justice as an end and as a means, although the Soviet Constitution states only that "justice is administered by" various courts. The use of the same word, however, does not guarantee agreement in meaning, e.g., G. F. Kennan mentions as "shocking" the use of "justice under law" in an American-Russian agreement to recognize the German judicial system (*Memoirs*, Boston [1967], p. 259). Whether or not ideas can shape the world, justice seems to be a terminological, if not ideological, necessity in such major documents.

A recurrent and universal idea of justice may therefore be assumed, even while the method of its seeking and its content may be questioned; that is to say, justice as a term which embodies the idea is used, even though its source or its definition is not clear and its substance is rejected by many. For example, Lao-Tzu uses the word "Tao" to denote the invisible, formless, nothing and nonbeing, which to him represented the "way" that anteceded the world and even Ti, the supreme god of the Chinese.

So the idea or term "justice" has also been popularly thought of as constant and absolute, at least in one aspect of a possible definition. Nevertheless, neither such an absolute nor any operative ideal has developed or been applied in a strict uniform fashion. Rather, the idea and the ideal have somewhat surged and circled, and have been subjected to a degree of cross-fertilization. In many respects ideals are part of the institutionalized substructure of cherished ideas, beliefs, and prejudices into which Western man is born, but the jelled climate of opinion so passively received is itself in constant change. This is not to imply that the idea itself is necessarily a constantly fluctuating one, since the ambiguous term has retained an ideological permanence which has made it an article of faith (slogan) or, in Holmesian language, a fighting word; e.g., the Romans warred in the name of justice, as still do modern nations, with the conquered then denouncing the wars as unjust. Or, in the middle sixties, and even though nationalism enters, the turmoil created in many countries and throughout the world because of the suppression of dissent, the form of government, the unequal distribution of resources, or the type of (legal) justice granted, illustrates further the compelling urge to achieve justice.

4. Sources and Content of the Idea of Justice. The idea of justice thus seems to have been a part of the Western, if not the civilized, world's heritage since its pagan inception. It has been, however, the ascertainment of the course and the analysis of the very meaning of the idea which, as we have seen, have simultaneously been the *desideratum* and the *bête noire* of philosophers, lawmakers, and others. These individuals have proposed a variety of sources, as distinguished from the content, of the idea of justice, and both source and content may be separately recapitulated even though interacting and necessarily determining each other to some undisclosed extent.

The source of the idea of justice has been sought by many philosophers. Some of these have already been mentioned, e.g., the Platonic idea or ethical "pattern of it" which "is laid" in "heaven . . . which he who desires may behold." The somewhat theocratic (Augustinian) aspect follows in this vein, and also the logically extended divine reason, although in contrast with the impersonal Stoics' absolute reason. There is an ambivalence in the view that utility is the only fount

of (legal) justice and its only basis, or that the basis lies in the concept of reciprocity which leads into a contract theory between God and man (the Hebraic approach) or among men (with king or state, as in Locke or with other men, as in the Mayflower Compact). Man himself and his legal needs provide another source, with respect to the governance of his actions and relations, avoiding injustice, and otherwise resolving disputes. So, too, the source may be found in history, custom, or the spirit of the people (*Volksgeist*), as in Maine, Savigny, or Herder; or, as Cicero put it, "the origin of Justice is to be found in Law" (*De legibus*, I. vi, 19), or even, as A. Brecht suggests, "Sometimes a voice within us claims to know" what is just and unjust. Brecht also lists twelve types of views of justice which he examines and then concludes, "One who changes from one conviction [source] to another will thenceforth have a different idea of justice."

The choice of one or more of these sources of the idea of justice is not required of the individual. Heraclitus, for one, would not approve, and Aristotle, for another, would insist upon distinctions, that is, should an economic, political, or other factor influence the source most closely approximating it; but if one's interests determine the choice, this permits the basis for the choice itself to return to the enumerated sources themselves, and now this circular reasoning requires another Alexander to cut the apocryphal knot. Aristotle's view of man as a social-political animal permits a multiplicity and combination of choices to be made, for modern pluralism stresses the variety of man's interests, associations, and not only social solidarity (Duguit) but even individualism (Laski), while Protagorean humanism and some correlative forms of pragmatism permit freedoms in choices almost without stint.

The very many elements which enter into the definition or content of the idea of justice cannot, of course, be systematically classified through an arbitrary arrangement of the components, for this presupposes the possibility of discrete, analytical distinctions, nor can it or they be subjected to content analysis. Any such effort can only disclose what the term "justice" variously connotes rather than what the content of the idea of justice itself contains. The content of the idea may, nevertheless, be understood, if not defined, by both positive and negative characteristics, and also by means of illustrations; the terms, however, vary with different thinkers' usages, as when Cairns refers to Plato's view of justice as "doing one's own business and not being a busybody," or as M. R. Cohen sums up Plato ". . . as saying that justice is the health of the body politic" (*Reason and Law*, Glencoe, Ill. [1950], p. 92), or when M. Radin refers to social, spiritual, etc., aspects of life and concludes that "out of these factors there has been created a social emotion which we call a sense of justice" ("The Chancellor's Foot," *Harvard Law Review*, **49** [1935], 48).

The following characteristics which permit justice broad latitude therefore merely indicate, and are not exhaustive of, the meanings of the idea. Foremost is the principle that the like be treated alike (equality, impartiality, to each his own due), and other versions of the idea refer to: harmony (ethics, morality); righteousness (equity, fairness); reason (man, divine, religion); reciprocity (contract, eye-for-eye); utility (pleasure, pain); custom (group, tribe, polis); man, his interests and needs, especially of order, and see also Leibniz' mature definition of justice as *caritas sapientis*, the charity of the wise man which, R. J. Mulvaney believes, "is without verbal antecedent . . . in the entire history of Western moral philosophy" (*Journal of the History of Ideas*, **29** [1968], p. 53).

The idea of justice can also be understood by means of historically concrete illustrations, e.g., in the bases used for making judicial decisions, or in the political treatment of minorities which is allegedly the mark of a civilized society. So also it may be understood in a negative aspect, e.g., as in diplomatic practice or in international claims procedures which use the phrase "denial of justice" to indicate a departure from some sort of international standard. This negative approach, however, is better disclosed where treatment based upon color, national origin, etc., is labeled as unjust, e.g., the "slaughter by command" of millions during World War II which resulted in Nuremberg's condemnation of such unquestioning obedience (although compare this type of obedience with the concept of *nomos* applied at Thermopylae in 480 B.C. where Leonidas and the Spartans voluntarily met their death; so did Socrates in 399 B.C.). This slaughter by command illustrates an unjust act or conduct, i.e., that injustice flows from certain facts; there are, of course, other variations of this negative terminology. This sense of injustice in effect creates a series of negative criteria which, by contrast, reveal the positive content of the idea of Justice more clearly.

BIBLIOGRAPHY

Works on jurisprudence, political theory, social philosophy, and those of particular authors mentioned contain discussions of justice. Of special interest are the following, most of which also contain references or bibliographies.

Aristotle, *Nicomachean Ethics*, and Plato, *Republic*, and their other works, any edition. E. K. Allen, *Aspects of Justice* (London, 1958). O. A. Bird, *The Idea of Justice* (New York, 1967). E. Bodenheimer, *Jurisprudence* (New York, 1940), p. 47. A. Brecht, *Political Theory* (Princeton, N.J., 1959), pp. 136, 155. E. N. Cahn, *The Sense of Injustice* (New York, 1940). H. Cairns, *Legal Philosophy from Plato to Hegel* (Baltimore, 1949), p. 551. T. N. Carver, *Essays in Social Justice* (Cambridge, Mass., 1932). L. Duguit, *Law in the Modern State*, trans. F. and H. Laski (New York, 1919). D. E. Emmet, "Justice and Equality," *Philosophy*, **14** (1939), 46–58. E. N. Garlan, *Legal Realism and Justice* (New York, 1941). D. R. Hillers, *Covenant: The History of a Biblical Idea* (Baltimore, 1969). L. T. Hobhouse, *Elements of Social Justice* (London, 1922). R. Jaffe, "The Pragmatic Conception of Justice," *Univ. of California Publications in Philosophy*, **34** (Berkeley, 1960). W. Kaufmann, "The Origin of Justice," *Review of Metaphysics*, **23** (1969), 209–39. H. Kelsen, *What is Justice?* (Berkeley, 1957). H. D. F. Kitto, *The Greeks*, rev. ed. (New York, 1957; reprint, 1965), p. 176. J. H. Muirhead, *The Platonic Tradition in Anglo-Saxon Philosophy* (London, 1931). H. J. Muller, trilogy of *Freedom in the Ancient World* (1961); *Western World* (1963); and *Modern World* (New York, 1966). F. A. Olfason, ed., *Justice and Social Policy* (Englewood Cliffs, N.J., 1961). C. Perelman, *The Idea of Justice and the Problem of Argument*, trans. J. Petrie (London, 1963); idem, *Justice* (New York, 1967). Plato, *Republic*, trans. B. Jowett, 3rd ed. (Oxford, 1888; New York, 1901). H. Potter, *The Quest for Justice* (London, 1951). R. Pound, "Social Justice and Legal Justice," *Century Law Journal*, **75** (1912), 455–63. J. H. Randall, Jr., "Plato's Treatment of the Theme of the Good Life . . . ," *Journal of the History of Ideas*, **28** (1967), 307, 319. A. Ross, *On Law and Justice* (London, 1958). H. Spencer, *Justice* (New York, 1891). R. Stammler, "The Idea of Justice," *Univ. of Pennsylvania Law Review*, **71** (1923), 303–17; idem, *The Theory of Justice*, trans. I. Husik (New York, 1925), pp. 89f. F. M. Stawell, "The Modern Conception of Justice," *International Journal of Ethics*, **19** (1908), 44–60. J. Stone, *The Province and Function of Law* (Cambridge, Mass., 1950); idem, *Human Law and Human Justice* (Stanford, 1965). G. del Vecchio, *Justice*, trans. Lady Guthrie, ed. A. H. Campbell (New York, 1953). A. Verdross, *Abendländische Rechtsphilosophie* (Vienna, 1958). J. H. Wigmore, *A Panorama of the World's Legal Systems*, 3 vols. (St. Paul, Minn., 1928). E. Zeller, *Outlines of the History of Greek Philosophy*, trans. L. R. Palmer, 13th ed., rev. (London, 1931; reprints, 1948, 1955).

MORRIS D. FORKOSCH

[See also **Equity**; Law, Ancient Greek, Due Process, **Equal Protection, Natural**; Platonism; Pre-Platonic Conceptions.]

STUDY OF LANGUAGE

I. BACKGROUND

IN ALL cultures men learn to speak at roughly the same age, starting in the first or second year of life, mastering most of the grammar of their language by the age of six, but increasing their vocabulary all through their lives. This means that we learn to speak long before we are able consciously to reflect on language. Speaking comes naturally to human beings, like breathing or walking. It is not necessary to give children formal instruction in how to speak: it is sufficient for them to grow up in a normal human environment. In this respect speaking differs from other intellectual activities such as mathematics, or practical activities such as ploughing or driving an automobile. We acquire these abilities by conscious efforts, while the complicated mechanism of language develops within us without our being in the least aware of it.

At a very early age most English children are able to use correctly the auxiliary verb *do*, or the definite and indefinite article, thereby showing that they master a set of quite complicated rules and classifications. Yet neither they nor (for the most part) their parents have the slightest conscious knowledge of those rules. Contrast with this the inability of most of us to multiply, say, 537 by 894 without using pencil and paper. Yet the rules for this arithmetical operation are far simpler than the ones governing the use of the *do*-auxiliary. In the language of the electronic computer, it seems as if our brain is pre-programmed to assimilate the kinds of rules that are needed for language, while a special program has to be fed into it for the rules of arithmetic. The contrast is the same as that between walking and driving. Walking involves an extremely complicated series of coordinated muscular movements and sensory feedback, which are undoubtedly very largely pre-programmed. Driving an automobile is in almost all respects far simpler, but has to be learned before it becomes automatic, going on without conscious control.

As the rules of language are normally not conscious, they are difficult to study. Indeed, the ordinary man has difficulty in realizing that the rules exist—just as he has difficulty in realizing that air can have weight. It is no wonder, therefore, that the study of language seems to be a late development in all cultures. It is not easy to visualize any utilitarian motive for studying language. To study arithmetic brings immediate rewards by increasing the ability to carry out arithmetical operations. But to study language does not necessarily increase the ability to speak, since we know how to speak without instruction. It must generally seem about as futile as instruction in how to walk. An incentive to study language therefore hardly arises until the language causes difficulty. There are two conditions, in particular, where this occurs. First, when the language in question is a foreign one. Second, when it represents a peculiar dialect of our native tongue.

The number of different languages spoken in the world at the present time runs into hundreds, if not thousands. There is little reason to suppose that the number has ever been much smaller. Judging from fossil remains, the human species has had basically its present physical characteristics for several hundred thousand years. In all probability language has been a characteristic of the species during most of this period. We know from the evidence of recorded history that it takes only a few thousand years for isolated dialects of what was once a single language (or nearly so) to become mutually incomprehensible and hardly recognizable as similar: witness Hindu and Gaelic, Greek and Swedish. Even if, at one time, the whole human species consisted of just a single tribe, living in a very limited area (and there is little reason to believe this), it would not take long for different languages to develop, as the species expanded over the face of the earth.

We may therefore assume that occasions for learning foreign tongues have existed in practically all human communities. In fact, ability to cope with more than one language may even have been a condition for survival in small nomadic communities like those of many American Indian tribes. This does not mean, of course, that complete bilingualism or multilingualism has ever been a common phenomenon. At the present day, bilingual states, like Switzerland, Belgium, or Finland, are the exception rather than the rule. And even there the overwhelming majority of the individuals grow up with one language as very definitely their first and most important vehicle of communication. Most people come to learn their second language considerably later and less well than their first. We may assume that this has always been the case.

It is for this reason that language is one of the most powerful instruments for tightening the coherence of a community. In this respect it may be considered as on a par with such species-forming vehicles as, say, the courtship behavior of animals. It is surely no mere accident that *nation* and *language community* tend on the whole to become coextensive terms. A common language and a common literary heritage have at all times been among the most powerful factors for creating a feeling for national unity.

But though in nearly all communities, there have always existed individuals who have learned to speak more than one language, an increased awareness of the nature of language has not always resulted. There are at least two explanations for this. In the first place, to learn a language sufficiently to use it as a means of communication is far more a question of practice than of theory. The appearance of pidgin languages all over the world shows that it is possible to understand and make oneself understood, even if the grammatical niceties that differentiate languages from one another are left out of account. In fact, language contacts of this kind may merely have strengthened the naïve idea that language is essentially just a collection of names for things and activities, and that learning a new language is just to learn a set of new names. The insufficiency of such a view naturally becomes apparent to those who try to speak their second language as well as the natives do. But such complete mastery is seldom attempted, except when the second language has a higher prestige.

This leads us to the second reason why the study of language has not in general grown out of contacts between different languages. Those who have had to go through the process of learning a second language completely and well have not, in the main, belonged to the dominant culture of the time. The attitude of the ancient Greeks is quite typical. They did not consider the languages of the barbarians (whose speech sounded as *bar-bar*) as worth their attention. The Chinese have felt the same, and it is no coincidence that the English have accepted with equanimity the charge of being "bad linguists" in the popular sense of that word.

In view of all this it is perhaps not surprising to find that the study of language has practically everywhere originated from problems concerning the interpretation of an old literary or religious tradition in the language of the dominant culture, rather than from problems arising out of a confrontation with foreign peoples. This also means that the appearance of linguistic studies is closely linked up with the creation of a writing system. It is only when writing has been created that it is possible to preserve an older stage of the language with such accuracy that an objective statement of the linguistic problems can be attempted. The nature of the writing system is not unimportant either. An alphabetical or syllabic script obviously gives a far more detailed representation of the outward form of the language than does an ideographic one. Hence it is not surprising that the contribution of the Chinese to the development of linguistics is far less than that of the Greeks and the Indians.

It should not be thought, however, that the study of language has been wholly subordinated to the practical or supposedly practical object of understanding old texts. Language is not only a means of communication among men, it is also a most important instrument of thought. Hence the study of language also becomes a natural concomitant of philosophy. Such branches of philosophy as logic and epistemology have been and are still regarded by many philosophers as branches of language study. The intimate connection between philosophy and linguistics is especially apparent in ancient Greece. In the Western world it is emphasized again in medieval scholasticism, in the

seventeenth and eig... age. European lingu... twentieth centuries, o... terized as more scienti... concerned far more wit... than with the connectio... external world, a problem... philosopher above all oth...

II. GENERA...

The study of language ha... main fields: the origin of lan... tween language and reality, an... guage. The first is bound up wit... or cosmogony, the second is epist... third may be called the field of... grammar. The fields are, however,... outlining the history of language stu... ble to treat them all together.

We shall start our account with G... including the Latin grammarians. Th... with Plato (ca. 400 B.C.) and ends with... A.D. 500). After that, we shall describe the... in Europe, noticing first the Schoolmen a... general grammarians of the seventeenth and... centuries. The last section will deal with the... and twentieth centuries, including a brief a... Indian linguistics. As Chinese and Japanese li... have hardly contributed to the mainstream of li... thought outside their native countries, they a... dealt with here.

III. ANTIQUITY: GREECE AND ROME

The Greek study of language may be said to st... with Plato and Aristotle. Both of them approach la... guage from a philosophical point of view. They ar... concerned with the nature of language and its relation... to thought and reality, rather than with the more technical matter of providing an exact description of linguistic forms. Such questions were later to be taken up by the Hellenistic grammarians of Alexandria, who were mainly concerned with establishing correct editions of Homer and other classical poets, and with preserving the purity of the Greek language as it became the common vehicle of communication throughout the eastern half of the Roman empire.

The history of Western linguistics ever since has been characterized by this double heritage: philosophical and philological. On the whole Western linguists have continued to be somewhat stronger on the philosophical than on the formal side, until the discovery of Sanskrit and Indian grammar, which enriched the Western grammatical tradition in the direction of descriptive accuracy and power.

661

Plato's views on language are chiefly put forth [in the] dialogue *Cratylus*. He discusses the relation [between] words (rather: names, as Plato consistently [refers] to the basic elements as *onómata*). Plato's view, [put in] the mouth of Socrates in the dialogue, seems [to be] that words may indeed to a certain extent give [clue] to the nature of reality, but that the guidance [they] provide is very uncertain. Even if a name (*ónoma*) [was] given at one time by the wisest of philosophers, [in full] conformity with the nature of the thing, it is [later] exposed to all the vicissitudes of chance and the [whims] of ordinary speakers. Hence no safe conclusions [can] be drawn from the etymology of the name to the [nature] of the thing the name stands for. On the whole, [therefore], Plato's attitude towards the study of language is rather unfavorable. Language does not, to him, provide the key to the realm of true reality.

Before arriving at this somewhat negative conclusion, however, Plato gives considerable attention to two ideas which unfortunately have exerted a disastrous influence on linguistic thought ever since. The first is the idea that there is some inner fitness connecting the name and the thing it stands for. The second concerns the way in which the fitness of the name should be ascertained. Here Plato applies an extremely loose and ad hoc method of etymologizing in which (to use Voltaire's quip made two thousand years later) the consonants counted for little and the vowels for nothing at all. The reasoning is often so ridiculously flippant that later commentators have assumed that Plato really meant to hold up the method to scorn. There is no doubt an element of playful irony in some of the wilder flights of etymological fancy in the dialogue. But though Plato certainly saw that the etymological approach he exemplified so copiously might be, and was, misused, it seems quite clear that in principle he considered it a natural and valid way of analyzing the meaning of a word. In any case, Plato's etymologies in *Cratylus* set more or less the pattern for Western scholars down to the beginning of the nineteenth century.

Let us consider Plato's discussion of the name "Poseidon":

Socrates: I think Poseidon's name was given by him who first applied it, because the power of the sea restrained him as he was walking and hindered his advance: it acted as a bond (*desmós*) of his feet (*podōn*). So he called the lord of this power Poseidon, regarding him as a foot-bond (*posi-desmon*). The *e* is inserted perhaps for euphony. But possibly that may not be right: possibly two *l*'s were originally pronounced instead of the *s*, because the god knew (*eidótos*) many (*pollá*) things. Or it may be that from his shaking he was called the Shaker (*ho seíōn*), and that the *p* and *d* are additions" (fol. 402–03; Plato, *Works*, trans. of Vol.

IV, H. N. Fowler, London and Cambridge, Mass. [1926], p. 169).

It will be seen that Plato is by no means dogmatic. Not infrequently he is quite willing to accept the possibility that several different derivations of a name may all be considered as valid. The underlying assumption is that names were consciously invented by an original name-giver, who may well have had more than one reason for a certain choice. The nearest analogy to Plato's name-giver would in fact be a modern inventor of trade names, who indeed works on the principle that the name should vaguely suggest those ideas that he believes the customers ought to associate with the product.

In his search for the smallest elements making up the names, Plato also considers the idea of sound symbolism. He finds that *r* should stand for swift movements, *l* for softness, and *i* for smallness. But then, he asks, how can we justify a word like *sklērós* ("hard"), which contains an *l*, a sign for softness? In the end, therefore, Plato arrives at the conclusion that it is futile to try to discover the truth of things by analyzing the names. That does not mean, however, that he condemns his previous argument altogether. It is only when compared with the high standard of perfect knowledge that the method of etymology falls short. Plato would also argue that the kind of knowledge that we get through our sensory organs is imperfect, compared with the ideal knowledge that purely intellectual contemplation gives.

In the controversy that occupied the Greeks so much, as to whether language was the product of *thésis* ("convention", another term was *nómos* "order") or *phúsis* ("nature"), Plato therefore seems to have taken a middle position. Though he concludes that the meanings of names are in large part determined by custom or convention, he seems to look upon this as due either to corruption or to the ignorance of the name-givers. Most of his discussion is carried on with the assumption that, at least in an ideal language, there is a fundamental fitness connecting the name with the thing. Such an idea leads to confusing the form and the content of the linguistic sign, and was to form the basis of both weak linguistics and bad metaphysics.

More important, however, is the fact that *Cratylus* gave its sanction to such a disastrous pattern for analyzing words. It is not only that the majority of the etymologies are wrong, if considered as statements of word history or derivation. The worst of it is that the method as such was perverse. By allowing sounds to be changed, dropped, or added in a perfectly haphazard way, in order to make a suggested etymology fit, one gave up in advance the possibility of finding a consistent pattern of word-formation in the language. It may have been this cavalier attitude towards sound changes in words that prevented the Greeks—and the Romans—from making consistent use of such a fundamental distinction as that between stem and ending, between root and affix. The Sanskrit grammarians did immensely better in this respect. It must be admitted, though, that the Greek language is unusually intractable to etymology. Indeed, it may even be said to favor the kind of analysis where sounds can be exchanged without limit. The declension and conjugation systems provide examples of almost every sort of change. We find the "addition" of letters in *gígās*, gen. *gígantos* "giant"; *ónoma*, gen. *onómatos* "name". We find "loss" of letters in *kúōn*, gen. *kunós* "dog"; and alteration of vowels as in *hēdús*, gen. *hēdéos* "sweet." Finally the verbal system yields a rich harvest: *gígnomai* "I am born," *gegénēmai*, *gégona* "I was born." It was not easy to discover any organizing principle in such a variable material.

Aristotle. What Aristotle has to say on linguistic topics is almost wholly incidental to his concern with logic. We find it chiefly in his treatises on the *Categories* and on *Interpretation* (*Perì hermeneías*). Scattered remarks are also to be found in the *Rhetoric* and *Poetics*.

What he says is brief, to the point, and generally sound. Aristotle does not dabble in etymology, though he recognizes that words may be connected with each other: "Things are said to be named derivatively, which derive their name from some other name, but differ from it in termination. Thus the grammarian derives his name from the word grammar, and the courageous man from the word courage" (*Categories*, 1; *Works . . .* , ed. W. D. Ross, Vol. I, trans. E. M. Edghill, Oxford [1928]). Here Aristotle was on the point of discovering the difference between base and derivation morpheme, but he never developed the idea any further.

Aristotle comes down squarely on the side of *thésis* in the *phúsis-thésis* controversy. Words, he also says, are "significant by convention" (*On Interpretation*, 16). He has no patience with the Platonic idea that a word, as such, may be "true": "Nouns and verbs . . . as isolated terms, are not yet either true or false" (ibid.). Truth or falsity can be predicated of propositions only.

His explanation of the relation between writing, speech, and meaning is admirably clear: "Spoken words are the symbols of mental experience and written words are the symbols of spoken words. Just as all men have not the same writing, so all men have not the same speech sounds, but the mental experiences, which these directly symbolize, are the same for all, as also are those things of which our experiences are the images" (ibid.). The later part of this quotation is the foundation of general grammar.

Aristotle's main contribution to linguistics is his careful definition of some important syntactic terms. Thus he distinguishes between a proposition, such as *the man runs*, which expresses a fact and hence may be either true or false, and single expressions, such as *a man*, or *runs*, or *a footed animal with two feet*. Not all sentences are propositions, though. A prayer, for instance, is not a proposition. The word *sentence* itself is defined, somewhat weakly, as "a significant portion of speech, some parts of which have an independent meaning" (ibid.).

Finally, Aristotle defines the principal parts of speech, *ónoma* (noun—or subject) and *rhēma* (verb—or predicate). An *ónoma* is "a sound significant by convention, which has no reference to time" (ibid.). A *rhēma* is "that which, in addition to its proper meaning, carries with it the notion of time . . . it is a sign of something said of something else" (ibid.).

It will be seen that Aristotle defines the parts of speech with reference to their function and meaning, rather than with reference to their form. The categories he has in mind should really be called sentence constituents. The second part of the verb definition clearly refers to the predicate of a sentence rather than to a word class. It is significant that the oblique cases of nouns are not looked upon by Aristotle as *onómata*, since, as he says, they cannot form propositions together with a *rhēma*. More surprisingly Aristotle accepts only the present tense forms as true verbs. Past and future forms are "not verbs, but tenses of verbs."

The analysis of the phrase as consisting of a combination of *ónoma* and *rhēma* is not Aristotle's invention. We find it previously in Plato, who hints vaguely at it in *Cratylus*, but is somewhat more explicit in the *Sophist* (fol. 262). Like Aristotle, Plato defines the terms as sentence constituents rather than as word classes. The *ónoma* indicates the performer of an action, the *rhēma* the action itself. And every complete sentence has to contain both an *ónoma* and a *rhēma*. Unlike Aristotle, however, Plato does not count time indication as essential to the verb.

The Grammarians. Neither Plato nor Aristotle were primarily concerned with linguistics proper, with questions having to do with the formal structure of language. If they analyzed expressions and sentences, it was in order better to understand what they stood for—ideas and propositions. Plato discussed language because of the light it might shed on the nature of knowledge; Aristotle because of its importance to logic.

During the following centuries more and more emphasis was given to the formal side of the discourse. But the logical and semantic foundation that had been laid was never abandoned. That might be a weakness from the point of view of theoretical consistency. On the other hand, thanks to this double base the linguistic theory of antiquity was flexible enough to be adapted to the description not only of Greek, but also of Latin, and later of the modern languages as well. It is no coincidence that the *ónoma-rhēma* (noun-verb) dichotomy has provided a starting-point for most attempts that have been made to formulate a general grammar.

The first to elaborate the parts of speech theory further seem to have been the Stoics. They recognized four parts: the noun (*ónoma*), the verb (*rhēma*), the conjunction (*súndesmos*), and the article (*árthron*). The latter two terms are also to be found in Aristotle, but the Stoics clarified the difference between them. The conjunctions are undeclinable, while the articles are declined for case.

The term case (*ptōsis*) was also redefined by the Stoics. While Aristotle had used it for both nouns and verbs, the Stoics restricted it to the noun. They also gave currency to the case names that are still in use: *onomastikē* ("nominative"), *genikē* ("genitive"), *dotikē* ("dative") and *aitiatikē* ("accusative," a mistranslation for "effective" or "causative").

The Stoics also tried to make a systematic description of the very complicated Greek verb conjugations. According to Aristotle's definition of the verb, time indication was essential to it. The Stoics, when pushing the analysis further, discovered that the Greek verb forms also had other functions: to indicate aspect (i.e., completed or incompleted action), mood (indicative, subjunctive, optative, imperative), and voice (active, medial, or passive). As far as we know—no complete account of the Stoic philosophy has come down to us—they did not quite succeed in unravelling the interrelation of these concepts. Perhaps because they held on to the view that time indication was the fundamental verbal function, they did not manage to disentangle the aspect and tense functions. The mood concept was treated as belonging to the sentence type rather than to the verb form. There is nothing surprising about the Stoic's failure on these points. After all, they were not chiefly concerned with linguistic form. Their interest, like Plato's and Aristotle's, was philosophical rather than grammatical.

While the philosophers analyzed language in order to understand reality, the grammarians were interested in language for its own sake. Or rather, they needed a correct description of the language system in order to judge and interpret the visible products of that system, whether classical literary texts that needed explanation, or spoken language that needed supervision so as to conform to a standard model. Both objects were of importance in Hellenistic times. The Homeric text, which was the foundation of all Greek literary

education, was becoming more and more remote from ordinary Greek, and the spread of Greek culture and Greek language all around the Eastern Mediterranean created a demand for pure *hellēnismós*, as the phrase was. The time was ripe for the grammarians.

One of the outcomes of the search for a standard was the struggle between *anomalists* and *analogists*. The analogists stressed the regularity of language. They tried to reduce its apparent chaos to order by establishing analogies: paradigms and schemas for the declension of words. The anomalists insisted that language was not determined by rules, but by custom. While naturally not denying that analogies could be established, they maintained that the assignment of words to different declension classes or conjugations was largely haphazard.

When faced with textual obscurities and difficulties, the analogists tended to emend the text by analogy with more common forms. The anomalists were more prone to accept the text as it stood. In their attitude to the standard language analogists took a normative stand, while anomalists would bow to custom and good usage. Analogists were authoritarian (Caesar published a pamphlet on the analogist side); anomalists were, if not democrats, at least liberal conservatives. The debate continued for several centuries. Out of it classical grammar developed. The only way for the analogists to prove their case was to show that it was indeed possible to reduce the apparent chaos of language to some sort of order. And all the time the anomalists compelled their adversaries to improve their descriptions by pointing to cases which did not fit the rules. In this way it was the language as such, not the philosophical uses of it, that occupied the center of the stage.

The work of the Greek grammarians, of whom Aristarchus of Alexandria (fl. ca. 160 B.C.) was the most famous, has come down to us in two versions, the grammars of Dionysius Thrax (fl. ca. 100 B.C.) and of Apollonius Dyscolus (fl. ca. A.D. 180). The former is a brief compendium of some twenty pages, which contains little more than definitions and explanations of the chief grammatical terms. The latter, which uses essentially the same terminology, is considerably longer and has a large separate section on syntax, which is entirely absent in Dionysius' book.

Dionysius defines grammar as having to do with pronunciation, explanation of textual difficulties and stylistic features, etymology, and, as he puts it, "the discovery of analogies." His approach is entirely philological and literary. This is a reflection of the fact that grammar had arisen out of the study of the old texts, and especially Homer. The wider, philosophical questions of the nature of language and the relation between language and thought were not touched upon at all by Dionysius.

Dionysius' "discovery of analogies," i.e., his morphology, introduces practically the whole of the conceptual apparatus of what was later to become traditional grammar. Like Aristotle, Dionysius recognizes two main parts of speech, noun and verb. His definition of them vaguely recalls Aristotle's, but it is more formal. He definitely seeks to define a word as a member of a class, not as a constituent of a sentence. The noun is defined formally as having case inflection, semantically as signifying "a person or thing." The different cases are enumerated and named. This is one of the great achievements of the Greek grammarians (and philosophers), since it requires quite a high degree of linguistic abstraction, in view of the fact that the declension morphemes in Greek and Latin express not only case but also number and gender. They also differ from one declension to another, and—especially in Greek—undergo extensive changes in different environments. As the classical grammarians never recognized any smaller semantic unit than the word—they never spoke about morphemes or suffixes, only about word endings—their task was made all the more difficult. All through antiquity the noun class included the adjectives. The adjective was not even recognized as one of the major subdivisions of the noun class. Dionysius' major subdivision is a formal one: original words (like *earth, white*) as against derived ones (like *earthly, whiteness*). The failure to separate the adjective class was obviously due to the ancient grammarians' weakness in the field of syntax.

The verb is defined by Dionysius as being devoid of case, but having tense, mood, person, number, and "kind" (active or passive). This is the system of traditional grammar almost full-fledged. Where Dionysius was weak, no improvement was to be made until modern times. That concerns above all the tense system, which he mixed up with the aspect system.

The other word classes recognized by Dionysius are: *metochē* (participle; thus called because it had both case and tense inflection, and thus participated in both the noun and the verb class), *árthron* (article; a case-forming part preceding a noun), *antōnymía* (pronoun; used in place of a noun), *próthesis* (preposition; could occur before all parts of speech—prefixes like *ad-* in *adapt* were considered as prepositions), *epírrhēma* (adverb; says something about a verb), and *súndesmos* (conjunction; "links together our thoughts in a determined order").

The accidence expounded by Dionysius Thrax is found practically unchanged in Apollonius Dyscolus, and was taken over almost completely by such Roman grammarians as Donatus and Priscianus. A somewhat more independent position was taken by the Latin writer Varro in his book *De lingua latina*, of which only six of the twenty-five chapters have been preserved.

The main change introduced by the Latin authors was to drop the article as a special word class (as Latin has no articles), and to introduce the interjection in its stead. Minor changes were due to the obvious differences between the Greek and Latin accidence, for instance, the ablative case. But the rather fundamental differences between the Latin and Greek verb systems were not clearly recognized. Priscianus tried, for instance, to carry over the Greek distinction between the optative and the subjunctive to Latin, thus indicating that he had not firmly grasped the fundamental principle of basing the morphology on the formal distinctions made in the language. The same weakness can be found, down to the present time, in a host of traditional grammars of modern languages.

The ancient grammarians' work on syntax was far inferior to that on accidence. This is due to the fact that they did not develop any theory of the sentence and sentence constituency. To the philosophers, *ónoma* and *rhēma* had been sentence constituents rather than word classes. The grammarians, while retaining the terms, had changed their function. As a result they did not know how to start analyzing the constituents of sentences. To Apollonius Dyscolus, as to Priscianus who followed him, syntax was therefore a question of finding out how word classes and word forms could be combined with each other on the basis of their intrinsic characteristics. This approach can achieve a limited success—for instance, to explain the concord of adjectives and nouns in the noun phrase, and the government of prepositions. But it cannot succeed at all in explaining the internal constituency of the verb or noun phrase in general, nor the constituency of the simple sentence, nor the interconnection of sentences and clauses, or infinitival or participial clause-like construction.

Every classical grammar started out with an account of letters and their pronunciation. That the point of departure was the letter, not the speech sound (phoneme) was natural, as grammar had arisen out of the study of literary texts, not the spoken language. The consequence of this approach, however, was that the letter and not the sound continued to be the fundamental unit in terms of which the form of words was discussed. Moreover, writers were constantly mixing up the two concepts.

The phonetic theory of the ancients was very deficient. No even remotely exact articulatory phonetics was developed. (On the Indian achievement, see below.) It is true that a consistent distinction was made between vowels and non-vowels. But the consonants were not described very efficiently. The distinction between voiced and unvoiced consonants, such as *b* and *p*, was not stated with any accuracy. Great importance was attached to the distinction between stops and continuants. The latter were generally called semivowels, a group which accordingly contained not only *l*, *m*, *n*, *r*, but also *s* and *f*.

As regards etymology no real improvement was made on the state of things illustrated in *Cratylus*. Though the grammarians recognized several types of derivation of verbs and nouns, and accurately described the different declension and conjugation classes, they never arrived at a clear view of the concept of the morpheme, whether word-base, derivational affix, or case affix. As long as this was so, they could not establish the main connections between the words in their own language, let alone those between Latin and Greek. The ancients were of course aware that these two languages were related, but could not make the proper distinction between similarities due to common origin and regular change, and similarities due to word loans. They had no realistic idea of the mechanism of language changes. They tried to explain them as due either to chance or to conscious manipulation by the speakers. Words were changed, they thought, or appeared in irregular shapes, for reasons of euphony, or to avoid ambiguity, or for some metaphysical reason or other. For instance, an *e* might be changed into *a* because *a* is more "dignified," as it comes first in the alphabet.

Against such a background one should not be too surprised to find even the most ridiculous etymologies advanced quite seriously. *Lapis* "stone" was derived from *laedens pedem* "hurting the foot." Even more remarkably, *lucus* "forest" was derived from *lucere* "be bright" because of the lack of light in the forest. In the same vein, *bellum* "war" was derived from *bellus* "beautiful" because war is the opposite of beautiful. These and other similar "etymologies" kept reappearing all through the Middle Ages and later, until the Europeans learned better from the Indians.

IV. THE MIDDLE AGES

The Schoolmen. The first five or six centuries of the Middle Ages in Europe were an era of intellectual recession in all branches of learning. Latin continued to be studied, as it was the language of the Church, and the normal means of communication of all clerics. But knowledge of Greek almost disappeared in the Western part of the former Empire. The classical Latin authors were also largely neglected. Therefore, one of the chief incentives for grammatical study, namely, the interpretation of an old and difficult literature, was lacking. Under the circumstances the chief function of

grammar became the pedagogical one. The youngsters were to be taught to read and to write correctly. Donatus' *Ars grammatica* was widely used as an elementary textbook. In fact, the name of the grammarian eventually came to be used as an ordinary noun, *donet*, meaning "primer," in medieval England.

Everything that was written on grammatical subjects in the Middle Ages took the form of commentaries on Donatus or, even more, Priscianus. Some small advances were made in these commentaries. Thus the important distinction between noun and adjective (*nomen substantivum* and *nomen adjectivum*) was first made, it seems, in the tenth or eleventh century. Some advances were also made in syntax. Thus the subject-predicate dichotomy was definitely reintroduced into grammar under the names of *suppositum* and *appositum*, and the clause-like construction called *ablativus absolutus* was recognized and defined.

But the independent effort of the Middle Ages in the study of language was the doctrine of the *modi significandi*. That doctrine was developed in the twelfth and thirteenth centuries, and arose from a desire to raise the status of grammatical teaching by making it conform to the standards set by Aristotelian logic and metaphysics. Aristotelian philosophy had by this time completely taken hold of the Arts faculties in the schools, especially in the famous university in Paris. In order to qualify as a science, grammar should be deducible from first principles by the methods developed in the current scholastic philosophy. And the first principles of grammar, one held, were the *modi significandi*, "ways of signifying." These were considered to be similar in all languages. Thus the *Modistae*, as they were called, thought they were building up a truly general grammar. They also called their science *grammatica generalis* or *speculativa*. Basically, the *modi significandi* are an attempt to define the functions of the different parts of speech. For instance, words like *dolere*, "suffer," and *dolor*, "pain," were said to have the same *significatio*, namely, pain, but different *modi significandi*: one signifying *per modum fieri*, the other *per modum substantiae*. The parts of speech definitions of Priscianus were restated in terms of the new concept. Later the concept was also used to redefine the subclasses and the inflected forms. The modes were then used as a basis for explaining syntax. Such a system, of course, was bound to fail in the same way as Priscianus' syntax failed. An adequate syntax requires an adequate theory of sentence structure, whereas Priscianus and the *Modistae* had only a (deficient) theory of word classes.

In reality the *Modistae* did no more than translate Priscianus' rather haphazard and ad hoc grammatical concepts into a highly abstract and abstruse terminology. It had only one advantage: it could be easily tied up with the common metaphysical jargon of the time. But when metaphysical realism gave way to metaphysical nominalism in the fourteenth century, the *Modistae* became obsolete. By and large the grammarians returned to the more practical but somewhat humdrum explanations of Donatus and Priscianus.

At the same time the claim of the *Modistae* that grammar should be considered as a general science had to be abandoned. It was to be taken up again some centuries later by the Port-Royal grammarians in a far more adequate form, freed from the hampering medieval veneration for authorities and from the sterile verbalism of the Schoolmen, and based on a far broader foundation of factual knowledge of languages.

V. THE RENAISSANCE AND THE ENLIGHTENMENT

The rediscovery of ancient literature, and concurrently with it, the opening up of new intellectual horizons in the Renaissance both had effects on language study. The subtleties of the Schoolmen were discarded, the more willingly as they were formulated in what the humanists considered as barbarous Latin. Grammar again became ancillary to literature. Moreover, Greek again became necessary equipment for scholars and gentlemen, and Hebrew was studied extensively. The Renaissance men refused to take the medieval authorities on trust; they went back to the sources.

At the same time interest in the popular languages awakened all over Europe. In his *De vulgari eloquentia* (ca. 1300) Dante made an impassioned plea for the superiority of the mother tongue over the artificial language of the clerics that was the Latin of the Middle Ages. As more and more of the popular tongues of Europe became literary languages, awareness of the differences among the grammars also naturally increased.

However, no really revolutionary advances were made in linguistics by the humanists and their immediate followers, but there is a remarkable sanity and soberness about much that was written. Thus J. J. Scaliger published in 1599 a remarkably correct account of the languages of Europe and their relation to each other. Also knowledge of the Hebrew language led to a realization that the parts of speech theory of antiquity might be called in question: Hebrew grammarians recognized only three parts of speech, noun, verb, and particle. In phonetics progress was made by the Englishman John Wallis, who published *Grammatica linguae anglicanae* in 1653. The attention to facts and common sense rather than to authorities and metaphysics was bearing fruit.

General Grammar. The chief result of the Renais-

sance was not, strictly speaking, to give the moderns access to the civilization of the ancients. It was, above all, to make them realize how far the human spirit might reach. The moderns began to emulate the ancients, and then tried to surpass them. In the seventeenth century it was clear to most that that goal had been reached. Not because the moderns were better men, but because, as Francis Bacon and others put it, they were standing on the shoulders of their predecessors. Anyhow, an era that produced philosophers like Galileo, Descartes, and Newton did not have to feel inferior to any that had come before. The achievement of these thinkers was their own, and not merely an explication of the work of the ancients.

The *Grammaire générale et raisonnée* of the Port-Royal School in Paris, written by Antoine Arnauld and Claude Launcelot (1660), is a product of the same independent spirit. The avowed object of the book is to set forth what is common to all languages. It was based on a thorough knowledge of Hebrew, Greek, Latin, Romance languages, and German. This in itself was new. Few previous grammarians had had such a wide empirical base to work from. But even more remarkable is the thoroughly independent approach to the subject. The authors set out to explain language by reference to the constitution of the human mind. For the first time we meet with grammarians who draw the proper linguistic consequences of Aristotle's insight that though the words vary, the thoughts that they stand for are common to all. The human mind is said to have three fundamental operations: conceive, judge, and reason. As reasoning consists in the comparison of judgments, the first two operations are fundamental. People "speak in order to express judgments, and the judgments are made about things that they conceive." A judgment is normally expressed by means of a proposition, and a proposition, such as "the earth is round," had two fundamental terms, the subject (*the earth*) and the attribute (*round*). Moreover, there is the link or copula (*is*) which predicates or "affirms" the attribute of the subject.

There is little here that Aristotle had not said before. But Aristotle never developed these ideas in linguistic terms. Nor had the medieval Schoolmen done so. The *grammatica speculativa* of the *Modistae* consisted essentially in a superficial harmonizing of Priscianus and Aristotle.

The distinction between conceiving and judging is essential for defining the verb, whose function, according to the Port-Royal grammarians, is to affirm. It is not, as all previous authorities had said, to mark time. Tense is accidental, not essential to the verb. A language need only contain a single verb, namely, the verb *is*. All other verbs can be analyzed as containing *is*, as a mark of affirmation, and in addition some attribute, of whatever kind. *He runs* is as much as to say *he is running*.

Thus the Port-Royal grammarians based their linguistic analysis squarely on sentence constituency. All of their predecessors had tried to progress in the other direction, by trying to build up the whole of their syntax on the system of parts of speech. The Port-Royal grammarians' approach was a new departure, and it was to influence subsequent grammatical thinking in many important respects.

Universal Language. Whereas the Port-Royal grammarians were concerned with laying bare the common structure of actually existing languages, other thinkers of the age went on from analysis to synthesis, attempting to construct a completely new, artificial language, designed to serve as an ideal medium of communication and thinking. Two men deserve mention above all others: the English bishop John Wilkins, and the German philosopher G. W. Leibniz.

Wilkins published in 1668 a large volume entitled *An Essay towards a Real Character and a Philosophical Language*, under the auspices of the Royal Society. Wilkins' "real character" is a kind of ideographic script, constructed on completely rational principles, and hence maximally systematic. (Wilkins explicitly contrasted it with the Chinese script in this respect.) He introduced some forty main characters, representing the main fields of human experience. Each of these is further subdivided into genera (usually six) and species (usually ten). By such a system, forty main signs, plus six plus ten modifications of them, are capable of distinguishing $40 \times 6 \times 10 = 2,400$ different concepts. For further refinement, compounding may be resorted to. The main symbols with their modification stand for what Wilkins called "principal words," covering nouns, verbs, adjectives, and adverbs. Grammatical words or "particles" are represented by smaller symbols above, below, and between the main characters. Superficially, a page in Wilkins' script is not unlike a page of Arabic.

Though Wilkins' chief object was to create a means of universal written communication, he also invented a way of reading it. For just as any spoken language can be reduced to writing, so any written text can be translated into a spoken one. Wilkins maintained that his language would be far easier to learn than a natural language, because of its systematic structure:

Now in the way here proposed, the words necessary for communication are not three thousand, and those so ordered by the help of natural method, that they may be more easily learned and remembered than a thousand words otherwise disposed of; upon which account they may be reckoned but as one thousand. And as for such Rules as are natural to

Grammar, they were not charged in the former account, and therefore are not to be allowed for here. So that by this it appears, that in point of easiness betwixt this and the Latin, there is the proportion of one to forty . . . (pp. 453–54).

The sentence about grammar refers to Wilkins' thesis that any natural language has two sets of grammatical rules: those common to all and those peculiar to each. His own philosophical language is meant to include only the former kind; the natural, universal rules.

Leibniz read Wilkins' book a few years after its appearance, and valued it very highly. But Leibniz wished to go further than Wilkins. His ultimate aim was to create a language which should not only be a subsidiary vehicle of communication, but an instrument of thought. Leibniz had already revolutionized mathematics by his invention of the higher calculus. His *characteristica universalis* aimed at introducing a calculus covering the whole field of human knowledge. As he said to a correspondent:

. . . each line [written in this universal language] would be a demonstration as in Arithmetic or Algebra. Two persons disputing on a matter . . . would only have to say, let us calculate . . . for in this way all errors would be nothing but calculating errors, and easy to correct by means of proofs similar to those . . . in arithmetic (to Johann Friedrich, Duke of Hanover, ca. February 1679; *Sämtliche Schriften und Briefe*, ed. Preussische Akademie der Wissenschaften, First Series, Darmstadt [1927], 2, 156; trans. Alvar Ellegård).

In fact, Leibniz looked upon mathematics as simply a sample (*échantillon*) of this all-embracing philosophical language.

But in order to reach this high aim it was necessary to have absolutely exact definitions of the terms that were to be used. Wilkins had made a start by defining quite a respectable portion of the English vocabulary in terms of his own system. Leibniz made several attempts to go beyond Wilkins. But he never managed to bring his work to a conclusion: he realized that the task was superhuman.

In our own time part of Leibniz' dream has been realized in the language of symbolic logic. But in this language the "principal words," as Wilkins called them, are not included. Attempts to represent formally the semantic content of such words have, however, been made, partly in connection with work on mechanical translation, partly as a result of the reorientation of linguistics caused by the introduction of transformational grammar. Uriel Weinreich, J. Katz, and J. Fodor deserve special mention in this connection. But we have still achieved immensely less than Leibniz' grand design. Wilkins' practical object, on the other hand, has been pursued with some limited success by the creators of artificial languages like Esperanto, Ido, Volapük. None of these, however, even aims at the thoroughgoing semantic consistency that Wilkins tried to achieve, and that caught Leibniz' imagination.

The Origin of Language. The view that Plato expressed in *Cratylus* to the effect that language had been originally invented by philosophers, seems to have been implicit in most ancient thinking. In the Middle Ages the question of the origin of language was hardly discussed. The Bible's story of the creation of man, and of the confusion of men's tongues in Babel was not put in doubt. In any case the historical perspective was extremely short. The ancients looked upon Homer as a representative of the youth of mankind, and Christians naturally looked upon Hebrew as Adam's language and thus the original mother tongue of all.

Neither the Renaissance nor the bold philosophizing of the seventeenth century brought any changes in these matters. René Descartes did not discuss the origin of language, nor did the Port-Royal grammarians. Their whole argument, however, indicates an implicit assumption, similar to Plato's, that language was invented by rational men.

In the eighteenth century the time perspective was gradually lengthened. E. B. de Condillac attempted to outline the gradual development of language in human society. But he did not commit himself to any definite time scale. His more famous friend, J. J. Rousseau, carried on the discussion in his prize essay on "The Origin of the Inequality of Men" (1754). Rousseau stressed the paradox that while language presupposes society, the creation of human society presupposes the existence of language. He therefore concluded that to invent language in a state of nature must have taken an infinite time.

The question raised by Rousseau was given full-length treatment by James Burnett, Lord Monboddo, whose six-volume *Origin and Progress of Language* was published 1773–92. Monboddo also looked upon language as an invention; there was, accordingly, a time when man did not speak. Rousseau had tried to imagine what that hypothetical state of nature was like. Monboddo did better; he could actually show us man in a state of nature: the ourang-outang, who cannot speak, but has all the physical characteristics of man, and therefore should be reckoned as belonging to the human species.

Monboddo agreed with Rousseau that for a creature like the ourang-outang to invent language must have been extremely difficult. The first beginnings must have been very crude. Again, Monboddo thought he could produce actual illustrations, and held forth the language of the Huron tribe in America, which, he said, is so "irregular" that no grammar of it can be written. Against this background it is not surprising that Monboddo could not imagine that a language like Greek, of whose absolute superiority he was convinced, could have been created by ordinary or common people. He felt his views were confirmed when he considered Chinese, Sanskrit, and the language of the ancient Egyptians. All those, he believed, must be the creation of a literate community.

Monboddo admitted that there are barbarian peoples with a civilized language. But that could be accounted for by language mixture and corruption, similar to what happened when Latin developed into the Romance languages. In fact, Monboddo was inclined to think that the ancient Egyptian language is the ultimate origin of all the European languages—including Hebrew—as well as of Sanskrit, whose similarity with Greek he was aware of.

The work of Monboddo is a curious mixture of crankiness and common sense. But he is far from untypical of his age. Above all, his idea that the highly inflected languages, and especially Greek, represented the best and highest type, continued to be an article of faith among the Europeans all through their imperialistic nineteenth century. Sanskrit was admired because it was, if anything, even more perfect than Greek.

In the nineteenth century linguists turned away from speculations on the origin of language. That was due to the development of far more exact methods in comparative linguistics, concurrently with the development of a more empirical attitude. Further, it came to be realized that no extant language is grammatically primitive. And last, there was Darwin's theory of evolution, which led to the establishment of an immensely extended time-scale. Language ceased to be looked upon as an invention. It was the product of the biological evolution of our species.

VI. THE NINETEENTH CENTURY AND AFTER

The eighteenth century was a great era for the collection and publication of useful knowledge. Interest in exotic countries and peoples was increasing rapidly. The fruits of this interest, as far as linguistics is concerned, are compilations setting out to describe all the known languages of the world. One such work is the Spaniard Lorenzo Hervas' *Catalogue*, in six volumes (1800–05). Another is the three-volume *Mithridates* (1806–17) by the German A. C. Adelung. A third is the *Comparative Vocabulary* of how 285 concepts were expressed in 200 different languages, which Catherine of Russia had the German zoologist P. S. Pallas compile (1786).

These massive collections of material, however, were to have less influence on the development of linguistics than their originators had hoped. Of far greater importance was the theoretical reorientation that was caused by the close study of one single language, Sanskrit. Sporadic references to the similarity of Sanskrit and the European languages can be found at least from the sixteenth century onwards (e.g., Filippo Sassetti, 1588). But nobody at that time was in a position to appreciate the importance of that kind of information. As long as it was believed that languages could be invented and changed more or less at will, there was nothing remarkable in any resemblances that could be found. And, after all, it was commonly assumed that Hebrew was the common origin of all languages. But in the eighteenth century the whole Indian peninsula was subjected to French or English rule. Among the colonists and administrators there were many people with a thorough literary, or even linguistic, education. The literature of India was discovered, and with it the extent of the similarity between Sanskrit and the European languages.

But more important than the extent of the similarity was the nature of it. Europeans brought up on the classical heritage had been used to look upon the complicated inflexional system of Latin and Greek as a sure sign of superiority. Now the researches of, above all, Sir William Jones showed that in precisely this respect Sanskrit left even Greek behind. "The Sanskrit language, whatever be its antiquity, is of a wonderful structure, more perfect than the Greek, more copious than the Latin, and more exquisitely refined than either, yet bearing to both of them a stronger affinity, both in the roots of verbs and in the forms of grammar, than could possibly be produced by accident," wrote Jones in 1786.

Sanskrit had not only the appeal of the exotic, but also the fascination of offering to the Europeans an insight into what they believed to be the glorious youth of their own civilization. It was for these reasons that it caught their imagination and attracted brilliant students. A combination of these happy circumstances led to a complete reorientation of linguistic studies.

Indian Linguistics. The seminal influence of Sanskrit on European linguistics was in no small part due to the impact of the Indian grammatical tradition. That tradition was at least as old as the Greco-Roman, and completely different. While Western grammar can be represented as a never quite happy marriage of logical analysis and linguistic description, the Indian grammar, as codified by the great Pānini (fl. 350 B.C.?) was wholeheartedly formal and descriptive. Its achievements in these respects are far in advance of anything the Europeans had done. The Indians had analyzed the phonological system of their language with great accuracy, and had also devised a writing system that matched the analysis. But above all the Indians were far superior to the Europeans in analyzing the morphemic constitution of words. The (verbal) root was made the basic unit. The root is of course a more abstract kind of unit than the word, as it normally does not occur as a free form. By isolating the root it was possible to discover the important variations that it could undergo—above all, the phenomenon of vowel gradation that is so important in Indo-European languages, as in English *spin-span-spun*. Further, the isolation of the root carried with it the isolation of the affix morphemes. Prefixes, derivational suffixes, and inflexional affixes were accurately described and their function defined. By stating fully under what conditions the root changed and the affixes were used, and what modifications they underwent, the Indians constructed what is in effect a generative grammar of Sanskrit word formation. Pānini set forth these results in a concise, almost algebraic form.

To some extent the Indian grammarians were helped by the structure of Sanskrit, whose morpheme structure is undoubtedly less complicated than that of Greek. Moreover, the language they described was even in Pānini's time a partly artificial one, especially in the form used in religious recital and ritual. Its regularity may to some extent have been the result of the efforts of the grammarians themselves, analogists all of them, to use the Greek term. Whatever the reason, their achievement was remarkable, especially in the fields of phonetics and morphology. Pānini also included syntax within his survey, but his successors—including the Europeans two thousand years later—tended to neglect it.

Historical Linguistics. Concern for historical perspective is undoubtedly one of the chief characteristics of the nineteenth-century intellectual scene. Geology, paleontology, archaeology, political history, literary history—all of these branches of learning were either born, or thoroughly reformed, in the nineteenth century. The Darwinian evolution theory may be seen as the culmination of this trend. Thus the historical perspective introduced into linguistics was due not only to the discovery of Sanskrit but also to the general historical trend of the age, especially in Germany, which was to dominate the linguistic scene throughout the nineteenth century. The Romantic movement, with its veneration for what was old, organic, and of popular origin, and its rejection of what was new, artificial, and cultivated, strongly encouraged those who turned their attention to the past. In Germany particularly there was also a nostalgia for a great heroic antiquity, to compensate for the national setbacks in the Napoleonic era.

All of these factors were of importance for Jacob

Grimm, who may be looked upon as the founder of historical linguistics. His imagination was caught when he discovered that the language of the medieval German texts contained many inflectional forms of the kind for which "the Germans used to envy the Greeks and the Romans." In other words, German might once have been as "perfect" as Greek. The belief in the superiority of the past, and the hope to establish a connection with the glorious classical languages provided the impetus. Important discoveries followed. Grimm's main contribution was to insist on the systematic nature of the sound correspondences between the Germanic languages and the classical ones. That there were fairly regular such correspondences had been pointed out before, for instance, by one Kaspar Cruciger as early as 1616. What Grimm did was to reveal the pattern in the correspondences. There was a common factor in the change of *p* to *f*, of *t* to þ, and of *k* to *h*, namely, that the unvoiced plosives had become spirants, while retaining the same place of articulation. And there was a further pattern in the fact that as the original *p*, *t*, and *k* disappeared, the voiced plosives *b*, *d*, and *g* moved into their place by simply losing their voicing. Finally, all the aspirated plosives, represented in Greek by φ, ϑ, χ, lost their aspiration to become *b*, *d*, and *g* in the Germanic languages.

All of these correspondences had been pointed out by the Dane, Rasmus Rask, in a prize essay of 1814. But it was Grimm, in 1822, who brought out and stressed the beautiful symmetry, the movement of the sounds, as it were, in a perfect circle, one set moving out of a place which was then taken by another set. Moreover Grimm showed that a similar movement took place later in the development of High German.

Thus the "sound law" was born. Grimm did not use that term himself, though the developments he described have later been summarized as "Grimm's law." It was Franz Bopp, the writer of an epoch-making treatise on the *Conjugation System of Sanskrit* (1816), and of a *Comparative Grammar* of the main Indo-European languages (1833–52) who made the concepts of "sound law" the central one of historical linguistics. Bopp consciously tried to adapt the method of linguistics to what he conceived to be that of the natural sciences. He hypostatized language as an independent organism, developing according to equally hypostatized laws, independently of the speakers. The contrast with the ancient view, where the speaker had full control, could not have been greater.

In Grimm's "sound law" the linguists had an organizing principle with which to master the masses of material that they collected. By comparing languages with one another and looking for systematic correspondences, the whole linguistic history of the Indo-European nations was to be written. In that way the mechanism of language and language development was to be laid bare.

The study of Sanskrit had taught the Westerners how to analyze an individual language accurately. The notion of "sound law" introduced the same demand for strict accuracy in the comparison of languages. After two thousand years of etymological speculation they could begin to argue from facts and principles.

An important event in the development of the concept of "sound law" was the publication of the article by the Dane Karl Verner on what he called an "exception" to Grimm's law (1876). Grimm himself had noted that the change of *p*, *t*, *k* to *f*, þ, *h* did not always take place: the result was sometimes *b*, *d*, *g* instead. Verner managed to show that the exceptions were themselves systematic. The exceptional sounds only occurred under certain specified conditions, having to do with the old Indo-European accentuation. Encouraged by Verner's success, some brilliant young linguists (among them Karl Brugmann and Hermann Osthoff) chose to lay down as a postulate that the laws of sounds admit no exceptions. Apparent exceptions only proved that the "laws" were not stated accurately enough.

The *Junggrammatiker* ("young grammarians"), as they were called, met with strong opposition: it was the ancient struggle between anomalists and analogists all over again. Above all, several linguists were loath to accept the theory that the "sound laws" were completely autonomous, independent of the will—or the whims—of the speakers. But however justified the objections, it is obvious that the postulate of the *Junggrammatiker* led to a considerable tightening of the methodological discipline of the linguists.

The raising of the standards led to further progress in several directions. The search for the detailed mechanism of the "sound laws" led to advances in descriptive phonetics. The necessity for explaining apparent exceptions led to an intensified study of dialects. The creation of linguistic atlases, like Jules Gilliéron's *Atlas linguistique de la France* (1902–12) was one of the results. The focusing of interest on the detailed mechanism of linguistic change thus led to an intensified study of the living languages, which alone afford a full view of all the possible factors influencing language change.

Structural Linguistics. The wheel had come full circle. The search for a complete explanation of the history of language had again brought the linguists face to face with the living language. The main theorist of this development is the Swiss linguist Ferdinand de Saussure. He made his mark as a leading *Junggrammatiker*, but is important above all for his work on general linguistics, which was published posthumously by his pupils in 1916 as *Cours de linguistique générale*.

Language, says Saussure, has a double face. On one hand it manifests itself as *parole* ("speech"), which is the actual performance of speakers when they speak or write. On the other hand, it is also *langue* ("language"), which represents the knowledge or competence that all speakers possess of their language. All changes in language occur in *parole*, in the actual speech act. But only some of these changes become institutionalized in *langue*.

Language can be studied in two ways, either diachronically, following its changes through time, or synchronically, analyzing its condition at a given moment. Nineteenth-century linguistics had considered mainly the diachronic aspect. Saussure stressed the primacy of the synchronic view. A complete diachrony could only be achieved by comparing not only isolated facts, like sounds, but the whole state of the language at one period with that prevailing at another. Saussure insisted on the systematic nature of language. Language is a structure, a functioning whole in which the different parts are determined by one another. In fact, no linguistic sign means anything by itself: it only acquires value by being distinguished from other signs in the language.

These ideas of Saussure's were taken up by several other linguists, especially outside Germany, where the historical school continued to be strong. Among them we may mention L. Hjelmslev, the founder of the Danish glossematic school, and the Russian prince N. S. Troubetskoy, one of the founders of the Prague school of phonology in the 1930's. Applying Saussure's idea of language as a system of values, Troubetskoy turned his attention to the distinctive function of the language sounds. The linguist, whose chief concern was *langue* rather than *parole*, should investigate to what extent phonetic differences were used in the language in order to distinguish one linguistic sign from another. Thus the concept of the *phoneme* was born.

The methods used for the establishment of the elementary linguistic unit, the phoneme, were later carried over to work on the smallest meaningful element in the language, the *morpheme*, especially in America, where Leonard Bloomfield was the leading figure. On the whole, the ideas launched by Saussure, and their successful application above all in phonology, led to an increased methodological awareness among the linguists in the period between the two world wars and after. The success of nineteenth-century diachronic linguistics had to a large extent been due to the consistent use of the concept of "sound law." It was felt that twentieth-century synchronic linguistics also needed a leading principle around which to organize its work.

Transformational Grammar. It is noticeable that the structuralistic linguists of the thirties, forties, and fifties

have in the main focussed their attention on the external side of language, on phonology and morphology rather than on syntax. In this they followed in the footsteps of their nineteenth-century predecessors. The typical "historical grammar" of the last century was two-thirds phonology and one-third morphology. It is true that B. Delbrück wrote a *Comparative Syntax* of the main Indo-European languages, published 1893–1900, but in the main, syntax was neglected: one had no methodological tool, comparable to the "sound law," to treat it in a scientific way. The theoretical framework remained the traditional one. Many linguists expressed their dissatisfaction with it, but few had anything to put in its stead. An exception is the Dane, Otto Jespersen, who introduced, among other things, the distinction between *nexus* and *junction* expressions, which roughly equals that made by Aristotle between predicative and non-predicative expressions. Jespersen also elaborated a theory of rank, designed to explicate the idea of syntactic rules.

Structuralists in general felt that syntax—like semantics—would have to wait until a sure foundation for grammar had been built on phonology and morphology. That seemed natural, as "immediate constituent analysis" (Bloomfield's version of traditional parsing theory) had to be based on the morphemes as ultimate elements.

A dramatic change, however, took place in the fifties. Noam Chomsky, professor of linguistics at Massachusetts Institute of Technology, published in 1957 a little book called *Syntactic Structures*, in which he outlined a new approach not only to syntactic analysis, but to grammar and linguistics in general. It was followed in 1964 by a far more extensive treatment, *Aspects of the Theory of Syntax*. The new approach, generally called "transformational grammar," has had a tremendous impact, and has led to almost feverish activity in practically all linguistic fields during the late fifties and sixties. The number of publications influenced by Chomsky's ideas runs into thousands, and they appear in all parts of the world. It seems evident that linguistics is undergoing a change of orientation which is quite as spectacular as the one that led to the establishment of historical linguistics in the early nineteenth century.

The American structuralists in the Bloomfield tradition had carried to an extreme the empiricism and positivism that had prevailed in linguistics for over a century. Hence their neglect of the content side of language. Hence also their insistence on the observation and classification of the material—the text—as the chief object of linguistic analysis.

Chomsky made a clean break with these views. A theory of language, as of anything else, cannot be produced mechanically from the material, but has to be invented. The classification of the "surface" properties of the text is not likely to yield the most fruitful basic concepts of linguistic theory. Instead, the basic concepts may very well be highly abstract constructions, connected with the observable reality only in an extremely complicated fashion. The basic concepts of, say, nuclear physics, illustrate this point. In principle transformational theory aims at constructing a theory which stands to language as physical theory stands to the world of matter. One of its basic assumptions is that linguistic expressions—sentences—have not only a surface structure, but also an underlying deep structure which is not immediately available for inspection. Roughly speaking the deep structure of a sentence represents its content, the surface structure its form.

Chomsky has himself pointed out that the notion of deep structure may be said to be implicit in the seventeenth-century idea of general grammar, an idea that had been almost totally eclipsed for a century and a half. But there is at least one important difference between the Port-Royal grammarians and Chomsky. The seventeenth-century grammarians left it to the intuition of the intelligent reader to establish the connection between the general grammar and the actual grammars of the particular languages. But the modern transformationist aims at stating explicitly (i.e., formally, mathematically) how the deep structures of a language can be transformed into surface structures. Starting from a precise, postulated set of primitive terms and operations it should be possible to generate fully any grammatical sentence in the language. Such a grammar is called a "generative grammar," a term which is also sometimes used for the new approach as a whole.

Transformational grammar clearly bears the imprint of its own age. Like most linguistics in the twentieth century it is synchronic rather than diachronic. Its employment of postulates and abstract models recalls the contemporary models of the advanced natural sciences. Its insistence on strict formalization is natural in an era where the hard work of comparing the theory with the facts can be handed over to the electronic computer.

But at the same time, transformational grammar is also the product of more than two thousand years of thinking about language. The distinction made between deep structure and surface structure may be said to complete the work that the Port-Royal grammarians had started, namely, to utilize to the full the contribution of Aristotle and of the philosophers to language study. And it is clear that the formalization of transformational grammar could not have been attempted without the strict methods of analysis developed by structural linguists. They, in their turn, owed much of their acumen in these matters to the *Junggrammatiker*

and, ultimately, to the Sanskrit grammarians. Linguists, like all others, develop their science by standing on the shoulders of their predecessors.

BIBLIOGRAPHY

General works: Francis P. Dineen, *An Introduction to General Linguistics* (New York, 1967), provides the history of linguistics discussed mainly in the light of twentieth-century structural grammar. Hans Arens, *Sprachwissenschaft: Der Gang ihrer Entwicklung von der Antike bis zur Gegenwart* (Munich, 1969), provides extracts in German translation from works on language from Ancient Greece to modern times, with historical notes and a commentary connecting the extracts. Half the text is devoted to the nineteenth century—mainly Germany—one-fourth to the twentieth century. R. H. Robins, *A Short History of Linguistics* (New York, 1967), gives comparatively ample space to ancient linguistics and to transformational grammar.

Particular periods: H. Steinthal, *Geschichte der Sprachwissenschaft bei den Griechen und Römern*, 2nd ed. (Berlin, 1890; reprint 1961). R. H. Robins, "Dionysius Thrax and the Western Grammatical Tradition," *Transactions of the Philological Society* (1957), 67–106. Theodor Benfey, *Geschichte der Sprachwissenschaft und orientalischen Philologie in Deutschland* (Munich, 1869), the first 300 pages of which are a general history of linguistics, with about 65 pages devoted to Indian grammar. J. F. Staal and Paul Kiparsky, "Syntactic and Semantic Relations in Pānini," *Foundations of Language*, **5**, No. 1 (1969). Jan Pinborg, "Die Entwicklung der Sprachtheorie im Mittelalter," *Beiträge zur Geschichte der Philosophie und Theologie des Mittelalters*, **42**:2 (Münster, 1967), is chiefly concerned with the epistemological aspects of the *Modi Significandi* theory. Charles Thurot, *Notices et extraits des Manuscrits de la Bibliothèque Impériale*, Vol. 22:2 (Paris, 1868), consists of extracts from medieval manuscripts on grammar, with connecting commentary. Holger Pedersen, *Linguistic Science in the Nineteenth Century*, English trans. (Bloomington, 1959), is a popular introduction, written in 1924. John Lyons, *Introduction to Theoretical Linguistics* (New York, 1968), is a balanced account of modern linguistic theories.

ALVAR ELLEGÅRD

[See also Analogy; Evolutionism; Historicism; **Linguistics; Positivism in the Twentieth Century;** Renaissance; **Rhetoric; Structuralism.**]

ANCIENT GREEK IDEAS OF LAW

I

THE ABSENCE from ancient Greek, as from English, of a single word—and thus of a concept—to express that body of legal principles which the Romans termed *ius* as distinct from *lex* (cf. French *droit: loi*, German *Recht:*

Gesetz) constitutes only one feature which makes a discussion of Greek concepts of "law" difficult. A second problem arises from the scanty source material. We can speak of *Greek* concepts only for the early archaic period (ca. 750–ca. 600 B.C.) for which the Homeric poems provide approximately the same kind of evidence for Greek Asia Minor as Hesiod provides for the mainland. For the rise of independent city-states, each with its own legal system, militated against the development of one concept of law, valid for the entire Greek world; moreover, since our evidence for the later archaic (ca. 600–ca. 500 B.C.) and for the classical periods (ca. 500–323 B.C.) comes almost exclusively from Athens, we have reliable access only to Athenian concepts of law for these periods. This is less of a loss than it might seem, because it was Athens which bequeathed her concept of *nomos* to the Hellenistic world in the wake of the conquests of Alexander the Great. It is to these three periods, then, that our attention will be confined.

A third factor, while presenting a further difficulty, also provides a methodological key toward an understanding of the variety of concepts of "law" found in Greek antiquity. None of the Greek expressions for "law" either originated or is found in exclusively legal contexts, but in addition to their legal connotations they all played important parts also in such spheres as cosmology, religion, politics, personal conduct, and philosophy, and often in such a way that our compartmentalized concepts cannot exhaust their meanings. Therefore, an examination of the range of usage of each relevant concept will enable us to discover a basic idea inherent in it and thus to differentiate the various concepts from one another.

II. THE EARLY ARCHAIC PERIOD

Since written law, which contributes most decisively to separating the sphere of law from other aspects of human existence, did not make its appearance in most of the Greek world before the seventh century B.C. and in Athens not until Draco (traditional date: 624 B.C.), the concepts of *themis* and *dikē*, which dominate throughout the early archaic period what we would call "legal" thinking, denote concepts of law considerably wider and more comprehensive than any later terms. For that reason it is incorrect to apply our notions of "unwritten law" to them, for where the written law has not been conceived of, its opposite cannot have been conceived of either.

Although *themis* plays a larger part than *dikē* in the *Iliad* and *dikē* than *themis* in the *Odyssey* and in Hesiod, the two concepts complement rather than exclude each other. Both are part of a social order which views them as having existed from time im-

memorial and believes that they will continue to exist without change, since the permanence of the order is guaranteed by the gods. In fact, both *themis* and *dikē* are often treated as divine persons, and both are in many passages related to the supreme god, Zeus. While the *Iliad* regards Themis as an Olympian deity (*Iliad* 15. 87–95, 20. 4; cf. *Odyssey* 2. 68–69), Hesiod makes her the child of Earth (Gaia) and Heaven (Ouranos), born even before Kronos and thus older than the Olympian generation of gods (*Theogony* 135). After Zeus had consolidated his power, he took her as his second wife, and by him she became the mother of Dike (*Theog.* 901–02; cf. *Works and Days* 256). If this shows in a genealogical and personal form the interest Zeus takes in the social order, Zeus' interest in them is also evinced by many passages which do not treat them as persons: it is Zeus who has entrusted the king with his staff and *themistes* (*Il.* 2. 205–06, 9. 98–99), it is Zeus who is concerned that in judicial proceedings *themistes* be sorted out with straight *dikē* (*Il.* 16. 386–87; *W.& D.* 9), and it is the *themistes* of Zeus which are to decide whether a royal person may be killed (*Od.* 16. 403. See also for *themis*: *Il.* 1. 238–39; *Od.* 11. 568–69, 14. 56–58; and for *dikē*: *W.& D.* 36, 239, 268–69, 276–80; *Hymn to Hermes* 312, 324; Archilochus, frag. 94). Thus both *themis* and *dikē* are permanent and immutable; although they both have a beginning in cosmic time, there is never any suggestion that they are the creation of man, that they have a beginning in human society, or that they are merely transitory, that is, that today's *themis* or, to a slightly lesser extent, *dikē* will no longer be valid tomorrow.

A further characteristic shared in common by *themis* and *dikē* is that both operate only in the larger social group. They do not function in the *phratrē* or the family, the smaller groups of which society is composed. This is shown best in Nestor's definition of the lover of civil strife as a person "without *phratrē* without *themis*, and without a hearth" (*Il.* 9. 63–64) to indicate that he is rejected by every kind of association: being without *themis* means exclusion from society in the widest sense. According to Hesiod, *dikē* is confined within the city (*W.& D.* 269). Similarly, the Cyclopes are called *athemistoi* ("without *themis*") because they are food-gatherers and shepherds rather than peasants and because they live the solitary existence of mountain-cave dwellers (*Od.* 9. 106–15, 187–89). This is not contradicted by the statement that "each one wields *themis* over his own children and wives, and they do not concern themselves with one another" (*Od.* 9. 114–15), for the *themis* here is *themis* only by analogy with a normal society: the very absence of community life denies the possibility of genuine *themis*. For that very reason Polyphemus is described as "knowing neither *dikai* nor *themistes*" (*Od.* 9. 215).

But these similarities are rather general and may be attributed to the way in which a society that has not yet broken life into separate compartments regards itself. Within this framework there are, however, significant differences between *themis* and *dikē*, differences which can be articulated more readily in some cases than in others. *Themis* (derived from a stem meaning "set," "place," "establish") is the wider concept of the two and tends to define those aspects of the social structure which give order and regularity to the whole, whereas *dikē*, whose etymology links it to a stem meaning "show," "point in a given direction," usually describes the place assigned to individuals within human society: it seems originally to designate claims or rights which define the place a person occupies within a community, often with the connotation that this place is actually or potentially assigned by the verdict of a judge.

In view of this it is not surprising that *dikē* plays no part in what we would call the constitutional and religious aspects of law. Here *themis* holds the field alone. The position of the king, as the keystone of the political structure of society, is guaranteed by the staff and the *themistes* which Zeus has given him (*Il.* 2. 205–06). These impose on him not only the right to give counsel but also the obligation to take advice from others (*Il.* 9. 98–102; cf. the beginning of an early epic, the *Cypria*, in Proclus' *Chrestomathy* 1, where Zeus deliberates with Themis about starting the Trojan War). In short, the *themistes* constitute those rights, prerogatives, and obligations by virtue of which the king wields power. One of the prerogatives is exercised by Agamemnon when he claims for himself the right to tempt the troops by proposing flight (*Il.* 2. 73–74); but the other nobles have prerogatives, too, in that they may dispute his proposals in assembly (*Il.* 9. 32–33). The royal prerogatives impose on his dependents the obligation to offer gifts to the king, and these gifts, embodying the dual aspect of prerogative and obligation, are also called *themistes* (*Il.* 9. 156, 298). In return, it is the king's *themis* to be ever ready to receive men who may wish to consult with him on matters of policy (*Il.* 24. 652). In short, it is on his *themistes* that the king's singular status in the community is based. The fact that he has received them from Zeus does not mean, however, that royal decisions are divinely inspired or revealed by Zeus to the king, else it would not be *themis* to contradict the king in assembly (*Il.* 9. 32–33). But it shows that the royal position in the social and political order is sanctioned by the supreme god, and this sanction suggests that it will continue to be as it is for all time. If prerogatives are temporarily

denied, it is *themis* that they be restored or granted at a later time: this at least is implied by Zeus's promise to those who had been denied their honors and prerogatives in the reign of Kronos (*Theog.* 395–96).

The constitutional prerogatives of the kings are manifested primarily in the *agorē*, a term which denotes the institution of a political assembly as well as the place where it is convened, and the *agorē* is, therefore, closely associated with *themis*. Themis is ordered by Zeus to convoke an assembly of the gods (*Il.* 20. 4), and she also dissolves and seats the assemblies of men (*Od.* 2. 68–69), where alone it is *themis* to challenge the king (*Il.* 9. 32–33). Moreover, *agorē* and *themis* are closely related as places, the one for assembly meetings and the other as the place of judgment, in the *Iliad* (11. 807) and possibly also in the *Odyssey* (9. 112).

In religious ritual we hear of a number of specific commands and prohibitions which are described as *themis* or *ou themis* ("not *themis*") respectively to indicate that certain ritual practices are part of the established order of life. When a banquet is held in honor of a god, it is *themis* to pour a libation and pray to him (*Od.* 3. 45), and it is *themis* for men in their several habitations to worship the gods and to offer sacrifice at their altars (*W.& D.* 135–37). On the other hand, it is *ou themis* that water touch the head of Achilles before Patroclus' funeral rites are completed (*Il.* 23. 44–46) or that a person hated by the gods be helped on his way (*Od.* 10. 72–75). In this context, too, presumably belong the *themistes* of Phoebus Apollo which are proclaimed by Minoan Cnossus and the pronouncements which come from Apollo's oracular shrine at Telphusa (*Hymn to Apollo* 393–96, 252–53, 292–93). It will be noted that the ritual *themistes* are not prerogatives which have been entrusted to a person but rules which men are expected to observe and the observation of which is accepted without question as part of the way things are in the universe.

"Rule" seems also to be one of the connotations of *themis* in the administration of justice. This, at any rate, is suggested by the fact that the administration of justice rests with persons called *dikaspoloi* ("handlers of *dikē*") whom Zeus has entrusted with the guardianship of the *themistes* (*Il.* 1. 237–39; cf. *Od.* 11. 186), and that is presumably the reason why Hesiod once applies the term *themistopoloi* to kings (frag. 10). The *themistes* mentioned here cannot be identical with those that constitute the royal prerogatives of ruling and counselling; they look more like a body of legal rules or principles on which judicial decisions are based, rules which no doubt included procedural matters, such as taking an oath to confirm one's legal claim (*Il.* 23. 581–85). Although in Hesiod jurisdiction is one

675

of the functions of kings (*Theog.* 80–86; *W.& D.* 248–50, 263–64), there is no evidence to affirm or to deny that the Homeric *dikaspoloi* were identical with the kings, even if their *themistes*, like those of the kings, are derived from Zeus. Nor is there any reason to assume that the divine assignment of the *themistes* to the judge meant that his verdicts were regarded as divinely inspired. One passage in the *Odyssey*, it is true, has been adduced to support the contention that Zeus was regarded as a source of law: as the suitors deliberate about murdering Telemachus, Amphinomus proposes first to ascertain whether the *themistes* of Zeus approve the murder of a royal person (*Od.* 16. 403). Since we are not told in what way Amphinomus thought of conducting his inquiry, there is no need to assume that he meant to ask an oracle for a specific injunction. In fact, no other passage in early archaic literature attributes specific legislation to a god, and the role of the gods does not go beyond guaranteeing the existing order as a whole. In view of that, the most natural interpretation is that Amphinomus intended to address his question to some human expert, possibly a *dikaspolos*, knowledgeable about the rules prevailing in the Zeus-given social order, in order to obtain from him instructions how to act under the circumstances. An expert of this kind might be a person like Nereus, of whom Hesiod says that "he does not forget *themistes* but knows just and kindly counsels" (*Theog.* 235–36), that is, someone who fulfils among the living the function which Minos performs among the dead: a *themisteuōn* ("person who wields *themistes*") who is asked to issue *dikai* (*Od.* 11. 568–71).

In matters of jurisdiction *themis* is frequently found in conjunction with *dikē*. In such contexts it seems to refer not to legal principles upon which verdicts are based, but to denote a "legitimate claim," a "title," or a "right" which the verdict has conferred upon one or both of the contending parties in a lawsuit. This is shown by the standard expression δίκην κρίνειν θέμιστας ("to separate rights by means of a verdict") with which Hesiod regularly describes the activity of a judge. The purpose of a trial in the early archaic period was not to establish the facts of a case but to have each of the contending parties state his claim under oath and to have the judge pass on the validity of the opposing claims. The act of the judge is described by the verb *krinein*—"separate," "distinguish," "decide" (*Il.* 16. 387–88; *Theog.* 85–86, *W.& D.* 35–36, 221); *dikē* is the verdict by which a given claim is validated, and *themis* is the validated claim, the right, or the title. The fact that *dikē* is etymologically linked to a complex which indicates "pointing in a direction" explains why a just verdict is called "straight" and an unjust verdict "crooked" (*Il.* 18. 508; *Theog.* 85–86,

W.& D. 35–36, 219, 221, 225–26, 250, 262, frag. 286), and why the activity of issuing just verdicts is expressed by the verb *ithynein*—"straighten" (*W.& D.* 263–64). The adjectives "straight" and "crooked" are always applied to *dikē*, and only once do we hear of "crooked *themistes*" (*Il.* 16. 387), evidently because claims authenticated by crooked verdicts are thought of as being themselves crooked.

From its meaning "verdict" a number of other uses of *dikē* can be derived. One of these is its application to the occasion or place at which verdicts are given, that is, to the session of the law court where legal proceedings take place. Hesiod informs us, for example, that Hekate sits *en dikēi* with reverent kings (*Theog.* 434) and Solon appeals to Earth to be his witness before the court of time, ἐν δίκῃ χρόνου (Solon, frag. 24. 3; cf. frag. 27, which may mean "obey the magistrates both in court and out of court," but both the reading and the interpretation are uncertain). But the use of *dikē* to describe a claim is more common, a claim different, however, from that expressed by *themis*. For while *themis* is used invariably of a claim which has been authenticated by a verdict and which has thus been recognized as part of the established order, *dikē* denotes what is regarded by the claimant as a just claim but which has not yet been validated or whose legitimacy is or may be contested; a claim, in other words, which, though adjudicated, is looked upon as still open to dispute. For example, it is with a view to claims that Achilles might possibly still make that Odysseus urges Agamemnon not only to deliver publicly the promised gifts of reconciliation but also to invite him to a banquet, so that Achilles may "lack nothing of his *dikē*" (*Il.* 19. 180). Similarly, *dikē* is used of Antilochus' protest that the prize awarded to Eumelus in the funeral games for Patroclus is actually *his* due (*Il.* 23. 542), and Hesiod describes as *dikē* his claim against his brother, which has been submitted for adjudication to the "gift-devouring princes" (*W.& D.* 39). In the *Hymn to Hermes* we find for the first time the expression δίκην διδόναι καὶ δέχεσθαι to describe the claim and counterclaim which is to be submitted to adjudication, and which is, in this case, to be weighed on Zeus' "scales of *dikē*" (312, 324).

Closely related to this is the contestable kind of *dikē*, which comes close to the meaning of *themis* ("title," "right"), but differs from it in that the claim is open to criticism and is not thought of as properly belonging to the immutably established order. In Hesiod's statement that he does not want to be righteous (δίκαιος) if a less righteous person (ἀδικώτερος) has the greater *dikē* (*W.& D.* 271–72), we are evidently dealing with a claim of this kind. It seems to be a claim unfairly validated by a judgment and Hesiod protests against it. The same is implied in Theognis' contention that evil men are corrupting the people by giving *dikai* to the unrighteous—i.e., to those not entitled to them—in order to increase their own profit and power (44–46); and the converse, namely that an otherwise contestable *dikē* will not be challenged, underlies his belief that nobody will wish to deprive of respect and *dikē* a distinguished man as he grows old (938).

Derived from its judicial sense as "verdict" *dikē* also is the "punishment" or "retribution" assigned to the doer of evil, and it is a punishment the justice of which is never questioned. This meaning, which *dikē* retains into the classical period and beyond, is first found in Hesiod's warning that Zeus ordains *dikē* against those who indulge in "evil arrogance and works of wickedness" and that *dikē* will visit a city for the crooked verdicts (*dikai*) with which people oppress their fellow men (*W.& D.* 238–39, 248–51), and it assumes a central role in Solon as the personified power of Retribution (frags. 1. 7–8, 3. 14–16; cf. Anaximander, frag. 1, and Heraclitus, frag. 94). The justice inherent in the idea of *dikē* as retribution is positively expressed especially in those passages in which *dikē* is contrasted with *hybris*, as it is in Hesiod's exhortations to his brother to listen to *dikē* and not incur *hybris* and to forget violence because *dikē* will triumph over *hybris* in the end (*W.& D.* 213, 217, cf. 275), or in Theognis' belief that shamelessness and arrogance have vanquished *dikē* all over the earth (291–92). In the *Iliad* this kind of *dikē*, which may best be rendered as "justice," is said to be driven out by men who adjudicate crooked *themistes* (*Il.* 16. 387–88; cf. *W.& D.* 224), while in the *Odyssey* it is bracketed with all things good and proper as being honored by the gods (*Od.* 14. 83–84). Hesiod goes so far as to treat it as the differentia between man and beast: to beasts Zeus assigned a way of life which makes them devour one another, "since *dikē* is not among them, whereas to men he gave *dikē* which is the best by far" (*W.& D.* 276–80). Thus *dikē* becomes the distinguishing feature of human civilization, an aspect to which we shall return later.

Finally, some uses of *dikē* seem to reflect the view that verdicts establish legal norms which are valid for the community. Glaucus, the ruler of Lycia, preserved his country by his might and by his *dikai*, that is, by the norms he propounded through the verdicts he gave (*Il.* 16. 542). Minos is asked for *dikai* among the dead (*Od.* 11. 570), and in the Iron Age the norms of right and wrong (*dikē*) reside in brute force (*W.& D.* 192). The same *dikai* seem to be involved in Solon's conviction that the good order (*eunomiē*) which his reforms will create will "straighten out crooked *dikai*," and that after his reforms his laws will apply a "straight *dikē*" to each person (frags. 3. 36, 24. 19).

The distinctions we have been drawing between the use of *themis* and *dikē* in different spheres of human life obviously do violence to the cultural context in which they belong. For while we have to differentiate the constitutional, religious, legal, and social aspects of these terms in order to make them comprehensible to ourselves and to find equivalents for them within our conceptual framework, the differences among these areas of life were less distinct for the Greeks of the early archaic period. For them *themis* and *dikē* were each one concept, regardless of how they were applied in particular cases. The truth of this is particularly evident as we now turn to the uses of *themis* and *dikē* to describe certain social features of life and certain ways of human behavior. Both *themis* and *dikē* in this field treat behavioral norms as immutable and perennial parts of the universe within which man has been placed and without which community life would cease to function. But while in many instances no difference can be detected between the contexts in which one term is preferred over the other, there is a general tendency to find *themis* defining rules which govern the correct *relations* into which men enter with one another or with the gods, while *dikē* tends to describe the essential *characteristic* of a group on the basis of which a certain kind of conduct can be expected from the individual members belonging to that group.

Thus *themis* regulates human behavior toward the gods in the statement that it is *ou themis* to fight with Poseidon (*Il.* 14. 386) or to help on his way a person hated by the gods (*Od.* 10. 72–75), that it was *ou themis* that Achilles' helmet be defiled in the dust as long as a *theios anēr* ("godlike man") wore it (*Il.* 16. 796–99), or that it is *themis* for men in their several habitations to worship the gods and offer sacrifice at their altars (*W.& D.* 135–37). It governs relations within the family when we learn that it is *themis* that a wife weep for the husband she believes lost abroad (*Od.* 14. 130) or that a son embrace his returning father (*Od.* 11. 451); relations between the sexes in the statement that it is *themis anthrōpōn* ("themis for humans") that men and women have sexual intercourse (*Il.* 9. 133–34, 275–76); and relations between allies in Zeus's promise, as he was trying to gather allies for his fight against the Titans, to give honors and prerogatives to those gods from whom Kronos had withheld them (*Theog.* 395–96). The most frequent use of *themis* in the description of social norms concerns the relation of host and guest, that is, the relation of *xeinoi* to one another. The hospitable entertainment of strangers and the exchange of gifts with them is *themis* (*Il.* 11. 779; *Od.* 9. 268, 14. 56, 24. 286, cf. 20. 287); when a visiting stranger asks for information, it is *themis* to give him a truthful answer (*Od.* 3. 186–87); and when he is the

677

subject of a discussion, it is *themis* for him to participate in it (*Od.* 16. 91).

While *themis* thus describes the normal kind of behavior in various human relationships, implying a correct norm, deviations from which are possible but reprehensible, *dikē*, which is in social contexts usually accompanied by a genitive defining the group whose *dikē* it is, denotes an intrinsic natural characteristic from which certain modes of behavior can be expected; it does not automatically imply a relationship, and deviations from it, where possible, are not measured by the yardstick of right and wrong at all. When it is said of mortal men, for example, that it is their *dikē* that in death fire consumes their flesh and bones while their soul (*psychē*) flies off like a dream (*Od.* 11. 218–22) or of the Olympian gods that they are perceptible to men only as radiant light (*Od.* 19. 43), no relationship is implied, and what is predicated is no more than a simple fact of natural experience, namely, the way in which a given group naturally behaves. In the same vein, the *dikē* of old men is to sleep softly after a bath and a meal (*Od.* 24. 254–55), and the *dikē* of a man who has long been away from home is to be dejected when asked about his ancestry (*Od.* 19. 167–70). The fact that seafarers go ashore and eat a meal when their ship has landed is *dikē* (*Hymn to Apollo* 458–61), as is the fact that slaves, fearful of their new masters, give only small gifts to strange visitors (*Od.* 14. 58–61). Two passages are interesting because they describe deviations from *dikē:* Odysseus is said to have been a remarkably good ruler in that he did not follow the *dikē* of kings, whose treatment of people is determined by their likes and dislikes (*Od.* 4. 691–92), and the suitors are said to be extraordinarily wicked because they do not follow the *dikē* of suitors of former times, who used to provide a banquet and gifts for the bride and her family rather than consume her property (*Od.* 18. 275–80). In both passages it is significant that it is the deviation from the norm which elicits praise or blame; the norm itself remains merely descriptive and morally neutral.

Yet it is often hard to determine why, in some of the passages just discussed, *themis* is used in preference to *dikē*, although it must be observed at the same time that there seems to be no use of *dikē* for which *themis* would have been more appropriate. For instance, the *themis*, discussed above, that men and women have sexual intercourse with each other, or that a wife weep when she has lost her husband abroad, might just as well have been expressed by *dikē*, and this is particularly true of the statement that *hybris* is the *themis* (rather than *dikē*) of mortal men (*Hymn to Apollo* 541). We can only guess that in these cases, and perhaps in some others too, an option was open to the poet

to view the action either as something right and proper in terms of the relationship involved, or as a typical natural characteristic, and that he adopted the first alternative.

Closely related in sense to the use of *dikē* plus the genitive is its use, normally in the plural, as the object of the verb "to know." When Nestor's rich experience of life is described as "he knows *dikai* and mentality better than anyone else" (*Od.* 3. 244), he is credited with a knowledge of the different ways of people, and *dikai* seems to be used in exactly the same sense when we are told that the Cyclops lacks this kind of knowledge (*Od.* 9. 215). Theognis' complaint (54) that those who now hold power "knew formerly neither *dikai* nor proper forms of behavior (*nomoi*)" points in the same direction, for the implication is that the present rulers were not brought up to know the ways of social conduct needed for the proper functioning of society. In this context perhaps also belongs Hesiod's warning that Zeus will notice what kind of *dikē* a city practices (*W. & D.* 269), for, although the singular is used here, the passage suggests that different kinds of *dikē* exist, and the phrase "it does not escape his notice" is of course merely a different way of expressing knowledge.

Themis and *dikē* are the only terms in which a concept of law can be expressed in the early archaic period. But, as we have seen, they provide much more than merely a set of legal rules by which right and wrong are determined. They belong to a society which is convinced that its own stability is guaranteed everlastingly by gods, who have assigned to kings the prerogatives that make them rulers and to judges the principles by which disputes are to be adjudicated. The verdicts of these judges legitimatize claims and rights and establish binding norms for the community, and the behavior of the members of the society toward one another is regulated by a code which sanctions some actions and forbids others. They are the only equivalents of concepts of law in early archaic society; but "law" is too narrow a term to encompass them.

Since *themis* and *dikē* constitute the bonds which keep the structure of the larger society intact, they are the hallmarks of the civilized life of the community. The primitiveness and barbarity of the Cyclopes, a pastoral gathering and nonagricultural society of isolated mountain-dwellers, who know no authority other than that exercised by the head of the family, is brought out by their description as *athemistoi* and "knowing *athemistia*" and as "knowing neither *dikai* nor *themistes*" (*Od.* 9. 106–15, 187–89, 215, cf. 114–15. See also Theognis 54). In the *Iliad*, *themis* is opposed to forces destructive of society: the lover of civil strife is without *themis* (*Il.* 9. 63), and Ares, the god of destructive war, "knows no *themis*" (*Il.* 5. 761). Hesiod presents the positive side of the picture when he identifies *dikē* as a force conducive to the preservation of society. As the daughter of Zeus and Themis, she is the sister of Peace, *Eirēnē*, and Good Order, *Eunomiē* (*Theog.* 901–02). Zeus gave mankind *dikē* to differentiate it from the beasts (*W.& D.* 276–80), and that city will flourish in which straight *dikai* are given to citizens and strangers alike (*W.& D.* 225–27). Therefore also *dikē* is the implacable foe of that peculiar trespassing of the bounds of propriety which the Greeks called *hybris* (*W.& D.* 213, 238–39; Archilochus, frag. 94), and even though *hybris* may degrade *dikē* to violence in the Iron Age (*W.& D.* 190–93; cf. Theognis' complaints at 44–45 and 291–92), *dikē* will win out in the end (*W.& D.* 217–18).

Another enemy of *dikē* in early archaic literature is violence, *bia* (*Il.* 16. 386–88; *W.& D.* 275), but this enmity does not survive unmodified into the late archaic period. In a passage in which Solon boasts of the accomplishments of his cancellation of debts (*seisachtheia*), he attributes his liberation of the earth and of Athenian citizens from bondage to his use of his legitimate power (*kratos*) to fuse *bia* and *dikē* into one (frag. 24. 15–16). That *bia* refers to the coercive measures by which he made creditors give up their claims is clear. But what is the point of *dikē* here? That it does not refer to Solon's statutes emerges from the fact that the written legislation is mentioned as a separate and different achievement in the next sentence of this poem (18–20). Nor does the context allow us to interpret *dikē* as a verdict or norms established by a verdict, since that would make nonsense of its association with *bia*. In fact, although *dikē* in Solon may still describe claims established by crooked verdicts (frag. 3. 36), Solon no longer uses the term for the verdict itself. In our passage it evidently refers to the moral norm, justice, which has been redressed by means of violence through Solon's authority, and in some other passages, too, a moral rather than a legal aspect of *dikē* is emphasized by Solon: it is the retribution that will overcome the evildoer, late though it may come (frags. 1. 8, 3. 12–16). Still, this does not mean that *dikē* loses its legal connotations in Solon altogether, for it is still used of the "straight" claim which, he asserts, his legislation assures to each individual as his due (frag. 24. 19), and it is still applied to the legal proceedings in which justice is meted out (frag. 24. 3). But *dikē* no longer occupies the central place as a concept of law in the strict sense which it occupied together with *themis* in Homer and Hesiod.

These developments foreshadow the role played by *themis* and *dikē* after the end of the early archaic age. Unlike *dikē*, *themis* vanishes completely from current legal usage and is found only as an archaism, generally with religious overtones, in poetry and in elevated prose passages in Plato. *Dikē*, on the other hand, remained current in daily prose as well as in poetry, but no longer as a concept of law in the sense in which we have been concerned with it. For while it retained the sense which it had, mainly in the *Odyssey*, of an essential characteristic defining a group and continued its development along the moral lines to which Solon had pointed, the moral norm of justice and the idea of a quasi-divine retribution, its use in legal matters was narrowed to designate a private (as opposed to a public) lawsuit, judicial proceedings, a trial, and the punishment inflicted by the court. Thus it was deprived of the central part which it had played in Homer and especially in Hesiod, and whatever notions of "right" (*ius*) may originally have been inherent in it were taken over by the adjectival *to dikaion*, which, however, never developed into a technical judicial term. In short, *themis* and *dikē* as concepts of "law" come to an end with the early archaic age and new terms take their places.

III. THE LATE ARCHAIC PERIOD

The beginning of written legislation toward the end of the early archaic age constitutes the most decisive influence upon the formation of new concepts of law in the late archaic period, since it sets the stage for a distinction between those aspects of community life which can and those which cannot be reduced to precisely formulated written regulations. We have no certain knowledge of either the date or the place of the first enactment of written statutes, and we are also ignorant of the identity of the first giver of written laws. Draco, to whom Aristotle attributes the earliest written legislation in Athens (*Athenaion Politeia* 41. 2) and whose code is usually dated 624 B.C., was certainly not the first giver of written laws in Greece. Whatever the truth about Lycurgus and the date of his legislative activity may be, there is no doubt that the Greeks believed Sparta to have had some written statutes before Athens (but see Plutarch, *Lycurgus* 13). But again, we do not know whether any state preceded Sparta in the written publication of laws. We can be certain only that written legislation did not antedate the emergence of the city-state (*polis*) as the basic social and political unit in the Greek world.

We know a little more, however, about some new concepts of law which emerge with the development of written legislation, although our knowledge stands on rather feeble legs. The terminology used by different states to describe their statutes provides an important clue for the interpretation of their notion of "law." One element in such an interpretation is etymology, which tells us to what kind of root a given word for "law" is related; another element is the variety of contexts in which the terms for "law" may be used. Since for all cities, with the sole exception of Athens, however, the quantity of surviving writings is very meager indeed, we do not have a sufficient number of contexts to check the results obtained through etymology against actual usage of the relevant term. Accordingly, etymology is in most cases the only method by which we can get at the concepts of law prevailing in different states in the late archaic as well as in the classical period, and our interpretation will be subject to the rather narrow and often unreliable limits which etymology imposes.

Apart from the Athenian term *thesmos,* to be considered at greater length later, the earliest terms for "written statute" are commonly derived either from stems meaning "to speak," "utter," "pronounce," or from stems meaning "to write." To the first of these groups belongs *rhetra,* a term early applied to Lycurgus' enactments at Sparta (Plutarch, *Lyc.* 6), but attested from the early sixth century B.C. on also for such Dorian states as Tarentum, Heracleia, and later also Messenia, for Ionian Chios, for Olympia, and for Cyprus (for the evidence see Busolt-Swoboda 1. 456). From the same root *ta eirēmena* is derived, which appears as a term for "statute" in early fifth-century Mycenae (*Inscriptiones Graecae* 4. 493). The concept underlying these two expressions is evidently that of a pronouncement or an utterance authoritatively made, in most cases by a people or an assembly; but whether it was originally envisaged as the pronouncement of an individual or a group we cannot tell. Moreover, with the exception of the Lycurgan *rhetra,* which is said to have been an oracle from Delphi (Plutarch, *Lyc.* 6), all other *rhetrai* of which we know from literary or epigraphical sources seem to have been regarded as human pronouncements. It may well be that the idea underlying *rhetra* and *ta eirēmena* is similar to the idea behind *dikē* in its sense of "verdict"; but this association has no ancient evidence to support it and also lacks an etymological basis. And further, there is no reason to assume that either *rhetra* or *ta eirēmena* originated from the utterance of a judge rather than from that of some political organ.

Less problematic is that group of terms for "statute" which is associated with the stem of a "writing" (*to graphos*), which appears side by side with *rhetra* in some inscriptions of the sixth century from Olympia (Schwyzer, Nos. 410. 5, 413. 7, 412. 1–2, 418. 19) and *ta grammata,* or expressions such as "as it is written," with which the fifth-century code of Gortyn invariably refers to itself. The basic idea manifested in these expressions is that a special importance and validity attaches to regulations promulgated in written form.

More we cannot say, and we can only surmise that the people of Olympia and Gortyn may have thought of writing as lending permanence to their laws, which these would lack if they were not published in written form.

We are in a much better position to determine Athenian concepts of law both for the late archaic and for the classical period. For the former *thesmos* was the technical term for a written statute, occasionally in the adjectival formation *ta thesmia.* The date when this concept first appears in Athens cannot be firmly established. According to Aristotle (*Athenaion Politeia* 3. 4) one of the functions of the *thesmothetai* before the legislation of Draco consisted in keeping written records of *ta thesmia,* which, since he attributes the earliest written legislation to Draco (41. 2), cannot have been statutes but probably records of particular judicial decisions or statements of the principles underlying such decisions. That Draco called his written laws *thesmoi* is attested by the only survivor of his legislation, a republication of 409/8 B.C. of some of his laws on homicide (*Inscriptiones Graecae* 1². 115. 19–20), as well as by later references to his legislation (*Athenaion Politeia* 4. 1, 7. 1; Andocides 1. 83, etc.). In the case of Solon, we know from the poem discussed toward the end of the preceding section that next to his *seisachtheia* he regarded as his main achievement the enactment of written *thesmoi,* through which he gave each individual "a straight *dikē*," i.e., his proper due (frag. 24. 18–20, cf. Plutarch, *Solon* 3. 5); and at least one of his surviving statues refers to itself as a *thesmos* (Plutarch, *Solon* 19. 4). The term remained valid throughout the tyranny of Peisistratus (Herodotus 1. 59. 6), and its last official use appears in the prescript of a regulation from the time of the expulsion of the Peisistratids (511/10 B.C.), in which the old Draconian law against tyranny is described as *thesmia kai patria* (*Athenaion Politeia* 16. 10). After the end of the sixth century, *thesmos* is used only for antiquarian and not for substantive reasons.

There is nothing controversial about the etymology of *thesmos.* Like *themis* it is derived from a root meaning "set," "place," "establish"; but unlike *themis* it has in its legal sense no divine sanction and it is not conceived of as a manifestation of a general social and political order. The basic idea inherent in the term is of something imposed by an agent or an agency on a place or upon a group which is regarded as the recipient of the imposition and for whom (in the case of the group) it constitutes an obligation.

In the earliest occurrences of *thesmos* that have come down to use the "imposition" is taken in a very concrete and literal sense and refers to an object placed in some significant location. Thus, in the only Homeric passage in which it is found (*Od.* 23. 296) *thesmos* signifies the proper location of the marriage couch of Odysseus and Penelope; Pindar applies it to the wreaths placed upon the victor's brow (*Olympian Odes* 13. 29); in Demeter's attribute *thesmophoros* it refers to the bringing forth of ritual objects which had been deposited in a special place; and in Anacreon it denotes a treasure (frag. 61).

Much more commonly, however, the imposition is to be taken in a metaphorical sense. In Aeschylus' *Eumenides* (391–93) *thesmos* refers not only to the place in the universe assigned by the gods to the Erinyes but also to the establishment of an institution, such as the establishment of the Areopagus as a court to try cases of murder (484, 615) and the pronouncement which constitutes the founding act (681, cf. 571). The establishment of an institution is involved also in the *Supplices*, where sexual intercourse is called a *thesmos* of Aphrodite (1034), and in Pindar's naming the Olympic Games as a *tethmos* of Heracles and the Isthmian Games as a *tethmos* of Poseidon (*Olymp.* 6. 69; *Nemean Odes* 10. 33, cf. 11. 27; *Olymp.* 13. 40), and a founding act is described when the immortals established Aegina as a pillar for strangers from all the world (*Olymp.* 8. 25–27).

Thesmos (or more usually the plural *thesmoi* or the adjectival *thesmia*) is also the term for fundamental regulations governing different aspects of communal organization. Political regulations established by the rulers are called *thesmoi* in the ephebic oath (Tod, No. 204. 11–14); in Aristophanes (*Birds* 331) and in Herodotus (3. 31. 3, cf. 1. 59. 6) their antiquity is stressed. Social rules are involved in the laws safeguarding the institution of marriage (Sophocles, *Antigone* 800–01; cf. Euripides, *Medea* 494) and protecting the ancient order as such (Euripides, frag. 360. 45); and *thesmoi* are moral rules when they demand loyalty to constituted authority, reverence for parents, or prescribe that the doer must suffer (*Antigone* 802; Aeschylus, *Supplices* 708, *Agamemnon* 1564).

In some contexts *thesmos* is sanctioned less by external enforcement than by forces within the agent himself. The term then denotes basic rules of propriety and good conduct, as it does in Pindar's excuse that *tethmos* and the pressure of time prevent him from telling a story fully (*Nem.* 4. 33) and in his rule to praise the Aeacidae whenever he comes to Aegina (*Isthmian Odes* 6. 20). Similar *thesmoi* are honored by Bellerophon in Euripides' *Stheneboea* (15, in Page [1942]).

Of most immediate relevance to an understanding of the concept of law are specific political and religious *thesmoi*. The written statutes of Draco and Solon have already been mentioned. To them must be added a number of Locrian statutes called *tetthmoi* (Buck, Nos.

57, 59), and fifth-century regulations from Athens and Delphi (*Hesperia* 36 [1967], No. 15; Buck. No. 52). But there are a number of passages which show that writing is an accidental and not an essential attribute of *thesmos*. The instructions the centaur Nessus left about the use of his blood (Sophocles, *Trachinian Maidens* 682), the ritual *thesmia* performed by Ajax (Sophocles, *Ajax* 712), the *thesmia* of the Areopagus which the Erinyes fear (Aeschylus, *Eumenides* 491), and several other *thesmoi* and *thesmia* are not very likely to have been issued in writing. In other cases, such as Democritus' proposed *thesmos* for the protection of public officials (frag. 266) or Hecuba's question, which *nomos* or *thesmion* sanctioned Polyxena's sacrifice (Euripides, *Troades* 266–67), the problem of written legislation is hardly relevant to the issue. In short, although *thesmos* seems to have emerged no earlier than written statutes, and although it is the earliest term applied to them in Athens, the fact that the legislation is written is not an intrinsic part of the concept.

What does this discussion teach us about the concept of law in the late archaic period, which ends for our purposes with the last attested use of *thesmos* as a technical term for "law" in Athens in the prescript of a reenactment of Draco's law against tyranny in 511/10 B.C.? The basic idea underlying all the uses of *thesmos* is that of something imposed by some higher authority upon those for whom the thing imposed constitutes an obligation. In its application to the legal sphere it denotes, accordingly, a law enacted by a lawgiver and imposed either in writing or in a non-written form, upon a community which, though it is bound by the law, has not necessarily had a voice in formulating it. It resembles *themis* and *dikē* in that it constitutes a binding obligation for the members of the community, which by this time is the city-state. But, unlike *themis* and *dikē*, it is not part of a universal order, was never personified, and is always thought of as having had a beginning in human time. Moreover, unlike *dikē* it is not formulated by the pronouncement of judges but is logically prior to such utterances and forms their basis. It also differs from *nomos*, the concept of law which came to the fore at the beginning of the classical period in Athens and remained the technical term for "statute" in Greece to this day. To it we shall now turn our attention.

IV. THE CLASSICAL PERIOD

There is reason to believe that the change from *thesmos* to *nomos* as the official term for "statute" in Athens was sudden and that it was the result of a deliberate policy (Ostwald [1969], Part III). After 511/10 B.C. *thesmos* is no longer applied as a current term to the statutes that were enacted; and, although *nomos* appears before that date (but only outside Athens), it does not carry the meaning of "statute" before the fifth century B.C. Moreover, the use of *nomos* in the sense of statute is first attested in Aeschylus' *Supplices* (387–91), first performed in 464/3 B.C., so that the adoption of a new term to replace *thesmos* must fall within the period 511/10 and 464/3. That it is associated with the most important internal event in Athens during this period, the overthrow of the tyranny and the democratic reforms of Cleisthenes of 507/6, is corroborated by the fact that we find at the same period in the Harmodius songs the first emergence of the only early *nomos*-compound which has political overtones, *isonomos*, as a term which celebrates the establishment of a democratic form of government in Athens. It is likely, therefore, that the rise of *nomos* is closely linked with the rise of the Athenian democracy; and the uses of the term in extra-legal contexts both before and after 511/10 lend weight to this supposition.

Etymologically *nomos* is derived from the root *nem-*, which signifies a "distribution" or an "assigning" of some kind, seen less from the point of view of an agent making the assignment than from the standpoint of the person to whom the assignment has been made. But the idea of distribution does not go very far in explaining the basic concept underlying *nomos* as "law," and we depend on an examination of the different contexts, legal as well as nonlegal, in which it is used to determine its nature. Such an examination will lead us to the conclusion that *nomos* describes an order of some kind, which differs from the order expressed in the early archaic age by *themis* in that it sees its sanction in its acceptance by those who live under it and who acknowledge it as valid and binding for themselves. It is, therefore, not part of a universal order but of a limited social order, nor is it like *thesmos* something imposed by an external agent; even when it is attributed to a god or a lawgiver, the source of its validity always remains its general acceptance as a norm by those who constitute a given milieu.

In its widest sense, *nomos* denotes an order of living, a way of life, and it is in this sense that the word is first attested in Greek literature. According to a Hesiodic passage, discussed in a different connection above, Zeus ordained for men the *nomos* that they should live with *dikē*, while the beasts which live without it should devour one another (*W.& D.* 276–80, cf. *Theog.* 66). The point here is not that *nomos* is god-given, but that Zeus's arrangement is regarded as the valid norm by beasts as well as by men. For each kind *nomos* is their own way of life. Theognis uses *nomos* in this sense of the perverted norms with which the present rulers govern Megara (289–90); and in the fifth

century it is applied by Aristophanes to the ways of the birds (*Birds* 1344–45), by Euripides to the ways of the gods (*Hippolytus* 98) and of mortals (*Supplices* 377–78). A similar *nomos* describes specific institutions which make up the normal order of things. Thus it is *nomos* that the union of male and female will result in children (Aeschylus, *Agamemnon* 1207), that blood spilled will demand more blood (Aeschylus, *Choephoroe* 400), that all great things entail destruction (Sophocles, *Antigone* 613–14), or that men defend themselves against enemy attacks and kill their opponents in battle (Thucydides 3. 56. 2, 66. 2).

To this some uses of *nomos* are related which define the proper way in which something is done or the normal or proper conduct of an individual. For the former of these we may cite Hesiod's injunction to strip for sowing, ploughing, and harvesting (*W.& D.* 388), Aeschylus' description of the natural and proper formulation of a prayer (*Choephoroe* 93), Pindar's prescription for horse-breeding or the way of using drugs (*Isthm.* 2. 38, *Nem.* 3. 55), or Herodotus' tale of how the lake-dwellers build their houses (5. 16. 2). Normal human conduct under given circumstances or for a particular kind of individual is described as *nomos* frequently by Euripides, who applies the term, for example, to the new standards of behavior which a woman has to adopt after marriage (*Medea* 238), to the rule to help the shipwrecked (*Cyclops* 299), to the love which all living creatures have for their offspring (frag. 346), to the rule of the gods not to interfere in each other's province (*Hippolytus* 1328), and many more. In short, in these cases, too, *nomos* denotes a norm accepted by most people.

A rather different sense of *nomos* describes the source that issues and guarantees those norms which are regarded as an obligation by those whose norms they are. It is first found in Heraclitus' statement that all human *nomoi* are sustained "by one the divine" (frag. 114). The "human *nomoi*" refer evidently to the mores prevailing in the several city-states; but the "one the divine" seems to be a *nomos* which transcends them, being the source on which they depend. The same kind of *nomos* is apparently that of which the Erinyes complain that they have been deprived (Aeschylus, *Eumenides* 778–79 to 808–09) as well as the *nomos* which, they allege, Apollo transgressed in honoring Orestes (ibid. 171). The "ancient *nomoi*" of Zeus, too, mentioned by both Aeschylus and Sophocles (*Supplices* 670–73; *Oedipus at Colonus* 1382), must be the source of norms rather than the norms themselves; and when Creon states in the *Antigone* (177) that the ability of a man is not fully known until he has been tested ἀρχαῖς τε καὶ νόμοισιν, it is obvious that his authority in issuing regulations is meant.

A value judgment is attached to *nomos* when it

describes that state of law-and-order or of a civilized existence which results from the adherence to accepted norms by all members of the community. *Nomos* here has connotations similar to those which *eunomia* has elsewhere in Greek literature, and it takes the place assigned to *themis* in one of its uses in the early archaic period. For example, while in Homer the uncivilized state of the Cyclopes was expressed in the words "he knows well neither *dikai* nor *themistes*" (*Od.* 9. 215), Herodotus expresses the same lack of civilization of the Androphagi by saying that they do not practice *dikē* and use no *nomoi* whatever (4. 106). This use of *nomos,* also in juxtaposition with *dikē,* appears for the first time in Theognis (54) and is found frequently without *dikē* and in a positive sense throughout the fifth century. In Sophocles Ismene bases her refusal to support Antigone on the argument that it would be a violation of *nomos* to defy the tyrant's decree (*Antigone* 59), Orestes justifies his murder of Aegisthus by saying that anyone who transgresses *nomos* should be killed (*Electra* 1506), and Theseus boasts that Athens accomplishes nothing without *nomos* (*Oedipus at Colonus* 914). In Euripides, Jason cites the availability of *nomoi* as one of the benefits he bestowed upon Medea by bringing her to Greece (*Medea* 538); and among the prose authors the most interesting application of the term is found in Thucydides' report of the speech of the Thebans against the Plataeans, in which they describe the reestablishment in Thebes of an orderly government, opposed to tyranny as well as to a narrow oligarchy as τοὺς νόμους ἔλαβε (3. 62. 3–5).

From these *nomoi,* which are thought of as prevailing among all decent men and in all societies, we now turn to regulations whose validity is envisaged within a narrower compass, because they describe the mores of a particular community. In this category belong the many *nomoi* which all Greeks share in common (Herodotus 6. 86β. 2, 7. 102. 1; Euripides, *Orestes* 495, frag. 853; Thucydides 1. 41) and by which they are differentiated from the *nomoi* of non-Greeks (Euripides, *Andromache* 243, *Bacchae* 484) and also those *nomoi* which in Herodotus' account of Darius' experiment each people likes best, viz., its own (3. 38. 4). In this sense, too, *nomos* is applied to the mores of a particular city, e.g., Athens (Aeschylus, *Eumenides* 693; Thucydides 3. 34. 4, 37. 4), Sparta (Herodotus 7. 136. 1; Thucydides 5. 60. 2), Thebes (Sophocles, *Antigone* 191; Euripides, *Bacchae* 331), Samos (Tod, No. 96. 15–16), Thessaly (Pindar, *Pythian Odes* 10. 70–71), and the many tribes and peoples, Greek and non-Greek, whose *nomoi* fill the pages of Herodotus.

The use of the plural in *nomoi* ("mores") shows that these *nomoi* are the aggregate of a number of norms which a people regards as valid and binding in its social, religious, and political life, and for each of these

also *nomos* is the proper term. For social customs (*nomoi*) prevailing in different communities Herodotus is again our main source. To cite but a few: he likes the Persian *nomos* which prevents a father from seeing his child before the age of five, lest the child's untimely death bring him grief (1. 136. 2–137. 1), and the Babylonian *nomos* of auctioning off marriageable women (1. 196. 1–4); but he does not like the Babylonian custom of temple prostitution (1. 199. 1–5). Euripides speaks of *nomos* in this sense when he mentions the Greek custom of honoring athletes (frag. 282. 13), of the Aetolian practice of going to war with only one foot shod (frag. 530. 9), or of the Phoenician habit of bowing down before a royal person (*Phoenissae* 294). While in these examples *nomos* is treated as a valid and generally accepted norm, other uses of the term indicate that custom had come under attack: *nomos* is used of practices which, though current, are in some way reprehensible or at least not worthy of respect. This is the case, for example, when Euripides calls *nomos* the custom of heralds to give exaggerated reports (*Heraclidae* 292–93), or when Orestes justifies the murder of Clytemnestra by saying that he put an end to the *nomos* of wives to kill their husbands (*Orestes* 571). In these instances, the use of *nomos* is obviously facetious. But the very fact that it can be so used shows that it is no longer immune to attack.

The devaluation of *nomos* becomes especially common when the term denotes a belief conventionally held but which will not stand up to closer scrutiny. When *nomos* first appears in this sense in extant Greek literature, the fact that such a belief is commonly held still gives it validity. This is the case in Pindar's famous poem νόμος ὁ πάντων βασιλεύς (frag. 169), where the stature and reputation of Heracles are regarded as justifying even his most violent deeds (see Ostwald, op. cit., pp. 37–38), in the *nomoi* which sum up Creon's convictions about the nature of a good citizen in Sophocles' *Antigone* (178–79), or in the description of the repute which, Alcibiades claims, his Olympic victories had brought Athens (Thucydides 6. 16. 2). But when Empedocles (frag. 9. 5) says that, while it is more correct to speak of "mixture" and "separation" than of "birth" and "death," he himself uses the less correct terms *nomōi,* when he does not speak as a philosopher; or when Democritus (frags. 9, 125) distinguishes between the true nature and the conventional appellation of color, sweetness, and bitterness, *nomos* is assigned an inferior place. From here it is only a small step to its rejection, for example, in Euripides' statement that illegitimate children are only *nomōi,* but not in fact, inferior to legitimate offspring (frag. 141), and in Callicles' championing *physis* (nature) over against *nomos* (Plato, *Gorgias* 482e–484c).

The earliest application of *nomos* to religious ritual

is found in Hesiod (frag. 322, cf. *Theog.* 417); and thereafter this use becomes so common throughout classical Greek literature that a few examples must suffice. *Nomos* governs the deposition of a suppliant's bough and the worship of Hermes (Aeschylus, *Supplices* 241, 220), the proper burial of the dead (Sophocles, *Ajax* 1130, 1343; *Antigone* 24, 519; Herodotus 2. 36. 1, 3. 16. 3–4, 6. 58. 2; Thucydides 2. 52. 4), the granting of asylum (Herodotus 2. 113. 2–3), the inviolability of altars (Euripides, *Helen* 800, frag. 1049. 2), purification rites (Euripides, *Orestes* 429, *Hercules Furens* 1361, *Helen* 871), and many other religious practices and beliefs. Since we are not told by whom religious *nomoi* are given and since their observance seems to be more important than the sanction behind them, we are justified in interpreting these *nomoi* as defining what is generally accepted as the proper thing to do in relation to the gods.

Finally *nomos* denotes those political and judicial regulations which are our main concern here, since they include *nomos* as the classical expression of the Athenian concept of law. It is important to note, however, that although *nomos* in this sense is the proper technical term for a written statute, in the first half of the fifth century B.C. not every political or judicial *nomos* is written. That the earliest surviving use of *nomos* as "statute" occurs in Aeschylus' *Supplices* (387–91), where it is a law governing the claims of the next-of-kin over marriageable heiresses, has already been mentioned. Since regulations of this kind may have been part of Solon's legislation, we are justified in assuming that the reference is to written legislation. The same assumption is warranted in Herodotus' reference to Solon's *nomoi* (1. 29. 1–2); but it is extremely doubtful that the *nomos* which gave the Athenian polemarch at the time of Marathon the command of the right wing of the army (6. 111. 1) was embodied in a written document, and the same is true of the *nomos* which prevented the Corinthians from giving away ships without payment (6. 89). Similarly, in a law from Halicarnassus of ca. 460–455 B.C. (Meiggs and Lewis, No. 32): the fact that it refers to itself as *nomos* shows that the term was used to describe a written statute (lines 32, 34–35); but, when the same law (lines 19–20) stipulates an oath to be taken *nomōi* by jurors, we have no way of knowing whether the oath was incorporated in a written law. In short, in the early fifth century the question whether a given statute existed in writing or not was of less interest to the Greeks than that it was generally looked upon as valid and obligating.

A similar ambiguity pervades Thucydides' references to political *nomoi*. While he has Pericles ascribe the *nomos* of delivering funeral orations to a particular author, it is by no means clear whether or not he thought of it as laid down in a written law (2. 35. 1), and we are equally ignorant as regards the Corcyrean *nomos* which forbade the cutting of vine poles in the precinct of Zeus and Alcinous (3. 70. 5–6) or the *nomos* which prescribed the rules of succession to the priesthood of Hera of Argos (4. 133. 3). But there is ample evidence that during the last three decades of the fifth century *nomos* increasingly assumed the connotation of written positive law, which it kept as its primary meaning ever after. Our early evidence comes chiefly from Euripides and Aristophanes. Euripides explicitly praises written laws as a bulwark against tyranny (*Supplices* 433); but he also disparages them, just as he criticized social *nomoi*, as inhibiting freedom of action (*Hecuba* 864–67). Even when writing is not explicitly mentioned, Euripides' use of *nomos* in the political or judicial sense shows that he wrote against a background of written legislation. We hear, for example, of decrees through which laws are applied (*Ion* 1250–56, *Heraclidae* 141), of the *nomos* that a tie-vote of the Areopagus results in acquittal of the accused (*Electra* 1268–69), and the *nomoi* against murder (*Orestes* 941, *Hercules Furens* 1322, *Hecuba* 291). Aristophanes calls the Megarian Decree "written *nomoi*" (*Acharnians* 532), refers to the Solonian *nomoi* about inheritance and about the payment of debts on the first of the month (*Birds* 1650, 1655–56; *Clouds* 1183–87), and in one instance refers as *nomos* to the decree on public maintenance in the Prytaneion (*Frogs* 761–64), which survives in an inscription (*Inscriptiones Graecae* 1². 77).

This completes our account of the various connotations of *nomos* which had evolved by the end of the fifth century B.C. There is no need to go beyond that date, since no new connotations of the term arose in the fourth-century orators and philosophers or in Hellenistic times. On the contrary, although *nomos* never quite lost any of the meanings which it had up to the end of the fifth century, its primary use was henceforth as the technical term for "statute" not only in the forensic orators, such as Demosthenes, Aeschines, and Isaeus, where one would expect this use, but also in Plato and Aristotle.

What conclusion, then, can we draw from our discussion about the Athenian concept of law from the classical period on? The fact that *nomos* may be translated as both "custom" and "law" has led some scholars to the conclusion that the term originally signified "customary law," that is, customs and practices which in the course of time were given legal as well as social sanction by being embodied in a written code of laws. But this position is untenable. For not only does the Greek language fail to differentiate between "state" and "society," and not only is it impossible to reduce all *nomoi* to "customs"; but, as we have seen, "law" and "custom" are only two of about a dozen connotations of *nomos*. In addition to them it describes a way of life, norms of conduct and the source which guarantees them, the mores of a political or social group, law-and-order, conventional beliefs, and religious practices. It is not the idea of "custom" that ties all these connotations together, but the idea of an order which, contrary to *themis* and *thesmos*, derives its cohesion from the fact that it is, or ought to be, generally regarded as valid and binding by the members of the group in which it prevails. For that reason *nomos* is usually accepted as the valid norm; but even when it is disparaged and rejected, its nonacceptance is viewed as an isolated phenomenon and predicated upon the general acceptance which it enjoys in the community at large. As "law" it is, therefore, the ratification of what the general consensus of a people regards as a proper and valid norm for the conduct of its own affairs, and it is no wonder that the Athenians abandoned *thesmos* and chose *nomos* to express their idea of law after they had expelled their tyrants and established a democratic form of government.

BIBLIOGRAPHY

Citations of ancient authors are based on the Oxford Classical Texts or, where these are not available, on the Teubner texts. Citations from the fragments of Solon and Theognis are taken from E. Diehl, *Anthologia Lyrica Graeca*, 3rd ed. (Leipzig, 1954–55), of Hesiod from R. Merkelbach and M. L. West, eds. *Fragmenta Hesiodea* (Oxford, 1967), of the Pre-Socratic philosophers from H. Diels and W. Kranz, *Die Fragmente der Vorsokratiker*, 6th ed. (Berlin, 1951–52), of the tragedians from A. Nauck, *Tragicorum Graecorum Fragmenta*, 2nd ed. (Hildesheim, 1964), of inscriptions from E. Schwyzer, *Dialectorum Graecarum Exempla Epigraphica Potiora* (Leipzig, 1923), M. N. Tod, *A Selection of Greek Historical Inscriptions*, 2nd ed., Vol. 2 (Oxford, 1948), from C. D. Buck, *The Greek Dialects* (Chicago, 1955), and from R. Meiggs and D. Lewis, *A Selection of Greek Historical Inscriptions to the End of the Fifth Century* B.C. (Oxford, 1969), and of papyri from *Greek Literary Papyri*, ed. D. L. Page, Vol. 1 (London and Cambridge, Mass., 1942).

The following is a selection of works helpful for further study of Greek concepts of law: G. Busolt and H. Swoboda, *Griechische Staatskunde*, 2 vols. (Munich, 1920–26); V. Ehrenberg, *Die Rechtsidee im frühen Griechentum* (Leipzig, 1921); H. Fränkel, *Wege und Formen frühgriechischen Denkens* (Munich, 1960); F. Heinimann, *Nomos und Physis* (Basel, 1945); R. Hirzel, *Themis, Dike und Verwandtes* (Leipzig, 1907); J. W. Jones, *The Law and Legal Theory of the Greeks* (Oxford, 1956); E. Laroche, *Histoire de la racine NEM- en grec ancien* (Paris, 1949); K. Latte, "Der Rechtsgedanke im archaischen Griechentum," *Antike und Abendland*, 2 (1946), 63–76; Albin Lesky, "Wertdenken in der frühen griechischen Dichtung," *Gesammelte Schriften*, ed. W. Kraus (Bern and Munich, 1966), pp. 479–92; M. Ostwald, *Nomos and the Beginnings of the Athenian Democracy* (Oxford, 1969); T. A. Sinclair, *A History of Greek Political Thought* (London, 1951); H. Vos, ΘΕΜΙΣ (Assen, 1956); E. Wolf, *Griechisches Rechtsdenken* (Frankfurt, 1950–).

MARTIN OSTWALD

[See also Constitutionalism; Democracy; Justice; **Law, Ancient Roman, Concept of, Natural;** Right; State.]

ANCIENT ROMAN IDEAS OF LAW

IN A brief article the vast and complicated subject of the history and historical importance of Roman legal ideas must be presented in general fashion. For the classical Roman law, then, reference will be made only to the *Corpus Iuris Civilis;* that is, the codification of the common law of Rome made at the very end of the ancient Roman Empire. In 529–34 a commission of jurists, at the command of the Emperor Justinian, made collections of imperial laws (the *Codex,* referred to as *C.*), and of opinions of Republican and imperial jurisconsults (the *Digest, D*). They also compiled a textbook for the use of students in the law schools (the *Institutes, Inst.*). It was this *Corpus Iuris Civilis* which played the leading role in the great revival of the Roman law in the Middle Ages (ca. 1100–1300), in the "Reception" of the modern age, and in the medieval-modern development of legal science. (The reader should be familiar with one more reference that will occasionally appear in these pages, *Glos. ord.*, that is, the *Glossa ordinaria* of Accursius, ca. 1230, a great compilation of the opinions of the early professors of the Roman law at Bologna.) Despite later disagreements with many of the opinions in the glosses, the work of Accursius was disseminated throughout western Europe, was printed over and over again in the sixteenth century, and is itself massive evidence of the contribution of the *Corpus Iuris Civilis* to the medieval renaissance of Roman law and legal thought.

We must not glorify beyond measure the contributions of the Roman law and legal thought to the history of civilization. It is going too far to say that "it was the majestic and beneficent Roman law which more than any other single element brought civilization back to Europe following the barbaric deluge of the Dark Ages" (Sherman, I, 1). There is more justification for such a claim, however, than for the attitude of nineteenth-century British historians who

685

were almost obsessed with the belief that all that is constitutional and democratic and noble in the English common law and in the history of Parliament derives from early Germanic and Anglo-Saxon traditions. (It is a matter of irony that Tacitus, a Roman historian, was an important source of this romantic idealization of Germanic customs.) Bishop Stubbs said (*Letters*, p. 159), the Roman law has been "a most pliant tool of oppression . . . no nation using the Civil Law has ever made its way to freedom . . . wherever it has been introduced the extinction of popular liberty has followed sooner or later." Indeed, to this day some scholars attribute the rise of royal absolutism to the revival of the Roman law in the Middle Ages, as they attribute the growth of a limited or constitutional monarchy to the English common law and to feudalism.

There is, of course, some truth in this hostility to Roman legal ideas: one finds no democracy in the jurisconsults' treatment of the power or authority of the emperor; the Roman law sanctioned slavery; even free men could be tortured and deprived of the right of fair trial when suspected of treason; punishments for crime were cruel; and the Roman courts and judges were readier to help the rich than the poor. Medieval and modern supporters of the royal authority and absolutism have found inspiration in Roman legal thought. They deduced from the Roman laws on treason that it was just to deny the rules of fair trial to heretics as well as traitors; and thus they helped create the medieval Papal and the modern Spanish Inquisitions. Nevertheless, medieval and modern men have also found inspiration in the Roman laws dealing with the fundamental rights of the individual and with "constitutionalism." Our study of Roman legal ideas will show, indeed, that despite all shortcomings the Roman law was in sober fact one of the greatest achievements of the ancient world and one of the greatest contributions of Rome to medieval and modern European and American legal science.

The achievement was not, however, exclusively Roman. Just as the Anglo-American common law owes much to Roman and Germanic ideas and customs, so the Roman law drew abundantly from earlier Mediterranean laws and customs and legal thought and philosophy. During the thousand years of the history of the ancient Roman Republic and Empire, the common law of Rome gradually absorbed important legal principles and practices of the conquered peoples and civilizations. From Greek Stoicism Roman jurists borrowed their essential philosophy of natural reason and justice. From the maritime law of Rhodes they took many laws pertaining to trade and shipping. From the Near East came Tyrian and Syrian men of learning who, having a knowledge of the legal systems of the Phoenicians

and indirectly also of the earlier traditions of Hammurabi and Babylonia, became distinguished Roman jurisconsults in the second and third centuries A.D. From Egypt came ideas of property rights related to irrigation. And if Saint Paul was a Roman citizen and knew something about the Roman law, no doubt Jews in the Empire taught the Romans matters of value about Hebrew laws and customs. Yet the growing body of law remained essentially Roman, the creation of those practical Romans who conquered and learned how to govern Italy and the ancient Mediterranean world. By the end of the ancient Empire, Christianity was contributing its special influence. But the substance of the Roman law that was codified at the command of Justinian had developed as the common law of "pagan" Rome.

As for the ideas, one could simply follow Sherman's example (*Roman Law*) and list a great number of ideas whether in the realm of general principles or in the realm of private law on property, contracts, partnerships, corporations, and injuries, among other subjects. It seems better, however, to call attention principally to general theories of law and justice. Ideas belonging either to property rights or to crime are, after all, subordinate both to the general principles followed by the courts and to the public law of the state. But a few of these should be mentioned. The Roman law affirmed the private ownership of property, giving to the owner the full right to sell and lease without outside interference. The acquisition of property by purchase, gift, and inheritance, and by prescriptive right, was of course the subject of many laws. The law also recognized servitudes or easements, rights such as passage by path or road through lands of others, or the drawing of water. Naturally, contracts (*pacta*) relating to property rights were well protected, except that no contract was valid that was contrary to the public law and welfare. Property usually concerns families: the Roman law carefully regulated problems of marriage, such as dowries, the rights of women and children, wills, and inheritances. In the Republic the head of the family, *paterfamilias*, theoretically had absolute power over his wife and children. In the Empire, however, the wife and female heirs were given full recognition of their rights. It is evident, despite differences, that much of the American law on all these matters bears the impress of the Roman law.

Property rights belonged not only to natural but to corporate or juridical persons. The Roman law on corporations, in fact, is the foundation of medieval and modern corporate law. From it we retain the idea that what is done by the majority of the members of a corporation (in the Roman law, if two-thirds of the membership, a *quorum*, attended the meeting) was done as if it were by all the members and therefore by the corporation as a person. The corporation could act by means of representatives appointed with *plena potestas* ("full powers of attorney"). From this developed in the thirteenth century the idea that English shires and towns could be represented in Parliament; and indeed modern representation of communities is based on this principle, as it is based on another Roman principle, that any important business that affects the rights of natural and corporate persons should be treated in their hearing and concluded, in many circumstances, with their consent. Not only was the corporation or guild of artisans or merchants treated as a person, so also was the city and even the state. As a result, today the state itself is looked upon as a kind of juridical and moral person, having its own rights apart from and superior to the individual rights of all the members, whether viewed individually or collectively. In the thirteenth century canon lawyers advanced the theory that since only a natural person could have a soul and could be excommunicated, a juridical person or corporation was soulless and hence could not be punished. But the Roman idea persisted, and exists now, that while the corporation as a whole is not subject to punishment for a delict, the officers can be punished.

The Roman public law, as we have observed, made the public welfare ultimately superior to private rights. Does this mean that the Roman Empire was a "welfare" or social-welfare state? Not at all. Nonetheless, the Roman law considered problems of the public or common interest in relation to private rights of ownership. So we find laws that condemned the building of dwellings that deprived others of space and light, that condemned owners who allowed their buildings to become a public nuisance, and that required adequate drainage or sewage in towns. Further, there were laws that frowned on public charity for those who were healthy and able to work; the shiftless should not be supported by the state. (How these principles were reconciled with *panis* and *circenses* is too complicated to treat here. We may remark, however, that just as the Romans could reason that it was for the public welfare that the mob in the great cities should be fed, so it was for the public welfare or entertainment that gladiators be supported by the state and given the lawful right to kill others and die in glory.) On the whole, however, there was no theory that it was the duty of the state to furnish social security or to establish a system of socialized medicine. The state did not provide education for children; there were no public elementary and high schools. Only a few schools, centers of higher learning, chiefly in law, received public support by way of salaries for the professors.

Like all legal systems, the Roman law naturally dealt chiefly with problems associated with rights in material things, or with the protection of free men from crimes and injuries to their property rights. Yet there was a real concern for human rights. Influenced by the ideals of Stoicism, Ulpian and other great jurisconsults of the Golden Age of the Empire subjected all laws, private and public, to the natural law as a universal reason that should be observed in legislation and in all judicial decisions of courts. The natural brotherhood of all men demanded equality before the law and the right of free men to a fair trial according to principles of equity rather than the letter of the law. The relation of the higher law of nature to the science of law was stressed by Ulpian. Law and justice, he said (*D.* 1.1.1), are a sacred art, the professors of which can be called priests and true philosophers. (Medieval professors of the Roman law carried this idea further: as professors of a sacred science and a true philosophy they were the equals of priests and philosophers, and their science was the equal of Theology, the Queen of Sciences; and since Justinian spoke of how the Empire was armed by laws as well as military might, they pretended to an equality with feudal knights and lords—they were themselves noble; perhaps they prepared the way for the "nobility of the robe" in early modern France.)

Thus the higher law of nature or reason was the foundation of law and justice. (As Saint Augustine held, it was by the gift of reason that men are made in the image of God.) If the lower law of nature was animal instinct, the higher law of nature taught men to live free and equal, in a universal brotherhood, innocent of property rights and the need of a state and its laws. As a result of human greed and disorder, however, men could no longer live in this primitive, completely natural society. Separate peoples and their states resulted from the necessity of creating some law and order to protect good men from the wicked. Customs and laws arose that were common to all peoples, the *ius gentium*, a kind of international law which regulated the relations of peoples or states with each other in such matters as war and peace, slavery, commercial relations, and the rights of men belonging to one state who lived as foreigners in another state. In the *ius gentium* also were those principles of natural reason which approved the right of each society, people, or state to wage war in defense of its safety, which inspired men to revere the gods and obey their fatherland and their parents, and which demanded equity or natural reason in men's handling of problems of relations between their states. Indeed, some jurisconsults looked upon the *ius gentium* as the natural law itself insofar as it applied to mankind.

As a result of this, in the Middle Ages and in modern times the doctrine has arisen that if the *ius gentium* is an aspect of the law of nature, the state itself is natural, not a necessary convention or lesser evil as in Stoic thought. The Christian emphasis on God's approval of the state and of its government ("the powers that be are ordained of God"), on the king's ruling *Dei gratia*, reinforced this tendency. While the revival of Aristotle's *Politics* in the mid-thirteenth century added a secular emphasis on the naturalness of man as a political and social animal and on the naturalness of the state, the Roman-Christian *ius gentium* and natural reason were a significant support of the idea that the state is natural itself and a supreme moral value that, in times of great danger or necessity, "knows no law."

If, according to the Romans, the law of nature thus participated at least as an element in the *ius gentium*, its participation in the laws of each society or state was less apparent. Yet the natural law, as reason and equity, was presumed to subsist in the positive laws of the state, the civil law. To be sure, the civil law as the body of laws needed for law and order in the state could not perfectly imitate the higher law of nature; as Justinian said, the lower nature of men and society is constantly changing in relation to new situations, and new laws become necessary. Nevertheless, all laws and customs should contain reason. That is to say, whatever the needs of men because of their violence and greed, some natural reason must remain a kind of fundamental law which the laws of the state could not change—but could modify for the human environment. As Ulpian said (*D.* 1.1.6), the civil law neither departs altogether from the natural law, nor obeys it in all things.

Medieval legists and theologians offered their own solution. By the law of nature, all things are held in common; but the civil law, like the *ius gentium*, legalized private property rights. By the law of nature marriage and the rearing of children belong to the procreative instinct; but the divine law and positive laws of the state made marriage a human institution. From Saint Augustine on, Christian theologians went so far as to admit that some laws of the state were good, even when they seemed to be contrary to the natural law as the moral commands of God. Prostitution itself, though immoral, should be legalized by the state. As Nicholas of Lire said (early fourteenth century, in his preface to *Postilla*), the state can legalize prostitution lest the natural *libido* of men (belonging to lower nature) cause anarchy and destroy the public welfare.

The laws of the state must never completely violate the fundamental laws of nature. Natural reason demanded that human laws should not legalize injury to lawful rights as established in the courts, nor approve crimes that hurt the innocent and injured the state and its law and order. New laws could change punishments but never condone fraud, theft, murder, or adultery. (As for adultery, however, a late thirteenth-century philosopher held that if it was committed for the safety of the state, in order to wreck the plans of a tyrant, it was a lesser evil than the destruction of the public welfare.) Above all, natural reason commanded that equity or fairness should prevail in the administration of justice and the interpretation of the laws. Justice, as defined by Ulpian (*D.* 1.1.10—*ius suum cuique*), since it was related to many intangibles in human relations, could not perfectly obey natural reason. Given the complications of laws on slavery, property, and crime, and given special circumstances, it was difficult to determine what a man's *ius* or legal right was. Nonetheless, the Roman principle of justice in accordance with reason and equity and human rights has ultimately inspired medieval and modern concepts on the equal rights of all men.

The higher law of nature, therefore, demanded fair trial as a natural right. Judges themselves should be fully aware of their high duty; they should be impartial, never acting as judges in matters that concerned their own interests, always following the rules of reason and equity rather than the letter of the law, and avoiding undue severity in the decision of cases. By the late Empire they took an oath of office according to which they swore that they would respect both the laws of the state and the rights and welfare of all subjects of the emperor. (This oath, indeed, may be in part the background of the coronation oath of the medieval king: that he would do justice to all in accordance with the customs and laws of the kingdom.) In general, then, Roman judges should never be influenced by the great and powerful at the expense of the humble, nor should they accept bribes from the wealthy. (The practice did not always reflect the ideal. In the Middle Ages lawyers were to admit that a judge could accept gifts provided that he was not influenced by them—surely an anticipation of famous statements attributed to Sir Francis Bacon and Talleyrand.)

More important than the idea of the good judge were Roman laws on legal procedure which the courts should respect as a protection of the accused. When a man was accused of injuring another's rights in property or of committing a crime, he should be presumed to be good or innocent when he came to trial. He should be given the benefit of all legal means of defending himself against the accusation. (One recalls the words of Saint Paul, that as a Roman citizen he had the right to face his accusers.) But there were important qualifications of the ideal of the presumption of innocence and of fair trial. For once a man had by fair trial been declared guilty of a crime, such as theft, he was no longer presumed to be innocent when later accused of the same crime. As a medieval glossator said (to *D.* 48.2.7.2): "Once wicked, the accused (in the same kind of crime) is thereafter presumed to be wicked (*malus*)." (However, this is but the same popular attitude that is known today: a repeater is not always presumed to be innocent, whether by the police or by the courts.) A far more serious qualification must be emphasized. Slaves did not enjoy the benefits of the free citizen, and they could fear torture in ordinary cases. (Juvenal, *Satires*, VI, however, may express the feeling of the more enlightened jurisconsults: he condemned the arbitrariness of a lady who demanded that a slave be punished at once, without a hearing of his defense—the husband vainly pleaded for reason.) Moreover, not even a free man or citizen was given the benefit of the presumption of innocence if accused of treason to the emperor or to the state. To be suspected of treason was to be presumed guilty. Trial did take place, but the accused was deprived of the advantages of fair trial, and, subjected to torture, could be forced to confess (self-incrimination).

In the Middle Ages legists and canonists accepted both the presumption and the limitations. By the mid-thirteenth century the Papal Inquisition applied to heretics the Roman law on treason, for it was assumed that the accused could be guilty of the highest treason of all, namely, treason to God and the faith. Hence he was presumed to be guilty, was deprived of adequate legal defense, could not know and challenge his accusers, had no public trial, and was tortured if he refused to confess. Although the Papal Inquisition was never established in England, in the Tudor Age men accused of treason to the king suffered a similar kind of treatment. (No wonder that in reaction to this the maxim arose which later became a part of our Fifth Amendment: no man shall be compelled "to accuse himself" or "to be a witness against himself.")

Nonetheless it was the Roman law, not the English common law, which first laid down the principle that normally the man accused of a tort or a crime should be presumed innocent. Implied as it is in Magna Carta (c. 39), the presumption of innocence was first literally stated, it seems, by Jean Lemoine, a canonist and cardinal in the time of Pope Boniface VIII. Making use of Stoic-Roman-Christian ideas of natural, human, and public law, and of the ideas of legists and canonists, he declared that every man accused of a crime had the full right to public trial and to full legal defense by lawyers and documents and witnesses. For every man, he declared, "is presumed innocent until proved guilty" (*quilibet praesumitur innocens, nisi probetur nocens, Glossae* to *Extrav. Communes*, 161–65).

All ideas of private law, however much they are of direct interest to individuals and their rights, must finally be subordinated to the public law and the state. Ulpian (*D.* 1.1.2) defined the public law as the law that pertains to the "state of the Republic"—that is to say, it is the law concerning the "state of the State." Therefore it regulated all matters related to the public welfare and safety of people and state. To it belonged the magistracy or government and the public rights of legislation, jurisdiction, and administration. As Justinian and medieval legists said, without magistrates the laws are useless and the state cannot exist. Furthermore, as Ulpian and other jurisconsults held, all *sacra* (all things "religious," such as temples, objects used in the cult, and also everything relating to the cult of the Emperor Augustus) and priests are subjects of the public law and the state.

No separation of "Church and State" was recognized. Partly directly, partly indirectly, to repeat, the public law affected the private law and private rights. Legislation on private rights and jurisdiction over them belonged to the state and the government; and to the state belonged the right to prevent abuses of ownership in property. The "public welfare clause" was as serious an interference with absolute private ownership then as it is now. Above all, the necessity of the safety of the state and measures taken to assure it gave the imperial authority extraordinary powers in times of emergency or necessity. Private properties could be expropriated, though with compensation to the owners. In times of just wars waged in defense of the Empire, the emperor could demand patriotic loyalty and extraordinary sacrifices. *Urbs* and *orbis* constituted the common fatherland, the *patria communis*—for which, classical writers and jurists loved to say, it was glorious to fight and die.

Such theories of public law played a significant role in the rise of medieval-modern states and nationalism. In the twelfth century, urged on by advisers trained in the Roman law at Bologna, Frederick Barbarossa, German king and emperor, tried to make the medieval Empire truly Roman, calling it the Holy (*Sacrum*) Roman Empire, thus challenging the Holy Roman Church and the superior authority claimed by the pope. By the mid-thirteenth century, however, despite the brilliance of Frederick II, the Church triumphed over the Empire. Canonists declared that the pope was the true emperor, that the Holy Roman Church was

689

the true heir of the Roman Empire; and soon Pope Boniface VIII claimed that all kings and princes were subject to the papal authority. Indeed, the Church had become a great state, with its own public law taken largely from ancient Rome. The pope was more than a ghostly imitation of the ancient Augustus.

But the triumph of the Church was short-lived. English, French, and Spanish students of the Roman law at Bologna were already going home to become advisers of their kings or were writing treatises which transferred ideas of Roman public (and private) law to independent kingdoms. By 1200–60 they were saying that England and France were sovereign realms, and that the king who recognized no superior was the emperor in his kingdom (so Jean de Blanot in France and Bracton in England). Each kingdom became a "common fatherland," an Empire in itself; it was also an independent, sovereign state, governed by principles of public law. So, by the public law, the king enjoyed extraordinary powers when enemies threatened the safety of the people and the "state of the realm." In times of national emergency or in cases of dire necessity, it was both the duty and the public right of the king to make use of the right of eminent domain and to levy taxes to pay for the costs of defending the realm. To be sure, the king, like the Roman emperor normally limited by the laws, had to respect all private rights; and when he needed an extraordinary subsidy he consulted with and obtained the formal consent of his subjects in a representative assembly. Nevertheless, "right of state" and "reason of state" gave an able monarch the public right to demand consent. Both the royal authority and the state thus began to overcome old feudal rights.

From the thirteenth century on, therefore, despite the threat of privileged nobles and communities and despite civil and religious wars of the early modern age, the public law and the state gradually became predominant. Further, the Roman principle that the public law gave the ruler and the state control over religion, priests, and churches, reached its climax when Henry VIII declared in effect that the imperial crown and empire of England were completely independent of the Holy Roman Church. The modern national state, an empire in itself, the common fatherland of all people in its territory, had appeared. (One remark is necessary: the Constitution of the United States, while retaining other Roman principles of public law, departed from Rome altogether in separating Church from State.)

It is regrettable that the influence of the Roman law on literature as well as legal science cannot be discussed. Mention can be made, however, of how Shakespeare reflected the continuing role of the Roman

law in the education of English jurists in his time. For example, he was echoing a Roman maxim (*D.* 4.4.37; *C.* 6.30.22.12) in the words of Sicinius, that Coriolanus "hath resisted the law, and therefore the law shall scorn him further trial" (*Coriolanus* 3.1. 265–69)—a maxim which one finds also in medieval legists and canonists.

In conclusion, the few ideas discussed in this article surely illustrate the greatness, nobility, and practical usefulness of the Roman law to the medieval and modern world. The eager acceptance of its ideals and scientific character is witnessed by the stages of reception from the twelfth to the twentieth century. Unfortunately, in nineteenth-century Germany, and above all, more recently in Nazi Germany, extreme Germanic nationalism, allegations that the Roman law was Semitic (because of Near Eastern influences), and the Nazi denial of all decent principles of fair trial and of the rights of men, caused a reaction to the Roman, civilized ideas of law—a reaction that one finds in all totalitarian systems. It is fortunate indeed that the Roman achievement in legal thought still promises well for civilization wherever the Roman law is studied.

BIBLIOGRAPHY

The following sources were consulted: *Corpus Iuris Civilis*, ed. Mommsen, Krüger, et al., 12th ed., 3 vols. (Berlin, 1911); *Glossa ordinaria* of Accursius, to *C. I. C.*, 5 vols. (Lyon, 1604); Jean Lemoine, *Glossae* to *Extravagantes communes*, at end of the Lyon (1559), ed. of the *Liber sextus*; Nicholas of Lire, *Postilla* (Mantua, 1477); William Stubbs, *Letters*, ed. W. H. Hutton (London, 1904).

Among the many secondary works the following are important: C. P. Sherman, *Roman Law in the Modern World*, 2nd ed., 3 vols. (New York, 1924), the most detailed account; Fritz Schulz, *Principles of Roman Law* (Oxford, 1936); W. W. Buckland and A. D. McNair, *Roman Law and Common Law* (Cambridge, 1936); Paul Koschaker, *Europa und das römische Recht* (Munich and Berlin, 1947), the best general interpretation of the medieval and modern "Receptions" of the Roman law; C. H. McIlwain, *Constitutionalism: Ancient and Modern* (New York, 1940), partly about Roman contributions to theories of limited monarchy; E. Kantorowicz, *The King's Two Bodies* (Princeton, 1957; rev. ed., 1968), makes good use of Roman law on medieval theories of kingship; G. Post, *Studies in Medieval Legal Thought, Public Law and the State* (Princeton, 1964), emphasizes the influence of the Roman law on medieval representation and consent, and on the origins of the medieval-modern state; P. Vinogradoff, *Roman Law in Medieval Europe*, 2nd ed. by F. de Zulueta (Oxford, 1929), gives a general history, not of ideas, but of the revival of the study of Roman law.

GAINES POST

[See also **Constitutionalism**; Equity; Justice; **Law, Ancient Greek, Natural**; **Property**; **State**; Stoicism.]

COMMON LAW

COMMON LAW is a category of the jurisprudence of every legal system that has reached a certain level of complexity. The term indicates a body of rules which is contrasted with some other body of rules belonging to the same legal system but having a special character. The special character of the other body of rules may arise because the rules have a particular origin, because they are applied by a particular court, or because they apply exclusively to a particular group of people or within a particular territorial area. The common law is the body of rules which apply generally, outside the particular category, and its precise content depends on the nature of the contrast being made. Common law is thus a relative notion, with no constant content, and the various possible specifications of the category in any legal system can only be explained historically.

In the terminology of Roman law, which has been more influential than that of any other legal system, the expression *ius commune* occurs principally in two such contrasts. The jurist Gaius (second century A.D.), as cited in Justinian's *Digest* (1.1.9), says that "all nations governed by laws and customs use partly law which is peculiar to themselves and partly law common to all mankind (*ius commune omnium hominum*)." He goes on to explain that the former is called civil law (*ius civile*) and the latter, "which natural reason has laid down for mankind in general," is called the law of nations (*ius gentium*). Thus within the Roman legal system some institutions and rules, which were considered to be dictated by common sense and to be shared by all legal systems, were ascribed to the latter category, while others were the special property of the Romans exclusively.

From another point of view the Roman lawyers distinguished between those rules of Roman law—irrespective of whether they belonged to all legal systems or were peculiar to Roman law—which applied to citizens generally (rules which they called *ius commune*), and those which they called *ius singulare*). Examples of the latter are the rules which allowed soldiers to make wills in informal ways not open to other citizens and the rules applicable to heretics as opposed to orthodox Christians.

The first of these conceptions of *ius commune* may be regarded as the parent of the Continental common law, and the second of the English common law.

By the end of its classical period (roughly the first two centuries A.D.), the remedies of Roman law were available to all free residents of the Empire, without regard to whether they were Roman citizens or not. However the Germanic tribes, which formed the bar-barian successor states after the collapse of the Roman Empire in the West, held to the personal principle in legal matters. They regarded their own tribal laws as applicable only to themselves and therefore continued to apply a form of Roman law to their Gallo-Roman subjects. The most enlightened of their kings provided compilations of Roman law for this purpose, the most important being the *Lex romana visigothorum* (A.D. 506), which was the main source for Roman law during the next five hundred years. Justinian's *Corpus iuris civilis*, which was compiled later in the sixth century in Byzantium, was hardly studied in the West before the eleventh century.

The personal principle gradually gave way to the territorial principle, whereby all those living in a certain area were subject to its law, irrespective of their national origin. The different populations were fusing together, and the distinction between Roman and Goth or Frank was no longer clear. So the personal laws disappeared in favor of the custom of the region. In those areas where the Romanized population was the strongest element, such as Italy and southern France, this custom was in effect a barbarized Roman law. Just as the Germanic languages gave way before dialects of Latin, so in these areas the Germanic tribal laws submitted to Roman law, which was no longer looked on as the law of the conquered subject people but as a general law for all the inhabitants. Even in the areas where the custom was predominantly Germanic, Roman law was not without influence, since even these Germanic laws were written in Latin and adopted many Roman legal terms.

In 800 Charlemagne revived the idea of the Roman Empire and by asserting their succession to the old Empire he and his successors claimed for themselves the position and powers of the old Roman emperors. They were thus able to exploit a widespread emotional feeling for the cultural legacy of Rome and assert that Roman law still applied to the inhabitants of the universal empire as it had done in the fifth century.

However, the full recognition of Roman law as the common law of Europe was the product of the revival of the study of the texts of Justinian's compilation, which began at Bologna at the beginning of the twelfth century. The first expositors of this law were the Glossators. They concentrated on mastering the Justinianic texts, which they regarded as a gift of God and treated as having an almost sacred authority. In the course of the twelfth and the first half of the thirteenth century, they subjected the whole compilation to a dialectical analysis, the results of which were synthesized about 1240 in the Great Gloss of Accursius. During this period Bologna became a "legal Mecca," to which students flocked from all parts of Europe.

The Commentators who built on the work of the Glossators treated the Gloss as having as much authority as the texts which it interpreted. "What the Gloss does not recognize, the Court does not recognize." In the course of the fourteenth century they began to adapt the material presented by the Glossators to the needs of the times in which they lived. In northern Italy each town had its own statutes. Under the leadership of their greatest figure, Bartolus, the Commentators established the principle that "a statute must be interpreted according to the *ius commune*," in the sense of the principles (*rationes*) derived from the law of the *Corpus iuris* as expounded by the Glossators. Moreover, wherever local law in the sense of the municipal statutes did not deal specifically with a matter, the law which was presumed to apply was this common law. From the fifteenth century onwards, doubts as to what constituted the common law were resolved by reference to the "common opinion of the doctors" (*communis opinio doctorum*), which was essentially the dominant view among those jurists who had written treatises for practical, forensic purposes.

It was gradually recognized that the justification for regarding this law as the common law of Europe was not so much its formal authority as the law of the Holy Roman Empire as its substantial superiority and comprehensive character compared with any possible rival. It was said to be a universal law not by reason of the Empire but by the empire of Reason, and its doctrines came to be regarded as "reason in writing" (*ratio scripta*). As such it was the only secular system of law to be taught in European universities side by side with the canon law of the universal Church. To distinguish it from the latter it was called the civil law. As long as the only secular law available in law faculties was the civil law taught in Latin, the learned lawyers in all countries of necessity shared a common legal culture, and often studied law in a country other than their own.

The movement by which the civil law superseded the local laws and became in fact accepted as the common law of all the countries of Europe, except England and Scandinavia, is known as the Reception. It took different forms and occurred at different times from country to country, but always it was associated with the development of a learned legal profession and courts of professional judges.

In Italy, the only secular rival to Roman law apart from the local statutes, which, as we have noted, were subordinated to Roman law, was the feudal land law. Here the civil lawyers executed a neat take-over by incorporating the *Libri feudorum* ("Books of the Feus"), the standard collection of feudal law (mid-twelfth century), into the *Corpus iuris*, of which they were henceforth considered a part.

In France, the southern part of the country, known as the *pays de droit écrit*, already recognized the barbarized Roman law of the *Lex romana visigothorum* as the principal element of its regional custom, and the new learning derived from Bologna was readily received there. The French civil lawyers proposed to treat the French customary laws like the Italian statutes, as particular laws over which the civil law enjoyed a higher authority. Where a definite rule applicable to the case in hand was lacking or where the customs were obscure, they held that the civil law applied as the residuary common law.

In the north, the *pays de droit coutumier*, where Germanic custom prevailed, Roman doctrines were drawn on to fill gaps in the customs. The lawyers of this part of France often used a Roman rule "not in its proper and logical sense, but in order to confirm or to prove some opinion of their own, which possibly did not fit in exactly with the concrete rule brought forward to support it" (Vinogradoff, p. 94). Thus they constructed their own systems partly out of Roman and partly out of native materials. They also held a view different from that prevailing in the south as to what constituted the common law. Already in the thirteenth century they were aware of a fundamental unity lying behind the apparently diverse customs. In the prologue to the *Coutumes de Beauvaisis* (ca. 1280), Philippe de Beaumanoir speaks of a common law of the kingdom of France, by which he means certain general principles, usually expressed in the form of an adage or maxim, which were accepted by all collections of customary law and were therefore regarded as having almost universal validity. There was a strong presumption against any deviation from these principles.

Whereas in France the Reception was a more or less gradual and voluntary process, extending over several centuries, in Germany it was wholesale and sudden. In the fourteenth century the German Empire was a loose confederation of countless principalities and free cities, each having its own customary law. In addition there were separate systems of law for particular social groups, such as knights, guilds, and peasants. Except in Saxony, there was little attempt to systematize the customs on a professional basis. In the fifteenth century only the civil law, as glossed and explained by the Commentators, provided the required centripetal force to counteract these particularistic tendencies.

The practice grew up of submitting disputes, when they were beyond the ability of lay judges of the local courts to solve them, to the German law faculties for their opinions, and the professors naturally applied the "learned law." In 1495 the central Imperial court, the Reichskammergericht, officially adopted the modernized Roman law as the common law of the Empire.

The influence of the Commentators, although it was delayed in Germany by contrast with Italy or France, was all the stronger and more dramatic and the local laws rapidly succumbed. Being mainly an upper-class movement, the common law (*gemeines Recht*) encountered much opposition from the lower orders, who were attached to the old customs that it was superseding. But the professional counterattack of Germanism against Romanism in law was a product of the nineteenth century. From the sixteenth to the eighteenth century inclusive, the civil law was scarcely challenged as the common law of the German-speaking states.

In Scotland the first permanent central court, the Court of Session, established in 1532, followed the common pattern by adopting the civil law whenever a case could not be settled by recourse to established native law. An Act of the Scots Parliament of 1583 (cap. 98) refers to a Roman law rule as "the disposition of the common law." Lord Stair in his *Institutions of the Law of Scotland* ([1681], I.1.11,12), recognized that in Scotland the civil law was considered to be common law in the sense of law "which in some sort is common to many nations," but emphasized that it was "not acknowledged as a law binding for its authority, yet being, as a rule, followed for its equity."

The civil law was received as common law throughout Europe out of a mixture of motives. In the political field, it expressed the idea of the State, superior to feudal groupings and local interests. It was therefore attractive to territorial princes, who appealed to the Roman maxim, "the will of the prince has the force of law." From the economic point of view, it provided the elements of a commercial law, especially with regard to contracts, which was urgently required by the rising merchant class, but which the local customs lacked. Lastly from the jurisprudential point of view, "it asserted itself as soon as there reappeared theoretical reflection of legal subjects. And when the elaboration of common law became a social necessity, the Roman system grew to be a force not only in the schools, but also in the courts" (Vinogradoff, p. 144). To be effective, the Continental common law had to be accepted by the courts, but its mouthpieces remained the academics rather than the practitioners, the jurists rather than the judges.

The seventeenth- and eighteenth-century movement in favor of rationalist systems of natural law shows how entrenched a position the civil law had achieved. For when the systems are examined, the rules dictated by natural reason usually turn out to be just the rules of the civil law purged of their more antiquarian aspects. Also in the seventeenth century, however, national deviations from the common law begin to be formally recognized by the use of such terms as Roman-Dutch law and Roman-German law. These laws were regarded as variations on the same theme until the publication of national codes at the end of the eighteenth century. The French Civil Code of 1804, by its association with the Revolution, marked a particularly sharp break with the past. Thereafter, although uncodified *gemeines Recht* existed in Germany until the enactment of the German Civil Code in 1900, the notion of a common law of Europe became increasingly a fiction. The romantic movement and the historical school of jurisprudence stressed national differences in law and the positivists urged the importance of legislation as a medium of law reform.

In England the situation was very different. Immediately after the Norman Conquest, William I began to impose on the country a centralized structure of government, and his policy of strengthening the administrative organs in the control of the king against the local institutions was continued by his successors, especially Henry II in the twelfth century. During this period there were many courts administering justice— shire courts, feudal courts, borough courts, church courts—and the king's court, the *curia regis*, was just one among them. The growth of the English common law is bound up with the gradual take-over by the king's court of the main work of these other courts and the corresponding submission of the laws applied by these courts to the law of the king's court. Already in Henry II's time it had become a permanent court of professional judges, who had their main seat at Westminster, but who traversed the whole country on regular circuits. The royal court (*curia regis*) was able to supersede its rivals because of the superiority of its procedure. In civil actions this procedure had two noteworthy features which distinguished it from its rivals: first, actions were begun by writ, a royal command in writing addressed to a sheriff or other royal officer bidding him bring a certain person before the royal court to answer the claim against him, and secondly (although at first only in disputes involving land), proof of matters of fact could be by the evidence of neighbors rather than by ordeal or battle, which were the normal methods of proof in the local courts.

By the end of Henry II's reign there were seventy-five stereotyped forms of writ, each with its own title indicating its function, such as writ of debt, writ of trespass, writ of mort d'ancestor, and the clerks of the royal Chancery would issue them as a matter of course to anyone who could pay for them. It is in these writs that we should seek the germ of the idea of a common law available to all Englishmen, whether of Norman or of Saxon stock, and wherever they happened to live.

The evident superiority of its justice naturally increased the popularity of the king's court and resulted in its splitting into three: King's Bench, Common Pleas, and Exchequer. The latter, although primarily an administrative body, had jurisdiction in all cases involving Crown debtors.

The substance of the common law was created by the judges of these three courts. The materials with which they worked were of customary origin, some going back to Anglo-Saxon England or pre-Conquest Normandy, but were mainly the product of the feudal conditions applicable to the larger landholders. Like their contemporaries in the regional courts of northern France, the English judges used Roman materials to eke out the exigencies of the native customs. Since most of the judges until well into the fourteenth century were ecclesiastics, they were well acquainted with the civil law. However, they were distinguished from their French colleagues by the fact that their courts had not a regional but a national jurisdiction. The victory of the national law created by the king's courts over the local customary laws was gradual, and the vitality of the latter is often underestimated. If a local custom could be proved to exist, the king's courts had to apply it; and as late as the end of the fourteenth century, for example, a defendant in the court of Common Pleas could plead that the common law did not apply to him, because the case was covered by the custom of the small Yorkshire village of Selby, which was different from the common law.

The first literary exponent of the new law of the king's court was Rannulf Glanvil, whose *Tractatus de legibus et consuetudinibus regni Angliae* ("Treatise on the Laws and Customs of England") was in effect a commentary on the main forms of writ current in the king's court. The emphasis on procedure is also evident in the main medieval work of English law, Bracton's *De legibus et consuetudinibus Angliae* ("Laws and Customs of England," ca. 1250). He made considerable use of decided cases, and also incorporated a good deal of the Roman law of the Glossators. He went to great pains to show that England had laws just as Continental countries did, even though these laws were not "written" in the Romanist sense of being declared in authoritative texts. The rules established by general custom were declared not by a single judge alone but by the whole court of the king, which represented the magnates of the kingdom; but there was no authorized version of these rules.

The term "common law," used to describe the law of the king's courts, was taken over from the exponents of canon laws of the Church. From the beginning of the thirteenth century the canonists used the term *ius commune* to distinguish the general law of the whole Church both from those rules which were peculiar to a particular provincial church and also from papal privileges, which granted special dispensations from the general canon law to particular favored groups. Thus Pope Innocent III in a decretal ascribes a certain ruling to "both the common law and the general custom of the English church." Maitland has shown (Pollock and Maitland, I, 176–77) that the term passed from the ecclesiastical courts to the secular courts. The Dialogue of the Exchequer, written about the same time as Glanvil's treatise, contrasts the common law of the realm with the forest laws, which are the product of the king's will. By the end of the thirteenth century the usual phrase for the common law was *lex communis* in Latin (or *commune lei* in Norman-French). The earliest Year Books (the series of notes of cases argued in the king's courts from about 1270 until the sixteenth century) use the phrase to indicate the general law by contrast with local custom and with the law merchant, which applied only among merchants and which was international in scope, and also to indicate the ancient unenacted law by contrast with the statute law laid down by Parliament and with the royal prerogative. But at this time the term did not have the emotive force which it later acquired.

Until the middle of the fourteenth century while the common law was fairly flexible, the judges of the king's court had adopted a free and accommodating attitude towards parliamentary legislation. They looked on statutes as merely settling the details of the common law and did not regard them as a distinct source of law. Thereafter, however, they made a sharp distinction between legislation and adjudication, and interpreted statutes strictly so as to interfere as little as possible with the ancient usages which constituted the common law. Henceforward the term "common law" bears the connotation of unwritten law of customary origin, declared by the judges of the king's court, by contrast with the authoritative texts of the statutes enacted by Parliament. The judges purported to declare what had always been the law; Parliament made new law and abrogated old law.

In the fourteenth and fifteenth centuries the law of the king's courts became increasingly rigid and technical. The judges no longer included ecclesiastics, who could contribute an experience of other legal systems. The bench consisted entirely of secular judges appointed by the king from the ranks of practicing barristers. The latter were organized in Inns of Court, which served the purpose of universities, providing both a collegiate environment for communal living with many cultural activities and also a system of education in the common law, which apprentices to the law were made to follow. It is this theoretical exposition of the common law in the Inns of Court, under the control of professional practitioners of the law, that distinguished it from the customary laws of the Continent, which were not taught systematically in any such equivalent to a law faculty. (Even in England, Oxford and Cambridge taught only civil and canon law until the middle of the eighteenth century.) This teaching gave the common law a scientific structure which was generally lacking in other systems of customary law and which enabled the common lawyers effectively to resist the influence of the Roman civil law. In Maitland's phrase "law schools make tough law."

For two and a half centuries after Bracton, foreign influence on English law was slight. When, at the end of the fifteenth century, Sir John Fortescue wrote his book *De laudibus legum Angliae* ("In Praise of the Laws of England," ca. 1470), he showed that the common law had become a system which rested on historical foundations of its own, a parallel system to the canon law of the Church but lacking the obvious features of the civil law which was having so considerable an influence on the Continent. Fortescue's book also manifested some of the spirit of nationalism and insularity which was henceforth to be a feature of the English common law.

The very technicality which enabled the common law to resist the influence of the civil law, together with the possibility of tampering with its juries, led to growing dissatisfaction with the common law courts among litigants. They therefore petitioned the King's council for remedies outside those of the common law. These petitions were dealt with by the Chancellor, who dispensed a discretionary equity which softened the effects of the now-rigid common law. By granting a common injunction, the Chancellor could prohibit a litigant who had been successful in an action at common law, under pain of penalty, from enforcing his judgment, if in the circumstances it would be unfair for him to do so, as for example if he had been guilty of fraud. Gradually the Court of Chancery established itself as having a jurisdiction parallel to that of the common law courts and as administering a body of rules which were collectively known as "equity" and which in the course of time became almost as rigid as those of the common law. Equity never, however, constituted a complete system in itself. It remained "a gloss on the common law," and most of its doctrines presupposed institutions of the common law.

By the sixteenth century, the idea was established that the common law was a set of customs which had stood the test of time and had acquired an absolute quality, which made them the equivalent of justice itself. Christopher St. Germain, a barrister of the Inner Temple and a cosmopolitan scholar familiar with other legal systems, wrote in his treatise on *Doctor and Student* (1532, Ch. vii):

Because the said customs be neither against the law of God nor the law of reason, and have always been taken to be good and necessary for the commonwealth of all the realm, therefore they have obtained the strength of a law, insomuch that he that doth against them doth against justice: and these be the customs that properly be called the common law.

As examples of such fundamental customs, St. Germain mentioned, *inter alia*, the system of courts, trial by jury, freedom from arbitrary imprisonment, feudal customs, and especially the principle of primogeniture, and the form of conveyance of land known as feoffment with livery of seisin.

The figure who in the eyes of subsequent generations seemed to personify the common law was Sir Edward Coke (1552–1634), who in his three *Institutes* and in some crucial judgments delivered as Chief Justice, first of Common Pleas and later of the King's Bench, restated the medieval common law as it was to be found in the cases reported in the Year Books, of whose contents he was the acknowledged master. Urging that "out of the old fields must come the new corn," he provided continuity between the medieval law and the law of modern times. But he also ensured that the common law would be highly technical and resistant to change. Uninterested in any law but that of the Year Books, he assumed that the common law was the only law that had ever prevailed in England and held that it was law because it was immemorial custom, and that law of this kind constituted an artificial reason, which only the judges could expound. One of Coke's contemporaries, Sir John Davies, argued that the common law of England was "so framed and fitted to the nature and disposition of this people as we may properly say it is connatural to the Nation, so as it cannot possibly be ruled by any other law" (preface to *Irish Reports*, 1612).

In the seventeenth-century struggle between Parliament and the Crown, the common lawyers threw their weight onto the side of Parliament and this alliance "made a clear issue between tradition, common law and the medieval view [that the king was under God and the law] on one hand and, on the other, the newer idea of statecraft, absolutism and a supreme royal equity" (Plucknett, p. 283).

The idea that the law which had begun life as the custom of the king's court was in fact the result of some indwelling of fundamental legal principles in the life of the English people reaches its supreme statement in the *Commentaries* of William Blackstone (1765). For him common law was synonymous with unwritten law in the sense of all law not set down in a statute or ordinance, and he even describes as common law the customs of a particular district or local court.

Nineteenth-century historical jurisprudence caused this view to be abandoned. Today common law indicates the form of uncodified law adopted by those countries deriving their legal traditions from England, particularly the United States, Canada, Australia, and New Zealand, and is sometimes designated Anglo-American. It connotes the case by case method of building up the law through judicial decisions as opposed to systematic legislative enactment. It is characterized first by the doctrine of the supremacy of law, which subjects the sovereign and its agencies to the law and obliges them to act according to principles and not by arbitrary will. In the United States, although not in England, a corollary of this doctrine is the power of the courts to declare legislation invalid. Its other basic feature is the doctrine of judicial precedent, which aims to combine certainty with the possibility of growth. The doctrine thus enshrines the apparent paradox of the common law, in that it is sometimes spoken of as something fixed and unalterable from time immemorial, while at other times, it is presented as a set of customary rules capable of developing, in a way that statutory rules are not, to meet new social necessities.

The strength of the modern common law lies in its treatment of concrete disputes rather than in the logical development of general principles and it is this feature which distinguishes the common law systems from the civil law systems, descended from the Continental *ius commune*. As a body of law the common law has inspired an intensely emotional loyalty in its adherents: "Her soul is founded in an order older than the gods themselves, but the joy of strife is not strange to her, nor yet the humours of the crowd" (Pollock, p. 2).

BIBLIOGRAPHY

For the notion of *ius commune*, see F. Calasso, *Medio Evo del diritto* (Milan, 1954), and most recently, L. Lombardi, *Saggio sul diritto giurisprudenziale* (Milan, 1967). For its spread throughout Europe, see P. Vinogradoff, *Roman Law in Medieval Europe*, 2nd ed. (Oxford, 1929); P. Koschaker, *Europa und das römische Recht* (Munich and Berlin, 1953); H. Coing, "Die europäische Privatrechtsgeschichte der neueren Zeit als einheitliches Forschungsgebiet," *Ius Commune*, 1 (Frankfurt, 1967), 1–33. For the medieval French notion, see P. Petot, "Le droit commun en France suivant les coutumiers," *Revue historique de droit français et étranger*, 4th sér., **38** (1960), 412–29. For English common law generally, see C. K. Allen, *Law in the Making*, 7th ed. (Oxford, 1964); S. F. C. Milsom, *Historical Foundations of the Common Law* (London, 1969); T. F. T. Plucknett, *Concise History of the Common Law*, 5th ed. (London, 1956). For its origins, F. Pollock and F. W. Maitland, *History of English Law Before the Time of Edward I*, 2nd ed. (Cambridge, 1898), and for recent studies, G. W. Keeton, *The Common Law and the Norman Conquest* (London and New York, 1966). For the crisis of the sixteenth century, F. W. Maitland, "English Law and the Renaissance," *Historical Essays* (Cambridge, 1957), pp. 133–51 (somewhat exaggerating the alien threats to English law); J. G. A. Pocock, *The Ancient Constitution and the Feudal Law* (Cambridge, 1957). For the main elements of the common law system, O. W. Holmes, Jr., *The Common Law* (Boston, 1881). For modern notions, see R. Pound, *The Spirit of the Common Law* (Boston, 1921); more romantic, F. Pollock, *The Genius of the Common Law* (New York, 1912).

PETER STEIN

[See also **Equity;** Heresy; Historicism; Justice; **Law, Ancient Roman, Natural;** Positivism; Romanticism.]